Fodor's 2023

ESSENTIAL
ITALY

Welcome to Italy

Italy is the kind of destination you return to over and over again. It boasts awe-inspiring art and architecture and stunning historical ruins—as well as some of the world's best food and wine. Also beckoning are sun-kissed olive groves and vineyards, and the beautiful sparkling waters of the Mediterranean Sea. As you plan your travels to Italy, please confirm that places are still open and let us know when we need to make updates by writing to us at: editors@fodors.com.

TOP REASONS TO GO

★ **Food:** Italy is a pasta lover's paradise; but don't forget the pizza and the gelato.

★ **Romance:** Whether you're strolling atmospheric Venice or sipping wine, Italy enchants.

★ **History:** The ruins of ancient Pompeii and the Leaning Tower of Pisa breathe antiquity.

★ **Art:** The big hitters—Botticelli, Michelangelo, Raphael, Caravaggio, and more.

★ **Shopping:** Few things say quality or style like "made in Italy."

★ **Stunning landscapes:** Tuscany, the Amalfi Coast, the Cinque Terre, to name just a few.

Contents

Fodor's Features

Chapter 1

EXPERIENCE ITALY

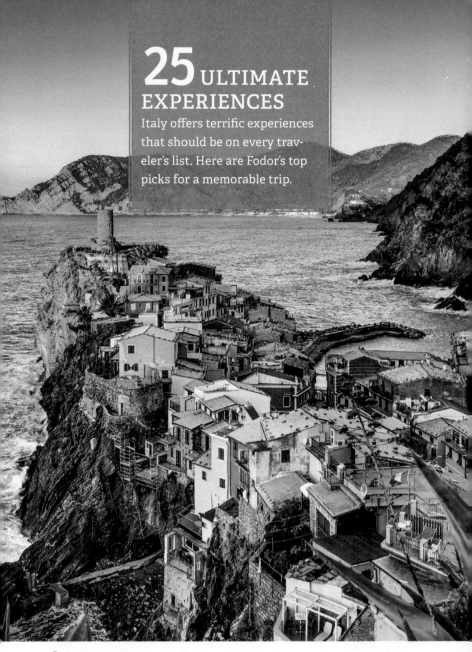

25 ULTIMATE EXPERIENCES

Italy offers terrific experiences that should be on every traveler's list. Here are Fodor's top picks for a memorable trip.

1 Hike the Cinque Terre

Walk the scenic footpaths that connect the five former fishing villages that make up the Cinque Terre; each one appears to hang off the cliffs, allowing for absolutely stunning views of the vineyards above and blue waters below. *(Ch. 10)*

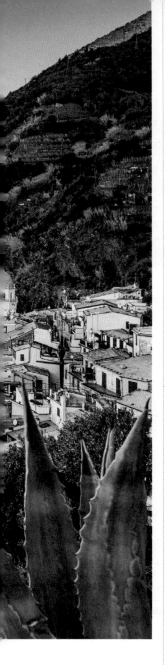

2 People-Watch in Venice

Venice's Piazza San Marco (St. Mark's Square), flanked by the gorgeous Basilica di San Marco, is certainly one of the world's loveliest squares for people-watching. *(Ch. 5)*

3 Shop in Milan

In Italy's fashion capital of Milan, you'll find the highest of high-end designers in the Quadrilatero della Moda district, north of the Duomo. *(Ch. 8)*

4 See Assisi's Frescoes

The peaceful medieval town of Assisi is home to enormous Basilica di San Francesco, which includes 28 frescoes showing the life of St. Francis. *(Ch. 14)*

5 Sail Away to Capri

This fabled island off the coast of Naples has long stood for glitz and glamour. It's a lovely place to escape to. *(Ch. 15)*

6 Ponder *The Last Supper*

Restoration work has returned *The Last Supper* to its original glory, so the painting is amazingly clear and luminous. *(Ch. 8)*

7 Roam a Medieval City

Perhaps Italy's best-preserved medieval city, Siena's narrow streets are fun to explore. The Piazza del Campo is one of the most beautiful squares in the country. *(Ch. 13)*

8 Discover Ravello

Wander the Amalfi Coast's refined mountaintop village and discover lush, hidden gardens, medieval fountains, and sweeping Mediterranean views. *(Ch. 15)*

9 Rent a Villa in Tuscany

One of the supreme pleasures of a visit to the countryside of Tuscany is the chance to stay in a villa—preferably one with a swimming pool and vineyard views. *(Ch. 13)*

10 Admire the Architecture

The city of Lecce is a jewel of Baroque architecture, but that is by no means its only style. Stand in Piazza Sant'Oronzo to best see and appreciate the blend. *(Ch. 16)*

11 Marvel at Mosaics

Some of the greatest Byzantine mosaics can be found in the unassuming city of Ravenna. You can view the most elaborate ones in the 5th-century Mausoleo di Galla Placidia. *(Ch. 11)*

12 Go Wine Tasting

The Barolo region produces excellent wine and is filled with hill towns and vistas. Make an appointment for a tour and tasting at one of the many wineries. *(Ch. 9)*

13 Explore Lava Fields

The largest and highest volcano in Europe, Sicily's Mt. Etna, has moonlike dunes that you can walk across, or view from the comfort of a cable car (the Funivia dell'Etna). *(Ch. 17)*

14 Enjoy Magical Views

Nowhere inspires as many oohs and aahs as the magnificent town of Positano, with its pastel-color houses seemingly spilling off the mountainside. *(Ch. 15)*

15 See Great Art

Florence's Galleria deglia Uffizi contains the collection of art from the Medicis, including Botticelli's *Birth of Venus*, Michelangelo's *Doni Tondo*, and Caravaggio's *Bacchus*. *(Ch. 12)*

16 Relax by the Sea

The lovely village of Portofino hugs the coast of the Italian Riviera, with the Santa Margherita cliffs on one side and the Ligurian Sea on the other. *(Ch. 10)*

17 Feel Romantic

Set on the shores of beautiful Lake Como, Bellagio is often considered one of the loveliest towns in Italy. Its steep streets, lined with cobblestones, are supremely romantic. *(Ch. 8)*

18 Visit a Volcanic Island

Just a ferry away from Sicily's northeast coast sit the Aeolian Islands, seven volcanic islands offering dramatic scenery and wonderful snorkeling and scuba diving. *(Ch. 17)*

19 Hit the Slopes

The gorgeous craggy peaks of the Dolomites make the perfect place for an unforgettable ski holiday in the winter or a rejuvenating hike in the spring and summer. *(Ch. 7)*

20 Toss a Coin in Trevi Fountain

The can't-miss Trevi Fountain, in Rome, is a Baroque fantasy of sea beasts, seashells, and mermaids in front of a triumphal arch. *(Ch. 3)*

21 Step Back in Time

The best-preserved excavated site in the world, the commercial center of Pompeii was frozen in time when Vesuvius erupted in AD 79. (*Ch. 15*)

22 Explore a Hill Town

Wander the narrow winding streets of the walled city of San Gimignano, which is filled with 14 soaring medieval towers (originally there were more than 70). (*Ch. 13*)

23 Enjoy the Coastline

In Italy's southernmost region of Puglia, around the heel of the boot, is a wonderfully dramatic coastline, with sandstone cliffs crashing into the ocean. (*Ch. 16*)

24 Lounge on a Beach

Sardinia is justly famed for its white-sand beaches. Spend the day soaking up the sun on these beautiful strands. (*Ch. 18*)

25 Stand in Awe

Dominating Florence's skyline, the magnificent Duomo is an architectural marvel that took almost 600 years to complete. *(Ch. 12)*

WHAT'S WHERE

1 Rome. Italy's capital is one of the greatest cities in Europe. It's a busy, modern metropolis where you'll encounter powerful evocations of its storied and spectacular past, from the Colosseum to St. Peter's.

2 Side Trips from Rome. The Eternal City is surrounded by intriguing towns and villages where you can explore without the crowds.

3 Venice. One of the world's most unusual—and beautiful—cities, Venice has canals instead of streets, along with an atmosphere of faded splendor.

4 The Veneto and Friuli–Venezia Giulia. The green plains stretching west of Venice hold three of northern Italy's most artistically significant midsize cities: Padua, Vicenza, and Verona. Farther north and east, Alpine foothills are dotted with welcoming villages and some of Italy's finest vineyards.

5 The Dolomites. Along Italy's northeast border, the Dolomites are the country's finest mountain playground,

Elevation	
15,577	4,748
10,825	3,300
9,840	3,000
8,860	2,700
7,875	2,400
6,900	2,100
5,900	1,800
4,920	1,500
3,940	1,200
2,920	900
1,970	600
980	300
490	150
250	75
100	30
feet	meters

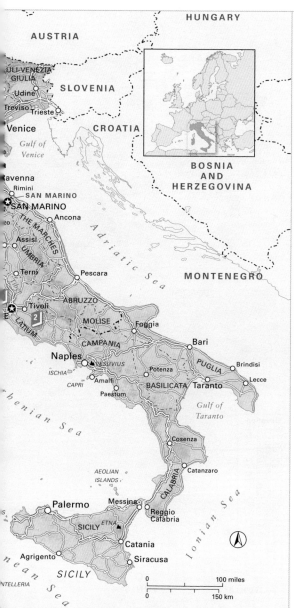

with gorgeous cliffs, curiously shaped peaks, lush meadows, and crystalline lakes.

6 Milan, Lombardy, and the Lakes. The lakes of Lombardy have been attracting vacationers since the days of ancient Rome. At the center of Lombardy is Milan, Italy's second-largest city and its business capital. It's also the hub of Italian fashion and design.

7 Piedmont and Valle d'Aosta. Here you'll find great Alpine peaks, one of the most highly esteemed food-and-wine cultures in Italy, and an elegant regional capital in Turin.

8 The Italian Riviera. Northern Italy's most attractive coastline runs along the Italian Riviera in the region of Liguria. The best beaches and temperate winter climate are west of Genoa, but the main appeal lies to the east, where fishing villages dot the seaside cliffs and coves.

9 Emilia-Romagna. Many of Italy's signature foods come from the Emilia-Romagna region. Bologna is a significant cultural center, and the mosaics of Ravenna are glittering Byzantine treasures.

WHAT'S WHERE

10 Florence. The hub of the 15th-century Renaissance, Florence is awash with artistic treasures, exceptional restaurants, and first-rate shopping, as well as a never-ending stream of tourists.

11 Tuscany. Nature outdid herself in Tuscany. The central Italian region has Florence as its principal city and many other interesting midsize towns, but the region's greatest appeal lies in the smaller towns, often perched on hilltops and not significantly altered since the Middle Ages.

12 Umbria and the Marches. A number of the smaller towns, particularly Assisi, Perugia, Spoleto, and Orvieto, are fun to explore, and Umbria's Roman past is everywhere—expect to see Roman villas, aqueducts, and temples. Urbino's Ducal Palace reveals more about the Renaissance than a shelf of art history books.

13 Naples and Campania. Campania is the gateway to southern Italy. Dream away two magical weeks on

Elevation	
15,577	4,748
10,825	3,300
9,840	3,000
8,860	2,700
7,875	2,400
6,900	2,100
5,900	1,800
4,920	1,500
3,940	1,200
2,920	900
1,970	600
980	300
490	150
250	75
100	30
feet	meters

the pint-size islands of Capri and Ischia and at the fabled resorts of the Amalfi Coast. Or explore the past at the archaeological ruins of Pompeii, Herculaneum, and Paestum. Naples is a fun, chaotic metropolis.

14 Puglia, Basilicata, and Calabria. The southernmost regions of the peninsula—Puglia, Basilicata, and Calabria—are known for their laid-back medieval villages, shimmering seas, and varied landscapes. The coastline of Puglia, along the heel of Italy's boot, is popular with beachgoers, but for the most part you're off the beaten path here.

15 Sicily. The breezes are sultry and everyday life is without pretense, as witnessed in the workaday stalls of the fish markets in ports all along the Tyrrhenian and Ionian coasts, bursting with tuna, swordfish, and sardines.

16 Sardinia. The beaches here rank among the Mediterranean's finest, and ancient sites, including the Carthaginian and Roman settlements of Nora and Tharros, add to the island's distinctive character.

Italy Today

ENDURING CUISINE

The old joke goes that three-quarters of the food and wine served in Italy is good—and the rest is amazing. In some sense, that's still true, and the "good" 75% has gotten even better. Those pundits would claim that ingredients that in the past were available only to the wealthy can now be found even in the remotest parts of the country at reasonable prices. Dishes originally conceived to make the most of inferior cuts of meat or the least flavorful part of vegetables are now made with the best.

But many Italians would say that the food in Italy is getting worse. There's a proliferation of fast-food establishments, and increasing tourism has allowed many restaurants to lower their standards while raising their prices. This is true not only in Rome, but in most other tourist centers as well. The good news is Italy is home to one of the world's greatest cuisines, and its traditional favorites still put meat on bones and smiles on faces. Italian restaurateurs seem determined to make the most of the country's reputation for good food. Although quaint, family-run trattorias with checkered tablecloths, traditional dishes, and an informal atmosphere are still common if on the decline, nearly every town has a newer eatery with matching flatware, a proper wine list, and an innovative menu.

This also holds for Italian wine. Today, through investment and experimentation, Italy's winemakers are figuring out how to get the most from their gorgeous vineyards. It's fair to say that Italy now produces more types of high-quality wine from more different grape varieties than any other country in the world.

SOCCER RULES

Soccer (or, as the Italians say, *calcio*—which means "kick") stands without rival as the national sport of Italy, though some complain that big-money influence and loose financial regulations are polluting the beautiful game. That aside, Italy did win its fourth World Cup in 2006 giving the country more world titles than any other this side of Brazil. More recently, Italy won the prestigious UEFA Euro 2020 championship (though due to COVID-19 it was played in 2021). Although the game is still played at a high level, its teams have not fared as well in European club competitions recently. More games in the schedule and a dwindling fan base mean fewer people are seen at the stadium. Still, fans can't stop watching the game on television. Indeed the allure of its famed teams like Juventus, Inter, and Napoli and their *ultras* (vociferous fans) means the top league, *Serie A,* has a worldwide following.

AN AGING POPULATION

Italy's population is the oldest in Europe (as percentage of population)—the result of its low birth rate and one of the highest life-expectancy rates in the world. The median age of an Italian in 2020 was 46; projections for 2050 exceed 50. Chronic underfunding of the public health-care system has left older Italians particularly vulnerable to COVID-19.

Italy's famously stable population is now aging and set to contract according to recent estimates, putting a strain on the country's pension system and on families because elderly family members are likely to live with their children or grandchildren in a country where retirement homes are rare.

The trend also has an impact in other areas, including politics (where older politicians are eager to promote policies aimed at older voters), the popular culture (where everything from fashion to television programming takes older consumers into consideration), and a kind of far-reaching nostalgia. Thanks to a long collective memory, it's common to hear even younger Italians celebrate or rue something that happened 50 or 60 years earlier as if it had just taken place.

THE BLACK-MARKET ECONOMY

Nobody knows how big Italy's black-market economy is, though experts all agree it's massive. The presence of the black market isn't obvious to the casual observer, but whenever a customer isn't given a printed receipt in a store or restaurant, tobacco without a tax seal is bought from a street seller, or a product or service is exchanged for another product or service, that means the transaction goes unrecorded, unreported, and untaxed. But that's all penny-ante stuff compared to what many professionals evade by neglecting to declare all they earn.

Austerity measures imposed in 2012 have led to much disgruntlement among the population; now most shopkeepers insist that you take a receipt. If you don't, you could be fined, as could the shopkeeper. These measures remain in place, but the country still struggles to meet the 3% limit to its budget deficit as mandated by European Union (EU) agreements, and it is pretty certain that Italy will continue to struggle to meet it in coming years.

A GROWING PARKS SYSTEM

Italy has 25 national parks covering a total of around 1½ million hectares (5,800 square miles), or about 6% of the entire surface area of the country—more than twice as much as 25 years ago.

Part of the reason for the expansion has been a growing environmental movement in Italy, which has lobbied the government to annex undeveloped land for parks, thus protecting against development. But the trend is a boon for visitors and nature lovers, who can enjoy huge expanses of unspoiled territory.

STAYING HOME IN AUGUST

Italy used to be the best example of Europe's famous August exodus, when city dwellers would spend most of the month at the seaside or in the mountains, leaving the cities nearly deserted. Today the phenomenon is less prevalent, as economic pressures have forced companies to keep operating through August. As a result, vacations are more staggered and more modest.

The loss of shared vacation time for Italian workers means good things for visitors: in August there's a little more room on beaches and mountains; in addition, cities promote events for nonvacationing natives. Summers in Italy now offer a plethora of outdoor concerts and theatrical events, extended museum hours, and local festivals.

MUSEI DIFFUSI

In recent years the idea of promoting tourism away from Italy's increasingly clogged destinations has spurred the idea of Musei Diffusi or "Scattered Museums." COVID regulations and social-distancing measures have only accelerated the need to support local communities and encourage visitors to seek out art and linger in sleepy, overlooked hilltop *borghi* instead of queuing for hours to glimpse Botticelli's *Venus*. The trend has evolved from Strade dei Vini (Wine Roads) and theme itineraries: now grand collections like the Uffizi are launching curator-led online exhibition tours and dusting off artworks in storage destined for display in municipal collections.

Best Hilltop Villages in Tuscany and Umbria

ORVIETO, UMBRIA

Although medieval architectural wonders adorn Orvieto, the labyrinth of subterranean tunnels beneath the town is even more fascinating. Orvieto is also recognized for its white and red wines, its olive oils, and its culinary classics—from boar and dove to pastas and pastries.

PITIGLIANO, TUSCANY

Although most Italian villages are overflowing with impressive churches, Pitigliano may be most famous for its synagogue, drawing attention to its rich history of Jewish settlement and giving the old town its nickname of Little Jerusalem. Of course, countless churches dot the rest of this Tuscan village. There's also a smattering of museums and other historic gems like the Palazzo Orsini, a Renaissance palace built on the ruins of medieval fortresses and containing both art and archaeological museums of its own.

SAN GIMIGNANO, TUSCANY

Most medieval towers have given way to war and erosion through the centuries, but San Gimignano retains so many that it has been dubbed the Town of Fine Towers and its historic center is a UNESCO World Heritage site. Although it's packed with immaculate examples of medieval architecture, this village is among the more tourist-minded, with contemporary events like music festivals and art exhibitions and plenty of modern conveniences and services for travelers. San Gimignano even has its own app.

VOLTERRA, TUSCANY

Twelve miles from the better-known village of San Gimignano is the less visited (less crowded) Volterra. Although there are some serious medieval remnants in this village, especially its narrow streets in the town center, it's much more famous for the historical periods before and after. Some of its ancient Etruscan fortification walls still surround Roman ruins, including an impressive amphitheater worth exploring (there are also remains of ancient Roman baths and a forum). The Florentine influence of the Medici family left behind some dazzling Renaissance art and architecture throughout the once bustling mercantile village. The alabaster trade remains strong today and provides beautiful souvenirs of this Tuscan treasure.

SORANO, TUSCANY

Ham it up in Sorano, where the local ham is so revered that the town holds a festival for it every August. If you don't eat pork, don't worry; there are plenty of other local specialties highlighted during the event, particularly dairy products, including sheep's milk ricotta cheese, as well as oranges and other fruits and the ever-popular Italian liqueur, *limoncello*. Don't miss the Masso Leopoldina (sometimes called the Rocca Vecchia). It was once central to the defense of the town but is now a fabulous terrace that's a good place to enjoy panoramic views of Tuscany—and, perhaps, yet another limoncello.

VINCI, TUSCANY

Yes, *that* Vinci. Established in the early Middle Ages among the rolling hills of Montalbano and with Arno Valley views, Vinci's claim to fame is Leonardo da Vinci (that, "Leonardo from Vinci"). The town is filled with tributes to him—like the imposing wooden sculpture, *Vitruvian Man,* by Mario Ceroli; the Biblioteca Leonardiana, an archive of his manuscripts and drawings; Santa Croce, the church where he was baptized; and the Museo Leonardiano Vinci, which houses his inventions and anatomical research, including drawings, studies, and replicas, in two buildings. You can also visit the birth home of this true Renaissance man in the nearby village of Anchiano. It's accessible via a 3-km (1.8-mile) walk up the *strade verde* (a dirt path with valley views) or by car or bus.

TODI, UMBRIA

Compact and ancient Todi is a hilltop citadel town with a beautiful patchwork of architecture that includes three sturdy walls, begun by the 3rd-century Etruscans followed by Roman and medieval dynasties. Starting at the café-community hub Piazza del Popolo, with an imposing 12th-century Romanesque-Gothic Duomo built upon a Roman temple, a maze of cobbled lanes and steep staircases fans out, inviting leisurely exploration. For grandstand views over roofs and the Umbrian hills beyond, climb the campanile of San Fortunato. Leafy walks abound in the Parco della Rocca, the city-wall park.

ASSISI, UMBRIA

Assisi claims history as ancient as 1000 BC and is probably best known for its most famous resident, St. Francis, whose 13th-century basilica is now a UNESCO World Heritage site, as is the entire village itself. Plenty of other impressive churches, Roman ruins, and not one but two castles top the extensive list of the town's architectural offerings. From ceramics to medieval weaponry, Assisi's artisan history is also strong. Cured meats and chocolate are popular here, so grab a snack between sword fights, and refuel on the Assisi ribbon-type pasta *stringozzi,* often served with Norcia black truffles, asparagus, or *piccante* (spicy) tomato sauce.

Best Beaches in Italy

TORRE GUACETO, PUGLIA

The color palate at Torre Guaceto is classic and calming: blue waters lapping chalky sands near the so-called Città Bianca (White City) of Ostuni. The beach is part of a marine reserve that extends 12 miles along the coast and 4 miles inland.

CALA GOLORITZÉ, SARDINIA

The beach's gleaming-white limestone pebbles, limpid waters, and dramatic geological formations make it a paradisiacal summer playground. The pinnacle towering over the cove is often dotted with climbers; dozens of nearby marine caves have wonderful natural light effects; and the surrounding mountain-ous national park is laced with challenging trails.

BAIA DEL SILENZIO, LIGURIA

Line a curvy bay with a sandy beach and warm-hued build-ings, and you have Baia del Silenzio, one of Liguria's most captivating seaside amphitheaters. This very popular spot in the resort town of Sestri Levante is a fabulous place to people-watch.

CALA DEL GESSO, TUSCANY

Gorgeous Cala del Gesso is nestled in a relatively sheltered nook on southern Tuscany's Monte Argentario peninsula. Stake out a spot early in high season: the beach's shiny limestone pebbles and crystal clear turquoise waters draw sun worshippers and snorkelers aplenty.

ROCA VECCHIA, PUGLIA

A big draw at Roca Vecchia is the Grotta della Poesia (Cave of Poetry)—a natural ovoid sinkhole-pool set into limestone along the stunning Salento Coast. Swimmers like to dive in (a 16-foot drop), and scuba divers like to swim in (via an underwater sea cave).

TONNARA DI SCOPELLO, SICILY

Rustic houses, a church, medieval towers on craggy cliffs, and sea-stack rock formations make Tonnara di Scopello on the Golfo del Castellammare one of Sicily's most picturesque beaches.

SPIAGGIA NERA–CALA JANNITA, BASILICATA

Maratea is one of the Tyrrhenian coast's most alluring towns, where the fabulous Spiaggia Nera (Black Beach) has limpid waters and dramatic scenery. Spread your towel out on the dark volcanic gravel, and float amid igneous boulders.

SPIAGGIA DELLA MARINELLA, CAMPANIA

Near the town of Palinuro on the oft-overlooked Cilento Coast, stunning Spiaggia della Marinella mixes pebbles and volcanic sand against a backdrop of otherworldly rock formations.

MARASUSA, CALABRIA

The area around the lovely town of Tropea has some of Calabria's most recognizable seascapes, including those on Marasusa, where the water is a remarkable greenish-blue, the sand light-hued and ultrafine, and buildings seem to grow from the rock atop sheer cliffs.

SPIAGGIA DI FEGINA, LIGURIA

Hikers tackling the famous Cinque Terre often take a breather on the beautiful, pebbly Spiaggia di Fegina. If you're feeling sprightly, clamber over *faraglioni* (sea stacks) amid the waves or trek down to one end of the beach to see the 46-foot Statua del Gigante (Giant Statue) hewn into the rock.

Best Vineyard and Wine-Tasting Experiences in Tuscany

Castiglion del Bosco

ANTINORI

Antinori (⊕ *www.antinori. it*) produces one of the best-known Super Tuscans, called Tignanello, a blend of Sangiovese with Cabernet Sauvignon and Cabernet Franc. It offers several winery/cellar tours, all of them followed by a tasting, across its different wineries in Tuscany. If you're inspired to buy a bottle (or two), the wineshop is well stocked.

AVIGNONESI

A 16th-century manor house surrounded by vineyards in Montepulciano is the setting for Avignonesi (⊕ *www.avignonesi. it*). On tours, which are followed by tastings, you'll learn about biodynamic wine making and visit the vin santo aging cellar, drying room, and barrel tunnel. Cooking classes are sometimes offered, too.

BADIA A COLTIBUONO

In Gaiole in Chianti, options at Badia a Coltibuono (⊕ *www.coltibuono.com/ en*), which also produces olive oil, include visiting the former crypt where Chianti Classico is aged, cooking classes, or walking tours of the vineyards, about a 20-minute drive from the abbey.

Castello di Ama

BARONE RICASOLI

Situated in Gaiole in Chianti, Barone Ricasoli (⊕ *www. ricasoli.com/en*) is Italy's oldest winery. Indeed, Bettino Ricasoli, the "Iron Baron," is said to have developed the original formula for Chianti wine in 1872. Book a winery tour, or visit the wineshop for a tasting.

CAPEZZANA

Make reservations to tour the cellars, olive oil mill, and vin santo aging cellar at Capezzana (⊕ www.capez-zana.it) in Prato. Afterward, enjoy both wine and olive oil tastings. Cooking classes are also available, as are eight charming *agriturismo* guest rooms.

CASTELLARE DI CASTELLINA

In addition to its panoramic views, Castellare di Castel-lina (⊕ *www.castellare.it/ en*) in Castellina in Chianti

is known for its sustainably produced I Sodi di S. Niccolò Super Tuscan, Chianti Classico, and vin santo dessert wine. Book ahead for the hour-long cellar tour followed by a tasting.

CASTELLO DI AMA

Ninety-minute visits to Gaiole in Chianti's Castello di Ama (⊕ *www.castel-lodiama.com/en*), which must be booked in advance, include tastings and tours of the property's cellars, 18th-century villas, and gardens. You can also spend the night in one of the Villa Ricucci suites.

CASTIGLION DEL BOSCO

Castiglion del Bosco, in Montalcino, is part of a luxury Rosewood (⊕ *www. rosewoodhotels.com*) resort. Private tours, by appointment only, include visits to the cellars and vineyards plus tastings.

FONTODI

At Fontodi (⊕ *www.fontodi. com*), in Panzano, appointment-only tours highlight the winery, cellars (where some wines are aged in terra-cotta pots), and bottling process, ending with a tasting. If you're with a group, look into staying at one of the villas here.

SALCHETO

Overlooking the hill town of Montepulciano, Salcheto (⊕ *salcheto.it/en*) is a biodynamic winery that follows fully sustainable practices, including generating energy from renewable sources and purifying and recycling wastewater. The property also has a wine bar that serves food, and six farmhouse guest rooms.

Best Ancient Sites in Rome

COLOSSEUM

Perhaps the monument most symbolic of ancient Rome, the Colosseum is one of the city's most fascinating—and popular—tourist attractions. It officially opened in AD 80 with 100 days of games, including wild-animal fights and gladiatorial combat.

FORO DI TRAIANO

Trajan's Forum was the last of imperial Rome's forums—and the grandest. Comprising a basilica, two libraries, and a colonnade surrounding a piazza, it's connected to a market that once bustled with commercial activity.

PANTHEON

Built as a pagan temple to the gods, the Pantheon is Rome's best-preserved ancient site, perhaps because it was later consecrated as a church. Step inside and you'll be amazed at its perfect proportions and the sunlight streaming in from the 30-foot-wide oculus. It's truly a wonder of ancient engineering.

ROMAN FORUM

One of the Eternal City's most emblematic sites, the Roman Forum stretches out between the Capitoline and Palatine Hills. This vast area filled with crumbling columns and the ruins of temples, palaces, and shops was once the hub of the ancient world and the center of political, commercial, and religious life in the city.

CIRCUS MAXIMUS

It might be hard to imagine now, but the grassy area between the Palatine and Aventine Hills was once the site of the largest hippodrome in the Roman Empire. The huge oval course was rebuilt under Julius Caesar and later enlarged by subsequent emperors. During its heyday, it hosted epic chariot races and competitions that sometimes lasted as long as 15 days.

BOCCA DELLA VERITÀ

Legend has it the mouth in this ancient stone face will bite off the hand of a liar, and tourists line up to stick their hand inside the mouth and put it to the test. (Gregory Peck's character tricks Audrey Hepburn's Princess Ann into thinking he lost a hand inside it in a scene from *Roman Holiday*.) You'll find the enigmatic face in the portico of the Church of Santa Maria in Cosmedin, near the Circus Maximus.

The Roman Forum

TEATRO MARCELLO

It may look a bit like a smaller version of the Colosseum, but the Teatro Marcello was once ancient Rome's largest and most important theater. Julius Caesar ordered the land for the theater to be cleared, but he was murdered before it was built. It was inaugurated in AD 12 by Augustus and hosted performances of drama and song. It's kept that purpose even today, at least during the summer, when it hosts concerts.

APPIA ANTICA

Head to the southeastern edge of the city to Appia Antica Park and you can walk on the same stones that ancient Roman soldiers and citizens once trod—which are incredibly well-preserved. This ancient thoroughfare once stretched all the way to Brindisi, some 300 miles away on the Adriatic Coast. Today, the first 10 miles are part of a regional park, and it's a perfect spot for bike rides and picnics in the grass under the shadow of Rome's emblematic umbrella pines.

ARA PACIS AUGUSTAE

Now housed in a modern glass-and-travertine building designed by renowned American architect Richard Meier, the Ara Pacis Augustae has some of the most incredible reliefs you'll see on any ancient monument. It was commissioned to celebrate the Emperor Augustus's victories in battle and the Pax Romana, a peaceful period that followed. It's centrally located on the Tiber River and definitely worth a visit.

BATHS OF CARACALLA

A testament to ancient Rome's bathing culture, this site was essentially a massive spa, with saunas, baths, what would be an Olympic-size pool, and two gymnasiums for boxing, weightlifting, and wrestling.

The Best Places to Discover Volcanoes

Ischia

CRATER RIM OF VESUVIUS

Peering over the edge into the 650-foot-deep crater you can glimpse and even taste the acrid, sulfuric menace of Vesuvio's steamy fumaroles. Hearts may skip a beat after the odd, unnerving earth tremor. Up here the views of the bay and the surrounding area below—Pompeii, Herculaneum, Oplontis—hint at its immense eruptive might.

POMPEII'S PLASTER-CAST FIGURES

To get an idea of the merciless nature of Vesuvius, visit Pompeii to see the plaster-cast ghosts of some of its AD 79 victims. Archaeologist Giuseppe Fiorelli's casts freeze the positions of the incinerated Pompeians: a chilling reminder of how the earth's awesome natural power can take lives in an instant.

CAMPI FLEGREI

The Campi Flegrei, or Fiery Fields, is a complex caldera volcano that some scientists now deem to be Europe's largest supervolcano.

FUMAROLES AND THERMAL SPRINGS OF ISCHIA

The island of Ischia sits within the Campi Flegrei caldera, whose gargantuan

Pompeii's plaster-cast figures

magma chambers fuel the hydrothermal springs and fumaroles that soothe and heal thousands of spa goers each day.

VILLA ROMANA

Although the Amalfi Coast is a limestone spur of the Apennines, without a fumarole or lava flow in sight, the communities some 13 miles from Vesuvius have been shaped by volcanology. By descending into the Villa Romana ruins by the beach at Positano, you are traveling through the volcanic debris spewed by the eruption of AD 79.

SOLFATARA CRATER

In this land scarred by constant tectonic activity, there is one steamy, fumarole-fizzing, and mud-bubbling 4,000-year-old crater that has become an emblem for volcanism in this part of the world.

Solfatara was a bathing curiosity on the Grand Tour and has appeared in numerous movies and music videos, including Rossellini's *Journey to Italy* and Pink Floyd's *Live at Pompeii*.

BAIA

Down at the shoreline of Baia, the sea has swallowed part of the town, and at nearby Pozzuoli, marine mollusk boreholes 20 feet up the Roman columns indicate that the sea was once much higher. These two towns attest to the shifting water levels—the rise and fall of the land surface caused by the constant emptying and filling of the magma chambers below.

HERCULANEUM

Walking down the sloping path into the Herculaneum archaeological site, you are struck by the enormity of

the eruption that buried Pompeii. Scientists believe that Herculaneum was seared by a 900°F pyroclastic surge that roared down the mountain at 250 mph.

SAN SEBASTIANO

In 1944, liquid lava enveloped buildings and took off the church cupola, while walls of cooler lava crushed buildings. Today the curious can walk on those lava flows and enter modern buildings built in the 1950s and 1960s atop the lava and half-destroyed main street, Via Roma.

OSSERVATORIO VESUVIANO

Vesuvius remains the most closely monitored volcano on the planet; the research here started the science of volcanology.

Fantastic Cooking Classes in Italy

TASTE BOLOGNA (BOLOGNA, EMILIA-ROMAGNA)

Any cook worth their *sale* (salt) should spend time in Italy's foodie capital, and Taste Bologna provides a fulsome introduction to its riches. Combine their Classic Bologna Tour with the Cooking Class to get a feel for life in the market and in the kitchen.

MONTESE COOKING EXPERIENCE (SAN GIMIGNANO, TUSCANY)

Situated just outside San Gimignano, the well-loved Montese Cooking Experience is blessed with fabulous facilities, chefs, and views. The intensive four-hour Pasta Fatta in Casa session highlights not only long pastas, but also stuffed varieties.

TASTING SARDINIA: THE CENTENARIANS MEAL (CAGLIARI, SARDINIA)

The enlightening Centenarians Meal session, one of many offerings from Tasting Sardinia, takes its premise—that cooking with fresh ingredients is essential to living long and well—straight from the island's centenarians.

BUCA DI BACCO (POSITANO, CAMPANIA)

The venerable Hotel Buca di Bacco opened in the 1950s, but tucked within is the even older, eponymous restaurant, established in 1916, which hosts Buca di Bacco cooking classes. You'll learn about pizza and pasta making, as well as the restaurant's signature antipasto: *gamberetti alla Clark*. The dish was created for U.S. General Clark, who was stationed here at the end of World War II. When he requested a prawn cocktail, the chef combined shrimp, lettuce, and a sauce to create a version that reflected the local climate and wartime larder.

COOKING TAORMINA (TAORMINA, SICILY)

In addition to helping you hone your cooking skills, the animated young chef at Cooking Taormina explains the many exotic influences that shaped *la cucina siciliana*. The first part of the lesson stimulates the senses on a visit to Taormina's produce and fish market. Afterward, you'll use your fresh ingredients in classic Sicilian specialties.

MAMA ISA'S COOKING SCHOOL (PADUA, VENETO)

In Padua, a 30-minute drive inland from Venice, Mama Isa and family offer a tempting array of courses—from half-day introductory lessons to six-day extravaganzas—covering many of the Veneto region's culinary traditions. There are weeks' worth of classes, including bread and pasta making, vegan and vegetarian cooking, and dessert

Bari Walking Tour in Puglia

and pastry creation—even how to prepare the perfect risotto.

BARI WALKING TOUR WITH PASTA-MAKING (BARI, PUGLIA)

Deep in Bari's atmospheric *centro storico*, you'll learn about the art of making orecchiette, which is still practiced on the city's streets. The two-hour Bari Walking Tour with Pasta-Making starts with a tour of the city and its food market before heading to the chef's house to get fiddly with the dough. By the end of the session, you will have created hundreds of edible "little ears" to enjoy with a few bottles of Puglia's red Primitivo wine during the all-important tasting lunch.

ITALIANNA COOKING CLASS (ALBA, PIEDMONT)

Renowned for its rich tradition of food and wine, greatly influenced by nearby France, Piedmont is a fine destination for a foodie adventure. Itali-Anna's beginner pasta-making class, for example, is fun, flour filled, and interactive—and just one of their offerings.

SLOW COOKING CLASS (PACIANO, UMBRIA)

The family-run Country Slow Living is based in an organic olive press, Il Fontanaro. Its most popular offering involves a tour of the mill, a rummage around the verdant market garden to select ingredients, and then a chance to get messy: mixing and kneading dough, shaping pasta, and creating the accompanying *sugo* (sauce) from scratch.

COOK WITH US IN ROME (ROMA, LAZIO)

The enthusiasm of the two Roman chefs who conduct the Cook with Us in Rome classes is contagious, making it truly fun to learn about the city's food in a morning or afternoon session.

Architectural Wonders in Venice

PONTE DI RIALTO
The iconic Ponte di Rialto was completed in 1591. Its generous arch, central portal, and Renaissance arcade make it appear so beautifully balanced that Palladio himself would surely have approved.

SAN FRANCESCO DELLA VIGNA
The harmonious combination of architectural designs by two Renaissance maestri and the tranquil neighborhood setting make this church a wonderful place to escape the crowds.

MOLINO STUCKY
This behemoth, neo-Gothic warehouselike building, formerly a flour mill and pasta factory, on the western end of the Giudecca certainly stands out on the Venetian skyline.

SANTA MARIA DELLA SALUTE
One of the city's most beloved and iconic churches, La Salute was built to mark the end of the 1630 plague that took almost 50,000 Venetian lives.

PUNTA DELLA DOGANA
There has been a Punta della Dogana (Sea Customs House) situated between the Grand and Giudecca Canals since the 15th century, although the building you see today was designed in the 1860s. Above the entrance tower, two Atlases lift a bronze sphere topped by the figure of Fortune.

ARSENALE
For centuries, the colossal Arsenale complex of shipyards, warehouses, and armories was Europe's largest military-industrial compound. Although many areas are still cordoned off as military zones, the southern side is open to the public during the Biennale Arte.

JEWISH GHETTO
Originally the site of a foundry (*geto* in the local dialect), both the atmosphere and the architecture set the Jewish Ghetto apart: palazzi and *case* are taller here than elsewhere, with story upon story piled on high in an effort to make the best use of limited space.

Palazzo Ducale

PALAZZO DUCALE

Adorned with a series of soaring Gothic arches topped by an ornately columned arcade, the labyrinthine Doge's Palace has a wedding-cake-like delicacy when viewed from the Piazza San Marco or the waterside Bacino di San Marco.

MADONNA DELL'ORTO

An alluring, redbrick Gothic church with ornate marble decoration, it was dedicated to St. Christopher, the patron saint of travelers, until a Madonna statue was found in a nearby *orto* (kitchen vegetable garden).

CA' DA MOSTO

As you drift along the Grand Canal, you'll see palazzi far more eye-catching than the Ca' da Mosto, but none more enduring—the crumbling Byzantine-style palace has been here since the 13th century. The ground and first floors are an example of a *casa-fondaco*.

What to Watch and Read

ITALIAN FOLKTALES BY ITALO CALVINO

In 1956 the celebrated, Cuban-born and Liguria-raised, magical realist published this fabulous collection of some 200 traditional folktales from across the archipelago. The prose in the 800-page *Fiabe italiane* tome is simple yet evocative, and the stories appeal to young and old alike. They're largely fantastical morality tales involving love, loss, revenge, and adventure on the part of kings, princesses, saints, and peasants. The book is a fabulous bedtime or beach read.

AMARCORD, DIRECTED BY FEDERICO FELLINI

Amarcord ("I remember," in the Romagnol dialect) is filled with comic archetypes and dreamlike excursions inspired by Fellini's 1930s adolescence in Rimini. The rosy-cheeked protagonist, Titta, and his pals have humorous encounters with authority figures—pompous schoolteachers, frustrated fathers, cruel Fascist officials—as well as with the buxom hairdresser, Gradisca. The 1973 movie, which won the Oscar for Best Foreign Language Film, offers poignant, entertaining, and often bonkers insight into the Italian psyche, family dynamics, and interwar society. Nino Rota's wistful soundtrack adds to the feeling of nostalgia.

THE ITALIANS BY JOHN HOOPER

In this 2015 book, longtime Rome correspondent John Hooper addresses the complexities of contemporary Italy, attempting to reveal "what makes the Italian tick." Here you'll learn the lexicon needed to negotiate and understand Italian culture. Of course, food, sex, and the weather—among other things—are heartily embraced in everyday life, but there is also an *amaro* (bitter) side. Hooper illustrates how the power of the *famiglia* (family) and the *chiesa* (church) has produced a society in which *furbizia* (cunning) is rewarded and meritocracy is replaced with *raccomandazioni* (favors) to get ahead in the world.

THE LEOPARD BY GIUSEPPE TOMASI DI LAMPEDUSA

Il gattopardo, an Italian literary classic, chronicles the tumultuous, revolutionary years of the Risorgimento (1860s–early 20th century). Lampedusa was the last in a line of minor princes, and the novel, borne of a lengthy depression, was published in 1958, a year after his death. Set in Sicily, the epic story of decay amid a changing society centers on the ebbing influence and power of Don Fabrizio, Prince of Salina, and his family, and hints at the emergence of the Mafia. One particularly insightful quote in the book—spoken by the prince's young nephew, Tancredi—sheds light on how Italy adapts to shifting political forces and class struggle: "For everything to stay the same, everything must change."

COSA NOSTRA BY JOHN DICKIE

Journalist and academic John Dickie packs a lot of gruesome detail into this fast-paced history of the Mafia. He traces the Cosa Nostra's origins during the Risorgimento years, its infiltration and corruption of the First Republic, and the curious and notorious role of the town of Corleone in its development. Dickie also recounts the organization's birth and rise in America, the Mafia Wars, and the recent crises and tragedies connected to Italy's corrupt political system.

THE CONFORMIST, DIRECTED BY BERNARDO BERTOLUCCI

Il conformista, Bertolucci's stylish psychological thriller set in 1930s Fascist Italy, is considered a postwar cinematic classic. As its name suggests, the 1970 film tackles the issue of conformity through the lens of the cruel, febrile political atmosphere created by Mussolini and his followers. Despite its dark themes, the movie is beautifully lit and shot, filled with vibrant colors, exquisite costuming, and atmospheric locations. It has inspired many directors of the American New Wave and beyond, including Martin Scorsese, Francis Ford Coppola, and the Coen brothers.

DELIZIA! BY JOHN DICKIE

If you think you know all there is to know about Italian food, you'll think again after reading this book. Dickie's gastronomic journey across the regions of Italy through the ages covers everything from *pastasciutta* in 12th-century Palermo to today's Slow Food movement in Turin. Carry this book with you as you travel, so you can compare your menu to, say, that for a 1529 Ferrara banquet, which featured "105 soused sea bream" and "15 large salted eels" for starters, followed by "104 roasted capon livers" and "sweet pastry tarts deep-filled with the spleens of sea bass, trout, pike and other fish." *Che delizia!*

THE GREAT BEAUTY, DIRECTED BY PAOLO SORRENTINO

Although directed by a Neapolitan, this Oscar-winning 2013 film is set in Rome and serves as a kind of contemporary *La Dolce Vita*. The lead character in *La grande bellezza*, Jep Gambardella (Toni Servillo), is an aging hedonistic journalist, who, while pining for his glory days, comes to realize the superficiality of his bourgeois lifestyle. Beset by Roman ennui after his raucous rooftop 65th-birthday bash, Jep goes in search of beauty beyond the vanity of his milieu.

THE NEAPOLITAN NOVELS

Elena Ferrante's novels (2012–15) and the HBO TV series bring multilayered postwar Naples to life, going beyond postcard beauty to portray the grim, savage reality of growing up in a rough *rione* (district). The four books explore the complexities of friendship and Italian society. With vivid depictions—mixing the palatial and the squalid—the pseudonymous author details the lifetime bond and inner lives of Elena and Lila and their interactions with a cast of characters across Italy as well as in Naples.

1992, 1993, AND 1994

The 10-episode television series *1992* and its follow-ups, *1993* and *1994*, (originally aired in 2015, 2017, and 2019, respectively) are political dramas that follow the intertwined lives of six people amid the tumult of early-1990s Italy. Massive cracks appear in the postwar political compromise, with the *Mani Pulite* (Clean Hands) investigation led by prosecutor Antonio Di Pietro initiating the fall of the First Republic. As the country is rocked by the so-called *Tangentopoli* (Bribesville) scandal, marketing man Stefano Accorsi sees an opportunity for an outside figure to seize power. And so up steps media tycoon Silvio Berlusconi and his populist Forza Italia party. Sound familiar?

STANLEY TUCCI: SEARCHING FOR ITALY (2021)

Italian-American actor Stanley Tucci goes on a culinary and cultural adventure around the Italian regions in this CNN TV production. In the first series he visits six regions, their urban centers, and fecund hinterlands. In Naples and the Amalfi Coast he visits a San Marzano tomato farm on the shadows of Vesuvius and discovers the art of mozzarella making. In Rome he samples imaginative *quinto-quarto* offal creations and Roman classics rigatoni *all'amatriciana* and *guanciale*-laden *carbonara*. Trips to Tuscany, Bologna, and Milan yield engaging encounters and mouthfuls of *bistecca alla Fiorentina*, the most sought-after Parmigiana-Reggiano cheese, and a cool hangout for an *aperitivo Milanese*. Tucci rounds off the series meeting young female vintner Arianna Occhipinti in Sicily.

Making the Most of Your Euros

TRANSPORTATION

Italy's state-sponsored train system has been given a run for its money by a private company. Sadly, the competitor (Italo) only operates major, high-speed connections (such as Rome to Naples, Florence to Venice, Milan to Bologna) and not local routes. Because of the competition, Trenitalia and Italo engage in price wars, which only plays to the consumer's advantage; depending on time of day and how far in advance you purchase the tickets, great bargains can be had.

No such good news exists for the *regionali* trains. These are trains connecting cities, highly frequented by commuters and used often by visitors who want to get to less visible towns. These trains are habitually late and almost always crowded. Patience is a virtue, and much needed when taking them, particularly during high season.

FOOD AND DRINK

Always remember, when you enter a bar, that there is almost always a two-tier pricing system: one if you stand, and one if you sit. It's always cheaper to stand, but sometimes sitting is not only necessary, but fun: you can relax and watch the world go by.

Italians love a good sandwich for lunch. Seek out popular sandwich shops (long lines signify that the place is worth visiting) or go to a *salumeria* (delicatessen) and have them make a sandwich for you. It will be simple—cheese and/or cold cuts with bread, no trimmings—but it will be made while you wait, fresh, delicious, and inexpensive.

SIGHTS

There are plenty of free wonderful things to see. Visit the Musei Vaticani, the Uffizi, and the Accademia in Florence (book ahead whenever possible), but don't forget that many artistic gems are found in churches, most of which can be visited with no charge (some of Caravaggio's best work can be found in various churches in Rome). Also, consider renting audio guides if you want direction to any specific place; if you find the idea of joining an organized tour daunting, most museums sell official guidebooks that can help you target what to see. Walking in *centri storici* (historic centers) is also a joy, and free. Seek out piazzas, climb towers, and look for views.

LODGING

High season in Italy runs from Easter to mid-October. If you want to have Florence practically to yourself, come in November or February (most Italian cities are very crowded during the Christmas holidays, which begin around Christmas and finish on January 6). Many hotels in cities offer bargain rates in July and August because most people are off to the beach or the mountains. Remember to factor in great heat and massive crowds, along with the money you'll save. If you decide to travel then, ensure that you have access to a pool and/or air-conditioning.

A great budget-conscious way to travel is via Airbnb (⊕ *www.airbnb.com*). You can sleep on someone's couch, rent a private room in an apartment (sometimes with en suite bathroom), or spread out in an entire apartment or house. One of the best things about Airbnb is that many of these accommodations come with refrigerators and kitchens, which means you don't have to spend all your money eating out.

In general, whatever your lodging choice, book sooner rather than later. You'll often find better deals that way.

Chapter 2

TRAVEL SMART

Updated by
Nick Bruno

★ **CAPITAL:**
Rome

✦ **POPULATION:**
58,983,122

💬 **LANGUAGE:**
Italian

$ **CURRENCY:**
Euro

☎ **COUNTRY CODE:**
39

⚠ **EMERGENCIES:**
112

🚗 **DRIVING:**
On the right

⚡ **ELECTRICITY:**
220v/50 cycles; electrical plugs have two round prongs

🕑 **TIME:**
6 hours ahead of New York

🌐 **WEB RESOURCES:**
www.italia.it
www.beniculturali.it

Know Before You Go

A TALE OF TWO COUNTRIES

Italy as we know it is just over 160 years old, united by Giuseppe Garibaldi in 1861, and traditions and customs die hard. Differences and rivalries between the wealthier north and the more relaxed south abound, but you will need to spend time in both for the full Italian experience.

DRINK YOUR FILL

Bottled water is available everywhere but often at an inflated price. Carry a refillable bottle and fill up for free at the strategically placed water fountains in cities. In restaurants you can ask for tap water (*acqua del rubinetto*), although you may have to insist.

GO FOOTBALL CRAZY

Soccer—*calcio*—is taken very seriously in Italy, with rivalries running deep. A little knowledge of a local team's performance makes for great conversation. Just avoid wearing your Juventus shirt in Naples if you want to make new friends. To get a taste for the football fervor, its songs and excitement, visit the *stadio* of the local *squadra* (team) and join the *tifosi* on the *curve* (in the stands).

BOOK IN ADVANCE

Avoid waiting in line for hours by buying museum tickets online before your visit. Also, the earlier you buy train tickets, the less expensive they're likely to be. Trenitalia and Italo offer substantial first-come, first-served discounts on high-speed services; check

their websites, and prepare to be flexible with your travel times. Discounts aren't offered on regional trains, and neither is seat reservation. Unless bought online, tickets for regional trains must be stamped before boarding.

TAKE THE BACK ROADS

So you've rented a car. Why stick to the highways? Much of Italy's beauty is along winding mountain roads or coastal secondary routes, so take your time and wander a little. Not only will you save on tolls, but you'll save on fuel, too, as gas prices are generally lower than on the *autostrade*. Also, if you're renting a car between November 15 and April 15, remember to ask for snow chains (obligatory on many roads).

EAT FOR (NEARLY) NOTHING

The *aperitivo* is a staple of many areas of the north, where, for little more than the price of a drink, you can partake of a vast buffet to substitute for your evening meal. Bars vie with each other to provide the best array of pasta dishes,

pizzette, and panini , so check out a few of them before sitting down. Look out for signs like "Aperitvo Happy Hour" and "Stuzzichini": there are bite-size snacks like *patatine* (potato chips), olives, and *grissini* (breadsticks) either served with your drink at the table, or else in a buffet-style spread replete with pasta, rice, and other dishes.

PLAN YOUR DAY

Although breakfast (*la colazione*) is generally served from 7 to 10:30, other mealtimes vary by region. In the north, lunch (*il pranzo*) is noon to 2, whereas restaurants in the south often serve it until 3. You may have difficulty finding dinner (*la cena*) in the north after 9 pm, when most southerners are just sitting down to eat (restaurants there tend not to open until 7:30). And shoppers take note: many stores close from 1 to 4:30.

LACE UP YOUR WALKING SHOES

The best—and often the only—way to see a city is on foot. Public transport works well (albeit generally better in the north), and in recent years many city and town centers have been pedestrianized. Parking costs and fines can add up (avoid ZTL or limited traffic zones), so when possible don your most comfortable shoes and prepare to pound the pavement. Fall in with a weekend afternoon *passeggiata* in smaller towns, where Italians stroll the main street dressed in their Sunday best.

DRINK LOCAL

Italy offers a vast array of fine wines, with each region boasting its own appellation. While you may see Chianti on a wine list in Catania, it will probably be no different to what you find at home; for a more authentic taste of the area, try a local Sicilian wine instead.

YOU GET A COFFEE IN A BAR

Coffee culture is different here. Italians take their single-shot espresso standing at a bar—where snacks and alcoholic drinks are also served, and which usually closes in the evening. Pay the cashier, then set your receipt on the counter and place your order. If you choose to sit, there is usually a surcharge, whether there is table service or not. Also, if you order a latte you'll get a glass of milk.

NEVER PASS A RESTROOM

Public restrooms in train stations usually cost €1, and bars frown on the use of theirs without making a purchase, so before you leave the hotel, restaurant, or museum, use the facilities.

DAY-TRIPPER

Lodging in tourist hot spots is at a premium during high season, but deals can be found a little farther from the action. Consider booking outside town and taking a local train or bus to see the sights—you might miss the evening atmosphere, but you'll have more to spend on lunch.

TAKE YOUR TIME

The Italian experience differs from region to region. Try to plan an itinerary that leaves time to explore each destination at leisure. Sure, quick in-and-out visits to cities will allow you to see the major sights, but rushing things means missing out on each area's unique atmosphere.

BE ITALIAN

Food is one of Italy's defining features, and locals continue to be horrified by the idea of pineapple on pizza or (heaven forbid!) ketchup on pasta. You don't need a knife to eat spaghetti (although using a spoon to help wind the pasta around a fork is allowed), and it's fine to pick your pizza up. Most restaurants set a per-person fee for *pane e coperto* (bread and cover charge), although waiters also appreciate a tip—which is standard (around 10%) in the south.

BEWARE OF SCAMS

Larger train stations are notorious for porters insisting on carrying your bags, then charging a fee, so be firm if you're not interested. Also, be careful where you store your wallet and valuables and avoid purchasing from illegal street vendors.

LOOK INTO SIGHT PASSES

Many cities and towns sell multiday passes for access to different museums and sights. These offer great savings if you plan to visit several attractions; some include deals on public transport.

LEARN THE LINGO

Most Italians have some command of English, although this isn't a fail-safe rule, particularly in the south. You can get by on hand gestures and pointing, but a *grazie* or *buongiorno* here and there can't hurt.

SPECIAL SUNDAYS FOR CULTURE

A fabulous Ministero della Cultura initiative, "Domenica al Museo," allows free entry to state-run museums, galleries, and archaeological sites throughout Italy on the first Sunday of the month. For the latest upcoming "Sunday at the Museum" details consult the list of participating institutions at ⊕ *cultura.gov.it/domenicalmuseo* and look out for the hashtag #DomenicaAl-Museo. Naturally, there are lots of crowds and families on these days.

FOOD-SHOP SAVVY

Save money on restaurant and hotel food, and pricey drinks bills, by seeking out stores to stock up. Head to the a *limentari,*the local food and general store to buy groceries, cheese, cold cuts, and essential refreshments for hot days out such as water in bottles. The *supermercato* has a wider selection and may stock interesting housewares and other items that make fab gifts to take home. For picnic supplies the *panificio*or *fornaio* is essential for fresh bakery goods such as *pane* (bread) and *panini* (rolls).

Getting Here and Around

Air

Most nonstop flights between North America and Italy serve Rome's Aeroporto Internazionale Leonardo da Vinci (FCO), better known as Fiumicino, and Milan's Aeroporto Malpensa (MXP), though the airports in Venice, Pisa, and Naples also accommodate nonstop flights from the United States. Flying time to Milan or Rome is approximately 8–8½ hours from New York, 10–11 hours from Chicago, and 11½ hours from Los Angeles.

Alitalia has direct flights from London to Milan and Rome, while British Airways and smaller budget carriers provide services between Great Britain and other locations in Italy. EasyJet connects London's Gatwick and Stansted airports with a dozen or so Italian destinations. Ryanair flies from Stansted to even more airports. Since tickets are frequently sold at discounted prices, investigate the cost of flights within Italy (even one-way) where you're faced with a long, multichange train journey—a potentially time-saving alternative (although less green) way to travel.

You can take the Ferrovie dello Stato Italiane (FS) airport train or bus to Rome's Termini station or to Cadorna or Centrale in Milan; from the latter you can then catch a train to any other location in Italy. It will take about 40 minutes to get from Fiumicino to Roma Termini, less than an hour from Malpensa to Milano Centrale.

A helpful website for information (location, phone numbers, local transportation, etc.) about all of the airports in Italy is ⊕ *www.italianairportguide.co*m.

Bus

Italy's far-reaching regional bus network, often operated by private companies, isn't as attractive an option as in other European countries, partly due to convenient train travel. Schedules are often drawn up with commuters and students in mind and can be sketchy on weekends. But, car travel aside, regional bus companies often provide the only means of getting to out-of-the-way places. Even when this isn't the case, buses can be faster and more direct than local trains, so it's worth taking time to compare bus and train schedules. Busitalia–Sita Nord covers Tuscany, Umbria, Campania, and the Veneto. Sita Sud caters to travelers in Puglia, Basilicata, and Campania. FlixBus offers a low-cost long-distance service.

All buses, even those on long-distance routes, offer a single class of service. Cleanliness and comfort levels are high on private motor coaches, which have plenty of legroom, sizable seats, luggage storage, and usually toilets. Smoking isn't permitted on buses. Private lines usually have a ticket office in town or allow you to pay when you board.

Major Italian cities have inexpensive urban bus service. Although some city buses have ticket machines on board, generally you buy tickets from newsstands or tobacconists and have them validated on board. Buses can get packed during busy travel periods, school commutes, and rush hours.

Car

Italy has an extensive network of *auto-stradas* (toll highways), complemented by equally well-maintained but free *super-stradas* (expressways). You'll need your autostrada ticket from entry to pay the toll when you exit; on some shorter auto-stradas, you pay the toll when you enter. The condition of provincial roads varies, but maintenance is generally good.

Most gas stations have self-service options. Those on autostradas are open 24 hours; others are generally open Monday through Saturday 7–7, with a break at lunchtime. Automobile Club Italiano offers 24-hour road service. To call the police in an emergency, dial 112. Autogrill provides decent highway catering across the country.

PARKING

Curbside spaces are marked by blue lines; pay at a nearby *parcometro* machine, and leave the printed ticket on your dashboard. Fines for violations are high, and towing is common. You often need a permit to enter historic centers with a vehicle—violating this strictly enforced rule can also result in hefty fines. It's best to park in designated (preferably attended) lots; even small towns often have them just outside their historic centers.

RULES OF THE ROAD

You can rent a car with a U.S. driver's license, but Italy also requires non-Europeans to carry an International Driver's Permit (IDP), available for a nominal fee via the AAA website (⊕ *www.aaa.com*). Speed limits are generally 130 kph (80 mph) on autostradas, 90 kph (55 mph) on state roads, and 50 kph (30 mph) in towns; this can drop to 10 kph (6 mph) in congested areas. Exceed the speed limit by more than 60 kph (37 mph), and your license could be confiscated.

Right turns on red lights are forbidden. Headlights must be kept on outside municipalities, and you must wear seat belts. Fines for using mobile phones while driving can exceed €1,000. The blood alcohol limit is 0.05% (stricter than in the United States).

Train

The fastest trains on the Ferrovie dello Stato Italiane (FS), or Italian State Railways, are the *Frecciarossa*. Their privately owned competitor, Nuovo Trasporto Viaggiatori (NTV), or Italo, also runs high-speed service between all major northern cities and as far as Reggio Calabria in the south. Seat reservations are mandatory for these bullet trains, just as they are for the Eurostar and slower Intercity (IC) trains; tickets for the latter are about half the price of those for the faster trains.

You can buy your tickets at machines in the station or on ⊕ *www.trenitalia.com*—consider downloading the Trenitalia app. Reservations are not available on *Regionale* and *Espresso* trains, which are slower, make more stops, and are less expensive. For these trains, you must validate your ticket before boarding by punching it at a wall- or pillar-mounted yellow or green box—if you forget to do this, find a conductor immediately. Fines for attempting to ride a train without a ticket are €200.

TRAIN PASSES

A rail pass can save you money on train travel, but it's good to compare the cost with actual fares to make sure. Generally, the more often you plan to travel long distances on high-speed trains, the more sense a rail pass makes. Keep in mind that even with a rail pass you still need to reserve seats on the trains that require them.

Travel Times
by Train and Ferry

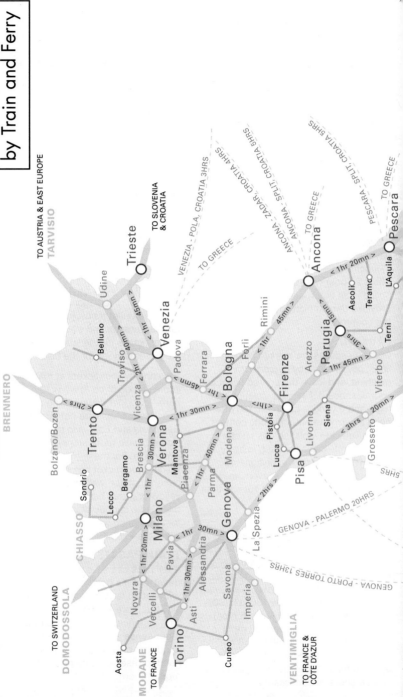

TO AUSTRIA & EAST EUROPE
TARVISIO

TO SLOVENIA
& CROATIA

TO AUSTRIA & GERMANY
BRENNERO

TO SWITZERLAND
DOMODOSSOLA

MODANE
TO FRANCE

VENTIMIGLIA
TO FRANCE &
CÔTE D'AZUR

CHIASSO

Aosta
Torino
Cuneo
Asti
Alessandria
Novara
Vercelli
Pavia
Milano
Lecco
Bergamo
Sondrio
Bolzano/Bozen
Trento
Brescia
Verona
Mantova
Piacenza
Parma
Modena
Bologna
Ferrara
Padova
Vicenza
Treviso
Belluno
Udine
Venezia
Trieste
Genova
Savona
Imperia
La Spezia
Lucca
Pistoia
Pisa
Livorno
Firenze
Arezzo
Siena
Grosseto
Viterbo
Terni
Perugia
Ascoli
Teramo
L'Aquila
Ancona
Pescara
Forlì
Rimini

< 1hr 20mn >
< 1hr 30mn >
< 1hr
< 30mn >
< 1hr
< 1hr 40mn >
< 1hr 30mn >
< 2hrs >
< 2hr
40mn >
< 1hr 45mn >
< 1hr
< 1hr
< 45mn
< 1hr
< 1hr 45mn >
15mn
45mn >
< 1hr 20mn >
3hrs
< 3hrs >
20mn >

VENEZIA - POLA, CROATIA 3HRS
TO GREECE
ANCONA - ZADAR, CROATIA 4HRS
ANCONA - SPLIT, CROATIA 6HRS
TO GREECE
PESCARA - SPLIT, CROATIA 5HRS
TO GREECE
GENOVA - PALERMO 20HRS
GENOVA - PORTO TORRES 13HRS
5HRS
10 HRS

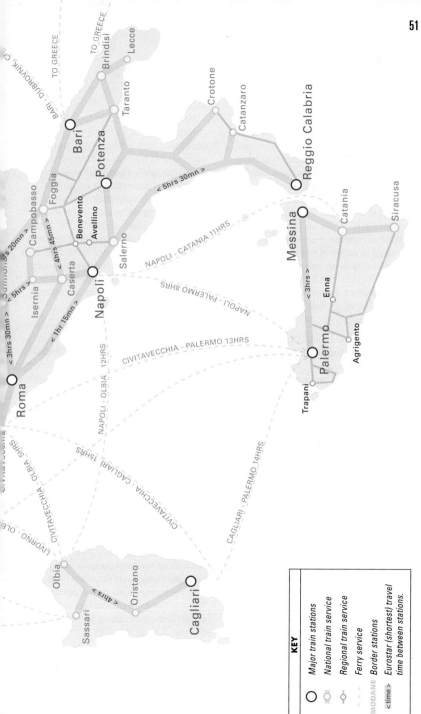

KEY

◯ Major train stations

National train service

Regional train service

- - - Ferry service

MODANE Border stations

<time> Eurostar (shortest) travel
time between stations.

Essentials

Hotels

Many Italian lodgings, some quite luxurious, are in palazzi, villas, monasteries, and smaller historic buildings that have been restored to blend modern comforts with original atmosphere. Another option is renting a vacation property—although, in addition to budget, you should keep in mind location (street noise and neighborhood ambience in cities and towns, degree of isolation in the countryside), the availability of an elevator or the number of stairs, the utility costs, and what's supplied (furnishings, including pots and linens, as well as sundries like dish detergent).

If you're intrigued by the "locavore" movement, ask local tourism offices about *agriturismo* accommodations. Rural farm-stay properties range from luxury villas to farmhouses with basic facilities.

The lodgings we list are the cream of the crop in each price category. Properties are assigned price categories based on the rate for two people sharing a standard double room in high season, including tax and service.

Restaurants

Italian cuisine is still largely regional, so try spaghetti *alla carbonara* (with cured pork jowl and egg yoke) in Rome, pizza in Naples, *cinghiale* (wild boar) in Tuscany, or *tartufi* (truffles) in Piedmont. Nowadays, vegetarian and gluten-free options are widely available. Still, if you have dietary restrictions, ask about ingredients; not everything is listed in menu descriptions.

The restaurants we list are the finest in each price category. Unless otherwise noted, they're open for lunch and dinner, closing one or two days a week.

MEALS

Although the distinction has blurred, *ristoranti* tend to be more elegant and expensive than trattorias or *osterie*, which serve traditional, home-style fare. Meals generally consist of an *antipasto* (starter) followed by a *primo* (first course), a *secondo* (main course) or *contorno* (vegetable side dish), and *dolce* (dessert). You can, of course, eat less (perhaps just a primo or secondo and a dolce). Single dishes are more the norm at an enoteca or pizzeria, and you can grab affordable snacks at bars, cafés, and spots for pizza *al taglio* (by the slice).

WINES, BEER, AND SPIRITS

The grape has been cultivated here since the time of the Etruscans, with Tuscany, Piedmont, the Veneto, Puglia, Calabria, Sicily, Le Marche, and Umbria among the renowned areas. Beer is readily available, and Italy has some excellent microbreweries, so ask about local brews. In addition, Italians are imaginative with their cocktails, so consider trying the *aperitivo della casa* (house aperitif). The minimum drinking age in Italy is 16.

Health/Safety
EMERGENCIES

No matter where you are in Italy, dial 112 for all emergencies. Key words to remember for emergency situations are *aiuto* for "help" (pronounced "aye- you-toh") and *pronto soccorso,* which means "first aid." When confronted with a health emergency, head straight for the Pronto Soccorso department of the nearest hospital or dial 118. To call a Red Cross *ambulanza* (ambulance), dial 800/065510. If you just need a doctor, ask for *un medico.* Ask the physician for *una fattura* (an invoice) to present to your insurance company for reimbursement.

HEALTH

Smoking is banned inside all public places, so sit indoors (where there's also often air-conditioning) if the smoke in outdoor seating areas bothers you.

It's always best to travel with your own trusted medications. Should you need prescription medication while in Italy, speak with a physician to ensure it's the proper kind. Aspirin (*l'aspirina*) can be purchased at any pharmacy, as can over-the-counter medicines, such as ibuprofen or acetaminophen.

COVID-19

COVID-19 brought travel to a virtual standstill for most of 2020 and into 2021, but vaccinations have made travel possible and more safe. However, each destination (and each business within that destination) may have its own requirements and regulations. Travelers may expect to continue to wear an FFP2 mask in some places and obey any other rules (and unvaccinated travelers may face certain restrictions). Given how abruptly travel was curtailed at the onset of the pandemic, it is wise to consider protecting yourself by purchasing a travel insurance policy that will reimburse you for cancellation costs related to COVID-19. Not all travel insurance policies protect against pandemic-related cancellations, so always read the fine print.

$ Money

Of Italy's major cities—where, as in other countries, prices are higher than in the countryside—Milan is by far the most expensive. Resort areas like Capri, Portofino, and Cortina d'Ampezzo cater to wealthy vacationers and also charge top prices. Good value can be found in the scenic Trentino–Alto Adige region of the Dolomites and in Umbria and Le Marche. With a few exceptions, southern Italy and Sicily also offer bargains for those who do their homework before they leave home.

Item	Average Cost
Cup of Coffee	€1–€1.50
Soft Drink (glass/can/bottle)	€1.70–€3
Glass of Beer	€3–€6
Sandwich	€3–€5.50
2-km (1-mile) Taxi Ride in Rome	€9

$ Tipping

In restaurants a service charge of 10%–15% may appear on your check, but it's not a given that your server will receive this; consider leaving a tip of 5%–10% (in cash) for good service. At a hotel bar, tip €1 and up for a round or two of drinks. In the south when taking your morning caffè it's customary to place some eurocents with the *scontrino* (receipt) on the counter, then tell the *barista*your order. Taxi drivers also appreciate a euro or two, particularly if they help with luggage.

In hotels, give the *portiere* (concierge) about 10% of the bill for services or €3–€5 for help with dinner reservations and such. In moderately priced hotels, leave chambermaids about €1 per day, and tip a minimum of €1 for valet or room service. In expensive hotels, double these amounts. Sightseeing guides should receive €1.50 at least per person for a half-day group tour, more if the tour is longer and/or they're especially knowledgeable.

Essentials

🌐 Passports

A U.S. passport is relatively simple to obtain and is valid for 10 years. You must apply in person if you're getting a passport for the first time; if your previous passport was lost, stolen, or damaged; or if it has expired and was issued more than 15 years ago or when you were under 16. The cost of a new passport is $165 for adults, $135 for children under 16; renewals are $130. Allow four to six weeks for processing.

▨ TIP → **Before your trip, make two copies of your passport's data page (one for someone at home and another for you to carry separately). Alternatively, scan the page and email it to someone at home and/ or yourself.**

🪪 Visa

When staying for 90 days or less, U.S. citizens aren't required to obtain a visa prior to traveling to Italy. A recent law requires that you fill in a declaration of presence within eight business days of your arrival—the stamp from passport control at the airport substitutes for this. If you plan to travel or live in Italy or the European Union for longer than 90 days, you must acquire a valid visa from the Italian consulate serving your state *before you leave the United States.* The process of obtaining a visa will take at least 30 days, and the Italian government doesn't accept applications submitted by visa expediters.

🖥 U.S. Embassy/Consulate

In addition to the embassy in Rome, the United States has consulates general in Florence, Milan, and Naples. (Note: you aren't allowed to bring laptops into any of these facilities.) If you're arrested or detained, ask Italian officials to notify the embassy or nearest consulate immediately. Consider participating in the U.S. Department of State's Smart Traveler Enrollment Program (STEP) (⊕ *step.state. gov/step*) to receive alerts and make it easier to locate you in an emergency.

📅 When to Go

High Season: June through September is expensive and busy. In August, most Italians take their own summer holidays; cities are less crowded, but many shops and restaurants close. July and August can be uncomfortably hot.

Low Season: Unless you're skiing, winter offers the least appealing weather, although it's the best time for airfare and hotel deals and to escape the crowds. Temperatures in the south can be mild.

Value Season: By late September, temperate weather, saner airfares, and more cultural events can make for a happier trip. October is also great, but November is often rainy. March and early April weather is changeable. From late April to early May, the masses have not yet arrived.

Contacts

Air

**AIRLINE SECURITY
ISSUES** Transportation
Security Administration.
(*TSA*). ☎ *866/289–9673*
⊕ *www.tsa.gov.*

AIRPORT INFORMATION
Aeroporto di Bologna.
(*BLQ, aka Guglielmo
Marconi*). ☎ *051/6479615*
⊕ *www.bologna-airport.
it.* **Aeroporto di Cagliari.**
(*CAG, aka Elmas*). ⊠ *Via
dei Trasvolatori, Elmas,*
☎ *070/211211* ⊕ *www.
sogaer.it.* **Aeroporto di
Catania.** (*CTA, aka Fontanarossa*). ☎ *095/7239111*
⊕ *www.aeroporto.catania.
it.* **Aeroporto di Firenze.** (*FLR, aka Amerigo
Vespucci or Peretola*).
☎ *055/3061830* ⊕ *www.
aeroporto.firenze.it.* **Aeroporto di Milan Linate.** (*LIN*).
☎ *02/232323* ⊕ *www.
milanolinate-airport.com.*
Aeroporto di Palermo.
(*PMO, aka Falcone e
Borsellino or Punta Raisi*).
☎ *091/7020273* ⊕ *www.
aeroportodipalermo.it.* **Aeroporto di Pisa.** (*PSA, aka
Aeroporto Galileo Galilei*).
⊠ ☎ *050/849111* ⊕ *www.
pisa-airport.com.* **Aeroporto
di Roma Ciampino.** (*CIA*).
⊠ ☎ *06/65951* ⊕ *www.*

*adr.it/web/aeroporti-di-ro-
ma-en/pax-cia-ciampino.*
Aeroporto di Venezia.
(*VCE, aka Marco Polo*).
☎ *041/2609260* ⊕ *www.
veneziaairport.it.* **Aeroporto
di Roma Fiumicino.** (*FCO,
aka Leonardo da Vinci*).
☎ *06/65951* ⊕ *www.adr.
it.* **Aeroporto Internazionale
di Napoli.** (*NAP, aka Capodichino*). ☎ *081/7896111
8–4* ⊕ *www.aeroporto-
dinapoli.it.* **Aeroporto di
Milano Malpensa.** (*MXP*).
⊠ ☎ *02/232323* ⊕ *www.
milanomalpensa-airport.
com.* **Aeroporto Orio al Serio
- Milan Bergamo (BGY).**
⊠ *Via Orio al Serio 49/51*
☎ *035/326323* ⊕ *www.
milanbergamoairport.it.*

Bus

ANM. ⊠ *Via G. Marino 1,*
☎ *800/639525 toll-free in
Italy* ⊕ *www.anm.it.* **ATAC.**
☎ *06/0606* ⊕ *www.atac.
roma.it.* **Autolinee Toscane.**
⊠ *Via Santa Caterina da
Siena 17,* ☎ *800/142424*
⊕ *www.at-bus.it.* **ATM.**
☎ *02/48607607* ⊕ *www.
atm.it.* **Busitalia-Sita Nord.**
⊠ *Viale dei Cadorna,
105,* ☎ *80075/373760
toll-free* ⊕ *www.*

fsbusitalia.it. **Dolomiti
Bus.** ⊠ *Via Col da Ren 14,*
☎ *0437/217111* ⊕ *www.
dolomitibus.it.* **Marino Bus.**
☎ *080/3112335* ⊕ *www.
marinobus.it.* **Sita Sud.**
⊠ *Via S. Francesco d'As-
sisi 1,* ☎ *080/5790900*
⊕ *www.sitasudtrasporti.it.*
ACTV. ⊠ *Venice* ☎ *041/041
call center* ⊕ *actv.avmspa.
it.*

Train

TRAIN INFORMATION
NTV Italo. ☎ *892020
Call Center* ⊕ *www.
italotreno.it.* **FS-Trenitalia.**
☎ *06/68475475 from
outside Italy (English),
892021 in Italy* ⊕ *www.
trenitalia.com.*

CONTACTS Eurail. ⊕ *www.
eurail.com.* **RailPass.**
☎ *877/3757245 toll-
free from U.S.* ⊕ *www.
railpass.com.* **Italia Rail.**
☎ *877/375–7245 in U.S.,
06/97632451 in Italy*
⊕ *www.italiarail.com.* **Rail
Europe.** ⊕ *www.raileurope.
com.*

Helpful Italian Phrases

BASICS

Yes/no	Sí/No	see/no
Please	Per favore	pear fa-**vo**-ray
Thank you	Grazie	**grah**-tsee-ay
You're welcome	Prego	**pray**-go
I'm sorry (apology)	Mi dispiace	mee dis-pee-**atch**-ay
Excuse me, sorry	Scusi	**skoo**-zee
Good morning/ afternoon	Buongiorno	bwohn-**jor**-no
Good evening	Buona sera	**bwoh**-na **say**-ra
Good-bye	Arrivederci	a-ree-vah-**dare**-chee
Mr. (Sir)	Signore	see-**nyo**-ray
Mrs. (Ma'am)	Signora	see-**nyo**-ra
Miss	Signorina	see-nyo-**ree**-na
Pleased to meet you	Piacere	pee-ah-**chair**-ray
How are you?	Come sta?	**ko**-may-**stah**
Hello (phone)	Pronto?	**proan**-to

NUMBERS

one-half	mezzo	**mets**-zoh
one	uno	**oo**-no
two	due	**doo**-ay
three	tre	Tray
four	quattro	**kwah**-tro
five	cinque	**cheen**-kway
six	sei	Say
seven	sette	**set**-ay
eight	otto	**oh**-to
nine	nove	**no**-vay
ten	dieci	dee-**eh**-chee
eleven	undici	**oon**-dee-chee
twelve	dodici	**doh**-dee-chee
thirteen	tredici	**trey**-dee-chee
fourteen	quattordici	kwah-**tor**-dee-chee
fifteen	quindici	**kwin**-dee-chee
sixteen	sedici	**say**-dee-chee
seventeen	dicissette	dee-chah-**set**-ay
eighteen	diciotto	dee-chee-**oh**-to
nineteen	diciannove	dee-chee-ahn-**no**-vay
twenty	venti	**vain**-tee
twenty-one	ventuno	**vent**-oo-no
thirty	trenta	**train**-ta
forty	quaranta	kwa-**rahn**-ta
fifty	cinquanta	cheen-**kwahn**-ta
sixty	sessanta	seh-**sahn**-ta
seventy	settanta	seh-**tahn**-ta
eighty	ottanta	o-**tahn**-ta
ninety	novanta	no-**vahn**-ta
one hundred	cento	**chen**-to
one thousand	mille	**mee**-lay
one million	un milione	oon **mill**-oo-nay

COLORS

black	Nero	**nair**-ro
blue	Blu	bloo
brown	Marrone	ma-**rohn**-nay
green	Verde	**ver**-day
orange	Arancione	ah-rahn-**cho**-nay
red	Rosso	**rose**-so
white	Bianco	bee-**ahn**-koh
yellow	Giallo	**jaw**-low

DAYS OF THE WEEK

Sunday	Domenica	do-**meh**-nee-ka
Monday	Lunedi	loo-ne-**dee**
Tuesday	Martedi	mar-te-**dee**
Wednesday	Mercoledi	**mer**-ko-le-**dee**
Thursday	Giovedi	jo-ve-**dee**
Friday	Venerdì	ve-ner-**dee**
Saturday	Sabato	**sa**-ba-toh

MONTHS

January	Gennaio	jen-**ay**-o
February	Febbraio	feb-**rah**-yo
March	Marzo	**mart**-so
April	Aprile	a-**pril**-ay
May	Maggio	**mahd**-joe
June	Giugno	**joon**-yo
July	Luglio	**lool**-yo
August	Agosto	a-**gus**-to
September	Settembre	se-**tem**-bre
October	Ottobre	o-**toh**-bre
November	Novembre	no-**vem**-bre
December	Dicembre	di-**chem**-bre

USEFUL WORDS AND PHRASES

Do you speak English?	Parla Inglese?	**par**-la een-**glay**-zay
I don't speak Italian	Non parlo italiano	non **par**-lo ee-tal-**yah**-no
I don't understand	Non capisco	non ka-**peess**-ko
I don't know	Non lo so	non lo **so**
I understand	Capisco	ka-**peess**-ko
I'm American	Sono Americano(a)	**so**-no a-may-ree-**kah**-no(a)
I'm British	Sono inglese	so-no een-**glay**-zay
What's your name?	Come si chiama?	**ko**-may see kee-**ah**-ma
My name is ...	Mi chiamo...	mee kee-**ah**-mo
What time is it?	Che ore sono?	kay **o**-ray **so**-no
How?	Come?	**ko**-may
When?	Quando?	**kwan**-doe
Yesterday/today/ tomorrow	Ieri/oggi/domani	**yer**-ee/ **o**-jee/ do-**mah**-nee

This morning	Stamattina/Oggi	sta-ma-**tee**-na/ o-jee
Afternoon	Pomeriggio	po-mer-**ee**-jo
Tonight	Stasera	sta-**ser**-a
What?	Che cosa?	kay **ko**-za
What is it?	Che cos'è?	kay ko-**zey**
Why?	Perchè?	pear-**kay**
Who?	Chi?	**Kee**
Where is ...	Dov'è...	doe-**veh**
the train station?	la stazione?	la sta-tsee-**oh**-nay
the subway?	la metropolitana?	may-tro-po-lee-**tah**-na
the bus stop?	la fermata dell'autobus?	la fer-**mah**-ta del-ow-tor-**booss**
the airport	l'aeroporto	la-er-roh-**por**-toh
the post office?	l'ufficio postale	loo-**fee**-cho po-**stah**-lay
the bank?	la banca?	la **bahn**-ka
the hotel?	l'hotel...?	lo-**tel**
the museum?	Il museo	eel moo-**zay**-o
the hospital?	l'ospedale?	lo-spay-**dah**-lay
the elevator?	l'ascensore	la-shen-**so**-ray
the restrooms?	...il bagno	eel **bahn**-yo
Here/there	Qui/là	kwee/la
Left/right	A sinistra/a destra	a see-**neess**-tra/a **des**-tra
Is it near/far?	È vicino/lontano?	ay vee-**chee**-no/ lon-**tah**-no
I'd like ...	Vorrei...	vo-**ray**
a room	una camera	**oo**-na **kah**-may-ra
the key	la chiave	la kee-**ah**-vay
a newspaper	un giornale	oon jore-**nah**-vay
a stamp	un francobollo	oon frahn-ko-**bo**-lo
I'd like to buy ...	Vorrei comprare...	vo-**ray** kom-**prah**-ray
a city map	una mappa della città	**oo**-na **mah**-pa **day**-la chee-**tah**
a road map	una carta stradale	**oo**-na **car**-tah stra-**dahl**-lay
a magazine	una revista	**oo**-na ray-**vees**-tah
envelopes	buste	**boos**-tay
writing paper	carta de lettera	**car**-tah dah **leyt**-ter-rah
a postcard	una cartolina	**oo**-na car-tog-**leen**-ah
a ticket	un biglietto	oon bee-**yet**-toh
How much is it?	Quanto costa?	**kwahn**-toe **coast**-a
It's expensive/ cheap	È caro/ economico	ay **car**-o/ ay-ko-**no**-mee-ko
A little/a lot	Poco/tanto	**po**-ko/**tahn**-to
More/less	Più/meno	pee-**oo**/**may**-no

Enough/too (much)	Abbastanza/ troppo	a-bas-**tahn**-sa/tro-po
I am sick	Sto male	sto **mah**-lay
Call a doctor	Chiama un dottore	kee-**ah**-mah-oondoe-**toe**-ray
Help!	Aiuto!	a-**yoo**-to
Stop!	Alt!	ahlt

DINING OUT

A bottle of ...	Una bottiglia di...	**oo**-na bo-**tee**-lee-ah dee
A cup of ...	Una tazza di...	**oo**-na **tah**-tsa dee
A glass of ...	Un bicchiere di...	oon bee-key-**air**-ay dee
Beer	La birra	la **beer**-rah
Bill/check	Il conto	eel **cone**-toe
Bread	Il pane	eel **pah**-nay
Breakfast	La prima colazione	la **pree**-ma ko-la-**tsee**-oh-nay
Butter	Il burro	eel **boor**-roh
Cocktail/aperitif	L'aperitivo	la-pay-ree-**tee**-vo
Dinner	La cena	la **chen**-a
Fixed-price menu	Menù a prezzo fisso	may-**noo** a **pret**-so **fee**-so
Fork	La forchetta	la for-**ket**-a
I am vegetarian	Sono vegetariano(a)	**so**-no vay-jay-ta-ree-**ah**-no/a
I cannot eat ...	Non posso mangiare	non **pose**-so mahn-gee-**are**-ay
I'd like to order	Vorrei ordinare	vo-**ray** or-dee-**nah**-ray
Is service included?	Il servizio è incluso?	eel ser-**vee**-tzee-o ay een-**kloo**-zo
I'm hungry/ thirsty	Ho fame/sede	oh **fah**-meh/**sehd**-ed
It's good/bad	È buono/cattivo	ay **bwo**-bo/ka-**tee**-vo
It's hot/cold	È caldo/freddo	ay **kahl**-doe/**fred**-o
Knife	Il coltello	eel kol-**tel**-o
Lunch	Il pranzo	eel **prahnt**-so
Menu	Il menu	eel may-**noo**
Napkin	Il tovagliolo	eel toe-va-lee-**oh**-lo
Pepper	Il pepe	eel **pep**-peh
Plate	Il piatto	eel pee-**aht**-toe
Please give me ...	Mi dia...	mee **dee**-a
Salt	Il sale	eel **sah**-lay
Spoon	Il cucchiaio	eel koo-kee-ah-yo
Tea	tè	tay
Water	acqua	**awk**-wah
Wine	vino	**vee**-noh

Great Itineraries

Northern Italy

Northern Italy is a region with high fashion, big wines, and beautiful lakes.

DAY 1: MILAN

Start off in **Milan,** Italy's capital of art, fashion, and design. Explore elegant shops around the **Duomo** and **Via Montenapoleone.** Some of Europe's great art treasures are housed in the **Brera Gallery.** The elegant **Basilica di Santa Maria presso San Satiro** is about a 20-minute walk from **Santa Maria delle Grazie,** where Leonardo's stunning *Last Supper* is housed. Spend a night at the opera in **La Scala,** Italy's most illustrious opera house.

Logistics: Central Milan is compact, with excellent public transportation.

DAY 2: BELLAGIO

Lake Como combines some of Italy's most beautiful scenery with elegant historic villas and gardens, making it truly worthy of a full-day excursion. **Bellagio** is a pretty village from which you can ferry to other points along the lake, take walking tours, hike, or just sit on a terrace watching the light play on the sapphire water and the snowcapped mountains.

Logistics: Como's San Giovanni station is just one hour by train from Milan, and Bus C10 leaves hourly from here for the 70-minute lakeside journey to Bellagio. In Bellagio you won't need a car, since most of your touring will be on foot, by ferry, or by bus.

DAYS 3 TO 5: VERONA/ MANTUA/VICENZA

Take an early train to **Verona** (90 minutes from Milan) and settle into your hotel. Start your exploration of northern Italy's three most important art cities with Verona's ancient Roman arena, theater, and city gates; its brooding medieval palaces

and castle; and its graceful bridge spanning the Adige.

The next day, make the 30- to 45-minute train trip to **Mantua,** arriving in time for lunch featuring a local specialty: *tortelli di zucca* (pumpkin-filled ravioli) served with sage butter and Parmesan cheese. Check out the Mantegna frescoes in the **Palazzo Ducale,** or visit Giulio Romano's **Palazzo Te,** a 16th-century pleasure palace. Take the train back to Verona in time for dinner and, perhaps, an opera in the Roman amphitheater.

On Day 3, head to **Vicenza** (30 minutes by train) to see the palaces, villas, and public buildings of the lion of late-16th-century architecture, Andrea Palladio. Don't miss his **Teatro Olimpico** and his famous villa, **La Rotonda,** slightly out of town. If time allows, try to see the frescoes by Gianbattista and Giandomenico Tiepolo in the **Villa Valmarana ai Nani,** near La Rotonda. For lunch, try *baccalà alla vicentina,* the local salt-cod dish.

DAY 6: PADUA

Most people visit this important art and university center on a day trip out of Venice, but then they miss one of **Padua** 's main attractions: the nightlife that goes on in the city's wine bars and cafés from evening until quite late. See the Giotto frescoes in the **Cappella degli Scrovegni** and the **Basilica di Sant'Antonio** before lunch, then spend a relaxing afternoon at the **Villa Pisani,** enjoying its gardens and important Tiepolo fresco.

Logistics: Trains run frequently to Padua from Verona (1 hour) and Vicenza (30 minutes); you don't really have to schedule ahead.

DAY 7: VENICE

The first things you'll probably want to do in **Venice** are to take a vaporetto ride down the **Grand Canal** and see **Piazza San Marco.** After that, move on to the

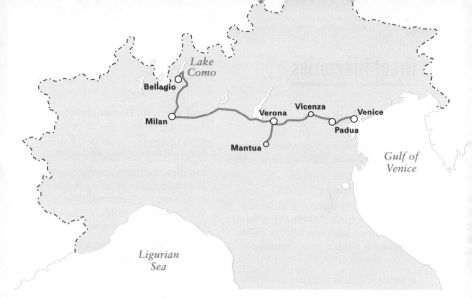

adjacent **Palazzo Ducale** and Sansovino's **Biblioteca Marciana,** across the piazzetta.

For lunch, take Vaporetto No. 1 to Ca' Rezzonico, and have a sandwich and a *spritz* in **Campo Santa Margherita.** From here, make your way to the **Galleria dell'Accademia** and spend a few hours taking in its wonderful collection of Venetian paintings. In the evening, walk up the Zattere and have a drink at one of the cafés overlooking the **Canale della Giudecca.**

Logistics: Seeing the Grand Canal and Piazza San Marco in relative tranquillity will be your reward for getting up at the crack of dawn (arrive at the vaporetto before 8:30 to avoid the rush) and doing a little extra planning.

DAY 8: VENICE
If the Galleria dell'Accademia has whetted your appetite for Venetian painting, start the day by visiting churches and institutions where you can see more. If your taste runs to modern art, head to the **Peggy Guggenheim Collection** and, down the street, the Pinault Collection in the refashioned **Punta della Dogana.**

In the afternoon, head for the Fondamenta Nuova station to catch a vaporetto to the outer islands: **Murano,** where you can shop for Venetian glass and visit a glass museum and workshops; **Burano,** known for lace making and colorful houses; and **Torcello,** Venice's first inhabited island and home to a beautiful cathedral.

DAY 9: VENICE
Pay a visit to the **Rialto,** one of Europe's largest and most varied fish markets, where Venetians also buy their fruit and vegetables as well as, of course, their fish. Note that the Rialto Market is closed on Sunday and Monday; since there is no fishing on Sunday, there can be no fresh fish available on Monday.

Have lunch in one of the excellent market-area restaurants. Then, on your last afternoon in Venice, leave time to sit with a coffee or spritz in a lively square or in a café along the **Fondamenta della Misericordia** in Cannaregio. Alternatively, visit Tullio Lombardo's lyrical **Miracoli,** a short walk from the San Marco end of the Rialto Bridge, or Palladio's masterpiece, the **Redentore** church on **Giudecca.**

DAY 10: VENICE/DEPARTURE
Take one last vaporetto trip up the Grand Canal to **Piazzale Roma** and, after saying good-bye to Venice, catch Bus No. 5 or an ATVO (private line) bus to the airport.

Great Itineraries

Central Italy

Visit central Italy for the great art, sumptuous countryside, and outstanding food and wine.

DAY 1: FLORENCE

If you're coming in on an international flight, you'll probably settle in Florence in time for an afternoon stroll or siesta (depending on your jet-lag strategy) before dinner.

Logistics: Begin anticipating the first dinner of your trip. Look for a place near your hotel, and when you arrive, reserve a table (or have your concierge do it for you). Making a meal the focus of your first day is a great way to ease into Italian life.

DAY 2: FLORENCE

Begin at the **Uffizi Gallery,** whose extensive collection will occupy much of your morning. Next, take in the neighboring **Piazza della Signoria,** then head a few blocks north to the **Duomo** to check out Ghiberti's famous bronze doors on the **Battistero** (actually high-quality copies; the originals are in the **Museo dell'Opera del Duomo**). Climb up Brunelleschi's cathedral dome to the cupola. Spend the afternoon wandering Florence's medieval streets; or head out to **Fiesole** to see the ancient amphitheater.

Logistics: It's a good idea to reserve Uffizi tickets online ahead of your visit; climbs up Brunelleschi's dome must be reserved in advance.

DAY 3: FLORENCE

Spend your morning seeing Michelangelo's *David* at the **Galleria dell'Accademia,** the **Medici Chapels,** the **Palazzo Pitti** and **Boboli Gardens,** and the churches of **Santa Maria Novella** and **Santa Croce.** If it's a clear day, spend the afternoon making

your way up to **Piazzale Michelangelo** for sweeping views of the idyllic Florentine countryside. Recharge with a dinner featuring *bistecca alla fiorentina.*

Logistics: You can reach Piazzale Michelangelo by taxi or by taking Bus No. 12 or 13 from the Lungarno. Otherwise, do your best to get around on foot; Florence is a brilliant city for walking.

DAY 4: SAN GIMIGNANO

After breakfast, pick up your car and make the lazy drive from Florence to **San Gimignano.** Upon arriving in town, you'll no doubt be awed by its towers—medieval skyscrapers that provided security and served as symbols of wealth and power. After finding your way to a hotel in the old town, set out on foot to check out the city's turrets and alleyways, then enjoy a leisurely dinner.

Logistics: San Gimignano is only 57 km (35 miles) to the southwest. Consider taking a detour on the SS222 (Strada Chiantigiana) to a winery in one of the Chianti wine towns.

DAY 5: SIENA

In the morning, set out for nearby **Siena,** which is known worldwide for its Palio, a horse race involving the city's 17 *contrade* (medieval neighborhoods). You will be blown away by the precious medieval streets and memorable fan-shape **Piazza del Campo.** Don't miss the spectacular **Duomo,** the **Battistero,** and the **Spedale di Santa Maria della Scala,** an old hospital and hostel that now contains an underground archaeological museum.

Logistics: Parking can be a challenge. Look for the stadio (soccer stadium), where there's a parking lot that often has space.

Adriatic Sea

Ligurian
Sea

Florence
San Gimignano
Arezzo
Cortona
Siena
Assisi
Spoleto

Elba

CORSICA
(FRANCE)

Rome

DAY 6: AREZZO/CORTONA

From Siena you'll first head to **Arezzo,** home to the **Basilica di San Francesco,** which contains important frescoes by Piero della Francesca. Check out the **Piazza Grande** along with its beautiful Romanesque church of **Santa Maria della Pieve.** Try to do all of this before lunch, after which you'll head straight to **Cortona.** Cortona is a town for walking and relaxing, not sightseeing, so enjoy yourself as you wander through the **Piazza della Repubblica** and **Piazza Signorelli,** perhaps doing a bit of shopping.

Logistics: Siena to Arezzo is 70 km (43½ miles) on the SS715 and A1 autostrada. From Arezzo to Cortona, it's just 30 km (18 miles)—take SR71.

DAY 7: ASSISI

Cross over into Umbria and see **Assisi,** the home of St. Francis that today hosts many religious pilgrims. After arrival and check-in, head straight for the **Basilica di San Francesco,** which displays the tomb of St. Francis and some unbelievable frescoes. From here, take Via San Francesco to **Piazza del Comune** and see the **Tempio di Minerva.** Break for lunch and then see **San Rufino,** the cathedral, before returning through the piazza to Corso Mazzini and **Santa Chiara.**

Logistics: From Cortona, take the SR71 to the A1 autostrada toward Perugia. After about 40 km (24 miles), take the Assisi exit (E45), and it's another 14 km (8 miles) to Assisi.

DAY 8: SPOLETO

This morning takes you to the walled city of **Spoleto,** renowned for its summer arts festival; its wonderful **Duomo;** its impressive **La Rocca** fortress; and its marvelous **Ponte delle Torri,** the 14th-century bridge that separates the town from Monteluco. Save your appetite for a serious last dinner in Italy. Try to sample black truffles, a proud product of the region, especially from mid-November to mid-March.

Logistics: The trip from Assisi to Spoleto is a pretty 47-km (29-mile) drive (SS75 to SS3) that should take less than an hour.

DAY 9: SPOLETO/DEPARTURE

It's a fair distance from Spoleto to the Florence airport, your point of departure. One alternative is to fly out of the tiny airport in Perugia. If you prefer to drive, get an early start and allow at least 2½ hours for the trip along the A1 autostrada.

Great Itineraries

Southern Italy

Come for the archaeological wonders, azure sea, and excellent Neapolitan fare.

DAY 1: NAPLES

Fly into Naples's **Aeroporto Capodichino,** a scant 5 km (3 miles) from the city. Naples is classic Italy, and many visitors end up falling in love with its alluring palazzi and spectacular pizza. If you can get over the shock of the initial cacophony and its sketchy reputation, you'll likely get hooked on its lively characters and irresistibly languid, stop-start rhythm.

Recharge with a nap and, after that, a good caffè—Naples has some of the world's best. You should be back on your feet in time for an evening stroll down the city's bustling shopping street, Via Toledo, to Piazza Plebiscito, before dinner and bed.

DAY 2: NAPLES

Start the day at the **Museo Archeologico Nazionale,** budgeting at least two hours for its collection, before stopping for coffee at a café in Piazza Bellini. From here, head down Via dei Tribunali, crossing Via Duomo to see Caravaggio's *The Seven Works of Mercy* at **Pio Monte della Misericordia.** Make your way back along Spaccanapoli with a brief stop at the **Cappella Sansevero** for a look at the pinnacle of Masonic sculpture. Continue on to the port and the **Castel Nuovo** and then past the **Teatro San Carlo** to the enormous **Palazzo Reale** in **Piazza Plebiscito.** Just beyond this is the **Santa Lucia** waterfront area, with the **Castel dell'Ovo.** Join the passeggiata along *lungomare* by the sea here as far as Mergellina, soaking up the atmosphere, spectacular views, and perhaps grab an aperitivo or gelato. Return to your hotel for a short rest before dinner and perhaps a night out at one of Naples's lively bars or clubs.

Logistics: This entire day is easily done on foot.

DAY 3: POMPEII/SORRENTO

After breakfast, pack your luggage, and head from Naples to **Pompeii,** one of Europe's true archaeological gems. If it's summer, be prepared for sweltering heat as you make your way through the incredible preserved ruins of a city that was devastated by the whims of **Mt. Vesuvius** nearly 2,000 years ago. You'll see the houses of noblemen and merchants, brothels, political graffiti, and more. **Sorrento,** the beginning of the fabled Amalfi Coast, is touristy, but it may well be the Italian city of your imagination: cliff hanging, cobblestone paved, and graced with an infinite variety of fishing ports and coastal views. Stop here for a relaxing dinner of fish and white wine.

Logistics: Rather than rent a car, take the Circumvesuviana, a twice-hourly train to Sorrento that stops near the ruins at Pompeii's Villa dei Misteri.

DAY 4: POSITANO/RAVELLO

Positano, your next stop, is one of Italy's most visited towns for good reason: its blue-green seas, stairs "as steep as ladders," and white Moorish-style houses are all memorable. Walk, gaze, and eat (lunch), before heading on to the less visited, yet even loftier town of **Ravello.** This aerie "closer to the sky than it is to the sea" is an Amalfi Coast dream come true. Don't miss the **Duomo, Villa Rufolo,** and **Villa Cimbrone** before settling in for dinner in the sky.

Logistics: Sorrento to Positano is a slow 15-km (9½-mile) jaunt, and then Ravello is another 26 km (16 miles) to the east, with the winding roads drawing it out for the better part of an hour. The SITA bus is your best option. Motorists should be prepared to use low gears if driving a stick shift.

DAY 5: MATERA

Those with a car will have a bit of a drive from the Amalfi Coast; leaving Campania and entering Basilicata is generally a lonely experience. Little-traveled roads, wild hills, and distant farms are the hallmarks of this province, which has perfected the art of peasant food and the deep, dark *aglianico* wines to go with it. The lengthy journey to **Matera** is worthwhile, however, to see this beautiful ancient city full of Paleolithic **Sassi** (cave-like dwellings hewn out of rock). Spend the afternoon exploring them, then enjoy a relaxing dinner at one of Matera's excellent restaurants.

Logistics: It's a long haul from Ravello to Matera—if using public transportation you may find it easier to return first to Naples—but the effort is worth it, as Basilicata's landscape is so pretty.

DAY 6: LECCE

Get an early start for your journey to the Baroque city of **Lecce,** which will mark your introduction to Puglia, the heel of Italy's boot. It's one of the country's best-kept secrets, as you'll soon find out upon checking out the spectacular church of **Santa Croce,** the ornate **Duomo,** and the harmonious **Piazza Sant'Oronzo.**

The shopping, the food, and the evening passeggiata are all great.

Logistics: It's not far from Matera to Lecce as the crow flies, but the 2½-hour trip is more involved than you might think; patience is required. Those without a car should head to Bari, then take the train south. The best driving route is via Taranto, *not* up through Bari.

DAY 7: BARI

It is a two-hour drive from Lecce to **Bari,** and many make a pit stop halfway at the beautiful hilltop town of **Ostuni.** Spend the day wandering through Bari's historic center and finish with a good fish dinner.

Logistics: Take a direct train or the coastal SS16 for 154 km (95 miles) until you hit Bari.

DAY 8: BARI/DEPARTURE

Bari's Aeroporto Karol Wojtyla is small but quite serviceable, with frequent connections through Rome and Milan.

Logistics: Bari hotels offer easy airport transfers; take advantage of them.

Great Itineraries

Venice, Florence, Rome, and Highlights in Between

Think of this itinerary as a rough draft for you to revise according to your interests and time constraints.

DAY 1: VENICE

Arrive in Venice's Marco Polo Airport, and hop on the bus to the city's main bus station. Check into your hotel, get out, and get lost along the canals for a couple of hours before dinner.

Logistics: At the main bus station, you can immediately transfer to the most delightful "bus" in the world: the vaporetto. Enjoy your first ride up the Grand Canal, and make sure you're paying attention to the *fermata* (stop) where you need to get off.

DAY 2: VENICE

Have coffee at a real Italian coffee bar before taking in the top sights, including the **Basilica di San Marco, Palazzo Ducale,** and **Galleria dell'Accademia.** Don't forget **Piazza San Marco**: the intense anticipation as you near the giant square climaxes in a stunning view of the piazza. Stop for lunch, sampling the traditional Venetian specialty *sarde in saor* (sardines in a mouthwatering sweet-and-sour preparation with onions and raisins), and check out the fish market at the foot of the **Rialto Bridge**; then see the sunset at the **Zattere** before dinner. Later, stop at a bar on the **Campo San Luca** or **Campo Santa Margherita,** where you can toast to being free of automobiles.

Logistics: Venice is best seen on foot, with the occasional vaporetto ride. Always carry a city map: it's very easy to get totally lost here.

Tips

■ The itinerary can also be completed by car on the autostradas. Obviously, it's best to pick up your car on Day 3, when you leave Venice.

■ The sights along this route can be crowded; you'll have a better time if you make the trip outside the busy months of June, July, and August.

DAY 3: FERRARA/BOLOGNA

The ride to **Ferrara,** your first stop in Emilia-Romagna, is about 90 minutes. Visit the **Castello Estense** and **Duomo** before grabbing lunch. Wander Ferrara's cobblestone streets, then hop on the train to **Bologna** (less than an hour away). Check into your hotel, and walk around **Piazza Maggiore** before dinner. Later check out some of Italy's best nightlife.

Logistics: The train station lies a bit outside the center of Ferrara, so you may want to take a taxi or a less expensive city bus into town.

DAY 4: BOLOGNA/FLORENCE

After breakfast, visit some of Bologna's churches and piazzas, and climb the leaning **Torre degli Asinelli** for a red-rooftop-studded panorama. After lunch, take the short train ride to **Florence.** You'll arrive in time for an afternoon siesta and an evening passeggiata.

DAY 5: FLORENCE

Start with the **Uffizi Gallery,** where you'll see Botticelli's *Primavera* and *Birth of Venus,* among other works. Next, walk to **Piazza del Duomo,** site of Brunelleschi's spectacular dome, which you can climb for an equally spectacular view. After a simple trattoria lunch, either devote the afternoon to art or hike up to **Piazzale Michelangelo,** which overlooks the

city. Finish the evening in style with a traditional bistecca alla fiorentina (grilled T-bone steak with olive oil).

Logistics: It's best to reserve Uffizi Gallery tickets in advance; you *must* reserve in advance to climb Brunelleschi's dome.

DAY 6: LUCCA/PISA

After breakfast, board a train for a 90-minute ride to the walled medieval city of **Lucca**. Don't miss the Romanesque **Duomo** or a walk along the city's ramparts. Have lunch at a trattoria before continuing on to **Pisa** (30 minutes away) and its **Campo dei Miracoli**, where you'll spend an afternoon seeing the **Leaning Tower,** along with the **Duomo** and **Battistero.** Walk down to the banks of the Arno River and dine at one of the inexpensive local restaurants in the real city center.

Logistics: Lucca's train station is conveniently situated just outside the walled city. Although across town from the Leaning Tower, Pisa's train station isn't far from the city center.

DAY 7: ROME

Take a high-speed train bound for **Rome,** a 90-minute trip from Florence, or three hours from Pisa. Although the Eternal City took millennia to build, on this whirlwind trip you'll have just two days to tour it. Make your way to your hotel and relax for a bit before heading to the **Piazza Navona, Campo de' Fiori,** and **Trevi Fountain**—it's best in the evening—and have a stand-up aperitivo (Campari and soda is a classic) at an unpretentious local bar. For dinner, you can't go wrong at any of Rome's popular local pizzerias.

DAY 8: ROME

In the morning, head to the **Vatican Museums** to see Michelangelo's glorious frescoes at the **Sistine Chapel.** Visit **St. Peter's Basilica and Square** before heading for lunch near the Pantheon. Next, visit the magnificent **Pantheon,** and then the **Colosseum,** stopping along Via dei Fori Imperiali to check out the **Roman Forum** from above. From the Colosseum, walk or take a taxi to **Piazza di Spagna,** a good place to shop at stylish boutiques.

Logistics: Avoid lines and waits by buying tickets online.

DAY 9: ROME/DEPARTURE

Head by taxi to Termini station and catch the train to Fiumicino airport.

Logistics: For most people, the train from Termini station is preferable to a taxi ride.

Great Itineraries

Rome in 3 Days

Rome wasn't built in a day—so don't try to see it all in a day. Three days is a doable, if jam-packed, amount of time to visit the ancient city's major attractions.

Logistics: Much of the city shuts down on Sunday (including the Vatican Museums, except for the last Sunday of the month), and many restaurants and state museums are closed on Monday. To skip lines and better enjoy your experiences, reservations are a good idea at the Colosseum and the Vatican Museums; they're required for the Galleria Borghese.

DAY 1: ANCIENT ROME

Spend your first day in Rome exploring the likes of the **Roman Forum, Musei Capitolini,** and the **Colosseum.** This area is pretty compact, but you can easily spend a full morning and afternoon exploring its treasures. It's best to try and beat the crowds at the Colosseum by getting there right when it opens at 8:30 am (advance tickets help, too). A guided tour of the Forum is also a good way to make the most out of your afternoon. After your day of sightseeing, stop for a classic Roman dinner in nearby Monti.

DAY 2: THE VATICAN AND PIAZZA NAVONA

Another full day of sightseeing awaits when you make your way to the city-state known as the **Vatican.** You'll once again want to try and avoid the biggest crowds here, especially for a glimpse of the Sistine Chapel (the best way to do this is to make online reservations ahead of time). Booking a tour of the **Vatican Museums** is a good way to take full advantage of the site; most tours last two hours. Be sure to stop in and marvel at **St. Peter's Basilica,** too. Stop for lunch in nearby Prati, but after you're done with the Vatican, cross the river to **Piazza Navona.** Spend some time exploring this glorious piazza and its sculptures, but make sure to stop by the **Pantheon** before heading to Campo de' Fiori for dinner at an outdoor restaurant. Afterward, there are plenty of nearby bars to keep you occupied.

DAY 3: PIAZZA DI SPAGNA, VILLA BORGHESE, AND TRASTEVERE

Start your morning with breakfast near the **Trevi Fountain,** before doing some window-shopping up Via Condotti and along the many surrounding backstreets as you make your way to the **Spanish Steps.** Pose for some postcard-worthy photos there before heading to nearby **Villa Borghese.** If you're sick of museums, feel free to explore Rome's main park and enjoy the great views; if you're up for some more art, the **Galleria Borghese** is one of the city's best art museums. Afterward, head to trendy Trastevere for dinner, and soak in the cobblestone streets and charming medieval houses as you barhop your last night in town.

IF YOU HAVE MORE TIME

If you want to make the most of your time in the city itself, take your time exploring the many churches and cathedrals, like **Sant'Ignazio** or **San Clemente.** You can also stop by to explore gorgeous palaces, like the **Palazzo Doria Pamphilij,** and check out lesser known but just as impressive museums, like the MAXXI or the MACRO. Visiting the ancient Roman road known as the Via Appia Antica and its spooky yet mesmerizing catacombs is a great way to spend an afternoon immersed in Roman history. Make time for some shopping: early evenings are a good time to saunter around the big-label boutiques of Piazza di Spagna and historic independents of Piazza Navona. For flea market bargains check out the Mercato di Porta Portese.

On the Calendar

Winter

Festa di Santa Lucia. The feast of Siracusa's patron, Santa Lucia, is held from December 13 to 20 at the Church of Santa Lucia alla Badia. A splendid silver statue of the saint is carried from the church to the Duomo: a torchlight procession and band music accompany the bearers, while local families watch from their balconies. ⊕ *www.basilicasantalucia.com.*

Sagra del Mandorlo in Fiore. In late February and early March, when most of the almond trees are in blossom, Agrigento hosts the Sagra del Mandorlo in Fiore, with international folk dances, a costumed parade, and the sale of marzipan and other sweet treats made from almonds. ⊕ *www.mandorloinfiore.online.*

Sant'Orso Fair. On the last weekend of January, the streets of Aosta are brightened by an arts-and-crafts market that brings artisans from all over the Valle d'Aosta. All the traditional techniques are featured: wood carving and sculpture, soapstone work, wrought iron, leather, wool, lace, and household items of all kinds. Food and wine are sold at outdoor stands and wandering minstrels enliven the whole event. ⊕ *www.fieradisantorso.it.*

Spring

Biennale di Venezia. Come springtime every two years (the even-numbered) the contemporary art world and the curious descend on the Giardini pavilions, Arsenale dockside warehouses, and scattered palazzi. In odd years it's the turn of the world's leading architects to display their creations. ⊕ *www.labiennale.org.*

Carnevale. Venice earned its international reputation as the "city of Carnevale" in the 18th century, when partying would begin several months before Lent and the city seemed to be one continuous masquerade. The celebration was revived for good in the 1970s, and each year over the 15- to 17-day Carnevale period (ending on the Tuesday before Ash Wednesday), more than a half-million people attend concerts, theater and street performances, masquerade balls, historical processions, fashion shows, and contests.

If you're not planning on joining in the revelry, you'd be wise to choose another time to visit Venice. Crowds throng the streets (which become one-way, with police directing foot traffic; bridges are designated "no-stopping" zones to avoid gridlock, and prices skyrocket. ⊕ *www.carnevale.venezia.it.*

Carnevale di Acireale. With fantastical floats and entertaining parades, Acireale's carnival celebrations are known as being the best in Sicily. The exact dates depend on Easter, but events are held over the course of three weekends before the start of Lent (Ash Wednesday), when thousands of revelers pack the streets of the coastal town. ⊕ *carnevaleacireale.eu.*

Festa della Madonna a Cavallo. In Scicli, southern Italy, the last Saturday in May brings the festival of the town's savior, Madonna delle Milizie (Virgin Mary of Militias), celebrating the supposed moment in the 11th century when the Virgin Mary descended on horseback to rescue the Norman-ruled town from a Saracen invasion. The weekend festival includes parading a statue of the Madonna on horseback through the main piazza to intervene in a mock battle before reveling in salvation by indulging in a sweet pastry towering with whipped cream, known as a *testa di turco.*

Festa di Sant'Efisio. On May 1, thousands of costumed villagers parade through town during Sardinia's greatest annual

On the Calendar

festival, the Festa di Sant'Efisio, named after the martyred saint who saved the city from the plague in the 17th century. The saint's statue is carried aloft through Cagliari's flower-lined streets, part of a four-day procession from Cagliari to Nora and back again (64 km [40 miles] round-trip), and is accompanied by colorful costumed groups from throughout the island in an enthusiastic celebration of traditional culture. Ask at Cagliari's tourist office about viewing the grand spectacle along the main route in Cagliari. From April on, you can find tickets at ⊕ *www. boxofficesardegna.it*.

Milan Design Week. For a week in April Italy's northern powerhouse city hosts the biggest gathering of the design world. Pride of place in the calendar is the Salone di Mobile, a furniture fair like no other, staged in the cavernous Fiera Milano exhibition center and in dozens of venues across this design-mad city.

Sagra del Pesce. The highlight of the festival of San Fortunato is held on the second Sunday of May each year. It's a crowded, colorful, and free-to-the-public feast of freshly caught fish, cooked outside at the port in a 12-foot frying pan. ⊕ *www.camogliturismo.it*.

Scoppio del Carro (Explosion of the Cart). On Easter Sunday, Florentines and foreigners alike flock to the Piazza del Duomo to watch as the Scoppio del Carro, a monstrosity of a carriage pulled by two huge oxen decorated for the occasion, makes its way through the city center and ends up in the piazza. Through an elaborate wiring system, an object representing a dove is sent from inside the cathedral to the baptistery across the way. The dove sets off an explosion of fireworks that come streaming from the carriage. You have to see it to believe it.

Vinitaly. This widely attended international wine and spirits event takes place for a few days in April. Recent gatherings have attracted more than 4,000 exhibitors from two dozen countries. The festivities kick off with Opera Wine, a showcase for the top 100 Italian wines as chosen by *Wine Spectator* magazine, which takes place in the Palazzo della Gran Guardia, in Piazza Bra. ⊕ *www.vinitaly.com*.

Summer

Arena di Verona Opera Festival. Milan's La Scala and Naples's San Carlo offer performances more likely to attract serious opera fans, but neither offers a greater spectacle than the Arena di Verona. During the venue's summer season (June to August), as many as 16,000 attendees sit on the original stone terraces or in modern cushioned stalls. Most of the operas presented are big and splashy, like *Aida* or *Turandot*, demanding huge choruses, lots of color and movement, and, if possible, camels, horses, or elephants. Order tickets by phone or through the arena website: if you book a spot on the cheaper terraces, be sure to take or rent a cushion—four hours on a 2,000-year-old stone bench can be an ordeal (from €27 for general admission). ⊕ *www.arena.it*.

Estate Fiesolana. From June through August, Estate Fiesolana, a festival of theater, music, dance, and film, takes place in Fiesole's churches and in the Roman amphitheater—demonstrating that the ancient Romans knew a thing or two about acoustics. ⊕ *www.estate-fiesolana.it*.

Festa del Redentore. On the third Sunday in July, crowds cross the Canale della Giudecca by means of a pontoon bridge, built every year to commemorate the doge's annual visit to Palladio's Chiesa del Santissimo Redentore to offer thanks for the end of a 16th-century plague. The evening before, Venetians—accompanied each year by an increasing number of tourists—set up tables and chairs along the canals. As evening falls, practically the whole city takes to the streets and tables, and thousands more take to the water. Boats decorated with colored lanterns (and well provisioned with traditional Redentore meals) jockey for position to watch the grand event. Half an hour before midnight, Venice kicks off a fireworks display over the Bacino, with brilliant reflections on its waters. You'll find good viewing anywhere along the Riva degli Schiavoni; you could also try Zattere, as close to Punta Dogana as you can get, or on the Zitelle end of the Giudecca. After the fireworks, join the young folks and stay out all night, greeting the sunrise on the Lido beach, or rest up and make the procession to mass on Sunday morning. If you're on a boat, allow a couple of hours to dislodge yourself from the nautical traffic jam when the festivities break up. ⊕ www.redentorevenezia.it.

Festa di San Giovanni (Feast of St. John the Baptist). On June 24 Florence mostly grinds to a halt to celebrate the Festa di San Giovanni in honor of its patron saint. Many shops and bars close, and at night a fireworks display lights up the Arno and attracts thousands.

Festival dei Due Mondi. Each summer Umbria hosts one of Italy's biggest arts festivals: Spoleto's Festival of the Two Worlds. Starting out as a classical music festival, it has now evolved into one of Italy's brightest gatherings of arts aficionados. Running from late June through mid-July, it features modern and classical music, theater, dance, and opera. Increasingly there are also a number of small cinema producers and their films. ⊕ www.festivaldispoleto.com.

Luminaria. Pisa is at its best during the Luminaria feast day, on June 16. The day honors St. Ranieri, the city's patron saint. Palaces along the Arno are lit with white lights, and there are plenty of fireworks.

Ravenna Festival. Orchestras from all over the world perform in city churches and theaters during this renowned music festival, which takes place in June and July, as well as during a few days at the beginning of November. ⊕ www.ravennafestival.org.

Ravello Festival. First staged in 1953 and partly inspired by composer Richard Wagner's declaration on setting foot in Villa Rufolo grounds: "The magical garden of Klingsor is found!" Sitting in this lofty terrace in serene Ravello, the striking Oscar Niemeyer Auditorium is the breathtaking venue for wonderful concerts. For the most uplifting musical experience secure a seat at the much-sought-after Sunrise Concert each August, where the dawning sun, divine sounds, and Costiera Amalfitana vistas intertwine.

Taormina Film Festival. Sicily's famous festival takes place in late June and early July. ⊕ www.taorminafilmfest.it.

Umbria Jazz Festival. Perugia is hopping for 10 days in July, when more than a million people flock to see famous names in contemporary music perform at the Umbria Jazz Festival. In recent years the stars have included Wynton Marsalis, Sting, Eric Clapton, Lady Gaga, Tony Bennett, Jeff Beck, and Elton John. There's also a shorter Umbria Jazz Winter Festival from late December to early January. ⊕ www.umbriajazz.com

On the Calendar

Fall

Douja d'Or National Wine Festival. For 10 days in mid-September, Asti is host to a popular wine festival—an opportunity to see Asti and celebrate the product that made it famous. ⊕ *www.doujador.it.*

Eurochocolate Festival. If you've got a sweet tooth and are visiting in fall, book early and head to Perugia for the Eurochocolate Festival. This is one of the biggest chocolate festivals in the world, with a million visitors, and is held over a week in late October. From 2021 there's a new International Chocolate Exhibition event in late March–early April. ⊕ *www.eurochocolate.com.*

Fiera Internazionale del Tartufo Bianco (International White Truffle Fair). From early October to early December, Alba hosts an internationally famous truffle fair. Merchants, chefs, and other aficionados of this pungent yet delicious fungus come from all over the world to buy and taste white truffles at the height of their season. The fourth Sunday of September sees the **Palio degli Asini**, a hilarious donkey race, a lampoon of Asti's eminently serious horse race. Tickets to watch this competition between Alba's districts, with riders dressed in medieval garb astride their stubborn beasts, can be hard to get. ■TIP→ **Hotel and restaurant reservations for October and November should be made well in advance.** ⊕ *www.fieradeltartufo.org.*

Palio di Asti. September is a month of fairs and celebrations in Asti, and this horse race that runs through the streets of town is the highlight. First mentioned in 1275, this annual event has been going strong ever since. After an elaborate procession in period costumes, nine horses and jockeys representing different sections of town vie for the honor of claiming the *palio*, a symbolic flag of victory. The race happens on a Sunday at the beginning of September each year. ⊕ *www.paliodiasti.com.*

Sagra Musicale Umbra. Held mid-September, the Sagra Musicale Umbra celebrates sacred music in Perugia and in several towns throughout the region. ⊕ *www.perugiamusicaclassica.com.*

Chapter 3

ROME

Updated by
Laura Itzkowitz
and Natalie Kennedy

⊙ Sights	🍴 Restaurants	🛏 Hotels	🛍 Shopping	🍸 Nightlife
★★★★★	★★★☆☆	★★★★★	★★★★☆	★★★★☆

WELCOME TO ROME

TOP REASONS TO GO

★ **The Vatican:** Although its population numbers only in the hundreds, the Vatican makes up for it with the millions who visit each year. Marvel at Michelangelo's Sistine Chapel and St. Peter's Basilica.

★ **The Colosseum:** The largest amphitheater of the Roman world was begun by Emperor Vespasian and inaugurated by his son Titus in AD 80.

★ **Piazza Navona:** You couldn't concoct a more Roman street scene: crowded café tables at street level, wrought-iron balconies above, and, at the center, Bernini's Fountain of the Four Rivers and Borromini's Sant'Agnese.

★ **Roman Forum:** This fabled labyrinth of ruins variously served as a political playground, a center of commerce, and a place where justice was dispensed during the Roman Republic and Empire.

★ **Trastevere:** This neighborhood is a maze of jumbled alleyways, traditional Roman trattorias, cobblestone streets, and medieval houses.

1 Ancient Rome with Monti and Celio. The Forum and Palatine Hill were once the hub of Western civilization.

2 The Vatican with Borgo and Prati. St. Peter's Basilica and the Sistine Chapel draw millions.

3 Piazza Navona, Campo de' Fiori, and the Jewish Ghetto. This is the heart of the historic quarter. The Ghetto still preserves the flavor of Old Rome.

4 Piazza di Spagna. Travel back to the days of the Grand Tour in this area.

5 Repubblica and the Quirinale. These areas house government offices, churches, and sights.

6 Villa Borghese and Environs. Rome's most famous park is home to the Galleria Borghese.

7 Trastevere. Rome's left bank has kept its authentic roots.

8 Aventino and Testaccio. Aventino is a posh residential area, and Testaccio is more working class.

9 Esquilino and Via Appia Antica. These neighborhoods have plenty of ancient sights and churches.

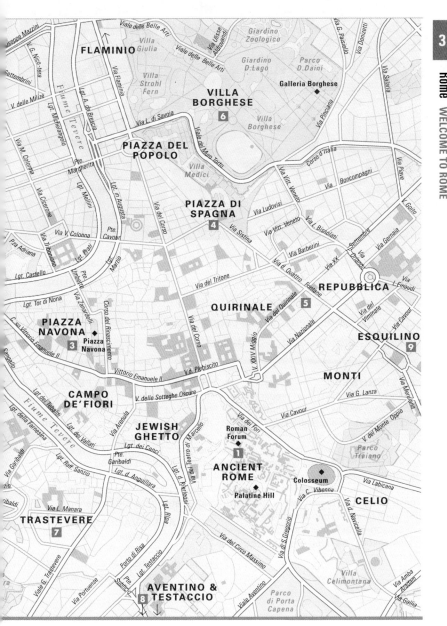

FLAMINIO

Viale delle Belle Arti

Villa Giulia

Giardino Zoologico

Viale delle Belle Arti

Giardino D.Lago

Parco D.Daini

Galleria Borghese ◆

VILLA BORGHESE

6

Villa Strohl Fern

Villa Borghese

PIAZZA DEL POPOLO

Villa Medici

Corso d'Italia

PIAZZA DI SPAGNA

4

Via Ludovisi

Via Boncompagni

QUIRINALE

REPUBBLICA

5

ESQUILINO

9

PIAZZA NAVONA ◆

3

Piazza Navona

MONTI

Vittorio Emanuele II

CAMPO DE'FIORI

JEWISH GHETTO

Roman Forum ◆

Via Cavour

ANCIENT ROME

Colosseum ◆

Parco Traiano

Palatine Hill ◆

CELIO

TRASTEVERE

7

AVENTINO & TESTACCIO

8

Villa Celimontana

Parco di Porta Capena

EAT LIKE A LOCAL IN ROME

In Rome, tradition is the dominant feature of the cuisine, with a focus on freshness and simplicity, so when Romans continue ordering the standbys, it's easy to understand why. That said, the influx of residents to the capital from other regions has yielded many variations on the staples.

ARTICHOKES

There are two well-known preparations of *carciofo*, or artichoke, in Rome. Carciofi *alla romana* are stuffed with wild mint, garlic, and pecorino, then braised in olive oil, white wine, and water. Carciofi *alla giudia* (Jewish-style) are whole artichokes, deep-fried twice, so that they open like a flower, the outer leaves crisp and golden brown, while the heart remains tender. When artichokes are in season—late winter through the spring—they're served everywhere.

BUCATINI ALL'AMATRICIANA

It might look like spaghetti with red sauce, but there's much more to *bucatini all'amatriciana*. It's a spicy, rich, and complex dish that owes its flavor to *guanciale*, or cured pork jowl, as well as tomatoes and crushed red pepper flakes. It's often served over bucatini, a hollow, spaghetti-like pasta, and topped with grated pecorino Romano.

CODA ALLA VACCINARA

Rome's largest slaughterhouse in the 1800s was in the Testaccio neighborhood, and that's where you'll find dishes like *coda alla vaccinara*, or "oxtail in the style of the cattle butcher." This dish is made from ox or veal tails stewed with tomatoes, carrots, celery, and wine, and it's usually seasoned with cinnamon. It's simmered for hours and then finished with raisins and pine nuts or bittersweet chocolate.

GELATO

Its consistency is often said to be a cross between regular American ice cream and soft-serve. The best versions of gelato are extremely flavorful, and almost always made fresh daily. When choosing a *gelateria*, watch for signs that say *gelato artigianale* (artisan- or homemade); otherwise, keep an eye out for the real deal by avoiding gelato that looks too bright or fluffy.

PIZZA

There are two kinds of Roman pizza: *al taglio* (by the slice) and *tonda* (round pizza). The former has a thicker, focaccia-like crust and is cut into squares; these are sold by weight and generally available all day. The typical Roman pizza tonda has a very thin crust and is served almost charred. Because they're so hot, the ovens are usually fired up only in the evening, which is why Roman *pizzerie* tend to open for dinner only.

CACIO E PEPE

The name means "cheese and pepper," and this is a simple pasta dish from the *cucina povera*, or rustic cooking, tradition. It's a favorite Roman primo, usually made with *tonnarelli* (fresh egg pasta a bit thicker than spaghetti), which is coated with a pecorino-cheese sauce and lots of freshly ground black pepper. Some restaurants serve the dish in an edible bowl of paper-thin baked cheese.

FRITTI

The classic Roman starter in a trattoria and especially at the pizzeria, is *fritti*: an assortment of fried treats, usually crumbed or in batter. Often, before selecting a pizza, locals will order their fritti: *filetti di baccalà* (salt cod in batter), *fiori di zucca* (zucchini flowers, usually stuffed with anchovy and mozzarella), *supplì* (rice balls stuffed with mozzarella and other ingredients), or *olive ascolane* (stuffed olives).

LA GRICIA

This dish is often referred to as a "white amatriciana" because it's precisely that: pasta (usually spaghetti or rigatoni) served with pecorino cheese and guanciale—thus amatriciana without the tomato sauce. It's a lighter alternative to carbonara in that it doesn't contain egg, and its origins date back further than the amatriciana.

The timeless city to which all roads lead, Mamma Roma enthralls visitors today as she has since time immemorial. Here the ancient Romans made us heirs-in-law to what we call Western Civilization; where centuries later Michelangelo painted the Sistine Chapel; and where Gian Lorenzo Bernini's Baroque nymphs and naiads still dance in their marble fountains.

Today the city remains a veritable Grand Canyon of culture. Ancient Rome rubs shoulders with the medieval, the modern runs into the Renaissance, and the result is like nothing so much as an open-air museum.

But always remember: "*Quando a Roma vai, fai come vedrai*" (When in Rome, do as the Romans do). Don't feel intimidated by the press of art and culture. Instead, contemplate the grandeur from a table at a sun-drenched café on Piazza della Rotonda; let Rome's colorful life flow around you without feeling guilty because you haven't seen everything. It can't be done, anyway. There's just so much here that you'll have to come back, so be sure to throw a coin in the Trevi Fountain.

Planning

Addresses

In the *centro storico* (old town/historic center), most street names are posted on ceramic-like plaques on the sides of buildings, which can make them hard to see. Addresses are fairly straightforward:

the street name is followed by the street number, but it's worth noting that Roman street numbering, even in the newer outskirts of town, can be erratic. Usually numbers are even on one side of the street and odd on the other, but sometimes numbers are in ascending consecutive order on one side of the street and descending order on the other side.

Etiquette

Although you may find Rome much more informal then many other European cities, Romans will nevertheless appreciate attempts to abide by local etiquette. When entering an establishment, the key words to know are: *buongiorno* (good morning), *buona sera* (good evening), and *buon pomeriggio* (good afternoon). These words can also double as a good-bye upon exit. Italians greet friends with a kiss, usually first on the right cheek, and then on the left. When you meet a new person, shake hands and say *piacere* (*pee*-ah-*chair*-ay).

Getting Around

Although most of Rome's sights are in a relatively circumscribed area, the city is too large to be seen solely on foot. Try to avoid rush hour when taking the Metro (subway) or a bus, as public transport can be extremely crowded. Midmorning or midday through early afternoon tends to be less busy. Otherwise, it's best to take a taxi to the area you plan to visit if it is across town. You should always expect to do a lot of walking in Rome, especially considering how little ground the subway actually covers, so plan on wearing a pair of comfortable, sturdy shoes to cushion the impact of the *sampietrini* (cobblestones). You can get free city and transit maps at municipal information booths.

METRO

Rome's integrated transportation system includes buses and trams (ATAC), the Metropolitana (the subway, or Metro), suburban trains and buses (COTRAL), and the commuter rail run by the state railway (Trenitalia). A ticket (BIT), valid for 100 minutes on any combination of buses and trams and one entrance to the Metro, costs €1.50. Tickets are sold at tobacco shops, newsstands, some coffee bars, automatic ticket machines in Metro stations, some bus stops, in machines on some buses, and at ATAC ticket booths. You can purchase individual or multiple tickets. It's always a good idea to have a few tickets handy so you don't have to hunt for a vendor when you need one. All tickets must be validated by time-stamping in the yellow meter boxes aboard buses and in Metro stations, immediately prior to boarding. Failure to validate your ticket will result in a fine of €54.90. You can now pay for fines on the ATAC website. Pay immediately, or the fine will increase to €104.90 if you pay after five days. You can also pay fines in post offices, authorized shops, or by wire transfer. Do not pay the ticket inspectors

in cash; some may be equipped for payment by mobile POS.

A Roma24H ticket, or *biglietto integrato giornaliero* (integrated daily ticket), is valid for 24 hours (from the moment you stamp it) on all public transit and costs €7. You can also purchase a Roma48H (€12.50), a Roma72H (€18), and a CIS (Carta Integrata Settimanale), which is valid for one week (€24). Each option gives unlimited travel on ATAC buses, COTRAL urban bus services, trains for the Lido and Viterbo, and Metro. There's an ATAC kiosk at the bus terminal in front of Termini station. If you're going farther afield, or planning to spend more than a week in Rome, think about getting a BIRG (daily regional ticket) or a CIRS (weekly regional ticket) from the railway station. These give you unlimited travel on all state transport throughout the region of Lazio. This can take you as far as the Etruscan city of Tarquinia or medieval Viterbo.

BUS AND TRAM

Although not as fast as the Metro, bus and tram travel is more scenic. With reserved bus lanes and numerous tram lines, surface transportation is surprisingly efficient, given the volume of Roman traffic. At peak times, however, buses can be very crowded. If the distance you have to travel is not too great, walking can be a more comfortable alternative. ATAC city buses are red or gray; trams are green. Remember to board at the rear and to exit at the middle: some bus drivers may refuse to let you out the front door, leaving you to scramble through the crowd to exit the middle or rear doors. Don't forget that you must buy your ticket before boarding, and be sure to stamp it in a machine as soon as you enter. The ticket is good for a transfer and one Metro trip within the next 100 minutes. Buses and trams run 5:30 am–midnight, after which time there's an extensive network of night buses with service throughout the city.

The bus system is a bit complicated to navigate due to the number of lines, but ATAC has a website (⊕ *www.atac.roma.it*) that will help you calculate the number of stops and bus route needed, and even give you a map directing you to the appropriate stops. To navigate the site, look for the British flag in the upper right-hand corner to change the website into English. Or do as the locals do and use the Moovit app.

Restaurants

In Rome, simple yet traditional cuisine reigns supreme. Most chefs prefer to follow the mantra of freshness over fuss, and simplicity of flavor and preparation over complex cooking techniques. Rome has been known since antiquity for its grand feasts and banquets, and dining out has always been a favorite Roman pastime. Until recently, the city's *buongustaii* (gourmands) would have been the first to tell you that Rome is distinguished more by its enthusiasm for eating out than for a multitude of world-class restaurants—but this is changing. There is an ever-growing promotion of slow-food practices, a focus on sustainably and locally sourced produce. The economic crisis forced the food industry in Rome to adopt innovative ways to maintain a clientele who were increasingly looking to dine out but wanting to spend less; the result has been the rise of "street food" restaurants, selling everything from inexpensive and novel takes on the classic *supplì* (Roman fried-rice balls) to sandwich shops that use a variety of organic ingredients.

Generally speaking, Romans like Roman food, and that's what you'll find in many of the city's trattorias and wine bars. For the most part, today's chefs cling to the traditional and excel at what has taken hundreds, sometimes thousands, of years to perfect. This is why the basic trattoria menu is more or less the same wherever you go. And it's why even the top Roman chefs feature their versions of simple trattoria classics like carbonara, sometimes in a "deconstructed" or slightly varied way. To a great extent, Rome is still a town where the Italian equivalent of "What are you in the mood for?" still gets the answer, "Pizza or pasta."

Nevertheless, Rome is the capital of Italy, and because people move here from every corner of the Italian peninsula, there are more variations on the Italian theme in Rome than you'd find elsewhere in Italy: Sicilian, Tuscan, Pugliese, Bolognese, Marchegiano, Sardinian, and northern Italian regional cuisines are all represented. And reflecting the increasingly cosmopolitan nature of the city, you'll find a growing number of good-quality international foods here as well—particularly Japanese, Indian, and Ethiopian.

Oddly enough, though, for a nation that prides itself on *la bella figura* ("looking good"), most Romans don't fuss about music, personal space, lighting, or decor. After all, who needs flashy interior design when so much of Roman life takes place outdoors, when dining alfresco in Rome can take place in the middle of a glorious ancient site or a centuries-old piazza?

Prices in the dining reviews are the average cost of a main course at dinner, or, if dinner is not served, at lunch. Restaurant reviews have been shortened. For full information, visit Fodors.com.

Hotels

When it comes to accommodations, Rome offers a wide selection of high-end hotels, bed-and-breakfasts, and designer boutique hotels—options that run the gamut from whimsical to luxurious. Whether you want a simple place to rest your head or a complete cache of exclusive amenities, you have plenty to choose from.

Luxury hotels are justly renowned for sybaritic comfort: postcard views over Roman rooftops, silver flatware on white linen atop a groaning breakfast-buffet table, and the fluffiest towels. But in more modest categories, very often Rome's hotels are not up to the standards of space, comfort, quiet, and service taken for granted in the United States: you'll still find places with tiny rooms, lumpy beds, and anemic air-conditioning. The good news: if you're flexible, there are happy mediums aplenty.

One thing to figure out before you arrive is which neighborhood you want to stay in. There are obvious advantages to staying in a hotel within easy walking distance of the main sights. If a picturesque location is your main concern, stay in one of the small hotels around Piazza Navona or Campo de' Fiori. If luxury is a high priority, head for Piazza di Spagna or beyond the city center, where quality/price ratios are higher and some hotels have swimming pools.

Prices in the lodging reviews are the lowest cost of a standard double room in high season. Hotel reviews have been shortened. For full information, visit Fodors.com.

What it Costs in Euros			
$	$$	$$$	$$$$
RESTAURANTS			
under €15	€15–€24	€25–€35	over €35
HOTELS			
under €125	€125–€200	€201–€300	over €300

Roman Hours

In Italy, almost nothing starts on time except for (sometimes) a theater, opera, or movie showing. Italians even joke about a "15-minute window" before actually being late somewhere. In

addition, the day starts a little later than normal here, with many shops not opening until 10 am, lunch never happens before 1 pm, and dinner rarely starts before 8 pm. On Sunday, Rome virtually shuts down, and on Monday, most state museums and exhibition halls, plus many restaurants, are closed. Daily food shop hours generally run 10 am–1 pm and 4 pm–7:30 pm or 8 pm; but other stores in the center usually observe continuous opening hours. Pharmacies tend to close for a lunch break and keep night hours (*ora rio notturno*) in rotation. As for churches, most open at 8 or 9 in the morning, close noon–3 or 4, then reopen until 6:30 or 7. St. Peter's, however, has continuous hours 7 am–7 pm (until 6 pm in the fall and winter); and the Vatican Museums are open Monday but closed Sunday (except for the last Sunday of the month).

Roma Pass

In addition to single- and multiday transit passes, a three-day Roma Pass (📧 *€52*) covers unlimited use of buses, trams, and the Metro, plus free admission to two museums or archaeological sites of your choice and discounted entrance to others. A two-day pass is €32 and includes one museum. The pass also allows you to skip the line at the Colosseum and Castel Sant'Angelo. Purchase the pass at either of Rome's airports, at tourist information offices, or at any of the participating attractions.

Tours

Some might consider them kitsch, but guided bus tours can prove a blissfully easy way to enjoy a quick introduction to the city's top sights—if you don't feel like being on your feet all day. Sitting in a bus, with friendly tour-guide commentary (and even friendlier fellow sightseers from every country under the sun), can make for a fun experience—so give one a whirl even if you're an old Rome hand. Of course, you'll want to savor these incredible sights at your own leisure later on.

The least expensive organized sightseeing tour of Rome is the one run by **CitySightseeing Roma**. Double-decker buses leave from Via Marsala, beside Termini station, but you can pick them up at any of their nine stopping points. A day ticket costs €24 and allows you to get off and on as often as you like. The price includes an audio guide system in six languages. The total tour takes about two hours and covers the Colosseum, Piazza Navona, St. Peter's, the Trevi Fountain, and Via Veneto. Tickets can be bought on board. Two- and three-day tickets are also available. Tours leave from Termini station every 20 minutes 9–7:30.

All operators can provide a luxury car for up to three people, a limousine for up to seven, or a minibus for up to nine, all with an English-speaking driver, but guide service is extra. Almost all operators offer "Rome by Night" tours, with or without dinner and entertainment. You can book tours through travel agents.

Visitor Information

The Department of Tourism in Rome, called Roma Capitale, staffs green information kiosks (with multilingual personnel) near important sights, as well as at Termini station and Leonardo da Vinci Airport.

When to Go

Spring and fall are the best times to visit, with mild temperatures and many sunny days. Summers are often sweltering, so come in July and August if you like, but we advise doing as the Romans do—get up and out early, seek refuge from the afternoon heat, resume activities in early evening, and stay up late to enjoy the nighttime breeze.

Most attractions are closed on major holidays. Come August, many shops and restaurants shutter as locals head out for vacation. Remember that air-conditioning is still a relatively rare phenomenon in this city, so carrying a small paper fan in your bag can work wonders. Roman winters are relatively mild, with persistent rainy spells.

Ancient Rome with Monti and Celio

Time has reduced ancient Rome to fields of silent ruins, but the powerful impact of what happened here, of the genius and power that made Rome the center of the Western world, echoes across the millennia. In this one compact area of the city, you can step back into the Rome of Cicero, Julius Caesar, and Virgil. You can walk along the streets they knew, cool off in the shade of the Colosseum that loomed over the city, and see the sculptures poised over their piazzas. Today, this part of Rome, more than any other, is a perfect example of the layering of historic eras, the overlapping of ages, of religions, of a past that is very much a part of the present.

Outside the actual ancient sites, you'll find neighborhoods like Monti and Celio, *riones* that are just as much part of Rome's history as its ruins. These are the city's oldest neighborhoods, and today they are a charming mix of the city's past and present. Once you're done exploring ancient Rome, these are the easiest places to head for a bite to eat or some shopping.

GETTING HERE AND AROUND
The Colosseo Metro station is right across from the Colosseum and a short walk from both the Roman and the Imperial Forums, as well as the Palatine Hill.

Walking from the very heart of the historic center will take about 20 minutes, much of it along the wide Via dei Fori Imperiali. The little electric Bus No. 117 from the center or No. 85 from Termini will also deliver you to the Colosseum's doorstep. Any of the following buses will take you to or near the Roman Forum: Nos. 60, 75, 85, and 170.

◉ Sights

Arco di Costantino (*Arch of Constantine*)
RUINS | This majestic arch was erected in AD 315 to commemorate Constantine's victory over Maxentius at the Milvian Bridge. It was just before this battle, in AD 312, that Constantine—the emperor who converted Rome to Christianity—legendarily had a vision of a cross and heard the words, "In this sign thou shalt conquer." Many of the costly marble decorations for the arch were scavenged from earlier monuments, both saving money and placing Constantine in line with the great emperors of the past. It is easy to picture ranks of Roman centurions marching under the great barrel vault. ⊠ *Piazza del Colosseo, Monti* Ⓜ *Colosseo.*

Basilica di Santa Maria di Aracoeli
CHURCH | Sitting atop 124 steps, Santa Maria di Aracoeli perches on the north slope of the Capitoline Hill. The church rests on the site of the temple of Juno Moneta (Admonishing Juno), which also housed the Roman mint (hence the origin of the word "money"). According to legend, it was here that the Sibyl, a prophetess, predicted to Augustus the coming of a Redeemer. He in turn responded by erecting an altar, the Ara Coeli (Altar of Heaven). This was eventually replaced by a Benedictine monastery, and then a church, which was passed in 1250 to the Franciscans, who restored and enlarged it in Romanesque-Gothic style. Today, the Aracoeli is best known for the Santo Bambino, a much-revered olivewood figure of the Christ Child (today a copy of

the 15th-century original that was stolen in 1994). At Christmas, everyone pays homage to the "Bambinello" as children recite poems from a miniature pulpit. In true Roman style, the church interior is a historical hodgepodge, with classical columns and large marble fragments from pagan buildings, as well as a 13th-century cosmatesque pavement. The richly gilded Renaissance ceiling commemorates the naval victory at Lepanto in 1571 over the Turks. The first chapel on the right is noteworthy for Pinturicchio's frescoes of St. Bernardino of Siena (1486). ⊠ *Via del Teatro di Marcello, at top of long, steep stairway, Piazza Venezia* ☎ *06/69763839* Ⓜ *Colosseo.*

★ **The Campidoglio**
PLAZA/SQUARE | Your first taste of ancient Rome should start from a point that embodies some of Rome's earliest and greatest moments: the Campidoglio. Here, on the Capitoline Hill (which towers over the traffic hub of Piazza Venezia), a meditative Edward Gibbon was inspired to write his 1764 tome, *The History of the Decline and Fall of the Roman Empire.* Of Rome's famous seven hills, the Capitoline is the smallest and the most sacred. It has always been the seat of Rome's government, and its Latin name echoes in the designation of the national and state capitol buildings of every country in the world. While there are great views of the Roman Forum from the terrace balconies to either side of the Palazzo Senatorio, the best view is from the 1st-century BC Tabularium, now part of the Musei Capitolini. The museum café is on the Terrazza Caffarelli, with a magical view toward Trastevere and St. Peter's, and is accessible without a museum ticket. ⊠ *Piazza del Campidoglio, including the Palazzo Senatorio and the Musei Capitolini, the Palazzo Nuovo, and the Palazzo dei Conservatori, Piazza Venezia* Ⓜ *Colosseo.*

Circo Massimo (*Circus Maximus*)

RUINS | From the belvedere of the Domus Flavia on the Palatine Hill, you can see the Circus Maximus; there's also a great free view from Piazzale Ugo La Malfa on the Aventine Hill side. The giant space where once 300,000 spectators watched chariot races while the emperor looked on is ancient Rome's oldest and largest racetrack; it lies in a natural hollow between the two hills. The oval course stretches about 650 yards from end to end; on certain occasions, there were as many as 24 chariot races a day and competitions could last for 15 days. The charioteers could amass fortunes rather like the sports stars of today. (The Portuguese Diocles is said to have totted up winnings of 35 million sestertii.) The noise and the excitement of the crowd must have reached astonishing levels as the charioteers competed in teams, each with their own colors—the Reds, the Blues, etc. Betting also provided Rome's majority of unemployed with a potentially lucrative occupation. The central ridge was the site of two Egyptian obelisks (now in Piazza del Popolo and Piazza San Giovanni in Laterano). Picture the great chariot race scene from MGM's *Ben-Hur* and you have an inkling of what this all looked like. ✉ *Between Palatine and Aventine Hills, Aventino* 🎫 *€16 24-hour ticket required* Ⓜ *Circo Massimo.*

★ **Colosseum** (*Colosseo*)

RUINS | The most spectacular extant edifice of ancient Rome, the Colosseum has a history that is half gore, half glory. Once able to house 50,000 spectators, it was built to impress Romans with its spectacles involving wild animals and fearsome gladiators from the farthest reaches of the empire. Senators had marble seats up front and the vestal virgins took the ringside position, while the plebs sat in wooden tiers at the back, then the masses above on the top tier. Looming over all was the amazing velarium, an ingenious system of sail-like awnings rigged on ropes and maneuvered by sailors from the imperial fleet, who would unfurl them to protect the arena's occupants from sun or rain. All visitors must book a combination ticket (with the Roman Forum and Palatine Hill) in advance online for a €2 surcharge. If you have a Roma Pass, you can use it. Aim for early or late slots to minimize lines, as even the preferential lanes get busy in the middle of the day. If you wish to see the arena or the underground, you must purchase a special timed ticket with those features, though they do not cost extra with the Full Experience ticket. ✉ *Piazza del Colosseo, Colosseo* ☎ *06/39967700* 🌐 *www.coopculture.it* 🎫 *Requires either the €16 24-hour ticket or the €22 Full Experience ticket (can include the arena and underground areas for no additional fee, but they must be specified during the purchase)* ⚠ *Requires a timed ticket purchased in advance* Ⓜ *Colosseo.*

Domus Aurea (*Golden House of Nero*)

RUINS | Legend has it that Nero famously fiddled while Rome burned. Fancying himself a great actor and poet, he played, as it turns out, his harp to accompany his recital of "The Destruction of Troy" while gazing at the flames of Rome's catastrophic fire of AD 64. Anti-Neronian historians propagandized that Nero, in fact, had set the Great Fire to clear out a vast tract of the city center to build his new palace. Today's historians discount this as historical folderol (going so far as to point to the fact that there was a full moon on the evening of July 19, hardly the propitious occasion to commit arson). But legend or not, Nero did get to build his new palace, the extravagant Domus Aurea (Golden House)—a vast "suburban villa" that was inspired by the emperor's pleasure palace at Baia on the Bay of Naples. His new digs were huge and sumptuous, with a facade of pure gold; seawater piped into the baths; decorations of mother-of-pearl, fretted ivory, and other precious materials; and vast gardens. It was said that after completing this gigantic house, Nero exclaimed,

"Now I can live like a human being!" Note that access to the site is exclusively via guided tours that use virtual reality headsets for part of the presentation. Booking ahead is essential. ✉ *Viale della Domus Aurea 1, Monti* ☎ *06/39967700 booking information* ⊕ *www.coopculture.it* 💳 *€14 including booking fee and guided visit* 👟 *Reservations essential* Ⓜ *Colosseo.*

Fori Imperiali

RUINS | A compound of five grandly conceived complexes flanked with colonnades, the Fori Imperiali contain monuments of triumph, law courts, and temples. The complexes were tacked on to the Roman Forum, from the time of Julius Caesar in the 1st century BC until Trajan in the very early 2nd century AD, to accommodate the ever-growing need for administrative buildings as well as grand monuments.

From Piazza del Colosseo, head northwest on Via dei Fori Imperiali toward Piazza Venezia. Now that the road has been closed to private traffic, it's more pleasant for pedestrians (it's closed to all traffic on Sunday). On the walls to your left, maps in marble and bronze, put up by Benito Mussolini, show the extent of the Roman Republic and Empire (at the time of writing, these were partially obstructed by work on Rome's new subway line, Metro C). The dictator's own dreams of empire led him to construct this avenue, cutting brutally through the Fori Imperiali and the medieval and Renaissance buildings that had grown upon the ruins, so that he would have a suitable venue for parades celebrating his expected military triumphs. Among the Fori Imperiali along the avenue, you can see the Foro di Cesare (Forum of Caesar) and the Foro di Augusto (Forum of Augustus). The grandest was the Foro di Traiano (Forum of Trajan), with its huge semicircular Mercati di Traiano and the Colonna Traiana (Trajan's Column). You can walk through part of Trajan's Markets on the Via Alessandrina and visit the Museo dei Fori Imperiali, which presents the Imperial Forums and shows how they would have been used through ancient fragments, artifacts, and modern multimedia. ✉ *Via dei Fori Imperiali, Monti* ☎ *06/0608* ⊕ *www.mercatiditraiano.it* 💳 *Museum €11.50* Ⓜ *Colosseo.*

Foro di Traiano (*Forum of Trajan*)

RUINS | Of all the Fori Imperiali, Trajan's was the grandest and most imposing, a veritable city unto itself. Designed by architect Apollodorus of Damascus, it comprised a vast basilica, two libraries, and a colonnade laid out around the square—all at one time covered with rich marble ornamentation. Adjoining the forum were the Mercati di Traiano (Trajan's Markets), a huge, multilevel brick complex of shops, taverns, walkways, and terraces, as well as administrative offices involved in the mammoth task of feeding the city. The Museo dei Fori Imperiali (Imperial Forums Museum) takes advantage of the Forum's soaring vaulted spaces to showcase archaeological fragments and sculptures while presenting a video re-creation of the original complex. In addition, the series of terraced rooms offers an impressive overview of the entire forum. A pedestrian walkway, the Via Alessandrina, also allows for an excellent (and free) view of Trajan's Forum.

To build a complex of this magnitude, Apollodorus and his patrons clearly had great confidence, not to mention almost unlimited means and cheap labor at their disposal (readily provided by slaves captured in Trajan's Dacian Wars). The complex also contained two semicircular lecture halls, one at either end, which are thought to have been associated with the libraries in Trajan's Forum. The markets' architectural centerpiece is the enormous curved wall, or *exedra*, that shores up the side of the Quirinal Hill excavated by Apollodorus's gangs of laborers. Covered galleries and streets were constructed

Rome Metro and Suburban Railway

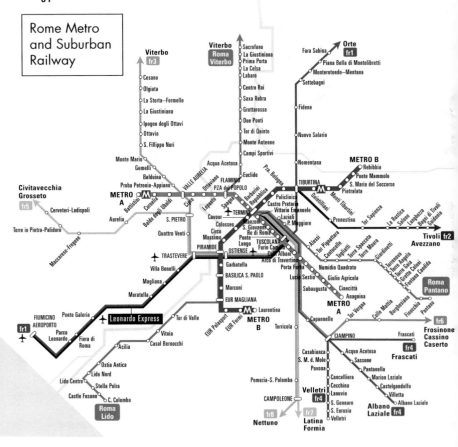

Tickets

A ticket (BIT) valid for 100 minutes on any combination of buses and trams and one entrance to the metro costs €1.50. Tickets are sold at newsstands, some coffee bars, ticket machines in metro stations, and ATAC and COTRAL ticket booths. Time-stamp your ticket when boarding the first vehicle, and stamp it again when boarding for the last time within 75 minutes. You stamp the ticket at Metro sliding electronic doors, and in the little yellow machines on buses and trams.

Fare fees	Price
Single fare	€1.50
Biglietto integrato giornaliero (Integrated Daily Ticket) BIG	€6
Biglietto turistico integrato (Three-Day Pass) BTI	€16.50
Weekly pass	€24
Monthly unlimited pass	€35

at various levels, following the exedra's curves and giving the complex a strikingly modern appearance.

As you enter the markets, a large, vaulted hall stands in front of you. Two stories of shops and offices rise up on either side. Head for the flight of steps at the far end that leads down to Via Biberatica. (*Bibere* is Latin for "to drink," and the shops that open onto the street are believed to have been taverns.) Then head back to the three retail and administrative tiers that line the upper levels of the great exedra and look out over the remains of the Forum. Empty and bare today, the cubicles were once ancient Rome's busiest market stalls. Though it seems to be part of the market, the Torre delle Milizie (Tower of the Militia), the tall brick tower that is a prominent feature of Rome's skyline, was actually built in the early 1200s. ✉ *Via IV Novembre 94, Monti* ☎ *06/0608* ⊕ *www.mercatiditraiano.it* ⌨ *€11.50* Ⓜ *Cavour.*

★ Musei Capitolini

ART MUSEUM | Surpassed in size and richness only by the Musei Vaticani, this immense collection was the world's first public museum. A greatest hits of Roman art through the ages, from the ancients to the Baroque, it's housed in the Palazzo dei Conservatori and the Palazzo Nuovo, which mirror one another across Michelangelo's famous piazza. The collection was begun by Pope Sixtus IV (the man who built the Sistine Chapel) in 1473, when he donated a room of ancient statuary to the people of the city. This core of the collection includes the She Wolf, which is the symbol of Rome, and the piercing gaze of the Capitoline Brutus.

Buy your ticket and enter the Palazzo dei Conservatori where, in the first courtyard, you'll see the giant head, foot, elbow, and imperially raised finger of the fabled seated statue of Constantine, which once dominated the Basilica of Maxentius in the Forum. Upstairs is the resplendent Sala degli Orazi e Curiazi (Hall of the Horatii and Curatii), decorated with a magnificent gilt ceiling, carved wooden doors, and 16th-century frescoes depicting the history of Rome's legendary origins. At each end of the hall are statues of two of the most important popes of the Baroque era, Urban VIII and Innocent X.

The heart of the museum is the modern Exedra of Marcus Aurelius (Esedra di Marco Aurelio), which displays the spectacular original bronze statue of the Roman emperor whose copy dominates the piazza outside. To the right, the room segues into the area of the Temple of Jupiter, with the ruins of part of its vast base rising organically into the museum space. A reconstruction of the temple and the Capitoline Hill from the Bronze Age to the present day makes for a fascinating glimpse through the ages. On the top floor, the museum's *pinacoteca,* or painting gallery, has some noted Baroque masterpieces, including Caravaggio's *The Fortune Teller* and *St. John the Baptist.*

To get to the Palazzo Nuovo section of the museum, take the stairs or elevator to the basement of the Palazzo dei Conservatori, where the corridor uniting the two contains the Epigraphic Collection, a poignant assembly of ancient gravestones. Just over halfway along the corridor, and before going up into the Palazzo Nuovo, be sure to take the staircase to the right to the Tabularium gallery and its unparalleled view over the Forum.

On the stairs inside the Palazzo Nuovo, you'll be immediately dwarfed by Mars in full military rig and lion-topped sandals. Upstairs is the noted Sala degli Imperatori, lined with busts of Roman emperors, and the Sala dei Filosofi, where busts of philosophers sit in judgment—a fascinating who's who of the ancient world. Within these serried ranks are 48 Roman emperors, ranging from Augustus to Theodosius. Nearby are rooms filled with sculptural masterpieces, including the famed *Dying Gaul*, the *Red Faun* from Hadrian's Villa, and a *Cupid and Psyche*. ⊠ *Piazza del Campidoglio 1, Piazza Venezia* ☎ *06/0608* ⊕ *www.museicapitolini.org* ✉ *€11.50 (€22 with exhibitions); €16 with access to Centrale Montemartini; €7 audio guide* Ⓜ *Colosseo*.

★ Palatine Hill

RUINS | Just beyond the Arch of Titus, the Clivus Palatinus gently rises to the heights of the Colle Palatino (Palatine Hill)—the oldest inhabited site in Rome. Despite its location overlooking the Forum's traffic and attendant noise, the Palatine was the most coveted address for ancient Rome's rich and famous. Augustus was born on the hill, and the Houses of Livia and Augustus are today the hill's best-preserved structures, replete with fabulous frescoes. Later emperors built even bigger, and much of what we see today dates from the reign of Domitian, in the late 1st century AD. ⊠ *Entrances at Piazza del Colosseo and Via di San Gregorio 30, Monti* ☎ *06/39967700* ⊕ *www.coopculture.it* ✉ *€18 combined ticket, includes single entry to Palatine Hill–Forum site and single entry to Colosseum (if used within 24 hours); S.U.P.E.R. ticket €22 (€24 with online reservation) includes access to the Houses of Augustus and Livia, the Palatine Museum, Aula Isiaca, Santa Maria Antiqua, and Temple of Romulus* Ⓜ *Colosseo*.

★ The Roman Forum

RUINS | Whether it's from the main entrance on Via dei Fori Imperiali or by the entrance at the Arch of Titus, descend into the extraordinary archaeological complex that is the Foro Romano and the Palatine Hill, once the very heart of the Roman world. The Forum began life as a marshy valley between the Capitoline and Palatine Hills—a valley crossed by a mud track and used as a cemetery by Iron Age settlers. Over the years, a market center and some huts were established here, and after the land was drained in the 6th century BC, the site eventually became a political, religious, and commercial center: the Forum.

Hundreds of years of plunder reduced the Forum to its current desolate state. But this enormous area was once Rome's pulsating hub, filled with stately and extravagant temples, palaces, and shops and crowded with people from all corners of the empire. Adding to today's confusion is the fact that the Forum developed over many centuries; what you see today are not the ruins from just one period but from a span of almost 900 years, from about 500 BC to AD 400. Nonetheless, the enduring romance of the place, with its lonely columns and great broken fragments of sculpted marble and stone, makes for a quintessential Roman experience.

There is always a line at the Colosseum ticket office for the combined Colosseum/Palatine/Forum ticket, but in high season, lines sometimes also form at the Forum and Palatine entrances. Those who don't want to risk waiting in line can book their tickets online in advance, for a €2 surcharge. Choose the print-at-home option (a PDF on a smartphone works, too) and avoid the line to pick up tickets. Your ticket is valid for one entrance to the Roman Forum and the Palatine Hill, which are part of a single continuous complex. Certain sites within the Forum require a S.U.P.E.R. ticket. ⊠ *Entrance at Via dei Fori Imperiali, Monti* ☎ *06/39967700* ⊕ *www.coopculture.it* ✉ *€18 combined ticket, includes single entry to Palatine Hill–Forum site and single entry to Colosseum (if used within 24 hours); S.U.P.E.R. ticket €22 (€24 with online reservation) includes access to the Houses of Augustus and Livia, the Palatine Museum, Aula Isiaca, Santa Maria Antiqua, and Temple of Romulus; audio guide €5* Ⓜ *Colosseo*.

★ San Clemente

CHURCH | One of the most impressive archaeological sites in Rome, San Clemente is a historical triple-decker. A 12th-century church was built on top of a 4th-century church, which had been built over a 2nd-century pagan temple to the god Mithras and 1st-century Roman apartments. The layers were uncovered in 1857, when a curious prior, Friar Joseph Mullooly, started excavations beneath the present basilica. Today, you can descend to explore all three.

In the left nave, the Castiglioni chapel holds frescoes painted around 1400 by the Florentine artist Masolino da Panicale (1383–1440), a key figure in the introduction of realism and one-point perspective into Renaissance painting. Note the large Crucifixion and scenes from the lives of Saints Catherine, Ambrose, and Christopher, plus the Annunciation (over the entrance). ⊠ *Via Labicana 95, Celio* ☎ *06/7740021* ⊕ *www.basilicasanclemente.com* 🖾 *Archaeological area €10* Ⓜ *Colosseo.*

★ Santa Maria Maggiore

CHURCH | Despite its florid 18th-century facade, Santa Maria Maggiore is one of the oldest churches in Rome, built around 440 by Pope Sixtus III. One of the four great pilgrimage churches of Rome, it's also the city center's best example of an early Christian basilica—one of the immense, hall-like structures derived from ancient Roman civic buildings and divided into thirds by two great rows of columns marching up the nave. The other three major basilicas in Rome (San Giovanni in Laterano, St. Peter's, and St. Paul Outside the Walls) have been largely rebuilt. Paradoxically, the major reason why this church is such a striking example of early Christian design is that the same man who built the undulating exteriors circa 1740, Ferdinando Fuga, also conscientiously restored the interior, throwing out later additions and, crucially, replacing a number of the great columns.

The Cappella Sistina (Sistine Chapel), in the right-hand transept, was created by architect Domenico Fontana for Pope Sixtus V in 1585. Elaborately decorated with precious marbles "liberated" from the monuments of ancient Rome, the chapel includes a lower-level museum with some 13th-century sculptures by Arnolfo da Cambio that survived the Sack of Rome in 1527. Borgia popes Paul V and Clement VIII are buried here, as is Gian Lorenzo Bernini, under a simple engraved slab as humble as the tombs of his patrons are grand. The outside mosaic of Christ raising his hand in blessing is one of Rome's most beautiful sights, especially when lighted at night. ⊠ *Piazza di Santa Maria Maggiore, Monti* ☎ *06/69886802* Ⓜ *Termini.*

 Restaurants

Li Rioni

$ | **PIZZA** | **FAMILY** | This busy pizzeria conveniently close to the Colosseum has been serving real-deal Roman-style pizza—super thin and cooked to a crisp— since the mid-1980s. The magic might be due to the fact that they let their pizza dough rise 24–48 hours before baking to guarantee an extra-light pizza, said to be more easily digested than others. **Known for:** homemade tiramisu; pizza margherita; olive ascolane (fried, breaded olives stuffed with sausage). Ⓢ *Average main: €12* ⊠ *Via dei Santi Quattro 24, Celio* ☎ *06/70450605* ⊕ *www.lirioni. it* ⊗ *Closed Tues. and 2 wks in Aug. No lunch* Ⓜ *Colosseo.*

Terra e Domus della Provincia di Roma

$ | **ITALIAN** | It's hard to find genuinely good food in this area, but this wine bar next to Trajan's Column is an exception. Ideal for coffee, a late lunch, early supper, or just an *aperitivo* (aperitif), it's run by the Province of Rome to showcase local produce and is a great spot to rest after wandering amid the ruins. **Known for:** tourist-friendly Roman classics; daily specials; local wines. Ⓢ *Average main: €14*

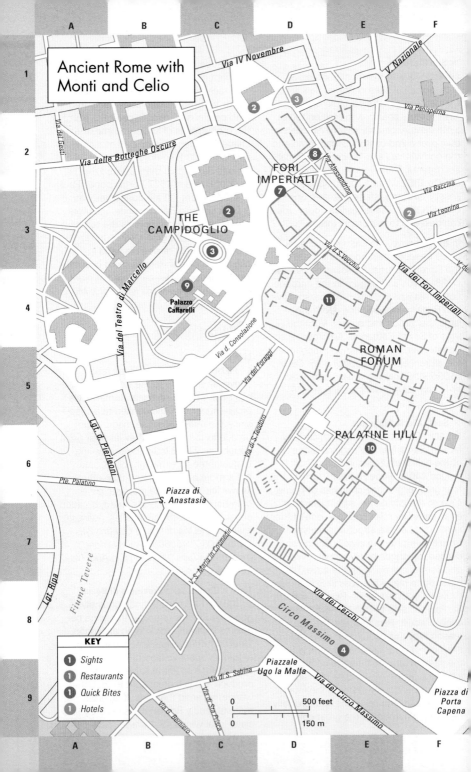

Ancient Rome with Monti and Celio

Via IV Novembre

V. Nazionale

Via Panisperna

Via del Gesù

Via delle Botteghe Oscure

FORI
IMPERIALI

Via Alessandrina

Via Baccina

Via Leonina

THE
CAMPIDOGLIO

Via d. S. Vecchia

Via dei Fori Imperiali

V. de

Palazzo
Caffarelli

Via del Teatro di Marcello

Via d. Consolazione

Via d. Foraggi

ROMAN
FORUM

Lgt. d. Pierleoni

Via di S. Teodoro

PALATINE HILL

Pte. Palatino

Piazza di
S. Anastasia

Lgt. Ripa

Fiume Tevere

V. S. Maria in Cosmedin

Via dei Cerchi

Circo Massimo

KEY

- Sights
- Restaurants
- Quick Bites
- Hotels

Via di S. Sabina

Piazzale
Ugo la Malfa

Via del Circo Massimo

Piazza di
Porta
Capena

Via di Sta Prisca

Via G. Bernardo

0   500 feet

0   150 m

3

Rome ANCIENT ROME WITH MONTI AND CELIO

✉ *Foro Traiano 82, Monti* ☎ *06/69940273* 🌐 *www.palazzovalentini.it/terre-domus* [M] *Cavour, Colosseo.*

★ **Urbana 47**

$$$ | **MODERN ITALIAN** | This restaurant serving lunch and dinner embodies the *kilometro zero* concept, highlighting hyper-local food from the surrounding Lazio region. The local boho crowd comes for tasty lunch and dinner options like fried calamari or cheeseburgers (with free Wi-Fi) in an industrial-chic space. **Known for:** hyper-local produce; aperitivo and tapas; industrial-chic design. [$] *Average main: €30* ✉ *Via Urbana 47, Monti* ☎ *06/47884006* 🌐 *www.urbana47.it* ⏲ *Closed Tues.* [M] *Cavour.*

Coffee and Quick Bites

★ **Fatamorgana Monti**

$ | **ICE CREAM** | The emphasis is on all-natural ingredients at this woman-owned gelateria, which has several locations in Rome. Flavors change often but might include favorites like stracciatella and hazelnut as well as more unusual flavors like matcha or carrot cake. **Known for:** gluten-free with many vegan options; unusual flavors; all natural ingredients. [$] *Average main: €3* ✉ *Piazza degli Zingari 5, Monti* ☎ *06/48906955* 🌐 *www.gelateriafatamorgana.com* [M] *Cavour.*

Hotels

Hotel Celio

$$ | **HOTEL** | There's much more to brag about than proximity to the Colosseum at this chic boutique hotel. **Pros:** beautiful rooftop garden; comfortable beds; nice decor. **Cons:** breakfast not that substantial; service can be iffy; very small bathrooms. [$] *Rooms from: €180* ✉ *Via dei Santissimi Quattro 35/c, Celio* ☎ *06/70495333* 🌐 *www.hotelcelio.com* 🛏 *22 rooms* 🍴 *Free Breakfast* [M] *Colosseo.*

Hotel Forum

$$ | **HOTEL** | A longtime favorite, this converted 18th-century convent has a truly unique setting on one side of the Fori Imperiali, with cinematic views of ancient Rome across the avenue so impressive that it has drawn celebrities and socialites. **Pros:** bird's-eye view of ancient Rome; discounted rates can be found from time to time; "American" bar on rooftop terrace. **Cons:** food and drinks are expensive; outdated decor; small rooms. [$] *Rooms from: €180* ✉ *Via Tor de' Conti 25–30, Monti* ☎ *06/6792446* 🌐 *www.hotelforum.com* 🛏 *80 rooms* 🍴 *No Meals* [M] *Cavour, Colosseo.*

NH Collection Roma Fori Imperiali

$$ | **HOTEL** | It would be hard to find a modern hotel closer to the Roman Forum—the ancient ruins are practically right outside the door. **Pros:** incredible views of ancient Rome; restaurant Oro Bistrot by renowned chef Natale Giunta; rooftop bar serves a great aperitivo. **Cons:** no spa or gym; not much public space; breakfast foods are pre-packaged. [$] *Rooms from: €200* ✉ *Via di Santa Eufemia 19, Piazza Venezia* ☎ *06/697689911* 🌐 *www.nh-collection.com/it/hotel/nh-collection-roma-fori-imperiali* 🛏 *42 rooms* 🍴 *No Meals* [M] *Cavour.*

Palazzo Manfredi

$$$$ | **HOTEL** | If you dream of waking up to head-on views of the Colosseum, look no further. **Pros:** incredible views; excellent restaurant and cocktail bar; unparalleled location. **Cons:** no meals included; not pet-friendly; not all rooms have views of the Colosseum. [$] *Rooms from: €506* ✉ *Via Labicana 125, Colosseo* ☎ *06/77591380* 🌐 *www.palazzomanfredi.com* 🛏 *20 rooms* 🍴 *No Meals* [M] *Colosseo.*

Y Nightlife

★ Ai Tre Scalini

WINE BARS | An ivy-covered wine bar in the center of Monti, Rome's trendiest 'hood, Ai Tre Scalini has a warm and cozy menu of delicious antipasti and light entrées to go along with its enticing wine list. After about 8 pm, if you haven't booked, be prepared to wait—this is one extremely popular spot with locals. ⊠ *Via Panisperna 251, Monti* ☎ *06/48907495* ⊕ *www.aitrescalini.org* Ⓜ *Cavour.*

★ The Court

COCKTAIL LOUNGES | For a winning combination of creative cocktails and incredible views of the Colosseum, this bar in Palazzo Manfredi can't be beat. Bar manager Matteo "Zed" Zamberlan cut his teeth in New York's top bars and here his creativity is on full display. The cocktails are pricey, but they come with a bounty of snacks from the hotel's acclaimed restaurant. ⊠ *Via Labicana 125, Colosseo* ☎ *06/77591380* ⊕ *www.palazzomanfredi. com* Ⓜ *Colosseo.*

Shopping

★ Sacripante

WOMEN'S CLOTHING | This tiny Monti art gallery/boutique/bar houses some of the most sophisticated retro-inspired fashion garments around Rome. Its owner, Wilma Silvestri, cleverly combines vintage and contemporary fabrics for her label Le Gallinelle, evolving them into stylish clothing with a modern edge made for everyday wear. ⊠ *Via Panisperna 59, Monti* ☎ *06/48903495* ⊕ *www.facebook. com/sacripantegallery* Ⓜ *Cavour.*

The Vatican with Borgo and Prati

Climbing the steps to St. Peter's Basilica feels monumental, like a journey that has reached its climactic end. Suddenly, all is cool and dark … and you are dwarfed by the gargantuan nave and its magnificence. Above is a ceiling so high it must lead to heaven itself. Great, shining marble figures of saints frozen mid-whirl loom from niches and corners. And at the end, a throne for an unseen king whose greatness, it is implied, must mirror the greatness of his palace. For this basilica is a palace, the dazzling center of power for a king and a place of supplication for his subjects. Whether his kingdom is earthly or otherwise may lie in the eye of the beholder.

For good Catholics and sinners alike, the Vatican is an exercise in spirituality, requiring patience but delivering joy. Some come here for a transcendent glimpse of a heavenly Michelangelo fresco; others come in search of a direct connection with the divine. But what all visitors share, for a few hours, is an awe-inspiring landscape that offers a famous sight for every taste: rooms decorated by Raphael, antique sculptures like the Apollo Belvedere, famous paintings by Giotto and Bellini, and, perhaps most of all, the Sistine Chapel—for the lover of beauty, few places are as historically important as this epitome of faith and grandeur.

The Borgo and Prati are the neighborhoods immediately surrounding the Vatican, and it's worth noting that, while the Vatican may well be a priority, these neighborhoods are not the best places to choose a hotel, as they're quite far from other top sights in the city.

GETTING HERE AND AROUND

Metro stop Cipro or Ottaviano will get you within about a 10-minute walk of the entrance to the Musei Vaticani. Or, from Termini station, Bus No. 40 Express or the famously crowded No. 64 will take you to Piazza San Pietro. Both routes swing past Largo Argentina, where you can also get Bus No. 46.

A leisurely meander from the centro storico, across the exquisite Ponte Sant'Angelo, will take about a half hour.

 # Sights

★ Basilica di San Pietro

CHURCH | The world's largest church, built over the tomb of St. Peter, is the most imposing and breathtaking architectural achievement of the Renaissance (although much of the lavish interior dates to the Baroque). No fewer than five of Italy's greatest artists—Bramante, Raphael, Peruzzi, Antonio da Sangallo the Younger, and Michelangelo—died while striving to erect this new St. Peter's. The history of the original St. Peter's goes back to AD 326, when the emperor Constantine completed a basilica over the site of the tomb of St. Peter, the Church's first pope. The original church stood for more than 1,000 years, undergoing a number of restorations and alterations, until, toward the middle of the 15th century, it was on the verge of collapse. In 1452, a reconstruction job began but was abandoned for lack of money. In 1503, Pope Julius II instructed the architect Bramante to raze all the existing buildings and build a new basilica, one that would surpass even Constantine's for grandeur. It wasn't until 1626 that the new basilica was completed and consecrated.

Highlights include the Loggia delle Benedizioni (Benediction Loggia), the balcony where newly elected popes are proclaimed; Michelangelo's *Pietà*; and Bernini's great bronze baldacchino, a huge, spiral-columned canopy—at

100,000 pounds, perhaps the largest bronze object in the world—as well as many other Bernini masterpieces. There are also the collection of Vatican treasures in the Museo Storico-Artistico e Tesoro, and the Grotte Vaticane crypt. For views of both the dome above and the piazza below, take the elevator or stairs to the roof; those with more stamina (and without claustrophobia) can then head up more stairs to the apex of the dome. ■ TIP→ **The basilica is free to visit, but a security check at the entrance can create very long lines. Arrive before 8:30 or after 5:30 to minimize the wait and avoid the crowds.** ⌧ *Piazza San Pietro, Vatican* ⊕ *www.vatican.va* ☉ *Closed during Papal Audience (Wed. until 1 pm) and during other ceremonies in piazza* Ⓜ *Ottaviano.*

★ Cappella Sistina (*Sistine Chapel*)

ART MUSEUM | In 1508, the redoubtable Pope Julius II commissioned Michelangelo to fresco the more than 10,000 square feet of the Sistine Chapel's ceiling. The task took four years, and it's said that for many years afterward Michelangelo couldn't read anything without holding it over his head. The result, however, was the greatest artwork of the Renaissance. A pair of binoculars helps greatly, as does a small mirror—hold the mirror facing the ceiling and look down to study the reflection. More than 20 years after his work on the ceiling, Michelangelo was called on again, this time by Pope Paul III, to add to the chapel's decoration by painting the *Last Judgment* on the wall over the altar. By way of signature on this, his late great fresco, Michelangelo painted his own face on the flayed-off human skin in St. Bartholomew's hand.

■ TIP→ **The chapel is entered through the Musei Vaticani, and lines are much shorter after 2:30 (reservations are always advisable)—except free Sundays, which are extremely busy and when admissions close at 12:30.** ⌧ *Musei Vaticani, Vatican* ⊕ *www.museivaticani.va* 🎫 *€17 (part of*

the Vatican Museums) ⊙ *Closed Sun.*
M *Ottaviano.*

Castel Sant'Angelo
CASTLE/PALACE | FAMILY | Standing
between the Tiber and the Vatican,
this circular castle has long been one
of Rome's most distinctive landmarks.
Opera lovers know it well as the setting
for the final scene of Puccini's *Tosca*.
Started in AD 135, the structure began
as a mausoleum for the emperor Hadrian
and was completed by his successor,
Antoninus Pius. From the mid-6th century the building became a fortress, a place
of refuge for popes during wars and
sieges. Its name dates to AD 590, when
Pope Gregory the Great, during a procession to plead for the end of a plague,
saw an angel standing on the summit of
the castle, sheathing his sword. Taking
this as a sign that the plague was at an
end, the pope built a small chapel at the
top, placing a statue next to it to celebrate his vision—thus the name, Castel
Sant'Angelo.

In the rooms off the Cortile dell'Angelo,
look for the Cappella di Papa Leone X
(Chapel of Pope Leo X), with a facade by
Michelangelo. In the Pope Alexander VI
courtyard, a wellhead bears the Borgia
coat of arms. The stairs at the far end of
the courtyard lead to the open terrace for
a view of the Passetto, the fortified corridor connecting Castel Sant'Angelo with
the Vatican. In the *appartamento papale*
(papal apartment), the Sala Paolina (Paul-
ine Room) was decorated in the 16th
century by Perino del Vaga and assistants
with lavish frescoes of scenes from the
Old Testament and the lives of St. Paul
and Alexander the Great. ⊠ *Lungotevere
Castello 50, Prati* ☎ *06/6819111 central
line, 06/6896003 tickets* ⊕ *castelsan-
tangelo.beniculturali.it* 🖾 *€13* ⊙ *Closed
Mon.* ⚹ *Online reservations recommended* M *Lepanto.*

★ **Musei Vaticani** (*Vatican Museums*)
ART MUSEUM | Other than the pope and
his papal court, the occupants of the
Vatican are some of the most famous
artworks in the world. The Vatican Palace,
residence of the popes since 1377,
consists of an estimated 1,400 rooms,
chapels, and galleries. The pope and his
household occupy only a small part; most
of the rest is given over to the Vatican
Library and Museums. Beyond the glo-
ries of the Sistine Chapel, the collection
is extraordinarily rich: highlights include
the great antique sculptures (including
the celebrated Apollo Belvedere in the
Octagonal Courtyard and the Belvedere
Torso in the Hall of the Muses); the
Stanze di Raffaello (Raphael Rooms),
with their famous gorgeous frescoes;
and the Old Master paintings, such as
Leonardo da Vinci's beautiful (though
unfinished) *St. Jerome in the Wilderness*,
some of Raphael's greatest creations,
and Caravaggio's gigantic *Deposition in
the Pinacoteca* ("Picture Gallery").

For those interested in guided visits
to the Vatican Museums, tours start at
€34, including entrance tickets, and can
also be booked online. Other offerings
include a regular two-hour guided tour
of the Vatican gardens; call or check
online to confirm. For more information,
call ☎ *06/69884676* or go to ⊕ *musei-
vaticani.va.* For information on tours,
call ☎ *06/69883145* or ⊠ *06/69884676;*
visually impaired visitors can arrange
tactile tours by calling ☎ *06/69884947.*
⊠ *Viale Vaticano, near intersection with
Via Leone IV, Vatican* ☎ *06/69883145*
⊕ *www.museivaticani.va* 🖾 *€17*
⊙ *Closed Sun. and church holidays*
M *Cipro–Musei Vaticani or Ottaviano–San
Pietro; Bus 64 or 40.*

Necropoli Vaticana (*Vatican Necropolis*)
CEMETERY | With advance notice you can
take a 1½-hour guided tour in English of
the Vatican Necropolis, under the Basilica
di San Pietro, which gives a rare glimpse

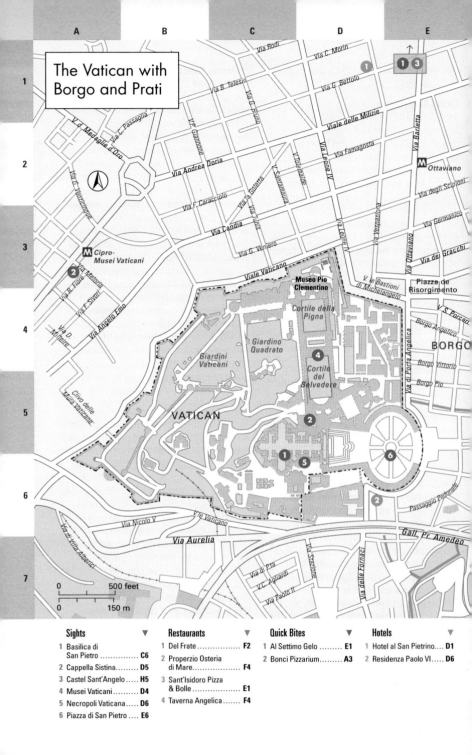

The Vatican with Borgo and Prati

Sights ▼
1 Basilica di San Pietro **C6**
2 Cappella Sistina **D5**
3 Castel Sant'Angelo **H5**
4 Musei Vaticani **D4**
5 Necropoli Vaticana **D6**
6 Piazza di San Pietro **E6**

Restaurants ▼
1 Del Frate **F2**
2 Properzio Osteria di Mare **F4**
3 Sant'Isidoro Pizza & Bolle **E1**
4 Taverna Angelica **F4**

Quick Bites ▼
1 Al Settimo Gelo **E1**
2 Bonci Pizzarium **A3**

Hotels ▼
1 Hotel al San Pietrino.... **D1**
2 Residenza Paolo VI **D6**

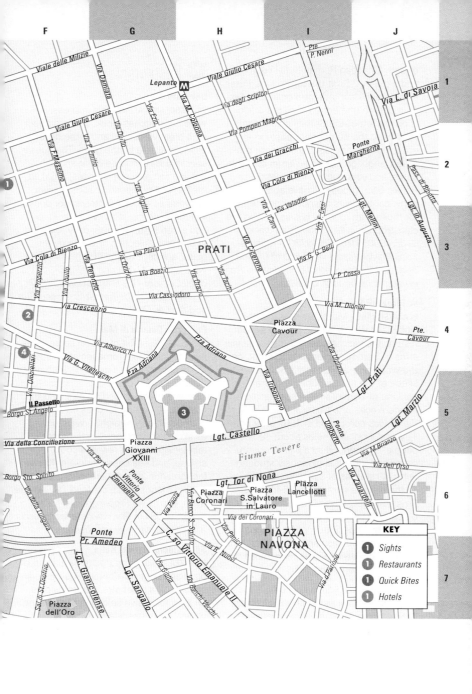

of early Christian Roman burial customs and a closer look at the tomb of St. Peter. Apply via the contact form online, by fax, or in person (the entrance to the office is on the left of the Bernini colonnade), specifying the number of people in the group (all must be age 15 or older), preferred language, preferred time, available dates, and your contact information in Rome. Each group will have about 12 participants. Visits are not recommended for those with mobility issues or who are claustrophobic. ✉ *Ufficio Scavi, Vatican* ☎ *06/69885318, 06/69873017 reservations* 🌐 *www.scavi.va* 🎫 *€13* 🕒 *Closed Sun. and Roman Catholic holidays* ✍ *Reservations required* [M] *Ottaviano.*

★ **Piazza di San Pietro**

PLAZA/SQUARE | Mostly enclosed within high walls that recall the papacy's stormy history, the Vatican opens the spectacular arms of Bernini's colonnade to embrace the world only at St. Peter's Square, scene of the pope's public appearances. One of Bernini's most spectacular masterpieces, the elliptical Piazza di San Pietro was completed in 1667 after only 11 years' work and holds about 100,000 people. Surrounded by a pair of quadruple colonnades, it is gloriously studded with 140 statues of saints and martyrs. At the piazza's center, the 85-foot-high Egyptian obelisk was brought to Rome by Caligula in AD 37 and moved here in 1586 by Pope Sixtus V. The famous Vatican post offices can be found on both sides of St. Peter's Square and inside the Vatican Museums complex.

■ **TIP→ The main Information Office is just left of the basilica as you face it.** ✉ *Piazza di San Pietro, Vatican* 🌐 *www.vaticanstate.va* [M] *Ottaviano.*

🍴 Restaurants

Del Frate

$$ | **MODERN ITALIAN** | This impressive wine bar matches sleek, modern decor with creative cuisine and three dozen wines available by the glass. The house specialty is marinated meat and fish, but you can also get cheeses, smoked meats, and composed salads. **Known for:** wide selection of after-dinner drinks, including mezcal (smoky agave liquor) and amari (bitter cordial); daily aperitivo with a nice selection of wines by the glass; adjacent to one of Rome's noted wine shops. [$] *Average main: €23* ✉ *Via degli Scipioni 118, Prati* ☎ *06/3236437* 🌐 *www.enotecadelfrate.it* 🕒 *Closed Sun. and Aug.* [M] *Ottaviano.*

Properzio Osteria di Mare

$$ | **SEAFOOD** | A bit of a local secret, this new osteria has a romantic atmosphere that's perfect for a date night, with stone walls, a wooden ceiling, chairs painted seafoam green, gilded mirrors, and fresh flowers. The menu focuses on seafood, with deliciously straightforward dishes like roasted octopus with broccoli rabe, linguine with raw and cooked shrimp, and sea bass meunière. **Known for:** romantic atmosphere; affordable tasting menus; fresh seafood. [$] *Average main: €18* ✉ *Via Properzio 20-24, Prati* ☎ *06/68308471* 🌐 *www.osteriaproperzio.it* 🕒 *Closed Mon.* [M] *Ottaviano.*

Sant'Isidoro Pizza & Bolle

$ | **PIZZA** | Taking the traditional pairing of pizza and beer up a notch, this modern pizzeria on a quiet street pairs its pies with an extensive selection of sparkling wines. More upscale than a typical pizzeria but casual enough for a weeknight, this place serves classic flavor combinations as well as some creative options, like a pizza topped with stracciatella, raw shrimp, lemon peel, and mint. **Known for:** chic modern design; creative pizzas;

wide selection of sparkling wines. $ *Average main: €12* ✉ *Via Oslavia 41, Prati* ☎ *06/89822607* ⊕ *www.pizzaebolle.it* ◷ *No lunch Sat.* Ⓜ *Lepanto.*

Taverna Angelica

$$ | **MODERN ITALIAN** | The Borgo area near St. Peter's Basilica hasn't been known for culinary excellence, but this is starting to change, and Taverna Angelica was one of the first refined restaurants in this part of town. The dining room is small, which allows the chef to create a menu that's inventive without being pretentious. **Known for:** ravioli with salt cod in arrabbiata oil spiced with red chili; elegant surroundings; eclectic Italian dishes. $ *Average main: €22* ✉ *Piazza Amerigo Capponi 6, Borgo* ☎ *06/6874514* ⊕ *www.tavernaangelica.com* ◷ *Closed Mon.* Ⓜ *Ottaviano.*

☕ Coffee and Quick Bites

Al Settimo Gelo

$ | **ICE CREAM** | The unusual flavors of gelato scooped up here include cinnamon and ginger and fig with cardamom and walnut, but the classics also get rave reviews. Ask for a taste of the *passito* flavor, if it's available; it's inspired by the popular sweet Italian dessert wine. **Known for:** completely gluten-free shop; homemade whipped cream; organic Sicilian lemon sorbetto. $ *Average main: €5* ✉ *Via Vodice 21/a, Prati* ☎ *06/3725567* ⊕ *www.alsettimogelo.it* ◷ *Closed Mon., and 1 wk in Aug.* Ⓜ *Lepanto.*

Bonci Pizzarium

$ | **PIZZA** | This tiny storefront by famed pizzaiolo Gabriele Bonci is the city's most famous place for pizza al taglio (by the slice). It serves more than a dozen flavors, from the standard margherita to slices piled high with prosciutto and other tasty ingredients. **Known for:** long lines; over a dozen flavors; Rome's best pizza al taglio. $ *Average main: €5* ✉ *Via della Meloria 43, Prati* ☎ *06/39745416* ⊕ *www. bonci.it* ◷ *Closed Mon.* Ⓜ *Cipro.*

Hotels

Hotel al San Pietrino

$ | **HOTEL** | This simple budget hotel on the third floor of a 19th-century palazzo offers rock-bottom rates at a five-minute walk from the Vatican. **Pros:** heavenly rates near the Vatican; free parking nearby; air-conditioning and Wi-Fi. **Cons:** no bar; flat pillows and basic bedding; a couple of Metro stops from the centro storico. $ *Rooms from: €40* ✉ *Via Giovanni Bettolo 43, Prati* ☎ *328/3416714 WhatsApp, 06/3700132* ⊕ *www.hotelsanpietrino.it* ⇆ *11 rooms* ⑪ *Free Breakfast* Ⓜ *Ottaviano.*

Residenza Paolo VI

$$ | **HOTEL** | Set in a former monastery—still an extraterritorial part of the Vatican—magnificently abutting Bernini's colonnade of St. Peter's Square, the Paolo VI (pronounced "Sesto," a reference to Pope Paul VI) is unbeatably close to St. Peter's, with comfortable and amazingly quiet guest rooms. **Pros:** direct views of St. Peter's from the rooftop terrace; lovely staff and service; quiet rooms. **Cons:** far away from Rome's historical attractions; bathrooms are a tight space; some rooms are really small. $ *Rooms from: €139* ✉ *Via Paolo VI 29, Borgo* ☎ *06/684870* ⊕ *www.residenzapaolovi.com* ⇆ *35 rooms* ⑪ *Free Breakfast* Ⓜ *Ottaviano.*

☉ Nightlife

Bukowski's Bar

COCKTAIL LOUNGES | This cozy spot outside the Vatican is furnished like a familiar living room with a giant leather sofa and armchairs, making it easy to meet the people sitting next to you. In addition to a strong cocktail and wine menu, the owners regularly host art, theater, and shopping events. *Aperitivo* (Italian happy hour) is served every evening, with a selection of drinks and the option of adding a small plate for €5. ✉ *Via Degli Ombrellari 25, Borgo* ☎ *351/7139892* Ⓜ *Ottaviano.*

Continued on page 106

HEAVENS ABOVE:
THE SISTINE CEILING

Forming lines that are probably longer than those waiting to pass through the Pearly Gates, hordes of visitors arrive at the Sistine Chapel daily to view what may be the world's most sublime example of artistry:

Michelangelo: *The Creation of Adam*, Sistine Chapel, The Vatican, circa 1511.

Michelangelo's Sistine Ceiling. To paint this 12,000-square-foot barrel vault, it took four years, 343 frescoed figures, and a titanic battle of wits between the artist and Pope Julius II. While in its typical fashion, Hollywood focused on the element of agony, not ecstasy, involved in the saga of creation, a recently completed restoration of the ceiling has revolutionized our appreciation of the masterpiece of masterpieces.

By Martin Bennett

View of the Cappella Sistina

MICHELANGELO'S
MISSION IMPOSSIBLE

Designed to match the proportions of Solomon's Temple described in the Old Testament, the Sistine Chapel is named after Pope Sixtus VI, who commissioned it as a place of worship for himself and as the venue where new popes could be elected. Before Michelangelo, the barrel-vaulted ceiling was an expanse of azure fretted with golden stars. Then, in 1504, an ugly crack appeared. Bramante, the architect, managed do some patchwork using iron rods, but when signs of a fissure remained, the new Pope Julius II summoned Michelangelo to cover it with a fresco 135 feet long and 44 feet wide.

Taking in the entire span of the ceiling, the theme connecting the various participants in this painted universe could be said to be mankind's anguished waiting. The majestic panel depicting the Creation of Adam leads, through the stages of the Fall and the expulsion from Eden, to the tragedy of Noah found naked and mocked by his own sons; throughout all runs the underlying need for man's redemption. Witnessing all from the side and end walls, a chorus of ancient Prophets and Sibyls peer anxiously forward, awaiting the Redeemer who will come to save both the Jews and the Gentiles.

APOCALYPSE NOW

The sweetness and pathos of his *Pietà*, carved by Michelangelo only ten years earlier, have been left behind. The new work foretells an apocalypse, its congregation of doomed sinners facing the wrath of heaven through hanging, beheading, crucifixion, flood, and plague. Michelangelo, by nature a misanthrope, was already filled with visions of doom thanks to the fiery orations of Savonarola, whose thunderous preachments he had heard before leaving his hometown of Florence. Vasari, the 16th-century art historian, coined the word "terribilità" to describe Michelangelo's tension-ridden style, a rare case of a single word being worth a thousand pictures.

Michelangelo wound up using a Reader's Digest condensed version of the stories from Genesis, with the dramatis personae overseen by a punitive and terrifying God. In real life, poor Michelangelo answered to a flesh-and-blood taskmaster who was almost as vengeful: Pope Julius II. Less vicar of Christ than latter-day Caesar, he was intent on uniting Italy under the power of the Vatican, and was eager to do so by any means, including riding into pitched battle. Yet this "warrior pope" considered his most formidable adversary to be Michelangelo. Applying a form of blackmail, Julius threatened to wage war on Michelangelo's Florence, to which the artist had fled after Julius canceled a commission for a grand papal tomb unless Michelangelo agreed to return to Rome and take up the task of painting the Sistine Chapel ceiling.

MICHELANGELO, SCULPTOR

A sculptor first and foremost, however, Michelangelo considered painting an inferior genre—"for rascals and sissies" as he put it. Second, there was the sheer scope of the task, leading Michelangelo to suspect he'd been set up by a rival, Bramante, chief architect of the new St. Peter's Basilica. As Michelangelo was also a master architect, he regarded this fresco commission as a Renaissance mission-impossible. Pope Julius's powerful will prevailed—and six years later the work of the Sistine Ceiling was complete. Irving Stone's famous novel *The Agony and the Ecstasy*—and the granitic 1965 film that followed—chart this epic battle between artist and pope.

THINGS ARE LOOKING UP

To enhance your viewing of the ceiling, bring along opera-glasses, binoculars, or just a mirror (to prevent your neck from becoming bent like Michelangelo's). Note that no photos are permitted. Insiders know the only time to get the chapel to yourself is during the papal blessings and public audiences held in St. Peter's Square. Failing that, get there during lunch hour. Admission and entry to the Sistine Chapel is only through the Musei Vaticani (Vatican Museums).

SCHEMATIC OF THE SISTINE CEILING

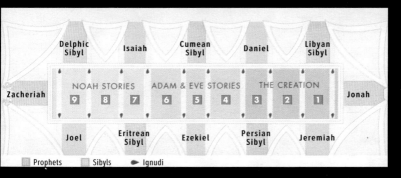

PAINTING
THE BIBLE

The ceiling's biblical symbols were ideated by three Vatican theologians, Cardinal Alidosi, Egidio da Viterbo, and Giovanni Rafanelli, along with Michelangelo. As for the ceiling's

painted "framework," this quadratura alludes to Roman triumphal arches because Pope Julius II was fond of mounting "triumphal entries" into his conquered cities (in imitation of Christ's procession into Jerusalem on Palm Sunday).

THE CENTER PANELS
Prophet turned art-critic or, perhaps doubling as ourselves, the ideal viewer, Jonah the prophet (painted at the altar end) gazes up at the Creation, or Michelangelo's version of it.

1 The first of three scenes taken from the Book of Genesis: God separates Light from Darkness.

2 God creates the sun and a craterless pre-Galilean moon while the panel's other half offers an unprecedented rear view of the Almighty creating the vegetable world.

3 In the panel showing God separating the Waters from the Heavens, the Creator tumbles towards us as in a self-made whirlwind.

4 Pausing for breath, next admire probably Western Art's most famous image—God giving life to Adam.

5 The Creation of Eve from Adam's rib leads to the sixth panel.

6 In a sort of diptych divided by the trunk of the Tree of Knowledge of Good and Evil, Michelangelo retells the Temptation and the Fall.

7 Illustrating Man's fallen nature, the last three panels narrate, in un-chronological order, the Flood. In the first Noah offers a pre-Flood sacrifice of thanks.

8 Damaged by an explosion in 1794, next comes Michelangelo's version of Flood itself.

9 Finally, above the monumental Jonah, you can just make out the small, wretched figure of Noah, lying drunk—in pose, the shrunken anti-type of the majestic Adam five panels down the wall.

THE CREATION OF ADAM

Michelangelo's Adam was partly inspired by the Creation scenes Michelangelo had studied in the sculpted doors of Jacopo della Quercia in Bologna and Lorenzo Ghiberti's Doors of Paradise in Florence. Yet in Michelangelo's version Adam's hand hangs limp, waiting God's touch to impart the spark of life. Facing his Creation, the Creator—looking a bit like the pagan god Jupiter—is for the first time ever depicted as horizontal, mirroring the Biblical "in his own likeness." Decades after its completion, a crack began to appear, amputating Adam's fingertips. Believe it or not, the most famous fingers in Western art are the handiwork, at least in part, of one Domenico Carnevale.

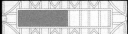

Emerald's Bar

COCKTAIL LOUNGES | This classy cocktail bar a few blocks from the Vatican makes you feel transported to a cozy salon in New York or London. The bartenders shake up reliably good classics, including an excellent dirty martini, and also some original creations. ✉ *Via Crescenzio 91C, Prati* ☎ *06/88654275* Ⓜ *Ottaviano.*

Shopping

★ Castroni

FOOD | Opening its flagship shop near the Vatican in 1932, this gastronomic paradise has long been Rome's port of call for decadent delicacies from around the globe; there are now 13 locations throughout the city. Jonesing expats and study-abroad students pop in for local sweets, 300 types of tea, and even some good old-fashioned Kraft Macaroni & Cheese. If you're just doing a little window-shopping, be sure to try their in-house roasted espresso, some of the best coffee in Rome. ✉ *Via Cola di Rienzo 196/198, Prati* ☎ *06/6874383* ⊕ *www.castronicoladirienzo.com* Ⓜ *Lepanto, Ottaviano.*

Savelli Arte e Tradizione

CRAFTS | Here you'll find a fully stocked selection of religious gifts: everything from rosaries and crosses to religious artwork and Pope Francis memorabilia. Founded in 1898, this family business provides a place for pilgrims to pick up a souvenir from the Holy See and also specializes in mosaics. The store has another location at the Self-Service Restaurant in Piazza del Sant'Uffizio 6/7. It's closed on Sunday afternoon. ✉ *Via Paolo VI 27–29, Borgo* ☎ *06/68307017* ⊕ *www.savellireligious.com* Ⓜ *Ottaviano.*

Piazza Navona, Campo de' Fiori, and the Jewish Ghetto

Set between Via del Corso and the Tiber bend, these time-burnished districts are some of the city's most beautiful. They're filled with airy piazzas, half-hidden courtyards, and narrow streets bearing curious names. Some of Rome's most coveted residential addresses are nestled here. So, too, are the ancient Pantheon and the Renaissance square of Campo de' Fiori, but the spectacular, over-the-top Baroque monuments of the 16th and 17th centuries predominate.

The hub of the district is the queen of squares, Piazza Navona—a cityscape adorned with the most jaw-dropping fountain by Gian Lorenzo Bernini, father of the Baroque. Streets running off the square lead to many historic must-sees, including noble churches by Borromini and Caravaggio's greatest paintings at San Luigi dei Francesi. This district has been an integral part of the city since ancient times, and its position between the Vatican and Lateran palaces, both seats of papal rule, put it in the mainstream of Rome's development from the Middle Ages onward. Craftsmen, shopkeepers, and famed artists toiled in the shadow of the huge palaces built to consolidate the power of leading figures in the papal court. Artisans and artists still live here, but their numbers are diminishing as the district becomes increasingly posh and—so critics say—"Disneyfied." But three of the liveliest piazzas in Rome—Piazza Navona, Piazza della Rotonda (home to the Pantheon), and Campo de' Fiori—are lodestars in a constellation of some of the city's finest cafés, stores, and wine bars.

Although today most of Rome's Jews live outside the Ghetto, the area remains the spiritual and cultural home of Jewish

Rome, and that heritage permeates its small commercial area of Judaica shops, kosher bakeries, and restaurants. The Jewish Ghetto was established by papal decree in the 16th century. It was by definition a closed community, where Roman Jews lived under lock and key until Italian unification in 1870. In 1943–44, the already small Jewish population there was decimated by deportations. Today there are a few Judaica shops and kosher groceries, bakeries, and restaurants (especially on Via di Portico d'Ottavia), but the neighborhood mansions are now being renovated and much coveted by rich and stylish expats.

GETTING HERE AND AROUND

The Piazza Navona and Campo de' Fiori are an easy walk from the Vatican or Trastevere, or a half-hour stroll from the Spanish Steps. From Termini or the Vatican, take Bus No. 40 Express or the No. 64 to Largo Torre Argentina; then walk 10 minutes to either piazza. Bus No. 62 winds from Piazza Barberini past the Trevi Fountain to Campo de' Fiori.

From the Vatican or the Spanish Steps, it's a 30-minute walk to the Jewish Ghetto, or take the No. 40 Express or the No. 64 bus from Termini station to Largo Torre Argentina.

 Sights

Chiesa del Gesù

CHURCH | The mother church of the Jesuits in Rome is the prototype of all Counter-Reformation churches, and its spectacular interior tells a great deal about an era of religious triumph and turmoil. Its architecture influenced ecclesiastical buildings in Rome for more than a century (the overall design was by Vignola, the facade by della Porta) and was exported by the Jesuits throughout the rest of Europe. Though consecrated in 1584, the interior of the church wasn't fully decorated for another 100 years. It was originally intended that the interior

be left plain to the point of austerity— but, when it was finally embellished, the mood had changed and no expense was spared. Its interior drips with gold and lapis lazuli, gold and precious marbles, gold and more gold, all covered by a fantastically painted ceiling. Unfortunately, the church is also one of Rome's most crepuscular, so its visual magnificence is considerably dulled by lack of light.

The architectural significance of Il Gesù extends far beyond the splendid interior. As the first of the great Counter-Reformation churches, it was put up after the Council of Trent (1545–63) had signaled the determination of the Roman Catholic Church to fight back against the Reformed Protestant heretics of northern Europe. The church decided to do so through the use of overwhelming pomp and majesty, in an effort to woo believers. As a harbinger of ecclesiastical spectacle, Il Gesù spawned imitations throughout Italy and the other Catholic countries of Europe as well as the Americas.

The most striking element is the ceiling, which is covered with frescoes that swirl down from on high to merge with painted stucco figures at the base, the illusion of space in the two-dimensional painting becoming the reality of three dimensions in the sculpted figures. Baciccia, their painter, achieved extraordinary effects in these frescoes, especially in the *Triumph of the Holy Name of Jesus*, over the nave. Here, the figures representing evil are cast out of heaven and seem to be hurtling down onto the observer. To appreciate in detail, the spectacle is best viewed through a specially tilted mirror in the nave.

The founder of the Jesuit order himself is buried in the Chapel of St. Ignatius, in the left-hand transept. This is surely the most sumptuous Baroque altar in Rome; as is typical, the enormous globe of lapis lazuli that crowns it is really only a shell of lapis over a stucco base—after all, Baroque decoration prides itself on achieving stunning effects and illusions. The heavy, bronze altar rail by architect Carlo Fontana is in keeping with the surrounding opulence. ⊠ *Via degli Astalli 16, Campo de' Fiori* ☎ *06/697001* ⊕ *www.chiesadelgesu.org.*

Crypta Balbi

RUINS | The fourth component of the magnificent collections of the Museo Nazionale Romano, this museum is unusual because it represents several periods of Roman history. The crypt is part of the Balbus Theater complex (13 BC), and other parts of the complex are from the medieval period, up through the 20th century. The written explanations accompanying the well-lit exhibits are excellent, and this museum is a popular field trip for teachers and school groups. ⊠ *Via delle Botteghe Oscure 31, Jewish Ghetto* ☎ *06/39967701* ⊕ *www.coopculture.it* 🎫 *€10 Crypta Balbi only; €14 includes three other Museo Nazionale Romano sites over a 1-wk period (Palazzo Altemps, Palazzo Massimo, Museo Diocleziano)* ⊘ *Closed Mon.* Ⓜ *Bus Nos. 64 and 40, Tram No. 8.*

Fontana delle Tartarughe

FOUNTAIN | Designed by Giacomo della Porta in 1581 and sculpted by Taddeo Landini, this fountain, set in pretty Piazza Mattei, is one of Rome's most charming. The focus of the fountain is four bronze boys, each grasping a dolphin spouting water into a marble shell. Bronze turtles held in the boys' hands drink from the upper basin. The turtles were added in the 17th century by Bernini. ⊠ *Piazza Mattei, Jewish Ghetto.*

Galleria Spada

ART MUSEUM | In this neighborhood of huge, austere palaces, Palazzo Spada strikes an almost frivolous note, with its pretty ornament-encrusted courtyard and its upper stories covered with stuccoes and statues. While the palazzo houses an impressive collection of Old Master paintings, it's most famous for its trompe-l'oeil garden gallery, a delightful example of the sort of architectural games rich Romans of the 17th century found irresistible. Even if you don't go into the gallery, step into the courtyard and look through the glass window of the library to the colonnaded corridor in the adjacent courtyard. See—or seem to see—a 26-foot-long gallery quadrupled in depth, a sort of optical telescope taking the Renaissance's art of perspective to another level, as it stretches out for a great distance with a large statue at the end. In fact the distance is an illusion: the corridor grows progressively narrower and the columns progressively smaller as they near the statue, which is just 2 feet tall. The Baroque period is known for special effects, and this is rightly one of the most famous. It was long thought that Borromini was responsible for this ruse; it's now known that it was designed by an Augustinian priest, Giovanni Maria da Bitonto. Upstairs is a seignorial picture gallery with the paintings shown as they would have been, piled on top of each other clear to the ceiling. Outstanding works include Brueghel's *Landscape with Windmills,* Titian's *Musician,* and Andrea del Sarto's *Visitation.* Look for the fact sheets that have descriptive notes about the objects in each room. ⊠ *Piazza Capo di Ferro 13, Campo de' Fiori* ☎ *06/6874896* ⊕ *www.galleriaspada.beniculturali.it* 🎫 *€5* ⊘ *Closed Tues.*

★ Palazzo Altemps

CASTLE/PALACE | Containing some of the finest ancient Roman statues in the world, Palazzo Altemps is part of the Museo Nazionale Romano. The palace's sober exterior belies a magnificence that appears as soon as you walk into the majestic courtyard, studded with statues and covered in part by a retractable awning. The restored interior hints at the Roman lifestyle of the 16th–18th centuries while showcasing the most illustrious pieces from the Museo Nazionale, including the collection of the Ludovisi noble family. In the frescoed salons you can see the *Galata Suicida,* a poignant sculptural work portraying a barbarian warrior who chooses death for himself and his wife, rather than humiliation by the enemy. Another highlight is the large Ludovisi sarcophagus, magnificently carved from marble. In a place of honor is the *Ludovisi Throne,* which shows a goddess emerging from the sea and being helped by her acolytes. For centuries this was heralded as one of the most sublime Greek sculptures, but, today, at least one authoritative art historian considers it a colossally overrated fake. Look for the framed explanations of the exhibits that detail (in English) how and exactly where Renaissance sculptors, Bernini among them, added missing pieces to the classical works. In the lavishly frescoed loggia stand busts of the Caesars. In the wing once occupied by early-20th-century poet Gabriele d'Annunzio (who married into the Altemps family), three rooms host the museum's Egyptian collection. ✉ *Piazza di Sant'Apollinare 46, Piazza Navona* ☎ *06/684851* ⊕ *museonazionaleromano. beniculturali.it* ✆ *€8; €12 combined ticket includes three other Museo Nazionale Romano sites over one week (Crypta Balbi, Palazzo Massimo alle Terme, and Museo delle Terme di Diocleziano)* ☉ *Closed Mon. and Tues.*

★ Pantheon

RELIGIOUS BUILDING | The best-preserved ancient building in the city, this former Roman temple is a marvel of architectural harmony and proportion. It was entirely rebuilt by the emperor Hadrian around AD 120 on the site of an earlier Pantheon (from the Greek: *pan,* all, and *theon,* gods) erected in 27 BC by Augustus's right-hand man and son-in-law, Agrippa.

The most striking thing about the Pantheon is not its size, immense though it is, nor even the phenomenal technical difficulties posed by so massive a construction; rather, it's the remarkable unity of the building. The diameter described by the dome is exactly equal to its height.

It's the use of such simple mathematical balance that gives classical architecture its characteristic sense of proportion and its nobility. The opening at the apex of the dome, the *oculus,* is nearly 30 feet in diameter and was intended to symbolize the "all-seeing eye of the heavens." On a practical note, this means when it rains, it rains inside: look out for the drainage holes in the floor.

Although little is known for sure about the Pantheon's origins or purpose, it's worth noting that the five levels of trapezoidal coffers (sunken panels in the ceiling) represent the course of the five then-known planets and their concentric spheres. Ruling over them is the sun, represented symbolically and literally by the 30-foot-wide eye at the top. The heavenly symmetry is further paralleled by the coffers: 28 to each row, the number of lunar cycles. In the center of each would have shone a small bronze star. Down below, the seven large niches were occupied not by saints, but, it's thought, by statues of Mars, Venus, the deified Caesar, and the other "astral deities," including the moon and sun, the "sol invictus." (Academics still argue, however, about which gods were most probably worshipped here.)

One of the reasons the Pantheon is so well preserved is the result of it being consecrated as a church in AD 608. (It's still a working church today.) No building, church or not, though, escaped some degree of plundering through the turbulent centuries of Rome's history after the fall of the empire. In 655, for example, the gilded bronze covering the dome was stripped. The Pantheon is also one of the city's important burial places. Its most famous tomb is that of Raphael (between the second and third chapels on the left as you enter). Mass takes place on Sunday and on religious holidays at 10:30; it's open to the public, but you are expected to arrive before the beginning and stay

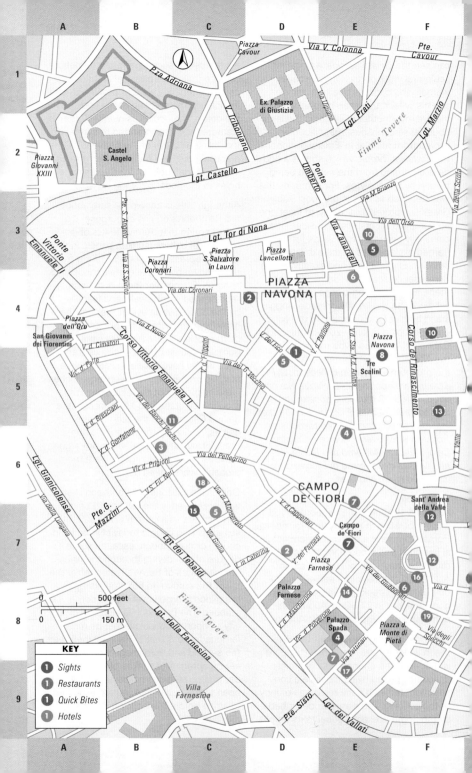

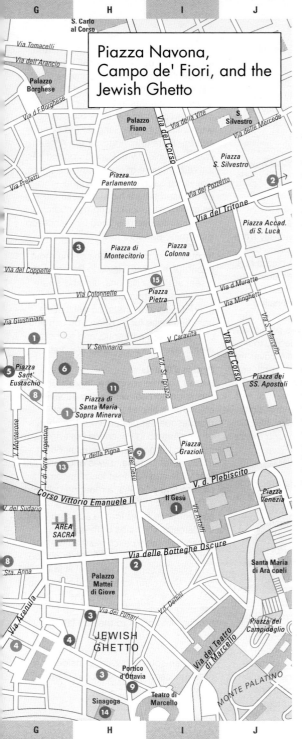

Piazza Navona, Campo de' Fiori, and the Jewish Ghetto

3

Rome PIAZZA NAVONA, CAMPO DE' FIORI, AND THE JEWISH GHETTO

until the end. General access usually resumes at about 11:30.

On weekends and public holidays, you must register in advance (only for the next upcoming weekend or holiday) for a free timed entry slot. Each guest can register up to six people at ⊕ *pantheon. cultura.gov.it.* ✉ *Piazza della Rotonda, Piazza Navona* ☎ *06/68300230* ⊕ *www. pantheonroma.com* 🎫 *Free; audio guide €8.50.*

Piazza Campo de' Fiori

MARKET | A bustling marketplace in the morning (Monday through Saturday from 8 to 2) and a trendy meeting place the rest of the day and night, this piazza has plenty of down-to-earth charm. Just after lunchtime, all the fruit and vegetable vendors disappear, and this so-called *piazza trasformista* takes on another identity, becoming a circus of bars particularly favored by study-abroad students, tourists, and young expats. Brooding over the piazza is a hooded statue of the philosopher Giordano Bruno, who was burned at the stake here in 1600 for heresy, one of many victims of the Roman Inquisition. ✉ *Intersection of Via dei Baullari, Via Giubbonari, Via del Pellegrino, and Piazza della Cancelleria, Campo de' Fiori.*

★ Piazza Navona

PLAZA/SQUARE | Always camera-ready, the beautiful Baroque plaza known as Piazza Navona has Bernini sculptures, three gorgeous fountains, and a magnificently Baroque church (Sant'Agnese in Agone), all built atop the remains of a Roman athletics track. Pieces of the arena are still visible near the adjacent Piazza Sant'Apollinare, and the ancient spirit of entertainment lives on in the buskers and artists who populate the piazza today.

The piazza took on its current look during the 17th century, after Pope Innocent X of the Pamphilj family decided to make over his family palace (now the Brazilian embassy and an ultra-luxe hotel) and the rest of the piazza. Center stage is the Fontana dei Quattro Fiumi, created for Innocent by Bernini in 1651. Bernini's powerful figures of the four rivers represent the longest rivers of the four known continents at the time: the Nile (his head covered because the source was unknown); the Ganges; the Danube; and the Plata (the length of the Amazon was then unknown). Popular legend has it that the figure of the Plata—the figure closest to Sant'Agnese in Agone—raises his hand before his eyes because he can't bear to look upon the church's "inferior" facade designed by Francesco Borromini, Bernini's rival.

If you want a café with one of the most beautiful, if pricey, views in Rome, grab a seat at Piazza Navona. Just be aware that all the restaurants here are heavily geared toward tourists, so while it's a beautiful place for a coffee, you can find cheaper, more authentic, and far better meals elsewhere. ✉ *Piazza Navona.*

Portico d'Ottavia

RUINS | Looming over the Jewish Ghetto, this huge portico, with a few surviving columns, is one of the area's most picturesque set pieces, with the church of Sant'Angelo in Pescheria built right into its ruins. Named by Augustus in honor of his sister Octavia, it was originally 390 feet wide and 433 feet long, encompassed two temples, a meeting hall, and a library, and served as a kind of grandiose entrance foyer for the adjacent Teatro di Marcello. The ruins of the portico became Rome's *pescheria* (fish market) during the Middle Ages. A stone plaque on a pillar (a copy; the original is in the Musei Capitolini) states in Latin that the head of any fish surpassing the length of the plaque was to be cut off "up to the first fin" and given to the city fathers, or else the vendor was to pay a fine of 10 gold florins. The heads were used to make fish soup and were considered a great delicacy. ✉ *Via Portico d'Ottavia 29, Jewish Ghetto.*

★ San Luigi dei Francesi

CHURCH | A pilgrimage spot for art lovers, San Luigi's Contarelli Chapel (the fifth and last chapel on the left, toward the main altar) is adorned with three stunningly dramatic works by Caravaggio (1571–1610), the Baroque master of the heightened approach to light and dark. They were commissioned for the tomb of Mattheiu Cointerel in one of Rome's French churches (San Luigi is St. Louis, patron saint of France). The inevitable coin machine will light up his *Calling of Saint Matthew, Saint Matthew and the Angel,* and *Martyrdom of Saint Matthew* (seen from left to right), and Caravaggio's mastery of light takes it from there. When painted, they caused considerable consternation among the clergy of San Luigi, who thought the artist's dramatically realistic approach was scandalously disrespectful. A first version of the altarpiece was rejected; the priests were not particularly happy with the other two, either. Time has fully vindicated Caravaggio's patron, Cardinal Francesco del Monte, who secured the commission for these works and stoutly defended them. ⊠ *Piazza di San Luigi dei Francesi, Piazza Navona* ☎ *06/688271* ⊕ *www.saintlouis-rome.net.*

★ Santa Maria sopra Minerva

CHURCH | The name of the church reveals that it was built *sopra* (over) the ruins of a temple of Minerva, the ancient goddess of wisdom. Erected in 1280 by Dominicans along severe Italian Gothic lines, it has undergone a number of more or less happy restorations to the interior. Certainly, as the city's major Gothic church, it provides a refreshing contrast to Baroque flamboyance. Have a €1 coin handy to illuminate the Cappella Carafa in the right transept, where Filippino Lippi's (1457–1504) glowing frescoes are well worth the small investment, opening up the deepest azure expanse of sky where musical angels hover around the Virgin. Under the main altar is the tomb of St. Catherine of Siena, one of Italy's patron saints. Left of the altar you'll find Michelangelo's *Risen Christ* and the tomb of the gentle artist Fra Angelico. Bernini's unusual and little-known monument to the Blessed Maria Raggi is on the fifth pier of the left-hand aisle. In front of the church, Bernini's *Elephant and Obelisk* is perhaps the city's most charming sculpture. An inscription on the base references the church's ancient patroness, reading something to the effect that it takes a strong mind to sustain solid wisdom. ⊠ *Piazza della Minerva, Piazza Navona* ☎ *06/792257* ⊕ *www.santamariasopraminerva.it.*

Sant'Andrea della Valle

CHURCH | Topped by the highest dome in Rome after St. Peter's (designed by Maderno), this huge and imposing 17th-century church is remarkably balanced in design. Fortunately, its facade, which had turned a sooty gray from pollution, has been cleaned to a near-sparkling white. Use one of the handy mirrors to examine the early-17th-century frescoes by Domenichino in the choir vault and those by Lanfranco in the dome. One of the earliest ceilings done in full Baroque style, its upward vortex was influenced by Correggio's dome in Parma, of which Lanfranco was also a citizen. (Bring a few coins to light the paintings, which can be very dim.) The three massive paintings of St. Andrew's martyrdom are by Mattia Preti (1650–51). Richly marbled and decorated chapels flank the nave, and in such a space, Puccini set the first act of *Tosca.* ⊠ *Piazza Vidoni 6, Corso Vittorio Emanuele II, Campo de' Fiori* ☎ *06/6861339.*

Sant'Ivo alla Sapienza

CHURCH | The main facade of this eccentric Baroque church, probably Borromini's best, is on the stately courtyard of an austere building that once housed Rome's university. Sant'Ivo has what must surely be one of the most delightful "domes" in all of Rome—a dizzying spiral said to have been inspired by a bee's stinger. The apian symbol is a reminder that Borromini built the church on commission from the Barberini pope Urban VIII (a swarm of bees figure on the Barberini family crest), although it was completed by Alexander VII. The interior, open only for three hours on Sunday morning, is worth a look, especially if you share Borromini's taste for complex mathematical architectural idiosyncrasies. "I didn't take up architecture solely to be a copyist," he once said. Sant'Ivo is certainly the proof. ⊠ *Corso del Rinascimento 40, Piazza Navona* ☏ *06/6864987* ⊗ *Closed Mon.–Sat. and Aug.*

Sinagoga

RELIGIOUS BUILDING | This synagogue has been the city's largest Jewish temple, and a Roman landmark with its aluminum dome, since its construction in 1904. The building also houses the Jewish Museum, with its precious ritual objects and other exhibits, which document the uninterrupted presence of a Jewish community in the city for nearly 22 centuries. Until the 16th century, Jews were esteemed citizens of Rome. Among them were bankers and physicians to the popes, who had themselves given permission for the construction of synagogues. But in 1555, during the Counter-Reformation, Pope Paul IV decreed the building of the walls of the Ghetto, confining the Jews to this small area and imposing a series of restrictions, some of which continued to be enforced until 1870. For security reasons, entrance is via guided visit only, and tours in English are available twice a day but should be booked online ahead of time; entrance to the synagogue is through the museum located in Via Catalana (⊠ *Largo 16 Ottobre 1943*). ⊠ *Lungotevere de' Cenci 15, Jewish Ghetto* ☏ *06/68400661* ⊕ *www. museoebraico.roma.it* 🎫 *€11* ⊗ *Museum closed Sat. and Jewish holidays.*

★ Via Giulia

STREET | Still a Renaissance-era diorama and one of Rome's most exclusive addresses, Via Giulia was the first street in Rome since ancient times to be deliberately planned. Straight as a die, it was named for Pope Julius II (of Sistine Chapel fame), who commissioned it in the early 1500s as part of a scheme to open up a grandiose approach to St. Peter's Basilica, and it is flanked with elegant churches and palaces. Although the pope's plans to change the face of the city were only partially completed, Via Giulia became an important thoroughfare in Renaissance Rome. Today, after more than four centuries, it remains the "salon of Rome," address of choice for Roman aristocrats, although controversy has arisen about a recent change—the decision to add a large parking lot along one side of the street—that meant steamrolling through ancient and medieval ruins underneath. A stroll will reveal elegant palaces and churches (one, San Eligio, on the little side street Via di Sant'Eligio, was designed by Raphael himself). The area around Via Giulia is wonderful to wander through and get the feel of daily life as carried on in a centuries-old setting. Among the buildings that merit your attention are Palazzo Sacchetti (Via Giulia 66), with an imposing stone portal (inside are some of Rome's grandest staterooms, still, after 300 years, the private quarters of the Marchesi Sacchetti), and the forbidding brick building that housed the Carceri Nuove (New Prison; Via Giulia 52), Rome's prison for more than two centuries and now the offices of Direzione Nazionale Antimafia. Near the bridge that arches over the southern end of Via Giulia is the church of Santa Maria dell'Orazione e Morte (Holy Mary of Prayer and Death), with stone skulls on its door. These are a symbol of a confraternity that was charged with burying the bodies of the unidentified dead found in the city streets. Home since 1927 to the Hungarian Academy, the Palazzo Falconieri (⊠ *Via Giulia 1* ☏ *06/68896700*) was designed by Borromini—note the architect's rooftop belvedere adorned with statues of the family "falcons," best viewed from around the block along the Tiber embankment. (The Borromini-designed salons and loggia are sporadically open as part of a guided tour; call the Hungarian Academy for information.) Remnant of a master plan by Michelangelo, the arch over the street was meant to link massive Palazzo Farnese, on the east side of Via Giulia, with the building across the street and a bridge to the Villa Farnesina, directly across the river. Finally, on the right and rather green with age, dribbles that star of many a postcard, the Fontana del Mascherone. ✉ *Via Giulia, between Piazza dell'Oro and Piazza San Vincenzo Palloti, Campo de' Fiori.*

🍴 Restaurants

★ Armando al Pantheon

$$ | **ROMAN** | In the shadow of the Pantheon, this small family-run trattoria, open since 1961, delights tourists and locals alike. There's an air of authenticity to the Roman staples here, and the quality of the ingredients and the cooking mean booking ahead is a must. **Known for:** good wine list; spaghetti alla gricia (with guanciale, pecorino cheese, and black pepper); beautifully executed traditional Roman cooking. [$] *Average main: €16* ✉ *Salita dei Crescenzi 31, Piazza Navona* ☎ *06/68803034* 🌐 *www.armandoalpantheon.it* 🕒 *Closed Sun. and Aug.*

★ Ba'Ghetto

$$ | **ITALIAN** | **FAMILY** | This hot spot on the main promenade in the Jewish Ghetto has been going strong for years, with pleasant indoor and outdoor seating. The kitchen is kosher (many places featuring Roman Jewish fare are not) and serves meat dishes (so no dairy) from the Roman Jewish tradition as well as from elsewhere in the Mediterranean; down the street is Ba'Ghetto Milky (✉ *Via del Portico d'Ottavia 2/a*), the kosher dairy version of the original. **Known for:** outside tables on the pedestrianized street; casual family atmosphere; carciofi alla giudia (deep-fried artichokes) and other Roman Jewish specialties. [$] *Average main: €22* ✉ *Via del Portico d'Ottavia 57, Jewish Ghetto* ☎ *06/68892868* 🌐 *www.baghetto.com* 🕒 *Dinner Fri. and lunch Sat. are strictly for those who observe Shabbat with advance payment.*

BellaCarne

$$ | **ROMAN** | *Bellacarne* means "beautiful meat," and that's the focus of the menu here, though the double entendre is that it's also what a Jewish Italian grandmother might say while pinching her grandchild's cheek. The kosher kitchen makes its own pastrami, though the setting is definitely more fine dining than deli. **Known for:** outside seating; deep-fried artichokes; homemade pastrami. [$] *Average main: €17* ✉ *Via Portico d'Ottavia 51, Jewish Ghetto* ☎ *06/6833104* 🌐 *www.bellacarne.it* 🕒 *No dinner Fri. No lunch Sat.*

★ Cul de Sac

$ | **WINE BAR** | This popular wine bar near Piazza Navona is among the city's oldest and offers a book-length selection of wines from Italy, France, the Americas, and elsewhere. Offering great value and pleasant service a stone's throw from Piazza Navona, it's open all afternoon, making it a lovely spot for a late lunch or an early dinner when most restaurants aren't open yet. **Known for:** relaxed atmosphere and outside tables; eclectic Italian and Mediterranean fare; great wine list (and wine bottle–lined interior). [$] *Average main: €14* ✉ *Piazza di Pasquino 73, Piazza Navona* ☎ *06/68801094* 🌐 *www.enotecaculdesacroma.it.*

Da Francesco

$ | **ROMAN** | **FAMILY** | For good, hearty, Roman cuisine in an area filled with mediocre touristy restaurants, head to this authentic trattoria that's been on the scene since the late 1950s. Foodwise, stick to the classics: start off with a mixed salumi plate (with Parma ham and buffalo mozzarella cheese), then hit the *primi* (first course)—the gricia and the amatriciana (the famous Roman pasta with tomato sauce, guanciale, and pecorino cheese) are usually the standouts. **Known for:** outside tables in summer; traditional Roman cooking; informal atmosphere. $ *Average main: €13* *Piazza del Fico 29, Piazza Navona* *06/6864009* *www.dafrancesco.it.*

Dar Filettaro a Santa Barbara

$ | **ITALIAN** | The window reads "Filetti di Baccalà," but the official name of this small restaurant that specializes in one thing—deliciously battered and deep-fried fillets of salt cod—is Dar Filettaro a Santa Barbara. The location, down the street from Campo de' Fiori in a little piazza in front of the beautiful Santa Barbara church, practically begs you to eat at one of the outdoor tables, where service is brusque. **Known for:** tables outside on the pretty square; functional "hole-in-the-wall" interior; filetti di baccalà. $ *Average main: €6* *Largo dei Librari 88, Campo de' Fiori* *06/6864018* *Closed Sun. and Aug.*

Ditirambo

$$ | **ITALIAN** | Don't let the country-kitchen setting fool you: at this little spot off Campo de' Fiori, the constantly changing selection of offbeat takes on Italian classics makes this a step beyond the ordinary. There are several good options for vegetarians. **Known for:** good vegetarian options; hearty meat and pasta dishes; cozy and casual atmosphere. $ *Average main: €16* *Piazza della Cancelleria 74, Campo de' Fiori* *06/6871626* *www.ristoranteditirambo.it* *Closed Aug.*

★ Emma

$$$ | **ROMAN** | **FAMILY** | With dough by Rome's renowned family of bakers, the Rosciolis, this large, sleek, modern pizzeria is smack in the middle of the city, with the freshest produce right outside the door. The wine list features many local Lazio options. **Known for:** tasty fritti (classic fried Roman pizzeria appetizers); thin-crust Roman pizza; light and airy, casual atmosphere. $ *Average main: €25* *Via Monte della Farina 28–29,* *Campo de' Fiori* *06/64760475* *www.emmapizzeria.com.*

Enoteca Corsi

$ | **ITALIAN** | Very convenient for a good-value lunch in the centro storico, this trattoria is undeniably old-school—it's been renovated, but you wouldn't know it—and that's all part of the charm. It's packed at lunch with a mix of civil servants from the nearby government offices, construction workers, and in-the-know tourists, when a few specials—classic pastas, a delicious octopus salad, and some *secondi* (second course) like roast veal with peas—are offered. **Known for:** brusque but friendly service; Roman specialties; casual atmosphere. $ *Average main: €12* *Via del Gesù 88, Piazza Navona* *06/6790821* *www.enoteca-corsi.com* *Closed Sun., and 3 wks in Aug. No dinner Sat. and Mon.*

★ Il Convivio Troiani

$$$$ | **MODERN ITALIAN** | In a tiny, nondescript alley north of Piazza Navona, the three Troiani brothers—Angelo in the kitchen, and brothers Giuseppe and Massimo presiding over the dining room and wine cellar—have been quietly redefining the experience of Italian *alta cucina* (haute cuisine) since 1990 at this well-regarded establishment. Service is attentive without being overbearing, and the wine list is exceptional. **Known for:** amazing wine cellar and a great sommelier; inventive modern Italian cooking with exotic touches; fine dining in elegant surroundings. $ *Average main: €38* *Vicolo dei Soldati 31, Piazza Navona* *06/6869432* *www.ilconviviotroiani.it* *Closed Sun., and 1 wk in Aug. No lunch.*

Il Pagliaccio

$$$$ | **MODERN ITALIAN** | Some of the most innovative interpretations of Roman fine dining can be found in this starkly chic restaurant on a backstreet between upscale Via Giulia and the popular Campo de' Fiori. Chef Anthony Genovese was born in France to Calabrese parents, and

spent time cooking in Japan and Thailand, so it's no surprise that the food he turns out makes use of nontraditional spices, ingredients, and preparations—all of which have gained him a loyal following and multiple accolades. **Known for:** discreet location close to Piazza Navona; elegant surroundings; fine dining, including elaborate tasting menus. $ *Average main: €55* ⊠ *Via dei Banchi Vecchi 129a, Piazza Navona* ☏ *06/68809595* ⊕ *www. ristoranteilpagliaccio.com* ⊗ *Closed Sun., Mon., and Aug. No lunch Tues. and Wed.*

Il Sanlorenzo

$$$$ | SEAFOOD | This gorgeous space, with its chandeliers and soaring original brickwork ceilings, houses one of the best seafood restaurants in the Eternal City. Order à la carte, or if you're hungry, the eight-course tasting menu is extremely tempting—it might include the likes of cuttlefish-ink tagliatelle with mint, artichokes, and roe, or shrimp from the island of Ponza with rosemary, bitter herbs, and porcini mushrooms—and, given the quality of the fish, a relative bargain at €90. **Known for:** elegant surroundings; spaghetti con ricci (sea urchins); top-quality fish and seafood. $ *Average main: €36* ⊠ *Via dei Chiavari 4/5, Campo de' Fiori* ☏ *06/6865097* ⊕ *www.ilsanlorenzo.it* ⊗ *Closed Sun. and 2 wks in Aug. No lunch Sat. and Mon.*

La Ciambella

$$ | ITALIAN | A large glass wall to the kitchen and massive skylight in the dining room hint at the contemporary leanings of this restaurant built atop the ruins of the Baths of Agrippa behind the Pantheon. The emphasis here is on high-quality ingredients and classic Italian culinary traditions interpreted for modern diners. **Known for:** great location near the Pantheon; sophisticated Italian cuisine; elegant setting. $ *Average main: €17* ⊠ *Via dell'Arco della Ciambella 20, Piazza Navona* ☏ *06/6832930* ⊕ *www.la-ciambella.it* ⊗ *Closed Mon.*

L'Angolo Divino

$ | WINE BAR | There's something about this cozy wine bar that feels as if it's in a small university town instead of a bustling metropolis. The walls are lined with a tempting array of bottles from around the Italian peninsula, and the counter is stocked with cheese and salumi that can be sliced and piled on plates to order. **Known for:** late-night snacks; cozy atmosphere; excellent wine selection and advice. $ *Average main: €13* ⊠ *Via dei Balestrari 12, Campo de' Fiori* ☏ *06/6864413* ⊕ *www.angolodivino. it* ⊗ *Closed 2 wks in Aug.*

Osteria dell'Ingegno

$$ | MODERN ITALIAN | This casual, trendy place is a great spot to enjoy a glass of wine or a gourmet meal in an ancient piazza in the city center, but the modern interior—vibrant with colorful paintings by local artists—brings you back to the present day. The simple but innovative menu includes dishes like Roman artichokes with baccalà, beef *tagliata* (sliced grilled steak) with a red-wine reduction, and a perfectly cooked duck breast with red fruit sauce. **Known for:** outdoor seating with views of ancient ruins; a great spot both for aperitifs and/or a meal; beautiful location on a pedestrian square. $ *Average main: €22* ⊠ *Piazza di Pietra 45, Piazza Navona* ☏ *06/6780662* ⊕ *www.osteriadellingegno.com* ⊗ *Closed Mon.*

Pesci Fritti

$$ | SOUTHERN ITALIAN | This cute jewel box of a restaurant sits on the seating of the ancient Theatre of Pompey just behind Campo de' Fiori (note the curve of the street). Step inside, and the whitewashed walls with touches of pale sea blue will make you feel like you've escaped to the Mediterranean for seafood favorites. **Known for:** cozy setting; spaghetti with clams; fried fish and seafood choices. $ *Average main: €18* ⊠ *Via di Grottapinta 8, Campo de'*

Fiori ☎ *06/68806170* ⊕ *www.pescifritti.it* ⊕ *Closed Mon. and Aug.*

★ Pianostrada

$$ | **MODERN ITALIAN** | This gourmet restaurant has an open kitchen, where you can watch the talented women owners cook up a storm of inventive delights—this is a "kitchen *lab*," after all, where top local ingredients are whipped into delicious plates. The spaghetti with tomato sauce, smoked ricotta, parmigiano, basil, and lemon peel is one of the signature dishes, and the amped-up traditional recipe is a delicious indication of how interesting the food can get. **Known for:** secret garden seating; creative burgers and salads; freshly baked focaccia with various toppings. $ *Average main: €20* ⊠ *Via delle Zoccolette 22, Campo de' Fiori* ☎ *06/89572296* ⊕ *Closed Mon. No lunch Tues.*

★ Pierluigi

$$$ | **ITALIAN** | This popular seafood restaurant is a fun spot on balmy summer evenings, with tables out on the pretty Piazza de' Ricci. As at most Italian restaurants, fresh fish is sold per hectogram (100 grams, or about.3.5 ounces), so you may want to double-check the cost after it's been weighed. **Known for:** elegant atmosphere with great service; tables on the pretty pedestrianized piazza; top-quality fish and seafood. $ *Average main: €30* ⊠ *Piazza de' Ricci 144, Campo de' Fiori* ☎ *06/6861302* ⊕ *www.pierluigi.it* ⊕ *Closed Mon.*

★ Roscioli Salumeria con Cucina

$$ | **WINE BAR** | The shop in front of this wine bar will beckon you in with top-quality comestibles like hand-sliced cured ham from Italy and Spain, more than 300 cheeses, and a dizzying array of wines—but venture farther inside to try an extensive selection of unusual dishes and interesting takes on the classics. There are tables in the cozy wine cellar downstairs, but try and bag a table at the back on the ground floor (reserve well ahead; Roscioli is very popular). **Known**

for: best prosciutto in town; arguably Rome's best spaghetti alla carbonara; extensive wine list. $ *Average main: €22* ⊠ *Via dei Giubbonari 21, Campo de' Fiori* ☎ *06/6875287* ⊕ *www.salumeriaroscioli. com* ⊕ *Closed 1 wk in Aug.*

☕ Coffee and Quick Bites

Bar del Fico

$ | **ITALIAN** | **FAMILY** | Everyone in Rome knows Bar del Fico, located right behind Piazza Navona, so if you're looking to hang out with the locals, this is the place to come for a drink or something to eat at any time of day or night. In the mornings, chess players sit at tables outside playing under the shade of the fig tree that gives the bar its name. **Known for:** buzzy atmosphere; Italian-style brunch; outside tables in a pretty square. $ *Average main: €10* ⊠ *Piazza del Fico 26, Piazza Navona* ☎ *06/68891373* ⊕ *www. bardelfico.com.*

★ Gelateria Del Teatro

$ | **ICE CREAM** | **FAMILY** | In a window next to the entrance of this renowned gelateria, you can see the fresh fruit being used in the laboratory to create the flavors of the day, which highlight the best of Italy, from Amalfi lemons to hazelnuts from Alba. In addition to traditional flavors, they serve a few interesting combinations, like raspberry and sage or white chocolate with basil. **Known for:** charming location on a cobblestone street; seasonal, all natural ingredients; sublime gelato. $ *Average main: €3* ⊠ *Via dei Coronari 65/66, Piazza Navona* ☎ *06/45474880* ⊕ *www.gelateriadelteatro.it.*

★ Giolitti

$ | **ICE CREAM** | **FAMILY** | Open since 1900, Giolitti near the Pantheon is Rome's old-school gelateria par excellence. Pay in advance at the register by the door and take your receipt to the counter, where you can choose from dozens of flavors, including chocolate, cinnamon, and pistachio. **Known for:** wide selection of flavors;

old-school setting; excellent gelato. $ *Average main: €3* ⊠ *Via degli Uffici del Vicario 40, Piazza Navona* ☎ *06/6991243* ⊕ *www.giolitti.it.*

Pasticceria Boccione

$ | **BAKERY** | This tiny, old-school bakery is an institution in the Ghetto area and is famed for its Roman-Jewish sweet specialties. Service is brusque, choices are few, what's available depends on the season, and when it's sold out, it's sold out. **Known for:** old-school bakery, so no frills and no seats; pizza ebraica ("Jewish pizza," a dense baked sweet rich in nuts and raisins); ricotta and cherry tarts. $ *Average main: €4* ⊠ *Via del Portico d'Ottavia 1, Jewish Ghetto* ☎ *06/6878637* ⊘ *Closed Sat.*

Sant'Eustachio il Caffè

$ | **CAFÉ** | Frequented by tourists and government officials from the nearby Senate alike, this café is considered by many to make Rome's best coffee. Take it at the counter Roman-style: servers are hidden behind a huge espresso machine, where they vigorously mix the sugar and coffee to protect their "secret method" for the perfectly prepared cup (if you want your caffè without sugar here, ask for it *senza zucchero*). **Known for:** 1930s interior; old-school Roman coffee bar vibe; gran caffè (large sugared espresso). $ *Average main: €2* ⊠ *Piazza Sant'Eustachio 82, Piazza Navona* ☎ *06/68802048* ⊕ *caffesanteustachio.com.*

 Hotels

Albergo Santa Chiara

$$$ | **HOTEL** | If you're looking for a good location and top-notch service at great rates—not to mention comfortable beds and a quiet stay—look no further than this historic hotel, run by the same family for some 200 years. **Pros:** great location near the Pantheon; lovely sitting area in front, overlooking the piazza; free Wi-Fi. **Cons:** street-side rooms can be noisy; Wi-Fi can be slow; some rooms

are on the small side and need updating. $ *Rooms from: €210* ⊠ *Via Santa Chiara 21, Piazza Navona* ☎ *06/6872979* ⊕ *www.albergosantachiara.com* ⊋ *96 rooms* ○ *Free Breakfast.*

Casa di Santa Brigida

$ | **B&B/INN** | The friendly sisters of Santa Brigida oversee simple, straightforward, and centrally located accommodations in one of Rome's loveliest convents, with a rooftop terrace overlooking Palazzo Farnese. **Pros:** insider papal tickets; free Wi-Fi; large library and sunroof. **Cons:** far from a Metro stop; no TVs in the rooms (though there is a common TV room); weak air-conditioning. $ *Rooms from: €50* ⊠ *Piazza Farnese 96, Campo de' Fiori* ☎ *06/68892596* ⊕ *www.brigidine.org* ⊋ *20 rooms* ○ *Free Breakfast.*

D.O.M Hotel Roma

$$$$ | **HOTEL** | In an old convent on Via Giulia, one of Rome's romantic ivy-covered streets, the D.O.M (Deo Optimo Maximo) is an ultrachic luxury hotel that resembles an aristocratic *casa nobile.* **Pros:** complimentary Acqua di Parma toiletries; hip decor; heated towel racks. **Cons:** standard rooms are small for a five-star hotel; delicious but expensive cocktails; an armed guard at the anti-terrorism headquarters opposite the hotel may be off-putting for some. $ *Rooms from: €390* ⊠ *Via Giulia 131, Campo de' Fiori* ☎ *06/6832144* ⊕ *www.domhotelroma.com* ⊋ *18 rooms* ○ *Free Breakfast.*

Hotel Chapter Roma

$$$ | **HOTEL** | This hip new member of Design Hotels has an edgy, of-the-moment design that juxtaposes plush midcentury Italian furnishings with street art murals and industrial touches. **Pros:** trendy design; lively rooftop bar in summer; coworking space available. **Cons:** service can be a bit spotty; no spa; no gym. $ *Rooms from: €230* ⊠ *Via di Santa Maria de' Calderari 47, Jewish Ghetto* ☎ *06/89935351* ⊕ *www.chapter-roma.com* ⊋ *47 rooms* ○ *Free Breakfast.*

Hotel de' Ricci

$$$$ | **HOTEL** | This intimate boutique hotel from the team behind Pierluigi is a top spot for wine lovers. **Pros:** excellent wine cellar and wine tastings; perks include complimentary aperitivo and priority reservations at Pierluigi; great location on a quiet street. **Cons:** there's no spa or gym; there is a weekend crowd for the brunch; there's a charge of €50 per day to bring pets. [$] *Rooms from: €350* ✉ *Via della Barchetta 14, Campo de' Fiori* ☎ *06/6874775* 🌐 *www.hoteldericci.com* 🛏 *8 rooms* 🍴 *No Meals.*

Hotel Genio

$$ | **HOTEL** | Just off one of Rome's most beautiful piazzas—Piazza Navona—this pleasant hotel has a lovely rooftop terrace perfect for enjoying a cappuccino or a glass of wine while taking in the view. **Pros:** breakfast buffet is abundant; spacious, elegant bathrooms; free Wi-Fi. **Cons:** beds can be too firm for some; spotty Internet; rooms facing the street can be noisy. [$] *Rooms from: €160* ✉ *Via Giuseppe Zanardelli 28, Piazza Navona* ☎ *06/6833781* 🌐 *www.hotelgenioroma.it* 🛏 *60 rooms* 🍴 *Free Breakfast.*

Hotel Ponte Sisto

$$$ | **HOTEL** | Situated in a remodeled Renaissance palazzo with one of the prettiest patio-courtyards in Rome, this hotel is a relaxing retreat close to Trastevere and Campo de' Fiori. **Pros:** rooms with views (and some with balconies and terraces); beautiful courtyard garden; luxury bathrooms. **Cons:** carpets starting to show signs of wear; some upgraded rooms are small and not worth the price difference; street-side rooms can be a bit noisy. [$] *Rooms from: €250* ✉ *Via dei Pettinari 64, Campo de' Fiori* ☎ *06/6863100* 🌐 *www.hotelpontesisto.it* 🛏 *106 rooms* 🍴 *Free Breakfast.*

The Pantheon Iconic Rome Hotel, Autograph Collection

$$$ | **HOTEL** | A member of Marriott's Autograph Collection, this boutique hotel is a sleek retreat in the center of the action. **Pros:** modern design and amenities; Marriott Bonvoy members can use and redeem points; restaurant by one of the city's best chefs. **Cons:** design might be considered a bit cold and corporate; no spa or gym; some rooms lack external views. [$] *Rooms from: €250* ✉ *Via di Santa Chiara 4A, Piazza Navona* ☎ *06/87807070* 🌐 *www.thepantheonhotel.com* 🛏 *79 rooms* 🍴 *No Meals.*

Nightlife

Enoteca al Parlamento Achilli

WINE BARS | The proximity of this traditional *enoteca* (wine bar) to Montecitorio, the Italian Parliament building, makes it a favorite with journalists and politicos, who often stop in for a glass of wine after work. But it's the tantalizing smell of truffles from the snack counter, where a sommelier waits to organize your tasting, that will probably lure you inside. There's also a celebrated restaurant where you can book a table and enjoy a parade of elegant Italian plates. Don't forget to check out their wine shop to take home a bottle of your favorite wine. ✉ *Via dei Prefetti 15, Piazza Navona* ☎ *06/6873446* 🌐 *www.achilli.restaurant.*

Il Goccetto

CAFÉS | A historic wine bar with a copious amount of elusive vintages, Il Goccetto specializes in wines from smaller vineyards from Sicily to Venice. Stay for a snack—its carefully chosen menu of Italian delicacies (meats and cheeses) represents the entire Italian peninsula. The burrata with sun-dried tomatoes is a perennial favorite. The tiny bar is well designed but is always busy and never accepts reservations. ✉ *Via dei Banchi Vecchi 14, Campo de' Fiori* ☎ *06/6864268* 🌐 *www.ilgoccetto.com.*

Jerry Thomas Project

COCKTAIL LOUNGES | One of just a handful of hidden bars in Rome, this intimate bar looks like a Prohibition-era haunt and serves the kind of classic cocktails you find in New York speakeasies. It's seating room only, so reservations must be made in advance. Upon booking, you'll receive a password via email. Serious cocktail aficionados can also purchase specialty bitters and mixology tools at the Emporium across the alley from the drinks spot. ⊠ *Vicolo Cellini 30, Piazza Navona* ☎ *370/1146287* ⊕ *www.thejerrythomasproject.it.*

The Sofa Bar & Roof Terrace Restaurant
BARS | The romantic rooftop terrace at Sofa has a 360-degree view of the Eternal City, so it's no surprise that it's a prime spot for a late-afternoon cocktail (weather permitting). Head downstairs in the cooler months for a wide selection of craft beers on tap inside the Hotel Indigo. ⊠ *Hotel Indigo Rome—St. George, Via Giulia 62, Campo de' Fiori* ☎ *06/686611* ⊕ *www.hotelindigorome.com.*

Vinoteca Novecento
WINE BARS | A lovely, tiny enoteca with a very old-fashioned vibe, Vinoteca Novecento has a seemingly unlimited selection of wines, proseccos, vini santi, and grappe, along with salami-and-cheese tasting menus. Inside is standing-room only; in good weather, sit outside on one of the oak barriques on a quiet cobblestone street leading to one of Rome's prettiest small squares. ⊠ *Piazza delle Coppelle 47, Piazza Navona* ☎ *06/6833078.*

Performing Arts

★ Teatro Argentina
THEATER | A gorgeous 18th-century theater, the Teatro Argentina evokes glamour and sophistication with its velvet upholstery, large crystal chandeliers, and beautifully dressed theatergoers, who come to see international productions of stage and dance performances. ⊠ *Largo di Torre Argentina 52, Campo de' Fiori* ☎ *06/684000314* ⊕ *www.teatrodiroma.net.*

Shopping

BEAUTY
Antica Erboristeria Romana
OTHER HEALTH & BEAUTY | Complete with hand-labeled wooden drawers holding more than 200 varieties of herbs, flowers, and tinctures, Antica Erboristeria Romana has maintained its old-world apothecary feel (it's the oldest shop of its kind in Rome, dating back to 1752). The shop stocks an impressive array of teas and herbal infusions, more than 700 essential oils, bud derivatives, and powdered extracts. ⊠ *Via Torre Argentina 15, Piazza Navona* ☎ *06/6879493* ⊕ *www.anticaerboristeriaromana.it.*

CERAMICS AND DECORATIVE ARTS
★ IN.OR. dal 1952
CRAFTS | For more than 50 years, IN.OR. dal 1952 has served as a trusty friend for Romans in desperate need of an exclusive wedding gift or those oh-so-perfect china place settings for a fancy Sunday dinner. Entrance is via a secluded 15th-century courtyard and up a flight of stairs. The store specializes in work handcrafted by the silversmiths of Pampaloni and Bastianelli in Florence. ⊠ *Via della Stelletta 23, Piazza Navona* ☎ *06/6878579* ⊕ *www.inor.it.*

CLOTHING
★ L'Archivio di Monserrato
WOMEN'S CLOTHING | This airy, spacious boutique curated by Soledad Twombly (daughter-in-law of painter Cy Twombly) showcases her original designs as well as a sophisticated mix of antique Turkish and Indian textiles, jewelry, shoes, and small housewares picked up on her travels. Tailored jackets trimmed with exotic fabrics, dresses in eclectic prints and bold colors, and smart linen suits are some of Twombly's signatures. ⊠ *Via di Monserrato 150, Campo de' Fiori* ☎ *06/45654157* ⊕ *www.soledadtwombly.com.*

Le Tartarughe

WOMEN'S CLOTHING | A familiar face on the catwalks of Rome's fashion shows, designer Susanna Liso, a Rome native, adds suggestive elements of playful experimentation to her haute couture and ready-to-wear lines, which are much loved by Rome's aristocracy and intelligentsia. With intense, enveloping designs, she mixes raw silks or cashmere and fine merino wool together to form captivating garments that combine seduction and linear form. ⊠ *Via Piè di Marmo 17, Piazza Navona* ☎ *06/6792240.*

Morgana

WOMEN'S CLOTHING | When strolling down Via del Governo Vecchio, a street popular for funky and edgy clothing boutiques, you can't help but stop and stare inside this shop's windows where the family-run business displays some of its best hippie-chick and bridal-chic gowns. Designer Luciana Iannace creates these highly original and highly sought-after clothes and accessories that many of Rome's ladies are desperate to get their hands on. In addition to her own designs, she also sources inventive items from Paris and Florence. ⊠ *Via del Governo Vecchio 27, Piazza Navona* ☎ *06/6879995.*

Vestiti Usati Cinzia

MIXED CLOTHING | Vintage-clothes hunters, costume designers, and stylists alike love browsing through the racks at Vestiti Usati Cinzia. The shop is fun and very inviting and stocked with wall-to-wall funky 1960s and '70s apparel and loads of goofy sunglasses. There's definitely no shortage of flower-power bell-bottoms and hippie shirts, embroidered tops, trippy and psychedelic boots, and other awesome accessories that will take you back to the days of peace and love. ⊠ *Via del Governo Vecchio 45, Piazza Navona* ☎ *06/6832945.*

FOOD AND WINE

Moriondo e Gariglio

CANDY | Not exactly Willy Wonka (but in the same vein), Moriondo e Gariglio is a chocolate lover's paradise, churning out some of the finest chocolate delicacies in town. The shop dates back to 1850 and adheres strictly to family recipes passed on from generation to generation. Whether you favor marrons glacés or dark-chocolate truffles, you'll delight in choosing from more than 80 delicacies. ⊠ *Via Piè di Marmo 21, Piazza Navona* ☎ *06/6990856* ⊕ *www.moriondoegariglio.com.*

JEWELRY

Massimo Maria Melis

JEWELRY & WATCHES | Drawing heavily on ancient Roman and Etruscan designs, Massimo Maria Melis jewelry will carry you back in time. Working with 21-carat gold, he often incorporates antique coins in many of his exquisite bracelets and necklaces. Some of his pieces are done with an ancient technique, much loved by the Etruscans, in which tiny gold droplets are fused together to create intricately patterned designs. ⊠ *Via dell'Orso 57, Piazza Navona* ☎ *06/6869188* ⊕ *www.massimomariamelis.com.*

Quattrocolo

JEWELRY & WATCHES | This historic shop dating to 1938 showcases exquisite antique micro-mosaic jewelry painstakingly crafted in the style perfected by the masters at the Vatican mosaic studio. You'll also find 18th- and 19th-century cameos and beautiful engraved stones as well as contemporary jewelry handmade in the studio. The small works were beloved by cosmopolitan clientele of the Grand Tour age and offer modern-day shoppers a taste of yesteryear's grandeur. ⊠ *Via della Scrofa 48, Piazza Navona* ☎ *06/68801367* ⊕ *www.quattrocolo.com.*

SHOES AND ACCESSORIES

★ Chez Dede

OTHER SPECIALTY STORE | Husband-and-wife duo Andrea Ferolla and Daria Reina (he's a fashion illustrator, she's a photographer) curate an edited selection of clothes, bags, vintage jewelry, books, home decor, and anything else you might need in this cult favorite lifestyle-concept shop.

Their signature bags are designed to go from the plane straight to the beach, and they regularly release collectible items featuring Ferolla's whimsical illustrations. ✉ *Via di Monserrato 35, Campo de' Fiori* ☎ *06/83772934* ⊕ *www.chezdede.com.*

Ibiz

LEATHER GOODS | In business since 1972, this family team creates colorful, stylish leather handbags, belts, and sandals near Piazza Campo de' Fiori. Choose from the premade collection or order something in the color of your choice; their workshop is visible in the boutique. ✉ *Via dei Chiavari 39, Campo de' Fiori* ☎ *06/68307297* ⊕ *www.ibizroma.it.*

★ Maison Halaby

HANDBAGS | Lebanese designer and artist Gilbert Halaby was featured in fashion magazines like *Vogue* and created jewelry for Lady Gaga before giving up the rat race and opening his own shop, where the ethos is all about slow fashion. He designs boldly colored leather handbags incorporating suede, python, fringe, raffia, or jeweled handles, as well as silk scarves printed with his original watercolors, which he sells in this small boutique that feels like an extension of his home, with a velvet sofa, plenty of books and plants, and his own paintings on the walls. The shop is mainly open by appointment, but if Gilbert is there when you pass by, ring the bell and he'll invite you in for coffee or Campari. Open by appointment. ✉ *Via di Monserrato 21, Campo de' Fiori* ☎ *06/96521585* ⊕ *www. maisonhalaby.com.*

STATIONERY
★ Cartoleria Pantheon dal 1910

STATIONERY | Instead of sending a postcard home, head to the simply sumptuous Cartoleria Pantheon dal 1910 for fine handmade paper to write that special letter. In addition to simple, stock paper and sheets of handcrafted Amalfi paper, there are hand-bound leather journals in an extraordinary array of colors and sizes. The store has two locations in the neighborhood. ✉ *Via della Maddalena 41, Piazza Navona* ☎ *06/6795633* ⊕ *www. cartoleriapantheon.it.*

TOYS
Al Sogno

TOYS | FAMILY | If you're looking for quality toys that encourage imaginative play and learning, look no further than Al Sogno. With an emphasis on the artistic as well as the multisensory, the shop has a selection of toys that are both discerning and individual, making them perfect for children of all ages. Carrying an exquisite collection of fanciful puppets, collectible dolls, masks, stuffed animals, and illustrated books, this Navona jewel, around since 1945, is crammed top to bottom with beautiful, well-crafted playthings. If you believe that children's toys don't have to be high-tech, you will adore reliving some of your best childhood memories here. ✉ *Piazza Navona 53, corner of Via Agonale, Piazza Navona* ☎ *06/6864198* ⊕ *www.alsogno.com.*

★ Bartolucci

TOYS | FAMILY | This shop opened in the '90s, but the Bartolucci family has been making whimsical, handmade curiosities out of pine, including clocks, bookends, bedside lamps, and wall hangings, since 1936. You can even buy a child-size motorbike entirely made of wood (wheels, too). Don't miss the life-size Pinocchio pedaling furiously on a wooden bike. ✉ *Via dei Pastini 98, Piazza Navona* ☎ *06/69190894* ⊕ *www.bartolucci.com.*

Piazza di Spagna

In spirit (and in fact) this section of the city is its most grandiose. The overblown Vittoriano monument, the labyrinthine treasure-chest palaces of Rome's surviving aristocracy, even the diamond-draped denizens of Via Condotti's shops—all embody the exuberant ego of a city at the center of its own universe. Here's where you'll see ladies in furs gobbling pastries at café tables and walk through a thousand snapshots as you climb the famous Spanish Steps, admired by generations from Byron to Versace. Cultural treasures abound around here: gilded 17th-century churches, glittering palazzi, and the greatest example of portraiture in Rome, Velázquez's incomparable *Innocent X* at the Galleria Doria Pamphilj. Have your camera ready—along with a coin or two—for that most beloved of Rome's landmarks, the Trevi Fountain.

GETTING HERE AND AROUND

Piazza di Spagna is a short walk from Piazza del Popolo, the Pantheon, and the Trevi Fountain. One of Rome's handiest subway stations, Spagna, is tucked just left of the steps. Buses No. 117 (from the Colosseum) and No. 119 (from Piazza del Popolo) hum through the area; the latter tootles up Via del Babuino, famed for its shopping.

 # Sights

★ Ara Pacis Augustae

(*Altar of Augustan Peace*)
MONUMENT | In a city better known for its terra-cotta–colored palazzi, this pristine monument sits inside one of Rome's newer architectural landmarks: a gleaming, rectangular glass-and-travertine structure designed by American architect Richard Meier. Overlooking the Tiber on one side and the ruins of the marble-clad Mausoleo di Augusto (Mausoleum of Augustus) on the other, the result is a serene, luminous oasis right in the center of Rome. The altar itself dates back to 13 BC; it was commissioned to celebrate the Pax Romana, the era of peace ushered in by Augustus's military victories. Like all ancient Roman monuments of this kind, you have to imagine its spectacular and moving relief sculptures painted in vibrant colors, now long gone. The reliefs on the short sides portray myths associated with Rome's founding and glory; the long sides display a procession of the imperial family. It's

fun to try to play "who's who"—although half of his body is missing, Augustus is identifiable as the first full figure at the procession's head on the south-side frieze—but academics still argue over exact identifications of most of the figures. This one splendid altar is the star of the small museum downstairs, which hosts rotating exhibits on Italian culture, with themes ranging from design to film. ✉ *Lungotevere in Augusta, at the corner of Via Tomacelli, Piazza di Spagna* ☎ *06/0608* ⊕ *www.arapacis.it* 💶 *€10.50, €13 when there's an exhibit* Ⓜ *Flaminio.*

★ Galleria d'Arte Moderna

ART MUSEUM | The city of Rome's modern art gallery is housed in a former convent on the opposite side of Villa Borghese, from the entrance above the Spanish Steps. The 18th-century building in this quiet corner of Rome is the perfect spot for more than 3,000 19th- and 20th-century paintings, drawings, prints, and sculptures by artists including Giorgio de Chirico, Gino Severini, Scipione, Antonio Donghi, and Giacomo Manzù. In fact, the permanent collection is too large to be displayed at once, so exhibits rotate. A trip out to the museum offers a look at modern Roman art as well as at another side of the city—one where, in the near-empty halls, tranquility and contemplation reign. ✉ *Via Francesco Crispi 24, Piazza di Spagna* ☎ *06/0608* ⊕ *www. galleriaartemodernaroma.it* 💶 *€7.50* ⊘ *Closed Mon.* Ⓜ *Spagna.*

Keats-Shelley Memorial House

HISTORIC HOME | Sent to Rome in a last-ditch attempt to treat his consumptive condition, English Romantic poet John Keats lived—and died—in this house at the foot of the Spanish Steps. At the time, this was the heart of the colorful bohemian quarter of Rome that was especially favored by English expats. He took his last breath here on February 23, 1821, and is now buried in the Non-Catholic Cemetery in Testaccio. Even before his death, Keats was celebrated for such poems as "Ode to a Nightingale" and "Endymion." In this "Casina di Keats," you can visit his final home and see his death mask, though all his furnishings were burned after his death as a sanitary measure by the local authorities. You'll also find a rather quaint collection of memorabilia of English literary figures of the period—Lord Byron, Percy Bysshe Shelley, Joseph Severn, and Leigh Hunt, as well as Keats—and an exhaustive library of works on the Romantics. ✉ *Piazza di Spagna 26, Piazza di Spagna* ☎ *06/6784235* 🌐 *www.keats-shelley-house.org* 🎟 *€6* 🕓 *Closed Sun.* Ⓜ *Spagna.*

Mausoleo di Augusto

TOMB | The largest circular tomb in the world, the mausoleum certainly made a statement about the glory of Augustus, Julius Caesar's successor. He was only 35 years old when he commissioned it following his victory over Marc Antony and Cleopatra. Though the ruins we see now are brick and stone, it was originally covered in marble and travertine, with evergreen trees planted on top, a colossal statue of the emperor at the summit, and a pair of bronze pillars inscribed with his achievements at the entrance. The mausoleum's innermost sepulchral chamber housed the ashes of several members of the Augustan dynasty, but it was subsequently raided and the urns were never found. Between the 13th and 20th centuries, it lived several other lives as a garden, an amphitheater that hosted jousting tournaments, and a concert hall, which Mussolini tore down in 1936 in a bid to restore the monument to its imperial glory. His plans were interrupted by World War II, after which the mausoleum was all but abandoned until a recent restoration reopened it to the public. Booking online as far in advance as possible is recommended because of the limited number of visitors allowed inside at any one time. A new public piazza is currently being constructed around it. ✉ *Piazza Augusto Imperatore, Piazza di Spagna* ☎ *06/0608* 🌐 *www.mausoleodiaugusto.it* 🎟 *€4* Ⓜ *Spagna.*

Monumento a Vittorio Emanuele II, or Altare della Patria (*Victor Emmanuel II Monument, or Altar of the Nation*)

MONUMENT | The huge white mass known as the "Vittoriano" is an inescapable landmark that has been likened to a huge wedding cake or an immense typewriter. Present-day Romans joke that you can only avoid looking at it if you are standing on it, but it was the source of great civic pride at the time of its construction at the turn of the 20th century. To create this elaborate marble monster and the vast piazza on which it stands, its architects blithely destroyed many ancient and medieval buildings and altered the slope of the Campidoglio (Capitoline Hill), which abuts it. Built to honor the unification of Italy and the nation's first king, Victor Emmanuel II, it also shelters the eternal flame at the tomb of Italy's Unknown Soldier, killed during World War I. You can't miss the Monumento, so enjoy neo-imperial grandiosity at its most bombastic.

The underwhelming exhibit inside the building tells the history of the country's unification, but the truly enticing feature of the Vittoriano is its rooftop terrace, which offers some of the best panoramic views of Rome. The only way up is by elevator (the entrance is located several flights of stairs up on the right as you face the monument). ✉ *Entrances on Piazza Venezia, Piazza del Campidoglio, and Via di San Pietro in Carcere, Piazza di Spagna* ☎ *06/0608* 🌐 *vittoriano.beniculturali.it* 🎟 *Free main building, €10 for the terrace* Ⓜ *Colosseo.*

★ **Palazzo Colonna**

HISTORIC HOME | Rome's grandest family built themselves Rome's grandest private palace, a fusion of 17th- and 18th-century buildings that has been occupied by the Colonna family for more than 20 generations. The immense palatial residence faces Piazza dei Santi Apostoli on one side and the Quirinale (Quirinal Hill) on the other (with a little bridge over Via della Pilotta linking to the gardens on the hill). The palazzo is still home to some Colonna patricians, but it also holds an exquisite art gallery, which is open to the public on Saturday morning (or by guided tour on Friday morning). The gallery is itself a setting of aristocratic grandeur; you might recognize the Sala Grande as the site where Audrey Hepburn meets the press in *Roman Holiday*. An ancient red marble column (*colonna* in Italian), which is the family's emblem, looms at one end, but the most spectacular feature is the ceiling fresco of the Battle of Lepanto painted by Giovanni Coli and Filippo Gherardi beginning in 1675. Adding to the opulence are works by Poussin, Tintoretto, and Veronese, and a number of portraits of illustrious members of the family, such as Vittoria Colonna, Michelangelo's muse and longtime friend. There are guided tours in English included in the entrance fee and can help you to navigate through the array of madonnas, saints, goddesses, popes, and cardinals to see Annibale Carracci's lonely *Beaneater,* spoon at the ready and front teeth missing. The gallery also has a café with a pleasant terrace. ⊠ *Via della Pilotta 17, Piazza di Spagna* ☎ *06/6784350* ⊕ *www.galleriacolonna. it* 🎟 *€15 for gallery and gardens, €25 to also visit the Princess Isabelle Apartment* ⊙ *Closed Sun.–Fri.* Ⓜ *Barberini.*

★ Palazzo Doria Pamphilj

HISTORIC HOME | Along with the Palazzo Colonna and the Galleria Borghese, this dazzling 15th-century family palace provides the best glimpse into aristocratic Rome. The main attractions are the legendary Old Master paintings, including treasures by Velázquez and Caravaggio, the splendor of the halls themselves, and a unique suite of private family apartments. The palace passed through several hands before becoming the property of the Pamphilj family, who married into the famous seafaring Doria family of Genoa in the 18th century. The picture gallery contains 550 paintings, including three by Caravaggio—a young St. John the Baptist, Mary Magdalene, and the breathtaking *Rest on the Flight to Egypt*. Off the eye-popping Galleria degli Specchi (Gallery of Mirrors)—a smaller version of the one at Versailles—are the famous Velázquez *Pope Innocent X,* considered by some historians as the greatest portrait ever painted, and the Bernini bust of the same. ⊠ *Via del Corso 305, Piazza di Spagna* ☎ *06/6797323* ⊕ *www.doriapamphilj.it* 🎟 *€14* ⊙ *Closed the 3rd Wed. of the month* ⚓ *Reservations required* Ⓜ *Barberini.*

★ Sant'Ignazio

CHURCH | Rome's second Jesuit church, this 17th-century landmark set on a rococo piazza harbors some of the city's most magnificent trompe l'oeils. To get the full effect of the marvelous illusionistic ceiling by priest-artist Andrea Pozzo, stand on the small yellow disk set into the floor of the nave. The heavenly vision above you, seemingly extending upward almost indefinitely, represents the *Allegory of the Missionary Work of the Jesuits* and is part of Pozzo's cycle of works in this church exalting the early history of the Jesuit order, whose founder was the reformer Ignatius of Loyola. The saint soars heavenward, supported by a cast of thousands, creating a jaw-dropping effect that was fully intended to rival the glorious ceiling produced by Baciccia in the nearby mother church of Il Gesù. Be sure to have coins handy for the machine that switches on the lights so you can marvel at the false dome, which is actually a flat canvas—a trompe l'oeil trick Pozzo used when the architectural budget drained dry. The dazzling church hardly stops there: scattered around the nave are several awe-inspiring altars; their soaring columns, gold-on-gold decoration, and gilded statues are pure splendor. The church is often host to concerts of sacred music performed by choirs from all over the world. Look for posters by the main doors or check the website for more information. ✉ *Via del Caravita 8A, Piazza Navona* ☎ *06/6794406* 🌐 *www.chiesasantignazio.it.*

★ The Spanish Steps

NOTABLE BUILDING | FAMILY | That icon of postcard Rome, the Spanish Steps (often called simply *la scalinata,* or "the staircase," by Italians) and the Piazza di Spagna from which they ascend both get their names from the Spanish Embassy to the Vatican on the piazza—even though the staircase was built with French funds in 1723. In honor of a diplomatic visit by the king of Spain, the hillside was transformed by architect Francesco de Sanctis to link the church of Trinità dei Monti at the top with the Via Condotti below. In an allusion to the church, the staircase is divided by three landings (beautifully lined with potted azaleas from mid-April to mid-May). Bookending the bottom of the steps are two beloved holdovers from the 18th century, when the area was known as the "English Ghetto": the 18th-century Keats-Shelley House and Babington's Tea Rooms, both beautifully redolent of the Grand Tour era. ✉ *Piazza di Spagna* [M] *Spagna.*

★ Trevi Fountain

FOUNTAIN | Alive with rushing waters commanded by an imperious sculpture of Oceanus, the Fontana di Trevi has been all about theatrical effects from the start; it is an aquatic marvel in a city filled with them. The fountain's unique drama is largely due to its location: its vast basin is squeezed into the tight confluence of three little streets (the *tre vie,* which may give the fountain its name), with cascades emerging as if from the wall of Palazzo Poli. The dream of a fountain emerging full force from a palace was first envisioned by Bernini and Pietro da Cortona from Pope Urban VIII's plan to rebuild an older fountain, which had earlier marked the end point of the ancient Acqua Vergine aqueduct, created in 18 BC by Agrippa. Three popes later, under Pope Clement XIII, Nicola Salvi finally broke ground with his winning design. Unfortunately, Salvi did not live to see his masterpiece of sculpted seashells, roaring sea beasts, and diva-like mermaids completed; he caught a cold and died while working in the culverts of the aqueduct 11 years before the fountain was finally finished in 1762.

Everyone knows the famous legend that if you throw a coin into the Trevi Fountain you will ensure a return trip to the Eternal City, but not everyone knows how to do it the right way. You must toss a coin with your right hand over your left shoulder, with your back to the fountain. One coin means you'll return to Rome; two, you'll return *and* fall in love; three, you'll return, find love, and marry. The fountain grosses some €600,000 a year, with every cent going to the Italian Red Cross, which is why Fendi was willing to foot the bill and fully funded the Trevi's marvelous recent restoration.

Tucked away in a little alley nearby (✉ *Vicolo del Puttarello 25*), visitors can pay €8 for a tour that descends into a newly uncovered subterranean area that gives a glimpse at the underground water source that keeps the fountain running. ✉ *Piazza di Trevi, Piazza di Spagna* [M] *Barberini.*

🍴 Restaurants

Baccano

$$$ | BRASSERIE | There are plenty of options for good food at reasonable prices around the Trevi Fountain, but this large brasserie is a good bet, and is open for lunch and dinner and everything in between. The extensive menu with a focus on seafood has something for everyone, from salads to pasta and entrées. **Known for:** champagne menu; tasty burgers; oyster bar. [$] *Average main: €28* ✉ *Via delle Muratte 23, Piazza di Spagna* ☎ *06/69941166* 🌐 *www.baccanoroma.com* [M] *Barberini.*

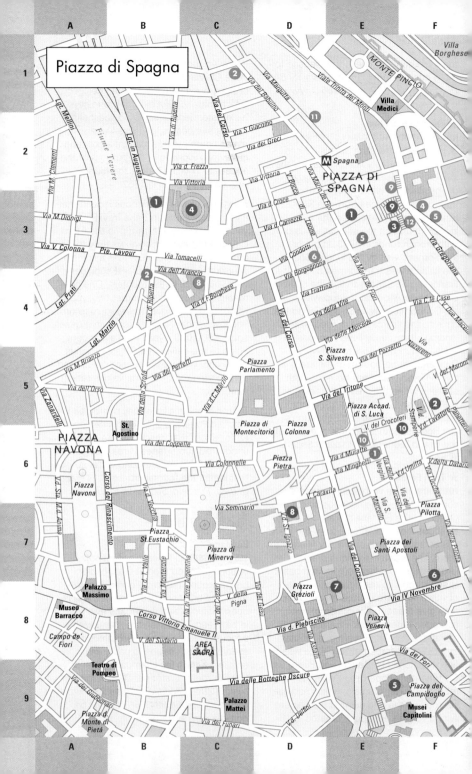

G H I J

Via del Muro Torto
Viale del Muro Torto
V. Lazio
V. Pta Pinciana
Via Pta Pinciana
Via Toscana
Via Marche
Via Sicilia
Via Abruzzi
Via Piemonte
Via Boncompagni
Via Vitt. Veneto
Via Emilia
Via Lombardia
Via Aurora
Via Lucullo
Via Salustiana
Via F.Crispi
Via Ludovisi
V. Liguria
Via Vitt. Veneto
Via Umbria
Via G. Carducci
Via Versilia
Via Leonida Bissolati
Via Purificazione
Santa di S. Nicola da Tolentino
Piazza di San Bernardo
Via Sistina
M Barberini
Piazza Barberini
Via Barberini
V. degli Avignonesi
Via d. Quattro Fontane
Via Venti Settembre
V. Rasella
Via del Giardin
t. Scuderie
Giardini del Quirinale
MONTE QUIRINALE
Via del Quirinale
Via d.s. Vitale
Via Ferrara
Via Piacenza
Via XXIV Maggio
Via Milano
Via Nazionale
Via Palermo
Via della Consulta
Via del Boschetto
Villa Colonna
Via Mazzarino
Via Milano
Via Panisperna
Via Cimarra
Via Urbana
V. d. Conti
Via di St Agata d.Goti
Via Baccina
Via Madonna dei Monti
Via Cavour

0 ——— 500 feet
0 ——— 150 m

Rome PIAZZA DI SPAGNA

3

Sights ▼

1. Ara Pacis Augustae **B3**
2. Galleria d'Arte Moderna **G4**
3. Keats-Shelley Memorial House... **E3**
4. Mausoleo di Augusto **C3**
5. Monumento a Vittorio Emanuele II, or Altare della Patria **E9**
6. Palazzo Colonna **F7**
7. Palazzo Doria Pamphilj............ **E8**
8. Sant'Ignazio **D7**
9. The Spanish Steps................. **E3**
10. Trevi Fountain **F5**

Restaurants ▼

1. Baccano............................ **E6**
2. Il Marchese **B4**
3. Mirabelle **G2**
4. Moma **I3**
5. Ristorante Nino **E3**
6. Settimo............................ **G2**

Quick Bites ▼

1. Antico Caffè Greco **E3**
2. Il Gelato di San Crispino **F5**

Hotels ▼

1. Aleph Rome Hotel **H3**
2. Babuino 181 .... **C1**
3. Baglioni Hotel Regina **H2**
4. The Hassler........................ **F3**
5. Hotel de la Ville **F3**
6. Hotel d'Inghilterra **D3**
7. Hotel Eden......................... **G2**
8. Hotel Vilòn **C4**
9. Il Palazzetto **E2**
10. Maalot Roma **E6**
11. Margutta 19 .... **D2**
12. Scalinata di Spagna............... **F3**

KEY

1 Sights
1 Restaurants
1 Quick Bites
1 Hotels

★ Il Marchese

$$ | **ITALIAN** | This rustic-meets-glamorous bistro attracts locals for its flawless execution of Roman classics (many served photogenically in metal cooking pans) as well as original dishes. Its bar is known among amaro connoisseurs for having the largest selection in Rome, and the bitter liquors are the stars of the expertly crafted cocktail menu. **Known for:** extensive selection of amaros and great cocktails; well-executed classics; beautiful design. $ *Average main: €18* ⊠ *Via di Ripetta 162, Piazza di Spagna* ☎ *06/90218872* ⊕ *www. ilmarcheseroma.it* Ⓜ *Spagna.*

Mirabelle

$$$$ | **MODERN ITALIAN** | Old-world elegance is the name of the game here—think white-jacketed waiters who attend to your every need, classic decor, and impeccable dishes, which are the most modern thing about this restaurant on the seventh floor of the Hotel Splendide Royal. Be sure to request a table on the terrace, which boasts panoramic views of leafy Villa Borghese and the center of Rome. **Known for:** top-notch food and service; panoramic terrace; romantic atmosphere. $ *Average main: €54* ⊠ *Hotel Splendide Royal, Via di Porta Pinciana 14, Piazza di Spagna* ☎ *06/42168838* ⊕ *www.mirabelle.it* 🏛 *business casual* Ⓜ *Spagna, Barberini.*

★ Moma

$$$ | **MODERN ITALIAN** | In front of the American embassy, a favorite of the design *trendoisie*, modern, Michelin-starred Moma attracts well-heeled businessmen at lunch but turns into a more intimate affair for dinner. The kitchen turns out hits as it creates *alta cucina* (haute cuisine) made using Italian ingredients sourced from small producers. **Known for:** affordable fine dining; creative presentation; pasta with a twist. $ *Average main: €25* ⊠ *Via San Basilio 42/43, Piazza di Spagna* ☎ *06/42011798* ⊕ *www.ristorantemoma.it* ⊙ *Closed Sun.* Ⓜ *Barberini.*

Ristorante Nino

$$$ | **ITALIAN** | Almost more of a landmark than an eatery, Nino has been a favorite among international journalists and the rich and famous since the 1930s and does not seem to have changed at all over the decades. The interior is Tuscan country rustic , and the menu, accordingly, sticks to the classics. **Known for:** ribollita (Tuscan bean soup); upscale old-school Italian vibe; warm crostini spread with pâté. $ *Average main: €26* ⊠ *Via Borgognona 11, Piazza di Spagna* ☎ *06/6786752* ⊕ *www.ristorantenino.it* ⊙ *Closed Sun. and Aug.* Ⓜ *Spagna.*

Settimo

$$$ | **ITALIAN** | Crowning the Sofitel Rome Villa Borghese hotel, this chic restaurant serves fancified takes on Rome's *cucina povera* (peasant cooking) in a chic space with graphic punches of color. The terrace offers fantastic views that stretch from Villa Borghese to the dome of St. Peter's, but the interior dining room, with its floor-to-ceiling windows and terrazzo-inspired floors, is lovely, too. **Known for:** terrace with great views; colorful, modern design; amped-up version of classic Roman recipes. $ *Average main: €26* ⊠ *Sofitel Rome Villa Borghese, Via Lombardia 47, Piazza di Spagna* ☎ *06/478021* ⊕ *www.settimoristorante. it* Ⓜ *Barberini.*

☕ Coffee and Quick Bites

Antico Caffè Greco

$ | **CAFÉ** | Pricey Antico Caffè Greco is a national landmark and Rome's oldest café; its red-velvet chairs, marble tables, and marble busts have seen the likes of Byron, Shelley, Keats, Goethe, and Casanova. Add to this the fact that it's in the middle of the shopping madness on the upscale Via Condotti, and you won't be surprised that the place is often filled with tourists. **Known for:** crystal goblets and high prices to match; perfect espresso; lavish historic design. $ *Average main: €12* ⊠ *Via dei Condotti 86, Piazza di*

Spagna ☎ *06/6791700* 🌐 *www.caffegreco.shop* [M] *Spagna.*

Il Gelato di San Crispino

$ | ICE CREAM | Many people say this is the best gelato in Rome, and though it's hard to pick just one, this is definitely the place to go if you want a delicious iced treat around the corner from the Trevi Fountain. The shop even had a cameo in the movie *Eat, Pray, Love* and is known for keeping its gelato hidden under metal covers in order to best preserve the quality. **Known for:** offering only cups and no cones; wine-based gelato; seasonal fruit flavors. [$] *Average main: €4* ✉ *Via della Panetteria 42, Piazza di Spagna* ☎ *06/6793924* 🌐 *www.ilgelatodisancrispino.it* [M] *Barberini.*

Hotels

Aleph Rome Hotel

$$$$ | HOTEL | Fashionable couples tend to favor the Aleph, a former bank–turned–luxury Rome hotel, where the motto seems to be "more marble, everywhere." Now part of Hilton's Curio Collection, the hotel has ample facilities that include two pools (one in the spa and one on the roof), a cigar lounge, a cocktail bar, and two restaurants, one on the ground floor and one on the rooftop. **Pros:** free access to the spa for hotel guests; terrace with pool; award-winning design. **Cons:** buffet breakfast not included; rooftop views don't showcase Rome's most flattering side; rooms are too petite for the price. [$] *Rooms from: €380* ✉ *Via San Basilio 15, Piazza di Spagna* ☎ *06/4229001* 🌐 *alephrome.com* 🛏 *88 rooms* 🍴 *No Meals* [M] *Barberini.*

Babuino 181

$$$ | HOTEL | On chic Via del Babuino, known for its high-end boutiques, jewelry stores, and antiques shops, this discreet and stylish hotel is an ideal Roman pied à terre that has spacious rooms spread over two historic buildings. **Pros:** spacious suites; iPhone docks and other handy in-room amenities; luxury Frette linens. **Cons:** annex rooms feel removed from service staff; breakfast is nothing special; rooms can be a bit noisy. [$] *Rooms from: €250* ✉ *Via del Babuino 181, Piazza di Spagna* ☎ *06/32295295* 🌐 *www.romeluxurysuites.com/babuino* 🛏 *24 rooms* 🍴 *Free Breakfast* [M] *Flaminio, Spagna.*

Baglioni Hotel Regina

$$$$ | HOTEL | The former home of Queen Margherita of Savoy, the Baglioni Hotel Regina, which enjoys a prime spot on the Via Veneto, is still a favorite among today's international jet-setters. **Pros:** nice decor; excellent on-site restaurant and bar; luxury on-site spa. **Cons:** location isn't as prestigious as it once was; service is hit-or-miss; some rooms are noisy. [$] *Rooms from: €319* ✉ *Via Veneto 72, Piazza di Spagna* ☎ *06/421111* 🌐 *www.baglionihotels.com/rome* 🛏 *114 rooms* 🍴 *No Meals* [M] *Barberini.*

★ The Hassler

$$$$ | HOTEL | When it comes to million-dollar views, the best place to stay in the whole city is the Hassler, so it's no surprise many rich and famous (Tom Cruise, Jennifer Lopez, and the Beckhams among them) are willing to pay top dollar for a room at this exclusive hotel atop the Spanish Steps. **Pros:** prime location and panoramic views; sauna access included with each reservation; private rooftop with bar service upon request. **Cons:** rooms are updated on a rolling basis, leaving some feeling dated; gym and wellness area is tiny; VIP rates (10% VAT not included). [$] *Rooms from: €1010* ✉ *Piazza Trinità dei Monti 6, Piazza di Spagna* ☎ *06/699340, 800/223–6800 in U.S.* 🌐 *www.hotelhasslerroma.com* 🛏 *87 rooms* 🍴 *Free Breakfast* [M] *Spagna.*

★ Hotel de la Ville

$$$$ | HOTEL | Occupying a prime position at the top of the Spanish Steps, the sister property to the beloved Hotel de Russie is the most glamorous new hotel in town. **Pros:** must-visit rooftop bar with panoramic views; pampering spa uses

signature made-in-Italy organic products; prestigious location atop the Spanish Steps. **Cons:** no pets allowed; service can be a bit slow at the bar; some rooms are a bit small. $ *Rooms from: €594* ✉ *Via Sistina 69, Piazza di Spagna* ☎ *06/977931* ⊕ *www.roccofortehotels.com* ⤳ *104 rooms* ⦿ *No Meals* Ⓜ *Spagna.*

Hotel d'Inghilterra

$$$$ | **HOTEL** | Situated in a stately 16th-century building and founded in 1845, Hotel d'Inghilterra has a long, storied history: it has been used as a guesthouse for aristocratic travelers visiting a noble family who once lived across the cobblestone street and has been the home away from home for various monarchs and movie stars, like Elizabeth Taylor, not to mention some of the greatest writers of all time—Lord Byron, John Keats, Mark Twain, and Ernest Hemingway among them. **Pros:** distinct character and opulence; excellent in-house restaurant; turndown service (with chocolates). **Cons:** some rooms badly in need of renovations and maintenance; the location, despite soundproofing, is still noisy; elevator is small. $ *Rooms from: €400* ✉ *Via Bocca di Leone 14, Piazza di Spagna* ☎ *06/699811* ⊕ *www.starhotelscollezione.com/en/our-hotels/hotel-d-inghilterra-rome* ⤳ *84 rooms* ⦿ *Free Breakfast* Ⓜ *Spagna.*

★ Hotel Eden

$$$$ | **HOTEL** | Once a favorite haunt of Ingrid Bergman, Ginger Rogers, and Fellini, this superlative hotel combines dashing elegance, exquisitely lush decor, and stunning vistas of Rome with true Italian hospitality to create one of the city's top luxury lodgings. **Pros:** gorgeous rooftop terrace restaurant; 24-hour room service; tranquil spa facilities. **Cons:** some rooms overlook an unremarkable courtyard; gym is standard but small; breakfast not included (and very expensive, at €45). $ *Rooms from: €780* ✉ *Via Ludovisi 49, Piazza di Spagna* ☎ *06/478121* ⊕ *www.dorchestercollection.com* ⤳ *98 rooms* ⦿ *No Meals* Ⓜ *Spagna.*

★ Hotel Vilòn

$$$$ | **HOTEL** | This intimate hotel in the 16th-century mansion annexed to Palazzo Borghese might be Rome's best-kept secret. **Pros:** gorgeous design; fantastic location; attentive staff. **Cons:** not much communal space; some rooms are a bit small; no spa or gym. $ *Rooms from: €460* ✉ *Via dell'Arancio 69, Piazza di Spagna* ☎ *06/878187* ⊕ *www.hotelvilon.com* ⤳ *18 rooms* ⦿ *Free Breakfast* Ⓜ *Spagna.*

Il Palazzetto

$$$ | **B&B/INN** | Once a retreat for one of Rome's richest noble families, this 15th-century house is one of the most intimate and luxurious hotels in Rome, with gorgeous terraces and a rooftop bar where you can watch the never-ending theater of the Spanish Steps. **Pros:** location and view; guests have full access to the Hassler's services; free Wi-Fi. **Cons:** breakfast is served in the main building at the Hassler; bedrooms do not access communal terraces; often books up far in advance, particularly in high season. $ *Rooms from: €290* ✉ *Vicolo del Bottino 8, Piazza di Spagna* ☎ *06/69934560* ⊕ *www.ilpalazzettoroma.com* ⤳ *4 rooms* ⦿ *Free Breakfast* Ⓜ *Spagna.*

Maalot Roma

$$$ | **HOTEL** | This new boutique hotel inside the former residence of opera composer Gaetano Donizetto aims to be a restaurant with rooms above rather than a hotel with a restaurant. **Pros:** great food at Don Pasquale restaurant; central location just steps from the Trevi Fountain; chic design with original art. **Cons:** no spa; service can be a bit slow; some rooms look directly onto the McDonald's across the street. $ *Rooms from: €280* ✉ *Via delle Murate 78, Piazza di Spagna* ☎ *06/878087* ⊕ *www.hotelmaalot.com* ⤳ *30 rooms* ⦿ *Free Breakfast* Ⓜ *Barberini.*

Margutta 19

$$$$ | **HOTEL** | Tucked away on a quiet, leafy street known for its art galleries, this 22-suite property is like your very own hip, New York–style loft in the center of old-world Rome, with top-drawer amenities, contemporary design, and a restaurant with a verdant terrace. **Pros:** studio-loft feel in center of town; deluxe furnishings; complete privacy. **Cons:** no elevator in the annex to reach rooms on higher floors; entry-level rooms lack views; no spa or gym. $ Rooms from: €520 ⊠ Via Margutta 19, Piazza di Spagna ☎ 06/97797979 ⊕ www.romeluxurysuites.com ⤏ 22 suites ⦿ Free Breakfast Ⓜ Spagna.

Scalinata di Spagna

$ | **B&B/INN** | Perched atop the Spanish Steps, this charming boutique hotel makes guests fall in love over and over again—so popular, in fact, it's often booked far in advance. **Pros:** friendly and helpful concierge; free Wi-Fi throughout; fresh fruit in guest rooms. **Cons:** no porter and no elevator; small rooms; hike up the hill to the hotel. $ Rooms from: €116 ⊠ Piazza Trinità dei Monti 17, Piazza di Spagna ☎ 06/45686150 ⊕ www.hotelscalinata.com ⤏ 30 rooms ⦿ Free Breakfast Ⓜ Spagna.

 Nightlife

Antica Enoteca

WINE BARS | Piazza di Spagna's staple wine bar literally corners the market on prime people-watching. Cozy up to the counter to sip a drink under the charming frescoes or snag a coveted outdoor table. In addition to a vast selection of wine, Antica Enoteca has delectable antipasti, perfect for a snack or a light lunch, as well as a full menu of pastas and pizzas. ⊠ Via della Croce 76/b, Piazza di Spagna ☎ 06/6790896 ⊕ www.anticaenoteca.com Ⓜ Spagna.

Wine Bar at the Palazzetto

WINE BARS | The prize for perfect aperitivo spot goes to the Palazzetto, with excellent drinks and appetizers, as well as a breathtaking view of Rome's domes and rooftops—all from its fifth-floor rooftop overlooking the comings and goings on the Spanish Steps. Reach it by climbing the monumental staircase that it overlooks, or getting a lift from the elevator inside the Spagna Metro station. ⊠ Vicolo del Bottino 8, Piazza di Spagna ⤖ The main entrance is a small gate at the top of the Spanish Steps ☎ 06/69934560 ⊕ www.ilpalazzettoroma.com Ⓜ Spagna.

 Shopping

ACCESSORIES

Furla

HANDBAGS | Furla very well might be the best deal in Italian leather, selling high-end quality handbags and purses at affordable prices. There are multiple locations throughout the Eternal City (including one at Fiumicino Airport), but its flagship store can be found in the heart of Piazza di Spagna. Be prepared to fight your way through crowds of passionate handbag lovers, all anxious to possess one of the delectable bags, wallets, or whimsical key chains in trendy sherbet hues or timeless bold color combos. ⊠ Piazza di Spagna 22, Piazza di Spagna ☎ 06/6797159 ⊕ www.furla.com Ⓜ Spagna.

CLOTHING

★ **Brioni**

MEN'S CLOTHING | Founded in 1945, Brioni is hailed for its impeccable craftsmanship in creating made-to-measure menswear. The classic brand hires the best men's tailors in Italy, who design bespoke suits to exacting standards, measured to the millimeter and completely personalized from a selection of more than 5,000 spectacular fabrics. A single made-to-measure wool suit will take a minimum of 32 hours to create. Their prêt-à-porter line is also praised for peerless cutting and stitching. Past and present clients include Clark Gable, Barack Obama, and, of course, James Bond. ✉ *Via Condotti 21A, Piazza di Spagna* ☎ *06/6783428* ⊕ *www.brioni.com* Ⓜ *Spagna.*

Dolce & Gabbana

MIXED CLOTHING | Dolce and Gabbana met in 1980 when both were assistants at a Milan fashion atelier, and they opened their first store in 1982. With a modern aesthetic that screams sex appeal, the brand has always thrived on excess and is known for its bold, creative designs. The Rome store has a glass ceiling above a sparkling chandelier to allow natural light to spill in, illuminating the marble floors, antique brass accents, and (of course) the latest lines for men, women, and even children, plus an expansive accessories area. ✉ *Via Condotti 49–51, Piazza di Spagna* ☎ *06/69924999* ⊕ *www.dolcegabbana.com* Ⓜ *Spagna.*

Elena Mirò

WOMEN'S CLOTHING | Elena Mirò is a high-end brand that specializes in sophisti-cated, beautifully feminine clothes for curvy, European-styled women size 46 (U.S. size 12, U.K. size 14) and up. There are several locations in Rome, including one on Via Nazionale. ✉ *Via Frattina 11, Piazza di Spagna* ☎ *06/6784367* ⊕ *www. elenamiro.com* Ⓜ *Spagna.*

Fendi

MIXED CLOTHING | Fendi has been a fixture of the Roman fashion landscape since "Mamma" Fendi first opened shop with her husband in 1925. With an eye for crazy genius, she hired Karl Lagerfeld, who began working with the group at the start of his career. His furs and runway antics made him one of the most influ-ential designers of the 20th century and brought international acclaim to Fendi along the way. The atelier, now owned by the Louis Vuitton group, continues to symbolize Italian glamour at its finest, though the difference in ownership is noticeable. It's also gotten new life in the Italian press for its "Fendi for Fountains" campaign, which included funding the restoration of Rome's Trevi Fountain, and for moving its global headquarters to a striking Mussolini-era building known as the "square Colosseum" in the city's EUR neighborhood. The flagship store in Rome can be found on the ground floor of Palazzo Fendi. The upper floors are home to the brand's seven private suites (the first ever Fendi hotel), and the rooftop hosts Zuma, a modern Japanese restaurant with an oh-so-cool bar that has sweeping views across Rome. ✉ *Largo Carlo Goldoni 420, Piazza di Spagna* ☎ *06/33450896* ⊕ *www.fendi.com* Ⓜ *Spagna.*

Giorgio Armani

MIXED CLOTHING | One of the most influ-ential designers of Italian haute couture, Giorgio Armani creates fluid silhouettes and dazzling evening gowns with sexy peek-a-boo cutouts; his signature cuts are made with the clever-handedness and flawless technique achievable only by working with tracing paper and Italy's finest fabrics over the course of a life-time. His menswear collection uses tra-ditional textiles like wide-ribbed corduroy and stretch jersey in nontraditional ways while staying true to a clean, masculine aesthetic. The iconic Italian brand has an Emporio Armani shop on Via del Babuino, but the flagship store is the best place to find pieces that range from exotic runway-worthy masterpieces to more wearable collections emphasizing casual Italian elegance with just the right touch of whimsy and sexiness. ✉ *Via dei Con-dotti 77, Piazza di Spagna* ☎ *06/6991460* ⊕ *www.armani.com* Ⓜ *Spagna.*

Gucci

MIXED CLOTHING | Guccio Gucci opened his first leather shop selling luggage in Florence in 1921, and as the glamorous fashion label celebrates its centennial, the success of the double-G trademark is unquestionable. Tom Ford joined as creative director in 1994, helping the fashion house move into a new era that continues today, maintaining the label's trendiness while bringing in a breath of fresh air, thanks to old-school favorites like reinterpreted horsebit styles and Jackie Kennedy scarves. Now helmed by Alessandro Michele, Gucci remains a fashion must for virtually every A-list celebrity, and their designs have moved from heart-stopping sexy rock star to something classically subdued and retrospectively feminine, making the handbags and accessories more covetable than ever. ⊠ *Via Condotti 6–8, Piazza di Spagna* ☎ *06/6790405* ⊕ *www.gucci. com* Ⓜ *Spagna.*

★ Laura Biagiotti

WOMEN'S CLOTHING | Until her death in 2017, Laura Biagiotti was a worldwide ambassador of Italian fashion. Considered the Queen of Cashmere, her soft-as-velvet pullovers have been worn by Sophia Loren, and her snow-white cardigans were said to be a favorite of the late pope John Paul II. Princess Diana even sported one of Biagiotti's cashmere maternity dresses. In addition to stocking the luxe clothing line, the flagship store has a bold red lounge where shoppers can indulge in sampling her line of his-and-her perfumes or sip a Campari cocktail while purchases are customized with Swarovski crystals. ⊠ *Via Belsiana 57, Piazza di Spagna* ☎ *06/6791205* ⊕ *www. laurabiagiotti.it* Ⓜ *Spagna.*

★ Patrizia Pepe

WOMEN'S CLOTHING | One of Florence's best-kept secrets for up-and-coming designs, Patrizia Pepe first emerged on the scene in 1993 with an aesthetic that's both minimalist and bold, combining classic styles with low-slung jeans and jackets with oversize lapels that are bound to draw attention. Her line of shoes is hot-hot-hot for those who can walk on stilts. As a relative newcomer to the crowded Italian fashion scene, the brand's stand-alone fame is still under the radar, but take a look at this shop

before the line becomes the next fast-tracked craze. ⊠ *Via Frattina 44, Piazza di Spagna* ☎ *06/6781851* ⊕ *www.patrizia-pepe.com* Ⓜ *Spagna.*

Prada

MIXED CLOTHING | Besides the devil, plenty of serious shoppers wear Prada season after season, especially those willing to sell their souls for one of their ubiquitous handbags. If you are looking for that blend of old-world luxury with a touch of fashion-forward finesse, you'll hit it big here. Mario Prada first founded the Italian luggage brand in 1913, but it has been his granddaughter, Miuccia, who updated the designs into the timeless investment pieces of today. You'll find the Rome store more service-oriented than the New York City branches—a roomy elevator delivers you to a series of thickly carpeted salons where a flock of discreet assistants will help you pick out dresses, shoes, lingerie, and fashion accessories. The men's store is located at Via Condotti 88/90, while the women's is down the street at 92/95. ⊠ *Via dei Condotti 88/90 and 92/95, Piazza di Spagna* ☎ *06/6790897* ⊕ *www.prada. com* Ⓜ *Spagna.*

Schostal

MIXED CLOTHING | A Piazza di Spagna fixture since 1870, the shop was once the go-to place for women looking to stock up on corsets, bonnets, stockings, and petticoats. Today, it's the place to stop for those essential basics that are increasingly difficult to find, like fine-quality shirts, underwear, and handkerchiefs made of wool and pure cashmere at affordable prices. ⊠ *Via della Fontanella di Borghese 29, Piazza di Spagna* ☎ *06/6791240* ⊕ *www.schostalroma1870.com* ⊙ *Closed Sun.* Ⓜ *Spagna.*

Valentino

MIXED CLOTHING | Since taking the Valentino reins, creative director Pierpaolo Piccioli has faced numerous challenges, the most basic of which is keeping Valentino true to Valentino after the designer's retirement in 2008. He served as accessories designer under Valentino for more than a decade and understands exactly how to make the next generation of Hollywood stars swoon. Valentino has taken over most of Piazza di Spagna, where he lived for decades in a lovely palazzo next to one of the multiple boutiques showcasing his eponymous designs with a romantic edginess; think studded heels or a showstopping prêt-à-porter evening gown worthy of the Oscars. Rock stars and other music lovers can also have their Valentino guitar straps personalized when they buy one at this enormous boutique. ⊠ *Piazza di Spagna 38, Piazza di Spagna* ☎ *06/94515710* ⊕ *www.valentino.com* Ⓜ *Spagna*.

Versace

MIXED CLOTHING | Versace's Rome flagship is a gem of architecture and design, with Byzantine-inspired mosaic floors and futuristic interiors with transparent walls, not to mention, of course, fashion: here shoppers will find apparel, jewelry, watches, fragrances, cosmetics, and home furnishings in designs every bit as flamboyant as Donatella and Allegra (Gianni's niece), drawing heavily on the sexy rocker gothic underground vibe. ⊠ *Piazza di Spagna 12, Piazza di Spagna* ☎ *06/6784600* ⊕ *www.versace.com* Ⓜ *Spagna*.

DEPARTMENT STORES

★ La Rinascente

DEPARTMENT STORE | Italy's best-known department store is located in a dazzling space that has seven stories packed with the best luxury goods the world has to offer. Here, one can find oodles of cosmetics on the ground floor, as well as a phalanx of ready-to-wear designer sportswear and blockbuster handbags and accessories, and kitchen and housewares in the basement. Even if you're not planning on buying anything, the basement excavations of a Roman aqueduct and the roof terrace bar with its splendid view are well worth a visit.

There's also a location at Piazza Fiume. ⊠ *Via del Tritone 61, Piazza di Spagna* ☎ *02/91387388* ⊕ *www.rinascente.it* Ⓜ *Barberini*.

HEALTH & BEAUTY

Modàfferi Barber Shop

OTHER HEALTH & BEAUTY | Run by two friendly brothers, who took over the business from their father, this barbershop is preferred by actors performing at the nearby Teatro Sistina. It was founded in the 1970s and still has charmingly retro decor. They offer haircuts, beard care, manicures, pedicures, facials, and massages and have their own line of products. For extra privacy, you can request the private room. ⊠ *Via dei Cappuccini 11, Piazza di Spagna* ☎ *06/4817077* ⊕ *www.modafferibarbershop.it* Ⓜ *Barberini*.

JEWELRY

Bulgari

JEWELRY & WATCHES | Every capital city has its famous jeweler, and Bulgari is to Rome what Tiffany is to New York and Cartier to Paris. The jewelry giant has developed a reputation for meticulous craftsmanship melding noble metals with precious gems. In the middle of the 19th century, the great-grandfather of the current Bulgari brothers began working as a silver jeweler in his native Greece and is said to have moved to Rome with less than 1,000 lire in his pocket. The recent makeover of the store's temple-inspired interior pays homage to the brand's ties to both places. Today the mega-brand emphasizes colorful and playful jewelry as the principal cornerstone of its aesthetic. Popular collections include Bulgari-Bulgari and B.zero1. ⊠ *Via dei Condotti 10, Piazza di Spagna* ☎ *06/6792487* ⊕ *www.bulgari.com* Ⓜ *Spagna*.

SHOES

A. Testoni

SHOES | Amedeo Testoni, the brand's founder and original designer, was born in 1905 in Bologna, the heart of Italy's shoe-making territory. In 1929, he opened his first shop and began producing shoes as artistic as the Cubist and Art Deco artwork of the period. His shoes have adorned the feet of Fred Astaire, proving that lightweight footwear can be comfortable and luxurious and still turn heads. Today the Testoni brand includes a line of enviable handbags and classically cool leather jackets, plus dreamy calfskin sneakers and chic messenger bags—all found at this Roman boutique. ⊠ *Via Borgognona 21, Piazza di Spagna* ☎ *06/6787718* ⊕ *www.testoni.com* Ⓜ *Spagna.*

★ Braccialini

HANDBAGS | Founded in 1954 by Florentine stylist Carla Braccialini and her husband, Robert, Braccialini makes bags that are authentic works of art in bright colors and delightful shapes, such as London black cabs or mountain chalets. The adorably quirky tote bags have picture-postcard scenes of luxury destinations made of brightly colored appliquéd leather. Be sure to check out their eccentric Temi (Theme) creature bags; the snail-shaped handbag made out of python skin makes an unforgettable fashion statement. ⊠ *Via Frattina, 117, Piazza di Spagna* ☎ *06/62286871* ⊕ *www.braccialini.it* Ⓜ *Spagna.*

Fausto Santini

SHOES | Shoe lovers with a passion for minimalist design flock to Fausto Santini to get their hands on his nerdy-chic shoes with their statement-making lines. Santini has been in business since 1970 and caters to a sophisticated, avant-garde clientele looking for elegant, classic shoes with a kick and a rainbow color palette. An outlet at Via Cavour 106, named for Fausto's father, Giacomo, sells last season's shoes at a big discount. ⊠ *Via Frattina 120, Piazza di Spagna* ☎ *06/6784114* ⊕ *www.faustosantini.com* Ⓜ *Spagna.*

★ Tod's

SHOES | First founded in the 1920s, Tod's has grown from a small family brand into a global powerhouse so wealthy that its owner Diego Della Valle donated €20 million to the Colosseum restoration project. The shoe baron's trademark is his simple, classic, understated designs and butter-soft leather. Sure to please are his light and flexible slip-on Gommino driving shoes with rubber-bottomed soles for extra driving-pedal grip. There is also a location on Via Condotti. ⊠ *Via della Fontanella di Borghese 56a–57, Piazza di Spagna* ☎ *06/68210066* ⊕ *www.tods.com* Ⓜ *Spagna.*

Repubblica and the Quirinale

This sector of Rome stretches down from the 19th-century district built up around the Piazza della Repubblica—originally laid out to serve as a monumental foyer between the Termini train station and the rest of the city—and over the rest of the Quirinale. The highest of ancient Rome's famed seven hills, the Quirinale is crowned by the massive Palazzo Quirinale, home to the popes until 1870 and now Italy's presidential palace. Along the way, you can see ancient Roman sculptures, early Christian churches, and highlights from the 16th and 17th centuries, when Rome was conquered by the Baroque—and by Bernini.

Although Bernini's work feels omnipresent in much of the city center, the Renaissance-man range of his creations is particularly notable here. The artist as architect considered the church of Sant'Andrea al Quirinale one of his best; Bernini the urban designer and water worker is responsible for the muscle-bound sea god who blows his conch so provocatively in the fountain at the center of whirling Piazza Barberini.

And Bernini the master gives religious passion a joltingly corporeal treatment in what is perhaps his greatest work, the *Ecstasy of St. Teresa,* in the church of Santa Maria della Vittoria.

GETTING HERE AND AROUND

Located between Termini station and the Spanish Steps, this area is about a 15-minute walk from either. Bus No. 40 will get you from Termini to the Quirinale in two stops; from the Vatican take Bus No. 64. The very central Repubblica Metro stop is on the piazza of the same name.

Sights

Capuchin Museum

RELIGIOUS BUILDING | Devoted to teaching visitors about the Capuchin order, this museum is mainly notable for a crypt visitable at the end of the museum circuit. Not for the easily spooked, the crypt under the church of Santa Maria della Concezione holds the bones of some 4,000 dead Capuchin monks. With bones arranged in odd decorative designs around the shriveled and decayed remains of their kinsmen, a macabre reminder of the impermanence of earthly life, the crypt is strangely touching and beautiful. As one sign proclaims: "What you are, we once were. What we are, you someday will be." Upstairs in the church, the first chapel on the right contains Guido Reni's mid-17th-century *Archangel St. Michael Trampling the Devil.* The painting caused great scandal after an astute contemporary observer remarked that the face of the devil bore a surprising resemblance to Pope Innocent X, archenemy of Reni's Barberini patrons. Compare the devil with the bust of the pope that you saw in the Palazzo Doria Pamphilj and judge for yourself. ✉ *Via Veneto 27, Quirinale* ☎ *06/88803695* ⊕ *www.cappuccinviaveneto.it* 🎟 *€8.50* Ⓜ *Barberini.*

Fontana delle Api (*Fountain of the Bees*)

FOUNTAIN | Decorated with the famous heraldic bees of the Barberini family, the upper shell and the inscription are from a fountain that Bernini designed for Pope Urban VIII; the rest was lost when the fountain was moved to make way for a new street. The inscription was the cause of a considerable uproar when the fountain was first built in 1644. It said that the fountain had been erected in the 22nd year of the pontiff's reign, although in fact the 21st anniversary of Urban's election to the papacy was still some weeks away. The last numeral was hurriedly erased, but to no avail—Urban died eight days before the beginning of his 22nd year as pope. The superstitious Romans, who had immediately recognized the inscription as a foolhardy tempting of fate, were vindicated. ✉ *Piazza Barberini, Quirinale* Ⓜ *Barberini.*

MACRO

ART MUSEUM | Formerly known as Rome's Modern and Contemporary Art Gallery, and before that as the Peroni beer factory, this redesigned industrial space has brought new life to the gallery and museum scene of a city hitherto hailed for its "then," not its "now." The collection here covers Italian contemporary artists from the 1960s through today. The goal is to bring current art to the public in innovative spaces and, not incidentally, to give support and bring recognition to Rome's contemporary art scene, which labors in the shadow of the city's artistic heritage. After a few days—or millennia—of dusty marble, it's a breath of fresh air. ■ TIP→ **Check the website for occasional late-night openings and events.** ✉ *Via Nizza 138, Repubblica* ☎ *06/696271* ⊕ *www.museomacro.it* 🎟 *Free* ☾ *Closed Mon.* Ⓜ *Castro Pretorio.*

★ Palazzo Barberini/Galleria Nazionale d'Arte Antica

ART MUSEUM | One of Rome's most splendid 17th-century buildings, the Palazzo Barberini is a landmark of the Roman Baroque style. The grand facade was designed by Carlo Maderno (aided by his nephew, Francesco Borromini), but when Maderno died, Borromini was passed over in favor of his great rival, Gian Lorenzo Bernini. Now home to the Galleria Nazionale d'Arte Antica, the palazzo holds a splendid collection that includes Raphael's *La Fornarina,* a luminous portrait of the artist's lover (a resident of Trastevere, she was reputedly a baker's daughter). Also noteworthy are Guido Reni's portrait of the doomed *Beatrice Cenci* (beheaded in Rome for patricide in 1599)—Hawthorne called it "the saddest picture ever painted" in his Rome-based novel, *The Marble Faun*—and Caravaggio's dramatic *Judith Beheading Holofernes.*

The showstopper here is the palace's Gran Salone, a vast ballroom with a ceiling painted in 1630 by the third (and too-often-neglected) master of the Roman Baroque, Pietro da Cortona. It depicts the *Glorification of Urban VIII's Reign* and has the spectacular conceit of glorifying Urban VIII as the agent of Divine Providence, escorted by a "bomber squadron" (to quote art historian Sir Michael Levey) of huge Barberini bees, the heraldic symbol of the family. ⊠ *Via delle Quattro Fontane 13, Quirinale* ☎ *06/4814591* ⊕ *www.barberinicorsini. org* ◺ *€12, includes Galleria Corsini* ☉ *Closed Mon.* Ⓜ *Barberini.*

★ Palazzo Massimo alle Terme

ART MUSEUM | Come here to get a real feel for ancient Roman art—the collection rivals even the Vatican's. The Museo Nazionale Romano, with a collection ranging from striking classical Roman paintings to marble bric-a-brac, has four locations: Palazzo Altemps, Crypta Balbi, the Museo delle Terme di Diocleziano, and this, the Palazzo Massimo alle Terme. This vast structure holds the great ancient treasures of the archaeological collection and also the coin collection. Highlights include the *Dying Niobid*, the famous bronze *Boxer at Rest*, and the *Discobolus Lancellotti*. But the best part of the museum are the ancient frescoes on view on the top floor, stunningly set up to "re-create" the look of the homes they once decorated. These include stuccoes and wall paintings found in the area of the Villa Farnesina (in Trastevere) and the legendary frescoes from Empress Livia's villa at Prima Porta, delightful depictions of a garden in bloom and an orchard alive with birds. Their colors are remarkably well preserved. These delicate decorations covered the walls of cool, sunken rooms in Livia's summerhouse outside the city. ⊠ *Largo di Villa Peretti 2, Repubblica* ☎ *06/39967700* ⊕ *www.museonazionaleromano.beniculturali.it* ◺ *€8, or €12 for a combined ticket including access to Crypta Balbi, Museo delle Terme di Diocleziano, and Palazzo Altemps (valid for 1 wk)* ☉ *Closed Mon.* ◁ *Reservations required* Ⓜ *Repubblica, Termini.*

Piazza del Quirinale

PLAZA/SQUARE | This strategic location atop the Quirinale has long been of great importance. It served as home of the Sabines in the 7th century BC—at that time, deadly enemies of the Romans, who lived on the Campidoglio and Palatino (all of 1 km [½ mile] away). Today, it's the foreground for the presidential residence, Palazzo del Quirinale, and home to the Palazzo della Consulta, where Italy's Constitutional Court sits. The open side of the piazza has an impressive vista over the rooftops and domes of central Rome and St. Peter's. The Fontana di Montecavallo, or Fontana dei Dioscuri, comprises a huge Roman statuary group and an obelisk from the tomb of the emperor Augustus. The group of the Dioscuri trying to tame two massive marble steeds was found in the Baths of Constantine, which occupied part

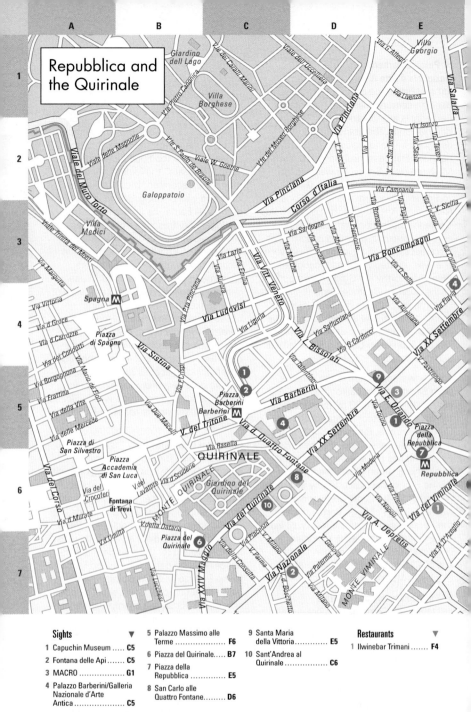

Repubblica and the Quirinale

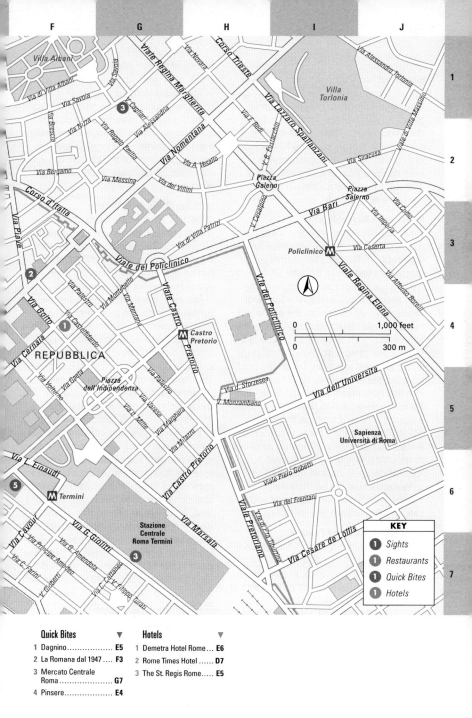

of the summit of the Quirinale. Unlike just about every other ancient statue in Rome, this group survived the Dark Ages intact and accordingly became one of the city's great sights, especially during the Middle Ages. Next to the figures, the ancient obelisk from the Mausoleo di Augusto (Tomb of Augustus) was put here by Pope Pius VI at the end of the 18th century. ⊠ *Piazza del Quirinale, Quirinale* Ⓜ *Barberini.*

Piazza della Repubblica

PLAZA/SQUARE | Often the first view that spells "Rome" to weary travelers walking from Termini station, this round piazza was laid out in the late 1800s and follows the line of the caldarium of the vast ancient public baths, the Terme di Diocleziano. At its center, the exuberant Fontana delle Naiadi (Fountain of the Naiads) teems with voluptuous bronze ladies happily wrestling with marine monsters. The nudes weren't there when the pope unveiled the fountain in 1888—sparing him any embarrassment—but when the figures were added in 1901, they caused a scandal. It's said that the sculptor, Mario Rutelli (grandfather of Francesco Rutelli, former mayor of Rome), modeled them on the ample figures of two musical-comedy stars of the day. The colonnades now house the luxe hotel Palazzo Naiadi and various shops and cafés. ⊠ *Repubblica* Ⓜ *Repubblica.*

San Carlo alle Quattro Fontane

CHURCH | Sometimes known as San Carlino because of its tiny size, this is one of Borromini's masterpieces. In a space no larger than the base of one of the piers of St. Peter's Basilica, he created a church that is an intricate exercise in geometric perfection, with a coffered dome that seems to float above the curves of the walls. Borromini's work is often bizarre, definitely intellectual, and intensely concerned with pure form. In San Carlo, he invented an original treatment of space that creates an effect of rippling movement, especially evident in the double-S

curves of the facade. Characteristically, the interior decoration is subdued, in white stucco with no more than a few touches of gilding, so as not to distract from the form. Don't miss the cloister: a tiny, understated Baroque jewel, with a graceful portico and loggia above, echoing the lines of the church. ⊠ *Via del Quirinale 23, Quirinale* 🕾 *06/48907729* Ⓜ *Barberini.*

★ Santa Maria della Vittoria

CHURCH | Designed by Carlo Maderno, this church is best known for Bernini's sumptuous Baroque decoration of the Cappella Cornaro (Cornaro Chapel, the last on the left as you face the altar), which houses his interpretation of divine love, the *Ecstasy of St. Teresa.* Bernini's masterly fusion of sculpture, light, architecture, painting, and relief is a multimedia extravaganza, with the chapel modeled as a theater, and one of the key examples of the Roman High Baroque. The members of the Cornaro family meditate on the communal vision of the great moment of divine love before them: the swooning saint's robes appear to be on fire, quivering with life, and the white marble group seems suspended in the heavens as golden rays illuminate the scene. An angel assists at the moment of Teresa's vision as the saint abandons herself to the joys of heavenly love. Bernini represented this mystical experience in what, to modern eyes, may seem very earthly terms. Or, as the visiting French dignitary Charles de Brosses put it in the 18th century, "If this is divine love, I know all about it." ⊠ *Via XX Settembre 17, Largo Santa Susanna, Repubblica* 🕾 *06/42740571* Ⓜ *Repubblica.*

Sant'Andrea al Quirinale

CHURCH | Designed by Bernini, this small church is one of the triumphs of the Roman Baroque period. His son wrote that Bernini considered it his best work and that he used to come here occasionally, just to sit and contemplate. Bernini's simple oval plan, a classic form in Baroque architecture, is given drama and movement by the church's decoration, which carries the story of St. Andrew's martyrdom and ascension into heaven, starting with the painting over the high altar, up past the figure of the saint above, to the angels at the base of the lantern and the dove of the Holy Spirit that awaits on high. ⊠ *Via del Quirinale 30, Quirinale* ☎ *06/4819399* ⊕ *santandrea.gesuiti.it* ⊙ *Closed Mon.* Ⓜ *Barberini.*

Restaurants

Ilwinebar Trimani

$$$ | **WINE BAR** | This wine bar is run by the Trimani family of wine merchants, whose shop next door has been in business for nearly two centuries. Hot food is served at lunch and dinner in the minimalist interior, and it is also perfect for an aperitif or an early supper (it opens for evening service at 6 pm). **Known for:** 5,000 wines from around the world; torte salate (savory tarts); candlelit second floor for sipping. Ⓢ *Average main: €30* ⊠ *Via Cernaia 37/b, Repubblica* ☎ *06/4469630* ⊕ *www.trimani.com* ⊙ *Closed Sun. and 3 wks in Aug.* Ⓜ *Castro Pretorio, Repubblica.*

🍵 Coffee and Quick Bites

Dagnino

$ | **BAKERY** | Hidden inside a covered arcade, this Sicilian pasticceria, which opened in 1955 and proudly wears its midcentury modern design, boasts pastry cases filled with sweets like cannoli, cassata, cakes, and marzipan. Go for breakfast and try the cornetto filled with ricotta and chocolate chips—this is one of the few places in Rome where you can find it. **Known for:** cornetti filled with ricotta and chocolate chips; midcentury modern design; Sicilian desserts. Ⓢ *Average main: €3* ⊠ *Via Vittorio Emanuele Orlando 75, Repubblica* ☎ *06/4818660* ⊕ *www. pasticceriadagnino.com* Ⓜ *Repubblica.*

La Romana dal 1947

$ | **ICE CREAM** | In summertime, the line at this gelateria stretches out the door and around the corner. Though it's a franchise that originated in Rimini, La Romana is loved by Romans for its rich, creamy gelato made with organic milk, fresh fruit, nuts, and chocolate. **Known for:** big portions; reasonably priced; modern decor. Ⓢ *Average main: €3* ⊠ *Via XX Settembre 60, Repubblica* ☎ *06/42020828* ⊕ *www.gelateriaromana. com* Ⓜ *Repubblica.*

Mercato Centrale Roma

$ | **ITALIAN** | This gourmet food hall is in the last place you'd expect: inside Termini station. It's great for a quick bite even if you're not catching a train. **Known for:** Sicilian specialties; trapizzino (stuffed triangle-shaped pizza) outpost; gourmet food hall. Ⓢ *Average main: €5* ⊠ *Termini Station, Via Giovanni Giolitti 36, Repubblica* ☎ *06/46202900* ⊕ *www. mercatocentrale.it* Ⓜ *Termini.*

Pinsere

$ | **PIZZA** | **FAMILY** | In Rome, you'll usually find either pizza tonda (round) or pizza al taglio (by the slice), but there's also pizza *pinsa*: it's an oval-shaped individual pie, and a little thicker than the classic Roman pizza. Pinsere is mostly a take-out shop, with people eating on the street for their lunch break, so it's the perfect quick meal. **Known for:** mortadella and pistachio pizzas; seasonal toppings; budget-friendly options. Ⓢ *Average main: €6* ⊠ *Via Flavia 98, Repubblica* ☎ *06/42020924* ⊙ *Closed weekends and 2 wks in Aug.* Ⓜ *Castro Pretorio.*

🛏 Hotels

Demetra Hotel Rome

$$ | **HOTEL** | This hotel near the glorious Santa Maria Maggiore Basilica is also close to Termini station, and has modern comforts and a great concierge—all at moderate rates. **Pros:** free Wi-Fi; excellent central location; soundproof rooms. **Cons:**

rooms can be on the small side; not a picturesque area, so views can be drab; basic breakfast buffet. $ *Rooms from: €180* ✉ *Via del Viminale 8, Repubblica* ☎ *06/45494943* ⊕ *www.demetrahotel-rome.com* 🛏 *27 rooms* ⦿ *Free Breakfast* Ⓜ *Repubblica.*

Rome Times Hotel

$$ | HOTEL | This modern hotel has large, soundproofed rooms with contemporary furnishings, hardwood floors, and huge fluffy beds. **Pros:** free minibar on arrival and late checkout if booked through site; large bright bathrooms; free use of Samsung smartphone for calls and Internet during your stay. **Cons:** lighting in rooms is not optimal; rooms in the annex don't come with all the benefits of the main hotel; lower floors can be noisy. $ *Rooms from: €180* ✉ *Via Milano 42, Quirinale* ☎ *06/99345101* ⊕ *www.rometimeshotel.com* 🛏 *81 rooms* ⦿ *No Meals* Ⓜ *Repubblica.*

The St. Regis Rome

$$$$ | HOTEL | Originally opened by César Ritz in 1894, this grande dame is looking fabulous thanks to a $40 million renovation completed in 2018. **Pros:** recently underwent a complete renovation; the library lounge serves a lovely afternoon tea; every room comes with 24/7 butler service. **Cons:** the restaurant feels more like a lounge than a proper restaurant; breakfast is not included; food and drinks are pricey. $ *Rooms from: €650* ✉ *Via Vittorio E. Orlando 3, Repubblica* ☎ *06/47091* ⊕ *www.stregisrome.com* 🛏 *161 rooms* ⦿ *No Meals* Ⓜ *Repubblica.*

🎭 Performing Arts

★ Teatro dell'Opera

OPERA | Long considered a far younger sibling of La Scala in Milan and La Fenice in Venice, the company commands an audience during its mid-November–May season. In the hot summer months, they move to the Terme di Caracalla for its outdoor opera series. As can be expected, the oft-preferred performance is *Aida,* for its spectacle, which once included real elephants. The company has lately taken a new direction, using projections atop the ancient ruins to create cutting-edge sets. ✉ *Piazza Beniamino Gigli 1, Repubblica* ☎ *06/481601, 06/4817003 tickets* ⊕ *www.operaroma.it* Ⓜ *Repubblica.*

Villa Borghese and Environs

Touring Rome's artistic masterpieces while staying clear of its hustle and bustle can be, quite literally, a walk in the park. Some of the city's finest sights are tucked away in or next to green lawns and pedestrian piazzas, offering a breath of fresh air for weary sightseers, especially in the Villa Borghese park. One of Rome's largest, this park can alleviate gallery gout by offering an oasis in which to cool off under the ilex, oak, and umbrella pine trees. If you feel like a picnic, have an *alimentari* (food shop) make you some panini before you go; food carts within the park are overpriced.

GETTING HERE AND AROUND

The Metro stop for Piazza del Popolo is Flaminio on Line A. The Villa Giulia, the Galleria Nazionale d'Arte Moderna e Contemporanea, and the Bioparco in Villa Borghese are accessible from Via Flaminia, 1 km (½ mile) from Piazza del Popolo. Tram No. 19 and Bus No. 3 stop at each. Bus No. 160 and No. 628 connect Piazza del Popolo to Piazza Venezia. Bus No. 116 goes into Villa Borghese.

Sights

★ Galleria Borghese

ART MUSEUM | The villa built for Cardinal Scipione Borghese in 1612 houses one of the finest collections of Baroque sculpture anywhere in the world. One of the most famous works in the collection is Canova's neoclassical sculpture of Pauline Borghese as *Venus Victrix*. The next three rooms hold three key early Baroque sculptures: Bernini's *David, Apollo and Daphne,* and *Rape of Proserpina*. The Caravaggio Room houses works by this hotheaded genius; upstairs, the Pinacoteca (Picture Gallery) boasts paintings by Raphael (including his moving *Deposition*), Pinturicchio, Perugino, Bellini, and Rubens. Probably the gallery's most famous painting is Titian's allegorical *Sacred and Profane Love*, a mysterious and yet-unsolved image with two female figures, one nude, one clothed. ■TIP➔ **Admission to the Galleria is by reservation only. Visitors are admitted in two-hour shifts 9–5. Prime-time slots usually sell out days in advance, so reserve directly through the museum's website.** ⊠ *Piazzale Scipione Borghese 5, off Via Pinciana, Villa Borghese* ☎ *06/32810 reservations, 06/8413979 info* ⊕ *www.galleriaborghese.it* ⊠ *€15, including €2 reservation fee; increased fee during temporary exhibitions* ⊙ *Closed Mon.* ⌂ *Reservations required.*

MAXXI—Museo Nazionale delle Arti del XXI Secolo (*National Museum of 21st-Century Arts*)
ART MUSEUM | Designed by the late Iraqi-British starchitect Zaha Hadid, this modern building plays with lots of natural light, curving and angular lines, and big open spaces, all meant to question the division between "within" and "without" (think glass ceilings and steel staircases that twist through the air). The MAXXI hosts temporary exhibitions of art, architecture, film, and more. The permanent collection, exhibited on a rotating basis, boasts more than 350 works from modern and contemporary artists, including Andy Warhol, Francesco Clemente, and Gerhard Richter. ⊠ *Via Guido Reni 4/A, Flaminio* ☎ *06/3201954* ⊕ *www.maxxi.art* ⊠ *€12* ⊙ *Closed Mon.* Ⓜ *Flaminio, then Tram No. 2 to Apollodoro.*

★ **Piazza del Popolo**
PLAZA/SQUARE | With its obelisk and twin churches, this immense square is a famed Rome landmark. It marks what was for centuries the northern entrance to the city, where all roads from the north converge and where visitors, many of them pilgrims, would get their first impression of the Eternal City. The desire to make this entrance to Rome something special had been a pet project of popes and their architects for more than three centuries. The piazza, crowded with fashionable carriages and carnival revelers in the past, is a pedestrian zone today. At election time, it's the scene of huge political rallies, and on New Year's Eve, Rome stages a mammoth alfresco party here. ⊠ *Piazza del Popolo* Ⓜ *Flaminio.*

★ **Santa Maria del Popolo**
CHURCH | Standing inconspicuously in a corner of the vast Piazza del Popolo, this church often goes unnoticed, but the treasures inside make it a must for art lovers. Bramante enlarged the apse, which was rebuilt in the 15th century on the site of a much older place of worship. Inside, in the first chapel on the right, you'll see some frescoes by Pinturicchio from the mid-15th century; the adjacent Cybo Chapel is a 17th-century exercise in decorative marble. Raphael designed the famous Chigi Chapel, the second on the left, with vault mosaics—showing God the Father in Benediction—as well as statues of Jonah and Elijah. More than a century later, Bernini added the oval medallions on the tombs and the statues of Daniel and Habakkuk. Finally, the Cerasi Chapel, to the left of the high altar, holds two Caravaggios: *The Crucifixion of St. Peter* and *The Conversion of St. Paul*. Exuding drama and realism, both are key early Baroque works that show how "modern" 17th-century art can appear. Compare their style with the much more restrained and classically "pure" *Assumption of the Virgin* by Annibale Carracci, which hangs over the altar of the chapel. ⊠ *Piazza del Popolo 12,*

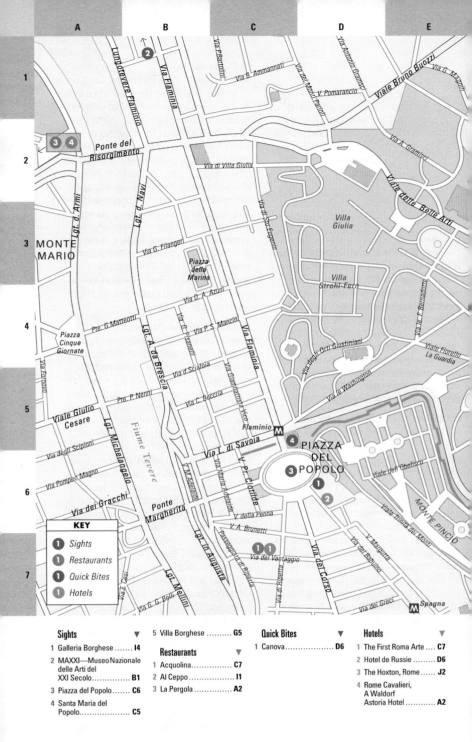

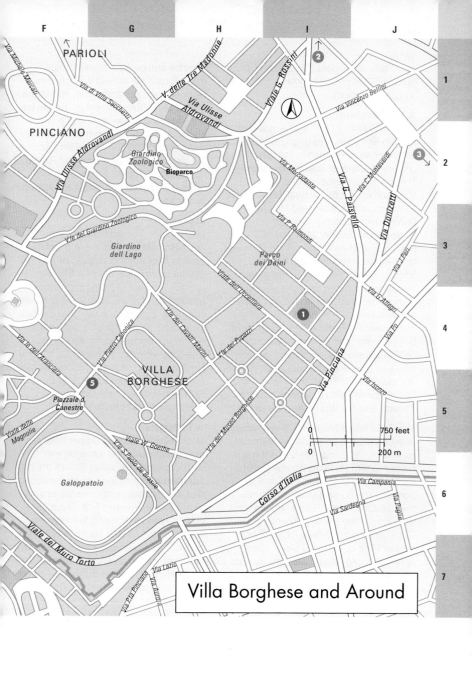

Villa Borghese and Around

near Porta del Popolo, Piazza del Popolo ☎ *3923612243* ⊕ *www.smariadelpopolo. com/it* Ⓜ *Flaminio.*

★ Villa Borghese

CITY PARK | FAMILY | Rome's Central Park, the Villa Borghese was originally laid out as a recreational garden in the early 17th century by Cardinal Scipione Borghese. The word "villa" was used to mean suburban estate, of the type developed by the ancient Romans and adopted by Renaissance nobles. Today's gardens cover a much smaller area—by 1630, the perimeter wall was almost 5 km (3 miles) long. At the end of the 18th century, Scottish painter Jacob More remodeled the gardens into the English style popular at the time. In addition to the gloriously restored Galleria Borghese, the highlights of the park are Piazza di Siena, a graceful amphitheater, and the botanical garden on Via Canonica, where there is a pretty little lake as well as the neoclassical faux–Temple of Aesculapius, the Biopark zoo, Rome's own replica of London's Globe Theatre, and the Villa Giulia museum.

The Carlo Bilotti Museum (⊕ *www.museocarlobilotti.it*) is particularly attractive for Giorgio de Chirico fans, and there is more modern art in the nearby Galleria Nazionale d'Arte Moderna e Contemporanea. The 63-seat children's movie theater, Cinema dei Piccoli, shows films for adults in the evening. There's also Casa del Cinema, where film buffs can screen films or sit at the sleek, cherry-red, indoor-outdoor café (you can find a schedule of events at ⊕ *www.casadelcinema.it.* ✉ *Main entrances at Porta Pinciana, the Pincio, Piazzale Flaminio (Piazza del Popolo), Viale delle Belle Arti, and Via Mercadante, Villa Borghese* Ⓜ *Flaminio.*

 Restaurants

Acquolina

$$$$ | MODERN ITALIAN | This Michelin-starred restaurant turns out delicious and high-quality seafood dishes that surprise and evoke a sensory experience. Tortelli are served with cheese, black pepper, eel, and onion, and all the dishes are artfully presented. **Known for:** sophisticated desserts; linguine with clams; elaborate tasting menus. Ⓢ *Average main: €50* ✉ *The First Roma Arte, Via del Vantaggio 14, Piazza del Popolo* ☎ *06/3201590* ⊕ *www.acquolinaristorante.it* ♥ *Closed Sun. and Tues. No lunch* Ⓜ *Flaminio.*

Al Ceppo

$$$ | ITALIAN | The well-heeled, the business-minded, and those of refined palates frequent this outpost of tranquility. The owners hail from Le Marche, the region northeast of Rome that encompasses inland mountains and the Adriatic coastline, and these ladies dote on their customers as you'd wish a sophisticated Italian mamma would. **Known for:** excellent wine list; authentic Le Marche cuisine; grilled meat and fish. Ⓢ *Average main: €30* ✉ *Via Panama 2, Villa Borghese* ☎ *06/8419696* ⊕ *www.ristorantealceppo. it* ♥ *Closed 3 wks in Aug.*

★ La Pergola

$$$$ | MODERN ITALIAN | Dinner here is a truly spectacular and romantic event, with incomparable views across the city matched by a stellar dining experience that includes top-notch service as well as sublimely inventive fare. The difficulty comes in choosing from among Michelin-starred chef Heinz Beck's alta cucina (high cuisine) specialties. **Known for:** weekend reservations that book up three months in advance; award-winning wine list; fagotelli La Pergola stuffed with pecorino, eggs, and cream with guanciale and zucchini. Ⓢ *Average main: €69* ✉ *Rome Cavalieri, A Waldorf Astoria Resort, Via Alberto Cadlolo 101, Monte Mario* ☎ *06/35092152* ⊕ *www.romecavalieri.com/lapergola.php* ♥ *Closed Sun. and Mon., 3 wks in Aug., and Jan. No lunch* ⍟ *Jacket for gentlemen.*

Coffee and Quick Bites

Canova

$$ | **ITALIAN** | Esteemed director Federico Fellini, who lived around the corner on Via Margutta, used to come here all the time and even had an office in the back. His drawings and black-and-white stills from his films remain on display in the hallway that leads to the interior dining room, but the best place to sit for people-watching with a coffee, light lunch, or aperitivo is on the terrace out front. **Known for:** Fellini's old hangout; sandwiches and other light fare; great people-watching on Piazza del Popolo. [$] *Average main: €15* ✉ *Piazza del Popolo 16, Piazza del Popolo* ☎ *06/3612231* 🌐 *www.canovapiazzadel-popolo.it* [M] *Flaminio.*

Hotels

The First Roma Arte

$$$$ | **HOTEL** | Set in a 19th-century neo-classical palace, this cozy boutique hotel was remodeled to feature high-tech, elegant guest rooms while keeping the core structure, including unique windows and tall ceilings, intact. **Pros:** fitness room with Technogym equipment; more than 200 works of art on display from Galleria Mucciaccia; incredible staff that is eager to please. **Cons:** not a lot of in-room storage for luggage; many rates don't include breakfast; some rooms can be a bit dark. [$] *Rooms from: €450* ✉ *Via del Vantaggio 14, Piazza del Popolo* ☎ *06/45617070* 🌐 *www.thefirsthotel.com/arte* 🛏 *29 rooms* 🍴 *No Meals* [M] *Flaminio.*

★ **Hotel de Russie**

$$$$ | **HOTEL** | Occupying a 19th-century hotel that once hosted royalty, Picasso, and Cocteau, the Hotel de Russie is now the first choice in Rome for government bigwigs and Hollywood high rollers seeking ultimate luxury in a secluded retreat. **Pros:** big potential for celebrity sightings; excellent Stravinskij cocktail bar also has tables in the garden; well-equipped gym and world-class spa with hydropool Jacuzzi, steam room, and sauna. **Cons:** expensive; breakfast not included; faster Internet comes at a fee. [$] *Rooms from: €710* ✉ *Via del Babuino 9, Piazza del Popolo* ☎ *06/328881* 🌐 *www.roccofortehotels.com/hotels-and-resorts/hotel-de-russie* 🛏 *120 rooms* 🍴 *No Meals* [M] *Flaminio.*

The Hoxton, Rome

$$ | **HOTEL** | British brand The Hoxton's first foray into Italy is a design lover's dream filled with 1970s-inspired bespoke furniture, art tomes, and plants that transform the large lobby into intimate seating nooks perfect for socializing and coworking. **Pros:** stylish design; great food and drinks; friendly staff. **Cons:** no gym or spa; rooms have little storage space for clothes; location far from tourist sites, with no Metro nearby. [$] *Rooms from: €189* ✉ *Largo Benedetto Marcello 220, Parioli* ☎ *06/94502700* 🌐 *www.thehoxton.com/rome* 🛏 *192 rooms* 🍴 *No Meals.*

Rome Cavalieri, A Waldorf Astoria Hotel

$$$ | **RESORT** | A hilltop oasis in a quiet residential neighborhood a short ride from the centro storico, the Rome Cavalieri comes with magnificent views, three outdoor pools, one indoor pool, and a palatial spa perched atop the Monte Mario amid 15 acres of lush Mediterranean parkland. **Pros:** famed art collection, including a Tiepolo triptych from 1725; impressive on-site restaurant; complimentary shuttle to city center. **Cons:** not all rooms have great views; outside the city center; you definitely pay for the luxury of staying here—everything is expensive. [$] *Rooms from: €300* ✉ *Via Alberto Cadlolo 101, Monte Mario* ☎ *06/35091* 🌐 *www.rome-cavalieri.com* 🛏 *370 rooms* 🍴 *No Meals.*

Nightlife

★ **Stravinskij Bar at the Hotel de Russie**

COCKTAIL LOUNGES | The Stravinskij Bar, in the Hotel de Russie's gorgeous garden, is the best place to catch a glimpse of la dolce vita. Celebrities, blue bloods, and VIPs hang out in the private courtyard garden where mixed drinks and cocktails are well above par. There are also healthy smoothies and bites if you need to refuel. ✉ *Hotel de Russie, Via del Babuino 9, Piazza del Popolo* ☎ *06/328881* ⊕ *www. roccofortehotels.com* Ⓜ *Flaminio.*

 Performing Arts

★ Auditorium Parco della Musica

CONCERTS | Architect Renzo Piano conceived and constructed the Auditorium Parco della Musica, a futuristic complex made up of three enormous, pod-shaped concert halls, which have hosted some of the world's greatest music acts. The Sala Santa Cecilia is a massive hall for grand orchestra and choral concerts; the Sala Sinopoli is more intimately scaled for smaller troupes; and the Sala Petrassi was designed for alternative events. All three are arrayed around the Cavea (amphitheater), a vast outdoor Greco-Roman-style theater. The Auditorium also hosts seasonal festivals, including the Rome Film Fest. ✉ *Viale Pietro de Coubertin 30, Flaminio* ☎ *06/80241281* ⊕ *www.auditorium.com* Ⓜ *Flaminio, then Tram No. 2 to Apollodoro.*

Teatro Olimpico

THEATER | Part of Rome's theater circuit, the 1930s-era Teatro Olimpico is one of the main venues for cabaret, contemporary dance companies, visiting international ballet companies, and touring Broadway shows. ✉ *Piazza Gentile da Fabriano 17, Flaminio* ☎ *06/32659916* ⊕ *www.teatroolimpico.it* Ⓜ *Flaminio, then Tram 2 to Mancini.*

Shopping

★ Il Marmoraro

ANTIQUES & COLLECTIBLES | This tiny shop is a holdout of Via Margutta's days as a street full of artists and artisans. Sandro Fiorentino's father opened the shop in 1969 (he carved plaques like the one that marks Federico Fellini's house up the street) and Sandro still engraves the

marble by hand. The shop is packed full of plaques, many with clever phrases, which make a great souvenir. Sandro will also engrave a message of your choice upon request. ✉ *Via Margutta 53B, Piazza del Popolo* ☎ *06/3207660* Ⓜ *Spagna.*

Trastevere

Across the Tiber from the Jewish Ghetto is Trastevere (literally "across the Tiber"), long cherished as Rome's Greenwich Village and now subject to rampant gentrification. In spite of this, Trastevere remains about the most tightly knit community in the city, the Trasteverini proudly proclaiming their descent from the ancient Romans. Ancient bridges—the Ponte Fabricio and the Ponte Cestio—link Trastevere and the Ghetto to Isola Tiberina (Tiber Island), a diminutive sandbar and one of Rome's most picturesque sights.

GETTING HERE AND AROUND

From the Vatican or Spanish Steps, expect a 30- to 40-minute walk to reach Trastevere. From Termini station, take Bus No. 40 Express or No. 64 to Largo di Torre Argentina, where you can switch to Tram No. 8 to get to Trastevere. If you don't feel like climbing the steep Gianicolo, take Bus No. 115 from Largo dei Fiorentini, then enjoy the walk down to the northern reaches of Trastevere or explore the leafy residential area of Monteverde Vecchio on the other side of the hill.

Sights

Isola Tiberina (*Tiber Island*)

ISLAND | It's easy to overlook this tiny island in the Tiber, but you shouldn't. In terms of history and sheer loveliness, charming Isola Tiberina—shaped like a boat about to set sail—gets high marks. Cross onto the island via Ponte Fabricio, Rome's oldest remaining bridge, constructed in 62 BC; on the north side of the island crumbles the romantic ruin of the Ponte Rotto (Broken Bridge), which dates back to 179

BC. Descend the steps to the lovely river embankment to see a Roman relief of the intertwined-snakes symbol of Aesculapius, the great god of healing. In imperial times, Romans sheathed the entire island with marble to make it look like Aesculapius's ship, replete with a towering obelisk as a mast. Amazingly, a fragment of the ancient sculpted ship's prow still exists. You can marvel at it on the downstream end of the embankment. Today, medicine still reigns here. The island is home to the hospital of Fatebenefratelli (literally, "Do good, brothers"). Nearby is San Bartolomeo, built at the end of the 10th century by the Holy Roman Emperor Otto III and restored in the 18th century. ⊠ *Trastevere* ✛ *Isola Tiberina can be accessed by Ponte Fabricio or Ponte Cestio.*

Palazzo Corsini

ART MUSEUM | A brooding example of Baroque style, the palace (once home to Queen Christina of Sweden) is across the road from the Villa Farnesina and houses part of the 16th- and 17th-century sections of the collection of the Galleria Nazionale d'Arte Antica. Among the star paintings in this manageably sized collection are Rubens's *St. Sebastian Healed by Angels* and Caravaggio's *St. John the Baptist.* Stop in if only to climb the 17th-century stone staircase, itself a drama of architectural shadows and sculptural voids. Behind, but separate from, the palazzo is the University of Rome's Orto Botanico, home to 3,500 species of plants, with various greenhouses around a stairway/fountain with 11 jets. ⊠ *Via della Lungara 10, Trastevere* ☎ *06/68802323 Galleria Corsini, 06/32810 Galleria Corsini tickets, 06/49917107 Orto Botanico* ⊕ *www.barberinicorsini.org* ⊠ *€12 Galleria Corsini, including entrance to Palazzo Barberini; €13 Orto Botanico* ☉ *Closed Mon.*

★ Santa Cecilia in Trastevere

CHURCH | This basilica commemorates the aristocratic St. Cecilia, patron saint of musicians. One of ancient Rome's most celebrated early Christian martyrs, she was most likely put to a supernaturally long death by the Emperor Diocletian just before the year AD 300. After an abortive attempt to suffocate her in the baths of her own house (a favorite means of quietly disposing of aristocrats in Roman days), she was brought before the executioner. But not even three blows of the executioner's sword could dispatch the young girl. She lingered for several days, converting others to the Christian cause, before finally dying. In 1595, her body was exhumed—it was said to look as fresh as if she still breathed—and the heart-wrenching sculpture by eyewitness Stefano Maderno that lies below the main altar was, the sculptor insisted, exactly how she looked. Time your visit in the morning to enter the cloistered convent to see what remains of Pietro Cavallini's *Last Judgment,* dating to 1293. It's the only major fresco in existence known to have been painted by Cavallini, a contemporary of Giotto. To visit the frescoes, ring the bell of the convent to the left of the church entrance between 10 am and 12 pm. ⊠ *Piazza di Santa Cecilia 22, Trastevere* ☎ *06/5899289* ⊕ *www.benedettinesantacecilia.it/htm/Basilica.html* ⊠ *Frescoes €2.50, underground €2.50* ☉ *Access to frescoes closed in the afternoon.*

★ Santa Maria in Trastevere

CHURCH | Originally built during the 4th century and rebuilt in the 12th century, this is one of Rome's oldest and grandest churches. It is also the earliest foundation of any Roman church to be dedicated to the Virgin Mary. With a nave framed by a processional of two rows of gigantic columns (22 in total) taken from the ancient Baths of Caracalla, and an apse studded with gilded mosaics, the interior conjures the splendor of ancient Rome better than any other in the city. Overhead is Domenichino's gilded ceiling (1617). The 18th-century portico draws attention to the facade's 800-year-old mosaics, which represent the parable

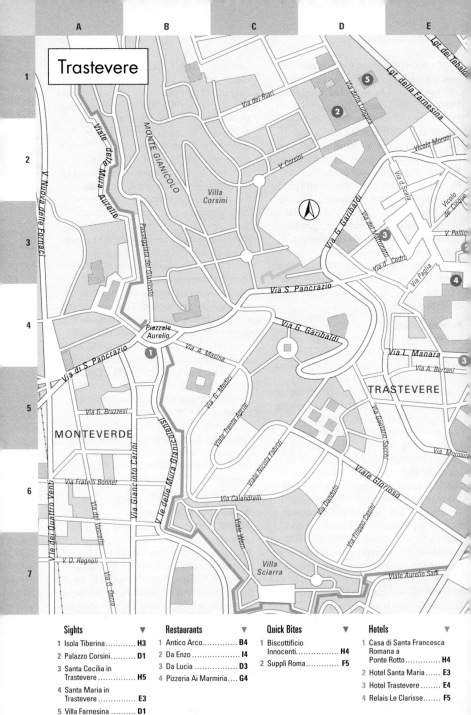

Trastevere

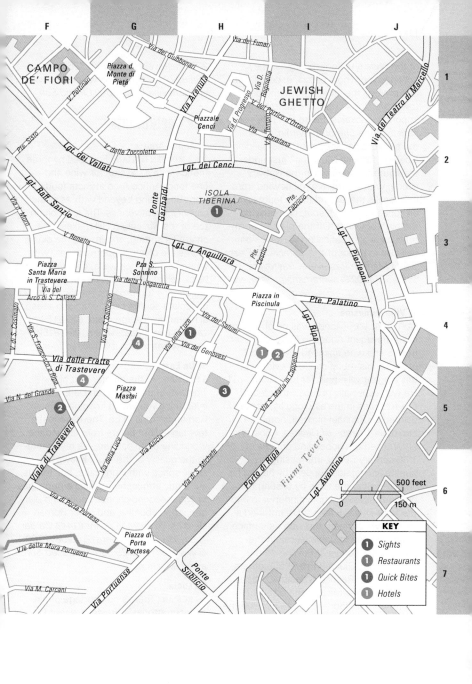

of the Wise and Foolish Virgins. They enhance the whole piazza, especially at night, when the church front and bell tower are illuminated. The church's most important mosaics, Pietro Cavallini's six panels of the *Life of the Virgin,* cover the semicircular apse. Note the building labeled "Taberna Meritoria" just under the figure of the Virgin in the Nativity scene, with a stream of oil flowing from it; it recalls the legend that a fountain of oil appeared on this spot, prophesying the birth of Christ. Off the piazza's northern side is a street called Via delle Fonte dell'Olio in honor of this miracle. ✉ *Piazza Santa Maria in Trastevere, Trastevere* ☎ *06/5814802* 🌐 *santamariaintrastevere.it.*

★ Villa Farnesina

CASTLE/PALACE | Money was no object to the extravagant Agostino Chigi, a banker from Siena who financed many papal projects. His munificence is evident in this elegant villa, built for him about 1511. He was especially proud of the decorative frescoes in the airy loggias, some painted by Raphael himself, notably a luminous *Triumph of Galatea.* Agostino entertained the popes and princes of 16th-century Rome, impressing his guests at riverside suppers by having his servants clear the table by casting the precious silver and gold dinnerware into the Tiber (indeed, nets were unfurled a foot or two beneath the water's surface to retrieve the valuable ware). In the magnificent Loggia of Psyche on the ground floor, Giulio Romano and others worked from Raphael's designs. Raphael's lovely *Galatea* is in the adjacent room. On the floor above you can see the trompe-l'oeil effects in the aptly named Hall of Perspectives by Peruzzi. Agostino Chigi's bedroom, next door, was frescoed by Il Sodoma with the *Wedding of Alexander and Roxanne,* which is considered to be the artist's best work. The palace also houses the Gabinetto Nazionale delle Stampe, a treasure trove of old prints and drawings. ✉ *Via della Lungara 230, Trastevere* ☎ *06/68027268 info, 06/68027397 tour reservations* 🌐 *www.villafarnesina.it* 🎫 *€10* 🕒 *Closed Sun.*

🍴 Restaurants

★ Antico Arco

$$$ | MODERN ITALIAN | Founded by three friends with a passion for wine and fine food, Antico Arco attracts foodies from Rome and beyond with its refined culinary inventiveness. The location on top of the Janiculum Hill makes for a charming setting, and inside, the dining rooms are plush, modern spaces, with whitewashed brick walls, dark floors, and black velvet chairs. **Known for:** private dining options for romantic meals; molten chocolate soufflé cake; changing seasonal menu. [$] *Average main: €29* ✉ *Piazzale Aurelio 7, Trastevere* ☎ *06/5815274* 🌐 *www.anticoarco.it* 🕒 *Closed Tues.*

★ Da Enzo

$ | ROMAN | In the quieter part of Trastevere, the family-run Da Enzo is everything you would imagine a classic Roman trattoria to be. There are just a few tables, but diners from around the world line up to eat here—a testament to the quality of the food. **Known for:** small space with long waits; boisterous, authentic atmosphere; cacio e pepe (pasta with pecorino-cheese sauce and black pepper), carbonara, and other Roman classics. [$] *Average main: €14* ✉ *Via dei Vascellari 29, Trastevere* ☎ *06/5812260* 🌐 *www.daenzoal29.com* 🕒 *Closed Sun. and 2 wks in Aug.*

Da Lucia

$ | ROMAN | There's no shortage of old-school trattorias in Trastevere, but Da Lucia has a strong following among them. Both locals and expats enjoy the brusque but "authentic" service and the hearty Roman fare; snag a table outside in warm weather for the true Roman experience of cobblestone-terrace dining. **Known for:** beef rolls (involtini); spaghetti cacio e pepe; bombolotti (a tubular pasta) all'amatriciana. $ Average main: €14 ✉ Vicolo del Mattonato 2, Trastevere ☎ 06/5803601 ⊘ Closed Mon. and Aug.

Pizzeria Ai Marmiria

$ | PIZZA | FAMILY | This place is about as lively as it gets—it's packed pretty much every night with diners munching on crisp pizzas that come out of the wood-burning ovens at top speed. It's best not to go during peak dining hours, so go early or late if you don't want to wait. **Known for:** open until midnight for a late-night bite; fried starters such as supplì (breaded fried rice balls); excellent wood-oven pizzas. $ Average main: €12 ✉ Viale Trastevere 53, Trastevere ☎ 06/5800919 ⊘ Closed Wed. and 3 wks in Aug. No dinner Sun.

Coffee and Quick Bites

Biscottificio Innocenti

$ | ITALIAN | FAMILY | The scent of cookies wafts out into the street as you approach this family-run bakery, where a small team of bakers makes sweet treats the old-school way in an oven bought in the 1960s. There are dozens of varieties of baked goods, mostly sweet but some savory. **Known for:** brutti ma buoni ("ugly but good") cookies; dozens of varieties of baked goods; old-school family-run bakery. $ Average main: €3 ✉ Via della Luce 21, Trastevere ☎ 06/5803926 ⊘ Closed 2 wks in Aug.

Supplì Roma

$ | ROMAN | Trastevere's best supplì have been served at this hole-in-the-wall take-out spot since 1979. At lunchtime, the line spills out onto the street with locals who've come for the namesake treats, as well as fried baccalà fillets and stuffed zucchini flowers. **Known for:** classic fried risotto ball with ragù or cacio e pepe; gnocchi on Thursday (the traditional day for it in Rome); old-fashioned baked pizza with zucchini and stracciatella cheese. $ Average main: €5 ✉ Via di San Francesco a Ripa 137, Trastevere ☎ 06/5897110

⊕ www.suppliroma.it ⊘ Closed Sun. and 2 wks in Aug.

Hotels

Casa di Santa Francesca Romana a Ponte Rotto

$ | HOTEL | In the heart of Trastevere but tucked away from the hustle and bustle of the medieval quarter, this cheap, clean, comfortable hotel in a former monastery is centered on a lovely green courtyard. **Pros:** rates can't be beat; away from rowdy tourist side of Trastevere; excellent restaurants nearby. **Cons:** spotty Wi-Fi; few amenities besides TV room and reading room; a bit far from Metro, but there are tram and bus stops nearby. $ Rooms from: €98 ✉ Via dei Vascellari 61, Trastevere ☎ 06/5812125 ⊕ www.sfromana.it ⇆ 37 rooms ◉ Free Breakfast.

Hotel Santa Maria

$ | HOTEL | A Trastevere treasure with a pedigree going back four centuries, this ivy-covered, mansard-roof, rosy-brick-red, erstwhile Renaissance-era convent—just steps away from the glorious Santa Maria in Trastevere church and a few blocks from the Tiber—has sweet and simple guest rooms: a mix of brick walls, "cotto" tile floors, oak furniture, and matching bedspreads and curtains. **Pros:** a quaint and pretty oasis in a central location; lovely rooftop terrace; free bicycles to use during your stay. **Cons:** some rooms can be noisy; not the best value for money; tricky to find. $ Rooms from: €120 ✉ Vicolo del Piede 2, Trastevere ☎ 06/5894626 ⊕ www.hotelsantamariatrastevere.it ⇆ 20 rooms ◉ Free Breakfast.

Hotel Trastevere

$$ | HOTEL | This hotel captures the villagelike charm of the Trastevere district and offers basic, clean, comfortable rooms. **Pros:** good rates for location; friendly staff; convenient to tram and bus. **Cons:** standard rooms are quite

small; few amenities; rooms are a little worn on the edges. $ *Rooms from: €130* ✉ *Via Luciano Manara 24/a, Trastevere* ☎ *06/5814713* ⊕ *www.hoteltrastevere. net* ⤶ *14 rooms* ⦿ *Free Breakfast.*

Relais Le Clarisse
$$ | **B&B/INN** | Set within the former cloister grounds of the Santa Chiara order, with beautiful gardens, Le Clarisse makes you feel like a personal guest at a friend's villa, thanks to the comfortable size of the guest rooms and personalized service. **Pros:** spacious rooms with comfy beds; complimentary high-speed Wi-Fi; high-tech showers/tubs with good water pressure. **Cons:** no restaurant or bar; check when booking as you may be put in neighboring building; this part of Trastevere can be noisy at night. $ *Rooms from: €140* ✉ *Via Cardinale Merry del Val 20, Trastevere* ☎ *06/58334437* ⊕ *www. leclarissetrastevere.com* ⤶ *17 rooms* ⦿ *Free Breakfast.*

 Nightlife

★ Freni e Frizioni
CAFÉS | This hipster hangout has a cute artist vibe, and is great for an afternoon coffee, tea, or aperitivo, or for late-night socializing. Though the vibe is laid-back, the bartenders take their cocktails seriously—and have the awards to prove it. In warmer weather, the crowd overflows into the large terrazzo overlooking the Tiber and the side streets of Trastevere. ✉ *Via del Politeama 4, Trastevere* ☎ *06/45497499* ⊕ *www.freniefrizioni. com.*

 Shopping

BOOKSTORES
Almost Corner Bookshop
BOOKS | Bursting at the seams with not an inch of space left on its shelves, this tiny little bookshop is a favorite meeting point for English speakers in Trastevere. Irish owner Dermot O'Connell goes out of his way to find what you're looking for, and if he doesn't have it in stock he'll make a special order for you. The shop carries everything from popular best sellers to translated Italian classics, as well as lots of good books about Rome. ✉ *Via del Moro 45, Trastevere* ☎ *06/5836942.*

FLEA MARKETS
Porta Portese
MARKET | One of the biggest flea markets in Italy, Porta Portese welcomes visitors in droves every Sunday from 7 am to 2 pm. Treasure seekers and bargain hunters love scrounging around tents for new and used clothing, antique furniture, used books, accessories, and other odds 'n' ends. Bring your haggling skills, and cash (preferably small bills—it'll work in your favor when driving a bargain); many stallholders don't accept credit cards, and the nearest ATM is a hike. ✉ *Via Portuense and adjacent streets between Porta Portese and Via Ettore Rolli, Trastevere.*

SPECIALTY STORES
Polvere di Tempo
OTHER SPECIALTY STORE | Collectors with a passion for rare and decorative timepieces should consider taking a stroll over to Polvere di Tempo. The owner and craftsman, Adrian Rodriguez, has a deep adoration for decorative sundials, watches, and even hourglasses—all entirely made by hand. Stop in at his store, and he'll tell you a story about how monks used candles to tell time and other interesting anecdotes related to timepieces. ✉ *Via del Moro 59, Trastevere* ☎ *06/5880704* ⊕ *www.polvereditempo.com.*

Aventino and Testaccio

The **Aventino** district is somewhat rarefied, where some houses still have their own bell towers and private gardens are called "parks," without exaggeration. Like the emperors of old on the Palatine, the fortunate residents here look out over the Circus Maximus and the river, winding its way far below. **Testaccio** is perhaps the world's only district built on broken pots: the hill of the same name was born from discarded pottery used to store oil, wine, and other goods loaded from nearby Ripa, when Rome had a port and the Tiber was once a mighty river to an empire. It's quiet during the day, but on Saturday buzzes with the loud music from rows of discos and clubs.

Sights

★ Centrale Montemartini

ART MUSEUM | A decommissioned power plant (Rome's first electricity plant) was reopened as a permanent exhibition space in 2005 and today houses the overflow of ancient art from the Musei Capitolini collection. After strolling Rome's medieval lanes, the Centrale Montemartini's early-20th-century style can feel positively modern. A 15-minute walk from the heart of Testaccio in one direction will lead you past walls covered in street art to the urban district of Ostiense. Head southwest and saunter under the train tracks to admire buildings bedecked with four-story-high murals until you reach the Centrale Montemartini. With Roman sculptures and mosaics set against industrial machinery and pipes, nowhere else in Rome is the contrast between old and new more apparent or enjoyable. A pleasure, too, is the fact that you're likely to be one of the few visitors here, making it the perfect stop for those feeling claustrophobic from Rome's crowds. Unusually, the collection is organized by the area in which the ancient pieces were found. Highlights include the former boiler room filled with ancient marble statues that once decorated Rome's private villas, such as the beautiful *Esquiline Venus*, as well as a large mosaic of a hunting scene. ⊠ *Via Ostiense 106, Testaccio* ☎ *06/0608* ⊕ *www.centralemontemartini.org* ⤳ *€10* ☉ *Closed Mon.* Ⓜ *Garbatella.*

★ Piazza dei Cavalieri di Malta

GARDEN | Peek through the keyhole of the Priorato di Malta, the walled compound of the Knights of Malta, and you'll get a surprising eyeful: a picture-perfect view of the dome of St. Peter's Basilica, far across the city. The top of the church is flawlessly framed by trimmed hedges that lie beyond a nondescript, locked green door. The square and the priory within the walls are the work of Giovanni Battista Piranesi, an 18th-century engraver who is more famous for etching Roman views than for orchestrating them, but he fancied himself a bit of an architect and did not disappoint. As for the Order of the Knights of Malta, it is the world's oldest and most exclusive order of chivalry, founded in the Holy Land during the Crusades. Though nominally ministering to the sick in those early days—a role that has since become the order's raison d'être—the knights amassed huge tracts of land in the Middle East. From 1530 they were based on the Mediterranean island of Malta, but in 1798 Napoléon expelled them, and, in 1834, they established themselves in Rome. Tours with a private guide are usually available on Friday mornings if you would like to go inside; email for more information (tours must be prebooked by email). ⊠ *Via Santa Sabina and Via Porta Lavernale, Aventino* ⤳ *From €5 per person (min. of 10 people), plus the cost of the required guide, €80 in Italian, €100 in any other language. If a group has already formed, then anyone may join for the regular entry fee* ⚇ *Reservations required* Ⓜ *Circo Massimo; Tram No. 3.*

★ Santa Maria in Cosmedin

CHURCH | **FAMILY** | Although this is one of Rome's oldest churches, with a haunting interior, it plays second fiddle to the renowned artifact installed out in the portico. The Bocca della Verità (Mouth of Truth) is in reality nothing more than an ancient drain cover, unearthed during the Middle Ages. Legend has it, however, that the teeth will clamp down on a

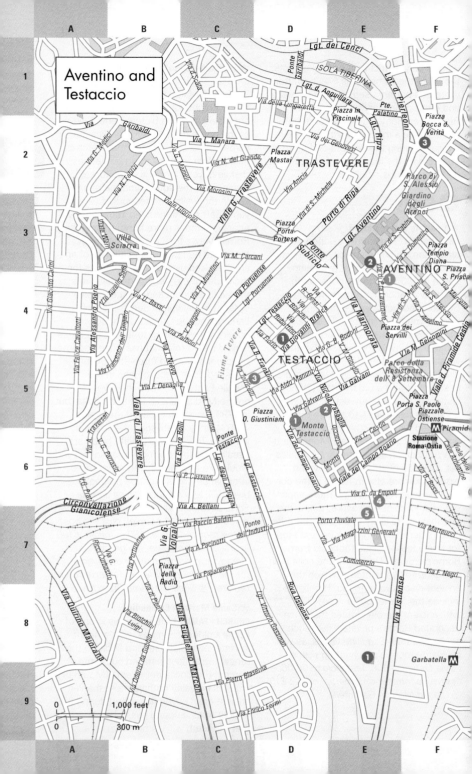

Aventino and Testaccio

ISOLA TIBERINA

Lgt. dei Cenci

Ponte Garibaldi

Lgt. d. Anguillara

Via della Lungaretta

Piazza in Piscinula

Pte. Palatino

Lgt. d. Pierleoni

Piazza Bocca d. Verità ❸

Via L. Manara

Via N. del Grande

Piazza Mastai

Via dei Genovesi

Lgt. Ripa

TRASTEVERE

Via Morosini

Via Amalia

Via di S. Michele

Parco di S. Alessio

Giardino degli Aranci

Viale Glorioso

Villa Sciarra

Via M. Carcani

Piazza Porta Portese

Ponte Sublicio

Lgt. Aventino

Via di S. Sabina

Via S. Domenico

Piazza Tempio Diana

Piazza S. Prisca

Via Aurelio Saffi

Via U. Bassi

Via Portuense

Lgt. Portuense

Lgt. Testaccio

❷ **AVENTINO** ❶

Via di S. Melania

Via S. Anselmo

Via Marcella

Via Parboni

Via P. Cossa

Via B. Bodoni

Via G.-B. Bodoni

Via Marmorata

Piazza dei Servilli

Via M. Gelsomini

Fiume Tevere

Via B. Franklin

Via Florio

Via Giovanni Branca

TESTACCIO

Via Aldo Manuzio

Via N. Zabaglia

Via Galvani

Parco della Resistenza dell'8 Settembre

Viale G. Baccelli

Viale di Trastevere

Via Niemec

Via F. Denaglia

❸

Via Galvani

❶ ❷

Piazza Porta S. Paolo

Piazzale Ostiense

Lgt. degli Artigiani

Ponte Testaccio

Piazza O. Giustiniani

❶ Monte Testaccio

Via di Monte Testaccio

Viale del Campo Boario

Via C. Cestia

Viale J. Piramide Cestia

Ⓜ Piramid

Stazione Roma-Ostia

Via P. Castaldi

Monte

Viale del Campo Boario

Via B. Bossi

Circonvallazione Gianicolense

Via A. Bellani

Via G. da Empoli

❹

Via G. Volpato

Via Baccio Baldini

Ponte dell'Industria

Porto Fluviale

❺

Via Magazzini Generali

Via Matteucci

Via A. Pacinotti

Commercio

Via Ostiense

Via F. Negri

Piazza della Radio

Via Papareschi

Lgt. Vittorio Gassman

Riva Ostiense

Via Durino Majorana

Via di Pietra

Via Biolchini Lungo

Viale Guglielmo Marconi

❶

Garbatella Ⓜ

Via Pietro Blaserna

Via Enrico Fermi

0 — 1,000 feet

0 — 300 m

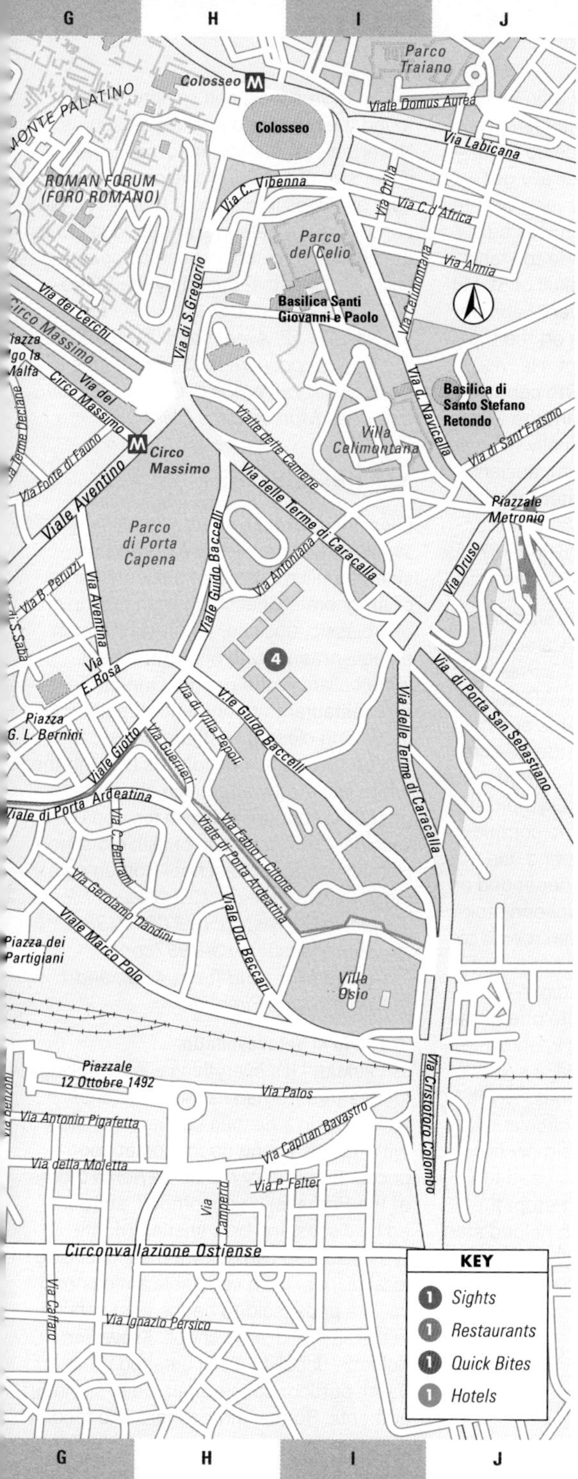

Sights ▼

1 Centrale Montemartini..............**E8**
2 Piazza dei Cavalieri di Malta **E3**
3 Santa Maria in Cosmedin..........**F2**
4 Terme di Caracalla.................**H4**

Restaurants ▼

1 Checchino dal 1887................**D5**
2 Flavio al Velavevodetto **D5**
3 La Torricella **C5**
4 Marigold **E6**
5 Porto Fluviale.......................**E7**

Quick Bites ▼

1 Trapizzino **D4**

Hotels ▼

1 Hotel San Anselmo **E4**

Rome AVENTINO AND TESTACCIO

3

KEY

1 *Sights*
1 *Restaurants*
1 *Quick Bites*
1 *Hotels*

liar's hand if they dare to tell a fib while holding their fingers up to the fearsome mouth. Hordes of tourists line up to take the test every day (kids especially get a kick out of it), but there is never a wait to enter the church itself, which was built in the 6th century. Head inside to stand before the flower-crowned skull of St. Valentine, who is celebrated every February 14th, but go ahead and pass on the trip down to the tiny, empty crypt. Heavily restored at the end of the 19th century, the church stands across from the Piazza della Bocca della Verità, originally the location of the Forum Boarium, ancient Rome's cattle market, and later the site of public executions. ✉ *Piazza della Bocca della Verità 18, Aventino* ☎ *06/6787759* 🌐 *www.cosmedin.org* [M] *Circo Massimo.*

Terme di Caracalla (*Baths of Caracalla*)
RUINS | **FAMILY** | The Terme di Caracalla are some of Rome's most massive—yet least visited—ruins. Begun in AD 206 by the emperor Septimius Severus and completed by his son, Caracalla, the 28-acre complex could accommodate 1,600 bathers at a time. Along with an Olympic-size swimming pool and baths, the complex also had two gyms, a library, and gardens. The impressive baths depended on slave labor, particularly the unseen stokers who toiled in subterranean rooms to keep the fires roaring in order to heat the water. Rather than a simple dip in a tub, Romans turned "bathing" into one of the most lavish leisure activities imaginable. A bath began in the sudatoria, a series of small rooms resembling saunas, which then led to the caldarium, a circular room that was humid rather than simply hot. Here a strigil, or scraper, was used to get the dirt off the skin. Next stop: the warm(-ish) tepidarium, which helped start the cool-down process. Finally, it ended with a splash around the frigidarium, a chilly swimming pool.

Today, the complex is a shell of its former self. Some black-and-white mosaic fragments remain, but most of the opulent mosaics, frescoes, and sculptures have found their way into Rome's museums. Nevertheless, the towering walls and sheer size of the ruins give one of the best glimpses into ancient Rome's ambitions. If you're here in summer, don't miss the chance to catch an open-air opera or ballet in the baths, put on by the Teatro dell'Opera di Roma. ✉ *Viale delle Terme di Caracalla 52, Aventino* ☎ *06/39967702* 🌐 *www.coopculture.it* 🎟 *€8 (includes Villa dei Quintili and Tomba di Cecilia Metella)* 🕓 *Closed Mon.* [M] *Circo Massimo.*

🍴 Restaurants

Checchino dal 1887
$$ | **ROMAN** | Literally carved into the side of a hill made up of ancient shards of amphorae, Checchino is an example of a classic, upscale, family-run Roman establishment, with one of the best wine cellars in the region. One of the first restaurants to open near Testaccio's (now long closed) slaughterhouse, they still serve classic offal dishes (though the white-jacketed waiters can also suggest other options). **Known for:** coda alla vaccinara (Roman-style oxtail); old-school Roman waiters; old-school Roman cooking. [$] *Average main: €23* ✉ *Via di Monte Testaccio 30, Testaccio* ☎ *06/5743816* 🌐 *www.checchino-dal-1887.com* 🕓 *Closed Mon. and Tues., Aug., and 1 wk at Christmas* [M] *Piramide.*

★ **Flavio al Velavevodetto**
$$ | **ROMAN** | It's everything you're looking for in a true Roman eating experience: authentic, in a historic setting, and filled with Italians eating good food at good prices. In this very *romani di Roma* (Rome of the Romans) neighborhood, surrounded by discos and bars sharing Monte Testaccio, you can enjoy a meal of classic local dishes, from vegetable antipasto to cacio e pepe (said to be the best version in the city) and lamb chops. **Known for:** polpette di bollito (fried breaded meatballs); outdoor covered terrace in summer; authentic Roman atmosphere and food.

$ Average main: €16 ⊠ Via di Monte Testaccio 97, Testaccio ☎ 06/5744194 ⊕ www.ristorantevelavevodetto.it Ⓜ Piramide.

La Torricella
$$ | SEAFOOD | FAMILY | This family-run institution has been serving seafood in the working-class Testaccio neighborhood for more than 40 years, and if you visit the local market early enough you may spot the owner on his daily rounds to select the freshest fish, which mainly arrives from Gaeta, south of Rome. The seafood menu changes every day, but look for house specialties like *paccheri* (a very large, tubular pasta) with *totani* (baby calamari), pasta with *telline* (small clams), and the wondrously simple spaghetti with lobster. **Known for:** relaxed but refined setting with outdoor seating; polpette di pesce al sugo (fish balls in tomato sauce); fresh, local seafood. $ *Average main: €18* ⊠ *Via Evangelista Torricelli 2/12, Testaccio* ☎ *06/5746311* ⊕ *www.la-torricella.com* Ⓜ *Piramide.*

Marigold
$ | SCANDINAVIAN | Run by a husband-and-wife team (she's Danish, he's Italian), this hip restaurant blends the best of both their cultures with a Scandinavian-meets-Italian design and menu. It draws a young, international crowd who come for the sourdough, cinnamon buns, and veggie-forward dishes. **Known for:** minimalist design; weekend brunch; Danish breads and baked goods. $ *Average main: €13* ⊠ *Via Giovanni da Empoli 37, Testaccio* ☎ *06/87725679* ⊕ *www.marigoldroma.com* ⊗ *Closed Mon., Tues., and 3 wks in Aug. No dinner* Ⓜ *Ostiense.*

Porto Fluviale
$ | ITALIAN | This massive structure takes up the better part of a block on a street that's gone from gritty clubland to popular nightspot, thanks largely to Porto Fluviale. The place pulls double duty as a bar, café, pizzeria, lunch buffet, and lively evening restaurant. **Known for:** cicheti (Venetian-style tapas); pizza from wood-burning oven; good cocktails.

$ Average main: €13 ⊠ Via del Porto Fluviale 22, Testaccio ☎ 06/5743199 ⊕ www.portofluviale.com Ⓜ Piramide.

Coffee and Quick Bites

Trapizzino
$ | ROMAN | FAMILY | Stefano Callegari is one of Rome's most famous pizza makers, but at Trapizzino he's doing something a bit different. The name of the restaurant is derived from the Italian words for sandwich (*tramezzino*) and pizza, and the result is something like an upscale pizza pocket, stuffed on the spot with local specialties like chicken alla cacciatore, or *trippa* (tripe), or roast pumpkin, pecorino, and almonds. **Known for:** Italian craft beer; eggplant parmigiana and meatball sandwiches; casual setting, with seating available next door. $ *Average main: €4* ⊠ *Via Giovanni Branca 88, Testaccio* ☎ *06/43419624* ⊕ *www.trapizzino.it* ⊗ *Closed 1 wk in Aug.* Ⓜ *Piramide.*

Hotels

Hotel San Anselmo
$ | HOTEL | This refurbished 19th-century villa is a romantic retreat from the city, set in a *molto* charming garden atop the Aventine Hill. **Pros:** free Wi-Fi; garden where you can enjoy breakfast; historic building with artful interior. **Cons:** no full restaurant; limited public transportation; some rooms are quite small. $ *Rooms from: €80* ⊠ *Piazza San Anselmo 2, Aventino* ☎ *06/570057* ⊕ *www.aventinohotels.com* ⊅ *34 rooms* ⏆ *Free Breakfast* Ⓜ *Circo Massimo.*

ⓨ Nightlife

Ketumbar
CAFÉS | FAMILY | One of Rome's few "organic" happy hours, the price of a drink will buy you a spread of healthy and organic vegetarian appetizers. Aperitivo (happy hour) starts daily at 6:30 pm, but the modern minimalist restaurant

also serves a great weekend brunch with a kids' area that includes a free babysitter. ✉ *Via Galvani 24, Testaccio* ☎ *06/57305338* ⊕ *www.ketumbar.it.*

★ Tram Depot

CAFÉS | A coffee stand by day and cocktail bar by night, this outdoor establishment began life as a city tram car back in 1903. Now the historic carriage has been converted to a kiosk permanently stationed on a park corner with retro tables and garden seating. A trendy crowd descends at sunset, and seats are at a premium until the wee hours of the morning. But since it is entirely outside, Tram Depot is mainly open in the warmer months of the year (April through November). ✉ *Via Marmorata 13, Testaccio* Ⓜ *Piramide.*

Shopping

★ Volpetti

FOOD | A Roman institution for more than 40 years, Volpetti sells excellent cured meats and salami from its buzzing deli counter. The rich aromas and flavors are captivating from the moment you enter the store. The food selection also includes genuine buffalo-milk mozzarella, fresh pasta, Roman pecorino, olive oils, balsamic vinegars, and fresh bread. It's also a great place for assembling gift baskets, and they offer worldwide shipping. ✉ *Via Marmorata 47, Testaccio* ☎ *06/5742352* ⊕ *www.volpetti.com* Ⓜ *Piramide.*

Esquilino and Via Appia Antica

Esquilino, covering Rome's most sprawling hill—the Esquiline—lies at the edge of the tourist maps, near the Termini station. Today, culturally diverse inhabitants of different nationalities live and work in the area. It's not the cobblestone-street atmosphere that most think of when they think of Rome. Far south lies catacomb country—the haunts of the fabled underground graves of Rome's earliest Christians, arrayed to either side of the Queen of Roads, the Via Appia Antica (Appian Way). Strewn with classical ruins and dotted with grazing sheep, the road stirs images of chariots and legionnaires returning from imperial conquests. It was completed in 312 BC by Appius Claudius, who laid it out to connect Rome with settlements in the south, in the direction of Naples. Though time and vandals have taken their toll on the ancient relics along the road, the catacombs remain to cast their spirit-warm spell. Today, the dark, gloomy catacombs contrast strongly with the Appia Antica's fresh air, verdant meadows, and evocative classical ruins.

GETTING HERE AND AROUND

The Esquilino Hill can be reached via the Vittorio Emanuele subway station, one stop from Termini station. Bus No. 150F runs from Piazza del Popolo to Esquilino.

The initial stretch of the Via Appia Antica is not pedestrian-friendly—there is fast, heavy traffic and no sidewalk all the way from Porta San Sebastiano to the Catacombe di San Callisto. To reach the catacombs, take Bus No. 218 from San Giovanni in Laterano. Alternatively, take Metro Line A to Colli Albani and then Bus No. 660 to the Tomba di Cecilia Metella.

⊙ Sights

Catacombe di San Callisto

(*Catacombs of St. Calixtus*)
CEMETERY | Burial place of several very early popes, this is Rome's oldest and best-preserved underground cemetery. One of the (English-speaking) friars who acts as custodian of the catacomb will guide you through its crypts and galleries, some adorned with early Christian frescoes. Watch out for wrong turns: this catacomb is five stories deep! ■TIP→ **The large parking area means this is favored by large groups; it can get busy.** ✉ *Via Appia Antica 110, Via Appia Antica*

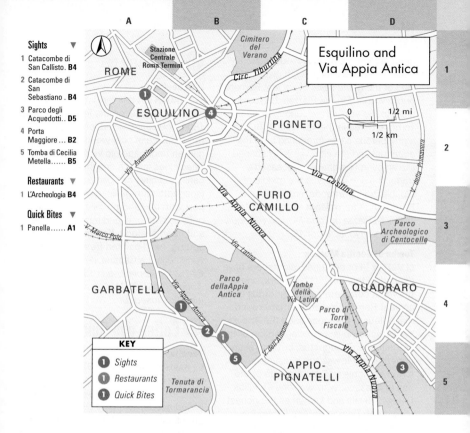

Esquilino and
Via Appia Antica

KEY

① Sights

① Restaurants

① Quick Bites

☎ 06/5130151 ⊕ www.catacombe.roma.it
☜ €8 ☾ Closed Wed. and mid-Jan.–Feb.

★ Catacombe di San Sebastiano

(*Catacombs of St. Sebastian*)
CEMETERY | The 4th-century church was
named after the saint who was buried in
the catacomb, which burrows underground
on four different levels. This was the only
early Christian cemetery to remain accessible during the Middle Ages, and it was
from here that the term "catacomb" is
derived—it's in a spot where the road dips
into a hollow, known to the Romans as
catacumba (Greek for "near the hollow").
⊠ *Via Appia Antica 136, Via Appia Antica*
☎ 06/7850350 ⊕ www.catacombe.org
☜ €8 ☾ Closed Thurs. and Dec.

Parco degli Acquedotti

CITY PARK | **FAMILY** | This massive park was
named for the six remaining aqueducts
that formed part of the famously elaborate
system that carried water to ancient Rome.
It's technically part of the Parco dell'Appia Antica and you can indeed walk on a
piece of an ancient Roman road that once
went all the way to Benevento, a city near
Naples. The park has some serious film
cred: it was featured in the opening scene
of *La Dolce Vita* and in a rather memorable scene depicting some avant-garde
performance art in *La Grande Bellezza*. On
weekends, it's a popular place for locals
to picnic, exercise, and bring their kids or
dogs. ⊠ *Via Lemonia 221, Via Appia Antica*
⊕ *www.parcodegliacquedotti.it* Ⓜ *Giulio
Agricola, Subaugusta.*

Porta Maggiore (*Great Gate*)

RUINS | The massive 1st-century-AD arch
was built as part of the original Aqua Clau-
dia and then incorporated into the walls
hurriedly erected in the late 3rd century
as Rome's fortunes began to decline; the

great arch of the aqueduct subsequently became a *porta* (city gate). It gives an idea of the grand scale of ancient Roman public works. On the Piazzale Labicano side, to the east, is the curious Baker's Tomb, erected in the 1st century BC by a prosperous baker (predating both the aqueduct and the city walls); it's shaped like an oven to signal the deceased's trade. The site is now in the middle of a public transport node, and is close to Rome's first tram depot (going back to 1889). ✉ *Piazza di Porta Maggiore, Esquilino* [M] *Tram No. 5, 14, or 19.*

Tomba di Cecilia Metella

CEMETERY | For centuries, sightseers have flocked to this famous landmark, one of the most complete surviving tombs of ancient Rome. One of the many round mausoleums that once lined the Appian Way, this tomb is a smaller version of the Mausoleum of Augustus, but impressive nonetheless. It was the burial place of a Roman noblewoman: the wife of the son of Crassus, who was one of Julius Caesar's rivals and known as the richest man in the Roman Empire (infamously entering the English language as "crass"). The original decoration includes a frieze of bulls' skulls near the top. The travertine stone walls were made higher and the medieval-style crenellations were added when the tomb was transformed into a fortress by the Caetani family in the 14th century. An adjacent chamber houses a small museum of the area's geological phases. Entrance to this site also includes access to the splendid Villa dei Quintili, but you can get a super view without going in. ✉ *Via Appia Antica 161, Via Appia Antica* ☎ *06/7886254* 🌐 *www.parcoarcheologicoappiaantica.it* 🎫 *€10, includes all the sites in the Parco dell'Appia Antica (Villa dei Quintili, Antiquarium di Lucrezia Romana, Complesso di Capo di Bove, Tombe della Via Latina, and the Villa dei Setti Bassi)* 🕓 *Closed Mon.*

🍴 Restaurants

L'Archeologia

$$ | **ITALIAN** | In this farmhouse just beyond the catacombs, founded around 1804, you can dine indoors beside the fireplace in cool weather or in the garden under age-old vines in summer. Specialties include spaghetti *aglio* (with garlic and olive oil), *olio e pepperoncini* (spaghetti with garlic, olive oil, and pepper) with raw shrimp, fillet of beef with onions, potatoes, and hazelnut sauce, and fresh seafood. **Known for:** romantic setting; hand-painted frescoes; ancient wine cellar La Cantina. [$] *Average main: €24* ✉ *Via Appia Antica 139, Via Appia Antica* ☎ *06/7880494* 🌐 *www.larcheologia.it* 🕓 *Closed Tues. No lunch weekdays.*

☕ Coffee and Quick Bites

Panella

$ | **BAKERY** | Opened in 1929, this nearly century-old spot is one of Rome's best bakeries and sells both sweet and savory baked goods, including over 70 types of bread. Line up for the pizza al taglio (by the slice) at lunchtime or sit down at one of the outdoor tables for a cappuccino and cornetto or an aperitivo replete with mini sandwiches made on homemade buns. **Known for:** over 70 types of bread; crostata, tartlets, and other sweet treats; one of Rome's best bakeries. [$] *Average main: €10* ✉ *Via Merulana 54, Esquilino* ☎ *06/4872435* 🌐 *www.panellaroma.com* [M] *Vittorio Emanuele.*

Chapter 4

SIDE TRIPS FROM ROME

Updated by
Natalie Kennedy

 Sights
★★★★☆

 Restaurants
★★☆☆☆

 Hotels
★☆☆☆☆

 Shopping
★☆☆☆☆

 Nightlife
★★★☆☆

WELCOME TO SIDE TRIPS FROM ROME

TOP REASONS TO GO

★ **Ostia Antica:** This excavated port city of ancient Rome is brimming with ruins, mosaics, and structures, which convey a picture of everyday life in the empire.

★ **Tivoli's Villa d'Este:** Hundreds of fountains cascading and shooting skyward (one even plays music on organ pipes) will delight you at this spectacular garden.

★ **Castelli Romani:** Enjoy a raucous Roman lunch and an escape to the ancient hilltop wine towns on the city's doorstep.

★ **Viterbo:** This town may be modern, but it has a Gothic papal palace, a Romanesque cathedral, and the magical medieval quarter of San Pellegrino. It's also the gateway to the *terme* (hot springs) closest to Rome.

★ **Bizarre and beautiful gardens:** The 16th-century proto-Disneyland Parco dei Mostri (Monster Park) is famed for its fantastic sculptures; the stately Villa Lante, a few miles away, is a postcard-perfect Renaissance garden of swirling, manicured hedges.

1 **Viterbo.** The capital of Tuscia and a 13th-century time capsule with papal connections.

2 **Bagnaia.** The site of a 16th-century cardinal's summer home.

3 **Caprarola.** A quiet village that is also home to the huge Palazzo Farnese.

4 **Bomarzo.** The town with the eccentric Monster Park garden.

5 **Ostia Antica.** An ancient Roman port, now an archaeological site.

6 **Tivoli.** A fitting setting for the regal Villa Adriana and the unforgettable Villa d'Este, a park filled with gorgeous fountains.

7 **Palestrina.** Originally an ancient pagan sanctuary and home to the father of musical counterpoint.

8 **Frascati.** A historic getaway amid the Alban Hills and famed for its wine.

9 **Castel Gandolfo.** A lakeside town otherwise known as the pope's summer retreat.

10 **Ariccia.** Home to the grand Palazzo Chigi.

11 **Nemi.** A pretty hamlet, with an eagle's-nest perch above a volcanic lake.

Tuscania

Tarquinia

Civitavecchia

Santa Marinella

Tyrrhenian Sea

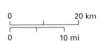

| 0 | | 20 km |
| 0 | | 10 mi |

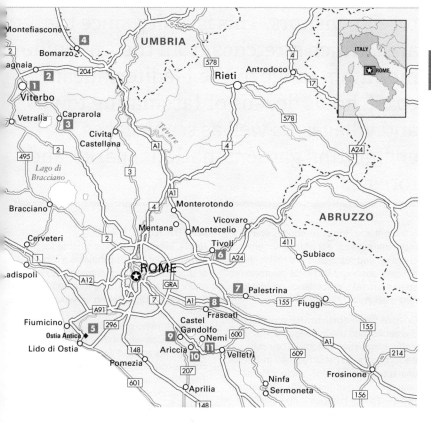

Less well known than neighboring Tuscany, Lazio, the region that encompasses Rome, is often bypassed by foreign visitors. This is a pity, since the area, which stretches from the Apennine mountain range to the Mediterranean coast, holds dozens of fascinating towns and villages, as well as scenic lakes, enchanting gardens, national parks, and forests.

A trip outside Rome introduces you to a more intimate aspect of Italy, where local customs and feast days are still enthusiastically observed and local gastronomic specialties take precedence on restaurant menus.

Despite these small towns' proximity to the capital and the increased commuter traffic congestion of today, they still each manage to preserve their individual character. Ostia Antica, ancient Rome's seaport, is one of the region's top attractions—it rivals Pompeii in the quality of its preservation, and it easily outshines the Roman Forum thanks to its beautiful setting and expansive, inspiring view on the past. Emperors, cardinals, and popes have long escaped to verdant retreats in nearby Tivoli, Viterbo, and the Alban Hills, and their amazing villas, palaces, and gardens add to nature's allure. So if the nonstop Vespa traffic and long lines at the Colosseum start to wear on you, do as the Romans do: get out of town. There's plenty to explore and experience.

MAJOR REGIONS

Tuscia. Tuscia (the modern name for the Etruscan domain of Etruria) is a region of dramatic beauty punctuated by deep, rocky gorges and thickly forested hills, with dappled light falling on wooded paths. This has been a preferred locale for the retreats of wealthy Romans for ages, a place where they could build grand villas and indulge their sometimes-eccentric gardening tastes. The provincial capital, Viterbo, which overshadowed Rome as a center of papal power for a time during the Middle Ages, lies in the heart of Tuscia. The farmland east of Viterbo conceals small quarries of the dark, volcanic *peperino* stone, which shows up in the walls of many buildings here. Lake Bolsena lies in an extinct volcano, and the sulfur springs still bubbling up in the modern spas were once used by the ancient Romans. Bagnaia and Caprarola are home to palaces and gardens; the garden statuary at Bomarzo is in a league of its own—somewhere between the beautiful and the bizarre. The ideal way to explore this region is by car. From Rome you can reach Viterbo by train and then get to Bagnaia by local bus. If you're traveling by train or bus, check schedules carefully; you may have to allow for an overnight if you want to do a round of the region's sights.

Tivoli and Palestrina. Tivoli is a five-star draw, its main attractions being its two villas. There's an ancient one in which Hadrian reproduced the most beautiful monuments in the then-known world, and a Renaissance one, in which Cardinal Ippolito d'Este created a water-filled wonderland. Unfortunately, the Via Tiburtina from Rome to Tivoli passes through miles of industrial areas with chaotic traffic, so whether you are driving or taking the bus, take the A24 motorway to avoid it. Or take the train, which offers a slightly more scenic journey. Whichever way you decide to go, persevere and it'll be worth it for the small but charming city center, expansive park, and Tivoli's two gems that are rightly world-famous. You'll know you're close to Tivoli when you see vast quarries of travertine marble and smell the sulfurous vapors of the little spa, Bagni di Tivoli. Both sites in Tivoli are outdoors and entail walking. With a car, you can continue your loop through the mountains east of Rome, taking in the ancient pagan sanctuary at Palestrina, spectacularly set on the slopes of Mt. Ginestro.

The Castelli Romani. These *castelli* aren't really castles, as their name would seem to imply. Rather, they're little towns that are scattered on the slopes of the Alban Hills just to the southeast of Rome. And the Alban Hills aren't really hills, but extinct volcanoes. There were castles here in the Middle Ages, however, when each of these towns, fiefs of rival Roman lords, had its own fortress to defend it. Some centuries later, the area was given over to villas and retreats, notably the pope's summer residence at Castel Gandolfo and the 17th- and 18th-century villas that transformed Frascati into the Beverly Hills of Rome. Arrayed

around the rim of an extinct volcano that encloses two crater lakes, the string of picturesque towns of the Castelli Romani are surrounded by vineyards, olive groves, and chestnut woods—no wonder overheated Romans have always loved to escape here.

In addition to their lovely natural settings, the Castelli have also been renowned for their wine since the ancient Roman times. In the narrow, medieval alleyways of the oldest parts of the various villages, you can still find old-fashioned taverns where the locals sit on wooden benches, quaffing the golden nectar straight from the barrel. Traveling around the countryside, you can also pop into some of the local vineyards, where they will be happy to give you a tasting of their wines. Exclusive local gastronomic specialties include the bread of Genzano, baked in traditional wood-fired ovens, the *porchetta* (roast suckling pig) of Ariccia, and the *pupazza* biscuits of Frascati, shaped like women or mermaids with three or more breasts (an allusion to ancient fertility goddesses). Each town has its own feasts and saints' days, celebrated with costumed processions and colorful events. Some are quite spectacular, like the annual Marino Wine Festival in October, where the town's fountains flow with wine; or the Flower Festival of Genzano in June, when an entire street is carpeted with millions of flower petals, arranged in elaborate patterns.

Planning

Making the Most of Your Time

Ostia Antica is in many ways an ideal day trip from Rome: it's fascinating, it's not far from the city, it's reachable by public transit, and it takes about half a day to do. Villa d'Este and Villa Adriana in Tivoli

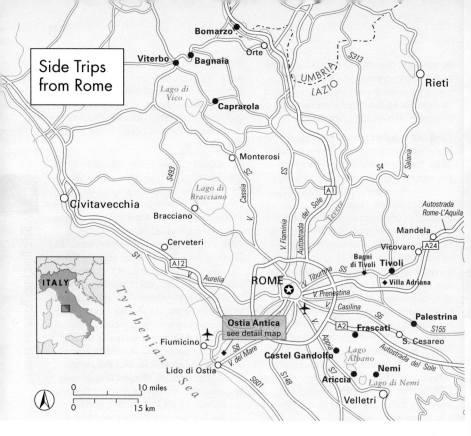

Side Trips
from Rome

also make for a manageable, though fuller, day trip. There's so much to see at these two sights alone, but also be sure to visit Tivoli's picturesque gorge, which is strikingly crowned by an ancient Roman temple to Vesta (which is now a part of the incomparable outdoor terrace at the famed Sibilla restaurant). Other destinations can be visited in a day, but you'll get more out of them if you stay the night.

One classic five-day itinerary that takes in the area's grand villas, ancient ruins, and pretty villages begins with Ostia Antica, the excavated port town of ancient Rome. You can then head north to explore Viterbo's medieval streets on Day 2. On Day 3, take in the hot springs or the gardens of Bomarzo, Bagnaia, and Caprarola. For Day 4, head to Tivoli's

delights. Then on Day 5 take a relaxing trip to the Castelli Romani, where Frascati wine is produced. Admire the sparkling volcanic lakes, find a spot at a family-style local restaurant, and explore the narrow streets of these small hill towns.

Getting Here and Around

There's reliable public transit from Rome to Ostia Antica, Frascati, Tivoli, and Viterbo. Castel Gandolfo is also reachable by train—so long as you don't mind a short uphill walk from the station. COTRAL is the regional bus company. For other destinations, having a car is a big advantage—going by bus or Trenitalia can add hours to your trip, and the routes and schedules are often puzzling.

CONTACTS COTRAL. ✉ *Via Bernardino Ali-mena 105* ☎ *800/174471* ⊕ *www.cotral-spa.it.* **Trenitalia.** *(Italian National Railway System)* ☎ *199/892021, 06/68475475* ⊕ *www.trenitalia.com.*

Restaurants

You certainly won't go hungry when you're exploring the Roman countryside. Whether you choose a five-star establishment or a simple eatery, you can be sure of a fresh, clean tablecloth and friendly, attentive service. Odds are that the ingredients will come from down the road and the owner will be in the kitchen, personally preparing the time-honored dishes that have made Italian cuisine so famous.

Prices in the dining reviews are the average cost of a main course at dinner, or, if dinner is not served, at lunch. Restaurant reviews have been shortened. For full information, visit Fodors.com.

Hotels

Former aristocratic villas with frescoed ceilings, *agriturismi* farmhouses, luxury spas, and cozy bed-and-breakfasts in the village center are just a few of the lodging options here. You won't find much in the way of big chain hotels, though.

Prices in the reviews are the lowest cost of a standard double room in high season. Hotel reviews have been shortened. For full information, visit Fodors.com.

What it Costs in Euros

	$	$$	$$$	$$$$
RESTAURANTS				
	under €15	€15–€24	€25–€35	over €35
HOTELS				
	under €125	€125–€200	€201–€300	over €300

Visitor Information

Tourist information kiosks, which are scattered around Rome's main squares and tourist sights, can give you information about the Castelli Romani, Ostia Antica, and Tivoli. The Tuscia area is served by the central tourist office in Viterbo.

CONTACT Visit Lazio. ⊕ *www.visitlazio.com.*

Viterbo

104 km (64 miles) northwest of Rome.

Viterbo's moment of glory was in the 13th century, when it became the seat of the papal court. The medieval core of the city still sits within 12th-century walls. Its old buildings, with window boxes bright with geraniums, are made of dark peperino, the local stone that colors the medieval part of Viterbo a deep gray, contrasted here and there with the golden tufa rock of walls and towers. Peperino is also used in the characteristic and typically medieval exterior staircases that you see throughout the old town.

Viterbo has blossomed into a regional commercial center, and much of the modern city is loud and industrial. Nevertheless, in Viterbo's San Pellegrino district you'll get the feel of the Middle Ages—artisan shops and bottegas still operate in a setting that has remained practically unchanged over the centuries. The Papal Palace and the cathedral, which sit at the heart of the oldest part of the city, enhance the effect. The city has remained a renowned spa center for its natural hot springs just outside town, which have been frequented by popes and mere mortals alike since medieval times.

GETTING HERE AND AROUND

Viterbo is well served by public transport from Rome. Direct train service from Stazione Trastevere takes one hour and 40 minutes, making frequent stops in the capital's more rural suburbs. Try to avoid peak hours, as many commuters live in towns along the line. By road, take either the old Roman consular road, the Via Cassia, which passes near Caprarola, or, if you are in a hurry, the A1 toll highway to the Orte exit and then the 204 highway, with a detour to Bomarzo. The trip can take a couple of hours or more, depending on traffic.

VISITOR INFORMATION

CONTACT Viterbo Tourism Office. ⊠ *Piazza Martiri D'Ungheria,* ☎ *0761/226427* ⊕ *www.promotuscia.it.*

 # Sights

Cattedrale di San Lorenzo

CHURCH | Viterbo's Romanesque cathedral was built over the ruins of the ancient Roman Temple of Hercules. During World War II, the roof and the vault of the central nave were destroyed, and you can still see the mark the shrapnel left on the columns closest to the pulpit. Subsequently, the church was rebuilt to its original medieval design, but it still has many original details, including a beautiful Cosmati floor that dates back to the 13th century. Three popes are buried here, including Pope Alexander IV (1254–61), whose body was hidden so well by the canons, out of fear that it would be desecrated, that it has never been found. The adjoining Museo del Colle del Duomo has a collection of 18th-century reliquaries, Etruscan sarcophagi, and a painting of the Crucifixion that has been attributed to Michelangelo. The ticket to the museum also grants you entrance to the Palazzo Papale, located on the same square. ⊠ *Piazza San Lorenzo, Viterbo* ☎ *320/7911328* ⊕ *www.archeoares.it* ✉ *€9, includes tour of Cattedrale di San Lorenzo, Palazzo dei Papi, and Museo del Colle del Duomo.*

Palazzo dei Papi (*Papal Palace*)

CASTLE/PALACE | This Gothic palace was built in the 13th century as a residence for popes looking to get away from the city. At the time, Rome was notoriously ridden with malaria and the plague, not to mention rampaging factions of rival barons. In 1271 the palace was the scene of a novel type of rebellion. A conclave held that year to elect a new pope dragged on for months. The people of Viterbo were exasperated by the delay, especially as custom decreed that they had to provide for the cardinals' board and lodging for the duration of the conclave. To speed up the deliberations, the townspeople tore the roof off the great hall where the cardinals were meeting, and put them on bread and water. A new pope—Gregory X—was elected in short order. Today, you can visit the great hall, step out on the pretty loggia, and admire the original frescoes in the small adjoining room. ■TIP→ **An audio guided tour is free with the purchase of a ticket and lasts 45 minutes, starting from Museo del Colle del Duomo.** ⊠ *Piazza San Lorenzo, Viterbo* ☎ *393/0916060* ⊕ *www.archeoares.it* ✉ *€9, includes tour of Cattedrale di San Lorenzo, Palazzo dei Papi, and Museo del Colle del Duomo.*

San Pellegrino

HISTORIC DISTRICT | One of the best-preserved medieval districts in Italy, San Pellegrino has charming vistas of arches, vaults, towers, exterior staircases, worn wooden doors on great iron hinges, and tiny hanging gardens. You pass many antiques shops and craft workshops, as well as numerous restaurants, as you explore the little squares and byways. The Fontana Grande in the piazza of the same name is the largest and most extravagant of Viterbo's Gothic fountains. ⊠ *Via San Pellegrino, near Palazzo dei Papi and Cattedrale di San Lorenzo, Viterbo* ⊕ *www.promotuscia.it.*

★ Terme dei Papi
HOT SPRING | Viterbo has been a spa town for centuries, and this excellent spa not far removed continues the tradition, providing the usual health and beauty treatments with an Etruscan twist: try a facial with local volcanic mud, or a steam bath in an ancient cave, where scalding hot mineral water direct from the spring splashes down a waterfall to a pool beneath your feet. The Terme dei Papi's main draw, however, comes from the terme themselves: a 21,000-square-foot outdoor limestone pool, into the shallow end of which Viterbo's famous hot water pours at 59°C (138°F)—and gives a jolt with its sulfurous odor. Floats and deck chairs are for rent, but bring your own bathrobe and towel unless you're staying at the hotel. Tickets tend to sell out but can be booked online up to five days ahead of your visit. **■ TIP→ Shuttle buses operate between Rome's Piazza del Popolo and the Terme on weekends and holidays. Round-trip tickets cost €12; call or check website for travel times.** ✉ *Strada Bagni 12, 5 km (3 miles) west of town center, Viterbo* ☎ *0761/3501* 🌐 *www.termedeipapi.it* 🎟 *Pool €18 weekdays, €25 weekends* 🕒 *Closed Tues.*

🍴 Restaurants

★ Osteria del Vecchio Orologio
$ | ITALIAN | Tucked away in a side street off the medieval Piazza delle Erbe, the Osteria del Vecchio Orologio offers top-quality Tuscia specialties in a warm and informal atmosphere. They're a member of the Slow Food movement, with a menu that changes according to the season. **Known for:** extensive wine list; local ingredients; cute, cupboard-lined walls. [$] *Average main: €14* ✉ *Via Orologio Vecchio 25, Viterbo* ☎ *335/337754* 🌐 *www.alvecchioorologio.it* 🕒 *No lunch Mon. Closed Tues.*

Taverna Etrusca
$$ | ITALIAN | FAMILY | Located between the heart of San Pellegrino and Porta Romana, this friendly trattoria is known for its excellent home cooking and pizza. Be sure to admire the Etruscan-inspired decorations and check out the dessert—all the excellent gelato is made on-site. **Known for:** excellent gelato; tagliolini (ribbon pasta) with lemon; homemade pasta alla viterbese (spicy red sauce with fennel). [$] *Average main: €15* ✉ *Via Annio 8, Viterbo* ☎ *0761/226694* 🌐 *www.tavernaetrusca.it* 🕒 *Closed Sun.*

Tre Re
$$ | ITALIAN | Viterbo's oldest restaurant—and one of the most ancient in Italy—has been operating in the *centro storico* (historic center) since 1622. The small, wood-paneled dining room, chummily packed with tables, was a favorite haunt of movie director Federico Fellini and, before that, of British and American soldiers during World War II. **Known for:** locals touch the Tre Re (Three Kings) sign outside for luck; roasted suckling pig; traditional local dishes. [$] *Average main: €15* ✉ *Via Macel Gattesco 3, Viterbo* ☎ *0761/304619* 🌐 *www.ristorantetrere.com* 🕒 *Closed Thurs.*

Bagnaia

5 km (3 miles) east of Viterbo.

The quiet village of Bagnaia is the site of the 16th-century cardinal Alessandro Montalto's summer retreat, which is quite an extravaganza.

GETTING HERE AND AROUND

Local buses from Viterbo are one way to get here. By local train, it's 10 minutes beyond the Viterbo stop—few local trains actually do stop, though, so be sure to check beforehand. If you prefer to drive, take the A1 to the exit for Orte and follow signs for Bagnaia. There is free parking across the bridge from the main square.

Sights

Villa Lante

CASTLE/PALACE | The main draw in this otherwise sweet but underwhelming village is the hillside garden and park that surround the two small, identical residences built by different owners in the 16th century, more than 30 years apart. The first belonged to Cardinal Gianfrancesco Gambara, but it was Cardinal Alessandro Montalto who built the second and soon commissioned the creation of a stunning garden filled with grottoes, fountains, and immaculately manicured hedges. The garden and the park were designed by the virtuoso architect Giacomo Barozzi (circa 1507–73), known as Vignola, who later worked with Michelangelo on St. Peter's. On the lowest terrace a delightful Italian garden has a centerpiece fountain fed by water channeled down the hillside. On another terrace, a stream of water runs through a groove carved in a long stone table where the cardinal entertained his friends alfresco, chilling wine in the running water. That's only one of the most evident of the whimsical water games that were devised for the cardinal. The symmetry of the formal gardens contrasts with the wild, untamed park adjacent to it, reflecting the paradoxes of nature and artifice that are the theme of this pleasure garden. ⊠ *Via Jacopo Barozzi 71, Bagnaia* ☎ *07/61288008* ⊕ *www.polomuseale-lazio.beniculturali.it/index.php?it/243/villa-lante* 🖾 *€5* 🕑 *Closed Mon.*

Caprarola

21 km (13 miles) southeast of Bagnaia, 19 km (12 miles) southeast of Viterbo.

The wealthy and powerful Farnese family took over this sleepy village in the 1500s and had the architect Vignola design a huge palace and gardens to rival the great residences of Rome. He also rearranged the little town of Caprarola to enhance the palazzo's setting.

GETTING HERE AND AROUND
Caprarola is served by COTRAL bus, leaving from Rome's Saxa Rubra station on the Roma Nord suburban railway line.

Sights

★ **Palazzo Farnese**

CASTLE/PALACE | When Cardinal Alessandro Farnese, Pope Paul III's grandson, retired to Caprarola, he intended to build a residence that would reflect the family's grandeur. In 1559, he entrusted the task to the leading architect Giacomo Barozzi da Vignola, who came up with some innovative ideas. A magnificent spiral staircase, lavishly decorated with allegorical figures, mythical landscapes, and grotesques by Antonio Tempesta, connected the main entrance with the cardinal's apartments on the main floor. The staircase was gently inclined, with very deep but low steps, so that the cardinal could ride his horse right up to his bedchamber. A tour of the five-sided palatial villa includes the Hall of Farnese Triumphs, the Hercules Room, and the Antechamber of the Council of Trent, all painted by the Zuccari brothers. Of special interest is the Hall of the Maps, with the ceiling depicting the zodiac and the walls frescoed with maps of the world as known to 16th-century cartographers. The palace is surrounded by a formal Renaissance garden. ⊠ *Piazza Farnese 1, Caprarola* ☎ *0761/646052* ⊕ *www.polomusealelazio.beniculturali.it* 🖾 *€5, includes garden* 🕑 *Closed Mon.*

🍴 Restaurants

Antica Trattoria del Borgo

$$ | ROMAN | FAMILY | Visitors to Caprarola's landmark Palazzo Farnese often round out the experience with a hearty meal at this celebrated trattoria. There's a cozy, familial atmosphere inside, and when the weather permits, a pleasant seating area

outside. **Known for:** homemade desserts; expansive wine cellar; local salumi (cured) and grilled meat. [$] *Average main: €20* ✉ *Via Borgo Vecchio 107, Caprarola* ☎ *0761/645252* 🌐 *www.anticatrattoriadelborgo.it* 🕒 *Closed Mon. No dinner Sun., Tues., or Wed.*

Bomarzo

15 km (9 miles) northeast of Viterbo.

Once a fief of the powerful Orsini family, Bomarzo is home to the Parco dei Mostri, the town's main attraction, which was created to amuse and astound the Orsinis' guests. The 16th-century Palazzo Orsini is now the seat of the town council. Inside, there is a princely hall, frescoed by Pietro da Cortona, the famous Italian Baroque fresco painter and architect.

GETTING HERE AND AROUND

Bomarzo is easily reached by car from the A1 autostrada. If you want to go there directly, carry on to the Attigliano exit. Parco dei Monstri is some 6 km (4 miles) from that point. Alternatively, come out at Orte and branch off at Casalone on the Viterbo road. A COTRAL bus also goes here, from Viterbo.

👁 Sights

Parco dei Mostri (*Monster Park*)
GARDEN | FAMILY | This eerie fantasy, originally known as the Village of Marvels, or the Sacred Wood, was created in 1552 by Prince Vicino Orsini, with the aid of the famous artist Pirro Ligorio. The surreal park is populated with weird and fantastic sculptures of mythical creatures intended to astonish illustrious guests. The sculptures, carved in outcroppings of mossy stone in shady groves and woodland, include giant tortoises and griffins and an ogre's head with an enormous gaping mouth and a table with chairs set inside. Children love it, and there are photo ops galore. The park has a self-service café (open Sunday only, in winter) and a gift shop. ✉ *Localita Giardino, 1½ km (1 mile) west of Bomarzo, Bomarzo* ☎ *0761/924029* 🌐 *www.sacrobosco.it* 🎟 *€13.*

Ostia Antica

30 km (19 miles) southwest of Rome.

Founded around the 4th century BC, Ostia served as Rome's port city for several centuries until the Tiber changed course, leaving the town high and dry. What has been excavated here is a remarkably intact Roman town. To get the most out of a visit, fair weather and good walking shoes are essential. To avoid the worst extremes of hot days, be here when the gates open or go late in the afternoon. A visit to the excavations takes two to three hours, including 20 minutes for the museum. Inside the site, there's a snack bar and a bookshop, but the best idea is to plan to have lunch outside the archaeological area, in the town's nearby medieval quarter.

GETTING HERE AND AROUND

The best way to get to Ostia Antica is by train. The Ostia Lido train leaves every 15 minutes from the Porta San Paolo station adjacent to Rome's Piramide Line B Metro station, stopping off at Ostia Antica en route; the trip takes 35 minutes. By car, take the Via del Mare that leads off from Rome's EUR district. Be prepared for heavy traffic, especially at peak hours, on weekends, and in summer.

👁 Sights

Castello di Giulio II
CASTLE/PALACE | The distinctive castle, easily spotted as you come off the footbridge from the train station and part of the medieval *borgo* (old town), was built in 1483 by the future Pope Julius II when he was the cardinal bishop of Ostia. The structure's triangular form is unusual for

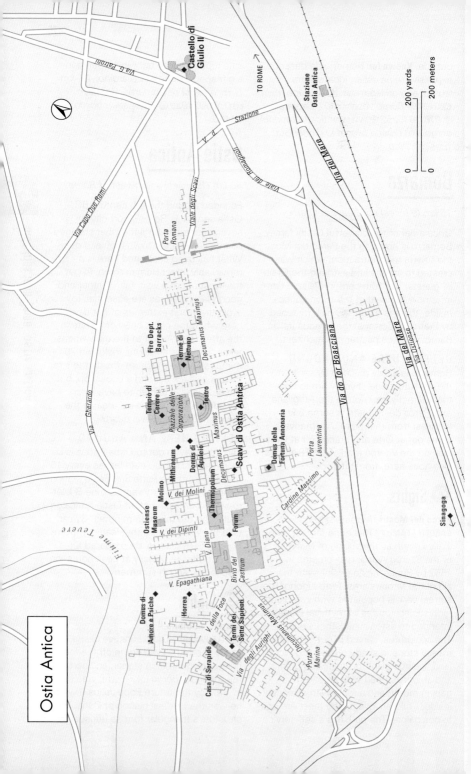

Ostia Antica

military architecture. The castle is typically open on the weekends, but it is best to check updated days and available times for visits, listed on the official website. Even if you can't get inside, its towers and walls add to the atmosphere of the charming old town. ✉ *Piazza della Rocca 13, Ostia Antica* 🌐 *www.ostiaantica.beniculturali.it* 🎫 *Free* ⏲ *Closed weekdays.*

★ **Scavi di Ostia Antica**
(*Ostia Antica Excavations*)
RUINS | Today some of Rome's most impressive ruins, the ancient port town was covered by tidal mud and windblown sand and lay buried until the 19th century, when it was extensively excavated. The massive archaeological site can be explored on foot and is brimming with curious corners, mosaic floors, fallen columns, and a huge Roman amphitheater. At its peak, it was home to a cosmopolitan population of rich businessmen, wily merchants, sailors, slaves, and their respective families. Great warehouses were built here in the 2nd century AD to handle goods that passed through the town, notably huge shipments of grain from Africa; the port did so much business that it necessitated the construction of *insulae* (apartment buildings) to provide housing for the city's growing population. The increasing importance of nearby Portus and the inexorable decline of the Roman Empire eventually led to the port's abandonment. Over the last two millennia the coastline has retreated, and a 16th-century flood diverted the course of the Tiber, so only a glimpse of the river (near the café) can be seen today. The on-site Museo Ostiense displays sculptures, mosaics, and objects of daily use found here. There's a cafeteria on-site. ■ **TIP→ The recently excavated ports of Tiberius and Claudius are nearby and also well worth visiting.** ✉ *Viale dei Romagnoli 717, Ostia Antica* ☎ *06/56358099* 🌐 *www.ostiaantica.beniculturali.it* 🎫 *€12, includes Museo Ostiense (small increase if there is an exhibition); free 1st Sun. of month* ⏲ *Closed Mon.*

🍴 Restaurants

Arianna al Borghetto
$$ | **ROMAN** | **FAMILY** | This cozy trattoria is tucked away in the charming walled medieval borgo of Ostia Antica next to the Castello di Giulio II. A short walk from the excavations, it's an ideal spot to restore your energy with some seasonal dishes and Roman specialties. **Known for:** charming outdoor seating; homemade pastas; traditional Roman food. [$] *Average main: €15* ✉ *Via del Forno 11, Ostia Antica* ☎ *06/56352956* ⏲ *Closed Mon. No dinner Sun.*

Tivoli

36 km (22 miles) northeast of Rome.

In ancient times, just about anybody who was anybody had a villa in Tivoli, including Crassus, Trajan, Hadrian, Horace, and Catullus. Tivoli fell into obscurity in the medieval era until the Renaissance, when popes and cardinals came back to the town and built villas showy enough to rival those of their extravagant predecessors.

Nowadays Tivoli is small but vibrant, with winding streets and views over the surrounding countryside. The deep Aniene River gorge runs through the center of town and comes replete with a romantically sited bridge, cascading waterfalls, and two jewels of ancient Roman architecture that crown its cliffs—the round Temple of Vesta (or the Sybil, the prophetess credited with predicting the birth of Christ) and the ruins of the rectangular temple of the hero-god Tibur, the mythical founder of the city. These can be viewed across the gorge from the Villa Gregoriana Park, named for Pope Gregory XVI, who saved Tivoli from chronic river damage by diverting the river through a tunnel, weakening its flow. An unexpected side effect was the creation of the Grande Cascata (Grand

Cascade), a waterfall formed by the huge jet of water that shoots picturesquely into the valley below. You may also want to set your sights on the Antico Ristorante Sibilla, set up against the Temple of Vesta. From its dining terrace you can take in one of the most memorably romantic landscape views in Italy.

GETTING HERE AND AROUND

Unless you have nerves of steel, it's best to skip the drive to Tivoli. Hundreds of businesses line the Via Tiburtina from Rome and bottleneck traffic is nearly constant. You can avoid some, but not all, of the congestion by taking the Roma–L'Aquila toll road. Luckily, there's abundant public transport (although leaving your own car behind does make it slightly more inconvenient to visit Hadrian's Villa). Buses leave every 15 minutes from the Ponte Mammolo stop on Metro Line B; the ride takes an hour. Regional Trenitalia trains connect from both Termini and Tiburtina stations and will have you in Tivoli in about an hour, or 30 minutes if you plan to take one of the few express trains each day. Villa d'Este is in the town center, and there is a bus service from Tivoli's main square to Hadrian's Villa.

VISITOR INFORMATION

CONTACT PIT (Punto Informativo Turistico). (*Tivoli Tourist Office*) ✉ *Piazzale Nazioni Unite,* ☎ *0774/313536* ⊕ *www.visittivoli. eu.*

Sights

★ **Villa Adriana** (*Hadrian's Villa*)

RUINS | An emperor's theme park, this astonishingly grand 2nd-century villa was an exclusive retreat below the ancient settlement of Tibur, where the marvels of the classical world were reproduced for a ruler's pleasure. Hadrian, who succeeded Trajan as emperor in AD 117, was a man of genius and intellectual curiosity, fascinated by the accomplishments of the Hellenistic world. From AD 125 to 134, architects, laborers, and artists

worked on his dreamy villa, re-creating some of the monuments and sights that the emperor had seen on his travels in Egypt, Asia Minor, and Greece. During the Middle Ages, the site was sacked by barbarians and Romans alike, and many of the statues and architectural features ended up in the Vatican Museums. Nonetheless, the colossal remains are impressive: the ruins rise in a garden setting of green lawns framed with oleanders, pines, and cypresses. Not surprisingly, Villa Adriana is a UNESCO World Heritage site, and it's one that has not yielded up all its secrets. Archaeologists recently discovered the site of the Temple of Isis, complete with several sculptures, including one of the falcon-headed god Horus. ■ TIP➡ **A visit to the villa, which sits outside town, takes at least two hours (carry water on hot days); maps dispensed at the ticket office will help you get your bearings.** ✉ *Largo Margherite Yourcenar 1, 6 km (4 miles) southwest of Tivoli, Tivoli* ☎ *0774/382733* ⊕ *www.levillae. com/en* 💶 *€10; free 1st Sun. of month Oct.–Mar.*

★ **Villa d'Este**

GARDEN | One of Italy's UNESCO World Heritage sites, Villa d'Este was created by Cardinal Ippolito d'Este in the 16th century. This villa in the center of Tivoli was the most amazing pleasure garden of its day, and it still stuns modern visitors with its beauty. Cardinal d'Este (1509–72), a devotee of the Renaissance celebration of human ingenuity over nature, was inspired by the excavation of nearby Villa Adriana. He paid architect Pirro Ligorrio an astronomical sum to create an extraordinary garden filled with nymphs and grottoes. But water is the true artistic centerpiece here, and the Aniene River had to be diverted to water the garden and feed the several hundred fountains that cascade, shoot skyward, imitate birdsong, and simulate rain. The musical Fontana dell'Organo has been restored to working order: the water dances to an organ tune every two hours starting at 10:30 am. Romantics will love the night tour of the gardens and floodlit fountains that takes place on Friday and Saturday in summer. **■ TIP→ Allow at least an hour for a visit, which involves steep inclines and many stairs. There are vending machines for refreshments by the bookshop.** ✉ *Piazza Trento 5, Tivoli* ☎ *0774/332920* 🌐 *www.levillae.com/en* 🎟 *€10; free 1st Sun. of month Oct.–Mar.*

🍴 Restaurants

★ Antico Ristorante Sibilla

$$ | **ITALIAN** | Founded as a hotel and restaurant in 1720 beside the striking Roman Temple of Vesta and the Sanctuary of the Sybil, the idyllic wisteria-draped terrace has a spectacular view over the deep gorge of the Aniene River, with the thundering waters of the waterfall in the background. Standards are high, and the trip to Tivoli is worth it even if you do nothing more than order a lunch of upscale versions of local dishes in this unforgettable setting. **Known for:** homemade pasta with seasonal ingredients; special take on fried zucchini blossoms; beautiful terrace with a super view. [$] *Average main: €20* ✉ *Via della Sibilla 50, Tivoli* ☎ *0774/335281* 🌐 *www.ristorantesibilla.com* ⏲ *Closed Mon.*

🛏 Hotels

Torre Sant'Antonio

$ | **B&B/INN** | Set inside a tower that dates back to the 1300s, this small but cozy hotel offers two private rooms on the edge of the historic center. **Pros:** historic setting; easy walk to most major sites; modern interior design. **Cons:** no 24-hour front desk; old windowpanes let in some street noise; limited parking nearby. [$] *Rooms from: €80* ✉ *Vicolo Sant'Antonio 35, Tivoli* ☎ *347/8037983* 🌐 *www.torresantantoniotivoli.it* 🛏 *2 rooms* 🍴 *No Meals.*

Palestrina

27 km (17 miles) southeast of Tivoli, 37 km (23 miles) east of Rome.

Except to students of ancient history and music lovers, Palestrina is little known outside Italy. Set on a steep hillside, Romans flock to the small town of sherbet-colored houses in summer, when its country breezes offer a refreshing break from the hot city. In addition to the relatively cooler weather, the town is best known for its most famous native son, Giovanni Pierluigi da Palestrina, born here in 1525, and considered the master of counterpoint and polyphony. He composed 105 Masses, as well as madrigals, Magnificats, and motets. There is a small museum dedicated to his life and work in the town center.

Ancient Praeneste (modern Palestrina) flourished much earlier than Rome. It was the site of the Temple of Fortuna Primigenia, which dates from the 2nd century BC. This was one of the largest, richest, most frequented temple complexes in all antiquity—people came from far and wide to consult its famous oracle. In modern times no one had any idea of the extent of the complex until World War II bombings exposed ancient foundations occupying huge artificial terraces, which stretch from the upper part of the town as far downhill as its central duomo.

GETTING HERE AND AROUND

COTRAL buses leave from the Anagnina terminal on Rome's Metro Line A and from the Tiburtina railway station. Alternatively, you can take a train to Zagarolo, where a COTRAL bus takes you on to Palestrina. The total trip takes 40 minutes. By car, take the A1 (Autostrada del Sole) to the San Cesareo exit and follow the signs to Palestrina. The drive takes about an hour.

Sights

Palazzo Barberini

RUINS | A bomb blast during World War II exposed the remains of the immense Temple of Fortune that covered the entire hillside under the present town. Large arches and terraces are now visible and you can walk or take a local bus up to the imposing Palazzo Barberini, which crowns the highest point. The palace was built in the 17th century along the semicircular lines of the original Roman temple. It now contains the Museo Nazionale Archeologico di Palestrina, with material found on the site that dates from throughout the classical period. There is a well-labeled collection of Etruscan bronzes, pottery, and terra-cotta statuary as well as Roman artifacts, but all of these take a distant second place to the main event, a massive 1st-century BC mosaic depicting a buzzing scene on the Nile River, complete with ancient Egyptian boats, waving palm trees, and intricately crafted African animals. This highly colorful and detailed work is worth the trip to Palestrina by itself. But there's more: a model of the temple as it was in ancient times helps you appreciate the immensity of the original construction. ✉ *Piazza della Cortina 1, Palestrina* ☎ *06/9538100* 🌐 *www.polomusealelazio.beniculturali.it* 🎟 *€5.*

Restaurants

Il Piscarello

$$ | **ITALIAN** | **FAMILY** | Tucked away at the bottom of a steep side road, this elegant dining room immersed in a garden comes as a bit of a surprise. Specialties of the house include meat carpaccio and fish, seafood, and meat dishes with white and black truffles, and the pasta can even be made gluten-free if you call at least one day ahead of time. **Known for:** outdoor seating in summer; fresh seafood; truffle-topped dishes. [$] *Average main: €20* ✉ *Via delle Pratarine 2, Palestrina* ☎ *06/9574326* 🌐 *www.ristoranteilpiscarello.it* 🕘 *Closed Mon. No lunch Tues.–Thurs. No dinner Sun.*

Frascati

20 km (12 miles) south of Rome.

Frascati is one of the easiest villages of the Castelli Romani to get to from Rome, as well as one of the most enjoyable to navigate. After climbing the stairs from the train station or driving uphill to the entrance of the town, it's worth taking a stroll through Frascati's lively old center. Via Battisti, leading away from the looming presence of Villa Aldobrandini, takes you into Piazza San Pietro with its imposing gray-and-white cathedral. Inside is the cenotaph of Prince Charles Edward, last of the Scottish Stuart dynasty, who tried unsuccessfully to regain the British Crown and died an exile in Rome in 1788. A little arcade beside the monumental fountain at the back of the piazza leads into Market Square, where the smell of fresh baking will entice you into the Purificato family bakery to see the traditional honey-flavored pupazza biscuits, modeled on old pagan fertility symbols.

Take your pick from the café and trattorias fronting the central Piazzale Marconi, or do as the locals do: buy fruit from the market gallery at Piazza del Mercato, then get a huge slice of porchetta from one of the stalls, a hunk of *casareccio* bread, and a few *ciambelline frascatane* (ring-shaped cookies made with wine), and take your picnic to any one of the nearby *cantine* (homey wine bars) to settle in for some sips of tasty, inexpensive vino. Or continue on to nearby Grottaferrata to take in its one-of-a-kind abbey.

GETTING HERE AND AROUND

An hourly train service along a single-track line through vineyards and olive groves takes you to Frascati from Stazione Termini. The trip takes 45 minutes. By car, take the Via Tuscolano, which branches off the Appia Nuova road just after St. John Lateran in Rome, and drive straight up.

VISITOR INFORMATION

CONTACT Frascati Point (Tourism Office). ✉ *Piazza G. Marconi 5,* ☎ *06/94184406* 🌐 *www.comune.frascati.rm.it.*

👁 Sights

Abbey of San Nilo Grottaferrata

CHURCH | In Grottaferrata, a busy village a couple of miles from Frascati, the main attraction is a walled citadel founded by St. Nilo, who brought his group of Basilian monks here in 1004, when he was 90. The order is unique in that it's Roman Catholic but observes Greek Orthodox rites. It is the last surviving Byzantine-Greek monastery in Italy, and has a distinctive blend of art and architecture. The fortified abbey with its soaring bell tower, considered a masterpiece of martial architecture, was restructured in the 15th century by Antonio da Sangallo for the future Pope Julius II. The abbey church, inside the second courtyard, is a jewel of Oriental opulence, with glittering Byzantine mosaics and a revered icon of Mary with child set into a marble tabernacle designed by Bernini. The Farnese chapel, leading from the right nave, contains a series of frescoes by Domenichino. If you make arrangements in advance you can visit the library, which is one of the oldest in Italy. The abbey also has a famous laboratory for the restoration of antique books and manuscripts, where Leonardo's *Codex Atlanticus* was restored in 1962 and more than a thousand precious volumes were saved after the disastrous Florence flood in 1966. ✉ *Corso del Popolo 128, Grottaferrata* ☎ *06/9459309* 🎫 *Free.*

★ Poggio Le Volpi

WINERY | Lazio's wines may not be as famous as those of Tuscany or Piedmont, but this award-winning family-run winery is leading the way for the region. The family's wine-making roots stretch back to 1920, but it was third-generation winemaker Felice Mergè who turned the winery into a destination with two restaurants: the casual Epos bistro and the fine-dining Barrique, where a tasting menu is served in the barrel aging room. Tours of the winery are available by appointment only, but the best way to experience this place is to book a table at one of the restaurants and request a tour. ✉ *Via Fontana Candida 3/C, Monte Porzio Catone* ☎ *06/9426980* 🌐 *www.poggiolevolpi.com* 🎫 *Tours available by appointment* 🕒 *Closed Mon.*

🍴 Restaurants

Antica Fontana

$$ | **ROMAN** | Across the road from the Abbey of San Nilo, this is one of Grottaferrata's most esteemed restaurants, and it tends to be slightly higher priced than other nearby eateries. Run by the Consoli family since 1989, the decor is rustic but stylish, with plants hanging from the ceiling and rows of polished antique copper pans and molds decorating the walls. **Known for:** pleasant outdoor terrace; fettuccine with porcini; homemade pizza with excellent dough. $ *Average main: €22* ✉ *Via Domenichino 24, Grottaferrata* ☎ *347/4044492* 🕒 *Closed Mon.*

★ Cacciani

$$ | **ITALIAN** | The Cacciani family has been running this stylish restaurant in the heart of Frascati old town since 1922, when it was a popular hangout for the likes of Clark Gable and Gina Lollobrigida. Perched high on a rise overlooking the town and the Roman plain, there are spectacular views from the Cacciani terrace, but you can also keep an eye on the gorgeous food being prepared in the open kitchen. **Known for:** welcoming, family-run vibe; great views; tonnarelli cacio e pepe (prepared with a pecorino-cheese sauce and black pepper) prepared at the table. $ *Average main: €18* ✉ *Via Armando Diaz 13, Frascati* ☎ *06/9420378*

⊕ *www.cacciani.it* ⊘ *Closed Mon. No dinner Sun.*

Il Grottino Frascati

$$ | **ITALIAN** | This former wine cellar just beyond Frascati's market square is now an old-fashioned and cheerful trattoria serving traditional Roman dishes and pizza. In summer you can sit under an awning outside and enjoy the sweeping view over the plain toward Rome. **Known for:** extensive wine list; casual atmosphere; pasta alla gricia (with pecorino cheese, black pepper, and guanciale). $ *Average main: €15* ✉ *Viale Regina Margherita 41–43, Frascati* ☎ *06/94289772.*

★ Osteria del Fico Vecchio

$$ | **ITALIAN** | Only a couple of miles outside Frascati, this 16th-century coaching inn has a tastefully renovated dining room and an old fig tree (its namesake) that shades the restaurant's charming garden filled with outdoor tables. Long known for its excellent cooking, the classic restaurant still prepares typical Roman dishes, among them *pollo al diavolo* (spicy braised chicken) and *abbacchio allo scottadito* (sizzling grilled lamb). **Known for:** typical Roman dishes; classic cacio e pepe; pretty garden for outdoor dining. $ *Average main: €20* ✉ *Via Anagnina 257, Grottaferrata* ☎ *06/9459261* ⊕ *www.alfico.it* ⊘ *No lunch Thurs.*

Hotels

★ Park Hotel Villa Grazioli

$ | **HOTEL** | One of the region's most famous residences, this patrician villa halfway between Frascati and Grottaferrata is now a first-class hotel, though the standard-issue guest rooms are a bit of a letdown amid the impressive frescoed salons of the main building. **Pros:** incredible frescoes in the main building; wonderful views of the countryside; elegant atmosphere. **Cons:** Wi-Fi connection can be poor; not all rooms are in the main building; situated at the end of a long, narrow lane. $ *Rooms from: €120* ✉ *Via Umberto Pavoni 19, Grottaferrata* ⊹ *Narrow turnoff from the SP216 road going from Grottaferrata roundabout to Frascati* ☎ *06/945400* ⊕ *www.villa-grazioli.it* ⇥ *62 rooms* ⦿ *Free Breakfast.*

Castel Gandolfo

8 km (5 miles) southwest of Frascati, 25 km (15 miles) south of Rome.

This scenic little town has been the preferred summer retreat of popes for centuries. It was the Barberini Pope Urban VIII who first headed here, eager to escape the malarial miasmas that afflicted summertime Rome; before long, the city's princely families also set up country estates around here.

The 17th-century Villa Pontificia has a superb position overlooking Lake Albano and is set in one of the most gorgeous gardens in Italy. Fortunately, these treasures are now open to the public as papal audiences are no longer held at Castel Gandolfo. There's a fountain on the little square in front of the palace by Bernini, who also designed the nearby Church of San Tommaso da Villanova, which has works by Pietro da Cortona.

The village has a number of interesting craft workshops and food purveyors, in addition to the souvenir shops on the square. On the horizon, the silver astronomical dome belonging to the Specola Vaticana observatory—one of the first in Europe—where the scientific Pope Gregory XIII indulged his interest in stargazing, is visible for miles around.

GETTING HERE AND AROUND

There's an hourly train service for Castel Gandolfo from Termini station (Rome–Albano line). Otherwise, buses leave frequently from the Anagnina terminal of Metro Line A. The trip takes about 40 minutes, and the village is reachable by a 10-minute uphill walk from the station. By car, take the Appian Way from San

Giovanni in Rome and follow it straight to Albano, where you branch off for Castel Gandolfo (about an hour, depending on traffic).

VISITOR INFORMATION

CONTACT PIT Tourist Office Castel Gandolfo. ✉ *Via Massimo D'Azeglio,* ⊕ *A green kiosk on your right as you walk up the road, just outside the town walls* ⊕ *www. comune.castelgandolfo.rm.it.*

Sights

Lakeside Lido

BEACH | FAMILY | This waterside promenade below the pretty town is lined with restaurants, ice cream parlors, and cafés and is a favorite spot for Roman families to relax on summer days. No motorized craft are allowed on the lake, but you can rent paddleboats and kayaks. In summer, you can also take a short guided boat trip to learn about the geology and history of the lake, which lies at the bottom of an extinct volcanic crater. The deep sapphire waters are full of swans, herons, and other birds, and there is a nature trail along the wooded end of the shore for those who want to get away from the crowds. Deck chairs are available for rent; you might also want to stop for a plate of freshly prepared pasta or a gigantic Roman sandwich at one of the little snack bars under the oak and alder trees. There's also a small permanent fairground for children, and local vendors often set up temporary shops selling crafts, toys, and snacks on the warmer weekends. ✉ *Lake Albano, Castel Gandolfo* 🎫 *Free.*

Palazzo Apostolico di Castel Gandolfo

CASTLE/PALACE | For centuries the Apostolic Palace of Castel Gandolfo was the summer retreat of popes, who kept the papal villa and extensive grounds completely private. Luckily for tourists, Pope Francis decided that he was too busy to use it and had it opened to the public. Inside you can view the Gallery of

Pontifical Portraits, ceremonial garments, and the imposing papal throne in the Sala degli Svizzeri. The private area of the palace with the pope's bedchamber, his library, study, and offices are also open to visitors. ✉ *Piazza della Libertà, Castel Gandolfo* 🎫 *06/69863111* ⊕ *www.museivaticani.va* 🎫 *€11* ⊘ *Closed Sun. and on Catholic holidays.*

★ Pontifical Gardens Villa Barberini

GARDEN | In 2016 Pope Francis opened the 136-acre pontifical estate and its glorious gardens to the public. Once rarely accessible, the pontifical gardens of Villa Barberini can now be visited in a 60-minute tour by an eco-friendly electric vehicle. The tour takes in the landscaped gardens as well as the archaeological remains of the palace of the Roman Emperor Domitian (dating back to the 1st century AD) and the home farm, which supplies the Vatican with fresh dairy products and eggs. Multilingual audio guides are included in the price. ✉ *Via Massimo D'Azeglio (entrance gate), Castel Gandolfo* ⊕ *www.museivaticani.va* 🎫 *€20 Villa Barberini gardens with minibus tour; €12 gardens only; €19 gardens and Apostolic Palace* ⊘ *Closed Sun.* 🚲 *Reservations required.*

Restaurants

Antico Ristorante Pagnanelli

$$$ | ITALIAN | One of the most refined restaurants in the Castelli Romani has been in the same family since 1882. Its dining-room windows open onto a breathtaking view across Lake Albano to the conical peak of Monte Cavo. **Known for:** famous wine cellar and wine museum in basement; elegant and cozy interior with an open fire in winter; homemade gnocchetti with clams and black truffles. 🟷 *Average main: €30* ✉ *Via Gramsci 4, Castel Gandolfo* 🎫 *06/9360004* ⊕ *www. pagnanelli.it.*

Hotels

Hotel Castelgandolfo

$ | **HOTEL** | Overlooking the volcanic crater of Lake Albano and a minute's walk from the Apostolic Palace, this intimate hotel in the heart of Castel Gandolfo makes an ideal retreat for romantics. **Pros:** convenient location; ideal for romantics; intimate. **Cons:** stunning terrace sometimes closed for private events; balconies are small and narrow; some rooms have street views. $ *Rooms from: €120* ⊠ *Via De' Zecchini 27, Castel Gandolfo* 🕾 *06/9360521* ⊕ *www.hotelcastelgandolfo.com* 🛏 *18 rooms* ❙⊙❙ *Free Breakfast.*

Ariccia

8 km (5 miles) southwest of Castel Gandolfo, 26 km (17 miles) south of Rome.

Ariccia is a gem of Baroque town planning. When Fabio Chigi, scion of the superwealthy banking family, became Pope Alexander VII, he commissioned Gian Lorenzo Bernini to redesign his country estate to make it worthy of his new station. Bernini restructured not only the existing 16th-century palace, but also the town gates, the main square, with its graceful loggias and twin fountains, and the round church of Santa Maria dell'Assunzione (the dome is said to be modeled on the Pantheon). The rest of the village was coiled around the apse of the church down into the valley below.

Ariccia's splendid heritage was largely forgotten in the 20th century, and yet it was once one of the highlights of every artist's and writer's Grand Tour. Corot, Ibsen, Turner, Longfellow, and Hans Christian Andersen all came to stay here.

GETTING HERE AND AROUND

For Ariccia, take the COTRAL bus from the Anagnina terminal of Metro Line A. Buses on the Albano–Genzano–Velletri line stop under the monumental bridge that spans the Ariccia Valley, where an elevator whisks you up to the main town square. If you take a train to Albano Laziale, you can proceed by bus to Ariccia or go on foot through the first town and over the bridge (it's just under 1½ km [1 mile]). If you're driving, follow the Via Appia Nuova to Albano and carry on to Ariccia.

Sights

★ Palazzo Chigi

CASTLE/PALACE | This is a true rarity: a Baroque residence whose original furniture, paintings, drapes, and decorations are largely intact. The Italian film director Luchino Visconti used the villa, which sits just at the end of Ariccia's famous bridge, for most of the interior scenes in his 1963 film *The Leopard*. The rooms of the *piano nobile* (main floor)—which, unlike Rome's Palazzo Chigi, does open to the public, but only on guided tours—contain intricately carved pieces of 17th-century furniture, as well as textiles and costumes from the 16th to the 20th century. The Room of Beauties is lined with paintings of the loveliest ladies of the day, and the Nuns' Room showcases portraits of 10 Chigi sisters, all of whom took the veil. You can get a close look at Le Stanze del Cardinale (Cardinal's Rooms), the suites occupied by the pleasure-loving Cardinal Flavio Chigi, with a guide on most days. ⊠ *Piazza di Corte 14, Ariccia* 🕾 *06/9330053* 🛅 *€19 full villa tour (when possible), €8 piano nobile, €6 Cardinal's Rooms, €6 Baroque Museum, €6 park* 🕙 *Palazzo closed Mon. Park closed Oct.–Mar.*

Santa Maria Assunta in Cielo (Church of the Assumption)

CHURCH | Directly across from Palazzo Chigi is the Church of the Assumption, with its distinctive blue dome and round shape designed by none other than Gian Lorenzo Bernini. The artistic architect had his best students execute most of the work of building and decorating the Pantheon-inspired church, creating porticoes

The Monumental Bridge connects Ariccia to Albano and offers beautiful views of Palazzo Chigi and Santa Maria Assunta.

outside and an intricately plastered cupola inside, which steals the show in the otherwise simple interior. ✉ *Piazza di Corte, Ariccia* 🌐 *www.chiesediariccia.it.*

🍴 Restaurants

A visit to Ariccia isn't complete without tasting the local gastronomic specialty: porchetta, a delicious roast whole pig stuffed with herbs, that is best with a side of local Romanella wine. The shops on the Piazza di Corte will make up a sandwich for you, or you can do what the Romans do: head for one of the *fraschetta* (a casual, boisterous countryside restaurant) wine cellars, which also serve cheese, cold cuts, pickled vegetables, olives, and sometimes a plate of pasta. Pass Palazzo Chigi and turn left under the arch to find several in a long row on the other side of the street. Take your pick and ask for a seat on a wooden bench at a trestle table covered with simple white paper; be ready to make friends and maybe join in a sing-along.

L'Aricciarola

$ | ITALIAN | FAMILY | This fraschetta around the corner from Palazzo Chigi is great for people-watching, which you can do while enjoying a platter of cold cuts and mixed cheeses, washed down with a carafe of local Castelli wine. Order your own appetizers and slices of porchetta at the counter near the door, snag a table on the patio, flag down a waiter if you want to order pasta, and then settle into the rustic setting surrounded by Roman families who've come to enjoy the local food. **Known for:** very casual and friendly atmosphere; local cold cuts; classic porchetta. [$] *Average main: €12* ✉ *Via Borgo S. Rocco 9, Ariccia* ☎ *06/9334103* 🌐 *osterialaricciarola.it* 🕒 *Closed Mon. and 2 wks in Jan.*

Nemi

8 km (5 miles) east of Ariccia, 34 km (21 miles) south of Rome.

A bronze statue of Diana the Huntress greets you at the entrance to Nemi, the smallest and prettiest village of the Castelli Romani. It's perched on a spur of rock 600 feet above the little oval-shaped lake of the same name, which is formed from a volcanic crater. Nemi has an eagle's-nest view over the rolling Roman countryside as far as the coast, some 18 km (11 miles) away. The one main street, Corso Vittorio Emanuele, takes you the quaint Piazza Umberto I, lined with outdoor cafés serving desserts made with the town's famous tiny wild strawberries which are harvested from the woodlands that line the crater bowl.

GETTING HERE AND AROUND

Nemi is difficult to get to unless you come by car. COTRAL buses from the Anagnina station on Metro Line A go to the town of Genzano, where a local bus travels to Nemi every two hours. If the times aren't convenient, you can take a taxi or walk the 5 km (3 miles) around Lake Nemi. By car, take the panoramic route known as the Via dei Laghi (Road of the Lakes). Follow the Appia Nuova from St. John Lateran and branch off on the well-signposted route after Ciampino airport. Follow the Via dei Laghi toward Velletri until you see signs for Nemi.

Sights

Museo delle Navi Romane (*Roman Ship Museum*)
HISTORY MUSEUM | In the 1930s, the Italian government drained Nemi's lake to recover two magnificent ceremonial ships, loaded with sculptures, bronzes, and art treasures, that were submerged for 2,000 years. The Museo delle Navi Romane, on the lakeshore, was built to house the ships, but they were burned during World War II. Inside are scale models and finds from the Bronze Age Diana sanctuary and the area nearby. There's also a colossal statue of the infamous and extravagant Roman emperor Caligula, who had the massive barges built on the pretty lake. Italian police once snatched the marble sculpture back from tomb robbers just as they were about to smuggle it out of the country. ✉ *Via del Tempio di Diana 13, Nemi* ☎ *06/9398040* 🌐 *www.beniculturali.it* 🎫 *€4* 🕒 *Closed Mon.*

🍴 Restaurants

★ La Fiocina
$$ | ITALIAN | With its privileged position on the tranquil shores of Lake Nemi next to the Roman Ship Museum, La Fiocina has been serving local specialties, including lake fish and homemade gnocchi with wild boar sauce, for more than 50 years. The dining room is elegant and welcoming, and there's a terrace on which you can dine alfresco, overlooking the small lakeside garden. **Known for:** tiny wild Nemi strawberries; garden terrace with lake views; coregone lake fish. [$] *Average main: €15* ✉ *Via delle Navi di Tiberio 9, Nemi* ☎ *06/9391120* 🕒 *Closed Mon. and Tues.*

Locanda Specchio di Diana
$ | ITALIAN | Halfway down the main street on the left is the town's most historic inn, where Byron stayed when visiting the area. Today it is a wine bar and café on street level, and a full restaurant on the second floor with marvelous views over the lake. **■ TIP→ It also has several small apartments and rooms available to rent by the night in the village center.** **Known for:** local Nemi strawberries when in season; spectacular lake views; fettuccine al sugo di lepre (hare sauce). [$] *Average main: €14* ✉ *Corso Vittorio Emanuele 13, Nemi* ☎ *06/9368714* 🌐 *www.albergodiffusonemi.it.*

Chapter 5

VENICE

Updated by
Liz Humphreys,
Nick Bruno and
Erla Zwingle

👁 **Sights**   🍴 **Restaurants**   🛏 **Hotels**   🛍 **Shopping**   🍸 **Nightlife**

★★★★★   ★★★★☆   ★★★★★   ★★★☆☆   ★★☆☆☆

WELCOME TO VENICE

TOP REASONS TO GO

★ **Cruising the Grand Canal:** The beauty of its palaces, enhanced by the play of light on the water, make a trip down Venice's "Main Street" unforgettable.

★ **Basilica di San Marco:** Don't miss the gorgeous mosaics inside—they're worth standing in line for.

★ **Santa Maria Gloriosa dei Frari:** Its austere, cavernous interior houses Titian's *Assumption*—one of the world's most beautiful altarpieces—plus several other spectacular art treasures.

★ **Gallerie dell'Accademia:** Legendary masterpieces of Venetian painting will overwhelm you in this fabled museum.

★ **Sipping wine and snacking at a bacaro:** For a sample of tasty local snacks and excellent Veneto wines in a uniquely Venetian setting, head for one of the city's many wine bars.

1 San Marco. The neighborhood at the center of Venice is filled with fashion boutiques, art galleries, and grand hotels.

2 Dorsoduro. This graceful residential area is home to renowned art galleries; the Campo Santa Margherita is a lively student hangout.

3 San Polo and Santa Croce. These bustling *sestieri* (districts) have all sorts of shops, several major churches, and the Rialto fish and produce markets.

4 Cannaregio. This sestiere has some of the sunniest open-air canalside walks in town; the Jewish Ghetto has a fascinating history.

5 Castello. With its gardens, park, and narrow, winding walkways, it's the sestiere least influenced by Venice's tourist culture.

6 San Giorgio Maggiore and the Giudecca. San Giorgio is graced with its magnificent namesake church, and the Giudecca has wonderful views of Venice.

7 Islands of the Lagoon. Each island in Venice's northern lagoon has its own allure.

EATING AND DRINKING WELL IN VENICE

The catchword in Venetian restaurants is "fish." How do you learn about the catch of the day? A visit to the Rialto's *pescheria* (fish market) is more instructive than any book, and when you're dining at a well-regarded restaurant, ask for a recommendation.

Traditionally, fish is served with a bit of salt, maybe some chopped parsley, and a drizzle of olive oil—no lemon; lemon masks the flavor. Ask for an entire wild-caught fish; it's much more expensive than its farmed cousin, but certainly worth it. Antipasto may be prosciutto *di San Daniele* (from the Veneto region) or *sarde in saor* (fresh panfried sardines marinated with onions, raisins, and pine nuts). Risotto, cooked with shellfish or veggies, is a great first course. Pasta? Enjoy it with seafood: this is *not* the place to order spaghetti with tomato sauce. Other pillars of regional cooking include *pasta e fagioli* (thick bean soup with pasta); polenta, often with *fegato alla veneziana* (liver with onion); and that dessert invented in the Veneto, tiramisu.

GOING BACARO

You can sample regional wines and scrumptious *cicheti* (small snacks) in *bacari* (wine bars), a great Venetian tradition. Crostini and *polpette* (meat, fish, or vegetable croquettes) are popular cicheti, as are small sandwiches, seafood salads, *baccalà mantecato* (creamy, whipped salt cod), and toothpick-speared items like roasted peppers, marinated artichokes, and mozzarella balls.

SEAFOOD

Granseola (crab), *moeche* (tiny, locally caught soft-shell crabs), sweet *canoce* (mantis shrimp), *capelunghe* (razor clams), calamari, and *seppie* or *seppioline* (cuttlefish) are all prominently featured, as well as *rombo* (turbot), *branzino* (sea bass), *San Pietro* (John Dory), *sogliola* (sole), *orate* (gilthead bream), and *triglia* (mullet). Trademark dishes include sarde in saor, *frittura mista* (tempura-like fried fish and vegetables), and baccalà mantecato.

RISOTTO, PASTA, POLENTA

As a first course, Venetians favor the creamy rice dish risotto *all'onda* ("undulating," as opposed to firm), prepared with vegetables or shellfish. When pasta is served, it's generally accompanied by seafood sauces, too: *pasticcio di pesce* is lasagna-type pasta baked with fish, and *bigoli* is a strictly local whole-wheat pasta shaped like thick spaghetti, usually served *in salsa* (an anchovy-onion sauce with a dash of cinnamon), or with *nero di seppia* (cuttlefish-ink sauce). *Pasta e fagioli* is another classic first course, and polenta is a staple—served creamy or fried in wedges, generally as an accompaniment to stews or *seppie in nero* (cuttlefish in black ink).

VEGETABLES

The larger islands of the lagoon are known for their legendary vegetables, such as the Sant'Erasmo *castraure*, sinfully expensive but heavenly tiny white artichokes that appear for a few days in spring. Spring treats include the fat white asparagus from neighboring Bassano or Verona, and artichoke bottoms (*fondi*), usually sautéed with olive oil, parsley, and garlic. From December to March the prized local radicchio *di Treviso* is grilled and frequently served with a bit of melted Taleggio cheese from Lombardy. Fall brings small wild mushrooms called *chiodini* and *zucca di Mantova*, a yellow squash with a gray-green rind used in soups, puddings, and ravioli stuffing.

SWEETS

Tiramisu lovers will have ample opportunity to sample this creamy delight made from ladyfingers soaked in espresso and rum or brandy and covered with mascarpone cream and cinnamon. Gelato, *sgroppino* (prosecco, vodka, and lemon sorbet), and *semifreddo* (soft homemade ice cream) are other sweets frequently seen on Venetian menus, as are almond cakes and dry cookies served with dessert wine. Try *focaccia veneziana,* a sweet raised cake made in the late fall and winter.

Venice is often called La Serenissima, or "the most serene," a reference to the majesty, wisdom, and power of this city that was for centuries a leader in trade between Europe and Asia and a major center of European culture. Built on water by people who saw the sea as defender and ally, and who constantly invested in its splendor with magnificent architectural projects, Venice is a city unlike any other.

No matter how often you've seen it in photos and films, the real thing is more dreamlike than you could ever imagine. Its most notable landmarks, the Basilica di San Marco and the Palazzo Ducale, are exotic mixes of Byzantine, Romanesque, Gothic, and Renaissance styles, reflecting Venice's ties with the rest of Italy and with Constantinople to the east. Shimmering sunlight and silvery mist soften every perspective here; it's easy to understand how the city became renowned in the Renaissance for its artists' use of color. It's full of secrets, inexpressibly romantic, and frequently given over to pure, sensuous enjoyment.

You'll see Venetians going about their daily affairs in vaporetti, in the *campi* (squares), and along the *calli* (narrow streets). Despite their many challenges (including more frequent flooding and overcrowding), they are proud of their city and its history and are still quite helpful to those who show proper respect for Venice and its way of life.

Planning

Making the Most of Your Time

The hordes of tourists here are legendary, especially in spring and fall but during other seasons too—there's really no "off-season" in Venice. Unfortunately, tales of impassable tourist-packed streets and endless queues to get into the Basilica di San Marco are not exaggerated. A little bit of planning, however, will help you avoid the worst of the crowds.

Most tourists do little more than take the vaporetto down the Grand Canal to Piazza San Marco, see the piazza and the basilica, and walk up to the Rialto and back to the station. You'll want to visit these areas, too, but do so in the early morning, before most tourists have finished their breakfast cappuccinos.

Because many tourists are other Italians who come for a weekend outing, you can further decrease your competition for Venice's pleasures by choosing to visit the city on weekdays.

Away from San Marco and the Rialto, the streets and quays of Venice's beautiful medieval and Renaissance residential districts receive only a moderate amount of traffic. Besides the Grand Canal and the Piazza San Marco, and perhaps Torcello, the other historically and artistically important sites are seldom overcrowded. Even on weekends you probably won't have to queue up for the Gallerie dell'Accademia.

Getting Oriented

Venice proper is quite compact, and you should be able to walk across it in a couple of hours, even counting a few minutes for getting lost. Vaporetti will save wear and tear on tired feet, but won't always save you much time.

Venice is divided into six sestieri: Cannaregio, Castello, Dorsoduro, San Marco, San Polo, and Santa Croce. More sedate outer islands float around them—San Giorgio Maggiore and the Giudecca just to the south; beyond them the Lido, the barrier island; and to the north, Murano, Burano, and Torcello.

Getting Here and Around

AIR
CONTACT Aeroporto Marco Polo.
☎ 041/2609260 ⊕ www.veniceairport.it.

LAND TRANSFERS
CONTACT ATVO. ☎ 0421/5944 ⊕ www.atvo.it.

WATER TRANSFERS
From Marco Polo terminal, it's a mostly covered seven-minute walk to the dock where boats depart for Venice's historic center. The ride is in a closed boat so you

won't get much of a view; plus, it's more expensive and generally slower than the bus to Piazzale Roma (unless your hotel is near a boat station).

CONTACT Alilaguna. ☎ 041/2401701 ⊕ www.alilaguna.it.

CAR
Venice is at the end of the SR11, just off the east–west A4 autostrada. There are no cars in Venice; if possible, return your rental when you arrive.

A warning: don't be waylaid by illegal touts, often wearing fake uniforms, who try to flag you down and offer to arrange parking and hotels; use one of the established garages, mainly clustered at Piazzale Roma. Consider reserving a space in advance. The **Autorimessa Comunale** (☎ 041/2722394) costs €26 for 24 hours. **Garage San Marco** (☎ 041/5232213) costs €15 from 5 pm to 5 am, and €39 for 24 hours with online reservations. For brief stays, opt for **Parcheggio Sant'Andrea** (☎ 041/2722384), where up to two hours costs €7. On its own island, **Isola del Tronchetto** (☎ 041/5207555) charges €22 for 24 hours. Watch for signs coming over the bridge—you turn right just before Piazzale Roma.

Many hotels and the casino have guest discounts with the San Marco or Tronchetto garages. A cheaper, and perfectly convenient, alternative is to park in Mestre, on the mainland, and take a train (10 minutes, €1) or bus into Venice. The garage across from the station and the Bus 2 stop costs €12 for up to 24 hours.

PUBLIC TRANSPORTATION
WATER BUSES
CONTACT ACTV. ☎ 041/041 041 ⊕ www.actv.it.

WATER TAXIS
A *motoscafo* isn't cheap: you'll spend about €70 for a short trip in town, €90 to the Lido, and €100 or more per hour to visit the outer islands. It is strongly suggested to book

through the **Consorzio Motoscafi Venezia** (📞 041/5222303 🌐 www.motoscafivenezia.com) to avoid an argument with your driver over prices. A water taxi can carry up to 10 passengers, with an additional charge of €10 per person for more than five people, so if you're traveling in a group, it may not be that much more expensive than a vaporetto.

TRAIN

Venice has rail connections with many major cities in Italy and Europe. Note that Venice's train station is **Venezia Santa Lucia,** not to be confused with Venezia Mestre, which is the mainland stop prior to arriving in the historic center. Some trains don't continue beyond the Mestre station; in such cases you can catch the next Venice-bound train. Get a ticket on the Trenitalia app or a paper ticket from the kiosk on the platform and validate it (in the yellow time-stamp machine) to avoid a fine.

Restaurants

Dining options in Venice range from ultra-high-end establishments, where jackets are required, to very casual eateries. Once staunchly traditional, many restaurants have revamped their dining rooms and their menus, creating dishes that blend classic elements with ingredients and methods less common to the region. Mid- and upper-range restaurants often offer innovative options as well as mainstays like sarde in saor and fegato alla veneziana.

Unfortunately, Venice also has its share of overpriced, mediocre eateries. Restaurants catering to tourists have little motivation to maintain quality since most diners are one-time patrons. You are better off at a restaurant frequented by locals, who are interested in the food, not the views. Avoid places with cajoling waiters outside, as well as those that don't display their prices or have showy tourist menus translated into a dozen

languages. For the same €15–€20 you'd spend at such places, you could do better at a bacaro making a meal of cicheti.

Prices in the dining reviews are the average cost of a main course at dinner, or, if dinner is not served, at lunch. Restaurant listings have been shortened. For full information, visit Fodors.com.

What it Costs in Euros			
$	$$	$$$	$$$$
AT DINNER			
under €15	€15–€24	€25–€35	over €35

Hotels

Venetian magic lingers when you retire for the night, whether you're staying in a grand hotel or budget *locanda* (inn). Hotels usually occupy very old buildings, often without elevators or lounge areas. It's not at all unusual for each room to be different, even on the same floor: windows overlooking charming canals and bleak alleyways are both common. Venice is one of the most popular destinations on Earth—so book your lodging as far in advance as possible.

In terms of location, the area in and around San Marco is the most crowded and expensive. Still convenient but more tranquil areas include Dorsoduro, Santa Croce, and Cannaregio (though the area around the train station can be hectic), or even Castello in the area beyond the Pietà church. Also take into consideration the proximity of a vaporetto stop, especially if you have heavy baggage. Regardless of where you stay, it's essential that you have detailed directions to your hotel: note not only its street address but also its sestiere as well as a nearby landmark or two. Even if you arrive by water taxi, you may still have a bit of a walk.

Prices in the reviews are the lowest cost of a standard double room in high season. Hotel reviews have been shortened. For full information, visit Fodors.com.

What it Costs in Euros			
$	$$	$$$	$$$$
LODGING FOR TWO			
under €125	€125– €200	€201– €300	over €300

Nightlife

Nightlife offerings in Venice are, even by rather sedate standards, fairly tame. Most bars must close by midnight, especially those that offer outdoor seating. Piazza San Marco is a popular meeting place in nice weather, when the cafés stay open relatively late and all seem to compete to offer the best live music. The younger crowd, Venetians and visitors alike, tend to gravitate toward the area around the Ponte di Rialto, with Campi San Bartolomeo and San Luca on one side and Campo Rialto Nuovo on the other. Especially popular with university students and young people from the mainland are the bars around Campo Santa Margherita.

Performing Arts

Visit ⊕ www.agendavenezia.org for a preview of musical, artistic, and sporting events. Venezia News (VENews), available at newsstands, has similar information but also includes in-depth articles about noteworthy events. The tourist office publishes a handy, free quarterly Calendar in Italian and English, listing daily events and current museum and venue hours. Venezia da Vivere (⊕ www. veneziadavivere.com/en) is a seasonal guide listing cool cultural happenings and places. And don't ignore the posters you see plastered on the walls as you walk—often they contain the most up-to-date information you can find.

■ TIP→ **For more information on festivals in Venice, see On the Calendar in Travel Smart.**

CARNEVALE

Although Carnevale has traditionally been associated with the time leading up to the Roman Catholic period of Lent, it originally started out as a principally secular annual period of partying and feasting to celebrate Venice's victory over Ulrich II, Patriarch of Aquileia, in 1162. To commemorate the annual tribute Ulrich was forced to pay, a bull and 12 pigs were slaughtered in Piazza San Marco each year on the day before Lent. Since then, the city has marked the days preceding Quaresima (Lent) with abundant feasting and wild celebrations. The word carnevale is derived from the words carne (meat) and levare (to remove), as eating meat was restricted during Lent. The use of masks for Carnevale was first mentioned in 1268, and its direct association with Lent was not made until the end of the 13th century.

Venice earned its international reputation as the "city of Carnevale" in the 18th century, when partying would begin several months before Lent and the city seemed to be one continuous masquerade. During this time, income from tourists became a major source of funds in La Serenissima's coffers. With the Republic's fall in 1797, Carnevale was prohibited by the French and the Austrians. From Italian reunification in 1866 until the fall of Fascism in the 1940s, the event was alternately allowed or banned, depending on the government's stance.

It was revived for good in the 1970s, when residents began taking to the calli and campi in their own impromptu celebrations. It didn't take long for the tourist industry to embrace Carnevale as a means to stimulate business in low season. And their faith is well placed: each year over the 10- to 12-day Carnevale period (ending on the Tuesday before Ash Wednesday), more than a half-million people attend concerts, theater and street performances, masquerade balls, historical processions, fashion shows, and contests. Since 2008 Carnevale has been organized by **Venezia Marketing & Eventi** (⊕ *www.carnevale.venezia.it*). *A Guest in Venice* is also a complete guide to public and private Carnevale festivities. Stop by the **tourist office** (☎ *041/2424* ⊕ *www.veneziaunica.it*) or the Venice Pavilion for information, but be aware they can be mobbed. If you're not planning on joining in the revelry, you'd be wise to choose another time to visit Venice. Crowds throng the streets (which become one-way, with police directing foot traffic), bridges are designated "no-stopping" zones to avoid gridlock, and prices skyrocket.

Shopping

Alluring shops abound in Venice. You'll find countless vendors of such trademark wares as glass, lace, and high-end textiles. The authenticity of some goods can be suspect, but they're often pleasing to the eye, regardless of origin. You will also find interesting craft and art studios with high-quality, one-of-a-kind articles. Antiques, especially antique Venetian glass, are almost invariably cheaper outside of Venice, because Venetians are ready to pay high prices for their own heritage.

The San Marco area is full of shops and couture boutiques, such as Armani, Missoni, Valentino, Fendi, and Versace. Leading from Piazza San Marco, you'll find some of Venice's busiest shopping streets—Le Mercerie, the Frezzeria, Calle dei Fabbri, and Calle Larga XXII Marzo. Other good shopping areas surround Calle del Teatro and Campi San Salvador, Manin, San Fantin, and San Bartolomeo. You can find somewhat less expensive, more varied, and more imaginative

shops between the Ponte di Rialto and San Polo and in Santa Croce, and art galleries in Dorsoduro from the Salute to the Accademia. Regular store hours are usually 9 to 12:30 and 3:30 or 4 to 7:30; some stores close Saturday afternoon or Monday morning.

Passes and Discounts

Avoid lines and hassle with the online **Venezia Unica City Pass** (⊕ *www.veneziaunica.it*). This all-in-one pass can be used for public transportation and entry to museums, churches, and other attractions; you only pay for the services you wish to add. You'll receive an email with the pass, which you can show for entry at sights, though you'll still need to physically collect your transportation pass at an ACTV automatic ticket machine or ticket point located around the city.

Fifteen of Venice's most significant churches covered by the Venezia Unica City Pass are part of the **Chorus Foundation** umbrella group (☎ *041/2750462* ⊕ *www.chorusvenezia.org*), which coordinates their administration, hours, and admission fees. Churches in this group are open to visitors all day except Sunday morning. Single church entry costs €3; you have a year to visit all 15 with the €12 Chorus Pass, which you can get at any participating church or online.

The Museum Pass (€35) from **Musei Civici** (☎ *041/2405211* ⊕ *www.visitmuve.it/en/tickets*) includes single entry to 12 Venice city museums for six months.

Tours

Venice has a variety of tours with expert guides; just be sure to choose a guide that's authorized if you book a private tour. Some excursions also include a boat tour as a portion of a longer walking tour.

PRIVATE TOURS
A Guide in Venice
GUIDED TOURS | This popular company offers a wide variety of innovative, entertaining, and informative themed tours—including master artisan, art, and architecture tours—for groups of up to eight people. Individual tours are also available and generally last two to three hours. The guide fee is €75 per hour, which does not include admissions or transportation fees. Small group tours running May–October are also available at €62.50 per person. ☎ *0348/5927974* ⊕ *www.aguideinvenice.com.*

See Venice
GUIDED TOURS | Luisella Romeo is a delightful guide capable of bringing to life even the most convoluted aspects of Venice's art and history. She can customize tours depending on guests' areas of interest, including Murano and glass art, music in Venice, and photography tours. ☎ *0349/0848303* ⊕ *www.seevenice.it.*

Walks Inside Venice
GUIDED TOURS | For a host of particularly creative group and private tours—from history to art to gastronomy—check out Walks Inside Venice. The maximum group size is six, and tour guides include people with advanced university degrees and published authors. ☎ *0347/2530560, 0335/5229714* ⊕ *www.walksinside-venice.com.*

Visitor Information

The multilingual staff of the **Venice tourism office** (☎ *041/2424* ⊕ *www.veneziaunica.it*) can provide directions and up-to-the-minute information. Branches can be found at Marco Polo Airport; the Venezia Santa Lucia train station; Garage Comunale, on Piazzale Roma; and at Piazza San Marco near Museo Correr at the southwest corner. The train station branch is open daily 7–9; other branches have similar hours.

San Marco

Extending from Piazza San Marco (St. Mark's Square) to the Ponte di Rialto, this sestiere is the historical and commercial heart of Venice. Restaurants in its eponymous square—the only one in Venice given full stature as a "piazza" and, hence, often referred to simply as "the Piazza"—heave with tourists, but enjoying an *aperitivo* here is an unforgettable experience.

This sestiere is also graced with some of Venice's loveliest churches, best-endowed museums, and finest hotels (often with Grand Canal views). In addition, it's the city's main shopping district. Some of the famous Venetian glass producers from Murano have boutiques in San Marco, as do many Italian designers. Its mazes of streets are also lined with shops that sell elegantly wrought jewelry among other items.

TIMING
You can easily spend several days seeing the historical and artistic monuments in and around Piazza San Marco alone, but at a bare minimum, plan on at least an hour for the basilica and its wonderful mosaics. Add on another half hour if you want to see its Pala d'Oro, Galleria, and Museo di San Marco. You'll want at least an hour to appreciate the Palazzo Ducale. Leave another hour for the Museo Correr, through which you also enter the archaeological museum and the Libreria Sansoviniana. If you choose to simply take in the piazza itself from a café table at an establishment with an orchestra, keep in mind there will be an additional charge for the music.

Continued on page 205

THE BASILICA DI SAN MARCO
Venice's Cultural Mosaic

Standing at the heart of Venice, the spectacular Basilica di San Marco has been, for about a millennium, the city's religious center. Like other great churches—and even more so—it's also an expression of worldly accomplishments and aspirations. As you take in the shimmering mosaics and elaborate ornamentation, you begin to grasp the pivotal role Venice has played for centuries in European culture.

Above, 17th century stamp of the winged lion, symbol of Venice

Below, facade of Basilica di San Marco

ORIGINS. The basilica began as a political statement. The original church, consecrated in 832, was built to house the body of St. Mark. According to legend, the saint's body had been stolen from Alexandria by two Venetians in 828. The whole enterprise was intended to establish Venice's prominence over neighboring Aquileia, a city with a glorious Roman past that claimed to have been founded by St. Mark.

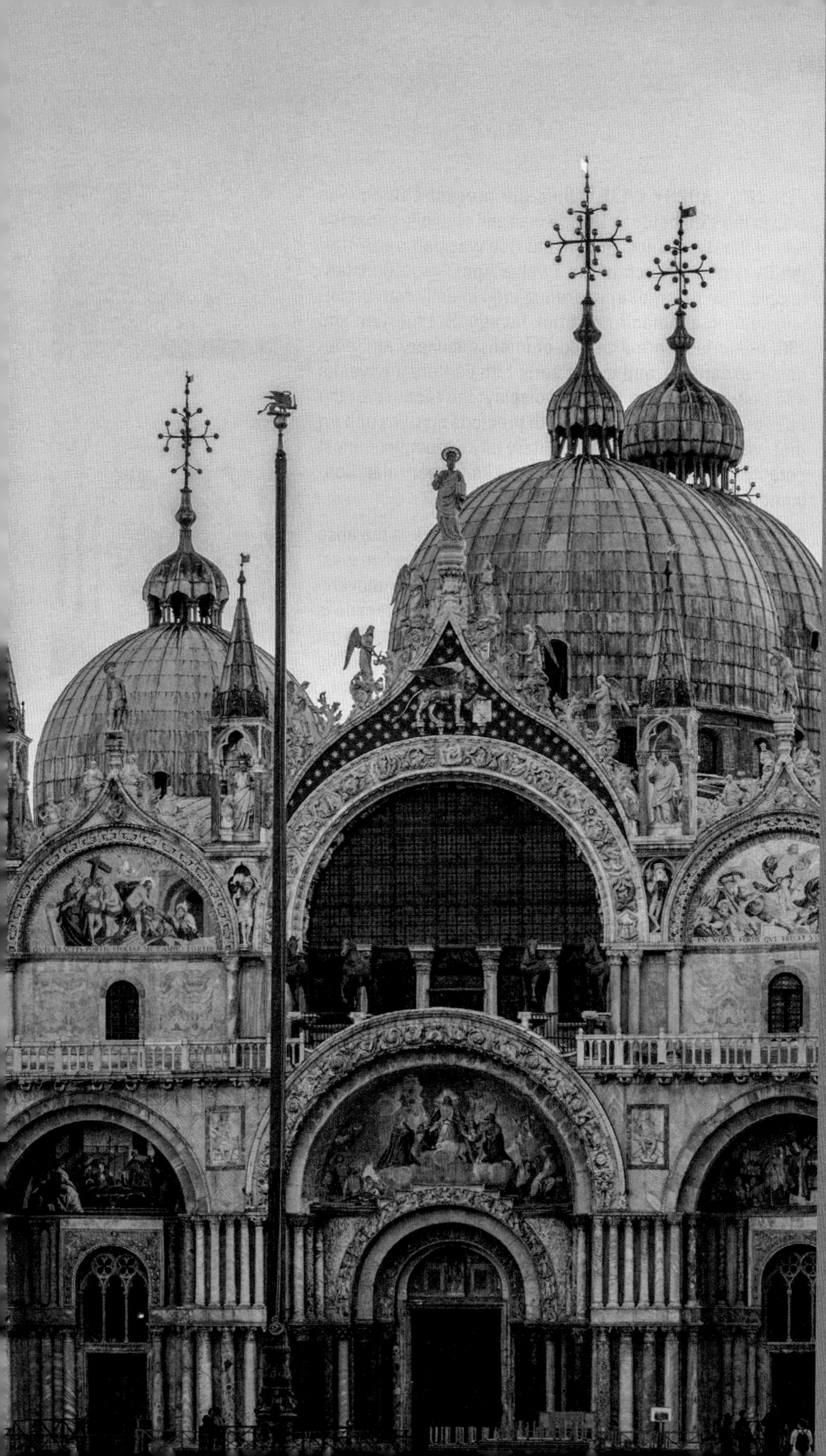

THE BASILICA'S FACADES

VENICE'S TROPHY CASE. When the present church was built in the 11th century, Venice was still officially under the rule of the Byzantium, and the basilica was patterned after the Byzantine Church of the Twelve Apostles in Constantinople. The external appearance was initially rather simple, bearing an unadorned brick facade. But the 12th and 13th centuries were a period of intense military and economic expansion, and by the early 13th century the wealth and power of Venice were on display: the facades of the basilica were being adorned with precious marbles and art that were trophies from the military city's triumphs—most notably the conquest and sacking ot its former ruler, Constantinople, in 1204.

St. Mark and lion, main portal

PORTAL OF SANT ALIPIO. Be sure to take a look at the apse of the portal of Sant Alipio, the farthest north of the five west facade portals. It bears a 13th-century mosaic showing how the church looked at that time. Note how the facade is already decorated with marble columns and the famous gilt bronze ancient Roman horses, taken by the Venetians during the sack of Constantinople.

Main portal entrance

The portal of Sant Alipio is typical of many parts of the basilica in that it contains elements that far predate the construction of the church. The base of the pointed arch beneath the mosaic, for example, dates from the 5th century, and the Byzantine capitals of the precious marble columns, as well as the window screens, are mostly from the 7th century. The use of these elements, most of them pillaged from raids and conquests, testifies to Venetian daring and power, and they create the illusion of an ancient heritage that Venice itself lacked and looked upon with envy.

Detail of bas-relief

Portal of Sant Alipio with 13th-century mosaic of the basilica

Bronze horses, facade

The details of lunette

THE MAIN PORTAL. By the time these ancient trophies were put into place, Venice had both the wealth and the talent to create its own, new decoration. On the inner arches of the main portal, look for the beautiful and fascinating Roman-esque and early Gothic allegorical, biblical, and zodiac bas-reliefs.

THE TETRARCHS. The Christian relevance of some of the trophies on the basilica is scant. For a fine example of pride over piety, take a look at the fourth-century group of four soldiers in red porphyry on the corner of the south facade. It's certain that this was taken from Constanti-nople, because a missing fragment of one of the figures' feet can still be found attached to a building in Istanbul. The current interpretation is that they are the Tetrarchs, colleagues of the Emperor Diocletian, having little if any religious significance.

The incorporation of art from many different cultures into Venice's most important building is a sign of imperial tri-umph, but it also indicates an embrace of other cultures that's a fundamental part of Venetian character. (Think of Marco Polo, who was on his way to China only a few years after the first phase of decoration of the facade of the basil-ica began.) Venice remains, even today, arguably the most tolerant and cosmopolitan city in Italy.

Statues of tetrarchs

TREASURES INSIDE THE BASILICA

THE MOSAICS. The glory of the basilica is its brilliant, floor-to-ceiling mosaics, especially those dating from the medieval period.

The mosaics of the atrium, or porch, represent the Old Testament, while those of the interior show the stories of the Gospel and saints, ending with the image of Christ in Glory (a Renaissance copy) in the apse. Many of the mosaics of the New Testament scenes are actually somewhat earlier (mid-12th century), or contemporaneous with the 13th-century mosaics of the atrium. You wouldn't know it from the style: the figures of the atrium still bear the late classical character of the early Christian manuscript, brought to Venice after the sack of Constantinople, that inspired them. In the mosaics of the church proper, notice the flowing lines, elongated figures, and stern expressions, all characteristics of high Byzantine art. Look especially for the beautiful 12th-century mosaics in the dome of the Pentecost, the first dome in the nave of the basilica as you enter the main part of the church, and for the 12th-century mosaics in the dome of the Ascension, considered the masterpiece of the Venetian school.

The choir

Above, detail of the nave
Below, detail of mosaic

The centerpiece of the basilica is, naturally, **❶ THE SANTUARIO (SANCTUARY)**, the main altar built over the tomb of St. Mark. Its green marble canopy, lifted high on carved alabaster columns, is another trophy dating from the fourth century. Perhaps even more impressive is the **❷ PALA D'ORO**, a dazzling gilt silver screen encrusted with 1,927 precious gems and 255 enameled panels. Originally commissioned (976–978) in Constantinople, it was enlarged and embellished over four centuries by master craftsmen and wealthy merchants.

❸ THE TESORO (TREASURY), part of the Museo di San Marco and entered from the right transept, contains treasures carried home from conquests abroad. Climb the stairway to the Galleria and the Museo di San Marco for the best overview of the basilica's interior. From here you can step out for a sweeping panorama of Piazza San Marco and across the lagoon to San Giorgio. The highlight is a close-up view of the original gilt bronze horses that were once on the outer gallery.

Right, detail of ceiling mosaics of the atrium

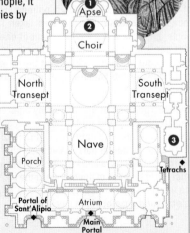

Did You Know?

The mosaics of the basilica are illuminated one hour a day, from 11:30 to 12:30. Visit then to see them at their most magnificent.

PLANNING YOUR VISIT

Be aware that guards at the basilica door turn away anyone with bare shoulders, midriff, or knees: no shorts, short skirts, or tank tops are allowed. Free guided tours in English were suspended during the COVID pandemic; call to get more information about whether they've started again.

■ TIP→ To skip the line at the basilica entrance, reserve your arrival—at no extra cost—on the basilica Web site (choose "Booking" on the homepage). If you have luggage, you'll need to store it at the nearby bag facility at Piazza San Marco 315 (from €1.99 per locker).

✉ Piazza San Marco

☎ 041/2708318 (9:30 am -3:30 pm weekdays)

🌐 www.basilicasan-marco.it

🎟 Basilica €3, Sanctuary and Pala d'Oro €5, Museum €7, Bell Tower €10

🕐 Mon.-Sat. 9:30 am-5:15 pm, Sun. 2 pm-5:15 pm (museum and bell tower open from 9:30 am); last admission 4:45 pm

Above, Piazza San Marco
Left, Crowds gather around the basilica

◉ Sights

★ Basilica di San Marco

(*St. Mark's Basilica*)

CHURCH | The Basilica di San Marco is not only the religious center of a great city, but also an expression of the political, intellectual, and economic aspiration and accomplishments of a place that, for centuries, was at the forefront of European culture. It is a monument not just to the glory of God, but also to the glory of Venice. The basilica was the doges' personal chapel, linking its religious function to the political life of the city, and was endowed with all the riches the Republic's admirals and merchants could carry off from the Orient (as the Byzantine Empire was then known), earning it the nickname "Chiesa d'Oro" (Golden Church). When the present church was begun in the 11th century, rare colored marbles and gold-leaf mosaics were used in its decoration. The 12th and 13th centuries were a period of intense military expansion, and by the early 13th century, the facades began to bear testimony to Venice's conquests, including gilt-bronze ancient Roman horses taken from Constantinople in 1204.

The glory of the basilica is, of course, its medieval mosaic work; about 30% of the mosaics survive in something close to their original form. The earliest date from the late 12th century, but the great majority date from the 13th century. The taking of Constantinople in 1204 was a deciding moment for the mosaic decoration of the basilica. Large amounts of mosaic material were brought in, and a Venetian school of mosaic decoration began to develop. Moreover, a 4th- or 5th-century treasure—the Cotton Genesis, the earliest illustrated Bible—was brought from Constantinople and supplied the designs for the exquisite mosaics of the Creation and the stories of Abraham, Joseph, and Moses that adorn the narthex (entrance hall). They are among the most beautiful and best preserved in all the basilica.

Remember that this is a sacred place: guards may deny admission to people in shorts, sleeveless dresses, and tank tops. ⊠ *Piazza San Marco, San Marco 328, San Marco* ☎ *041/2708311* ⊕ *www.basilicasanmarco.it* ☑ *Basilica €3, sanctuary and Pala d'Oro €5, museum €7* Ⓜ *Vaporetto: Zaccaria, Vallaresso.*

Campanile di San Marco (*St. Mark's Bell Tower*)

VIEWPOINT | Construction of Venice's famous brick bell tower (325 feet tall, plus the angel) began in the 9th century; it took on its present form in 1514. During the 15th century, the tower was used as a place of punishment: immoral clerics were suspended in wooden cages from the tower, some forced to subsist on bread and water for as long as a year; others were left to starve. In 1902, the tower unexpectedly collapsed, taking with it Jacopo Sansovino's marble loggia (1537–49) at its base. The largest original bell, called the Marangona, survived. The crushed loggia was promptly reconstructed, and the new tower, rebuilt to the old plan, reopened in 1912. Today, on a clear day the stunning view includes the Lido, the lagoon, and the mainland as far as the Alps, but strangely enough, none of the myriad canals that snake through the city. ⊠ *Piazza San Marco, San Marco* ☎ *041/2708311* ⊕ *www.basilicasanmarco.it* ☑ *€10* Ⓜ *Vaporetto: San Zaccaria, Vallaresso.*

★ Museo Correr

HISTORY MUSEUM | This museum of Venetian art and history contains an important sculpture collection by Antonio Canova and important paintings by Giovanni Bellini, Vittore Carpaccio (Carpaccio's famous painting of the Venetian courtesans is here), and other major local painters. There are nine sumptuously decorated Imperial Rooms, where the Empress of Austria once stayed, and several rooms convey the city's proud naval history through highly descriptive paintings and numerous maritime objects, including

San Marco

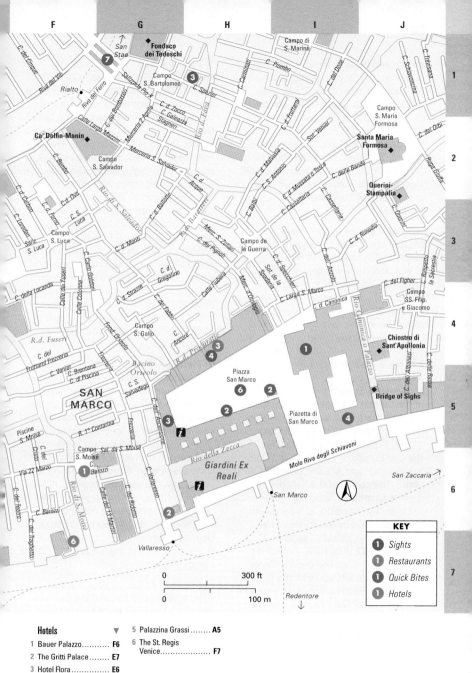

ships' cannons and some surprisingly large iron mast-top navigation lights. ✉ *Piazza San Marco 52, Ala Napoleonica, opposite Basilica, San Marco* ☎ *041/2405211* ⊕ *correr.visitmuve.it* 🎫 *Museums of San Marco Pass €25, includes Museo Correr, Museo Archeologico, Biblioteca Nazionale Marciana, and Palazzo Ducale. Museum Pass €36, includes all four museums plus eight civic museums* Ⓜ *Vaporetto: San Zaccaria, Vallaresso.*

★ **Palazzo Ducale** (*Doge's Palace*)

CASTLE/PALACE | Rising majestically above Piazzetta San Marco, this Gothic fantasia of pink-and-white marble—the doges' residence from the 10th century and the central administrative center of the Venetian Republic—is a majestic expression of Venetian prosperity and power. Upon entering, you'll find yourself in an immense courtyard with some of the first evidence of Venice's Renaissance architecture, including Antonio Rizzo's 15th-century Scala dei Giganti (Stairway of the Giants). The palace's sumptuous chambers have walls and ceilings covered with works by Venice's greatest artists. In the Anticollegio you'll find *The Rape of Europa* by Veronese and Tintoretto's *Bacchus and Ariadne Crowned by Venus*. The ceiling of the Sala del Senato (Senate Chamber), featuring *The Triumph of Venice* by Tintoretto, is magnificent, but it's dwarfed by his masterpiece *Paradise* in the Sala del Maggiore Consiglio (Great Council Hall), the world's largest oil painting. The popular Secret Itineraries tour lets you visit the doge's private apartments and hidden passageways. ✉ *Piazza San Marco 1, San Marco* ☎ *041/42730892 tickets* ⊕ *palazzoducale. visitmuve.it* 🎫 *Museums of San Marco Pass €25, includes Palazzo Ducale, Museo Correr, Museo Archeologico, and Biblioteca Nazionale Marciana. Museum Pass €36, includes all four museums plus eight civic museums. Secret Itineraries tour €28* Ⓜ *Vaporetto: San Zaccaria, Vallaresso.*

★ **Palazzo Grassi**

ART MUSEUM | Built between 1748 and 1772 by Giorgio Massari for a Bolognese family, this palace is one of the last of the great noble residences on the Grand Canal. Once owned by auto magnate Gianni Agnelli, it was bought by French businessman François Pinault in 2005 to showcase his highly esteemed collection of modern and contemporary art (which has now grown so large that Pinault rented the Punta della Dogana, at the entryway to the Grand Canal, for his newest acquisitions). Pinault brought in Japanese architect Tadao Ando to remodel the Grassi's interior. Check online for a schedule of temporary art exhibitions. ✉ *Campo San Samuele 3231, San Marco* ☎ *041/5231680* ⊕ *www.palazzograssi. it* 🎫 *€18, includes Punta della Dogana* 🕐 *Closed Tues.* Ⓜ *Vaporetto: San Samuele, Sant'Angelo.*

★ **Piazza San Marco** (*St. Mark's Square*)

PLAZA/SQUARE | FAMILY | One of the world's most beautiful squares, Piazza San Marco (St. Mark's Square) is the spiritual and artistic heart of Venice, a vast open space bordered by an orderly procession of arcades marching toward the fairy-tale cupolas and marble lacework of the Basilica di San Marco. From midmorning on, it is generally packed with tourists. (If Venetians have business in the piazza, they try to conduct it in the early morning, before the crowds swell.) At night the piazza can be magical, especially in winter, when mists swirl around the lampposts and the campanile.

Facing the basilica, on your left, the long, arcaded building is the Procuratie Vecchie, renovated to its present form in 1514 as offices and residences for the powerful procurators, or magistrates.

On your right is the Procuratie Nuove, built half a century later in a more imposing, classical style. It was originally planned by Venice's great Renaissance architect Jacopo Sansovino (1486–1570), to carry on the look of his Libreria

Let's Get Lost

Getting around Venice presents some unusual problems: the city's layout has few straight lines; house numbering seems nonsensical; and the six sestieri of San Marco, Cannaregio, Castello, Dorsoduro, Santa Croce, and San Polo all duplicate each other's street names. What's more, addresses in Venice are given by sestiere rather than street, making them of limited help in getting around. Venetians commonly give directions by pinpointing a major landmark, such as a church, and telling you where to go from there.

The numerous vaporetto lines can be bewildering, too, and often the only option for getting where you want to go is to walk. Yellow signs, posted on many busy corners, point toward the major landmarks—San Marco, Rialto, Accademia, and so forth—but don't count on finding such markers once you're deep into residential neighborhoods. Even buying a good map at a newsstand—the kind showing all street names and vaporetto routes—won't necessarily keep you from getting lost. To make matters worse, map apps on smart phones, for some reason, give frequently erroneous results for Venice.

Fortunately, as long as you maintain your patience, getting lost in Venice can be a pleasure. For one thing, being lost is a sign that you've escaped the tourist throngs. And although you might not find the Titian masterpiece you'd set out to see, you could wind up coming across an ageless bacaro (a traditional wine bar) or a quirky shop that turns out to be the highlight of your afternoon. Opportunities for such serendipity abound. Keep in mind that the city is self-contained: sooner or later, perhaps with the help of a patient native, you can rest assured you'll regain your bearings.

Sansoviniana (Sansovinian Library), but he died before construction on the Nuove had begun. Vincenzo Scamozzi (circa 1552–1616), a pupil of Andrea Palladio (1508–80), completed the design and construction. Still later, the Procuratie Nuove was modified by architect Baldassare Longhena (1598–1682), one of Venice's Baroque masters.

When Napoléon (1769–1821) entered Venice with his troops in 1797, he expressed his admiration for the piazza and promptly gave orders to alter it. His architects demolished a church with a Sansovino facade in order to build the Ala Napoleonica (Napoleonic Wing), or Fabbrica Nuova (New Building), which linked the two 16th-century procuratie and effectively enclosed the piazza.

Piazzetta San Marco is the "little square" leading from Piazza San Marco to the waters of Bacino San Marco (St. Mark's Basin); its *molo* (landing) once served as the grand entrance to the Republic. Two imposing columns tower above the waterfront. One is topped by the winged lion, a traditional emblem of St. Mark that became the symbol of Venice itself; the other supports St. Theodore, the city's first patron, along with his dragon. (A third column fell off its barge and ended up in the bacino before it could be placed alongside the others.) Although the columns are a glorious vision today, the Republic traditionally executed convicts here—and some superstitious Venetians still avoid walking between them. ✉ *San Marco* Ⓜ *Vaporetto: San Zaccaria, Vallaresso.*

★ Ponte di Rialto (*Rialto Bridge*)

BRIDGE | FAMILY | The competition to design a stone bridge across the Grand Canal attracted the best architects of the late 16th century, including Michelangelo, Palladio, and Sansovino, but the job went to the less famous (if appropriately named) Antonio da Ponte (1512–95). His pragmatic design, completed in 1591, featured shop space and was high enough for galleys to pass beneath. Putting practicality and economy over aesthetic considerations—unlike the classical plans proposed by his more famous contemporaries—da Ponte's bridge essentially followed the design of its wooden predecessor. But it kept decoration and cost to a minimum at a time when the Republic's coffers were low, due to continual wars against the Turks and competition brought about by the Spanish and Portuguese opening of oceanic trade routes. Along the railing you'll enjoy one of the city's most famous views: the Grand Canal vibrant with boat traffic. ⊠ *San Marco* Ⓜ *Vaporetto: Rialto.*

 Restaurants

Enoteca al Volto

$$ | VENETIAN | A short walk from the Ponte di Rialto, this bar has been around since 1936, and the satisfying cicheti and primi have a lot to do with its staying power. Grab a table out front, or take refuge in one of the two small, dark rooms with a ceiling plastered with wine labels that provide a classic backdrop for simple fare, including a delicious risotto that is served daily from noon, plus a solid wine list of both Italian and foreign vintages. **Known for:** fantastic main courses, including risotto and pasta with seafood; tasty and inexpensive cicheti; great local and international wine selection. Ⓢ *Average main: €17* ⊠ *Calle Cavalli, San Marco 4081, San Marco* ☎ *041/5228945* ⊕ *enotecaalvolto.com* Ⓜ *Vaporetto: Rialto.*

★ Harry's Bar

$$$$ | VENETIAN | For those who can afford it, lunch or dinner at Harry's Bar is as much a part of a visit to Venice as a walk across Piazza San Marco or a vaporetto ride down the Grand Canal. Inside, the suave, subdued beige-on-white decor is unchanged from the 1930s, and the classic Venetian fare is carefully and excellently prepared. **Known for:** signature crepes flambées and famous Cipriani chocolate cake; see-and-be-seen atmosphere; being the birthplace of the Bellini cocktail. Ⓢ *Average main: €58* ⊠ *Calle Vallaresso, San Marco 1323, San Marco* ☎ *041/5285777* ⊕ *www.cipriani.com* Ⓜ *Vaporetto: Vallaresso.*

★ Ristorante Quadri

$$$$ | VENETIAN | Although the lavish interior has been updated by designer Philippe Starck, this restaurant above the famed café of the same name is still steeped in Venetian ambience and history (it was where Turkish coffee was introduced to the city in the 1700s). When the Alajmo family (of the celebrated Le Calandre near Padua) took over, they put their accomplished sous-chef from Padua in charge of the kitchen, resulting in the addition of dishes—best sampled with a tasting menu—that are complex and sophisticated, with a wonderful wine list to match. **Known for:** revitalized designer decor; seasonal tasting menus; sophisticated and modern Italian cuisine. Ⓢ *Average main: €60* ⊠ *Piazza San Marco 121, San Marco* ☎ *049/630303* ⊕ *alajmo.it* ⊙ *Closed Mon. and Tues., and late Jan.–mid-Feb. No lunch Wed.–Fri.* Ⓜ *Vaporetto: Giardinetti, Vallaresso.*

☕ Coffee and Quick Bites

Bar all'Angolo

$ | CAFÉ | This corner of Campo Santo Stefano is a pleasant place to sit and watch the Venetian world go by. The café staff are in constant motion, so you'll receive your coffee, spritz, *panino* (a sandwich warmed on a griddle), or *tramezzino* (sandwich on untoasted white bread, usually with a mayonnaise-based filling) in short order; consume it at your leisure at one of the outdoor tables, at the bar, or at the tables in the back. **Known for:** good people-watching; tasty homemade desserts, including tiramisu and cakes; simple yet satisfying fare, like tramezzini and panini. $ *Average main: €10 ⊠ Campo Santo Stefano, San Marco 3464, just in front of Santo Stefano church, San Marco* 🕾 *041/5220710* ⊗ *Closed Sun. and Jan.* Ⓜ *Vaporetto: Sant'Angelo.*

★ Caffè Florian

$$ | **CAFÉ** | Florian is not only Italy's first café (1720), but also one of its most beautiful, with glittering, neo-Baroque decor and 19th-century wall panels depicting Venetian heroes. The coffee, drinks, and snacks are good, but most people—including Venetians from time to time—come for the atmosphere and history: this was the only café to serve women during the 18th century (hence Casanova's patronage); it was frequented by artistic notables like Wagner, Goethe, Goldoni, Lord Byron, Marcel Proust, and Charles Dickens; and it was the birthplace of the international art exhibition that became the Venice Biennale. **Known for:** hot chocolate, coffee, and quick nibbles; beautiful, historic interior; prime location on St. Mark's Square. $ *Average main: €16 ⊠ Piazza San Marco 57, San Marco* 🕾 *041/5205641* ⊕ *www.caffeflorian.com* ⊗ *Closed early Jan.* Ⓜ *Vaporetto: Giardinetti, Vallaresso.*

Gelatoteca Suso

$ | **ICE CREAM** | **FAMILY** | Try this fun shop for gelato that's out of the ordinary: think walnut cream with caramelized fig, or vanilla with rum raisins and Malaga wine. Sorbets and milkshakes are also on offer. **Known for:** unusual flavors; convenient location on way to Rialto Bridge; vegan ice cream options. $ *Average main: €5 ⊠ Sotoportego de la Bissa, San Marco 5453, San Marco* 🕾 *0348/5646545* ⊕ *tastesu.so* Ⓜ *Vaporetto: Rialto.*

★ Gran Caffè Quadri

$$ | **CAFÉ** | Come for breakfast, a predinner aperitivo, or anything in between at this always lively historic coffeehouse—opened in 1775 and taken over by the famous culinary Alajmo family in 2011—in the center of the action on Piazza San Marco. Choose from a wide selection of pastries at breakfast (though the cappuccino and brioche combo is always a classic), pizzas at lunch, and tramezzini all day long, including one with lobster. **Known for:** prime people-watching; celebrity owners; extensive (though pricey) aperitivo. $ *Average main: €17 ⊠ Piazza San Marco 121, San Marco* 🕾 *049/630303* ⊕ *alajmo.it* Ⓜ *Vaporetto: Giardinetti, Vallaresso.*

 Hotels

Bauer Palazzo

$$$$ | **HOTEL** | This palazzo with an ornate 1930s neo-Gothic facade facing the Grand Canal has large (by Venetian standards), lavishly decorated guest rooms with high ceilings, tufted walls of Bevilacqua and Rubelli fabrics, Murano glass, marble bathrooms, damask drapes, and reproduction antique furniture. **Pros:** pampering service; Venice's highest rooftop terrace; high-end luxury. **Cons:** no spa on-site; furnishings are, as is the facade, an imitation; decor could be a bit dark and old-fashioned for some. $ *Rooms from: €301 ⊠ Campo San Moisè, San Marco 1459, San Marco* 🕾 *041/5207022* ⊕ *www.bauervenezia.com* ⊅ *191 rooms* ⦿ *No Meals* Ⓜ *Vaporetto: Vallaresso.*

★ The Gritti Palace

$$$$ | **HOTEL** | With handblown chandeliers, sumptuous textiles, and sweeping canal views, this grande dame (whose history dates from 1525, when it was built as the residence of the prominent Gritti family) represents aristocratic Venetian living at its best. **Pros:** truly historical property; classic Venetian experience; Grand Canal location. **Cons:** few spa amenities; food served at the hotel gets

mixed reviews; major splurge. $ *Rooms from: €1470* ✉ *Campo Santa Maria del Giglio 2467, San Marco* ☎ *041/794611* ⊕ *www.thegrittipalace.com* ⤴ *82 rooms* ⏣ *No Meals* Ⓜ *Vaporetto: Giglio.*

Hotel Flora

$$ | **HOTEL** | The elegant and refined facade announces a charming, and reasonably priced, place to stay; the hospitable staff, the tastefully decorated rooms, and the lovely garden, where guests can breakfast or drink, do not disappoint. **Pros:** central location; excellent breakfast; peaceful hidden garden. **Cons:** old-fashioned lobby doesn't invite hanging out; no water views; some rooms can be on the small side. $ *Rooms from: €160* ✉ *Calle Bergamaschi, San Marco 2283/A, San Marco* ☎ *041/5205844* ⊕ *www.hotelflora.it* ⤴ *40 rooms* ⏣ *Free Breakfast* Ⓜ *Vaporetto: Vallaresso.*

★ Novecento

$$ | **HOTEL** | A stylish yet intimate retreat tucked away on a quiet *calle* (street) midway between Piazza San Marco and the Accademia Bridge offers exquisite rooms tastefully decorated with original furnishings and tapestries from the Mediterranean and Far East. **Pros:** intimate, romantic atmosphere; complimentary afternoon tea; unique design sensibility. **Cons:** some rooms can be noisy; no elevator; most rooms only have showers, not tubs. $ *Rooms from: €184* ✉ *Calle del Dose, San Marco 2683/84, San Marco* ☎ *041/2413765* ⊕ *www.novecento.biz* ⤴ *9 rooms* ⏣ *Free Breakfast* Ⓜ *Vaporetto: Santa Maria del Giglio.*

Palazzina Grassi

$$$$ | **HOTEL** | The only hotel in Italy outfitted by famed French designer Philippe Starck boasts a clubby atmosphere, over-the-top contemporary rooms lined with Murano glass, and so-close-you-can-touch-them Grand Canal views. **Pros:** next door to Palazzo Grassi art space and walking distance to St. Mark's; fun, modern take on Venetian design; friendly, helpful service. **Cons:** food in restaurant not up to par; bathrooms smaller than they should be; can be loud when parties are in full swing. $ *Rooms from: €495* ✉ *Ramo Grassi, San Marco* ☎ *041/5284644* ⊕ *www.palazzinagrassi.com* ⤴ *26 rooms* ⏣ *No Meals* Ⓜ *Vaporetto: San Samuele.*

★ The St. Regis Venice

$$$$ | **HOTEL** | Whimsical design details evoking the Venetian landscape abound in this elegant, contemporary hotel constructed from five historic palazzi with phenomenal views onto the Grand Canal. **Pros:** wonderful central location; St. Regis butler service for all guests; terraces with unbeatable views. **Cons:** few spa amenities (no pool or saunas); standard rooms on the small side; sleek modern style not for fans of Venetian opulence. $ *Rooms from: €931* ✉ *San Marco 2159, San Marco* ☎ *041/2400001* ⊕ *www.marriott.com* ⤴ *169 rooms* ⏣ *Free Breakfast* Ⓜ *Vaporetto: Vallaresso.*

Nightlife

Bacarando in Corte dell'Orso

WINE BARS | It is easy to see why this place is popular with the locals, offering fairly priced cocktails, a reasonable assortment of cicheti, and a good selection of Italian wine, but the warm ambience, friendly staff, and occasional live jazz are the main draws. The kitchen stays open until late. ✉ *Corte Dell'Orso, San Marco 5495, San Marco* ✛ *Tucked away in alley across from Church of San Giovanni Grisostomo* ☎ *041/5238280* ⊕ *www.bacarando.com* Ⓜ *Vaporetto: Rialto.*

Bacaro Jazz

BARS | This Venetian-style dive bar has strong cocktails, a jazz soundtrack, and hundreds of bras hanging from the ceiling. The lively daily happy hour is a great time to visit. ✉ *San Marco 5546, San Marco* ☎ *041/5285249* ⊕ *bacarojazz.it* Ⓜ *Vaporetto: Rialto.*

★ Bar Longhi

BARS | The Gritti Palace is home to one of the most exclusive watering holes in town (though thankfully open to the public), lined with 18th-century paintings and Murano chandeliers. You can also enjoy your cocktail on the patio with prime views onto the Grand Canal. ✉ The Gritti Palace, Campo Santa Maria del Giglio, San Marco 2467, San Marco ☎ 041/794611 ⊕ www.thegrittipalace. com Ⓜ Vaporetto: Giglio.

🛍 Shopping

★ Al Duca d'Aosta

MIXED CLOTHING | The most stylish of Venetians and visitors alike come here for women's and men's designer labels for every taste. Brands include Burberry, Givenchy, Jil Sander, Lanvin, Moncler, and many others; be prepared to be wowed. ✉ San Marco 284, San Marco ☎ 041/5220733 ⊕ www.alducadaosta. com Ⓜ Vaporetto: San Marco, Zaccaria.

★ Atelier Segalin di Daniela Ghezzo

SHOES | This artist turned master shoemaker produces one-of-a-kind creations from exotic leathers. Though the shoes start at €650 and usually take at least six weeks to finish, you'll truly feel like you're wearing a masterpiece. ✉ Calle dei Fuseri, San Marco 4365, San Marco ☎ 041/5222115 ⊕ www.danielaghezzo.it Ⓜ Vaporetto: Rialto.

★ Bevilacqua

FABRICS | This renowned studio has kept the weaving tradition alive in Venice since 1875, using 18th-century hand looms for its most precious creations. Its repertoire of 3,500 different patterns and designs yields a ready-to-sell selection of hundreds of brocades, Gobelins, damasks, velvets, taffetas, and satins. You'll also find tapestry, cushions, and braiding. ✉ Campo di Santa Maria del Giglio, San Marco 2520, San Marco ☎ 041/2410662 main retail outlet, 041/5287581 retail outlet behind Basilica, 041/721566 Santa

Croce production center ⊕ bevilacquatessuti.com Ⓜ Vaporetto: Giglio.

★ Dittura Massimo

SHOES | Run by a second-generation shoemaker, this shop is one of the only places left in the city still producing Venice's iconic friulane slippers, invented in the 19th century and handstitched from velvet and rubber. The shoes are still worn by gondoliers today. ✉ Calle Fiubera, San Marco 943, San Marco ☎ 041/5231163 ⊕ ditturamassimo.it Ⓜ Vaporetto: San Marco.

★ Giuliana Longo

HATS & GLOVES | A hat shop that's been around since 1901 offers an assortment of Venetian and gondolier straw hats, Panama hats from Ecuador, caps and berets, and some select scarves of silk and fine wool; there's even a special corner dedicated to accessories for antique cars. ✉ Calle del Lovo, San Marco 4813, San Marco ☎ 041/5226454 ⊕ www.giulianalongo.com Ⓜ Vaporetto: San Marco.

★ Jesurum Venezia 1870

FABRICS | A great deal of so-called Burano Venetian lace is now machine-made in China—and there really is a difference. Unless you have some experience, you're best off going to a trusted place. Jesurum has been the major producer of handmade Venetian lace since 1870. Its lace is, of course, all modern production, but if you want an antique piece, the people at Jesurum can point you in the right direction. ✉ Calle Veste, San Marco 2024, San Marco ☎ 041/5238969 ⊕ www. jesurum.it Ⓜ Vaporetto: Vallaresso.

★ MuranoVitrum

GLASSWARE | You'll find Murano-made glassworks, including glasses, vases, chandeliers, mirrors, and sculptures, in this friendly family-owned shop. ✉ San Marco 1229, San Marco ☎ 041/5206358 ⊕ www.muranovitrum.com Ⓜ Vaporetto: Vallaresso.

Venetian Art Glass

The glass of Murano is Venice's number one product, and you'll be confronted by mind-boggling displays of traditional and contemporary glassware—much of it kitsch and not made in Venice. Traditional Venetian glass is hot blown glass, not lead crystal; it comes in myriad forms that range from the classic ornate goblets and chandeliers, to beads, vases, sculpture, and more. Beware of paying "Venetian" prices for glass made elsewhere. A piece claiming to be made in Murano may guarantee its origin, but not its value or quality; the prestigious Venetian glassmakers—like Venini, Seguso, Salviati, and others—sign their pieces, but never use a "made in Murano" label. To make a smart purchase, take your time and be selective. You can learn a great deal without sales pressure at the Museo del Vetro (⊕ *museovetro.visitmuve. it*) on Murano; unfortunately, you'll likely find the least attractive glass where public demonstrations are offered. Although prices in Venice and on Murano are comparable, shops in Venice with wares from various glassworks may charge slightly less.

■TIP➜ A "free" taxi to Murano always comes with sales pressure. Take the vaporetto included in your transit pass, and, if you prefer, a private guide who specializes in the subject but has no affinity to any specific furnace.

T Fondaco dei Tedeschi

DEPARTMENT STORE | This 15th-century Renaissance commercial center served as Venice's main post office for many years, but was remodeled and returned to its historical roots as a luxury department store. Here you can find a large assortment of high-end jewelry, clothing, and other luxury items, plus fabulous views from the rooftop terrace; book online for a free 15-minute visit. ⊠ *Calle Fondaco dei Tedeschi, near San Marco end of Ponte di Rialto, San Marco* ☏ *041/3142000* ⊕ *www.dfs.com* Ⓜ *Vaporetto: Rialto.*

Dorsoduro

The sestiere Dorsoduro (named for its "hard back" solid clay foundation) is across the Grand Canal to the south of San Marco. It is a place of meandering canals, the city's finest art museums, monumental churches, and *scuole* (Renaissance civic institutions) filled with works by Titian, Veronese, and Tiepolo,

and a promenade called the Zattere, where on sunny days you'll swear half the city is out for *passeggiata* (a stroll). The eastern tip of the peninsula, the Punta della Dogana, is capped by the dome of Santa Maria della Salute and was once the city's customs point; the old customs house is now a museum of contemporary art.

TIMING

You can easily spend a full day in the neighborhood. Devote at least a half hour to admiring the Titians in the imposing and monumental Santa Maria della Salute, and another half hour for the wonderful Veroneses in the peaceful, serene church of San Sebastiano. The Gallerie dell'Accademia demands a few hours, but if time is short an audio guide can help you cover the highlights in about an hour. Ca' Rezzonico deserves at least an hour, as does the Peggy Guggenheim Collection.

Venice's Scuola Days

An institution you'll inevitably encounter from Venice's glory days is the *scuola*. These weren't schools, as the word today translates, but important fraternal institutions. The smaller ones (*scuole piccole*) were established by different social groups—enclaves of foreigners, tradesmen, followers of a particular saint, and parishioners. The *scuole grandi*, however, were open to all citizens and included people of different occupations and ethnicities. They formed a more democratic power base than the Venetian governmental Grand Council, which was limited to nobles.

For the most part secular, despite their devotional activities, the scuole concentrated on charitable work, either helping their own membership or assisting the city's neediest citizens. The tradesmen's and servants' scuole formed social-security nets for elderly and disabled members. Wealthier scuole assisted orphans or provided dowries so poor girls could marry.

By 1500 there were more than 200 minor scuole in Venice but only six scuole grandi, some of which contributed substantially to the arts. The Republic encouraged their existence—the scuole kept strict records of the names and professions of contributors to the brotherhood, which helped when it came time to collect taxes.

◉ Sights

★ Ca' Rezzonico

HISTORY MUSEUM | Designed by Baldassare Longhena in the 17th century, this gigantic palace was completed nearly 100 years later by Giorgio Massari and became the last home of English poet Robert Browning (1812–89). Stand on the bridge by the Grand Canal entrance to spot the plaque with Browning's poetic excerpt, "Open my heart and you will see graved inside of it, Italy…" on the palace's left side. The eye-popping Grand Ballroom has hosted some of the grandest parties in the city's history, from its 18th-century heyday to the 1969 Bal Fantastica (a Save Venice charity event that attracted notables from Elizabeth Taylor to Aristotle Onassis) to balls re-created for Heath Ledger's 2005 film *Casanova*. Today the upper floors of the Ca' Rezzonico are home to the especially delightful Museo del Settecento (Museum of Venice in the 1700s), decorated with period furniture and tapestries in gilded salons, as well as Tiepolo ceiling frescoes and oil paintings. ✉ *Fondamenta Rezzonico, Dorsoduro 3136, Dorsoduro* ☎ *041/2410100* ⊕ *carezzonico.visitmuve.it* 🎫 *€10 (free with Museum Pass)* ⊗ *Closed Mon.–Wed.* Ⓜ *Vaporetto: Ca' Rezzonico.*

Campo Santa Margherita

PLAZA/SQUARE | Lined with cafés and restaurants generally filled with students from the two nearby universities, Campo Santa Margherita also has produce vendors and benches where you can sit and take in the bustling local life of the campo. Also close to Ca' Rezzonico and the Scuola Grande dei Carmini, and only a 10-minute walk from the Gallerie dell'Accademia, the square is the center of Dorsoduro social life. It takes its name from the church to one side, closed since the early 19th century and now used as an auditorium. On weekend evenings, especially in the summer, it attracts hordes of students, even from the mainland. ✉ *Campo Santa Margherita,*

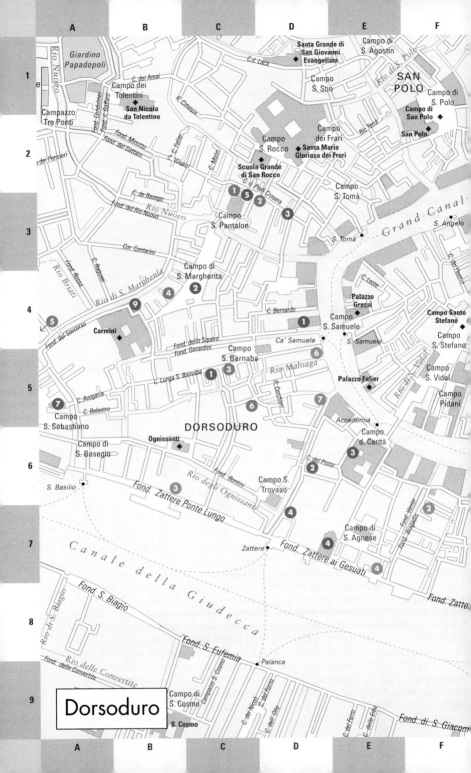

Sights ▼

Restaurants ▼

Quick Bites ▼

Hotels ▼

Dorsoduro Ⓜ *Vaporetto: Zattere, Ca' Rezzonico.*

★ Gallerie dell'Accademia

ART MUSEUM | The greatest collection of Venetian paintings in the world hangs in these galleries founded by Napoléon in 1807 on the site of a religious complex he had suppressed. The galleries were carefully and subtly restructured between 1945 and 1959 by the renowned Venetian architect Carlo Scarpa. Highlights include works by Jacopo Bellini, the father of the Venetian Renaissance, as well as the richly colored paintings of his more accomplished son Giovanni; *The Tempest* by Giorgione, a revolutionary work that has intrigued viewers and critics for centuries; *Feast in the House of Levi,* which got Veronese summoned to the Inquisition; and several of Tintoretto's finest works. Don't miss the views of 15th- and 16th-century Venice by Carpaccio and Gentile Bellini, Giovanni's brother—you'll recognize many places you've seen on your walks. Booking tickets in advance isn't essential but only costs an additional €1.50. Valid certificate of vaccination against COV-ID-19 is required in all Italian museums. ⊠ *Campo de la Carità, Dorsoduro 1050, Campo della Carità just off Accademia Bridge, Dorsoduro* ☎ *041/5222247, 041/5243354 reservations when calling from outside Italy* ⊕ *www.gallerieacca-demia.it/en* 🎫 *€12; subject to increases for special exhibitions* Ⓜ *Vaporetto: Accademia, Zattere.*

Gesuati (Church of Santa Maria del Rosario)

CHURCH | When the Dominicans took over the church of Santa Maria della Visitazione from the suppressed order of Gesuati laymen in 1668, Giorgio Massari, the last of the great Venetian Baroque architects, was commissioned to build this structure between 1726 and 1735. It has an important Gianbattista Tiepolo (1696–1770) illusionistic ceiling and several other of his works, plus those of

his contemporaries Giambattista Piazzetta (1683–1754) and Sebastiano Ricci (1659–1734). Outside on the right-hand wall above a small staircase is a bronze door decorated with a series of panels showing scenes from the life of Jesus by noted Venetian sculptor Francesco Scarpabolla. ⊠ *Fondamenta Zattere ai Gesuati, Dorsoduro* ☎ *041/2750462 Chorus Foundation, 041/5205921 church office* ⊕ *www.chorusvenezia.org* 🎫 *€3 (free with Chorus Pass)* ⊘ *Closed Sun.* Ⓜ *Vaporetto: Zattere.*

Peggy Guggenheim Collection

ART MUSEUM | FAMILY | Housed in the incomplete but nevertheless charming Palazzo Venier dei Leoni, this choice selection of 20th-century painting and sculpture represents the taste and extraordinary style of the late heiress Peggy Guggenheim. Through wealth, social connections, and a sharp eye for artistic trends, Guggenheim (1898–1979) became an important art dealer and collector from the 1930s through the 1950s, and her personal collection here includes works by Picasso, Kandinsky, Pollock, Motherwell, and Ernst (her onetime husband). The museum serves beverages, snacks, and light meals in its refreshingly shady and artistically sophisticated garden. ⊠ *Fondamenta Venier dei Leoni, Dorsoduro 701-704, Dorsoduro* ☎ *041/2405411* ⊕ *www.gug-genheim-venice.it* 🎫 *€15* ⊘ *Closed Tues.* ☞ *Timed tickets must be purchased online in advance. Weekend tickets must be booked at least one day ahead* Ⓜ *Vaporetto: Accademia, Salute.*

★ Punta della Dogana

ART MUSEUM | Funded by the billionaire who owns a major share in Christie's Auction House, the François Pinault Foundation commissioned Japanese architect Tadao Ando to redesign this fabled customs house—sitting at the *punta,* or point of land, at the San Marco end of the Grand Canal—now home to a changing roster of works from Pinault's renowned collection of contemporary art. The streaming light, polished surfaces, and clean lines of Ando's design contrast beautifully with the massive columns, sturdy beams, and brick of the original Dogana. Even if you aren't into contemporary art, a visit is worthwhile just to see Ando's amazing architectural transformation. Be sure to walk down to the punta for a magnificent view of the Venetian basin. Check online for a schedule of temporary exhibitions. ⊠ *Punta della Dogana, Dorsoduro* ☎ *041/2401308* ⊕ *www.palazzograssi.it* ✉ *€15 with Palazzo Grassi* ☉ *Closed Tues.* Ⓜ *Vaporetto: Salute.*

★ San Sebastiano

CHURCH | Paolo Veronese (1528–88), though still in his twenties, was already the official painter of the Republic when he began the ceiling oil panels and wall frescoes at San Sebastiano in 1555. For decades he continued to embellish the church with very beautiful illusionistic scenes. The cycles of scenes in San Sebastiano are considered to be his supreme accomplishment. His three oil paintings in the center of the ceiling depict scenes from the life of Esther, a rare theme in Venice. Veronese is buried beneath his bust near the organ. ⊠ *Campazzo San Sebastiano, Dorsoduro* ☎ *041/2750462* ⊕ *www.chorusvenezia.org* ✉ *€3 (free with Chorus Pass)* ☉ *Closed Sun.* Ⓜ *Vaporetto: San Basilio.*

★ Santa Maria della Salute

CHURCH | The most iconic landmark of the Grand Canal, La Salute (as this church is commonly called) is best viewed from the Riva degli Schiavoni at sunset or from the Accademia Bridge by moonlight. Baldassare Longhena (later Venice's most important Baroque architect) won a competition in 1631 to design a shrine honoring the Virgin Mary for saving Venice from a plague that over two years (1629–30) killed 47,000 residents, or one-third of the city's population. Outside, this ornate white Istrian stone octagon is topped by a colossal cupola with snail-like ornamental buttresses. ⊠ *Punta della Dogana, Dorsoduro* ☎ *041/2743928* ⊕ *basilicasalutevenezia.it* ✉ *Church free, sacristy €4* Ⓜ *Vaporetto: Salute.*

Scuola Grande dei Carmini

HISTORIC SIGHT | When the order of Santa Maria del Carmelo commissioned Baldassare Longhena to finish the work on the Scuola Grande dei Carmini in the 1670s, their confraternity was one of the largest and wealthiest in Venice. Little expense was spared in the stuccoed ceilings and carved wooden paneling, and the artwork is remarkable. The paintings by Gianbattista Tiepolo that adorn the Baroque ceiling of the **Sala Capitolare** (Chapter House) are particularly alluring. In what many consider his best work, the artist's nine canvases vividly transform some rather conventional religious themes into dynamic displays of color and movement. ⊠ *Campo dei Carmini, Dorsoduro 2617, Dorsoduro* ☎ *041/5289420* ⊕ *www.scuolagrandecarmini.it* ✉ *€7* Ⓜ *Vaporetto: Ca' Rezzonico.*

🍴 Restaurants

★ Estro Vino e Cucina

$$$$ | MODERN ITALIAN | Wine lovers shouldn't miss this cozy and compact eatery run by the Spezzamonte brothers, which offers a fantastic selection of organic wines along with modern takes on classic Venetian dishes, such as *scampi in saor* (marinated langoustines) and grilled local amberjack. If you can't choose, let the helpful servers suggest the perfect vino from their list of more than 700 bottles to pair with your à la carte dishes or tasting menu. **Known for:** vibrant atmosphere; ambitious local cuisine; extensive natural wine list. 💲 *Average main: €38* ⊠ *Crosera San Pantalon, Dorsoduro 3778, Dorsoduro* ☎ *041/4764914* ⊕ *www.estrovenezia.com* ☉ *Closed Tues.* Ⓜ *Vaporetto: San Tomà.*

Impronta

$$$ | **VENETIAN** | This sleek café is a favorite lunchtime haunt for professors from the nearby university and local businesspeople, when you can easily have a beautifully prepared *primo* (first course) or *secondo* (second course), plus a glass of wine, for a reasonable price; there's also a good selection of sandwiches and salads. Unlike most local eateries, this spot is open from breakfast through late dinner, and you can dine well in the evening on imaginative pasta, seafood, and meat dishes. **Known for:** all-day dining; contemporary decor; imaginative dishes. [$] *Average main: €25* ✉ *intersection of Calle Crosera and Calle San Pantalon, Dorsoduro 3815, Dorsoduro* ☎ *041/2750386* 🌐 *www.improntacafevenice.com* 🕒 *Closed Sun. and 2 wks in Aug.* [M] *Vaporetto: San Tomà.*

★ **La Bitta**

$$$ | **NORTHERN ITALIAN** | For a break from all the fish and seafood options in Venice, this is your place; the meat- and veggie-focused menu (inspired by the cuisine of the Venetian mainland) presents a new temptation at every course, and market availability keeps the dishes changing almost every day. The homemade desserts are all luscious (it's been said that La Bitta serves the best panna cotta in town), and you can trust the owner's selections from her excellent wine and grappa lists, which tend to favor small local producers. **Known for:** friendly and efficient service; seasonally inspired menus; meat dishes (no seafood). [$] *Average main: €25* ✉ *Calle Lunga San Barnaba, Dorsoduro 2753/A, Dorsoduro* ☎ *041/5230531* 🌐 *facebook.com/LaBittaVenezia* 💳 *No credit cards* 🕒 *Closed Sun. No lunch* [M] *Vaporetto: Ca' Rezzonico, Zattere.*

★ **Osteria alla Bifora**

$$ | **VENETIAN** | A beautiful and atmospheric bacaro, Alla Bifora has such ample, satisfying fare that most Venetians consider it a full-fledged restaurant. Offerings include overflowing trays of cold, sliced meats and cheeses; various preparations of baccalà (cod); and Venetian classics, such as polpette (croquettes), sarde in saor, and marinated anchovies. **Known for:** warm and friendly owners; seppie in nero con polenta (cuttlefish in ink with polenta); good selection of regional wines by the glass. [$] *Average main: €18* ✉ *Campo Santa Margherita, Dorsoduro 2930, Dorsoduro* ☎ *041/5236119* 🕒 *Closed Jan. and Aug.* [M] *Vaporetto: Ca' Rezzonico.*

Osteria Bakan

$$$$ | **VENETIAN** | Outstanding fish, from the simplest steamed sea bass to decadent swordfish ravioli, is served at Bakan, its name a reference to the part of the lagoon near Sant'Erasmo that's popular for swimming and clamming. You'll see more students and locals than tourists here, and there are tables outside. **Known for:** local patrons; outdoor seating; seafood classics like baccalà mantecato. [$] *Average main: €50* ✉ *Corte Mazor, Dorsoduro 2314/A, Dorsoduro* ☎ *041/5647658* 🕒 *Closed Mon. and Tues.* [M] *Vaporetto: San Basilio, Piazzale Roma.*

★ **Osteria Enoteca ai Artisti**

$$$ | **VENETIAN** | Pop into this canal-side restaurant at lunch for a satisfying primo or come for dinner to sample fine and fresh offerings; the candlelit tables that line the *fondamenta* (quay) suggest romance, and the service is friendly and welcoming. The posted menu—with choices like tagliatelle with porcini mushrooms and tiger prawns, or a filleted John Dory with tomatoes and pine nuts—changes daily (spot the date at the top) and seasonally. **Known for:** truly helpful service; superlative tiramisu; delicious pasta and seafood offerings. [$] *Average main: €25* ✉ *Fondamenta della Toletta, Dorsoduro 1169a, Dorsoduro* ☎ *041/5238944* 🌐 *www.enotecaartisti.com* 🕒 *Closed Sun. and Mon.* [M] *Vaporetto: Ca' Rezzonico, Zattere.*

Coffee and Quick Bites

Caffè Ai Artisti

$ | **CAFÉ** | Caffè Ai Artisti gives locals, students, and travelers alike good reason to pause and refuel. The location is central, pleasant, and sunny—perfect for people-watching and taking a break before the next destination—and the hours are long. **Known for:** chilling with the locals; evening Aperol spritz or wine; relaxing with a coffee. [$] *Average main: €8* ✉ *Campo San Barnaba, Dorsoduro 2771, Dorsoduro* ☎ *3939680135, 041/5238994* [M] *Vaporetto: Ca' Rezzonico.*

★ **Cantine del Vino già Schiavi**

$ | **WINE BAR** | A mainstay for anyone living or working in the area, this beautiful, family-run, 19th-century bacaro across from the *squero* (gondola boatyard) of San Trovaso has original furnishings and one of the city's best wine cellars, and the walls are covered floor to ceiling with bottles for purchase. The cicheti here are some of the most inventive—and freshest—in Venice (feel free to compliment the signora, who makes them up to twice a day); everything's eaten standing up, as there's no seating. **Known for:** boisterous local atmosphere; plenty of wine choices; excellent quality cicheti. [$] *Average main: €8* ✉ *Fondamenta Nani, Dorsoduro 992, Dorsoduro* ☎ *041/5230034* 🌐 *www.cantinaschiavi.com* 🕒 *Closed Sun. and 3 wks in Aug.* [M] *Vaporetto: Accademia, Zattere.*

Imagina Cafè

$ | **ITALIAN** | This friendly café and art gallery, located between Campo Santa Margherita and Campo San Barnaba, is a great place to stop for a spritz, or even for a light lunch or dinner. The highlights are the freshly made salads, but their panini and tramezzini (sandwiches) are also among the best in the area. **Known for:** pleasant outdoor seating; good wines and cocktails; tasty sandwiches and salads. [$] *Average main: €10* ✉ *Rio Terà Canal, Dorsoduro 3126, Dorsoduro* ☎ *041/2410625* 🌐 *www.imaginacafe.it/english.html* [M] *Vaporetto: Ca' Rezzonico.*

Osteria al Squero

$$ | **ITALIAN** | It wasn't long after this lovely little wine bar (not, as its name implies, a restaurant) appeared across from Squero San Trovaso that it became a neighborhood—and citywide—favorite. The Venetian owner has created a personal vision of what a good bar should offer: a variety of sumptuous cicheti, panini, and cheeses to be accompanied by just the right regional wines (ask for his recommendation). **Known for:** pretty canal views; good veggie options; tasty cicheti. [$] *Average main: €20* ✉ *Fondamenta Nani, Dorsoduro 943/944, Dorsoduro* ☎ *335/6007513* 🌐 *osteriaalsquero.wordpress.com* 🕒 *Closed Sun.* [M] *Vaporetto: Zattere, Accademia.*

Pasticceria Tonolo

$ | **BAKERY** | One of Venice's premier confectioneries has been in operation since 1886. During Carnevale it's still one of the best places in town for *frittelle,* or fried doughnuts (traditional raisin or cream-filled), and at Christmas and Easter, this is where Venetians order their focaccia veneziana, the traditional raised cake—well in advance. **Known for:** can't-miss doughnuts; excellent coffee; arguably the best pastries in Venice. [$] *Average main: €5* ✉ *Calle San Pantalon, Dorsoduro 3764, Dorsoduro* ☎ *041/5237209* 🌐 *pasticceria-tonolo-venezia.business.site* 🕒 *Closed Mon.* [M] *Vaporetto: San Tomà.*

Hotels

★ **Ca' Maria Adele**

$$$$ | **HOTEL** | One of the city's most intimate and elegant getaways blends terrazzo floors, dramatic Murano chandeliers, and antique-style furnishings with contemporary touches, particularly in the African-wood reception area and breakfast room. **Pros:** quiet and romantic; tranquil yet convenient spot near Santa Maria della Salute; imaginative decor.

Cons: no restaurant (just breakfast room); bathrooms on the small side; no elevator and lots of stairs. $ *Rooms from: €462* ✉ *Campo Santa Maria della Salute, Dorsoduro 111, Dorsoduro* ☎ *041/5203078* ⊕ *www.camariaadele.it* ⊘ *Closed 3 wks in Jan.* ⇄ *14 rooms* ⦿ *Free Breakfast* Ⓜ *Vaporetto: Salute.*

Hotel American Dinesen

$$ | **HOTEL** | If you're in Venice to see art, you can't beat the location of this hotel, where all the spacious rooms have brocade fabrics and Venetian-style lacquered furniture. **Pros:** wonderfully located near Gallerie dell'Accademia, Peggy Guggenheim Collection, and Punta della Dogana; some rooms have canal-view terraces; on a bright, quiet, exceptionally picturesque canal. **Cons:** bathrooms can feel cramped; style could be too understated for those expecting Venetian opulence; canal-view rooms are more expensive. $ *Rooms from: €171* ✉ *Fondamenta Bragadin, Dorsoduro 628, Dorsoduro* ☎ *041/5204733* ⊕ *www.hotelamerican.it* ⇄ *34 rooms* ⦿ *No Meals* Ⓜ *Vaporetto: Accademia, Salute, Zattere.*

Il Palazzo Experimental

$$$ | **HOTEL** | Of-the-moment Parisian designer Dorothée Meilichzon composed the striped pastel color palette at this hip boutique hotel— the first Experimental Group property in Italy—hidden inside a Renaissance palazzo facing the Giudecca Canal. **Pros:** fun, whimsical decor; trendy cocktail bar on-site; quiet location away from the Venice crowds. **Cons:** no gym; little storage space in bathrooms; not all rooms have water views. $ *Rooms from: €270* ✉ *Fondamenta Zattere Al Ponte Lungo, Dorsoduro 1411, Dorsoduro* ☎ *041/0980200* ⊕ *www.palazzoexperimental.com* ⇄ *32 rooms* ⦿ *No Meals* Ⓜ *Vaporetto: Zattere, San Basilio.*

La Calcina

$$ | **HOTEL** | Many notables (including Victorian-era art critic John Ruskin) have stayed at this hotel, though they might not recognize it after its series of upscale renovations; it has an enviable location along the sunny Zattere, as well as comfy rooms and apartments with parquet floors, original 19th-century furniture, and firm beds. **Pros:** panoramic views from some rooms; well-regarded restaurant with terrace over the Giudecca Canal; quiet, peaceful atmosphere. **Cons:** most rooms on the small side; no elevator; not for travelers who prefer ultramodern surroundings. $ *Rooms from: €130* ✉ *Zattere, Dorsoduro 780, Dorsoduro* ☎ *041/5206466* ⊕ *www.lacalcina.com* ⇄ *25 rooms* ⦿ *Free Breakfast* Ⓜ *Vaporetto: Zattere.*

Locanda Ca' Zose

$$ | **HOTEL** | The idea that the Campanati sisters named the 15 rooms in their renovated 17th-century locanda after the stars and constellations of the highest magnitude in the Northern Hemisphere says something about how personally this place is run. **Pros:** quiet but convenient location; canal views; efficient, personal service. **Cons:** no outdoor garden or terrace; no Wi-Fi in rooms (but free in lounge, as is computer use); unimpressive breakfast. $ *Rooms from: €165* ✉ *Calle del Bastion, Dorsoduro 193/B, Dorsoduro* ☎ *041/5226635* ⊕ *www.hotelcazose.com* ⇄ *15 rooms* ⦿ *Free Breakfast* Ⓜ *Vaporetto: Salute.*

★ Palazzo Stern

$$ | **HOTEL** | This opulently refurbished neo-Gothic palazzo features marble-column arches, terrazzo floors, frescoed ceilings, mosaics, and a charming carved staircase, and some rooms have tufted walls and parquet flooring. **Pros:** excellent hotel service; modern renovation retains historic ambience; lovely views from many rooms. **Cons:** no restaurant, gym, or spa; Grand Canal–facing rooms can be a bit noisy; standard rooms don't have views. $ *Rooms from: €192* ✉ *Calle del Traghetto, Dorsoduro 2792, Dorsoduro* ☎ *041/2770869* ⊕ *www.palazzostern.com* ⇄ *24 rooms* ⦿ *Free Breakfast* Ⓜ *Vaporetto: Ca' Rezzonico.*

Pensione Accademia Villa Maravege

$$ | HOTEL | Behind iron gates in one of the most densely packed parts of the city is this renowned Gothic-style villa with gardens and charmingly decorated accommodations with Venetian-style antique reproductions and fine tapestry. **Pros:** a unique villa in the heart of Venice; complimentary drinks and snacks at the bar; two gardens where guests can breakfast, drink, and relax. **Cons:** no restaurant; bathrooms can be on the small side; no guest rooms have Grand Canal views. $ *Rooms from: €128* ✉ *Fondamenta Bollani, Dorsoduro 1058, Dorsoduro* ☎ *041/5210188* ⊕ *www.pensioneaccademia.it* 🛏 *27 rooms* ⊙ *Free Breakfast* Ⓜ *Vaporetto: Accademia.*

Nightlife

Al Chioschetto

BARS | Although this popular place consists only of a kiosk set up to serve some outdoor tables, it is located on the Zattere and thus provides a wonderful view of the Giudecca Canal. It's a handy meet-up spot for locals, especially students from the nearby university, and a useful stop-off for tourists in nice weather for a spritz or a panino. Keep in mind, though, that "the kiosk" exists for quick refreshments and not for lingering. The view and the sunshine (and especially the sunset) are the main draw; the food and drink, while acceptable, are not exceptional. ✉ *Fondamenta delle Zattere, Dorsoduro 1406/A, Dorsoduro* ☎ *348/3968466* Ⓜ *Vaporetto: San Basilio, Zattere.*

★ **Il Caffè Rosso** (*Bar Rosso*)

BARS | The sign above the door simply says "CAFFÈ," but it has long since been called "Bar Rosso" for its bright-red exterior. The ideal people-watching spot on one of the busiest campos, it has far more tables outside than inside. A favorite with students and faculty from the nearby university, it's a good place to start the day with coffee and croissant, or to enjoy a drink. ✉ *Campo Santa*

Margherita, Dorsoduro 2963, Dorsoduro ☎ *041/5287998* ⊕ *facebook.com/cafferosso.venezia* Ⓜ *Vaporetto: Ca' Rezzonico.*

Orange

BARS | Modern, hip, and complemented by an internal garden, this welcoming bar anchors the south end of Campo Santa Margherita, the liveliest campo in Venice. You can have *piadine* (thin flatbread) sandwiches, salads, and drinks while watching soccer games on a massive screen inside, or sit at the tables facing the campo. Despite being close to the university, Orange is frequented primarily by young working people from the mainland and tourists. ✉ *Campo Santa Margherita, Dorsoduro 3054/A, Dorsoduro* ☎ *041/5234740* ⊕ *facebook.com/OrangeVenezia/* Ⓜ *Vaporetto: Ca' Rezzonico.*

Venice Jazz Club

LIVE MUSIC | Owner Federico is on the piano while his band plays live jazz, in styles including classic, modern, Latin jazz, and bossa nova, at this intimate venue. Concerts usually start at 9 pm every night except Thursday and Sunday, and dinner is available beforehand for an extra charge. ✉ *Ponte dei Pugni, Dorsoduro 3102, Dorsoduro* ☎ *041/5232056, 3401504985* ⊕ *venicejazzclub.weebly.com* 🛏 *€20 entrance fee includes 1 drink* Ⓜ *Vaporetto: Ca' Rezzonico.*

Shopping

Il Grifone

HANDBAGS | Of Venice's few remaining artisan leather shops, Il Grifone is the standout with respect to quality, tradition, and the guarantee of an exquisite product. For more than 30 years, Antonio Peressin has been making bags, purses, belts, and smaller leather items that have a wide following because of his precision and attention to detail. His goods remain reasonably and accessibly priced. ✉ *Fondamenta del Gafaro, Dorsoduro 3516, Dorsoduro* ☎ *041/5229452* ⊕ *www.ilgrifonevenezia.it* Ⓜ *Vaporetto: Piazzale Roma.*

Marina and Susanna Sent

JEWELRY & WATCHES | The beautiful and elegant glass jewelry of Marina and Susanna Sent has been featured in *Vogue*. Look also for vases and other exceptional design pieces. Other locations are on the Fondamenta Serenella on Murano and in San Polo under the Sotoportego dei Oresi at Rialto. ✉ *Campo San Vio, Dorsoduro 669, Dorsoduro* ☎ *041/5208136 for Dorsoduro, 041/5210016 for San Polo, 041/5274665 for Murano* ⊕ *www.marinaesusannasent.com* Ⓜ *Vaporetto: Salute, Accademia, Zattere.*

San Polo and Santa Croce

The two smallest of Venice's six sestieri, San Polo and Santa Croce, were named after their main churches, although the Chiesa di Santa Croce was demolished in 1810. The city's most famous bridge, the Ponte di Rialto, unites San Marco (east) with San Polo (west). The Rialto takes its name from Rivoaltus, the high ground on which it was built. You'll find some of Venice's most lauded restaurants here, and shops abound in the area surrounding the Ponte di Rialto. On the San Marco side you'll find fashion, on the San Polo side, food.

TIMING

To do the area justice requires at least half a day. If you want to take part in the food shopping, come early to beat the crowds. Campo San Giacomo dell'Orio, west of the main thoroughfare that takes you from the Ponte di Rialto to Santa Maria Gloriosa dei Frari, is a peaceful place for a drink and a rest. The museums of Ca' Pesaro are a time commitment—you'll want at least two hours to see them both.

Sights

Ca' Pesaro

ART MUSEUM | Baldassare Longhena's grand Baroque palace, begun in 1676, is the beautifully restored home of two impressive collections. The Galleria Internazionale d'Arte Moderna has works by 19th- and 20th-century artists, such as Klimt, Kandinsky, Matisse, and Miró. It also has a collection of representative works from the Venice Biennale that amounts to a panorama of 20th-century art. The pride of the Museo Orientale is its collection of Japanese art—and especially armor and weapons—of the Edo period (1603–1868). It also has a small but striking collection of Chinese and Indonesian porcelains and musical instruments. ✉ *Fondamenta Pesaro, Santa Croce 2076, Santa Croce* ☎ *041/721127 Galleria, 041/5241173 Museo Orientale* ⊕ *capesaro.visitmuve.it* 🎟 *€10, includes both museums* ⊗ *Closed Mon.–Wed.* Ⓜ *Vaporetto: San Stae.*

Campo San Polo

PLAZA/SQUARE | Only Piazza San Marco is larger than this square, and the echo of children's voices bouncing off the surrounding palaces makes the space seem even bigger. Campo San Polo once hosted bullfights, fairs, military parades, and packed markets, and now comes especially alive on summer nights, when it's home to the city's outdoor cinema.

The Chiesa di San Polo has been restored so many times that little remains of the original 9th-century church, and the 19th-century alterations were so costly that, sadly, the friars sold off many great paintings to pay bills. Although Gianbattista Tiepolo is represented here, his work is outdone by 16 paintings by his son Giandomenico (1727–1804), including the *Stations of the Cross* in the oratory to the left of the entrance. The younger Tiepolo also created a series of expressive and theatrical renderings of the saints. Look for altarpieces by Tintoretto and Veronese that managed to escape auction.

San Polo's bell tower (begun 1362), across the street from the entrance to the church, remained unchanged over the centuries—don't miss the two lions, playing with a disembodied human head and a serpent, on the wall just above the tower's doorway. Tradition has it that the head refers to that of Marino Faliero, the doge executed for treason in 1355. ⊠ *Campo San Polo, San Polo* ☎ *041/2750462 Chorus Foundation* ⊕ *www.chorusvenezia.org* ✉ *Chiesa di San Polo €3 (free with Chorus Pass)* ☉ *Closed Sun.* Ⓜ *Vaporetto: San Silvestro, San Tomà.*

San Giacomo dall'Orio

PLAZA/SQUARE | This lovely square was named after a laurel tree (*orio*), and today trees lend it shade and character. Add benches and a fountain (with a drinking bowl for dogs), and the pleasant, oddly shaped campo becomes a welcoming place for friendly conversation and neighborhood kids at play. The church of San Giacomo dall'Orio was founded in the 9th century on an island still populated (the legend goes) by wolves. The current church dates from 1225. ⊠ *Campo San Giacomo dall'Orio, Santa Croce* ☎ *041/2750462 Chorus Foundation* ⊕ *www.chorusvenezia.org* ✉ *Church €3 (free with Chorus Pass)* ☉ *Church closed Sun.* Ⓜ *Vaporetto: San Stae, Riva de Biasio.*

San Giovanni Elemosinario

CHURCH | Storefronts make up the facade, and market guilds—poulterers, messengers, and fodder merchants—built the altars at this church intimately bound to the Rialto markets. The original church was completely destroyed by a fire in 1514 and rebuilt in 1531 by Scarpagnino, who had also worked on the Scuola di San Rocco. During a more recent restoration, workers stumbled upon a frescoed cupola by Pordenone (1484–1539) that had been painted over centuries earlier.

Don't miss Titian's *St. John the Almsgiver* and Pordenone's *Sts. Catherine, Sebastian, and Roch.* ⊠ *Rialto Ruga Vecchia San Giovanni, San Polo 480, San Polo* ☎ *041/2750462 Chorus Foundation* ⊕ *www.chorusvenezia.org* ✉ *€3 (free with Chorus Pass)* ☉ *Closed Mon.–Sat. after 1:15 and Sun.* Ⓜ *Vaporetto: San Silvestro, Rialto Mercato.*

San Stae

CHURCH | The church of San Stae—the Venetian name for Sant'Eustachio (St. Eustace)—was reconstructed in 1687 by Giovanni Grassi and given a new facade in 1707 by Domenico Rossi. Renowned Venetian painters and sculptors of the early 18th century decorated this church around 1717 with the legacy left by Doge Alvise II Mocenigo, who's buried in the center aisle. San Stae affords a good opportunity to see the early works of Gianbattista Tiepolo, Sebastiano Ricci, and Piazzetta, as well as those of the previous generation of Venetian painters, with whom they had studied. ⊠ *Campo San Stae, Santa Croce* ☎ *041/2750462 Chorus Foundation* ⊕ *www.chorusvenezia.org* ✉ *€3 (free with Chorus Pass)* ☉ *Closed Sun.* Ⓜ *Vaporetto: San Stae.*

★ Santa Maria Gloriosa dei Frari

CHURCH | Completed in 1442, this immense Gothic church of russet-color brick, known locally as "I Frari," is famous worldwide for its array of spectacular Venetian paintings and historic tombs. In the sacristy, see Giovanni Bellini's 1488 triptych *Madonna and Child with Saints,* painted for precisely this spot. The Corner Chapel is graced by Bartolomeo Vivarini's altarpiece *St. Mark Enthroned* and *Saints John the Baptist, Jerome, Peter, and Nicholas.* In the first south chapel of the chorus, there is a fine sculpture of St. John the Baptist by Donatello, dated 1438, with a psychological intensity rare for early Renaissance sculpture. ⊠ *Campo dei Frari, San Polo* ☎ *041/2728618, 041/2750462 Chorus Foundation* ⊕ *www. basilicadeifrari.it* ✉ *€3 (free with Chorus*

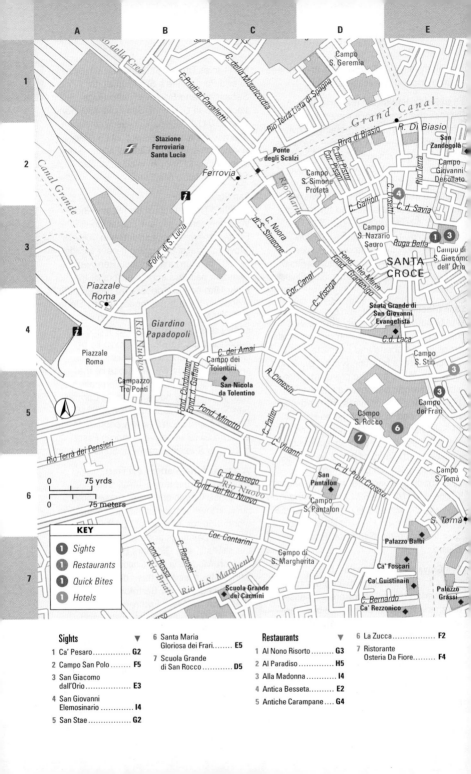

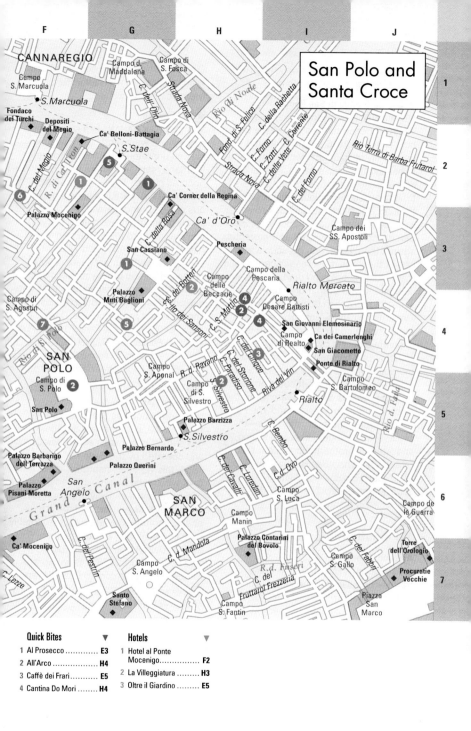

San Polo and Santa Croce

CANNAREGIO

Campo
S. Marcuola

Fondaco
dei Turchi
Depositi
del Megio
Ca' Belloni-Battagia
S.Marcuola
Campo d.
Maddalena
Campo di
S. Fosca

S.Stae
Ca' Corner della Regina
Ca' d'Oro
Campo dei
SS. Apostoli

Palazzo Mocenigo

San Cassiano
Pescheria
Campo della
Pescaria
Rialto Mercato

Palazzo
Muti Baglioni
Campo
delle
Beccarie
Campo
Cesare Battisti
San Giovanni Elemosinario
Ca dei Camerlenghi
San Giacometto

Campo di
S. Agostin
Campo
di Realto
Ponte di Rialto

SAN
POLO
Campo
S. Aponal
Campo
S. Bartolomeo

Campo di
S. Polo
Campo
di S.
Silvestro
Riva del Vin
Rialto

San Polo
Palazzo Barzizza
S. Silvestro

Palazzo Bernardo
Palazzo Querini

Palazzo Barbarigo
dell Terrazza
San
Angelo Canal
Campo
S. Luca
Campo de
la Guerra

Palazzo
Pisani-Moretta
Grand Canal
SAN
MARCO
Campo
Manin

Ca' Mocenigo
Palazzo Contarini
del Bovolo
Torre
dell'Orologio

Campo
S. Angelo
Campo
S. Gallo
Procuratie
Vecchie

Santo
Stefano
Campo
S. Fantin
Piazza
San
Marco

Pass), €1.50 for students under 30 with ID card Ⓜ *Vaporetto: San Tomà.*

★ Scuola Grande di San Rocco

ART MUSEUM | This elegant example of Venetian Renaissance architecture was built between 1516 and 1549 for the essentially secular charitable confraternity bearing the saint's name. The Venetian scuole were organizations that sometimes had loose religious affiliations, through which the artisan class could exercise some influence upon civic life. San Rocco was venerated as a protector against the plague, and his scuola was one of the city's most magnificent. While the building is bold and dramatic outside, its contents are even more stunning—a series of more than 60 paintings by Tintoretto. In 1564, Tintoretto edged out competition for a commission to decorate a ceiling by submitting not a sketch, but a finished work, which he moreover offered free of charge, calculating correctly that a gift could not be rejected. *Moses Striking Water from the Rock, The Brazen Serpent,* and *The Fall of Manna* represent three afflictions—thirst, disease, and hunger—that San Rocco, and later his brotherhood, sought to relieve. ⊠ *Campo San Rocco, San Polo 3052, San Polo* ☎ *041/5234864* ⊕ *www.scuolagrandesanrocco.it* 🎫 *€10* Ⓜ *Vaporetto: San Tomà.*

 **Restaurants**

Al Nono Risorto

$$$ | **VENETIAN** | **FAMILY** | This friendly trattoria popular with the locals is only a short walk from the Rialto markets. The pizza—not a Venetian specialty, generally speaking—is pretty good here, but the star attractions are the generous appetizers and excellent shellfish pastas. **Known for:** pretty outdoor garden seating; quite tasty pizzas; traditional starters and pastas. Ⓢ *Average main: €25* ⊠ *Sotoportego de Siora Bettina, Santa Croce 2338, Santa Croce* ☎ *041/5241169*

⊕ *alnonorisortovenezia.com* ⊗ *Closed Wed. and Jan.* Ⓜ *Vaporetto: Rialto Mercato.*

★ Al Paradiso

$$$$ | **MODERN ITALIAN** | In a small dining room made warm and cozy by its pleasing and unpretentious decor, proprietor Giordano makes all diners feel like honored guests. Unlike many elegant restaurants, Al Paradiso serves generous portions, and many of the delicious antipasti and primi are quite satisfying; you may want to follow the traditional Italian way of ordering and wait until you've finished your antipasto or your *primo* before you order your secondo. **Known for:** central location near the Ponte di Rialto; tasty meat and fish mains; large appetizer and pasta portions. Ⓢ *Average main: €40* ⊠ *Calle del Paradiso, San Polo 767, San Polo* ☎ *041/5234910* ⊕ *www.ristorantealparadiso.com* ⊗ *Closed 3 wks Jan.–Feb.* Ⓜ *Vaporetto: San Silvestro.*

Alla Madonna

$$$ | **VENETIAN** | "The Madonna" used to be world-famous as *the* classic Venetian trattoria, but in recent decades has settled into middle age. Owned and operated by the Rado family since 1954, this Venetian institution looks like one, with wood beams, stained-glass windows, and a panoply of paintings on white walls. **Known for:** old-time atmosphere; traditional Venetian cuisine; freshly prepared seafood. Ⓢ *Average main: €30* ⊠ *Calle della Madonna, San Polo 594, San Polo* ☎ *041/5223824* ⊕ *www.ristoranteallamadonna.com* ⊗ *Closed Wed. and Jan.* Ⓜ *Vaporetto: San Silvestro, Rialto Mercato.*

Antica Besseta

$$$ | **VENETIAN** | Tucked away in a quiet corner of Santa Croce, with a few tables under an ivy shelter, the Antica Besseta dates from the 19th century, and it retains some of its old feel. The menu focuses on vegetables and fish, according to what's at the market, with some pasta and meat dishes, too. **Known**

for: charming old-fashioned feel; simple menu of fish and meat choices; classic Italian pastas, like spaghetti con vongole (with clams). $ *Average main: €35 ⊠ Salizzada de Ca' Zusto, Santa Croce 1395, Santa Croce* ☎ *041/721687* ⊕ *www.anticabesseta.it* ☾ *Closed Tues.* Ⓜ *Vaporetto: Riva de Biasio.*

★ Antiche Carampane

$$$$ | **SEAFOOD** | Judging by its rather modest and unremarkable appearance, you wouldn't guess that Piera Bortoluzzi Librai's trattoria is among the finest fish restaurants in the city both because of the quality of the ingredients and because of the chef's creative magic. You can choose from a selection of classic dishes with a modern and creative touch. **Known for:** popular with visitors and locals (so book ahead); modernized Venetian dishes; superlative fish and seafood. $ *Average main: €40* ⊠ *Rio Terà delle Carampane, San Polo 1911, San Polo* ☎ *041/5240165* ⊕ *www.antichecarampane.com* ☾ *Closed Sun. and Mon., 10 days in Jan., and 3 wks July–Aug.* Ⓜ *Vaporetto: Rialto Mercato, San Silvestro.*

La Zucca

$$$ | **NORTHERN ITALIAN** | Simple place settings, wood lattice walls, and a mélange of languages make La Zucca (The Pumpkin) feel much like a typical, somewhat sophisticated vegetarian restaurant that you could find in any European city. What makes La Zucca special is simply great cooking and the use of fresh, local ingredients—many of which, like the particularly sweet zucca itself, aren't normally found outside northern Italy. **Known for:** flan di zucca, a luscious pumpkin pudding topped with aged ricotta cheese; home-style Italian cooking; seasonal vegetarian-focused dishes. $ *Average main: €25* ⊠ *Calle del Tentor, at Ponte del Megio, Santa Croce 1762, Santa Croce* ☎ *041/5241570* ⊕ *www. lazucca.it* ☾ *Closed Sun.* Ⓜ *Vaporetto: San Stae.*

★ Ristorante Osteria Da Fiore

$$$$ | **VENETIAN** | The understated atmosphere, simple decor, and quiet elegance featured alongside Da Fiore's modern take on traditional Venetian cuisine certainly merit its international reputation. With such beautifully prepared cuisine, you would expect the kitchen to be run by a chef with a household name; however, the kitchen is headed by owner Maurizio Martin's wife, Mara, who learned to cook from her grandmother. **Known for:** reservations required; delicious tasting menus; sophisticated traditional Venetian dishes. $ *Average main: €50* ⊠ *Calle del Scaleter, San Polo 2202, San Polo* ☎ *041/721308* ⊕ *www. ristorantedafiore.com* ☾ *Closed 3 wks in Jan. and Sun. No dinner Fri. and Sat.* Ⓜ *Vaporetto: San Tomà, San Silvestro.*

☕ Coffee and Quick Bites

Al Prosecco

$$ | **WINE BAR** | Locals drop into this friendly bacaro to explore wines from this region and elsewhere in Italy, which accompany a carefully chosen selection of meats, cheeses, and other food from small, artisanal producers, used in tasty panini like the *porchetta romane verdure* (roasted pork with greens) and in elegant cold platters. A young, friendly staff reel off the day's specials with ease. **Known for:** outdoor seating on the lively campo; lovely meat and cheese platters; great selection of biodynamic wines, including prosecco. $ *Average main: €20* ⊠ *Campo San Giacomo dall'Orio, Santa Croce 1503, Santa Croce* ☎ *041/5240222* ⊕ *www.alprosecco.com* ☾ *Closed Sun.* Ⓜ *Vaporetto: San Stae.*

All'Arco

$ | **WINE BAR** | Just because it's noon and you only have enough time between sights for a sandwich doesn't mean that it can't be a satisfying, even awe-inspiring, one. There's no menu at All'Arco, but a scan of what's behind the glass counter is all you need; order what entices you, or have Roberto or Matteo (father and son) suggest a cicheto or panino. **Known for:** friendly and helpful service; platters of meats and cheeses; top-notch cicheti. Ⓢ *Average main: €8* ✉ *Calle Arco, San Polo 436, San Polo* ☎ *041/5205666* ☯ *Closed Wed.* Ⓜ *Vaporetto: Rialto Mercato, San Silvestro.*

Caffè dei Frari

$ | **CAFÉ** | Just over the bridge in front of the Frari church is this old-fashioned place where you'll find an assortment of sandwiches and snacks, but it is the atmosphere, and not the food, that is the main attraction. Established in 1870, it's one of the last Venetian tearooms with its original decor, and while prices are a bit higher than in cafés in nearby Campo Santa Margherita, the vibe and the friendly "retro" atmosphere make the added cost worthwhile. **Known for:** quality cicheti; well-made cocktails; lovely historic setting. Ⓢ *Average main: €8* ✉ *Fondamenta dei Frari, San Polo 2564, San Polo* ☎ *347/8293158* ⊕ *www.ilmercantevenezia.com/il-locale* ☯ *Closed Sun and Mon. No dinner* Ⓜ *Vaporetto: San Tomà.*

Cantina Do Mori

$ | **WINE BAR** | This is the original bacaro, in business continually since 1462; cramped but warm and cozy under hanging antique copper pots, it has served generations of workers from the Rialto markets. In addition to young local whites and reds, the well-stocked cellar offers reserve labels, many available by the glass; between sips you can choose to munch the wide range of cicheti on offer, or a few tiny well-stuffed tramezzini, appropriately called *francobolli* (postage stamps). **Known for:** delicious baccalà mantecato, with or without garlic and parsley; fine selection of cicheti and sandwiches; good choice of wines by the glass. Ⓢ *Average main: €8* ✉ *Calle dei Do Mori, San Polo 429, San Polo* ☎ *041/5225401* ☯ *Closed Sun.* Ⓜ *Vaporetto: Rialto Mercato.*

 ## Hotels

★ Hotel al Ponte Mocenigo

$ | **HOTEL** | At this hotel—once home to the Santa Croce branch of the Mocenigo family, which counts a few doges in its lineage—a columned courtyard welcomes you, and guest room decor nods to the building's history, with canopied beds, striped damask fabrics, lustrous terrazzo flooring, and gilt-accented furnishings. **Pros:** fantastic value; enchanting courtyard (the perfect spot for an aperitivo); friendly and helpful staff. **Cons:** rooms in the annex can be noisy; standard rooms are small; beds are on the hard side. Ⓢ *Rooms from: €110* ✉ *Salizzada San Stae, Santa Croce 1985, Santa Croce* ☎ *041/5244797* ⊕ *www.alpontemocenigo.com* ⇲ *11 rooms* ⦿l *Free Breakfast* Ⓜ *Vaporetto: San Stae.*

La Villeggiatura

$ | **HOTEL** | If eclectic Venetian charm is what you seek, this luminous residence near the Rialto has it: each of the individually decorated guest rooms has its own theater-theme wall painting by a local artist. **Pros:** relaxed atmosphere and friendly, personalized service; well located near markets, artistic monuments, and restaurants; meticulously maintained. **Cons:** no restaurant (though breakfast is served); no view to speak of, despite the climb; no elevator and lots of stairs. Ⓢ *Rooms from: €104* ✉ *Calle dei Botteri, San Polo 1569, San Polo* ☎ *041/5244673* ⊕ *www.lavilleggiatura.it* ⇲ *6 rooms* ⦿l *Free Breakfast* Ⓜ *Vaporetto: Rialto Mercato.*

★ Oltre il Giardino

$$$ | **HOTEL** | Behind a brick wall, just over the bridge from the Frari church, this palazzo is hard to find but well worth the effort: a sheltered location, large garden, and individually decorated guest rooms make it feel like a country house. **Pros:** peaceful, gracious, and convenient setting; friendly owners happy to share their Venice tips; glorious walled garden. **Cons:** no in-house restaurant

(though breakfast served); rooms book up quickly; a beautiful, but not particularly Venetian, ambience. [$] *Rooms from: €218* ✉ *Fondamenta Contarini, San Polo 2542, San Polo* ☎ *041/2750015* 🌐 *www.oltreilgiardino-venezia.com* 🕐 *Closed Jan.* 🛏 *6 rooms* 🍴 *Free Breakfast* [M] *Vaporetto: San Tomà.*

Nightlife

★ Il Mercante

COCKTAIL LOUNGES | When the clock strikes 6 pm, historic Caffè dei Frari transforms into this lively craft cocktail bar that will dazzle your inner adventurer. Relax on a velvet sofa while savoring remarkably inventive drinks paired with flavorful small bites. Each pairing has a distinctive name; "Amatriciana" is composed of vodka, dry vermouth, and black tea, served with Parmesan foam, pineapple gel, and balsamic vinegar (billed as "strong, smoky, tasty"). ✉ *Fondamenta dei Frari, San Polo 2564, San Polo* ☎ *347/8293158* 🌐 *www.ilmercantevenezia.com* [M] *Vaporetto: San Tomà.*

Naranzaria

BARS | At the friendliest of the several bar-restaurants that line the Erbaria, near the Rialto markets, enjoy a cocktail outside, along the Canal Grande, or at a cozy table inside the renovated 16th-century warehouse. Although the food is acceptable, the ambience is really the main attraction. After the kitchen closes at 10:30, light snacks are served until midnight, and there is live music (usually jazz, Latin, or rock) occasionally on Sunday evening. On summer evenings, especially the weekend, the market area draws crowds of young people from Venice, the lagoon islands, and the mainland. ✉ *L'Erbaria, San Polo 130, San Polo* ☎ *041/7241035* 🌐 *www.naranzaria.it* [M] *Vaporetto: Rialto Mercato.*

Shopping

Gilberto Penzo

CRAFTS | The gondola and lagoon boat expert in Venice creates scale models of a wide variety of Venetian boats in his nearby *laboratorio* (workshop). (If the retail shop is closed, a sign posted on the door will explain how to find Signor Penzo.) When he's not busy sawing and sanding, Mr. Penzo writes historical and technical books about traditional Venetian boats, including the gondola. Here you'll also find gondola model kits, as well as some *forcole* (Venetian rowing oarlocks). ✉ *Calle Seconda dei Saoneri, San Polo 2681, San Polo* ☎ *041/5246139* 🌐 *www.veniceboats.com* [M] *Vaporetto: San Tomà.*

★ Il Tabarro San Marco di Monica Daniele

OTHER SPECIALTY STORE | This petite shop is the best place in town to find traditional Venetian wool capes, known as *tabarro*, and classic hats, such as the Ezra Pound (curved hat with a brim), the *tricorno* (three-cornered hat), and the *cilindro* (top hat). ✉ *Calle del Scaleter, San Polo 2235, San Polo* ☎ *041/5246242, 375/5355420* 🌐 *www.monicadaniele.com* [M] *Vaporetto: San Stae, San Silvestro.*

Laberintho

JEWELRY & WATCHES | A tiny bottega near Campo San Polo is run by a team of young goldsmiths and jewelry designers specializing in inlaid stones. The work on display in their shop is exceptional, and they also create customized pieces. ✉ *Calle del Scaleter, San Polo 2236, San Polo* ☎ *041/710017* 🌐 *www.laberintho.com* [M] *Vaporetto: San Stae, San Silvestro.*

Cannaregio

Seen from above, this part of town seems like a wide field plowed by several long, straight canals linked by perpendicular streets—not typical of Venice, where the shape of the islands usually defines the shape of the canals. Cannaregio's main thoroughfare, the Strada Nova (New Street, as it was converted from a canal in 1871), is the longest street in Venice; it runs parallel to the Grand Canal.

TIMING

Although it's more residential and less sight-rich than other Venice neighborhoods, you'll still need several hours here to explore the Ca' d'Oro palace and Madonna dell'Orto and Santa Maria dei Miracoli churches, and to wander the Jewish Ghetto. Cannaregio is a great place to spend a morning before taking the vaporetto to Murano and Burano, which departs from the Fondamente Nove stop.

 # Sights

★ Ca' d'Oro

HISTORY MUSEUM | One of the classic postcard sights of Venice, this exquisite Venetian Gothic palace was once literally a "Golden House," when its marble tracery and ornaments were embellished with gold. It was created by Giovanni and Bartolomeo Bon between 1428 and 1430 for the patrician Marino Contarini, who had read about the Roman emperor Nero's golden house in Rome, the Domus Aurea, and wished to imitate it as a present to his wife. Her family owned the land and the Byzantine *fondaco* (palace-trading house) previously standing on it; you can still see the round Byzantine arches incorporated into the Gothic building's entry porch. ⊠ *Calle Ca' d'Oro, Cannaregio 3933, Cannaregio* ☎ *041/5200345* ⊕ *www.cadoro.org* ⊠ *€6* Ⓜ *Vaporetto: Ca' d'Oro.*

★ Gesuiti (*Chiesa di Santa Maria Assunta*)

CHURCH | The interior walls of this early-18th-century church (1715–30) resemble brocade drapery, and only touching them will convince skeptics that rather than embroidered cloth, the green-and-white walls are inlaid marble.

This trompe-l'oeil decor is typical of the late Baroque's fascination with optical illusion. Toward the end of his life, Titian tended to paint scenes of suffering and sorrow in a nocturnal ambience. A dramatic example of this is on display above the first altar to the left: Titian's daring *Martyrdom of St. Lawrence* (1578), taken from an earlier church that stood on this site. Titian's *Assumption* (1555), originally commissioned for the destroyed Crociferi church, demands reverence. The Crociferi's surviving Oratory features some of Palma Giovane's best work, painted between 1583 and 1591. ⊠ *Campo dei Gesuiti, Cannaregio* ☎ *041/5286579* ⊠ *Gesuiti €1; oratory €3* ⊗ *Oratory closed Mon.–Wed., Jan.–mid-Feb., and Sept.–Oct.* Ⓜ *Vaporetto: Fondamente Nove.*

★ Jewish Ghetto

HISTORIC DISTRICT | The neighborhood that gave the world the word *ghetto* is today a quiet place surrounding a large campo. The area has Europe's highest density of Renaissance-era synagogues, and visiting them is interesting not only culturally but also aesthetically. In 1516, relentless local opposition forced the Senate to confine Jews to an island in Cannaregio, named for its *geto* (foundry). The term "ghetto" also may come from the Hebrew "ghet," meaning separation or divorce. Gates at the entrance were locked at night, and boats patrolled the surrounding canals. In the 16th century, the community grew with refugees from the Inquisition. Although the gates were pulled down after Napoléon's 1797 arrival, the ghetto was reinstated during the Austrian occupation. Full freedom wasn't realized until 1866 with the founding of the Italian state. Many Jews fled Italy as a result of Mussolini's 1938 racial laws. During World War II, the remaining 247 were deported by the Nazis; only eight returned. ⊠ *Campo del Ghetto Nuovo, Cannaregio.*

★ Madonna dell'Orto

CHURCH | Though built toward the middle of the 14th century, this church takes its character from its beautiful late-Gothic facade, added between 1460 and 1464; it's one of the most beautiful Gothic churches in Venice. Tintoretto lived nearby, and this, his parish church, contains some of his most powerful work. Lining the chancel are two huge (45 feet by 20 feet) canvases, *Adoration of the Golden Calf* and *Last Judgment.* In glowing contrast to this awesome spectacle is Tintoretto's *Presentation of the Virgin at the Temple* and the simple chapel where he and his children, Marietta and Domenico, are buried. Paintings by Domenico, Cima da Conegliano, Palma Giovane, Palma Vecchio, and Titian also hang in the church. A chapel displays a photographic reproduction of a precious *Madonna with Child* by Giovanni Bellini. The original was stolen one night in 1993. Don't miss the beautifully austere, late-Gothic cloister (1460), which you enter through the small door to the right of the church; it is frequently used for exhibitions but may be open at other times as well. ⊠ *Campo della Madonna dell'Orto, Cannaregio* ☏ *041/795993* 🎫 *€3, free with Chorus Pass* Ⓜ *Vaporetto: Orto.*

Museo Ebraico (*Jewish Museum*)

SYNAGOGUE | The small but well-arranged museum highlights centuries of Venetian Jewish culture with splendid silver Hanukkah lamps and Torahs and beautifully decorated wedding contracts handwritten in Hebrew. Tours of the ghetto and its five synagogues in Italian and English leave from the museum hourly (on the half hour). ⊠ *Campo del Ghetto Nuovo, Cannaregio 2902/B, Cannaregio* ☏ *041/715359* ⊕ *www.museoebraico. it* 🎫 *€8* ⊘ *Closed Sat.* Ⓜ *Vaporetto: San Marcuola, Guglie.*

Palazzo Vendramin-Calergi

CASINO | Hallowed as the site of Richard Wagner's death and today Venice's most glamorous casino, this magnficent edifice found its fame centuries earlier: Venetian star architect Mauro Codussi (1440–1504) essentially invented Venetian Renaissance architecture with this design. Built for the Loredan family around 1500, Codussi's palace married the fortresslike design of the Florentine Alberti's Palazzo Rucellai with the lightness and delicacy of Venetian Gothic. Note how Codussi beautifully exploits the flickering light of Venetian waterways to play across the building's facade and to pour in through the generous windows. Consult the website for upcoming free guided tours of the small Museo Wagner upstairs, where an archive, events, and concerts may interest Wagnerians.

Venice has always prized the beauty of this palace. In 1652 its owners were convicted of a rather gruesome murder, and the punishment would have involved, as was customary, the demolition of their palace. The murderers were banned from the Republic, but the palace, in view of its beauty and historical importance, was spared. Only a newly added wing was torn down. ⊠ *Cannaregio 2040, Cannaregio* ☏ *041/5297111* ⊕ *www.casinovenezia.it* 🎫 *Casino €5–€10; free for visitors staying at a Venice hotel* Ⓜ *Vaporetto: San Marcuola.*

★ Santa Maria dei Miracoli

CHURCH | Tiny yet harmoniously proportioned, this Renaissance gem, built between 1481 and 1489, is sheathed in marble and decorated inside with exquisite marble reliefs. Architect Pietro Lombardo (circa 1435–1515) miraculously compressed the building to fit its lot, then created the illusion of greater size by varying the color of the exterior, adding extra pilasters on the building's canal side and offsetting the arcade windows to make the arches appear deeper. The church was built to house *I Miracoli,* an image of the Virgin Mary by Niccolò di Pietro (1394–1440) that is said to have performed miracles—look for it on the high altar. ⊠ *Campo Santa Maria*

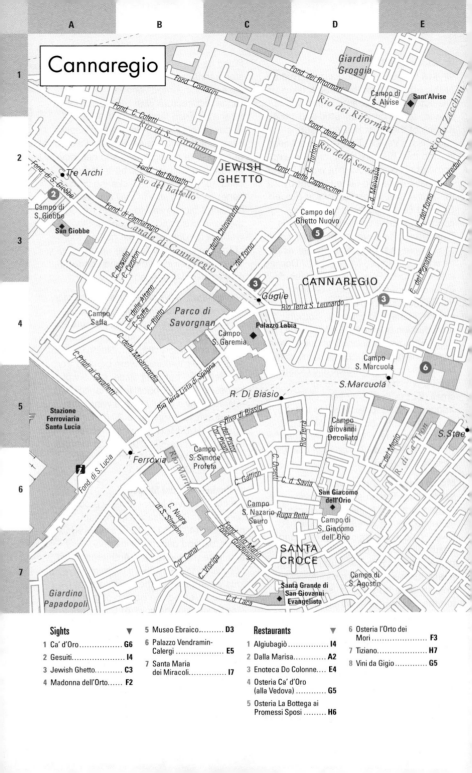

Cannaregio

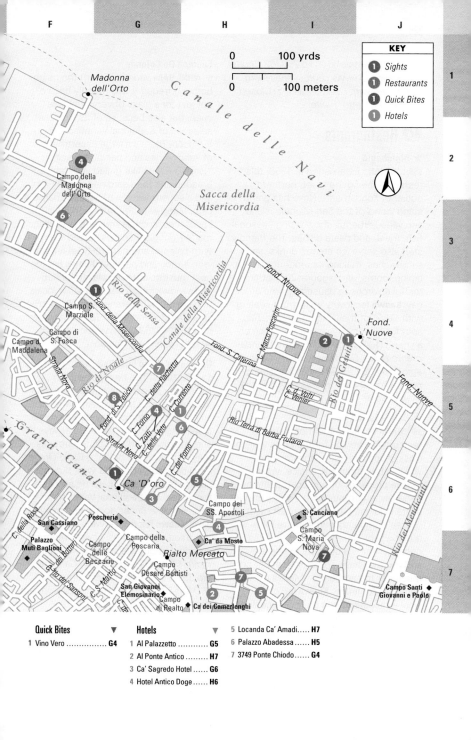

KEY

- **1** Sights
- **1** Restaurants
- **1** Quick Bites
- **1** Hotels

Madonna dell'Orto

Canale delle Navi

Campo della Madonna dell'Orto

Sacca della Misericordia

Fond. Nuove

Fond. Nuove

Campo S. Marziale

Campo di S. Fosca

Campo d. Maddalena

Strada Nova

Rio di Noale

Fond. della Misericordia

Canale della Misericordia

Fond. S. Caterina

C. Marco Foscarini

Rio della Racchetta

C. della Racchetta

C. Correrte

Fond. di S. Felice

C. Forno

C. Zotti

C. delle Vere

C. del Forno

Strada Nova

Rio Terra di Barba Frutarol

C. d. Volti

C. Venier

Grand Canal

Ca 'D'oro

Campo dei SS. Apostoli

S. Canciano

Campo S. Maria Nova

C. della Rosa

San Cassiano

Pescheria

Campo della Pescaria

Ca' da Mosto

Rialto Mercato

Palazzo Muti Baglioni

C. dei Botteri

Campo delle Beccarie

Campo Cesare Battisti

C. S. Maria

San Giovanni Elemosinario

Campo di Rialto

Ca dei Camerlenghi

Campo Santi Giovanni e Paolo

C. Larga dei Sansoni

Rio dei Mendicanti

Nova, Cannaregio ☎ 041/2750462 Chorus Foundation ⊕ www.chorusvenezia.org 🎫 €3 (free with Chorus Pass) ⊘ Closed Sun. Ⓜ Vaporetto: Rialto.

 Restaurants

★ Algiubagiò

$$$ | **ITALIAN** | Established in 1950, this restaurant along the quiet, northern outlier of Fondamente Nove has grandstand views of the San Michele island and various menus showcasing seasonal fish, meat, and pasta dishes. The friendly staff also serve ice cream, drinks, and sandwiches, making its modern bar, chic dining rooms, and lagoon-side platform restful environs to pause any time of day. **Known for:** lovely waterfront seating with views of the Dolomites; romantic spot for dinner; airy respite for lunch or a snack. Ⓢ Average main: €33 ✉ Fondamente Nove, Cannaregio 5039, Cannaregio ☎ 041/5236084 ⊕ www.algiubagio. net ⊘ Closed Tues. Ⓜ Vaporetto: Fondamente Nove.

★ Dalla Marisa

$$ | **ITALIAN** | This is the most famous restaurant in Venice for the city's working class; if you can get a table for lunch, you'll eat, without any choice, what Marisa prepares for her local clientele—generally, enormous portions of excellent pasta followed by a hearty roast meat course (frequently game, more infrequently fish), for an inexpensive fixed price. Dinner is a bit more expensive, and you may have some choice, but not much; for the authentic "Marisa experience," go for lunch. **Known for:** genuine local atmosphere and gruff service; limited menu choices and cramped inside; Venetian classics like baccalà mantecato. Ⓢ Average main: €15 ✉ Fondamenta di San Giobbe 652B, Cannaregio ☎ 041/720211 ⊘ No dinner Sun.–Tues.

Enoteca Do Colonne

$ | **WINE BAR** | Venetians from the neighborhood frequent this friendly bacaro, not just for a glass of very drinkable wine, but also because of its excellent selection of traditional Venetian cicheti for lunch. There's a large assortment of sandwiches and panini, as well as luscious tidbits like grilled vegetables, breaded and fried sardines and shrimp, and a superb version of baccalà mantecato, along with Venetian working-class specialties, such as *musetto* (a sausage made from pigs' snouts served warm with polenta) and *nervetti* (veal tendons with lemon and parsley). **Known for:** the best musetto in town; classic cicheti and sandwiches; a cozy place for locals to hang out. Ⓢ Average main: €10 ✉ Rio Terà Cristo, Cannaregio 1814, Cannaregio ☎ 041/5240453 ⊕ www.docolonne.it Ⓜ Vaporetto: San Marcuola.

Osteria Ca' d'Oro (alla Vedova)

$ | **VENETIAN** | "The best polpette in town," you'll hear fans of the venerable Vedova say, and that explains why it's an obligatory stop on any *giro d'ombra* (bacaro tour); the polpette are always hot and crunchy—and also gluten-free, as they're made with polenta. Ca' d'Oro is a full-fledged trattoria as well, but make sure to reserve ahead: it's no secret to those seeking traditional Venetian fare at reasonable prices, locals and travelers alike. **Known for:** house wine served in tiny traditional glasses; classic Venetian cuisine; famous polpette. Ⓢ Average main: €13 ✉ Calle del Pistor, Cannaregio 3912, off Strada Nova, Cannaregio ☎ 041/5285324 ⊘ Closed Thurs. and Sun. morning Ⓜ Vaporetto: Ca' d'Oro.

Osteria La Bottega ai Promessi Sposi

$$ | **VENETIAN** | Join locals at the *banco* (counter) premeal for an *ombra* (small glass of wine) and cicheti like polpette or violet eggplant rounds, or reserve a table for a full meal in the dining room or the intimate courtyard. A varied, seasonal menu includes local standards like calf's liver or grilled canestrelli, along with creative variations on classic Venetian fare, such as homemade ravioli stuffed with radicchio di Treviso or orecchiette with a scrumptious minced-duck sauce. **Known for:** friendly, helpful service; regularly changing menu with both traditional and modern choices; creative cicheti and wine. [$] *Average main: €19* ✉ *Calle de l'Oca, just off Campo Santi Apostoli, Cannaregio 4367, Cannaregio* ☎ *041/2412747* 🕒 *No lunch Mon.* [M] *Vaporetto: Ca' d'Oro.*

Osteria l'Orto dei Mori

$$$ | **ITALIAN** | This small, popular neighborhood osteria—located canal-side, just under the nose of the campo's famous corner statue—specializes in creative versions of classic Italian (but not necessarily Venetian) dishes; don't skip dessert, as the tiramisu wins raves. Dine in the artsy and atmospheric interior or outside in the intimate, echoing square for a truly memorable experience. **Known for:** buzzing atmosphere with locals and tourists alike; choice local wine selection; traditional Italian dishes with modern accents. [$] *Average main: €26* ✉ *Campo dei Mori, Fondamenta dei Mori, Cannaregio 3386, Cannaregio* ☎ *041/5243677* 🌐 *www.osteriaortodeimori.com* 🕒 *Closed Tues. and Wed.* [M] *Vaporetto: Orto, Ca' d'Oro, San Marcuola.*

Tiziano

$ | **ITALIAN** | A fine variety of excellent tramezzini (sandwiches made of untoasted white bread triangles) lines the display cases at this *tavola calda* (roughly the Italian equivalent of a cafeteria) on the main thoroughfare from the Rialto to Santi Apostoli; inexpensive salad plates and daily pasta specials are also served. This is a great place for a light meal or snack before a performance at the nearby Teatro Malibran. **Known for:** efficient (if occasionally grumpy) service; modest prices; quick meals or snacks, especially tramezzini. [$] *Average main: €8* ✉ *Salizada San Giovanni Crisostomo, Cannaregio 5747, Cannaregio* ☎ *041/5235544* [M] *Vaporetto: Rialto.*

★ Vini da Gigio

$$$ | **VENETIAN** | A brother-sister team run this refined trattoria, where you're made to feel as if you've been personally invited to lunch or dinner. Indulge, perhaps, in rigatoni with duck sauce or arugula-stuffed ravioli, seafood risotto made to order, or sesame-encrusted tuna. Just note, though, that it's the meat dishes that steal the show: the steak with red-pepper sauce and the *tagliata di agnello* (sautéed lamb fillet with a light, crusty coating) are both superb, and you'll never enjoy a better *fegato alla veneziana*. **Known for:** helpful and professional service; one of the city's best wine cellars; superb meat dishes like fegato alla veneziana. [$] *Average main: €25* ✉ *Fondamenta San Felice, Cannaregio 3628/A, Cannaregio* ☎ *041/5285140* 🌐 *www.vinidagigio.com* 🕒 *Closed Mon., Tues., and 2 wks in Aug.* [M] *Vaporetto: Ca' d'Oro.*

☕ Coffee and Quick Bites

★ Vino Vero

$ | **WINE BAR** | Swing by this pint-sized wine bar for cicheti and crostini that are just a bit different and fresher than what you'll find elsewhere, along with a fine selection of natural wines. Though there's not much space inside, try to snag one of the coveted seats by the canal. **Known for:** pretty canal-side seating; delectable small bites; large selection of both Italian and international natural wines. [$] *Average main: €12* ✉ *Fondamenta de la Misericordia, Cannaregio 2497, Cannaregio* ☎ *041/2750044* 🌐 *vinovero.wine* 🕒 *No lunch Mon.* [M] *Vaporetto: Madonna dell'Orto, Ca' d'Oro.*

Hotels

Al Palazzetto

$$ | **B&B/INN** | **FAMILY** | Understated Venetian decor, original exposed-beam ceilings and terrazzo flooring, and large rooms suitable for families or small groups are hallmarks of this intimate, family-owned guesthouse. **Pros:** authentic 18th-century palace; good value; clean and quiet. **Cons:** a bit rough around the edges; not many amenities; old-fashioned decor. [$] *Rooms from: €149* ✉ *Calle delle Vele, Cannaregio 4057, Cannaregio* ☎ *041/2750897* 🌐 *www.guesthouse.it* 🛏 *5 rooms* 🍴 *Free Breakfast* [M] *Vaporetto: Ca' d'Oro.*

★ Al Ponte Antico

$$$$ | **HOTEL** | This hospitable 16th-century palace inn has lined its Gothic windows with tiny white lights, creating an inviting glow that's emblematic of the luxurious, distinctively Venetian warmth inside. **Pros:** upper-level terrace overlooks Grand Canal; excellent service; family-run warmth. **Cons:** books up quickly; beds a little hard for some; in one of the busiest areas of the city (although not particularly noisy). [$] *Rooms from: €330* ✉ *Calle dell'Aseo, Cannaregio 5768, Cannaregio* ☎ *041/2411944* 🌐 *www.alponteantico.com* 🛏 *9 rooms* 🍴 *Free Breakfast* [M] *Vaporetto: Rialto.*

Ca' Sagredo Hotel

$$$ | **HOTEL** | This expansive palace has been the Sagredo family residence since the mid-1600s and has the decor to prove it: a massive staircase has Longhi wall panels soaring above it; large common areas are adorned with original art by Tiepolo, Longhi, and Ricci; and a traditional Venetian style dominates guest rooms, many of which have canal views and some of which have original art and architectural elements. **Pros:** excellent location; rooftop terrace and indoor bar; some of the city's best preserved interiors. **Cons:** no coffee- or tea-making facilities in rooms; heat in rooms controlled by front desk; more opulent than intimate. [$] *Rooms from: €280* ✉ *Campo Santa Sofia, Cannaregio 4198/99, Cannaregio* ☎ *041/2413111* 🌐 *www.casagredohotel.com* 🛏 *42 rooms* 🍴 *No Meals* [M] *Vaporetto: Ca' d'Oro.*

Hotel Antico Doge

$$$ | **HOTEL** | Once the home of Marino Faliero, a 14th-century doge who was executed for treason, this palazzo has been attentively "modernized" in elegant 18th-century Venetian style: all rooms are adorned with brocades, damask-tufted walls, gilt mirrors, and parquet floors—even the breakfast room has a stuccoed ceiling and Murano chandelier. **Pros:** romantic, atmospheric decor; some rooms have whirlpool tubs; convenient to the Rialto and beyond. **Cons:** area outside hotel can get very busy; no elevator; no outdoor garden or terrace. [$] *Rooms from: €230* ✉ *Campo Santi Apostoli, Cannaregio 5643, Cannaregio* ☎ *041/2411570* 🌐 *www.anticodoge.com* 🛏 *20 rooms* 🍴 *Free Breakfast* [M] *Vaporetto: Ca' d'Oro, Rialto.*

Locanda Ca' Amadi

$$ | **HOTEL** | A historic 13th-century palazzo near the Rialto markets is a welcome retreat on a tranquil *corte,* (court) and individually decorated rooms have tufted walls and views of a lively canal or a quiet courtyard. **Pros:** classic Venetian style; handy for sightseeing; some canal-view rooms. **Cons:** reception staff not always helpful or available; no restaurant (simple continental breakfast served, though); rooms vary a lot in size and quality. [$] *Rooms from: €130* ✉ *Corte Amadi, Cannaregio 5815, Cannaregio* ☎ *041/5285210* 🌐 *www.caamadi.it* 🛏 *6 rooms* 🍴 *Free Breakfast* [M] *Vaporetto: Rialto.*

★ Palazzo Abadessa

$$ | **HOTEL** | At this late-16th-century palazzo, you can experience warm hospitality, a luxurious atmosphere, a lush private garden, and unusually spacious guest rooms well appointed with antique-style furniture, frescoed or stuccoed ceilings,

and silk fabrics. **Pros:** enormous walled garden, a rare and delightful treat in crowded Venice; superb guest service; unique and richly decorated guest rooms. **Cons:** Wi-Fi can be iffy; no restaurant (buffet breakfast served); some bathrooms are small and plain. [$] *Rooms from: €160* ✉ *Calle Priuli, Cannaregio 4011, Cannaregio* ☎ *041/2413784* 🌐 *www.abadessa.com* 🕓 *Closed last 2 wks in Jan.* 🛏 *15 rooms* 🍴 *Free Breakfast* [M] *Vaporetto: Ca' d'Oro.*

3749 Ponte Chiodo

$ | **B&B/INN** | Spending time at this charming guesthouse near the Ca' d'Oro vaporetto stop is like staying with a friend: service is warm and helpful, with lots of suggestions for dining and sightseeing. **Pros:** highly attentive service; pretty private garden; relaxed atmosphere. **Cons:** not for those looking for large-hotel amenities (no spa or gym); no restaurant, though breakfast is served in the garden; some bathrooms are smallish. [$] *Rooms from: €105* ✉ *Calle Racheta, Cannaregio 3749, Cannaregio* ☎ *041/2413935* 🌐 *www.pontechiodo.it* 🛏 *6 rooms* 🍴 *Free Breakfast* [M] *Vaporetto: Ca' d'Oro.*

Nightlife

El Sbarlefo

WINE BARS | The odd name is Venetian for "smirk," although you'll be hard-pressed to find one at this cheery, familiar bacaro with a wine selection as ample as the cicheti on offer. The spread of delectables ranges from classic polpette of meat and tuna to tomino cheese rounds to speck and robiola rolls, and the selection of wines is equally intriguing. There's often live jazz and blues on Friday and Saturday nights. El Sbarlefo has a second location in Dorsoduro, in the calle just behind the church of San Pantalon. ✉ *Salizada del Pistor, off Campo Santi Apostoli, Cannaregio 4556/C, Cannaregio* ☎ *041/5246650* 🌐 *www.elsbarlefo.it* [M] *Vaporetto: Ca' d'Oro.*

TiME Social Bar

COCKTAIL LOUNGES | The seasonal cocktails at this charming mixology bar, many of which use fruit and homemade bitters, win rave reviews from visitors and locals alike. There are also small nibbles on offer if hunger strikes. ✉ *Rio Terà Farsetti, Cannaregio 1414, Cannaregio* ☎ *0338/3636951* 🌐 *timesocialbar.it* [M] *Vaporetto: San Marcuola Casino.*

Un Mondo di Vino

WINE BARS | Recharge with some wine or a cicheto or two—meat, fish, and vegetarian choices are on offer—at this cozy, friendly spot near the Miracoli church. Numerous wines are available by the glass, and the helpful servers are often happy to crack open a bottle for sampling if there's something you fancy. ✉ *Salizzada San Cancian, Cannaregio* ☎ *041/5211093* 🌐 *www.bacarounmondodivino.it* [M] *Vaporetto: Rialto, Ca' d'Oro.*

Shopping

★ **Gianni Basso Stampatore**

STATIONERY | Beloved of artists and celebrities, this traditional printer creates handmade business cards, stationery, and invitations using vintage letterpress machinery. You can choose from the selection on offer, or have your own custom-designed and shipped to you at home. ✉ *Calle del Fumo, Cannaregio 5306, Cannaregio* ☎ *041/5234681* [M] *Vaporetto: Fondamente Nove.*

Vittorio Constantini

ANTIQUES & COLLECTIBLES | **FAMILY** | This glass artist's workshop features unusual, intricate pieces inspired by nature—birds, butterflies, beetles, and other insects—appreciated by adults and children alike. ✉ *Calle del Fumo, Cannaregio 5311, Cannaregio* ☎ *041/5222265* 🌐 *www.vittoriocostantini.com* [M] *Vaporetto: Fondamente Nove.*

Castello

Castello, Venice's largest sestiere, includes all of the land from east of Piazza San Marco to the city's easternmost tip. Its name probably comes from a fortress that once stood on one of the eastern islands. Not every well-off Venetian family could find a spot or afford to build a palazzo on the Grand Canal. Many who couldn't instead settled in western Castello, taking advantage of its proximity to the Rialto and San Marco, and built the noble palazzi that today distinguish this area from the fisher's enclave in the more easterly streets of the sestiere. During the days of the Republic, eastern Castello was the primary neighborhood for workers in the shipbuilding Arsenale located in its midst and now home to the Venice Biennale. Foodies flock here for some of the city's most creative modern Italian cuisine.

TIMING

Unless you're here during the Biennale—in which case, you'll be spending at least a full day or two at the Arsenale—you can check out the neighborhood's three gorgeous churches (San Francesco della Vigna, Santi Giovanni e Paolo, and San Zaccaria), as well as the lovely rooms in the Scuola di San Giorgio degli Schiavoni (if it's open, which it isn't always), in half a day.

Sights

Arsenale

MILITARY SIGHT | Visible from the street, the Porta Magna (1460), an impressive Renaissance gateway designed by Antonio Gambello, was the first classical structure to be built in Venice. It is guarded by four lions—war booty of Francesco Morosini, who took the Peloponnese from the Turks in 1687. The Arsenale is said to have been founded in 1104 on twin islands. The immense facility that evolved—it was the largest industrial complex in Europe built prior to the Industrial Revolution—was given the old Venetian dialect name *arzanà*, borrowed from the Arabic *darsina'a*, meaning "workshop." At the height of its activity, in the early 16th century, it employed as many as 16,000 *arsenalotti*, workers who were among the most respected shipbuilders in the world. The Arsenale developed a type of pre–Industrial Revolution assembly line, which allowed it to build ships with astounding speed and efficiency. The Arsenale's efficiency was confirmed time and again—whether building 100 ships in 60 days to battle the Turks in Cyprus (1597) or completing one perfectly armed warship, start to finish, while King Henry III of France attended a banquet. ⊠ *Campo de la Tana 2169, Castello* Ⓜ *Vaporetto: Arsenale.*

★ San Francesco della Vigna

CHURCH | Although this church contains some interesting and beautiful paintings and sculptures, it's the architecture that makes it worth the hike through a lively, middle-class residential neighborhood. The Franciscan church was enlarged and rebuilt by Jacopo Sansovino in 1534, giving it the first Renaissance interior in Venice; its proportions are said to reflect the mystic significance of the numbers three and seven dictated by Renaissance neo-Platonic numerology. The soaring but harmonious facade was added in 1562 by Palladio. The church represents a unique combination of the work of the two great stars of 16th-century Veneto architecture. ⊠ *Campo di San Francesco della Vigna, Castello* ☎ *041/5206102* Ⓜ *Vaporetto: Celestia.*

★ San Zaccaria

CHURCH | More a museum than a church, San Zaccaria has a striking Renaissance facade, with central and upper portions representing some of Mauro Codussi's best work. The lower portion of the facade and the interior were designed by Antonio Gambello. The original structure of the church was 14th-century Gothic, with its facade completed in 1515, some years after Codussi's death in 1504, and it retains the proportions of the rest of the essentially Gothic structure. Inside is one of the great treasures of Venice, Giovanni Bellini's celebrated altarpiece, *La Sacra Conversazione,* easily recognizable in the left nave. Completed in 1505, when the artist was 75, it shows Bellini's ability to incorporate the aesthetics of the High Renaissance into his work. ⊠ *Campo San Zaccaria, 4693 Castello, Castello* ☎ *041/5221257* ⊠ *Church free, chapels and crypt €2* ⊘ *Closed Sun. morning* Ⓜ *Vaporetto: San Zaccaria.*

★ Santi Giovanni e Paolo

CHURCH | This gorgeous Italian Gothic church of the Dominican order, consecrated in 1430, looms over one of the most picturesque squares in Venice: the Campo Giovanni e Paolo, centered around the magnificent 15th-century equestrian statue of Bartolomeo Colleoni by the Florentine Andrea Verrocchio. Bartolomeo Bon's portal, combining Gothic and classical elements, was added between 1458 and 1462, using columns salvaged from Torcello. The 15th-century Murano stained-glass window near the side entrance is breathtaking for its beautiful colors and figures. ⊠ *Campo dei Santi Giovanni e Paolo, Castello* ☎ *041/5235913* ⊕ *www.santigiovannie-paolo.it* ⊠ *€3.50* ⊘ *Closed weekends* Ⓜ *Vaporetto: Fondamente Nove, Rialto.*

★ Scuola di San Giorgio degli Schiavoni

HISTORIC SIGHT | Founded in 1451 by the Dalmatian community, this small scuola, or confraternity, was, and still is, a social and cultural center for migrants from what is now Croatia. It contains one of Italy's most beautiful rooms, harmoniously decorated between 1502 and 1507 by Vittore Carpaccio. Although Carpaccio generally painted legendary and religious figures against backgrounds of contemporary Venetian architecture, here is perhaps one of the first instances of "Orientalism" in Western painting.

■ TIP→ **Opening hours are quite flexible. Since this is a must-see site, book in advance so you won't be disappointed.** ⊠ *Calle dei Furlani, Castello 3259/A, Castello* ☎ *041/5228828* ⊕ *www.scuo-ladalmatavenezia.com* ⊠ *€5* Ⓜ *Vaporetto: Arsenale, San Zaccaria.*

 ## Restaurants

Al Covo

$$$ | VENETIAN | For years, Diane and Cesare Binelli's Al Covo has set the standard of excellence for traditional, refined Venetian cuisine; the Binellis are dedicated to providing their guests with the freshest, highest-quality fish from the Adriatic, and vegetables, when at all possible, from the islands of the Venetian Lagoon and the fields of the adjacent Veneto region. Although their cuisine could be correctly termed "classic Venetian," it always offers surprises, like the juicy crispness of their legendary *fritto misto* (fried mixed seafood and vegetables)—reliant upon an unconventional secret ingredient in the batter—or the heady aroma of their fresh anchovies marinated in wild fennel, an herb somewhat foreign to Veneto. **Known for:** Diane's chocolate cake for dessert; top-notch local ingredients; sophisticated Venetian flavors. Ⓢ *Average main: €28* ⊠ *Campiello Pescaria, Castello 3968, Castello* ☎ *041/5223812* ⊕ *www. ristorantealcovo.com* ⊘ *Closed Tues. and Wed., 3 wks. in Jan., and 10 days in Aug.* Ⓜ *Vaporetto: Arsenale.*

★ Alle Testiere

$$$ | VENETIAN | The name is a reference to the old headboards that adorn the walls of this tiny, informal restaurant, but the food (not the decor) is undoubtedly the focus. Local foodies consider this one of the most refined eateries in the city thanks to chef Bruno Gavagnin's gently creative take on classic Venetian fish dishes; the chef's artistry seldom draws attention to itself, but simply reveals new dimensions of familiar fare, creating

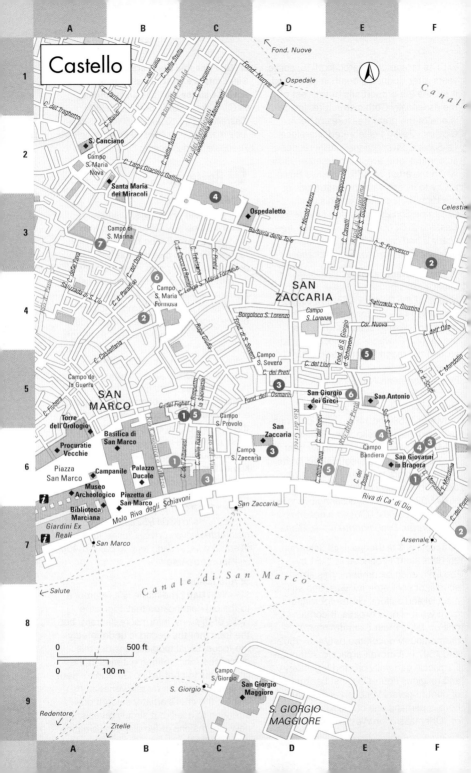

KEY

1 *Sights*
1 *Restaurants*
1 *Quick Bites*
1 *Hotels*

Sights ▼

1 Arsenale **I7**
2 San Francesco della Vigna **F3**
3 San Zaccaria **D6**
4 Santi Giovanni e Paolo **C3**
5 Scuola di San Giorgio
  degli Schiavoni **E5**

Restaurants ▼

1 Al Covo **F6**
2 Alle Testiere **B4**
3 Corte Sconta **F6**
4 CoVino **F6**
5 Il Ridotto **C5**
6 Local **E5**
7 Osteria di Santa Marina **A3**

Quick Bites ▼

1 Aciugheta **C5**
2 El Rèfolo **H8**
3 Wine Bar 5000 .... **D5**

Hotels ▼

1 Ca' dei Dogi **B6**
2 Ca' di Dio **F7**
3 Hotel Danieli **C6**
4 Hotel La Residenza **E6**
5 Metropole **E6**
6 Ruzzini Palace Hotel **B4**

elle Fondamento Nuove

Bacini →

nd Casa Nuova

dell'Oratorio
mpo
ella
éstia

Canale delle Galeazze

◆Arsenale

Darsena
Grande

Darsena Arsenale Vecchio

Campo
dell'
arsenale

CASTELLO

Tana

Rio di S. Daniele

Campo della Tana

Rio della Tana

Fond. della Tana

C. dei Preti

Cor. Nuova

Fond. S. Gioacchino
Fond. di S. Anna

Via Giuseppe Garibaldi

C. del Santi

C. dei Pister

C. Caboto

C. Vechia

Via Giuseppe Garibaldi

C. Nicoli

C. delle Ancore

C. delle Eufalie

C. della Stra

C. Sarestin

Riva S. Biagio

C. S. Biagio

Cor. Colonne

Cor. Schiavona

C. di S. Domenico

Secco Marina

Riva dei Sette Martiri

Giardini
Garibaldi

Fond. di S. Giuseppe

Campo di
S. Giuseppe

Viale Trento

Giardini
Pubblici

S. Elena ↘

Giardini •

dishes that stand out for their lightness and balance. **Known for:** wonderful wine selection; excellent pasta with seafood; daily changing fish offerings, based on what's fresh at the market. [$] *Average main: €28* ✉ *Calle del Mondo Novo, Castello 5801, Castello* ☎ *041/5227220* 🌐 *www.osterialletestiere.it* 🕒 *Closed Sun. and Mon., 3 wks in Jan.–Feb., and 4 wks in July–Aug.*

★ Corte Sconta

$$$ | **SEAFOOD** | The heaping seafood antipasti alone is reason enough to visit this classic seafood-focused eatery close to the Biennale—think tuna and swordfish carpaccio, spider crab, clams, crab pâté, and a variety of fish. But you'll also want to stay for the excellent mains, particularly soft-shell crab, mixed grilled fish, and spaghetti vongole, plus the lovely courtyard setting. **Known for:** service with a sense of humor; charming atmosphere with outdoor seating; some of the best seafood in town. [$] *Average main: €25* ✉ *Calle del Pestrin, Castello 3886, Castello* ☎ *041/5227024* 🌐 *www.cortescontavenezia.com* 🕒 *Closed Sun. and Mon.* [M] *Vaporetto: Arsenale.*

CoVino

$$$$ | **ITALIAN** | A charming new concept in Venetian eateries, diminutive CoVino offers a fixed-price, three-course menu, from which you'll choose among several traditionally inspired antipasti, secondi, and desserts with innovative—and satisfying—twists. At this Slow Food presidio, you can watch the cook construct your sliced tuna dressed with Bronte pistachios and eggplant; Bra sausage "imported" from the Piedmont alla Valpolicella with tiny green beans; or perhaps even fresh gazpacho. **Known for:** wine selection; light lunch option for €30; locally sourced ingredients. [$] *Average main: €42* ✉ *Calle del Pestrin, Castello 3829a-3829, Castello* ☎ *041/2412705* 🌐 *www.covinovenezia.com* 💳 *No credit cards* 🕒 *Closed Tues. and Wed. No lunch Thurs.* [M] *Vaporetto: Arsenale.*

★ Il Ridotto

$$$$ | **MODERN ITALIAN** | Longtime restaurateur Gianni Bonaccorsi (proprietor of the popular Aciugheta nearby) has established an eatery where he can pamper a limited number of lucky patrons with his imaginative cuisine and impeccable taste in wine. *Ridotto* means "small, private place," which this very much is, evoking an atmosphere of secrecy and intimacy; the innovative menus tend toward lighter but wonderfully tasty versions of classic dishes. **Known for:** extensive wine recommendations; excellent five- or seven-course tasting menus; some of the most creative cuisine in Venice. [$] *Average main: €40* ✉ *Campo SS. Filippo e Giacomo, Castello 4509, Castello* ☎ *041/5208280* 🌐 *www.ilridotto.com* 🕒 *Closed Wed., no lunch Tues. and Thurs.* [M] *Vaporetto: San Zaccaria.*

★ Local

$$$$ | **VENETIAN** | In a simple yet charming setting with beamed ceilings and terrazzo floors, a sister and brother team oversee their "New Venetian Cuisine," where local ingredients are used to prepare reinvented traditional dishes, often with Japanese influences. It's tasting-menu only, with seven or nine courses (or a less expensive three-course option at weekday lunch), and wine pairings from their extensive list are a recommended treat. **Known for:** highly attentive staff; ingredients from Italian producers and daily catch; tiramigiù dessert: coffee, marsala, and mascarpone. [$] *Average main: €110* ✉ *Salizzada dei Greci, Castello 3303, Castello* ☎ *041/2411128* 🌐 *www.ristorantelocal.com* 🕒 *Closed Tues. and Wed.* [M] *Vaporetto: San Zaccaria.*

★ Osteria di Santa Marina

$$$ | **VENETIAN** | The candlelit tables on this romantic campo are inviting enough, but it's the intimate restaurant's imaginative kitchen that's likely to win you over; you can order consistently excellent pasta, fish, or meat dishes à la carte or opt for one of the rewarding

tasting menus. The wine list is ample and well thought out, and the service is gracious, warm, and professional. **Known for:** wonderful wine pairings; charming setting; innovative and artfully presented modern Venetian food. $ *Average main: €30* ⊠ *Campo Santa Marina, Castello 5911, Castello* ☎ *041/5285239* ⊕ *www. osteriadisantamarina.com* ☉ *Closed Sun. and 2 wks in Aug. No lunch Mon.* Ⓜ *Vaporetto: Rialto.*

Coffee and Quick Bites

Aciugheta
$$ | **WINE BAR** | Almost an institution, the "Tiny Anchovy" (as the name translates) doubles as a pizzeria-trattoria, but the real reason for coming is the bar's tasty cicheti (finger foods), like the eponymous anchovy minipizzas, the *arancioni* (stuffed fried rice balls), and the polpette (meatballs or croquettes). Wines by the glass change daily, but there is always a good selection of local wines on hand, as well as some Tuscan and Piedmontese choices thrown in for good measure. **Known for:** good selection of Italian wines by the glass; mix of traditional and more modern cicheti; pizzetta con l'acciuga (minipizza with anchovy). $ *Average main: €15* ⊠ *Campo SS. Filippo e Giacomo, Castello 4357, Castello* ☎ *041/5224292* ☉ *Closed Mon.* Ⓜ *Vaporetto: San Zaccaria.*

El Rèfolo
$$ | **WINE BAR** | At this contemporary cantina and hip hangout in a very Venetian neighborhood, the owner pairs enthusiastically chosen wines and artisanal beers with select meat, savory cheese, and seasonal vegetable combos. With outside-only seating (not particularly comfortable), it's more appropriate for an aperitivo and a light meal. **Known for:** boisterous atmosphere outside in nice weather; filling meat and cheese plates; good selection of wine and beer. $ *Average main: €16* ⊠ *Via Garibaldi, Castello 1580, Castello* ☎ *344/1636759* ⊕ *www.elrefolo. it* ☉ *Closed Mon.* Ⓜ *Vaporetto: Arsenale.*

Wine Bar 5000
$ | **WINE BAR** | Nibble on a selection of cicheti or a cheese or meat plate at this cozy wine bar on Campo San Severo, near the Basilica dei Frari. You can either dine inside the brick-walled, Murano glass–chandeliered space, or watch the gondolas sail by at a table outdoors next to the quiet adjacent Severno canal. **Known for:** small but well-prepared choice of cicheti; lovely outdoor seating area; large wine list, including biodynamic options. $ *Average main: €10* ⊠ *Campo San Severo, Castello 5000, Castello* ☎ *041/5201557* ⊕ *www.lunasentada.it/ winebar5000* ☉ *Closed Tues. and Wed.* Ⓜ *Vaporetto: San Zaccaria.*

🛏 Hotels

★ Ca' dei Dogi
$ | **HOTEL** | A quiet courtyard secluded from the San Marco melee offers an island of calm in six guest rooms and two apartments (some with private terraces overlooking the Doge's Palace, one with a Jacuzzi), which are individually decorated with contemporary furnishings and accessories. **Pros:** amazing location close to Doge's Palace and Piazza San Marco; traditional Italian restaurant on-site; balconies with wonderful views. **Cons:** bathrooms can feel cramped; no elevator and lots of stairs; rooms are on the small side. $ *Rooms from: €116* ⊠ *Corte Santa Scolastica, Castello 4242, Castello* ☎ *041/2413751* ⊕ *www. cadeidogi.it* ☉ *Closed 3 wks. in Dec.* ↴ *6 rooms* ⦿ *Free Breakfast* Ⓜ *Vaporetto: San Zaccaria.*

Ca' di Dio
$$$$ | **HOTEL** | Housed in a palace dating from 1272, with interiors updated by of-the-moment architect Patricia Urquiola, this deluxe hotel offers rooms with views of San Giorgio Maggiore island, two restaurants, and two internal courtyards, all within striking distance of the Venice Biennale grounds. **Pros:** on-site gym and spa; convenient to the

Biennale; most guest rooms are suites. **Cons:** quite expensive; a walk from traditional Venetian sights; not for fans of traditional design. $ *Rooms from: €565* ✉ *Riva Ca' di Dio, Castello 5866, Castello* ☎ *041/0980238* ⊕ *vretreats.com/en/ca-di-dio* ⇴ *66 rooms* ⦿ *Free Breakfast* Ⓜ *Vaporetto: Arsenale.*

★ Hotel Danieli

$$$$ | HOTEL | One of the city's most famous lodgings—built in the 14th century and run as a hotel since 1822—lives up to its reputation: the chance to explore the wonderful, highly detailed lobby is itself a reason to book an overnight stay, plus the views along the lagoon are fantastic, the rooms gorgeous, and the food fabulous. **Pros:** historical and inviting lobby; tasty cocktails at Bar Dandolo; amazing rooftop views. **Cons:** service can be indifferent; some rooms feel dated; lots of American tourists. $ *Rooms from: €500* ✉ *Riva degli Schiavoni, Castello 4196, Castello* ☎ *041/5226480* ⊕ *www.marriott.com/hotels/travel/vcelc-hotel-danieli-a-luxury-collection-hotel-venice* ⇴ *210 rooms* ⦿ *No Meals* Ⓜ *Vaporetto: San Zaccaria.*

Hotel La Residenza

$$$ | HOTEL | Set in a quiet campo, this renovated 15th-century Gothic-Byzantine palazzo has simple but spacious rooms and lovely public spaces filled with chandeliers, 18th-century paintings, and period reproduction furnishings. **Pros:** lavish salon and breakfast room; affordable rates; quiet residential area, steps from Riva degli Schiavoni and 10 minutes from Piazza San Marco. **Cons:** sparse breakfast; basic guest rooms; no elevator. $ *Rooms from: €210* ✉ *Campo Bandiera e Moro (or Bragora), Castello 3608, Castello* ☎ *041/5285315* ⊕ *www.venicelaresidenza.com* ⇴ *15 rooms* ⦿ *No Meals* Ⓜ *Vaporetto: Arsenale.*

★ Metropole

$$$$ | HOTEL | Atmosphere prevails in this labyrinth of opulent, intimate spaces featuring classic Venetian decor combined with Eastern influences: the owner—a lifelong collector of unusual objects—has filled the common areas and sumptuously appointed guest rooms with an assortment of antiques and curiosities. **Pros:** hotel harkens back to the gracious Venice of a bygone era; great food and cocktails in the gorgeous Oriental Bar & Bistrot; suites have private roof terraces with water views. **Cons:** quirky, eccentric collections on display not for everyone; rooms with views are considerably more expensive; one of the most densely touristed locations in the city. $ *Rooms from: €400* ✉ *Riva degli Schiavoni, Castello 4149, Castello* ☎ *041/5205044* ⊕ *www.hotelmetropole.com* ⇴ *67 rooms* ⦿ *Free Breakfast* Ⓜ *Vaporetto: San Zaccaria.*

Ruzzini Palace Hotel

$$$ | HOTEL | Renaissance- and Baroque-style common areas are soaring spaces with Venetian terrazzo flooring, frescoed and exposed beam ceilings, and Murano chandeliers; guest rooms tastefully mix historical style with contemporary furnishings and appointments. **Pros:** a luminous, aristocratic ambience; great buffet breakfast (not included in all rates); located on a lively Venetian campo not frequented by tourists. **Cons:** no restaurant on-site; relatively far from a vaporetto stop; plain bathrooms. $ *Rooms from: €250* ✉ *Campo Santa Maria Formosa, Castello 5866, Castello* ☎ *041/2410447* ⊕ *www.ruzzinipalace.com* ⇴ *28 rooms* ⦿ *No Meals* Ⓜ *Vaporetto: San Zaccaria, Rialto.*

Nightlife

Bar Dandolo

COCKTAIL LOUNGES | Even if you're not staying at Hotel Danieli, it's worth a stop to marvel at its bar's over-the-top decor inside a 14th-century palace. Though pricey, it's a highly atmospheric place to sample their signature Vesper martini or another cocktail of your choice, usually accompanied by live piano music. ✉ *Hotel Danieli, Riva degli Schiavoni, Castello*

4196, Castello ☎ 041/5226480 ⊕ *www.
marriott.com* Ⓜ *Vaporetto: San Zaccaria.*

Zanzibar

CAFÉS | This kiosk bar is very popular on
warm summer evenings with Venetians
and tourists. Although there's food, it's
mostly limited to conventional Venetian
sandwiches and commercial ice cream.
The most interesting thing about the
place is its location with a view of the
church of Santa Maria Formosa, which
makes it a pleasant place for a drink
and a good place for people-watching.
⊠ *Campo Santa Maria Formosa, Castello
5840, Castello* ☎ *345/9423998* Ⓜ *Vaporetto: San Zaccaria.*

Shopping

★ **Banco Lotto No. 10**

WOMEN'S CLOTHING | All the one-of-a-
kind clothes and bags on sale at this
vintage-inspired boutique were designed
and created by residents of the women's
prison on Giudecca island. ⊠ *Salizada
Sant'Antonin, Castello 3478/A, Castello* ☎ *041/5221439* Ⓜ *Vaporetto: San
Zaccaria.*

★ **Papier Mache—Laboratorio
di Artigianato Artistico**

OTHER SPECIALTY STORE | FAMILY | If you're
looking for an authentic Venetian mask,
this is the place to come. Owner Stefano
and his talented team of artists create
exquisite handmade masks that can be
custom-ordered if you don't see what
you want, as well as shipped worldwide.
⊠ *Calle Lunga Santa Maria Formosa,
Castello 5174/B, Castello* ☎ *041/5229995
⊕ www.papiermache.it* Ⓜ *Vaporetto:
Ospedale.*

San Giorgio Maggiore and the Giudecca

Beckoning travelers across St. Mark's
Basin is the island of San Giorgio Maggiore, separated by a small channel from
the Giudecca. A tall brick campanile on
that distant bank nicely complements
the Campanile of San Marco. Beneath
it looms the stately dome of one of
Venice's greatest churches, San Giorgio
Maggiore, the creation of Andrea Palladio. To the west, on the Giudecca, is
Palladio's other masterpiece, the church
of the Santissimo Redentore.

You can reach San Giorgio Maggiore via
Vaporetto Line 2 from San Zaccaria. The
next three stops on the line take you to
the Giudecca. The island's past may be
shrouded in mystery, but despite recent
gentrification by artists and well-to-do
bohemians, it's still down-to-earth and
one of the city's few remaining primarily
working-class neighborhoods. Interest-
ingly, you find that most Venetians don't
even consider the Giudecchini Venetians
at all.

TIMING

A half day should be plenty of time to
visit the area. Allow about a half hour to
see each of the churches and an hour or
two to look around the Giudecca.

Sights

★ **Fondazione Giorgio Cini**
(*Cini Foundation*)

OTHER MUSEUM | Adjacent to San Giorgio
Maggiore is a complex that now houses
the Cini Foundation, established in
1951 as a cultural center dedicated
to humanist research. It contains a
beautiful cloister designed by Palladio
in 1560, his refectory, a library designed
by Longhena, and various archives. In
a woodland area you can wander amid
10 "Vatican Chapels" created for the
2018 Architecture Biennale by renowned

Did You Know?

The nobility in Venice used to be extremely competitive about their gondolas, decorating them in flamboyant colors and over-the-top ornaments. A law in the 16th century put an end to that. Today, all gondolas in Venice must be painted boring black, though they are allowed three flourishes: a curly tail, a pair of seahorses, and a multi-pronged prow.

architects, including Norman Foster. Another stunning feature is the Borges Labyrinth, a 1-km (½-mile) path through a boxwood hedge that allows visitors to take a 45-minute contemplative walk. It was designed by Randoll Coate and inspired by the Jorge Luis Borges short story "The Garden of Forking Paths." An evocative audio guide, composed by Antonio Fresa and performed by Teatro La Fenice's orchestra, may accompany your pensive stroll. Guided tours are given daily (except Wednesday, November through mid-March), and reservations are required. ☒ *Isola di San Giorgio Maggiore, San Giorgio Maggiore* ☎ *366/4202181 WhatsApp for info and guided tours reservations* ⊕ *www.cini. it* ☒ *€14 for guided tour of either the Foundation buildings or the Vatican Chapels; €18 for guided tour of both the Foundation buildings and the Vatican Chapels* ⊗ *Closed Wed. Nov.–mid-Mar.* ⊠ *Reservations required* Ⓜ *Vaporetto: San Giorgio.*

★ **San Giorgio Maggiore**

CHURCH | There's been a church on this island since the 8th century, with the addition of a Benedictine monastery in the 10th. Today's refreshingly airy and simply decorated church of brick and white marble was begun in 1566 by Palladio and displays his architectural hallmarks of mathematical harmony and classical influence. *The Last Supper* and the *Gathering of Manna,* two of Tintoretto's later works, line the chancel. To the right of the entrance hangs *The Adoration of the Shepherds* by Jacopo Bassano (1517–92); affection for his home in the foothills, Bassano del Grappa, is evident in the bucolic subjects and terra-firma colors. If they have time, monks are happy to show Carpaccio's *St. George and the Dragon,* which hangs in a private room. The campanile (bell tower) dates from 1791, the previous structures having collapsed twice. ■**TIP→ Climb to the top of the campanile for unparalleled 360-degree views of the lagoon, islands,** and Venice itself. ☒ *Isola di San Giorgio Maggiore, San Giorgio Maggiore* ☎ *041/5227827 San Giorgio Maggiore* ⊕ *www.abbaziasangiorgio.it* ☒ *Church free, campanile €6* Ⓜ *Vaporetto: San Giorgio.*

Santissimo Redentore

CHURCH | After a plague in 1576 claimed some 50,000 people—nearly one-third of the city's population (including Titian)—Andrea Palladio was asked to design a commemorative church. The Giudecca's Capuchin friars offered land and their services, provided the building's design was in keeping with the simplicity of their hermitage. Consecrated in 1592, after Palladio's death, the Redentore (considered Palladio's supreme achievement in ecclesiastical design) is dominated by a dome and a pair of slim, almost minaretlike bell towers. Its deceptively simple, stately facade leads to a bright, airy interior. There aren't any paintings or sculptures of note, but the harmony and elegance of the interior makes a visit worthwhile. ☒ *Fondamenta San Giacomo, Giudecca* ☎ *041/5231415, 041/2750462 Chorus Foundation* ⊕ *www.chorusvenezia.org* ☒ *€3 (free with Chorus Pass)* ⊗ *Closed Sun.* Ⓜ *Vaporetto: Redentore.*

🍴 Restaurants

Cip's Club & Oro

$$$$ | VENETIAN | Located on the water's edge, looking out at the Venice skyline, the Belmond Cipriani's exclusive outdoor-indoor Cip's Club bar and Oro restaurant is best known for its breathtaking views, but the exquisite tasting menu of Venetian classics and extensive wine list certainly don't play second fiddle. Taking the complimentary 10-minute boat ride to and from San Marco also adds to the thoroughly James Bond sense of drama and romance. **Known for:** relaxing lunch destination; sophisticated service; sublime Venice vistas with a Bellini. Ⓢ *Average main: €100* ☒ *Belmond Hotel Cipriani, Giudecca 10, Giudecca*

☎ *041/240801* 🌐 *www.belmond.com/hotels/europe/italy/venice/belmond-hotel-cipriani/dining* 👔 *Oro: elegant informal (no shorts, sleeveless shirts, or flip-flops)* [M] *Vaporetto: Zitelle.*

★ La Palanca

$$ | ITALIAN | It's all about the views at this classic, informal wine bar–restaurant, where tables perched on the water's edge are often filled with chatty patrons, particularly at lunchtime. The homemade pasta and fish dishes are highly recommended, and although they don't really serve dinner, a filling selection of cicheti is offered in the evening. **Known for:** superlative views; good, affordable wine list; sea bass ravioli, grilled seafood, and baccalà. [$] *Average main: €16* ✉ *Isola della Giudecca 448, Giudecca* ☎ *041/5287719* ⏲ *Closed Sun.* [M] *Vaporetto: Palanca.*

Hotels

★ Belmond Hotel Cipriani

$$$$ | HOTEL | With amazing service, wonderful rooms, fab restaurants, and a large pool and spa—all just a five-minute boat ride from Piazza San Marco (the hotel water shuttle leaves every 15 minutes, 24 hours a day)—the Cipriani is Venetian luxe at its best. **Pros:** old-world charm meets modern luxury; Michelin-starred restaurant; Olympic-size heated saltwater pool. **Cons:** gym not open 24 hours; may be too quiet for some; very expensive. [$] *Rooms from: €967* ✉ *Giudecca 10, Giudecca* ☎ *041/240801* 🌐 *belmond.com* ⏲ *Closed mid-Nov.–late Mar.* 🛏 *96 rooms* 🍴 *Free Breakfast* [M] *Vaporetto: Zitelle.*

Hilton Molino Stucky Venice

$$$ | HOTEL | FAMILY | Wooden beams and iron columns are some of the original details still visible in this redbrick former flour mill-turned-hotel, which also features sublime views across the lagoon to Venice, particularly from the lively rooftop bar. **Pros:** extremely helpful staff; ample breakfast buffet; shuttle boat to San Marco. **Cons:** food offerings on the pricey side; hotel itself a bit confusing to navigate; can hear noise from other rooms. [$] *Rooms from: €215* ✉ *Giudecca 810, Giudecca* ☎ *041/2723311* 🌐 *www.hilton.com* 🛏 *379 rooms* 🍴 *No Meals* [M] *Vaporetto: Palanca.*

Nightlife

★ Skyline Rooftop Bar

COCKTAIL LOUNGES | For arguably the best views of Venice anywhere, visit this buzzy eighth-floor hotel cocktail bar. There are regular DJ and live music events during the summer months. ✉ *Hilton Molino Stucky Venice, Giudecca 810, Giudecca* ☎ *041/2723316* 🌐 *www.skylinebarvenice.it* [M] *Vaporetto: Palanca.*

Shopping

Fortuny Tessuti Artistici

FABRICS | The original Fortuny textile factory, built on former convent grounds, has been converted into a showroom. Prices are over-the-top, but it's worth a trip to see the extraordinary colors and textures of their hand-printed silks and velvets. Call in advance to arrange a tour of the buildings and gorgeous gardens. ✉ *Fondamenta San Biagio, Giudecca 805, Giudecca* ☎ *041/5287697, 393/8257651* 🌐 *fortuny.com* [M] *Vaporetto: Palanca.*

Islands of the Lagoon

The perfect vacation from your Venetian vacation is an escape to Murano, Burano, and sleepy Torcello, the islands of the northern lagoon, or to the Lido, Venice's barrier island that forms the southern border of the Venetian Lagoon. Torcello is legendary for its beauty and breathing room, and makes a wonderful destination for a picnic (be sure to pack a lunch). Burano, which has a long history of lace production, is an island

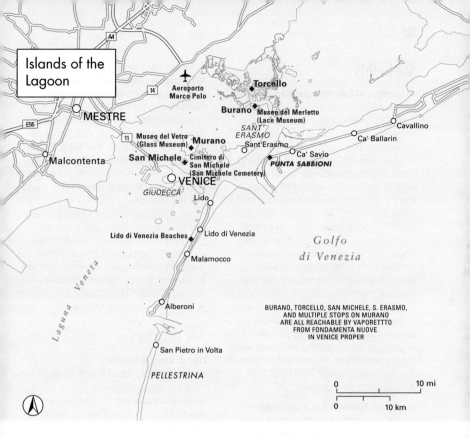

Islands of the Lagoon

MESTRE

Aeroporto Marco Polo

Torcello

Burano Museo del Merletto (Lace Museum)

Museo del Vetro (Glass Museum) **Murano**

SANT' ERASMO

Sant'Erasmo

San Michele
Cimitero di San Michele (San Michele Cemetery)

Ca' Savio

PUNTA SABBIONI

Malcontenta

Ca' Ballarin

Cavallino

VENICE

GIUDECCA

Lido

Laguna Veneta

Lido di Venezia Beaches

Lido di Venezia

Golfo di Venezia

Malamocco

Alberoni

BURANO, TORCELLO, SAN MICHELE, S. ERASMO, AND MULTIPLE STOPS ON MURANO ARE ALL REACHABLE BY VAPORETTO FROM FONDAMENTA NUOVE IN VENICE PROPER

San Pietro in Volta

PELLESTRINA

0   10 mi

0   10 km

of fishing traditions and houses painted in a riot of colors—blue, yellow, pink, ocher, and dark red. Murano is renowned for its glass, and you can tour a glass factory here, but be warned that you will be pressured to buy. San Michele, a vaporetto stop on the way to Murano, is the cemetery island of Venice, the resting place of many international artists who have chosen to spend eternity in this beautiful city. Finally, the Lido, which protects Venice from the waters of the Adriatic, forms the beach of Venice, and is home to a series of elegant bathing establishments.

TIMING

Hitting all the sights on all the islands takes a busy, full day. If you limit yourself to Murano and San Michele, you can easily explore for an ample half day; the same goes for Burano and Torcello. In summer

the express Vaporetto Line 7 will take you to Murano from San Zaccaria (the Jolanda landing) in 25 minutes; Line 3 will take you from Piazzale Roma to Murano via the Canale di Cannaregio in 21 minutes; otherwise, local Line 4.1 makes a 45-minute trip from San Zaccaria every 20 minutes, circling the east end of Venice, stopping at Fondamente Nove and San Michele on the way. To see glassblowing, get off at Colonna; the Museo stop will put you near the Museo del Vetro.

Line 12 goes from Fondamente Nove direct to Murano and Burano every 30 minutes (from there, Torcello is a five-minute ferry ride on Line 9); the full trip takes 45 minutes each way. To get to Burano and Torcello from Murano, pick up Line 12 at the Faro stop (Murano's lighthouse). Line 1 runs from San Marco to the Lido in about 20 minutes.

Sights

★ Cimitero di San Michele (San Michele Cemetery)

CEMETERY | It's no surprise that serenity prevails on San Michele in Venice's northern lagoon. The city's island cemetery is surrounded by ocher brick walls and laced with cypress-lined pathways amid plots filled with thousands of graves; there's also a modern extension completed by British architect David Chipperfield in 2017. Among those who have made this distinctive island their final resting place are such international arts and science luminaries as Igor Stravinsky, Sergei Diaghilev, Ezra Pound, and the Austrian mathematician Christian Doppler (of the Doppler effect). You're welcome to explore the grounds if you dress respectfully and adhere to a solemn code of conduct. Photography and picnicking are not permitted. ⊠ *Isola di San Michele, San Michele* ☎ *041/7292841* ⛴ *Free* Ⓜ *Vaporetto: San Michele.*

Museo del Merletto (Lace Museum)

HISTORY MUSEUM | **FAMILY** | Home to the Burano Lace School from 1872 to 1970, the palace of Podestà of Torcello now houses a museum dedicated to the craft for which this island is known. Detailed explanations of the manufacturing process and Burano's distinctive history as a lace-making capital provide insight into displays that showcase everything from black Venetian Carnival capes to fingerless, elbow-length "mitten gloves" fashionable in 17th-century France. Portraits of Venice's aristocracy as well as embroidered silk and brocade gowns with lace embellishments provide greater societal context on the historical use of lace in European fashion. You can also watch interesting lace-making demonstrations. ⊠ *Piazza Galuppi 187, Burano* ☎ *041/730034* ⊕ *museomerletto. visitmuve.it* ⛴ *€6* ⊗ *Closed Mon.–Wed.* Ⓜ *Vaporetto: Burano.*

★ Museo del Vetro (Glass Museum)

ART MUSEUM | **FAMILY** | This compact yet informative museum displays glass items dating from the 3rd century to today. You'll learn all about techniques introduced through the ages (many of which are still in use), including 15th-century gold-leaf decoration, 16th-century filigree work that incorporated thin bands of white or colored glass into the crystal, and the 18th-century origins of Murano's iconic chandeliers. A visit here will help you to understand the provenance of the glass you'll see for sale—and may be tempted to buy—in shops around the island. ⊠ *Fondamenta Marco Giustinian 8, Murano* ☎ *041/739586* ⊕ *museovetro. visitmuve.it* ⛴ *€11* ⊗ *Closed Mon.–Wed.* Ⓜ *Vaporetto: Murano Museo.*

Beaches

Lido di Venezia Beaches

BEACH | **FAMILY** | Most hotels on the Lido have access to charming beach clubs with cabanas, striped umbrellas, and chaise longues—all of which are often available for nonguests to use for a fee. On either end of the long barrier island, the public beaches offer a more rustic but still delightful setting for nature lovers to dig their toes in the sand. **Amenities:** food and drink; lifeguards; showers; toilets. **Best for:** swimming; walking. ⊠ *Lido di Venezia, Lido* Ⓜ *Vaporetto: Lido.*

Restaurants

Acquastanca

$$$ | **VENETIAN** | Grab a seat among locals at this charming, intimate eatery—the perfect place to pop in for a lunchtime primo or to embark on a romantic evening. The name, referring to the tranquility of the lagoon at the turn of the tide, reflects this restaurant's approach to food and service, and you'll find such tempting seafood-based dishes as gnocchi with scallops and zucchini and curried scampi with black venere rice; tasteful decor sets the mood, with exposed brick, iron, and glass accents, and charming fish sculptures. **Known for:** relaxing atmosphere; focus on seafood dishes; light and fresh traditional food. [$] *Average main: €26* ✉ *Fondamenta Manin 48, Murano* ☎ *041/3195125* 🌐 *www.acquastanca.it* 🕒 *Closed Sun. No dinner Tues.–Thurs.* [M] *Vaporetto: Murano Colonna, Murano Faro.*

Busa alla Torre da Lele
$$ | **VENETIAN** | If you're shopping for glass on Murano and want to sample some first-rate home cooking for lunch, you can't do better than stopping in this unpretentious trattoria in the island's central square. Friendly waiters will bring you ample portions of pasta, with freshly made seafood-based sauces, and a substantial variety of carefully grilled or baked fish. **Known for:** outdoor dining on a square; reliable lunch stop in Murano; tasty local fish and seafood. [$] *Average main: €20* ✉ *Campo Santo Stefano 3, Murano* ☎ *041/739662* 🕒 *No dinner* [M] *Vaporetto: Murano Colonna.*

Locanda Cipriani Restaurant
$$$ | **VENETIAN** | A nearly legendary restaurant—Hemingway came here often to eat, drink, and brood under the veranda's greenery—established by a nephew of Giuseppe Cipriani (the founder of Harry's Bar), this inn profits from its idyllic location on the island of Torcello. The food is not exceptional, especially considering the high prices, but dining here is more about getting lost in Venetian magic; the menu features pastas and lots of seafood. **Known for:** a peaceful lunch choice when you want to get away from Venice; traditional Venetian cuisine, with a focus on seafood; wonderful historic atmosphere. [$] *Average main: €31* ✉ *Piazza Santa Fosca 29, Torcello* ☎ *041/730150* 🌐 *www.locandacipriani.com* 🕒 *Closed Tues. and early Jan.–mid-Feb.* [M] *Vaporetto: Torcello.*

Trattoria Al Gatto Nero
$$$ | **SEAFOOD** | Around since 1965, Al Gatto Nero offers the best fish on Burano. No matter what you order, though, you'll savor the pride the owner and his family have in their lagoon, their island, and the quality of their *cucina* (maybe even more so when enjoying it on the picturesque fondamenta). **Known for:** tagliolini (thin spaghetti) with spider crab; risotto Burano style, using local ghiozzi fish; the freshest fish and seafood around. [$] *Average main: €33* ✉ *Fondamenta della Giudecca 88, Burano* ☎ *041/730120* 🌐 *www.gattonero.com* 🕒 *Closed Mon., 1 wk in July, and 3 wks in Nov. No dinner Sun. or Wed.* [M] *Vaporetto: Burano.*

★ **Venissa**
$$$$ | **MODERN ITALIAN** | Stroll across the bridge from Burano to the islet of Mazzorbo to see some of the Venetian islands' only working vineyards, amid which sits this charming restaurant where seasonal dishes incorporate vegetables, herbs, and flowers fresh from the garden and fish fresh from the lagoon, served in seven- to nine-course tasting menus (there's also a more casual osteria). To accompany your meal, pick out a local wine like the Dorona di Venezia, made with the island's native grape. **Known for:** perfect wine pairings; relaxed setting with tables overlooking the vines; creative, sometimes avant-garde dishes. [$] *Average main: €140* ✉ *Fondamenta Santa Caterina 3, Mazzorbo* ☎ *041/5272281* 🌐 *www.venissa.it* 🕒 *Closed Tues., Wed., and Dec.–mid-Mar. No lunch* [M] *Vaporetto: Mazzorbo.*

🛏 Hotels

Hotel Excelsior Venice Lido Resort
$$$$ | **HOTEL** | **FAMILY** | Built in 1908, this grand hotel with Moorish decor has old-fashioned charm and loads of amenities—from a private beach with white cabanas and a seasonal bar and restaurant to a swimming pool, gym, and tennis courts (though, oddly, no spa).

Pros: lovely beachfront location; friendly, welcoming staff; convenient water shuttle every 30 minutes to and from Venice proper. **Cons:** can get very busy in summer and around the Venice Film Festival; restaurants on the expensive side; could do with a refresh. $ *Rooms from: €610* ⊠ *Lungomare Marconi 41, Lido* ☎ *041/5260201* ⊕ *www.hotelex-celsiorvenezia.com* 🛏 *196 rooms* ⦿ *No Meals* Ⓜ *Vaporetto: Lido.*

★ Hyatt Centric Murano Venice
$$ | HOTEL | Befitting its location on Murano, this well-situated hotel is in a former glassmaking factory and has vitreous works of art throughout; it also has spacious, contemporary guest rooms with dark-wood floors and brown-and-cream color schemes. **Pros:** excellent breakfast buffet; easy walk to restaurants and shops; vaporetto stop right outside the hotel, free airport transfers. **Cons:** extra charge for using wellness center; gym is basic; most rooms have no views. $ *Rooms from: €153* ⊠ *Riva Longa 49, Murano* ☎ *041/2731234* ⊕ *www.hyatt.com* 🛏 *119 rooms* ⦿ *No Meals* Ⓜ *Vaporetto: Murano Museo.*

★ JW Marriott Venice Resort & Spa
$$$$ | RESORT | Once you get a taste of the resort's lush gardens, fabulous spa, and fantastic pools—all set on an exclusive island called Isole Delle Rose, a 20-minute boat ride from Venice—you may find yourself quickly settling in to la dolce vita. **Pros:** relaxed vibe; loads of amenities; spacious rooms. **Cons:** extra charge for spa; not much Venetian style in rooms; getting to and from Venice can feel like a hassle. $ *Rooms from: €647* ⊠ *Isola delle Rose, Laguna di San Marco, Venice* ☎ *041/8521300* ⊕ *www.jwvenice.com* ◷ *Closed mid-Nov.–Feb.* 🛏 *266 rooms* ⦿ *Free Breakfast.*

🛍 Shopping

★ Davide Penso
JEWELRY & WATCHES | This Venice-born, Murano-based artist makes gorgeous glass necklaces, earrings, and bracelets using the lampwork technique, where he shapes colored glass rods over a flame. ⊠ *Fondamenta Riva Longa 48, Murano* ☎ *041/739819* ⊕ *www.davidepenso.info* Ⓜ *Vaporetto: Museo Murano.*

★ Emilia Burano
FABRICS | This is not your grandmother's lace—these fourth-generation lace makers have updated their designs to produce exquisite bed linens, lampshades, and other items. ⊠ *Piazza Galuppi 205, Burano* ☎ *041/735245* ⊕ *emiliaburano.it* Ⓜ *Vaporetto: Burano.*

★ MaMa Salvadore Murano
GLASSWARE | To see more of glassmaking's artistic side, visit this gallery/shop that highlights works from international contemporary glass artists. ⊠ *Fondamenta da Mula 148, Murano* ☎ *0331/6224359* ⊕ *www.mamamurano.com* Ⓜ *Vaporetto: Murano.*

★ Salviati
GLASSWARE | One of the oldest and most prestigious Italian glassmakers (founded in 1859), Salviati partners with renowned international designers, including Tom Dixon, to create beautiful contemporary pieces. ⊠ *Fondamenta Radi 16, Murano* ☎ *041/5274085* ⊕ *www.salviati.com* Ⓜ *Vaporetto: Murano Museo, Murano Navagero.*

★ Simone Cenedese
GLASSWARE | This talented second-generation glass master produces intricately designed and often whimsical glass chandeliers and sculptures. ⊠ *Calle Bertolini 6, Murano* ☎ *041/5274455* ⊕ *simonecenedese.it* Ⓜ *Vaporetto: Murano Faro, Murano Colonna.*

Chapter 6

THE VENETO AND FRIULI–VENEZIA GIULIA

Updated by
Nick Bruno

 Sights
★★★☆☆

 Restaurants
★★★★★

 Hotels
★★★★☆

 Shopping
★★☆☆☆

 Nightlife
★☆☆☆☆

WELCOME TO THE VENETO AND FRIULI–VENEZIA GIULIA

TOP REASONS TO GO

★ **Giotto's frescoes in the Cappella degli Scrovegni:** In this Padua chapel, Giotto's expressive and innovative frescoes foreshadowed the Renaissance.

★ **Villa Barbaro in Maser:** Master architect Palladio's graceful creation meets Veronese's splendid frescoes in a one-time-only collaboration.

★ **Opera in Verona's ancient arena:** The performances may not be top-notch, but even serious opera fans can't resist the spectacle of these shows.

★ **Roman and early Christian ruins at Aquileia:** Aquileia's beautiful ruins offer a glimpse of the transition from pagan to Christian Rome and are almost entirely free of tourists.

★ **The wine roads north of Treviso:** A series of routes takes you through beautiful hillsides to some of Italy's finest wines.

1 Padua. An old university city brimming with art and history, Padua is most noted for Giotto's Cappella degli Scrovegni frescoes.

2 Verona. One of the best preserved and most beautiful cities in Italy.

3 Vicenza. This elegant art city bears the signature of the great 16th-century architect Andrea Palladio.

4 Marostica. A small hilltop-citadel town renowned for a biennial human-scale chess game.

5 Asolo. The "City of a Hundred Horizons" is in the wine-producing hills.

6 Treviso. This town with beguiling canals has more than a touch of Venetian style.

7 Udine. This city has medieval and Renaissance splendors, including works by Tiepolo.

8 Cividale del Friuli. The Natisone River and ravine and the Julian Alps provide a ravishing backdrop to this town.

9 Aquileia. This was a pivotal port town in Augustus's Rome.

10 Trieste. This port city has Belle Époque cafés and palaces.

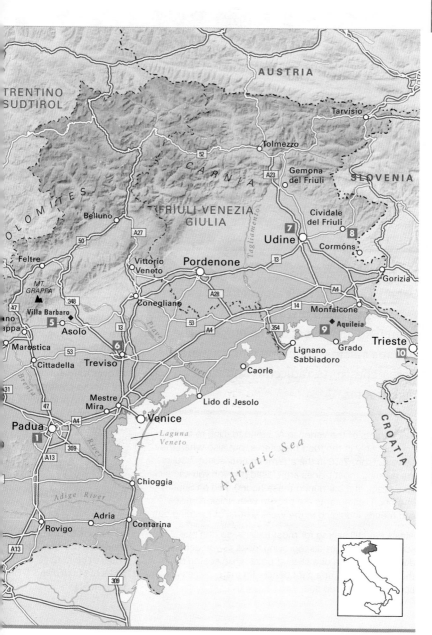

EATING AND DRINKING WELL IN THE VENETO AND FRIULI–VENEZIA GIULIA

With the decisive seasonal changes of the Venetian Arc, it's little wonder that many restaurants shun printed menus. Elements from field and forest define much of the region's cuisine, including white asparagus, herbs, chestnuts, radicchio, and wild mushrooms.

Restaurants of the Venetian Arc tend to cling to tradition, not only in the food they serve, but also when they serve it. From 2:30 in the afternoon until about 7:30 in the evening most places are closed (though you can pick up a snack at a bar during these hours), and on Sunday afternoon restaurants are packed with Italian families and friends indulging in the weekly ritual of lunching out.

Meals are still sacred for most Italians, so don't be surprised if you get disapproving looks as you gobble down a sandwich or a slice of pizza while seated on the church steps or a park bench. (In many places it's actually illegal to do so.)

THE BEST IN BEANS

Pasta e fagioli (a thick bean soup with pasta, served slightly warm or at room temperature) is made all over Italy. Folks in the Veneto, though, take special pride in their version, made from particularly fine beans grown around the village of Lamon, near Belluno. *Il fagiolo di Lamon* derives from the *Borlotto di Vigevano* bean and was first introduced by a monk in the 1500s via the Spanish court's colonial links to Mexico and Guatemela.

FISH

The catch of the day is always a good bet, whether it's sweet and succulent Adriatic shellfish, sea bream, bass, or John Dory, or freshwater fish from Lake Garda, near Verona. A staple in the Veneto is *baccalà*: this is dried salt cod, which, alongside *stoccafisso*, air-dried cod, was introduced to Italy during the Renaissance by northern European traders. Dried cod is soaked in water or milk and then prepared in a different way in each city. In Vicenza, baccalà *alla vicentina* confusingly uses stoccafisso, which is cooked with onions, milk, and cheese, and is generally served with polenta.

MEAT

In the Veneto, traditional dishes feature offal as much as the prime cuts. Beef (including veal), pork, rabbit, horse, and donkey meat are standard, while goose, duck, and guinea fowl are common poultry options. In Friuli–Venezia Giulia, menus show the influence of Austria-Hungary: you may find deer and hare on the menu, as well as Eastern European–style goulash. One unusual treat served throughout the Veneto is *nervetti*—cubes of gelatin from a calf's knee prepared with onions, parsley, olive oil, and lemon.

PASTA, RISOTTO, POLENTA

For *primi* (first courses), the Veneto dines on *bigoli* (thick whole-wheat pasta), generally served with an anchovy-onion sauce delicately flavored with cinnamon, or creamy risotto flavored with vegetables or shellfish. Polenta is everywhere, whether it's a stiff porridge topped with Gorgonzola, or a stew, or a patty grilled and served alongside meat or fish.

RADICCHIO DI TREVISO

In fall and winter be sure to try the radicchio di Treviso, a red endive grown near that town but popular all over the region. Cultivation is very labor-intensive, so it can be expensive. It's best in a veal or chicken stew, in a risotto, or just grilled or baked with a drizzle of olive oil and perhaps a little Taleggio cheese from neighboring Lombardy.

WINE

The Veneto produces more D.O.C. (Denominazione di Origine Controllata) wines than any other region in Italy. Amarone, the region's crowning achievement, is a robust, full-bodied red. The best of the whites are Soave, prosecco, and *pinot bianco* (pinot blanc). In Friuli–Venezia Giulia, local wines include *friulano*, a dry, lively white made from the sauvignon vert grape, and *picolit*, a dessert wine.

The arc around Venice—stretching from Verona to Trieste, encompassing the Veneto and Friuli–Venezia Giulia regions—is indisputably one of the most culturally rich areas in Italy, an intellectual and spiritual feast of architecture, painting, and sculpture. Since the 16th century, the art, architecture, and way of life here have all reflected Venetian splendor.

It wasn't always this way. Back in the Middle Ages, Padua and Verona were independent cities that developed substantial cultural traditions of their own, leaving behind many artistic treasures. And even while it was under Venice's political domination, 16th-century Vicenza contributed more to the cultural heritage of La Serenissima than it took from her—in large part because of its master architect, Andrea Palladio.

This region is primarily flat, green farmland. As you move inland, though, you encounter low hills, which swell and rise in a succession of plateaus and high meadows, culminating in the snowcapped Dolomite Alps. Much of the pleasure of exploring here comes from discovering the variations on the Venetian theme that give a unique character to each of the towns. Some, such as Verona, Treviso, and Udine, have a solid medieval look at their heart. Padua, with its narrow arcaded streets and tree-lined canals, is romantic. Vicenza, ennobled by the architecture of Palladio, is more elegant. Udine, in Friuli–Venezia Giulia, is a genteel, intricately sculpted city that's

home to the first important frescoes by Gianbattista Tiepolo. In Trieste, once the main port of the Austro-Hungarian Empire, you can find survivors of those days in its Viennese-inspired coffeehouses and *buffets*—hole-in-the-wall eateries serving sausages and other pork dishes.

Unlike the western regions of northern Italy, the Veneto and Friuli–Venezia Giulia were slow to move from an agricultural to an industrial economy, and even now the region depends upon small- and medium-size businesses, many of which are still family-run. The area, therefore, has attracted far fewer migrants from elsewhere in Italy and thus maintained its cultural identity; local dialects, for example, may have all but died out in places like Milan and Turin, but they still thrive in the Veneto and Friuli–Venezia Giulia. Even when residents speak standard Italian, it is frequently laced with local words and pronounced with a distinctive nasal-sounding musicality.

MAJOR REGIONS

The **Veneto,** for centuries influenced by the city of Venice on the marshy Adriatic coast, is a prosperous region dotted by fortified cities with captivating history and undulating vineyards. Padua's alluring architecture, art, and canal network may reflect the Venetian influence as the closest terra firma dominion, but its ancient, pioneering university—famed for its humanist alumni—creates a beguiling buzz of cycling students, food markets, and commerce. With the cooling Dolomite Alpine waters of the Adige River snaking through its medieval, Roman, and Venetian heart, Verona combines splendor with intimacy. Perfectly formed and wealthy Vicenza is where the peerless Palladio put his harmonious architectural plans into bricks, mortar, and gleaming marble. Heading north toward the snowcapped Dolomites, Marostica draws visitors moved by commanding views and an annual human-scale game of chess on a colossal board. Set amid verdant hills, Asolo dines out on its 19th-century heyday as an idyllic village muse for artists and poets. Moated and medieval Treviso retains a thriving and tranquil air in arcaded streets and leafy canals.

Heading northeast of the Veneto, the atmosphere of the **Friuli–Venezia Giulia** region derives from its fascinating mix of Italian, Slavic, and Central European influences. Sitting atop foothills below the Carnic Alps, the university city of Udine mixes semirural provincial charms with the grandeur of Venetian architecture and the rococo riches of 18th-century artist Gianbattista Tiepolo. A short hop east and set amid scenic wooded valleys, Cividale del Friuli brims with Roman, Celtic, and Lombard archaeological artifacts. Following the Natisone River down to tranquil Aquileia, you'll hear echoes of ancient Rome in this erstwhile port and spot signs of early Christianity in its mosaics. Bordering Slovenia, the strategic Adriatic port city of Trieste mixes Eastern, Central, and Western European cultures, giving it a liminal atmosphere of nostalgia and intrigue, beloved by writers and artists.

Planning

When to Go

The towns and services of the Veneto and Friuli–Venezia Giulia are generally busy all year, with all but a few attractions accessible to visitors. Summer months are generally very humid but dry and hot. The most precipitation and fog fall between November and March, although these months can be rewarding for city sightseeing and immersion in local culture and seasonal food. Toward the foothills of the Dolomites, there are cooler summers and snowfall in winter, while the northeast Adriatic corner around the Gulf of Trieste can have year-round breezy days from eastern winds.

Planning Your Time

Lined up in a row west of Venice are Padua, Vicenza, and Verona—three prosperous small cities that are worth at least one day each on a northern Italy itinerary. Verona has the most grandeur and most varied attractions, as well as the widest selection of hotels and restaurants. It's probably the best choice for a base in the area, even though it also draws the most tourists. The hills north of Venice make for good driving, with appealing villages set in a visitor-friendly wine country.

East of the Veneto, the region of Friuli–Venezia Giulia is off the main tourist circuit. You probably won't go here on a first trip to Italy, but by your second or third visit you may be drawn by its caves and castles, its battle-worn hills, and its mix of Italian and Central European culture. The port city of Trieste, famous for its elegant cafés, has a quiet character that some people find dull but others find alluring.

Note that several of the most interesting and important sights in the Venetian Arc require reservations or are open only at limited times, so plan ahead. For instance, reservations are now required 24 hours in advance to see the Giotto frescoes in Padua's Cappella degli Scrovegni. On the outskirts of Vicenza, the Villa della Rotonda, one of Palladio's masterpieces, is not open in winter and has very limited hours when it is open. Another important Palladian conception, Villa Barbaro near Maser, also has limited hours.

Getting Here and Around

BUS

There are interurban and interregional connections throughout the Veneto and Friuli–Venezia Giulia, handled by nearly a dozen private bus lines. To figure out which line will get you where, the best strategy is to seek assistance from local tourist offices.

CAR

Padua, Vicenza, and Verona are on the highway (and train line) between Venice and Milan. Seeing them without a car isn't a problem; in fact, having a car can even complicate matters. The cities sometimes limit automobile access, permitting cars only with plates ending in an even number on even days, odd on odd, or prohibiting them altogether on weekends. There's no central source for information about these sporadic traffic restrictions; the best strategy is to check with your hotel before arrival for an update. You will need a car to get the most out of the hill country that makes up much of the Venetian Arc, and it will be particularly useful for visiting Aquileia, a rather interesting archaeological site with limited public transportation.

The two main access roads to the Venetian Arc from southern Italy are both linked to the A1 (Autostrada del Sole), which connects Bologna, Florence, and Rome. They are the A13, which ends in Padua, and the A22, which passes through Verona running north–south. Linking the region from east to west is the A4, the primary route from Milan to Trieste, skirting Verona, Padua, and Venice along the way. The distance from Verona to Trieste via the A4 is 263 km (163 miles; 2½ hours), with one break in the autostrada near Venice/Mestre. Branches link the A4 with Treviso (A27) and Udine (A23).

TRAIN

Trains on the main routes from the south stop twice hourly in Verona, Padua, and Venice. From northern Italy and the rest of Europe, trains usually enter via Milan or through Porta Nuova in Verona. Treviso and Udine both lie on the main line from Venice to Tarvisio. Unfortunately, there are no daytime express trains between Venice and Tarvisio, only the slower interregional and regional service. There is now a regional through-train service between Trieste and the neighboring Slovenian capital Ljubljana (Lubiana in Italian). To the west of Venice, the main line running across the north of Italy stops at Padua (30 minutes from Venice), Vicenza (1 hour), and Verona (1½ hours); to the east is Trieste (2 hours). Local trains link Vicenza to Treviso (1 hour) and Udine to Trieste (1 hour).

Be sure to take Regionale Veloce (fast regional) trains whenever possible; a local "milk run" or Regionale that stops in every village along the way can take considerably longer. The fastest trains are the Frecce, but reservations are mandatory and fares are much higher than on regional services.

TRAIN CONTACT Trenitalia. ☎ *892021* ⊕ *www.trenitalia.com.*

Restaurants

Although the Veneto is not considered one of Italy's major culinary destinations, the region offers many opportunities for exciting gastronomic adventures. The fish offerings are among the most varied and freshest in Italy (and possibly Europe), and the vegetables from the islands in the Venetian lagoon are considered a national treasure. Take a break from pasta and try the area's wonderful, creamy risottos and hearty polenta.

Prices in the dining reviews are the average cost of a main course at dinner, or, if dinner is not served, at lunch. Restaurant reviews have been shortened. For full information, visit Fodors.com.

Hotels

Rates tend to be higher in Padua and Verona; in Verona especially, seasonal rates vary widely and soar during trade fairs and the opera season. There are fewer good lodging choices in Vicenza, perhaps because overnighters are drawn to the better restaurant scenes in Verona and Padua. *Agriturismo* (farm stay) information is available at tourist offices and sometimes on their websites. Ask about weekend discounts, often available at hotels catering to business clients. Substantial savings can sometimes be had by booking through reservation services on the Internet.

Prices in the reviews are the lowest cost of a standard double room in high season. Hotel reviews have been shortened. For full information, visit Fodors.com.

What it Costs in Euros

	$	$$	$$$	$$$$
RESTAURANTS				
	under €15	€15–€24	€25–€35	over €35
HOTELS				
	under €125	€125–€200	€201–€300	over €300

Padua

42 km (25 miles) west of Venice.

A romantic warren of arcaded streets, Padua has long been one of the major cultural centers of northern Italy. It has first-rate artistic monuments and, along with Bologna, is one of the few cities in the country where you can catch a glimpse of student life.

Its university, founded in 1222 and Italy's second oldest, attracted such cultural icons as Dante (1265–1321), Petrarch (1304–74), and Galileo Galilei (1564–1642), thus earning the city the sobriquet *La Dotta* (The Learned). Padua's Basilica di Sant'Antonio, begun around 1238, attracts droves of pilgrims, especially on his feast day, June 13. Three great artists—Giotto (1266–1337), Donatello (circa 1386–1466), and Mantegna (1431–1506)—left significant works in Padua, with Giotto's Scrovegni Chapel being one of the best-known, and most meticulously preserved, works of art in the country. Today, a cycle-happy student body—some 60,000 strong—flavors every aspect of local culture. Don't be surprised if you spot a *laurea* (graduation) ceremony marked by laurel leaves, mocking lullabies, and X-rated caricatures.

GETTING HERE AND AROUND

The train trip between Venice and Padua is short, and regular bus service originates from Venice's Piazzale Roma. By car from Venice, Padua is on the Autostrada Torino–Trieste A4/E70. Take the

San Carlo exit and follow Via Guido Reni to Via Tiziano Aspetti into town. Regular bus service connects Venice's Marco Polo airport with downtown Padua.

Padua is a walker's city. If you arrive by car, leave your vehicle in one of the parking lots on the outskirts or at your hotel. Unlimited bus service is included with the PadovaCard (€16 or €21, valid for 48 or 72 hours), which allows entry to all the city's principal sights (€1 extra for a Scrovegni Chapel reservation). It's available at tourist information offices and at some museums and hotels.

VISITOR INFORMATION

CONTACT Padua Tourism Office. ⊠ *Piazzale Stazione,* ☎ *049/5207415* ⊕ *www.turismopadova.it.*

 ## Sights

Abano Terme

HOT SPRING | A very popular hot-springs spa town about 12 km (7 miles) southwest of Padua, Abano Terme lies at the foot of the Euganean Hills among hand-tilled vineyards. If a bit of pampering sounds better than traipsing through yet another church or castle, indulge yourself with a soak, a massage, stone therapy, a skin peel, or a series of mud treatments, which are especially recommended for joint aches. A good-value day pass (€35) is available at the central and well-equipped Hotel Antiche Terme Ariston Molino Buja (⊕ *aristonmolino.it*). For a longer stay check out the latest offers on the Abano spa hotel hub website (⊕ *www.abano*.it).

The nearest railway stop on the Bologna–Padua line is Terme Euganee–Montegrotto. Alternatively, you can board a train on the Milan–Venice line, disembark at Padua, and board an Abano-bound bus in front of the train station. The trip takes about half an hour. ⊠ *Abano Terme* ⊹ *Take Padua West exit off A4, or Terme Euganee exit off A13* ⊕ *www.abano.it; aristonmolino.it.*

★ Basilica di Sant'Antonio

(*Basilica del Santo*)

CHURCH | Thousands of faithful make the pilgrimage here each year to pray at the tomb of St. Anthony, while others come to admire works by the 15th-century Florentine master Donatello. His equestrian statue (1453) of the condottiere Erasmo da Narni, known as Gattamelata, in front of the church is one of the great masterpieces of Italian Renaissance sculpture. It was inspired by the ancient statue of Marcus Aurelius in Rome's Campidoglio. Donatello also sculpted the series of bronze reliefs in the imposing interior illustrating the miracles of St. Anthony, as well as the bronze statues of the Madonna and saints on the high altar.

The huge church, which combines elements of Byzantine, Romanesque, and Gothic styles, was probably begun around 1238, seven years after the death of the Portuguese-born saint. It underwent structural modifications into the mid-15th century. Masses are held in the basilica almost constantly, which makes it difficult to see these artworks. More accessible is the restored Cappella del Santo (housing the tomb of the saint), dating from the 16th century. Its walls are covered with impressive reliefs by important Renaissance sculptors. ⊠ *Piazza del Santo, Padua* ☎ *049/8225652* ⊕ *www.basilicadelsanto.it* ⊠ *Basilica free, museum complex €7* ⊙ *Museum complex closed Mon.*

Burchiello Excursion, Brenta Canal

BODY OF WATER | During the 16th century the Brenta was transformed into a mainland version of Venice's Grand Canal with the building of nearly 50 waterside villas. Back then, boating parties viewed them from *burchielli*—beautiful river barges. Today the Burchiello excursion boat makes full- and half-day tours along the Brenta in season, departing from Padua and Venice; tickets can also be bought at travel agencies. You visit three houses, including the Villas Pisani and Foscari, with a lunchtime break in Oriago (€23 or €30 extra). Note that most houses are on the left side coming from Venice, or the right from Padua. ⊠ *Via Porciglia 34, Padua* ☎ *049/8760233* ⊕ *www.ilburchiello.it* 🎫 *€70 half day, €99 full day; lunch extra* ⊘ *Closed Mon. and Nov.–Feb.*

★ Cappella degli Scrovegni
(*The Arena Chapel*)
CHURCH | The spatial depth, emotional intensity, and naturalism of the frescoes illustrating the lives of Mary and Jesus in this world-famous chapel broke new ground in Western art. Enrico Scrovegni commissioned these frescoes to atone for the sins of his deceased father, Reginaldo, the usurer condemned to the Seventh Circle of the Inferno in Dante's *Divine Comedy.* Giotto and his assistants worked on the frescoes from 1303 to 1305, arranging them in tiers to be read from left to right. Opposite the altar is a *Last Judgment,* most likely designed and painted by Giotto's assistants.

To preserve the artwork, doors are opened only every 15 minutes. A maximum of 25 visitors must spend 15 minutes in an acclimatization room before making a 15-minute chapel visit (20 minutes in certain months). Tickets should be picked up at least one hour before your reservation. It's sometimes possible to buy admission on the spot. A good place to get some background before visiting the chapel is the multimedia room. ⊠ *Piazza Eremitani 8, Padua* ☎ *049/2010020 reservations* ⊕ *www.cappelladegliscrovegni.it* 🎫 *€14, includes Musei Civici and Palazzo Zuckermann.*

Chiesa degli Eremitani
CHURCH | This 13th-century church houses substantial fragments of Andrea Mantegna's frescoes (1448–50), which were damaged by Allied bombing in World War II. Despite their fragmentary condition, Mantegna's still beautiful and historically important depictions of the martyrdom of St. James and St. Christopher show the young artist's mastery of extremely

complex problems of perspective. ⊠ *Piazza Eremitani, Padua* ☎ *049/8756410.*

Montegrotto Terme
HOT SPRING | At this spa town about 13 km (8 miles) southwest of Padua, you can luxuriate in thermal mineral pools. Montegrotto Terme has several hotels whose treatments vary from simple massage and thermal and mud baths to hydrokinetic therapy. Scuba enthusiasts head here for the world's deepest indoor pool, Y-40 Deep Joy. The nearest railway stop, on the Bologna–Padua line, is Terme Euganee–Montegrotto. Taxis are available outside the station. ⊠ *Montegrotto Terme* ⊹ *Terme Euganee exit off A13* ⊕ *www.visitabanomontegrotto.com.*

★ Musei Civici degli Eremitani
(*Civic Museum*)
OTHER MUSEUM | Usually visited along with the neighboring Cappella degli Scrovegni, this former monastery houses a rich array of exhibits and has wonderful cloister gardens with a mix of ancient architectural fragments and modern sculpture. The Pinacoteca displays works of medieval and modern masters, including some by Tintoretto, Veronese, and Tiepolo. Standouts are the *Giotto Crucifix,* which once hung in the Cappella degli Scrovegni, and the *Portrait of a Young Senator,* by Giovanni Bellini (1430–1516). Among the archaeological finds is an intriguing Egyptian section, while the Gabinetto Fotografico is an important collection of photographs. Set aside at least 60–90 minutes to appreciate the scope of this fabulous museum complex. ⊠ *Piazza Eremitani 8, Padua* ☎ *049/8204551* 🎫 *€10, €14 with Scrovegni Chapel and Palazzo Zuckermann; free with PadovaCard* ⊘ *Closed Mon.*

Orto Botanico (*Botanical Garden*)
GARDEN | The Venetian Republic ordered the creation of Padua's botanical garden in 1545 to supply the university with medicinal plants, and it retains its original layout. You can stroll the arboretum—still part of the university—and wander

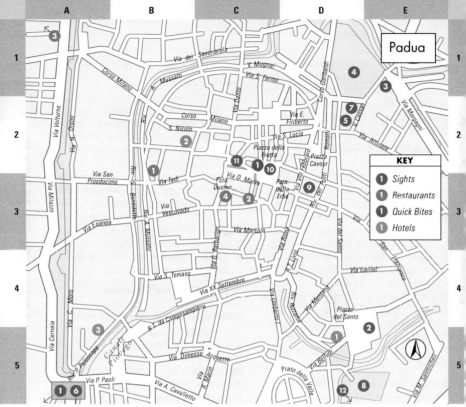

Padua

KEY
- 🔵 Sights
- 🔵 Restaurants
- 🔵 Quick Bites
- 🔵 Hotels

The Venetian Arc, Past and Present

Long before Venetians made their presence felt on the mainland in the 15th century, Ezzelino III da Romano (1194–1259) laid claim to Verona, Padua, and the surrounding lands and towns. He was the first of a series of brutal and aggressive rulers who dominated the cities of the region until the rise of Venetian rule. Because of Ezzelino's cruel and violent nature, Dante consigned his soul to Hell.

After Ezzelino was ousted, powerful families such as Padua's Carrara and Verona's della Scala (Scaligeri) vied throughout the 14th century to dominate these territories. Venetian rule ushered in a time of relative peace, when noble families from the lagoon and the mainland commissioned Palladio and other accomplished architects to design their palazzi and villas. This rich classical legacy, superimposed upon medieval castles and fortifications, is central to the identities of present-day Padua, Vicenza, and Verona.

The region remained under Venetian control until the Napoleonic invasion and the fall of the Venetian Republic in 1797. The Council of Vienna ceded it, along with Lombardy, to Austria in 1815. The region revolted against Austrian rule and joined the Italian Republic in 1866.

Friuli–Venezia Giulia has been marched through, fought over, hymned by patriots, and romanticized by writers that include James Joyce, Rainer Maria Rilke, Pier Paolo Passolini, and Jan Morris. The region has seen Fascists and Communists, Romans, Habsburgs, and Huns. It survived by forging sheltering alliances—Udine beneath the wings of San Marco (1420), Trieste choosing Duke Leopold of Austria (1382) over Venetian domination.

Some of World War I's fiercest fighting took place in Friuli–Venezia Giulia, where memorials and cemeteries commemorate hundreds of thousands who died before Italian troops arrived in 1918 and liberated Trieste from Austrian rule. Trieste, along with the whole of Venezia Giulia, was annexed to Italy in 1920. During World War II the Germans occupied the area and placed Trieste in an administrative zone along with parts of Slovenia. The only Nazi extermination camp on Italian soil, the Risiera di San Sabba, was in a suburb of Trieste. After the war, during a period of Cold War dispute, Trieste was governed by an allied military administration; it was officially reannexed to Italy in 1954, when Italy ceded the Istrian peninsula to the south to Yugoslavia. These arrangements were not finally ratified by Italy and Yugoslavia until 1975.

through hothouses and beds of plants that were introduced to Italy in this late-Renaissance garden. A St. Peter's palm, planted in 1585, inspired Goethe to write his 1790 essay, "The Metamorphosis of Plants."⌑ *Via Orto Botanico 15, Padua* ☎ *049/8273939* ⊕ *www.ortobotanicopd.it* ⌑ *€10 (€5 with PadovaCard)* ⊙ *Closed Mon. May–Mar.*

★ Palazzo del Bo

CASTLE/PALACE | The University of Padua, founded in 1222, centers on this predominantly 16th-century palazzo with an 18th-century facade. It's named after the Osteria del Bo (*bo* means "ox"), an inn that once stood on the site. It's worth a visit to see the perfectly proportioned anatomy theater (1594), the beautiful Old Courtyard, and a hall with a lectern used by Galileo. You can enter only as part of a guided tour; weekend/public holiday tours allow access to other parts of the university; most guides speak English, but it is worth checking ahead by phone. ✉ *Via 8 Febbraio, Padua* ☎ *049/8275111 university switchboard, 049/8273939* 🌐 *www.unipd.it* 🎟 *€7; €12 extended tour weekends and public holidays.*

Palazzo della Ragione

CASTLE/PALACE | Also known as Il Salone, the spectacular arcaded reception hall in Padua's original law courts is as notable for its grandeur—it's 85 feet high—as for its colorful setting, surrounded by shops, cafés, and open-air fruit and vegetable markets. Nicolò Miretto and Stefano da Ferrara, working from 1425 to 1440, painted the frescoes after Giotto's plan, which was destroyed by a fire in 1420. The stunning space hosts art shows, and an enormous wooden horse, crafted for a public tournament in 1466, commands pride of place. It is patterned after the famous equestrian statue by Donatello in front of the Basilica di Sant'Antonio, and may, in fact, have been designed by Donatello himself in the last year of his life. ✉ *Piazza della Ragione, Padua* ☎ *049/8205006* 🎟 *€7 (free with PadovaCard)* 🕒 *Closed Mon.*

Piazza dei Signori

PLAZA/SQUARE | Some fine examples of 15th- and 16th-century buildings line this square. On the west side, the **Palazzo del Capitanio** (facade constructed 1598–1605) has an impressive **Torre dell'Orologio,** with an astronomical clock dating from 1344 and a portal made by Falconetto in 1532 in the form of a Roman triumphal arch. The 12th-century **Battistero del Duomo** (Cathedral Baptistry), with frescoes by Giusto de' Menabuoi (1374–78), is a few steps away. ✉ *Piazza dei Signori, Padua* ☎ *049/656914* 🌐 *www.battisteropadova.it* 🎟 *Battistero €5 (free with PadovaCard).*

Villa Pisani

CASTLE/PALACE | **FAMILY** | Extensive grounds with rare trees, ornamental fountains, and garden follies surround this extraordinary palace in Stra, 13 km (8 miles) southeast of Padua. Built in 1721 for the Venetian doge Alvise Pisani, it recalls Versailles more than a Veneto villa. This was one of the last and grandest of many stately residences constructed along the Brenta River from the 16th to 18th centuries by wealthy Venetians for their villeggiatura escape from midsummer humidity. Gianbattista Tiepolo's (1696–1770) spectacular fresco on the ballroom ceiling, *The Apotheosis of the Pisani Family* (1761), alone is worth the visit. For a relaxing afternoon, explore the gorgeous park and maze. To get here from Padua, take the SITA bus, or from Venice or Padua, take AVTV Bus No. 53E. The villa is a five-minute walk from the bus stop in Stra. **■ TIP→ Mussolini invited Hitler here for their first meeting, but they stayed only one night because of the mosquitoes, which continue to be a nuisance. If visiting on a late afternoon in summer, carry bug repellent.** ✉ *Via Doge Pisani 7, Stra* ☎ *049/502074* 🌐 *www.villapisani.beniculturali.it* 🎟 *€8, €5 park only* 🕒 *Closed Mon.*

🍴 Restaurants

★ Enoteca dei Tadi

$$ | **ITALIAN** | In this cozy and atmospheric cross between a wine bar and a restaurant, you can put together a fabulous, inexpensive dinner from various classic dishes from all over Italy. Portions are small, but prices are reasonable—just follow the local custom and order a selection, perhaps starting with fresh *burrata* (mozzarella's creamier cousin) with tomatoes, or a selection of prosciutti or salami. **Known for:** bountiful wine and grappa list; intimate and rustic setting; several kinds of lasagna. [$] *Average main: €22* ✉ *Via dei Tadi 16, Padua* ☎ *049/8364099, 388/4083434 mobile*

🌐 *www.enotecadeitadi.it* ⏲ *Closed Mon., 2 wks in Jan., and 2 wks late June–July. No dinner Sun.*

L'Anfora

$$ | **WINE BAR** | This mix between a traditional *bacaro* (wine bar) and an osteria is a local institution, opened in 1922. Stand at the bar with a cross section of Padovano society, from construction workers to professors, and peruse the reasonably priced menu of simple *casalinga* (home-cooked dishes), plus salads and a selection of cheeses. **Known for:** very busy at lunchtime; no-nonsense traditional Veneto food; atmospheric art-filled osteria with wood interior. [$] *Average main: €19* ✉ *Via Soncin 13, Padua* ☎ *049/656629* 🌐 *osteria-lanfora.eatbu.com* ⏲ *Closed Sun. (except in Dec.), 1 wk in Jan., and 1 wk in Aug.*

Le Calandre

$$$$ | **MODERN ITALIAN** | Traditional Veneto recipes are given a highly sophisticated and creative treatment here, and the whole theatrical tasting-menu experience and gorgeous table settings can seem by turns revelatory or overblown at this high-profile place. Owner-chef Massimiliano Alajmo's creative, miniscule-portion dishes, passion for design (bespoke lighting, carved wooden tables, and quirky plates), and first-class wine list make this an option for a pricey celebratory meal. **Known for:** reservations essential; playful (or to some pretentious) touches; theatrical, sensory dining experience. [$] *Average main: €150* ✉ *Via Liguria 1, Sarmeola* ✥ *7 km (4 miles) west of Padua* ☎ *049/630303* 🌐 *www.calandre.com* ⏲ *Closed Sun., Mon., and Jan. 1–20. No lunch Tues.*

Osteria dal Capo

$$ | **VENETIAN** | Located in the heart of what used to be Padua's Jewish ghetto, this friendly trattoria serves almost exclusively traditional Veneto dishes, and it does so with refinement and care. Everything from the well-crafted dishes to the unfussy ship's dining cabin–like decor and elegant plates reflect decades of Padovano hospitality. **Known for:** limited tables mean reservations essential; liver and onions with grilled polenta; intimate and understated dining at decent prices. [$] *Average main: €23* ✉ *Via degli Obizzi 2, Padua* ☎ *049/663105* 🌐 *www.osteriadalcapo.it* ⏲ *Closed Sun. No lunch Mon.*

☕ Coffee and Quick Bites

Bar Romeo

$ | **NORTHERN ITALIAN** | Deep in the atmospheric Sotto Salone market, this busy bar does a fab selection of filled *tramezzini* (triangular sandwiches), panini, and other snacks. It's a great place to hear the local dialect and mingle with the market workers and shoppers any time of day; grab a breakfast coffee and brioche, a glass of Falanghina, or a bit later—after 11 am perhaps—an apertivo with snacks. **Known for:** superb selection of wine by the glass; friendly staff and Padovano vibe; good-value sandwiches. [$] *Average main: €5* ✉ *26 Sotto Salone, Padua* ☎ *340/556 0611.*

🛏 Hotels

Al Fagiano

$ | **HOTEL** | The refreshingly funky surroundings in this self-styled art hotel include sponge-painted walls, brush-painted chandeliers, and views of the spires and cupolas of the Basilica di Sant'Antonio. **Pros:** great for art lovers or those after a unique ambience; convenient location; relaxed, quirky, homey atmosphere. **Cons:** lots of stairs; some find the way-out-there (some risqué) art a bit much; not all rooms have views. [$] *Rooms from: €99* ✉ *Via Locatelli 45, Padua* ☎ *049/8750073* 🌐 *www.alfagiano.com* 🛏 *40 rooms* 🍴 *No Meals.*

Albergo Verdi

$ | **HOTEL** | One of the best-situated hotels in the city provides understated modern rooms and public areas that tend toward the minimalist without being severe, while the intimate breakfast room with stylish Eames Eiffel chairs and adjoining terrace is a tranquil place to start the day. **Pros:** excellent location close to Piazza dei Signori; 24-hour bar service; attentive staff. **Cons:** steep stairs and small elevator; few views; student noise in piazza-facing rooms. $ Rooms from: €90 ⊠ Via Dondi dell'Orologio 7, Padua ☎ 049/8364163 ⊕ www.albergoverdipadova.it ⤷ 14 rooms ❍ Free Breakfast.

Methis Hotel & Spa

$ | HOTEL | Four floors of sleekly designed guest rooms reflect nature's elements at this modern spa hotel: there are gentle earth tones and fiery red in the Classic rooms; watery, cool blues in Superior rooms; and airy white in the top-floor suites. **Pros:** superb canal walks nearby; gym, sauna, Turkish bath, and spa treatments; better views of canal across road from front rooms. **Cons:** tired decor and unkempt corners; public spaces lack some character; 15-minute walk from major sights and restaurants. $ Rooms from: €120 ⊠ Riviera Paleocapa 70, Padua ☎ 049/8725555 ⊕ www.methishotel.it ⤷ 59 rooms ❍ Free Breakfast.

Nightlife

CAFÉS AND WINE BARS

★ **Caffè Pedrocchi**

CAFÉS | No visit to Padua is complete without taking time to sit in this historic café and iconic Padovano venue, patronized by luminaries like the French novelist Stendhal in 1831. Nearly 200 years later, it remains central to the city's social life. The café was built in the Egyptian Revival style, and it's now famed for its innovative aperitivi and signature mint coffee. The accomplished, innovative restaurant serves breakfast, lunch, and dinner. The grand salons and terrace provide a backdrop for the occasional jazz, swing, and cover bands. ⊠ Piazzetta Pedrocchi, Padua ☎ 049/8781231 ⊕ www.caffepedrocchi.it.

Cocktail Hour on Padua's Piazzas

One of Padua's greatest traditions is the outdoor en masse consumption of aperitifs: a spritz mixing Aperol or Campari with soda water and wine, prosecco (sparkling wine), or wine. It all happens in Piazza delle Erbe and Piazza delle Frutta. Several bars there provide drinks in plastic cups, so you can take them outside and mingle among the crowds. The ritual, practiced primarily by students, begins at 6 or so, at which hour you can also pick up a snack from one of the outdoor vendors.

👜 Shopping

★ **Mercato Sotto il Salone**

FOOD | Under the Salone there's an impressive food market where shops sell choice salami and cured meats, local cheeses, wines, coffee, and tea. With the adjacent Piazza delle Erbe fruit and vegetable market, you can pick up all the makings of a fine picnic. On weekends and public holidays, the piazza is often filled with fabulous street food, as well as wine and beer stalls. ⊠ Piazza della Ragione, Padua ⊕ mercatosottoilsalone.it.

Zotti Antiquariato

ANTIQUES & COLLECTIBLES | Owned by antiques dealer Pietro Maria Zotti—who has worked for more than 40 years in the trade—this always-changing shop has fascinating finds from Venetian artworks to stylish midcentury furniture, plus lots of smaller, more affordable items, including books, prints, jewelry, militaria, and coins. ⊠ Selciato San Nicolò 5, Padua ☎ 338/2930830 ⊕ www.zottiantiquariato.it.

Activities

HelloVeneto Tours

WALKING TOURS | **FAMILY** | HelloVeneto runs numerous tours around the region, including a Giotto-theme walk and a Gardens and Castles excursion that explores Villa Barbarigo and Castello del Catajo. ✉ *Via Martiri d'Ungheria 60, Padua* ⊕ *Abano Terme* ☎ *0444/886737* ⊕ *www. helloveneto.it* ✇ *From €90.*

Verona

114 km (71 miles) west of Venice, 60 km (37 miles) west of Vicenza.

On the banks of the fast-flowing River Adige, enchanting Verona has timeless monuments, a picturesque town center, and a romantic reputation as the setting of Shakespeare's *Romeo and Juliet.* With its lively Venetian air and proximity to Lake Garda, it attracts hordes of tourists, especially Germans and Austrians. Tourism peaks during summer's renowned season of open-air opera in the arena and during spring's Vinitaly, one of the world's most important wine expos. For five days you can sample the wines of more than 3,000 wineries from dozens of countries.

Verona grew to power and prosperity within the Roman Empire as a result of its key commercial and military position in northern Italy. With its Roman arena, theater, and city gates, it has the most significant monuments of Roman antiquity north of Rome. After the fall of the empire, the city continued to flourish under the guidance of barbarian kings, such as Theodoric, Alboin, Pepin, and Berenger I, reaching its cultural and artistic peak in the 13th and 14th centuries under the della Scala (Scaligero) dynasty. (Look for the *scala,* or ladder, emblem all over town.) In 1404 Verona traded its independence for security and placed itself under the control of Venice. (The other

recurring architectural motif is the lion of St. Mark, a symbol of Venetian rule.)

If you're going to visit more than one or two sights, it's worth purchasing a VeronaCard, available at museums, churches, and tobacconists for €20 (for 24 hours) or €25 (48 hours). It buys a single admission to most of the city's significant museums and churches, plus you can ride free on city buses. If you're mostly interested in churches, a €6 cumulative ticket is sold at Verona's major houses of worship and gains you entry to the Duomo, San Fermo Maggiore, San Zeno Maggiore, and Sant'Anastasia. Note that Verona's churches strictly enforce their dress code: no sleeveless shirts, shorts, or short skirts.

GETTING HERE AND AROUND

Verona is midway between Venice and Milan. Several trains per hour depart from any point on the Milan–Venice line. By car, from Venice, take the Autostrada Trieste–Torino A4/E70 to the SS12 and follow it north into town.

VISITOR INFORMATION

CONTACT Verona Tourism Office (IAT Verona). ✉ *Via degli Alpini 9,* ☎ *045/8068680* ⊕ *www.veronatouristoffice.it/en.*

◉ Sights

In addition to ancient Verona's famous Roman theater and arena, two of its city gates (Porta dei Leoni and Porta dei Borsari) and a beautiful triumphal arch (Arco dei Gavi) have survived. These graceful and elegant portals provide an idea of the high aesthetic standards of their time. Look, too, beyond the main sights of the Città Antica (historic center): take time to wander the streets, and be sure not to miss out on the many leafy stretches of the riverside Lungadige. Away from the crowds there's a wealth of varied architecture from ancient Rome to the Fascist era to the contemporary, as well as tranquil spots for feeding the ducks.

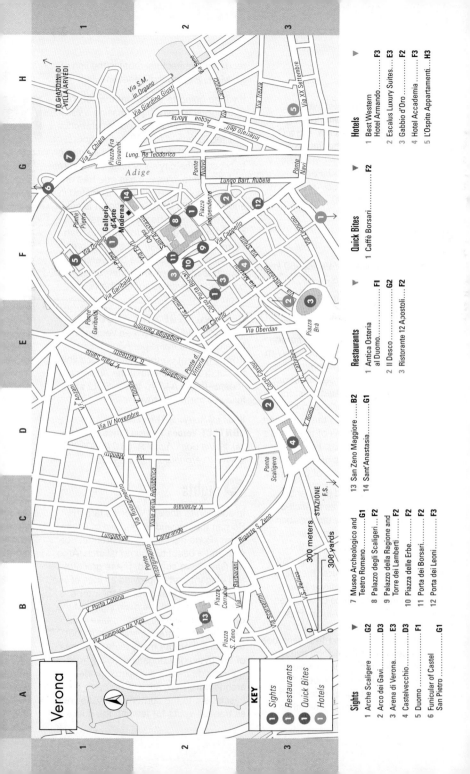

Verona

KEY

- ▶ Sights
- ▶ Restaurants
- ▶ Quick Bites
- ▶ Hotels

Sights

1 Arche Scaligere **G2**
2 Arco dei Gavi **D3**
3 Arena di Verona **E3**
4 Castelvecchio **D3**
5 Duomo **F1**
6 Funicular of Castel
  San Pietro **G1**
7 Museo Archeologico and
  Teatro Romano **G1**
8 Palazzo degli Scaligeri ... **F2**
9 Palazzo della Ragione and
  Torre dei Lamberti **F2**
10 Piazza delle Erbe **F2**
11 Porta dei Borsari **F2**
12 Porta dei Leoni **F3**
13 San Zeno Maggiore **B2**
14 Sant'Anastasia **G1**

▶ Restaurants

1 Antica Osteria
  al Duomo **F1**
2 Il Desco **G2**
3 Ristorante 12 Apostoli **F2**

▶ Quick Bites

1 Caffè Borsari **F2**

▶ Hotels

1 Best Western
  Hotel Armando **F3**
2 Escalus Luxury Suites ... **E3**
3 Gabbio d'Oro **F2**
4 Hotel Accademia **F3**
5 L'Ospite Appartamenti ... **H3**

Arche Scaligere

TOMB | On a little square off Piazza dei Signori are the fantastically sculpted Gothic tombs of the della Scala family, who ruled Verona during the late Middle Ages. The 19th-century English traveler and critic John Ruskin described the tombs as graceful places where people who have fallen asleep live. The tomb of Cangrande I (1291–1329) hangs over the portal of the adjacent church and is the work of the Maestro di Sant'Anastasia. The tomb of Mastino II, begun in 1345, has an elaborate baldachin, originally painted and gilded, and is surrounded by an iron grillwork fence and topped by an equestrian statue. The latest and most elaborate tomb is that of Cansignorio (1375), the work principally of Bonino da Campione. The major tombs are all visible from the street. ⊠ *Via Arche Scaligere, Verona.*

★ Arco dei Gavi

RUINS | This stunning structure is simpler and less imposing, but also more graceful, than the triumphal arches in Rome. Built in the 1st century by the architect Lucius Vitruvius Cerdo to celebrate the accomplishments of the patrician Gavia family, it was highly esteemed by several Renaissance architects, including Palladio. ⊠ *Corso Cavour, Verona.*

Arena di Verona

RUINS | FAMILY | Only Rome's Colosseum and Capua's arena would dwarf this amphitheater, built for gymnastic competitions, choreographed sacrificial rites, and games involving hunts, fights, battles, and wild animals. Although four arches are all that remain of the arena's outer arcade, the main structure is complete and dates from AD 30. In summer, you can join up to 16,000 for spectacular opera productions and pop or rock concerts (extra costs for these events). ■ TIP➔ **The opera's the main thing here: when there is no opera performance, you can still enter the interior, but the arena is less impressive inside than the** Colosseum or other Roman amphitheaters. ⊠ *Piazza Bra 5, Verona* ☎ *045/8003204 visit, 045/8005151 performance tickets* ⊕ *www.arena.it* ⊠ *€10 (free with VeronaCard); €11 includes entrance to nearby Museo Lapidario Maffeiano.*

★ Castelvecchio

CASTLE/PALACE | This crenellated, russet brick building with massive walls, towers, turrets, and a vast courtyard was built for Cangrande II della Scala in 1354 and presides over a street lined with attractive old buildings and palaces of the nobility. Only by going inside the **Museo di Castelvecchio** can you really appreciate this massive castle complex with its vaulted halls. You also get a look at a significant collection of Venetian and Veneto art, medieval weapons, and jewelry. The interior of the castle was restored and redesigned as a museum between 1958 and 1975 by Carlo Scarpa, one of Italy's most accomplished architects. Behind the castle is the Ponte Scaligero (1355), which spans the River Adige. ⊠ *Corso Castelvecchio 2, Verona* ☎ *045/8062611* ⊕ *museodicastelvecchio.comune.verona.it* ⊠ *€6 (free with VeronaCard)* ⊗ *Closed Mon.*

Duomo

CHURCH | The present church was begun in the 12th century in the Romanesque style; its later additions are mostly Gothic. On pilasters guarding the main entrance are 12th-century carvings thought to represent Oliver and Roland, two of Charlemagne's knights and heroes of several medieval epic poems. Inside, Titian's *Assumption* (1532) graces the first chapel on the left. ⊠ *Via Duomo, Verona* ☎ *045/592813* ⊕ *www.chieseverona.it* ⊠ *€3 (free with Church Cumulative Ticket or VeronaCard).*

★ Funicular of Castel San Pietro

VIEWPOINT | Opened in 2017, this funicular ride ascends 500 feet from near the Teatro Romano up to a panoramic terrace in just 90 seconds, affording fabulous Veronese views. For the adventurous, there's scope for long walks around the parkland paths and quiet lanes crisscrossing the elevated city walls. ✉ *Via Fontanelle S. Stefano, Verona* ☎ *342/8966695* ⊕ *www.funicolarediverona.it* 🎫 *€3 round-trip, €2 one-way.*

Museo Archeologico and Teatro Romano

HISTORY MUSEUM | The archaeological holdings of this museum in a 15th-century former monastery consist largely of the donated collections of Veronese citizens proud of their city's classical past. You'll find few blockbusters here, but there are some noteworthy pieces (especially among the bronzes), and it is interesting to see what cultured Veronese collected between the 17th and 19th centuries. The museum complex includes the Teatro Romano, Verona's 1st-century theater, which is open to visitors. ✉ *Rigaste del Redentore 2, Verona* ☎ *045/8000360* ⊕ *museoarcheologico.comune.verona.it* 🎫 *€5 (free with VeronaCard)* ⊗ *Closed Mon.*

Palazzo degli Scaligeri (*Palazzo di Cangrande*)

CASTLE/PALACE | The della Scala family ruled Verona from this stronghold built (over Roman ruins) at the end of the 13th century and then inhabited by Cangrande I. At that time Verona controlled the mainland Veneto from Treviso and Lombardy to Mantua and Brescia, hence the building's alternative name as a seat of Domini di Terraferma (Venetian administration): Palazzo del Podestà. The portal facing Piazza dei Signori was added in 1533 by the accomplished Renaissance architect Michele Sanmicheli. You have to admire the palazzo from the outside, as it's not open to the public. ✉ *Piazza dei Signori, Verona.*

★ Palazzo della Ragione and Torre dei Lamberti

VIEWPOINT | An elegant 15th-century pink-marble staircase leads up from the *mercato vecchio* (old market) courtyard to the magistrates' chambers in this 12th-century palace, built at the intersection of the main streets of the ancient Roman city. The interior now houses

exhibitions of art from the **Galleria d'Arte Moderna Achille Forti.** You can get the highest view in town from atop the attached 270-foot-high Romanesque Torre dei Lamberti. About 50 years after a lightning strike in 1403 knocked its top off, it was rebuilt and extended to its current height. ✉ *Piazza dei Signori, Verona* ☎ *045/9273027* ⊕ *torredeilamberti.it* 🎫 *Gallery and tower €8 (free with VeronaCard); €4 gallery only; €6 tower only* ⊗ *Gallery closed Mon.*

Piazza delle Erbe

PLAZA/SQUARE | Frescoed buildings surround this medieval square, where a busy Roman forum once stood; during the week it's still bustling, as vendors sell produce and trinkets, much as they have been doing for generations Eyes are drawn to the often sun-sparkling Madonna Verona fountain (1368) and its Roman statue (the body is from AD 380, with medieval additions). ✉ *Verona.*

★ Porta dei Borsari

RUINS | As its elegant decoration suggests, this is the main entrance to ancient Verona—dating, in its present state, from the 1st century. It's at the beginning of the narrow, pedestrianized Corso Porta Borsari, now a smart shopping street leading to Piazza delle Erbe. ✉ *Corso Porta Borsari, Verona.*

Porta dei Leoni

RUINS | The oldest of Verona's elegant and graceful Roman portals, the Porta dei Leoni (on Via Leoni, just a short walk from Piazza delle Erbe) dates from the 1st century BC, but its original earth-and-brick structure was sheathed in local marble during the early imperial era. It has become the focus of a campaign against violence—there are often flowers and messages by the monument—in memory of the murder of a young Veronese here in 2009. ✉ *Via Leoni, Verona.*

★ San Zeno Maggiore

CHURCH | One of Italy's finest Romanesque churches is filled with treasures, including a rose window by the 13th-century sculptor Brioloto that represents a wheel of fortune, with six of the spokes formed by statues depicting the rising and falling fortunes of mankind. The 12th-century porch is the work of Maestro Niccolò; it's flanked by marble reliefs by Niccolò and Maestro Gugliel-mo depicting scenes from the Old and New Testaments and from the legend of Theodoric. The bronze doors date from the 11th and 12th centuries; some were probably imported from Saxony, and some are from Veronese workshops. They combine allegorical representations with scenes from the lives of saints.

Inside, look for the 12th-century statue of San Zeno to the left of the main altar. In modern times it has been dubbed the "Laughing San Zeno" because of a misinterpretation of its conventional Romanesque grin. A famous *Madonna and Saints* triptych by Andrea Mantegna (1431–1506) hangs over the main altar, and a peaceful cloister (1120–38) lies to the left of the nave. The detached bell tower was finished in 1173. ☒ *Piazza San Zeno, Verona* ☎ *045/592813* ⊕ *www. chieseverona.it* 🎟 *€3 (free with Church Cumulative Ticket or VeronaCard).*

Sant'Anastasia

CHURCH | Verona's largest church, begun in 1290 but only consecrated in 1471, is a fine example of Gothic brickwork and has a grand doorway with elaborately carved biblical scenes. The main reason for visiting this church, however, is *St. George and the Princess* (dated 1434, but perhaps earlier) by Pisanello (1377–1455). It's above the Pellegrini Chapel off the main altar. As you come in, look also for the *gobbi* (hunchbacks) supporting the holy-water basins. ☒ *Piazza Sant'Ana-stasia, Verona* ☎ *045/592813* ⊕ *www. chieseverona.it* 🎟 *€3 (free with Church Cumulative Ticket or VeronaCard).*

🍴 Restaurants

★ Antica Osteria al Duomo

$$ | **NORTHERN ITALIAN** | This side-street eatery, lined with old wood paneling and decked out with musical instruments, serves traditional Veronese classics, like *bigoli* (thick whole wheat spaghetti) with donkey ragù and *pastissada con polenta* (horse-meat stew with polenta). Don't be deterred by the unconventional meats—they're tender and delicious, and this is probably the best place in town to sample them. **Known for:** rustic courtyard; occasional live music; blackboard menu, bar, and wooden interiors. $ *Average main: €20* ☒ *Via Duomo 7/A, Verona* ☎ *045/8004505* ⊕ *alduomoosteria.altervista.org* ⊙ *Closed Sun. except in Dec. and during wine fair.*

★ Il Desco

$$$$ | **MODERN ITALIAN** | Opened in 1981 by Elia Rizzo, the nationally renowned fine-dining Desco cuisine is now crafted by talented son Matteo. True to Italian and Rizzo culinary traditions, he preserves natural flavors through careful ingredient selection, adding daring combinations inspired by stints in kitchens around the world. **Known for:** pricey tasting menus; elegant, arty surroundings fit for a modern opera; inventive, colorful plates of food. $ *Average main: €95* ☒ *Via Dietro San Sebastiano 7, Verona* ☎ *045/595358* ⊕ *www.ristoranteildesco. it* ⊙ *Closed Sun. and Mon. (open for dinner Mon. in Dec.).*

Ristorante 12 Apostoli

$$$$ | **NORTHERN ITALIAN** | Run by the Gioco family for over a century, 12 Apostoli offers a fine-dining experience amid gorgeous frescoes and dramatically lit place settings. Near Piazza delle Erbe, this historic palazzo setting stands on the foundations of a Roman temple: you can view architectural fragments and a model in the wine cellar. **Known for:** innovative tasting menus; slow and sumptuous dining; elegant, atmospheric rooms and cantina. $ *Average main: €120* ⊠ *Vicolo Corticella San Marco 3, Verona* ☎ *045/596999* ⊕ *www.12apostoli.com* ⊘ *Closed Mon. No dinner Sun.*

☕ Coffee and Quick Bites

★ Caffè Borsari

$ | **NORTHERN ITALIAN** | This bustling café-bar is famed for its excellent creamy coffee and freshly made brioche—pre-COVID, it was cheek-by-jowl *al banco* (at the counter/bar), but for now the Veronese patrons must spill outside. The narrow space on the charming Corso Borsari cobbles is packed with coffee- and tea-making pots and cups, as are its walls with colorful gifts and oddities according to the time of year. **Known for:** fab staff may decorate your schiuma (froth); selection of coffee, tea, candies, and chocolates to take away; indulgent hot chocolate. $ *Average main: €4* ⊠ *Corso Portoni Borsari 15, Verona* ☎ *045/8031313.*

🛏 Hotels

Book hotels months in advance for spring's Vinitaly, usually the second week in April, and for opera season. Verona hotels are also very busy during the January, May, and September gold fairs in neighboring Vicenza. Hotels jack up prices considerably at all these times.

Best Western Hotel Armando

$$ | **HOTEL** | In a residential area a few minutes' walk from the Arena, this contemporary Best Western hotel offers respite from the busy city as well as easier parking. **Pros:** large rooms for Italy; free Wi-Fi; good breakfast. **Cons:** noise from neighboring restaurant; simple room decor; no parking valet. $ *Rooms from: €130* ⊠ *Via Dietro Pallone 1, Verona* ☎ *045/8000206* ⊕ *www.hotelarmando. it* ⊘ *Closed 2 wks late Dec.–early Jan.* ⇥ *28 rooms* ⦿| *Free Breakfast.*

Escalus Luxury Suites

$$$ | **HOTEL** | **FAMILY** | Near the Arena and Verona's marble-paved main shopping street, Via Mazzini, these suites and mini-apartments offer contemporary minimalist style in muted colors; the larger ones have handy kitchenettes, and all have swank bathrooms. **Pros:** chic location near sights and shopping; large showers; family-friendly Glamour Deluxe Suite with balcony. **Cons:** minimalist decor not to everyone's taste; constant passeggiata hum from Via Mazzini; checkout is before 11 am. $ *Rooms from: €275* ⊠ *Vicolo Tre Marchetti 12, Verona* ☎ *045/8036754* ⊕ *www. escalusverona.com* ⇥ *6 suites* ⦿| *Free Breakfast.*

Gabbia d'Oro

$$$$ | **HOTEL** | Occupying a historic building off Piazza delle Erbe in the ancient heart of Verona, this hotel is a romantic fantasia of ornamentation, rich fabrics, and period-style furniture. **Pros:** central location; romantic atmosphere; great breakfast. **Cons:** some guests may find the decor overly ornate, even stuffy; small bathrooms; some very small rooms, especially considering the price. $ *Rooms from: €375* ⊠ *Corso Porta Borsari 4/a, Verona* ☎ *045/8003060* ⊕ *www. hotelgabbiadoro.it* ⇥ *27 rooms* ⦿| *Free Breakfast.*

Hotel Accademia

$$$ | **HOTEL** | The Palladian facade of columns and arches here hint at the well-proportioned interior layout: expect an elegant contemporary take on Art Deco in public spaces and immaculate if impersonal traditional-style decor in guest rooms. **Pros:** central location; rooftop solarium; good fitness room. **Cons:** service can be patchy; some may find the decor lacking; expensive parking. $ *Rooms from: €286* ⊠ *Via Scala 12, Verona* ☎ *045/596222* ⊕ *www.hotelaccademiaverona.it* ⇥ *96 rooms* ⦿| *Free Breakfast.*

★ L'Ospite Appartamenti

$ | **APARTMENT** | Friendly and energetic Federica has transformed this three-story property, owned by her family (of De Rossi patisserie fame), into some of the most stylish contemporary apartments—and one of the best values—in Verona, complete with kitchenettes. **Pros:** great location in the Veronetta near the university and the Adige River; immaculately clean; helpful host offers tips and some cooking courses. **Cons:** books up early; on a busy road; narrow pavement outside. $ *Rooms from: €95* ⊠ *Via Venti Settembre 3, Verona* ☎ *045/8036994, 329/4262524 mobile* ⊕ *www.lospite. com* ☉ *Closed early Jan.* ⤳ *6 apartments* ❑ *No Meals.*

⏯ Performing Arts

★ Arena di Verona Opera Festival

OPERA | Milan's La Scala and Naples's San Carlo offer performances more likely to attract serious opera fans, but neither offers a greater spectacle than the Arena di Verona. During the venue's summer season (June to August), as many as 16,000 attendees sit on the original stone terraces or in modern cushioned stalls. Most of the operas presented are big and splashy, like *Aida* or *Turandot,* demanding huge choruses, lots of color and movement, and, if possible, camels, horses, or elephants. Order tickets by phone or through the arena website. If you book a spot on the cheaper terraces, be sure to take or rent a cushion—four hours on a 2,000-year-old stone bench can be an ordeal. ⊠ *Box office, Via Dietro Anfiteatro 6/b, Verona* ☎ *045/8005151* ⊕ *www.arena.it* 🎟 *From €35 (for general admission).*

Vinitaly

FESTIVALS | This widely attended international wine and spirits event takes place in Verona over four days in April. ⊠ *Fiera di Verona, Viale del Lavoro 8,* ☎ *045/8298111* ⊕ *www.vinitaly.com.*

🛍 Shopping

ANTIQUES

Sant'Anastasia

ANTIQUES & COLLECTIBLES | The area around the Gothic church of Sant'Anastasia has a smattering of antiques shops, some catering to serious collectors. Head to San Zeno on the first Sunday of the month for the Mercato dell'Antiquariato fair on the piazza. ⊠ *Corso Sant'Anastasia, Verona.*

BOOKS AND PRINTS

Libreria del Novecento

BOOKS | All bibliophiles should make a beeline to this small bookshop with its fascinating selection of secondhand volumes spanning many subjects. Have a rummage to unearth paperbacks with alluringly designed covers, collectibles, first editions, and intriguing art books. They also have a selection of vinyl records and CDs. ⊠ *Via Santa Maria in Chiavica 3/A, Verona* ☎ *045/8008108* ⊕ *www.libreriadelnovecento.it.*

★ Museo Conte—Antica Tipografia

ART GALLERIES | Look out for the striking Fascism-era signage typography above the door—TIPOGRAFIA—and enter Verona's oldest printing press, opened in 1750 and run by the Conte family since the '30s. Marvel at the well-oiled working machinery, tools, and rows of printing blocks before perusing their striking, colorful prints and stationery. Since 2000 it's become a nonprofit cultural association. ⊠ *Via Santa Maria in Chiavica 3, Verona* ☎ *045/8003392.*

FOOD AND WINE

De Rossi

FOOD | Opened in 1947, De Rossi is a Veronese institution producing oven-hot bread, cakes, pastries, biscotti, and other specialties like fresh pasta. ⊠ *Corso Porta Borsari 3, Verona* ☎ *045/8002489* ⊕ *www.derossi.it.*

Activities

★ Adige Rafting

RAFTING | FAMILY | Briefed by expert guides and issued with paddles and life jackets, the adventurous can set off on a *gommone* (dinghy) from the Chievo (eastern) area of town and navigate the cool waters of the Adige, finishing up at the picnic area of Boschetto. Along the 8-km (5-mile) stretch of river there are wonderful water-level views of Verona's architectural and natural riches. The trip takes around three hours, with two hours spent on the water, including a fun race along the way. ⊠ *Centro Sportivo Bottagisio, Via del Perloso 14/A, Verona* ☎ *347/8892498* ⊕ *adigerafting.it* ⊠ *€25.*

Vicenza

74 km (46 miles) west of Venice, 43 km (27 miles) west of Padua.

A visit to Vicenza is a must for any student or fan of architecture. This elegant, prosperous city bears the distinctive signature of the 16th-century architect Andrea Palladio, whose name has been given to the "Palladian" style of architecture. He emphasized the principles of order and harmony using the classical style of architecture established by Renaissance architects, such as Brunelleschi, Alberti, and Sansovino. He used these principles and classical motifs not only for public buildings but also for private dwellings. His elegant villas and palaces were influential in propagating classical architecture in Europe, especially Britain, and later in America—most notably at Thomas Jefferson's Monticello.

In the mid-16th century Palladio was commissioned to rebuild much of Vicenza, which had been greatly damaged during wars waged against Venice by the League of Cambrai (1505), an alliance of the papacy, France, the Holy Roman Empire, and several neighboring city-states. He made his name with the renovation of the basilica, begun in 1549 in the heart of Vicenza, and then embarked on a series of lordly buildings, all of which adhere to the same classicism and principles of harmony.

GETTING HERE AND AROUND

Vicenza is midway between Padua and Verona; several trains leave from Venice every hour. By car, take the Autostrada Brescia–Padova/Torino–Trieste A4/E70 to SP247 North directly into Vicenza.

VISITOR INFORMATION

CONTACT Vicenza Tourism Office. ⊠ *Piazza Giacomo Matteotti 12,* ☎ *0444/320854* ⊕ *www.vicenzae.org.*

Sights

Palazzo Barbaran da Porto (Palladio Museum)

CASTLE/PALACE | Palladio executed this beautiful city palace for the Vicentine noble Montano Barbarano between 1570 and 1575. The noble patron, however, did not make things easy for Palladio; the architect had to incorporate at least two pre-existing medieval houses, with irregularly shaped rooms, into his classical, harmonious plan. It also had to support the great hall of the *piano nobile* (moving floor) above the fragile walls of the original medieval structure. The wonder of it is that this palazzo is one of Palladio's most harmonious constructions; the viewer has little indication that this is actually a transformation of a medieval structure. The palazzo also contains a museum dedicated to Palladio and is the seat of a center for Palladian studies. ⊠ *Contrà Porti 11, Vicenza* ☎ *0444/323014* ⊕ *www.palladiomuseum. org* ⊠ *€8; €20 Vicenza Card, includes Palazzo Chiericati and Teatro Olimpico, plus others* ⊗ *Closed Mon. and Tues.*

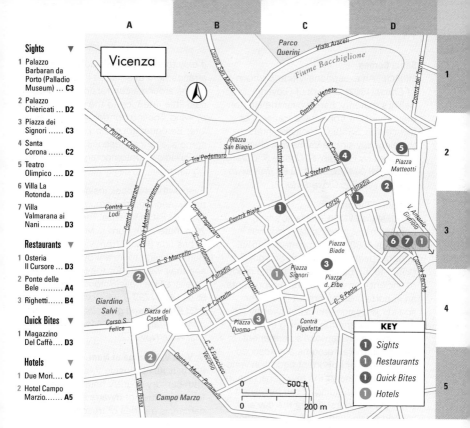

Vicenza

Sights ▼

1 Palazzo Barbaran da Porto (Palladio Museum) ... **C3**
2 Palazzo Chiericati ... **D2**
3 Piazza dei Signori **C3**
4 Santa Corona **C2**
5 Teatro Olimpico **D2**
6 Villa La Rotonda..... **D3**
7 Villa Valmarana ai Nani **D3**

Restaurants ▼

1 Osteria Il Cursore ... **D3**
2 Ponte delle Bele **A4**
3 Righetti...... **B4**

Quick Bites ▼

1 Magazzino Del Caffè.... **D3**

Hotels ▼

1 Due Mori.... **C4**
2 Hotel Campo Marzio....... **A5**

KEY
- ❶ Sights
- ❶ Restaurants
- ❶ Quick Bites
- ❶ Hotels

Palazzo Chiericati

CASTLE/PALACE | This imposing Palladian palazzo (1550) would be worthy of a visit even if it didn't house Vicenza's **Museo Civico.** Because of the ample space surrounding the building, Palladio combined elements of an urban palazzo with those he used in his country villas. The museum's important Venetian holdings include significant paintings by Cima, Tiepolo, Piazzetta, and Tintoretto, but its main attraction is an extensive collection of rarely found works by painters from the Vicenza area, among them Jacopo Bassano (1515–92) and the eccentric and innovative Francesco Maffei (1605–60), whose work foreshadowed important currents of Venetian painting of subsequent generations. ⊠ *Piazza Matteotti, Vicenza* ☎ *0444/222811* ⊕ *www.museicivicivicenza.it* 🎟 *€7; €20 Vicenza Card, includes*

Palazzo Barbaran da Porto and Teatro Olimpico, plus others ⊗ *Closed Mon.*

Piazza dei Signori

PLAZA/SQUARE | At the heart of Vicenza, this square contains the **Palazzo della Ragione** (1549), the project with which Palladio made his name by successfully modernizing a medieval building, grafting a graceful two-story exterior loggia onto the existing Gothic structure. Commonly known as Palladio's basilica, the palazzo served as a courthouse and public meeting hall (the original Roman meaning of the term *basilica*) and is now open only when it houses exhibits. The main point of interest, though, the loggia, is visible from the piazza. Take a look also at the **Loggia del Capitaniato,** opposite, which Palladio designed but never completed. ⊠ *Vicenza.*

Santa Corona

CHURCH | An exceptionally fine *Baptism of Christ* (1502), a work of Giovanni Bellini's maturity, hangs over the altar on the left, just in front of the transept of this church. Santa Corona also houses the elegantly simple Valmarana chapel, designed by Palladio. ✉ *Contrà S. Corona, Vicenza* ☎ *0444/320854* ⬛ *€3 (free with Vicenza Card)* ⊘ *Closed Mon.*

★ Teatro Olimpico

PERFORMANCE VENUE | Palladio's last, perhaps most spectacular work was begun in 1580 and completed in 1585, after his death, by Vincenzo Scamozzi (1552–1616). Based closely on the model of ancient Roman theaters, it represents an important development in theater and stage design and is noteworthy for its acoustics and the cunning use of perspective in Scamozzi's permanent backdrop. The anterooms are frescoed with images of important figures in Venetian history. One of the few Renaissance theaters still standing, it can be visited (with guided tours) during the day and is used for concerts, operas, and other performances. ✉ *Ticket office, Piazza Matteotti 12, Vicenza* ☎ *0444/964380* ⊕ *www.teatrolimpicovicenza.it* ⬛ *€11; €20 Vicenza Card, includes Palazzo Barbaran da Porto and Palazzo Chiericati, plus others* ⊘ *Closed Mon.*

★ Villa La Rotonda (*Villa Almerico Capra*)

HISTORIC HOME | Commissioned in 1556 as a suburban residence for Paolo Almerico, this beautiful Palladian villa is the purest expression of Palladio's architectural theory and aesthetic. More a villa-temple than a residence, it contradicts the rational utilitarianism of Renaissance architecture and demonstrates the priority Palladio gave to the architectural symbolism of celestial harmony over practical considerations. A visit to view the interior can be difficult to schedule—the villa remains privately owned, and visiting hours are limited and constantly change—but this is a worthwhile stop, if only to see how Palladio's harmonious arrangement of smallish interconnected rooms around a central domed space paid little attention to the practicalities of living. The interior decoration, mainly later Baroque stuccowork, contains some allegorical frescoes in the cupola by Palladio's contemporary, Alessandro Maganza.

Even without a peek inside, experiencing the exterior and the grounds is a must for any visit to Vicenza. The villa is a 20-minute walk from town or a cab (€12) or bus ride (No. 8) from Vicenza's Piazza Roma. Private tours are by appointment; see their website for the latest visiting details. ✉ *Via della Rotonda, Vicenza* ☎ *0444/321793* ⊕ *www.villalarotonda. it* ⬛ *€10 villa and grounds, €5 grounds only* ⊘ *Interior closed Mon.–Thurs. late Mar.–late Nov.*

★ Villa Valmarana ai Nani

HISTORIC HOME | Inside this 17th- to 18th-century country house, named for the statues of dwarfs adorning the garden, is a series of frescoes executed in 1757 by Gianbattista Tiepolo depicting scenes from classical mythology, *The Iliad*, Tasso's *Jerusalem Delivered*, and Ariosto's *Orlando furioso* (The Frenzy of Orlando). They include his *Sacrifice of Iphigenia*, a major masterpiece of 18th-century painting. The neighboring *foresteria* (guesthouse) is also part of the museum; it contains frescoes showing 18th-century life at its most charming and scenes of chinoiserie popular in the 18th century, by Tiepolo's son Giandomenico (1727–1804). The garden dwarfs are probably taken from designs by Giandomenico. You can reach the villa on foot by following the same path that leads to Palladio's Villa La Rotonda. ✉ *Via dei Nani 2/8, Vicenza* ☎ *0444/321803* ⊕ *www. villavalmarana.com* ⬛ *€11.*

🍴 Restaurants

★ Osteria Il Cursore

$$ | NORTHERN ITALIAN | This cozy 19th-century *locale storico* (historic hostelry) is steeped in Vicentina atmosphere, from the bar serving local wines and *sopressa* (premium salami) to the intimate dark-wood restaurant serving hearty classics. Grab a table out back for a sit-down meal of robust dishes like *bigoli* (thick, egg-enriched spaghetti) with duck, spaghetti with baccalà (cod), and, in spring, *risi e bisi* (rice with peas). **Known for:** buzzy atmosphere, especially on Vicenza soccer-match days; great-value pasta; quality wine and cold cuts. $ *Average main: €16* ⊠ *Stradella Pozzetto 10, Vicenza* ☎ *0444/323504* ⊕ *www.osteriacursore.it* ⊘ *Closed Tues.*

Ponte delle Bele

$$ | NORTHERN ITALIAN | Many of Vicenza's wealthier residents spend at least part of the summer in the Alps to escape the heat, and the dishes of this popular and friendly trattoria reflect the hearty Alpine influences on local cuisine. The house specialty, *stinco di maiale al forno* (roast pork shank), is wonderfully fragrant, with herbs and aromatic vegetables. **Known for:** mountain cheeses and cold cuts; unfussy, relaxed atmosphere and kitschy Alpine decor; hearty Vicentina classics, including baccalà served with polenta. $ *Average main: €15* ⊠ *Contrà Ponte delle Bele 5, Vicenza* ☎ *0444/320647* ⊕ *www.pontedellebele.it* ⊘ *Closed Sun. and 2 wks in Aug.*

Righetti

$ | ITALIAN | Vicentini of all generations gravitate to this popular self-service cafeteria for classic dishes that don't put a dent in your wallet. Expect hearty helpings of fare such as *orzo e fagioli* (barley and bean soup) and baccalà alla vicentina (stockfish Vicenza style). **Known for:** entertaining local atmosphere; very popular, especially for lunch; classic dishes.

$ *Average main: €12* ⊠ *Piazza Duomo 3, Vicenza* ☎ *0444/543135* ⊕ *www. selfrighetti.it* ⊘ *Closed weekends and 1 wk in Jan. and Aug.*

☕ Coffee and Quick Bites

Magazzino del Caffè

$ | NORTHERN ITALIAN | Il Magazzino is a great spot to grab a snack any time of day, as this well-run, modern place covers all the bases, from coffee and brioche breakfast fixes, to brunch panini and plates of pasta or risotto with a glass of wine later. Check out their fab selection of brioche pastries with novel fruit and nutty fillings, as well as heaped salads. **Known for:** aperitivi with snacks; tempting biscuits and gelato; friendly, youthful staff. $ *Average main: €10* ⊠ *Corso Palladio 152, Vicenza* ☎ *0444/212774.*

🛏 Hotels

During annual gold fairs in January, March, and September, it may be quite difficult to find lodging. If you're coming then, be sure to reserve well in advance and expect to pay higher rates.

★ Due Mori

$ | HOTEL | The public areas and guest rooms at one of the oldest (1883) hotels in the city, just off Piazza dei Signori, are filled with turn-of-the-20th-century antiques, and regulars favor the place because the high ceilings in the main building make it feel light and airy. **Pros:** comfortable, tastefully furnished rooms in central location; free Wi-Fi; rate same year-round. **Cons:** no TVs in rooms; no help with luggage; no a/c, although ceiling fans minimize the need for it. $ *Rooms from: €90* ⊠ *Contrà Do Rode 24, Vicenza* ☎ *0444/321886* ⊕ *www. albergoduemori.it* ⊘ *Closed 2 wks in early Aug. and 2 wks in late Dec.* ⇌ *30 rooms* ❌ *No Meals.*

Hotel Campo Marzio

$$ | HOTEL | Rooms at this comfortable full-service hotel—a five-minute walk from the train station and right in front of the city walls—are ample in size, with a mix of contemporary and traditional accents. **Pros:** great location; set back from the street, so it's quiet and bright; free bike hire. **Cons:** no in-room tea- or coffeemaking facilities; businesslike exterior; breakfast room a tad uninspiring. $ *Rooms from: €140* ⊠ *Viale Roma 21, Vicenza* ☎ *0444/5457000* ⊕ *www.hotelcampomarzio.com* ➽ *36 rooms* ⭕️ *Free Breakfast.*

Activities

Palladian Routes

CULTURAL TOURS | FAMILY | Based in the handsome Palazzo Valmarana Braga, this company offers a wealth of tours around the province of Vicenza. The most popular excursion is their two-day Vicenza and Odyssey around the lake by e-bike tour. Visit their office to pick up your bike with GPS and be guided by a narration app via smartphone around gorgeous landscapes, three villas, and the verdant shores of Lago di Fimon. ⊠ *Palazzo Valmarana Braga, Corso Fogazzaro 16, Vicenza* ☎ *0444/1270212* ⊕ *www.palladianroutes.com* ➽ *from €45 for e-bike rental; €59 e-bike tour.*

Marostica

26 km (16 miles) northeast of Vicenza, 93 km (58 miles) northwest of Venice.

From the 14th-century Castello Inferiore, where the town council still meets, an ancient stone wall snakes up the hill to enclose the Castello Superiore, which has commanding views. Marostica's most celebrated feature is the checkerboard-like square made with colored stone, Piazza Castello. The big annual event here, held in September in even-number years, is the Partita a Scacchi, a human-scale chess game.

GETTING HERE AND AROUND

There's no train station in Marostica. The closest rail connection is Bassano del Grappa, about 8 km (5 miles) away. There are regular bus connections from Vicenza's main station on FTV Bus No. 5; the trip takes about 45 minutes. By car, take the SS248 northeast from Vicenza, or southwest from Bassano.

VISITOR INFORMATION

CONTACT Associazione Pro Marostica. ⊠ *Piazza Castello 1,* ☎ *0424/72127* ⊕ *www.marosticascacchi.it.*

Sights

Castello di Marostica

CASTLE/PALACE | FAMILY | Sitting on the summit of Monte Pauso, the origins of fortifications here stretch back to the turn of the first millennium, and a guided tour of the castle delves into its bloody history, and the lives and tastes of its former residents. The fairy-tale-like castle form makes it a fine backdrop to the giant chess game staged outside the impressive drawbridge and crenellated, pitted walls. Legend has it that the moat was the watery, muddy realm of an Egyptian crocodile brought here by the town's most famous son, the physician and botanist Prospero Alpini (1553–1617). The atmospheric interiors house collections of court clothing including those of the Venetian Podestà, arms and armature, and a fresco attributed to Mantegna (1454–57). The Sale Espostive stages exhibitions and cultural events, and has a curious sculpture of doge Foscari kneeling before the lion of San Marco. ⊠ *Via Cansignorio della Scala 4, Marostica* ☎ *0424/72127* ⊕ *www.marosticascacchi.it* ➽ *Free* ➽ *Book a guided tour by phone or online.*

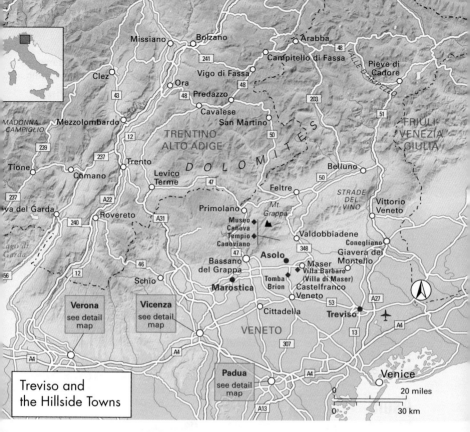

Treviso and
the Hillside Towns

🍴 Restaurants

Osteria Madonnetta

$ | VENETIAN | Opened in 1904, this
ever-reliable osteria serves hearty
traditional *cucina veneta* in wonderfully
homey, rustic surroundings. Take a seat
under the dark wooden beams or in the
leafy courtyard, and let the friendly staff
guide you through a menu, dominated
by meat dishes and seasonal soups, that
has barely changed in decades. **Known
for:** quirky, history-filled decor including a
chess-theme fireplace; sweet, grappa-in-
fused zaeti biscuits; baccalà alla vicentina. $ *Average main: €12* ✉ *Via Vajenti
21, Marostica* ☎ *0424/75859* ⊕ *www.
osteriamadonnetta.it.*

🛏 Hotels

Due Mori

$ | B&B/INN | Although this inn dates
from the 18th century, the interior is
minimalist and clean-lined—Rooms 7,
8, 11, and 12 redress the balance with
picture-perfect views of the town's upper
castle, while other windows look out
onto the city walls or olive-tree-filled
terraces. **Pros:** only hotel within the city
walls; great views of castle from some
rooms; train station transfers available.
Cons: bland decoration; noise from Corso
Mazzini–facing rooms; limited breakfast
choice. $ *Rooms from: €107* ✉ *Corso
Mazzini 73, Marostica* ☎ *0424/471777*
⊕ *www.duemori.com* ⇥ *12 rooms*
🍽 *Free Breakfast.*

🎭 Performing Arts

Partita a Scacchi

THEATER | FAMILY | A human-scale chess game known as the Partita a Scacchi is acted out by players in medieval costume on the second weekend in September in even-number years. The game dates from 1454 and originated as a peaceful way of settling a love dispute for the hand of the daughter of the lord of Marostica Castle. The orders are still given in the local Veneto dialect. A game is presented on Friday and weekend evenings as well as Sunday afternoon. If you book an evening show and do not have a hotel reservation in Marostica, be sure you have a way of getting back afterward. Buses do not run late in the evening, and taxis, if you can find one, may hike up their rates. Tickets go on sale in February; the tourist office can help with bookings. ✉ *Piazza Castello 1, Marostica* ☎ *0424/72127* ⊕ *www.marosticascacchi.it* 💳 *From €35.*

Asolo

27 km (17 miles) east of Marostica.

Once considered the most romantic and charming of Veneto towns, the hamlet of Asolo has unfortunately lost much of its appeal, now that it's given over completely to tourism and vacation houses, with almost no local population. It does still make a nice stop for lunch after a visit to the Palladian villa at Maser, but try to avoid it on weekends and holidays, when the crowds pour in.

Through the centuries, Veneto aristocrats built elegant villas on the hillside, and in the 19th century Asolo became the idyllic haunt of musicians, poets, and painters. Back then it was one of Italy's most perfectly situated villages, with views across miles of hilly countryside; now it bears some of the scars of modern development.

Asolo hosts a modest antiques market on the second Sunday of every month.

GETTING HERE AND AROUND

There's no train station in Asolo; the closest one is in Montebelluna, 12 km (7½ miles) away. Bus connections are infrequent, and buses are not coordinated with trains, making it about a 2½-hour trip from Venice via public transportation. The best option is to drive.

By car from Treviso, take Via Feltrina and continue onto Via Padre Agostino Gemelli (SR348). Follow SR348 about 16 km (10 miles), then turn left on SP667, which you follow for almost 4 km (2½ miles). At the roundabout, take the first exit, Via Monte Grappa (SP248), and follow it for 6½ km (4 miles) to Via Loredan, where you turn right and then left onto Via Biordo Vecchio. Asolo is less than 7 km (4½ miles) away from the Palladian Villa Barbaro at Maser.

VISITOR INFORMATION

CONTACT Asolo Tourism Office. ✉ *Piazza Maggiore 73 (aka Piazza Garibaldi),* ☎ *0423/529046* ⊕ *www.asolo.it.*

👁 Sights

★ **Museo Canova** (*Gypsoteca*)

ART MUSEUM | The most significant cultural monument in the Asolo area is this museum dedicated to the work of the Italian neoclassical sculptor Antonio Canova (1757–1822), whose sculptures are featured in many major European and North American cultural institutions. Set up shortly after the sculptor's death in his hometown, the village of Possagno, the museum houses most of the original plaster casts, models, and drawings made by the artist in preparation for his marble sculptures. In 1957 the Museo Canova was extended by the Italian architect Carlo Scarpa. ✉ *Via Canova 74, 13½ km (8¼ miles) northwest of Asolo, Possagno* ☎ *0423/544323* ⊕ *www.museocanova.it* 💳 *€10* ⊗ *Closed Mon.*

Museo Civico, Torre Civica, and La Rocca
HISTORY MUSEUM | In the Piazza Maggiore, the frescoed 15th-century Loggia del Capitano contains the Museo Civico, which displays a collection of eccentric memorabilia—the Italian actress Eleonora Duse's correspondence, the poet Robert Browning's spinet, and portraits of the noble Caterina Cornaro (1454–1510). There is also access to the nearby medieval tower, Torre Civica, partially rebuilt after an earthquake in 1685. It affords great views just above its handsome 18th-century clock, designed by Bartolomeo Ferracina, the genius engineer behind clocks in Venice's Piazza San Marco and Sant'Antonio da Padova. Temporary exhibitions are also staged in the tower, along with guided tours. Those after a woodland stroll should head up to the 1,000-foot Monte Ricco medieval hilltop fortress La Rocca—the views are fabulous but the structure itself is sometimes off-limits. ✉ *Piazza Maggiore, Asolo* ☎ *0423/952313* 🌐 *www.museoasolo.it* 🎫 *€5 Museo Civico; €3 Torre Civica; €3 La Rocca; €9 combined ticket* 🕒 *Closed weekdays.*

★ Tempio Canoviano
MONUMENT | One of the most impressive and historically significant neoclassical buildings in Italy, the Tempio Canoviano, a church, was designed by Canova in 1819 and finished in 1830, incorporating motifs from the rotunda of the Roman Pantheon and the pronaos of the Parthenon. The church contains several works by Canova, including his tomb, along with paintings by Luca Giordano, Palma il Giovane, and Il Pordenone. ✉ *Piazza Canova, Possagno* ✥ *16 km (10 miles) north of Asolo* ☎ *0423/544323* 🌐 *www.tempiocanoviano.it* 🎫 *Free.*

Tomba Brion
MONUMENT | One of the major monuments of contemporary Italian architecture, the Brion family tomb was designed and built by the architect Carlo Scarpa (1906–78) between 1970 and 1972. Combining Western rationalism with Eastern spirituality, Scarpa avoids the gloom and bombast of conventional commemorative monuments, creating, in his words, a secluded Eden. ✉ *SP6 (Via Castellana), about 7 km (4½ miles) south of Asolo, near village of San Vito di Altivole, Asolo* 🎫 *Free.*

🍴 Restaurants

Al Bacaro
$$ | **ITALIAN** | At this rustic, wood-rich family-style osteria, it's worth giving the robust local specialties, such as tripe, snails, or stewed game, a go—many of them served with polenta. Less adventurous diners can go for other homey options, such as goulash, polenta with cheese and mushrooms, or one of Bacaro's open-face sandwiches, generously topped with fresh salami, speck, or other cold cuts. **Known for:** seasonal vegetables and meat; jolly osteria crammed with local artifacts and patrons' hand-scribbled witticisms; good, meaty country fare. [$] *Average main: €17* ✉ *Via Browning 165, Asolo* ☎ *0423/55150* 🕒 *Closed Wed. No dinner weekends.*

★ Locanda Baggio
$$ | **ITALIAN** | A fabulous garden setting and warm yet unfussy country-style dining rooms elevate this family-run restaurant, renowned for Nino Baggio's elegant creative take on traditional cuisine. This is the finest restaurant in Asolo, and the prix-fixe menu (you can also order à la carte) delivers one of the best-value top-quality dining options in the Veneto. **Known for:** warm hospitality; white truffles and other seasonal specialties; inventive, tasty food. [$] *Average main: €23* ✉ *Via Bassane 1, Asolo* ☎ *0423/529648* 🌐 *www.locandabaggio.it* 🕒 *Closed Mon.*

🛏 Hotels

Albergo Al Sole
$$$ | **HOTEL** | This elegant pink-washed hotel in a 16th-century building overlooks the main square and has wide views over picturesque Asolo or its leafy hinterland.

Pros: central location with beautiful views; shuttle service to the surrounding area; free bike hire. **Cons:** expensive drinks and hidden extras; standard rooms have less interesting views than more expensive ones; huge rate increase in the high season. [$] *Rooms from: €234* ✉ *Via Collegio 33, Asolo* ☎ *0423/951332* 🌐 *www.albergoalsole.com* 🕒 *Generally closed early Jan.–mid-Feb.* 🛏 *23 rooms* 🍴 *Free Breakfast.*

Hotel Duse
$$ | **HOTEL** | A spiral staircase winds its way up this narrow, centrally located building—filled with traditional furnishings like gilded chairs—to rooms with grandstand-like views of the main square. **Pros:** simple but tasteful good-value rooms; bike rental and tours available; homey feel and central location. **Cons:** dated, garish decor in some rooms; not as much of a bargain when you add the cost of breakfast and parking; some street noise. [$] *Rooms from: €135* ✉ *Via Browning 190, Asolo* ☎ *0423/55241* 🌐 *www.hotelduse.com* 🕒 *Closed 3 wks in Jan. and Feb.* 🛏 *14 rooms* 🍴 *No Meals.*

Villa Cipriani
$$$ | **HOTEL** | From its 19th-century furnishings to a 21st-century spa and a romantic garden, this luxurious 16th-century villa turned hotel strives for opulence. **Pros:** incomparable views, including from the terrace; spa services and outdoor panoramic pool; truly elegant grounds. **Cons:** rooms in the annex are very small; exorbitant parking fees; small bathrooms. [$] *Rooms from: €270* ✉ *Via Canova 298, Asolo* ☎ *0423/523411* 🌐 *www.villacipriani-asolo.com* 🛏 *29 rooms* 🍴 *Free Breakfast.*

Treviso

37 km (23 miles) southeast of Asolo, 30 km (19 miles) north of Venice.

Treviso has been dubbed "Little Venice" because of its meandering, moss-bank canals. They can't really compare with Venice's spectacular waterways, but Treviso's historic center, with its medieval arcaded streets, does have a great deal of charm. Treviso is a fine place to stop for a few hours on the way from Venice to the wine country in the north or to the Palladian villas in the hinterland.

Allied bombing on Good Friday in 1944 destroyed half the city—it was bombed by mistake after a report that Hitler would be in Tarvisio, on the Austrian border, was misread. Despite this, Treviso managed to preserve what remained of its old town's narrow streets while introducing modernity far more gently than in many other parts of Italy. These days it's one of the wealthiest small cities in the country, with fashionable shops and boutiques at every turn in the busy city center.

GETTING HERE AND AROUND

Treviso is 30 minutes by train from Venice; there are frequent daily departures. By car from Venice, pick up the SS13 (Via Terraglio) in Mestre and follow it all the way to Treviso; the trip takes about 45 minutes.

VISITOR INFORMATION

CONTACT Treviso Tourism Office (IAT Treviso). ✉ *Piazza Borsa 4,* ☎ *0422/595780* 🌐 *www.visittreviso.it.*

👁 Sights

Conegliano
TOWN | This attractive town, with Venetian-style villas and arcaded streets, lies 23 km (14 miles) north of Treviso in wine-producing country and is known for its sparkling white wine, prosecco. Its other claim to fame is its connection with Gianbattista Cima—called Cima di Conegliano. Along with Giovanni Bellini, Cima is one of the greatest painters of the early Venetian Renaissance, and the town's elegant 14th-century Duomo houses an altarpiece he painted in 1492. The front of the Duomo is formed by the frescoed late-medieval facade and Gothic arcade of the Scuola dei Battuti. If you stop in town, be sure to taste the

prosecco, sold in local wine bars and shops. There is regular train service from Treviso. ⊠ *Conegliano.*

Duomo

CHURCH | The Cattedrale San Pietro Apostolo, or Duomo, was given a 19th-century neoclassical makeover but retains the Renaissance splendor of the Malchiostro Chapel, with an *Annunciation* by Titian (1520) and Pordenone's (1484–1539) *Adoration of the Magi* frescoes. The crypt has 12th-century columns. Bring a handful of coins for the coin-operated lights that illuminate the artwork. To the left of the Duomo is the Romanesque Battistero di San Giovanni (11th–12th centuries), which is probably quite similar in style to the medieval Duomo; it's open only for special exhibitions. ⊠ *Piazza del Duomo, Treviso* ☎ *0422/545720.*

La Pescheria

HISTORIC DISTRICT | A short walk east of Piazza dei Signori is the *pescheria* (fish market; opened in 1856), set on an island on Cagnan Grande, one of the small canals that flow through town. The picturesque, leafy setting here is completed by the surrounding handsome medieval buildings, including Ca' dei Carraresi, Ca' Brittoni, and the former convent of the Monache Camaldolesi. Seek out two beguiling female statues close to Trevisani hearts around these parts: *La Sirenetta* or Little Mermaid emerges from the Cagnan Grande; and on Vicolo Podestà, Fontana Delle Tette's serene-looking signorina spouts water— and on special occasions, *vino rosso* and *vino bianco*—from her breasts. ⊠ *Vicolo Podestà, Treviso.*

Piazza dei Signori

PLAZA/SQUARE | The center of medieval Treviso, this Piazza dei Signori remains the town's social hub, with outdoor cafés and some impressive public buildings. The most important of these, the Palazzo dei Trecento (1185–1268), was the seat of the city government, composed of the Council of 300, during the Middle Ages. It was rebuilt after bombing in 1944. Step inside to view its beautiful loggia, the Salone replete with impressive wooden roof trusts and elaborate frescoed walls. ⊠ *Treviso.*

San Nicolò

CHURCH | The most important church in Treviso, this huge Venetian Gothic structure from the early 14th century has an ornate vaulted ceiling and frescoes (circa 1350) of saints by Tommaso da Modena (circa 1325–79) on the columns. The depiction of St. Agnes on the north side is particularly interesting, combining the naturalism initiated a few decades earlier by Giotto with the grace and elegance of Gothic abstraction. Also worth examining are Tommaso's realistic portraits of 40 Dominican friars, found in the Sala del Capitolo of the seminary next door. They include the earliest known painting of a subject wearing eyeglasses, an Italian invention (circa 1280–1300). ⊠ *Seminario Vescovile, Via San Nicolò, Treviso* ☎ *0422/548626* ⊕ *www.sannicolotreviso. it* ⊘ *Closed Sun. except to worshippers.*

★ Villa Barbaro (Villa di Maser)

NOTABLE BUILDING | At the Villa Barbaro (1554) near the town of Maser, you can see the exquisite results of a onetime collaboration between two of the greatest artists of their age: Palladio was the architect, and Paolo Veronese did the interiors. You can easily spend a couple of hours here, so set aside time for lingering in the gorgeous grounds, admiring the honey-hue exterior and ornate statuary, including the dreamlike nymphaeum and pool. A visit is particularly immersive because the superb condition of the grounds and interior creates an uncanny atmosphere: nowhere else in the Veneto do you get such a vivid feeling for the combination of grandeur and leisure with a tangible whiff of a working farm.

Villa Barbaro, a short drive from Asolo, is most accessible by private car; the closest train station is Montebelluna. Buses leave for Maser from the bus station at Treviso, Montebelluna, or Bassano di Grappa. The

Traveling the Wine Roads

You'd be hard-pressed to find a more stimulating and varied wine region than northeastern Italy. From the Valpolicella, Bardolino, and Soave produced near Verona to the superlative whites of the Collio Goriziano region, wines from the Veneto and Friuli–Venezia Giulia earn more Denominazione di Origine Controllata (DOC) seals for uniqueness and quality than those of any other area of Italy.

You can travel on foot, by car, or by bicycle over hillsides covered with *cantine* (vineyards), each field nurturing subtly different grape varieties. Be advised that Italy has become more stringent about its driving regulations; designated drivers can help avoid the risk of fines, embarrassment, or worse.

In the stretch of country north of Treviso, you can follow designated wine roads—tours that blend a beautiful rural setting with the delights of the grape. Authorized wineshops, where you can stop and sample, are marked with a sign showing a triangular arrangement of red and yellow grapes. There are three routes to choose from, and you can do them all comfortably over the course of a day or two.

Montello and Asolo Hills

This route provides a good balance of vineyards and nonwine sights. It winds from Nervesa della Battaglia, 18 km (10 miles) north of Treviso, past two prime destinations in the area, the village of Asolo and the Villa Barbaro at Maser. Asolo produces good prosecco, while Montello, a hill near Nervesa, favors merlot and cabernet. Both areas also yield pinot noir and chardonnay.

Piave River

The circular route follows the Piave River and runs through orchards, woods, and hills. Among the area's gems are the dessert wines Torchiato di Fregona and Refrontolo Passito, both made according to traditional methods.

Raboso del Piave, renowned since Roman times, ages well and complements local dishes such as beans and pasta or goose stuffed with chestnuts. Other reds include merlot and cabernet sauvignon.

Prosecco

La Strada del Prosecco (Prosecco Road) runs for 47 km (29 miles) between Valdobbiadene and Conegliano, home of Italy's first wine institute, winding between knobby hills covered in grapevines. These hang in festoons on row after row of pergolas to create a thick mantle of green.

Turn off the main route to explore the narrower country lanes. They meander past numerous family wineries where you can taste and buy the wines. It's well worth setting aside time to explore the most scenic southern stretches: between Renfrontolo and Col San Martino there's the ancient San Vigilio church and the celebrated Follador winery; while the Cartizze hills afford breathtaking views. Spring is an excellent time to visit, with no fewer than 15 local wine festivals held between March and early June.

bus will leave you at a stop about 1½ km (1 mile) from Maser. Hours can vary, so check the website. ✉ *Via Cornuda 7, Maser, Treviso* ☎ *0432/923004* 🌐 *www.villadimaser.it* 🎟 *€9* 🕒 *Closed Mon., Wed., and Fri. Apr.–Oct. and weekdays Nov.–Mar.*

🍴 Restaurants

All'Antico Portico

$$ | **ITALIAN** | **FAMILY** | This little old brick trattoria on a beguiling piazza with views of the Santa Maria Maggiore church is a favorite among locals and tourists, who flock to its cozy wood-trimmed interior. The menu changes daily but always features well-executed versions of simple local dishes, from risottos and pastas to a variety of seafood and meat dishes. **Known for:** mamma's baccalà alla veneziana recipe; homemade pasta and white truffle; set under the 15th-century porticoes. [$] *Average main: €21* ✉ *Piazza Santa Maria Maggiore 18, Treviso* ☎ *0422/545259* 🌐 *www.anticoportico.it* 🕒 *Closed Tues. No dinner Mon.*

Beccherie

$$$ | **ITALIAN** | Adventurous foodies should book a table in this stylish blue-and-wood-accented dining room, located behind Treviso's Palazzo dei Trecento old meat market, for an experience that marries Trevigiano culinary traditions with contemporary elegance. The owner's parents, Alba and Ado, invented the famous dessert tiramisu in the 1960s, and the Beccherie, opened in 1939, still makes it to the original, feather-light recipe. **Known for:** reservations recommended for dinner; contemporary design above the canal; inventive food and special tiramisu. [$] *Average main: €28* ✉ *Piazza Ancilotto 10, Treviso* ☎ *0422/540871* 🌐 *www.lebeccherie.it* 🕒 *Closed Tues.*

Il Basilisco

$$ | **ITALIAN** | Gastronomically adventurous diners who visit this quirky restaurant filled with stylish midcentury furnishings will find *cucina povera* (peasant food) given an inventive twist. The chef is a passionate Slow Food champion, so expect local and seasonal meat and vegetables, as well as excellent seafood and an extensive wine list from Italy and farther afield. **Known for:** homemade pasta, cured meats, and antipasti; vibrant contemporary decor and design; inventive use of quinto quarto (offal). [$] *Average main: €20* ✉ *Via Bison 34, Treviso* ☎ *0422/541822* 🌐 *www.ristorantebasilisco.com* 🕒 *Closed Sun. No lunch Mon.*

Odeon alla Colonna

$$ | **NORTHERN ITALIAN** | Dine in the atmospheric arcaded canal-side *vicolo*on Odeon's superb-value pasta, meat, and seafood dishes, or amid the columns in the high-ceilinged *salone*. As befits the intriguing historic setting and interiors, the menu showcases traditional Trevisano ingredients with the occasional flavorsome twist. **Known for:** take-away dried pasta, risotto, and so on from their deli counter; special tasting menus and cultural gatherings; light lunches, heaped salads, and homemade pasta dishes. [$] *Average main: €15* ✉ *Vicolo Rinaldi 3, Treviso* ☎ *0422/541012* 🌐 *www.odeonlacolonna.it.*

Toni del Spin

$$ | **ITALIAN** | Wood-paneled and with a 1930s-style interior, this bustling trattoria has a wholesome menu based on local Veneto cooking. The *spin* in the restaurant's name refers to the spine of the baccalà, one of several justly famous specialties (served without the titular spine); also try the *sopa coada*, a pigeon-and-bread soup. ■ **TIP→ Reservations are essential, even for lunch, since the word is out that this is the best value in town.** **Known for:** terrazza dining in warmer months; idiosyncratic, sometimes brusque service; Veneto specialties and great wine choices. [$] *Average main: €18* ✉ *Via Inferiore 7, Treviso* ☎ *393/9863597* 🌐 *www.ristorantetonidelspin.com* 🕒 *Closed 3 wks in July and Aug. No lunch Mon.*

☕ Coffee and Quick Bites

Caffetteria Broli

$ | **NORTHERN ITALIAN** | This central coffee bar serves lots of different *espressi* and *cappuccini*—topped with chocolate and cream and other enhancements—as well as a cornucopia of great-value tramezzini sandwiches, *piadine* (Italian flat-bread wraps), and panini. Pop in most times of the day (closes at 7:30 pm) for a selection of classic pasta primi and secondi, as well as healthy juices and vegan options. **Known for:** vegan selection; insalatoni (heaped salads); brioche and other pastries topped with fruit. $ *Average main: €8* ✉ *Vicolo Broli 8/10, Treviso* ☎ *0422/582225.*

🛏 Hotels

Hotel San Nicolò

$ | **HOTEL** | Comfort combines with warm hospitality and distinctive decor—public areas are elegant with choice antiques, while each guest room is themed after a global city—at this well-run central hotel in a handsome palazzo near Chiesa di San Nicolò. **Pros:** individual character in each guest room; only a dozen steps up to rooms; warm, family-run customer service. **Cons:** no elevator; some rooms on the small size; road noise in some rooms. $ *Rooms from: €119* ✉ *Via Risorgimento 54, Treviso* ☎ *0422/590114* ⊕ *www.relais-sannicolo.com* ⇨ *10 rooms* ¶ *Free Breakfast.*

Udine

127 km (79 miles) northeast of Venice.

The main reason for devoting some time to Udine is to see works by Gianbattista Tiepolo (1696–1770), one of the greatest European painters of the 18th century. Distributed in several palaces and churches around town, this is the largest assembly of his art outside Venice. In fact, Udine calls itself "la città di Tiepolo."

The largest city on the Friuli side of the region, Udine has a provincial, genteel atmosphere and lots of charm. The city sometimes seems completely unaffected by tourism, and things are still done the way they were decades ago. In the medieval and Renaissance historical center of town, you'll find unevenly spaced streets with appealing wine bars and open-air cafés. Friulani are proud of their culture, with many restaurants featuring local cuisine, and street signs and announcements written in both Italian and Friulano (Furlan), which, although it is classified as a dialect, is really a separate language from Italian.

Commanding a view from the Alpine foothills to the Adriatic Sea, Udine stands on a mound that, according to legend, was erected so Attila the Hun could watch the burning of Aquileia, an important Roman center to the south. Although the legend is unlikely (Attila burned Aquileia about 500 years before the first historical mention of Udine), the view from Udine's castle across the alluvial plane down to the sea is impressive. In the Middle Ages Udine flourished, thanks to its favorable trade location and the right granted by the local patriarch to hold regular markets.

GETTING HERE AND AROUND

There's frequent train service from both Venice and Trieste; the trip takes about two hours from Venice, and a little over an hour from Trieste. By car from Venice, take the SR11 to the E55 and head east. Take the E55 (it eventually becomes the Autostrada Alpe Adria) to SS13 (Viale Venezia) east into Udine. Driving from Trieste, take the SS202 to the E70, which becomes the A4. Turn onto the E55 north, which is the same road you would take coming from Venice. Driving times are 1½ to 2 hours from Venice and 1 hour from Trieste.

VISITOR INFORMATION

The tourist office sells the FVG (Friuli Venezia Giulia) Card, which includes admission to most museums in Udine and other important sites in the region. Its price ranges from €25 (for 48 hours) up to €39 (for one week).

CONTACT Udine Tourism Office. ✉ *Piazza I Maggio 7,* ☎ *0432/295972* ⊕ *www. turismofvg.it.*

Sights

★ Castello and Musei Civici

CASTLE/PALACE | The hilltop castle (construction began in 1517) has panoramic views extending to Monte Nero (7,360 feet) in neighboring Slovenia, but head inside to see Udine's civic museums of art and archaeology, with myriad collections that can detain you for hours. On the ground floor are the Museo del Risorgimento (tracing the history of Italian unification) and Museo Archeologico; the third floor is the Museo della Fotografia, with fascinating 19th- and 20th-century images of the Friuli. Particularly worthwhile is the national and regional art collection in the Galleria d'Arte Antica, which has canvases by Venetians Vittore Carpaccio (circa 1460–1525) and Gianbattista Tiepolo, the recently restored (2020) *Il San Francesco Riceve le Stimmate* (St. Francis Receiving the Stigmata) by Caravaggio, and carefully selected works by lesser known but still interesting Veneto and Friuli artists. ■ TIP→ **The museum's small collection of drawings includes several by Tiepolo; some find his drawings even more moving than his paintings.** ✉ *Via Lionello 1, Udine* ☎ *0432/1272591* ⊕ *www.civicimuseiudine.it* 🎟 *€8, €10 Unico ticket also includes Casa Cavazzini and Museo Etnografico del Friuli (free with FVG Card)* ⊗ *Closed Mon.*

Duomo

CHURCH | A few steps from the Piazza della Libertà is Udine's 1335 Duomo, with some significant works by Tiepolo.

Its Cappella del Santissimo has important early frescoes by Tiepolo, and the Cappella della Trinità has a Tiepolo altarpiece. There is also a beautiful late Tiepolo *Resurrection* (1751) in an altar by the sculptor Giuseppe Toretti. Ask the Duomo's attendant to let you into the adjacent **Chiesa della Purità** to see more important late paintings by Tiepolo. ✉ *Piazza del Duomo 1, Udine* ☎ *0432/505302* ⊕ *www.cattedraleudine.it* 🎟 *Free.*

★ Museo d'Arte Moderna e Contemporanea–Casa Cavazzini

ART GALLERY | Udine's fine civic collection of modern and contemporary art is housed in the handsome and part-modernized 16th-century Casa Cavazzini, which retains some ornate apartment interiors. The first and second floors display the permanent collection: first-floor highlights include bold sculptural works by the three Udinese brothers Dino, Mirko, and Afro Basaldella, with a backdrop of 14th-century frescoes discovered during the 2012 refurbishing. There are also fine works by Giorgio Morandi, Renato Guttuso, and Carlo Carrà. Up a floor is the Collezione Astaldi, spanning the 1920s through the 1960s, and Collezione FRIAM, with '60s and '70s works. Worth seeking out are Giorgio de Chirico's *I Gladiatori* (1931) and pieces by 20th-century American icons Willem de Kooning, Roy Lichtenstein, and Sol LeWitt. Entry to themed temporary exhibitions costs extra. ✉ *Via Cavour 14, Udine* ☎ *0432/1273772* ⊕ *www.civicimuseiudine.it* 🎟 *€5 (€12 temporary shows), €10 Unico ticket also includes Castello and Museo Etnografico del Friuli (free with FVG Card)* ⊗ *Closed Mon.*

★ Museo Diocesano e Gallerie del Tiepolo

CASTLE/PALACE | The handsome Palazzo Patriarcale o Arcivescovile contains several rooms of frescoes by the young Gianbattista Tiepolo, painted from 1726 to 1732, which comprise the most important collection of early works by Italy's most brilliant 18th-century painter.

The Galleria del Tiepolo (1727) contains superlative Tiepolo frescoes depicting the stories of Abraham, Isaac, and Jacob. The *Judgment of Solomon* (1729) graces the Pink Room. There are also beautiful and important Tiepolo frescoes in the staircase, throne room, and palatine chapel of this palazzo. Even in these early works we can see the Venetian master's skill in creating an illusion of depth, not only through linear perspective, but also through subtle gradations in the intensity of the colors, with the stronger colors coming forward and the paler ones receding into space. Tiepolo was one of the first artists to use this method of representing space and depth, which reflected the scientific discoveries of perception and optics in the 17th century.

The Museo Diocesano here features sculptures from Friuli churches from the 13th through 18th centuries; and don't miss the magnificent library, the Biblioteca Arcivescovile Delfiniana. ✉ *Piazza Patriarcato 1, Udine* ☎ *0432/25003* 🌐 *www.musdioc-tiepolo.it* 🎟 *€8, includes Museo Diocesano (free with FVG Card)* 🕓 *Closed Tues.*

Piazza della Libertà

PLAZA/SQUARE | Udine was conquered by the Venetians in 1420, so there is a distinctly Venetian stamp on the architecture of the historic center, most noticeably here, in the large main square. The Loggia del Leonello, begun in 1428, dominates the square and houses the municipal government. Its similarity to the facade of Venice's Palazzo Ducale (finished in 1424) is clear, but there is no evidence that it is an imitation of that palace. It's more likely a product of the same architectural fashion. Opposite stands the Renaissance Porticato di San Giovanni (1533–35) and the Torre dell'Orologio, a 1527 clock tower with naked *mori* (Moors), who strike the hours on the top. ✉ *Udine.*

🍴 Restaurants

★ Hostaria alla Tavernetta

$$$ | **FRIULIAN** | The trusty Hostaria (open since 1954) has rustic fireside dining downstairs and more elegantly decorated rooms upstairs, where there's also an intimate terrace under the Duomo. It's a great place for sampling regional specialties such as *orzotto* (barley prepared like risotto), delicious *cjalzòns* (ravioli from the Carnia), and seasonal meat dishes, accompanied by a fabulous wine list. **Known for:** superb local Collio wine, grappa, and regional selections; Friulian ingredients and traditions; rustic yet sophisticated atmosphere. [$] *Average main: €25* ✉ *Via di Prampero 2, Udine* ☎ *0432/501066* 🌐 *www.allatavernetta.com* 🕓 *Closed Sun. and Mon. No lunch Sat.*

★ Vitello d'Oro

$$$ | **ITALIAN** | Udine's very chic landmark restaurant is the one reserved most by locals for special occasions, and the menu features the freshest meat and fish in sophisticated dishes served with moodily lit culinary stagecraft. You might start with an antipasto of assorted raw shellfish, including the impossibly sweet Adriatic scampi, followed by the fresh fish of the day. **Known for:** multicourse tasting menu; large terrace popular in summer; seafood served raw and cooked. [$] *Average main: €26* ✉ *Via Valvason 4, Udine* ☎ *0432/508982* 🌐 *www.vitellodoro.com* 🕓 *Closed Tues. No lunch Wed. and Thurs.*

☕ Coffee and Quick Bites

★ Grosmi Caffè

$ | **NORTHERN ITALIAN** | Under the porticoes of gorgeous Piazza Matteoti, with its vibrant student and dialect-speaking locals, Grosmi is a reliable choice for excellent coffee, pastries, and people-watching. Although the brioche filled with chocolate, custard, or fruit jam are staples, some opt for a small cake or

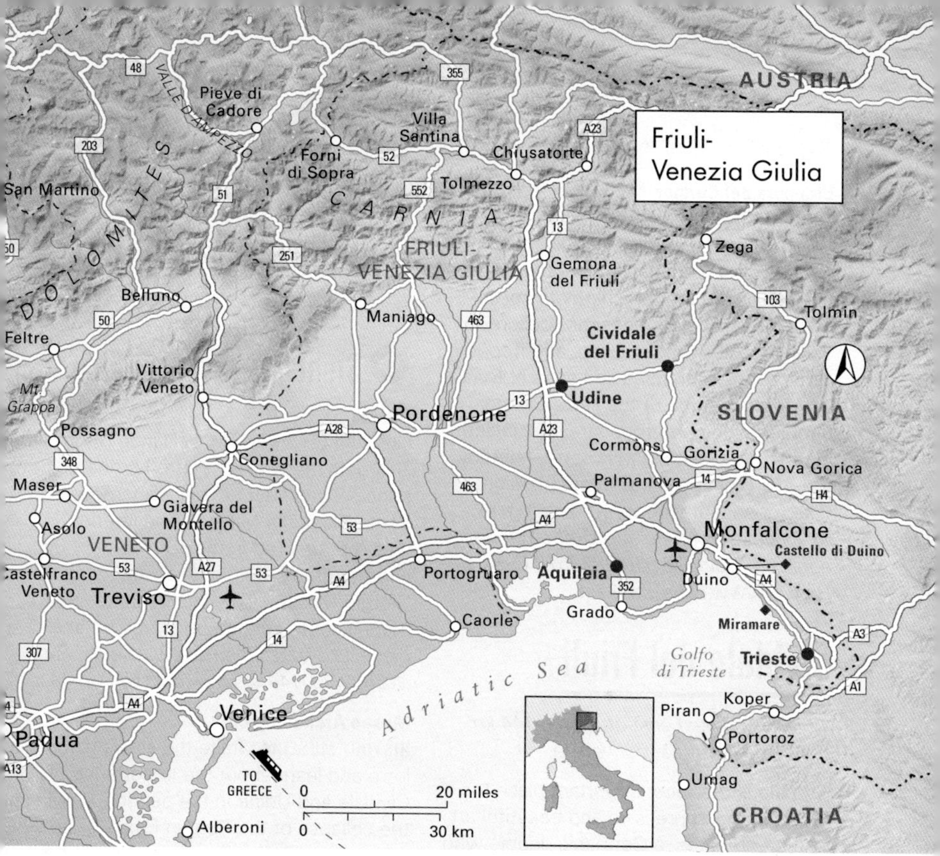

macaroon to accompany their caffeine fix. **Known for:** brioche, pastries, and cakes; tables on the piazza; selection of imported blends. [$] *Average main: €5* ✉ *Piazza Giacomo Matteotti 9, Udine* ☎ *0432/506411* 🌐 *biquadrocaffe.it.*

Hotels

Hotel Clocchiatti Next

$ | **HOTEL** | You have two smart and contrasting choices here: the 19th-century villa, with canopy beds and Alpine-style wood ceilings and paneling; and the "Next Wing," with rich colors and spare furnishings in starkly angular rooms. **Pros:** stylish, individually decorated rooms; a tranquil Zen-garden haven; excellent breakfast for €10 extra. **Cons:** no restaurant; small bathrooms; 10-minute drive from town center. [$] *Rooms from: €120* ✉ *Via Cividale 29, Udine* ☎ *0432/505047* 🌐 *www.hotelclocchiatti.it* 🛏 *27 rooms* 🍴 *No Meals.*

Hotel Ristorante Allegria

$$ | **HOTEL** | Renovation of this 15th-century building took a decidedly minimalist approach: the breakfast room, lounges, and guest rooms feature plenty of light wood, mood lighting, and sleek, angular design. **Pros:** well-appointed, neutral-hue rooms; easy walking distance to the center; easy access, secure garage. **Cons:** a/c can be unreliable; fee for parking; rooms may be too minimalist for some. [$] *Rooms from: €160* ✉ *Via Grazzano 18, Udine* ☎ *0432/201116* 🌐 *www.hotelallegria.it* 🛏 *21 rooms* 🍴 *Free Breakfast.*

Activities

L'Ippovia del Cormor

BIKING | L'Ippovia del Cormor is a 26-km (16-mile) path that allows walkers, cyclists, and horseback riders to immerse themselves in the rural hamlets north of Udine, including Tricesimo, Colloredo di Monte Albano, Cassacco, and Treppo Grande. The path rises and ends at Buja, where the source of the River Cormor bubbles with numerous streams, including the Rio Gelato, and is surrounded by the mountain peaks. Contact Cussigh Bike for suitably robust wheels to hire. ⊠ *Via del Lavoro, Feletto Umberto—Tavagnacco, Udine* ☏ *040/9828570 Cussigh Bike* ⊕ *www.cussighbike.it.*

Cividale del Friuli

17 km (11 miles) east of Udine, 144 km (89 miles) northeast of Venice.

Cividale is the most important place for taking in the impressive and beautiful art of the Lombards, a Germanic people who entered Italy in 568 and who ruled parts of Italy until the late 8th century. The city was founded in AD 53 by Julius Caesar, then commander of Roman legions in the area. Here you can also find Celtic, Roman, and medieval Jewish ruins alongside Venetian Gothic buildings, including the Palazzo Comunale. Strolling through the part of the city that now occupies the former Gastaldia, the Lombard ducal palace, gives you spectacular views of the medieval city and the river.

GETTING HERE AND AROUND

There's half-hourly train service from Udine. Since the Udine–Cividale train line isn't part of the Italian national rail system, you have to buy the tickets from the electronic machines, the MPL tobacconist, or the newsstand Edicola 103 within the Udine station. You can't buy a ticket through to Cividale from another city.

By car from Udine, take Via Cividale, which turns into SS54; follow SS54 into Cividale.

VISITOR INFORMATION

CONTACT Informacittà office. ⊠ *Piazza Duomo 5,* ☏ *0432/710460* ⊕ *www.cividale.com.*

 Sights

Duomo

CHURCH | Cividale's Renaissance Duomo is largely the work of Pietro Lombardo, principal architect of Venice's famous Santa Maria dei Miracoli. The interior was restructured in the 18th century by another prominent Venetian architect, Giorgio Massari. The church contains a magnificent 12th-century silver gilt altarpiece. ⊠ *Piazza Duomo, Cividale del Friuli* ☏ *0432/731144* ⊕ *www.duomocividale.it.*

Museo Archeologico

HISTORY MUSEUM | Trace the area's history here and learn about the importance of Cividale and Udine in the period following the collapse of the Roman Empire. The collection includes Roman mosaics and epigraphs as well as weapons and exquisite jewelry from 6th-century Lombard warriors, who swept through much of what is now Italy. ⊠ *Piazza Duomo 13, Cividale del Friuli* ☏ *0432/700700* ⊕ *www.museoarcheologicocividale. beniculturali.it* ☏ *€4; €9 combined ticket, includes Museo Archeologico and Museo Cristiano e Tesoro del Duomo (free with FVG Card).*

Museo Cristiano e Tesoro del Duomo

OTHER MUSEUM | Entered via a courtyard to the right of the Duomo, this museum contains two interesting, important, and surprisingly beautiful monuments of Lombard art: the Altar of Duke Ratchis (737–744) and the Baptistry of Patriarch Callisto (731–776). Both were found under the floor of the present Duomo in the early 20th century. The museum also has two fine paintings by Veronese, one by Il Pordenone, and a small collection of medieval and Renaissance vestments. ✉ *Via Candotti 1, Cividale del Friuli* ☎ *0432/730403* 🎫 *€4; €9 combined ticket, includes Museo Archeologico and Museo Cristiano e Tesoro del Duomo (free with FVG Card)* ⏲ *Closed Mon. and Tues.*

Palazzo de Nordis: Galleria d'Arte De Martiis

ART GALLERY | Opened in 2020 and housed in a magnificent historic palazzo, originally dating from the 15th century, the Gallery showcases the De Martiis family's exquisite collection of 20th-century art. Among the figurative works is a saucy Toulouse-Lautrec, and there are eye-popping Impressionist masterpieces by Karel Appel and Victor Vasarely. **■ TIP→ For tourist info visit the ground floor Sportello Informacittà.** ✉ *Piazza Duomo 5, Cividale del Friuli* ☎ *0432/710357* 🌐 *palazzodenordis.it* 🎫 *€10; free with FVG Card.*

★ Tempietto Longobardo
(*Lombard Church*)

CHURCH | Seeing the beautiful and historically important Tempietto Longobardo from the 8th century is more than enough reason to visit Cividale. Now inside the 16th-century Monastery of Santa Maria in Valle, the Tempietto was originally the chapel of the ducal palace, known as the Gastaldia. The west wall is the best-preserved example of the art and architecture of the Lombards, a Germanic people who entered Italy in 568. It has an archway with an exquisitely rendered vine motif, guarded by an 8th-century procession of female figures, showing the Lombard interpretation of classical forms that resembles the style of the much earlier Byzantine mosaics in Ravenna, a town that had passed briefly to Lombard rule in 737. The post-Lombard frescoes decorating the vaults and the east wall date from the 13th and 14th centuries, and the fine carved wooden stalls also date from the 14th century. ✉ *Via Monastero Maggiore, Cividale del Friuli* ☎ *0432/700867* 🌐 *www.tempiettolongobardo.it* 🎫 *€4; €9 combined ticket, includes Museo Archeologico and Museo Cristiano e Tesoro del Duomo (free with FVG Card).*

🍴 Restaurants

Alla Speranza

$$$ | **NORTHERN ITALIAN** | This well-thought-of osteria-trattoria lands the freshest seafood and creates exquisite, beautifully presented plates; the chefs constantly delight with new things to try such as homemade spirulina grissini, unusual flavor combos, and vibrant garnishes. Dine in the rustic yet refined dining room with its exposed stone, wooden beams, and coved ceilings, or outside on the gorgeous terrace with piazza views. **Known for:** fresh seafood with colorful flowers, herbs, and crunchy garnishes; crazy creations like the Tuna Rubik's Cube; innovative desserts and aperitivi. [$] *Average main: €26* ✉ *Piazza Foro Giulio Cesare 15, Cividale del Friuli* ☎ *0432/731131* 🌐 *www.allasperanza.net* ⏲ *Closed Mon. No lunch Tues.–Fri.*

🛏 Hotels

B&B dai Toscans

$ | **B&B/INN** | In a central location, this 15th-century palazzo, once home to the dukes of Tuscany, is now a charming and romantic bed-and-breakfast with parquet flooring throughout, a pleasant if unremarkable breakfast room, and large guest rooms furnished in antique style. **Pros:** large, well-appointed rooms; no- or low-fee nearby parking; triples for families. **Cons:** can be a struggle hauling luggage in this pedestrianized area; quirky decor not to everyone's taste; some noise from the street and the cathedral bells. [$] *Rooms from: €85* ✉ *Corso Mazzini 15/1, Cividale del Friuli* ☎ *3490/765288 mobile* 🌐 *daitoscans.it* 🛏 *5 rooms* 🍽 *Free Breakfast.*

Aquileia

123 km (77 miles) east of Venice, 42 km (25 miles) south of Udine.

This sleepy little town is refreshingly free of the tourists that you might expect at such a culturally historic place. In the time of Emperor Augustus, it was Italy's fourth-most-important city (after Rome, Milan, and Capua), as well as the principal northern Adriatic port of Italy and the beginning of Roman routes north. Aquileia's Roman and early Christian remains offer an image of the transition from pagan to Christian Rome.

GETTING HERE AND AROUND

Getting to Aquileia by public transportation is difficult but not impossible. There's frequent train service from Venice and Trieste to Cervignano di Friuli, which is 8 km (5 miles) away from Aquileia by taxi (about €25) or infrequent bus service. (Ask the newsstand attendant or the railroad ticket teller for assistance.) By car from Venice or Trieste, take Autostrada A4 (Venezia–Trieste) to the Palmanova exit and continue 17 km (11 miles) to Aquileia. From Udine, take Autostrada A23 to the Palmanova exit.

VISITOR INFORMATION

CONTACT Aquileia Infopoint. ⊠ *Via Giulia Augusta 11,* ☏ *0431/919491* ⊕ *www. turismofvg.it.*

 Sights

Aquileia Archaeological Site

RUINS | Roman remains of the forum, houses, cemetery, and port are surrounded by cypresses here, and the little stream was once an important waterway extending to Grado. Unfortunately, many of the excavations of Roman Aquileia could not be left exposed, because of the extremely high water table under the site, and had to be reburied after archaeological studies had been conducted; nevertheless, what remains aboveground, along with the monuments in the archaeological museum, gives an idea of the grandeur of this ancient city. The area is well signposted. ⊠ *Near basilica, Aquileia* 🎟 *Free.*

★ Basilica

CHURCH | The highlight here is the spectacular 3rd- to 4th-century mosaic covering the entire floor of the basilica and the adjacent crypt, which make up one of the most important early Christian monuments. Theodore, the basilica's first bishop, built two parallel basilicas (now the north and the south halls) on the site of a Gnostic chapel in the 4th century. These were joined by a third hall, forming a "U." The complex later accumulated the Romanesque portico and Gothic bell tower. The mosaic floor of the basilica is the remains of the floor of Theodore's south hall.

In his north hall, Theodore retained much of the floor of the earlier Gnostic chapel, whose mosaics represent the ascent of the soul, through the realm of the planets and constellations, to God, who is represented as a ram. (The ram, at the head of the zodiac, is the Gnostic generative force.) This integration of Gnosticism into a Christian church is interesting, since Gnosticism had been branded a heresy by early church fathers.

The 4th-century mosaics of the south hall (the present-day nave) represent the story of Jonah as prefiguring the salvation offered by the Church. Down a flight of steps, the Cripta degli Affreschi contains 12th-century frescoes. ⊠ *Piazza Capitolo 1, Aquileia* ☏ *0431/919719* ⊕ *www. fondazioneaquileia.it* 🎟 *€3 basilica and Cripta degli Affreschi, €5 with Cripta degli Scavi; €2 campanile; €10 whole complex; all sites free with FGV Card* ☉ *Campanile closed Oct.–Mar.*

Museo Archeologico

OTHER MUSEUM | The museum's wealth of material from Roman times includes portrait busts from the Republican era, semiprecious gems, amber—including preserved flies—and goldwork, and a fine glass collection. Beautiful pre-Christian mosaics are from the floors of Roman houses and palaces. ✉ *Via Roma 1, Aquileia* ☎ *0431/91016* ⊕ *www.museoarcheologicoaquileia.beniculturali.it* 🎫 *€7 (free with FGV card)* ⊘ *Closed Mon.*

Trieste

163 km (101 miles) east of Venice, 77 miles (48 km) east of Aquileia.

Trieste is Italy's only truly cosmopolitan city. In a country—perhaps even in a continent—where the amalgamation of cultures has frequently proved difficult, Trieste stands out as one of the few authentic melting pots. Not only do Italian, Slavic, and Central European cultures meet here, they actually merge to create a unique Triestino culture. To discover this culture, visiting Trieste's coffeehouses, local eateries, and piazzas is probably more important than visiting its churches and museums, interesting though they are.

Trieste is built along a fringe of coastline where the rugged Karst Plateau tumbles abruptly into the beautiful Adriatic. It was the only port of the Austro-Hungarian Empire and, therefore, a major industrial and financial center. In the early years of the 20th century, Trieste and its surroundings also became famous by their association with some of the most important names of Italian literature, such as Italo Svevo, and Irish and German writers. James Joyce drew inspiration from the city's multiethnic population, and Rainer Maria Rilke was inspired by the coast to the west.

The city has lost its importance as a port and a center of finance, but perhaps because of its multicultural nature, at the juncture of Latin, Slavic, and Germanic Europe, it's never fully lost its role as an intellectual center. In recent years the city has become a center for science and technology. The streets hold a mix of monumental neoclassical and Art Nouveau architecture, built by the Austrians during Trieste's days of glory, granting an air of melancholy stateliness to a city that lives as much in the past as the present.

Italian revolutionaries of the 1800s rallied their battle cry around Trieste, because of what they believed was foreign occupation of their motherland. After World War II the sliver of land including Trieste and a small part of Istria became an independent, neutral state that was officially recognized in a 1947 peace treaty. Although it was actually occupied by British and American troops for its nine years of existence, the Free Territory of Trieste issued its own currency and stamps. In 1954 a Memorandum of Understanding was signed in London, giving civil administration of Trieste to Italy.

GETTING HERE AND AROUND

Trains to Trieste depart regularly from Venice, Udine, and other major Italian cities. By car, it's the eastern terminus of the Autostrada Torino–Trieste (E70). The city is served by Trieste–Friuli Venezia Giulia Airport, which receives flights from major Italian airports and some European cities. The airport is 33 km (20½ miles) from the city; transfers into Trieste are by taxi or APT coach No. 51.

VISITOR INFORMATION

CONTACT Trieste Infopoint. ✉ *Via dell'Orologio 1,* ☎ *040/3478312* ⊕ *www. turismofvg.it.*

 Sights

Castello di Duino

CASTLE/PALACE | This 14th-century castle, the property of the Princes of Thurn and Taxis, contains a collection of antique furnishings and an amazing Palladian circular staircase, but the main attractions are the surrounding gardens and the spectacular views. In 1912 Rainer Maria Rilke wrote much of his masterpiece, the

Duino Elegies, here. The easy path along the seacoast from the castle toward Trieste has gorgeous views that rival those of the Amalfi Coast and the Cinque Terre. For more spectacular cliff-top views, visit the ruins of the nearby 11th-century Castelvecchio. ✉ *Frazione Duino 32, 12 km (7½ miles) from Trieste, Duino* ✈ *Take Bus No. 44 or 51 from Trieste train station to Duino* ☎ *040/208120* ⊕ *www. castellodiduino.it* ☐ *€10; €12 Castello di Duino and Castello Vecchio* ⊙ *Closed Tues.; closed weekdays Jan.–mid-Mar., Nov., and Dec.*

Castello di San Giusto

CASTLE/PALACE | This hilltop castle, built between 1470 and 1630, was constructed on the ruins of the Roman town of Tergeste. Given the excellent view, it's no surprise that 15th-century Venetians turned the castle into a shipping observation point; the structure was further enlarged by Trieste's subsequent rulers, the Habsburgs. The castle also contains the Civic Museum, which has a collection of furnishings, tapestries, and weaponry, as well as Roman artifacts in the atmospheric Lapidario Tergestino. ✉ *Piazza della Cattedrale 3, Trieste* ☎ *040/309362* ⊕ *www.castellodisangiustotrieste.it* ☐ *€5 includes all complex museums* ⊙ *Closed Mon. during winter months.*

Cattedrale di San Giusto

CHURCH | Dating from the 14th century and occupying the site of an ancient Roman forum, the cathedral contains remnants of at least three previous buildings, the earliest a hall dating from the 5th century. A section of the original floor mosaic still remains, incorporated into the floor of the present church. In the 9th and 11th centuries two adjacent churches were built—the Church of the Assumption and the Church of San Giusto. The beautiful apse mosaics of these churches, done in the 12th and 13th centuries by a Venetian artist, still remain in the apses of the side aisles of the present church. The mosaics in the main apse

date from 1932. In the 14th century the two churches were joined and a Romanesque-Gothic facade was attached, ornamented with fragments of Roman monuments taken from the forum. The jambs of the main doorway are the most conspicuous Roman element. ✉ *Piazza della Cattedrale 2, Trieste* ☎ *040/2600892* ⊕ *www.sangiustomartire.it.*

★ Miramare

CASTLE/PALACE | FAMILY | A 19th-century castle on the Gulf of Trieste, this is nothing less than a major expression of the culture of the decaying Austrian Habsburg monarchy: nowhere else— not even in Vienna—can you savor the decadent opulence of the last years of the empire. Maximilian of Habsburg, brother of Emperor Franz Josef and the retired commander of the Austrian Navy, built the seafront extravaganza between 1856 and 1860, complete with a throne room under a wooden ceiling shaped like a ship's keel. The rooms are generally furnished with copies of medieval, Renaissance, and French period furniture, and the walls are covered in red damask. In 1864 Maximilian became emperor of Mexico at the initiative of Napoléon III. He was executed three years later by a Mexican firing squad.

During the last years of the Habsburg reign, Miramare became one of the favorite residences of Franz Josef's wife, the Empress Elizabeth (Sissi). The castle was later owned by Duke Amedeo of Aosta. Changing exhibitions in the revamped Sala Progetti showcase the impressive museum archive. Tours in English are available by reservation. Surrounding the castle is a 54-acre park. To get here from central Trieste, take Bus No. 36 from Piazza Oberdan; it runs every half hour. ✉ *Viale Miramare, off SS14, Trieste* ✈ *7 km (4½ miles) northwest of Trieste* ☎ *040/224143* ⊕ *www.castello-miramare.it* ☐ *€10.*

Museo d'Antichità J. J. Winckelmann

HISTORY MUSEUM | On the hill near the Castello, this eclectic collection showcases statues from the Roman theater, mosaics, and a wealth of artifacts from Egypt, Greece, and Rome. There's also an assortment of glass and manuscripts. The Orto Lapidario (Lapidary Garden) has classical statuary, pottery, and a small Corinthian temple. The collection was renamed in 2018 after the pioneering art historian and Hellenist J. J. Winckelmann, who was murdered in Trieste in 1768. ⊠ *Via Cattedrale 1, Trieste* ☎ *040/310500* ⊕ *museoantichitawinckelmann.it* ▣ *Free* ⊘ *Closed Mon.*

★ Museo Revoltella–Galleria d'Arte Moderna

ART MUSEUM | Housed in three magnificent buildings and partly remodeled by influential Italian architect Carlo Scarpa, the Revoltella provides a stimulating survey of 19th- and 20th-century art and decoration. Building on the bequeathment of the grand palazzo and art of Triestino collector-industrialist Pasquale Revoltella (1795–1869), the institution has continued to add important artworks from the Venice Biennale by the likes of Carrà, Mascherini, Morandi, de Chirico, Manzù, Fontana, and Burri. In contrast, a gorgeous cochlear staircase connects the three floors of the museum: its history and 1850–60 cityscapes are on the ground floor; 19th-century classical statuary, portraits, and historic scenes take up the first; while the third preserves opulent *saloni.* ⊠ *Via Diaz 27, Trieste* ☎ *040/6754350* ⊕ *museorevoltella.it* ▣ *Free* ⊘ *Closed Tues.*

Piazza Unità d'Italia

PLAZA/SQUARE | The imposing square, ringed by grandiose facades, was set out as a plaza open to the sea, like Venice's Piazza San Marco, in the late Middle Ages. It underwent countless changes through the centuries, and its present size and architecture are essentially products of late-19th- and early-20th-century Austria. It was given its current name in 1955, when Trieste was finally given to Italy. On the inland side of the piazza, note the facade of the **Palazzo Comunale** (Town Hall), designed by the Triestino architect Giuseppe Bruni in 1875. It was from this building's balcony in 1938 that Mussolini proclaimed the infamous racial laws, depriving Italian Jews of most of their rights. The sidewalk cafés on this vast seaside piazza are popular meeting places in the summer months. ⊠ *Trieste.*

Risiera di San Sabba

HISTORIC SIGHT | In September 1943 the Nazi occupation established Italy's only concentration camp in this rice-processing factory outside Trieste. In April 1944 a crematorium was put into operation. The Nazis destroyed much of the evidence of their atrocities before their retreat, but a good deal of the horror of the place is still perceivable in the reconstructed museum (1975). The site, an Italian national monument since 1965, receives more than 100,000 visitors per year. ⊠ *Via Giovanni Palatucci 5, Trieste* ⊹ *Take municipal Bus No. 8 or 10; off the Autostrada A4, take exit Valmaura/ Stadio/Cimitero* ☎ *040/826202* ⊕ *www. risierasansabba.it* ▣ *Free.*

San Silvestro

CHURCH | This small Romanesque gem, dating from the 9th to the 12th centuries, is the oldest church in Trieste that's still in use and in approximately its original form. Its interior walls have some fragmentary remains of Romanesque frescoes. The church was deconsecrated under the secularizing reforms of the Austrian emperor Josef II in 1785 and was later sold to the Swiss Evangelical community; it then became, and is still, the Reformed Evangelical and Waldensian Church of Trieste. ⊠ *Piazza San Silvestro 1, Trieste* ☎ *040/632770* ⊕ *triestevangelica.org.*

Teatro Romano

RUINS | The ruins of this 1st-century amphitheater, near the Via Giuseppe Mazzini opposite the city's *questura* (police station), were discovered during 1938 demolition work. Its statues are now displayed at the Museo Civico, and the space is used for summer plays and concerts. ⊠ *Via del Teatro Romano, Trieste.*

 ## Restaurants

Al Bagatto

$$$ | SEAFOOD | At this warm and sophisticated seafood place, going strong since 1966 near Piazza Unità d'Italia, you'll find exquisite dishes that honor the traditions of the Mancussi family. Although now run by the Leonardi family, Roberto Mancussi's culinary ethos remains: integrating nouvelle ingredients without overshadowing the freshness of whatever local fish he bought in the market that morning. **Known for:** novel culinary experience; more than 300 wine labels and spirits; freshest seafood beautifully prepared. ⓢ *Average main: €28* ⊠ *Via Luigi Cadorna 7, Trieste* ☎ *040/301771* ⊕ *www.albagatto.it* ⊘ *Closed Sun. No lunch Mon.*

Buffet da Siora Rosa

$$ | NORTHERN ITALIAN | FAMILY | Serving delicious and generous portions of traditional Triestino buffet fare, such as boiled pork and sausages with savory sauerkraut, Siora Rosa is a bit more comfortable than many buffets. In addition to ample seating in the simple dining room, there are tables outside for when the weather is good. **Known for:** meat dishes galore; chatty locals speaking in dialect; well-loved Trieste institution (opened 1921). ⓢ *Average main: €19* ⊠ *Piazza Hortis 3, Trieste* ☎ *040/301460* ⊕ *buffetsiorarosa.it* ⊘ *Closed Sun. and Mon.*

Mare alla Voliga

$$ | SEAFOOD | Hidden halfway up the hill to the Castello di San Giusto, in what the Triestini call *Zità Vecia* (Old City), this informal little restaurant specializes in simply prepared seafood. Amid whitewashed wooden walls and nautical ephemera, you can sample the freshest catches—bluefish, sardines, mackerel, mussels, and squid—accompanied by salad, potatoes, polenta, and house wine. **Known for:** beach-hut decor and atmosphere; locals packed in like sarde; tasty fish and seafood. ⓢ *Average main: €16* ⊠ *Via della Fornace 1, Trieste* ☎ *040/309606* ⊕ *www.allavoliga.it* ⊘ *Closed Mon. and Tues.*

★ Suban

$$ | NORTHERN ITALIAN | An easy trip just outside town, this landmark trattoria—serving Triestino food with Slovene, Hungarian, and Austrian accents—has been in business since 1865. Sit by the dining room fire or relax on a huge terrace with a pergola, watching the sun set as you tuck into rich soups and roasts spiced with rosemary, thyme, and sweet paprika. ■ **TIP→ Portions tend to be small, so if you're hungry, order both a first and second course, as well as an antipasto.** **Known for:** warm hospitality; jota carsolina (a rich soup of cabbage, potatoes, and beans); smallish portions. ⓢ *Average main: €24* ⊠ *Via Comici 2, Trieste* ⊹ *Take Bus No. 35 from Piazza Oberdan* ☎ *040/54368* ⊕ *www.suban.it* ⊘ *Closed Tues. and 2 wks in early Jan.*

☕ Coffee and Quick Bites

★ Da Pepi

$ | NORTHERN ITALIAN | A Triestino institution, this is the oldest and most esteemed of the many "buffet" restaurants serving pork and sausages around town, with a wood-paneled interior and seating outside. It specializes in *bollito di maiale*, a dish of boiled pork and pork sausages accompanied by delicately flavored sauerkraut, mustard, and grated horseradish. **Known for:** good for a snack on the hoof; panino porzina (pork shoulder with mustard and kren [horseradish]); porky platter La Caldaia Da Pepi. ⓢ *Average main: €14* ⊠ *Via Cassa di Risparmio 3, Trieste* ☎ *040/366858* ⊕ *www.buffetdapepi.it* ⊘ *Closed Sun. and last 2 wks in July.*

🛏 Hotels

★ Duchi d'Aosta

$$$ | HOTEL | Bang smack in regal Piazza Unità d'Italia, this grande dame of a hotel is beautifully furnished in Venetian Renaissance style, with dark-wood antiques, rich carpets, and plush fabrics. **Pros:** lots of charm paired with modern convenience; sumptuous breakfast; outstanding indoor pool and spa on grand scale. **Cons:** expensive and inconvenient parking; restaurant overpriced; rooms overlooking the piazza can be very expensive. $ *Rooms from: €270 ⊠ Piazza Unità d'Italia 2/1, Trieste ☎ 040/7600011 ⊕ www.grandhotelduchidaosta.com ⤴ 55 rooms* ⦿ *Free Breakfast.*

Hotel Riviera & Maximilian's

$$$ | HOTEL | Set on gorgeous, verdant grounds with stunning sea views, this cliff-top hotel—a villa with a modern annex—offers a mix of traditional and minimalist rooms, many with private balconies. **Pros:** superb views of the Golfo di Trieste; spa facilities; area for swimming in sea. **Cons:** small spa; rooms on the small side; far from town. $ *Rooms from: €252 ⊠ Strada Costiera 22, Trieste ☎ 040/224551 ⊕ www.hotelrivierae-maximilian.com ⤴ 67 rooms* ⦿ *Free Breakfast.*

★ L'Albero Nascosto Hotel Residence

$$ | B&B/INN | There's plenty of architectural character mixed with contemporary, artsy warmth in the guest rooms of this central 18th-century building, while the nearby annex offers five spacious apartments. **Pros:** very central; great tea and coffee; spacious and simple but tasteful rooms. **Cons:** tricky parking nearby; street noise can be a problem (if noise sensitive, ask for a room in the back); no elevator. $ *Rooms from: €155 ⊠ Via Felice Venezian 18, Trieste ☎ 040/300188 ⊕ www.alberonascosto.it ⤴ 10 rooms* ⦿ *Free Breakfast.*

Victoria Hotel Letterario

$ | HOTEL | The former home of James Joyce is a real gem of a hotel—with stylish, unfussy traditional decor and a just-out-of-town location that's convenient for both local sightseeing and trips into the Karst mountains. **Pros:** large, pleasant, light-filled rooms; wellness center and spa; excellent two-bedroom apartments for longer stays. **Cons:** some rooms suffer from traffic noise; a bit removed and a stroll into town; parking fee. $ *Rooms from: €121 ⊠ Alfredo Oriani 2, Trieste ☎ 040/362415 ⊕ www.hotelvictoriatri-este.com ⤴ 44 rooms* ⦿ *No Meals.*

🍸 Nightlife

Trieste is justly famous for its coffee. The elegant civility of Trieste plays out beautifully in a café culture combining the refinement of Vienna with the passion of Italy. In Trieste, as elsewhere in Italy, ask for a caffè and you'll get a thimbleful of high-octane espresso. Your cappuccino here will come in the Viennese fashion, with a dollop of whipped cream. Many cafés are part of a *torrefazione* (roasting shop), so you can sample a cup and then buy beans to take with you.

Antico Caffè San Marco

CAFÉS | Few cafés in Italy can rival Antico Caffè San Marco for its historic and cultured atmosphere. Founded in 1914, it was largely destroyed in World War I and rebuilt in the 1920s, then restored several more times, but some of the original Art Nouveau interior remains. It became a meeting place for local intellectuals and was the haunt of the Triestino writers Italo Svevo and Umberto Saba. It remains open until midnight on Friday and Saturday, and light meals are available. ⊠ *Via Battisti 18, Trieste ☎ 040/2035357 ⊕ www.caffesanmarco.com.*

Caffè degli Specchi

CAFÉS | For a great view of the great piazza, you can't do better than this café, whose many mirrors make for engaging people-watching. Originally opened in 1839, it was taken over by the British Navy after World War II, and Triestini were not allowed in unless accompanied by someone British. Because of its location, the café—which stays open late—is heavily frequented by tourists. It's now owned by the Segafredo Zanetti coffee company, and some feel it has lost its local character. ⊠ *Piazza Unità d'Italia 7, Trieste* ☎ *040/368033* ⊕ *www.caffespecchi.it.*

Caffè Tommaseo

CAFÉS | Founded in 1830, this classic café is a comfortable place to linger, especially on weekend evenings and at lunchtime (11–1:30) on Sunday, when there's live music. Although you can still have just a coffee, Tommaseo has evolved into a restaurant, with an extensive menu. It's open nightly until 10:30. ⊠ *Piazza Tommaseo 4/C, Trieste* ☎ *040/362666* ⊕ *www.caffetommaseo.it.*

🎭 Performing Arts

Teatro Verdi

OPERA | Trieste's main opera house, built under Austrian rule in 1801, is of interest to aficionados of fine architecture as well as music lovers. Gian Antonio Selva, the architect of Venice's Teatro La Fenice, designed the interior, and Matteo Pertsch, responsible for Milan's Teatro alla Scala, designed the facade. You'll have to attend a performance to view Teatro Verdi's interior; guided tours aren't conducted for individuals. ■TIP→ **Opera season runs from October through May, with a brief operetta festival in July and August.** ⊠ *Piazza Verdi 1, Trieste* ☎ *040/6722298* ⊕ *www.teatroverdi-trieste.com.*

🛍 Shopping

Trieste has some 50 local dealers in jewelry, antiques, and bric-a-brac; the city's old center hosts an antiques and collectibles market on the third Sunday (Mercatino dell'Usato e dell'Antiquariato in Largo Granatieri) and fourth Saturday (Mercato dei Tritoni in Piazza Vittorio Veneto) of each month, and there's a large antiques fair, **Trieste Antiqua,** at the end of October. Trieste's busy shopping street, **Corso Italia,** is off Piazza della Borsa.

Katastrofa

ANTIQUES & COLLECTIBLES | Head to this bonkers emporium for an entertaining and eye-popping perusal of 20th-century antiques and ephemera, from vintage stereo equipment and funky furniture to quirky artworks and designer handbags. ⊠ *Via Armando Diaz 4, Trieste* ☎ *335/8298432 cell.*

Rigatteria

ANTIQUES & COLLECTIBLES | Opened in 1981, the fascinating Rigatteria is crammed with antiques, paintings, and a cornucopia of printed matter, including books, newspapers, and magazines, many documenting Triestina life over the decades. ⊠ *Via Malcanton 12, Trieste* ☎ *040/630866* ⊕ *www.rigatteria.com.*

Activities

Arawak Sailing Club

BOATING | FAMILY | Renowned for its fierce Bora breeze and the largest sailing regatta in the world, Barcolana, Trieste is the perfect spot for boating adventures. Arawak Sailing Club rents all sorts of craft, from skippered yachts and catamarans to kayaks and motorboats. They also run a number of courses, including beginner sailing lessons and more advanced instruction. ⊠ *Via della Geppa 19, Trieste* ☎ *040/2654315* ⊕ *www.arawak.it.*

Chapter 7

THE DOLOMITES

Updated by
Liz Humphreys

👁 **Sights**
★★★★☆

🍽 **Restaurants**
★★★★☆

🛏 **Hotels**
★★★★☆

🛍 **Shopping**
★☆☆☆☆

🍸 **Nightlife**
★★☆☆☆

WELCOME TO THE DOLOMITES

TOP REASONS TO GO

★ **Driving in the Dolomites:** Your Fiat rental will think it's a Ferrari on a gorgeous drive through the heart of the Dolomites.

★ **Hiking:** No matter your fitness level, there's an unforgettable walk in store for you here.

★ **Skiing:** The Dolomites are renowned as one of Europe's top locations for winter sports.

★ **Museo Archeologico dell'Alto Adige, Bolzano:** The impossibly well-preserved body of the iceman Ötzi, the star attraction at this museum, provokes countless questions about what life was like 5,000 years ago.

★ **Trento:** A graceful fusion of Austrian and Italian styles, this breezy frescoed town is famed for its imposing castle.

1 Trento. Piazza del Duomo is a highlight.

2 Rovereto. Enjoy the medieval center.

3 Madonna di Campiglio. A favorite for skiers and hikers.

4 Bolzano (Bozen). High-gabled houses are hallmarks.

5 Bormio. History, ski trails, and spa treatments.

6 Merano (Meran). Come here for the thermal waters.

7 Naturno (Naturns). Known for its hiking trails and castle museum.

8 Caldaro (Kaltern). The Strada del Vino runs through this wine town.

9 Bressanone (Brixen). The castle is a big draw.

10 Brunico (Bruneck). Don't miss the medieval quarter.

11 Misurina. The Three Peaks views are lovely.

12 Canazei. Come for the hiking and skiing.

13 Ortisei (St. Ulrich). Woodcarving workshops dot this town.

14 Corvara. Known for skiing and fine hotels.

15 Cortina d'Ampezzo. This ski resort has lots of summer activities.

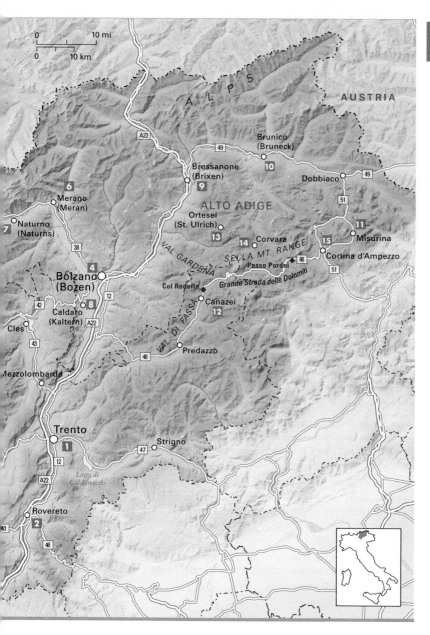

0 10 mi

0 10 km

A L P S

AUSTRIA

A22

49

Brunico
(Bruneck)

10

Bressanone
(Brixen)

9

Dobbiaco

49

51

6

Merano
(Meran)

ALTO ADIGE

Ortesei
(St. Ulrich)

13

14 Corvara

11 Misurina

15

7 Naturno
(Naturns)

38

VAL GARDENA

SELLA MT. RANGE

48

Cortina d'Ampezzo

4

Passo Pordoi

51

Bolzano
(Bozen)

12

Col Rodella

Grande Strada delle Dolomiti

8

Canazei

Caldaro
(Kaltern)

A22

12

Cles

VAL DI FASSA

43

48

Predazzo

Mezzolombardo

Trento

1

Strigno

47

12

*Lago di
Caldonazzo*

A22

Rovereto

2

40

46

EATING AND DRINKING WELL IN THE DOLOMITES

Everything in Alto Adige (and, to a lesser extent, Trentino) has more than a tinge of the Teutonic—and food is no exception. The rich and creamy cuisine here, including fondue, polenta, and barley soup, reflects the Alpine climate and Austrian and Swiss influences.

The quintessential restaurant is the wood-paneled Tyrolean *stube* (pub) serving hearty meat-and-dumpling fare, and there's also a profusion of pastry shops and lively beer halls.

Although the early dining schedule you'll find in Germany or Austria is somewhat tempered here, your options for late-night meals are more limited than they are in places farther south, where la dolce vita has a firmer grip.

Thankfully, the coffee is every bit as good as in parts south—just expect to hear "*danke, grazie*" when paying for your cappuccino.

BEST OF THE WURST

Not to be missed are the outdoor wurst carts. After placing your order you'll get a sheet of wax paper, followed by a dollop of mustard, a kaiser roll, and your chosen sausage. You can sometimes make your selection by pointing to whatever picture is most appealing; if not, pass on the familiar-sounding *Frankfurter* and try the local *Meraner*. Carts can reliably be found in Bolzano (try Piazza delle Erbe, or in front of the archaeological museum) and Merano (Piazza del Grano, or along the river).

POLENTA AND DUMPLINGS

Polenta is a staple in the region, in both creamy and firm renditions, often topped with cheese or mushrooms (or both). Dumplings also appear on many menus; the most distinctive to the region are *canederli* (also known as *Knödel*), pictured at right, made from seasoned bread in many variations, and served either in broth or with a sauce. Other dumplings to look for are the dense *strangolapreti* (literally, "priest-chokers") and *gnocchi di ricotta alla zucca* (ricotta and pumpkin dumplings).

CHEESE

Every isolated mountain valley in Trentino–Alto Adige seems to make its own variety of cheese, and the local specialty is often simply called *nostrano* (ours). The best known of them are the mild Asiago and *fontal,* as well as the more pungent *puzzone di Moena* (literally, "stinkpot"). Also try the *schiz*: fresh cheese that's sliced and fried in butter.

PASTRIES AND BAKED GOODS

Bakeries turn out a wide selection of crusty dark rolls and caraway-studded rye breads—maybe not typical Italian bread, but full of flavor. Pastries here are reminiscent of what you'd find in Vienna. Apple strudel is everywhere, and for good reason: the best apples in Italy are grown here. There are other exceptional fruits as well, including pears, plums, and grapes, which make their way into baked goods.

ALIMENTARI

If you're planning a picnic or getting provisions for a hike, you'll be well served by the fine *alimentari* (food shops) of Trentino and Alto Adige. They stock a bounty of regional specialties, including cheeses, pickles, salami, and smoked meats. These are good places to pick up a sample of *speck tirolese*, the salt-cured, cold-smoked deboned ham hock usually cut in paper-thin slices like prosciutto (though proud speck producers often bristle at the comparison).

WINE

Although Trentino and Alto Adige aren't as esteemed for their wines as many other Italian regions, they produce a wide variety of crisp, dry, and aromatic whites—*Kerner, Müller-Thurgau,* and *Traminer,* to name a few—not surprisingly, more like what you'd expect from German vineyards than Italian. Among the reds, look for *lagrein* and the native *teroldego,* a fruity, spicy variety produced only in the tiny valley north of Trento. The Trento D.O.C. appellation yields a marvelous sparkling wine in a class with Champagne.

The Dolomites, those inimitable craggy peaks Le Corbusier called "the most beautiful work of architecture ever seen," are never so arresting as at dusk, when the last rays of sun create a pink hue that languishes into purple—a magnificent transformation locals call the *enrosadira*. You can certainly enjoy this glow from a distance, but the Dolomites are such an appealing year-round destination precisely because of the many ways to get into the mountains themselves. And once there, in short order your perspective—like the peaks around you—will take on a rosy hue.

The Dolomites are strange, rocky pinnacles that jut straight up like chimneys; they are, in fact, the otherworldly pinnacles that Leonardo depicted in the background of his *Mona Lisa*. In spite of this incredible beauty, the vast mountainous domain of northeastern Italy has remained relatively undeveloped. Below the peaks, rivers meander through valleys dotted with peaceful villages, while pristine lakes are protected by picture-book castles. In the most secluded Dolomite vales, unique cultures have flourished: the Ladin language, an offshoot of Latin still spoken in the Val Gardena and Val di Fassa, owes its unlikely survival to centuries of topographic isolation.

The more accessible parts of Trentino–Alto Adige, on the other hand, have a history of near-constant intermingling of cultures. The region's Adige and Isarco Valleys make up the main access route between Italy and Central Europe, and as a result, the language, cuisine, and architecture are a blend of north and south. The province of Trentino is largely Italian-speaking, but Alto Adige is predominantly Germanic: until World War I the area was Austria's Südtirol. As you move north toward the famed Brenner Pass—through the prosperous valley towns of Rovereto, Trento, and Bolzano—the Teutonic influence is increasingly dominant; by the time you reach Bressanone, it's hard to believe you're in Italy at all.

MAJOR REGIONS

Trentino. Until the end of World War I, the Trentino–Alto Adige/Südtirol region was part of Austria-Hungary. Although today the province of Trentino remains unmistakably Italian, Germanic influences are palpable in its architecture, cuisine, culture, and language. Visitors are drawn by the historical sites and cosmopolitan nature of Trento, while numerous year-round mountain resorts, like the fashionable Madonna di Campiglio, can be found in the wings of this butterfly-shape region. Culture-hounds will want to visit Rovereto, a town just south of Trento known for its fine contemporary art museum.

Bolzano. With castles and steeples topping the landscape, this quiet city at the confluence of the Isarco (Eisack) and Talvera Rivers has retained its provincial appeal. Proximity to fabulous skiing and mountain climbing—not to mention the world's oldest preserved human body— make it a very worthwhile destination. And its streets are immaculate: after Milan, residents here have the highest per capita earnings of any city in Italy.

The Western Dolomites. The Parco Nazionale dello Stelvio extends through western Trentino and the Altoatesino area of Alto Adige and beyond into eastern Lombardy. It's named for the famed Stelvio, Europe's highest road pass and site of the highest battle fought during World War I. Even if you don't want to ski its trails or indulge in one of its renowned spa treatments, the well-preserved town of Bormio still merits a visit for its history and character.

Alto Adige. In the province of Alto Adige (Südtirol/South Tyrol), Germanic and Italian culture balance harmoniously, as do medieval and modern influences, with ancient castles regularly hosting contemporary art exhibitions. Prosperous valley towns, such as the famed spa center of Merano, the medieval town of Bressanone, and the wine village of Caldaro, entice those seeking both relaxation and the finer pleasures.

The Heart of the Dolomites. This area between Bolzano and the mountain resort Cortina d'Ampezzo is dominated by two major valleys, Val di Fassa and Val Gardena. Both share the spectacular panorama of the Sella mountain range. Along the scenic Grande Strada delle Dolomiti (Great Dolomites Road), you'll find Canazei, Ortisei, and Corvara, resort towns with skiing and hiking galore. The Tre Cime (Three Peaks), the best-known symbol of the Dolomites, are visible from the lakeside town of Misurina and worth a gander if not a hike.

Planning

Making the Most of Your Time

For a brief stay, your best choice for a base is vibrant Bolzano, where you can get a sense of the region's contrasts— Italian and German, medieval and modern. After a day or two in town, venture an hour south to history-laden Trento, north to the lovely spa town of Merano, or southwest to Caldaro and its Strada di Vino; all are viable day trips from Bolzano, and Trento and Merano make good places to spend the night as well.

If you have more time, you'll want to get up into the mountains, which are the region's main attraction. The trip on the Grande Strada delle Dolomiti through the Heart of the Dolomites from Bolzano to Cortina d'Ampezzo is one of Italy's most spectacular drives. Summer or winter, this is a great destination for mountain sports, with scores of trails for world-class hiking and skiing.

Be sure to look into the Südtirol Museumobil Card when planning your visit. Besides entry to more than 80 museums, the card allows you free use of the regional train system from Brennero to Trento, and the use of all public buses in Alto Adige (Südtirol/South Tyrol). The card is available for three days (€30) or seven days (€34). The Museumobil Card can be purchased at train stations, tourist offices, and some museums (⊕ www. suedtirolmobil.info). The Brixen Card (free with paid lodging in Bressanone) offers free transportation throughout Trentino and Alto Adige (Südtirol/South Tyrol) and entrance to nearly 90 museums, plus free guided tours and discounts at partner venues. See ⊕ www.brixen. org for a list of participating hotels and bed-and-breakfasts.

Detailed information about Vie Ferrate in the eastern Dolomites can be found at ⊕ www.dolomiti.org. Capable tour organizers include the **Scuola di Alpinismo** (Mountaineering School) in Madonna di Campiglio (☏ 0465/442634 ⊕ www. guidealpinecampiglio.it) and Cortina d'Ampezzo (☏ 0436/868505 ⊕ www. guidecortina.com).

Getting Here and Around

BUS
Regular bus service connects larger cities to the south (Verona, Venice, and Milan) with valley towns in Trentino–Alto Adige (Rovereto, Trento, Bolzano, and Merano). You'll need to change to less frequent local buses to reach resorts and smaller villages in the mountains beyond. At the time of this writing, masks must be worn on all buses.

If you're equipped with current schedules and don't mind adapting your schedules to theirs, it's possible to visit even the remotest villages by bus. ATVO provides year-round service to Cortina from Venice airport and Mestre train station daily. CortinaExpress has a fast winter bus connection from the same places, as well as connections to Treviso airport in high season. FlixBus connects Venice directly

with Bolzano and Trento. DolomitiBus covers the eastern Dolomites, including a number of small towns. SAD provides service from Bolzano and Bressanone. Trentino Trasporti offers buses within Trento and Rovereto. Südtirolmobil provides further information on local services.

BUS CONTACTS ATVO. ☏ 0421/5944 ⊕ www.atvo.it. **CortinaExpress.** ☏ 0436/867350 ⊕ www.cortinaexpress. it. **DolomitiBus.** ☏ 0437/217111 ⊕ www. dolomitibus.it. **SAD.** ☏ 0471/450111 ⊕ www.sad.it. **südtirolmobil.** ☏ 0471/220880 ⊕ www.suedtirolmobil. info. **Trentino Trasporti.** ☏ 0461/821000 ⊕ www.trentinotrasporti.it.

CAR
Driving is easily the most convenient way to travel in the Dolomites; it can be difficult to reach the ski areas (or any town outside of Rovereto, Trento, Bolzano, or Merano) without a car. Driving is also the most exhilarating way to get around, as you rise from broad valleys into mountains with narrow, winding roads straight out of a sports-car ad. The most important route in the region is the A22 autostrada, the main north–south highway linking Italy with Central Europe by way of the Brenner Pass. It connects Innsbruck with Bressanone, Bolzano, Trento, and Rovereto, and near Verona joins the A4, which runs east–west across northern Italy, from Trieste to Turin. By car, Trento is 3 hours from Milan and 2½ hours from Venice. Bolzano is another 45-minute drive to the north, with Munich 4 hours farther on.

Caution is essential (tap your horn in advance of hairpin turns), as are chains in winter, when roads are often covered in snow. Sudden closures are common, especially on high mountain passes, and can occur as early as September and as late as May. Even under the best conditions, expect to negotiate mountain roads at speeds no greater than 50 kph (30 mph).

TRAIN

The rail line following the course of the Isarco and Adige Valleys—from Munich and Innsbruck, through the Brenner Pass, and southward past Bressanone, Bolzano, Trento, and Rovereto en route to Verona—is well trafficked, making trains a viable option for travel between these towns. Eurocity trains on the Dortmund–Venice and Munich–Innsbruck–Rome routes stop at these stations, and you can connect with other Italian lines at Verona. Although branch lines from Trento and Bolzano do extend into some of the smaller valleys (including hourly service between Bolzano and Merano), most mountain attractions are beyond the reach of trains. At the time of this writing, masks must be worn on all trains.

TRAIN CONTACT Trenitalia. ☎ *892021 within Italy* ⊕ *www.trenitalia.com.*

Restaurants

When dining out in the Dolomites, it's evident you are in a part of Italy that was once part of Austria-Hungary. Although you can still find traditional Italian pasta and pizza, in this region there's a considerable amount of Austro-Germanic flair. Sausages, spaetzle, meats, cheeses, and polenta—foods that will sustain the body through a long day of skiing or hiking—can be found on nearly every menu, although you'll also find more contemporary restaurants using seasonal ingredients in a lighter style. Many restaurants either raise their own crops and livestock or have a direct relationship with their farmers and providers.

Prices in the dining reviews are the average cost of a main course at dinner, or, if dinner is not served, at lunch. Restaurant reviews have been shortened. For full information, visit Fodors.com.

Hotels

Classic Dolomite lodging includes restored castles, chalets, and stately 19th-century hotels. The small villages that pepper the Dolomites often have scores of flower-bedecked inns, many of them inexpensive. Hotel information offices at train stations and tourist offices can help if you've arrived without reservations. The Bolzano train station has a 24-hour hotel service, and tourist offices will give you a list of all the hotels in the area, arranged by location, stars, and price. Hotels at ski resorts cater to longer stays at full or half board. Many Italians come to the Dolomites every winter for their Settimana Bianca (White Week), and if you care to join them you should book ski vacations as packages well in advance. Most rural accommodations close from early November to mid- or late December, as well as for two months or so after Easter. The majority of *rifugi* (mountain huts) on hiking trails are operated by the **Club Alpino Italiano** (⊕ *www.cai.it*). Contact information for both CAI-run and private rifugi is available from local tourist offices; most useful are those in Madonna di Campiglio (⊕ *www.campiglio.com*), Cortina d'Ampezzo (⊕ *www.dolomiti.org*), Val di Fassa (⊕ *www.fassa.com*), and Val Gardena (⊕ *www.val-gardena.com*).

Prices in the reviews are the lowest cost of a standard double room in high season. Hotel reviews have been shortened. For full information, visit Fodors.com.

What it Costs in Euros			
$	$$	$$$	$$$$
RESTAURANTS			
under €15	€15–€24	€25–€35	over €35
HOTELS			
under €125	€125–€200	€201–€300	over €300

Trento

58 km (36 miles) south of Bolzano.

Trento is a prosperous, cosmopolitan university town that retains an architectural charm befitting its historical importance. It was here, from 1545 to 1563, that the structure of the Catholic Church was redefined at the Council of Trent, the starting point of the Counter-Reformation, which brought half of Europe back to Catholicism. Today, the word *consiglio* (council) appears everywhere in Trento—in hotel, restaurant, and street names, and even on wine labels. The Piazza del Duomo remains splendid, and its enormous medieval palazzo dominates the city landscape in virtually its original form.

The 24-hour Trentino Card (⊕ *www. visittrentino.* info) is given free (via email or text) to hotel guests, and grants free or discounted admission to museums as well as all public transportation. Non–hotel guests can make use of the 48-hour Museum Pass (€22), which allows unlimited access to all museums and castles in Trento and Rovereto as well as free public transportation in Trentino. It can be bought online (⊕ *www.visittrentino.info/en/experience/ museum-pass*), at tourist offices, or at participating museums, and can even be converted into a three-month card for no extra charge.

GETTING HERE AND AROUND
The A22 autostrada is the main highway to Trento. From the north, take the Trento Nord exit; from the south, take the Trento Sud exit. There are signs directing you to the city center. Trento is easily accessible from Venice (2½ hours) and Verona (just over an hour), and is only 4½ hours from Munich. The city center is pedestrian-friendly, or you can use the transit options in conjunction with the Trentino Card for discounts on the city buses.

TOURS
Guided Tours of Trento

GUIDED TOURS | FAMILY | Guided tours of Trento's city center depart from the tourist office on Saturday at 10 am, in Italian and English. Reserve your place on the tour by 2 pm the day before by email or online. ⊠ *Piazza Dante 24, Trento* ☎ *0461/216000* ⊕ *www.discovertrento. it* 🖃 *€10.*

VISITOR INFORMATION
CONTACT Trento Tourism Office. ⊠ *Piazza Dante 24,* ☎ *0461/216000* ⊕ *www. discovertrento.it.*

Sights

Belvedere di Sardagna
VIEWPOINT | FAMILY | Take the Funivia Trento–Sardagna cable car up to the Belvedere di Sardagna, a lookout point 1,200 feet above medieval Trento. ∎TIP→ **This is open year-round, but can close due to inclement weather.** ⊠ *Via Monte Grappa 1, Trento* ☎ *0461/232154* ⊕ *www.trentinotrasporti.it* 🖃 *€6 round-trip.*

★ Castello del Buonconsiglio
(Castle of Good Counsel)

CASTLE/PALACE | FAMILY | The position and size of this stronghold of the prince-bishops made it easier to defend than the Palazzo Pretorio. Look for the evolution of architectural styles: the medieval fortifications of the Castelvecchio section (on the far left) were built in the 13th century; the fancier Renaissance Magno Palazzo section (on the far right) wasn't completed until 300 years later. The 13th-century **Torre dell'Aquila** (Eagle's Tower) is home to the castle's artistic highlight, a 15th-century *ciclo dei mesi* (cycle of the months). The four-wall fresco is full of charming and detailed scenes of medieval life in both court and countryside. ⊠ *Via Bernardo Clesio 5, Trento* ☎ *0461/233770* ⊕ *www.buonconsiglio. it* 🖃 *€10; Torre Aquila €3* ⏱ *Closed Mon.* ⚓ *Timed visits must be booked online in advance.*

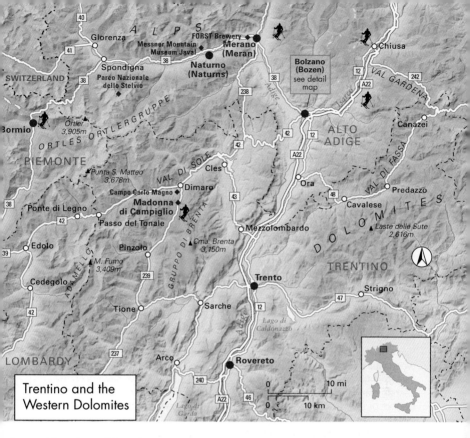

Trentino and the Western Dolomites

Duomo (*Cattedrale di San Vigilio*)
CHURCH | This massive Romanesque church, also known as the Cathedral of San Vigilio (St. Vigilius), forms the southern edge of the Piazza del Duomo. Locals refer to this square as the city's *salotto* (sitting room), as in fine weather it's always filled with students and residents drinking coffee, sipping an aperitif, or reading the newspaper. The Baroque Fontana del Nettuno presides over it all. When skies are clear, pause here to savor the view of the mountaintops enveloping the city.

Within the Duomo, unusual arcaded stone stairways border the austere nave. Ahead is the *baldacchino* (altar canopy), a copy of Bernini's masterpiece in St. Peter's in Rome. To the left of the altar is a mournful 16th-century crucifixion, flanked by the Virgin Mary and John

the Apostle. This crucifix, by German artist Sisto Frey, was a focal point of the Council of Trent: each decree agreed on during the two decades of deliberations was solemnly read out in front of it. Stairs on the left side of the altar lead down to the 4th-century Paleo-Christian burial vault. Outside, check out the bronze scale model of the city on the south side of the cathedral, then walk around to the back to see an exquisite display of 14th-century stonemason artistry, from the small porch to the intriguing knotted columns on the graceful apse. ⊠ *Piazza del Duomo, Trento* ☎ *0461/231293* ⊕ *www.cattedralesanvigilio.it* 🎟 *Free, burial vault €2* ⊙ *Burial vault closed Sun. morning and Tues.*

★ MUSE – Museo delle Scienze di Trento

(*Science Museum of Trento*)

SCIENCE MUSEUM | FAMILY | Extending over six floors, in a 41,000-foot space, this interactive science museum, designed by Renzo Piano, encourages families of all ages to explore science and nature. As befits the region, mountain imagery plays a big part in the displays, and is used to investigate the Dolomites' history and even life on earth. There's also a sensory experience room for younger kids up to five years old. ⊠ *Corso del Lavoro e della Scienza 3, Trento* ☎ *0461/270311* ⊕ *www.muse.it* 🎟 *€11* ⊗ *Closed Mon.*

Museo Diocesano Tridentino

HISTORY MUSEUM | Located inside the **Palazzo Pretorio,** the Museo Diocesano Tridentino is where you can see paintings and other objects that come from the treasury of the adjoining Cathedral of San Vigilio. This includes many carved wood altars and statues; an 11th-century sacramentary, or book of services; the seating plan of the prelates during the Council of Trent; and early-16th-century tapestries by Pieter van Aelst (1502–56), the Belgian artist who carried out Raphael's 15th-century designs for the Vatican tapestries. The palazzo itself was built in the 13th century and designed to seem like a wing of the Duomo; it became the fortified residence of the prince-bishops, who enjoyed considerable power and autonomy within the medieval hierarchy. The remarkable palazzo has lost none of its original splendor. Accessible through the museum, a subterranean archaeological area beneath the adjacent cathedral reveals remnants of the Early Christian Basilica of San Vigilio. ⊠ *Piazza del Duomo 18, Trento* ☎ *0461/234419* ⊕ *www. museodiocesanotridentino.it* 🎟 *€7, includes entrance to Duomo burial vault (free 1st Sun. of month)* ⊗ *Closed Tues.* ✍ *Recommended to purchase tickets online in advance.*

Santa Maria Maggiore

CHURCH | Many sessions of the Council of Trent met in this Renaissance church. Limited light enters through the simple rose window over the main door, so you have to strain to see the magnificent ceiling, an intricate combination of frescoes and stuccowork. The church is off the northwest side of the Piazza del Duomo, about 200 yards down Via Cavour. ⊠ *Vicolo Orsoline 1, Trento* ☎ *0461/230037* 🎟 *Free.*

Tridentum — Spazio Archeologico Sotterraneo del Sas (*S.A.S.S.*)

RUINS | FAMILY | The ancient Roman city of Tridentum lies beneath much of Trento's city center. Centuries of Adige River flooding buried ruins that only recently have been unearthed on public and private land. Beneath this piazza lies the largest of the archaeological sites, which reveals some marvels of Roman technology, such as underfloor heating and subterranean sewers complete with manhole covers. The Romans also used lead pipes for four centuries before recognizing it was hazardous to health. ⊠ *Piazza Cesare Battisti, Trento* ☎ *0461/230171* 🎟 *€3* ⊗ *Closed Mon.*

Via Belenzani

STREET | Locals refer to this street as Trento's outdoor gallery because of the frescoed facades of the hallmark Renaissance palazzi. It's an easy 50-yard walk up the lane behind the church of Santa Maria Maggiore. ⊠ *Trento.*

🍴 Restaurants

Orso-Grigio Ristorante & Pizza

$$ | NORTHERN ITALIAN | Located on a nondescript side street, this friendly family-run trattoria serves tasty regional dishes like *rufioi* (homemade ravioli stuffed with savoy cabbage) along with a fine selection of pizza. The wine list is also dominated by regional selections, which pair well with items on the menu. **Known for:** dining in a shady vine-covered courtyard when the weather is nice; generations of culinary expertise; congenial atmosphere. [$] *Average main: €17* ✉ *Via degli Orti 19, Trento* ☎ *0461/984400* 🌐 *www.orso-grigio.it* 🕓 *Closed Mon.*

Osteria a Le Due Spade

$$$ | **NORTHERN ITALIAN** | What started out as a Tyrolean tavern around the time of the Council of Trent is today an intimate restaurant that adeptly serves superb innovative dishes, using both local and international ingredients. The menu changes throughout the year and includes pasta such as *casoncello* stuffed with rabbit and local marinated pike with yuzu and chicory. **Known for:** cozy wood-paneled interior; knowledgeable, welcoming staff; creative fine dining. [$] *Average main: €25* ✉ *Via Rizzi 11, Trento* ☎ *0461/234343* 🌐 *www.leduespade.com* 🕓 *Closed Sun. No lunch Mon.*

Ristorante Al Vò

$ | **NORTHERN ITALIAN** | Trento's oldest trattoria (it's the descendant of a 14th-century tavern) remains one of its most popular lunch spots. Locals crowd into a simple, modern dining room to enjoy regional specialties like gnocchi with vegetables and *baccalà* (salt cod); an impressive (and inexpensive) selection of local wines is available. **Known for:** fine selection of wines; knowledgeable, welcoming staff; Trento's oldest eatery. [$] *Average main: €12* ✉ *Vicolo del Vò 11, Trento* ☎ *0461/985374* 🌐 *www.ristorantealvo.it* 🕓 *Closed Sun. No dinner.*

Scrigno del Duomo

$$ | **NORTHERN ITALIAN** | More than 30 wines by the glass, accompanied by an excellent selection of local cheeses, are served in this chic eatery, which has outside seating in the piazza. Salads and regional specialties are prepared in the open kitchen by gourmet chefs; the downstairs room features graffito murals from local artist Luigi Senesi, while the Roman wall running under the Duomo is also in clear view. **Known for:** local art and history; fine views of the cathedral; traditional food and local wine. [$] *Average main: €22* ✉ *Piazza del Duomo 29, Trento* ☎ *0461/220030* 🌐 *www.scrignodelduomo.com.*

Coffee and Quick Bites

Antica Birreria Pedavena

$ | **NORTHERN ITALIAN** | **FAMILY** | Come for the beer—several varieties are brewed in-house and served in this charismatic beer hall—and stay for the meals that include wursts, meat and cheese platters, pizzas, and huge salads. Smaller wood-paneled dining rooms and a summer terrace allow for more peaceful dining. **Known for:** enormous beer hall; typical Bavarian meats; fine selection of brewed-in-house beers. [$] *Average main: €12* ✉ *Piazza di Fiera 13, Trento* ☎ *0461/986255* 🌐 *www.birreriapedavena.com* 🕓 *Closed Tues.*

Hotels

Accademia Hotel Trento

$$ | **HOTEL** | Stylish, contemporary bedrooms with comfortable beds and handsome lithographs occupy an ancient, character-filled house close to the railway station and Piazza del Duomo. **Pros:** central location; helpful staff; beautiful courtyard. **Cons:** rather basic decor; no wellness area; breakfast could be better. [$] *Rooms from: €131* ✉ *Vicolo Colico 4, Trento* ☎ *0461/233600* 🌐 *www.accademiahotel.it* 🕓 *Closed 1 wk at Christmas* 🔑 *40 rooms* 🍴 *Free Breakfast.*

Castel Pergine

$$$ | **B&B/INN** | **FAMILY** | The stone and brick chambers, prison cells, and chapels in this labyrinthine 13th-century castle (occupied by Trento's prince-bishops in the 16th century) today contain spare, rustic guest rooms with carved-wood trim, lace curtains, and heavy wooden beds—some of them canopied. **Pros:** romantic setting; authentic castle experience; great restaurant. **Cons:** bathrooms are very small; need a car to get around;

simple accommodations. [$] *Rooms from: €230* ✉ *Via al Castello 10, Pergine Valsugana* ☎ *0461/531158* 🌐 *www.castelpergine.it* 🕘 *Closed Nov.–Mar.* 🛏 *20 rooms* 🍴 *Free Breakfast.*

Grand Hotel Trento

$ | **HOTEL** | This contemporary, rounded facade stands out among the ancient palazzi nearby, but inside you'll find a handsome marble-paved lobby, rich drapery in the restaurant, and ample rooms with clubby wood-trimmed furniture. **Pros:** near train station; wellness center; professional service. **Cons:** basic bathroom amenities; dated decor; busy neighborhood. [$] *Rooms from: €117* ✉ *Piazza Dante 20, Trento* ☎ *0461/271000* 🌐 *www.grandhoteltrento.com* 🛏 *136 rooms* 🍴 *Free Breakfast.*

Hotel Buonconsiglio

$ | **HOTEL** | Public areas in this hotel near the train station are decorated with contemporary paintings by the hotel's owner, and the well-kept guest rooms have sound-resistant windows. **Pros:** spacious rooms; good-size modern bathrooms; efficient service. **Cons:** some signs of wear; basic breakfast; outside the town center. [$] *Rooms from: €106* ✉ *Via Romagnosi 16, Trento* ☎ *0461/272888* 🌐 *www.hotelbuonconsiglio.com* 🛏 *47 rooms* 🍴 *Free Breakfast.*

Hotel Garni Venezia

$ | **B&B/INN** | For reasonably priced accommodations, it's hard to beat this *garni* (bed-and-breakfast) right on Piazza Duomo, where six of the simple rooms have wonderful views. **Pros:** great location; won't break the bank; friendly environs. **Cons:** guest rooms could use a refresh; not all rooms have private baths; piazza can be noisy. [$] *Rooms from: €85* ✉ *Via Belenzani 70, Piazza Duomo 45, Trento* ☎ *0461/234559* 🌐 *www.hotelvenezi-atrento.it* 🛏 *43 rooms* 🍴 *Free Breakfast.*

Imperial Grand Hotel Terme

$$ | **HOTEL** | If you're in the mood for some pampering, choose a grand room with a frescoed ceiling in the graciously restored golden-yellow palace in the nearby spa town of Levico Terme. **Pros:** beautiful park setting; interesting history; pleasant indoor pool. **Cons:** no a/c in some rooms; use of thermal baths costs extra; standard rooms are small. [$] *Rooms from: €135* ✉ *Via Silva Domini 1, Levico Terme* ☎ *0461/700512* 🌐 *www.hotel-imperial-levico.com* 🕘 *Closed Dec.–Mar.* 🛏 *81 rooms* 🍴 *Free Breakfast.*

Performing Arts

★ I Suoni delle Dolomiti

(*The Sounds of the Dolomites*)

FESTIVALS | **FAMILY** | Held from June through September high in the hills of Trentino, this series of free concerts offers the chance to enjoy chamber music performances amid grassy meadows. ✉ *Trento* ☎ *0461/219300* 🌐 *www.isuonidelledolomiti.it* 🎟 *Free, except for certain concerts.*

Shopping

Enoteca di Corso

FOOD | A bit outside the town center, this atmospheric shop is laden with wines, sweets, and other local products. ✉ *Corso 3 Novembre 64, Trento* ☎ *0461/916424.*

La Salumeria Lunelli

FOOD | This specialty food shop boasts an impressive array of sauces, as well as wines, grappas, and liqueurs. A picnic can be handily assembled from a huge assortment of local salamis and cheeses. ✉ *Via Mazzini 46, Trento* ☎ *0461/238053* 🌐 *www.lunelli.it.*

Panificio Pulin

FOOD | Whole-grain breads and delicate pastries are on offer in this fragrant bakery. There's a second location on

Via Suffragio. ⊠ *Via Cavour 23, Trento* ☎ *0461/234544* ⊕ *www.facebook.com/ PulinPanificio.*

Piazza Alessandro Vittoria

MARKET | You can pick up meats, cheeses, produce, local truffles, and porcini mushrooms at the small morning market in the square. ⊠ *Trento.*

Rovereto

24 km (15 miles) south of Trento, 75 km (47 miles) south of Bolzano.

A 15th-century Venetian castle dominates Rovereto's compact medieval *centro storico* (historic center), with one of Italy's finest contemporary art museums just steps away. ■ **TIP→ The Trento Museum Pass also includes entry to sites here in Rovereto.**

GETTING HERE AND AROUND

By car from Trento, take the A22/E45 for 28 km (17 miles) to Rovereto. Frequent trains run from Trento to Rovereto; the journey takes about 13 minutes.

VISITOR INFORMATION

CONTACT Rovereto Tourism Office. ⊠ *Corso Rosmini 21,* ☎ *0464/430363* ⊕ *www. visitrovereto.it.*

Sights

Mart Rovereto (*Museo di Arte Moderna e Contemporanea di Trento e Rovereto*)
ART MUSEUM | Most of the 20,000 works of contemporary and modern art in this collection are from the 20th century. Rotating exhibitions and special events throughout the year highlight still more contemporary art. ⊠ *Corso Bettini 43, Rovereto* ☎ *0464/438887* ⊕ *www. mart.tn.it* ⊠ *€11; free every 1st Sun. of month Oct.–Mar. (with prior reservation)* ⊗ *Closed Mon.*

Museo Storico Italiano della Guerra
(*Italian Historical War Museum*)
HISTORY MUSEUM | This museum was founded after World War I to commemorate the conflict—and to warn against repeating its atrocities. An authoritative exhibition of military artifacts is displayed in the medieval castle perched above Rovereto; the views alone warrant a visit. From May through October you can also see a collection of artillery from the Great War housed in a former air-raid shelter. ⊠ *Via Castelbarco 7, Rovereto* ☎ *0464/438100* ⊕ *www.museodellaguerra.it* ⊠ *€9* ⊗ *Closed Mon.*

Hotels

Hotel Rovereto

$ | **HOTEL** | The Zani family runs this modern, centrally located hotel, which has welcoming public spaces, warm-color guest rooms, and one of the city's most appealing restaurants; select from classic rooms or those with a more contemporary style. **Pros:** excellent restaurant; distinctive decor; unbeatable location. **Cons:** design choices, like sinks in some rooms, not to everyone's taste; small parking area; some rooms are on the small side. $ *Rooms from: €109* ⊠ *Corso Rosmini 82/D, Rovereto* ☎ *0464/435222* ⊕ *www.hotelrovereto.it* ⊗ *Restaurant closed Sun. No lunch Mon.–Wed.* 🛏 *49 rooms* ��◎❙ *No Meals.*

Bolzano (Bozen)

32 km (19 miles) south of Merano, 50 km (31 miles) north of Trento.

Bolzano (Bozen), capital of the autonomous province of Alto Adige, is tucked among craggy peaks in a Dolomite valley 77 km (48 miles) from the Brenner Pass and Austria. Tyrolean culture dominates Bolzano's language, food, architecture, and people. It may be hard to remember that you're in Italy when walking the city's colorful cobblestone streets and visiting its lantern-lighted cafés, where you may enjoy sauerkraut and a beer among a lively crowd of German speakers. That said, the fine Italian espresso and the boutiques will help to remind you where you are. The long, narrow arcades of Via dei Portici house shops that specialize in Tyrolean crafts and clothing, as well as many Italian designers.

The Bolzano Bozen Guestcard, free of charge at participating accommodations, grants free entry to 90 museums in Bolzano and Alto Adige, as well as free transport throughout the region and guided tours.

GETTING HERE AND AROUND
By car from Trento, take the A22 for 60 km (37 miles) to Bolzano Sud. The train station is just steps away from Piazza Walther and has regular service from Italy and Munich (four hours). The SASA bus can help you connect between Bolzano and other parts of the region. There is an airport in Bolzano, but its connections are not as convenient as the larger airports serving Venice, Verona, and Munich.

VISITOR INFORMATION
CONTACT Bolzano Tourism Office. ⊠ *Via Alto Adige 60,* ☎ *0471/307000* ⊕ *www. bolzano-bozen.it.*

 Sights

Assumption of Our Lady Cathedral (*Duomo*)
CHURCH | A lacy spire looks down on the mosaic-like roof tiles of the city's Gothic cathedral, built between the 12th and 14th centuries. Inside are 14th- and 15th-century frescoes and an intricately carved stone pulpit dating from 1514. Outside, don't miss the Porta del Vino (Wine Gate) on the northeast side facing the square; decorative carvings of grapes and harvest workers attest to the long-standing importance of wine to this region. ⊠ *Piazza della Parrocchia 27, Bolzano* ☎ *0471/978676* ⊴ *Free.*

Castel Roncolo (*Schloss Runkelstein*)
CASTLE/PALACE | Green hills and farmhouses north of town surround this meticulously kept castle (also called Runkelstein Castle, or Schloss Runkelstein in German) with a tiled roof. It was built in 1237, destroyed half a century later, and then rebuilt soon thereafter. The world's largest cycle of secular medieval frescoes, beautifully preserved, is inside. A tavern in the courtyard serves excellent local food and wines. To get here from Piazza Walther, take Bus No. 12 or 14; there's also a free shuttle bus that runs in the summer. Alternatively, it's a 45-minute walk from Piazza delle Erbe: head north along Via Francescani, continue through Piazza Madonna, connecting to Via Castel Roncolo. If you drive or take the bus, be advised that you'll still have a 5- to 10-minute walk up to the castle. ⊠ *Via San Antonio 15, Bolzano* ☎ *0471/329808 castle* ⊕ *www.runkelstein.info* ⊴ *€8* ⊗ *Closed Mon. and mid-Jan.–late Feb.*

Chiesa dei Domenicani
CHURCH | The 13th-century Dominican Church is renowned for its Cappella di San Giovanni, where frescoes from the Giotto school show the birth of a pre-Renaissance sense of depth and individuality. ⊠ *Piazza Domenicani, Bolzano* ☎ *0471/982027* ⊴ *Free.*

★ **Messner Mountain Museum Firmian**
ART MUSEUM | FAMILY | Perched on a peak overlooking Bolzano, the 10th-century Castle Sigmundskron is home to one of six mountain museums established by Reinhold Messner—the first climber to conquer Everest solo and the first to reach its summit without oxygen. The Tibetan tradition of *kora,* a circular pilgrimage around a sacred site, is an inspiration for the museum, where visitors contemplate the relationship between human and mountain, guided by images and objects Messner collected during his adventures. The museum is 3 km (2 miles) southwest of Bolzano, just off the Appiano exit on the highway

to Merano. ✉ *Sigmundskron Castle 53, Sigmundskronerstrasse, Bolzano* ☎ *0471/631264* ⊕ *www.messner-mountain-museum.it* 🎫 *€13* 🕔 *Closed Thurs. and mid-Nov.–mid-Mar.*

★ Museo Archeologico dell'Alto Adige

HISTORY MUSEUM | FAMILY | This museum has gained international fame for Ötzi, its 5,300-year-old iceman, discovered in 1991 and the world's oldest naturally preserved body. In 1998 Italy acquired it from Austria after it was determined that the body lay 100 yards inside Italian territory. The iceman's leathery remains are displayed in a freezer vault, preserved along with his longbow, ax, and clothing. The rest of the museum relies on models and artifacts from nearby archaeological sites, and exhibitions change regularly. An English audio guide leads you not only through Ötzi's Copper Age, but also into the preceding Mesolithic and Neolithic eras, and the Bronze and Iron Ages that followed. ✉ *Via Museo 43, Bolzano* ☎ *0471/320100* ⊕ *www.iceman.it* 🎫 *€13* 🕔 *Closed Mon. Jan.–June and Oct. and Nov.* 🖱 *Advance online reservations recommended.*

Passeggiata del Guncina

PROMENADE | FAMILY | An 8-km (5-mile) botanical promenade dating from 1892 ends with a panoramic view of Bolzano. Recent updates include signposting for various species of plants and trees, as well as benches and picnic tables. You can choose to return to town along the same path, or you can walk along the River Fago and end up back in the center of Bolzano. ✉ *Entrance near Vecchia Parrocchiale di Gries, across river and up Corsa Libertà, Bolzano* 🎫 *Free.*

Piazza delle Erbe

PLAZA/SQUARE | A bronze statue of Neptune, which dates from 1745, presides over this square's bountiful fruit and vegetable market. Stalls spill over with colorful displays of local produce; bakeries and grocery stores showcase hot breads, pastries, cheeses, and delicatessen meats—a complete picnic. Try the speck tirolese and the apple strudel. ✉ *Bolzano* 🎫 *Free.*

Piazza Walther

PLAZA/SQUARE | This pedestrians-only square is Bolzano's heart; in warmer weather it serves as an open-air living room where locals and tourists can be found at all hours sipping a drink (such as a glass of chilled Riesling). The piazza's namesake was the 12th-century German wandering minstrel Walther von der Vogelweide, whose songs lampooned the papacy and praised the Holy Roman Emperor. In the center of the piazza stands Heinrich Natter's white-marble, neo-Romanesque *Monument to Walther,* built in 1889. ✉ *Piazza Walther, Bolzano* 🎫 *Free.*

★ Renon (Ritten) Plateau

NATURE SIGHT | FAMILY | The earth pyramids of Renon Plateau are a bizarre geological formation where erosion has left a forest of tall, thin, needlelike spires of rock, each topped with a boulder. To get here, take the Soprabolzano cable car from Via Renon, about 300 yards left of the Bolzano train station. At the top, switch to the electric train that takes you to the plateau, which is in Collalbo, just above Bolzano. The cable car takes about 12 minutes and the train takes around 18 minutes. The final 30-minute hike along gentle Trail No. 24 is free. ✉ *Via Renon, Collalbo* ☎ *0471/356100* ⊕ *www.ritten. com* 🎫 *Cable car €10 round-trip, electric train €6 round-trip.*

Vecchia Parrocchiale di Gries

(*Old Parish Church*)

CHURCH | Visit this church, said to have been built in 1141, to see two medieval treasures: an 11th-century Romanesque crucifix and an elaborate 15th-century wooden altar, carved by Michael Pacher and a masterpiece of the Gothic style. ✉ *Via Martin Knoller, in Gries, Bolzano* ☎ *0471/283089* 🎫 *Free* 🕔 *Closed Nov.–Mar., and July and Aug. afternoons.*

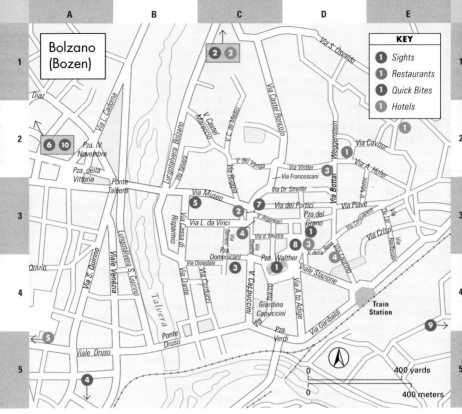

Bolzano (Bozen)

KEY

1 Sights
1 Restaurants
1 Quick Bites
1 Hotels

🍴 Restaurants

Batzen Häusl

$$ | **ECLECTIC** | Locals hold animated conversations over pints of beer in this modern take on a traditional stube. Tasty South Tyrolean specialties include *bierspeckknodeln* (homemade beer bacon dumplings) and *bauerngröstl* (beef, onion, and potato fry-up), and there's also a wide menu of salads, pastas, and burgers. ■ **TIP→ This is a good place for a late bite, as food is served until midnight. Known for:** late-night dining; home-brewed beer on tap; convivial atmosphere. [$] *Average main: €17* ✉ *Via Andreas Hofer 30, Bolzano* ☎ *0471/050950* 🌐 *www.batzen.it.*

Hopfen & Co.

$$ | **NORTHERN ITALIAN** | Fried white *Würstel* (sausage), sauerkraut, and grilled ribs complement the excellent home-brewed Austrian-style pilsner and wheat beer at this bustling pub-restaurant. Hopfen & Co. attracts Bolzano's students, young professionals, and tourists alike. **Known for:** traditional pub environment; bustling atmosphere; home-brewed beer. [$] *Average main: €17* ✉ *Piazza delle Erbe, Obstplatz 17, Bolzano* ☎ *0471/300788* 🌐 *www.boznerbier.it.*

Ristorante Cavallino Bianco

$$ | **NORTHERN ITALIAN** | A spacious, comfortable dining room near Via dei Portici is a dependable favorite with locals and visitors alike. A wide selection of Italian and German dishes are served to large tables of families enjoying their meals together. **Known for:** local dishes, such as canederli in brodo (bread dumplings in broth); crowded, friendly atmosphere; generations of cooking. [$] *Average main: €16* ✉ *Via Bottai 6, Bolzano* ☎ *0471/973267* 🌐 *www.weissesroessl.org* 🕓 *Closed Sun. No dinner Sat.*

★ Wirtshaus Vögele

$$ | **NORTHERN ITALIAN** | Ask locals where they like to dine out, and odds are they'll tell you Vögele, one of the area's oldest inns, where the menu features Tyrolean standards such as *canederli* (bread dumplings) with speck and venison. The classic wood-paneled dining room on the ground level is often packed, but don't despair—the restaurant has two additional floors. **Known for:** local dishes; late dining; friendly vibe. [$] *Average main: €20* ✉ *Goethestr 3, Bolzano* ☎ *0471/973938* 🌐 *www.voegele.it* 🕓 *Closed Sun. No dinner Sat.*

☕ Coffee and Quick Bites

★ Vögelino

$ | **ITALIAN** | The more casual little sister to long-standing favorite Vögele serves up coffee and croissants for breakfast, plus all manner of focaccia, ice cream and cake, and aperitivo (think *stuzzichini,* or savory Italian snacks, and Aperol spritz) all day long. The prime spot on bustling Piazza Walther is perfect for people-watching while catching some rays. **Known for:** focaccia of the day; pleasant central location; fine selection of wine and cocktails. [$] *Average main: €12* ✉ *Piazza Walther 2, Bolzano* ☎ *0338/8485646* 🌐 *www.voegelino.com* 🕓 *Closed Sun. No dinner.*

🛏 Hotels

Castel Hörtenberg

$$$$ | **HOTEL** | The modern and the ancient contrast beautifully in the contemporary interiors of this renovated palace, only about a 10-minute walk from lively Piazza Walther, but in a quiet neighborhood that seems a world away. **Pros:** lovely stone-walled restaurant in the old dungeon; large-size guest rooms; relaxing spa area with outdoor pool. **Cons:** service can be standoffish at times; no coffee- or tea-making facilities in the guest rooms; modern interior design a bit generic. [$] *Rooms from: €440* ✉ *Via Monte Tondo 4, Bolzano* ☎ *0471/1800355* 🌐 *www.castel-hoertenberg.com* 🛏 *24 rooms* 🍴 *Free Breakfast.*

★ Hotel Bad Schörgau

$$$ | **HOTEL** | You'll get a warm welcome at this charming family-run hotel in the Sarentino Valley, which has incorporated natural materials into the design and an innovative philosophy into the menus, including a substantial cellar of natural wines. **Pros:** delicious cuisine and wines; peaceful, relaxing surroundings; large, out-of-the-ordinary spa area. **Cons:** not much else around the immediate area; beds on the hard side; some rooms are carpeted. [$] *Rooms from: €286* ✉ *Via Ronco 24, Sarentino* ✣ *17 km (11 miles) north of Bolzano* ☎ *0471/623048* 🌐 *www.bad-schoergau.com* 🕒 *Closed Mar. and Apr.* 🛏 *22 rooms* 🍴 *Free Breakfast.*

★ Hotel Greif

$$$ | **HOTEL** | Individually designed guest rooms in a centuries-old Bolzano landmark feature modern furnishings with clean lines, as well as contemporary art paired with 19th-century paintings and sketches. **Pros:** elegant decor; central location; helpful staff. **Cons:** no on-site spa; some rooms have small windows; rooms vary in size. [$] *Rooms from: €264* ✉ *Piazza Walther 1, Bolzano* ☎ *0471/318000* 🌐 *www.greif.it* 🛏 *33 rooms* 🍴 *Free Breakfast.*

Parkhotel Laurin

$$$ | **HOTEL** | An exercise in Art Nouveau opulence, presiding over a large park in the middle of town, this elegant hotel features art-filled guest rooms, handsome public spaces, and an exceptional restaurant. **Pros:** convenient location; high standard of service; excellent restaurant. **Cons:** decor a bit old-fashioned; can be packed with business groups; rooms facing park can be noisy. [$] *Rooms from: €263* ✉ *Via Laurin 4, Bolzano* ☎ *0471/311000* 🌐 *www.laurin.it* 🛏 *100 rooms* 🍴 *Free Breakfast.*

Schloss Korb

$$$ | **B&B/INN** | This romantic 13th-century castle with crenellations and a massive tower is perched in a park amid vine-covered hills, viewed from some of the cozy guest rooms through Romanesque arched windows. **Pros:** romantic setting; very nice indoor and outdoor pools; charming traditional furnishings. **Cons:** a/c cannot be adjusted; need a car to get around; not all rooms are in the castle. [$] *Rooms from: €218* ✉ *Via Castel d'Appiano 5, Missiano* ☎ *0471/636000* 🌐 *www.schloss-hotel-korb.com* 🕒 *Closed Nov.–Mar.* 🛏 *49 rooms* 🍴 *Free Breakfast.*

Nightlife

Grifoncino

COCKTAIL LOUNGES | The Hotel Greif's sleek, modern cocktail bar (where the actual bar is made out of empty bottles) serves the best libations in town. The drinks menu betrays a particular fondness for gin, but the staff also excel at making cocktails tailored to your preferences. ✉ *Via della Rena 28, Bolzano* ☎ *0471/318000* 🌐 *www.grifoncino.it.*

Parkhotel Laurin Bar

LIVE MUSIC | The Laurin Bar hosts jazz combos on Friday between October and May and a jazz pianist every Saturday evening. In summer, the bar moves outside to the pretty garden, where a DJ spins tunes on Thursday night. ✉ *Via Laurin 4, Bolzano* ☎ *0471/311000* 🌐 *www.laurin.it.*

Shopping

CRAFTS

Artigiani Atesini

CRAFTS | This is the largest store for locally made handcrafted goods. ✉ *Via Portici 39, Bolzano* ☎ *0471/978590* 🌐 *www.facebook.com/suedtiroler.werkstaetten.*

MARKETS

Christkindlmarkt (*Christmas market*)

MARKET | **FAMILY** | From the end of November to the first week after New Year's there's a traditional Christkindlmarkt in Piazza Walther, with stalls selling all kinds of Christmas decorations and local handcrafted goods. ✉ *Piazza Walther, Bolzano* 🌐 *www.mercatinodinatalebz.it.*

Piazza della Vittoria
MARKET | A weekly flea market takes place Saturday morning in Piazza della Vittoria. ✉ *Piazza della Vittoria, Bolzano.*

Activities

BIKING

Südtirol Rad Bici Alto Adige
BIKING | **FAMILY** | If you're in decent shape, one great way to see some of the surrounding castles, lakes, and forested valleys of the Dolomites is by bike. Südtirol Rad can help with bike rentals from late April till the end of October. ✉ *Via Renon 45, Bolzano* ☎ *0473/201500* 🌐 *www.suedtirol-rad.com* 🎫 *Bike rental from €25 per day.*

Madonna di Campiglio

80 km (50 miles) northwest of Trento, 100 km (62 miles) southwest of Bolzano.

The winter resort of Madonna di Campiglio vies with Cortina d'Ampezzo as the most fashionable place for Italians to ski and be seen in the Dolomites. Madonna's popularity is well deserved, with 61 lifts connecting 156 km (97 miles) of well-groomed ski runs and equally good lodging and trekking facilities. The resort itself is a modest 5,000 feet above sea level, but the downhill runs, summer hiking paths, and mountain-biking trails venture high up into the surrounding peaks (including Pietra Grande at 9,700 feet).

GETTING HERE AND AROUND

By car from Trento, take the SS45 toward Vezzano. After Vezzano, continue to the SS237 until Ragoli, and turn onto the SP34. Follow the SP34 for 6 km (4 miles), and turn onto the SS239 for another 23 km (15 miles) until you arrive at Madonna di Campiglio. The more convenient railway station is at Trento; then you can ride the Trentino Trasporti bus for 2½ hours from Trento for €5.10 (five times daily).

VISITOR INFORMATION

CONTACT Madonna di Campiglio Tourism Office. ✉ *Via Pradalago 4,* ☎ *0465/447501* 🌐 *www.campigliodolomiti.it.*

Sights

Campo Carlo Magno
VIEWPOINT | The stunning pass at Campo Carlo Magno (5,500 feet) is 3 km (2 miles) north of Madonna di Campiglio. This is where Charlemagne is said to have stopped in AD 800 on his way to Rome to be crowned emperor. You, too, can stop here to gaze upon the whole of northern Italy. If you continue north, take the descent with caution—in the space of a mile or so, hairpin turns and switchbacks deliver you down more than 2,000 feet. ✉ *Madonna di Campiglio.*

Restaurants

Cascina Zeledria
$$ | **NORTHERN ITALIAN** | Although most of Madonna's visitors dine at resort hotels, Italians consider an on-mountain meal in a remote, rustic refuge like this one to be an indispensable part of a proper ski week. You can drive or hike up in summer months, but in winter, you ski, snowshoe, or are collected by a Sno-Cat and ferried 10 minutes up the slopes; once there, you'll sit down to grill your own meats and vegetables over stone griddles. ■ **TIP→ You must call in advance to reserve a table and arrange transportation.** **Known for:** local wine; house specialty mushrooms and polenta; authentic experience in a rural mountain setting. [$] *Average main: €22* ✉ *Località Zeledria, Madonna di Campiglio* ☎ *0465/440303* 🌐 *www.zeledria.it* 🕒 *Closed mid-Apr.–mid-June and mid-Sept.–Nov.*

Ferrari Spazio Bollicine Nabucco
$$$ | **WINE BAR** | Although it has a stylish black-and-white color scheme, this restaurant nevertheless has the feel of a rustic, intimate chalet. Settle into pleasant surroundings for an après-ski

aperitif or a light meal made with local ingredients and paired with the sparkling wines of Ferrari, a well-known Trentino vintner. **Known for:** central location; intimate atmosphere; predinner cocktails. [$] *Average main: €30* ✉ *Piazza Righi B3, Madonna di Campiglio* ☎ *0465/440756* 🌐 *www.ferraritrento.com* 🕒 *Closed May–Nov.*

Hotels

Hotel Casa del Campo

$$ | **HOTEL** | Just yards from both the downhill slopes and the *ski-fondo* (cross-country skiing) paths, this charming, Tyrolean-style hotel has an on-site restaurant as well as spacious guest rooms, complete with orthopedic mattresses, soaking tubs, regional wood-and-fabric decor, and tremendous views. **Pros:** good-size rooms; sheltered parking; great location for outdoor activities year-round. **Cons:** thin pillows; small TVs; some months have seven-night minimum stay. [$] *Rooms from: €135* ✉ *Passo Campo Carlo Magno, Madonna di Campiglio* ☎ *0465/443130* 🌐 *www.casadelcampo.it* 🛏 *15 rooms* 🍴 *Free Breakfast.*

★ Savoia Palace Hotel

$$ | **HOTEL** | At Madonna's most traditional lodging, guest rooms and lounges are full of carved-wood and mountain-style furnishings, and two fireplaces blaze away in the bar, where you can relax while recalling the day's exploits on the ski slopes. **Pros:** central location in town; nice spa; warm atmosphere. **Cons:** can be noisy; faces a busy street; breakfast is nothing special. [$] *Rooms from: €128* ✉ *Viale Dolomiti di Brenta 18, Madonna di Campiglio* ☎ *0465/441004* 🌐 *www.savoiapalace.it* 🕒 *Closed mid-Apr.–late June and mid-Sept.–Nov.* 🛏 *60 rooms* 🍴 *Free Breakfast.*

Style Hotel Grifone

$ | **HOTEL** | **FAMILY** | At this comfortable lodge with a distinctive wooden facade, flower-bedecked balconies catch the sun, and contemporary guest rooms and suites have views of the forested slopes. **Pros:** convenient location; complimentary afternoon snack; charming decor. **Cons:** mattresses can be uncomfortable; a bit out of town (but the Spinale cable car is nearby); lacks a/c. [$] *Rooms from: €105* ✉ *Via Vallesinella 7, Madonna di Campiglio* ☎ *0465/442002* 🌐 *www.stylehotelgrifone.it* 🕒 *Closed mid-Apr.–mid-June and Sept.–Nov.* 🛏 *40 rooms* 🍴 *Free Breakfast.*

TH Madonna di Campiglio Golf Hotel

$$ | **HOTEL** | **FAMILY** | You need to make your way north to the Campo Carlo Magno Pass to reach this grand hotel, the former summer residence of Habsburg emperor Franz Josef, replete with verandas, Persian rugs, and bay windows. **Pros:** attractive indoor pool; kids' club for children and teens; elegant rooms. **Cons:** rooms can be noisy; food not up to par; long walk into town. [$] *Rooms from: €135* ✉ *Via Cima Tosa 3, Madonna di Campiglio* ☎ *0465/441003, 049/2956411 for reservations* 🌐 *www.thcampiglio.it* 🕒 *Closed late Apr.–June and Sept.–early Dec.* 🛏 *109 rooms* 🍴 *Free Breakfast.*

Activities

GOLF

Campo Carlo Magno Golf Club

GOLF | The 9-hole Campo Carlo Magno course is one of the highest in Europe, at 5,400 feet. It's only open mid-June through mid-September. ✉ *Via Cima Tosa 16, near Golf Hotel, Madonna di Campiglio* ☎ *0465/440622* 🌐 *www.golfcampocarlomagno.it* 🎫 *€40; €70 late July–late Aug.* ⛳ *9 holes, 6090 yards, par 70.*

HIKING AND CLIMBING

The Madonna di Campiglio tourism office has maps of a dozen trails leading to waterfalls, lakes, and stupefying views.

Monte Spinale (*Spinale Peak*)

HIKING & WALKING | **FAMILY** | The cable car to 6,900-foot-high Monte Spinale offers magnificent views of the Brenta Dolomites in winter; it also runs during peak summer season and leads to many hikes at the vista. Alternatively, you can opt for an intermediate-level hike from town to the top, which takes around two hours to complete. ⊠ *Off Via Monte Spinale, Madonna di Campiglio* ☎ *0465/447744* ⊕ *www.ski.it* ⊠ *€14 round-trip.*

SKIING

⭐ **Campiglio Dolomiti di Brenta Skiarea**
SKIING & SNOWBOARDING | FAMILY | Miles of interconnecting ski runs—some of the best in the Dolomites—are linked by the cable cars and lifts of Campiglio Dolomiti di Brenta Skiarea. Advanced skiers will like the extremely difficult terrain found on certain mountain faces, and intermediate and beginner skiers will find many runs at their levels, all accessible from town. There are also plenty of off-piste opportunities. Passes can be purchased at the main *funivia* (cable car) in town, and multiday passes are available. ⊠ *Via Presanella 12, Madonna di Campiglio* ☎ *0465/447744* ⊕ *www.ski.it* ⊠ *Passes from €59 per day.*

Bormio

97 km (60 miles) northwest of Madonna di Campiglio, 100 km (62 miles) southwest of Merano.

At the foot of Stelvio Pass, Bormio is the most famous ski resort on the western side of the Dolomites, with 38 km (24 miles) of long pistes and a 5,000-plus-foot vertical drop. In summer its cool temperatures and clean air entice Italians away from cities on the humid Lombard plain. This dual-season popularity supports the plentiful shops, restaurants, and hotels in town. Bormio has been known for the therapeutic qualities of its waters since the Roman era, and there are numerous spas.

GETTING HERE AND AROUND
Take the SS239 North toward Dimaro. Turn onto the SS42 and follow it for 41 km (25 miles). Turn right onto Via Roma,

and, after 2 km (1 mile), turn right onto Via Valtellina for 24 km (15 miles), and then turn right at SP78. Merge onto the SS38, and follow it to Bormio. In the summertime, you can choose to turn off the SS42 at Ponte di Legno, onto the SS300, and follow it to the end in Bormio. This takes you through Stelvio National Park. The nearest railway is in Tirano, which is half an hour away by bus. Tirano is serviced by Trenitalia, as well as the UNESCO World Heritage–designated Rhaetian Railway.

VISITOR INFORMATION
CONTACT Bormio Tourism Office. ⊠ *Via Roma 131/B,* ☎ *0342/903300* ⊕ *www.bormio.eu.*

Sights

Parco Nazionale dello Stelvio
NATIONAL PARK | FAMILY | The Alps' (and Italy's) biggest national park is spread over 1,350 square km (520 square miles) and four provinces. Opened in 1935 to preserve flora and protect fauna, today it has more than 1,200 types of plants, 600 different mushrooms, and more than 160 species of animals, including the chamois, ibex, and roe deer. There are many entrances to the park and 11 visitor centers. ■**TIP→ Bormio makes a good base for exploring—the closest entrance to town is the year-round gateway at Torre Alberti.** ⊠ *Via Roma 131, Bormio* ☎ *0473/830430* ⊕ *www.parconazionale-stelvio.it* ⊠ *Free.*

Restaurants

Ristorante Caffe Kuerc
$$ | NORTHERN ITALIAN | FAMILY | This building was for centuries where justice was publicly served to accused witches, among others. Today, it's a great place to enjoy bewitching specialties like tasty pizza, bresaola with lemon and olive oil, or *pizzoccheri* (buckwheat pasta) with garlic and winter vegetables. **Known for:** pleasant location; delicious

pizza; interesting history. $ *Average main: €17* ✉ *Piazza Cavour 8, Bormio* ☎ *0342/910787* ⊕ *www.facebook.com/ ristorantekuerc* ⊗ *Closed Tues.*

Hotels

La Genzianella

$$ | **HOTEL** | **FAMILY** | Unpretentious Alpine chic meets contemporary decor, with warm pine, ceramics, rich textiles, and wood-beamed ceilings—and all but one of the guest rooms have balconies. **Pros:** great for bikers; excellent on-site restaurant; handy to slopes and town. **Cons:** rooms can be compact; some beds are two twins pushed together; no pool. $ *Rooms from: €197* ✉ *Via Zandilla 6, Bormio* ☎ *0342/904485* ⊕ *www.genzi-anella.com* ⊗ *Closed late Apr.–late May and mid-Sept.–Dec.* ⤶ *39 rooms* ⦶ *Free Breakfast.*

Activities

SKIING
Bormio Ski

SKIING & SNOWBOARDING | **FAMILY** | You can buy a ski pass and pick up a trail map at the base of the funivia (cable car), in the center of town (or buy the pass in advance online), before connecting to the Bormio 2000 station (6,600 feet) on Vallecetta, the main resort mountain. From there, you can ski down intermediate trails (the majority of Bormio's runs), use the extensive lift network to explore secondary ski areas, or get another funivia up to the Bormio 3000 station at Cima Bianca (9,800 feet) for more challenging terrain. The cable car also runs July to mid-September, when it is used by mountain bikers to reach long trails through breathtaking Alpine terrain; less ambitious visitors can wander around and then ride the cable car back down. ✉ *Via Battaglion Morbegno 25, Bormio* ☎ *0342/901451* ⊕ *www.bormioski. eu* ✉ *Ski pass €44 for 1 day. Cable car Bormio–Bormio 2000 €15 round-trip;*

cable car Bormio 2000–Cima Bianca €15 round-trip; cable car Bormio–Cima Bianca €22 round-trip.

SPAS
Bormio Terme

SPAS | **FAMILY** | From outdoor swimming pools to private baths, there are plenty of ways for the entire family to enjoy the healing qualities of the thermal waters. General admission gets you a full day in the pools, saunas, and Turkish baths. Spa and beauty treatments are also available; book ahead to avoid disappointment. You do not need to pay for the pools if you are only enjoying spa treatments. ✉ *Via Stelvio 14, Bormio* ☎ *0342/901325* ⊕ *www.bormioterme.it* ✉ *Entrance fee from €22, massages from €40, facials from €49.*

QC Terme Bagni Vecchi (*Old Baths*)

SPAS | Ancient Roman baths predate the thermal springs, caves, and waterfalls that are now known as the Bagni Vecchi. Leonardo da Vinci soaked here in 1493, and today you can also take the waters, as well as book massages and treatments. The spa complex includes thermal baths, saunas, aromatherapy, and a salt grotto. Bagni Vecchi only accepts those aged 14 or older. ✉ *Via Bagni Nuovi 7, Molina* ☎ *0289/747201* ⊕ *www.qcterme. com* ✉ *Admission fee from €44, massages from €48, facials from €44.*

Merano (Meran)

29 km (18 miles) north of Bolzano, 16 km (10 miles) east of Naturno.

The second-largest town in Alto Adige, Merano (Meran) was once the capital of the Austrian region of Tyrol. When the town and surrounding area were ceded to Italy as part of the 1919 Treaty of Versailles, Innsbruck became Tyrol's capital. Merano continued to be known as a spa town, attracting European nobility for its therapeutic waters and its "grape cure," which consists simply of eating

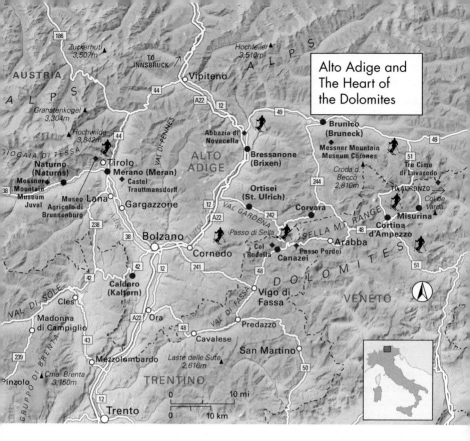

Alto Adige and The Heart of the Dolomites

the grapes grown on the surrounding hillsides. Sheltered by mountains, Merano has an unusually mild climate, with summer temperatures rarely exceeding 80°F (27°C) and winters that usually stay above freezing, despite the skiing within easy reach. Along the narrow streets of Merano's old town, houses have little towers and huge wooden doors, and the pointed arches of the Gothic cathedral sit next to neoclassical and Art Nouveau buildings. Merano serves as a good respite from mountain adventures, or from the bustle of nearby Trento and Bolzano.

GETTING HERE AND AROUND

By car from Bolzano, take the SP165 to the SP117 toward Merano (29 km [18 miles]). There is regular service by Trenitalia to the train station in Merano from many points in Italy.

VISITOR INFORMATION

CONTACT Merano Tourism Office. ⊠ *Corso Libertà 45,* ☎ *0473/272000* ⊕ *www. merano-suedtirol.it.*

◉ Sights

★ Castel Trauttmansdorff

GARDEN | FAMILY | This Gothic castle was restored in the 19th century and now serves as a museum that celebrates more than 200 years of tourism in South Tyrol. But the real draw is the expansive garden, where exotic flora is organized by country of origin. The castle is about 2 km (1 mile) southeast of town on the Sentiero di Sissi; you can walk in about 45 minutes from the center of Merano on Sissi's Path, or take Bus No. 4 or 1B from the Merano train station. ⊠ *Via Valentino 51a, Merano* ☎ *0473/255600*

🌐 *www.trauttmansdorff.it* 🎫 *€15* ⏲ *Closed mid-Nov.–Mar.*

Chiesa di San Nicolò (*Duomo*)
CHURCH | The 14th-century Gothic cathedral, with a crenellated facade and an ornate campanile, sits in the heart of the old town. The Capella di Santa Barbara, just behind the Duomo, is an octagonal church containing a 15th-century pietà. **TIP→ Mass is held in German only.** ✉ *Piazza del Duomo, Merano* ☎ *0473/230174* 🌐 *www.stadtpfarre-meran.it* 🎫 *Free.*

Museo Agricolo di Brunnenburg
HISTORY MUSEUM | **FAMILY** | Overlooking the town, atop Mt. Tappeinerweg, is Castel Fontana, which was the home of poet Ezra Pound from 1958 to 1964. Still in the Pound family, the castle now houses the Museo Agricolo di Brunnenburg, devoted to Tyrolean country life. Among its exhibits are a smithy and a room with Pound memorabilia. ✉ *Ezra Pound Strada 3, Tirolo* ✣ *Take Bus No. 3, which departs every hr on the hr from Merano to Dorf Tirol (20 mins)* ☎ *339/1803086* 🌐 *www.brunnenburg.net* 🎫 *€6* ⏲ *Closed Fri. and Sat.*

★ **Promenades**
PROMENADE | **FAMILY** | A stroll along one of Merano's well-marked, impossibly pleasant promenades may yield even better relaxation than time in its famous spa. **Passeggiata Tappeiner** (Tappeiner's Promenade) is a 3-km (2-mile) path with panoramic views from the hills north of the Duomo and diverse botanical pleasures along the way. **Passeggiata d'Estate** (Summer Promenade) runs along the shaded south bank of the Passirio River, and the **Passeggiata d'Inverno** (Winter Promenade), on the exposed north bank, provides more warmth and the Wandelhalle—a sunny area decorated with idyllic paintings of surrounding villages. The popular Austrian empress Sissi (Elisabeth of Wittelsbach, 1837–98) put Merano on the map as a spa destination; a trail named in her honor, the **Sentiero di Sissi** (Sissi's Walk), follows a path from Castel Trauttmansdorff to the heart of Merano. ✉ *Merano.*

🍴 Restaurants

Bistro 7
$$ | **ITALIAN** | A hip young crowd frequent the ground-floor bar of this modern bistro in the town's central arcade. Upstairs in the stylish dining room, an older crowd enjoys both contemporary cooking—heavy on beef, venison, and other meat specialties, including calf's liver—and attentive service. **Known for:** central location; fine wines; welcoming atmosphere. [$] *Average main: €24* ✉ *Lauben 232, Merano* ☎ *0473/210636* 🌐 *www.bistrosieben.it* ⏲ *Closed Sun.*

★ **Prezioso**
$$$$ | **MODERN ITALIAN** | South Tyrol native Egon Heiss uses ingredients from Castel Fragsburg's gardens as well as produce from nearby organic farms, and meat and fish from area producers, to create his beautiful versions of hyperlocal dishes. Delicious items on Prezioso's five-course tasting menus may include potato dumplings with alpine cheese, alpine salmon, and lamb from the Funes Valley—traditional cuisine elevated by modern preparations and artful presentations. **Known for:** refined local cuisine; mountainside setting; organic ingredients. [$] *Average main: €140* ✉ *Castel Fragsburg, Via Fragsburg 3, Merano* ✣ *8½ km (5 miles) southeast of Merano* ☎ *0473/244071* 🌐 *www.fragsburg.com* ⏲ *Closed Sun. and Mon. No lunch.*

Restaurant Sigmund
$$ | **ITALIAN** | Smack-dab on Merano's popular Corso della Libertà, this unassuming restaurant has an inviting terrace where you can people-watch and soak up some sun while enjoying specialties with seasonal twists, such as a springtime menu with all things asparagus. The interior's wood-beamed ceilings and candlelit tables make it the perfect setting for a romantic dinner. **Known for:** central location; well-prepared food with a mix of local and global ingredients; solid wine list. [$] *Average main: €22* ✉ *Freiheitsstr.*

2, Merano ☎ *0473/237749* 🌐 *www.restaurantsigmund.com* 🕓 *Closed Wed.*

Saxifraga

$$ | **ITALIAN** | To reach this charming eatery, which occupies an enviable position overlooking Merano and the peaks enveloping the town, climb the stairs behind the Duomo or hike up along the Passeggiata Tappeiner. The kitchen serves well-prepared dumplings, pasta, and other local specialties—just don't leave without trying the homemade breads. **Known for:** beautiful views; delicious desserts; charcuterie and cheeses. [$] *Average main: €20* ✉ *Via Monte San Zeno 33, Passeggiata Tappeiner (Tappeiner's Promenade), Merano* ☎ *0473/239249* 🌐 *www.saxifraga.it* 🕓 *Closed Tues. and Nov.–Mar. No dinner Oct. and Apr.–May.*

★ **Sissi**

$$$ | **NORTHERN ITALIAN** | The sterile surroundings of this restaurant, a short walk from Via dei Portici, belie its culinary delights—namely, rustic regional dishes re-energized and prepared with precision. Three-, five-, and seven-course tasting menus change according to the chef's whim and the season, but they usually include a modernized *vitello tonnato* (veal with tuna sauce), delightful homemade pasta and dumplings, and decadent meat dishes, such as veal stewed in Lagrein, the area's renowned red wine; vegetarian options are also available. **Known for:** highly polished service; fantastic wine list; varied tasting menu. [$] *Average main: €32* ✉ *Via Galilei 44, Merano* ☎ *0473/231062* 🌐 *sissi.andreafenoglio.com* 🕓 *Closed Mon. No lunch Tues.*

Coffee and Quick Bites

Vinothek Relax

$$ | **NORTHERN ITALIAN** | If you have difficulty choosing from the long list of tasty pizzas here, ask the friendly English-speaking staff for help with the menu. You're unlikely to find a better selection of wine, or a more pleasant environment for sampling; you can also buy bottles of the locally produced vintages to take home. **Known for:** helpful service; top-notch pizzas and local cuisine; large choice of wines. [$] *Average main: €15* ✉ *Via Cavour 31, opposite Palace Hotel, Merano* ☎ *0473/236735* 🌐 *www.weine-relax.it* 🕓 *Closed Sun. and 2 wks in Feb. and Mar.*

Hotels

★ **Castel Fragsburg**

$$$$ | **HOTEL** | For a taste of old-school Italian glamour just outside of Merano, you can't do better than this elegant Relais & Chateaux property high up in the mountains, set amid 4 acres of gardens and featuring a Michelin-starred restaurant and spa that both use products sourced from the land. **Pros:** wonderful spa concept; discreet, courteous service; beautiful landscape. **Cons:** classic decor not to everyone's taste; not a lot of indoor common space for relaxing; drive up to hotel not for faint of heart. [$] *Rooms from: €558* ✉ *Via Fragsburg 3, Merano* ✥ *8½ km (5 miles) southeast of Merano* ☎ *0473/244071* 🌐 *www.fragsburg.com* 🕓 *Closed mid-Nov.–early Apr.* 🛏 *20 rooms* 🍴 *Free Breakfast.*

★ **Hotel Terme Merano**

$$$$ | **HOTEL** | If you're in Merano to pamper yourself, you can't do much better than the Hotel Terme: as its name suggests, it's connected to the expansive Terme Merano (a stay here includes free, unlimited access via a "bathrobe tunnel"), and it also has the rooftop Sky Spa with indoor and outdoor pools and saunas. **Pros:** delicious breakfast offerings; very central location; well-equipped gym. **Cons:** staff can be unfriendly at times; accommodations above bar can be noisy; rooms on the plain side. [$] *Rooms from: €369* ✉ *Piazza Terme 1, Merano* ☎ *0473/259000* 🌐 *www.hoteltermemerano.it* 🛏 *139 rooms* 🍴 *Free Breakfast.*

★ Miramonti Boutique Hotel

$$$$ | HOTEL | FAMILY | Perched up in the hills 4,035 feet above Merano, this striking Alpine hotel takes full advantage of its superlative views with floor-to-ceiling windows in the guest rooms, a panoramic restaurant, and an infinity pool. **Pros:** tasty and well-presented food, at breakfast and dinner; second-to-none mountain views; kids' play area and dedicated splash time in the pool. **Cons:** no a/c in rooms; three-night minimum stay; spa not open till noon and forest sauna till 2 pm. $ *Rooms from: €396* ✉ *Via San Caterina 14, Avelengo ✚ 12 km (7½ miles) southeast of Merano* ☎ *0473/279335* ⊕ *www.hotel-miramonti. com* ☾ *Closed mid-Mar.–late Apr.* ⇌ *44 rooms* ⦿ *Free Breakfast.*

Shopping

Via dei Portici (*Laubengasse*)

NEIGHBORHOODS | Merano's narrow, arcaded main shopping street runs west from the cathedral. Here you can find regional products—wood carvings, Tyrolean-style clothing, embroidery, cheeses, salami, and fruit schnapps—alongside standard clothing-boutique stock. ✉ *Via dei Portici, Merano.*

Activities

BIKING

Sissi Tours

BIKING | Merano makes for a scenic place to explore by bike, and Sissi Tours offers guided day trips that include e-bike rental and helmet. Tours are usually held in German, so ask in advance if English is preferred. ✉ *Viale Europa, Merano* ☎ *0473/424344* ⊕ *www.sissitours.it* ☞ *Full-day guided bike tour €89.*

SPAS

★ Terme Merano

SPAS | FAMILY | This sprawling spa complex has 25 pools (15 indoor pools open year-round and 10 outdoor pools open from mid-May to mid-September) and six saunas (with an indoor "snow room" available for cooling down). Along with the family-friendly options for bathing, personalized services for grown-ups include traditional cures using local products, such as grape-based applications and hay baths. ✉ *Piazza Terme 9, Merano* ☎ *0473/252000* ⊕ *www.termemerano.it* ☞ *From €16 for 2 hrs in thermal baths; from €23 for 2 hrs in thermal baths and saunas; from €31 for full day's use of baths and saunas. Massages and facials from €69.*

Naturno (Naturns)

44 km (27 miles) northwest of Bolzano, 61 km (38 miles) east of Passo dello Stelvio.

As the name suggests, Naturno is a great location for a nature-based vacation; you can access a number of hiking trails to explore the area by foot. City planners have redesigned the town, reducing traffic and making the town more pedestrian-friendly. The locals take great pride in their produce; the fresh fruit, wine, and cheeses of this area are alone worth the drive.

GETTING HERE AND AROUND

By car from Bolzano, take the SS42 to the SS38 toward Merano. Naturno is 15 km (9 miles) past Merano. The town is very pedestrian-friendly, so talk to your hotel about where to leave your car, or head straight to a parking garage. Naturno is easily accessible by train from Bolzano or Merano.

VISITOR INFORMATION

CONTACT **Naturno Tourism Office.** ✉ *Via Municipio 1,* ☎ *0473/666077* ⊕ *www.merano-suedtirol.it.*

Sights

FORST Brewery

BREWERY | The source of the full-flavor beer served throughout the region is the striking FORST Brewery, on the road connecting Naturno and Merano. Tours

Stumbling on Ötzi

It was at the Similaun rifugio in September 1991 that a German couple arrived talking of a dead body they'd discovered near a "curious pickax." The couple, underestimating the age of the corpse by about 5,300 years, thought it was a matter for the police. This was to be the world's introduction to Ötzi, the oldest mummy ever found. World-famous mountaineers Reinhold Messner and Hans Kammerlander happened to be passing through the same rifugio during a climbing tour, and a few days later they were on the scene, freeing the iceman from the ice, and Ötzi's remarkable story was under way.

Today, you can see Ötzi on display, along with his longbow, ax, and clothes, at Bolzano's Museo Archeologico dell'Alto Adige, where he continues to be preserved at freezing temperatures.

can be arranged if you call ahead, but you can turn up between late May and September to sample the product line. In high season, cross a flower-lined covered wooden bridge to reach the delightful beer garden. ✉ *Via Venosta 10, Lagundo* ☎ *0473/221887* 🌐 *www.forst.it* 🎫 *Free* 🕒 *Closed late Sept.–late May.*

★ Messner Mountain Museum Juval
(*Castel Juval*)
ART MUSEUM | FAMILY | Since 1983 this 13th-century castle in the hills above the hamlet of Stava has been the summer home of the South Tyrolese climber and polar adventurer Reinhold Messner—the first climber to conquer Everest solo. Part of the castle has been turned into one of six in Messner's chain of mountain museums, where visitors can view his collection of Tibetan art and masks from around the world. You can download an app to use as a self-guided tour. It's a 10-minute shuttle ride from the parking lot below, plus a 15-minute walk up to the castle, or a 60- to 90-minute hike on local trails; wear sturdy shoes, even if you take the shuttle, as the paths are uneven. ✉ *Juval 3, Castelbello* ☎ *348/4433871, 0471/631264* 🌐 *www.messner-mountain-museum.it* 🎫 *€12, shuttle bus €5 round-trip* 🕒 *Closed Wed. and Nov.–late Mar.*

St. Prokulus Kirchlein
(*St. Proculus Church*)
CHURCH | Frescoes here are some of the oldest in the German-speaking world, dating from the 8th century. A small, modern museum offers multimedia installations (in Italian or German only) presenting four epochs in the region's history: ancient, medieval, Gothic, and the era of the Great Plague of 1636 (which claimed a quarter of Naturno's population, some of whom are buried in the church's cemetery). There are leaflets and other information in English on request. ✉ *Via San Procolo 1A, Naturno* ☎ *348/673139* 🌐 *www.merano-suedtirol.it* 🎫 *€6* 🕒 *Closed Mon., Wed., Fri., Sat., and Nov.–early Apr.*

🍴 Restaurants

★ Schlosswirt Juval
$$ | NORTHERN ITALIAN | Reinhold Messner's restored farmhouse, which is below Castel Juval, holds an old-style restaurant serving traditional local dishes. Not to be missed are the smoked hams and flavorful cheeses provided by the farm outside; they are well paired with the estate's Castel Juval wine. **Known for:** local wine; farm-to-table fare; mountaintop dining. [$] *Average main: €22* ✉ *Juval*

2, Castelbello ☎ 0473/668056 🌐 www.schlosswirtjuval.it 🕒 Closed Wed. and Nov.–mid-Mar.; dinner by reservation only.

Caldaro (Kaltern)

15 km (9 miles) south of Bolzano.

This vineyard village, with clear views of castles high up in the surrounding mountains, represents the centuries of division that forged the unique character of the area. Caldaro architecture is famous for the way it blends Italian Renaissance elements of balance and harmony with the soaring windows and peaked arches of the Germanic Gothic tradition—the church of Santa Caterina, on the main square, is a good example. The warmest bathing lake in the Alps is just 4 km (2½ miles) away.

GETTING HERE AND AROUND

By car from Bolzano, follow the SS42 south toward Caldaro. This road is famously known as the Strada del Vino (Wine Road), and you will pass several vineyards along the way. If you head straight to the Wine Museum in Caldaro, you can pick up maps and plan a route through the vineyards based on specific tastes.

VISITOR INFORMATION

CONTACT Caldaro Tourism Office. ✉ *Piazza Principale 8,* ☎ *0471/963169* 🌐 *www.kaltern.com.*

Sights

★ Elena Walch

WINERY | This sustainably farmed 148-acre property produces some of the region's most renowned wines, in paricular Gewürztraminer and Pinot Nero. It's overseen by Elena herself along with her daughters Julia and Karoline. Stop by their gorgeous Castel Ringberg site for tastings in their wine shop, a tour that includes a short vineyard hike (May through October, by reservation), or lunch at their Ostaria al Castello, which has panoramic views over the vines and down to Lake Caldaro. A second vineyard site closer to Tramin, with a wine shop and a bistro, is open daily year-round. ✉ *Castel Ringberg, San Giuseppe al Lago 1, Caldaro* ☎ *0471/860172* 🌐 *www.elenawalch.com* 🎟 *€20 for 2-hr vineyard tour with wine tasting* 🕒 *Castel Ringberg wine shop and osteria closed Tues. and Nov.–Apr.*

★ South Tyrolean Wine Museum

OTHER MUSEUM | Head here to learn how local wine has historically been made, stored, served, and worshipped, through a series of entertaining exhibits. ✉ *Via dell'Oro 1, near main square, Caldaro* ☎ *0471/963168* 🌐 *www.museo-del-vino.it* 🎟 *€6* 🕒 *Closed Sun., Mon., and mid-Nov.–Mar.*

Restaurants

★ Alois Lageder Paradeis

$$ | **NORTHERN ITALIAN** | Just off of the Strada del Vino (Wine Road), this charming eatery and wine bar lets you indulge in seasonal dishes while sampling some of the biodynamic wines produced by one of the Trentino area's most well-known vintners. When the weather's nice, dining in the pretty courtyard amongst lemon trees, with mountaintops visible just behind, really lives up to the "paradise" name. **Known for:** gorgeous garden-like setting; chance to sample older vintages for a great price; organic ingredients, including produce from their veggie garden. [$] *Average main: €22* ✉ *Via Casòn Hirschprunn 1, Margrè* ☎ *0471/809580* 🌐 *en.paradeis-aloislageder.eu* 🕒 *Closed Sun. No dinner.*

Bressanone (Brixen)

42 km (25 miles) northeast of Bolzano.

Bressanone is an important artistic center and was the seat of prince-bishops for centuries. Like their counterparts in Trento, these medieval administrators had the delicate task of serving two masters—the pope (the ultimate spiritual authority) and the Holy Roman Emperor (the civil and military power), who were virtually at war throughout the Middle Ages. Bressanone's prince-bishops became experts at tact and diplomacy.

The BrixenCard offers free transportation throughout Alto Adige (Südtirol/South Tyrol) and grants entry to almost 90 museums, plus free guided tours and discounts at partner venues; it's free to guests of local hotels.

GETTING HERE AND AROUND

Driving from Bolzano, follow the SS12 northeast 42 km (26 miles) to Bressanone. Trains run from Bolzano, as does SAD Bus No. 350.

VISITOR INFORMATION

CONTACT Bressanone Tourism Office. ✉ *Regensburger Allee 9,* ☎ *0472/275252* 🌐 *www.brixen.org.*

Sights

Abbazia di Novacella

CHURCH | This Augustinian abbey founded in 1142 has been producing wine for at least nine centuries and is most famous for the delicate stone-fruit character of its dry white Sylvaner. As you wander the delightful grounds, note the progression of Romanesque, Gothic, and Baroque building styles. Guided tours of the abbey, in various languages, depart daily, except Sunday. Guided tours of the vineyard are also available, in English, by reservation. ✉ *Via Abbazia 1, 3 km (2 miles) north of Bressanone, Varna* ☎ *0472/836189* 🌐 *www.kloster-neustift.it* 🎟 *Abbey visit €10; wine tastings with vineyard tour €15* 🕒 *Closed Sun., and Mon. Jan.–Mar.*

Duomo di Bressanone

CHURCH | The imposing town cathedral was built in the 13th century but acquired a Baroque facade 500 years later; its 14th-century cloister is decorated with medieval frescoes. ✉ *Piazza Duomo 1, Bressanone* ☎ *0472/834034* 🎟 *Free.*

Museo Diocesano (*Diocesan Museum*)

ART MUSEUM | The Bishop's Palace houses an abundance of local medieval art, in particular Gothic wood carvings—statues and liturgical objects collected from the cathedral treasury. During the Christmas season, curators arrange the museum's large collection of antique Nativity scenes; look for the shepherds wearing Tyrolean hats. ✉ *Palazzo Vescovile 2, Bressanone* ☎ *0472/830505* 🌐 *www.hofburg.it* 🎟 *€10.*

Restaurants

Fink

$$ | **NORTHERN ITALIAN** | This warm, wood-paneled upstairs dining room is under the arcades of the pedestrians-only town center; unlike most other restaurants in the region, Fink serves food all day long, with no break between lunch and dinner, just a slightly shortened menu. In addition to hearty Tyrolean specialties, such as dumplings and gröstl (meat, onion, and potato fry-up), there are affordable daily set meals. **Known for:** central location; bustling atmosphere; using regional and seasonal products. [$] *Average main: €23* ✉ *Kleine Lauben 4, Bressanone* ☎ *0472/834883* 🌐 *www.restaurant-fink.it* 🕒 *Closed Tues. before 2 pm and Wed.*

Hotels

★ **Hotel Elephant**

$$$ | **HOTEL** | At this cozy inn—over 500 years old and still one of the region's best—each room is unique, and many are filled with antiques and paintings. **Pros:** lovely ambience; lavish breakfast; good restaurants. **Cons:** some bathrooms are small; soundproofing in rooms could be better; rooms vary in size. [$] *Rooms from: €212* ✉ *Via Rio Bianco 4, Bressanone* ☎ *0472/832750* 🌐 *www.hotelelephant.com* 🛏 *44 rooms* 🍴 *Free Breakfast.*

Hiking the Dolomites

In 2009 UNESCO (the United Nations Educational, Scientific, and Cultural Organization) added the Dolomites to its list of natural heritage sites. The dramatic terrain, inspiring vistas, and impossibly pleasant climate are complemented by excellent facilities for enjoying the mountains.

Picking a Trail

The Dolomites have a well-maintained network of trails for hiking and rock climbing. As long as you're in reasonably good shape, the number of appealing hiking options can be overwhelming. Trails are well marked and designated by grades of difficulty: T for tourist path, H for hiking path, EE for expert hikers, and EEA for equipped expert hikers. On any of these paths you're likely to see carpets of mountain flowers between clutches of dense evergreens, with chamois and roe deer milling about.

If you're just out for a day in the mountains, you can leave the details of your walk open until you're actually on the spot; local tourist offices (especially those in Cortina and Madonna) can help you choose the right route based on trail conditions, weather, and desired exertion level.

Traveling the Vie Ferrate

If you're looking for an adventure somewhere between hiking and climbing, consider a guided trip along the Vie Ferrate (Iron Paths; *www.viefer-rate.it*). These routes offer fixed climbing aids (steps, ladders, bridges, safety cables) left by Alpine divisions of the Italian and Austro-Hungarian armies

and later converted for recreational use. Previous experience is generally not required, but vertigo-inducing heights do demand a strong stomach.

Bedding Down

One of the pleasures of an overnight adventure in the Dolomites is staying at a rifugio, one of the refuges that dot the mountainsides, often in remote locations. There are hundreds of them, and they range in comfort from spartan to posh. Most fall somewhere in between—they're cozy mountain lodges with dormitory-style accommodations. Pillows and blankets are provided (there's no need to carry a sleeping bag), but you have to supply your own sheet. Bathrooms are usually shared, with cold showers. Reservations are a must, especially in August, although Italian law requires rifugi to accept travelers for the night if there's insufficient time to reach other accommodations before dark.

Eating Well

Food is as much a draw at rifugi as location. The rustic dishes, such as salami, dumplings, and hearty stews, are all excellent—an impressive feat, made all the more remarkable when you consider that supplies often have to arrive by helicopter. Your bed for the night, with breakfast and dinner included, may cost from €45 to €75 per person. Snacks and packed lunches are available for purchase, but many opt to sit down for the midday meal. Multilingual stories are swapped, food and wine shared, and new adventures launched.

Brunico (Bruneck)

33 km (20 miles) east of Bressanone, 65 km (40 miles) northwest of Cortina d'Ampezzo.

Located in the heart of the Val Pusteria, this quiet and quaint town is divided by the Rienza River. The modern part of Brunico is on one side of the river, and on the other is the medieval quarter, nestled below a 13th-century bishop's castle.

GETTING HERE AND AROUND

From Bressanone follow the E66 east for 30 km (19 miles) to Brunico. If driving from Cortina d'Ampezzo, take the SR51 to Toblach and continue to the SS49 toward Brunico. There are bus (SAD) and train (Trenitalia) connections available at Bolzano.

VISITOR INFORMATION

CONTACT Brunico Tourism Office. ⊠ *Piazza Municipio 7,* ☎ *0474/555722* ⊕ *www. bruneck.com.*

 ## Sights

★ Lumen Museum

ART MUSEUM | Take a cable car to the top of Kronplatz to reach this 19,375-square-foot museum dedicated to mountain photography (actually, you have your choice of eight different cable cars, two from the town of Brunico). Once inside, you'll find pictures from alpine photography's early days all the way to the present, taken by photographers from mountainous regions throughout the world and displayed across four floors. Lumen also houses AlpiNN, a casual restaurant from critically acclaimed chef Norbert Niederkofler of St. Hubertus fame. Note that the museum can be difficult to access in winter if you're not a skier; it's down a slight, rather terrifying incline from the top of the mountain. Be aware that the museum closes at 4 pm (last admission at 3:30), so that you won't miss the last cable car back down. ⊠ *Kronplatz–Plan de Corones Mountain Station, Brunico* ⊕ *Take a cable car up to Kronplatz* ☎ *0474/431090* ⊕ *www.lumenmuseum. it* ⊠ *€17* ⊘ *Closed late Apr.–May and mid-Oct.–Nov.*

Messner Mountain Museum Corones

OTHER MUSEUM | High atop the Mountain Station Kronplatz–Plan de Corones, almost 7,500 feet above Brunico, the newest museum from mountaineer Reinhold Messner displays climbing equipment and other alpine paraphernalia from the 1800s until now. It also examines all facets of mountaineering through painting, sculpture, and other media. Equally interesting is the museum's Zaha Hadid–designed concrete building: its sloped roof makes it seem like a miniature mountain, and its outdoor lookout point affords magnificent vistas. Note that the museum closes at 4 pm (last admission at 3:30), so that you won't miss the last cable car back down. ⊠ *Kronplatz–Plan de Corones Mountain Station, Brunico* ⊕ *Take a cable car up to Kronplatz* ☎ *0474/501350* ⊕ *www.messner-mountain-museum.it* ⊠ *€12* ⊘ *Closed late Apr.–May and early–late Nov.*

★ Messner Mountain Museum Ripa

OTHER MUSEUM | **FAMILY** | This fascinating, comprehensive museum within the 13th-century Bruneck Castle looks at the lives of mountain-dwelling people from Europe, Asia, Africa, and South America through artifacts, tools, statues, paintings, living spaces, and more. Part of the experience is reaching the castle itself: it's a 15-minute hike up to it on a path accessed just off Brunico's pedestrian area. ⊠ *Schlossweg 2, Brunico* ☎ *0474/410220* ⊕ *www.messner-mountain-museum.it* ⊠ *€12* ⊘ *Closed Tues., late Apr.–mid-May, and Nov.–early Dec.*

South Tyrolean Folklore Museum

MUSEUM VILLAGE | **FAMILY** | A re-creation of a medieval rural village is built around a 300-year-old mansion. The wood-carving displays are especially interesting. ⊠ *Herzog-Diet-Strada 24, Brunico*

The craggy peaks around Canazei are particularly stunning at sunset.

☎ *0474/552087* 🌐 *www.volkskunde-museum.it* 🎟 *€9* 🕒 *Closed Mon. and Nov.–mid-Apr.*

🍴 Restaurants

★ Oberraut

$$ | **ITALIAN** | Drive up into the hills about 12 minutes northeast of Brunico to reach this charming chalet-style family-run eatery, which has an expansive terrace with great views overlooking the mountains. Hearty dishes use local ingredients—including meat from their farm, vegetables from their gardens and greenhouses, and grain from their own mill—and the delightful servers are happy to recommend seasonal specialties. **Known for:** deer and beef dishes; alpine vistas; zero-kilometer philosophy. [$] *Average main: €22* ✉ *Via Ameto 1, Brunico* ☎ *0474/559977* 🌐 *oberraut.it* 🕒 *Closed Thurs.*

🛏 Hotels

Das Majestic Hotel & Spa

$$$$ | **HOTEL** | Right in front of the Plan de Corones, this is a great base for a skiing or hiking vacation, with bus service to the ski slopes and a spa and pools on-site to unwind after a big day out. **Pros:** convenient for skiers and hikers; spacious rooms; nice indoor and outdoor pools. **Cons:** far from town center; no covered parking; meal portions are a little small. [$] *Rooms from: €304* ✉ *Via Im Gelände 20, Brunico* ☎ *0474/410993* 🌐 *www.hotel-majestic.it* 🕒 *Closed Easter–mid-May* 🛏 *60 rooms* 🍴 *Free Breakfast.*

Hotel Post

$$ | **HOTEL** | This homey hotel housed in a former post office dating from the 1880s is the most central, appealing lodging choice in town. **Pros:** professional staff; parking on-site; central location. **Cons:** small spa; simple breakfast; modern decor lacks historical charm. [$] *Rooms from: €167* ✉ *Via Bastioni 9, Brunico* ☎ *0474/834001*

🌐 *www.hotelpost-bruneck.com* 🛏 *39 rooms* 🍴 *No Meals.*

Misurina

115 km (71 miles) east of Bolzano.

Nestled on the shores of Lake Misurina, among the Dolomites, Misurina's high altitude, low air humidity, and total absence of dust mites and air pollution has some saying that the "Pearl of the Dolomites" has some of the purest air in the world. The town itself is rather small, but it's a perfect base to explore Lake Misurina and the Tre Cime of Lavaredo. The surrounding mountains are rich in history and artifacts from the First World War and earlier conflicts. Along some of the hikes and *vie ferrate* (mountain paths with steel cables and fixed anchors and ladders), you can explore caves and trenches complete with informational placards giving details about troop positions and fighting.

GETTING HERE AND AROUND

From Brunico, drive southeast on the SS49/E66 to Dobbiaco. Turn right onto SS51 and drive for 13 km (8 miles). Turn left onto SP49 in the direction of Auronzo. Arrive at Lago di Misurina in 6 km (4 miles).

VISITOR INFORMATION

CONTACT Misurina Tourism Office. ✉ *Via Monte Piana 2,* ☎ *0435/39016* 🌐 *auronzomisurina.it.*

Sights

★ Tre Cime di Lavaredo
MOUNTAIN | **FAMILY** | Without a doubt, the Three Peaks—Cima Piccola (9,373 feet), Cima Grande (9,839 feet), and Cima Ovest (9,753 feet)—are the symbols of the Dolomite UNESCO World Heritage site. From the town of Misurina, only two of the Tre Cime are visible. In order to get up close and personal, drive or take a bus along the dedicated toll road (open May through October; car parking €30). Once at the top, follow Footpath 101 from Rifugio Auronzo to Forcella Laveredo (easy) for about an hour. There are many other footpaths and vie ferrate which allow you to climb the cime and access the base. Rifugi offer hot meals without a reservation, as well as dorm-style lodging, which is best reserved in advance. ✉ *Parco Naturale Tre Cime, Auronzo di Cadore* ☎ *0474/710355* 🌐 *www.drei-zinnen.info.*

Restaurants

Malga Rin Bianco
$$$ | **NORTHERN ITALIAN** | **FAMILY** | For fresh, properly cooked regional food, this *malga* (Alpine hut) with great mountain views can't be beat—just make a reservation, especially in winter, when you must be transported over on a snowmobile by day and a shuttle at night (in summer, you can drive all the way). Salamis and cheeses are made on-site, and the bar serves both commercial and homemade grappas, many of which are brewed with local herbs; also try some *capriolo* (mountain goat stew), polenta, *skitz* (grilled cheese that doesn't melt), or fresh local mushrooms. **Known for:** great views; local food; scenic mountain location. [$] *Average main: €26* ✉ *Via Monte Piana 35, Strada Tre Cime, Misurina* ☎ *0320/5699375 for whatsapp reservations, 0435/39048* 🌐 *www.rinbianco.com.*

Hotels

Chalet Lago Antorno
$$ | **B&B/INN** | **FAMILY** | Located in a quiet, panoramic spot, this chalet is ideal for exploring the mountains or simply relaxing amid the beauty of the Alps. **Pros:** family-run; idyllic mountain setting; typical decor and regional flavor. **Cons:** some rooms are small; minimum night stays in peak season; away from town center. [$] *Rooms from: €140* ✉ *Località Lago Misurina, Misurina* ☎ *0320/9625700* 🌐 *www.lagoantorno.it* 🕓 *Closed*

Apr.–May and mid-Oct.–Nov. 🛏 *10 rooms* 🍴 *Free Breakfast.*

Grand Hotel Misurina

$$ | HOTEL | FAMILY | On the shores of beautiful Lake Misurina and just a few kilometers from renowned winter resort Cortina d'Ampezzo, this grand hotel has simply furnished rooms that range from standard fare to full apartments. **Pros:** located in town center; shuttle to ski areas; perfect for large groups. **Cons:** no Wi-Fi in rooms; dated decor; rooms have simple furnishings. [$] *Rooms from: €136* ✉ *Via Monte Piana 21, Misurina* ☎ *0435/39191* 🌐 *www.grandhotelmisurina.com* 🕒 *Closed Nov. and Apr.* 🛏 *125 rooms* 🍴 *Free Breakfast.*

Activities

BIKING

Cycling enthusiasts flock to the Dolomites for the challenging mountain terrain, and much of the region is used by Olympic athletes to train. In addition, several important cycling races (such as the Giro di Italia) take place in this area. Some of the descents along gravelly roads set off a rush of adrenaline, while others follow paved roads and bike paths. The Auronzo-Misurina Cycle Track provides about 32 km (20 miles) of bicycle path between the two towns.

SKIING

Two major ski lifts service the area: the Col de Varda lift in Misurina, and the Monte Agudo lift in Auronzo di Cadore (about a 30-minute drive from Misurina), which takes you from Taiarezze (2,952 feet) to Rifugio Monte Agudo (5,160 feet). The views from Auronzo differ from Misurina in that all Tre Cime are visible. Restaurants and maps are available at the top.

Col de Varda

SKIING & SNOWBOARDING | FAMILY | The major ski lift servicing the area from Misurina climbs to Col de Varda, with a summit of 6,909 feet. Rifugio Col de Varda, at the top, has a bar and restaurant, as well as rooms to rent. In the summer, the area is an excellent starting point for great hiking and biking excursions. At any time of the year, the views of Lake Misurina, Mt. Cristallo, the Sesto Dolomites, and the Cadini, Sorapiss, and Tofane massifs are breathtaking. ✉ *Misurina* ☎ *0435/39013* 🌐 *www.auronzomisurina.it* 🎟 *€13 round-trip.*

Monte Cristallo

SKIING & SNOWBOARDING | Some of the most impressive views (and steepest slopes) are on Monte Cristallo. ✉ *Misurina* ☎ *0436/861035* 🌐 *faloriacristallo.it* 🎟 *€46 for one-day pass.*

Canazei

45 km (28 miles) southwest of Misurina.

Of the year-round resort towns in the Val di Fassa, Canazei is the most popular. The mountains around this small town are threaded with hiking trails and ski slopes, set amid large clutches of conifers.

GETTING HERE AND AROUND

Bus service from Bolzano and Bressanone (the nearest train stations) is infrequent, and schedules are often interrupted or canceled. By car from the A22 autostrada, take the Bolzano Nord exit onto the SS241. Cross the Passo Costalunga into the Val di Fassa. From the town of Vigo, follow signs for Canazei.

VISITOR INFORMATION

CONTACT Canazei Tourism Office. ✉ *Strèda Roma 36,* ☎ *0462/609500* 🌐 *www.fassa.com.*

Sights

★ Col Rodella

VIEWPOINT | FAMILY | An excursion from Campitello di Fassa, about 4 km (2½ miles) west of Canazei, to the vantage point at Col Rodella has unmissable views. A cable car rises some 3,000 feet to a full-circle vista of the Heart of the Dolomites, including the Sasso Lungo and the rest of the Sella range. ✉ *Località Ischia 1, Canazei* ☎ *0462/608811* 🌐 *www.fassa.com* 🎫 *Col Rodella cable car €22 round-trip.*

Passo Pordoi

MOUNTAIN | FAMILY | At 7,346 feet, Passo Pordoi is the highest surface-road pass in the Dolomites. It connects Arabba, in Val Cordevole (Province of Belluno), with Canazei, in Val di Fossa (Province of Trento). Views from the top include the Sassolungo and Sella group of mountains, and even the Marmolada Glacier. There are several hotels and a ski school located at the pass, as well as some souvenir shops, restaurants, and snack carts. While the hotels are not glamorous, some do offer half-board packages at reasonable rates. The road up to the pass from Canazei has a few scenic and picnic pull-offs, plus 28 hairpin turns.

Skiing is available year-round. The most popular winter skiing areas are Belvedere and Sella Ronda, and much of the area is part of the Dolomiti Superski package. Even if the road for the pass is closed, many of the cable cars in neighboring valley towns will be running to various summits.

From Passo Pordoi you can get a cable car (May through October) to the Sass Pordoi, often called the Terrazza delle Dolomiti (Terrace of the Dolomites). At more than 9,100 feet, it offers myriad hiking trails and vie ferrate with varying degrees of difficulty (none of which are easy), leading to rifugi and the region's other peaks and passes. ✉ *Strada del Pordoi, Canazei* 🌐 *www.fassa.com* 🎫 *Sass Pordoi cable car €25 round-trip.*

Hotels

Alla Rosa

$$ | HOTEL | Ask for a room with a balcony: the view of the imposing Dolomites is the real attraction in accommodations that pleasantly blend rustic and contemporary furnishings. **Pros:** in the center of town; free parking nearby; great views. **Cons:** no tea or coffee facilities in room; busy neighborhood; sparse breakfast. [$] *Rooms from: €137* ✉ *Strada del Faure 18, Canazei* ☎ *0462/601107* 🌐 *www.hotelallarosa.com* 🛏 *49 rooms* 🍴 *Free Breakfast.*

Ortisei (St. Ulrich)

28 km (17 miles) northwest of Canazei.

Ortisei (St. Ulrich), the jewel in the crown of Val Gardena's resorts, is a hub of activity in both summer and winter; there are hundreds of miles of hiking trails and accessible ski slopes. Ortisei has been a family-friendly mountain vacation destination since the 1930s. The most famous cable car in the area, the Alpe di Siusi, operates in summer and winter. As the largest village in the Val Gardena, Ortisei makes a picturesque and practical base for exploring much of the heart of the Dolomites.

For centuries Ortisei has also been famous for the expertise of its wood carvers, and there are still numerous workshops. Apart from making religious sculptures—particularly the wayside calvaries you come upon everywhere in the Dolomites—Ortisei's carvers were long known for producing wooden dolls, horses, and other toys. As itinerant peddlers, they traveled every spring on foot with their loaded packs as far as Paris, London, and St. Petersburg. Shops in town still sell woodcrafts.

GETTING HERE AND AROUND

By car from Bolzano, take the SS12 to the SS242 in the direction of Ortisei. From Canazei, follow the SS242 north to Ortisei. Free bus service is available from participating accommodations on the Val Gardena network from Bolzano and Bressanone and other points around the region. The Gardena Card gives unlimited use of all the lifts (17) of the region for one price.

VISITOR INFORMATION

CONTACT Ortisei Tourist Office. ✉ *Via Rezia 1,* ☎ *0471/777600* 🌐 *www.valgardena.it.*

Sights

Alpe di Siusi Cable Car

TRANSPORTATION | **FAMILY** | First opened in 1935, the cable car from Ortisei to Alpe di Siusi climbs more than 6,100 feet to the widest plateau in Europe. There are more than 57 square km (22 square miles) of Alpine pastures lined with summertime hiking trails. In the winter, 20 ski lifts and cross-country ski paths keep active visitors happy. There is a restaurant at the top of the Mt. Seuc ski lift, or you can pick up a map at the tourist office in Ortisei listing the mountain huts and restaurants that can be reached on foot. Opening days and times depend on the season and daily weather conditions; check the website or call ahead to avoid disappointment. ✉ *Setil Strada 9, Ortisei* ☎ *0471/797897* 🌐 *www.funiviaortisei.eu* 🎟 *€24 round-trip.*

Museo della Val Gardena

ART MUSEUM | **FAMILY** | Fine historic and contemporary examples of local woodworking are on display here, as well as a retrospective on the life of local film director Luis Trenker. ✉ *Via Rezia 83, Ortisei* ☎ *0471/797554* 🌐 *www.museumgherdeina.it* 🎟 *€8* 🕒 *Closed mid-Apr.–mid-May and mid-Oct.–mid-Dec.; closed weekends mid-May–mid-Oct.*

Hotels

Cavallino Bianco Family Spa Grand Hotel

$$$$ | **RESORT** | **FAMILY** | With delicate wooden balconies and an eye-catching wooden gable, the pink Cavallino Bianco (Little White Horse) looks like a gigantic dollhouse, and it is, in fact, marketed toward families. **Pros:** excellent family facilities; laundry facilities; cheerful rooms. **Cons:** fixed arrival/departure dates in winter; some lower-level rooms face garage; in the busy town center. [$] *Rooms from: €536* ✉ *Via Rezia 22, Ortisei* ☎ *0471/783333* 🌐 *www.cavallino-bianco.com* 🕒 *Closed mid-Apr.–mid-May* 🛏 *104 rooms* 🍴 *All-Inclusive.*

Hotel Garni Planaces

$$ | **B&B/INN** | This clean and spacious B&B is just a short walk from ski lifts and the bus stop, and all guests have access to the spa and pool areas. **Pros:** very clean; good value for the area; well maintained. **Cons:** rooms can feel small with ski gear; fewer amenities than at higher-priced hotels; simple furnishings. [$] *Rooms from: €142* ✉ *Via Rezia 212, Ortisei* ☎ *0471/796159* 🌐 *www.garniplanaces.it* 🕒 *Closed Apr.–late June and mid-Oct.–early Dec.* 🛏 *9 rooms, 4 apartments* 🍴 *Free Breakfast.*

Hotel Grones

$$$ | **HOTEL** | **FAMILY** | The attention to detail at this family-run hotel, located just a few minutes' walk from the ski slopes or downtown, makes it a great base for a mountain vacation. **Pros:** friendly staff; spa with nice indoor pool; shuttle service to ski stations. **Cons:** bed linens/bath towels could be higher quality; pool and whirlpool not quite warm enough; it's an uphill walk from town. [$] *Rooms from: €280* ✉ *110 Stufan St., Ortisei* ☎ *0471/797040* 🌐 *www.hotelgrones.com* 🕒 *Closed Apr. and May and early Oct.–early Dec.* 🛏 *23 rooms* 🍴 *Free Breakfast.*

Activities

SKIING

With almost 600 km (370 miles) of accessible downhill slopes and more than 90 km (56 miles) of cross-country skiing trails, Ortisei is one of the most popular ski resorts in the Dolomites. Prices are good, and facilities are among the most modern in the region. In warmer weather, the slopes surrounding Ortisei are a popular hiking destination, as well as a playground for vehicular mountain adventures like biking, rafting, and paragliding.

Sella Ronda

SKIING & SNOWBOARDING | FAMILY | An immensely popular ski route, the Sella Ronda relies on well-placed chairlifts to connect 26 km (16 miles) of downhill skiing around the colossal Sella massif, passing through several towns along the way. You can ski the loop, which requires intermediate ability and a full day's effort, either clockwise or counterclockwise. Going with a guide is recommended. ⊠ *Ortisei* ⊕ *www.sella-ronda.info.*

Corvara

29 km (18 miles) east of Ortesei (St. Ulrich).

Corvara is the main town of the Alta Badia, known for its prime skiing and hiking location in the middle of the Sella Ronda. The first chairlift in Italy opened here in 1946, and today, there are two cable cars—the Col Alto and the Boè—along with 12 chairlifts, making Corvara a convenient base for an active holiday in winter or summer. Corvara is also the start of the First World War Ski Tour, a 49-mile route around Col di Lana that takes you past wartime relics like trenches and forts. The town itself is pleasant and walkable, with a smattering of restaurants, bars, and ski rental and sporting goods stores.

GETTING HERE AND AROUND

To get to Corvara from Bolzano, take the A22 north to Bressanone/Pusteral. Turn right on the SS244, and take it all the way to Corvara. From Ortisei, take the SS242 to the SS243 into Corvara. Buses arrive many times daily from Bolzano and Bressanone.

VISITOR INFORMATION

CONTACTS Corvara Tourist Office. ⊠ *Strada Col Alt 36,* ☎ *0471/836176* ⊕ *www. altabadia.org.*

 Sights

Boè Cable Car

TRANSPORTATION | FAMILY | This cable car takes hikers and skiers from Corvara up Piz Boè, the highest mountain of the Sella group, at 10,341 feet. Once at the first station, you can hike the Sella Ronda, ski back down, or ride a chairlift farther up to the Vallon Peak for more challenging skiing or hiking in the warmer months. Paragliding is also popular from the Vallon area. ⊠ *Strada Burjé* ☎ *0471/836073* ⊕ *www.moviment.it/en/boe-ski-lift-corvara.php* 🎫 *€19 round-trip.*

Col Alto Cable Car

TRANSPORTATION | FAMILY | The site of Italy's first chairlift in 1946 now has modern yellow eight-seater cable cars that ascend to a height of 6,562 feet. From there you have access to ski lifts that take you all over the Alta Badia region and, in summer, to trails that include a 6-mile route to the Rifugio Pralongià. You can rent skis and snowboards at the Ski Service Colalto, located at the bottom of the lift. ⊠ *Strada Col Alt 36, Corvara* ☎ *0471/836073* ⊕ *www.moviment.it/en/col-alt-ski-lift-corvara.php* 🎫 *€14 round-trip.*

 Restaurants

La Stüa de Michil

$$$$ | ITALIAN | You'll feel like you're dining in a traditional Alto Adige hut at the Perla hotel's critically acclaimed restaurant, which features wood-beamed ceilings. Menu items are complex, modern takes on regional cuisine: even a simple veal dish might be served with reserve Alpine cheese and black truffle. **Known for:** daring ingredient combinations; interesting wine pairings (not all Italian); romantic atmosphere. $ *Average main: €120* ✉ *Strada Col Alt 105, Corvara* ☎ *0471/831000* ⊕ *www.laperlacorvara. it* ⊗ *Closed Sun., Apr.–late June, and late Sept.–early Dec.*

★ Ristorante Refugio Col Alt

$$ | ECLECTIC | From town, take the Col Alt cable car—or a snowcat (by reservation only) for dinner on Wednesday and Friday—to this surprisingly modern restaurant with amazing panoramas from 6,562 feet. The wide-ranging menu features everything from salads to hearty fried potatoes, eggs, and bacon (perfect after a morning of skiing), and the interesting wine list is heavy on natural producers, since the affable owner is a fan and often has local winemakers in for tastings. **Known for:** memorable wines at affordable prices; an enormous terrace; unbeatable vistas. $ *Average main: €22* ✉ *Monte Cabinovia, Strada Col Alt 1, Corvara* ✛ *Take Col Alt cable car* ☎ *0471/836324* ⊕ *rifugiocolalt.it* ⊗ *Closed mid-Apr.–late June and late Sept.–early Dec.*

★ St. Hubertus

$$$$ | MODERN ITALIAN | In a laid-back, welcoming setting at the Rosa Alpina hotel, chef Norbert Niederkofler oversees one of the Alto Adige's most highly regarded restaurants, where seasonal products sourced exclusively from the region are transformed into delicacies on a 12-course tasting menu. Servers thoroughly explain the provenance of the seemingly simple yet multilayered dishes, which can be paired with wines from all over the world, though there's a slant toward small local producers. **Known for:** zero-waste philosophy, all parts of ingredients are used; bold use of fermentation; hyperlocal cuisine. $ *Average main: €320* ✉ *Hotel & Spa Rosa Alpina, Strada Micurá de Rü 20, 7½ km (4½ miles) east of Corvara, San Cassiano* ☎ *0471/849500* ⊕ *www.st-hubertus.it* ⊗ *Closed Mon., Tues., Apr.–early June, and late Sept.–early Dec.*

 Hotels

Ciasa Salares

$$$$ | HOTEL | FAMILY | This refined, amenities-filled hotel has a distinctly Germanic vibe and lots of mountain atmosphere—from its outdoor hot tub and sauna to its simple guest rooms, with light-wood paneling, white accents, and balconies, to its underground fondue room–wine cellar (24,000 bottles with a focus on biodynamic producers). **Pros:** a number of top-notch dining choices; more affordable than comparable hotels; lovely spa. **Cons:** not ski-in, ski-out; service can be standoffish; some rooms feel a bit cramped. $ *Rooms from: €340* ✉ *Strada Prè de Vi 31, San Cassiano* ☎ *0471/849445* ⊕ *www.ciasasalares.it* ⊗ *Closed Apr.–mid-June* ⤳ *50 rooms* ⦿ *Free Breakfast.*

★ Hotel & Spa Rosa Alpina

$$$$ | HOTEL | FAMILY | The Rosa Alpina offers everything you need for a relaxed mountain stay: chic yet homey Alpine decor, guest rooms with working fireplaces and balconies, a spa, both family and adults-only pools, and the St. Hubertus restaurant, one of the region's most renowned. **Pros:** perfect blend of refinement and mountain flavor; private cinema; bountiful breakfast selection. **Cons:** overnight guests not guaranteed St. Hubertus reservations; no a/c; can hear noise in rooms from outside and within hotel. $ *Rooms from: €650* ✉ *Strada Micurà de Rü 20, San Cassiano* ✛ *7½ km (4½ miles) east of Corvara*

☎ *0471/849500* 🌐 *www.rosalpina.it* ⏲ *Closed early Oct.–early Dec. and Apr.–early June* 🛏 *52 rooms* 🍴 *Free Breakfast.*

★ **La Perla**
$$$$ | **HOTEL** | Best described as "Alpine country chic," this luxe yet rustic family-run hotel has spacious wood-latticed rooms with mountain-view balconies, a spa, lots of cozy sitting areas, and a much-lauded restaurant. **Pros:** ski-in, ski-out; extremely friendly service; convenient location next to both the mountains and town. **Cons:** Wi-Fi can be iffy at times; expensive drinks; no minibar in rooms. [$] *Rooms from: €316* ✉ *Strada Col Alt 105, Corvara* ☎ *0471/831000* 🌐 *www.laperlacorvara.it* ⏲ *Closed Apr.–mid-June and late Sept.–early Dec.* 🛏 *50 rooms* 🍴 *All-Inclusive.*

Activities

HIKING

Corvara offers hikes for all levels, including the popular Col Alt Pralongià hike—an easy, level hike that passes through pasture lands—as well as a number of walks in the Puez-Odle nature reserve. Hikers looking for more challenging, steeper routes should start at the top of the Boè cable car.

SKIING

Alta Badia
SKIING & SNOWBOARDING | The Alta Badia ski area, which includes 53 ski lifts and 130 km (80 miles) of slopes, is cheaper and more Austrian in character than the more famous ski destinations in this region. Groomed trails for cross-country skiing (usually loops marked off by the kilometer) accommodate differing degrees of ability. Inquire at the local tourist office. ✉ *Corvara* ☎ *0471/836176 Corvara tourism office* 🌐 *www.altabadia.org* 🎫 *€62 Day Pass.*

Cortina d'Ampezzo

38 km (24 miles) east of Corvara.

The archetypal Dolomite resort, Cortina d'Ampezzo entices those seeking both relaxation and adventure. The town is the western gateway to the Strade Grande delle Dolomiti and actually crowns the northern Veneto region and an area known as Cadore in the northernmost part of the province of Belluno. Like Alto Adige to the west, Cadore (birthplace of the Venetian Renaissance painter Titian) was on the Alpine front during World War I, and was the scene of many battles that have been commemorated in refuges and museums. Although its appeal to younger Italians has been eclipsed by the steeper, sleeker Madonna di Campiglio, Cortina remains, for many, Italy's most idyllic incarnation of an Alpine ski town.

GETTING HERE AND AROUND

To drive to Cortina d'Ampezzo from Trento or Bolzano, take the A22 autostrada north to Bressanone/Pustertal. Turn right on the SS49/E66, then right on to the SS51 and follow it into Cortina. The Südtirolmobil site provides itineraries for train and bus arrivals from around the region. The town itself is pedestrian-friendly and has local bus service to area ski slopes. Beware of taxis, as the rates are very high—and the fare may begin from the taxi's point of origin, not necessarily where you get in the vehicle.

CONTACT Cortina d'Ampezzo Tourism Office. ✉ *Corso Italia 81,* ☎ *0436/869086* 🌐 *www.dolomiti.org.*

Sights

Surrounded by mountains and dense forests, the "Queen of the Dolomites" is in a lush meadow 4,000 feet above sea level. The town hugs the slopes beside a fast-moving stream, and a public park extends along one bank. Higher in the valley, luxury hotels and the villas of the rich are identifiable by their attempts to hide behind stands of firs and spruces. The bustling center of Cortina d'Ampezzo has little nostalgia, despite its alpine appearance, with its tone set by shops and cafés as chic as their well-dressed patrons. Unlike neighboring resorts that have a strong Germanic flavor, Cortina d'Ampezzo is unapologetically Italian and distinctly fashionable.

🍴 Restaurants

La Tavernetta

$$ | **NORTHERN ITALIAN** | These Tirolean-style wood-paneled dining rooms near the Olympic ice-skating rink are a Cortina institution. Join the local clientele in sampling terrific pizza along with house specialties such as pasta with pork, radicchio, and ricotta, and ravioli with beetroot. **Known for:** house-made desserts; nice wine selection; typical dishes. [$] *Average main: €15* ✉ *Via Castello 53, Cortina d'Ampezzo* ☎ *0436/868102.*

Ristorante Lago Pianozes di Alberti Massimo

$$$ | **NORTHERN ITALIAN** | The owner of this small, endearing establishment—just outside Cortina and beside picturesque Lago Pianozes—is friendly and knowledgeable, not only about the food and wine but also about the region. The menu varies according to the seasons, always incorporating local recipes—seating is limited, though, so reservations are recommended. **Known for:** friendly staff; local dishes; delightful location. [$] *Average main: €28* ✉ *Campo di Sotto Pianozes 1, Cortina d'Ampezzo* ☎ *366/3591737* ⏲ *Closed early May–late June, and Tues. and Thurs. Apr., Oct., and Nov.*

🛏 Hotels

★ Cristallo, a Luxury Collection Resort & Spa

$$$$ | **RESORT** | This luxury grande dame, now run by Marriott, is lauded for its service, spa, and more—the architecture was immortalized in 1963's *The Pink Panther*. **Pros:** stellar food and service; wonderful atmosphere; great spa. **Cons:** high parking fee; not accessible for all budgets; not in town. [$] *Rooms from: €546* ✉ *Via R. Menardi 42, Cortina d'Ampezzo* ☎ *0436/881111* 🌐 *www.cristallo.it* ⏲ *Closed Apr.–late May and early Oct.–mid-Dec.* 🛏 *74 rooms* 🍴 *Free Breakfast.*

Hotel Corona

$$ | **HOTEL** | Modern art adorns the small but comfortable pine-paneled rooms at this inviting lodge, once owned by noted ski instructor Luciano Rimoldi; ski slopes and the town center are a 10-minute walk away. **Pros:** quiet location; ski shuttle stops out front; friendly staff. **Cons:** dated decor; outside the town center; small rooms. [$] *Rooms from: €153* ✉ *Via Val di Sotto 12, Cortina d'Ampezzo* ☎ *0436/3251* 🌐 *www.hotelcorona.dolomiti.com* ⏲ *Closed Apr.–May and mid-Sept.–Nov.* 🛏 *44 rooms* 🍴 *Free Breakfast.*

Hotel De la Poste

$$ | **HOTEL** | Loyal skiers return year after year to this old-school mountain retreat, where each unique room has antiques in characteristic Dolomite style (almost all have wooden balconies) and the main terrace bar is one of Cortina's social centers. **Pros:** professional service; lively atmosphere; charging stations for electric cars. **Cons:** street noise can be an issue; dated furnishings; a bit stuffy. [$] *Rooms from: €198* ✉ *Piazza Roma 14, Cortina d'Ampezzo* ☎ *0436/4271* 🌐 *www.delaposte.it* ⏲ *Closed Apr.–May and mid-Oct.–early Dec.* 🛏 *72 rooms* 🍴 *Free Breakfast.*

Miramonti Majestic

$$$$ | **RESORT** | A touch of luxurious formality rather than rustic charm comes through in the imperial Austrian design of this century-old landmark tucked into a magnificent mountain valley. **Pros:** magnificent location; great pool and spa; loads of old-world charm in lounges and guest rooms alike. **Cons:** shows a few signs

of wear; Wi-Fi can be iffy; about 1 km (½ mile) outside town center. [$] *Rooms from: €318* ✉ *Località Peziè 103, Cortina d'Ampezzo* ☎ *0436/4201* 🌐 *www.mira-montimajestic.it* 🕓 *Closed Apr.–June and Sept.–mid-Dec.* 🛏 *122 rooms* 🍴 *Free Breakfast.*

Activities

HIKING AND CLIMBING

Gruppo Guide Alpine Cortina Scuola di Alpinismo (*Mountaineering School*)
HIKING & WALKING | This group organizes climbing trips and trekking adventures. ✉ *Corso Italia 69/a, Cortina d'Ampezzo* ☎ *0436/868505* 🌐 *www.guidecortina.com.*

SKIING

Dolomiti Superski Pass
SKIING & SNOWBOARDING | **FAMILY** | The Dolomiti Superski Pass provides access to the surrounding Dolomites, with 450 lifts and gondolas serving 1,200 km (750 miles) of trails. There's also a Dolomiti Supersummer Pass, good from mid-May to early November. Buy the passes at the ticket office next to the bus station and at other outlets in the Dolomites. ✉ *Via Marconi 15, Cortina d'Ampezzo* ☎ *0471/795397* 🌐 *www.dolomitisuperski.com* 🎫 *Superski: from €54 for one day, lower rates for longer durations. Supersummer: €51 for one day.*

Faloria Gondola
SKIING & SNOWBOARDING | **FAMILY** | The Faloria gondola runs from the center of town. From its top you can get up to most of the central mountains. ✉ *Via Ria de Zeta 10, Cortina d'Ampezzo* ☎ *0436/2517* 🌐 *www.faloriacristallo.it* 🎫 *€24 round-trip.*

Passo Falzarego
SKIING & SNOWBOARDING | The topography of the Passo Falzarego ski area, 16 km (10 miles) east of town, is dramatic. From here, a cable car takes you to one of the highest points in the Dolomites (Rifugio Lagazuoi)—where, on a clear day, you'll experience some of the best views. It's also easy to see why this was such a deadly area for soldiers in the Great War. Hiking is uneven in places, and there are vie ferrate that require the use of helmets and flashlights; other paths lead to tunnels that don't require helmets. ✉ *Cortina d'Ampezzo* ☎ *0436/5921* 🌐 *lagazuoi.it* 🎫 *Cable car €21 round-trip.*

Chapter 8

MILAN, LOMBARDY, AND THE LAKES

8

Updated by
Elizabeth Shemaria

 Sights
★★★★☆

 Restaurants
★★★★☆

 Hotels
★★★★☆

 Shopping
★★★★★

 Nightlife
★★★☆☆

WELCOME TO
MILAN, LOMBARDY, AND THE LAKES

TOP REASONS TO GO

★ **Lake Como, one of the most beautiful lakes in the world:** Ferries crisscross the waters, taking you from picture-book villages to stately villas to Edenic gardens—all against the backdrop of the snowcapped Alps.

★ **Leonardo's** *The Last Supper*: Behold one of the world's most famous works of art for yourself.

★ **The sky's no limit:** A funicular ride in Bergamo whisks you up to the magnificent medieval city.

★ **Milan alla moda:** As you window-shop the afternoon away in Milan's Quadrilatero shopping district, catch a glimpse of fashion's latest trends.

★ **A night at La Scala:** What the Louvre is to art, Milan's La Scala is to the world of opera.

★ **Lake Garda and Lake Maggiore:** The former is great for outdoors enthusiasts; the latter has plentiful islands to explore.

★ **Cremona's violins:** If you are in the market for a violin, you'll find the world's best here in more than 150 shops.

1 Milan. The international fashion capital.

2 Bergamo. A charming medieval quarter.

3 Pavia. See the 15th-century monastery.

4 Cremona. The birthplace of the violin.

5 Mantua. The Palazzo Ducale is a must.

6 Lake Iseo and Franciacorta. Lovely views and quaint restaurants.

7 Sirmione. A bustling spa town.

8 Malcesine. A favorite of sailors and hikers.

9 Riva del Garda. Stroll, sunbathe, or windsurf.

10 Gargnano. Don't miss the pleasant beach.

11 Gardone Riviera. A lovely town set against the Alps.

12 Bellagio. The belle of Lake Como.

13 Tremezzo. Explore two 18th-century villas.

14 Cernobbio. Villa d'Este hotel commands pride of place.

15 Como. A former silk town, with an urban vibe.

16 Stresa and the Isole Borromee. Grand hotels abound here.

17 Verbania. Gorgeous gardens and villas.

8

EATING WELL IN MILAN, LOMBARDY, AND THE LAKES

Lombardy may well offer Italy's most varied, rich, and refined cuisine. Local cooking is influenced by the neighboring regions of the north; foreign conquerors have left their mark; and today, business visitors, industrious immigrants, and well-traveled Milanese are likely to find more authentic ethnic cuisine in Milan than in any other Italian city.

Milan runs counter to many established Italian dining customs. A "real" traditional Milanese meal is a rarity; instead, Milan offers a variety of tastes, prices, and opportunities, from expense-account elegance in fancy restaurants to abundant *aperitivo*-hour nibbles. The city's cosmopolitan nature means trends arrive here first, and things move fast. Meals are not the drawn-out pastime they tend to be elsewhere in Italy. But the food is still consistently good: competition among restaurants is fierce and the local clientele is demanding, which means you can be reasonably certain that if a place looks promising, it won't disappoint.

THE COTOLETTA QUESTION

Everyone has an opinion on *cotoletta*, the breaded veal cutlet known across Italy as *una Milanese*. It's clearly related to Austria's Wiener schnitzel, but did the Austrians introduce it when they seized Milan, or did they take it home when they left? Some think it's best with fresh tomato and arugula on top; others find this sacrilege. Two things unite all camps: the meat must be well beaten until it's thin, and it must never leave a grease spot after it's fried.

REGIONAL SPECIALTIES

Ask an Italian what Lombards eat, and you're likely to hear *cotoletta, càsoeûla,* and *risotto giallo*—all dishes that reinforce Lombardy's status as the crossroads of Italy. *Cotoletta alla Milanese* may very well have Austrian roots. *Càsoeûla* is a cabbage-and-pork stew that resembles French cassoulet, though some say it has Spanish origins. *Risotto giallo* (also known as *risotto Milanese*) is colorful and perfumed with exotic saffron.

BUTTER AND CHEESE

Geography and a strong agricultural tradition mean that animal products are more common here than in southern Italy; butter and cream, for example, take the place of olive oil. One rare point of agreement about cotoletta is that it's cooked in butter, and the first and last steps of risotto making—toasting the rice, then letting it "repose" before serving—use ample amounts of butter. And the second-most-famous name in Italian cheese (after Parmesan) is likely Gorgonzola, named for a town near Milan; the best now comes from Novara.

RISOTTO

Rice is Lombardy's answer to pasta, and the region is the center of Italian (and European) rice production. From Milan's risotto giallo with its saffron tint, to Mantua's risotto with pumpkin or sausage, there's no end to the variety. Canonical risotto should be *all'onda,* flowing off the spoon like a wave. In keeping with the Italian tradition of wasting nothing, yesterday's risotto is flattened in a pan and fried in butter to produce *riso al salto,* which at its best has a crispy crust and a tender middle.

PANETTONE

Panettone, a tall, fluffy yeast bread, is flavored with sweet candied fruit. Invented in Milan, it graces nearly every table during the Christmas holiday. Consumption begins on December 7, Milan's patron saint's day, and goes until supplies run out at January's end.

WINE

The Franciacorta region around Brescia makes highly regarded sparkling wines, often called the "Champagne of Italy" since they're produced using the same labor-intensive method. The Valtellina area to the northeast of Milan produces two notable reds from the *nebbiolo* grape: Valtellina Superiore and the intense dessert wine Sforzato di Valtellina. Lake breezes yield crisp, smooth whites from the shores of Lake Garda.

Lombardy is one of Italy's most dynamic regions, offering everything from world-class ski slopes to summer lake resorts, and Milan is the pulse of the nation—commercial, fashionable, and forward-looking. The Renaissance cities of the Po Plain—Pavia, Cremona, and Mantua—offer the romantic Italy visitors dream about, embracing their past by preserving national treasures while keeping an eye on the present.

Topping any list of the region's attractions are the glacial lakes at the very feet of the Alps, praised as the closest thing to paradise by writers throughout the ages, from Virgil to Hemingway.

Millions of travelers have concurred: for sheer beauty, the lakes of northern Italy—Como, Maggiore, Garda, Iseo, and Orta—have few equals. Along their shores are 18th- and 19th-century villas, exotic formal gardens, sleepy villages, and dozens of Belle Époque–era resorts that were once Europe's most fashionable and that still retain a powerful allure.

Milan can be disappointingly modern and congested—a little too much like the place you've come to Italy to escape—but its historic buildings and art collections in many ways rival those of Florence and Rome. And if you love to shop, Milan is one of the world's great fashion centers, offering experiences and goods for every taste, from Corso Buenos Aires, which has a higher ratio of stores per square foot than anywhere else in Europe, to the edgy street style of Corso di Porta Ticinese and upscale Via Montenapoleone, where there's no limit on what you can spend. Milan is home to global fashion giants such as Armani, Prada, Versace, Salvatore Ferragamo, and Ermenegildo Zegna; behind them stand a host of less famous designers who help fill all those fabulous shops.

MAJOR REGIONS

Milan. Long the country's capital of commerce, finance, fashion, and media, Milan is also Italy's transport hub, with the biggest international airport, the most rail connections, and the best subway system.

The Po Plain, Lake Garda, and Lake Iseo. Italy's wealthiest, most populous region is home not only to Milan, but also to nearby medieval towns that once rivaled Milan in power. Bergamo, set against the Bergamese Alps, is a modern town connected by funicular to its lovely ancient counterpart. Pavia is celebrated for its extraordinarily detailed Carthusian monastery, and Cremona for its incomparable violin-making tradition. Picturesque Mantua was the home of the fantastically wealthy Gonzaga dynasty for almost 300 years.

An hour's drive from Milan, sleepy Lake Iseo merits a stop for waterfront eateries amid picture-postcard settings. It's also on the northern edge of the Franciacorta region, home to production of Italy's up-and-coming sparkling wine.

Lake Garda is the region's biggest and, by most accounts, cleanest lake. The terrain is flat at its southern base—home to the enchanting former Roman resort town of Sirmione—and mountainous at its northern tip, where dramatic Riva del Garda sits. Places of note include summer resort Malcesine, port town Gargnano (known for its association with Mussolini), and quaint 19th-century Gardone Riviera.

Lakes Como and Maggiore. Palatial villas, rose-laden belvederes, and majestic Alpine vistas are among the treasures of Lake Como—Europe's deepest lake. Many travelers head directly to boats for Bellagio and the *centro di lago,* the beautiful center region of the lake's three branches. Seasonal car ferries and vaporetti also make it easy to reach the towns of Cernobbio and Tremezzo. Don't bypass the walled city of Como, which has a medieval town center and pretty lakefront. Magnificently scenic Lake Maggiore has a unique geographical position: its mountainous western shore is in Piedmont, its lower eastern shore is in Lombardy, and its northern tip is in Switzerland. The better-known resort towns, Stresa and Verbania, are on its western shore, with access to the lake's Borromean Islands.

Planning

Making the Most of Your Time

Italy's commercial hub isn't usually at the top of the list for visiting tourists, but Milan is the nation's most modern city, with its own sophisticated appeal: its fashionable shops rival those of New York and Paris, its soccer teams are Italy's answer to the Yankees and the Mets, its opera performances set the standard for the world, and its art treasures are well worth the visit.

The biggest draw in the region, though, is the Lake District. Throughout history, the magnificently beautiful lakes of Como, Garda, Maggiore, Iseo, and Orta have attracted their fair share of well-known faces—from Winston Churchill and Russian royalty to George Clooney and Madonna. Each lake town has its own history and distinct character. If you have limited time, visit the lake you think best suits your style, but if you have time to spare, make the rounds to two or three to get a sense of their contrasts.

Getting Here and Around

AIR
The region's main international gateway airport is Aeroporto Malpensa (⊕ *www. milanomalpensa-airport.com*), 48 km (30 miles) northwest of Milan. Some international and domestic flights also fly into more central Aeroporto Linate (⊕ *www. milanolinate-airport.com*), 7 km (4 miles) east of Milan, while European low-cost carriers like Ryanair use Aeroporto Milano Bergamo Orio al Serio (⊕ *www. milanbergamoairport.it*), 55 km (34 miles) northeast of Milan and 5 km (3 miles) south of Bergamo.

BOAT

Frequent daily ferry and hydrofoil services link the lakeside towns and villages. Residents take them to get to work and school, while visitors use them for exploring the area. There are also special round-trip excursions, some with (optional) dining service on board.

CONTACTS Navigazione Laghi.
☎ *800/551801 within Italy* ⊕ *www.navigazionelaghi.it.*

BUS

Bus service isn't the best way to travel between cities here because trains are faster, cheaper, and more convenient. There's regular bus service for reaching and traveling between the small towns on the lakes. It's less convenient than going by boat or by car, and it's used primarily by locals (particularly schoolchildren), but sightseers can use it as well. The bus service around Lake Garda serves mostly towns on the western shore.

CONTACTS Arriva Italia. ☎ *035/289000 call center* ⊕ *www.arriva.it.* **Autostradale.** ☎ *02/30089000* ⊕ *www.autostradale.it.*

CAR

Getting almost anywhere by car is a snap, as several major highways intersect at Milan, all connected by the *tangenziale*, the city's ring road. The A4 autostrada runs west to Turin and east to Venice; the A1 leads south to Bologna, Florence, and Rome; the A7 angles southwest down to Genoa. The A8 goes northwest toward Lake Maggiore, and the A9 runs north past Lake Como and into Switzerland's southernmost tip.

To get around the lakes themselves by car, you have to follow secondary roads. The SP572 follows the southern and western shores of Lake Garda, the SS45bis edges the northernmost section of the western shore, and the SR249 runs along the eastern shore. Around Lake Como, follow the SS340 along the western shore, the SS36 on the eastern shore, and the SP583 on the lower arms. The SS33 and SS34 trace the western shore of Lake Maggiore. The SP469 runs on the western side of Lake Iseo, while the SP510 borders the east. Although the roads around the lakes can be beautiful, they're full of harrowing twists and turns, making for a slow, challenging drive—often with an Italian speed racer on your tail.

CONTACTS ACI (Automobile Club d'Italia). ☎ *803/116* ⊕ *www.aci.it.*

TRAIN

Milan's majestic Central Station (Milano Centrale), 3 km (2 miles) northwest of the Duomo, has frequent service within the region to Como, Bergamo, Brescia, Sirmione, Pavia, Cremona, and Mantua. There are plenty of signs to help you get around, but its sheer size requires considerable amounts of walking and patience, so allow for some extra time here.

Tickets bought without a reservation need to be validated by stamping them in yellow machines on the train platforms. Tickets with reservations don't require validation. When in doubt, validate—it can't hurt. For general information on trains and schedules, as well as online ticket purchases, visit the website of the Italian national railway, **Trenitalia**, also known as **Ferrovie dello Stato (FS)**.

CONTACTS Trenitalia. ☎ *892021 within Italy* ⊕ *www.trenitalia.com.*

Restaurants

You'll find lots of traditional northern Italian restaurants in this region, and can pretty much count on menus divided into pasta, fish, and meat options. As in the rest of Italy, it's common for dishes to feature seasonal and local ingredients. Meal prices in Milan tend to be higher than in the rest of the region (and quite high for European cities in general), though this is also where you'll see examples of the latest food trends and more adventurous choices on the menus.

Prices in the dining reviews are the average cost of a main course at dinner, or, if dinner is not served, at lunch. Restaurant reviews have been shortened. For full information, visit Fodors.com.

Hotels

Given that this is the wealthiest part of Italy, most hotels here cater to a clientele willing to pay for extra comfort. Outside Milan, many are converted villas with well-landscaped grounds. Most of the famous lake resorts are expensive; many smaller lakeside hotels are more reasonably priced. Local tourism offices throughout the region are an excellent source of information about affordable lodging.

Please note that the time for "high season" can vary here—in the lakes it's the height of summer, not surprisingly, but in Milan it depends on what fairs and exhibitions are being staged. Prices in almost all hotels can go up dramatically during Salone, the furniture and design fair in early April. Fashion, travel, and tech fairs also draw big crowds throughout the year, raising prices. In contrast to other cities in Italy, however, you can often find discounts on weekends. The lakes, including Maggiore and Garda, have little to offer except quiet from November to March, when most gardens, hotels, and restaurants are closed.

Prices in the lodging reviews are the lowest cost of a standard double room in high season. Hotel reviews have been shortened. For full information, visit Fodors.com.

What it Costs in Euros

	$	$$	$$$	$$$$
RESTAURANTS				
	under €15	€15–€24	€25–€35	over €35
HOTELS				
	under €125	€125–€200	€201–€300	over €300

Milan

Rome may be bigger and wield political power, but Milan and the affluent north are what really make the country go. Leonardo da Vinci's *The Last Supper* and other great works of art are here, as well as a spectacular Gothic Duomo, the finest of its kind. Milan even reigns supreme where it really counts (in the minds of many Italians), routinely trouncing the rest of the nation with its two premier soccer teams.

And yet, Milan hasn't won the battle for hearts and minds when it comes to tourism. Most visitors prefer Tuscany's hills and Venice's canals to Milan's hectic efficiency and wealthy indifference, and it's no surprise that in a country of medieval hilltop villages and skilled artisans, a city of grand boulevards and global corporations leaves visitors asking the real Italy to please stand up. They're right, of course: Milan is more European than Italian, a new buckle on an old boot, and although its old city can stand cobblestone to cobblestone against the best of them, seekers of Roman ruins and fairy-tale towns may pass. But Milan's secrets reveal themselves slowly to those who look. A side street conceals a garden complete with flamingos (Giardini Invernizzi, on Via dei Cappuccini, just off Corso Venezia; closed to the public, but you can still catch a glimpse), and a renowned 20th-century-art collection hides modestly behind an unspectacular facade a block from Corso Buenos Aires (the Casa-Museo Boschi di Stefano). Visitors tempted by world-class shopping will appreciate Milan's European sophistication while discovering unexpected facets of a country they may have only thought they knew.

Virtually every invader in European history—Gaul, Roman, Goth, Lombard, and Frank—as well as a long series of rulers from France, Spain, and Austria, took a turn at ruling the city. After being completely sacked by the Goths in AD 539 and by the Holy Roman Empire under Frederick Barbarossa in 1157, Milan became one of the first independent city-states of the Renaissance. Its heyday of self-rule proved comparatively brief. From 1277 until 1500 it was ruled first by the Visconti and then the Sforza dynasties. These families were known, justly or not, for a peculiarly aristocratic mixture of refinement, classical learning, and cruelty; much of the surviving grandeur of Gothic and Renaissance art and architecture is their doing. Be on the lookout in your wanderings for the Visconti family emblem—a viper, its jaws straining wide, devouring a child.

GETTING HERE AND AROUND

The city center is compact and walkable; trolleys and trams make it even more accessible, and the efficient Metropolitana (subway) and buses provide access to locations farther afield. Driving in Milan is difficult and parking a real pain, so a car is a liability. In addition, drivers within the second ring of streets (the *bastioni*) must pay a daily congestion charge on weekdays between 7:30 am and 7:30 pm (until 6 pm on Thursday). You can pay the charge at news vendors, tobacconists, Banca Intesa Sanpaolo ATMs, or with the EasyPark app ⊕ *www.easyparkitalia. it*; parking meters and parking garages in the area also include it in the cost. There is also a public bike sharing system called BikeMi (⊕ *www.bikemi.com*).

BICYCLE
CONTACT BikeMi. ☎ *02/48607607* ⊕ *www.bikemi.com.*

PUBLIC TRANSPORTATION
A standard public transit ticket within the central zones of Milan costs €2 and is valid for a 90-minute trip on a subway, bus, or tram. An all-inclusive subway, bus, and tram pass costs €11.50 for 24 hours or €17.50 for 48 hours. Another option is a Carnet (€18), good for 10 tram, bus, or subway rides. Individual tickets and passes can be purchased from news vendors, tobacconists, at ticket machines at all subway stops, at ticket offices at the Duomo and other subway stops, and on your phone via the ATM Milano app. You can also pay for a subway ride using a contactless credit card at the turnstile to avoid ticket purchasing lines.

Once you have your ticket, either stamp it or insert it into the slots in station turnstiles or on poles inside trolleys and buses. (Electronic tickets won't function if they become bent or demagnetized. If you have a problem, contact a station manager, who can usually issue a new ticket.) Trains run from 6 am to 12:30 am.

CONTACTS ATM. (*Azienda Trasporti Milanesi*) ☎ *02/48607607* ⊕ *www.atm. it/en.* **Radiobus.** ☎ *02/48034803* ⊕ *www. atm.it/en.*

TAXI
Taxi fares in Milan are higher than in American cities; a short ride can run about €15 during rush hour or fashion week. You can get a taxi at a stand with an orange "Taxi" sign, or by calling one of the taxi companies. Most also have apps you can download to order taxis from your phone; some let you text or use WhatsApp to hail a cab. Dispatchers may speak some English; they'll ask for the phone number you're calling from, and they'll tell you the number of your taxi and how long it'll take to arrive. If you're in a restaurant or bar, ask the staff to call a cab for you.

CONTACTS 026969. ☎ *02/6969*
⊕ *www.026969.it.* **Taxi028585.** ☎ *02/8585*
⊕ *www.028585.it.* **Taxiblu.** ☎ *02/4040*
⊕ *www.taxiblu.it.*

TOURS
CONTACT City Sightseeing Milano.
☎ *55/961237* ⊕ *www.city-sightseeing.it/
en/milan.*

VISITOR INFORMATION
CONTACT Milan Tourism Office. ✉ *Piazza
del Duomo 14, Duomo* ☎ *02/88455555*
⊕ *www.yesmilano.it.*

Duomo

Milan's main streets radiate out from the
massive Duomo, a late-Gothic cathedral
begun in 1386. Heading north is the
handsome Galleria Vittorio Emanuele II,
an enclosed shopping arcade that opens
at one end to the world-famous opera
house known as La Scala. Via Manzoni
leads northeast from La Scala to the
Quadrilatero della Moda, or fashion
district. Heading northeast from the Duomo is the pedestrian-only street Corso
Vittorio Emanuele II. Northwest of the
Duomo is Via Dante, at the top of which
is the imposing outline of the Castello
Sforzesco.

 Sights

Battistero Paleocristiano/Baptistry
of San Giovanni alle Fonti
CHURCH | More specifically known as
the Baptistry of San Giovanni alle Fonti,
this 4th-century baptistry is one of two
that lie beneath the Duomo. Although
opinion remains divided, it is widely
believed to be where Ambrose, Milan's
first bishop and patron saint, baptized
Augustine. Tickets also include a visit to
the Duomo and its museum. ✉ *Piazza del
Duomo, enter through Duomo, Duomo*
☎ *02/72023375* ⊕ *www.duomomilano.
it* 📷 *€10, including admission to Duomo*

and museum; €20, including Duomo,
museum, and roof with elevator, valid for
72 hrs Ⓜ *Duomo.*

★ Duomo
CHURCH | There is no denying that for
sheer size and complexity, the Duomo is
unrivaled in Italy. It is the second-largest
church in the country—the largest being
St. Peter's in Rome—and the fourth
largest in the world. This intricate Gothic
structure has been fascinating and exas-
perating visitors and conquerors alike
since it was begun by Gian Galeazzo Visconti III (1351–1402), first duke of Milan,
in 1386. Consecrated in the 15th or 16th
century, it was not completed until just
before the coronation of Napoléon as
king of Italy in 1809.

The building is adorned with 135 marble
spires and 2,245 marble statues. The
oldest part is the apse. Its three colossal
bays of curved and counter-curved
tracery—especially the bay adorning the
exterior of the stained-glass windows—
should not be missed. At the end of the
southern transept down the right aisle
lies the tomb of Gian Giacomo Medici.
The tomb owes some of its design to
Michelangelo but was executed by Leone Leoni (1509–90) and is generally considered his masterpiece; it dates from
the 1560s. Directly ahead is the Duomo's
most famous sculpture, the gruesome
but anatomically instructive figure of San
Bartolomeo (St. Bartholomew), who was
flayed alive. As you enter the apse to
admire those splendid windows, glance
at the sacristy doors to the right and
left of the altar. The lunette on the right
dates from 1393 and was decorated by
Hans von Fernach. The one on the left
also dates from the 14th century and is
ascribed jointly to Giacomo da Campio-
ne and Giovannino de' Grassi. ✉ *Piazza
del Duomo, Duomo* ☎ *02/36169340*
⊕ *www.duomomilano.it* 📷 *Cathedral €5;
museum €5; cathedral, museum, and*

8

Milan, Lombardy, and the Lakes MILAN

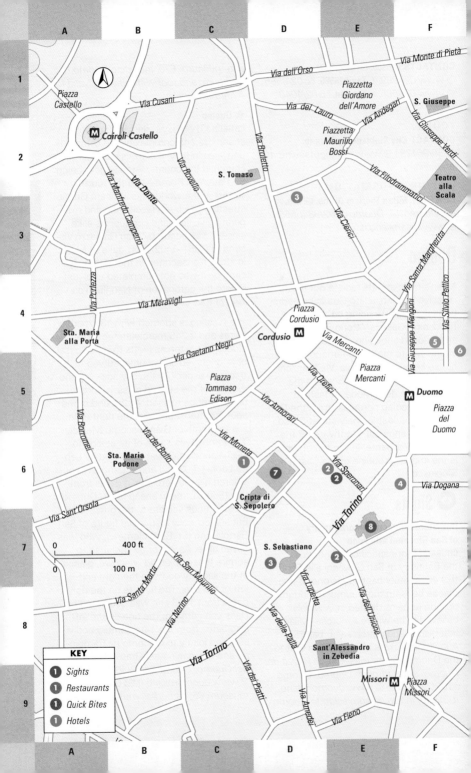

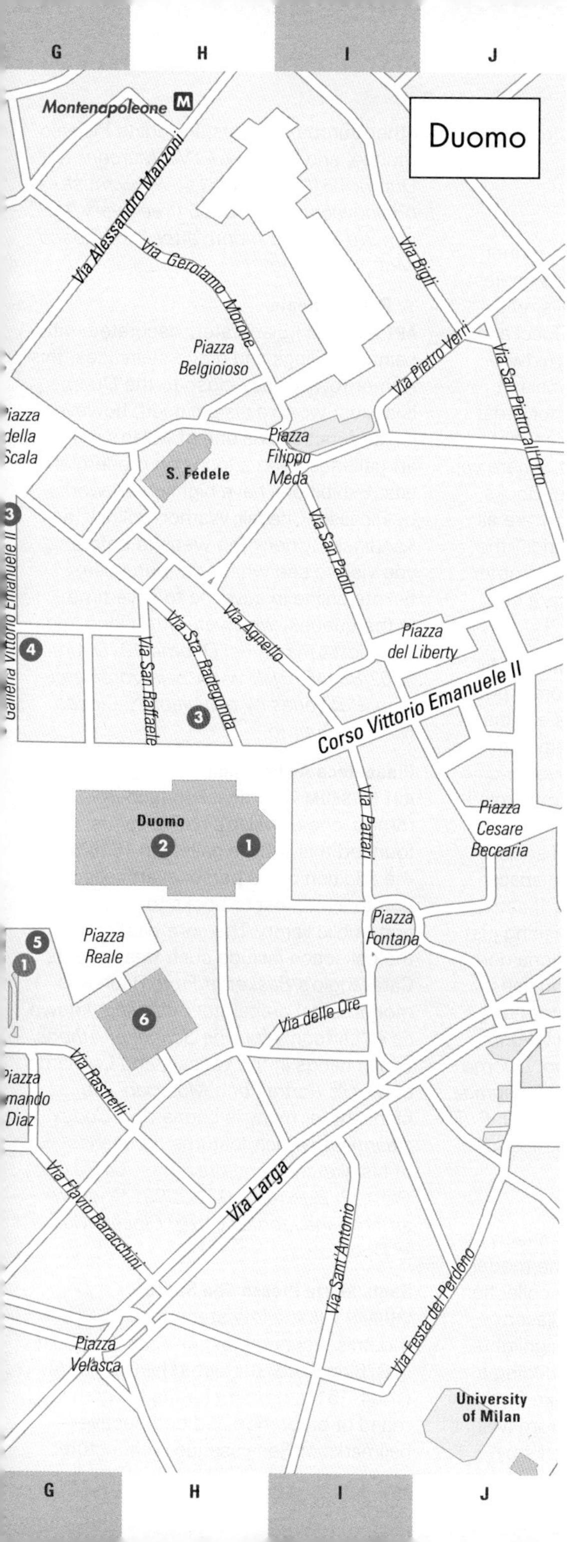

Montenapoleone Ⓜ

Duomo

Via Alessandro Manzoni

Via Gerolamo Morone

Via Bigli

Via Pietro Verri

Via San Pietro all'Orto

Piazza
Belgioioso

Piazza
della
Scala

Piazza
Filippo
Meda

S. Fedele

Via San Paolo

Galleria Vittorio Emanuele II

Via Sta. Radegonda

Via Agnello

Via San Raffaele

Piazza
del Liberty

④

③

Corso Vittorio Emanuele II

Piazza
Cesare
Beccaria

Duomo

Via Pattari

② **①**

⑤
①

Piazza
Reale

Piazza
Fontana

⑥

Via delle Ore

Via Rastrelli

Piazza
Armando
Diaz

Via Flavio Baracchini

Via Larga

Via Sant'Antonio

Via Festa del Perdono

Piazza
Velasca

University
of Milan

Sights ▼

1 Battistero Paleocristiano/
Battistry of San Giovanni
alle Fonti **H5**
2 Duomo **H5**
3 Galleria Vittorio
Emanuele II......................... **G3**
4 Milano Osservatorio—
Fondazione Prada **G4**
5 Museo del Novecento **G6**
6 Palazzo Reale **H7**
7 Pinacoteca Ambrosiana **D6**
8 Santa Maria Presso
San Satiro **E7**

Restaurants ▼

1 Giacomo Arengario................ **G6**
2 La Vecchia Latteria **E7**
3 Piz **D7**

Quick Bites ▼

1 Camparino in Galleria **G5**
2 Piccolo Peck **E6**
3 Rinascente Food Hall............. **H5**

Hotels ▼

1 Hotel Gran Duca di York.......... **C6**
2 Hotel Spadari al Duomo........... **E6**
3 Hotel Star **D3**
4 Maison Milano |
UNA Esperienze **F6**
5 Park Hyatt Milan................... **F4**
6 Room Mate Giulia................. **F5**

8

Milan, Lombardy, and the Lakes MILAN

archaeological area €10; stairs to roof
€15; elevator €20 Ⓜ Duomo.

★ **Galleria Vittorio Emanuele II**
STORE/MALL | This spectacular
late-19th-century Belle Époque tunnel
is essentially one of the planet's earliest
and most select shopping malls, with
upscale tenants that include Gucci and
Prada. This is the city's heart, midway
between the Duomo and La Scala. It
teems with life, which makes for great
people-watching from the tables that spill
out from bars and restaurants, where you
can enjoy an overpriced coffee. Books,
clothing, food, hats, and jewelry are all
for sale. Known as Milan's "parlor," the
Galleria is often viewed as a barometer
of the city's well-being. ⊠ Piazza del
Duomo, Duomo Ⓜ Duomo.

Milano Osservatorio—Fondazione Prada
OTHER MUSEUM | This contemporary pho-
tography and visual languages exhibition
space, developed in partnership with
Fondazione Prada, is spread over two
floors in the Galleria Vittorio Emanuele II.
Exhibitions, which rotate several times
a year, explore the cultural and social
implications of expression. The space
itself, bombed after World War II and
then fully restored, is worth visiting just
for the unique view of the Galleria dome
through the large windows. You can
reach the gallery via the elevator next
to the Prada store. ⊠ Galleria Vittorio
Emanuele II, Piazza del Duomo, Duomo
☎ 02/56662611 ⊕ www.fondazioneprada.
org/visit/milano-osservatorio 🎟 €10; €15,
including Fondazione Prada ⊘ Closed
Tues. Ⓜ Duomo.

Museo del Novecento
ART MUSEUM | Ascend a Guggenheim-es-
que spiral walkway to reach the modern
works at this petite yet dense collection
of Italian contemporary art, adjacent
to the Duomo. The museum highlights
20th-century Italian artists, including a
strong showing of Futurists, like Boccioni
and Severini, and sculptures from Marini,
along with a smattering of works by

other European artists, including Picasso,
Braque, and Matisse. ⊠ Via Marconi 1,
Duomo ☎ 02/88444061 ⊕ www.muse-
odelnovecento.org 🎟 €5 (free every 1st
and 3rd Tues. of month after 2) ⊘ Closed
Mon. Ⓜ Duomo.

★ **Palazzo Reale**
ART MUSEUM | Elaborately decorated with
painted ceilings and grand staircases, this
former royal palace close to the Duomo
is almost worth a visit in itself; however,
it also functions as one of Milan's major
art galleries, with a focus on modern artists. Exhibitions have highlighted works
by Picasso, Chagall, Warhol, Pollock, and
Kandinsky. Check the website before
you visit to see what's on; purchase
tickets online in advance to save time
in the queues, which are often long and
chaotic. ⊠ Piazza del Duomo 12, Duomo
☎ 02/88445181 ⊕ www.palazzorealemi-
lano.it 🎟 Varies by exhibition ⊘ Closed
Mon. Ⓜ Duomo.

Pinacoteca Ambrosiana
ART MUSEUM | Cardinal Federico Bor-
romeo, one of Milan's native saints,
founded this picture gallery in 1618 with
the addition of his personal art collection to a bequest of books to Italy's
first public library. The core works of
the collection include such treasures as
Caravaggio's Basket of Fruit, Raphael's
monumental preparatory drawing (known
as a "cartoon") for The School of Athens,
which hangs in the Vatican, and Leonardo
da Vinci's Portrait of a Musician. The
highlight for many is Leonardo's Codex
Atlanticus, which features thousands
of his sketches and drawings. ⊠ Piazza
Pio XI 2, Duomo ☎ 02/806921 ⊕ www.
ambrosiana.it/en 🎟 €15 ⊘ Closed Mon.
Ⓜ Duomo.

Santa Maria Presso San Satiro
CHURCH | Just a few steps from the Duo-
mo, this architectural gem was first built
in 876 and later perfected by Bramante
(1444–1514), demonstrating his command of proportion and perspective—
hallmarks of Renaissance architecture.

Bramante tricks the eye with a famous optical illusion that makes a small interior seem extraordinarily spacious and airy, while accommodating a beloved 13th-century fresco. ✉ *Via Torino 17–19, Duomo* ☎ *02/874683* [M] *Duomo; Tram No. 2, 3, 4, 12, 14, 19, 20, 24, or 27.*

🍴 Restaurants

Giacomo Arengario

$$$ | **ITALIAN** | Join businesspeople, ladies who lunch, and in-the-know travelers at this elegant restaurant atop the Museo del Novecento and with a glorious Duomo view (be sure to request a window table, though, or risk being relegated to a viewless back room). To complement the vistas, choose from a selection of well-prepared seafood, pasta, and meat courses for lunch and dinner; the servers are happy to recommend pairings from the extensive wine list. **Known for:** wine pairings; contemporary Milanese dishes; amazing Duomo views from tables by the windows. [$] *Average main: €30* ✉ *Via Marconi 1, Duomo* ☎ *02/72093814* 🌐 *www.giacomomilano.com* [M] *Duomo.*

La Vecchia Latteria

$$ | **VEGETARIAN** | In its two small dining rooms, this family-owned lunch spot serves an impressive amount of vegetarian cuisine. Nestled on a small street just steps away from the Duomo, it offers an array of freshly prepared seasonal selections from a daily-changing menu; try the *misto forno* (mixed plate), which offers a taste of several different small dishes. **Known for:** retro '50s atmosphere; varied menu; Italian-focused vegetarian cuisine. [$] *Average main: €15* ✉ *6 Via dell'Unione, Duomo* ☎ *02/874401* 🕒 *Closed Sun. No dinner* [M] *Duomo or Missori.*

★ **Piz**

$ | **PIZZA** | Fun, lively, and full of locals, this casual and inexpensive pizzeria on a side street near the Duomo has just three kinds of thin-crust pizza on the menu—luckily, all are excellent. Choose from margherita, bianca (white, with no tomato), and marinara (with no mozzarella); although you'll inevitably need to wait, you'll likely get a free glass of prosecco and a slice of pizza while you do. **Known for:** bustling vibe; free before- and after-dinner drinks; seasonal changing bianca pizza. [$] *Average main: €9* ✉ *Via Torino 34, Duomo* ☎ *02/86453482* [M] *Duomo; Tram No. 2, 3, or 14.*

☕ Coffee and Quick Bites

Camparino in Galleria

$$$ | **CAFÉ** | One thing has remained constant in the Galleria: the Camparino, whose inlaid counter, mosaics, and wrought-iron fixtures have been welcoming tired shoppers since 1867. In its latest incarnation, star chef Davide Oldani offers a menu of Pan'cot—roasted bread topped with veggies, fish, or meat, to be enjoyed with a Campari aperitif—served in pretty Bar di Passo downstairs, while a more extensive range of Campari cocktails paired with food for aperitivo or dinner is available in elegant Sala Spiritello upstairs. **Known for:** prime people-watching; high-end aperitivo; contemporary versions of Campari cocktails. [$] *Average main: €30* ✉ *Galleria Vittorio Emanuele, Piazza del Duomo 21, Duomo* ☎ *02/86464435* 🌐 *www.camparino.com* [M] *Duomo.*

Piccolo Peck

$$ | **SANDWICHES** | The café at this foodie paradise near the Duomo features Italian specialty foods such as excellent cheeses, charcuterie, vegetables in olive oil, seafood, and sandwiches. It also reinterprets classic dishes like Russian salad and pâté, which can be washed down with a fine selection of wines by the glass or a bottle from its cellar of global labels. **Known for:** casual atmosphere; delicious Italian treats from the famed Peck deli; wide bakery selection, including classic brioche. [$] *Average main: €20* ✉ *Via Spadari 9, Duomo* ☎ *02/8023161* 🌐 *www.peck.it/en/restaurants/piccolo-peck* [M] *Tram No. 2, 12, 14, 16, or 19.*

Rinascente Food Hall

$ | **ECLECTIC** | The seventh floor of this famous Italian department store is a gourmet food market surrounded by several small restaurants that can be a good option for lunch, an aperitivo overlooking the Duomo, or dinner after a long day of shopping. There are several places to eat, including the popular mozzarella bar Obica, God Save the Food for juices and healthy bowls, and the sophisticated Maio restaurant. **Known for:** terrace overlooking the Duomo; inexpensive meals and snacks; culinary gifts to take home. [$] *Average main: €10* ✉ *Piazza Duomo, Duomo* ☎ *02/8852454* 🌐 *www.rinascente.it* [M] *Duomo.*

Hotels

Hotel Gran Duca di York

$$$ | **HOTEL** | The spare but classically elegant and efficient rooms at this hotel are arranged around a courtyard—four have private terraces—and offer good value for pricey Milan. **Pros:** central location; good breakfast; friendly staff. **Cons:** showers can be tiny; many rooms on the small side; limited amenities (no restaurant or gym). [$] *Rooms from: €230* ✉ *Via Moneta 1, Duomo* ☎ *02/874863* 🌐 *www.ducadiyork.com* 🛏 *33 rooms* 🍴 *Free Breakfast* [M] *Cordusio or Duomo; Tram No. 2, 12, 14, 16, or 27.*

Hotel Spadari al Duomo

$$$ | **HOTEL** | That this chic city-center inn is owned by an architect's family comes through in details like the custom-designed furniture and paintings by young Milanese artists in the stylish guest rooms. **Pros:** good breakfast; attentive staff; central location. **Cons:** no restaurant; street noise can be a problem; some rooms on the small side. [$] *Rooms from: €250* ✉ *Via Spadari 11, Duomo* ☎ *02/72002371* 🌐 *www.spadarihotel.com* 🛏 *40 rooms* 🍴 *Free Breakfast* [M] *Duomo; Tram No. 2, 3, 12, 14, 16, 24, or 27.*

Hotel Star

$$ | **HOTEL** | The price is reasonable, the staff are helpful, and the rooms are well equipped and comfortable, some with touches like whirlpool tubs and balconies. **Pros:** centrally located near key attractions; breakfast is included; reasonably priced. **Cons:** some bathrooms are extremely small; street noise can be an issue; quirky animal prints in some rooms not for everyone. [$] *Rooms from: €141* ✉ *Via dei Bossi 5, Duomo* ☎ *02/801501* 🌐 *www.hotelstar.it* 🛏 *30 rooms* 🍴 *Free Breakfast.*

Maison Milano | UNA Esperienze

$$$ | **HOTEL** | Inside this faithfully restored palazzo dating from the early 1900s, spaciousness is accentuated with soft white interiors, muted fabrics and marble, and contemporary lines. **Pros:** the warmth of a residence and the luxury of a design hotel; friendly staff; lovely bathrooms. **Cons:** no restaurant or bar; not much of a lobby; breakfast not included. [$] *Rooms from: €215* ✉ *Via Mazzini 4, Duomo* ☎ *02/69826982* 🌐 *www.gruppouna.it/esperienze/maison-milano* 🛏 *27 rooms* 🍴 *No Meals* [M] *Duomo; Tram No. 2, 3, 12, 14, 16, 24, or 27.*

★ Park Hyatt Milan

$$$$ | **HOTEL** | Extensive use of warm travertine stone and modern art creates a sophisticated yet inviting backdrop at the Park Hyatt, where spacious, opulent guest rooms have walk-in closets and bathrooms with double sinks, glass-enclosed rain showers, and separate soaking tubs. **Pros:** central location; excellent restaurant; contemporary decor and amenities. **Cons:** some rooms showing a little wear; very expensive; not particularly intimate. [$] *Rooms from: €1024* ✉ *Via Tommaso Grossi 1, Duomo* ☎ *02/88211234* 🌐 *milan.park.hyatt.com* 🛏 *106 rooms* 🍴 *No Meals* [M] *Duomo; Tram No. 1.*

★ Room Mate Giulia

$$$ | **HOTEL** | For hip, design-focused lodging with a friendly feel and prime location right next to the Galleria and around the corner from the Duomo, you can't do much better than the city's first outpost from Spanish hotel chain Room Mate. **Pros:** amazing location; relatively affordable rates for the area; fresh, appealing design. **Cons:** busy location means some noise in rooms; gym on the small side; breakfast room a bit cramped. [$] *Rooms from: €269* ✉ *Via Silvio Pellico 4, Duomo* ☎ *02/80888900* 🌐 *www.room-matehotels.com/en/* 🛏 *85 rooms* 🍴 *No Meals* [M] *Duomo; Tram No. 1.*

Nightlife

Bar STRAF

BARS | This architecturally stimulating but dimly lit place has such artistic features as recycled fiberglass panels and vintage 1970s furnishings. The music is an eclectic mix of chill-out tunes during the daytime, with more upbeat and vibrant tracks pepping it up at night. Located on a quiet side street near the Duomo, STRAF draws a young and lively, if tourist-heavy, crowd. ✉ *Via San Raffaele 3, Duomo* ☎ *02/805081* 🌐 *www.straf.it/bar* [M] *Duomo.*

Performing Arts

Conservatorio

MUSIC | The two halls belonging to the Conservatorio host some of the leading names in classical music. Series are organized by several organizations, including the venerable chamber music society the **Società del Quartetto**. ✉ *Via del Conservatorio 12, Duomo* ☎ *02/762110, 02/795393 Società del Quartetto* 🌐 *www.consmilano.it* [M] *San Babila; Tram No. 9, 12, 23, or 27; Bus No. 60 or 73.*

★ Teatro alla Scala

OPERA | You need know nothing of opera to sense that La Scala is closer to a cathedral than a concert hall. Hearing opera sung in this magical setting is an unparalleled experience: it is, after all, where Verdi established his reputation and where Maria Callas sang her way into opera lore. It stands as a symbol—both for the performer who dreams of singing here and for the opera buff—and its notoriously demanding audiences are apt to jeer performers who do not measure up.

If you are lucky enough to be here during opera season, do whatever is necessary to attend. Tickets go on sale two months before the first performance and are usually sold out the same day. The opening gala is December 7, the feast day of Milan patron St. Ambrose, and performances run all year, except for the end of July and August, and major holidays. For tickets, visit the box office at Largo Ghiringhelli 1, Piazza della Scala, every day from noon to 6 pm and two hours before the beginning of each performance, for same-day shows. Tickets are also available online. Tickets purchased online can be presented at the entrance with your smartphone or tablet.

Although you might not get seats for the more popular operas with big-name stars, it is worth trying; ballets are easier. There are also 140 reduced-visibility balcony tickets available for each performance on a first-come, first-served basis; for evening operas and ballets, registration for the list begins at 1 pm, and ticket recipients (with a maximum of two tickets per person) are announced at 5:30 pm.

At the Museo Teatrale alla Scala you can admire an extensive collection of librettos, paintings of the famous names of Italian opera, posters, costumes, antique instruments, and design sketches for the theater. It is also possible to take a look at the theater itself. Special exhibitions reflect current productions. ✉ *Piazza della Scala, Largo Ghiringhelli 1, Duomo* ☎ *02/72003744 theater, 02/88797473 museum* 🌐 *www.teatroallascala.org* 🎫 *Museum €10* [M] *Duomo or Cordusio; Tram No. 1.*

Shopping

Borsalino

HATS & GLOVES | The kingpin of milliners, Borsalino has managed to stay trendy since it opened in 1857. ⊠ *Galleria Vittorio Emanuele II 92, Duomo* 🕾 *02/89015436* ⊕ *www.borsalino.com* Ⓜ *Duomo; Tram No. 1.*

Gucci

MIXED CLOTHING | This Florence-born brand attracts lots of fashion-forward tourists in hot pursuit of its monogrammed bags, shoes, and accessories. ⊠ *Galleria Vittorio Emanuele II, Duomo* 🕾 *02/8597991* ⊕ *www.gucci.com* Ⓜ *Duomo; Tram No. 1.*

La Rinascente

DEPARTMENT STORE | The flagship location of this always bustling and very central department store—adjacent to both the Duomo and the Galleria Vittorio Emanuele II—carries a wide range of Italian and international brands (both high-end and casual) for men, women, and children. There's also a fine selection of beauty and home products. ⊠ *Piazza Duomo, Duomo* 🕾 *02/91387388* ⊕ *www.rinascente.it* Ⓜ *Duomo; Tram No. 1, 2, 12, 14, 16, or 27.*

Trussardi

MIXED CLOTHING | This Milan-based label offers sleek, fashion-forward accessories, leather goods, and clothes. ⊠ *Galleria San Carlo angolo, Corso Europa, 6, Duomo* 🕾 *02/783909* ⊕ *www.trussardi.com* Ⓜ *Duomo; Tram No. 1.*

Castello

This 15th-century castle is home to crypts, battlements, tunnels, and an interesting array of museums.

Sights

Castello Sforzesco

HISTORIC SIGHT | Wandering the grounds of this tranquil castle and park near the center of Milan is a great respite from the often-hectic city, and the interesting museums inside are an added bonus. For the serious student of Renaissance military engineering, the Castello must be something of a travesty, so often has it been remodeled or rebuilt since it was begun in 1450 by the condottiere, or mercenary, who founded the city's second dynastic family: Francesco Sforza, fourth duke of Milan.

Since the turn of the 20th century, the Castello has been the depository of several city-owned collections of Egyptian and other antiquities. Highlights include the Sala delle Asse, a frescoed room attributed to Leonardo da Vinci (1452–1519), and Michelangelo's unfinished *Rondanini Pietà*, believed to be his last work. The *pinacoteca* (picture gallery) features 230 paintings from medieval times to the 18th century, and the Museo dei Mobili e delle Sculture Lignee (Furniture Museum) includes a delightful collection of Renaissance treasure chests. A single ticket purchased in the office in an inner courtyard admits visitors to these separate installations, which are dispersed around the castle's two immense courtyards. ⊠ *Piazza Castello, Castello* 🕾 *02/88463700* ⊕ *www.milanocastello.it* 🎫 *Castle free, museums €5 (free every 1st and 3rd Tues. of month after 2)* ⏱ *Museums closed Mon.* Ⓜ *Cadorna, Lanza, or Cairoli; Tram No. 1, 2, 4, 12, 14, or 19; Bus No. 18, 37, 50, 58, 61, or 94.*

Performing Arts

Teatro Dal Verme

CONCERTS | Frequent classical, rock, and jazz concerts by international artists are staged here from October to May. ⊠ *Via San Giovanni sul Muro 2, Castello*

02/87905 ⊕ *www.ipomeriggi.it* Ⓜ *Cairoli; Tram No. 1 or 4.*

Sempione

Just beyond the Sforzesco Castle grounds is a large park that holds an aquarium, the Triennale museum, and the Torre Branca.

◉ Sights

Acquario Civico di Milano
(*Civic Aquarium of Milan*)
AQUARIUM | FAMILY | The third-oldest aquarium in Europe, opened in 1906, is known as much for its Art Nouveau architecture as for its small but interesting collection of marine life. You'll find 36 pools that house more than 100 species of fish, including an emphasis on Italian freshwater fish and their habitat, and one tank of species from the Red Sea. ✉ *Viale Gerolamo Gadio 2, Sempione* 🕾 *02/88465750* ⊕ *www.acquariodimilano.it* 💶 *€5; free every 1st and 3rd Tues. of month after 2* 🕘 *Closed Mon.* Ⓜ *Lanza; Tram No. 2, 4, 12, or 14; Bus No. 57.*

Parco Sempione
CITY PARK | FAMILY | Originally the gardens and parade grounds of the Castello Sforzesco, this open space was reorganized during the Napoleonic era, when the arena on its northeast side was constructed, and then turned into a park during the building boom at the end of the 19th century. It is still the lungs of the city's fashionable western neighborhoods, and the **Aquarium** still attracts Milan's schoolchildren. The park became a bit of a design showcase in 1933 with the construction of the Triennale. ✉ *Sempione* 💶 *Free* Ⓜ *Cairoli, Lanza or Cadorna; Tram No. 1, 2, 4, 12, 14, 19, or 27; Bus No. 43, 57, 61, 70, or 94.*

Torre Branca
VIEWPOINT | It is worth visiting Parco Sempione just to see the Torre Branca. Designed by the architect Gio Ponti

(1891–1979), who was behind so many of the projects that made Milan the design capital that it is, this steel tower rises 330 feet over the Triennale. Take the elevator to get a nice view of the city, then have a drink at the glitzy Just Cavalli Restaurant and Club at its base. ✉ *Parco Sempione, Sempione* 🕾 *02/3314120* ⊕ *www.museobranca.it/torre-branca-2* 💶 *€6* 🕘 *Closed Mon., Tues., and Thurs.; and mid-May–mid-Nov.* Ⓜ *Cadorna; Tram No. 1; Bus No. 61.*

Triennale Design Museum
ART MUSEUM | In addition to honoring Italy's design talent, the Triennale also offers a regular series of exhibitions on design from around the world. A spectacular bridge entrance leads to a permanent collection, an exhibition space, and a stylish café and rooftop restaurant with expansive views. The Triennale also manages the fascinating museum-studio of designer Achille Castiglioni, in nearby Piazza Castello (hour-long guided tours Tuesday–Friday at 10, 11, and noon, and one Saturday a month; €15. Call or email in advance to book: 🕾 *02/8053606 info@achillecastiglioni.it*). ✉ *Via Alemagna 6, Sempione* 🕾 *02/72434244* ⊕ *www.triennale.org* 💶 *€12* 🕘 *Closed Mon.* Ⓜ *Cadorna; Bus No. 61.*

Brera

To the north of the Duomo lie the winding streets of this elegant neighborhood, once the city's bohemian quarter.

◉ Sights

★ Pinacoteca di Brera (*Brera Art Gallery*)
ART MUSEUM | The collection here is star-studded even by Italian standards. The museum has nearly 40 rooms, arranged in chronological order—so pace yourself. One highlight is the somber, moving *Cristo Morto* (Dead Christ) by Mantegna, which dominates Room VI with its sparse palette of umber and its foreshortened perspective.

Room XXIV offers two additional highlights of the gallery: Raphael's (1483–1520) *Sposalizio della Vergine* (Marriage of the Virgin), with its mathematical composition and precise, alternating colors, portrays the betrothal of Mary and Joseph. *La Vergine con il Bambino e Santi* (Madonna with Child and Saints), by Piero della Francesca (1420–92), is an altarpiece commissioned by Federico da Montefeltro (shown kneeling, in full armor, before the Virgin); it was intended for a church to house the duke's tomb. ✉ *Via Brera 28, Brera* ☎ *02/722631* ⊕ *www.pinacotecabrera.org* 🎟 *€15* 🕑 *Closed Mon.* Ⓜ *Montenapoleone or Lanza; Tram No. 1, 4, 12, 14, or 27; Bus No. 61.*

🍴 Restaurants

★ Cittamani
$$ | MODERN INDIAN | Celebrity chef Ritu Dalmia runs well-regarded Italian restaurants in India, so it's no surprise that her first restaurant in Italy offers a mash-up of modern Indian food with Italian and international ingredients; even the decor, with shelves of pottery and terrazzo floors, is a cultural combo. Look for unexpected flavors and a mix of small plates, more substantial mains, and utterly delicious fusion desserts. **Known for:** sleek contemporary setting; nontraditional naans; Indian food quite different from the norm. 💲 *Average main: €21* ✉ *Piazza Mirabello 5, Brera* ☎ *02/38240935* ⊕ *www.cittamani.com* 🕑 *Closed Mon.* Ⓜ *Moscova or Turati; Bus No. 43 or 94.*

Fioraio Bianchi Caffè
$$$ | MODERN ITALIAN | A French-style bistro in the heart of Milan, Fioraio Bianchi Caffè was opened more than 40 years ago by Raimondo Bianchi, a great lover of flowers; in fact, eating at this restaurant is a bit like dining in a Parisian boutique with floral decor. Despite the French atmosphere, the dishes have Italian flair and ensure a classy, inventive meal. **Known for:** great spot for morning coffee and pastries; creative Italian-style bistro food; charming, flower-filled, shabby-chic setting. 💲 *Average main: €28* ✉ *Via Montebello 7, Brera* ☎ *02/29014390* ⊕ *www.fioraiobianchicaffe.it* 🕑 *Closed Sun. and 3 wks in Aug.* Ⓜ *Turati.*

Coffee and Quick Bites

N'Ombra de Vin
$ | WINE BAR | This enoteca serves wine by the glass and, in addition to the plates of *salumi* (Italian cold cuts) and cheese nibbles, has light food and not-so-light desserts. It's a great place for people-watching on Via San Marco, while indoors offers a more dimly lit, romantic setting; check out the impressive vaulted basement, where bottled wines and spirits are sold. **Known for:** solid tapas dishes; Italian and French wines; atmospheric setting in an old Augustinian refectory. 💲 *Average main: €14* ✉ *Via S. Marco 2, Brera* ☎ *02/6599650* ⊕ *www.nombradevin.it* Ⓜ *Lanza, Turati, or Montenapoleone; Tram No. 1, 2, 4, 12, or 14.*

🛏 Hotels

Bulgari Hotel Milano
$$$$ | HOTEL | Housed in an 18th-century palazzo on a quiet street a short stroll from the shops of Brera and Montenapoleone, the Bulgari offers up chic yet restrained rooms, an enormous garden, and a celebrity-chef-helmed restaurant. **Pros:** excellent spa, with heated pool, sauna, and Jacuzzi; convenient location for sightseeing; trendy and fashionable guests. **Cons:** extremely expensive; service not quite up to par; rooms are a bit bland. 💲 *Rooms from: €950* ✉ *Via Privata Fratelli Gabba 7b, Brera* ☎ *02/8058051* ⊕ *www.bulgarihotels.com/en_US/milan* 🛏 *61 rooms* 🍽 *No Meals* Ⓜ *Montenapoleone.*

▼ Nightlife

Il Bar at Bulgari Hotel Milano

BARS | Having drinks or a light lunch at the Bulgari Hotel bar lets you step off the asphalt and into one of the city's most impressive private urban gardens—even indoors you seem to be outside, separated from the elements by a spectacular wall of glass. The Bar is a great place to run into international hotel guests and jet-setting Milanese, and the staff mix up a wide range of traditional and novel drinks—including the Bulgari Cocktail with gin, Aperol, and orange, pineapple, and lime juices. ⊠ *Via Privata Fratelli Gabba 7/b, Brera* ☎ *02/8058051* ⊕ *www.bulgarihotels.com/en_US/milan/ bar-and-restaurant/il-bar* Ⓜ *Montenapole-one; Tram No. 1.*

● Shopping

With its narrow streets and outdoor cafés, Brera is one of Milan's most charming neighborhoods. Wander through it to find smaller shops with some appealing offerings from lesser-known names that cater to the well-heeled taste of this upscale area. The densest concentration is along Via Brera, Via Solferino, and Corso Garibaldi.

Mercato di Via S. Marco

MARKET | The Monday- and Thursday-morning markets here cater to the wealthy residents of the central Brera neighborhood. In addition to food stands where you can get cheese, roast chicken, and dried beans and fruits, there are several clothing and shoe stalls that are important stops for some of Milan's most elegant women. ⊠ *Via San Marco, near Via Castelfidardo, Brera* Ⓜ *Lanza; Tram No. 2, 4, 12, or 14.*

Sant'Ambrogio

If the part of the city to the north of the Duomo is dominated by shopping, Sant'Ambrogio and other parts to the south are known for art. The most famous piece is *Il Cenacolo*—known in English as *The Last Supper*. If you have time for nothing else, make sure you see this masterpiece, which is housed in the refectory of Santa Maria delle Grazie. Reservations are required to see it, and you should make yours at least three weeks before you depart for Italy, so you can plan the rest of your time in Milan.

◉ Sights

Basilica di Sant'Ambrogio (*Basilica of St. Ambrose*)

CHURCH | Milan's bishop, St. Ambrose (one of the original Doctors of the Catholic Church) consecrated this church in AD 387. St. Ambroeus, as he is known in Milanese dialect, is the city's patron saint, and his remains—dressed in elegant religious robes, a miter, and gloves—can be viewed inside a glass case in the crypt below the altar. Until the construction of the more imposing Duomo, this was Milan's most important church. Much restored and reworked over the centuries (the gold-and-gem-encrusted altar dates from the 9th century), Sant'Ambrogio still preserves its Romanesque characteristics, including 5th-century mosaics. The church is often closed for weddings on Saturday. ⊠ *Piazza Sant'Ambrogio 15, Sant'Ambrogio* ☎ *02/86450895* ⊕ *www.basilicasantam-brogio.it* Ⓜ *Sant'Ambrogio; Bus No. 50, 58, or 94.*

Chiesa di San Maurizio al Monastero Maggiore

CHURCH | Next to the Museo Civico Archeologico, you'll find this little gem of a church, constructed starting in 1503 and decorated almost completely with magnificent 16th-century frescoes.

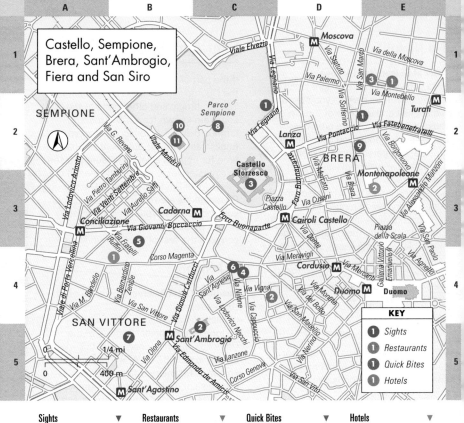

Castello, Sempione, Brera, Sant'Ambrogio, Fiera and San Siro

The modest exterior belies the treasures inside, including a concealed back room once used by nuns that includes a fascinating fresco of Noah loading the ark with animals, including two unicorns. ✉ *Corso Magenta 15, Sant'Ambrogio* ☎ *02/88445208* Ⓜ *Cadorna or Cairoli; Tram No. 16 or 27; Bus No. 50, 58, or 94.*

★ **The *Last Supper/Il Cenacolo*/Santa Maria delle Grazie**

CHURCH | Leonardo da Vinci's *The Last Supper,* housed in this church and former Dominican monastery, has had an almost unbelievable history of bad luck and neglect. Its near destruction in an American bombing raid in August 1943 was only the latest chapter in a series of misadventures, including—if one 19th-century source is to be believed—being whitewashed over by monks. Well-meant but disastrous attempts at restoration have done little to rectify the problem of the work's placement: it was executed on a wall unusually vulnerable to climatic dampness. Yet Leonardo chose to work slowly and patiently in oil pigments, which demand dry plaster, instead of proceeding hastily on wet plaster according to the conventional fresco technique. After years of restorers patiently shifting from one square centimeter to another, Leonardo's masterpiece is free of centuries of retouching, grime, and dust. Astonishing clarity and luminosity have been regained, helped by lighting, and a timed entry system where small groups are ushered into climate-controlled rooms with automatic glass doors, to prevent humidity. Before and after viewing the masterpiece you can read displays about the restoration process.

Despite Leonardo's carefully preserved preparatory sketches, in which the apostles are clearly labeled by name, there still remains some small debate about a few identities in the final arrangement. There can be no mistaking Judas, however—small and dark, his hand calmly reaching forward to the bread, isolated from the terrible confusion that has taken the hearts of the others. Art historian Frederick Hartt offers an elegantly terse explanation for why the composition works: it combines "dramatic confusion" with "mathematical order." Certainly, the amazingly skillful and unobtrusive repetition of threes—in the windows, in the grouping of the figures, and in their placement—adds a mystical aspect to what at first seems simply the perfect observation of spontaneous human gesture.

Reservations are required to view the work. Viewings are in 15-minute timed-entry slots, and visitors must arrive 30 minutes before their assigned time in order not to lose their place. Reservations can be made online. Reserve at least three weeks ahead if you want a Saturday slot, two weeks for a weekday slot. Some city bus tours include a visit in their regular circuit, which may be a good option.

The painting was executed in what was the order's refectory, which is now referred to as the Cenacolo Vinciano. Take a moment to visit Santa Maria delle Grazie itself. It's a handsome, completely restored church with a fine dome and a cloister, both of which Bramante added around the time Leonardo was commissioned to paint *The Last Supper.* ✉ *Piazza Santa Maria delle Grazie 2, off Corso Magenta, Sant'Ambrogio* ☎ *02/92800360 reservations, 02/4676111 church* ⊕ *www.cenacolovinciano.net* 🎟 *Last Supper €15* ⊘ *Closed Mon.* Ⓜ *Cadorna or Conciliazione; Tram No. 18.*

Museo Civico Archeologico

(*Municipal Archaeological Museum*)

HISTORY MUSEUM | Appropriately situated in the heart of Roman Milan, this museum housed in a former monastery displays everyday utensils, jewelry, silver plate, and several fine examples of mosaic pavement from Mediolanum, the ancient Roman name for Milan.

The museum opens into a garden that is flanked by the square tower of the Roman circus and the polygonal Ansperto tower, adorned with frescoes dating to the end of the 13th and 14th centuries that portray St. Francis and other saints receiving the stigmata. ⊠ *Corso Magenta 15, Sant'Ambrogio* ☎ *02/88445208* ⊕ *www.museoarcheologicomilano.it* ⊠ *€5 (free every 1st and 3rd Tues. of month after 2)* ⊗ *Closed Mon.* Ⓜ *Cadorna or Cairoli; Tram No. 16 or 27; Bus No. 50, 58, or 94.*

Museo Nazionale della Scienza e Tecnologia Leonardo da Vinci (*National Museum of Science and Technology*)

SCIENCE MUSEUM | FAMILY | This converted cloister is best known for the collection of models based on Leonardo da Vinci's sketches. One of the most visited rooms features interactive, moving models of the famous *vita aerea* (aerial screw) and *ala battente* (beating wing), thought to be forerunners of the modern helicopter and airplane, respectively. The museum also houses a varied collection of industrial artifacts, including trains, and several reconstructed workshops, including a watchmaker's, a lute maker's, and an antique pharmacy. ⊠ *Via San Vittore 21, Sant'Ambrogio* ☎ *02/02485551* ⊕ *www.museoscienza.org* ⊠ *€10, €18 including tour of submarine (€20 when reserved in advance)* ⊗ *Closed Mon.* Ⓜ *Sant'Ambrogio; Bus No. 50, 58, or 94.*

🍴 Restaurants

DaDa in Taverna

$$ | MODERN ITALIAN | This wood-paneled taverna (formerly known as Taverna Moriggi) near the stock exchange, within a house from the 14th century, was transformed into a contemporary restaurant and cocktail bar; it's the perfect spot to enjoy a mix of both traditional and more innovative fare. Pastas like a traditional carbonara and robust secondi like roasted leg of lamb are available at dinner. **Known for:** historical setting with a modern edge; fantastic wine and cocktail selection; inventive dishes. Ⓢ *Average main: €21* ⊠ *Via Morigi 8, Sant'Ambrogio* ☎ *02/36755232* ⊕ *www.dadaintaverna.com* ⊗ *No dinner Mon.* Ⓜ *Cairoli or Cordusio; Tram 1, 2, 4, 12, 14, 16, or 27.*

Hotels

Antica Locanda Leonardo

$$ | HOTEL | A feeling of relaxation prevails in this 19th-century building, and the neighborhood—the church that houses *The Last Supper* is a block away—is one of Milan's most desired and historic. **Pros:** very quiet and homey; friendly, helpful staff; breakfast is ample. **Cons:** breakfast is an extra fee; old-fashioned decor; more like a bed-and-breakfast than a hotel. Ⓢ *Rooms from: €150* ⊠ *Corso Magenta 78, Sant'Ambrogio* ☎ *02/48014197* ⊕ *www.anticalocandaleonardo.com* ⊗ *Closed 1st wk in Jan. and 3 wks in Aug.* ⌷ *24 rooms* ⫶Ⓞⶓ *No Meals* Ⓜ *Conciliazione, Sant'Ambrogio, or Cadorna; Tram No. 1, 16, 19, or 27.*

Fiera and San Siro

Fiera is a quiet suburb northwest of the city center. Neighboring San Siro is home to Stadio Meazza (commonly known as San Siro Stadium), where AC and Inter Milan play their home matches.

Activities

San Siro Stadium (Stadio Meazza)

SOCCER | AC Milan and Inter Milan, two of the oldest and most successful teams in Europe, vie for the heart of soccer-mad Lombardy. For residents, the city is *Milano* but the teams are *Milan,* a vestige of their common founding as the Milan Cricket and Football Club in 1899. When an Italian-led faction broke off in 1908, the new club was dubbed F. C. Internazionale (or "Inter") to distinguish it from the bastion of English exclusivity that would become AC Milan (or simply "Milan"). Since then, the picture has become more clouded: although Milan used to pride itself as the true team of the city and of its working class, and Inter more persuasively claimed pan-Italian support, the divide among the fan base is not so clear-cut.

AC Milan and Inter Milan share the use of San Siro Stadium (Stadio Meazza) during their August–May season. With more than 60,000 of the 80,000 seats appropriated by season-ticket holders and another couple of thousand allocated to visiting fans, tickets to Sunday games can be difficult to come by. You can purchase advance AC Milan tickets online at the club's website (🌐 *www.acmilan.com*), at the Casa Milan ticket office at Via Aldo Rossi 8, or at VivaTicket sales points. They're also sold at the stadium booth on match days. For true fans, the AC Milan headquarters, called Casa Milan, includes a museum with interactive exhibits, a store selling team merchandise, and a restaurant. Inter tickets are available on the club's website (🌐 *www.inter.it*).

If you're a soccer fan but can't get in to see a game, consider taking one of the stadium tours (🌐 *www.sansirostadium.com/en/museum-tour/tour*). ✉ *Piazzale Angelo Moratti, San Siro* ☎ *02/48798201* 🌐 *www.sansirostadium.com* [M] *San Siro Stadio; Tram No. 16; Bus No. 49.*

Quadrilatero

Via Manzoni, which lies northeast of La Scala, leads to Milan's Quadrilatero della Moda, or fashion district.

👁 Sights

Museo Bagatti Valsecchi

HISTORIC HOME | Glimpse the lives of 19th-century Milanese aristocrats in a visit to this lovely historic house museum, once the home of two brothers, Barons Fausto and Giuseppe Bagatti. Family members inhabited the house until 1974; it opened to the public as a museum in 1984. The house is decorated with the brothers' fascinating collection of 15th- and 16th-century Renaissance art, furnishings, and objects, including armor, musical instruments, and textiles. The detailed audio guide included with admission provides a thorough insight into the history of the artworks and intriguing stories of the family itself. ✉ *Via Gesu 5, Quadrilatero* ☎ *02/76006132* 🌐 *museobagattivalsecchi.org* 🎫 *€10* 🕒 *Closed Mon. and Tues.* [M] *Montenapoleone; Tram No. 1.*

Museo Poldi-Pezzoli

ART MUSEUM | This exceptional museum, opened in 1881, was once a private residence and collection, and contains not only pedigreed paintings but also porcelain, textiles, and a cabinet with scenes from Dante's life. The gem is undoubtedly *Portrait of a Lady*, by Piero del Pollaiolo (1431–98), one of the city's most prized treasures and the source of the museum's logo. The collection also includes masterpieces by Botticelli (1445–1510), Andrea Mantegna (1431–1506), Giovanni Bellini (1430–1516), and Fra Filippo Lippi (1406–69). ✉ *Via Manzoni 12, Quadrilatero* ☎ *02/794889* 🌐 *www.museopoldipezzoli.it* 🎫 *€14* 🕒 *Closed Tues.* [M] *Montenapoleone or Duomo; Tram No. 1.*

🍴 Restaurants

Don Carlos

$$$$ | **ITALIAN** | One of the few restaurants open after La Scala lets out, Don Carlos, in the Grand Hotel et de Milan, is nothing like its indecisive operatic namesake (whose betrothed was stolen by his father). Flavors are bold, presentation is precise and full of flair, service is attentive, and the walls are blanketed with sketches of the theater. **Known for:** late-night hours; homemade pasta; veal Milanese. [$] *Average main: €39* ✉ *Grand Hotel et de Milan, Via Manzoni 29, Quadrilatero* ☎ *02/72314640* 🕒 *No lunch* [M] *Montenapoleone; Tram No. 1 or 2.*

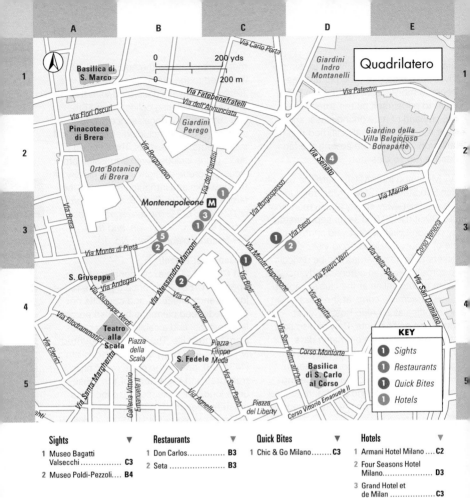

Sights ▼

1 Museo Bagatti
  Valsecchi **C3**
2 Museo Poldi-Pezzoli.... **B4**

Restaurants ▼

1 Don Carlos.............. **B3**
2 Seta **B3**

Quick Bites ▼

1 Chic & Go Milano........ **C3**

Hotels ▼

1 Armani Hotel Milano **C2**
2 Four Seasons Hotel
  Milano................... **D3**
3 Grand Hotel et
  de Milan **C3**
4 Hotel Senato **D2**
5 Mandarin Oriental,
  Milan **B3**

★ Seta

$$$$ | **MODERN ITALIAN** | Modern Italian cuisine made using interesting ingredients is the draw at this restaurant with sophisticated brown-and-turquoise decor in Milan's Mandarin Oriental Hotel. The best way to experience the intricate dishes is through the seven-course tasting menu; for a less expensive option, opt for the three-course "carte blanche" lunch menu. **Known for:** top-notch service; wonderful Italo-centric wine list; ultracreative dishes. $ Average main: €150 ⊠ Via Andegari 9, Quadrilatero ☎ 02/87318897 ⊕ www.mandarinoriental.com/milan/ la-scala/fine-dining/restaurants/italian-cuisine/seta ⊗ Closed Sun. and Mon.,1st wk of Jan., and 3 wks in Aug. Ⓜ Montenapoleone; Tram No. 1.

☕ Coffee and Quick Bites

Chic & Go Milano

$ | **MODERN ITALIAN** | Step into these stylish and trendy surroundings for a quick sandwich as exquisite as the fashions in the nearby shops. Though the lobster panini will run you a pretty penny, other top-notch items—like crab, salmon, prosciutto, Angus tartare, and mozzarella di bufala—are not a bad deal. **Known for:** convenient location near shopping; regional meats; gourmet sandwiches. $ Average main: €8 ⊠ Via Montenapoleone 25, Quadrilatero ☎ 02/782648 Ⓜ Montenapoleone; Tram No. 1.

🛏 Hotels

★ Armani Hotel Milano

$$$$ | **HOTEL** | Located in Milan's fashion district, this minimalist boutique hotel looks like it has been plucked from the pages of a sleek shelter magazine, and it should: it was designed by fashion icon Giorgio Armani to evoke the same sculptural, streamlined aesthetic—and tailored comfort—as his signature clothing. **Pros:** complimentary (except for alcohol) minibar; great location near major shopping

streets; lovely spa area and 24-hour gym. **Cons:** a few signs of wear and tear; some noise issues from neighboring rooms; breakfast (only included in some rates) not up to par. $ Rooms from: €860 ⊠ Via Manzoni 31, Quadrilatero ☎ 02/88838888 ⊕ www.armanihotelmilano.com ⌁ 95 rooms ⍾| No Meals Ⓜ Montenapoleone.

Four Seasons Hotel Milano

$$$$ | **HOTEL** | Built in the 15th century as a convent, with a colonnaded cloister, this sophisticated retreat in the heart of Milan's upscale shopping district certainly exudes a feeling that is anything but urban. **Pros:** quiet, elegant setting that feels removed from noisy central Milan; large rooms; friendly and helpful staff. **Cons:** expensive; breakfast isn't included in the rate; decor is a bit old-fashioned. $ Rooms from: €825 ⊠ Via Gesù 6–8, Quadrilatero ☎ 02/77088 ⊕ www.fourseasons.com/milan ⌁ 118 rooms ⍾| No Meals Ⓜ Montenapoleone; Tram No. 1.

Grand Hotel et de Milan

$$$$ | **HOTEL** | Only blocks from La Scala, you'll find everything you would expect from a traditionally elegant European hotel, where tapestries and persimmon velvet enliven a 19th-century look without sacrificing dignity and luxury. **Pros:** traditional and elegant; staff go above and beyond to meet guest needs; great location off Milan's main shopping streets. **Cons:** some small rooms; no spa; gilt decor may not suit those who like more modern design. $ Rooms from: €574 ⊠ Via Manzoni 29, Quadrilatero ☎ 02/723141 ⊕ www.grandhoteletdemilan.it ⌁ 72 rooms, 23 suites ⍾| No Meals Ⓜ Montenapoleone.

Hotel Senato

$$$ | **HOTEL** | The central courtyard of this boutique hotel near Milan's fashion district is covered in a layer of water, a cheeky nod to the Naviglio Grande canal that once ran in front of the 19th-century palace, which now has a sleek, minimalist design and artsy touches like brass ginkgo biloba–leaf lamps, serpentine

mosaic floor patterns, and flowers and music selected by "curators." Relatively simple white-on-white guest rooms have black and gray accents, high ceilings, oak parquet floors, and white Carrara marble bathrooms; try for a room with a private terrace overlooking the peaceful courtyard. **Pros:** cool designer touches; convenient location; lovely breakfast buffet with local products. **Cons:** basic gym facilities; noise can be an issue; some rooms on the small side. [$] *Rooms from: €250* ✉ *Via Senato 22, Quadrilatero* ☎ *02/781236* 🌐 *www.senatohotelmilano.it* 🛏 *43 rooms* 🍴 *Free Breakfast* [M] *Turati or Palestro; Tram No. 1; Bus No. 61 or 94.*

★ Mandarin Oriental, Milan

$$$$ | **HOTEL** | **FAMILY** | A sense of refined luxury pervades the guest rooms and public spaces of this sophisticated hotel, located just off the main Via Montenapoleone shopping street; from the elegant bedrooms with supercomfortable beds and oversize bathrooms with underfloor heating to the highly rated restaurant and one of the largest spas in Milan (9,700 square feet), you'll be taken care of here. **Pros:** wonderful and attentive service; top restaurant on-site; tranquil spa and 24-hour fitness center. **Cons:** can be difficult to find; only some rooms have views; very expensive. [$] *Rooms from: €700* ✉ *Via Andegari 9, Quadrilatero* ☎ *02/87318888* 🌐 *www.mandarinoriental.com* 🛏 *70 rooms, 34 suites* 🍴 *No Meals* [M] *Montenapoleone; Tram No. 1.*

Nightlife

Armani/Bamboo Bar

BARS | With high ceilings, louvered windows, and expansive views of the city's rooftops, this modern architectural marvel is a great spot to enjoy a relaxing cup of tea or a predinner aperitivo. ✉ *Via Manzoni 31, Quadrilatero* ☎ *02/88838703* 🌐 *www.armanihotelmilano.com/dine/armani-bamboo-bar* [M] *Montenapoleone; Tram No. 1.*

Shopping

The heart of Milan's shopping reputation is the Quadrilatero della Moda district, north of the Duomo. Here the world's leading designers compete for shoppers' attention, showing off their ultrastylish clothes in stores that are works of high style themselves. It's difficult to find any bargains, but regardless of whether you're making a purchase, the area is a great place for window-shopping and people-watching.

Armani Megastore

OTHER SPECIALTY STORE | Armani Junior, Emporio Armani, Armani Fiori (flowers), Armani Dolci (chocolate), and Armani Libri (books) are all under this monumental store's roof. ✉ *Via Manzoni 31, Quadrilatero* ☎ *02/62312600* 🌐 *www.armani.com* [M] *Montenapoleone; Tram No. 1.*

★ DMAG Outlet

MIXED CLOTHING | This store has some of the best prices in the area for luxury items, such as Prada, Gucci, Lanvin, and Cavalli. DMAG has two other locations, at Via Forcella 13 and Via Bigli 4. ✉ *Via Manzoni 44, Quadrilatero* ☎ *02/36514365* 🌐 *www.dmag.eu* [M] *Montenapoleone; Tram No. 1.*

★ Dolce & Gabbana

MIXED CLOTHING | This fabulous duo has created an empire based on sultry designs for men and women. The gorgeous three-story flagship store features clothing for both, plus accessories. ✉ *Via della Spiga 2, Quadrilatero* ☎ *02/795747* 🌐 *www.dolcegabbana.it* [M] *San Babila; Tram No. 61 or 94.*

Dondup

MIXED CLOTHING | Started in 1999, Dondup is a Milanese brand that has captured the essence of casual chic. But it's no longer just a brand for denim lovers: its flagship store houses menswear, women's wear, accessories, and shoe collections. ✉ *Via della Spiga 50, Quadrilatero*

☎ *02/20242232* ⊕ *www.dondup.com* Ⓜ *Montenapoleone; Tram No. 1.*

Giorgio Armani

MIXED CLOTHING | Find Armani's apparel and accessories for both men and women in the brand's newest boutique. ✉ *Via Sant'Andrea 9, Quadrilatero* ☎ *02/76003234* ⊕ *www.armani.com* Ⓜ *San Babilo.*

Missoni

MIXED CLOTHING | Famous for their kaleidoscope-pattern knits, this family-run brand sells whimsical designs for men and women. ✉ *Via Sant'Andrea, angolo Via Bagutta, Quadrilatero* ☎ *02/76003555* ⊕ *www.missoni.com* Ⓜ *Montenapoleone or San Babila; Tram No. 1.*

Miu Miu

MIXED CLOTHING | Prada's more upbeat, youthful brand has a wide offering of boldly printed women's fashions and accessories. ✉ *Via Sant'Andrea 21, Quadrilatero* ☎ *02/76001799* ⊕ *www.miumiu.com* Ⓜ *Montenapoleone, San Babila, or Palestro; Tram No. 1.*

Moschino

MIXED CLOTHING | Known for its bold prints, colors, and appliqués, Moschino is a brand for daring fashionistas. ✉ *Via Sant'Andrea 25, Quadrilatero* ☎ *02/76022639* ⊕ *www.moschino.com* Ⓜ *Montenapoleone, San Babila, or Palestro; Tram No. 1.*

Prada

MIXED CLOTHING | Founded in Milan in 1913 selling steamer trunks and handbags, Prada has several locations throughout the city. Its stores on Via Montenapoleone showcase its women's (Via Montenapoleone 8) and men's fashions (Via Montenapoleone 6). ✉ *Via Montenapoleone 8, Quadrilatero* ☎ *02/7771771* ⊕ *www.prada.com* Ⓜ *Montenapoleone, San Babila, or Palestro; Tram No. 1.*

Roberto Cavalli

MIXED CLOTHING | Famous for his wild-animal prints, Roberto Cavalli creates sexy designs for men and women. ✉ *Via Montenapoleone 6, Quadrilatero* ☎ *02/7630771* ⊕ *www.robertocavalli.com* Ⓜ *San Babila.*

Salvatore Ferragamo Donna

LEATHER GOODS | This Florence-based brand is a leader in leather goods and accessories, and carries designs for women in this store. ✉ *Via Montenapoleone 3, Quadrilatero* ☎ *02/76000054* ⊕ *www.ferragamo.com* Ⓜ *San Babila.*

Salvatore Ferragamo Uomo

LEATHER GOODS | Ferragamo's men's accessories, leather goods, and ties are a staple for Milan's male fashion set. ✉ *Via Montenapoleone 20/4, Quadrilatero* ☎ *02/76006660* ⊕ *www.ferragamo.com* Ⓜ *Montenapoleone; Tram No. 1.*

Tod's

LEATHER GOODS | This leather-goods leader sells luxury handbags as well as a variety of shoes for men and women. It also offers men's and women's clothing. ✉ *Via Montenapoleone 13, Quadrilatero* ☎ *02/76002423* ⊕ *www.tods.com* Ⓜ *Montenapoleone, San Babila, or Palestro; Tram No. 1.*

Valentino

MIXED CLOTHING | Even after the departure of its founding father, Valentino Garavani, this fashion brand still flourishes. ✉ *Via Montenapoleone 20, Quadrilatero* ☎ *02/76006182* ⊕ *www.valentino.com* Ⓜ *Montenapoleone; Tram No. 1.*

Versace

MIXED CLOTHING | Run by flamboyant Donatella Versace and known for its rock-and-roll styling, the first store of this fashion house opened on Via della Spiga in 1978, not far from its current location in the Quadrilatero della Moda shopping district. ✉ *Via Monte Napoleone, 11, Quadrilatero* ☎ *02/76008528* ⊕ *www.versace.com* Ⓜ *San Babila or Montenapoleone.*

8

Milan, Lombardy, and the Lakes MILAN

Porta Garibaldi

This stylish, upscale, and buzzing district is home to the emblematic 10 Corso Como concept store and the colorful and lively Piazza Gae Aulenti, which is a study in Milan's modern architecture, including the 757-foot UniCredit Tower. New construction, stylish restaurants, and urban parks provide a modern break from historical sightseeing.

Sights

ADI Design Museum Compasso d'Oro
OTHER MUSEUM | More than 350 of the most renowned Italian industrial design objects from the last 65 years are showcased in this former Enel electricity plant (with two original transformers still visible in one gallery), which opened as a museum in 2021. The items in the permanent collection were selected during biennial judging for *Compasso d'Oro* (golden compass) awards from 1954 until today. Some of the exhibits are grouped by category, like cars (1960 Abarth-Fiat Monza Zagato, 1959 Fiat 500, and 2014 Ferrari F12berlinetta) and coffeemakers (Alessi's 9090 from 1979 and Napoletana from 1981). There's even a 1960 Flying Dutchman boat from Alpa. ✉ *Piazza Compasso d'Oro, 1, Garibaldi* ☎ *02/36693790* 🌐 *www.adidesignmuseum.org* 🎟 *€12* 🕒 *Closed Mon.* ☞ *Tickets may be purchased online, or at the museum with a credit card or mobile wallet (no cash accepted)* [M] *Garibaldi.*

Piazza Gae Aulenti
PLAZA/SQUARE | Welcome to the modern era. The piazza named for the famed Italian female architect is a stroll into the future of architectural design. Here you'll find Italy's tallest skyscraper (the 757-foot mirrored and spired UniCredit Tower), IBM Studios (a curved and wood-slatted innovation lab), a Tesla dealership, and an LED tree surrounded by reflective pools. Nearby are Bosco Verticale—two apartment buildings covered in more than 900 hanging trees—part of Stefano Boeri's "Vertical Forest" project, which launched in 2014 to improve air quality in cities (the studio has since created similar structures in more than 20 locations across the globe). Linger through a botanical garden, Biblioteca degli Alberi (library of trees), and join locals picnicking when the weather cooperates. ✉ *Piazza Gae Aulenti, Garibaldi* [M] *Garibaldi.*

Restaurants

★ **Ceresio 7 Pools & Restaurant**
$$$$ | **CONTEMPORARY** | Book well in advance for one of Milan's most fashionable eateries, where the tables are lacquered red and modern artwork crowds the walls—exactly what you'd expect from the twin brothers, Dean and Dan Caten, behind the fashion label Dsquared2. The food cred matches the scene—with fresh, creative, sophisticated pastas and other dishes. **Known for:** swimming pools and terrace views; place for seeing and being seen; luxe ingredients like lobster, king crab, and truffles. [$] *Average main: €37* ✉ *Via Ceresio 7, Garibaldi* ☎ *02/31039221* 🌐 *www.ceresio7.com* [M] *Garibaldi; Tram No. 2, 4, 12, or 14; Bus No. 37 or 190.*

Ratanà
$$ | **NORTHERN ITALIAN** | Chef Cesare Battisti infuses the Milanese dishes of his childhood with a contemporary twist at this lively restaurant. Its two patios face a park with skyline views, and its dining room is decorated with vintage items (like an Olivetti typewriter and Scandalli accordion). **Known for:** more than 500 wines; setting in a former historical house; meat- and fish-focused menu with contemporary and traditional dishes. [$] *Average main: €24* ✉ *Via Gaetano de Castillia, 28, Garibaldi* ☎ *02/87128855* 🌐 *www.ratana.it* 🕒 *Closed 2 wks in Aug. and 2 wks in Dec.* [M] *Gioia.*

Coffee and Quick Bites

Zàini

$ | BAKERY | The Zàini family opened its chocolate factory here in 1913, on a side street off Corso Como. Today, its black-and-white marble-tile–floored and chandelier-lit café, is found just past flagship stores for Dsquared2 and Moschino. **Known for:** elegant breakfast or aperitivo spot; artfully wrapped chocolate gifts; decadent hot chocolate. $ *Average main: €10 ⊠ Via Carlo de Cristoforis, 5, Garibaldi ☎ 02/694914449 ⊕ www.zainispa.com* Ⓜ *Garibaldi.*

Hotels

Hotel Viu Milan

$$$ | HOTEL | A short walk from trendy Corso Como and the historic Cimitero Monumentale, this sleek business-focused hotel features vertical gardens outside and contemporary Italian-designed furnishings within—but its true pièce de résistance is an inviting rooftop pool with panoramic views. **Pros:** stylish modern decor; high-quality food; spacious bathrooms. **Cons:** rooftop terrace sometimes not useable due to events; hotel has a signature scent, which may bother perfume-averse guests; out-of-the-way location for central Milan. $ *Rooms from: €252 ⊠ Via Aristotile Fioravanti 6, Garibaldi ☎ 02/80010910 ⊕ www.hotelviumilan. com ⊅ 124 rooms* ⊙ *No Meals* Ⓜ *Monumentale; Tram No. 10, 12, or 14.*

Ⓨ Nightlife

★ Blue Note

LIVE MUSIC | The first European branch of the famous New York nightclub features regular performances by some of the most famous names in jazz, as well as blues and rock concerts. Dinner is also available. ⊠ *Via Borsieri 37, Garibaldi ☎ 02/69016888 ⊕ www.bluenotemilano. com* Ⓜ *Isola; Tram No. 7, 31, or 33.*

Dry Milano

BARS | A hot spot for both classic and creative cocktails, this trendy industrial space packed with hip locals has a pizza joint in the back if you get hungry. There's a second location at Viale Vittorio Veneto 28. ⊠ *Via Solferino 33, Garibaldi ☎ 02/63793414 ⊕ www.drymilano.it* Ⓜ *Moscova, Turati, or Repubblica; Tram No. 1, 9, or 33; Bus No. 37.*

Shopping

★ 10 Corso Como

OTHER SPECIALTY STORE | A shrine to Milan's creative fashion sense, the concept store 10 Corso Como was founded by the former fashion editor and publisher Carla Sozzani. The clothing and design establishment also includes a restaurant-café, gallery, bookstore, and small hotel. ⊠ *Corso Como 10, Corso Como ☎ 02/29013581 ⊕ www.10corsocomo. com* Ⓜ *Porta Garibaldi.*

Repubblica

Some of the city's best hotels can be found around the Piazza della Repubblica.

Ⓒ Coffee and Quick Bites

★ Pavè

$ | BAKERY | Your main problem at Pavè will be deciding what to order among rows of cakes, tarts, classic Italian brioches (with sweet fillings like cream and jam), and other pastries. When everything is this drool-worthy, your best strategy is to come with friends and share your favorites. **Known for:** sandwiches and crostini on house-made bread; vegan pastries; chocolate and fruit-filled tarts. $ *Average main: €10 ⊠ Via Felice Casati, 27, Repubblica ☎ 02/37905491 ⊕ www.pavemilano.com* ⊙ *No dinner* Ⓜ *Repubblica.*

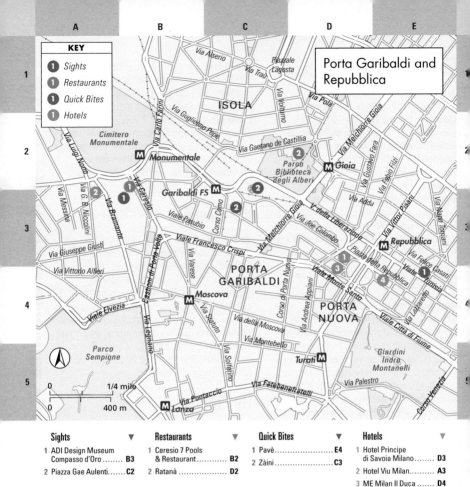

Porta Garibaldi and Repubblica

Sights	▼	Restaurants	▼	Quick Bites	▼	Hotels	▼
1 ADI Design Museum Compasso d'Oro **B3**		1 Ceresio 7 Pools & Restaurant **B2**		1 Pavè **E4**		1 Hotel Principe di Savoia Milano **D3**	
2 Piazza Gae Aulenti **C2**		2 Ratanà **D2**		2 Zàini **C3**		2 Hotel Viu Milan **A3**	
						3 ME Milan Il Duca **D4**	
						4 Westin Palace **E4**	

Hotels

Hotel Principe di Savoia Milano

$$$$ | **HOTEL** | Milan's grande dame has all the exquisite trappings of a traditional luxury hotel: lavish mirrors, drapes, and carpets; limousine services; and some of the city's largest guest rooms, outfitted with eclectic fin de siècle furnishings. **Pros:** substantial health club–spa; shuttle to Duomo and shopping district; close to Central Station. **Cons:** showing a bit of wear and tear; breakfast and other meals overly expensive; located in a not-very-attractive neighborhood; not near major sites. [$] *Rooms from: €450* ✉ *Piazza della Repubblica 17, Repubblica* ☎ *02/62301* 🌐 *www.dorchestercollection.com/en/milan/hotel-principe-di-savoia* 🛏 *301 rooms* 🍴 *No Meals* [M] *Repubblica; Tram No. 1, 9, or 33.*

ME Milan Il Duca

$$$ | **HOTEL** | The first Italian outpost of the Spanish hotel brand ME by Meliá has a lively party atmosphere, with rousing music playing in the lobby, a design-conscious vibe, and a happening rooftop bar with panoramic city views. **Pros:** great rooftop bar; young, vibrant atmosphere; spacious rooms. **Cons:** can be noisy; may feel overdesigned to some; no spa. [$] *Rooms from: €284* ✉ *Piazza della Repubblica 13, Repubblica* ☎ *02/35403218* 🌐 *www.melia.com/en/hotels/italy/milan/me-milan-il-duca/index.htm* 🛏 *132 rooms* 🍴 *No Meals* [M] *Repubblica; Tram No. 1, 5, 9, 10, or 33.*

Westin Palace

$$$ | **HOTEL** | Don't be fooled by the functional 1950s-era exterior of one of Milan's premier business addresses: inside, rooms have a contemporary look with soothing gray walls and marble bathrooms. **Pros:** full-service hotel with extensive amenities; good-size gym open 24/7; renovated rooms in both modern and more traditional styles. **Cons:** Wi-Fi can be spotty in some rooms; not in the most central or attractive location; lacking in local character. [$] *Rooms from: €220* ✉ *Piazza della Repubblica 20, Repubblica* ☎ *02/63361* 🌐 *www.marriott.com/hotels/travel/milwi-the-westin-palace-milan* 🛏 *231 rooms* 🍴 *No Meals* [M] *Repubblica; Tram No. 1, 5, 9, or 33.*

Nightlife

Radio Rooftop Bar

COCKTAIL LOUNGES | Some of Milan's most beautiful people congregate for an Aperol spritz and a selection of international tapas on this terrace with panoramic views of the city. Located at the top of the ME Milan Il Duca, the bar has heat lamps to keep visitors here even in cooler weather. ✉ *Piazza della Repubblica 13, Repubblica* ☎ *02/84220109* 🌐 *www.melia.com/en/hotels/italy/milan/me-milan-il-duca/restaurants.htm* [M] *Repubblica; Tram No. 1, 5, 9, 10, or 33.*

Shopping

Antonioli

MIXED CLOTHING | Antonioli raises the bar for Milan's top trendsetters. Uniting the most cutting-edge looks of each season, it is among the fashion-forward concept stores in the city. Aside from Italian brands like Valentino, it also stocks a competitive international array of designers, like Ann Demeulemeester, Rick Owens, Givenchy, Maison Margiela, and Vetements. ✉ *Via Pasquale Paoli 1, Centro Direzionale* ☎ *02/36561860* 🌐 *www.antonioli.eu* [M] *Porta Genova; Tram No. 2; Bus No. 47 or 74.*

Cinque Giornate

Located just east of the city center, Cinque Giornate marks the location of the Five Days revolt against Austrian rule in Milan.

🍴 Restaurants

Da Giacomo
$$$ | **ITALIAN** | The fashion and publishing crowds, as well as international bankers and businesspeople, favor this Milanese-Ligurian restaurant. The emphasis is on fish, and with its tile floor and bank of fresh seafood, the place has a refined neighborhood-bistro style. **Known for:** extensive wines, cocktails, and after-dinner drinks; specialty gnocchetti alla Giacomo (with seafood and tomato); sophisticated dining. [$] *Average main: €32* ✉ *Via P. Sottocorno 6, entrance in Via Cellini, Cinque Giornate* ☎ *02/76023313* 🌐 *www.giacomomilano.com* [M] *Tram No. 9, 12, 23, or 27; Bus No. 60 or 73.*

☕ Coffee and Quick Bites

De Santis
$ | **ITALIAN** | Whether you want to grab a quick sandwich, or linger with a glass of wine, since 1964, De Santis is the spot if you're hungry, any time of day. There's a selection of traditional sandwiches like Friulano with prosciutto, basil, tomato, and soft cow's milk cheese, and the Doralice with mortadella, fontina, and tomato. **Known for:** inventive sandwich fillings; sandwiches made-to-order; late-night quick meals and drinks. [$] *Average main: €12* ✉ *Via Cesare Battisti 19, Cinque Giornate* ☎ *02/72095124* 🌐 *www.paninidesantis.it* 🕒 *Closed Sun.*

Palestro

Nestled just below the Giardini Pubblici Indro Montanelli park, Palestro is filled with galleries, museums, and historical landmarks.

👁 Sights

GAM: Galleria d'Arte Moderna/Villa Reale
HISTORIC HOME | One of the city's most beautiful buildings is an outstanding example of neoclassical architecture, built between 1790 and 1796. After it was donated to Napoléon, who lived here briefly with Empress Josephine, it became known as the Villa Reale. The collection consists of works donated by prominent Milanese art collectors. It emphasizes 18th- and 19th-century Italian works, but also has a smattering of 20th-century Italian pieces. ✉ *Via Palestro 16, Palestro* ☎ *02/88445947* 🌐 *www.gam-milano.com* 🎟 *€5 (free every 1st and 3rd Tues. of month after 2)* 🕒 *Closed Mon.* [M] *Palestro or Turati; Tram No. 1 or 2; Bus No. 94 or 61.*

Villa Necchi Campiglio
NOTABLE BUILDING | In 1932, architect Piero Portaluppi designed this sprawling estate in an Art Deco style, with inspiration coming from the decadent cruise ships of the 1920s. Once owned by the Necchi Campiglio industrial family, the tasteful and elegant three-level home and garden—which sits on Via Mozart, one of Milan's most exclusive streets—is a reminder of the refined, modern culture of the nouveaux riches who accrued financial power in Milan during that era. There is also a café on the grounds that is open 10 am–6 pm. ■ **TIP→ Tours of the estate last about one hour; English-speaking tours are offered Wednesday–Saturday between 10:30 am and 2:15 pm.** ✉ *Via Mozart 14, Palestro* ☎ *02/76340121* 🌐 *www.fondoambiente.it/villa-necchi-campiglio-eng* 🎟 *From €14 for guided visits; garden-only €4.* 🕒 *Closed Mon. and Tues.* [M] *Palestro, San Babila, or Montenapoleone; Bus No. 54, 61, or 94.*

Porta Venezia

This district is home to parks and gardens, museums, galleries, and one end of the famed Corso Buenos Aires shopping street.

Sights

Giardini Pubblici Indro Montanelli (*Public Gardens Indro Montanelli*)
GARDEN | FAMILY | Giuseppe Piermarini, architect of La Scala, laid out these gardens across Via Palestro from the Villa Reale in 1770. Designed as public pleasure gardens, today they are still popular with families who live in the city center. Generations of Milanese have taken pony rides and gone on the miniature train and merry-go-round. The park also contains a small planetarium and the **Museo Civico di Storia Naturale** (Municipal Natural History Museum). ✉ *Corso Venezia 55, Porta Venezia* ☎ *02/88463337* 🎟 *Gardens free, museum €5 (free every 1st and 3rd Tues. of month after 2 and 1st Sun. of month)* ⏲ *Museum closed Mon.* [M] *Palestro; Tram No. 9, 29, or 30.*

Restaurants

Joia
$$$$ | VEGETARIAN | At this hushed, haute-cuisine vegetarian haven near Piazza della Repubblica, delicious dishes—all without eggs and many without flour—are served in a minimalist beige room that puts the focus solely on the artistry of the food. Vegetarians, who often get short shrift in Italy, will marvel at the variety of culinary offerings made from many organic and biodynamic ingredients. **Known for:** well-thought-out wine selection; ever-changing menu; imaginative presentations. [$] *Average main: €40* ✉ *Via Panfilo Castaldi 18, Porta Venezia* ☎ *02/29522124* ⏲ *Closed Sun. and Mon., 2 wks in Aug., and Dec. 24–Jan. 6* [M] *Repubblica or Porta Venezia; Tram No. 1, 5, 9, or 33.*

LùBar
$$ | SICILIAN | Dining at LùBar, which was started by three children of Milan fashion designer Luisa Beccaria and which is tucked into the side of the Galleria d'Arte Moderna, feels like eating inside a greenhouse—only with fashionable people among the trees and plants. The cozy, chic environs lend themselves perfectly to nibbling on small plates of modern Sicilian food—for lunch, an afternoon snack, or a light dinner—many served on Caltagirone ceramics straight from Sicily. **Known for:** charming, relaxed atmosphere; LùBar Spritz made with Amara, a Sicilian blood orange amaro; Sicilian street food like arancini and polpette (meatballs). [$] *Average main: €16* ✉ *Via Palestro 16, Porta Venezia* ☎ *02/83527769* 🌐 *www.lubar.it* [M] *Palestro or Turati; Tram No. 1 or 2; Bus No. 94 or 61.*

Coffee and Quick Bites

Égalité
$ | FRENCH | The 15 different types of daily breads along with tarts, croissants, and a decadent selection of other desserts have a French influence at this bakery with robin's-egg blue sidewalk tables and chairs and a viewing window into the bakers behind the scenes of it all. Grab an easy breakfast, lunch, or aperitif as you soak up the aroma of fresh-baked baguettes. **Known for:** aperitif dishes with cheeses, meats, pickles, and jams; hearty sandwiches; bread made with Moulin Céard French flour. [$] *Average main: €12* ✉ *Via Melzo 22, Porta Venezia* ☎ *02/91763465* 🌐 *www.egalitemilano.it* ⏲ *Closed Mon.*

Shopping

Milan has several shopping streets that serve nearby residential areas. **Corso Buenos Aires** begins in the Porta Venezia area, and runs northeast from the Giardini Pubblici. The wide and busy street is lined with affordable shops. It

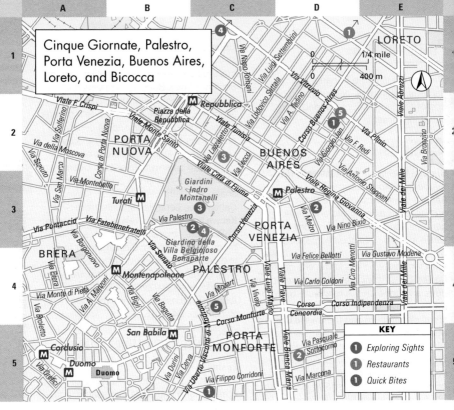

Cinque Giornate, Palestro, Porta Venezia, Buenos Aires, Loreto, and Bicocca

has one of the highest concentrations of clothing stores in Europe, so be prepared to give up halfway. Avoid weekends after 3, when it seems the entire city is here looking for bargains.

Buenos Aires

This street in northeastern Milan is one of the busiest in the city and has over 350 stores and outlets to choose from.

◉ Sights

Casa-Museo Boschi di Stefano (*Boschi di Stefano House and Museum*)
HISTORIC HOME | To most people, Italian art means Renaissance art, but the 20th century in Italy was also a time of artistic achievement. An apartment on the second floor of a stunning Art Deco building designed by Milan architect Portaluppi houses this collection, which was donated to the city of Milan in 2003 and is a tribute to the enlightened private collectors who replaced popes and nobles as Italian patrons. The walls are lined with the works of postwar greats, such as Fontana, de Chirico, and Morandi. Along with the art, the museum holds distinctive postwar furniture and stunning Murano glass chandeliers. ⌂ *Via Jan 15, Buenos Aires* ☎ *02/88463614* ⊕ *www.casamuseoboschidistefano.it* ⌂ *Free* ⊘ *Closed Mon.* Ⓜ *Lima; Tram No. 33; Bus No. 60.*

🍴 Restaurants

★ **Marghe**
$ | NEOPOLITAN | At Marghe, crafting Neapolitan-style pizza is art—as the line of people outside the restaurant each night suggests. Put your name down (they don't accept reservations), or better, arrive right before they open at 7:30 pm to grab a table in the rustic and lively dining room with exposed concrete walls, floral-tiled floors, and pendant lights, where pizzas are delivered quickly and piping hot. **Known for:** pizza made from type 1 flour and dough that rises for 48 hours; local atmosphere; ingredients from Naples and the Amalfi Coast. $ *Average main: €10* ⌂ *Via Plinio 6, Buenos Aires* ☎ *02/2047117* ⊕ *www.marghepizza.com* Ⓜ *Lima.*

Loreto

Located in the northeastern part of the city, Piazzale Loreto has a rather grim recent history: In August 1944, the Gestapo in Milan publicly executed 15 Italian resistance fighters here. Less than a year later, Benito Mussolini and a number of other high-ranking fascists, were captured and shot, with their bodies displayed here. There are no placards or signs to mark this history.

🍴 Restaurants

Da Abele
$ | ITALIAN | The superb risotto dishes at this neighborhood trattoria change with the season; you'll find at least three on the menu—meat, fish, and vegetarian—and it's tempting to try them all. The setting is relaxed and the service is informal. **Known for:** reasonable prices; cozy neighborhood favorite; meat-focused main courses like tripe. $ *Average main: €13* ⌂ *Via Temperanza 5, Loreto* ☎ *02/2613855* ⊘ *Closed Mon. No dinner weekdays and Sun.* Ⓜ *Pasteur.*

Bicocca

This university and business district plays host to musicals and concerts as well as art installations.

Sights

Pirelli HangarBicocca

ARTS CENTER | Anselm Kiefer's *The Seven Heavenly Palaces*—seven cement towers extending 43–52 feet high, along with five of Kiefer's large-scale paintings—is the must-see permanent installation at this impressive gallery in a former train factory. There are also temporary exhibitions of contemporary art throughout the year; check the website for the latest showings. ✉ *Via Chiese 2, Bicocca* ☎ *02/66111573* ⊕ *www.hangarbicocca. org* 🎟 *Free* ⊘ *Closed Mon.–Wed.* Ⓜ *Via Chiese; Bus No. 87 or 51.*

Porta Romana

Porta Romana is a hip and vibrant neighborhood.

Sights

★ Fondazione Prada

ART MUSEUM | New structures of metal and glass and revamped buildings once part of a distillery from the 1910s now contain this museum's roughly 205,000 square feet. The modern art showcased here is not for the faint of heart. Permanent pieces, such as *Haunted House,* featuring works by Louise Bourgeois and Robert Gober, are avant-garde and challenging, and temporary exhibitions highlight cutting-edge Italian and international artists. Don't hesitate to ask one of the helpful, knowledgeable staffers for guidance navigating the expansive grounds, which can be confusing. And don't miss the Wes Anderson–designed café, Bar Luce, for a drink or snack, or the restaurant Torre for an aperitivo or a full meal with panoramic views from on high. The Fondazione is a hike from the city center; expect a 10-minute walk from the metro station to the galleries. ✉ *Largo Isarco 2, Porta Romana* ☎ *02/56662611* ⊕ *www.fondazioneprada. org* 🎟 *€15 for full visit admission, which*

Formula 1 Racing

Italian Grand Prix. Italy's Formula 1 fans are passionate and huge numbers converge in early September for the Italian Grand Prix, held 15 km (9 miles) northeast of Milan in Monza. The racetrack was built in 1922 within the **Parco di Monza**. Check the website for dates, as well as for special category races, like classic cars and motorcycles. Visitors are allowed to zoom around the track on certain days—guided by a professional driver, of course. ✉ *Monza Eni Circuit, Via Vedano 5, Parco di Monza, Monza* ⊕ *www. monzanet.it.*

includes a ticket to Milano Osservatorio ⊘ *Closed Tues.* Ⓜ *Lodi TIBB; Tram No. 24; Bus No. 65.*

🍴 Restaurants

Pastamadre

$$ | **MODERN ITALIAN** | Mobiles and natural-wood lanterns decorate this cozy restaurant where house-made pasta is the main event. Start with crusty sourdough bread and small dishes of seasonal salads, vegetables, and fish served on plates crafted in a Milan ceramics studio. **Known for:** intimate setting; vegetarian options; pasta made in-house. 🅢 *Average main: €17* ✉ *Via Bernardino Corio, 8, Porta Romana* ☎ *02/55190020* ⊕ *www. pastamadremilano.it* ⊘ *Closed Mon. No dinner Sun.*

U Barba

$ | **NORTHERN ITALIAN** | Simple, fresh, authentic Ligurian (in that region's dialect the name means "the uncle") specialties will take you back to lazy summer days on the Italian Riviera—even during Milan's gray winters. Such coastal classics as *trofie al pesto* (an egg-free pasta served with pesto) and *bagnun di acciughe* (anchovy soup), coupled with a basket of warm focaccia, or a side of *farinata* (a chickpea pancake) reign supreme in this Milan favorite. **Known for:** seasonal changing menu; charming setting with vintage furniture; fresh pasta, also available to take home. $ *Average main: €14* ✉ *Via Pier Candido Decembrio 33, Porta Romana* ☎ *02/45487032* 🌐 *www.ubarba.it* 🕑 *Closed Mon. No lunch Tues.–Fri.* [M] *Lodi TIBB; Tram No. 16; Bus No. 90.*

Coffee and Quick Bites

Marlà

$ | **BAKERY** | Whether you stop for a cappuccino and one of their gigantic brioche (similar to a croissant) filled with jam, cream, or an unconventional salted-caramel for breakfast, an afternoon break with a selection of minicakes, or to eat a quick sandwich, any craving can be satisfied at Marlà—the acronym for the first names of the two owners, Marco Battaglia and Lavinia Franco. Keep in mind that you may not have room for dinner if you stop by this sea green–and–white modern café in the afternoon. **Known for:** specialty desserts from Tuscany, Lombardy, and Sicily; minisize cheesecakes and tiramisu; wide selection of breakfast pastries. $ *Average main: €10* ✉ *Corso Lodi 15, Porta Romana* ☎ *02/36536410* 🌐 *www.marlapasticceria.it/* 🕑 *Closed Mon. and Sun. afternoon.*

Ticinese

This boho district is also home to the Basilica di San Lorenzo Maggiore and the Basilica di Sant'Eustorgio.

Sights

San Lorenzo Maggiore alle Colonne

CHURCH | Sixteen ancient Roman columns line the front of this sanctuary; remnants of 4th-century Paleo-Christian mosaics survive in the Cappella di Sant'Aquilino (Chapel of St. Aquilinus). ✉ *Corso di Porta Ticinese 35, Ticinese* ☎ *02/89404129* 🌐 *www.sanlorenzomaggiore.com* 🎫 *Mosaics €2* [M] *Missori.*

Restaurants

★ **[bu:r] di Eugenio Boer**

$$$$ | **MODERN ITALIAN** | Named after the phonetic spelling of the Dutch-Italian chef's last name, this innovative, high-concept restaurant, whose quiet dining rooms are done up in gray and gold, offers a choice of interesting tasting menus and à la carte options. Boer's contemporary Italian food is beautifully presented and full of complex flavors, and the well-matched wines lean toward the natural. **Known for:** helpful and well-informed service; traditional dishes with an ultramodern spin; personalized cuisine. $ *Average main: €65* ✉ *Via Mercalli ang. Via SF D'Assisi, Ticinese* ☎ *02/62065383* 🌐 *www.restaurantboer.com* 🕑 *Closed Sun. No lunch* [M] *Crocetta; Tram No. 15; Bus No. 94.*

Hotels

★ **Aethos Milan**

$$ | **HOTEL** | The decor in this eclectic, extremely hip hotel at the foot of the lively Corso di Porta Ticinese and by the Navigli canals features sports memorabilia from golf, horseback riding, boxing, and others. **Pros:** contemporary flair; very friendly staff; interesting location near many restaurants and bars. **Cons:** bar noise can be heard in some rooms; about a half-hour hike from the Duomo and central attractions; lacking some of the amenities of large hotels. $ *Rooms from: €189* ✉ *Piazza XXIV Maggio 8,*

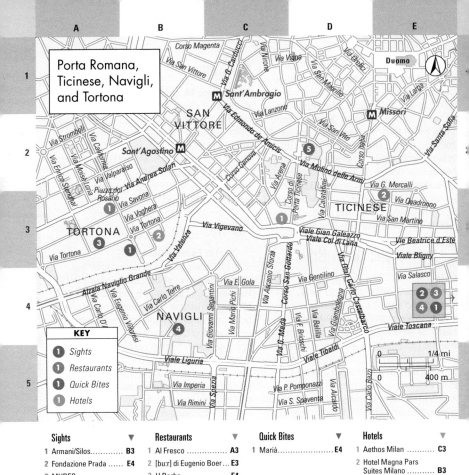

Porta Romana,
Ticinese, Navigli,
and Tortona

KEY
1 Sights
1 Restaurants
1 Quick Bites
1 Hotels

Porta Ticinese ☎ *02/89415901* ⊕ *www. aethoshotels.com/milan/* ↝ *32 suites* ⦿ *No Meals* Ⓜ *Tram No. 3 or 9.*

Navigli

One of the oldest neighborhoods in the city, Navigli is a quiet, artistic hub during the weekdays and a lively hot spot on nights and weekends.

Sights

★ Navigli District

HISTORIC DISTRICT | In medieval times, a network of *navigli*, or canals, criss-crossed the city. Almost all have been covered over, but two—Naviglio Grande and Naviglio Pavese—are still navigable. The area's chock-full of boutiques, art galleries, cafés, bars, and restaurants, and at night the Navigli serves up a scene about as close as you will get to southern Italian–style street life in Milan. On weekend nights, it is difficult to walk among the youthful crowds thronging the narrow streets along the canals. Check out the antiques fair on the last Sunday of the month from 9 to 6.

■ TIP→ **During the summer months, be sure to put on some mosquito repellent.** ⊠ *South of Corso Porta Ticinese, Navigli* Ⓜ *Porta Genova; Tram No. 2, 3, 9, 14, 15, 29, or 30.*

Nightlife

Rita

BARS | Though it's a bit difficult to find, on a side street in the popular aperitivo haunt of Navigli, the expertly mixed cocktails, well-prepared snacks, and excellent playlist make this classic worth the hunt. It also serves burgers, sand-wiches, and more substantial plates for dinner. ⊠ *Via Angelo Fumagalli 1, Navigli* ☎ *02/8372865* Ⓜ *Porta Genova; Tram No. 2.*

"Let's Go to the ⊚ Columns"

Andiamo al Le Colonne, in Milanese youthspeak, is the cue to meet up at the sober Roman columns in front of the Basilica San Lorenzo Maggiore. Attracted to the Corso di Porta Ticinese by its bars and shops, hipsters spill out on the street to chat and drink. Neighbors may complain about the noise and confusion, but students and nighthawks find it indispensable for socializing at all hours. It's a street—no closing time.

★ Ugo Bar

BARS | Flanked by a long bar and tables lit by candles, and featuring floral wallpaper and eclectic framed paintings of animals, this bar has a moody living-room vibe. It's a charming place for a drink, if you can squeeze past the crowds. There is also a handful of outdoor tables for prime peo-ple-watching. ⊠ *Via Corsico 12, Navigli* ☎ *02/39811337* ⊕ *www.ugobar.it* Ⓜ *Porta Genova; Tram No. 9 or 10.*

⬤ Performing Arts

Auditorium di Milano Fondazione Cariplo

CONCERTS | This modern hall, known for its excellent acoustics, is home to the **Orchestra Sinfonica di Milano Giuseppe Verdi** (Symphonic Orchestra) and **Coro Sinfonico di Milano Giuseppe Verdi** (Sym-phonic Choir). The season, which runs from September to June, includes many top international performers and rotating guest conductors. ⊠ *Largo Gustav Mahler, at Corso San Gottardo, Navigli* ☎ *02/83389401* ⊕ *www.laverdi.org* Ⓜ *Tram No. 3 or 15; Bus No. 59 or 91.*

Did You Know?

The oldest canal in Milan, the Naviglio Grande was built between 1177 and 1257. It's more than 50 km long and was primarily used for transporting goods. Today, the area around the canal is hopping with charming boutiques, galleries, cafés, and restaurants. Take a boat tour down the waterway and take in the neighborhood.

Tortona

Tortona's former factories, warehouses, and workshops are now a creative hub packed with shops, studios, and the MUDEC, a museum with modern and contemporary art and special exhibitions.

Sights

Armani/Silos

OTHER MUSEUM | About 600 pieces, from about 1980 to the present, by famed Milanese fashion designer Giorgio Armani are displayed on four floors of this airy 48,000-square-foot museum, housed in a 1950s building that was formerly a Nestlé cereal storage facility. The collection is divided by theme: Ethnicities; Androgynous, including many of Armani's famous suits; and Stars, with clothes worn to the Oscars and other celebrity-studded events. A digital archive lets you explore Armani's full body of work, and a café lets you stop for a restorative espresso. Temporary exhibitions explore photography, architecture, and other themes related to design. ✉ *Via Bergognone 40, Ticinese* ☎ *02/91630010* 🌐 *www.armanisilos.com* 🎫 *€12* 🕒 *Closed Mon. and Tues.* [M] *Sant'Agostino or Porta Genova; Tram No. 2 or 14; Bus No. 68 or 90/91.*

MUDEC (Museo delle Culture)

ART MUSEUM | Home to a permanent collection of ethnographic displays as well as temporary exhibitions of big-name artists such as Basquiat and Miró, MUDEC is in the vibrant Zona Tortona area of the city. British architect David Chipperfield designed the soaring space in a former factory. The permanent collection includes art, objects, and documents from Africa, Asia, and the Americas. Book in advance for the most popular temporary exhibits. There's also a highly rated restaurant, Enrico Bartolini Mudec, as well as a more casual bistro. ✉ *Via Tortona 56, Ticinese* ☎ *02/54917* 🌐 *www.mudec.it* 🎫 *Permanent collection free, special exhibitions from €10* 🕒 *Closed Mon. until 2:30 pm* [M] *Sant'Agostino or Porta Genova; Tram No. 2 or 14; Bus No. 68 or 90/91.*

Restaurants

Al Fresco

$$$ | **MODERN ITALIAN** | In Italian, *al fresco* means open-air, and when the weather cooperates you can dine in the candlelit garden of this restaurant converted from a former factory. The string lights and wooden tables create a romantic setting, while indoors, a greenhouse with terra-cotta floors is decorated with seasonal floral arrangements, chandeliers, and pendant lights to add to the 19th-century charm. **Known for:** fish and tempura courses; extensive menu and many vegetarian options; garden setting. [$] *Average main: €25* ✉ *Via Savona 50, Milan* ☎ *02/49533630* 🌐 *www.alfrescomilano.it* 🕒 *No lunch Mon.*

Hotels

Hotel Magna Pars Suites Milano

$$$$ | **HOTEL** | This ultrastylish all-suites boutique hotel in a former perfume factory has Italian-designed furnishings; paintings by local Brera Academy artists; and sleek, white accommodations—each with its own signature scent (such as fruity, woodsy, or floral) and all overlooking one of two tranquil courtyards. **Pros:** modern, design-y feel; wonderful food at the attached restaurant; attentive service. **Cons:** perfumed rooms not for everyone; a bit of a trek to central attractions; spa on the small side. [$] *Rooms from: €330* ✉ *Via Forcella 6, Tortona* ☎ *02/8338371* 🌐 *www.magnapars.it* 🛏 *60 suites* 🍴 *Free Breakfast* [M] *Porta Genova; Tram No. 2, 9, or 19.*

The medieval town of Bergamo at sunrise

Bergamo

52 km (32 miles) northeast of Milan.

If you're driving from Milan to Lake Garda, the perfect deviation from your autostrada journey is the lovely medieval town of Bergamo, which is also a wonderful side trip by train from Milan. With direct service from Milan, you'll be whisked from the restless pace of city life to the medieval grandeur of Bergamo Alta in less than an hour.

From behind a set of battered Venetian walls high on an Alpine hilltop, Bergamo majestically surveys the countryside. Behind are the snowcapped Bergamese Alps, and two funiculars connect the modern **Bergamo Bassa** (Lower Bergamo) to the ancient **Bergamo Alta** (Upper Bergamo). Bergamo Bassa's long arteries and ornate piazzas speak to centuries of prosperity, but it's nonetheless overshadowed by Bergamo Alta, whose magnificent architecture has a fairy-tale allure.

GETTING HERE AND AROUND

Bergamo is along the A4 autostrada. By car from Milan, take the A51 out of the city to pick up the A4; the drive is 52 km (32 miles) and takes about 45 minutes. By train, Bergamo is about one hour from Milan and 1½ hours from Desenzano del Garda-Sirmione station.

VISITOR INFORMATION

CONTACTS Bergamo Tourism Office. ⊠ *Via Gombito 13,* ☎ *035/242226* ⊕ *www. visitbergamo.net.*

Sights

Accademia Carrara

ART MUSEUM | Bergamo is home to an art collection that's surprisingly rewarding given its size and remote location. Many of the Venetian masters are represented—Mantegna, Bellini, Carpaccio (circa 1460–1525/26), Tiepolo (1727–1804), Francesco Guardi (1712–93), and Canaletto (1697–1768), as well as Botticelli (1445–1510). ⊠ *Piazza Carrara 82, Bergamo Bassa, Bergamo* ☎ *035/234396* *weekdays, 035/4122097 weekends* 🌐 *www.lacarrara.it* 🎫 *€10* ⏲ *Closed Tues.*

Campanone

VIEWPOINT | The massive 13th-century Torre Civica (Civic Tower), known as the Campanone, offers a great view of the two cities. Climb the stairs or take an elevator to the top of the tower, where the bells ring every half hour and then 100 times each night at 10 to commemorate the closure of the city gates during Venetian rule. ✉ *Piazza Vecchia, Bergamo Alta, Bergamo* ☎ *035/247116* 🎫 *€5* ⏲ *Closed Mon.*

Cappella Colleoni

CHURCH | Bergamo's **Duomo** and **Battistero** are the most substantial buildings in Piazza Duomo. But the most impressive structure is the Cappella Colleoni, which boasts a kaleidoscope of marble decoration and golden accents. ✉ *Piazza Duomo, Bergamo Alta, Bergamo* ☎ *035/210061* ⏲ *Closed Mon.*

🍴 Restaurants

★ Al Donizetti

$$ | **NORTHERN ITALIAN** | Find a table in the back of this central, cheerful restaurant before choosing local cured meats and cheeses to accompany your wine. A few versions of polenta, daily pastas, and other heartier dishes are also available; just save room for the desserts, which go well with the sweet wines. **Known for:** chocolate desserts; 900-bottle wine selection with many by the glass; beef tartare. [$] *Average main: €20* ✉ *Via Gombito 17/a, Bergamo Alta, Bergamo* ☎ *035/242661* ⏲ *Closed Tues.*

Da Ornella

$$ | **NORTHERN ITALIAN** | The vaulted ceilings of this popular trattoria on the upper town's main street are marked with ancient graffiti, created by (patiently) holding candles to the stone overhead. The house specialties are simple but tasty: polenta *taragna* (with buckwheat flour) cooked with butter and cheese and served with rabbit, chicken, or sliced mushrooms with oil, garlic, and parsley. **Known for:** casoncelli (meat-filled pasta from Lombardy) dell'Ornella; historical setting; local salame. [$] *Average main: €18* ✉ *Via Gombito 15, Bergamo Alta, Bergamo* ☎ *035/232736* ⏲ *Closed Thurs.*

Vineria Cozzi

$$ | **WINE BAR** | The wine list at this romantic but informal *vineria* (wine bar) is exceptional—both by the glass and by the bottle—and there's also an array of flavorful foods, from snacks to sumptuous full-course meals typical of the region. The atmosphere is warm and charming, harking back more than 150 years to when the spot was first established in Bergamo as a lively meeting place. **Known for:** polenta dishes as starters and mains; cellar with more than 300 wines; quirky historical decorations. [$] *Average main: €18* ✉ *Via B. Colleoni 22, Bergamo Alta, Bergamo* ☎ *035/238836* 🌐 *www.vineriacozzi.it* ⏲ *Closed Wed.*

☕ Coffee and Quick Bites

La Marianna

$ | **ICE CREAM** | **FAMILY** | Stracciatella gelato—a creamy combination of milk, egg yolks, vanilla, sugar, and dark chocolate shavings—is Italy's answer to chocolate-chip ice cream. While you'll see the flavor in gelaterie across Italy, one pastry shop, and city, Bergamo, claims it as its own. **Known for:** decorated seasonal cookies and cakes; upscale gelateria atmosphere; outdoor courtyard away from the crowds of Città Alta. [$] *Average main: €10* ✉ *Largo Colle Aperto, 4, Bergamo* ☎ *035/237027* 🌐 *www.lamarianna.it.*

Panificio Tresoldi

$ | **BAKERY** | The Tresoldi family began baking bread in Bergamo in 1946 and the tradition continues with pizza, focaccia, pastries, and the local dessert Polenta e Osei—a sweet polenta-and-marzipan concoction decorated with chocolate that comes in sizes from small to large. The walls are lined with portraits of Bergamo's elite and with just a few bar stools the spot is ideal if you need a quick snack or lunch on the go. **Known for:** local desserts and breakfast pastries; loaves of bread as well as pizza by the slice; friendly service. [$] *Average main: €10* ✉ *Via Bartolomeo Colleoni, 13a, Bergamo* ☎ *035/243960* 🌐 *www.panetteriatresoldi.it.*

Hotels

Excelsior San Marco

$ | **HOTEL** | Some of the comfortable (if generic) rooms at this Bergamo Bassa hotel a short walk from the funicular have balconies with amazing upper town views. **Pros:** convenient location with parking; panoramic views from rooftop restaurant; modern surroundings. **Cons:** many bathrooms on the small side; rooms a little dated; hotel decor is nothing special. [$] *Rooms from: €105* ✉ *Piazza della Repubblica 6, Bergamo* ☎ *035/366111* 🌐 *www.hotelsanmarco.com* 🛏 *154 rooms* 🍴 *Free Breakfast.*

Mercure Bergamo Centro Palazzo Dolci

$ | **HOTEL** | Set in a restored 19th-century palazzo, this Bergamo Basso hotel has modern comforts and a friendly, efficient staff, making it a good choice for both business and leisure travelers. **Pros:** convenient to train station, airport, and some shopping; bountiful breakfast buffet; good value. **Cons:** no restaurant; no parking on-site; basic rooms. [$] *Rooms from: €104* ✉ *Viale Papa Giovanni XXIII 100, Bergamo* ☎ *035/227411* 🌐 *mercure-bergamocentropalazzodolci.com-hotel.com* 🛏 *92 rooms* 🍴 *Free Breakfast.*

Relais San Vigilio

$$$ | **HOTEL** | Brothers Gigi and Paolo Zani transformed a castle and soldiers' barracks dating from the Middle Ages into a retreat just above the Città Alta. **Pros:** quiet location away from the crowds; hotel layout in two buildings offers extra privacy among rooms; lovely views and spacious garden with many sitting areas. **Cons:** expensive on-site parking in small garage with narrow driveway; 10-minute walk or quick funicular ride to Città Alta; some bathrooms are small. [$] *Rooms from: €250* ✉ *Via al Castello 7/9, Bergamo* ☎ *035/2650987* 🌐 *www.relaissanvigilio.it* 🛏 *9 rooms* 🍴 *Free Breakfast.*

Pavia

40 km (25 miles) south of Milan.

Pavia was once Milan's chief regional rival. The city dates from at least the Roman era and was the capital of the Lombard kings for two centuries (572–774). It was at one time known as "the city of a hundred towers," but only a few have survived the passing of time. Its prestigious university was founded in 1361 on the site of a 10th-century law school, but it has roots that can be traced to antiquity.

GETTING HERE AND AROUND

By car from Milan, start out on the A7 autostrada and exit onto the A53 as you near Pavia; the drive is 40 km (25 miles) and takes about 45 minutes. Pavia is 30–40 minutes by train from Milan and 1½ hours (by slower regional service) from Cremona. The Certosa is 30 minutes by train from Milan Rogoredo station.

VISITOR INFORMATION

CONTACT Pavia Tourism Office. ✉ *Piazza della Vittoria 20/d,* ☎ *0382/399790* 🌐 *www.visitpavia.com.*

Sights

Castello Visconteo di Pavia

CASTLE/PALACE | The town's 14th-century fortress-castle now houses the local Museo Civico (Municipal Museum), with a Romanesque and Renaissance sculpture gallery, an archaeological collection, and a large picture gallery displaying works by Correggio, Bellini, Tiepolo, Hayez, Pellizza da Volpedo, and la Foppa, among others. ✉ *Viale XI Febbraio 35, near Piazza Castello, Pavia* ☎ *0382/399770* 🌐 *www.museicivici.pavia.it* 🎟 *€10* 🕒 *Closed Tues.*

Certosa di Pavia (*Carthusian monastery*)
HISTORIC SIGHT | The main draw in Pavia is its *certosa* (Carthusian monastery), 9 km (5½ miles) north of the city center and a 15-minute walk from the Certosa di Pavia train station. Its elaborate facade shows the same relish for ornamentation as Milan's Duomo. The Certosa di Pavia's extravagant grandeur was due in part to the plan to have it house the tombs of the family of the first duke of Milan, Gian Galeazzo Visconti (who died during a plague, at age 49, in 1402). The best marble was used, taken undoubtedly by barge from the quarries of Carrara, roughly 240 km (150 miles) away. Although the floor plan is Gothic—a cross shape divided into a series of squares—the gorgeous fabric that rises above it is triumphantly Renaissance. On the facade, in the lower frieze, are medallions of Roman emperors and Eastern monarchs; above them are low reliefs of scenes from the life of Christ and from the career of Gian Galeazzo Visconti. ✉ *Certosa, Località Monumento 4, 9 km (5½ miles) north of Pavia, Pavia* ☎ *0382/925613* 🌐 *www.certosatourism.it* 🎟 *Free* 🕒 *Closed Mon.*

San Pietro in Ciel d'Oro
CHURCH | This basilica, a Romanesque masterpiece, houses the tomb of Christianity's most celebrated convert, St. Augustine (354–430), who rests in an intricately carved white-marble Gothic ark on the high altar. ✉ *San Pietro in Ciel d'Oro 2, Pavia* ☎ *0382/303036* 🌐 *santagostinopavia.wordpress.com* 🕒 *Closed daily noon–3.*

🍴 Restaurants

Locanda Vecchia Pavia al Mulino
$$$ | **NORTHERN ITALIAN** | Amid sophisticated Art Nouveau surroundings, you can order creative versions of traditional Lombard cuisine. All fish dishes are done with verve, as are the *lasagnette di pasta fresca alla robiola spinaci* (lasagna with soft cheese and spinach), *nocette d'agnello* (noisette of lamb), and veal-shank stew, which earned the restaurant a Michelin star in 2019. **Known for:** veranda (summer only) with a view of Certosa di Pavia; Pavese wines; tasting menu with Lombard dishes and homemade pasta. [$] *Average main: €35* ✉ *Via al Monumento 5, Certosa di Pavia* ☎ *0382/925894* 🌐 *www.vecchiapaviaalmulino.it* 🕒 *Closed Mon., Aug., and Jan. No dinner Sun.*

Cremona

85 km (53 miles) east of Pavia, 100 km (62 miles) southeast of Milan.

Cremona is a classical-music lover's dream. With violin shops on every block along its crooked old streets, it is where the world's best violins are crafted. Andrea Amati (1510–80) invented the modern instrument here in the 16th century. Though cognoscenti continue to revere the Amati name, it was an apprentice of Amati's nephew for whom the fates had reserved wide and lasting fame. In a career that spanned an incredible 68 years, Antonio Stradivari (1644–1737) made more than 1,200 instruments—including violas, cellos, harps, guitars, and mandolins, in addition to his fabled violins. They remain the most coveted, most expensive stringed instruments in the world.

Cremona's other claim to fame is *torrone* (nougat), which is said to have been created here in honor of the marriage of Bianca Maria Visconti and Francesco Sforza, which took place in October 1441.

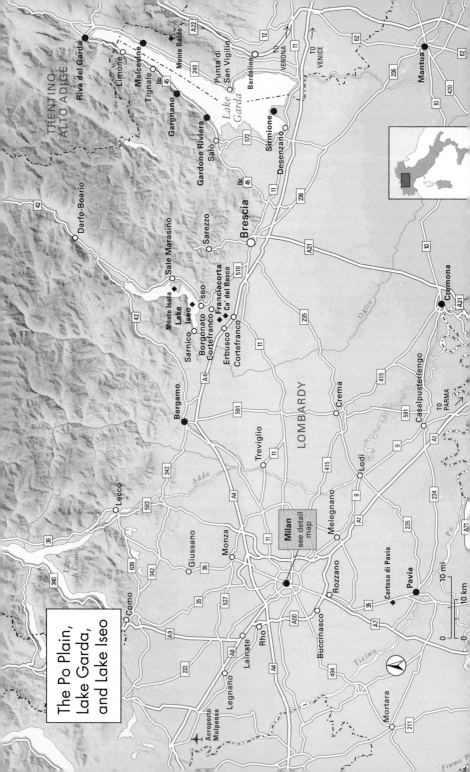

The Po Plain, Lake Garda, and Lake Iseo

The new confection, originally prepared by heating almonds, egg whites, and honey over low heat, and shaped and named after the city's tower, was created in symbolic celebration. The annual Festa del Torrone is held in the main piazza over the third or fourth week of November.

GETTING HERE AND AROUND

By car from Milan, start out on the A1 autostrada and switch to the A21 at Piacenza; the drive is about 100 km (62 miles) and takes about 1½ hours. From Pavia, take the SP617 to the A21; the trip is 85 km (53 miles) and takes about an hour. By train, Cremona is about an hour from Milan and 1½ hours from Desenzano, near Sirmione on Lake Garda.

VISITOR INFORMATION

CONTACT Cremona Tourism Office. ⊠ *Piazza del Comune 5,* ☎ *0372/407081* ⊕ *www.turismocremona.it.*

Sights

Duomo

CHURCH | Cremona's Romanesque Duomo was consecrated in 1190. It's an impressive structure in a breathtaking piazza, and certainly one of the most beautiful churches in Italy. Here you can find the *Story of the Virgin Mary and the Passion of Christ,* the central fresco of an extraordinary cycle commissioned in 1514 and featuring the work of local artists, including Boccaccio Boccaccino, Giovanni Francesco Bembo, and Altobello Melone. ⊠ *Piazza del Comune, Cremona* ☎ *0373/406391* ⊕ *www.cattedraledicremona.it.*

★ Museo del Violino

OTHER MUSEUM | At this lovely and informative museum dedicated to all things violin, even those not already enamored by the instrument will find something to appreciate. Historic violins made in Cremona by masters, including Stradivari, are presented as works of art; be sure to get the audio guide included with admission to listen to recordings as you stroll. An audio chamber lets you hear a musical performance in "3D audio"—and if you're lucky, there will be a live concert going on at the innovative on-site auditorium, where the seats wrap around the stage and musicians for an immersive experience. ⊠ *Palazzo dell'Arte, Piazza Marconi 5, Cremona* ☎ *0372/801801, 0372/080809 tickets* ⊕ *www.museodelviolino.org* ⊠ *€12* ◷ *Closed Mon. and Tues.*

No. 1 Piazza Roma

PLAZA/SQUARE | Legendary violin maker Antonio Stradivari lived, worked, and died near the verdant square at Piazza Roma 1 (not open to the public). According to local lore, Stradivari kept each instrument in his bedroom for a month before varnishing it, imparting part of his soul before sealing and sending it out into the world. In the center of the park is a copy of Stradivari's tombstone, while the original is in the Violin Museum. ⊠ *Piazza Roma 1, Cremona.*

Piazza del Comune

PLAZA/SQUARE | The Duomo, tower, baptistery, and Palazzo Communale (city hall) surround this distinctive and harmonious square: the combination of old brick, rose- and cream-color marble, terra-cotta, and old copper roofs brings Romanesque, Gothic, and Renaissance together with unusual success. ⊠ *Piazza del Comune 8, Cremona.*

Torrazzo (*Big Tower*)

NOTABLE BUILDING | Dominating Piazza del Comune is perhaps the tallest campanile in Italy, visible for a considerable distance across the Po Plain. The tower's astronomical clock is the 1583 original. Climb the 500-plus steps to the top for amazing views; along the way, you can stop at the Museo Verticale for informative displays on astronomy and ancient methods of measuring time. ⊠ *Piazza del Comune, Cremona* ☎ *0372/495011* ⊕ *museoverticale.it* ⊠ *€5 (€6 with baptistery)* ◷ *Closed Mon. and daily 1–2:30.*

 Restaurants

La Sosta

$$ | **NORTHERN ITALIAN** | This osteria looks to the 16th century for culinary inspiration, with excellent homemade salami and two popular primi—*gnocchi vecchia Cremona* (stuffed with sausage and baked with poppy seeds, sesame, and Parmigiano-Reggiano) and *marubini Cremonesi ai tre brodi* (stuffed meat ravioli in broth)—made according to time-tested recipes. Order the tiramisu and an accompanying dessert wine for a perfect finish. **Known for:** extensive wine cellar with dessert wines; Cremonese sausage and veal osso buco; cheese tasting menu. $ *Average main: €22* ✉ *Via Sicardo 9, Cremona* ☎ *0372/456656* ⊕ *www. osterialasosta.it* ⊘ *Closed Mon. and 3 wks in Aug. No dinner Sun.*

Coffee and Quick Bites

★ Pasticceria Duomo

$ | **CAFÉ** | This portal to the past opened in 1883 and still serves up such handmade local delights as *pan torrone* (a loaf cake made with chunks of nougat) and *torta cremona* (a cake made with almond flour and filled with Amarena cherries). A relaxing stop between visiting museums, it's the perfect place to have a cappuccino and sit by the fireplace. **Known for:** seasonal decorated cakes and pastries; old-world charm; torrone (nougat) in many shapes and sizes. $ *Average main: €10* ✉ *Via Boccaccino 6, Cremona* ☎ *0372/22273* ⊕ *www.pasticceriaduomo. it* ⊘ *Closed Tues.*

Hotels

Delle Arti Design Hotel

$$ | **HOTEL** | With modern interiors and eclectic but comfortable designer furniture, this aptly named hotel makes a nice counterpoint to the historical surroundings of Cremona. **Pros:** convenient central location; good breakfast options; friendly staff. **Cons:** starting to show its age; hallways can be a little dark; small bathrooms. $ *Rooms from: €143* ✉ *Via Bonomelli 8, Cremona* ☎ *0372/23131* ⊕ *www.dellearti.com* ⇱ *33 rooms* ❖ *Free Breakfast.*

Hotel Impero

$ | **HOTEL** | Just a few minutes' walk from the Duomo and the Museo del Violino, this comfortable hotel with functional yet pleasant rooms (the best of which overlook the piazza) is well equipped to satisfy both leisure and business travelers. **Pros:** central location; spacious rooms; highly professional staff. **Cons:** breakfast is basic; outside noise can be a problem, especially on weekends; rooms are a little bland and outdated. $ *Rooms from: €108* ✉ *Piazza della Pace 21, Cremona* ☎ *0372/413013* ⊕ *www.hotelimpero.cr.it* ⇱ *51 rooms* ❖ *Free Breakfast.*

Shopping

Sperlari

FOOD | Sperlari and parent company Fieschi have grown into a confectionery empire, but it all started at this handsome shop, which has been selling Cremona's famous nougat and its best *mostarda* (a preserved-fruit condiment served alongside meat and cheese) since 1836. While shopping for these items— as well as teas, marmalades, and other Italian delights—be sure to check out the historical product display at the back of the store. ✉ *Via Solferino 25, Cremona* ☎ *0372/22346* ⊕ *www.sperlari1836.com.*

Mantua

192 km (119 miles) southeast of Milan.

Mantua (Mantova in Italian) stands tallest among the ancient walled cities of the Po Plain; it may not be flashy or dramatic, but its beauty is subtle and deep, hiding a rich trove of artistic, architectural, and cultural gems beneath its slightly somber facade. Its fortifications are circled on three sides by the passing Mincio River, which long provided Mantua with protection, fish, and a steady stream of river tolls on its meandering way from Lake Garda to the Po.

Mantua first came to prominence in Roman times as the home of Virgil, but its grand monuments date from the glory years of the Gonzaga dynasty. From 1328 until 1708, when the Austrian Habsburgs sacked the city, Gonzaga dukes and marquesses reigned over a wealthy independent commune, and the arts thrived in the relative peace. Raphael's star pupil, Andrea Mantegna, who served as court painter for 50 years, was the best known of a succession of the artists and architects who served Mantua through the years; some of his finest work, including his only surviving fresco cycle, can be seen here. Giulio Romano (circa 1499–1546), Mantegna's apprentice, built his masterpiece, Palazzo Te, on an island in the river. Leon Battista Alberti (1404–72), who designed two impressive churches in Mantua, was widely emulated later in the Renaissance.

GETTING HERE AND AROUND

Mantua is 5 km (3 miles) west of the A22 autostrada. The drive from Milan, following the A4 to the A22, takes a little more than two hours. The drive from Cremona, along the SP10, is 1¼ hours. Most trains arrive in just under two hours from Milan, depending on the type of service, and in about 1½ hours from Desenzano, near Sirmione on Lake Garda, via Verona.

VISITOR INFORMATION

CONTACT Mantua Tourism Office. ⊠ *Piazza Sordello 23,* ☎ *0376/288208* ⊕ *www. turismo.mantova.it.*

 Sights

Be sure to pick up a Mantova Sabbioneta Card (⊕ *www.mantovacard.it*) at the tourism office, the Palazzo Ducale, or the Palazzo Te. It entitles you to visit 11 museums for one price and also includes access to city buses.

Casa del Mantegna

HISTORIC HOME | Serious Mantegna aficionados will want to visit the house the artist designed and built around an intriguing circular courtyard, which is usually open to view. The exterior is interesting for its unusual design, and the interior, with its hidden frescoes, can be seen by appointment or during occasional art exhibitions. Hours and prices vary depending on the exhibition. ⊠ *Via Acerbi 47, Mantua* ☎ *0376/360506* ⊕ *www.casadelmantegna.it* ⊠ *Varies by exhibition.*

★ Palazzo Ducale

CASTLE/PALACE | The 500-room palace that dominates the Mantua skyline was built for the Gonzaga family, though much of the art within the castle was sold or stolen as the dynasty waned in power and prestige. A glimpse of past grandeur can still be spotted in the Camera degli Sposi (literally, the "Wedded Couple's Room") where Duke Ludovico and his wife held court. Mantegna painted the hall over a nine-year period at the height of his power, finishing at age 44. Only 25 people at a time are allowed in the room and for only five minutes at a time (though sometimes longer in low season); reservations are recommended, either by phone or online (⊕ *www.ducalemantova.org*). ⊠ *Piazza Sordello 40, Mantua* ☎ *041/2411897* ⊕ *www.mantovaducale. beniculturali.it* ⊠ *€15* ⊗ *Closed Mon.*

★ Palazzo Te

CASTLE/PALACE | One of the greatest of all Renaissance palaces, built between 1525 and 1535 by Federico II Gonzaga, is the Mannerist masterpiece of artist-architect Giulio Romano, who created a pavilion where the strict rules of courtly behavior could be relaxed for libertine pastimes. Romano's purposeful breaks with classical tradition are lighthearted and unprecedented; note, for example, the "slipping" triglyphs along the upper edge of the inside courtyard. Two highlights are the Camera di Amore e Psiche (Room of Cupid and Psyche), which depicts a wedding set among lounging nymphs, frolicking satyrs, and even a camel and an elephant; and the gasp-inducing Camera dei Giganti (Room of the Giants) that shows Jupiter expelling the Titans from Mount Olympus. The scale of the latter is overwhelming; the floor-to-ceiling work completely envelops the viewer. The room's rounded corners, and the river rock covering the original floor, were meant to make it seem cavelike. It is a "whisper chamber" in which words softly uttered in one corner can be heard in the opposite one. Note the graffiti from as far back as the 17th century. ✉ *Viale Te 13, Mantua* ☎ *0376/323266* 🌐 *www.palazzote.it* 🎫 *€15.*

Sant'Andrea

CHURCH | Mantegna's tomb is in the first chapel to the left in this basilica, most of which was built in 1472. The current structure, a masterwork by the architect Alberti, is the third built on this spot to house the relic of the Precious Blood: the crypt holds two reliquaries containing earth believed to be soaked in the blood of Christ, brought to Mantua by Longinus, the soldier who pierced his side. They are displayed only on Good Friday. ✉ *Piazza di Mantegna 1, Mantua* ☎ *0376/320220* 🌐 *www.parrocchiasantanselmomantova.it.*

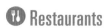

🍴 Restaurants

Ambasciata

$$$$ | **NORTHERN ITALIAN** | Heralded as one of Italy's classic gourmet restaurants, Ambasciata (Italian for "embassy") emphasizes elegance in tiny Quistello, 20 km (12 miles) southeast of Mantua. Those who are willing to make the trek (and pay the bill) can opt for the tasting menu with an ever-changing array of traditionally inspired creations, such as the famed *tortelli di zucca* (pumpkin tortelli with pumpkin cream and Parmigiano-Reggiano), or mains like guinea fowl with mostarda (a sweet-and-sour mustard from Mantua) and roast pigeon with 25-year reserve balsamic vinegar. **Known for:** attentive service; whimsical setting; intricate cuisine coupled with classics. [$] *Average main: €55* ✉ *Piazzetta Ambasciatori del Gusto 1, Quistello* ☎ *376/619169* 🌐 *www.ristorantelambasciata.eu* ⏲ *Closed Tues. No dinner Mon.*

🛏 Hotels

Casa Poli

$$ | **HOTEL** | **FAMILY** | A refreshing minimalist influence, attention to detail, and creative touches (like the room number projected onto the hall floor) create a welcoming ambience with contemporary flair. **Pros:** attentive staff; families welcome; tasteful and modern. **Cons:** no on-site restaurant; some traffic noise in front-facing rooms; although convenient, not in the absolute center of the city. [$] *Rooms from: €125* ✉ *Corso Garibaldi 32, Mantua* ☎ *0376/288170* 🌐 *www.hotelcasapoli.it* 🛏 *27 rooms* 🍴 *Free Breakfast.*

Lake Iseo and Franciacorta

108 km (67 miles) northeast of Milan.

The lesser known of Lombardy's lakes, Iseo is a haven for cyclists and sailors around Monte Isola. With 117 cellars and more than 7,783 acres of vineyards across 124 miles, for wine lovers, Franciacorta is a region not to be missed.

GETTING HERE AND AROUND

Frequent trains make the hour-long trip from Milano Centrale to Brescia. From there, hourly trains run to the town of Iseo (about half an hour) and then up Lake Iseo's eastern shore. You'll need a car to reach the western side or the Franciacorta wine region just south of the lake.

To drive from Milan or Bergamo, take the A4/E64; exit at Rovato on SP51 in the direction of Iseo. The trip takes about one hour and 20 minutes from Milan and 30 minutes from Bergamo. Ferries run from Sulzano, Sale Marasino, Iseo, and Tavernola Bergamasca to Monte Isola.

VISITOR INFORMATION

CONTACTS Lake Iseo and Franciacorta Tourism Office. ✉ *Lungolago Marconi 2/c* ☎ *030/980209* 🌐 *www.visitlakeiseo.info.*

Sights

Ca' del Bosco

WINERY | Modern sculptures adorn the grounds of this respected Franciacorta winery (one of the largest in the region). Enjoyable hour-long cellar tours conclude with a 30-minute tasting; information about tour availability can be requested online. ✉ *Via Albano Zanella 13, Erbusco* ☎ *030/7766111* 🌐 *www.cadelbosco.com* 🎟 *From €35* 🕒 *Closed weekdays 12:30–2.*

★ Monte Isola

ISLAND | The largest island within any European lake, Monte Isola allows no cars (except authorized vehicles), making it the perfect place for leisurely walks and bike rides. The main towns are Siviano, with medieval mansions; Peschiera Maraglio, an old fishing village with 16th-century homes and the Church of St. Michele; and Carzano, with the 18th-century San Giovanni Battista church. Walk around the water and stop at the many restaurants and gelaterie, or, for more exercise, trek uphill to admire the views back to the shore. Frequent ferries from Sulzano stop at Peschiera Maraglio, and ferries from Sale Marasino arrive at Carzano; there are less frequent ferries from Iseo and Tavernola Bergamasca. ✉ *Monte Isola* 🌐 *www.navigazionelagoiseo.it.*

Restaurants

★ Due Colombe Ristorante Al Borgo Antico

$$$ | **NORTHERN ITALIAN** | Visitors to Lake Iseo would do well to follow the locals' lead by sampling the delightful cooking at this cozy restaurant just south of the lake. The elegant dining area, with wood-beam ceilings and stone walls, is juxtaposed with the thoroughly modern menu, which offers a selection of "classic" and "creative" dishes. **Known for:** more than 900 wines to select from; countryside setting; Franciacorta sauces. [$] *Average main: €25* ✉ *Via Foresti 13, Borgonato* ☎ *030/9828227* 🌐 *www.duecolombe.com* 🕒 *Closed Mon.–Wed. No dinner Sun. No lunch Thurs.*

Hotels

★ L'Albereta

$$$$ | **HOTEL** | Set in an early-20th-century villa amid Franciacorta's hilly vineyards, this Relais & Chateaux property is a true sanctuary, with an enormous spa, a botanical garden, and vast, sculpture-filled grounds to explore. **Pros:** cozy, calm, and luxurious atmosphere; beautiful surroundings; excellent on-site restaurants. **Cons:** breakfast not included; not all rooms have Lake Iseo views; rooms quite varied in terms of size and level of renovation. [$] *Rooms from: €351* ✉ *Via Vittorio Emanuele 23, Erbusco* ☎ *030/7760550* 🌐 *www.albereta.it* 🛏 *57 rooms* 🍴 *No Meals.*

Sirmione

138 km (86 miles) east of Milan.

Dramatically rising out of Lake Garda is the enchanting town of Sirmione. "*Paene insularum, Sirmio, insularumque ocelle,*" wrote Catullus in a homecoming poem: "It is the jewel of both peninsulas and islands." The forbidding Castello Scaligero stands guard behind the small bridge connecting Sirmione to the mainland;

beyond, cobbled streets wind their way through medieval arches past lush gardens, stunning lake views, and gawking crowds. Originally a Roman resort town, Sirmione served under the dukes of Verona and later Venice as Garda's main point of defense. It has now reclaimed its original function, bustling with visitors in summer. Cars aren't allowed into town; parking is available by the tourist office at the entrance.

GETTING HERE AND AROUND

The town of Sirmione, at the south end of the lake, is 10 km (6 miles) from Desenzano, which has regular train service; it's about one hour and 20 minutes by train from Milan and 25 minutes from Verona. The A4 autostrada passes to the south of the lake, and the A22 runs north–south about 10 km (6 miles) from the eastern shore.

VISITOR INFORMATION

CONTACT Sirmione Tourism Office. ✉ *Viale Marconi 8,* ☎ *349/8183452* 🌐 *www.sirmionebs.it.*

Sights

Bardolino

TOWN | This small town—one of the most popular summer resorts on the lake—is 32 km (20 miles) north of Sirmione along Lake Garda's eastern shore, at the wider end. It's most famous for its red wine, which is light, dry, and often slightly sparkling; the Festa dell'Uva e del Vino (Grape and Wine Festival), held here in early October, is a great excuse to indulge in the local product. Bardolino has two handsome Romanesque churches, both near the center: San Severo, from the 11th century, and San Zeno, from the 9th. ✉ *Bardolino* 🌐 *www.visitbardolino.it.*

Castello Scaligero di Sirmione

CASTLE/PALACE | As hereditary rulers of Verona for more than a century before they lost control of the city in 1402, the Della Scala counted Garda among their possessions. It was they who built this lakeside redoubt, along with almost all the other castles on the lake. You can go inside to take in a lake view from the tower, or you can swim at the nearby beach. ✉ *Piazza Castello, Sirmione* ☎ *030/916468* 🎟 *€6* 🕒 *Closed Mon.*

Grotte di Catullo (*Grottoes of Catullus*)

RUINS | Locals will almost certainly tell you that these romantic lakeside ruins were once the site of the villa of Catullus (87–54 BC), one of the greatest pleasure-seeking poets of all time. Modern-day archaeology, however, does not concur, and there is some consensus that this was the site of two villas of slightly different periods, dating from about the 1st century AD. But never mind—the view through the cypresses and olive trees is lovely, and even if Catullus didn't have a villa here, he is closely associated with the area and undoubtedly did have a villa nearby. The ruins are at the top of the isthmus and are poorly signposted: walk through the historic center and past the various villas to the top of the spit; the entrance is on the right. A small museum offers a brief overview of the ruins (on the far wall). ✉ *Piazzale Orti Manara, Sirmione* ☎ *030/916157* 🌐 *www.grottedicatullo.beniculturali.it* 🎟 *€8* 🕒 *Closed Mon.*

Restaurants

La Rucola 2.0

$$$$ | **MODERN ITALIAN** | Next to the castle and tucked into three charming rooms, this elegant, intimate restaurant is considered by many to be Sirmione's finest. Its creative menu has an appealing mix of fish (from the lake or the sea), meat, and vegetarian dishes, all accompanied by a good choice of wines; opt for one of the three-, five-, or seven-course tasting menus to fully experience the chef's sophisticated creations. **Known for:** fantastic wine list; open kitchen; meat, fish, and carte blanche tasting menus. [$] *Average main: €85* ✉ *Vicolo Strentelle 3, Sirmione* ☎ *030/916326* 🌐 *www.*

ristorantelarucola.it ⏲ *Closed Thurs. No lunch Fri.*

Ristorante Al Pescatore

$$ | **SEAFOOD** | Freshwater fish is the specialty at this simple, popular restaurant in Sirmione's historic center. Try the grilled trout with a bottle of local white, and then settle your meal with a walk in the nearby park. **Known for:** inexpensive meals; extensive variety of pasta and seafood; grilled fresh fish from the lake. [$] *Average main: €18* ✉ *Via Giovanni Piana 20/22, Sirmione* ☎ *030/916216* 🌐 *www.ristorantealpescatore.com* ⏲ *Closed Thurs.*

Hotels

Hotel Sirmione e Promessi Sposi

$$ | **HOTEL** | A homey feel with comfortable beds and upholstered furnishings with matching drapery, along with a luxurious thermal spa, keeps many guests returning year after year. **Pros:** next to the lake and near Castello; nice spa area; beautiful grounds. **Cons:** service can be indifferent; hotel could use a refresh; not all rooms have lake views. [$] *Rooms from: €169* ✉ *Piazza Castello 19, Sirmione* ☎ *030/916331, 030/9904922 booking* 🌐 *www.termedisirmione.com* 🛏 *102 rooms* 🍴 *Free Breakfast.*

★ **Palace Hotel Villa Cortine**

$$$$ | **HOTEL** | This former private villa in a secluded park would be ostentatious if it weren't for the bucolic lakeside setting, the charming decor of the older rooms, and the accommodating staff. **Pros:** an opulent experience; beautiful grounds; lovely pool area. **Cons:** no gym; no spa at hotel but thermal baths a short walk away; very expensive. [$] *Rooms from: €393* ✉ *Viale C. Gennari 2, Sirmione* ☎ *030/9905890* 🌐 *www.hotelvillacortine.com* ⏲ *Closed mid-Oct.–Apr.* 🛏 *54 rooms* 🍴 *Free Breakfast.*

Malcesine

63 km (39 miles) northeast of Sirmione, 180 km (112 miles) northeast of Milan.

Malcesine is one of the loveliest areas along the upper eastern shore of Lake Garda. It's principally known as a summer resort, with sailing and windsurfing schools. It tends to be crowded, but there are nice walks from the town toward the mountains. In winter, several lifts and more than 11 km (7 miles) of runs of varying degrees of difficulty serve skiers.

GETTING HERE AND AROUND

By car from Milan follow A4 to Pescheria del Garda to SR249. The drive is 181 km (112 miles) and takes about three hours.

VISITOR INFORMATION

CONTACT Malcesine Tourism Office. ✉ *Via Gardesana 238,* ☎ *045/6589904* 🌐 *www.visitmalcesine.com.*

Sights

Castello di Malcesine

CASTLE/PALACE | Dominating the town is a 12th-century castle built by Verona's dynastic Della Scala family. It now contains a small museum of natural history. ✉ *Via Castello 39, Malcesine* ☎ *045/6570333* 🎟 *€6* ⏲ *Closed early Nov.–mid-Mar.*

Monte Baldo

MOUNTAIN | The futuristic *funivia* (cable car), which zips visitors to the top of Monte Baldo (7,276 feet), is unique because it rotates. After a 10-minute ride, you're high in Veneto where you can take a stroll and enjoy spectacular views of the lake. Ride the cable car down or bring along a mountain bike (or even a hang glider) for the descent. In the winter, there's skiing, snowboarding, and snowshoeing. ✉ *Via Navene Vecchia 12, Malcesine* ☎ *045/7400206* 🌐 *www.funiviedelbaldo.it* 🎟 *€25 round-trip (Malcesine–Monte Baldo).*

Riva del Garda

18 km (11 miles) north of Malcesine, 180 km (112 miles) northeast of Milan.

Riva del Garda is set on the northern tip of Lake Garda, against a dramatic backdrop of jagged cliffs and miles of beaches. The old city, surrounding a pretty harbor, was built up during the 15th century, when it was a strategic outpost of the Venetian Republic.

GETTING HERE AND AROUND

Riva del Garda is along Lake Garda's scenic SS45bis. By car from Milan, head to the A35 from SP14. The drive is 167 km (103 miles) and takes approximately three hours.

VISITOR INFORMATION

CONTACT Riva del Garda Tourism Office. ✉ *Largo Medaglie d'Oro al Valor Militare 5,* ☎ *0464/554444* 🌐 *www.gardatrentino.it.*

Sights

Piazza III Novembre

PLAZA/SQUARE | This lakeside piazza, the heart of Riva del Garda, is surrounded by medieval palazzi. Standing there and looking out over the lake, you can understand why Riva del Garda has become a windsurfing destination: air currents ensure good breezes on even the most sultry midsummer days. ✉ *Piazza III Novembre, Riva del Garda.*

Torre Apponale

VIEWPOINT | Predating the Venetian period by three centuries, this sturdy tower looms above the medieval residences of the main square; its crenellations recall its defensive purpose. You can climb the 165 steps to see the view from the top. ✉ *Piazza III Novembre, Riva del Garda* ☎ *0464/573869* 🌐 *www.gardatrentino.it* 🎫 *€2* 🕒 *Closed Mon.*

Restaurants

Ristorante Castel Toblino

$$$ | NORTHERN ITALIAN | A lovely stop for a drink or a romantic dinner, this 16th-century castle is right on a lake in Sarche, about 20 km (12 miles) north of Riva toward Trento. Dishes highlight seasonal local ingredients, including mountain cheeses, salmon, trout, duck, and deer. **Known for:** wine list featuring Trentino varieties; fish tasting menu; castle setting. [$] *Average main: €26* ✉ *Localita' Castel Toblino 1, Sarche* ☎ *0461/864036* 🌐 *www.casteltoblino.com* 🕒 *Closed mid-Oct.–late Mar.*

Coffee and Quick Bites

★ Eta Beta

$ | ICE CREAM | FAMILY | Matteo Mutti's gelato flavors have personality. Like cheesecake with red pepper, rosemary, and pineapple, which might sound strange, but leaves a delightful impression on your taste buds. **Known for:** gelato flavors that you won't find elsewhere; wide selection of cones, sundaes, and sizes; fun atmosphere. [$] *Average main: €5* ✉ *Via Disciplini 14, Riva del Garda* ☎ *0464/554614* 🕒 *Closed Nov.–Mar.*

Hotels

Du Lac et du Parc Grand Resort

$$ | RESORT | FAMILY | Highly personalized service and well-appointed guest rooms (including bungalows perfect for families) are among the hallmarks of Riva's largest resort; another is the beautifully manicured 17-acre garden with more than 200 species of plants. **Pros:** lush, expansive grounds with two swimming pools, plus kids' pool; lovely spa area; pampering and indulgent staff. **Cons:** can hear noise in some rooms; no beach of its own; not that cozy. [$] *Rooms from: €179* ✉ *Viale Rovereto 44, Riva del Garda* ☎ *0464/566600* 🌐 *www.dulacetduparc.*

com ⏲ *Closed mid-Nov.–late Mar.* 🛏 *163 rooms* 🍴 *Free Breakfast.*

Hotel Sole

$$ | **HOTEL** | A 15th-century palazzo in the center of town is the setting for this classic, comfortable, and relatively affordable hotel, where front rooms have terraces with breathtaking lake views and the rooftop terrace is a perfect retreat from summer's crowded beaches. **Pros:** prime location on the lake; comfortable beds; modern hotel conveniences. **Cons:** food gets mixed reviews; not for those looking for ultracontemporary design; sometimes taken over by tour groups. [$] *Rooms from: €133* ✉ *Piazza III Novembre 35, Riva del Garda* ☎ *0464/552686, 0464/557809 booking office* 🌐 *www.hotelsoleriva.it* ⏲ *Closed Nov.–Dec. 21 and early Jan.–Mar.* 🛏 *80 rooms* 🍴 *Free Breakfast.*

Lido Palace

$$$$ | **HOTEL** | In a 19th-century lakeside palace, Riva's most chic hotel has a high-end spa; sleek public spaces with turquoise mod couches and classic floor-to-ceiling windows; and contemporary guest rooms, where slate floors and brown-and-gray color schemes are offset by crisp white linens. **Pros:** friendly service; top-notch food; gorgeous spa and pools. **Cons:** coffee- or tea-making facilities in room only on request; on the pricey side; not all rooms have lake views or balconies. [$] *Rooms from: €326* ✉ *Viale Carducci 10, Riva del Garda* ☎ *0464/021899* 🌐 *www.lido-palace.it* ⏲ *Closed mid-Jan.–late Mar.* 🛏 *44 rooms* 🍴 *Free Breakfast.*

★ Luise

$ | **HOTEL** | **FAMILY** | Outdoor perks here include a big garden, a large swimming pool, and free bikes to explore paths around the lake; interior draws include unique design touches—such as the lobby's collection of vintage luggage labels—and spacious rooms, all with comfy beds and a playful vibe and some with a whirlpool tub and a balcony. **Pros:** pleasant service; great for kids; reasonably priced. **Cons:** no gym; 10-minute walk to center of Riva; some rooms can be noisy. [$] *Rooms from: €89* ✉ *Viale Rovereto 9, Riva del Garda* ☎ *0464/550858* 🌐 *www.hotelluise.com* ⏲ *Closed mid-Nov.–late Mar.* 🛏 *68 rooms* 🍴 *Free Breakfast.*

Gargnano

30 km (19 miles) southwest of Riva del Garda, 144 km (89 miles) northeast of Milan.

This small port town was an important Franciscan center in the 13th century. Today, it comes alive in the summer, when German tourists, many of whom have villas here, crowd the small pebble beach. An Austrian flotilla bombarded the town in 1866, and some of the houses still bear marks of cannon fire. Mussolini owned two houses in Gargnano: one is the luxury hotel Villa Feltrinelli.

GETTING HERE AND AROUND

Gargnano is about a 30-minute drive south of Riva del Garda along the SS45bis.

VISITOR INFORMATION

CONTACT Gargnano Tourism Office. ✉ *Piazza Boldini 2,* ☎ *0365/791243* 🌐 *www.gargnanosulgarda.it.*

🍴 Restaurants

La Tortuga

$$$ | **NORTHERN ITALIAN** | This rustic trattoria is more sophisticated than it first appears: not only does it serve local dishes with novel twists, but it also has an extensive wine cellar. *Capesante scottate con salse ai diversi sapori* (seared scallops with different sauces) and *palette di piccoli campioni di lago e di mare* (mixed lake and sea fish) are worthy introductions to regional delights. **Known for:** delightful service; extensive cheese selection; fish and meat tasting menu.

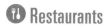

ⓈⒶ *Average main: €35* ✉ *Via XXIV Maggio 5, Gargnano* ☎ *0365/71251* ⊕ *www. ristorantelatortuga.it* ⊘ *Closed Tues. and Dec.–Mar.*

 ## Hotels

Garni Bartabel

$ | **HOTEL** | The small rooms at this cozy main-street inn—where breakfast is served on an elegant lake-view terrace—have attractive Venetian-style furnishings and pastel color schemes. **Pros:** attractive lake views; delicious breakfast; a bargain for this area. **Cons:** can hear road noise; not all rooms have lake views or terraces; few luxuries. Ⓢ *Rooms from: €86* ✉ *Via Roma 39, Gargnano* ☎ *0365/71300* ⊕ *www.hotelbartabel.it* ⊘ *Closed Nov.–Mar.* ⇥ *11 rooms* ⦿ *Free Breakfast.*

Lefay Resort & Spa Lago di Garda

$$$$ | **RESORT** | The first thing you'll notice about this elegant resort in the hills above Gargnano are the stupendous lake and mountain views; the second thing will be its enormous spa, which is so filled with amenities (heated indoor-outdoor pool, saunas, well-equipped lake-view gym, extensive treatment menu) that you might just want to stay all day—and some guests do. **Pros:** fabulously relaxing spa; delicious breakfast buffet; lovely location. **Cons:** prices for food and drink excessively high; restaurant not up to standards of rest of hotel; village of Gargnano is down a steep and twisty road. Ⓢ *Rooms from: €590* ✉ *Via Angelo Feltrinelli 136, Gargnano* ☎ *0365/241800* ⊕ *lagodigarda.lefayresorts.com* ⊘ *Closed early Jan.–early Feb.* ⇥ *93 rooms* ⦿ *Free Breakfast.*

Villa Feltrinelli

$$$$ | **HOTEL** | This 1892 Art Nouveau villa hotel, named for the Italian publishing family who once vacationed here, has attracted the likes of Winston Churchill, D.H. Lawrence, and Benito Mussolini to its private lake-view gardens; extensive library; sumptuous and palatial rooms (as

befits the final bill); and overall opulent interior of fresco ceilings, wood paneling, and antique ceramics. **Pros:** first-class luxury hotel; amazing service including laundry and valet services, and in-room bar; like stepping into a bygone era. **Cons:** some find the attitude a bit arrogant; no gym; one of the most expensive hotels on the lake (or elsewhere). Ⓢ *Rooms from: €1450* ✉ *Via Rimembranza 38/40, Gargnano* ☎ *0365/798000* ⊕ *www.villafeltrinelli.com* ⊘ *Closed mid-Oct.–mid-Apr.* ⇥ *20 suites* ⦿ *Free Breakfast.*

Gardone Riviera

12 km (7 miles) southwest of Gargnano, 139 km (86 miles) northeast of Milan.

Now pleasantly faded, this once fashionable 19th-century resort is best known these days for the hilltop estate of the poet Gabriele D'Annunzio, made as an elaborate memorial to himself. The middle-European appearance of its towers and palaces helps set this lakeside town apart from the rest of Italy. With the Italian Alps in the background and crystalline lake views in the summer, it's a gorgeous, albeit underappreciated, destination.

GETTING HERE AND AROUND

Gardone Riviera is about 22 km (13 miles) east of Brescia and 126 km (78 miles) east of Milan. By car from Milan, head for the A35 autostrada from SP14.

VISITOR INFORMATION

CONTACTS Gardone Riviera Tourism.
✉ *Corso Repubblica 1, Gardone Riviera* ☎ *030/3748736.*

 ## Sights

★ Heller Garden

GARDEN | This 2½-acre garden is a place to get lost on a scavenger hunt while navigating stepping stones over lily ponds, climbing rock formations, and walking across wooden bridges. The treasures to be found are nearly 100 different Alpine, subtropical, and Mediterranean plant species and 30 modern art installations by the likes of Roy Lichtenstein, Joan Miró, and Auguste Rodin. A former vineyard, Heller Garden was first cultivated in 1903 by Austrian dentist and botanist Arthur Hruska, and bought in 1988 by artist Andrè Heller (although he is no longer the owner) who collaborated with artists to transform the garden into an open-air contemporary art gallery. There are dozens of places to sit and contemplate the merger of art and nature through a whimsical arrangement of plants by color to complement the art on display. A small café at the top of the garden offers panoramic views of Lake Garda. ⊠ *Via Roma 2, Gardone Riviera* ☏ *0366/410877* ⊕ *www.hellergarden. com* ✉ *€12* ⊘ *Closed Nov.–Feb.*

Il Vittoriale

HISTORIC HOME | The estate of the larger-than-life Gabriele D'Annunzio (1863–1938)—one of Italy's major modern poets, and later war hero and supporter of Mussolini—is filled with the trappings of his conquests in art, love, and war. His eccentric house crammed with quirky memorabilia can only be seen during a 35-minute guided tour (available in English), and the extensive gardens are definitely worth a stroll, particularly to see the curious full-size warship's prow. There's also an imposing mausoleum, made of white marble, along with three museums showcasing personal items from D'Annunzio's exploits, including one devoted to his cars. ⊠ *Via Vittoriale 12, Gardone Riviera* ☏ *0365/296511* ⊕ *www. vittoriale.it* ✉ *€18 for park, museums, and guided tour of house; €12 for park only* ⊘ *House closed Mon. Nov.–Feb.*

Salò Market (Mercato Di Salò)

MARKET | Four kilometers (2½ miles) south of Gardone Riviera is the enchanting lakeside town of Salò, which history buffs may recognize as the capital of the ill-fated Social Republic, set up in 1943 by the Germans after they liberated Mussolini from the Gran Sasso. Every Saturday morning an enormous market is held in the Piazza Mario Pedrazzi, with bargains on household goods, clothing, food, and other items. In August or September a vendor often sells locally foraged *tartufi neri* (black truffles) at affordable prices. ⊠ *Piazza Mario Pedrazzi, Salò.*

Restaurants

★ Ristorante Lido 84

$$$$ | **MODERN ITALIAN** | Dining in this bright, airy space feels like enjoying a meal in a fabulous friend's modern lake cottage—if the friend had floor-to-ceiling windows overlooking Lake Garda and a top-notch chef on hand. For an adventure in flavors from across the country, choose from two tasting menus (either "the classics" or one with "surprise" dishes chosen by the chef) and complement your meal with Italian or international wines in four- or five-glass pairings. **Known for:** exquisite lake setting; rose cake with zabaglione; unusual ingredients from all across Italy. $ *Average main: €40* ⊠ *Corso Zanardelli 196, Gardone Riviera* ☏ *0365/20019* ⊕ *www.ristorantelido84. com* ⊘ *Closed Tues., Wed., and early Jan.–mid-Feb.*

Hotels

★ Grand Hotel Fasano

$$$ | **HOTEL** | Used as a hunting lodge in the 19th century, the Fasano has matured into a seasonal hotel with high standards, opulent rooms, and many amenities—including an Aveda Destination Spa and a well-regarded restaurant, Il Fagiano, in addition to three more casual eateries (one a short walk away). **Pros:** exquisitely stylish rooms; gorgeous spa; relaxing surroundings. **Cons:** food gets mixed reviews; staff can seem indifferent; not all rooms have lake views. $ *Rooms from: €240* ⊠ *Corso Zanardelli 190, Gardone Riviera* ☏ *0365/290220*

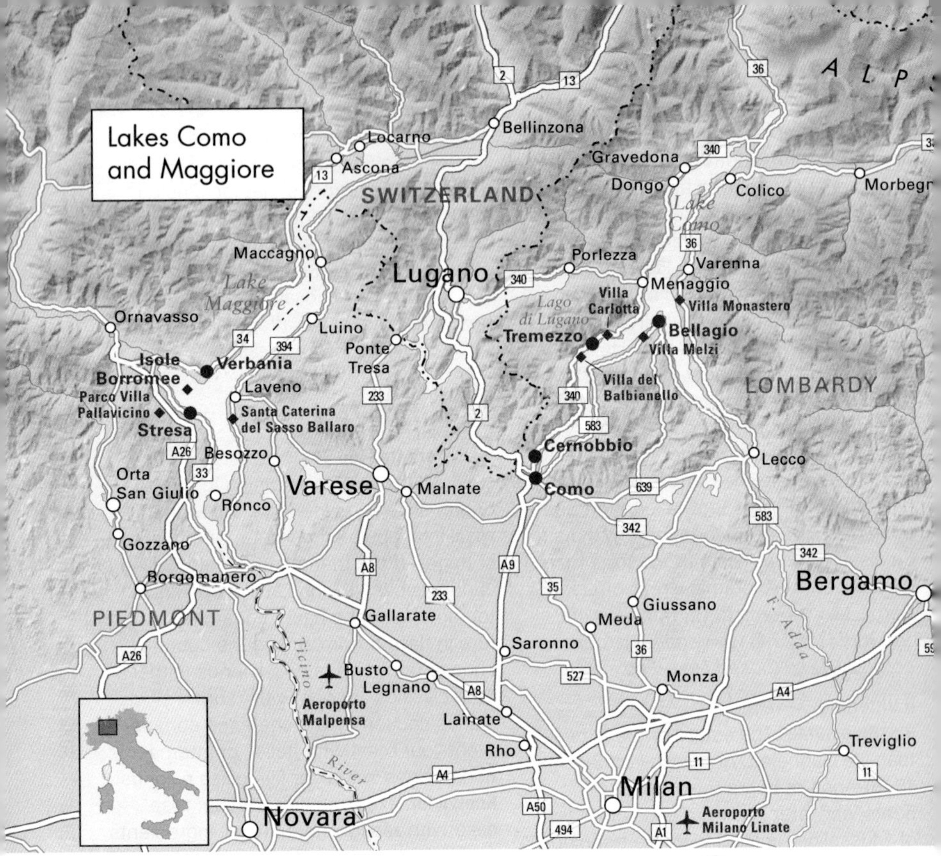

🌐 *www.ghf.it* ⏱ *Closed Nov.–Mar.* 🛏 *79 rooms* 🍴 *Free Breakfast.*

Grand Hotel Gardone

$$$ | **HOTEL** | Attractive gardens surround this majestic 1800s palace, where the service is top-notch, many of the rooms have balconies overlooking the water, and a large pool and terrace sit near the gorgeous lake. **Pros:** well-appointed; lakeside pool; expansive, well-manicured grounds. **Cons:** service can be hit-or-miss; some rooms could use an update; not much to do in the immediate area. [$] *Rooms from: €263* ✉ *Via Zanardelli 84, Gardone Riviera* ☎ *0365/20261* 🌐 *www.grandhotelgardone.it* ⏱ *Closed mid-Oct.–Apr.* 🛏 *167 rooms* 🍴 *Free Breakfast.*

Villa del Sogno

$$$$ | **HOTEL** | A narrow winding road takes you from town to this imposing villa, now a luxurious hotel retreat thanks to its valley and lake views and its peaceful grounds, which have an outdoor pool and a tennis court. **Pros:** endless amenities; expansive terrace overlooking the lake; individually decorated rooms. **Cons:** staff can be indifferent; remote location; food gets mixed reviews. [$] *Rooms from: €329* ✉ *Via Zanardelli 107, Gardone Riviera* ☎ *0365/290181* 🌐 *www.villadelsogno.it* ⏱ *Closed Nov.–mid-Apr.* 🛏 *38 rooms* 🍴 *Free Breakfast.*

Villa Fiordaliso

$$$ | **HOTEL** | A fine restaurant and five tastefully furnished guest rooms are housed in the pink-and-white lakeside villa given to Benito Mussolini's mistress, Claretta Petacci, by Il Duce himself—indeed, the expensive Claretta Suite is probably where they conducted their affair. **Pros:** combines cinematic charm with the intimacy of a B&B; elaborate breakfast spread; amazing setting on the lake. **Cons:** may be too small for some people; can sometimes be noisy; short on amenities (no spa or pool). $ *Rooms from: €300 ☒ Corso Zanardelli 150, Gardone Riviera ☎ 0365/20158 ⊕ www. villafiordaliso.it ⊘ Closed mid.-Oct.-mid-Mar. ⥂ 5 rooms ⦿⧵ Free Breakfast.*

Bellagio

30 km (19 miles) northeast of Como, 56 km (35 miles) northwest of Bergamo.

Sometimes called the prettiest town in Europe, Bellagio always seems perfectly adorned, with geraniums ablaze in every window and bougainvillea veiling its staircases, or *montées*. At dusk Bellagio's nightspots—including the wharf, where an orchestra may be serenading dancers under the stars—beckon you to come and make merry. It's an impossibly enchanting location, one that inspired the French composer Gabriel Fauré to call Bellagio "a diamond contrasting brilliantly with the sapphires of the three lakes in which it is set."

GETTING HERE AND AROUND

Boats can take you from here to Tremezzo, where Napoléon's worst Italian enemy, Count Sommariva, resided at Villa Carlotta; and a bit farther south of Tremezzo, to Villa del Balbianello via Lenno. Check timetables at ⊕ *www. navigazionelaghi.it.*

VISITOR INFORMATION

CONTACT Bellagio Tourism Office. ☒ *Piazza della Chiesa 14, ☎ 031/951555 ⊕ www. bellagiolakecomo.com.*

Sights

Villa Melzi

GARDEN | The famous gardens of the Villa Melzi were once a favorite picnic spot for Franz Liszt, who advised author Louis de Ronchaud in 1837, "When you write the story of two happy lovers, place

them on the shores of Lake Como. I do not know of any land so conspicuously blessed by heaven." The gardens are open to the public, and though you can't get into the 19th-century villa, don't miss the lavish Empire-style family chapel. The Melzi were Napoléon's greatest allies in Italy (the family has passed down the name "Josephine" to the present day). Guided tours are available with advance booking. ☒ *Lungo Lario Manzoni, Bellagio ☎ 031/950318 guided tour bookings ⊕ www.giardinidivillamelzi.it ⊠ €8 ⊘ Closed Nov.-late Mar.*

Villa Monastero

GARDEN | By ferry from Bellagio it's a quick trip across the lake to Varenna. The principal sight here is the spellbinding garden of the Villa Monastero, which, as its name suggests, was originally a monastery. There's also a house museum where you can admire 18th-century furnishings, as well as an international science and convention center. ☒ *Viale Giovanni Polvani 4, Varenna ☎ 0341/295450 ⊕ www.villamonastero. eu ⊠ Garden €8, garden and house €10 ⊘ Garden and house closed Mon.-Sat. early Nov.-Feb. (except Dec 26-Jan. 6). House also closed Mon.-Thurs. in Mar. and Apr., Mon.-Wed. in May, and Mon. in June, Sept., and Oct.*

Villa Serbelloni Garden

GARDEN | This property of the Rockefeller Foundation has celebrated gardens on the site of Pliny the Elder's villa, overlooking Bellagio. There are only two 1½-hour-long guided visits per day, at 11 am and 3:30 pm, with a maximum of 30 people each, and in May they tend to be booked by whole groups. It's wise to arrive early to sign up at the starting point, at the Bellagio tourist office in the medieval tower in St. Giacomo Square. The garden also closes due to bad weather, so call in advance. ☒ *Piazza della Chiesa 14, Bellagio ☎ 031/951555 ⊕ www.bellagiolakecomo.com/en/bellagio-lake-como-italy/POI-points-of-interest/*

villa-serbelloni-garden 🚇 *€10* 🕙 *Closed Mon. and early Nov.–mid-Mar.*

 Restaurants

★ Ristorante La Punta

$$ | ITALIAN | When tourist-heavy Bellagio starts to wear you down, seek respite at this charming restaurant located on the town's very northernmost point, a scenic 10-minute walk from the center, with amazing lake views of Varenna to the north and Tremezzo to the west. As you might expect, the menu is heavy on lake fish; although the dishes aren't innovative, they're fresh and well prepared, and the view makes the experience even better. **Known for:** friendly service; superlative Lake Como views; superfresh fish. $ *Average main: €23* ✉ *Via Eugenio Vitali 19, Bellagio* ☎ *031/951888* ⊕ *www.ristorantelapunta.it* 🕙 *Closed Nov.–Feb.*

Hotels

Du Lac

$$ | HOTEL | Most of the modern, inviting guest rooms at this comfortable, good-value old hotel—owned by an Anglo-Italian family and right in the center of Bellagio's action—have lake and mountain views, and the rooftop terrace garden is a perfect spot for drinks or dozing. **Pros:** pleasant on-site restaurant; friendly service; fabulous buffet breakfast. **Cons:** the boat dock right in front of the hotel can be noisy; some of the decor could use a refresh; beds too hard for some. $ *Rooms from: €195* ✉ *Piazza Mazzini 32, Bellagio* ☎ *031/950320* ⊕ *www.bellagiohoteldulac.com* 🕙 *Closed Nov.–Mar.* ⤴ *42 rooms* ⦿ *Free Breakfast.*

★ Grand Hotel Villa Serbelloni

$$$$ | HOTEL | The 19th-century luxury at this grand lake hotel—originally designed to cradle nobility and still a refined haven for the discreetly wealthy—has not so much faded as mellowed: guest rooms remain immaculate and plush; public areas are still awash with gilt ornamentation and marble; and breakfast is served in a ballroom. **Pros:** old-world grandeur; great pools; lovely gardens. **Cons:** expensive food and drink; staff helpfulness varies widely; could use some sprucing up. $ *Rooms from: €525* ✉ *Via Roma 1, Bellagio* ☎ *031/950216* ⊕ *www.villaserbelloni.com* 🕙 *Closed Nov.–early Apr.* ⤴ *94 rooms* ⦿ *Free Breakfast.*

Hotel Belvedere

$$$$ | HOTEL | FAMILY | In Italian, belvedere means "beautiful view," and it's an apt name for this enchanting spot, where the modern rooms have classic touches such as antique furniture, decorative tiles, and marble bathrooms. **Pros:** attention to detail; has a spa and a lovely pool; great views. **Cons:** fewer on-site amenities than other similarly priced hotels; must request a lake-view balcony room in advance; a climb from the waterfront. $ *Rooms from: €470* ✉ *Via Valassina 31, Bellagio* ☎ *031/950410* ⊕ *www.belvederebellagio.com* 🕙 *Closed Nov.–Mar.* ⤴ *63 rooms* ⦿ *Free Breakfast.*

Hotel Florence

$$ | HOTEL | Most of the large and comfortable rooms in this 1880s villa across from the ferry stop are furnished with interesting antiques and have splendid views of the lake. **Pros:** central location; lovely bar with outdoor lake-facing seating; appealing public spaces. **Cons:** hotel could use an update; some baths only have handheld showers; location may feel too central if you're looking to get away from it all. $ *Rooms from: €166* ✉ *Piazza Mazzini 46, Bellagio* ☎ *031/950342* ⊕ *www.hotelflorencebellagio.it* 🕙 *Closed mid-Oct.–Apr.* ⤴ *30 rooms* ⦿ *Free Breakfast.*

Tremezzo

34 km (21 miles) north of Cernobbio, 78 km (48 miles) north of Milan.

The dreamy lakeside town of Tremezzo is close to two outstanding and magical villas, as well as sprawling gardens and one of the lake's grandest hotels.

GETTING HERE AND AROUND

Tremezzo is along the SS340. By car from Milan, the drive is 80 km (50 miles) following the A8 autostrada and takes about 90 minutes.

VISITOR INFORMATION

CONTACTS Tremezzo Tourist Office. ✉ *Via Statale Regina 3, Tremezzo* ☎ *0344/40493.*

Sights

Villa Carlotta

GARDEN | If you're lucky enough to visit Tremezzo in late spring or early summer, you will find the magnificent Villa Carlotta a riot of color, with more than 14 acres of azaleas and dozens of varieties of rhododendrons in full bloom. The height of the blossoms is late April to early May. The villa was built between 1690 and 1743 for the luxury-loving marquis Giorgio Clerici. The garden's collection is remarkable, particularly considering the difficulties of transporting delicate plants before the age of aircraft. Palms, banana trees, cacti, eucalyptus, a sequoia, orchids, and camellias are among the more than 500 species.

The villa's interior is worth a visit, particularly if you have a taste for the romantic sculptures of Antonio Canova (1757–1822). The best known is his *Cupid and Psyche,* which depicts the lovers locked in an odd but graceful embrace, with the young god above and behind, his wings extended, while Psyche awaits a kiss that will never come. The villa can be reached by boat from Bellagio and Como. ✉ *Via Regina 2, Tremezzo* ☎ *0344/40405* 🌐 *www.villacarlotta.it* 🎫 *€12* 🕒 *Closed early Nov.–Mar.*

★ Villa del Balbianello

HISTORIC HOME | The relentlessly picturesque Balbianello may be the most magical house in all of Italy; you probably know it from cameos in the movies *Casino Royale* and *Star Wars Episode II: Attack of the Clones*. It sits on its own little promontory, Il Dosso d'Avedo, around the bend from the tiny fishing village of Ossuccio. The villa is composed of loggias, terraces, and *palazzini* (tiny palaces), all spilling down verdant slopes to the shore, where you'll find an old Franciscan church, a magnificent stone staircase, and a statue of San Carlo Borromeo blessing the waters.

The villa is usually reached from Como and Bellagio by boat, which leaves you at the village of Lenno. From there, marked signs lead you to the villa—it's either accessible by foot via a 20-minute walk or a more challenging 45-minute hike. ✉ *Via Guido Monzino 1, Lenno* ✥ *5 km (3 miles) southwest of Tremezzo* ☎ *0344/56110* 🌐 *www.fondoambiente.it/luoghi/villa-del-balbianello* 🎫 *€22 villa and gardens, includes 1-hr guided tour; €11 gardens only* 🕒 *Closed Mon., Wed., and early Jan.–mid-Mar.*

Hotels

★ Grand Hotel Tremezzo

$$$$ | **RESORT** | Creature comforts in this turn-of-the-20th-century building—one of the top grand hotels on the lake—include a lush park, three heated swimming pools (one of them floats on pontoons on the lake), a small private beach, and sumptuous guest rooms where old-world style meets modern amenities. **Pros:** lakeside location with beautiful views; gracious service; attractive spa. **Cons:** somewhat busy road between hotel and lake; very expensive; not well situated if you're looking for shopping or nightlife. [$] *Rooms from: €820* ✉ *Via Regina 8, Tremezzo* ☎ *0344/42491* 🌐 *www.grandhoteltremezzo.com* 🕒 *Closed mid-Nov.–early Apr.* 🛏 *90 rooms* 🍴 *Free Breakfast.*

Hotel Rusall

$$ | **B&B/INN** | Amid a large garden on the hillside above Tremezzo, this hotel offers small, private, comfortably simple rooms; a pool with a nice view; and a popular restaurant that serves tasty Italian classics. **Pros:** lovely walks into town and in the countryside; good on-site restaurant; more intimate than grander lake hotels. **Cons:** air-conditioning can be an issue in rooms and common areas; rooms are fairly basic; takes some effort to reach and walk to town. [$] *Rooms from: €135* ✉ *Via San Martino 2, Tremezzo* ☎ *0344/40408* 🌐 *www.rusallhotel.com* 🕓 *Closed Jan. and Feb.* 🛏 *23 rooms* 🍴 *Free Breakfast.*

Cernobbio

5 km (3 miles) north of Como, 53 km (34 miles) north of Milan.

The legendary resort of Villa d'Este is reason enough to visit this jewel on the lake, but the town itself is worth a stroll. The place still has a neighborhood feel to it, especially on summer evenings and weekends, when the piazza is full of families and couples strolling.

GETTING HERE AND AROUND

Cernobbio is on the SS340, 6 km (4 miles) north of the city of Como; from Milan take the A9 and follow signs for Como. The drive is 53 km (32 miles) and takes about one hour.

VISITOR INFORMATION

CONTACT Cernobbio Tourism Office. ✉ *Largo Alfredo Campanini 1,* ☎ *347/8818532* 🌐 *www.mylakecomo.co/en/cernobbio.*

🍴 Restaurants

Il Gatto Nero

$$$ | **NORTHERN ITALIAN** | Reservations are a good idea for this longtime favorite in the hills above Cernobbio. The lake view is splendid, and specialties include homemade pastas and fish dishes with a dash of international flair. **Known for:** lovely terrace; high-end wine selection; classic (veal) and nonclassic (tuna) cotoletta alla Milanese. [$] *Average main: €32* ✉ *Via Monte Santo 69, Cernobbio* ☎ *031/512042* 🌐 *www.ristorantegattonero.it* 🕓 *Closed Mon. and Jan.–mid-Mar. No lunch weekdays mid- to late Mar.*

Il Giardino

$$ | **NORTHERN ITALIAN** | "The Garden" has an expansive patio that's a shady respite from the summer sun. Though mainly known for its pizza, the restaurant also has an extensive menu of fish and meat dishes. **Known for:** fun vibe; tasty pizza; extensive outdoor seating. [$] *Average main: €16* ✉ *Via Regina 73, Cernobbio* ☎ *031/511154* 🌐 *www.giardinocernobbio.com* 🕓 *Closed Wed. Nov.–Feb.*

Lido di Cernobbio

$$$ | **ITALIAN** | Right next to the Cernobbio ferry stop, this pretty restaurant offers a nice selection of local wines and, whenever possible, uses local ingredients in its pizza, pasta, fish, and meat dishes. Though the modern gray interior is pleasant, try for a table on the terrace, and note that, in season, you can rent a sunbed and use the pools (one for adults and one for kids) before or after your meal. **Known for:** family-friendly atmosphere; solid Italian dishes; lovely lake scenery. [$] *Average main: €25* ✉ *Piazza Risorgimento 5, Cernobbio* ☎ *031/4446437* 🌐 *www.lidodicernobbio.com* 🕓 *Closed Wed. and Nov.–Mar.*

★ **Materia**

$$$ | **MODERN ITALIAN** | This aesthetically simple bistro-style restaurant, spruced up with modern art, draws a mainly local crowd for some of the most inventive food creations and presentation in the Como region. The imaginative Asian-inspired cuisine (think steamed partridge with smoked eel butter), makes good use of local ingredients like lake fish, and the frequently changing surprise five-, seven-, or twelve-course tasting menus are a particular delight, especially when paired with

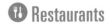

the mostly natural wines on offer. **Known for:** Italian and international wines from small producers; seasonally changing dishes; use of organic herbs and vegetables from their greenhouse. $ *Average main: €30* ⊠ *Via Cinque Giornate 32, Cernobbio* ☎ *031/2075548* ⊕ *www.ristorantemateria. it* ⊗ *Closed Mon. and Tues.*

Hotels

★ Villa d'Este

$$$$ | **HOTEL** | Europe's rich and famous have long favored this hotel, one of Italy's grandest, where rooms are done in Empire style; a broad veranda sweeps out to the lakefront; a swimming pool extends above the water; a restaurant offers top-notch views and cuisine; there are four private villas; and pavilions, miniature forts, and other follies ensure whimsical garden walks. **Pros:** fine service; excellent restaurant; amazing grounds. **Cons:** all this grandness comes with a hefty price tag; not all rooms have lake views; may feel too formal for some. $ *Rooms from: €970* ⊠ *Via Regina 40, Cernobbio* ☎ *031/3481* ⊕ *www. villadeste.it* ⊗ *Closed mid-Nov.–mid-Mar.* ⭧ *152 rooms, 4 private villas* ❙○❙ *Free Breakfast.*

Como

5 km (3 miles) south of Cernobbio, 30 km (19 miles) southwest of Bellagio, 49 km (30 miles) north of Milan.

Como commands the south shore of the lake. In its center, elegant cobblestone pedestrian streets wind their way past parks and bustling cafés. However, it's only partly a resort: the city also has an industrial heritage, deeply rooted in the production of textiles, particularly silk and the silk trade. If traveling by car, leave it at the edge of the town center in the well-lit underground parking facility right on the lake.

GETTING HERE AND AROUND

Como is easily reachable by regional trains from Milan from Porta Garibaldi and Milano Centrale stations, and the ride is about one hour. If driving from Milan, take the A9 and follow signs for Como; the journey is 50 km (31 miles) and takes about one hour.

VISITOR INFORMATION

CONTACT Como Tourism Office. ⊠ *Via Albertolli 7, Como* ☎ *031/304137, 031/4493068, 031/269712* ⊕ *www. visitcomo.eu/en.*

Sights

Duomo

CHURCH | The splendid 15th-century Renaissance-Gothic Duomo was begun in 1396. The facade was added in 1455, and the transepts were completed in the mid-18th century. The dome was designed by Filippo Juvarra (1678–1736), chief architect of many of the sumptuous palaces of the royal house of Savoy. The facade has statues of two of Como's most famous sons, Pliny the Elder and Pliny the Younger, whose writings are among the most important documents from antiquity. Inside, the works of art include Luini's *Holy Conversation,* a fresco cycle by Morazzone, and the *Marriage of the Virgin Mary* by Ferrari. ⊠ *Piazza del Duomo, Como* ☎ *031/3312275* ⊕ *www. cattedraledicomo.it.*

Museo della Seta (*Silk Museum*)

OTHER MUSEUM | From silkworm litters to textile finishing machinery to temporary exhibitions, this small but complete collection preserves the history of a manufacturing region that continues to supply a large proportion of Europe's silk. The friendly staffers will give you an overview of the museum; they are also happy to provide brochures and information about local retail shops. The location isn't well marked: follow the textile school's driveway around to the low-rise concrete building on the left, and take the shallow ramp down to the entrance. ✉ *Via Castelnuovo 9, Como* ☎ *031/303180* 🌐 *www.museosetacomo.com* 🎫 *€10* 🕒 *Closed Mon.*

San Fedele

CHURCH | At the heart of Como's medieval quarter, the city's first cathedral is well worth a peek. The apse walls and ceiling are completely frescoed, as are the ceilings above the altar. ✉ *Piazza San Fedele, Como* ☎ *031/3868316* 🌐 *www.parrocchiasanfedelecomo.it.*

Sant'Abbondio

CHURCH | If you head into Como's industrial quarter, you will come upon this church, a gem of Romanesque architecture begun by Benedictine monks in 1013 and consecrated by Pope Urban II in 1095. Inside, the five aisles converge on a presbytery with a semicircular apse decorated with a cycle of 14th-century frescoes by Lombard artists heavily influenced by the Sienese school. To see them, turn right as you enter. In the nave, the cubical capitals are the earliest example of this style in Italy. ✉ *Via Regina Teodolinda 35, Como* ☎ *031/304518* 🌐 *www.santabbondio.eu* 🎫 *Free.*

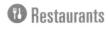

🍴 Restaurants

★ Feel Como

$$$ | **MODERN ITALIAN** | Your palate will travel from the lakes (eel with leek) to the countryside (hay risotto) to the mountains (tripe), all from the comfort of your table, at this cozy stone-arched eatery tucked into Como's commercial district. Expect creative takes on Italian cuisine, like deconstructed ravioli, using both local and more exotic ingredients, best sampled with a tasting menu focused on either fish, meat, vegetables, or a mix. **Known for:** extensive wine list; gorgeous platings; witty variations on local cuisine. [$] *Average main: €30* ✉ *Via Generale Armando Diaz 54, Como* ☎ *0334/7264545* 🌐 *www.feelcomo.com* 🕒 *Closed Mon. and Tues. No lunch Wed.–Fri.*

Rivenoteca

$$$ | **NORTHERN ITALIAN** | A former 17th-century convent is now a lively enoteca run by Alberto and Catia Rivetti, with more than 600 wines, as well as spirits and beers—all from northern Italy. Old and new merge in this warm and friendly spot with sage and rose walls, an original decorative ceiling, and a hallway with an automatic dispenser with more than 30 wines available on demand—get up from your seat to taste as many wines as you'd like using a prepaid card. **Known for:** entirely Lombard-focused cuisine; dispenser for wines "on demand" in three sizes, or by the bottle; local wines and spirits, including from the owners' Rivetti winery. [$] *Average main: €28* ✉ *Via A. Diaz 56, Como* ☎ *335/6688743* 🌐 *www.rivenoteca.it* 🕒 *Closed Sun. No lunch weekdays.*

🛏 Hotels

Albergo Terminus

$$$$ | **HOTEL** | In addition to Lake Como panoramas, this early-20th-century Art Nouveau landmark has marbled public spaces and guest rooms with floral fabrics, walnut wardrobes, and silk-covered sofas. **Pros:** old-world charm; bountiful breakfast; right on the lake. **Cons:** noise from the restaurant and outside can be an issue; decor in some rooms seems dated; limited number of lake-view rooms. [$] *Rooms from: €310* ✉ *Lungo Lario Trieste 14, Como* ☎ *031/329111* 🌐 *www.albergoterminus.it* 🛏 *50 rooms* 🍴 *Free Breakfast.*

★ Il Sereno Lago di Como

$$$$ | **HOTEL** | Throughout this, the first European outpost of the luxe Il Sereno Hotel in St. Barths, you'll find floor-to-ceiling lake-view windows and an understated retro-mod aesthetic, with a muted palette of browns and grays complementing a panoply of wood, stone, leather, and copper accents. **Pros:** cool modern design; fabulous views; hushed elegance throughout. **Cons:** can be

difficult to find; not for lovers of historical villas; extremely expensive. $ *Rooms from: €1250* ✉ *Via Torrazza 10, Torno* ☎ *031/5477800* ⊕ *www.ilsereno.com* ◷ *Closed Nov.–mid-Mar.* ⌦ *40 suites* ¶◎¶ *Free Breakfast.*

Mandarin Oriental, Lago di Como

$$$$ | HOTEL | The nine 19th-century villas that comprise this Lake Como outpost of the extravagant Mandarin chain have been thoroughly updated for the 21st century, offering a quiet setting (just north of the busy town of Como) and luxurious amenities that include a 14,000-square-foot spa and a swimming pool that "floats" above the lake. **Pros:** amazingly peaceful setting; complimentary minibar; fabulous wellness facilities. **Cons:** service can be haphazard; food not up to par; location a bit isolated from other towns. $ *Rooms from: €850* ✉ *Via E. Caronti 69, Blevio* ☎ *031/32511* ⊕ *www.mandarinoriental.com/lake-como/blevio/luxury-hotel* ◷ *Closed mid-Nov.–mid-Mar.* ⌦ *75 rooms* ¶◎¶ *Free Breakfast.*

Posta Design Hotel

$$ | HOTEL | Just a block from the lake, on downtown Como's pedestrian-only Piazza Volta, this boutique hotel has a minimalist modern interior that's in perfect keeping with its exterior—the 1931 building that houses it was designed by Rationalist architect Giuseppe Terragni. **Pros:** central location; friendly service; comfortable rooms. **Cons:** Internet must be logged into each time; sparse amenities (no minibars in rooms, no breakfast, no gym); rooms on lower floors can be noisy. $ *Rooms from: €129* ✉ *Via Garibaldi 2, Como* ☎ *031/2769011* ⊕ *www.postadesignhotel.com* ⌦ *14 rooms* ¶◎¶ *No Meals.*

Vista Palazzo Lago di Como

$$$$ | HOTEL | A 19th-century lakefront palazzo steps from pedestrian-only Piazza Cavour has been transformed into an elegant in-town hotel, where a sweeping staircase leads to spacious, sophisticated white-and-gray guest rooms that have pops of color, parquet floors, walk-in closets, and sumptuous marble bathrooms with deep soaking tubs. **Pros:** great central location; friendly and helpful service; lovely views from most rooms. **Cons:** not everyone wants to stay in Como town; breakfast can be a bit sparse; lakefront rooms can be noisy. $ *Rooms from: €814* ✉ *Piazza Cavour 24, Como* ☎ *031/5375241* ⊕ *vistalagodicomo.com* ⌦ *18 rooms* ¶◎¶ *Free Breakfast.*

Activities

Lake Como has lots of ways to stay active and outdoors, from windsurfing at the lake's northern end, to boating, sailing, and Jet Skiing at Como and Cernobbio. The lake is also quite swimmable in summer. For hikers there are lovely paths all around the lake. For an easy trek, take the funicular up to Brunate, and walk along the mountain to the lighthouse for a stunning view of the lake.

Stresa and the Isole Borromee

80 km (50 miles) northwest of Milan.

One of the better known resorts on the western shore, Stresa is a tourist town, which provided Hemingway with one of the settings in *A Farewell to Arms*. It has capitalized on its central lakeside position, though the luxurious elegance that distinguished its heyday has faded; grand hotels are still grand, but traffic now encroaches on their parks and gardens.

The best way to escape to yesteryear is to head for the Isole Borromee (Borromean Islands) in Lake Maggiore. Boats to the three islands depart every 15–30 minutes from the dock at Stresa's Piazza Marconi, as well as from Piazzale Lido at the northern end of the promenade. There's also a boat from Verbania; check locally for the seasonal schedule.

Although you can hire a private boat, it's cheaper and just as convenient to use the regular service. Make sure you buy a ticket allowing you to visit all the islands—Bella, Superiore dei Pescatori, and Madre. The islands take their name from the Borromeo family, which has owned them since the 12th century.

GETTING HERE AND AROUND

Trains run regularly from Milan to the town of Stresa on Lake Maggiore; the trip takes 1–1½ hours, depending on the type of train. By car from Milan to Stresa, take the A8 autostrada to the A8dir, and from the A8dir take the A26; the drive is about 1¼ hours.

VISITOR INFORMATION

CONTACTS Stresa and Isole Borromee Information. ⊠ *Piazza Marconi 16,* ☎ *0323/933478* ⊕ *www.isoleborromee.it.*

 # Sights

Isola Bella (*Beautiful Island*)

ISLAND | The most famous of the three Isole Borromee (Borromean Islands), is named after Isabella, whose husband, Carlo III Borromeo (1538–84), built the palace and terraced gardens here for her as a wedding present. Before Count Carlo began his project, the island was rocky and almost devoid of vegetation; the soil for the garden had to be transported from the mainland. For a splendid view of the lake, wander up the 10 terraces of Teatro Massimo. In the gardens, white peacocks roam among the scented shrubs, statues, and fountains. Visit Palazzo Borromeo to see the rooms where famous guests—including Napoléon and Mussolini—stayed in 18th-century splendor. Those three interlocked rings on walls and even streets represent the powerful Borromeo, Visconti, and Sforza families. ⊠ *Isola Bella* ☎ *0323/933478* ⊕ *www.isoleborromee. it* ☜ *Garden and palazzo €20* ⊙ *Closed early Nov.–mid-Mar.*

★ **Isola Madre** (*Mother Island*)

GARDEN | All of this Borromean island is a botanical garden, with a season that stretches from late March to late October due to the climatic protection of the mighty Alps and the tepid waters of Lake Maggiore. The cacti and palm trees here, so far north and so near the border with Switzerland, are a beautiful surprise. Take time to see the profusion of exotic trees and shrubs running down to the shore in every direction. Two special times to visit are April, for the camellias, and May, for azaleas and rhododendrons. Also on the island is a 16th-century palazzo, where the Borromeo family still lives for part of the year. The palazzo has an antique puppet theater on display, complete with string puppets, prompt books, and elaborate scenery designed by Alessandro Sanquirico, who was a scenographer at La Scala in Milan. ⊠ *Isola Madre* ☎ *0323/933479* ⊕ *www.isoleborromee. it* ☜ *€17 (palace and garden)* ⊙ *Closed early Nov.–mid Mar.*

Isola Superiore dei Pescatori (*Island of the Fishermen*)

ISLAND | Stop for lunch at the smallest Borromean island, less than 100 yards wide and only about ½ km (¼ mile) long. It's an ideal place to visit before, after, or in between visiting the other two islands. Of the 10 or so restaurants on this island the two worth visiting are Ristorante Il Verbano (☎ *0323/31226*) and Ristorante Belvedere (☎ *0323/32292*). The island's little lanes strung with fishing nets and dotted with shrines to the Madonna make it a crowded place filled with souvenir stands and shops in high season. ⊠ *Isola dei Pescatori.*

Parco Villa Pallavicino

GARDEN | FAMILY | As you wander around the palms and semitropical shrubs, don't be surprised if you're followed by a peacock or even an ostrich: they're part of the zoological garden and are allowed to roam almost at will. From the top of the hill on which the villa stands you can see the gentle hills of the Lombardy shore of Lake Maggiore and, nearer and to the left, the jewel-like Isole Borromee. In addition to a bar and restaurant, the grounds also have picnic spots and there is a farm that's popular with children. ✉ *Via Sempione 8, Stresa* ☎ *0323/933478* 🌐 *www.isoleborromee.it* 🎫 *€13* 🕓 *Closed early Nov.–mid-Mar.*

🍴 Restaurants

★ Ristorante Lastresa

$$ | **NORTHERN ITALIAN** | The nondescript exterior of this buzzy eatery off one of Stresa's main streets belies its chic, stylish interior. Dishes made with seasonal ingredients dominate the menu, but, no matter the season, you'll find local lake fish, both marinated and panfried, as well as a solid list of wines from throughout the region and across Italy. **Known for:** Piedmont dessert sampler; friendly, knowledgeable waitstaff; locals' favorite. [$] *Average main: €20* ✉ *Via Principessa Margherita 22, Stresa* ☎ *0323/33240* 🌐 *www.ristorantelastresa.it* 🕓 *Closed Mon. and Tues. Sept.– Mar.*

Trattoria due Piccioni

$$ | **MODERN ITALIAN** | In a town with an overabundance of touristy pizza and pasta places, this unassumingly modern family-run bistro raises the bar. Although the shabby-chic decor and friendly service entice, the real draw is the short but smart menu of creative Italian dishes and vegetarian options. **Known for:** attentive service; intriguing desserts; inventive local cuisine. [$] *Average main: €16* ✉ *Via P. Tommaso 61, Stresa* ☎ *0323/934556* 🌐 *www.duepiccioni.it* 🕓 *Closed Wed.*

☕ Coffee and Quick Bites

Cicinin panini al metro

$ | **SANDWICHES** | Pick a sandwich size (from a few inches to 40—or a meter—as the name *al metro* implies) to match your appetite, at this paninoteca off of Piazza Luigi Cadorna. There are just four inventive sandwich types on offer each day, with ingredients changing daily and seasonally like lentil cream, fennel, ricotta salata, and orange; or mortadella, pistachio cream, and Toma cheese. **Known for:** curated menu of local ingredients; portions for any appetite; friendly service. [$] *Average main: €7* ✉ *Via Principe Tomaso, 10, Stresa* ☎ *334/1627769* 🕓 *Closed Thurs.*

Pasticceria Marcolini

$ | **BAKERY** | Margheritine cookies were first baked in Stresa for Margherita of Savoy in 1857 while she was still a princess. Named for the first queen of Italy as well as for their shape like a daisy (*margherita* in Italian) the biscuits' recipe includes cooked egg yolk and an abundant supply of powdered sugar making them crumble effortlessly in your mouth. **Known for:** gift boxes to take cookies home; sweets made following traditional Stresa recipes; locals' spot for breakfast and special occasions. [$] *Average main: €10* ✉ *Via Vincenzo de Vit, 14, Stresa* ☎ *0323/30364* 🕓 *Closed Tues.*

🛏 Hotels

★ Grand Hotel des Iles Borromees

$$$$ | **HOTEL** | This palatial, Liberty-style hotel has catered to a demanding European clientele since 1863, and although its spacious salons and guest rooms still have lavish turn-of-the-last-century furnishings, there are signs of modernity, including a redesigned bar (Hemingway Bar), low-calorie and gluten-free options at the restaurant, and extensive wellness treatments. **Pros:** bygone-era grace and style plus modern amenities; nice pool and spa selection; sumptuous rooms, particularly the fabulous Hemingway Suite. **Cons:** Internet can be on the slow side; decor may be over the top for some; bathrooms could use a refresh. [$] *Rooms from: €314* ✉ *Corso Umberto I 67, Stresa* ☎ *0323/938938* 🌐 *www.borromees.com* 🕓 *Closed Dec. and Jan.* 🛏 *179 rooms* 🍴 *Free Breakfast.*

Verbania

16 km (10 miles) north of Stresa, 95 km (59 miles) northwest of Milan.

The quaint town of Verbania is across the Gulf of Pallanza from its more touristy neighbor, Stresa. It is known for the Villa Taranto, which has magnificent botanical gardens. With its majestic gardens and greenery, Verbania is often called the Garden of Lake Maggiore.

GETTING HERE AND AROUND

By car from Milan take the A8 to Lago Maggiore, traveling 100 km (63 miles); Verbania is on SS34 and the drive takes about one hour and 45 minutes.

VISITOR INFORMATION

CONTACTS Verbania Tourism. ✉ *Piazza Daniele Ranzoni 40, Verbania* ☎ *0323/503249.*

Sights

Santa Caterina del Sasso Ballaro
CHURCH | Near the town of Laveno, this beautiful lakeside hermitage was constructed in the 12th century by a local merchant to express his gratitude for having been saved from the wrath of a storm. Seemingly carved out of its supporting cliff, it's particularly striking as you approach it by boat or ferry, although, after docking, you'll need to climb 80 steps to reach the hermitage. Alternatively, park in the lot above and walk down a 268-step staircase; there's also an elevator, though it's not as scenic an option. ✉ *Via Santa Caterina 13, Leggiuno* ☎ *0332/647014* 🌐 *www.eremosantacaterina.it* 🎫 *€5.*

Villa Taranto
GARDEN | FAMILY | The Villa Taranto was acquired in 1931 by Scottish captain Neil McEachern, who helped make the magnificent gardens here what they are today, adding terraces, waterfalls, more than 3,000 plant species from all over the world—including 300 varieties of dahlias—and broad meadows sloping gently to the lake. While the gardens can be visited, the villa itself is not open to the public. ✉ *Via Vittorio Veneto 111, Verbania* ☎ *0323/556667* 🌐 *www.villataranto.it* 🎫 *€12* 🕒 *Closed early Nov.–early Apr.*

Hotels

Il Chiostro
$ | HOTEL | Using space formed from a 17th-century monastery merged with an adjoining 19th-century textile factory, this hotel offers plain, functional rooms, some overlooking a lovely garden. **Pros:** friendly, efficient staff; affordable for the area; lovely breakfast. **Cons:** small bathrooms; limited amenities; rooms are fairly plain. [$] *Rooms from: €95* ✉ *Via Fratelli Cervi 14, Verbania* ☎ *0323/404077* 🌐 *www.chiostrovb.it* 🛏 *100 rooms* 🍴 *Free Breakfast.*

Il Sole di Ranco
$$ | HOTEL | For more than 170 years the same family has run this elegant inn—about an hour's drive from Verbania on the banks of the lake opposite Stresa—where guest rooms are in two late-19th-century villas surrounded by a garden and the chef does the family proud in the exceptional restaurant. **Pros:** classic lake setting; lovely pool area; tranquil grounds. **Cons:** restaurant a bit pricey; decor on the old-fashioned side; far from the tourist center (hotel offers tours with private drivers). [$] *Rooms from: €190* ✉ *Piazza Venezia 5, Ranco* ☎ *0331/976507* 🌐 *www.ilsolediranco.it* 🕒 *Closed Jan.–early Feb.* 🛏 *14 rooms* 🍴 *Free Breakfast.*

Chapter 9

PIEDMONT AND THE VALLE D'AOSTA

9

Updated by
Liz Humphreys

 Sights
★★★☆☆

 Restaurants
★★★★★

 Hotels
★★★★☆

 Shopping
★★☆☆☆

 Nightlife
★☆☆☆☆

WELCOME TO
PIEDMONT AND THE VALLE D'AOSTA

TOP REASONS TO GO

★ **Sacra di San Michele:** Explore one of the country's most spectacularly situated religious monuments.

★ **Castello di Fénis:** This castle transports you back in time to the Middle Ages.

★ **Monte Bianco:** A cable-car ride over a snowcapped mountain will take your breath away.

★ **Turin's Museo Egizio:** A surprising treasure—one of the world's richest collections of Ancient Egyptian art outside Cairo, Egypt.

★ **Regal wines:** Some of Italy's most revered reds—led by Barolo, the "king of wines"—come from the hills of southern Piedmont.

★ **Turin's Galleria Sabauda:** Witness to the regal splendor of the reigning House of Savoy, this museum is famed for its spectacular collection of Old Masters.

1 Turin. Neoclassical piazzas and Baroque palazzi have been restored in grand style.

2 Asti. Home of its namesake *spumante*, a sweet sparkling wine.

3 Alba. A city that's renowned for its truffles and mushrooms.

4 The Barolo Region. This is where nebbiolo grapes become celebrated wines.

5 Bard. A strategic medieval town with an impressive fortress.

6 Breuil-Cervinia/The Matterhorn. This skier's paradise straddles the Swiss border.

7 Castello di Fénis. Castello di Fénis is embellished with many towers.

8 Aosta. This is one of Italy's most livable cities.

9 Courmayeur/Monte Bianco. A cozy mountain town, popular with skiers and hikers.

10 Venaria Reale. An expansive 16th-century Savoy palace.

11 Rivoli. The storybook town of Rivoli is a highlight.

12 Sacra di San Michele. This 11th-century abbey once controlled 176 churches in Italy, France, and Spain.

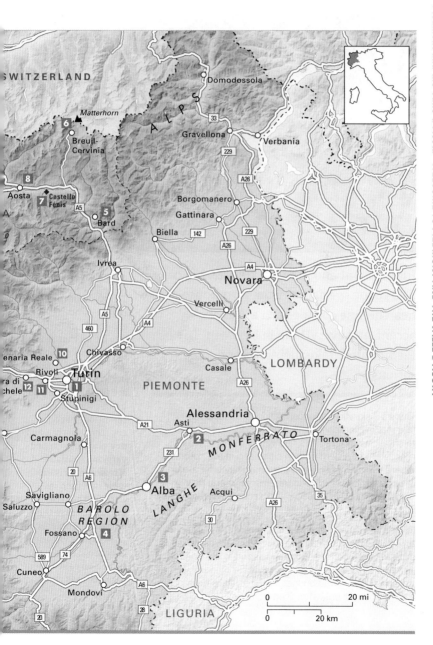

SWITZERLAND

Domodossola

Matterhorn

6 Breuil-Cervinia

A L P S

33

Gravellona

Verbania

229

8

A26

Aosta

7 Castello
Fénis

Borgomanero

Gattinara

A5

5 Bard

229

Biella

142

A26

Ivrea

A4

Novara

A5

460

A4

Vercelli

Chivasso

enaria Reale **10**

Casale

LOMBARDY

Rivoli

A26

ra di
chele **12** **11**

Turin **1**

PIEMONTE

Stupinigi

Alessandria

Carmagnola

A21

Asti

2 *M O N F E R R A T O*

Tortona

231

Saluzzo

Savigliano

20   A6

3 Alba

Acqui

A26

35

*B A R O L O
R E G I O N*

L A N G H E

30

Fossano

4

589   74

Cuneo

A6

Mondovì

A26

28

20

LIGURIA

0   20 mi

0   20 km

EATING AND DRINKING WELL IN PIEDMONT AND THE VALLE D'AOSTA

In Piedmont and the Valle d'Aosta you can find rustic specialties from farmhouse hearths, fine cuisine with a French accent, and everything in between. The Piedmontese take their food and wine very seriously.

There's a significant concentration of upscale restaurants in Piedmont, with refined cuisine designed to showcase the region's fine wines. Wine-oriented menus are prevalent both in cities and in the country, where even simply named trattorias may offer a *menu di degustazione* (a multicourse tasting menu that highlights the chef's specialties) accompanied by wine pairings.

In Turin the ritual of the *aperitivo* (aperitif) has been finely tuned, and most cafés from the early evening onward provide lavish buffets that are included in the price of a cocktail—a respectable substitute for dinner if you're traveling on a limited budget. As a result, restaurants in Turin tend to fill only after 9 pm.

GREAT GRISSINI

Throughout the region—and especially in Turin—you'll find that most meals are accompanied by *grissini* (bread sticks). When they are freshly made and hand-rolled, these renditions are a far cry from the thin and dry, plastic-wrapped versions available elsewhere. Grissini were invented in Turin in the 17th century to ease the digestive problems of little Prince Vittorio Amedeo II (1675–1730). Napoléon called them *petits batons* and was supposedly addicted to them.

TRUFFLES

The *tartufo* (truffle) is a peculiar delicacy—a gnarly clump of fungus that grows wild in forests a few inches underground. It's hunted down using truffle-sniffing dogs. The payoff is a powerful, perfume flavor that makes gourmets swoon and for which they are willing to pay a small fortune. Although truffles are more abundant farther south in Umbria, the most coveted ones are the *tartufi bianchi* (white truffles) from Alba in Piedmont. A thin shaving of truffle often tops pasta dishes; they're also used to flavor soups and other dishes.

POLENTA AND PASTA

The area's best-known dish is probably polenta, creamy cornmeal served with *carbonada* (a meat stew), melted cheese, or wild mushrooms. *Agnolotti*—crescent-shape pasta stuffed with meat filling—is another specialty, often served with the pan juices of roast veal. Agnolotti *del plin* is a smaller version topped with melted butter and shaved truffles.

CHEESE

In keeping with their northern character, Piedmont and the Valle d'Aosta are both known for *fonduta*, a version of fondue made with melted cheese, eggs, and sometimes grated truffles.

Fontina and ham also often deck out the ubiquitous French-style crepes *alla valdostana,* served casserole-style.

MEAT

The locally raised beef of Piedmont is some of Italy's most highly prized; it's often braised or stewed with the region's hearty red wine. In winter, *bollito misto* (various meats, boiled and served with a rich sauce) shows up on many menus, and *fritto misto,* a combination of fried meats and vegetables, is another specialty.

DESSERTS AND SWEETS

Although desserts here are less sweet than in some other Italian regions, treats like *panna cotta* (a puddinglike cooked cream), *torta di nocciole* (hazelnut torte), and *bonet* (a pudding made with hazelnuts, cocoa, milk, and macaroons) are delights. Turin is renowned for its delicate pastries and fine chocolates—especially for *gianduiotti,* made with hazelnuts.

WINE

Piedmont is one of Italy's most important wine regions, producing full-bodied reds, such as Barolo, Barbaresco, freisa, barbera, and the lighter dolcetto. Asti Spumante, a sweet sparkling wine, comes from the region, while the Valle d'Aosta is famous for brandies made from fruits or herbs.

Northwest Italy's Piedmont and Valle d'Aosta regions come with a large dose of mountain splendor, bourgeois refinement, culinary achievement, and scenic beauty. Two of Europe's most famous peaks, Monte Bianco (Mont Blanc) and Monte Cervino (the Matterhorn), straddle the Valle d'Aosta's borders with France and Switzerland, and the region draws skiers and hikers from all over.

To the south, the mist-shrouded lowlands skirting the Po River are home to Turin, a city that may not have the artistic treasures of Rome or the cutting-edge style of Milan, but has developed a sense of urban sophistication that makes it a pleasure to visit. The first capital of unified Italy and the fourth-largest city in the country, it was once overlooked on tourist itineraries as a mere industrial center (Fiat is based here), but the 2006 Winter Olympic Games put Turin on many tourists' map. Still, despite its higher profile and its many excellent museums, cafés, and restaurants, Turin never feels overrun.

Farther south, vineyards carpet the rolling hills of the Langhe and Monferrato regions, where Barolo, Barbaresco, and Asti Spumante wines—some of Italy's finest—are produced. It's here, as well, that the prized white truffle of Alba is found and celebrated during an autumn fair.

Piedmont has the longest border with France of any region, and the fact of its having been ruled by the French Savoy for centuries is revealed in a Gallic influence in all walks of life—especially in food and architecture. Turin's mansard roofs and porticoed avenues can make a walk through its streets feel like a stroll down a Parisian boulevard. Food is richer, creamier, and perhaps more refined than in many other parts of Italy, and the standard of service, even in simple restaurants, is often very high.

MAJOR REGIONS

Southeast of Turin—in the hilly, wooded Monferrato area, and farther south in the Langhe near Alba—the landscape is a patchwork of vineyards and dark woods, dotted with hill towns, castles like medieval Castello di Fénis, and fortresses like the one in Bard. This area produces some of Italy's most famous red wines, as well as sparkling whites like Asti Spumante. And in those dark woods are secret places where hunters and their dogs unearth the precious aromatic truffles that are worth their weight in gold at Alba's truffle fair.

In the Valle d'Aosta, a semiautonomous bilingual region near the French–Swiss border, the unspoiled beauty of the Alps' highest peaks, the Matterhorn and Mont Blanc, competes with the magnificent scenery of Italy's oldest national park, Gran Paradiso. Luckily, the region is so small that you don't have to choose—you can fit skiing, après-ski in the villages of Breuil-Cervinia or Courmayeur, and viewing wild ibex into one memorable trip. Aosta is also known as one of Italy's most livable cities.

The main Aosta Valley, largely on an east–west axis, is hemmed in by high mountains where glaciers have gouged out 14 tributary valleys, six to the north and eight to the south. A car is helpful, but although distances are relatively short as the crow flies, steep slopes and winding roads add to your mileage and travel time. Coming up from Turin, beyond Ivrea, the road takes you through steep ravines guarded by brooding, romantic castles. Pont St. Martin, about 18 km (11 miles) north of Ivrea, is the beginning of bilingual (Italian and French) territory.

As you head west from Turin into the Colline ("little hills"), castles and medieval fortifications begin to pepper the former dominion of the House of Savoy, and the Alps come into better and better view. In this region lie the storybook medieval town of Rivoli; 12th-century abbeys like Sacra di San Michele; a 16th-century Savoy hunting lodge, Venaria Reale; and, farther west in the mountains, the ski resort of Sestriere, one of the venues used during the 2006 Winter Games.

Planning

Making the Most of Your Time

Turin needs at least two or three days to visit properly. If you have extra time, visit one of the magnificent palaces built by the Savoy family. They surround Turin in the so-called *corona di delizie* (crown of delights) and make for an easy day trip.

Plan on several days to visit the Langhe and Monferrato areas. The towns of Alba and Asti should not be missed, but neither should the smaller wine towns that dot the rolling hills of both regions. You'll need your own car here, but the rewards are great views, great food, and great wine. If coming in September and October, when there are festivals in both Alba and Asti, make sure to book your trip well in advance.

Unless you are planning on a skiing or hiking holiday, the Valle d'Aosta requires less time to visit. The emphasis here is on the natural beauty of the mountains, but if you are driving between France and Italy, the region certainly merits a one- or two-night stopover, in either Courmayeur or Aosta; be sure not to miss Castello di Fénis and the Forte di Bard on your way.

Getting Here and Around

BUS

Turin's main bus station is on the corner of Corso Inghilterra and Corso Vittorio Emanuele. There's also a major bus station at Aosta, across the street from the train station.

CONTACTS GTT. ☎ *800/019152 toll-free in Italy* ⊕ *www.gtt.to.it/cms.* **Arriva Italia.** ☎ *035/289000* ⊕ *torino.arriva.it.*

CAR

Like any mountainous region, the Italian Alps can be tricky to navigate by car. Roads that look like highways on the map can be narrow and twisting, with steep slopes and cliff-side drops. Generally, roads are well maintained, but the distance covered by all of those curves tends to take longer than you might expect, so it's best to figure in extra time for getting around. This is especially true in winter, when weather conditions can slow traffic and close roads. Check with local tourist offices or, in a pinch, with the police to make sure roads are passable and safe.

For travel across the French, Swiss, and Italian borders in Piedmont and the Valle d'Aosta, only a few routes are usable year-round: the 12-km (7-mile) Mont Blanc tunnel connecting Chamonix with Courmayeur; the Colle del Gran San Bernardo/Col du Grand-Saint-Bernard (connecting Martigny to Aosta on Swiss highway E27 and Italian highway SS27, with 6 km [4 miles] of tunnel); and the Traforo del Fréjus (between Modane and Susa, with 13 km [8 miles] of tunnel). Other passes become increasingly unreliable between November and April.

TRAIN

Turin is on the main Paris–Rome TGV express line and is also connected with Milan, 60 minutes away on the fast train. The fastest (Frecciarossa) trains cover the 667-km (414-mile) trip to Rome in just over four hours; other trains take between five and seven hours.

Services to the larger cities east of Turin are part of the extensive and reliable train network of the Lombard Plain. In the mountains to the west of the region's capital, however, train service begins to peter out in favor of bus connections; information about train-bus mountain services can be obtained from train stations and tourist information offices, or by contacting FS–Trenitalia, the Italian national train service.

CONTACTS Italo. ☎ *892020* ⊕ *www. italotreno.it/en.* **Trenitalia.** ☎ *892021 toll-free in Italy* ⊕ *www.trenitalia.com.*

Restaurants

In this region's restaurants you'll taste a difference between the mountain and the city, but the hearty peasant fare served in tiny stone villages and the French-accented delicacies of the plain are both eminently satisfying.

Prices in the dining reviews are the average cost of a main course at dinner, or, if dinner is not served, at lunch. Restaurant reviews have been shortened. For full information, visit Fodors.com.

Hotels

High standards and good service are characteristic of Turin's better hotels, and the same is true at top mountain resorts. Hotels in Turin and other major towns are generally geared to business travelers; make sure to ask whether lower weekend rates or special deals for two- or three-night stays are available.

Summer vacationers and winter skiers keep occupancy rates and prices high at resorts during peak seasons. Many mountain hotels require guests to pay for either half or full board and insist on a stay of several nights; some have off-season rates that can reduce the cost by a full price category. If you're planning to ski, ask about packages that give you a discount on lift tickets.

Prices in the reviews are the lowest cost of a standard double room in high season. Hotel reviews have been shortened. For full information, visit Fodors.com.

What it Costs in Euros

	$	$$	$$$	$$$$
RESTAURANTS				
	under €15	€15–€24	€25–€35	over €35
HOTELS				
	under €125	€125–€200	€201–€300	over €300

Turin

Turin (Torino, in Italian) is roughly in the center of Piedmont–Valle d'Aosta and 128 km (80 miles) west of Milan; it's on the Po River, on the edge of the Po Plain, which stretches east all the way to the Adriatic. Turin's flatness and wide, angular, tree-lined boulevards are a far cry from Italian *metropoli* to the south; the region's decidedly northern European bent is quite evident in its nerve center. Aside from its role as northwest Italy's major industrial, cultural, intellectual, and administrative hub, Turin also has a reputation as Italy's capital of black magic and the supernatural. This distinction is enhanced by the presence of Turin's most famous and controversial relic, the Sacra Sindone (Shroud of Turin), still believed by many Catholics to be Christ's burial shroud. (For its part, the Vatican has not taken an official position on its authenticity.)

GETTING HERE AND AROUND

Turin is well served by the Italian auto-strada system and can be reached easily by car from all directions: from Milan on the A4 (two hours); from Bologna (four hours) and Florence (five hours) on the A1 and A21; from Genoa on the A6 (two hours). Bus service to and from other major Italian cities is also plentiful, and Turin can be reached by fast train service from Paris in less than six hours. Fast train service also connects the city with Milan, Genoa, Bologna, Venice, Florence, and Rome.

VISITOR INFORMATION

The city's tourist office organizes group and personal guided tours. It also provides maps and details about a wide range of thematic self-guided walks through town. The Torino+Piemonte Card, which provides discounts on transportation and museum entrances for one-, two-, three-, or five-day visits, can be purchased here.

CONTACT Turin Tourist Information Center.
✉ *Piazza Castello,* ☎ *011/535181* ⊕ *www.turismotorino.org.*

👁 Sights

DOWNTOWN TURIN

Many of Turin's major sights are clustered around Piazza Castello, and others are on or just off the portico-lined Via Roma, one of the city's main thoroughfares, which leads 1 km (½ mile) from Piazza Castello south to Piazza Carlo Felice, a landscaped park in front of the train station. First opened in 1615, Via Roma was largely rebuilt in the 1930s, during the Mussolini era.

Duomo di San Giovanni

CHURCH | The most impressive part of Turin's 15th-century cathedral is the shadowy black-marble-walled **Cappella della Sacra Sindone** (Chapel of the Holy Shroud), where the famous relic is housed in a sealed casket. The chapel was designed by the priest and architect Guarino Guarini (1604–83), a genius of the Baroque style who was official engineer and mathematician to the court of Duke Carlo Emanuele II of Savoy.

The Sacra Sindone is a 12-foot-long sheet of linen, thought by millions to be the burial shroud of Christ, bearing the light imprint of his crucified body. The shroud first made an appearance around the middle of the 15th century, when it was presented to Ludovico of Savoy in Chambéry. In 1578 it was brought to Turin by another member of the Savoy royal family, Duke Emanuele Filiberto. It

426

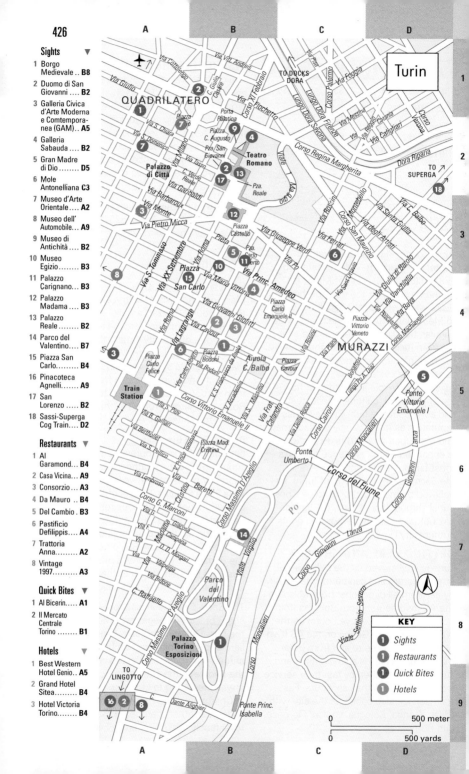

was only in the 1990s that the Catholic Church began allowing rigorous scientific study of the shroud. Not surprisingly, the results have been hazy, bolstering both sides of the argument. On one hand, three separate university teams—in Switzerland, Britain, and the United States—have concluded, as a result of carbon-14 analysis, that the cloth dates from between 1260 and 1390. On the other hand, they are unable to explain how medieval forgers could have created the shroud's image, which resembles a photographic negative, and how they could have had the knowledge or means to incorporate traces of Roman coins covering the eyelids and endemic Middle Eastern pollen woven into the cloth. Either way, the shroud continues to be revered as a holy relic, exhibited to the public on very rare occasions. ⊠ *Piazza San Giovanni, Centro* ☎ *011/4361540.*

Galleria Civica d'Arte Moderna e Contemporanea (GAM)

ART MUSEUM | In 1863 Turin was the first Italian city to begin a public collection devoted to contemporary art. Housed in a modern building on the edge of downtown, a permanent display of more than 600 paintings, sculptures, and installation pieces provides an exceptional glimpse of how Italian contemporary art has evolved since the late 1800s. The Futurist, Pop, neo-Dada, and Arte Povera movements are particularly well represented, and the gallery has a fine video and art film collection. ⊠ *Via Magenta 31, Centro* ☎ *011/5211788* ⊕ *www.gamtorino.it* ☛ *€10* ⊗ *Closed Mon.*

Galleria Sabauda

ART MUSEUM | Housed in the restored Manica Nuova (new wing) of the Palazzo Reale, the gallery displays some of the most important paintings from the vast collections of the house of Savoy. The collection is particularly rich in Dutch and Flemish paintings: note the *Stigmate di San Francesco* (*St. Francis Receiving the Stigmata*) by Jan van Eyck (1395–1441),

in which the saint receives the marks of Christ's wounds while a companion cringes beside him. ⊠ *Piazzetta Reale 1, Centro* ☎ *011/19560449* ⊕ *museireali. beniculturali.it* ☛ *€15, includes Palazzo Reale, Armeria Reale, and the Cappella della Sindone* ⊗ *Closed Mon.*

Mole Antonelliana

NOTABLE BUILDING | You can't miss the unusual square dome and thin, elaborate spire of this Turin landmark above the city's rooftops. This odd structure, built between 1863 and 1889, was intended to be a synagogue, but costs escalated and eventually it was bought by the city. In its time it was the tallest brick structure in the world. You can take the crystal elevator to reach the terrace at the top of the dome for an excellent view of the city, the plain, and the Alps beyond. ⊠ *Via Montebello 20, Centro* ☎ *011/8138563* ⊕ *www.museocinema. it* ☛ *Museum €11, elevator €8; combination ticket €15* ⊗ *Closed Tues.*

Museo d'Arte Orientale

ART MUSEUM | Housed in the magnificently renovated 17th-century Palazzo Mazzonis, this is a beautifully displayed collection of Southeast Asian, Chinese, Japanese, Himalayan, and Islamic art, including sculptures, paintings, and ceramics. Highlights include a towering 13th-century wooden statue of the Japanese temple guardian Kongo Rikishi and a sumptuous assortment of Islamic manuscripts. ⊠ *Via San Domenico 11, Centro* ☎ *011/4436932* ⊕ *www.maotorino.it* ☛ *€10* ⊗ *Closed Mon.*

Museo di Antichità

HISTORY MUSEUM | A small but fascinating collection of artifacts found at archaeological sites in and around Turin is displayed here. A spiral ramp winds down through the subterranean museum; and, as in a real archaeological site, the deeper you go, the older the objects on display. A life-size silver bust of the Roman emperor Lucius Verus (AD 161–169) is one of the masterpieces of the collection. ⊠ *Via XX Settembre 88, Centro* ☎ *011/19560449* ⊕ *museireali. beniculturali.it* 🎫 *€15, includes Galleria Sabauda, Armeria Reale, and Palazzo Reale* ⊗ *Closed Mon.*

★ Museo Egizio

HISTORY MUSEUM | The Egyptian Museum's superb collection includes statues of pharaohs and mummies and entire frescoes taken from royal tombs—it's one of the world's finest and largest museums of its kind. The striking sculpture gallery, designed by the Oscar-winning production designer Dante Ferretti, is a veritable who's who of ancient Egypt. Look for the magnificent 13th-century BC statue of Ramses II and the fascinating Tomb of Kha. The latter was found intact with furniture, supplies of food and clothing, writing instruments, and a complete set of personal cosmetics and toiletries. The museum is housed in the **Palazzo dell'Accademia delle Scienze,** a Baroque tour de force designed by the priest and architect Guarino Guarini. ⊠ *Via Accademia delle Scienze 6, Centro* ☎ *011/4406903* ⊕ *www.museoegizio.it* 🎫 *€15* ⊗ *Closed Mon. afternoon.*

Palazzo Carignano

HISTORY MUSEUM | Half of this building is the Baroque triumph of Guarino Guarini, the priest and architect who designed many of Turin's most noteworthy buildings. Built between 1679 and 1685, his redbrick palace later played an important role in the creation of the modern-day nation. Vittorio Emanuele II of Savoy (1820–78), the first king of a united Italy, was born here, and, after a 19th-century neoclassical extension, Italy's first parliament met here between 1860 and 1865. The palace now houses the Museo del Risorgimento, a museum honoring the 19th-century movement for Italian unity. ⊠ *Via Accademia delle Scienze 5, Centro* ⊕ *Entrance at Piazza Carlo Alberto 8* ☎ *011/5621147* ⊕ *www.museorisorgimentotorino.it* 🎫 *€10* ⊗ *Closed Mon.*

Palazzo Madama

HISTORY MUSEUM | In the center of Piazza Castello, this castle was named for the Savoy queen Maria Cristina, who made it her home in the 17th century. The building incorporates the remains of a Roman gate with late-medieval and Renaissance additions, and the monumental Baroque facade and grand entrance staircase were added by Filippo Juvarra (1678–1736). The palace now houses the Museo Civico d'Arte Antica, whose collections comprise more than 30,000 items dating from the Middle Ages to the Baroque era. ⊠ *Piazza Castello 10, Centro* ☎ *011/5211788 tickets, 011/4433501* ⊕ *www.palazzomadamatorino.it* 🎫 *Staircase and courtyard free, museum €10* ⊗ *Closed Tues.*

★ Palazzo Reale

CASTLE/PALACE | **FAMILY** | This 17th-century palace, a former Savoy royal residence, is an imposing work of brick, stone, and marble that stands on the site of one of Turin's ancient Roman city gates. In contrast to its sober exterior, the two main floors of the palace's interior are swathed in luxurious rococo trappings, including tapestries, gilt ceilings, and sumptuous 17th- to 19th-century furniture. The gardens were laid out in the late 17th century by André Le Nôtre, landscape designer at Versailles and the Armeria Reale (Royal Armory) wing holds one of Europe's most extensive collections of arms and armor. ⊠ *Piazzetta Reale 1, Centro* ☎ *011/4361455* ⊕ *museireali.beniculturali.it* 🎫 *€15, includes Armeria Reale, Galleria Sabauda, and Museo Archeologico* ⊗ *Closed Mon.*

Piazza San Carlo

PLAZA/SQUARE | Surrounded by shops, arcades, fashionable cafés, and elegant Baroque palaces, this is one of the most beautiful squares in Turin. In the center stands a statue of Duke Emanuele Filiberto of Savoy, the victor at the battle of San Quintino, in 1557. The melee heralded the peaceful resurgence of Turin under the Savoy after years of bloody dynastic fighting. The fine bronze statue erected in the 19th century is one of Turin's symbols. At the southern end of the square, framing the continuation of Via Roma, are the twin Baroque churches of San Carlo and Santa Cristina. ⊠ *Piazza San Carlo, Centro*.

San Lorenzo

CHURCH | Architect, priest, and mathematician Guarino Guarini was in his mid-sixties when he began this church in 1668. The masterful use of geometric forms and the theatrical control of light and shadow show him working at his mature and confident best. ■TIP➔ **Stand in the center of the church and look up into the cupola to appreciate the full effect.** ⊠ *Via Palazzo di Città 4, Centro* ☎ *011/4361527* ⊕ *www.sanlorenzo.torino.it* ⊙ *Closed noon–3:30 pm Mon.–Sat.*

ALONG THE PO

The Po River is narrow and unprepossessing here in Turin, only a hint of the broad waterway that it becomes as it flows eastward toward the Adriatic. It's flanked, however, by formidable edifices, a park, and a lovely pedestrian path.

Borgo Medievale

TOWN | FAMILY | Along the banks of the Po, this complex, built for a General Exhibition in 1884, is a faithful reproduction of a typical Piedmont village in the Middle Ages. Craft shops, houses, a church, and stores are clustered in the narrow lanes, and in the center of the village is the Rocca Medievale, a medieval castle that's its main attraction, but is closed until at least 2023 for major restorations. ⊠ *Viale Virgilio 107, San Salvario* ☎ *011/01167101* ⊕ *www.borgomedievaletorino.it* ⊠ *Village free, Rocca Medievale and garden €6* ⊙ *Rocca closed Mon.–Thurs.*

Gran Madre di Dio

CHURCH | On the east bank of the Po, this neoclassical church is modeled after the Pantheon in Rome. It was built between 1827 and 1831 to commemorate the return of the house of Savoy to Turin after the fall of Napoléon's empire. ⊠ *Piazza Gran Madre di Dio 4, Borgo Po* ☎ *011/8193572*.

★ Museo dell'Automobile

OTHER MUSEUM | FAMILY | No visit to this motor city would be complete without a pilgrimage to see the perfectly preserved Bugattis, Ferraris, and Isotta Fraschinis at this museum. Here you can get an idea of the importance of Fiat—and cars in general—to Turin's economy. There's a collection of antique cars from as early as 1896, and displays show how the city has changed over the years as a result of the auto industry. ⊠ *Corso Unità d'Italia 40, Millefonti* ☎ *011/677666* ⊕ *www. museoauto.com* ⊠ *€15* ⊙ *Closed Mon. after 2 pm*.

Parco del Valentino

CITY PARK | FAMILY | This pleasant riverside park is a great place to stroll, bike, or jog. Originally the grounds of a relatively simple hunting lodge, the park owes its present arrangement to Madama Maria Cristina of France, who received the land and lodge as a wedding present after her marriage to Vittorio Amedeo I of Savoy. With memories of 16th-century French château in mind, she converted the lodge into a magnificent palace, the Castello del Valentino. The building, now home to the University of Turin's Faculty of Architecture, is not open to the public. ⊠ *Viale Mattioli 25, San Salvario* ☎ *011/6705970 botanical gardens* ⊕ *www.comune.torino.it* ⊠ *Botanical gardens €5* ⊙ *Botanical gardens closed Nov.–mid-Apr.*

★ Pinacoteca Agnelli

ART MUSEUM | This gallery was opened by Gianni Agnelli (1921–2003), the head of Fiat and patriarch of one of Italy's most powerful families, just four months before his death. There are four magnificent scenes of Venice by Canaletto (1697–1768); two splendid views of Dresden by Canaletto's nephew, Bernardo Bellotto (1720–80); several works by Manet (1832–83), Renoir (1841–1919),

Matisse (1869–1954), and Picasso (1881–1973). The gallery is on the top floor of the Lingotto, a former Fiat factory that was completely transformed between 1982 and 2002 by architect Renzo Piano. ⊠ *Via Nizza 230, Lingotto* ☎ *011/0925011* ⊕ *www.pinacoteca-agnelli.it* ⊠ *€10* ⊘ *Closed Mon.*

Sassi-Superga Cog Train

TRAIN/TRAIN STATION | **FAMILY** | The 18-minute ride from Sassi up the Superga hill is a real treat on a clear day. The view of the Alps is magnificent at the hilltop **Parco Naturale Collina Torinese,** a tranquil retreat from the bustle of the city. If you feel like a little exercise, you can walk back down to Sassi (about two hours) on one of the well-marked wooded trails that start from the upper station. Other circular trails lead through the park and back to Superga. Note that a bus replaces the train on Wednesday, although the ride up the hill is still just as lovely. ⊠ *Piazza G. Modena, Sassi* ☎ *011/0672000* ⊕ *www.gtt.to.it* ⊠ *€4 one-way and €6 round-trip on weekdays, €6 one-way and €9 round-trip on weekends* ⊘ *Closed Wed.*

🍴 Restaurants

★ Al Garamond

$$$ | **PIEDMONTESE** | The well-spaced tables and the ancient brick vaulting in this small, bright space set the stage for game, meat, fish, and seafood dishes served with creative flair. The level of service is very high, even by demanding Turin standards. **Known for:** merging Sicilian and Piedmontese cuisine; mix of traditional and inventive dishes; chef's table experience. $ *Average main: €26* ⊠ *Via G. Pomba 14, Centro* ☎ *011/8122781* ⊕ *www.algaramond.it* ⊘ *Closed Sun., Aug., and Jan. 7–14. No lunch Mon., Tues., and Sat.*

★ Casa Vicina

$$$$ | **PIEDMONTESE** | Tucked away on the third floor of the Green Pea sustainable retail venture (next to Eataly Lingotto), one of Turin's top destinations for fine dining is run by the fourth generation of the Vicina family, with Claudio and wife Anna leading the kitchen and Stefano managing the front of house. Excellent quality traditional Piedmontese dishes are served up with creative style, and the wine list is an encyclopedia, featuring not only the top Barolo producers but also many other small but notable wineries. **Known for:** layered bagna càuda served in a martini glass; fixed-price tasting and gastronomic menus; fresh agnolotti pasta. $ *Average main: €45* ⊠ *Via Ermanno Fenoglietti 20/B, 3rd fl. of Green Pea, Lingotto* ☎ *011/19506840* ⊕ *www.casavicina.com* ⊘ *Closed Mon. No dinner Sun.*

Consorzio

$$ | **PIEDMONTESE** | Extremely popular for lunch during the week, this lively and informal osteria is in Turin's business district. The service is relaxed, the decor is low-key, the menu highlights organic meats and vegetables from Piedmont, and there's a good selection of natural wines. **Known for:** creative presentation; Piedmont dishes like agnolotti gobbi (stuffed pasta); wide selection of cheeses from across Europe. $ *Average main: €20* ⊠ *Via Monte di Pietà 23, Centro* ☎ *011/2767661* ⊕ *ristoranteconsorzio.it* ⊘ *Closed Sun. No lunch Mon.*

Da Mauro

$$ | **TUSCAN** | After a flux of Tuscan migrants moved to Turin in the '60s, Da Mauro was one of the first restaurants to cater to their tastes, mixing Tuscan dishes into the largely Piedmontese menu. Service is brisk and efficient for a local crowd at lunch and dinner—it's not the place to come for a slow-paced meal. **Known for:** Tuscan specialties; affordable, daily-changing menu; fresh pasta dishes like agnolotti al ragù. $ *Average main: €15* ⊠ *Via Maria Vittoria 21, Centro* ☎ *0349/1513068* ⊕ *ristorante-da-mauro.business.site* ⊘ *Closed Mon.*

★ **Del Cambio**

$$$$ | **PIEDMONTESE** | Set in a palace dating from 1757, this is one of Europe's most beautiful and historic restaurants, with decorative moldings, mirrors, and hanging lamps contrasted with ultra-modern takes on Piedmontese cuisine from young Michelin-starred chef Matteo Baronetto. Order inventive dishes such as the Piedmontese salad, with around 24 artfully composed ingredients, or the umbrine fish in three ways, or opt for the four-, six-, or nine-course tasting menu to sample more of the chef's innovative cooking. **Known for:** well-selected wine pairings; elegant atmosphere; beautifully presented plates. [$] *Average main: €43* ✉ *Piazza Carignano 2, Centro* ☎ *011/546690* 🌐 *delcambio.it* 🕒 *Closed Mon. No lunch Tues.–Thurs. No dinner Sun.*

Pastificio Defilippis

$$ | **PIEDMONTESE** | Famous for freshly made seasonal pasta dishes since 1872, this shop serves a packed lunch crowd all week long, with outdoor seating in the summer. Secondi and dolci are also available, but pasta is the main event. **Known for:** wide variety of pasta from Piedmont and across Italy; vegetarian, meat, and seafood sauces; traditional agnolotti. [$] *Average main: €18* ✉ *Via Lagrange 39, Centro* ☎ *011/542137* 🌐 *www.pastificio-defilippis.it.*

Trattoria Anna

$ | **SEAFOOD** | If you are hankering for something different from the usual meat-based Piedmontese cuisine, give this simple, extremely popular family-run spot a try. They serve only seafood, and they do it well. **Known for:** mixed grilled fish; linguine Trattoria Anna, with prawns, pesto, and cherry tomatoes; Ligurian-style dishes. [$] *Average main: €14* ✉ *Via Gian Francesco Bellezia 20, Centro* ☎ *011/4362134* 🌐 *trattorianna.com* 🕒 *Closed Sun., Mon., and 2 wks in Aug. No lunch.*

★ **Vintage 1997**

$$$ | **NORTHERN ITALIAN** | The first floor of an elegant town house in the center of Turin makes a fitting location for this sophisticated restaurant. There's an excellent wine list with regional, national, and international vintages well represented, and tasting menus, including a nine-course feast that covers the full range of the restaurant's cuisine and desserts. **Known for:** tasting menus from three to nine courses; selection of rare cheeses; Piedmontese roasted veal. [$] *Average main: €32* ✉ *Piazza Solferino 16/h, Centro* ☎ *011/535948* 🌐 *www.vintage1997.com* 🕒 *Closed Sun. No lunch Sat.*

Coffee and Quick Bites

★ **Al Bicerin**

$ | **CAFÉ** | **FAMILY** | A chocolate lover's pilgrimage to Turin inevitably leads to this café where Nietzsche, Puccini, Dumas, and the political reformer Cavour have all sipped. If you order the house specialty, *bicerin* (a hot drink with layers of chocolate, coffee, and cream), or a flavored *zabaioni* (warm eggnog), and browse the collection of chocolate goodies including chocolate-flavored pasta, you'll understand why. **Known for:** wide assortment of creative sweet drinks; traditional Gianduiotto chocolates; elegant presentation. [$] *Average main: €6* ✉ *Piazza della Consolata 5, Centro* ☎ *011/4369325* 🌐 *bicerin.it* 🕒 *Closed Wed. and Aug.*

★ **Il Mercato Centrale Torino**

$ | **INTERNATIONAL** | **FAMILY** | When you're not in the mood for an Italian-style lunch or dinner (read: leisurely), head to the Mercato Centrale for a choice of foods—from more than 20 food stands—like fresh pasta, fish, roast meats, pizza, and fried dishes, along with more international choices including ramen and Peruvian plates, along with a good choice of cocktails, wines, and beer. But don't fill up on the mains, as you'll also find a delightful selection of baked goods and, of course, gelato, for a sweet finish. **Known for:**

lively crowds; wide selection of dishes; late-night hours (open daily till midnight). $ *Average main: €10* ⊠ *Piazza della Repubblica 25, Centro* ☏ *011/0898040* ⊕ *www.mercatocentrale.com/turin.*

 Hotels

The Turin Tourist Information Center provides a booking service for accommodations in the city and throughout the region. Book hotels through them at least 48 hours in advance, B&Bs at least seven days in advance.

Best Western Hotel Genio

$ | HOTEL | Although they're just steps away from the main train station, these spacious and tastefully decorated rooms are a quiet haven from the bustle of the city. **Pros:** convenient location; spacious rooms and bathrooms; abundant breakfast. **Cons:** entrance and lobby area could be updated; neighborhood is a bit seedy; street noise in some rooms. $ *Rooms from: €95* ⊠ *Corso Vittorio Emanuele II 47, Centro* ☏ *011/6505771* ⊕ *www.hotel-genio.it* ⟿ *113 rooms* ｜○｜ *No Meals.*

★ Grand Hotel Sitea

$$ | HOTEL | One of the city's finest hotels, the Sitea is in the historic center and decorated in a warm classical style; the common areas and guest rooms are elegant, spacious, and comfortable. **Pros:** central location; large bathrooms; well-appointed rooms. **Cons:** bathrooms could use a refresh; carpets are a little worn; air-conditioning and street noise can be loud in some rooms. $ *Rooms from: €167* ⊠ *Via Carlo Alberto 35, Centro* ☏ *011/5170171* ⊕ *www.grandhotelsitea.it* ⟿ *120 rooms* ｜○｜ *No Meals.*

Hotel Victoria Torino

$$ | HOTEL | Style, attention to detail, and comfort are hallmarks of this retreat that's furnished like a refined English home. **Pros:** tranquil location in the center of town; wonderful breakfast; good spa facilities. **Cons:** no gym; no on-site restaurant; standard rooms are small. $ *Rooms*

from: €195 ⊠ *Via Nino Costa 4, Centro* ☏ *011/5611909* ⊕ *www.hotelvictoria-torino.com* ⟿ *106 rooms* ｜○｜ *Free Breakfast.*

 Nightlife

Two areas of Turin are enormously popular nightlife destinations: the Quadrilatero, to the north of the city center, and the Murazzi embankment, near the Ponte Vittorio Emanuele I. The center of town is also popular, especially earlier in the evening.

Caffè Elena

CAFÉS | This café/bar is a trendy place for an aperitif or for a drink before going out to a show or dancing. It's in the large piazza at the end of Via Po. ⊠ *Piazza Vittorio Veneto 5, Centro* ☏ *0329/5767414* ⊕ *www.caffeelena.it.*

Pastis

GATHERING PLACES | The Quadrilatero Romano, which roughly corresponds to the grid pattern of Roman Turin near Piazza della Repubblica, is a hopping area filled with nightclubs and ethnic restaurants. Places open and close with startling frequency here, but Pastis has shown considerable staying power. ⊠ *Piazza Emanuele Filiberto 9b, Centro* ☏ *011/5211085* ⊕ *pastistorino.com.*

 Performing Arts

MUSIC
★ Lingotto Musica

MUSIC | Classical music concerts are held at this theater designed by Renzo Piano in the renovated Lingotto building; internationally famous conductors and orchestras are frequent guests. ⊠ *Via Nizza 280, Lingotto* ☏ *011/6313721* ⊕ *www.lingottomusica.it.*

MITO Settembre Musica Festival

MUSIC | Running for three weeks in September, this popular festival of classical music is held in a variety of venues around town. The program of performances and tickets becomes available

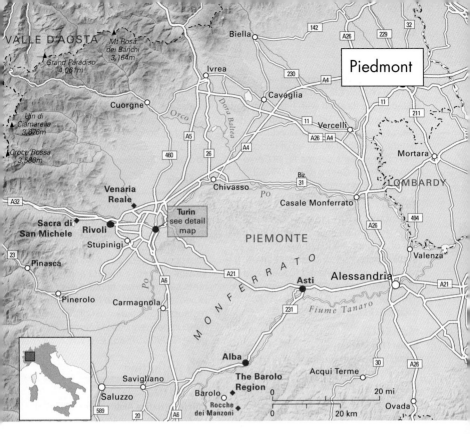

in June each year. ⊠ *Urban Lab, Piazza Palazzo di Città 8/F, ticket office, Turin* ☎ *011/24787* ⊕ *www.mitosettembremusica.it.*

OPERA

Teatro Regio

OPERA | Premieres at the Teatro Regio, one of Italy's leading opera houses, sell out well in advance. You can buy tickets for most performances at the box office or on the website, where discounts are often offered on the day of the performance. The season runs from October through July. ⊠ *Piazza Castello 125, Centro* ☎ *011/8815241* ⊕ *www.teatroregio.torino.it.*

Shopping

Many people know that Turin produces the vast majority of Italy's cars, but they're often unaware that it's also a hub for clothing manufacturing. Top-quality boutiques stocking local, national, and international lines are clustered along Via Roma and Via Garibaldi. Piazza San Carlo, Via Po, and Via Maria Vittoria are lined with antiques shops, some of which specialize in 18th-century furniture and domestic items.

CHOCOLATE

The Italian tradition of making chocolate began in Turin during the early 17th century. Chocolate at that time was an aristocratic drink, but in the 19th century a Piedmontese invention made it possible to further refine cocoa to create solid bars and candies.

★ Peyrano

CHOCOLATE | FAMILY | The most famous of all Turin chocolates is the wedge-shape gianduiotto, flavored with hazelnuts and first concocted in 1867. The tradition has been continued at this family-run shop, where more than 80 types of chocolates and other sweets are made. ✉ *Corso Moncalieri 47, Centro* ☎ *011/6602202* ⊕ *www.peyrano.com.*

Stratta

CHOCOLATE | FAMILY | In business since 1836, this famed shop sells confectionery of all kinds—not just the chocolates in the lavish window displays but also fancy cookies, rum-laced fudges, and magnificent cakes. ✉ *Piazza San Carlo 191, Centro* ☎ *011/547920* ⊕ *www.stratta1836.it.*

MARKETS

Balon Flea Market

MARKET | Go to this famous market for bargains on secondhand books, antiques, and clothing. There is good browsing to be had among the stands, which spill out of Borgo Dora onto the surrounding side streets. During the second weekend of every month, the market extends its hours into Sunday, becoming the so-called Gran Balon. (Be aware, however, that the market is also famous for its pickpockets.) ✉ *Borgo Dora, Centro* ⊕ *www.balon.it.*

★ Mercato di Porta Palazzo

MARKET | For food lovers, people-watchers, or anyone interested in the lively local scene, the immensely popular market in this huge square to the north of town is not to be missed. Outdoors, the keepers of hundreds of vegetable stands vie with one another to create the most appetizing displays. Indoors, the meat vendors provide an equally tantalizing array of local products, while the fishmongers proudly display the fresh catch of the day. ✉ *Piazza della Repubblica, Centro* ⊕ *www.scopriportapalazzo.com.*

SPECIALTY FOOD AND DELIS

★ Borgiattino

FOOD | Specialty food stores and delicatessens abound in central Turin, but for a truly spectacular array of cheeses and other delicacies, this should be your first stop. ✉ *Corso Vinzaglio 29, Centro* ☎ *011/5629075* ⊕ *www.borgiattino.com.*

★ Eataly

FOOD | Now with branches in Milan, Florence, Bologna, New York, and Tokyo, the original home of Eataly is probably Turin's most famous food emporium. In addition to the market, there are kitchenware and cookbook stores, plus a wine bar and several different counters and restaurants serving pizza, haute cuisine (Giù da Guido, a branch of the Michelin-starred restaurant Guido da Costigliole), and lots more in between. ✉ *Via Nizza 230, Lingotto* ☎ *0800/975880* ⊕ *www.eataly.net.*

🏃 Activities

BICYCLING

Ufficio Iniziative Ambientali (*Office for Environmental Initiatives*)

BIKING | Turin has about 160 km (100 miles) of bike paths running through the city and its parks. Bicycles are available for daily rental at stands throughout the city year-round. ✉ *Piazza San Giovanni 5, Madonna di Campagna* ☎ *011/4420177* ⊕ *www.comune.torino.it.*

Asti

60 km (37 miles) southeast of Turin.

Asti is best known outside Italy for its wines—excellent reds as well as the famous sparkling white *spumante*. The town itself has some impressive reminders of the days when its strategic position on trade routes between Turin, Milan, and Genoa gave it broad economic power. In the 12th century Asti began to develop as a republic, at a time when other Italian cities were also flexing their

Skiing is the major sport in both Piedmont and the Valle d'Aosta. Excellent facilities abound at resort towns such as Courmayeur and Breuil-Cervinia. The so-called Via Lattea (Milky Way)—five skiing areas near Sestriere with 400 km (almost 250 miles) of linked runs and more than 100 ski lifts—provides practically unlimited skiing. Lift tickets, running around €40 for a day's pass, are a good deal compared to those at major U.S. resorts.

To Italian skiers, a weeklong holiday on the slopes is known as a *settimana*

bianca (white week). Ski resort hotels in Piedmont and the Valle d'Aosta encourage these getaways by offering six- and seven-day packages, and though they're designed with the domestic market in mind, you can get a bargain by taking advantage of them. The packages usually (though not always) include half or full board.

You should have your passport with you if you plan a day trip into Switzerland—although the odds are that you won't be asked to show it.

economic and military muscles. It flourished in the following century, when the inhabitants began erecting lofty towers (west end of Corso Vittorio Alfieri) for its defense. As in Pavia, near Milan, this gave rise to the medieval nickname "City of a Hundred Towers." In the center of Asti some of these remain, among them the 13th-century **Torre Comentina** and the well-preserved **Torre Troyana,** a tall, slender tower attached to the **Palazzo Troya.** The 18th-century church of **Santa Caterina** has incorporated one of Asti's medieval towers, the **Torre Romana** (itself built on an ancient Roman base), as its bell tower. Corso Vittorio Alfieri is Asti's main thoroughfare, running west–east across the city. This road, known in medieval times as Contrada Maestra, was built by the Romans.

GETTING HERE AND AROUND

Asti is less than an hour away from Turin by car on the A21 autostrada. Train service from Turin to Asti is frequent and fast, and Itabus service directly connects the two towns.

VISITOR INFORMATION
CONTACT Asti Tourism Office. ✉ *Piazza Alfieri 34, Asti* ☎ *0141/530357* ⊕ *www.visitlmr.it.*

Sights

Collegiata di San Secondo
CHURCH | This Gothic church is dedicated to Asti's patron saint, believed by some to have been decapitated by the Emperor Hadrian on this very spot. San Secondo is also the patron of the city's favorite folklore and sporting event, the annual Palio di Asti, a colorful medieval-style horse race that's similar to Siena's. It's held each year on a Sunday in early September in the vast Campo del Palio to the south of the church. ✉ *Piazza San Secondo, south of Corso Vittorio Alfieri, Asti* ☎ *0141/530066* 🎟 *Free.*

Duomo (*Cattedrale di Santa Maria Assunta*)
CHURCH | Dedicated to the Assumption of the Virgin, the Duomo is an object lesson in Italian Gothic architecture. Completed in the early 14th century, it is decorated so as to emphasize geometry and verticality: pointed arches and narrow vaults

are completely covered with frescoes that direct your gaze upward. The porch on the south side of the cathedral facing the square was built in 1470; it represents the Gothic style at its most florid and excessive. ✉ *Piazza Cattedrale, Asti* ☎ *0141/592924* 🌐 *www.diocesiasti.it* 🎟 *Free.*

🍴 Restaurants

★ Il Cavallo Scosso

$$$ | **MODERN ITALIAN** | In a contemporary villa built entirely of wood on the outskirts of Asti, chef Enrico Pivieri uses a mix of local and international ingredients to create new takes on traditional dishes with a global flair. The Shaken Horse is especially strong in seafood—rare for meat-heavy Piedmont—with such creative plates as gnocchi with cuttlefish ink in miso broth with smoked sardines and fried Sicilian anchovies with giardiniera (pickled vegetables in vinegar). **Known for:** modern interpretations of meat and seafood dishes; choice of three tasting menus; beef tartare marinated with citrus fruits, seared scampi, and beetroot. [$] *Average main: €26* ✉ *Via Al Duca 23/D, Asti* ☎ *0141/211435* 🌐 *www.ilcavalloscosso.it* 🕒 *Closed Mon.*

L'Angolo del Beato

$$ | **PIEDMONTESE** | At this Asti institution, in a building that dates to the 12th century (as you'll see from the exposed brick walls and original wood-beamed ceiling), you'll find that regional specialties are the main attractions. There's also an extensive list of several hundred Piedmont wines. **Known for:** risotto with barbera wine; roasted meats; tonno di coniglio (rabbit marinated in olive oil and garlic) antipasto. [$] *Average main: €16* ✉ *Vicolo Cavalleri 2, Asti* ☎ *0141/531668* 🌐 *www.angolodelbeato.it* 🕒 *Closed Sun., 1st wk of Jan., and 10 days in Aug.*

🛏 Hotels

Relais Sant'Uffizio

$$ | **HOTEL** | You may be surprised to learn that this now delightfully peaceful and elegant retreat—with a luxurious spa and swimming pool, surrounded by vineyards and rolling hills—was once home to the Inquisition in the 16th century. **Pros:** tranquil and beautiful location; good value for the amenities; excellent spa and exercise facilities. **Cons:** soundproofing could be better in some rooms; some rooms are a walk from the main building; a bit isolated, 20 km (12 miles) north of Asti. [$] *Rooms from: €136* ✉ *Strada Sant Uffizio 1, Asti* ☎ *0141/916292* 🌐 *www.relaissantuffizio.com* 🛏 *41 rooms* 🍽 *Free Breakfast.*

Alba

30 km (18 miles) southwest of Asti.

This small town has a gracious atmosphere and a compact core, studded with medieval towers and Gothic buildings. In addition to being a wine center for the region, Alba is known as the "City of the White Truffle" for delicious little tubers that cost as much as €2,200 a pound. For picking out your truffle and having a few wisps shaved on top of your food, expect to shell out an extra €16 or so—definitely worth doing for a second-to-none foodie experience.

For the true truffle experience, visit during the annual Fiera Internazionale Tartufo Bianco D'Alba (International Alba White Truffle Fair; 🌐 *www.fieradeltartufo.org*) every October and November for a truffle market, cooking shows, food with truffles, wine tasting, and even educational games for kids.

GETTING HERE AND AROUND

By car from Turin follow the A6 autostrada south to Marene and then head east on the A33, which connects Asti and Alba. GTT offers frequent bus service between Alba and Turin—the journey takes approximately 1½ hours. Direct trains run to Alba from Turin's Lingotto station; the trip takes about an hour.

VISITOR INFORMATION

CONTACT Alba Tourism Office. ✉ *Piazza Risorgimento 2, Alba* ☎ *0173/35833* 🌐 *www.visitlmr.it.*

Sights

★ Castello di Neive

WINERY | This family-run, 160-acre wine estate produces wine from seven vineyards in the Langhe region. Barbaresco is their star wine, and they also make fine barbera and dolcetto. Visitor tours, by appointment only, include a look inside their 18-century castle, including the wine cellars, as well as a tasting of three wines. ✉ *Piazzetta Demaria 1, Neive* ☎ *0329/2125171* 🌐 *www.castellodineive.it* 🎟 *Tour and tasting from €10* 🕒 *Closed Tues.* ✍ *Reservations required.*

Restaurants

★ Guido da Costigliole

$$$$ | NORTHERN ITALIAN | Inside atmospheric stone-walled ancient cellars, the latest incarnation of Guido—which began in 1961 in Costigliole d'Asti—is now managed by the son of the original owners. It serves up excellent preparations of traditional dishes best sampled with one of the three tasting menus (classic, vegetables, or fish), along with superlative pairings of wine from the surrounding regions. **Known for:** agnolotti pasta filled with meat; gelato of the moment; wonderful wine list. [$] *Average main: €45* ✉ *Relais San Maurizio, Località San Maurizio 59, Santa Stefano Belbo* ✥ *22 km (14 miles) east of Alba* ☎ *0340/4728569* 🌐 *www.guidodacostigliole.it* 🕒 *Closed Sun. No lunch.*

La Libera

$$ | PIEDMONTESE | Modern and subdued, this small spot on a quiet backstreet is conducive to a leisurely meal while trying a huge selection of Barolo wines. On the menu you'll find Piedmontese starters and pastas and a variety of tasty meat dishes, and there's also a superb selection of local cheeses. **Known for:** locally sourced meat and produce; Piedmontese wines and cheeses; tajarin al ragù. [$] *Average main: €20* ✉ *Via Elvio Pertinace 24a, Alba* ☎ *0173/293155* 🌐 *www.lalibera.com* 🕒 *Closed Sun., 3 wks in Aug., and late Dec.–mid-Jan. No lunch Mon.*

★ L'inedito: Vigin Mudest

$$ | PIEDMONTESE | Delicious regional specialties with tartufo-focused and fixed-price tasting menus are served at this bustling family-run restaurant in the center of Alba. Seasonal recipes emphasize local vegetables, nuts (particularly hazelnuts), and meats like rabbit and venison. **Known for:** braised beef marinated in Barolo; fresh tajarin (tagliolini with egg dough); agnolotti del plin (stuffed ravioli) with truffles. [$] *Average main: €18* ✉ *Via Vernazza 11, Alba* ☎ *0173/441701* 🌐 *www.lineditoviginmudest.it* 🕒 *Closed Wed.*

Osteria dell'Arco

$$ | PIEDMONTESE | Delicious, hearty dishes using local ingredients are served here in a lovely setting with wine bottles lining the walls. In addition to lots of game meats, you'll find a nice selection of seafood dishes with a hint of Liguria. **Known for:** meat and fish crudos; Slow Food movement cooking; house-made pastas. [$] *Average main: €16* ✉ *Piazza Savona 5, Alba* ☎ *0173/363974* 🌐 *www.osteriadelarco.it* 🕒 *Closed Sun. Dec.–Sept.*

Vincafè

$$ | WINE BAR | This excellent *enoteca,* with a contemporary casual atmosphere, has a whole range of Piedmont specialties to pair with local wines. You'll find more than 60 labels, as well as grappas and liqueurs, on the menu. **Known for:** late-night dining; Piedmontese crudos; Langhe wine pairings. $ *Average main: €16* ⊠ *Via Emanuele 12, Alba* ☎ *0173/364603* ⊕ *www.vincafe.com.*

 Hotels

La Meridiana

$ | **B&B/INN** | This lovely manor house is on a hill overlooking the historic center, surrounded by dolcetto and nebbiolo vines. **Pros:** friendly, family atmosphere; nice views from the many terraces and balconies; in a secluded setting convenient for exploring the Langhe. **Cons:** the road to the hotel is winding and a bit dark at night; no a/c in some rooms; long walk to nearest restaurants (some units have kitchens). $ *Rooms from: €102* ⊠ *Località Altavilla 9, Alba* ☎ *0338/4606527* ⊕ *www.villalameridianaalba.it* 📞 *10 rooms* ⦿ *Free Breakfast.*

Locanda del Pilone

$$$ | **B&B/INN** | It would be hard to imagine a more commanding position for these simply but tastefully decorated accommodations and the Michelin-starred restaurant above Alba. **Pros:** spectacular location with a 360-degree view; abundant breakfast; excellent restaurant. **Cons:** rooms near common areas can be noisy; parking can be challenging; while not far from Alba, you do need a car to get around. $ *Rooms from: €235* ⊠ *Località Madonna di Como 34, Alba* ☎ *0173/366616* ⊕ *www.locandadelpilone. com* ⊘ *Closed Jan.–Apr.* 📞 *6 rooms* ⦿ *Free Breakfast.*

★ Nordelaia

$$$$ | **HOTEL** | A stay at this charming, rural-chic hotel surrounded by vineyards is like visiting a stylish friend's country home—one with impeccably good taste in design and cuisine. **Pros:** gorgeous environs; luxe yet homey atmosphere; friendly service. **Cons:** a little out of the way from Piedmont's main wine region; terrace pool is unheated; prices on the high side. $ *Rooms from: €400* ⊠ *Via Piazze 14–16, Cremolino* ✛ *71 km (44 miles) east of Alba* ☎ *0143/038045* ⊕ *nordelaia.com* ⊘ *Closed mid-Jan.–mid-Mar.* 📞 *12 rooms* ⦿ *Free Breakfast.*

★ Relais San Maurizio

$$$$ | **HOTEL** | **FAMILY** | The first luxury hotel in Piedmont, opened in 2002 inside a 17th-century monastery, is still one of the most extravagant places to stay in Piedmont, with a 10,764-square-foot spa, an outdoor swimming pool, tennis courts, and a Michelin-star restaurant. **Pros:** wonderful dining options; ultrarelaxing spa area with unique treatments; elegant, old-fashioned charm. **Cons:** some rooms on the small side; bathrooms could use an update; breakfast choices could be more extensive. $ *Rooms from: €453* ⊠ *Località San Maurizio 39, Santa Stefano Belbo* ✛ *22 km (14 miles) east of Alba* ☎ *0141/841900* ⊕ *www.relaissanmaurizio. it* 📞 *36 rooms* ⦿ *Free Breakfast.*

Villa Beccaris

$$$ | **HOTEL** | This beautiful property consists of an old villa and two newer buildings in the heart of one of the Langhe's most charming villages. **Pros:** lovely gardens and pool area; nice views; located in a village with good restaurants. **Cons:** no elevator; some rooms are noisy; the classic rooms are on the small side. $ *Rooms from: €225* ⊠ *Via Bava Beccaris 1, Monforte d'Alba* ☎ *0173/78158* ⊕ *www.villabeccaris.com* ⊘ *Closed Jan. 8–Feb. 8* 📞 *23 rooms* ⦿ *Free Breakfast.*

★ Villa La Madonna

$$$$ | **HOTEL** | This art-filled boutique hotel (one of the two sister-owners is a photographer) surrounded by vineyards exudes a sense of casual luxury and a modern design aesthetic, from the sitting room with an open fireplace to the lively outdoor pool with retro snack bar. **Pros:** cozy, comfortable feel; delicious food at the in-house eatery; all rooms have outdoor spaces. **Cons:** no TVs or phones in rooms; minimum-night stays in some seasons; some rooms rather

small. $ *Rooms from: €385* ⊠ *Regione Madonna 21, Monastero Bormida* ✛ *45 km (28 miles) southeast of Alba* ☎ *0348/8366141* ⊕ *villamadonna.com* ⊗ *Closed mid-Nov.–late Mar.* ⊅ *18 rooms* ❍❙ *Free Breakfast.*

The Barolo Region

17 km (11 miles) southwest of Alba, 72 km (45 miles) southeast of Turin.

The Langhe district produces some of the top wines in Italy (Barolo and Barbaresco), along with the less-famous but well-regarded dolcetto (from Dogliani) and arneis and nebbiolo (from Roero). Try to schedule a day trip to one or several of the wine estates here.

GETTING HERE AND AROUND
The easiest way to reach Barolo and its wineries is to drive from Alba.

Sights

Famiglia Anselma
WINERY | This winery is known for its steadfast commitment to producing only Barolo—nothing else. The winemaker here, Maurizio Anselma, is something of a prodigy in the Barolo world, and he's quite open to visitors. Contact them by email or phone in advance for an appointment. ⊠ *Località Castello della Volta, Barolo* ☎ *0173/560511* ⊕ *www.anselma.it* ⚲ *Reservations essential.*

Marchesi di Barolo
WINERY | Right in the town of Barolo, this wine estate makes an easy, if touristy, option for getting to know the local wines. In the estate's user-friendly enoteca you can taste wine, buy some of the thousands of bottles from vintages going way back, and look at display bottles, including an 1859 Barolo. Marchesi di Barolo's *cantine* (wine cellars), at Via Roma 1, are open daily; book tours and tastings in advance online. ⊠ *Via Roma 1, Barolo* ☎ *0173/564419* ⊕ *marchesibarolo.*

com ⚼ *From €15 for tour and tasting* ⚲ *Reservations essential.*

Rocche dei Manzoni
WINERY | A good, accessible example of the new school of Barolo wine making (small oak barrels, blended wines) is this estate, about 6 km (4 miles) south of Barolo. The facade of the cantina (wine cellar) is like a Roman temple of brick, complete with imposing columns. Rocche dei Manzoni's reds include Barolo, dolcetto, Langhe Rosso, and barbera. Visits take about two hours and include a guided tour of the wine cellar plus a tasting of three wines; reserve in advance online. ⊠ *Località Manzoni Soprani 3, Monforte d'Alba* ☎ *0173/78421* ⊕ *www.barolobig.com* ⚼ *From €25 for tour and tasting* ⊗ *Closed Dec. 24–Jan. 6; week of Aug. 15; and weekends in July and Aug.* ⚲ *Reservations required.*

WiMu—Il Museo del vino a Barolo
OTHER MUSEUM | **FAMILY** | Spread over three floors of the Barolo Castle, this quirky wine museum looks at the emotions behind the region's top tipple. The entertaining interactive exhibits explore such themes as the moon in harmony, the geometry of life, and the history of wine, through films, displays, and art— just don't expect a glass of Barolo at the end. ⊠ *Castello Comunale Falletti, Piazza Falletti, Barolo* ☎ *0173/386697* ⊕ *www.wimubarolo.it* ⚼ *€9* ⊗ *Closed Feb.*

🍴 Restaurants

★ **Massimo Camia**
$$$ | **PIEDMONTESE** | Chef Massimo Camia's restaurant is in an elegant and modern space, with views of the Barolo vineyards that surround the Damilano winery; the service is impeccable and the food is divine. The restaurant is outside the town of La Morra, a 20-minute drive to the southwest of Alba. **Known for:** amuse-bouche and wine pairings; extensive cheese menu; inventive meat, seafood, and game dishes. $ *Average main:*

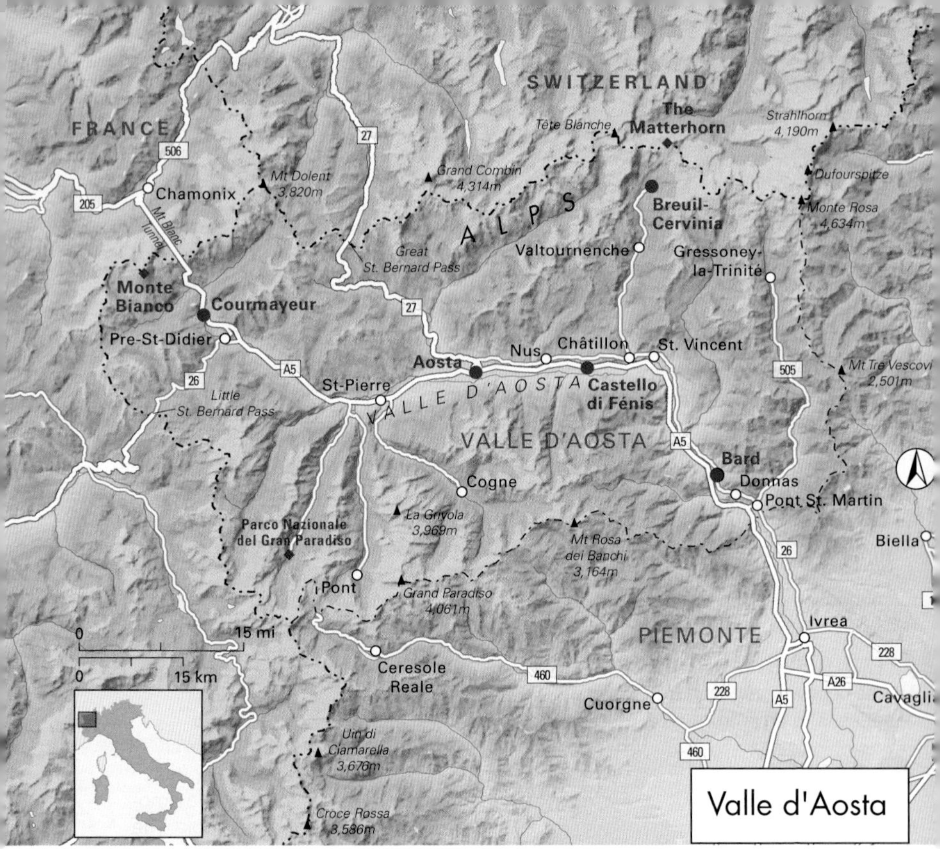

€35 ✉ *SP122 (Alba–Barolo), La Morra* ☎ *0173/56355* 🌐 *www.massimocamia.it* 🕒 *Dec.–Aug.: closed Tues. and Wed.; Sept.–Nov.: closed Tues. No lunch Wed.*

Hotels

Casa di Langa

$$$$ | **HOTEL** | Billed as the first sustainable luxury hotel in Barolo, Casa di Langa uses local materials in its architecture, organic ingredients in its restaurant, and recycled water to irrigate the 104 acres of vineyards and land on its property. **Pros:** fabulous outdoor heated pool; tasty restaurant food; convenient location for Barolo area wine tasting. **Cons:** decor rather on the plain side; not all rooms have views; service not up to par. [$] *Rooms from: €396* ✉ *Località Talloria 1, Cerreto Langhe* ☎ *0173/520520* 🌐 *www.casadilanga.com* 🛏 *39 rooms* 🍴 *Free Breakfast.*

Bard

65 km (40 miles) north of Turin.

This small medieval town clings to a rocky crag that almost completely blocks the entrance to the Valle d'Aosta from Piedmont. Recognized for its strategic importance since prehistoric times, the location was first fully fortified by the Romans, and then by the Ostrogoths in the 6th century. As befits its military heritage, the village is rather gray and somber, but the magnificent fortress that sits atop it makes a visit well worthwhile.

GETTING HERE AND AROUND

Bard is just off the A5 autostrada, which runs north from Turin into the Valle d'Aosta—by car the trip takes about an hour. There are trains about every two hours from Turin and more regular service to and from Aosta. Traveling to Bard by bus is not a viable option.

Sights

★ Forte di Bard

OTHER MUSEUM | FAMILY | A few minutes beyond the French-speaking village of Pont St. Martin, you pass through the narrow Gorge de Bard to reach the fortress that has stood guarding the valley entrance for more than eight centuries. In 1800, Napoléon entered Italy through this valley, using the cover of darkness to get his artillery units past the castle unnoticed. Ten years later he remembered this inconvenience and had the fortress destroyed. It was rebuilt in the 19th century and now houses five museums: the lavishly multimedia Museo delle Alpi, dedicated to the history and culture of the Alps and the Valle d'Aosta region; Le Prigioni, an interactive walk through the former prisons; Museo delli Fortificazioni, which looks at defense techniques (fortifications) over the centuries; Museo delle Frontiere, which examines the political, economic, and cultural meaning of borders; and the children's museum, Le Alpi dei Ragazzi (closed at the time of this writing, so check before you go). Forte di Bard also hosts occasional art exhibitions, accessible for an extra charge. ⌂ *Bard* ☎ *0125/833811* ⊕ *www.fortedibard.it* ✉ *€8 for one museum, €15 for two museums, €24 for all museums* ⊗ *Closed Mon. Sept.–July.*

Breuil-Cervinia/ The Matterhorn

50 km (30 miles) north of Bard, 116 km (72 miles) north of Turin.

Sitting in a huge natural basin at the foot of the Matterhorn, this town, once a high Alpine pasture, grew to become one of Europe's most famous ski areas when a road connecting it to the Valle d'Aosta

Road to Gaul

Between Bard and the town of Donnas, 5 km (3 miles) south along the SS26, you can walk a short but fascinating stretch of a 1st-century Roman consular road that passed this way en route to France. Still showing the deeply worn tracks left by the passage of cart and chariot wheels, this section includes an archway carved through solid rock (used during the Middle Ages as the Donnas city gate) and a milestone ("XXXVI," counting 36 Roman miles from Aosta).

was completed in 1934. It bustles in the winter and has become a popular spot for hikers in the summer, but it's sleepy for much of the rest of the year.

GETTING HERE AND AROUND
From Aosta take the A5 autostrada and then the SR46 (1 hour); from Turin take the A5 and then the SR46 (90 minutes). SADEM has regular bus service from Turin; FlixBus travels here from Milan. Breuil-Cervinia isn't on a train line.

Sights

★ Matterhorn (*Monte Cervino in Italian; Mont Cervin in French*)

MOUNTAIN | FAMILY | The famous peak straddles the border between Italy and Switzerland, and all sightseeing and skiing facilities are operated jointly. Splendid views of the peak can be seen from Plateau Rosa, which can be reached by cable car from the center of Breuil-Cervinia. The cable car gives access to climbing and off-trail skiing on ridges that were once inaccessible. A cable car from Cervinia directly to Zermatt is expected to open in the fall of 2022. ⌂ *Breuil-Cervinia* ⊕ *www.cervinia.it* ✉ *€13 round-trip from Breuil-Cervinia to Plateau Rosa.*

The mighty Matterhorn straddles Switzerland and Italy and has one of the highest summits in Europe.

Hotels

Cime Bianche

$$$ | B&B/INN | This calm, quiet mountain lodge offers commanding views of the Matterhorn and surrounding peaks from the balconies of its simply furnished wood-paneled guest rooms (price includes two meals). **Pros:** next to the ski slopes; lovely views; great restaurant. **Cons:** location is far from everything but the slopes; busy during the ski season; lobby is showing wear. $ *Rooms from: €240 ⊠ Frazione La Vieille 44, Breuil-Cervinia ⊕ Near ski lift ☎ 0166/949046 ⊕ www.hotelcimebianche.com ☉ Closed May and June ⇆ 13 rooms ❍❙ Free Breakfast.*

★ Hermitage

$$$$ | RESORT | The entryway's marble relief of St. Theodolus reminds you that this was once a hermitage, but asceticism has given way to comfort and elegance—a fire is always glowing in the enormous hearth, the dining room is candlelit, the bright bedrooms have balconies, and the suites have antique fireplaces and 18th-century furnishings. **Pros:** superlative staff; frequent shuttle service into town and to ski lifts; refined atmosphere. **Cons:** expensive for the area; books up quickly; located 2 km (1 mile) from the town center. $ *Rooms from: €427 ⊠ Via Piolet 1, Breuil-Cervinia ☎ 0166/948998 ⊕ www.hotelhermitage. com ☉ Closed May, June, and Sept.–late Nov. ⇆ 47 rooms ❍❙ Free Breakfast.*

Les Neiges d'Antan

$$$$ | B&B/INN | In an evergreen forest at Perrères, just outside Cervinia, this family-run inn is quiet and cozy, with three big fireplaces and a nice view of the Matterhorn. **Pros:** secluded and beautiful setting; well-designed spa facilities; wonderful restaurant. **Cons:** no elevator; entrance and lobby areas are showing some wear; 5 km (3 miles) outside Breuil-Cervinia (a car is essential). $ *Rooms from: €316 ⊠ Frazione Cret de Perrères 10, Breuil-Cervinia ☎ 0166/948775 ⊕ le-sneigesdantan.it ☉ Closed mid–late May ⇆ 24 rooms ❍❙ Free Breakfast.*

Activities

CLIMBING

Serious climbers can make the ascent of the Matterhorn from Breuil-Cervinia after registering with the local mountaineering officials at the tourist office. This ascent is for experienced climbers only. Less demanding hikes follow the lower slopes of the Marmore river valley, south of town.

Società Guide Alpine del Cervino

SNOW SPORTS | FAMILY | The Society's guides are available to accompany you on treks and also lead skiing, snowshoeing, ice-climbing, and rock-climbing excursions. ⊠ *Via Circonvallazione 2, Breuil-Cervinia* ☎ *0166/948169* ⊕ *www. guidedelcervino.com* ⌦ *Ski touring, ice climbing, and rock climbing from €380 per person per day; group snowshoeing from €25 per person for 2 hrs; private snowshoeing from €100 per person for 2 hrs.*

SKIING

About 60 lifts and a few hundred miles of ski runs, ranging from beginner to expert, make Breuil-Cervinia Valtournenche one of the best and most popular resort areas in Italy. Because the slopes border a glacier, there's skiing year-round.

Castello di Fénis

34 km (21 miles) northwest of Bard, 104 km (65 miles) north of Turin.

The tiny town of Fénis owes its origins to the presence of the medieval castle that once provided shelter for the local peasants who lived nearby. Today, the population of the town is less than 2,000, most either farmers or part of the tourist industry.

GETTING HERE AND AROUND

To reach the castle by car, take the Nus exit from the A5 autostrada. SAVDA buses provide infrequent service between Aosta

and Fénis. It's about a 10-minute train ride from Aosta to the train station in Nus, a 2-km (1-mile) walk from the castle.

◉ Sights

★ Castello di Fénis

CASTLE/PALACE | FAMILY | The best-preserved medieval fortress in Valle d'Aosta, this many-turreted castle was built in the mid-14th century by Aimone di Challant, a member of a prolific family related to the Savoys. The castle, which used a double ring of walls for its defense, would make a perfect setting for a fairy tale, given its pointed towers, portcullises, and spiral staircases. The 15th-century courtyard surrounded by wooden balconies is elegantly decorated with well-preserved frescoes. Inside you can see the kitchen, with an enormous fireplace that provided central heat in winter; the armory; and the spacious, well-lighted rooms used by the lord and lady of the manor. If you have time to visit only one castle in the Valle d'Aosta, this should be it. ⊠ *Località Chez-Sapin 1, Fénis* ☎ *0165/764263* ⊕ *www.regione.vda. it* ⌦ *€7* ⊗ *Closed Mon.*

Aosta

12 km (7 miles) west of Castello di Fénis, 113 km (70 miles) north of Turin.

Aosta stands at the junction of two of the important trade routes that connect France and Italy, the valleys of the Rhône and the Isère. Its significance as a trading post was recognized by the Romans, who built a garrison here in the 1st century BC, and the present-day layout of the streets is the clearest example you'll find of Roman urban planning in Italy. Well-preserved Roman walls form a perfect rectangle around the center, and the regular pattern of streets reflects its role as a military stronghold. Although its gray-stone buildings and slate roofing give the town a rather cold feeling, Aosta has appeared on several lists as one of the most livable towns in Italy.

GETTING HERE AND AROUND

Aosta is off the A5 autostrada and can easily be reached by car or bus from Milan and Turin. SAVDA buses regularly travel to and from Milan, Turin, and Chamonix in France. Train service is also available from Turin (two hours) and from Milan (three hours), but you'll have to transfer.

VISITOR INFORMATION

CONTACT Aosta Tourism Office. ⊠ *Piazza Porta Praetoria 3, Aosta* ☎ *0165/236627* ⊕ *www.lovevda.it.*

 Sights

Arco di Augusto

HISTORIC SIGHT | At the eastern entrance to town, and commanding a fine view over Aosta and the mountains, stands the Arco di Augusto (Arch of Augustus), built in 25 BC to mark Rome's victory over the Celtic Salassi tribe. (The sloping roof was added in 1716 in an attempt to keep rain from seeping between the stones.) ⊠ *Piazza Arco d'Augusto, Aosta.*

Cattedrale di Santa Maria Assunta (*Duomo*)

CHURCH | Aosta's cathedral dates from the 10th century, but all that remains from that period are the bell towers. The decoration inside is primarily Gothic, but the main attraction of the cathedral predates that era by 1,000 years: among the many ornate objects housed in the treasury is a carved ivory diptych from AD 406 portraying the Roman emperor Honorius. ⊠ *Piazza Papa Giovanni XXIII, Aosta* ☎ *0165/40251* ⊕ *www.cattedraleaosta.it* ⊠ *Duomo free, treasury €5.*

Collegiata di Sant'Orso

CHURCH | This church has layers of history literally visible in its architecture. Originally there was a 6th-century chapel on this site, founded by the Archdeacon Orso, a local saint. Most of the structure was destroyed or hidden when an 11th-century church was erected over it. That church, in turn, was encrusted with Gothic and, later, Baroque features, resulting in a jigsaw puzzle of styles that surprisingly manage to work together. The 11th-century features are almost untouched in the crypt, and if you go up the stairs on the left from the main church you can see the 11th-century frescoes (ask the sacristan, who'll let you in). These restored frescoes depict the life of Christ and the apostles; although only the tops are visible, you can see the expressions on the faces of the disciples. Take the outside doorway to the right of the main entrance to see the church's crowning glory, its 12th-century cloister, enclosed by some 40 stone columns with masterfully carved capitals depicting scenes from the Old and New Testaments and the life of St. Orso. The turrets and spires of Aosta peek out above. ⊠ *Via Sant'Orso 14, Aosta* ☎ *0165/262026* ⊕ *www.diocesiaosta.it* ⊠ *Free.*

Porta Pretoria (*Roman Gate*)

HISTORIC SIGHT | This huge gateway, regally guarding the city, is a remarkable relic from the Roman era. The area between the massive inner and outer walls was used as a small parade ground for the changing of the guard. ⊠ *West end of Via Sant'Anselmo, Aosta* ⊕ *www.lovevda.it.*

Teatro Romano

RUINS | The 72-foot-high ruin of the facade of the Teatro Romano guards the remains of the 1st-century-BC amphitheater, which once held 20,000 spectators. Only a bit of the outside wall and seven of the amphitheater's original 60 arches remain. The latter, once incorporated into medieval buildings, are being brought to light by ongoing archaeological excavations. ⊠ *Via Porta Praetoria at Via Baillage,* ☎ *0165/231665* ⊕ *www.lovevda.it* ⊠ *€10, includes church of San Lorenzo, archaeological museum, and crypt.*

🍴 Restaurants

Trattoria Praetoria
$$ | **NORTHERN ITALIAN** | Just outside the Porta Pretoria, this simple and unpretentious restaurant serves hearty local dishes, including homemade pastas and desserts. They're also well-known for their tasty gluten-free recipes. **Known for:** savory crepes; apple tart with vanilla sauce; polenta with a variety of sauces and accompaniments. [$] *Average main: €20* ✉ *Via Sant'Anselmo 9, Aosta* ☎ *0165/35473* 🌐 *www.trattoriapraetoria.it* 🕒 *Closed Wed.*

★ **Vecchio Ristoro**
$$$ | **NORTHERN ITALIAN** | Chef Filippo Oggioni took over this traditional restaurant in 2019, adding freshness and creative versions of regional recipes and decadent desserts, available both à la carte or as five- or seven-course tasting menus. The elegant, intimate spaces of this converted mill are furnished with antiques, and a traditional ceramic stove provides additional warmth in cool weather. **Known for:** game dishes; wonderful wine pairings; regional tasting menus. [$] *Average main: €35* ✉ *Via Tourneuve 4, Aosta* ☎ *0165/33238* 🌐 *ristorantevecchioristoro.it* 🕒 *Closed Sun. No dinner Mon.*

🛏 Hotels

★ **Hotel Milleluci**
$$ | **B&B/INN** | At this small and inviting family-run hotel overlooking Aosta, guest rooms are bright and charmingly decorated; some have balconies and all have splendid views of the city and mountains. **Pros:** panoramic views; cozy and traditionally decorated rooms; great spa amenities. **Cons:** small bathrooms; no a/c; 1 km (½ mile) north of town, so a car is needed to get around. [$] *Rooms from: €200* ✉ *Località Porossan Roppoz 15, Aosta* ☎ *0165/235278* 🌐 *www.hotelmilleluci.com* 🛏 *28 rooms* 🍽 *Free Breakfast.*

Le Miramonti
$$ | **B&B/INN** | On the banks of a branch of the Dora Baltea River, this establishment offers the alpine interiors, traditional furnishings, and homey comforts needed for a relaxing evening after a day of strenuous activity. **Pros:** friendly, efficient service; spa and swimming pool; excellent location for outdoor sports. **Cons:** some rooms and bathrooms are small; rooms near the river may seem noisy to some; isolated location in a small village. [$] *Rooms from: €147* ✉ *Via Piccolo San Bernardo 3, La Thuile* ☎ *0165/883084* 🌐 *www.alpissima.it* 🕒 *Closed mid-Apr.–early July and mid-Sept.–early Dec.* 🛏 *40 rooms* 🍽 *Free Breakfast.*

Courmayeur/ Monte Bianco

35 km (22 miles) northwest of Aosta, 150 km (93 miles) northwest of Turin.

The main attraction of Courmayeur is a knock-'em-dead view of Europe's highest peak, Monte Bianco. The celebrities and the wealthy who come here these days are following a tradition that dates back to the late 17th century, when Courmayeur's natural springs first began to attract visitors. The spectacle of the Alps gradually surpassed the springs as the biggest draw: the Alpine letters of the English poet Percy Bysshe Shelley were almost advertisements for the region. Since 1965, when the Mont Blanc Tunnel opened, ever-increasing numbers of travelers have passed through the area, and it's now hugely popular with both skiers in winter and hikers during the summer. Planners have managed to keep some restrictions on wholesale development within the town, and its angled rooftops and immaculate cobblestone streets maintain a cozy feeling.

GETTING HERE AND AROUND

Courmayeur is on the A5 autostrada and can easily be reached by car from both Turin and Milan by way of Aosta. There is FlixBus service from Milan and SAVDA buses run regularly from both Turin and Milan. Train service isn't available.

VISITOR INFORMATION

CONTACT Courmayeur Tourism Office. ✉ *Piazzale Monte Bianco 15, Courmayeur* ☎ *0165/842060* 🌐 *www.lovevda.it.*

Sights

★ **Monte Bianco** (*Mont Blanc*)

MOUNTAIN | Monte Bianco's attraction is not so much its shape, which is much less distinctive than that of the Matterhorn, as is its expanse and the awesome vistas from the top. You can reach the summit via a cable car that ascends from Entrèves, just below the Mont Blanc Tunnel. In summer, if so inclined, you can then switch cable cars and descend into Chamonix, in France. In winter you can ski parts of the route off-piste. The Funivia Entrèves whisks you up first to the Pavillon du Mont Fréty in just four minutes—a starting point for many beautiful hikes—and then in six minutes to the spectacular viewing platform at **Punta Helbronner** (more than 11,000 feet), which is also the border post with France.

The next stage up (in summer only) is on the **Télépherique de l'Aiguille du Midi,** as you pass into French territory. The trip is particularly impressive; you dangle over a huge glacial snowfield (more than 2,000 feet below) and make your way slowly to the viewing station above Chamonix. It's one of the most dramatic rides in Europe. From this point you're looking down into France, and if you change cable cars at the Aiguille du Midi station, you can make your way down into Chamonix itself. ✉ *SS26, Courmayeur* ☎ *0165/89196 in Courmayeur, 0450/532275 in Chamonix* 🌐 *www.montebianco.com* 🎫 *€25 round-trip to Pavillon du Mont Fréty, €55 round-trip to Punta Helbronner; additional €69 from Helbronner to Chamonix* 🕑 *Closed Nov., May, and depending on weather conditions and demand.*

Parco Nazionale del Gran Paradiso

NATIONAL PARK | **FAMILY** | Cogne, 52 km (32 miles) southeast of Courmayeur, is the gateway to this huge park, which was once the domain of King Vittorio Emanuele II (1820–78). Bequeathed to the nation after World War I, it is one of Europe's most rugged and unspoiled wilderness areas, with wildlife and many plant species protected by law. The park is one of the few places in Europe where you can see the ibex (a mountain goat with horns up to 3 feet long) and the chamois (a small antelope). The park, which is 703 square km (271 square miles), is open free of charge throughout the year; there's an information office in Cogne. **■ TIP→ Try to visit in May, when spring flowers are in bloom and most of the meadows are clear of snow.** ✉ *Villaggio Cogne 81, Cogne* ☎ *011/8606233* 🌐 *www.pngp.it* 🎫 *Free.*

Hotels

Auberge de la Maison

$$$ | **HOTEL** | Most guest rooms here have balconies with spectacular views of Monte Bianco, and the plush fabrics, wood-burning stoves, and Alpine prints on the walls give the feeling of a cozy country inn. **Pros:** secluded location in the center of Entrèves; charming decor; hotel spa. **Cons:** spa and pool can be crowded and loud in high season; not all standard rooms have views of Monte Bianco; minimum stay in high seasons (summer and winter). [$] *Rooms from: €280* ✉ *Via Passerin d'Entrèves 16, Courmayeur* ☎ *0165/869811* 🌐 *www.aubergemaison.it* 🕑 *Closed May and Nov.* 🛏 *33 rooms* 🍴 *Free Breakfast.*

Grand Hotel Royal e Golf

$$$ | HOTEL | With wide terraces and wood paneling, this longtime landmark in the center of Courmayeur is one of the most elegant spots in town, and the cheery guest rooms have plenty of amenities. **Pros:** central location on main traffic-free street; abundant breakfast buffet; panoramic views. **Cons:** no a/c; fee for spa and swimming pool; standard rooms can be small and outdated. $ *Rooms from: €254* ⊠ *Via Roma 87, Courmayeur* ☎ *0165/831611* ⊕ *www.hotelroyalegolf. com* ⊗ *Closed Easter–mid-June and mid-Sept.–Nov.* ⥲ *86 rooms* ❙⊙❙ *Free Breakfast.*

Hotel Croux

$$ | HOTEL | Half the guest rooms at this bright and comfortable hotel have balconies, the other half have great views of the mountains, and all have contemporary furnishings. **Pros:** central location; shuttle to ski lifts; great views. **Cons:** some rooms are noisy; on a busy road; rooms are simple and could use a revamp. $ *Rooms from: €130* ⊠ *Via Croux 8, Courmayeur* ☎ *0165/846735* ⊕ *www.hotelcroux.it* ⊗ *Closed mid-Apr.– mid-June, Oct., and Nov.* ⥲ *28 rooms* ❙⊙❙ *Free Breakfast.*

★ Villa Novecento Romantic Hotel

$$ | HOTEL | Run with friendly charm and efficiency, the Novecento is a peaceful haven with the style of a comfortable mountain lodge, complete with a log fire in winter, traditional fabrics, wooden furnishings, and early-19th-century prints. **Pros:** frequent shuttle to the slopes and town; away from the main tourist area; good restaurant and excellent breakfast. **Cons:** spa is modest; no a/c; parking is limited. $ *Rooms from: €136* ⊠ *Viale Monte Bianco 64, Courmayeur* ☎ *0165/843000* ⊕ *www.villanovecento. it* ⊗ *Closed Nov. and mid-Apr.–mid-May* ⥲ *22 rooms* ❙⊙❙ *Free Breakfast.*

☖ Activities

SKIING

Courmayeur Mont Blanc

SNOW SPORTS | Courmayeur pales in comparison to its French neighbor, Chamonix, in both the quality and the number of its ski runs. But with good natural snow cover, the trails and vistas are spectacular. A huge gondola leads from the center of Courmayeur to Plan Chécrouit, where other gondolas and lifts lead to the slopes. The skiing around Monte Bianco is particularly good, and the off-piste options are among the best in Europe. The routes from Cresta d'Arp (the local peak) to Dolonne, and from La Palud into France, should be done with a guide. Contact the Courmayeur tourist office for complete information about lift tickets, ski runs, and weather conditions. ⊠ *Strada Dolonne La Villette 1, Courmayeur* ☎ *0165/846658* ⊕ *www. courmayeur-montblanc.com* ⊠ *1-day ski pass €51.*

Società delle Guide Alpine

(*Alpine Guide Society*) **SKIING & SNOWBOARDING** | The society provides Alpine guide services year-round. ⊠ *Strada Villair 2, Courmayeur* ☎ *0165/842064* ⊕ *www.guidecourma-yeur.com* ⊠ *Guides from €215 for 1 day.*

Venaria Reale

10 km (6 miles) northwest of Turin.

This immense palace was built in the 16th century as a hunting lodge.

GETTING HERE AND AROUND

Starting in Turin, from the north side of Piazza della Repubblica, take Bus No. 11 to reach Venaria; the trip takes approximately 60 minutes. By car, follow Corso Regina Margherita to the A55 autostrada. Head north and leave the highway at the Venaria exit, following signs for the Venaria Reale.

Sights

★ Reggia di Venaria Reale

ART MUSEUM | **FAMILY** | Extensive Italianate gardens surround this 16th-century hunting lodge built for Carlo Emanuele II of Savoy. Inside, its Great Gallery is worthy of Versailles. The basements now house a historical exhibition that relates the story of the House of Savoy. The upper floors are reserved for changing exhibitions. ✉ *Piazza della Repubblica 4, Venaria Reale* ☎ *011/4992333* ⊕ *www. lavenaria.it* 🎟 *€20* ⊘ *Closed Mon.*

★ Museo d'Arte Contemporanea

(*Museum of Contemporary Art*)

ART MUSEUM | The Baroque castle of Rivoli now houses a fascinating museum of contemporary art. The building was begun in the 17th century and then redesigned, but never finished, by Juvarra in the 18th century; it was finally converted into a museum in the late 20th century by the minimalist Turin architect Andrea Bruno. ✉ *Piazzale Mafalda di Savoia, Rivoli* ☎ *011/9565222* ⊕ *www.castello-dirivoli.org* 🎟 *€10 (varies for temporary exhibitions)* ⊘ *Closed Mon.–Wed.*

Rivoli

16 km (10 miles) southwest of Venaria, 13 km (8 miles) west of Turin.

The Savoy court was based in Rivoli in the Middle Ages, and the town retains several remnants from that richly dramatic period.

GETTING HERE AND AROUND

GTT buses and trams regularly link central Turin with Rivoli; the journey takes just over one hour. By car, follow Corso Francia from central Turin all the way to Rivoli; unless there's a lot of traffic, the trip should take a half hour.

Sights

Casa del Conte Verde (*House of the Green Count*)

HISTORIC HOME | The richly decorated House of the Green Count, in the oldest part of Rivoli, attests to the wealth and importance of its onetime owner, Amedeo VI of Savoy (1334–83). Legend has it that the count attended tournaments dressed all in green, hence the name. Inside, a small gallery occasionally hosts temporary exhibitions, which may increase the entrance fee. ✉ *Via Fratelli Piol 8, Rivoli* ☎ *011/9563020* ⊕ *www. comune.rivoli.to.it* 🎟 *€5 (varies with exhibitions)* ⊘ *Closed Mon.*

Sacra di San Michele

26 km (17 miles) west of Rivoli, 43 km (27 miles) west of Turin.

Perhaps best known as inspiration for the setting of Umberto Eco's novel *The Name of the Rose,* this abbey was built on Monte Pirchiriano in the 11th century so it would stand out: it occupies the most prominent location for miles around, hanging over a 3,280-foot bluff.

GETTING HERE AND AROUND

From Turin, take the train to Avigliana and then a 14-km (9-mile) taxi ride or uphill hike from the station. By car take the Avigliana Est exit from the A32 autostrada (Torino–Bardonecchia).

Sights

Sacra di San Michele

CHURCH | To reach the church, you must climb 150 steps, from the Porta dello Zodiaco, a splendid Romanesque doorway decorated with the signs of the zodiac. On the left side of the interior are 16th-century frescoes representing New Testament themes; on the right are depictions of the founding of the church. ✉ *Via Sacra di San Michele 14, Sant'Ambrogio di Torino* ☎ *011/939130* ⊕ *www. sacradisanmichele.com* 🎟 *€8.*

Chapter 10

THE ITALIAN RIVIERA

Updated by
Patricia Rucidlo

⊙ **Sights**
★★★☆☆

🍴 **Restaurants**
★★★★☆

🛏 **Hotels**
★★★★☆

🛍 **Shopping**
★☆☆☆☆

🍸 **Nightlife**
★☆☆☆☆

WELCOME TO THE ITALIAN RIVIERA

TOP REASONS TO GO

★ **The Cinque Terre:** Hike the famous Cinque Terre trails past gravity-defying vineyards, colorful, rock-perched villages, and the deep blue Mediterranean Sea.

★ **Portofino:** See the world through rose-tinted sunglasses at this glamorous little harbor village.

★ **Genoa's historical center and port:** From the palaces of Via Garibaldi to the labyrinthine backstreets of the old city to the world-class aquarium, the city is full of surprising delights.

★ **Giardini Botanici Hanbury:** A spectacular natural setting harbors one of Italy's largest, most exotic botanical gardens, near Bordighera.

★ **Pesto:** The basil-rich sauce was invented in Liguria, and it's never been equaled elsewhere.

1 Riomaggiore. The first of the Cinque Terre villages has a small harbor and coastal views.

2 Manarola. Terraced vineyards, olive trees, and pastel houses fill the town.

3 Corniglia. Climb (365 steps) to the most remote Cinque Terre town.

4 Vernazza. Enjoy its lively piazza and a postcard-worthy port view.

5 Monterosso al Mare. Come here for festivals, beaches, clear water, and plentiful accommodations.

6 Lerici. White-sand beaches, hiking trails, and seaside cafés are memorable.

7 La Spezia. This busy port city has outdoor markets and palm-lined streets.

8 Portovenere. Quaint passageways and a castle distinguish the port town.

9 Levanto. This makes an ideal base for diving, surfing, hiking, and day trips around Liguria.

10 Sestri Levante. The small seaside village is framed by two bays.

11 Chiavari. Ancient, twisting streets give character to this fishing town.

12 Santa Margherita Ligure. Palm trees, attractive hotels, and a yacht-filled marina add appeal.

13 Portofino. This vacation spot for the rich and famous has a castle, cliff-side gardens, and fancy boutiques.

14 Camogli. Multicolor houses and a picturesque historical fishing port are draws here.

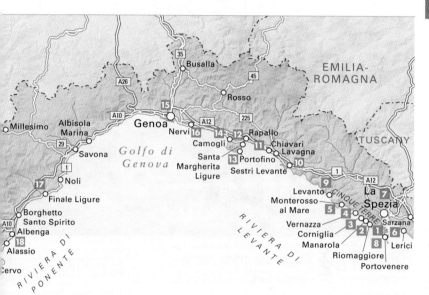

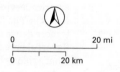

15 Genoa. Palaces, superb pesto, and a rich maritime history mark the birthplace of Christopher Columbus.

16 Nervi. A promenade and parks enhance this resort near busy Genoa.

17 Finale Ligure. Explore the Riviera di Ponente in the villages of Finalmarina, Finalpia, and Finalborgo.

18 Albenga. Narrow Roman-era streets, a Romanesque cathedral, and quaint shops and cafés fill this medieval town.

19 Imperia. This center of olive oil production has 17th- and 18th-century palaces.

20 San Remo. The largest resort in the Riviera di Ponente is known for its casino, glamorous hotels, and seaside promenades.

21 Bordighera. Its many English residents give this town a distinct personality, and it's near a famous botanical garden.

EATING AND DRINKING WELL IN THE ITALIAN RIVIERA

Ligurian cuisine might surprise you. As you'd expect, given the long coastline, it employs all sorts of seafood, but its real claim to fame is the exemplary use of vegetables and herbs.

Basil is practically revered in Genoa—the word is derived from the Greek *basileus,* meaning "king"—and the city is considered the birthplace of pesto, the basil-rich pasta sauce. This and other herbs (laurel, fennel, and marjoram) are cultivated, but also grow wild on the sun-kissed hillsides. Naturally, seafood plays a prominent role on the menu, appearing in soups, salads, and pasta dishes. Vegetables—particularly artichokes, eggplant, and zucchini—are abundant, and usually prepared with liberal amounts of olive oil and garlic.

Like much of Italy, Liguria has a wide range of eating establishments from cafeteria-like *tavole calde* to family-run trattorias to sophisticated *ristoranti.* Lunch is served between 12:30 and 2:30 and dinner between 7:30 and 11. Also popular, especially in Genoa, are *enoteche* (wine bars), which serve simply prepared light meals late into the night.

FABULOUS FOCACCIA

When you're hankering for a snack, turn to bakeries and small eateries serving focaccia. The flatbread is more dense and flavorful here than what's sold as focaccia in American restaurants—it's the region's answer to pizza, usually eaten on the go. It comes simply salted and drizzled with olive oil; flavored with rosemary and olives; covered with cheese or anchovies; and even *ripiena* (stuffed), usually with cheese or vegetables and herbs.

ANTIPASTI

Seafood antipasti are served in abundance at most Ligurian restaurants. Typical dishes include marinated anchovies from Monterosso, *cozze ripiene* (mussel shells stuffed with minced mussel meat, prosciutto, Parmesan, herbs, and bread crumbs), and *soppressata di polpo* (flattened octopus in olive oil and lemon sauce).

PASTA

Liguria's classic sauce is pesto, made from basil, garlic, olive oil, pine nuts, and hard cheese. It's usually served with *trenette* (similar to spaghetti) or the slightly sweet *testaroli* (a flat pasta made from chestnut flour). You can also find *pansotti* (triangular pockets filled with a cheese mixture), and *trofie* (short twists) with *salsa di noci,* a rich sauce of garlic, walnuts, and cream that, as with pesto, is ideally pounded with mortar and pestle. Spaghetti *allo scoglio* has an olive oil, tomato, and white-wine-based sauce containing an assortment of local *frutti di mare* (seafood) like shrimp, clams, mussels, and cuttlefish.

FISH AND MEAT

Fish is the best bet for a second course: the classic preparation is a whole grilled or baked whitefish—branzino and *orata* (dorado) are good

choices—served *alle Ligure,* with olives, potatoes, tomatoes, Ligurian spices, and a drizzle of olive oil. A popular meat dish is *cima alla Genovese,* a veal roll stuffed with a mixture of eggs and vegetables, served as a cold cut.

PANIGACCI

One of the real treats of the region is *panigacci.* Small, terra-cotta dishes known as *testine* are placed in a wood-burning oven or fire to heat at the highest of temperatures. Then balls of dough are laid in the dishes, which are stacked one on top of the other in order to flatten and cook the dough. Panigacci are usually served with *stracchino* cheese, pesto or nut sauce, and cold cuts.

WINE

Local vineyards produce mostly light and refreshing whites, such as *pigato* from the Ponente and *vermentino* from the Levante, although both light reds and appealing *rosato* (Italian rosé) are on the rise. Rossese di Dolceacqua, from near the French border, is considered the best red wine the region has to offer, but for a more robust accompaniment to meats, opt for the full-bodied reds of the neighboring Piedmont region. For a postdinner or dessert wine, try the *sciacchetrà,* made exclusively in the Cinque Terre.

Nestled between the south of France and the Tuscan border lies the region of Liguria, with verdant and lush mountains to the north and east, and the sapphire-blue Mediterranean to the south and west. In between is a land of lush vegetation, medieval hilltop hamlets, panoramic vistas, colorful seaside villages, pristine beaches, and one of Italy's most underrated cities, Genoa.

There is plenty to do—from hiking and biking, to water sports and fishing, to eating (very) well—and plenty to see, including some of Italy's most aesthetically pleasing architecture. It's also easy to just enjoy la dolce vita along this coast, better known as the Italian Riviera.

The Italian Riviera oozes charm and irresistible allure, with many seaside resort towns and colorful villages that stake intermittent claim to the rocky shores of the Ligurian Sea and seem like the long-lost cousins of newer seaside paradises found elsewhere. It has been a haven for artists, writers, celebrities, and royalty since the 1800s, and continues to fascinate visitors throughout the year due to its mild climate. Here the grandest palazzi share space with frescoed, angular *terratetti* (tall, skinny houses). The rustic and elegant, the provincial and chic, the small-town and cosmopolitan all collide here in a sun-drenched blend that defines the Italian side of the Riviera. There are chic resort towns such as San Remo and Portofino, the unique beauty and outdoor adventures of the Cinque Terre, numerous quaint seaside and hilltop villages to explore, plus the history and architectural charm of Genoa. Mellowed by balmy breezes blowing in from the sea, travelers bask in the sun, explore the picturesque fishing villages, and pamper themselves at the resorts that dot this ruggedly beautiful landscape.

MAJOR REGIONS

The beautiful **Cinque Terre** is the heart of the Italian Riviera. In their rugged simplicity, the five old fishing towns of **Monterosso al Mare, Vernazza, Corniglia, Manarola,** and **Riomaggiore** seem to mock the glitzy neighboring resorts. With a blue sea in the foreground, multicolor buildings emerge almost seamlessly from cliffs, and rocky mountains rise precipitously to vineyards and olive groves. The terrain is so steep that for centuries, footpaths were the only way to get around. Since its 1997 UNESCO World Heritage designation, the Cinque Terre have become one of Italy's most popular destinations. Eastward from Genoa to Lerici (encompassing the Cinque Terre and a naval port, **La Spezia**) stretches the **Riviera di Levante** (Riviera of the Rising Sun). It has a raw, unpolished feel, and its rugged coastline is dotted with colorful fishing villages like **Camogli, Portovenere, Chiavari,** and **Sestri Levante.** It also has one of Europe's well-known playgrounds for the rich and famous, the inlet of **Portofino,** and nearby **Santa Margherita Ligure** is popular with well-to-do Italians. From this area's twisting roads, the hills plummet sharply to the sea. Beaches tend to be rocky, yet there are some lovely sandy stretches in **Lerici,** Monterosso al Mare, **Levanto,** and Paraggi (near Portofino).

The seaside city of **Genoa** (Genova in Italian), birthplace of Christopher Columbus, has a long history as a major trading station, and in the Middle Ages and the Renaissance Genoa became a wealthy, prestigious commercial center. Its bankers, merchants, and princes adorned their city with palaces, churches, and impressive art collections. Today Genoa is a cultural center worth a look. Nearby **Nervi** is a stately resort town.

West of Genoa, the **Riviera di Ponente** (Riviera of the Setting Sun) covers the narrow strip of northwest Liguria from Genoa to the French border. The sapphire Mediterranean Sea to one side and the verdant foothills of the Alps on the other allow for temperate weather, which is why it's also called the Riviera dei Fiori (Riviera of the Flowers). There is also olive-growing in **Imperia.** Once filled with seaside villages and elegant homes, this area struggles to balance natural beauty with resort development, as in glitzy **San Remo.** Highly populated resorts and some overly industrialized areas are jammed into the thin stretch of white-sand and pebble beaches. There are still several worthwhile villages, like **Finale Ligure, Albegna,** and **Bordighera,** along the sea and hinterland. Bordighera is near Giardini Botanici Hanbury, one of Italy's most beautiful grouping of gardens. The Riviera di Levante may retain more of its natural beauty, but the Ponente remains popular with visitors looking for sunshine, nightlife, and relaxation.

Planning

When to Go

The Italian Riviera is extremely seasonal, apart from Genoa, a city with year-round cultural attractions. The region has a typical Mediterranean climate with warm summers and rainy winters, making high season (Easter and June–August in particular) the best time to visit, though it can be really crowded as well as lively. From April to October, the area bustles with shops, cafés, clubs, and restaurants that stay open late. The rest of the year, the majority of resorts close down, and you'll be hard-pressed to find accommodations or restaurants open.

Planning Your Time

Your first decision, particularly given limited time, is between the two Rivieras. The Riviera di Levante (east of Genoa) is more rustic and has a more distinct personality, with the unique Cinque Terre, ritzy Portofino, and the panoramic Gulf of Poets. The Riviera di Ponente (west of Genoa) is a classic European resort experience with many white-sand beaches and more nightlife and accommodation choices—similar to, but not as glamorous as, the French Riviera across the border.

In either case, your second decision is whether to visit Genoa. Despite its rough exterior and (diminishing) reputation as a seamy port town, Genoa's artistic and cultural treasures are significant—you won't find anything remotely comparable elsewhere in the region. Unless your goal is to avoid urban life entirely, consider a night or two in the city.

Getting Here and Around

BUS

Generally speaking, buses are a difficult way to come and go in Liguria. Although there are local buses that run between villages along the Riviera Ponente, it's not an extensive network and can be a challenge to navigate.

CONTACTS ATP. ☎ *0185/3731* ⊕ *www. atpesercizio.it.* **Volpibus.** ☎ *010/561661* ⊕ *www.gruppostat.com/autolinee-locali.*

CAR

With the freedom of a car, you could drive from one end of the Riviera to the other on the autostrada in about three hours. Two good roads run parallel to each other along the coast of Liguria. Closer to shore and passing through all the towns and villages is the SS1, or Via Aurelia, which was laid out by the ancient Romans and has excellent views at almost every turn. It gets very crowded in July and August. More direct and higher up than SS1 are autostradas A10, west of Genoa, and A12, to the south—engineering wonders with literally hundreds of long tunnels and towering viaducts. These routes save time on weekends, in summer, and on days when festivals slow traffic in some resorts to a standstill.

TRAIN

Train travel on the national railway, Ferrovie dello Stato, is by far the most convenient mode of transportation throughout the region. It takes 3½ hours for an express train to cover the entire Ligurian coast. Local trains take upward of five hours or more to get from one end of the coast to the other, stopping in or near all the towns along the way. For schedules, check ⊕ *www.trenitalia.com/en.*

Hiking

Walking Liguria's extensive network of trails while taking in the gorgeous views is a major outdoor activity and regional attraction. The mild climate and laid-back state of mind can lull you into underestimating just how strenuous such walks can be. Wear good shoes, use sunscreen, and carry plenty of water—you'll be glad you did. Trail maps are available from tourist information offices, or upon entry to the Cinque Terre National Park.

On the Portofino promontory, the relatively easy walk to the Abbazia di San Fruttuoso is popular, and there's a more challenging hike from Ruta to the top of Monte Portofino and back down to Camogli. From Genoa, you can take the Zecca–Righi funicular up to Righi and walk along the ring of fortresses that used to defend the city.

Walking tours can introduce you to lesser-known aspects of the region. For the Cinque Terre and the rest of the Province of La Spezia, the **Cooperativa Arte e Natura** (⊠ *Viale Amendola 172, La Spezia* ☎ *0187/739410* ⊕ *www.cinqueterrexperience.com*) is a good source for English-speaking and other foreign-language guides. A full day costs €255, and a three-hour tour is €170; these prices are for a group of up to 35 people.

Restaurants

While fine dining can be found in Liguria, you are more likely to enjoy a casual atmosphere, often with an amazing sea view. Expect both the decor and dishes to be simple but flavorful; fish and seafood are highlights here.

Restaurant prices are the average cost of a main course at dinner or, if dinner is not served, at lunch. Restaurant reviews have been shortened. For full information, visit Fodors.com.

Hotels

Liguria's lodging may be a step behind more developed areas like Positano and Taormina, so be sure to reserve its better accommodations (and the relatively limited options in the Cinque Terre) far in advance. Lodging tends to be pricey in high season, particularly June to August.

Hotel prices are the lowest cost of a standard double room in high season. Hotel reviews have been shortened. For full information, visit Fodors.com.

What it Costs in Euros

	$	$$	$$$	$$$$
RESTAURANTS				
	under €15	€15–€24	€25–€35	over €35
HOTELS				
	under €125	€125–€200	€201–€300	over €300

Riomaggiore

17 km (11 miles) southwest of La Spezia, 101 km (60 miles) southeast of Genoa.

At the eastern end of the Cinque Terre, Riomaggiore is built into a river gorge (hence the name, which means "major river") and is easily accessible from La Spezia by train or car. The landscape is terraced and steep—be prepared for many stairs!—and leads to a small harbor, protected by large slabs of alabaster and marble that serve as tanning beds for sunbathers. The harbor is also the site of several outdoor cafés with fine views. According to legend, the settlement of Riomaggiore dates as far back as the 8th century, when Greek religious refugees came here to escape persecution by the Byzantine emperor.

The village is divided into two parts. If you arrive by train, you will have to pass through a tunnel that flanks the train tracks to reach the historic side of town. To avoid the crowds and get a great view of the Cinque Terre coast, walk straight uphill as soon as you exit the station. This winding road takes you over the hill to the 14th-century **church of St. John the Baptist,** toward the medieval town center and the Genovese-style tower houses that dot the village. Follow Via Roma (the Old Town's main street) downhill, pass under the train tracks, and you'll arrive in the charming fishermen's port. Lined with traditional fishing boats and small trattorias, this is a lovely spot for a romantic lunch or dinner. Unfortunately, Riomaggiore doesn't have as much old-world charm as its sister villages; its easy accessibility has brought traffic and more construction here than elsewhere in the Cinque Terre.

GETTING HERE AND AROUND

The enormous parking problems presented by these cliff-dwelling villages have been mitigated somewhat by a large, covered parking structure at La Spezia Centrale station, which costs €2.30 per hour in summer. It's clean and secure (you cannot enter without a ticket code to open the door), and it's open 24/7. This is a good backup solution for those with cars, although others may choose to take a day trip from Pisa or Lucca and rely on bus and train services. Arrive early, as it can fill up by mid-morning, especially in high season.

 Sights

Riomaggiore

TOWN | This village at the eastern end of the Cinque Terre is built into a river gorge (hence the name, which means "river major"). It has a tiny harbor protected by large slabs of alabaster and marble, which serve as tanning beds for sunbathers, as well as being the site of several outdoor cafés with fine views. According to legend, the settlement of Riomaggiore dates as far back as the 8th century, when Greek religious refugees came here to escape persecution by the

Accessing Cinque Terre Trails

When to Go

The ideal times to visit the Cinque Terre are September and May, when the weather is mild and the summer tourist season isn't in full swing (June through August can be unbearably hot and crowded).

Getting Here and Around

There is now a local train between La Spezia and Levanto that stops at each of the Cinque Terre villages, and runs approximately every 30 minutes throughout the day. Tickets for each leg of the journey (€1.90–€2.20) are available at all five train stations. In Corniglia, the only one of the Cinque Terre that isn't at sea level, a shuttle service (€1.50) is provided for those who don't wish to climb (or descend) the 300-plus steps that link the train station with the cliff-top town.

Along the Cinque Terre coast two ferry lines operate. From June to September, Golfo Paradiso runs from Genoa and Camogli to Monterosso al Mare and Vernazza (a one-day ticket costs €38). The smaller but more frequent Golfo dei Poeti stops at each village from Lerici (east of Riomaggiore) to Monterosso, with the exception of Corniglia, four times a day (a one-day ticket costs €35).

Admission

Entrance tickets for using the trails are available at ticket booths located at the start of each section of Trail No. 2, and at information offices in the Levanto, Monterosso, Vernazza, Corniglia, Manarola, Riomaggiore, and La Spezia train stations. A one-day pass costs €7.50, which includes a trail map and an information leaflet; a two-day pass is €14.50.

The Cinque Terre Card combines park entrance fees with unlimited daily use of the regional train between La Spezia, the five villages, and Levanto just north of Monterosso, and costs €16 for a one-day pass and €29 for a two-day pass.

For More Information

www.cinqueterre.com; www.lecinqueterre.org; www.parconazionale-5terre.it; www.rebuildmonterosso.com; www.savevernazza.com; www.littleparadiso.com (blog).

Byzantine emperor. ⊠ *Stazione Ferroviaria, Riomaggiore* ☎ *0187/762187* ⊕ *www.turismoinliguria.it.*

 Restaurants

Dau Cila

$$$ | LIGURIAN | There's wonderful seaside dining on Riomaggiore harbor, with a menu of local Ligurian dishes and an extensive wine list. ■TIP→ On bad-weather days, take advantage of the lovely dining room with vaulted ceilings, built into the rock. **Known for:** local flavors; extensive wine list; sea views. $ *Average main: €28* ⊠ *Via San Giacomo 65, Riomaggiore* ☎ *0187/760032* ⊘ *Closed Tues.*

Manarola

16 km (10 miles) southwest of La Spezia, 117 km (73 miles) southeast of Genoa.

The enchanting pastel houses of Manarola spill down a steep hill overlooking a spectacular turquoise swimming cove

Continued on page 462

HIKING THE CINQUE TERRE

FIVE REMOTE VILLAGES MAKE ONE MUST-SEE DESTINATION

"Charming" and "breath-taking" are adjectives that get a workout when you're traveling in Italy, but it's rare that both apply to a single location. The Cinque Terre is such a place, and this combination of characteristics goes a long way toward explaining its tremendous appeal.

The area is made up of five tiny villages (Cinque Terre literally means "Five Lands") clinging to the cliffs along a gorgeous stretch of the Ligurian coast. The terrain is so steep that for centuries footpaths were the only way to get from place to place. It just so happens that these paths provide beautiful views of the rocky coast tumbling into the sea, as well as access to secluded beaches and grottoes.

Backpackers "discovered" the Cinque Terre in the 1970s, and its popularity has been growing ever since. Despite summer crowds, much of the original appeal is intact. Each town has maintained its own distinct charm, and views from the trails in between are as breathtaking as ever.

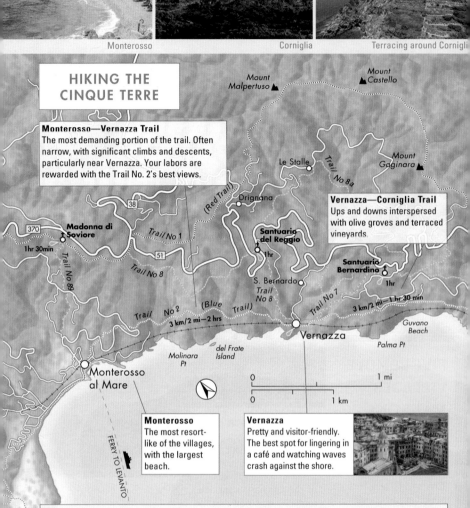

Monterosso

Corniglia

Terracing around Corniglia

HIKING THE CINQUE TERRE

Mount Malpertuso ▲

Mount Castello ▲

Monterosso—Vernazza Trail
The most demanding portion of the trail. Often narrow, with significant climbs and descents, particularly near Vernazza. Your labors are rewarded with the Trail No. 2's best views.

Le Stalle

Trail No 8a

Mount Gaginara ▲

(Red Trail)

Drignana

38

Vernazza—Corniglia Trail
Ups and downs interspersed with olive groves and terraced vineyards.

370

Madonna di Soviore

Trail No 1

Santuario del Reggio

1 hr 30 min

Trail No 89

51

Trail No 8

1hr

Santuario Bernardino

1hr

S. Bernardo
Trail No 8

Trail No 7

3 km/2 mi — 1 hr 30 min

Trail No 2 (Blue Trail)

3 km/2 mi — 2 hrs

Vernazza

Guvano Beach

del Frate Island

Molinara Pt

Palma Pt

Monterosso al Mare

0   1 mi

0   1 km

FERRY TO LEVANTO

Monterosso
The most resort-like of the villages, with the largest beach.

Vernazza
Pretty and visitor-friendly. The best spot for lingering in a café and watching waves crash against the shore.

THE CLASSIC HIKE

Hiking is the most popular way to experience the Cinque Terre, and Trail No. 2, the Sentiero Azzurro (Blue Trail), is the most traveled path. To cover the entire trail is a full day: it's approximately 13 km (8 miles) in length, takes you to all five villages, and requires about five hours, not including stops, to complete. The best approach is to start at the eastern-most town of Riomaggiore and warm up your legs on the easiest segment of the trail. As you work your way west, the hike gets progressively more demanding. Between Corniglia and Manarola take the ferry (which provides its own beautiful views) or the inland train running between the towns instead.

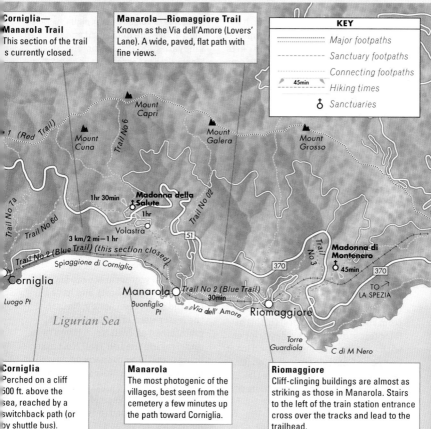

Manarola

Along Lovers' Lane

Via dell'Amore

Corniglia—Manarola Trail
This section of the trail is currently closed.

Manarola—Riomaggiore Trail
Known as the Via dell'Amore (Lovers' Lane). A wide, paved, flat path with fine views.

KEY

····················	Major footpaths
- - - - - - - - -	Sanctuary footpaths
– – – – – – – –	Connecting footpaths
45min	Hiking times
☗	Sanctuaries

Mount Capri

1 (Red Trail)

Mount Cuna

Trail No 6

Mount Galera

Mount Grosso

Trail No 7a

Trail No 6d

1hr 30min

Madonna della Salute ☗
1hr

Volastra

Trail No 02

3 km/2 mi—1 hr

51

Trail No 2 (Blue Trail) (this section closed)

Spiaggione di Corniglia

Corniglia

Luogo Pt

Trail No 3

Madonna di Montenero
☗ 45min

370

370

TO
LA SPEZIA

Manarola ☗

Trail No 2 (Blue Trail)
30min

Buonfiglio Pt

Via dell' Amore

Riomaggiore

Ligurian Sea

Torre Guardiola

C di M Nero

Corniglia
Perched on a cliff 500 ft. above the sea, reached by a switchback path (or by shuttle bus).

Manarola
The most photogenic of the villages, best seen from the cemetery a few minutes up the path toward Corniglia.

Riomaggiore
Cliff-clinging buildings are almost as striking as those in Manarola. Stairs to the left of the train station entrance cross over the tracks and lead to the trailhead.

BEYOND TRAIL NO.2

Trail No. 2 is just one of a network of trails crisscrossing the hills. If you're a dedicated hiker, spend a few nights and try some of the other routes. Trail No. 1, the Sentiero Rosso (Red Trail), climbs from Portovenere (east of Riomaggiore) and returns to the sea at Levanto (west of Monterosso al Mare). To hike its length takes from 9 to 12 hours; the ridge-top trail provides spectacular views from high above the villages, each of which can be reached via a steep path. Other shorter trails go from the villages up into the hills, some leading to religious sanctuaries. Trail No. 9, for example, starts from the old section of Monterosso and ends at the Madonna di Soviore Sanctuary.

Hiking the Cinque Terre

Though often described as relaxing and easy, the Cinque Terre also have several hiking options if you wish to exert yourself a little. Many people do not realize just how demanding parts of these trails can be—it's best to come prepared. We recommend bringing a Cinque Terre Card and cash (smaller shops, eateries, and the park entrances do not accept credit cards).

When all trails are completely open, a hike through the entire region takes about four to five hours; add time for exploring each village and taking a lunch break—it's an all-day, if not two-day, trek. We recommend an early start, especially in summer when midday temperatures can rise to 90°F. Note that only Sentiero Azzurro (Trail No. 2) requires the Cinque Terre Card. The other 20-plus trails in the area are free. All trails are well marked with a red-and-white sign. Trails from village to village get progressively steeper from south (Riomaggiore) to north (Monterosso). If you're a day-tripper with a car, use the underground lot at La Spezia Centrale train station (€2.30 per hour in summer) and take the train to Riomaggiore (6–8 minutes).

Our Favorites

Other trails to consider include **Monterosso to Santuario Madonna di Soviore**, a fairly strenuous but rewarding 1½ hours up to a lovely 8th-century sanctuary. There is also a restaurant and a priceless view. **Riomaggiore to Montenero and Portovenere** is one hour up to the sanctuary and another three hours to Portovenere, passing through some gorgeous, less-traveled terrain. **Manarola to Volastra to Corniglia** runs high above the main trail and through vineyards and lesser-known villages. **Monterosso to Levanto** is a good 2½-hour hike, passing over Punta Mesco with glorious views of the Cinque Terre to the south, Corsica to the west, and the Alps to the north.

Each town has something that passes for a beach (usually with lots of pebbles or slabs of terraced rock), but there is only one option for both sand and decent swimming—in Monterosso, just across from the train station. It's equipped with chairs, umbrellas, and snack bars.

Precautions

If you're hitting the trails, carry water with you, wear sturdy shoes (hiking boots are best), and have a hat and sunscreen handy. Note that the lesser-used trails aren't as well maintained as Trail No. 2. If you're undertaking the full Trail No. 1 hike, bring something to snack on as well as your water bottle. Note that currently the Via dell'Amore and the portion of Trail No. 2 between Manarola and Corniglia are closed indefinitely due to landslides.

■ TIP→ Check weather reports, especially in late fall and winter; thunderstorms can make shelterless trails slippery and dangerous. Rain in October and November can cause landslides and close trails altogether.

and a bustling harbor. The whole town is built on black rock. Above the town, ancient terraces still protect abundant vineyards and olive trees. This village is the center of wine and olive oil production in the region, and its streets are lined with shops selling local products.

Surrounded by steep terraced vineyards, Manarola's one road tumbles from the **Chiesa di San Lorenzo** (14th century) high above the village, down to the rocky port. Since the Cinque Terre wine cooperative is located in **Groppo,** a hamlet overlooking the village (reachable by foot or by the green park bus; ask at park offices for schedules), the vineyards are accessible. If you'd like to snap a shot of the most famous view of the town, you can walk from the port area to the cemetery above. Along the way you'll pass the town's playground, uncrowded bathrooms, and a tap with clean drinking water.

GETTING HERE AND AROUND

Though it's possible to drive and park (in a lot above town, which means walking down), it's much easier to arrive by often overly crowded train. Trains run from La Spezia or Levanto; both are very short journeys and cost about €5.

Sights

Manarola
TOWN | Enchanting pastel houses spill down a steep hill overlooking a spectacular turquoise swimming cove and a bustling harbor. The whole town is built on black rock. Above the town, ancient terraces still protect abundant vineyards and olive trees. This village is the center of the wine and olive oil production of the region, and its streets are lined with shops selling local products. ✉ *Manarola* 🌐 *www.turismoinliguria.it, www.parconazionale5terre.it.*

Hotels

★ **La Torretta**
$$$ | **HOTEL** | One of the Cinque Terre's few "boutique" hotels is in a 17th-century tower that sits high on the hill above the rainbow-hue village of Manarola, with truly lovely views of the terraced vineyards, colorful village homes, and the Mediterranean sea; inside, decor is chic, sleek, and antiques-bedecked. **Pros:** no-smoking policy; stellar staff; free luggage transfer. **Cons:** books up quickly; strict no-refund policy; steep walk up to the hotel. [$] *Rooms from: €250* ✉ *Vico Volto 20, Manarola* ☎ *0187/920327* 🌐 *www.torrettas.com* 🕒 *Closed Dec.–Feb.* 🛏 *15 rooms* 🍴 *Free Breakfast.*

Corniglia

27 km (17 miles) northwest of La Spezia, 100 km (60 miles) southeast of Genoa.

The buildings, narrow lanes, and stairways of Corniglia are strung together amid vineyards high on the cliffs. On a clear day, views of the entire coastal strip are excellent, from Elba in the south to the Italian Alps in the north. The high perch and lack of harbor make this farming community the most remote and therefore least crowded of the Cinque Terre. In fact, the 365 steps that lead up from the train station to the town center dissuade many tourists from making the hike to the village. You can also take the green park bus, but they run infrequently and are usually packed with tired hikers.

Corniglia is built along one road edged with small shops, bars, gelaterias, and restaurants. Midway along Via Fieschi is the **Largo Taragio,** the main square and heart of the village. Shaded by leafy trees and umbrellas, this is a lovely spot for a mid-hike gelato break. Here you'll find the 14th-century **Chiesa di San Pietro.** The church's rose window of marble imported from Carrara is impressive, particularly considering the work required to get it here!

GETTING HERE AND AROUND

This town has very limited parking and it's much simpler to take the train from either La Spezia or Levanto.

Sights

Corniglia

TOWN | Stone buildings, narrow lanes, and stairways are strung together amid vineyards high on the cliffs; on a clear day views of the entire coastal strip are excellent. The high perch and lack of harbor make this farming community the most remote of the Cinque Terre. ⊠ *Corniglia* ☎ *0187/762600* ⊕ *www.parconazionale-5terre.it.*

San Pietro

CHURCH | On a pretty pastel square sits the 14th-century church of San Pietro. The rose window of marble imported from Carrara is impressive, particularly considering the work required to get here. ⊠ *Main Sq., Corniglia.*

Vernazza

27 km (17 miles) west of La Spezia, 96 km (59 miles) southeast of Genoa.

With its narrow streets and small squares, Vernazza is arguably the most charming of the Cinque Terre towns, and usually the most crowded. Historically, it was the most important of them and—since Vernazza was the only one fortunate enough to have a natural port—the wealthiest, as evidenced by the elaborate arcades, loggias, and marble work lining Via Roma and Piazza Marconi.

The village's pink slate-roof houses and colorful squares contrast with the remains of the medieval fort and castle, including two towers, in the Old Town. The Romans first inhabited this rocky spit of land in the 1st century. Today, Vernazza

has a fairly lively social scene. **Piazza Marconi** looks out across Vernazza's small sandy beach to the sea, toward Monterosso. The numerous restaurants and bars crowd their tables and umbrellas on the outskirts of the piazza, creating a patchwork of sights and sounds that form one of the most unique and beautiful places in the world.

GETTING HERE AND AROUND

Driving to Vernazza is complicated, and it's much easier to take a short train ride from either La Spezia or Levanto. Trains run frequently.

Sights

If Mass is not going on (a cord blocks the entrance if it is), take a peek into the **church of St. Margaret of Antioch,** where little has changed since its enlargement in the 1600s. This 14th-century edifice has simple interiors but truly breathtaking views toward the sea: a stark contrast to the other, elaborate churches of the Cinque Terre.

On the other side of the piazza, stairs lead to a lookout **fortress and cylindrical watchtower,** built in the 11th century as protection against pirate attacks. For a small fee you can climb to the top of the tower for a spectacular view of the coastline.

Vernazza

TOWN | With narrow streets and small squares, the village that many consider to be the most charming of the five towns has the best access to the sea—a geographic reality that made the village wealthier than its neighbors, as evidenced by the elaborate arcades, loggias, and marble work. The village's pink, slate-roof houses and colorful squares contrast with the remains of the medieval fort and castle, including two towers, in the old town. The Romans first inhabited this rocky spit of land in the 1st century. Today, Vernazza has a fairly lively social scene. It's a great place to refuel with a hearty seafood lunch or linger in a café between links of the seaside hike. ✉ *Vernazza* 🌐 *www.turismoinliguria.it, www.parconazionale5terre.it.*

🍴 Restaurants

Gambero Rosso

$$$ | **LIGURIAN** | Relax on Vernazza's main square at this fine trattoria looking out onto the church of Santa Maria d'Antiochi. Enjoy such delectable dishes as shrimp salad, vegetable torte, and squid-ink risotto. **Known for:** pesto dishes; fresh seafood; piazza view. [$] *Average main: €33* ✉ *Piazza Marconi 7, Vernazza* ☎ *0187/812265* 🌐 *www.ristorantegamberorosso.net* 🕒 *Closed Thurs. and Nov.–Mar.*

★ **Ristorante Belforte**

$$ | **LIGURIAN** | High above the sea in one of Vernazza's remaining medieval stone towers is this unique spot serving delicious Cinque Terre cuisine such as branzino *sotto sale* (cooked under salt), stuffed mussels, and *insalata di polpo* (octopus salad). The setting is magnificent, so try for an outdoor table. **Known for:** lively atmosphere; octopus salad; incredible views. [$] *Average main: €20* ✉ *Via Guidoni 42, Vernazza* ☎ *0187/812222* 🌐 *www.ristorantebelforte.it* 🕒 *Closed Tues. and Nov.–Easter.*

🛏 Hotels

La Malà

$$ | **B&B/INN** | A cut above other lodging options in the Cinque Terre, these small guest rooms are equipped with flat-screen TVs, air-conditioning, marble showers, and comfortable bedding and have views of the sea or the port, which can also be enjoyed at their most bewitching from a shared terrace literally suspended over the Mediterranean. **Pros:** clean, fresh-feeling rooms; helpful, attentive staff; views. **Cons:** child-friendly (either a pro or a con); books up quickly; some stairs are involved. [$] *Rooms from: €160* ✉ *Giovanni Battista 29, Vernazza* ☎ *334/2875718* 🌐 *www.lamala.it* 🕒 *Closed Jan. 8–Mar. 1* 🛏 *4 rooms* 🍴 *Free Breakfast.*

Monterosso al Mare

32 km (20 miles) northwest of La Spezia, 89 km (55 miles) southeast of Genoa.

It's the combined draw of beautiful beaches, rugged cliffs, crystal clear turquoise waters, and plentiful small hotels and restaurants that has made Monterosso al Mare the largest of the Cinque Terre villages (population 1,800) and also the busiest in midsummer.

And Monterosso has festivals enough to match its size. They start with the Lemon Feast on the Saturday before Ascension Sunday. Then, on the second Sunday after Pentecost, comes the Flower Festival of Corpus Christi: during the afternoon, the streets and alleyways of the historic center are decorated with thousands of colorful flower petals, set in beautiful designs, over which an evening procession passes. Finally, the Salted Anchovy and Olive Oil Festival takes place each year during the second weekend of September.

GETTING HERE AND AROUND

The largest of the "Five Earths," it's possible to drive and park nearby, but it's best to take the train either from La Spezia or Levanto.

👁 Sights

Heading west from the train station, you pass through a tunnel and exit into the *centro storico* (historic center) of the village.

Monterossa al Mare

TOWN | Nestled into the wide valley that leads to the sea, Monterosso is built above numerous streams, which have been covered to make up the major streets of the village. Via Buranco, the oldest street in Monterosso, leads to the most characteristic piazza of the village, Piazza Matteotti. Locals pass through here daily to shop at the supermarket and butcher. This piazza also contains the oldest and most typical wineshop in the village, Enoteca da Eliseo—stop here between 6 pm and midnight to share tables with fellow tourists and locals over a bottle of Cinque Terre wine. There's also the **Chiesa di San Francesco**, built in the 12th century and an excellent example of the Ligurian Gothic style. Its distinctive black stripes and marble rose window make it one of the most photographed sites in the Cinque Terre.

Fegina, the newer side of the village (and site of the train station), has relatively modern homes ranging from the Liberty style (Art Nouveau) to the early 1970s. At the far eastern end of town, you'll run into a private sailing club sheltered by a vast rock carved with an impressive statue of Neptune. From here, you can reach the challenging trail to Levanto (a great 2½-hour hike). This trail has the added bonus of a five-minute detour to the **ruins of a 14th-century monastery**. The expansive view from this vantage point allowed the monks who were housed here to easily scan the waters for enemy ships that might invade the villages and alert residents to coming danger. Have your camera ready for this Cinerama-like vista.

The **local outdoor market** is held on Thursday and attracts crowds of tourists and villagers from along the coast to shop for everything from pots, pans, and underwear to fruits, vegetables, and fish. Often a few stands sell local art and crafts, as well as olive oil and wine. ✉ *Monterosso al Mare.*

🍴 Restaurants

★ Enoteca Internazionale

$ | **WINE BAR** | Located on the main street, this bar offers a large selection of wines, both local and from farther afield, plus delicious light fare; its umbrella-covered patio is a welcoming spot to recuperate after a day of hiking. Susanna, the owner, is a certified sommelier who's always forthcoming with helpful suggestions on pairing local wines with their tasty bruschettas. **Known for:** helpful staff; patio dining; extensive wine list. [$] *Average main: €13* ✉ *Via Roma 62, Monterosso al Mare* ☎ *0187/817278* 🌐 *www.enotecainternazionale.com* 🕓 *Closed Jan. and Feb.*

★ Miky

$$$ | **SEAFOOD** | This is arguably the best restaurant in Monterosso, specializing in tasty, fresh seafood dishes like grilled calamari and monkfish ravioli. If their *catalana* (poached lobster and shrimp with sliced raw fennel and carrot) happens to be on the menu, know that it's a winner. **Known for:** fine dining; fresh seafood; sunny seaside setting. [$] *Average main: €33* ✉ *Via Fegina 104, Monterosso al Mare* ☎ *0187/817608* 🌐 *www.ristorantemiky.it* 🕓 *Closed mid-Nov.–Easter.*

🛏 Hotels

Bellambra B&B

$$ | **B&B/INN** | Modern rooms with charm and comfort in the heart of the old town make this a terrific base for exploring the Cinque Terre. **Pros:** an apartment can sleep up to six people; location; spacious rooms and bathrooms. **Cons:** books up quickly; no elevator with steep, narrow stairs; can be a bit noisy. [$] *Rooms from: €200* ✉ *Via Roma 64, Monterosso al Mare* ☎ *39/3920121912* 🌐 *www.bellambra5terre.com* 🛏 *4 rooms* 🍽 *No Meals.*

★ Il Giardino Incantato

$$ | **B&B/INN** | With wood-beam ceilings and stone walls, the stylishly restored and updated rooms in this 16th-century

house in the historic center of Monterosso ooze comfort and old-world charm. **Pros:** spacious rooms; excellent hosts; gorgeous garden. **Cons:** there are only four rooms; books up quickly; no views. $ *Rooms from: €180* ⊠ *Via Mazzini 18, Monterosso al Mare* ☎ *0187/818315* ⊕ *www.ilgiardinoincantato.net* ⊗ *Closed Nov.–Easter* ⇆ *4 rooms* ❢◯❢ *Free Breakfast.*

Porto Roca

$$$$ | **HOTEL** | Far from the madding crowds, one of Cinque Terre's only high-end hotels is perched on the famous terraced cliffs right over the main beach, with large balconies to savor panoramic views of the magnificent sea. **Pros:** unobstructed sea views; shuttle bus into town (though walking there is eminently possible); tranquil location. **Cons:** somewhat removed from town; back-facing rooms can be a bit dark; two-night minimum stay for most weekends. $ *Rooms from: €380* ⊠ *Via Corone 1, Monterosso al Mare* ☎ *0187/817502* ⊕ *www.portoroca. it* ⊗ *Closed Nov.–Easter* ⇆ *43 rooms* ❢◯❢ *Free Breakfast.*

Lerici

106 km (66 miles) southeast of Genoa, 65 km (40 miles) west of Lucca.

Lerici, part of the Riviera di Levante, is on the spectacular Bay of La Spezia, otherwise known as the Gulf of Poets, and is famous for its natural beauty. Near Liguria's border with Tuscany, this picturesque village dates back to medieval times when, under the rule of Pisa, it fought cross-bay battles with the Genovese town of Portovenere, as well as with local pirates. The town is set on a magnificent coastline of gray cliffs jutting down into a crystal clear sea and surrounded by a national park that is like an unframed painting of pine forests, olive trees, and tiny colorful hamlets. The waterfront piazza is filled

with trompe-l'oeil frescoed buildings, and seaside cafés line a charming little harbor that holds sailboats and *gozzi,* the typical small fishing boats of the area.

Several white-sand beaches and bathing establishments dot the 2-km (1-mile) walk along the bay from the village center to nearby San Terenzo. From the village, you can also reach some beautiful hiking trails that head southeast to both seaside and hilltop villages like Fiascherino, Tellaro, and Montemarcello.

GETTING HERE AND AROUND

By car, Lerici is less than a 10-minute drive west from the A12, with plenty of blue signs indicating the way. There's a large parking lot (fee) about a 10-minute walk along the seaside promenade from the center. By train, the closest station is either Sarzana (10-minute drive) or La Spezia Centrale (20-minute drive) on the main north–south line between Genoa and Pisa.

VISITOR INFORMATION

CONTACT Lerici Tourism Office. ⊠ *Piazza Bacigalupi 9, Lerici* ☎ *0187/9601* ⊕ *www. comune.lerici.sp.it.*

 ## Sights

Castello di Lerici

CASTLE/PALACE | The promontory is dominated by this 13th-century Pisan castle, which now houses a museum of art and paleontology, a superb location for weddings—it overlooks the entire Gulf of Poets. ⊠ *Piazza S. Giorgio 1, Lerici* ⊠ *€5.*

Restaurants

Bonta Nascoste

$$ | **ITALIAN** | In the local dialect, *bonta nascoste* means "hidden goodness," a reference to its back-alleyway location and consistently delicious dishes, which include fresh pasta, local fish, and a handful of meat choices. There are only eight tables (and a couple more outside in summer), so reserve ahead. **Known**

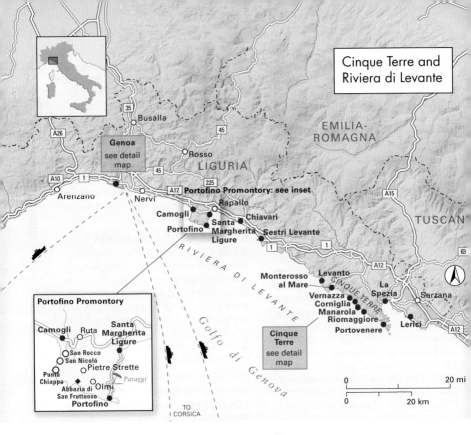

Cinque Terre and Riviera di Levante

Portofino Promontory

---

for: crudo; cozy atmosphere; inventive seafood dishes. $ *Average main: €20* ✉ *Via Cavour 52, Lerici* ☏ *0187/965500* ⊕ *www.bontanascoste.it* ⊙ *Closed Tues. No lunch Mon. and Wed.*

★ Locanda Miranda

$$$ | **LIGURIAN** | Perched amid the clustered old houses in seaside Tellaro, 4 km (2½ miles) southeast of Lerici, this small, unpretentious family-run restaurant with wooden tables and plenty of windows has become a foodie destination. The imaginative seafood-focused menu changes often, and the pretty building also houses a small inn with seven charming and comfortable rooms. **Known for:** pasta and risotto paired with seafood; cozy dining room; locally sourced fish. $ *Average main: €25* ✉ *Via Fiascherino 92, Tellaro* ☏ *0187/964012* ⊕ *www.locandamiranda.com* ⊙ *Closed Mon. and Nov.*

Hotels

★ Doria Park

$$ | **HOTEL** | **FAMILY** | Its location—set amid hills of olive trees yet steps from the village center—makes this hotel with bright rooms and contemporary furnishings one of the best places to stay in Lerici. **Pros:** sea views; free parking and convenient location near town and the beach; comfortable beds. **Cons:** fills up quickly; expensive restaurant; stairs, narrow paths, and elevator are not equipped for people with mobility issues. $ *Rooms from: €160* ✉ *Via Carpanini 9, Lerici* ☏ *0187/967124* ⊕ *www.doriaparkhotel.it* ⇥ *42 rooms* ⦿ *Free Breakfast.*

Florida

$$ | **HOTEL** | **FAMILY** | Prepare to relax at this family-run seaside establishment, where one pleasure is lounging on one

of the deck chairs on the hotel's rooftop solarium and enjoying its sea views. **Pros:** beachfront location; abundant breakfast; bay views from some rooms. **Cons:** small beds in some rooms; spotty Wi-Fi connection; some rooms have no view and can be noisy. $ *Rooms from: €190* ⊠ *Lungomare Biaggini 35, Lerici* ☏ *0187/967332* ⊕ *www.hotelflorida.it* ⊗ *Closed approximately Dec. 15–Jan. 15* ⇄ *40 rooms* ⦿ *Free Breakfast.*

La Spezia

11 km (7 miles) northwest of Lerici, 103 km (64 miles) southeast of Genoa.

La Spezia is sometimes thought of as nothing but a large, industrialized naval port en route to the Cinque Terre and Portovenere; it does possess some charm, however, and it also gives you a look at a less tourist-focused part of the Riviera. Its palm-lined promenade, fertile citrus parks, renovated Liberty-style palazzi, and colorful balcony-lined streets make parts of La Spezia surprisingly beautiful. Monday through Saturday morning, you can stroll through the fresh fish, produce, and local cheese stalls at the outdoor market on Piazza Cavour, and on Friday take part in the busy flea market on Via Garibaldi. There's also Porto Mirabello, a newly built tourist port with a pool club, shops, and several restaurants that overlook the fleet of superyachts.

GETTING HERE AND AROUND
By car, take the exit for La Spezia off the A12. La Spezia Centrale train station is on the main north–south railway line between Genoa and Pisa.

VISITOR INFORMATION
CONTACT La Spezia Tourism Office. ⊠ *Via del Prione 222, La Spezia* ☏ *0187/026152* ⊕ *www.myspezia.it.*

◉ Sights

Castello di San Giorgio
CASTLE/PALACE | FAMILY | The remains of this massive 13th-century castle, atop a small hill above the modern town, now house a small museum dedicated to local archaeology. ⊠ *Via XXVII Marzo, La Spezia* ☏ *0187/751142* ⊕ *museodelcastello.spezianet.it* ⊡ *€6* ⊗ *Closed Mon. afternoon and Tues.*

Restaurants

La Pia Centenaria
$ | **PIZZA** | Considered an institution, this white-walled, simply decorated *farinateria* and pizzeria dates back to 1887. During the lunch hour, you will probably find a line out the door, while inside—and on the patio in summer—locals munch on *farinata* (a chickpea pancake and a Ligurian delicacy) and thick-crust pizza served hot out of the wood-burning oven. **Known for:** variety of pizza toppings; traditional Ligurian recipes; affordable lunch menu. $ *Average main: €8* ⊠ *Via Magenta 12, La Spezia* ☏ *0187/739999* ⊕ *www.lapia.it.*

Portovenere

12 km (7 miles) south of La Spezia, 114 km (70 miles) southeast of Genoa.

The colorful facades and pedestrian-only *calata* (promenade) make Portovenere the quintessential Ligurian seaside village; it's often called the "sixth town" of the Cinque Terre—but with half the crowds. As a UNESCO World Heritage Site, Portovenere is lined with tall, thin *terratetto* houses (town houses), which date from as far back as the 11th century and which were connected in a wall-like formation to protect against attacks by Pisans and local pirates. Its tiny *carruggi* (alleylike passageways) lead to an array of charming shops, homes, and gardens, and eventually to the village's impressive

Castle Doria, high on the olive-tree-covered hill. To the west, standing guard over the Mediterranean, is the picturesque medieval **Chiesa di San Pietro**, once the site of a temple to Venus (Venere in Italian), from which Portovenere gets its name. Nearby, in a rocky area leading to the sea, is Byron's Cave, one of the poet's favorite spots for swimming out into the sea.

GETTING HERE AND AROUND

By car from the port city of La Spezia, follow the blue signs for Portovenere. It's about a 20-minute winding drive along the sea through small fishing villages. From La Spezia train station you can hire a taxi for about €30. By bus from Via Garibaldi in La Spezia (a 10-minute walk from the train station) it takes about 30 minutes.

VISITOR INFORMATION

CONTACT Portovenere Tourist Office. ✉ *Piazza Bastreri 7,* ☎ *0187/790691* 🌐 *www.portovenere.com.*

Sights

Grotto Arpaia

CAVE | Near the entrance to the huge, strange Grotto Arpaia, at the base of the sea-swept cliff, is a plaque recounting the strength and courage of Lord Byron (1788–1824) as he swam across the gulf to the village of San Terenzo, near Lerici, to visit his friend Shelley (1792–1822). The poet is said to have written his lengthy narrative poem *Childe Harold's Pilgrimage* in Portovenere. ✉ *Portovenere.*

★ San Pietro

CHURCH | With its black-and-white-striped exterior, this 13th-century Gothic church is a spectacular landmark recognizable from far out at sea and upon entering the village. It is built on the site of an ancient pagan shrine, on a formidable solid mass of rock above the Grotto Arpaia. There's a fantastic view of the Cinque Terre coastline from the front porch of the church. ✉ *Waterfront promenade, Portovenere* ☎ *0187/790691.*

Restaurants

★ Bacicio

$ | WINE BAR | This enoteca and antipasto bar is popular with locals and tourists looking for quality regional dishes, fresh fish, and a lengthy wine list. The owner designed the entire place, right down to the tables and chairs made from anchors and old boats. **Known for:** generous portions at reasonable prices; fresh fish crostini; anchovies cooked many ways. [$] *Average main: €13* ✉ *Via Cappellini 17, Portovenere* ☎ *0187/793031* 🕓 *Closed Thurs.*

★ Il Timone

$ | LIGURIAN | FAMILY | Find some of the best food in Portovenere at this airy, affordable, and casual portside restaurant. The menu is typical "Ligure," ranging from meat to pasta with seafood, and also offers farinata, focaccia, and pizza. **Known for:** Ligurian farinata and pizza; all-inclusive tasting menus; comfortable patio in summer. [$] *Average main: €11* ✉ *Via Olivo 29, Portovenere* ☎ *347/2601008* 🌐 *www.pizzeriailtimone.it* 🕓 *Closed Tues., Nov., and mid-Jan.–Feb.*

Locanda Lorena

$$$ | LIGURIAN | Across the small bay of Portovenere lies the rugged island of Palmaria, where there are only a few restaurants (making for high prices), including this place with lovely seafront views and headliners like fresh pasta and local fish. To get here, take the restaurant's free Riva boat from the Portovenere jetty. **Known for:** incredible Portovenere views; catch of the day specials; quaint seaside setting. [$] *Average main: €25* ✉ *Palmaria Island, Portovenere* ☎ *0187/792370* 🌐 *www.locandalorena.com* 🕓 *Closed Nov.*

Hotels

Grand Hotel Portovenere

$$$$ | HOTEL | This 13th-century Franciscan convent turned elegant hotel incorporates modern enhancements while retaining the structure's impressive rose facade, arches, and frescoes. **Pros:** excellent location and views; shuttle service to a private beach; comfortable beds and spacious rooms. **Cons:** expensive restaurant and bar; some room amenities are limited, no in-room tea or coffeemaker; updated rooms bring hefty rates. $ *Rooms from: €400 ⊠ Via Giuseppe Garibaldi 5, Portovenere* ☎ *0187/777751* ⊕ *www.portoveneregrand.com* ⊗ *Closed Nov.–Easter* ⌐ *48 rooms* ¦⊙¦ *Free Breakfast.*

Hotel Belvedere

$$ | HOTEL | True to its name (which means "nice view"), the best rooms in this sunny Liberty-style building face the bay of Portovenere, with lovely vistas of Palmaria Island and the Gulf of Poets. **Pros:** sea views from the terrace and some rooms; good value for the location despite plain decor; ideal location to reach town and ferry terminal. **Cons:** rooms facing the street are noisy; limited parking; parts of the hotel could use a makeover. $ *Rooms from: €150 ⊠ Via Giuseppe Garibaldi 26, Portovenere* ☎ *0187/790608* ⊕ *www.belvedereportovenere.it* ⊗ *Closed Nov.–Easter* ⌐ *17 rooms* ¦⊙¦ *Free Breakfast.*

Levanto

47 km (29 miles) northwest of Portovenere, 60 km (36 miles) southeast of Genoa.

Nestled at the end of a valley of pine forests, olive groves, vineyards, and medieval villages lies this sunny seaside town, an alternative and usually less expensive base for exploring the Cinque Terre and the Riviera di Levante.

GETTING HERE AND AROUND

By car, take the Carodanno/Levanto exit off the A12 for 25 minutes to the town center. By train, Levanto is on the main north–south railway, one stop north of Monterosso.

VISITOR INFORMATION

CONTACT Levanto Tourism Office. ⊠ *Piazza Cavour 1, Levanto* ☎ *0187/808125* ⊕ *www.visitlevanto.it.*

 Sights

Levanto

TOWN | With its long sandy beach, colorful old quarter, and breathtakingly beautiful hiking paths, Levanto has become a haven not only for sun worshippers but also for divers, surfers, and hikers. The path between Levanto and Monterosso al Mare, about a 2½-mile hike, is freely accessible. This is also an ideal starting point for day trips by train or boat to many interesting places along the Riviera, such as Portovenere, Lerici, Tellaro, and Fiascherino, in the direction of La Spezia; and Portofino, Santa Margherita, Camogli, and Sestri Levante, in the direction of Genoa. ⊠ *Levanto.*

Sestri Levante

37 km (22 miles) northwest of Levanto, 28 km (17 miles) southeast of Santa Margherita Ligure.

Halfway between the Cinque Terre and Portofino lies this lovely seaside resort. The old village is on a peninsula with the beautiful Baia del Silenzio on one side and the Baia delle Favole and promenade on the other. The Baia delle Favole (*favole* means "fairy tales") was named in honor of the Danish author Hans Christian Andersen, who visited Sestri for a short time.

GETTING HERE AND AROUND

By car, it is a five-minute drive off the A12. The Sestri Levante train station is on the main north–south train line between Genoa and Pisa; it's just a five-minute walk to the beach and old village.

VISITOR INFORMATION

CONTACT Sestri Levante Tourist Office. ✉ *Corso Colombo 50, Sestri Levante* ☎ *0185/478530* 🌐 *www.sestri-levante.net.*

Beaches

Baia del Silenzio

BEACH | The Bay of Silence is a sandy cove east of the pedestrian-only street in the old town, with pastel-color bars and restaurants edging the sand and bobbing boats dotting the horizon. It's a picture-postcard public beach and an idyllic setting for a dip in the Mediterranean, frequented mostly by locals and some visiting crowds in summer. You can also take a short walk up to the Convento dei Cappuccini, a church dedicated to the Virgin Mary. The monastery was built at the end of the 17th century and offers a spectacular panoramic view. **Amenities**: though food is available, packing a picnic lunch is a good idea. **Best for**: calming views. ✉ *Sestri Levante, Finale Ligure.*

Restaurants

Cantina del' Polpo

$$ | **LIGURIAN** | The Ballarini family runs three restaurants in Sestri Levante, and this cozy former cantina with wood paneling, a fireplace, local maritime memorabilia, and red-checkered tablecloths serves some of the best dishes in town. Using the bounty of the two bays that frame the village, they create inventive tasting menus and standout mains, which, in addition to expertly seasoned fish, include homemade pastas, like the gnocchi. **Known for:** hard-to-find regional wines; creative seafood-focused tasting menus at affordable prices; friendly staff. [$] *Average main: €22* ✉ *Via Camillo Benso Cavour 2, Sestri Levante* ☎ *0185/485296* 🌐 *www.cantinadelpolpo.it* 🕓 *Closed Wed.*

Hotels

Grand Hotel dei Castelli

$$$ | **B&B/INN** | You can see the Baia delle Favole from this castle-turned-hotel on a promontory, and you just might feel you've been transported to a fairy tale here. **Pros:** grand setting with spectacular views of the two bays; private inlet; beautiful grounds. **Cons:** a bit far from the train station, so a car is best; steep walk (or slow elevator) down to the beach; some rooms and public areas have a dated feel. [$] *Rooms from: €300* ✉ *Via Penisola di Levante 26* ☎ *0185/487020* 🌐 *www.hoteldeicastelli.it/en* 🕓 *Closed Nov.–mid-Mar.* 🛏 *50 rooms* 🍴 *Free Breakfast.*

Chiavari

8 km (5 miles) northwest of Sestri Levante, 38 km (23 miles) southeast of Genoa.

Chiavari is a fishing town (rather than village) of considerable character, with narrow, twisting streets and a good harbor. Chiavari's citizens were intrepid explorers, and many emigrated to South America in the 19th century. The town boomed, thanks to the wealth of the returning voyagers, but Chiavari retains many medieval traces in its buildings.

GETTING HERE AND AROUND

By car, take the Chiavari exit off the A12. The Chiavari train station is located on the main north–south train line between Genoa and Pisa.

VISITOR INFORMATION

CONTACT Chiavari Tourism Office. ✉ *Via della Cittadella, Chiavari* ☎ *0185/365400* 🌐 *www.chiavariturismo.it.*

Sights

Museo Archeologico

ART MUSEUM | A worthy collection in the town center displays objects from an 8th-century BC necropolis, or ancient cemetery, excavated nearby. ✉ *Via Costaguta 4, Chiavari* ☎ *0185/320829* 🌐 *www.musei.liguria.beniculturali.it/musei* 🎫 *€3* 🕒 *Closed Mon.*

Santa Margherita Ligure

21 km (13 miles) west of Chiavari, 31 km (19 miles) southeast of Genoa.

A beautiful old resort town favored by well-to-do Italians, Santa Margherita Ligure has everything a Riviera playground should have—plenty of palm trees and attractive hotels, cafés, and a marina packed with yachts. Some of the older buildings have trompe-l'oeil frescoed exteriors that are typical of this part of the Riviera. For many people, this pleasant, convenient base represents the perfect balance on the Italian Riviera: more spacious than the Cinque Terre; less glitzy than San Remo; more relaxing than Genoa and environs; and ideally situated for day trips, such as an excursion to Portofino.

GETTING HERE AND AROUND

By car, take the Rapallo exit off the A12 and follow the blue signs, about a 10-minute drive. The Santa Margherita Ligure train station is on the main north–south line between Genoa and Pisa.

VISITOR INFORMATION

CONTACT Santa Margherita Ligure Tourism Office. ✉ *Piazza Vittorio Veneto, Santa Margherita Ligure* ☎ *0185/287485* 🌐 *www.smlturismo.it.*

Restaurants

Oca Bianca

$$ | **EUROPEAN** | In a departure from the local norm, the menu at Oca Bianca has no seafood to offer; instead, meat dishes are the specialty, along with a few pastas. Choices may include mouthwatering preparations of beef, lamb, duck, and pork, and there is an extensive wine list from its next-door cantina. **Known for:** classic sauces for meat dishes; multiple steak preparations; lively outdoor seating in summer. [$] *Average main: €20* ✉ *Via XXV Aprile 21, Santa Margherita Ligure* ☎ *0185/288411* 🌐 *www.ristoranteocabianca.it* 🕒 *Closed Tues.*

★ **U Giancu**

$$ | **LIGURIAN** | Although the walls of Fausto Oneto's restaurant are covered in original cartoons, and a playground is the main feature of the outdoor seating area, this chef-owner is completely serious about his cooking, which follows the seasons. His own garden provides the freshest possible vegetables, the wine list (ask to visit the cantina) is excellent, and there are lively morning Ligurian cooking lessons. **Known for:** vegetables fresh from the restaurant's garden; creative and playful setting; lamb dishes. [$] *Average main: €20* ✉ *Via San Massimo 78, Località San Massimo* ☎ *0185/261212* 🌐 *www.ugiancu.it* 🕒 *Closed Wed. and Nov. No lunch weekdays.*

Hotels

Grand Hotel Miramare

$$$$ | **RESORT** | Classic Riviera elegance prevails at this palatial hotel overlooking the bay, where antique furniture and crystal chandeliers fill the high-ceiling rooms. **Pros:** top-notch service close to the beach; well-maintained rooms and marble bathrooms; spa and wellness center. **Cons:** beach is run by different managment than the hotel; sea access is down the grand entrance staircase and across a busy street; traffic in summer from the road in front of the hotel. [$] *Rooms from: €621* ✉ *Via Milite Ignoto 30, Santa Margherita Ligure* ☎ *0185/287013* 🌐 *www.grandhotelmiramare.it* 🕒 *Closed Jan. 7–Mar.* 🛏 *75 rooms* 🍴 *Free Breakfast.*

Hotel Continental

$$$$ | HOTEL | A stately seaside mansion surrounded by a lush garden shaded by tall palms and pine trees offers stylish accommodations done in a blend of classic furnishings, mostly inspired by the 19th century. **Pros:** lovely location; panoramic views from some rooms and the dining area; private beach. **Cons:** located off a road that gets busy in high season; beach access included in room rates, but lounge chairs and cabanas are extra; rooms in the annex need to be refurbished. $ *Rooms from: €323* ✉ *Via Pagana 8, Santa Margherita Ligure* ☎ *0185/286512* ⊕ *www.hotel-continental. it* ⊘ *Closed Jan. and Feb.* ⇌ *68 rooms* ⦿| *Free Breakfast.*

Hotel Jolanda

$$$ | HOTEL | They may not have sea views, but the stylish, comfortable, and spacious rooms here are decorated in a contemporary style, and some have large balconies. **Pros:** reasonable rates in a high-price area; spa and massage options; outdoor areas for dining and relaxing. **Cons:** indoor common areas feel cramped; breakfast costs extra; no sea view. $ *Rooms from: €202* ✉ *Via Luisito Costa 6, Santa Margherita Ligure* ☎ *0185/287512* ⊕ *www.hoteljolanda.it* ⇌ *45 rooms* ⦿| *No Meals.*

Santa Margherita Palace

$$$$ | HOTEL | Just a short walk from the old town, this well-kept and well-equipped hotel offers modern rooms with contemporary furnishings, an abundant breakfast, and two spas. **Pros:** nice-size rooms with plenty of storage; modern bathrooms (some rooms have Jacuzzis); helpful staff. **Cons:** outdoor spaces in common areas are a bit closed in due to the location; no beach access; the neighborhood is less charming than the old town and seaside. $ *Rooms from: €400* ✉ *Via Roma 9, Santa Margherita Ligure* ☎ *0185/287139* ⊕ *www. santamargheritapalace.com* ⇌ *53 rooms* ⦿| *No Meals.*

Portofino

5 km (3 miles) southeast of Santa Margherita Ligure, 36 km (22 miles) east of Genoa.

One of the most photographed villages along the coast, with a decidedly romantic and highly affluent aura, Portofino has long been a popular destination for the rich and famous. Once an ancient Roman colony and taken by the Republic of Genoa in 1229, it has also been ruled by the French, English, Spanish, and Austrians, as well as by marauding bands of 16th-century pirates. Elite British tourists first flocked to the lush harbor in the mid-1800s. Some of Europe's wealthiest drop anchor in Portofino in summer, but they stay out of sight by day, appearing in the evening after buses and boats have carried off the day-trippers.

There's not actually much to *do* in Portofino other than stroll around the wee harbor, see the castle, walk to Punta del Capo, browse at the pricey boutiques, and sip a coffee while people-watching. However, weaving through picture-perfect cliff-side gardens and gazing at yachts framed by the sapphire Ligurian Sea and the cliffs of Santa Margherita can make for quite a relaxing afternoon. There are also several tame, photo-friendly hikes into the hills to nearby villages.

Unless you're traveling on a deluxe budget, you may want to stay in Camogli or Santa Margherita Ligure rather than at one of Portofino's few very expensive hotels. Restaurants and cafés are good but also pricey: don't expect to have a beer here for much under €10.

GETTING HERE AND AROUND

By car, exit at Rapallo off the A12 and follow the blue signs (about a 20-minute drive mostly along the coast). Trying to reach Portofino by bus or car on the single narrow road can be a nightmare in summer and on holiday weekends.

The nearest train station is Santa Margherita Ligure. No trains go directly to Portofino: you must stop at Santa Margherita, then take public Bus No. 82 from there (€3). Alternatively, you can take a boat from Santa Margherita.

Portofino can be reached from Santa Margherita on foot: it's about a 60-minute walk along the sea, but be aware that many parts of the narrow road have no sidewalk.

VISITOR INFORMATION

CONTACT Portofino Tourism Office. ✉ *Via Roma 35, Portofino* ☎ *0185/269024* 🌐 *www.turismoinliguria.it.*

Sights

Abbazia di San Fruttuoso
(Abbey of San Fruttuoso)
CHURCH | A medieval stronghold built by the Benedictines of Monte Cassino protects a minuscule fishing village that can be reached only on foot or by water—a 20-minute boat ride from Portofino and also reachable from Camogli, Santa Margherita Ligure, and Rapallo. The restored abbey is now the property of a national conservation fund (FAI) and occasionally hosts temporary exhibitions; it also contains the tombs of some illustrious members of the Doria family. Plan on spending a few hours enjoying the abbey and grounds, and perhaps lunching at one of the modest beachfront trattorias nearby (open only in summer). Boatloads of visitors can make this place very crowded very fast; you might appreciate it most off-season. ✉ *Portofino* ✢ *15-min boat ride or 2-hr walk northwest of Portofino* ☎ *0185/772703* 🌐 *fondoambiente.it* 🎫 *€8* 🕒 *Closed Mon. Nov.–Feb.* ✍ *Reservations essential.*

San Giorgio
CHURCH | This small church, sitting on a ridge above Portofino, is said to contain the relics of its namesake, brought back from the Holy Land by the Crusaders. Portofino enthusiastically celebrates St. George's Day every April 23. ✉ *Above harbor, Salita San Giorgio, Portofino.*

Beaches

Paraggi
BEACH | The only sand beach near Portofino is at Paraggi, a cove on the road between Santa Margherita Ligure and Portofino. The bus will stop here on request. **Amenities:** umbrella and chair rentals, bars and restaurants on the beach. **Best for:** relaxing; snorkeling. ✉ *Via Strada Provinciale, Portofino.*

Punta Portofino
VIEWPOINT | Pristine views can be had from the deteriorating *faro* (lighthouse) at Punta Portofino, a 15-minute walk along the point that begins at the southern end of the port. Along the seaside path you can see numerous impressive, sprawling private residences behind high iron gates. **Amenities:** views. **Best for:** relaxing. ✉ *Viale Rainusso 1, Portofino.*

Restaurants

Canale
$ | BAKERY | If the staggering prices at virtually all of Portofino's cafés and restaurants are enough to ruin your appetite, join the long line outside this family-run bakery where you will find affordable and delicious eats worth waiting for. At this takeaway spot, the focaccia is baked on-site and served fresh, along with all kinds of sandwiches and other refreshments. **Known for:** delicious pastries; friendly staff; cash-only takeout. [$] *Average main: €10* ✉ *Via Roma 30, Portofino* ☎ *0185/269248* 🌐 *www.panificiocanale.it* 🕒 *Closed Wed. and Nov.*

Ristorante Puny
$$$ | LIGURIAN | If you want to be in the middle of everything and dine well, and don't mind spending a small fortune, then you'll want (and need) a reservation at this waterfront restaurant in Portofino. Quite simply, it's *the* place to be seen

while dining on baked fish and homemade pasta dishes. **Known for:** dining right on the port; baked mini octopus; pappardelle al portofino (with tomato and pesto sauce). [$] *Average main: €30* ✉ *Piazza Martiri dell'Olivetta 4–5, on harbor, Portofino* ☎ *0185/269037* 🌐 *punyportofino.it* 🕓 *Closed Thurs.*

Hotels

Belmond Hotel Splendido

$$$$ | **HOTEL** | **FAMILY** | This 1920s luxury hotel oozes charm, taste, and lovely scenery, with a particular attention to color—from the coordinated floral linens in corals and gold in the guest rooms to the fresh flowers in the reception rooms and on the large terrace. **Pros:** rooms have garden or sea views; attentive staff; lovely manicured grounds. **Cons:** location makes it a hike to get to the center of Portofino; pool and other common areas can be noisy because of the kid-friendly atmosphere; be prepared to spend upward of €100 for a simple lunch for two. [$] *Rooms from: €1000* ✉ *Salita Baratta 16, Portofino* ☎ *0185/267801* 🌐 *www.belmond.com/hotel-splendido-portofino* 🕓 *Closed Nov.–Mar.* 🛏 *108 rooms* 🍴 *Free Breakfast.*

Eight Hotel Portofino

$$$$ | **HOTEL** | At this intimate hotel, comfortable and soothingly designed guest rooms—some with canopy beds, pastel walls, and ultramodern bathrooms—are spread across two small 19th-century town houses on a quiet backstreet. **Pros:** walking distance to the harbor and village; comfortable beds and a choice of pillows; rooftop garden. **Cons:** some rooms are small; no sea views; some lower-level rooms don't receive much light. [$] *Rooms from: €830* ✉ *Via Del Fondaco 11, Portofino* ☎ *0185/26991* 🌐 *www.eighthotels.it* 🕓 *Closed Nov.–Easter* 🛏 *18 rooms* 🍴 *Free Breakfast.*

Activities

HIKING

If you have the stamina, you can hike to the Abbazia di San Fruttuoso from Portofino. It's a steep climb at first, and the walk takes about 2½ hours one-way. If you're extremely ambitious and want to make a day of it, you can hike another 2½ hours all the way to Camogli. Much more modest hikes from Portofino include a one-hour uphill walk to Cappella delle Gave, a bit inland in the hills, from where you can continue downhill to Santa Margherita Ligure (another 1½ hours); there is also a gently undulating paved trail leading to the beach at Paraggi (½ hour). Finally, there's a 2½-hour hike from Portofino that heads farther inland to Ruta, through Olmi and Pietre Strette. The trails are well marked, and maps are available at the tourist information offices in Rapallo, Santa Margherita Ligure, Portofino, and Camogli.

Camogli

15 km (9 miles) northwest of Portofino, 20 km (12 miles) southeast of Genoa.

Camogli, at the edge of the large promontory and nature reserve known as the Portofino Peninsula, has always been a town of sailors. By the 19th century it was leasing its ships throughout the continent. Today, multicolor houses, staircases with incredible sea views, and a massive 17th-century seawall mark this appealing harbor community, which is perhaps as beautiful as Portofino but without the glamour. When exploring on foot, don't miss the antiquated second harbor, reached through a narrow archway at the northern end of the first one.

GETTING HERE AND AROUND

By car, exit the A12 at Recco and follow the blue signs. There are several parking lots (fee) near the village center. Camogli is on the main north–south railway line between Genoa and La Spezia.

VISITOR INFORMATION

CONTACT Camogli Tourism Office. ✉ *Via XX Settembre 33/R, Camogli* ☎ *0185/7771066* 🌐 *www.camogliturismo.it.*

Sights

Ruta

TRAIL | The footpaths that leave from Ruta, 4 km (2½ miles) east of Camogli, thread through rugged terrain and contain a multitude of plant species. Weary hikers are sustained by stunning views of the Riviera di Levante from various vantage points along the way. ✉ *Camogli.*

San Rocco, San Nicolò, and Punta Chiappa

TOWN | From Camogli, you can reach these hamlets along the western coast of the peninsula either on foot or by boat. They're more natural and less fashionable than those facing south on the eastern coast. In the small Romanesque church at San Nicolò, sailors who survived dangerous voyages came to offer thanks. ✉ *Camogli.*

Restaurants

Vento Ariel

$$ | **SEAFOOD** | This small, friendly restaurant serves some of the best seafood in town on the covered terrace or the indoor patio with wicker chairs, where you can watch the bustling activity in the old port. Only the freshest catches are presented; try the mixed grilled fish or any of the pastas. **Known for:** relaxed atmosphere; spaghetti alle vongole (clams); outdoor seating with views. [$] *Average main: €20* ✉ *Calata Porticciolo 1, Camogli* ☎ *0185/771080* 🌐 *www.ventoariel.it* 🕒 *Closed weekdays Nov.–Jan.*

Coffee and Quick Bites

Revello

$ | **LIGURIAN** | You'll know this focacceria and pasticceria by the line out the door, as you walk along the beach before entering the archway to the old port. This tiny spot—where you can see focaccia being baked through a window into its kitchen—specializes in Liguria's favorite bread, farinata (baked late afternoons from October to March) and several flavors of *camogliesi* (rum-filled is the original), a sweet that the shop's owner, Giacomo, invented in 1970. **Known for:** no seating, so take your treats away; wide variety of focaccia flavors; camogliesi sweets. [$] *Average main: €5* ✉ *Via Giuseppe Garibaldi 183, Camogli* ☎ *0185/770777* 🌐 *www.revellocamogli.com* 🕒 *Closed 10 days in Jan.*

Hotels

Cenobio dei Dogi

$$ | **HOTEL** | Perched majestically above Camogli's beaches, the former summer palace of Genoa's doges features many guest rooms with expansive balconies and commanding vistas of the city's port. **Pros:** location and setting are wonderful; private beach; pool and gardens. **Cons:** neighborhood is less charming than the old town; old-fashioned decor; books quickly in high season. [$] *Rooms from: €170* ✉ *Via Nicolò Cuneo 34, Camogli* ☎ *0185/7241* 🛏 *100 rooms* 🍴 *Free Breakfast.*

★ **Locanda I Tre Merli**

$$ | **B&B/INN** | In a typical Ligurian terratetto on the old port, this charming *locanda,* or inn, is reminiscent of old-world voyages but with the amenities to make it a comfortable and relaxing stop for today's traveler. **Pros:** friendly staff; small spa with whirlpool tub and Turkish bath; quaint port location and views. **Cons:** narrow corridors; located right on the port, so you have to park a distance away; can be a bit noisy in the summer

months. $ *Rooms from: €190* ✉ *Via Scalo 5, Camogli* ☎ *0185/776752* ⊕ *www.locandaitremerli.com* ⮎ *5 rooms* ❚◎❙ *Free Breakfast.*

Villa Rosmarino

$$$ | **B&B/INN** | A beautiful Ligurian villa in the Camogli hills offers chic, contemporary, and comfortable accommodations, along with well-manicured gardens and outdoor sitting areas, arbors, and a welcoming pool. **Pros:** modern furnishings; friendly staff; pleasant outdoor pool and garden. **Cons:** parking can be challenging; the hike uphill is not ideal in summer months; some rooms are small and have minimal storage. $ *Rooms from: €290* ✉ *Via Figari 38, Camogli* ☎ *0185/771580* ⊕ *www.villarosmarino.com* ⊗ *Closed Nov.–Feb.* ⮎ *6 rooms* ❚◎❙ *Free Breakfast.*

Genoa

20 km (12 miles) northwest of Camogli, 144 km (89 miles) south of Milan.

Genoa (Genova in Italian) was the birthplace of Christopher Columbus, but the city's proud history predates the famous explorer by hundreds of years. Genoa was already an important trading station by the 3rd century BC, when the Romans conquered Liguria. The Middle Ages and the Renaissance saw it rise to become a jumping-off place for the Crusaders, a commercial center of tremendous wealth and prestige, and a strategic bone of international contention. A network of fortresses defending the city connected by a wall second only in length to the Great Wall of China was constructed in the hills above, and Genoa's bankers, merchants, and princes adorned the city with palaces, churches, and impressive art collections.

Crammed into a thin crescent of land between sea and mountains, Genoa expanded up rather than out, taking on the form of a multilayer wedding cake, with churches, streets, and entire residential neighborhoods built on others' rooftops. Public elevators and funiculars are as common as buses and trains.

With its impressive palaces and museums, the largest medieval city center in Europe, and an elaborate network of ancient hilltop fortresses, Genoa may be just the dose of culture you're looking for. Europe's biggest boat show, the annual Salone Nautico Internazionale, is held here. Fine restaurants are abundant, and classical dance and music are richly represented. The Teatro Carlo Felice is the local opera venue, and it's where the internationally renowned annual Niccolò Paganini Violin Contest takes place.

GETTING HERE AND AROUND

By car, take the Genoa Ovest exit off the A12 and take the upper bridge (*sopraelevata*) to the second exit, Genova Centro–Piazza Corvetto. Be forewarned: driving in Genoa is harrowing and best avoided whenever possible. If you want to see the city on a day trip, go by train; regular service operates from Genoa's two stations. If you're staying in the city, park in a garage or by valet and travel by foot and taxi throughout your stay.

The best way by far to get around Genoa is on foot, with the occasional assistance of public transportation. Many of the more interesting districts are either entirely closed to traffic, have roads so narrow that no car could fit, or are, even at the best of times, blocked by gridlock. Although it might seem a daunting task, exploring the city is made simple by its geography. The historical center of Genoa occupies a relatively narrow strip of land running between the mountains and the sea. You can easily visit the most important monuments in one or two days. The main bus station in Genoa is at Piazza Principe. Local buses operated by the municipal transport company, AMT, serve the steep valleys that run to some of the towns along the western coast. Tickets may be bought at local bus stations or at newsstands. (You must have a ticket before you board.) This company also operates the funicular railways and the elevators that service the steeper sections of the city.

CONTACTS AMT. ✉ *Palazzo Ducale, Molo* ☎ *010/5582414* ⊕ *www.amt.genova.it.* **Stazione Principe.** ✉ *Piazza del Principe, San Teodoro* ⊕ *www.trenitalia.com.*

VISITOR INFORMATION
CONTACTS Genoa Tourism Offices. ✉ *Via Garibaldi 12r, Maddalena* ☎ *010/5572903* ⊕ *www.visitgenoa.it.*

Sights

THE MEDIEVAL CORE AND POINTS ABOVE
Castelletto
VIEWPOINT | To reach this charming neighborhood high above the city center, you take one of Genoa's historical municipal elevators that whisk you skyward from Piazza del Portello, at the end of Galleria Garibaldi, for a spectacular view of the old city. ✉ *Piazza del Portello, Castelletto* ☎ *€2 for municipal elevator.*

Cimitero Monumentale di Staglieno
CEMETERY | One of the most famous of Genovese landmarks is this bizarrely beautiful cemetery; its fanciful marble and bronze sculptures sprawl haphazardly across a hillside on the outskirts of town. A pantheon holds indoor tombs and some remarkable works like an 1878 *Eve* by Villa. Don't miss Rovelli's 1896 **Tomba Raggio,** which shoots Gothic spires out of the hillside forest. The cemetery began operation in 1851 and has been lauded by such visitors as Mark Twain and Evelyn Waugh. It covers a good deal of ground (allow at least half a day to explore). Take Bus Nos. 13 or 14 from the Stazione Genova Brignole, Bus No. 34 from Stazione Principe, or a taxi. ✉ *Piazzale Resasco 2, Piazza Manin* ☎ *010/5576400* ⊕ *www.staglieno. comune.genova.it* ☎ *Free.*

Ferrovia Genova–Casella
TRAIN/TRAIN STATION | **FAMILY** | The Genova–Casella Railroad is a good way to get a sense of the rugged landscape around Genoa; the train departs about every hour. In operation since 1929, it runs from Piazza Manin in Genoa (follow Via Montaldo from the center of town, or take Bus No. 34 or 36 to the piazza) through the beautiful countryside above the city, arriving in the rural hill town Casella. The tiny train traverses precarious switchbacks that afford sweeping views of the Ligurian hills. In **Casella Paese** (the last stop) you can hike, eat lunch, or check out the view and ride back. **Canova** (two stops from the end of the line) is the start of two possible hikes: a two-hour (one-way) trek to a small sanctuary, **Santuario della Vittoria,** and a grueling four-hour hike to the hill town of **Creto.** Another worthwhile stop is **Sant'Olcese Tullo,** where you can take a half-hour (one-way) walk through the **Sentiero Botanico di Ciaé,** a botanical garden and forest refuge with a tiny medieval castle. ✉ *Piazza Manin* ☎ *010/5582414* ⊕ *www.ferroviagenova-casella.it* ☎ *€3 one-way.*

Galleria Nazionale di Palazzo Spinola
ART MUSEUM | Housed in the richly adorned Palazzo Spinola north of Piazza Soziglia, this beautiful museum contains masterpieces by Luca Giordano and Guido Reni. The *Ecce Homo,* by Antonello da Messina (1430–79), is a hauntingly beautiful painting, of historical interest because it was the Sicilian Antonello who first brought Flemish oil paints and techniques to Italy from his sojourns in the Low Countries. Or some contend. ✉ *Piazza Pelliceria 1, Maddalena* ☎ *010/2705300* ⊕ *www.palazzospinola.beniculturali.it* ☎ *€10* ⊙ *Closed Sun.–Tues.*

Granarolo Funicular
OTHER ATTRACTION | **FAMILY** | Take a cog railway up the steeply rising terrain to another part of the city's fortified walls. It takes 15 minutes to hoist you from Stazione

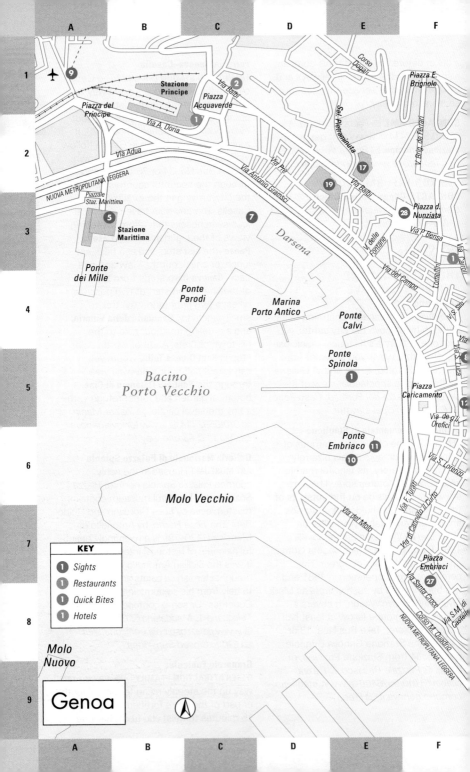

Sights ▼

1 Acquario di Genova E5
2 Castelletto H4
3 Childhood Home of Christopher
   Columbus I7
4 Cimitero Monumentale di
   Staglieno........................... J5
5 Consorzio Liguria Viamare........ B3
6 Ferrovia Genova-Casella J5
7 Galata Museo del Mare........... C3
8 Galleria Nazionale di Palazzo
   Spinola F5
9 Granarolo Funicular A1
10 The Harbor E6
11 Il Bigo E6
12 Loggia dei Mercanti............... F5
13 Mercato Orientale.................. J7
14 Museo d'Arte Orientale
   Chiossone I4
15 Museo dell'Accademia Ligustica
   di Belle Arti H6
16 Palazzo Bianco..................... G4
17 Palazzo dell'Università E2
18 Palazzo Ducale..................... H6
19 Palazzo Reale D2
20 Palazzo Tursi G4
21 Porta Soprana...................... H7
22 San Donato G7
23 San Lorenzo G6
24 San Matteo H6
25 San Siro............................. G4
26 Sant'Agostino G8
27 Santa Maria di Castello F7
28 Santissima Annunziata
   del Vastato......................... F3
29 Zecca-Righi Funicular............. G3

Restaurants ▼

1 Da Gaia F3
2 Da Gibbi ai Rolli I5
3 Farmer's Cooking Concept........ I5
4 I Cuochi H5
5 Il Genovese......................... J7

Quick Bites ▼

1 I Canovacci........................ H5
2 Spin Ristorante-Enoteca.......... J9

Hotels ▼

1 B&B Hotel Genova C2
2 Grand Hotel Savoia................. C1
3 Hotel Bristol Palace I7
4 Hotel Palazzo Grillo............... G5

Principe to **Porta Granarolo,** 1,000 feet above, where the sweeping view gives you a sense of Genoa's size. The funicular departs about every 40 minutes. ⊠ *Piazza del Principe, San Teodoro* ☎ *010/5582414* ⊕ *www.amt.genova.it* ⊴ *€2.*

Loggia dei Mercanti

MARKET | This merchants' row dating from the 16th century is lined with shops selling local foods and gifts, as well as flowers and vintage books and records. ⊠ *Piazza Banchi, Maddalena.*

Museo d'Arte Orientale Chiossone

ART MUSEUM | One of Europe's most note-worthy collections of Japanese, Chinese, and Thai objects is housed in galleries in the Villetta di Negro park on the hillside above Piazza Portello. There's also a fine view of the city from the museum's terrace. ⊠ *Piazzale Mazzini 4, Maddalena* ☎ *010/542285* ⊕ *www.museidigenova. it/it/content/museo-darte-orientale* ⊴ *€5* ⊙ *Closed Mon.*

Palazzo Bianco

CASTLE/PALACE | It's difficult to miss the splendid white facade of this town palace and museum as you walk down Via Garibaldi (also known as Strada Nuova), one of Genoa's most important streets. The building houses a fine collection of 16th- and 17th-century art, with the Spanish and Flemish schools well represented. There's also a textiles collection. ⊠ *Via Garibaldi 11, Maddalena* ☎ *010/5572193* ⊕ *www.museidigenova.it* ⊴ *€9, includes Palazzo Rosso and Palazzo Doria Tursi* ⊙ *Closed Mon.–Wed.*

Palazzo dell'Università

COLLEGE | Built in the 1630s as a Jesuit college, this has been Genoa's university since 1803. The exterior is unassuming, but climb the stairway flanked by lions to visit the handsome courtyard, with its portico of double Doric columns. ⊠ *Via Balbi 5, Pré* ☎ *010/20991* ⊕ *www.unige.it.*

★ Palazzo Reale

CASTLE/PALACE | Lavish rococo rooms provide sumptuous display space for paintings, sculptures, tapestries, and Asian ceramics. The 17th-century palace—also known as Palazzo Balbi Durazzo—was built by the Balbi family, enormously wealthy Genovese merchants. Its regal pretensions were not lost on the Savoy, who bought the palace and turned it into a royal residence in the early 19th century. The gallery of mirrors and the ballroom on the upper floor are particularly decadent. ■TIP→ **The formal gardens provide a welcome respite from the bustle of the city, as well as great views of the harbor.** ⊠ *Via Balbi 10, Pré* ☎ *010/2710236* ⊕ *www.palazzorealegenova.beniculturali. it* ⊴ *€4* ⊙ *Closed Sun.–Tues.*

Palazzo Tursi

GOVERNMENT BUILDING | In the 16th century, wealthy resident Nicolò Grimaldi had a palace built of pink stone quarried in the region, and today it has been reincarnated as Genoa's Palazzo Municipale (Municipal Building). Most of the goings-on inside are the stuff of local politics and weddings, but you can visit the richly decorated Sala Paganini, where the famous Guarnerius violin belonging to Niccolò Paganini (1782–1840) is typically displayed, and the gardens that connect the palace with the neighboring Palazzo Bianco. There is also a collection of five centuries worth of coins, as well as ceramics that were used in homes and pharmacies. ⊠ *Via Garibaldi 9, Maddalena* ☎ *010/2759185* ⊕ *www.museidigenova. it* ⊴ *€9, includes Palazzo Bianco and Palazzo Rosso* ⊙ *Closed Mon.–Wed.*

San Siro

CHURCH | Genoa's oldest church was a Benedictine monastery and the city's cathedral from the 4th to the 9th century. It was rebuilt in the 16th and 17th centuries, and you can see excellent examples of Caravaggism—works reflecting the style of Caravaggio (1571–1610)—in the frescoes that decorate its chapels. ⊠ *Via San Siro 3, Maddalena* ☎ *010/2461674.*

Santissima Annunziata del Vastato

CHURCH | Exuberantly frescoed vaults decorate the 16th- to 17th-century church, which is an excellent example of Genovese Baroque architecture. ⊠ *Piazza della Nunziata, Pré* ☎ *010/2465525.*

Zecca-Righi Funicular

OTHER ATTRACTION | A seven-stop commuter funicular begins at Piazza della Nunziata and ends at a high lookout on the fortified gates in the 17th-century city walls. Ringed around the circumference of the city are a number of huge fortresses; this gate was part of the city's system of defenses. From Righi you can undertake scenic all-day hikes from one fortress to the next. ⊠ *Piazza della Nunziata, Pré* ☎ *010/5582414* ⊕ *www.amt. genova.it* ✉ *€2.*

SOUTHERN DISTRICTS AND THE AQUARIUM

Inhabited since the 6th century BC, the oldest section of Genoa lies on a hill to the southwest of the Caruggi District. Today, apart from a section of 9th-century wall near Porta Soprana, there's little to show that an imposing castle once stood here. Though the neighborhood is quite run-down, some of Genoa's oldest churches make it a worthwhile excursion. Heading down the hill, you can stroll along the harbor. Once squalid and unsafe, the port was given a complete overhaul during Genoa's preparations for the Columbus quincentennial celebrations of 1992, and additional restorations in 2003 and 2004 have done much to revitalize the waterfront. You can easily reach the port on foot by following Via San Lorenzo downhill from Genoa's cathedral, Via delle Fontane from Piazza della Nunziata, or any of the narrow vicoli that lead down from Via Balbi and Via Pré.

Acquario di Genova

OTHER ATTRACTION | FAMILY | Europe's biggest aquarium is the third-most-visited museum in Italy and a must for children. Fifty tanks of marine species, including sea turtles, dolphins, seals, eels, penguins, jellyfish, and sharks, share space with educational displays, touch pools, and re-creations of marine ecosystems, among them a tank of coral from the Indian Ocean, and a wall that replicates a forest in Madagascar. The Aquarium Village complex (additional cost) includes two biospheres with tropical plants and birds, as well as a virtual reality room. If arriving by car, take the Genova Ovest exit from the autostrada. ⊠ *Ponte Spinola, Porto Vecchio* ☎ *010/2345678* ⊕ *www.acquariodigenova.it* ✉ *From €17.*

Childhood Home of Christopher Columbus

HISTORIC HOME | The ivy-covered remains of this fabled medieval house—just a very small portion of it—stand in the gardens below the Porta Soprana. A small collection of objects and reproductions relating to the life and travels of Columbus are on display inside. ⊠ *Piazza Dante, Molo* ☎ *010/4490128* ⊕ *www.museidigenova.it* ✉ *€11* ⊘ *Closed Mon.*

Consorzio Liguria Viamare

OTHER ATTRACTION | Boat tours of the harbor, operated by the Consorzio Liguria Viamare, launch from the aquarium pier and last about an hour. The tours include a visit to the breakwater outside the harbor, the Bacino delle Grazie, and the Molo Vecchio (Old Port). There are also daily excursions down the coast as far as the Cinque Terre and Portovenere. ⊠ *Via Marina d'Italia, Porto Vecchio* ☎ *010/256775* ⊕ *www. liguriaviamare.it* ✉ *€8.*

Galata Museo del Mare

OTHER MUSEUM | FAMILY | Devoted to the city's seafaring history, this museum is probably the best way, at least on dry land, to get an idea of the changing shape of Genoa's busy port. Highlighting the displays is a full-size replica of a 17th-century Genovese galleon. ⊠ *Calata de Mari 1, Ponte dei Mille* ☎ *010/2345655* ⊕ *www.galatamuseodelmare.it* ✉ *€12* ⊘ *Closed Mon.*

The Harbor

OTHER ATTRACTION | A boat tour (with Consorzio Liguria Viamare, for example) gives you a good perspective on the layout of the harbor, which dates to Roman times. The Genoa inlet, the largest along the Italian Riviera, was also used by the Phoenicians and Greeks as a harbor and a staging area from which they could penetrate inland to form settlements and to trade. The port is guarded by the Diga Foranea, a striking 5-km-long (3-mile-long) wall built into the ocean. The **Lanterna,** a lighthouse more than 360 feet tall, was built in 1544; it's one of Italy's oldest lighthouses and a traditional emblem of Genoa. ⊠ *Porto Vecchio.*

Il Bigo

VIEWPOINT | FAMILY | Designed by world-renowned architect Renzo Piano, this spiderlike white structure was erected in 1992 to celebrate the Columbus quincentenary. You can take its **Ascensore Panoramico Bigo** (Bigo Panoramic Elevator) up 650 feet for a 360-degree view of the harbor, city, and sea. In winter there's an ice-skating rink next to the elevator, in an area covered by sail-like awnings. Check the website for seasonal opening hours. ⊠ *Ponte Spinola, Porto Vecchio* ☎ *010/23451* ⊕ *www.acquariodigenova. it/bigo-panoramic* 🎫 *Elevator €4* ⏱ *See website for seasonal hrs.*

Mercato Orientale

MARKET | A bustling place, this produce, fish, and meat market in a former church cloister has added a second-floor bar, restaurant, and cooking school. Experience the sensory overload of colorful everyday Genovese life while watching the merchants and buyers banter over prices on the ground floor, and then head upstairs for a drink, a cooking lesson, or to try authentic Ligurian cuisine. ⊠ *Via XX Settembre, Portoria* ⊕ *www.moggenova. it* ⏱ *Closed Sun.*

Museo dell'Accademia Ligustica di Belle Arti

ART MUSEUM | Founded in 1751, the city's art school has a museum with a collection of paintings from the 16th to the 19th century. Genovese artists of the Baroque period are particularly well represented. ⊠ *Largo Pertini 4, Portoria* ☎ *010/506131* ⊕ *www.museo.accademialigustica.it* 🎫 *€5* ⏱ *Closed Sun. and Mon.*

Palazzo Ducale

ART GALLERY | This palace was built in the 16th century over a medieval hall, and its facade was rebuilt in the late 18th century and later restored. It now houses temporary exhibitions upstairs and a restaurant-bar serving fusion cuisine, as well as several other bars offering coffee and drinks. The amazingly large courtyard (which is free) is worth strolling through. ⊠ *Piazza Matteotti 9, Portoria* ☎ *010/8171600* ⊕ *www.palazzoducale.genova.it* 🎫 *Tickets from €12* ⏱ *Closed Mon.*

Porta Soprana

NOTABLE BUILDING | A striking 12th-century twin-tower structure, this medieval gateway stands on the spot where a road from ancient Rome entered the city. It is just steps uphill from Christopher Columbus's boyhood home. ⊠ *Piazza Dante, Molo.*

San Donato

CHURCH | Although somewhat marred by 19th- and 20th-century restorations, the 12th-century church of San Donato, with its original portal and octagonal campanile, is a fine example of Genovese Romanesque architecture. Inside, an altarpiece by the Flemish artist Joos van Cleve (circa 1485–1540) depicts the Adoration of the Magi. ⊠ *Piazza San Donato, Portoria* ☎ *010/2468869* ⊕ *www. sandonato.org.*

San Lorenzo

CHURCH | Contrasting black and white marble, so common in Liguria, embellishes the cathedral at the heart of medieval Genoa, inside and out. Consecrated in

1118, the church honors St. Lawrence, who passed through the city on his way to Rome in the 3rd century. For hundreds of years the building was used for state purposes, such as civic elections, as well as religious. Note the 13th-century Gothic portal, the fascinating twisted barbershop columns, and the 15th- to 17th-century frescoes inside. The last campanile dates from the early 16th century. The Museo del Tesoro di San Lorenzo (San Lorenzo Treasury Museum) inside has some stunning pieces from medieval goldsmiths and silversmiths, work for which medieval Genoa was renowned. ✉ *Piazza San Lorenzo, Molo* ☎ *010/2091863* 🌐 *www.museidigenova.it* 🎟 *Cathedral free, museum €6.*

San Matteo

CHURCH | This typically Genovese black-and-white-striped church dates from the 12th century; its crypt contains the tomb of Andrea Doria (1466–1560), the Genovese admiral who maintained the independence of his native city. The well-preserved Piazza San Matteo was, for 500 years, the seat of the Doria family, which ruled Genoa and much of Liguria from the 16th to the 18th century. The square is bounded by 13th- to 15th-century houses decorated with portals and loggias. ✉ *Piazza San Matteo, Maddalena* ☎ *010/2474361.*

Santa Maria di Castello

CHURCH | One of Genoa's most significant churches, this early Christian structure was rebuilt in the 12th century and finally completed in 1513. You can visit the adjacent cloisters and see the fine artwork in the museum. Hours vary during religious services. ✉ *Salita di Santa Maria di Castello 15, Molo* ☎ *347/9956740* 🌐 *www.santamariadicastello.it* 🎟 *Free.*

Sant'Agostino

CHURCH | This 13th-century Gothic church was damaged during World War II, but it still has a fine campanile with a Moorish inlaid marble design, and two well-preserved cloisters (one of which is the only triangular cloister in Europe) that house a museum displaying pieces of medieval architecture, sculptures, and frescoes. Highlights of the collection are the enigmatic fragments of a tomb sculpture by Giovanni Pisano (circa 1250–1315). ✉ *Piazza Sarzano 35/R, Molo* ☎ *010/2511263* 🌐 *www.museidigenova.it/it/content/museo-di-santagostino* 🎟 *€5* 🕒 *Closed Mon.*

🍴 Restaurants

Da Gaia

$ | **LIGURIAN** | For a truly Genovese experience, this unassuming restaurant, located in the basement of an old palazzo in the heart of the centro storico between Strada Nuova and the port, is just the place. You'll find some of the best, most authentic food in the city, with a focus on fish, meat dishes, and, of course, pesto. **Known for:** Genovese dishes; stuffed anchovies; cozy, old-world atmosphere. [$] *Average main: €14* ✉ *Vico dell'Argento, Maddalena* ☎ *010/2461629* 🕒 *Closed Sun.*

Da Gibbi ai Rolli

$ | **ITALIAN** | **FAMILY** | It bills itself as a pizzeria, focacceria (endemic in these parts), and an *insalateria.* The pizzas are magnificent, as are their first cousins the focaccia. But if you tire of this, their salads are worth a trip in themselves. **Known for:** superb rectangular pizzas; fine wine list (even by the glass); gracious staff. [$] *Average main: €13* ✉ *Salita Santa Caterina 4/r, Genoa* ☎ *010/2363947* 🕒 *Closed Mon.*

Farmer's Cooking Concept

$ | **ITALIAN** | Imagine having a swell glass of wine (their list is beyond foolproof) in a narrow, highly vaulted hall. The space may date to the 16th century, but some experts would argue it's earlier. **Known for:** top quality locally sourced ingredients; the room; superb cocktails. [$] *Average main: €14* ✉ *Salita Santa Caterina 34/r, Genoa* ☎ *010/2925426* 🌐 *www.*

The Art of the Pesto Pestle 🍴

You may have known Genoa primarily for its salami or its brash explorer, but the city's most direct effect on your life away from Italy may be through its cultivation of one of the world's best pasta sauces. The sublime blend of basil, extra-virgin olive oil, garlic, pine nuts, and grated pecorino and Parmigiano-Reggiano cheeses that forms *pesto alla Genovese* is one of Italy's crowning culinary achievements, a concoction that the late Italian food writer Marcella Hazan called "the most seductive of all sauces for pasta." Ligurian pesto is served usually over spaghetti, gnocchi, lasagna, or—most authentically—*trenette* (a flat, spaghetti-like pasta) or *trofie* (short, doughy pasta twists), typically mixed with boiled potatoes and green beans. Pesto is also occasionally used to flavor minestrone. Sometimes it appears in other tasty guises (like focaccia).

The small-leaf basil grown in the region's sunny seaside hills is considered by many to be the best in the world, and pesto sauce was invented primarily as a showcase for that singular flavor. The simplicity and rawness of pesto is one of its virtues, as cooking (or even heating) basil ruins its delicate flavor. In fact, pesto aficionados refuse even to subject the basil leaves to an electric blender; Genovese (and other) foodies insist that true pesto can be made only with mortar and pestle.

farmercookingconcept.it 🕒 *Closed weekends.*

I Cuochi
$$ | **LIGURIAN** | This cozy bistro-style restaurant is popular with locals and visitors alike for its refined, almost elegant menu of primarily seafood dishes, with a few pastas and meats. The decor is Art Nouveau with exposed brick walls, round tables with candles, and white tablecloths. **Known for:** contemporary Ligurian dishes; romantic setting; artistically presented seafood and desserts. [$] *Average main: €18* ✉ *Vico del Fieno 18r, Maddalena* ☎ *010/2476170* 🕒 *Closed Sun. and Mon. No lunch Tues.*

Il Genovese
$ | **LIGURIAN** | At this bright and friendly trattoria with a maritime theme, you can dine on some of the city's best pesto and Ligurian dishes in a casual, comfortable setting. The staff are knowledgeable about the region's specialties and the wines on the always interesting menu, and even if you don't order a pesto dish, they'll bring you some to sample before your meal. **Known for:** good value for the price; local atmosphere near Brignole station; award-winning pesto. [$] *Average main: €12* ✉ *Via Galata 35r, Brignole* ☎ *010/8692937* 🌐 *www.ilgenovese.com* 🕒 *Closed Sun.*

☕ Coffee and Quick Bites

I Canovacci
$ | **ITALIAN** | There's a steady crowd of regulars at this modern and homey lunch spot and dry goods store on a typical vicolo. The reasonably priced, good-value daily menu follows the seasons, with generous portions of fish and pasta, sandwiches, vegetables, and homemade desserts. **Known for:** vegetarian options; seasonal ingredients, some of which are also sold in its grocery store; efficient and friendly staff. [$] *Average main: €10* ✉ *Via dei Macelli di Soziglia 60, Maddalena* ☎ *010/0985417* 🕒 *Closed Sun. No dinner.*

Spin Ristorante-Enoteca

$$ | **LIGURIAN** | Dishes are created specifically to complement wines at this casually elegant enoteca with dark wood tables and bottle-lined walls in the heart of the modern town. The Ligurian menu varies daily, but the real draw is the vast wine list, including biodynamic selections. **Known for:** Ligurian seafood dishes; elegant setting in an otherwise brash part of town; wines take precedence. $ *Average main: €15* ⊠ *Via C. Barabino 120/R, Foce* ☎ *010/594513* ⊕ *www. spinristorante-enoteca.com.*

 Hotels

★ B&B Hotel Genova

$ | **B&B/INN** | **FAMILY** | This simple and utterly charming inn is a stone's throw away from the main train station (Piazza Principe), and is handily located near to most sights. **Pros:** location; charming staff; great value. **Cons:** might be too close to the train station for some; books up quickly; breakfast costs extra. $ *Rooms from: €90* ⊠ *Piazza Acquaverde 1, Genoa* ☎ *010/4030343* ⊕ *www.hotelbb.com* ⤴ *108 rooms* ⦿ *Free Breakfast.*

★ Grand Hotel Savoia

$ | **HOTEL** | As you enter this 1890s-vintage hotel above Piazza Acquaverde, you'll be transported from the modern city to a more glamorous era, thanks to details such as the original marble floors and lush gilt and richly colored velvet furniture in common areas. **Pros:** convenient location near Stazione Principe; comfortable rooms with luxury amenities; rooftop restaurant and bar. **Cons:** breakfast not included in all rates; rooms on lower floors face next-door buildings; Principe station area not the best in the city. $ *Rooms from: €119* ⊠ *Via Arsenale di Terra 5, Genoa* ☎ *010/27721* ⊕ *www. grandhotelsavoiagenova.it* ⤴ *117 rooms* ⦿ *Free Breakfast.*

Hotel Bristol Palace

$$ | **HOTEL** | One of Europe's gracious 19th-century grand hotels, the Bristol Palace guards its reputation for courtesy, service, and elegance, offering mostly spacious, handsomely furnished, high-ceilinged guest rooms and lovely public spaces. **Pros:** outdoor terrace is lovely in summer months; beautiful period details in some rooms; in the heart of the shopping district. **Cons:** some standard rooms are small; parking is a bit expensive; on a busy street that can be noisy. $ *Rooms from: €185* ⊠ *Via XX Settembre 35, Portoria* ☎ *010/592541* ⊕ *www.hotelbristol-palace.it* ⤴ *133 rooms* ⦿ *Free Breakfast.*

Hotel Palazzo Grillo

$$ | **HOTEL** | Formerly the Grillo family palace, this sumptuously comfortable boutique hotel integrates architectural details from the 1500s to the 1700s—like an original marble entryway and staircase, frescoed ceilings, and frieze details in some rooms—with clean-lined modern luxury. **Pros:** comfortable rooms with large bathrooms and high-end mattresses; terrace with cathedral views; modern furnishings and attention to aesthetic details. **Cons:** parking can be difficult in the old town; breakfast costs a lot extra; location on piazza and next to a church can be a bit noisy. $ *Rooms from: €175* ⊠ *Piazza delle Vigne 4, Maddalena* ☎ *010/2477356* ⊕ *www.hotelpalazzogrillo.it* ⤴ *25 rooms* ⦿ *No Meals.*

Performing Arts

Teatro Carlo Felice

OPERA | The World War II–ravaged opera house in Genoa's modern center, Piazza de Ferrari, was rebuilt and reopened in 1991 to host the fine Genovese opera company; its massive tower has been the subject of much criticism. Lavish productions of old favorites and occasional world premieres are staged from October to May. ⊠ *Piazza de Ferrari, Passo Eugenio Montale 4, Portoria* ☎ *010/5381* ⊕ *www.carlofelicegenova.it.*

Shopping

Liguria is famous for fine lace, silver-and-gold filigree work, and ceramics. Also look for bargains in velvet, macramé, olivewood, and marble. Genoa is the best spot to find all these specialties. In the heart of the medieval quarter, Via Soziglia is lined with shops selling handicrafts and tempting foods. Via XX Settembre and Via Roma are famous for their exclusive shops. High-end shops line Via Luccoli. The best shopping area for trendy-but-inexpensive Italian clothing is near San Siro, on Via San Luca.

CLOTHING AND LEATHER GOODS

Pescetto

MIXED CLOTHING | Look for designer clothes, perfumes, and fancy gifts like high-end soaps and silk scarves at Pescetto. ⊠ *Via Scurreria 8, Molo* ☎ *010/2473433* ⊕ *www.pescetto.it.*

JEWELRY

Codevilla

JEWELRY & WATCHES | Established in 1830, Codevilla is known as one of the best jewelers in the city. They sell top-of-the-line watches and custom jewelry. ⊠ *Via Roma 83/85r, Maddalena* ☎ *010/8938278* ⊕ *www.luigicodevilla.it/codevilla.*

WINES

Vinoteca Sola

WINE/SPIRITS | The owner of this shop specializes in discovering the best wines from across Italy. During the fall you can taste the latest wines, and all year you can purchase your favorites and have them shipped home. You can even buy futures for vintages to come. ⊠ *Piazza Colombo 13–15/R, near Stazione Brignole, Brignole* ☎ *010/561329* ⊕ *www.vinotecasola.it.*

Nervi: Side Trip from Genoa

11 km (7 miles) east of Genoa.

The identity of this stately late-19th-century resort, famous for its 1½-km-long

(1-mile-long) seaside **Passeggiata Anita Garibaldi,** its palm-lined roads, and its 300 acres of parks rich in orange trees, is given away only by the sign on the sleepy train station. Although Nervi is technically part of Genoa, its peace and quiet are as different from the city's hustle and bustle as its clear blue water is from the crowded port. From the centrally located train station, walk east along the seaside promenade to reach the beaches, a cliffside restaurant, and the 2,000 varieties of rose in the public **Parco Villa Grimaldi,** all the while enjoying one of the most breathtaking views on the Riviera. Nervi and the road between it and Genoa are known for their nightlife in summer.

GETTING HERE

By car, exit the A12 at Genova Nervi and follow the "Centro" signs. The Nervi train station is on the main north–south line, and you can also take the commuter trains from Genova Principe and Brignole. Nervi can also be reached on Bus No. 15 from Genoa's Piazza Cavour.

◉ Sights

GAM (Galleria d'Arte Moderna di Genova)

ART MUSEUM | Beautifully situated in a 16th century villa (with a garden and great views), this collection houses a vast amount of paintings, sculptures, and drawings from the very recent past. The artists are largely not household names, but a visit here is well worth it. (As are their contemporary exhibitions.) ⊠ *Villa Saluzzo Serra, Via Capolungo 3, Nervi* ☎ *010/3726025* ⊕ *www.museigenova.it* ⊡ *€6* ⊗ *Closed Mon.*

Wolfsoniana

ART MUSEUM | The private collection of businessman Mitchell Wolfson, Jr. has turned into an eclectic museum displaying his whims and caprices. ⊠ *Via Serra Gropolla 4, Nervi* ☎ *010/32313329* ⊕ *www.wolfsoniana.it* ⊡ *€5* ⊗ *Closed Mon.*

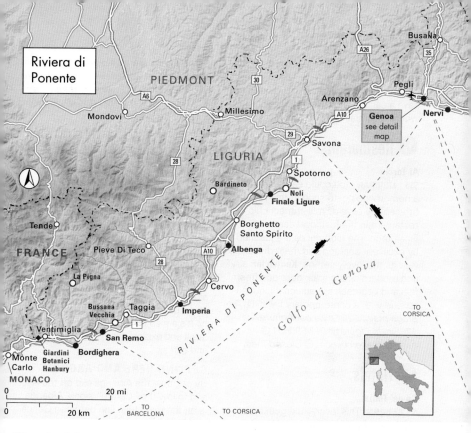

Riviera di Ponente

Finale Ligure

72 km (44 miles) southwest of Genoa.

Lovely Finale Ligure is actually made up of three small villages—Finalmarina, Finalpia, and Finalborgo—and makes a wonderful base for exploring the Riviera di Ponente. The former two have fine sandy beaches and a mix of traditional and modern resort amenities. Finalborgo, less than 1 km (½ mile) inland, is an attractive medieval walled village with nice shops and restaurants. Just above is a hauntingly well-preserved medieval settlement, planned to a rigid blueprint, with 15th-century walls. The surrounding countryside is pierced by deep, narrow valleys and caves; the limestone outcroppings provide the warm pinkish stone found in many buildings in Genoa. Rare reptiles lurk among the exotic flora.

GETTING HERE AND AROUND

By car, take the Finale Ligure exit off the A10 and follow the "Centro" signs. Finale Ligure is on the main train line between Genoa and France.

VISITOR INFORMATION

CONTACT Finale Ligure Tourism Office.
✉ *Via San Pietro 14,* ☎ *019/681019* ⊕ *tur-ismo.comunefinaleligure.it.*

Sights

Noli

TOWN | Just 9 km (5½ miles) northeast of Finale Ligure, the ruins of a castle loom benevolently over Noli, a tiny medieval gem. It's hard to imagine that this charming seaside village was—like Genoa, Venice, Pisa, and Amalfi—a prosperous maritime republic in the Middle Ages. Let yourself get lost among its labyrinth of cobblestone streets filled with shops and cafés or enjoy a day in the sun on its lovely stretch of beach. If you don't have a car, get a bus for Noli at Spotorno, where local trains stop. ✉ *Noli.*

🍴 Restaurants

Ai Torchi

$$$ | **LIGURIAN** | You could easily become a homemade-pesto snob at this restored 5th-century olive oil mill–turned–chic restaurant in the historical center of Finalborgo. The high prices are justified by excellent seafood and meat dishes as well as the lovely setting. **Known for:** airy and modern dining area; delicious fresh fish and vegetables; traditional Ligurian cuisine with a contemporary twist. [$] *Average main: €25* ✉ *Via dell'Annunziata 12, Finale Ligure* ☎ *019/690531* 🌐 *www.ristoranteaitorchi.com* 🕓 *Closed Tues.*

🛏 Hotels

Ca de' Tobia

$ | **B&B/INN** | This lovely little guesthouse on the seafront promenade of Noli is stylishly done with wood floors, splashes of bright colors, and modern decor. **Pros:** modern furniture and bathrooms; great breakfast and aperitivo; easy beach access. **Cons:** a bit more expensive than comparable hotels in town; parking can be a challenge; street noise. [$] *Rooms from: €100* ✉ *Via Aurelia 35, Noli* ☎ *019/7485845* 🌐 *www.cadetobia.it* 🛏 *6 rooms* 🍴 *Free Breakfast.*

Punta Est

$$$ | **HOTEL** | **FAMILY** | The grand former home of a musician and composer, this 18th-century villa perched on a fragrant hillside above white-sand beaches has since had a wing added, creating a wonderful retreat from the crowds at the water's edge. **Pros:** dining on the terrace with views; relaxing pool and gardens; close to the beach. **Cons:** some noisy rooms because of their proximity to the terrace; parking can be a challenge; some rooms are a bit outdated. [$] *Rooms from: €240* ✉ *Via Aurelia 1, Finale Ligure* ☎ *39/019600611* 🌐 *www.puntaest.com* 🕓 *Closed mid-Oct.–mid-Apr.* 🛏 *36 rooms* 🍴 *Free Breakfast.*

Albenga

20 km (12 miles) southwest of Finale Ligure, 90 km (55 miles) southwest of Genoa.

Albenga has a medieval core, with narrow streets laid out by the ancient Romans. A network of alleys is punctuated by centuries-old towers surrounding the 12th-century Romanesque cathedral, along with a late-14th-century campanile and a baptistery dating to the 5th century. It's a nice place to take an afternoon stroll and explore the many quaint shops and cafés.

GETTING HERE AND AROUND

By car, take the Albenga exit off the A10 and follow the "Centro" signs. Albenga is on the main train line between Genoa and France.

VISITOR INFORMATION

CONTACT Albenga Tourism Office. ✉ *Piazza San Michele 17, Albenga* ☎ *0182/5621* 🌐 *www.comune.albenga.sv.it.*

👁 Sights

Bardineto

TOWN | For a look at some of the Riviera's mountain scenery, make an excursion by car to this attractive village in the middle of an area rich in mushrooms, chestnuts, a wide variety of potatoes, and blueberries, as well as local cheeses. A ruined castle stands above the village. From Borghetto Santo Spirito (between Albenga and Finale Ligure), drive inland 25 km (15 miles). ✉ *Piazza della Chiesa 6, Bardineto* 🌐 *www.comune.bardineto.sv.it.*

Imperia

34 km (21 miles) southwest of Albenga, 116 km (71 miles) southwest of Genoa.

Imperia actually consists of two towns: Porto Maurizio, a medieval town built on a promontory, and Oneglia, now an industrial center for oil refining and pharmaceuticals. Porto Maurizio has a virtually intact medieval center, an intricate spiral of narrow streets and stone portals, and some imposing 17th- and 18th-century palaces. There's little of interest in modern Oneglia, except the olive oil museum.

GETTING HERE AND AROUND

By car, take the Imperia Est exit off the A10 and follow the signs for "Centro" or "Porto Maurizio." Both Imperia and Porto Maurizio are on the main rail line between Genoa and France.

Sights

Museo dell'Olivo

OTHER MUSEUM | Imperia is king when it comes to olive oil, and the story of the olive is the theme of this small museum. Displays of the history of the olive tree, farm implements, presses, and utensils show how olive oil has been made in many countries throughout history. A multilingual audio guide is also available. ⊠ *Via Garessio 13, Imperia* ☎ *0183/295762* ⊕ *www.museodellolivo. com* 🎫 *€5.*

San Remo

36 km (22 miles) southwest of Imperia, 146 km (90 miles) southwest of Genoa.

Once the crown jewel of the Riviera di Ponente, San Remo is still the area's largest resort, lined with polished hotels, exotic gardens, and seaside promenades. Renowned for its VIP crowd, glittering casino, annual music festival, and romantic setting, San Remo maintains remnants of its glamorous past from the late 19th century to World War II, but it also suffers from the same epidemic of overbuilding that has changed so much of the Ponente for the worse. Still, it continues to be a lively town, even in the off-season.

The Mercato dei Fiori, Italy's most important wholesale flower market, is held here in a market hall between Piazza Colombo and Corso Garibaldi, though it's open to dealers only. More than 20,000 tons of carnations, roses, mimosa flowers, and innumerable other kinds of cut flowers are dispatched from here each year. As the center of northern Italy's flower-growing industry, the town is surrounded by hills where verdant terraces are now blanketed with plastic to form immense greenhouses.

GETTING HERE AND AROUND

By car, take the San Remo exit off the A10 and follow the "Centro" signs. San Remo is on the main train line between Genoa and France.

VISITOR INFORMATION

CONTACT San Remo Tourism Office. ⊠ *Corso Garibaldi 1, San Remo* ☎ *0184/580500* ⊕ *www.turismoinliguria.it.*

Sights

Bussana Vecchia

TOWN | In the hills where flowers are cultivated for export, this self-consciously picturesque former ghost town is a flourishing artists' colony. The town was largely destroyed by an earthquake in 1877, when the inhabitants packed up and left en masse. For almost a century the houses, church, and crumbling bell tower were empty shells, overgrown by weeds and wildflowers. Since the 1960s, painters, sculptors, artisans, and bric-a-brac dealers have restored the dwellings as houses and studios. You need a car to visit the town. ⊠ *San Remo* ✛ *8 km*

(5 miles) east of San Remo ⊕ www.bussanavecchia.it.

Chiesa Russa Ortodossa

CHURCH | This domed Russian Orthodox church testifies to a long Russian presence on the Italian Riviera. Russian empress Maria Alexandrovna, wife of Czar Alexander I, built a summerhouse here, and in winter San Remo was a popular destination for other royal Romanovs. The church was consecrated in 1913. ⊠ *Via Nuvoloni 2, San Remo* ☎ *0184/531807* ⊕ *www.chiesarussasanremo.it* 🖾 *€1 donation.*

La Pigna (*The Pinecone*)

TOWN | San Remo's old town climbs upward to Piazza Castello, which offers a splendid view of the town and sea below. Some lovely old palazzi and squares have been restored, and the neighborhood gives you a sense of what it was like to live in San Remo centuries ago. ⊠ *Old Town, San Remo* ⊕ *www.turismoinliguria.it.*

San Remo Casinò

CASINO | In addition to gaming, this lovely 1905 Art Nouveau landmark offers two restaurants, bars, and a theater that hosts concerts. Admission is free, but if you want to try your luck at the gaming tables, bets begin at around €10, depending on the time of day or night. ■ TIP→ **Dress is elegant, with jacket and tie requested at the French gaming tables.** ⊠ *Corso Inglesi 18, San Remo* ☎ *0184/5951* ⊕ *www.casinosanremo.it.*

 Restaurants

Nuovo Piccolo Mondo

$ | LIGURIAN | Vintage wooden furniture evokes the homey charm of this small family-run trattoria. A faithful clientele keeps the kitchen busy, so get here early to grab a table and order Ligurian specialties—fresh pasta, pesto, and vegetable and seafood dishes. **Known for:** local atmosphere; polpo e patate (stewed octopus with potatoes); sciancui (flat pasta with beans, tomatoes, zucchini, and

pesto). $ *Average main: €14* ⊠ *Via Piave 7, San Remo* ☎ *0184/509012* ⊙ *Closed Sun.*

 Hotels

Hotel Paradiso

$$$ | HOTEL | There's an air of seclusion and a respite from hectic San Remo in these bright, well-equipped rooms—some with balconies and sea views—that face a quiet, palm-fringed garden and pool. **Pros:** nice pool and private beach; secluded yet near town; on-site restaurant and bar. **Cons:** some bathrooms are dated; paid parking; steep walk up some stairs and a hill from town. $ *Rooms from: €260* ⊠ *Via Roccasterone 12, San Remo* ☎ *0184/571211* ⊕ *www.paradisohotel.it* ⊙ *Closed mid-Oct.–Dec. 15* 🛏 *41 rooms* ⊚ *Free Breakfast.*

Royal Hotel San Remo

$$$ | HOTEL | With its heated seawater swimming pool in a tropical garden and guest rooms (some with sea views) with an attention to traditional design and modern amenities, this is considered one of Liguria's most luxurious resorts. **Pros:** the glamour of yesteryear with high-end amenities; relaxing pool open April through October; reasonable prices given the surroundings and closeness to casino. **Cons:** pool area can be crowded in high season; some bathrooms could be updated; expensive on-site meals and beverages. $ *Rooms from: €270* ⊠ *Corso Imperatrice 80, San Remo* ☎ *0184/5391* ⊕ *www.royalhotelsanremo.com* ⊙ *Closed mid-Nov.–Feb. 1* 🛏 *127 rooms* ⊚ *Free Breakfast.*

Bordighera

12 km (7 miles) southwest of San Remo, 155 km (96 miles) southwest of Genoa.

Bordighera is an attractive seaside resort with panoramas (on a clear day) from Genoa to Monte Carlo. A large English colony settled here in the second half of

Did You Know?

The gorgeous Hanbury Botanic Gardens were completely devastated in World War II. In 1960, Lady Hanbury sold the property to the State of Italy and in 1987, the University of Genoa began restoration. Today it's considered one of the most beautiful gardens in Italy.

the 19th century and is still very much in evidence today; you regularly find people taking afternoon tea in the cafés, and streets are named after Queen Victoria and Shakespeare.

GETTING HERE AND AROUND

By car, take the Bordighera exit off the A10 and follow the signs for "Centro," about a 10-minute drive. Bordighera is on the main railway line between Genoa and France.

VISITOR INFORMATION

CONTACT Bordighera Tourism Office. ✉ *Via Vittorio Emanuele 172, Bordighera* ☎ *0184/262882* 🌐 *www.bordighera.it.*

Sights

★ Giardini Botanici Hanbury

GARDEN | Mortola Inferiore is the site of the world-famous Hanbury Botanical Gardens, one of the largest and most beautiful in Italy. Planned and planted in 1867 by a wealthy English merchant, Sir Thomas Hanbury, and his botanist brother, Daniel, the terraced gardens contain species from five continents, including many palms and succulents. ✉ *Corso Montecarlo 43, Località Mortola Inferiore, Ventimiglia* ☎ *0184/229507* 🌐 *www.giardinihanbury.com* 🎟 *€9.*

Lungomare Argentina

PROMENADE | Running parallel to the ocean, Lungomare Argentina is a pleasant 1½-km (1-mile) promenade, which begins at the western end of the town and provides good views westward to the French Côte d'Azur. Most Thursdays it's also the site of a bustling outdoor market. ✉ *Bordighera.*

Restaurants

Buga Buga Bar

$$ | **ITALIAN** | It seems that most locals congregate at this lively bar/restaurant, and they often bring their dogs and children with them. In the morning, tasty brioches start off the festivities, and segues neatly into lunch. **Known for:** nice wines by the glass accompanied by lovely snacks; great staff; opens early, closes late. [$] *Average main: €17* ✉ *Corso Italia 13, Bordighera* ☎ *0184/998001.*

Burger e Stars

$$ | **BURGER** | As the name implies, this place is largely a burger joint. The toppings, however, are not (cheese in this case often means Gorgonzola and burrata). **Known for:** creative culinary combinations; killer desserts; burgers. [$] *Average main: €15* ✉ *Corso Italia 76, Bordighera* ☎ *340/9215469* 🕒 *Closed Mon. and Tues. No lunch Wed.–Sat.*

Magiargè

$$ | **LIGURIAN** | A mix of great charm and great food make this small, bustling osteria in the historic center an absolute dining delight. Dishes are Ligurian with a focus on local fish, and the list of local wines, including organic selections, is excellent. **Known for:** multicourse set menus of Ligurian specialties; salt cod with chickpea polenta; cozy dining room with curved archways. [$] *Average main: €18* ✉ *Via Dritta 2, Bordighera* ☎ *0184/262946* 🌐 *www.magiarge.it* 🕒 *Closed Mon. and Tues.*

Hotels

★ Villa Elisa

$$ | **HOTEL** | On a street filled with beautiful old villas, this Victorian-era former private residence has a relaxed and friendly atmosphere, beautiful gardens, a spa, and well-appointed rooms (some with balconies) at reasonable prices. **Pros:** gregarious staff; old-world charm; an amazing breakfast buffet. **Cons:** the spa costs extra; somewhat removed from the center of things; books up quickly. [$] *Rooms from: €180* ✉ *Via Romana 70, Bordighera* 🌐 *www.villaelisa.com* 🕒 *Closed mid-Oct.–Jan.* 🛏 *32 rooms* 🍴 *Free Breakfast.*

Chapter 11

EMILIA–ROMAGNA

Updated by
Patricia Rucidlo

11

😊 **Sights**
★★★★☆

🍴 **Restaurants**
★★★★★

🛏 **Hotels**
★★★★☆

🛍 **Shopping**
★★★☆☆

🍸 **Nightlife**
★☆☆☆☆

WELCOME TO EMILIA-ROMAGNA

TOP REASONS TO GO

★ **The signature food of Emilia:** This region's food—prosciutto crudo, Parmesan cheese, balsamic vinegar, and above all, pasta—makes the trip to Italy worthwhile.

★ **Mosaics that take your breath away:** The intricate tiles in Ravenna's Mausoleo di Galla Placidia, in brilliantly well-preserved colors, depict vivid portraits and pastoral scenes.

★ **Arguably Europe's oldest wine bar:** Nicolaus Copernicus tippled here while studying at Ferrara's university in the early 1500s—Enoteca al Brindisi, in the historic center, has been pouring wine since 1435.

★ **The nightlife of Bologna:** This red-roof city has had a lively student culture since the university—Europe's oldest—was founded in the late 11th century.

★ **The medieval castles of San Marino:** Its three castles dramatically perch on a rock more than 3,000 feet above the flat landscape of Romagna.

1 Piacenza. With its majestic piazzas, fine cathedral, and palatial museum, this town at Emilia's northwestern end makes a fitting introduction to the region.

2 Busseto. Opera aficionados visit to pay homage to one of Italy's greatest composers, Giuseppe Verdi.

3 Parma. Internationally known for its foodstuffs, Parma also boasts a battery of sights.

4 Modena. Endowed with a compact, beautifully preserved city center and a magnificent cathedral, this town repays a leisurely wander.

5 Bologna. Emilia's principal cultural and intellectual center is famed for its arcaded sidewalks, medieval towers, and sublime restaurants.

6 Ferrara. This prosperous, tidy town north of Bologna has a rich medieval past and distinctive cuisine.

7 Imola. There is plenty more to this place than its famous Formula One racetrack, including an attractive city center.

8 Faenza. This handsome setttlement has bequeathed its name to the majolica ceramics, or *faience*, for which it is best known.

9 Rimini. A beach resort on the Adriatic coast, Rimini has noteworthy Roman and Renaissance monuments.

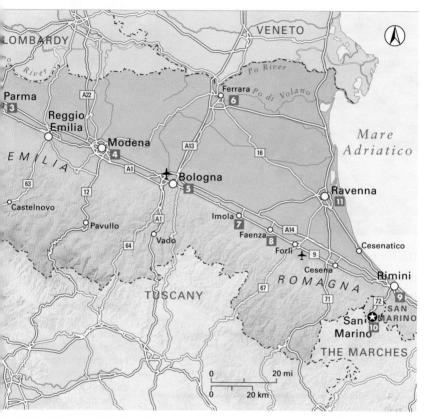

San Marino. Officially an independent republic, this quirky enclave is a tourist hot spot.

Ravenna. The main attractions of this well-preserved Romagna city are its mosaics—glittering treasures left from Byzantine rule.

EATING AND DRINKING WELL IN EMILIA-ROMAGNA

Italians rarely agree about anything, but many concede that some of the country's finest foods originated in Emilia-Romagna. Tortellini, fettuccine, Parmesan cheese, prosciutto crudo, and balsamic vinegar are just a few of the Italian delicacies born here.

One of the beauties of Emilia-Romagna is that its exceptional food can be had without breaking the bank. Many trattorias serve up classic dishes, mastered over the centuries, at reasonable prices. Cutting-edge restaurants and wine bars are often more expensive; their inventive menus are full of *fantasia*—reinterpretations of the classics. For the budget-conscious, Bologna, a university town, has great places for cheap eats.

Between meals, you can sustain yourself with the region's famous sandwich, the *piadina*. It's made with pitalike thin bread, usually filled with prosciutto or mortadella, cheese, and vegetables, then put under the grill and served hot, with the cheese oozing at the sides. These addictive sandwiches can be savored at sit-down places or ordered to go.

THE REAL RAGÙ

Emilia-Romagna's signature dish is *tagliatelle al ragù* (flat noodles with meat sauce), known as "spaghetti Bolognese" most everywhere else. This *primo* (first course) is on every menu, and no two versions are the same. The sauce starts in a sauté pan with finely diced carrots, onions, and celery. Purists add nothing but minced beef, but some use *guanciale* (pork cheek), sausage, veal, or chicken. Regular ministrations of broth are added, and sometimes wine, milk, or cream.

PORK PRODUCTS

It's not just mortadella and cured pork products like prosciutto crudo and *culatello* that Emilia-Romagnans go crazy for—they're wild about the whole hog. You'll frequently find cotechino and zampone, both *secondi* (second courses), on menus. *Cotechino* is a savory, thick, fresh sausage served with lentils on New Year's Eve (the combination is said to augur well for the new year) and with mashed potatoes year-round. *Zampone,* a stuffed pig's foot, is redolent of garlic and deliciously fatty.

BOLLITO MISTO

The name means "mixed boil," and they do it exceptionally well in this part of Italy. According to Emilia-Romagnans, *bollito misto* was invented here, although other Italians—especially those from Milan and Piedmont—might dispute this claim. Chicken, beef, tongue, and zampone are tossed into a stockpot and boiled; they're then removed from the broth and served with a fragrant *salsa verde* (green sauce), made with parsley and spiced with anchovies, garlic, and capers. This simple yet rich dish is usually served with mashed potatoes on the side, and savvy diners will mix some of the piquant salsa verde into the potatoes as well.

STUFFED PASTA

Among the many Emilian variations on stuffed pasta, *tortellini* are the smallest. *Tortelli* and *cappellacci* are larger pasta "pillows," about the size of a brussels sprout, but with the same basic form as tortellini. They're often filled with pumpkin or spinach and cheese. *Tortelloni* are, in theory, even bigger, although their size varies. Stuffed pastas are generally served simply, with melted butter, sage, and Parmigiano-Reggiano cheese or, in the case of tortellini, *in brodo* (in beef, chicken, or capon broth or some combination thereof), which brings out the subtle richness of the filling.

WINES

Emilia-Romagna's wines accompany the region's fine food rather than vying with it for accolades. The best-known is *Lambrusco,* a sparkling red produced on the Po Plain that has some admirers and many detractors. It's praised for its tartness and condemned for the same; it does, however, pair brilliantly with the local fare. The region's best wines include Sangiovese di Romagna (somewhat similar to Chianti), from the Romagnan hills, and barbera from the Colli Piacentini and Apennine foothills. Castelluccio, Bonzara, Zerbina, Leone Conti, and Tre Monti are among the region's top producers.

Gourmets the world over claim that Emilia-Romagna's greatest contribution to humankind has been gastronomic. Birthplace of fettuccine, tortellini, lasagna, prosciutto, balsamic vinegar, and Parmigiano-Reggiano cheese, the region has a spectacular culinary tradition.

But there are many reasons to come here aside from the desire to be well fed: Parma's Correggio paintings, Giuseppe Verdi's villa at Sant'Agata, the medieval splendor of Bologna's palaces, Ferrara's medieval alleys, the rolling hills of the Romagna countryside, and, perhaps foremost, the Byzantine beauty of mosaic-rich Ravenna—glittering as brightly today as it did 1,500 years ago.

As you travel through Emilia, the western half of the region, you'll encounter the sprawling plants of Italy's industrial food giants, like Barilla and Fini, standing side by side with the fading villas and farmhouses that have long punctuated the flat, fertile land of the Po Plain. Bologna, the principal city of Emilia, is a busy cultural and, increasingly, business center, less visited but in many ways just as engaging as the country's more famous tourist destinations—particularly given its acknowledged position as the leading city of Italian cuisine. The rest of the region follows suit: eating is an essential part of any Emilian experience.

The area's history is laden with culinary legends, such as how the original tortellino was modeled on the shape of Venus's navel and the original *tagliolini* (long, thin egg pasta) was served at the wedding banquet of Annibale Bentivoglio and Lucrezia d'Este—a marriage uniting two of the most powerful noble families in the region. You'll need to stay focused just to make sure you try all the basics: Parma's famed prosciutto and Parmigiano-Reggiano cheese, Modena's balsamic vinegar, the ragù whose poor imitations are known worldwide as "Bolognese"—and, of course, perhaps the best pasta in the world.

The historic border between Emilia to the west and Romagna to the east lies near the fortified town of Dozza. Emilia is flat, but just east of the Romagnan border the landscape gets hillier and more sparsely settled, in places covered with evergreen forests and steaming natural springs. Finally, it flattens again into the low-lying marshland of the Po Delta, which meets the Adriatic Sea. Each fall, in both Romagna and Emilia, the trademark fog rolls in off the Adriatic to hang over the flatlands in winter, coloring the region with a spooky, gray glow.

MAJOR REGIONS

The westernmost part of the region, **Emilia,** is richly redolent of the history and culture of northern Italy. The Via Emilia, an ancient Roman road, runs through Emilia's heart in a straight shot from medieval Piacenza, southeast of Milan, through Bologna, home to one of the world's first universities and still one of Italy's great cities, and ultimately to

Romagna and the Adriatic Coast. On the way you encounter many of Italy's cultural riches—notably the culinary and artistic treasures of Parma and Modena. Take time to veer into the countryside, with its ramshackle farmhouses and 800-year-old abbeys, and to detour north to the birthplace and home of Giuseppe Verdi at Busseto. Northeast of Bologna, explore the mist-shrouded tangle of streets in Ferrara's charismatic old town.

The mostly rural **Romagna** has rolling hills dotted with handsome farmhouses, giving way at its eastern end to the lively resorts and sandy beaches of the Adriatic coast. Imola, most famed for its Formula One racetrack, is traditionally regarded as the western gateway to Romagna. From here it's a short hop to Faenza, home to dozens of shops selling its well-known ceramics. Most visitors to Romagna make a beeline for Ravenna, the site of shimmering Byzantine mosaics, though you'll also find absorbing historical remnants at Rimini, a beach resort. The mini-state of San Marino, to the south, is a curiosity worth a brief detour for its castles.

Planning

When to Go

Extending along the valley of the River Po, Emilia-Romagna's predominantly flat and featureless landscape is subject to hot summers and cold, foggy winters. It's humid year-round, so rain is always a possibility and fairly common during the winter months. Tourism is mainly cultural in the region and thus isn't particularly subject to seasonal variations, though you can expect to see some resorts along the Romagna coast close in winter, particularly around Rimini.

Planning Your Time

Plan on spending at least two days in Bologna, the region's cultural and historical capital. You shouldn't miss Parma, with its stunning food and graceful public spaces. Also plan on visiting Ferrara, a misty, mysterious medieval city. If you have time, go to Ravenna for its memorable Byzantine mosaics and Modena for its harmonious architecture and famous balsamic vinegar.

If you have only a few days in the region, it's virtually impossible to do all five of those cities justice. If you're a dedicated gourmand (or *buona forchetta,* as Italians say), move from Bologna west along the Via Emilia (SS9) to Modena and Parma. If you're more interested in architecture, art, and history, choose the eastern route, heading north on the A13 to Ferrara and then southeast on the SS16 to Ravenna.

If you have more time, you won't have to make such tough choices. You can start in Milan, go east, and finish on the Adriatic—or vice versa.

Getting Here and Around

CAR

Driving is the best way to get around Emilia-Romagna. Roads are wide, flat, and well marked; distances are short; and beautiful farmhouses and small villages offer undemanding detours.

A car is particularly useful for visiting the spa towns of Romagna, which aren't well connected by train. Historic centers are off-limits to cars, but they're also quite walkable, so you may just want to park your car and get around on foot once you arrive.

Entering Emilia-Romagna by car is as easy as it gets. Coming in from the northwest on the Autostrada del Sole (A1), you'll first hit Piacenza, a mere

45-minute drive southeast of Milan. On the other side of the region, Venice is about an hour from Ferrara by car on the A13.

Bologna is on the autostrada, so driving between cities is a breeze, though take special care if you're coming from Florence, as the road is winding and the drivers speed. The Via Emilia (SS9), one of the oldest roads in the world, runs through the heart of the region. Although less scenic, the A1 autostrada, which runs parallel to the Via Emilia from Bologna, can get you where you're going about twice as fast. From Bologna, the A13 runs north to Ferrara, and the A14 takes you east to Ravenna. Much of the historic center of Bologna is closed off to cars daily from 7 am to 8 pm.

TRAIN

When it comes to public transportation in the region, trains are better than buses— they're fairly efficient and quite frequent, and most stations aren't too far from the center of town. The railroad track follows the Via Emilia (SS9). In Emilia it generally takes 30–60 minutes to get from one major city to the next. To reach Ferrara or Ravenna, you typically have to change to a local train at Bologna. Ferrara is a half hour north of Bologna on the train, and Ravenna is just over an hour east.

Bologna is an important rail hub for northern Italy and has frequent, fast service to Milan, Florence, Rome, and Venice. The routes from Bologna to the south usually go through Florence, about 40 minutes away on a high-speed train. The high-speed Frecciarossa train service cuts the time from Milan to Bologna to only one hour. On the northeastern edge of the region, Venice is 1½ hours east of Ferrara by train. Check the website of the state railway, the **Trenitalia** (aka Ferrovie dello Stato or FS; ⊕ *www.trenitalia.com/ en.html*), for information, or stop in a travel agency, as many sell train tickets (without a markup) and agents often speak English. **Italo** (⊕ *www.italotreno.*

it/en), a privately owned high-speed train line, competes with the state-sponsored service. Italo's Milan–Rome line makes stops in Reggio Emilia, Bologna, and Florence; the Venice–Naples line stops in Padua, Bologna, Florence, and Rome. Some of these also stop at secondary stations.

Restaurants

Dining options range from mom-and-pop-style informal trattorias to three-star Michelin restaurants. Food in Emilia-Romagna is not for the faint of heart (or those on diets): it is rich, creamy, and cheesy. Local wines pair remarkably well with this sumptuous fare. You may want to rethink Lambrusco, as it marries well with just about everything on the menu.

Restaurant prices are the average cost of a main course at dinner, or, if dinner is not served, at lunch. Restaurant reviews have been shortened. For full information, visit Fodors.com.

Hotels

Emilia-Romagna has a reputation for demonstrating a level of efficiency uncommon in most of Italy. Even the smallest hotels are usually well run, with high standards of quality and service. Bologna is very much a businessperson's city, and many hotels here cater to the business traveler, but there are smaller, more intimate hotels as well. It's smart to book in advance—the region hosts many fairs and conventions that can fill up hotels even during low season.

Hotel prices are the lowest cost of a standard double room in high season. Hotel reviews have been shortened. For full information, visit Fodors.com.

What it Costs in Euros

	$	$$	$$$	$$$$
RESTAURANTS				
	under €15	€15–€24	€25–€35	over €35
HOTELS				
	under €125	€125–€200	€201–€300	over €300

Piacenza

67 km (42 miles) southeast of Milan, 150 km (93 miles) northwest of Bologna.

Piacenza has always been associated with industry and commerce. Its position on the Po River has made it an important inland port since the Etruscans, and then the Romans, had thriving settlements here. As you approach the city today, you could be forgiven for thinking that it holds little of interest. Piacenza is surrounded by ugly industrial suburbs (with particularly unlovely concrete factories and a power station), but if you forge ahead you'll discover a well-preserved medieval center and an unusually clean city. Its prosperity is evident in the great shopping along Corso Vittorio Emanuele II.

GETTING HERE AND AROUND
Regional trains run often from Milan to Piacenza and take a little less than an hour, and Frecciarossa trains make it from Milan to Bologna in an hour. Services from Bologna to Piacenza take about 1½ hours and closer to 2 hours on some regional trains. Both have frequent service. Piacenza is easily accessible by car via the A1, either from Milan or from Bologna. If you're coming from Milan, take the Piacenza Nord exit; from Bologna, the Piacenza Est exit.

VISITOR INFORMATION
CONTACT Piacenza Tourism Office. ⊠ *Piazza Cavalli 10,* ☎ *0523/492001* ⊕ *www.comune.piacenza.it.*

Sights

Duomo
CHURCH | Attached like a sinister balcony to the bell tower of Piacenza's 12th-century Duomo is a *gabbia* (iron cage), where miscreants were incarcerated naked and subjected to the scorn of the crowd in the marketplace below. Inside the cathedral, less evocative but equally impressive medieval stonework decorates the pillars and the crypt, and there are extravagant frescoes in the dome of the cupola begun by Morazzone (1573–1626). Guercino (1591–1666) completed them upon Morazzone's death. If you're feeling strong, you can climb 136 steps to the cupola for a closer view. The Duomo can be reached by following Via XX Settembre from Piazza dei Cavalli. ⊠ *Piazza Duomo, Piacenza* ☎ *331/4606435* ⊕ *www.cattedralepiacenza.it* 🎫 *Free; cupola €10.*

Musei di Palazzo Farnese
ART MUSEUM | The eclectic city-owned museum of Piacenzan art and antiquities is housed in the vast Palazzo Farnese, a monumental palace commissioned by the ruling family that, although construction began in 1558, was never completed as planned. The highlight of the museum's collection is the tiny 2nd-century-BC Etruscan Fegato di Piacenza, a bronze tablet shaped like a *fegato* (liver), marked with the symbols of the gods of good and ill fortune. The collection also contains Botticelli's beautiful *Madonna and Child with St. John the Baptist.* ⊠ *Piazza Cittadella 29, Piacenza* ☎ *0523/492658* ⊕ *www.palazzofarnese.piacenza.it* 🎫 *€8* 🕑 *Closed Mon.*

Emilia-Romagna Through the Ages

Ancient History. Emilia-Romagna owes its beginnings to a road. In 187 BC the Romans built the Via Aemilia—a long road running northwest from the Adriatic port of Rimini to the central garrison town of Piacenza—and it was along this central spine that the primary towns of the region developed.

Despite the unifying factor of what came to be known as the Via Emilia, this section of Italy has had a fragmented history. Its eastern part, roughly the area from Faenza to the coast (known as Romagna), looked first to the Byzantine east and then to Rome for art, political power, and, some say, national character. The western part, from Bologna to Piacenza (Emilia), looked more to the north with its practice of self-government and dissent.

Bologna was founded by the Etruscans and eventually came under the influence of the Roman Empire. The Romans established a garrison here, renaming the old Etruscan settlement Bononia. It was after the fall of Rome that the region began its fragmentation. Romagna, centered in Ravenna, was ruled from Constantinople. Ravenna eventually became the capital of the empire in the west in the 5th century, passing to papal control in the 8th century. Even today, the city is filled with reminders of two centuries of Byzantine rule.

Family Ties. The other cities of the region, from the Middle Ages on, became the fiefdoms of important noble families—the Este in Ferrara and Modena, the Pallavicini in Piacenza, and the Bentivoglio in Bologna. Today all these cities bear the marks of their noble patrons. When in the 16th century the papacy managed to exert its power over the entire area, some of these cities were divided among the papal families—hence the stamp of the Farnese family on Parma and Piacenza.

A Leftward Tilt. Emilia-Romagna (and Bologna, in particular) has an established and hearty tradition of rebellion and dissent. The Italian socialist movement was born in this region, as was Benito Mussolini. In keeping with the political climate of his home state, he was a firebrand socialist during the early part of his career. Despite having Mussolini as a native son, Emilia-Romagna didn't take to Fascism: it was here that the anti-Fascist resistance was born, and during World War II the region suffered terribly at the hands of the Fascists and the Nazis.

Piazza dei Cavalli (*Square of the Horses*)
PLAZA/SQUARE | The hub of the city is the Piazza dei Cavalli, with the flamboyant equestrian statues from which the piazza takes its name. These are depictions of Ranuccio Farnese (1569–1622) and, on the left, his father, Alessandro (1545–92). The latter was a beloved ruler, enlightened and fair; Ranuccio, his successor, less so. Both statues are the work of Francesco Mochi, a master Baroque sculptor. Dominating the square is the massive 13th-century **Palazzo Pubblico,** also known as Il Gotico. This two-tone, marble-and-brick, turreted and crenellated building was the seat of town government before Piacenza fell under the iron fists of the ruling Pallavicini and Farnese families. ⊠ *Piazza dei Cavalli, Piacenza.*

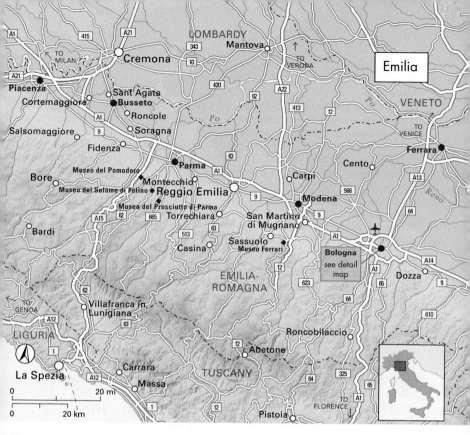

Busseto

30 km (19 miles) southeast of Piacenza, 25 km (16 miles) south of Cremona in Lombardy.

Sleepy Busseto's greatest claim to fame is local son Giuseppe Verdi (1813–1901), who was not exactly born here—he was born in Le Roncole, a stone's throw away. However, he always considered this town his home. It's in the middle of cultivated countryside, and was known since Carolingian times as Buxetum. In 1533 it attracted the attention of Habsburg emperor Charles V, who became lord of the city. Now it attracts opera lovers who wish to walk in the grand maestro's footsteps—either by hearing one of his works at the local theater or by touring either of his country estates.

GETTING HERE AND AROUND

If you're coming by car from Parma, drive along the A1/E35 and follow signs for the A15 in the direction of Milan/La Spezia. Choose the exit in the direction of Fidenza/Salsomaggiore Terme, following signs to the SP12, which connects to the SS9W. At Fidenza, take the SS588 heading north, which will take you into Busseto. If you're without a car, you'll have to take a bus from Piacenza or Parma, as there's no train service.

VISITOR INFORMATION

CONTACT Busseto Tourism Office. ⊠ *Piazza G. Verdi 10,* ☎ *0524/92487* ⊕ *www. bussetolive.com.*

Sights

Teatro Verdi

HISTORIC SIGHT | In the center of Busseto is the lovely Teatro Verdi, dedicated, as you might expect, to the works of the hamlet's famous son. Guided tours (in both English and Italian) of the well-preserved, ornate, 19th-century-style theater are offered every half hour. Check with the Busseto tourist office for the performance schedule. ⊠ *Piazza G. Verdi 10, Busseto* ☎ *0524/92487* ⊕ *www.bussetolive.com* ✆ *Tours €5* ⊘ *Closed Mon.*

Villa Verdi

HISTORIC HOME | For Verdi lovers, Villa Verdi (also known as Villa Sant'Agata) is a veritable shrine. It's the grand country home Verdi built for himself in 1849—and the place where some of his greatest works were composed. Visits are by tour only. ⊠ *Via Verdi 31, 4 km (2½ miles) north of Busseto on SS588, toward Cremona, Sant'Agata* ☎ *0523/830000* ⊕ *www.villaverdi.info* ✆ *Tours €9* ⊘ *Closed weekdays July.*

Parma

40 km (25 miles) southeast of Busseto, 97 km (60 miles) northwest of Bologna.

Parma stands on the banks of a tributary of the Po River. Despite damage during World War II, much of the stately historic center seems untouched by modern times. This is a prosperous city, and it shows in its well-dressed residents, clean streets, and immaculate piazzas.

Bursting with gustatory delights, Parma draws crowds for its sublime cured pork product, *prosciutto crudo di Parma* (known locally simply as "prosciutto crudo"). The pale-yellow Parmigiano-Reggiano cheese produced here and in nearby Reggio Emilia is the original—and best—of a class known around the world as Parmesan.

Almost every major European power has had a hand in ruling Parma at one time or another. The Romans founded the city— then little more than a garrison on the Via Emilia—after which a succession of feudal lords held sway. In the 16th century came the ever-conniving Farnese family, which died out in 1731 on the death of Antonio Farnese. It then went to the Spanish before falling into French hands in 1796. In 1805 Marie-Louise (better known to the Parmigiani as Maria Luigia), the wife of Napoléon, took command of the city. She was a much-beloved figure in her adopted town until her death in 1847.

GETTING HERE AND AROUND

Train service, via Frecciabianca, Intercity, and Regionale trains, runs frequently from Milan and Bologna. It takes around 1¼ hours from Milan and slightly less than an hour on fast trains from Bologna. By car, Parma is just off the A1 autostrada, halfway between Bologna and Piacenza.

VISITOR INFORMATION

CONTACT Parma Tourism Office. ⊠ *Piazza Garibaldi 1,* ☎ *0521/218889* ⊕ *www.parmawelcome.it.*

Sights

Battistero (*Baptistery*)

CHURCH | Baptisms still happen (one Saturday and one Sunday a month) in this baptistery, which has a simple pink-stone Romanesque exterior and an uplifting Gothic interior. The doors are richly decorated with figures, animals, and flowers, and inside, the building is adorned with stucco figures (probably carved by Antelami) showing the months and seasons. Early-14th-century frescoes depicting scenes from the life of Christ grace the walls. ⊠ *Piazza del Duomo, Parma* ☎ *0521/208699* ⊕ *www.piazzaduomoparma.com* ✆ *€12.*

★ Camera di San Paolo

HISTORIC SIGHT | This was the reception room for the erudite abbess Giovanna da Piacenza, who hired Correggio in 1519 to provide its decoration: mythological scenes are depicted in glorious frescoes of the *Triumphs of the Goddess Diana,* the *Three Graces,* and the *Three Fates.* ✉ *Via Melloni 3, off Strada Garibaldi, near Piazza Pilotta, Parma* ☎ *0521/287195* 💳 *€6* ◷ *Closed Wed.*

Duomo

CHURCH | The magnificent 12th-century cathedral has two vigilant stone lions standing guard beside the main door; inside is some notable art in styles from medieval to Mannerist. The arch of the entrance is decorated with a delicate frieze of figures representing the months of the year, a motif repeated inside the baptistery. Some of the church's original artwork still survives, notably the simple yet evocative *Descent from the Cross,* a carving in the right transept by Benedetto Antelami (active 1178–1230), whose masterwork is this cathedral's baptistery. It's an odd juxtaposition to turn from his austere work to the exuberant fresco in the dome, the *Assumption of the Virgin* by Antonio Allegri, better known to us as Correggio (1494–1534). The fresco was not well received when it was unveiled in 1530. "A mess of frogs' legs," the bishop of Parma is said to have called it. Today Correggio is acclaimed as one of the leading masters of Mannerist painting. ■TIP→ **The fresco is best viewed when the sun is strong, as this building is not particularly well lit.** ✉ *Piazza del Duomo, Parma* ☎ *0521/208699* ⊕ *www.piazzaduomoparma.com.*

Museo del Parmigiano Reggiano

OTHER MUSEUM | **FAMILY** | The trademark crumbly cheese is the focus of this museum, which is part of the collective known as Musei del Cibo whose goal is to showcase the region's most famous foods. There's a video that demonstrates the process of making Parmigiano-Reggiano and some 120 exhibits that explore the history of the cheese. Tastings are also offered, and cheese is available to purchase. ✉ *Corte Castellazzi, Via Volta 5, Soragna* ✛ *28 km (17 miles) northwest of Parma* ☎ *340/1939057* ⊕ *www.museidelcibo.it* 💳 *€5* ◷ *Closed weekdays, and Dec. 9–Feb. 28.*

Museo del Pomodoro

OTHER MUSEUM | **FAMILY** | It's hard to imagine what Italian cuisine would be like without the New World tomato. This museum in Collecchio, part of the collective known as Musei del Cibo, explains all the mysteries. There are about a hundred exhibits explaining the history of the tomato, its farming, and its processing. If you want to book a guided tour, it's necessary to call or email *prenotazioni.pomodoro@museidelcibo.it* at least 15 days in advance. ✉ *Corte di Giarola, Strada Giarola 11, Collecchio* ✛ *12 km (7 miles) from Parma* ☎ *340/1939057* ⊕ *www.museidelcibo.it* 💳 *€5* ◷ *Closed weekdays, and Dec. 9–Feb. 28.*

Museo del Prosciutto di Parma

OTHER MUSEUM | **FAMILY** | Part of the collective known as Musei del Cibo, which works to showcase the region's most famous foods, this museum offers an in-depth look at Italy's most famous cured pork product. It offers tastings, a bit of history on prosciutto, and a tour through the process of making it. A gift shop ensures that you can take some of this marvelous product home. ■TIP→ **Call or email prenotazioni.prosciutto@museidelcibo.it at least 48 hours ahead for a guided tour in English.** ✉ *C/o Ex Foro Boario, Via Bocchialini 7, Parma* ✛ *Langhirano, 22 km (13 miles) from Parma* ☎ *340/1939057* ⊕ *www.museidelcibo.it* 💳 *€5* ◷ *Closed Dec. 9–Feb. 28.*

Museo del Salame di Felino

OTHER MUSEUM | **FAMILY** | This museum, part of the Musei del Cibo collective that works to showcase the region's most famous food, is all about cured meats.

There are tastings, a bit of history, and a tour through the process of making these specialties. Guided tours in English are available upon request. **■ TIP→ Tours must be booked at least 48 hours in advance by emailing prenotazioni.salame@museidelcibo.it.** ✉ *Strada al Castello 1, Parma* ✣ *Near Castello di Felino, 17 km (10 miles) southwest of Parma* ☎ *340/1939057* 🌐 *www.museidelcibo.it* 🎟 *€2* 🕒 *Closed weekdays and Dec. 9–Feb 28.*

★ Pilotta Museums

ART GALLERY | With one ticket, you can visit the Pilotta museums. The Galleria Nazionale contains masterpieces by Correggio, Leonardo da Vinci, and Bronzino. The Baroque Teatro Farnese, built in 1617–18, is made entirely of wood—though largely destroyed in a 1944 Allied bombing raid, it's been flawlessly restored. In the Archeological Museum see Etruscan, Roman, and Egyptian artifacts; the Palatina Library houses more than 500 religious manuscripts; and the Bodoniano museum covers printmaking. ✉ *Piazza della Pilotta 15, Parma* ☎ *0521/220400* 🌐 *www.complessopilotta.it* 🎟 *€16* 🕒 *Closed Mon.*

Piazza del Duomo

PLAZA/SQUARE | **FAMILY** | This spacious cobblestone piazza contains the cathedral and the Battistero, plus the Palazzo del Vescovado (Bishop's Palace). Behind the Duomo is the Baroque church of San Giovanni Evangelista. ✉ *Parma.*

Piazza Garibaldi

PLAZA/SQUARE | **FAMILY** | This piazza is the heart of Parma, where people gather to pass the time of day, start their *passeggiata* (constitutional), or simply hang out; the square and nearby Piazza del Duomo make up one of the loveliest historic centers in Italy. Strada Cavour, leading off the piazza, is Parma's prime shopping street. It's also crammed with wine bars teeming with locals, so it's a perfect place to stop for a snack or light lunch or a drink. ✉ *Parma.*

San Giovanni Evangelista

CHURCH | Beyond the elaborate Baroque facade of San Giovanni Evangelista, the Renaissance interior reveals several works by Correggio: *St. John the Evangelist* (in the lunette above the door in the left transept) is considered among his finest. Also in this church are works by Parmigianino (1503–40), a contemporary of Correggio's. ✉ *Piazzale San Giovanni 1, Piazza del Duomo, Parma* ☎ *0521/235311* 🌐 *www.monasterosangiovanni.com.*

Santa Maria della Steccata

CHURCH | Dating from the 16th century, this delightful church has one of Parma's most recognizable domes. In the dome's large arch there's a wonderful decorative fresco by Francesco Mazzola, better known as Parmigianino. He took so long to complete it that his patrons briefly imprisoned him for breach of contract. ✉ *Piazza Steccata 9, off Via Dante near Piazza Garibaldi, Parma* ☎ *0521/380500* 🌐 *www.diocesi.parma.it.*

🍴 Restaurants

La Filoma

$$ | **EMILIAN** | **FAMILY** | The dining room here evokes the turn of the 19th century with its high ceilings, chandeliers, and damask drapes. The food shines, from the classic *anolini in brodo di manzo e cappone* (a local variation on tortellini in brodo) to the exquisite roast veal stuffed with prosciutto and Parmigiano-Reggiano. **Known for:** excellent wine list; Parmigiana di melanzane and other options for vegetarians; regional specialties that don't break the bank. [$] *Average main: €23* ✉ *Borgo XX Marzo 15, Parma* ☎ *0521/206181* 🌐 *www.ristorantelafiloma.it* 🕒 *Closed Wed. and 10 days in July.*

★ La Forchetta

$$ | **ITALIAN** | Sicily-born Parma transplant Angelo Cammarata makes magic in his small eatery on the ground floor of a 16th-century palazzo, where the menu teems with Parma classics as

well as modern takes on Sicilian dishes. Creatures from the sea play a starring role—try the terrific starter of blanched shrimp. **Known for:** lip-smacking cannoli; great fish dishes; cozy interior. $ *Average main: €22* ✉ *Borgo San Biagio 6/D, Parma* ☎ *0521/208812* ⊕ *www.laforchettaparma.it* ⊗ *No dinner Sun. Closed Mon.*

La Greppia

$$ | **EMILIAN** | Little-known by tourists but popular with locals in the know, this small and select restaurant just down the street from Palazzo della Pilotta in the historic center offers up traditional Parmesan cooking with stylistic flourishes. The chef has a nice touch with classics like *anolini ripieni di stracotto in brodo di cappone* (dumplings stuffed with stewed meat in a capon stock) but also prepares innovative dishes. **Known for:** superb antipasti and desserts; good gluten-free choices; impeccable service. $ *Average main: €17* ✉ *Strada Garibaldi 39, Parma* ☎ *0521/233686* ⊕ *facebook.com/lagreppiaparma* ⊗ *Closed Thurs.*

Ristorante Parizzi

$$$ | **EMILIAN** | Chef-owner Marco Parizzi is the third-generation cook in this elegant restaurant, originally his grandfather's *salumeria* (delicatessen), where he now serves a mix of Parmense classics and contemporary creations. The *anolini alla parmigiana in brodo di manzo e gallina* (pasta with Parmigiano-Reggiano in broth) is a more typical dish, while the *faraona in crosta di frutta secca* (guinea fowl cooked with dried fruits and mushroom sauce) is a flight of fancy. **Known for:** affordable, well-curated wine list; inventive terra (earth) and mare (sea) tasting menus; special menu with white truffles from Alba in autumn. $ *Average main: €26* ✉ *Strada della Repubblica 71, Parma* ☎ *0521/285952* ⊕ *www.ristoranteparizzi.it* ⊗ *Closed Mon., Aug., and Jan. 8–15.*

☕ Coffee and Quick Bites

Enoteca Antica Osteria Fontana

$ | **WINE BAR** | This old-school *enoteca* (wine bar) is one of Parma's liveliest, drawing in a mix of intellectuals and gregarious twentysomethings, who often spill out onto the street, wine glasses in hand. Grab a table inside and feast on inexpensive tartines or grilled panini, whose seemingly endless options include coppa, pancetta, and Gorgonzola. **Known for:** teeming with happy locals; wide selection of wine bottles to go; culatello cured ham. $ *Average main: €9* ✉ *Strada Farini 24/a, near Piazza Garibaldi, Parma* ☎ *0521/286037* ⊗ *Closed Sun. and Mon.*

★ Tabarro

$ | **EMILIAN** | Convivial, lively, and full of locals, this favorite little wine bar on one of Parma's main drags has a couple of keg tables outside, a few stools on the ground floor, and several more small tables upstairs. The menu is based largely on cheese and pork products (equine as well: people in this part of the world like to eat horse) and is designed to pair with, and accentuate, the fine wines on offer. **Known for:** the ebullient host; delicious crostini; international wine list. $ *Average main: €12* ✉ *Strada Farini 5/b, Parma* ☎ *0521/200223* ⊕ *www.tabarro. net* ⊗ *Closed Tues. No lunch Sun.–Fri.*

Hotels

★ Palazzo dalla Rosa Prati

$$ | **HOTEL** | Marchese Vittorio dalla Rosa Prati has converted part of his family's 15th-century palace on Piazza del Duomo into luxurious, self-catering accommodations, and those with connecting rooms are ideal for families. **Pros:** spacious, well-appointed rooms with small kitchenettes; apartments perfect for families or friends traveling together; historical setting. **Cons:** books up quickly; parking can sometimes be a problem; staff leave at 8 pm. $ *Rooms from: €130* ✉ *Strada al*

Duomo 7, Parma ☎ *0521/386429* 🌐 *www.palazzodallarosaprati.it* 🛏 *19 rooms* 🍴 *No Meals.*

Parizzi Suites and Studio

$ | **B&B/INN** | A 17th-century palace has been refurbished with 21st-century amenities to provide a lovely place to rest one's head: the suites are under the same management as the Parizzi restaurant (it's a shared entrance), so you can just glide downstairs for a marvelous meal. **Pros:** central location; breakfast served in rooms; great staff. **Cons:** somewhat removed from the center of things; might be too chic for some; no parking. [$] *Rooms from: €80* ✉ *Strada della Repubblica 71, Parma* ☎ *0521/207032* 🌐 *www.parizzisuite.com* 🛏 *13 suites* 🍴 *No Meals.*

Modena

56 km (35 miles) southeast of Parma, 38 km (24 miles) northwest of Bologna.

Modena is famous for local products: Maserati, Ferrari, and opera star Luciano Pavarotti, born near here and buried in his family plot in Montale Rangone in 2007. However, it's Modena's heavenly scented balsamic vinegar, aged up to 40 years, that's probably its greatest achievement. The town has become another Emilian food mecca, with terrific restaurants and salumerie (delicatessens) at every turn. Although surrounded by modern industrial sprawl, the city's small historic center is filled with narrow medieval streets, pleasant piazzas, and typical Emilian architecture.

GETTING HERE AND AROUND

Modena, on the Bologna–Milan line, is easily accessible by train, and it's an easy walk from the station to the *centro storico*. The Intercity connection from Florence takes about 90 minutes. By car, Modena is just off the A1 autostrada.

TOURS

Consorzio Produttori Aceto Balsamico Tradizionale di Modena

FOOD AND DRINK TOURS | Connoisseurs of balsamic vinegar can arrange visits to local producers through the Consorzio. It's best to contact the organization via its website to obtain a list of producers offering tours. ✉ *Strada Vaciglio Sud 1085/1, Modena* ☎ *059/395633* 🌐 *www.balsamico.it* 🎫 *Free.*

VISITOR INFORMATION

CONTACT Modena Tourism Office. ✉ *Piazza Grande 14,* ☎ *059/2032660* 🌐 *www.visitmodena.it.*

Sights

Duomo

CHURCH | Begun by the architect Lanfredo in 1099 and consecrated in 1184, the 12th-century Romanesque cathedral has medieval sculptures depicting scenes from Genesis on the facade, but walk around to the Piazza Grande side as well to see the building's marvelous arcading. It's a rare example of a cathedral having more than one principal view. The interior, completely clad in brick, imparts a sober and beautiful feel. An elaborate gallery has scenes of the Passion of Christ carved by Anselmo da Campione and his assistants circa 1160–80. The tomb of San Geminiano is in the crypt. The white-marble bell tower is known as **La Torre Ghirlandina** (the Little Garland Tower) because of its distinctive weather vane. ✉ *Piazza Grande, Modena* ☎ *059/216078* 🌐 *www.duomodimodena.it.*

★ **Mercato Storico Albinelli**

MARKET | Locals and visitors flock to this fruit, vegetable, meat, and fish market with good reason. Ingredients are of the finest and of the freshest, and visually the place is a glorious sight to behold. A restaurant inside (outside seating when the weather agrees) serves much of

Continued on page 516

EMILIA
ONE TASTE AT A TIME

4 towns, dozens of foods, and a mouthful of flavors you'll never forget

Imagine biting into the silkiest prosciutto in the world or the most delectable homemade tortellini you've ever tasted. In Emilia, Italy's most famous food region, you'll discover simple tastes that exceed all expectations. Beginning in Parma and moving eastward to Bologna, you'll find the epicenters of such world-renowned culinary treats as *prosciutto crudo*, Parmigiano-Reggiano, *aceto balsamico*, and tortellini. The secret to this region is not the discovery of new and exotic delicacies, but rather the rediscovery of foods you thought you already knew—in much better versions than you've ever tasted before.

TASTE 1 | PROSCIUTTO CRUDO

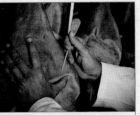
Quality testing

From Piacenza to the Adriatic, ham is the king of meats in Emilia-Romagna, but nowhere is this truer than in **Parma.**

Parma is the world's capital of *prosciutto crudo*, raw cured ham (*crudo* for short). Ask for *crudo di Parma* to signal its local provenance; many other regions also make their own crudo.

CRUDO LANGUAGE

It's easy to get confused with the terminology. Crudo is the product that Americans simply call "prosciutto" or the Brits might call "Parma ham." *Prosciutto* in Italian, however, is a more general term that means any kind of ham, including *prosciutto cotto*, or simply *cotto*, which means "cooked ham." Cotto is an excellent product and frequent pizza topping that's closer to (but much better than) what Americans would put in a deli sandwich.

Greasing the ham

Crudo is traditionally eaten in one of three ways: in a dry sandwich (*panino*); by itself as an appetizer, often with shaved butter on top; or as part of an appetizer or snack platter of assorted *salumi* (cured meats).

Fire branding

WHAT TO LOOK FOR

For the best crudo di Parma, look for slices, always cut to order, that are razor thin and have a light, rosy red color (not dark red). Don't be shy about going into a simple *salumeria* (a purveyor of cured meats) and ordering crudo by the pound. You can enjoy it straight out of the package on a park bench—and why not?

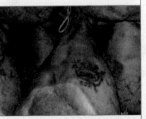
Quality trademark

BEST SPOT FOR A SAMPLE

You can't go wrong with any of Parma's famed salumerie, but **Salumeria Garibaldi** is one of the town's oldest and most reliable. You'll find not only spectacular prosciutto crudo, but also delectable cheeses, wines, porcini mushrooms, and more.

LEARN MORE

For more information on crudo di Parma, contact the **Consorzio del Prosciutto di Parma** through the tourist office, or stop by the famous store, La Prosciutteria.

A cut above

TASTE 2 | PARMIGIANO-REGGIANO

From Parma, it's only a half-hour trip east to **Reggio Emilia**, the birthplace of the crumbly and renowned Parmigiano-Reggiano cheese. Reggio (not to be confused with Reggio di Calabria in the south) is a charming little Emilian town that has been the center of production for this legendary cheese for more than 70 years.

Warming milk in copper cauldrons

SAY CHEESE

Grana is the generic Italian term for hard, aged, full-flavored cheese that can be grated. Certain varieties of Pecorino Romano, for example, or Grana Padano, also fall under this term, but Parmigiano-Reggiano, aged for as long as four years, is the foremost example.

Breaking up the curds

NOT JUST FOR GRATING

In Italy, Parmigiano-Reggiano is not only grated onto pasta, but also often served by itself in chunks, either as an appetizer—perhaps accompanied by local salumi (cured meats)—or even for dessert, when it might be drizzled with honey or Modena's balsamic vinegar.

MEET THE MAKERS

If you're a cheese enthusiast, you shouldn't miss the chance to take a free two-hour guided tour of a Parmigiano-Reggiano–producing farm. You'll witness the entire process and get to meet the cheesemakers. Tours can be arranged by contacting the **Consorzio del Formaggio Parmigiano-Reggiano** in Reggio Emilia at least 20 days in advance. (Ask specifically for an English-language tour if that's what you want.)

Placing cheese in molds

BEST SPOT FOR A SAMPLE

The production of Parmigiano-Reggiano is heavily controlled by the Consorzio del Formaggio, so you can buy the cheese at any store or supermarket in the region and be virtually guaranteed equal quality and price. For a more distinctive shopping experience, however, try buying Parmigiano-Reggiano at the street market on Reggio's central square. The market takes place on Tuesday and Friday from 8 AM to 1 PM year-round. You can pick up a small piece to eat while you're in Italy, or have larger pieces shrink-wrapped to take home.

Aging cheese wheels

Parmigiano-Reggiano

TASTE 3 | ACETO BALSAMICO DI MODENA

Modena is home to *Aceto Balsamico Tradizionale di Modena*, a kind of balsamic vinegar unparalleled anywhere else on Earth. The balsamic vinegar you've probably tried—even the pricier versions sold at specialty stores—may be good on salads, but it bears only a fleeting resemblance to the real thing.

Tasting tradizionale vinegar

HOW IS IT MADE?

The *tradizionale* vinegar that passes strict government standards is made with Trebbiano grape must, which is cooked over an open fire, reduced, and fermented from 12 to 25 or more years in a series of specially made wooden casks. As the vinegar becomes more concentrated, so much liquid evaporates that it takes more than 6 gallons of must to produce one quart of vinegar 12 years later. The result is an intense and syrupy concoction best enjoyed sparingly on grilled meats, strawberries, or Parmigiano-Reggiano cheese. The vinegar has such a complexity of flavor that some even drink it as an after-dinner liqueur.

Wooden casks for fermenting

BEST SPOT FOR A SAMPLE

The **Consorzio Produttori Aceto Balsamico Tradizionale di Modena** offers tours and tastings by reservation only. The main objective of the consortium is to monitor the quality of the authentic balsamic vinegar, made by only a few licensed restaurants and small producers.

The consortium also limits production, keeping prices sky high. Expect to pay €60 for a 100-ml (3.4 oz) bottle of tradizionale, which is generally aged 12 to 15 years, or €90 and up for the older tradizionale extra vecchio variety, which is aged 25 years.

But perhaps the best place to sample this vinegar, in its various stages and permutations, is in situ—that is, in any one of Modena's remarkable restaurants. You can have a simple trattoria meal at Ermes, whose recipes rely heavily on that liquid gold. Or you can splurge at Osteria Francescana, where three-starred Michelin chef Massimo Bottura works miracles with local ingredients.

OTHER TASTES OF EMILIA

■ **Cotechino:** a sausage made from pork and lard, a specialty of Modena

■ **Culatello de Zibello:** raw cured ham produced along the banks of the Po River, and cured and aged for more than 11 months

■ **Mortadella:** soft, smoked sausage made with beef, pork, cubes of pork fat, and seasonings, a specialty of Bologna

■ **Ragù:** a sauce made from minced pork and beef, simmered in milk, onions, carrots, and tomatoes

■ **Salama da sugo:** salty, oily sausage aged and then cooked, a specialty of Ferrara

■ **Tortelli and cappellacci:** pasta pillows with the same basic form as tortellini, but stuffed with cheese and vegetables

TASTE 4 | TORTELLINI

Simple beginnings

The venerable city of **Bologna** is called "the Fat" for a reason: this is the birthplace of tortellini, not to mention other specialties such as mortadella and ragù. Despite the city's new reputation for chic nightclubs and flashy boutiques, much of the food remains as it ever was.

You'll find the many Emilian variations on stuffed pasta all over the region, but they're perhaps at their best in Bologna, especially the native tortellini.

INSPIRED BY THE GODS

According to one legend, tortellini was inspired by the navel of Venus, goddess of love. As the story goes, Venus and some other gods stopped at a local inn for the night. A nosy chef went to their room to catch a glimpse of Venus. Peering through the keyhole, he saw her lying only partially covered on the bed. He was so inspired after seeing her perfect navel that he created a stuffed pasta, tortellini, in its image.

Stretching the dough

ON THE MENU

Tortellini is usually filled with beef (sometimes cheese), and is served two ways: *asciutta* is "dry," meaning it is served with a sauce such as ragù, or perhaps just with butter and Parmigiano. *Tortellini in brodo* is immersed in a lovely, savory beef broth.

Tortellini alla panna contains a meat filling and is sauced with cream. Aficionados, however, argue frequently about what to stuff into these little bundles, and probably no two cooks do it the same. Some purists insist that only beef will do; others mix it up with sausages, mortadella, spices, and cheese (usually Parmigiano).

Adding the filling

BEST SPOT TO BUY

Don't miss **Tamburini**, Bologna's best specialty food shop, where aromas of Emilia-Romagna's famous specialties waft out through the room and into the streets.

Shaping each piece

Tortellini di Bologna

what comes from the market. It's been around in this current incarnation since 1931, and it's pretty easy to see why. ✉ *via Luigi Albinelli 13, Modena* 🌐 *mercatoalbinelli.it* 🕓 *Closed Sun.*

Museo Enzo Ferrari

OTHER MUSEUM | FAMILY | The home of the much revered founder of the Ferrari automobile marque, Enzo Ferrari, has been imaginatively enlarged and converted into a museum dedicated to his life and work. Besides the various trophies and engines on display, visitors can view an absorbing video that tells the Ferrari story and see the restored workshop belonging to Enzo's father, Alfredo, and, in a futuristic pavilion built alongside, a grand array of contemporary and vintage cars. ■**TIP→ A joint ticket is available with the Museo Ferrari in Maranello.** ✉ *Via Paolo Ferrari 85, Modena* ☎ *059/4397979* 🌐 *www.ferrari.com* 🎫 *€17, combination ticket with Museo Ferrari in Maranello €24.*

Museo Ferrari

OTHER MUSEUM | FAMILY | This museum has become a pilgrimage site for auto enthusiasts. It takes you through the illustrious history of Ferrari, from early 1951 models to the present—the legendary F50 and cars driven by Michael Schumacher in Formula One victories being highlights. You can also take a look at the glamorous life of founder Enzo Ferrari (a re-creation of his office is on-site) and get a glance at the production process. ✉ *Via Dino Ferrari 43, Maranello* ✥ *In Maranello, 17 km (11 miles) south of Modena* ☎ *0536/949713* 🌐 *www.ferrari.com* 🎫 *€17, combination ticket with Museo Enzo Ferrari in Modena €24.*

🍴 Restaurants

Aldina

$$ | EMILIAN | On the second floor of a building across from the covered market, steps from the Piazza Grande, this simple, typical trattoria is in the very nerve center of the city. Here you'll find exemplary preparations of the region's crown jewels: tortellini in brodo, tagliatelle al ragù, and roasted meats. **Known for:** tortellini in brodo; authentically old-fashioned character; inexpensive regional food loved by locals. [$] *Average main: €20* ✉ *Via Albinelli 40, Modena* ☎ *059/236106* 🌐 *www.trattoriaaldina.it* 💳 *No credit cards* 🕓 *Closed Sun. Aug. No dinner Mon.–Thurs.*

★ Danilo

$$ | EMILIAN | Honest cooking doesn't get much better than this: host Danilo has been at the helm for decades, and oversees his restaurant with a keen eye and great spirit. The food here is local, terrific, and unpretentious. **Known for:** well-priced wine list; attentive and courteous staff; il filetto all'aceto balsamico (beef fillet with a sumptous balsamic sauce). [$] *Average main: €16* ✉ *Via Coltellini 31, Modena* ☎ *059/216691* 🌐 *www.ristorantedadanilo-modena.it* 🕓 *Closed Sun.*

★ Hosteria Giusti

$$$ | EMILIAN | In the back room of the Salumeria Giusti, established in 1605 and reportedly the world's oldest deli, you'll find just four tables in a room tastefully done with antique furnishings. You'll also find some of the best food in Emilia-Romagna—perfectly executed takes on traditional dishes such as *gnocco fritto* (fried dough) stuffed with pancetta or prosciutto, and *anolini in brodo di Cappone* (pasta in possibly the most fragrant broth in the world). **Known for:** popular and busy; cozy setting; gnocco fritto with prosciutto. [$] *Average main: €26* ✉ *Via Farini 75 and Vicolo Squallore 46, Modena* ☎ *059/222533* 🌐 *www.hosteriagiusti.it* 🕓 *Closed Sun. and Mon., Aug., and Dec. No dinner.*

★ Mon Café

$$ | ECLECTIC | Locals love this lively café because it does just about everything and does it well, beginning at 7 in the morning with excellent coffee and tasty breakfast pastries and ending long after dark with *aperitivi*, cocktails, and dinner. The fairly limited menu includes Italian tapas and starters and mains with vegetarian and fish options. **Known for:** atmospheric interior; excellent service; fresh fruit cocktails. [$] *Average main: €17* ✉ *Corso Canalchiaro 128, Modena* ☎ *059/223257* ⏲ *Closed Mon. No dinner Sun.*

★ Osteria Francescana
$$$$ | **EMILIAN** | Chef-proprietor Massimo Bottura has done stints with Adrià and Ducasse, takes inspiration from music and literature, and pours all these influences into creating some of the most memorable food in all of Italy while remaining true to his Modenese roots. The restaurant contains only 12 tables and although it's possible to order à la carte, most everyone opts for the 12-course tasting menu with the accompanying wine pairing. **Known for:** reservations required months in advance; five stages of Parmesan signature dish; a chef who makes food art. [$] *Average main: €130* ✉ *Via Stella 22, Modena* ☎ *059/223912* 🌐 *www.osteriafrancescana.it* ⏲ *Closed Sun., Mon., and 2 wks in Aug.*

☕ Coffee and Quick Bites

Archer
$ | **ITALIAN** | Bibliophile proprietor (she named her establishment after a Henry James heroine) Marina Bersani presides over this sleek wine bar. High ceilings provide plenty of places to store her vast collection of unique wines, and the short-but-sweet menu offers lots of traditional classics like *affettati misti* (sliced, cured pork products), as well as cheese plates. **Known for:** outdoor seating; crostini for snacking; unique wines. [$] *Average main: €14* ✉ *Via Cesare Battisti 54, Modena* ☎ *059/237656* ⏲ *Closed Mon. and 3 wks in Aug.*

★ Cibo Pasticceria
$ | **ITALIAN** | Just a handful of steps from Modena's beautiful cathedral, this lively place serves coffee, juices, fine wines by the glass, and lovely little sandwiches. But perhaps it's best to come here for a sweet, as they are luscious and delicious, and they're all made in-house. **Known for:** the short but well-priced wine list; their cannoli; tiny sandwiches, often on multi-grain bread. [$] *Average main: €6* ✉ *Corso Duomo 19, Modena* ☎ *059/3966345.*

🛏 Hotels

La Maison du Charme
$ | **B&B/INN** | Gracious host Maria Luisa Valentini has turned part of her family's early-20th-century villa into a charming bed-and-breakfast complete with period-appropriate furniture and bright aqua walls. **Pros:** quiet location, yet close to the center; historic ambience; intimate experience. **Cons:** steps to climb and no elevator; antique furniture not always practical or usable; books up quickly. [$] *Rooms from: €115* ✉ *Via Usiglio 12, Modena* ☎ *349/1984584* 🌐 *www.bblamaisonducharmemodena.it* 🛏 *2 suites* 🍴 *No Meals.*

Phi Hotel Canalgrande
$$ | **HOTEL** | In a calm location within easy walking distance of Modena's main tourist attractions, this hotel housed in an old palazzo has plenty of old-world character in the form of antique paintings, fancy plasterwork, and trompe l'oeil in the public rooms. **Pros:** great central position; secure garage parking; spacious gardens. **Cons:** inadequate soundproofing in some rooms; service is sometimes poor; dated in parts. [$] *Rooms from: €153* ✉ *Corso Canalgrande 6, Modena* ☎ *059/217160* 🌐 *www.hotelcanalgrandemodena.com* 🛏 *67 rooms* 🍴 *Free Breakfast.*

★ Quartopiano
$$ | **B&B/INN** | Proprietor Antonio di Resta shows his impeccable sense of style and love of all things French in a lovely little bed-and-breakfast just a few steps from the Duomo. **Pros:** intimate setup in the heart of town; owner provides helpful local advice; lovely bath products and fluffy towels. **Cons:** breakfast in a separate establishment; space a bit cramped;

with only two rooms, it books up quickly. [$] *Rooms from: €160* ✉ *Via Bonacorsa 27, Modena* ☎ *348/0189112* 🌐 *www.bbquartopiano.it* 🛏 *2 rooms* 🍴 *Free Breakfast.*

Bologna

Bologna, a city rich with cultural jewels, has long been one of the best-kept secrets in northern Italy. Tourists in the know bask in the shadow of its leaning medieval towers and devour the city's wonderful food.

The charm of the centro storico, with its red-arcaded passageways and sidewalks, can be attributed to wise city counselors who, at the beginning of the 13th century, decreed that roads couldn't be built without *portici* (porticoes). Were these counselors to return to town eight centuries later, they'd marvel at how little has changed.

Bologna, with a population of about 388,000, has a university-town vibe—and it feels young and lively in a way that many other Italian cities don't.

GETTING HERE AND AROUND

Frequent train service from Florence to Bologna makes getting here easy. The Italo and Frecciarossa and Frecciargento (high-speed trains) run several times an hour and take just under 40 minutes. Otherwise, you're left with the *regionale* (regional) trains, which putter along and get you to Bologna in around 1¾ hours. The historic center is an interesting and relatively effortless walk from the station—though it takes about 20 minutes.

If you're driving from Florence, take the A1, exiting onto the A14, and then get on the RA1 to Exit 7–Bologna Centrale. The trip takes about an hour. From Milan, take the A1, exiting to the A14 as you near the city; from there, take the A13 and exit at Bologna; then follow the RA1 to Exit 7–Bologna Centrale. The trip takes just under three hours.

VISITOR INFORMATION

CONTACTS Bologna Tourism Office ✉ *Piazza Maggiore 1/e, Bologna* ☎ *051/6583111* 🌐 *www.bolognawelcome.com*

Sights

Piazza Maggiore and the adjacent Piazza del Nettuno are the historic centers of the city. Arranged around these two squares are the imposing Basilica di San Petronio, the massive Palazzo Comunale, the Palazzo del Podestà, the Palazzo Re Enzo, and the Fontana del Nettuno—one of the most visually harmonious groupings of public buildings in the country. From here, sights that aren't on one of the piazzas are but a short walk away, along delightful narrow cobblestone streets or under the ubiquitous arcades that double as municipal umbrellas. Take at least a full day to explore Bologna; it's compact and lends itself to easy exploration, but there's plenty to see.

■ TIP→ **The first Sunday of the month is free at many museums.**

Basilica di San Petronio

CHURCH | Construction on this vast cathedral began in 1390; and the work, as you can see, still isn't finished more than 600 years later. The wings of the transept are missing and the facade is only partially decorated, lacking most of the marble that was intended to adorn it. The main doorway was carved in 1425 by the great Sienese master Jacopo della Quercia. Above the center of the door is a Madonna and Child flanked by Saints Ambrose and Petronius, the city's patrons. Michelangelo, Giulio Romano, and Andrea Palladio (among others), submitted designs for the facade, which were all eventually rejected.

The Bolognesi had planned an even bigger church—you can see the columns erected to support the larger version outside the east end—but had to tone down construction when the university seat was established next door in 1561. The Museo di San Petronio contains models showing how it was originally supposed to look. The most important art in the church is in the fourth chapel on the left: these frescoes by Giovanni di Modena date to 1410–15. ⊠ *Piazza Maggiore* ☎ *051/231415* ⊕ *www.basilicadisanpetronio.org* ✉ *Free* ⊘ *Museo di San Petronio closed Mon.*

Fontana del Nettuno

FOUNTAIN | Sculptor Giambologna's elaborate 1563–66 Baroque fountain and monument to Neptune occupying Piazza Nettuno has been aptly nicknamed "Il Gigante" (The Giant). Its exuberantly sensual mermaids and undraped god of the sea drew fire when it was constructed—but not enough, apparently, to dissuade the populace from using the fountain as a public washing stall for centuries. ⊠ *Piazza del Nettuno, next to Palazzo Re Enzo, Piazza Maggiore.*

Le Due Torri

NOTABLE BUILDING | FAMILY | Two landmark medieval towers, mentioned by Dante in *The Inferno,* stand side by side in the compact Piazza di Porta Ravegnana. Once, every family of importance had a tower as a symbol of prestige and power (and as a potential fortress). Now only 24 remain out of nearly 100 that once presided over the city. Torre Garisenda (late 11th century), which tilts 10 feet off perpendicular, was shortened to 157 feet in the 1300s and is now closed to visitors. Torre degli Asinelli (1119) is 318 feet tall and leans 7½ feet. If you're up to a serious physical challenge—and not claustrophobic—you may want to climb its 498 narrow, wooden steps to get the view over Bologna. ⊠ *Piazza di Porta Ravegnana, East of Piazza Maggiore* ⊕ *www.duetorribologna.com* ✉ *€5* ♿ *Reservations essential.*

MAMbo

ART MUSEUM | The museum—the name stands for Museo d'Arte Moderna di Bologna, or Bologna's Museum of Modern Art—houses a permanent collection of modern art (defined as post–World War II until five minutes ago) and stages a revolving series of temporary exhibitions by cutting-edge artists. All of this is set within a remarkable space: you might have a hard time telling that the sleek minimalist structure was built in 1915 as the Forno del Pane, a large bakery that made bread for city residents. A bookshop and a restaurant complete the complex, the latter offering Sunday brunch and delicious aperitivi. ⊠ *Via Don Minzoni 14, Bologna* ☎ *051/6496611* ⊕ *www.mambo-bologna.org* ✉ *€6* ⊘ *Closed Mon.*

Museo Internazionale e Biblioteca della Musica di Bologna

OTHER MUSEUM | The music museum in the spectacular Palazzo Aldini-Sanguineti, with its 17th- and 18th-century frescoes, offers among its exhibits a 1606 harpsichord and a collection of beautiful music manuscripts dating from the 1500s. ⊠ *Strada Maggiore 34, University area* ☎ *051/2757711* ⊕ *www.museibologna.it* ✉ *€5* ⊘ *Closed Mon.*

Palazzo Comunale

GOVERNMENT BUILDING | When Bologna was an independent city-state, this huge palace dating from the 13th to 15th century was the seat of government—a function it still serves today in a building that is a mélange of styles. Over the door is a statue of Bologna-born Pope Gregory XIII (reigned 1572–85), most famous for reorganizing the calendar. There are good views from the upper stories. The first-floor Sala Rossa (Red Room) and the Sala del Consiglio Comunale (City Council Hall) are open with advance request and during some exhibitions. Within the palazzo are two museums. The Collezioni Comunali d'Arte exhibits medieval paintings as well as some Renaissance works by Luca Signorelli (circa 1445–1523) and Tintoretto (1518–94). Underground caves and the foundations of the old cathedral can be visited by appointment; contact the tourist office. The old stock exchange, part of the Palazzo Comunale, which you

11

Emilia-Romagna BOLOGNA

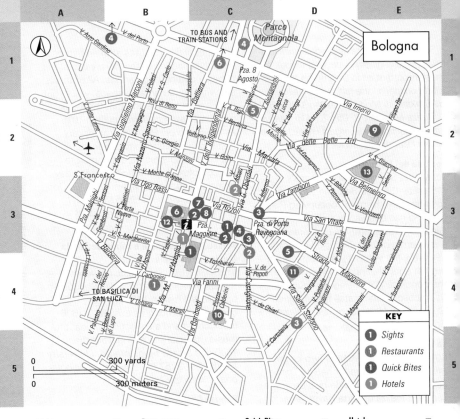

Bologna

Sights ▼

1 Basilica di
  San Petronio **B3**
2 Fontana del Nettuno..... **C3**
3 Le Due Torri.............. **C3**
4 MAMbo **B1**
5 Museo Internazionale
  e Biblioteca della
  Musica di Bologna **D4**
6 Palazzo Comunale **B3**
7 Palazzo del Podestà..... **C3**
8 Palazzo Re Enzo.......... **C3**
9 Pinacoteca Nazionale... **E2**
10 San Domenico **C4**
11 Santo Stefano **D4**
12 Torre dell'Orologio
   (Clock Tower)............ **B3**
13 Università di Bologna ... **E2**

Restaurants ▼

1 Da Cesari **B4**
2 Da Gianni a la Vecia
  Bulagna................... **C3**
3 Drogheria della Rosa... **D4**
4 Ristorante I Portici....... **C1**
5 Trattoria del Rosso....... **C2**
6 Trattoria di Via Serra **C1**

Quick Bites ▼

1 Eataly..................... **C3**
2 Mercato di Mezzo **C3**
3 Sfoglia Rina.............. **C3**
4 Tamburini **C3**

Hotels ▼

1 Art Hotel Orologio **B3**
2 Hotel Corona D'Oro...... **C3**

enter from Piazza Nettuno, has been turned into a library. Dubbed the Sala Borsa, it has an impressive interior courtyard. ⌧ *Piazza Maggiore 6, Piazza Maggiore* ☎ *051/2193998 Collezioni Comunali d'Arte, 051/2194400 Sala Borsa* ⊕ *www.museibologna.it* ⌧ *Collezioni Comunali d'Arte €6; Sala Borsa free* ⊗ *Collezioni Comunali d'Arte closed Mon.; Sala Borsa closed Sun.*

Palazzo del Podestà

NOTABLE BUILDING | This classic Renaissance palace facing the Basilica di San Petronio was erected from 1484–94, and attached to it is the soaring Torre dell'Arengo. The bells in the tower have rung whenever the city has celebrated, mourned, or called its citizens to arms. It's not open to the public. ⌧ *Piazza Maggiore 1, Piazza Maggiore.*

Palazzo Re Enzo

CASTLE/PALACE | Built in 1244, this palace became home to King Enzo of Sardinia, who was imprisoned here in 1249 after he was captured during the fierce battle of Fossalta. He died here 23 years later. The palace has other macabre associations as well: common criminals received last rites in the tiny courtyard chapel before being executed in Piazza Maggiore. The courtyard is worth a peek, but the palace merely houses government offices as well as special events. ⌧ *Piazza del Nettuno 1/c, Piazza Maggiore* ☎ *051/6583121.*

Pinacoteca Nazionale

ART GALLERY | Bologna's principal art gallery contains many works by the immortals of Italian painting; its prize possession is the *Ecstasy of St. Cecilia* by Raphael (1483–1520). There's also a beautiful polyptych by Giotto (1267–1337), as well as *Madonna with Child and Saints Margaret, Jerome, and Petronius* (altarpiece of St. Margaret) by Parmigianino (1503–40); note the rapt eye contact between St. Margaret and the Christ child. ⌧ *Via delle Belle Arti 56, University area* ☎ *051/4209411* ⊕ *www.pinacotecabologna.beniculturali.it* ⌧ *€6* ⊗ *Closed Mon.*

San Domenico

CHURCH | The tomb of St. Dominic, who died here in 1221, is called the **Arca di San Domenico,** and is found in this church in the sixth chapel on the right. Many artists participated in its decoration, notably Niccolò di Bari, who was so proud of his 15th-century contribution that he changed his name to Niccolò dell'Arca to recall this famous work. The young Michelangelo (1475–1564) carved the angel on the right and the image of San Petronio. In the right transept of the church is a tablet marking the last resting place of hapless King Enzo, the Sardinian ruler imprisoned in the Palazzo Re Enzo. The attached museum contains religious relics. ⌧ *Piazza San Domenico 13, off Via Garibaldi, South of Piazza Maggiore* ☎ *051/6400411* ⊕ *www.sandomenicobologna.it.*

★ Santo Stefano

CHURCH | This splendid and unusual basilica contains between four and seven connected churches (authorities differ). A 4th-century temple dedicated to Isis originally occupied this site, but much of what you see was erected between the 10th and 12th centuries. The oldest existing building is **Santi Vitale e Agricola,** parts of which date from the 5th century. The exquisite beehive-shape San Sepolcro contains a Nativity scene much loved by Bologna's children, who come at Christmastime to pay their respects to the Christ child. Just outside the church, which probably dates from the 5th century (with later alterations), is the **Cortile di Pilato** (Pilate's Courtyard), named for the basin in the center. Despite the fact that the basin was probably crafted around the 8th century, legend has it that Pontius Pilate washed his hands in it after condemning Christ. Also in the building are a museum displaying various medieval religious works and its shop, which sells honey, shampoos, and jams made by the monks. ✉ *Piazza Santo Stefano, Via Santo Stefano 24, University area* ☎ *320/9065699* 🌐 *www.santostefanobologna.it* 🕓 *Closed during services.*

Torre dell'Orologio (Clock Tower)

CLOCK | For a spectacular view of Piazza Maggiore and the Bolognesi hills from two terraces as well as a look at how Bologna's oldest clock keeps the city punctual, climb the Torre dell'Orologio, or d'Arccursio tower. Opened to the public in 2021, it was built in 1249 as University of Bologna law professor Accursio da Bagnolo's monumental timepiece for his home in the piazza. The clock mechanism you'll see dates from 1773, as found on the horologist's inscription "Rinaldo Gandofli Accademic Clementi Fece 1773," among the clock's movement, gears, and swinging pendulum. ✉ *Piazza Maggiore 6, Bologna* ☎ *051/6583111* 🌐 *www.bolognawelcome.com* 🎟 *€8* 🕓 *Closed Mon.* ✍ *Reservations required.*

Università di Bologna

COLLEGE | Take a stroll through the streets of the university area: a jumble of buildings, some dating as far back as the 15th century and most to the 17th and 18th. The neighborhood, as befits a college town, is full of bookshops, coffee bars, and inexpensive restaurants. Though not particularly distinguished, they're characteristic of student life in the city. Try eating at the *mensa universitaria* (cafeteria) if you want to strike up a conversation with local students (most speak English). Political slogans and sentiments are scrawled on walls all around the university and tend to be ferociously leftist, sometimes juvenile, and often entertaining. Among the university museums, the most interesting is the **Museo di Palazzo Poggi,** which displays scientific instruments plus paleontological, botanical, and university-related artifacts. ✉ *Via Zamboni 33, University area* ☎ *051/2099610 museum* 🌐 *www.museopalazzopoggi.unibo.it* 🎟 *€5 museum* 🕓 *Closed Mon.*

🍴 Restaurants

★ Da Cesari

$$ | **EMILIAN** | Host Paolino Cesari has been presiding over his eatery since 1962, and he and his staff go out of their way to make you feel at home. The food's terrific, and if you love pork products, try anything on the menu with *mora romagnola:* Paolino has direct contact with the people who raise this breed that nearly became extinct (he calls it "my pig"). **Known for:** traditional setting; wine list with lots of local bottles; pork dishes like flavorful salame. [$] *Average main: €18* ✉ *Via de' Carbonesi 8, South of Piazza Maggiore* ☎ *051/237710* 🌐 *www.da-cesari.it* 🕓 *Closed Sun., Aug., and 1 wk in Jan.*

★ Da Gianni a la Vecia Bulagna

$$ | **EMILIAN** | At the bottom of an alley off Piazza Maggiore, this unassuming place—known to locals as simply "Da Gianni"—is all about food. The usual starters are on hand—including a tasty tortellini in brodo—in addition to daily specials; bollito misto (mixed boiled meat) is a fine option here, and the cotechino *con puré di patate* (pork sausage with mashed potatoes) is elevated to sublimity by the accompanying salsa verde. **Known for:** busy local spot; efficient and friendly service; tortellini in brodo. [$] *Average main: €20* ✉ *Via Clavature 18, Piazza Maggiore* ☎ *051/229434* 🌐 *www.trattoria-gianni.it* 🕓 *Closed Mon. and 1 wk early Jan. No dinner Sun.*

Drogheria della Rosa

$$ | **EMILIAN** | Chef Emanuele Addone, who presides over his intimate little restaurant set in an ex-pharmacy, hits the food markets every day and buys what looks good, ensuring seasonality. He sauces his tortelli stuffed with *squacquerone* and *stracchino* (two creamy, fresh cow's-milk cheeses) with artichokes, zucchini flowers, or mushrooms, depending on the time of year. **Known for:** no written menu; seasonal filled tortelli; idiosyncratic surroundings. [$] *Average*

main: €18 ✉ *Via Cartoleria 10, University area* ☎ *051/222529* ⊕ *www.drogheriadellarosa.it* ⊘ *No dinner Sun. Closed Mon.*

Ristorante I Portici

$$$$ | EMILIAN | The frescoed ceiling, parquet flooring, and live classical music are clues that this sophisticated restaurant (part of the hotel of the same name) occupies a former theater and *café-chantant,* or musical venue, from the late 19th century. It's the perfect setting for an evening of fine dining featuring mainly Emilian-inspired dishes with modern touches and the vision of the young, award-winning chef Gianluca Renzi. **Known for:** refined and attentive service; sophisticated culinary offerings; sumptuous surroundings in a former theater. $ *Average main: €46* ✉ *Via dell'Indipendenza 69, North of Piazza Maggiore* ☎ *051/42185* ⊕ *www.iporticihotel.com* ⊘ *Closed Sun. and Mon. No lunch.*

Trattoria del Rosso

$ | EMILIAN | Here, in the mirrored interior, a mostly young crowd chows down on classic regional fare at affordable prices. Nimble staff bearing multiple plates sashay neatly between the closely spaced tables delivering such standards as tortellini in brodo and *cotoletta alla Bolognese* (veal with Parmigiano-Reggiano and prosciutto). **Known for:** fun atmosphere; affordable wine list; student haunt with great-value regional food. $ *Average main: €13* ✉ *Via Augusto Righi 30/A, University area* ☎ *051/236730* ⊘ *No dinner Sun.*

Trattoria di Via Serra

$$ | EMILIAN | At this simple trattoria off the main tourist circuit, much care has been taken with the decor: the rooms, overseen by host Flavio, are small and intimate, and the wooden walls painted a creamy whitish gray. Chef Tommaso gives equal care to the menu and deftly turns out Bolognese classics, as well as dishes with a modern twist—among the antipasti, his *tosone fresco avvolto nella pancetta* incorporates

Parmigiano-Reggiano, unsmoked bacon, and greens. **Known for:** convivial atmosphere; modern riffs on classic dishes; all locally sourced ingredients. $ *Average main: €18* ✉ *Via Serra 9B, Beyond the City Center* ☎ *051/6312330* ⊕ *www.trattoriadiviaserra.it* ⊘ *Closed Sun., Mon., and Aug.*

☕ Coffee and Quick Bites

Eataly

$ | ITALIAN | At this lively shop—the original location in the now international Italian cuisine empire—with an attached bookstore, you can grab a bite to eat or have a glass of wine while stocking up on high-quality olive oil, vinegar, cured meats, and artisanal pasta. On the top floor, you can have a full-fledged trattoria meal, but what you can't have is anything decaffeinated. **Known for:** adherence to top-notch ingredients; reliance on local producers as much as possible; its lively atmosphere and marvelous staff. $ *Average main: €10* ✉ *Via degli Orefici 19, Piazza Maggiore* ☎ *051/0952820* ⊕ *www.eataly.net.*

Mercato di Mezzo

$ | ITALIAN | FAMILY | This former fruit and vegetable market has morphed into a food hall. Various stalls offer the best that Bologna has to offer, and the Bolognesi are gobbling it up (as are visitors). **Known for:** great wines by the glass; full of locals; its pork products. $ *Average main: €13* ✉ *Via Clavature 12, Piazza Maggiore* ☎ *379/1855172* ⊘ *Closed Mon.*

Sfoglia Rina

$ | ITALIAN | FAMILY | The *pastaio* (pasta-maker) tradition in this bright honeycomb tiled pasta shop and restaurant—which often has a line around the block—started nearly 60 years ago in a town about 9½ km (6 miles) southwest of Bologna. There, Rina De Franceschi rolled *sfoglia* (dough) following family recipes. **Known for:** affordable and wide-ranging menu; weekly vegetarian-friendly specials; fresh pasta in many varieties. $ *Average main: €11* ✉ *Via Castiglione 5/b, Bologna* ☎ *051/9911710* ⊕ *www.sfogliarina.it.*

★ Tamburini

$ | **WINE BAR** | Two small rooms inside plus kegs and bar stools outside make up this lively, packed little spot. The overwhelming plate of *affettati misti* is crammed with top-quality local cured meats and succulent cheeses, and the adjacent salumeria offers many wonderful items to take away. **Known for:** lively atmosphere with a vast wine selection; abundant portions; cheese and cured meat plates. $ *Average main: €12* ✉ *Via Caprarie 1, Piazza Maggiore* ☎ *051/234726* ⊕ *www.tamburini.com.*

Hotels

★ Art Hotel Orologio

$$ | **HOTEL** | **FAMILY** | The location of this stylish and welcoming family-run hotel can't be beat: it's right around the corner from Piazza Maggiore on a quiet piazza. **Pros:** central location; welcomes all animals; family-friendly rooms. **Cons:** limited facilities; pet-friendly environment may not appeal to allergy sufferers; some street noise. $ *Rooms from: €129* ✉ *Via IV Novembre 10, Piazza Maggiore* ☎ *051/7457411* ⊕ *www.art-hotel-orologio.com* ⇨ *34 rooms* ◎ *Free Breakfast.*

Hotel Corona D'Oro

$$$$ | **HOTEL** | Elegance and historic charm are the keynotes of this central lodging, converted from a medieval palazzo and just a short stroll from Piazza Maggiore and all the main attractions. **Pros:** helpful, friendly staff; historic character; spacious and silent rooms. **Cons:** some rooms are small; no restaurant; steps on some floors are not ideal for anyone with mobility issues. $ *Rooms from: €319* ✉ *Via Oberdan 12, Bologna* ☎ *051/7457611* ⊕ *www.hco.it* ⇨ *40 rooms* ◎ *Free Breakfast.*

▼ Nightlife

As a university town, Bologna has long been known for its busy nightlife. By as early as 1300, it was said to have 150 taverns, and most of the city's current 200-plus pubs and bars are frequented by students and young adults—with the university area forming the hub. The pedestrian zone on Via del Pratello, lined with plenty of bars, also has a hopping nightlife scene, as does Via delle Moline, with its cutting-edge cafés and bars. A more upscale, low-key evening experience can be had at one of Bologna's many wine bars, where the *apericena* (snack accompaniments) are often substantial enough to constitute dinner.

BARS

Bar Calice

BARS | A year-round indoor-outdoor operation (with heat lamps), this bar is extremely popular with thirtysomethings, sometimes pushing baby carriages. Its large menu includes raw oysters. There's also a dining room upstairs. ✉ *Via Clavature 13, at Via Marchesana, Piazza Maggiore* ☎ *051/236523.*

Le Stanze

BARS | At Le Stanze you can sip an aperitivo or a late-night drink amid a young and noisy clientele. The decor includes 17th-century frescoes in what was once the private chapel of the Palazzo Bentivoglio. The adjoining restaurant offers a small selection of Bologna favorites. ✉ *Via del Borgo di San Pietro 1, University area* ☎ *051/228767* ⊕ *www.lestanze-cafe.it.*

★ Nu Lounge Bar

BARS | This high-energy tiki bar draws a cocktail-loving crowd that enjoys fun drinks such as "Hellvis," made with lime, agave syrup, rum, grenadine, ginger, and Angostura. ✉ *Via de' Musei 6, off Buca San Petronio, Piazza Maggiore* ☎ *051/222532* ⊕ *www.nuloungebar.com.*

★ Osteria del Sole

WINE BARS | Although "osteria" in an establishment's name suggests that food will be served, such is not the case here. This place is all about drinking wine; the entrance door has warnings such as "He who doesn't drink will please stay outside." It's been around since 1465, and locals pack in, bearing food from outside to accompany the wine. ✉ *Vicolo Ranocchi 1/d, Piazza Maggiore* ☎ *347/9680171* ⊕ *www.osteriadelsole.it.*

CAFÉS

★ Zanarini

CAFÉS | Chic Bolognesi congregate at this bar that serves coffee in the morning and swank aperitivi in the evening. Tasty sandwiches and pastries are also available. ✉ *Piazza Galvani 1, Piazza Maggiore* ☎ *051/2750041.*

MUSIC VENUES

Cantina Bentivoglio

LIVE MUSIC | With live music including jazz staged nearly every evening, Cantina Bentivoglio is one of Bologna's most renowned nightspots. You can enjoy light and more substantial meals here as well. ✉ *Via Mascarella 4/B, University area* ☎ *051/265416* ⊕ *www.cantinabentivoglio.it.*

Osteria Buca delle Campane

LIVE MUSIC | In a 13th-century building, this underground tavern has good, inexpensive food, and the after-dinner scene is popular with locals, including students, who come to listen to the live music on weekends and some other nights. The kitchen stays open until long past midnight. Reservations are strongly advised. ✉ *Via Benedetto XIV 4, University area* ☎ *051/220918* ⊕ *www.bucadellecampane.it.*

🎭 Performing Arts

MUSIC AND OPERA

Teatro Comunale

MUSIC | This 18th-century theater presents concerts by Italian and international orchestras throughout the year, but the highly acclaimed opera performances from January to July and October to December are the main attraction. Reserve seats for those performances well in advance. ✉ *Largo Respighi 1, University area* ☎ *051/529019* ⊕ *www.tcbo.it.*

🛍 Shopping

CLOTHING

Castel Guelfo The Style Outlets

OUTLET | If you don't feel like paying Galleria Cavour prices, this mall is about 20 minutes outside Bologna. It includes more than 50 stores, among them such top brands as Swarovski. ✉ *Via del Commercio 4/2, Loc. Poggio Piccolo, Castel Guelfo* ⊹ *Take the A14 toward Imola, Castel San Pietro Terme exit; 980 feet after tollbooth, turn right onto Via San Carlo* ☎ *0542/670765* ⊕ *www.thestyleoutlets.it.*

Galleria Cavour

MALL | One of the most upscale malls in Italy, the Galleria houses many of the fashion giants, including Armani, Gucci, Saint Laurent, and Tod's. ✉ *Via Luigi Carlo Farini, South of Piazza Maggiore* ⊕ *www.galleriacavour.it.*

WINE AND FOOD

Bologna is a good place to buy wine. Several shops have a bewilderingly large selection—to go straight to the top, ask the managers which wines have won the prestigious Tre Bicchieri (Three Glasses) award from Gambero Rosso's wine bible, *Vini d'Italia.*

Enoteca Italiana

WINE/SPIRITS | Consistently recognized as one of the best wine stores in the country, Enoteca Italiana lives up to its reputation—as it says, "every good bottle has a good story"—with shelves lined with excellent selections from all over Italy at reasonable prices. In addition, the delicious plates of cured meats served with wines by the glass, make a great light lunch. ✉ *Via Marsala 2/b, North of*

Piazza Maggiore ☎ 051/235989 ⊕ www.
enotecaitaliana.it.

La Baita Vecchia Malga

FOOD | Fresh tagliolini, tortellini, and other
Bolognese pasta delicacies are sold here,
along with sublime food to eat at small
tables here or take away. The cheese
counter is laden with superlative local
specimens. ⊠ Via Pescherie Vecchie 3/a,
Piazza Maggiore ☎ 051/223940 ⊕ www.
vecchiamalganegozi.com.

Majani

CANDY | Classy Majani has been produc-
ing chocolate since 1796. Its staying
power may be attributed to high-quality
confections that are as pretty to look at
as they are to eat. ⊠ Via de' Carbonesi 5,
Piazza Maggiore ☎ 051/234302 ⊕ www.
majani.it.

Mercato delle Erbe

FOOD | This food market and food hall
that opened in 1910 bustles year-round.
⊠ Via Ugo Bassi 23, Piazza Maggiore
☎ 335/4112427 ⊕ www.mercatodelleer-
be.it.

Paolo Atti & Figli

FOOD | This place has been producing
some of Bologna's finest pastas, cakes,
and other delicacies since 1868. There's
a second branch at Via Drapperie 6.
⊠ Via Caprarie 7, Piazza Maggiore
☎ 051/220425 ⊕ www.paoloatti.com.

★ Roccati

CANDY | Sculptural works of chocolate,
as well as basic bonbons and simpler
sweets, have been crafted here since
1909. ⊠ Via Clavature 17/a, Piazza Maggiore ☎ 051/261964 ⊕ www.roccaticioc-
colato.com.

Ferrara

47 km (29 miles) northeast of Bologna,
74 km (46 miles) northwest of Ravenna.

When the legendary Ferrarese filmmak-
er Michelangelo Antonioni called his
beloved hometown "a city that you can
see only partly, while the rest disap-
pears to be imagined," perhaps he was
referring to the low-lying mist that rolls in
off the Adriatic each winter and shrouds
Ferrara's winding knot of medieval
alleyways, turreted palaces, and ancient
wine bars—once frequented by the likes
of Copernicus—in a ghostly fog. But perhaps Antonioni was also suggesting that
Ferrara's striking beauty often conceals a
dark and tortured past.

Today you're likely to be charmed by
Ferrara's prosperous air and meticulous
cleanliness, its excellent restaurants and
chic bars (for coffee and any other liquid
refreshment), and its lively wine-bar
scene. You'll find aficionados gathering
outside any of the wine bars near the
Duomo even on the foggiest of week-
nights. Although Ferrara is a UNESCO
World Heritage site, the city draws
amazingly few tourists—which only adds
to its appeal.

GETTING HERE AND AROUND

Train service is frequent from Bologna (usually three trains per hour) and
takes either a half hour or 50 minutes,
depending on which train type you take.
It's around 35 minutes from Florence
to Bologna, and then about a half hour
from Bologna to Ferrara. The walk from
the station is easy (about 20 minutes)
and not particularly interesting. You can
also take Bus No. 1, No. 6, No. 9, or No.
11 from the station to the center; buy
your ticket at the newsagent inside and
remember to stamp your ticket upon
boarding the bus.

If you're driving from Bologna, take the
RA1 out of town, then the A13 in the
direction of Padua, exiting at Ferrara
Nord. Follow the SP19 directly into the
center of town. The trip should take
about 45 minutes.

VISITOR INFORMATION

CONTACT Ferrara Tourism Office. ⊠ *Piazza Castello,* ☎ *0532/209370* ⊕ *www.ferrarainfo.com.*

 Sights

Casa Romei

CASTLE/PALACE | Built by the wealthy banker Giovanni Romei (1402–83), this vast structure with a graceful courtyard ranks among Ferrara's loveliest Renaissance palaces. Mid-15th-century frescoes adorn rooms on the ground floor; the piano nobile contains detached frescoes from local churches as well as lesser-known Renaissance sculptures. The Sala delle Sibille has a very large 15th-century fireplace and beautiful coffered wood ceilings. ⊠ *Via Savonarola 30, Ferrara* ☎ *0532/234130* ⊕ *www.ferraraterraeacqua.it* ⌖ *€5.*

★ Castello Estense

CASTLE/PALACE | The former seat of Este power, this massive castle dominates the center of town, a suitable symbol for the ruling family: cold and menacing on the outside, lavishly decorated within. The public rooms are grand, but deep in the bowels of the castle are dungeons where enemies of the state were held in wretched conditions. The prisons of Don Giulio, Ugo, and Parisina have some fascinating features, like 15th-century graffiti. Lovers Ugo and Parisina (stepmother and stepson) were beheaded in 1425 because Ugo's father, Niccolò III, didn't like the fact that his son was cavorting with his stepmother.

The castle was established as a fortress in 1385, but work on its luxurious ducal quarters continued into the 16th century. Representative of Este grandeur are the Sala dei Giochi, painted with athletic scenes, and the Sala dell'Aurora, decorated to show the times of the day. The terraces of the castle and the hanging garden have fine views of the town and countryside. You can traverse the castle's drawbridge and wander through many of its arcaded passages whenever the castle gates are open. ⊠ *Piazza Castello, Ferrara* ☎ *0532/419180* ⊕ *www.castelloestense.it* ⌖ *€12* ⊗ *Closed Tues.*

Duomo

CHURCH | The magnificent Gothic cathedral, a few steps from the Castello Estense, has a three-tier facade of slender arches and beautiful sculptures over the central door. Work began in 1135 and took more than 100 years to complete. The interior was completely remodeled in the 17th century. At this writing, the facade is scaffolded and the interior closed as part of a major restoration. ⊠ *Piazza della Cattedrale, Ferrara* ☎ *0532/207449* ⊕ *www.cattedralediferrara.it.*

Museo della Cattedrale

ART MUSEUM | Some of the original decorations of the town's main church, the former church, and the cloister of San Romano reside in the Museo della Cattedrale, across the piazza from the Duomo. Inside you'll find 22 codices commissioned between 1477 and 1535; early-13th-century sculptures by the Maestro dei Mesi; a mammoth oil on canvas by Cosmè Tura from 1469; and an exquisite Jacopo della Quercia, the *Madonna della Melagrana*. Although this last work dates from 1403 to 1408, the playful expression on the Christ child seems very 21st century. ⊠ *Via San Romano 1, Ferrara* ☎ *0532/761299* ⊕ *www.artecultura.fe.it* ⌖ *€6* ⊗ *Closed Mon.*

Museo Nazionale dell'Ebraismo Italiano e della Shoah (*Museum of Italian Judaism and the Shoah*)

OTHER MUSEUM | The collection of ornate religious objects and multimedia installations at this museum (commonly known as MEIS) bears witness to the long history of the city's Jewish community. This history had its high points—1492, for example, when Ercole I invited the Jews to come over from Spain—and its lows, notably 1627, when Jews were enclosed within the ghetto, where they were forced to live until the advent of a united Italy in 1860. The triangular warren of narrow cobbled streets that made up the ghetto originally extended as far as Corso Giovecca (originally Corso Giudecca, or Ghetto Street). When it was enclosed, the neighborhood was restricted to the area between Via Scienze, Via Contrari, and Via di San Romano. The museum is located about a 15-minute walk from the former Jewish ghetto. Guided tours may be booked in advance by emailing or calling the museum. ✉ *Via Piangipane 81, Ferrara* ☎ *0532/769137* 🌐 *www.meisweb.it* 🎫 *€11* 🕒 *Closed Mon.*

Palazzina di Marfisa d'Este

CASTLE/PALACE | On the busy Corso Giovecca, this grandiose 16th-century palace belonged to a great patron of the arts. It has painted ceilings, fine 16th-century furniture, and a garden containing a grotto and an outdoor theater. ✉ *Corso Giovecca 170, Ferrara* ☎ *0532/244949* 🌐 *www.artecultura.fe.it* 🎫 *€4* 🕒 *Closed Mon.*

Palazzo dei Diamanti (*Palace of Diamonds*)

ART MUSEUM | Named for the 8,500 small pink-and-white marble pyramids (or "diamonds") that stud its facade, this building was designed to be viewed in perspective—both faces at once—from diagonally across the street. Work began in the 1490s and finished around 1504. Inside the palazzo is the Pinacoteca Nazionale and Modern and Contemporary Art Gallery, which host temporary exhibits. ✉ *Corso Ercole I d'Este 21, Ferrara* ☎ *0532/244949* 🌐 *www.palazzodiamanti.it* 🎫 *€6* 🕒 *Closed Mon.*

★ **Palazzo Schifanoia**

HISTORIC SIGHT | The oldest, most characteristic area of Ferrara is south of the Duomo, stretching between the Corso Giovecca and the city's ramparts. Here various members of the Este family built pleasure palaces, the best known of which is the Palazzo Schifanoia (*schifanoia* means "carefree" or, literally, "fleeing boredom"). Begun in the late 14th century, the palace was remodeled between 1464 and 1469. Inside is Museo Schifanoia, with its lavish interior—particularly the Salone dei Mesi, which contains an extravagant series of frescoes showing the months of the year and their mythological attributes. ✉ *Via Scandiana 23, Ferrara* ☎ *0532/244949* 🌐 *www.artecultura.fe.it* 🎫 *€12* 🕒 *Closed Mon.*

Via delle Volte

STREET | One of the best-preserved medieval streets in Europe, the Via delle Volte clearly evokes Ferrara's past. The series of ancient *volte* (arches) along the narrow cobblestone alley once joined the merchants' houses on the south side of the street to their warehouses on the north side. The street ran parallel to the banks of the Po River, which was home to Ferrara's busy port. ✉ *Ferrara.*

🍴 Restaurants

★ **Enoteca al Brindisi**

$ | WINE BAR | Ferrara is a city of wine bars, beginning with this one (allegedly Europe's oldest), which opened in 1435—Copernicus drank here while a student in the late 1400s, and the place still has an undergraduate aura. The twentysomething staff pours well-chosen wines by the glass, and they serve cappellacci di zucca (pasta stuffed with squash) with two different sauces (ragù or butter and sage). **Known for:** full of locals, students, and visitors; marvelous salads; set menus at great prices. [$] *Average main: €12* ✉ *Via Adelardi 11, Ferrara* ☎ *0532/473744* 🌐 *www.albrindisi.net* 🕒 *Closed Mon. and 1 wk late Jan.*

Il Mandolino

$$ | EMILIAN | At this idiosyncratic trattoria on the historic Via delle Volte try tearing your attention away from the countless paintings, photographs, and musical instruments that cover the walls, and instead focusing on the excellent fare on offer. Typical dishes include the classic *cappellacci di zucca* (pasta stuffed with squash in a meat sauce), and the lasagna may be one of the best you'll ever have. **Known for:** friendly staff; local home cooking like excellent lasagna; fascinating decor. [$] *Average main: €15* ✉ *Via delle Volte 52, Ferrara* ☎ *0532/760080* 🌐 *www.ristoranteilmandolino.it* 🕓 *Closed Tues.*

Il Sorpasso

$$ | **EMILIAN** | Named after a 1962 cult movie, *Il Sorpasso* (*The Easy Life*) serves terrific, honestly priced food in an unassuming space: white walls lined with movie posters, and white floors. No matter—the fine cooking and the sourcing of local ingredients whenever possible help this trattoria surpass many others. **Known for:** vegan and vegetarian options; using local ingredients whenever possible; excellent pastas and desserts. [$] *Average main: €16* ✉ *Via Saraceno 118, Ferrara* ☎ *0532/790289* 🌐 *www.trattoriailsorpasso.it* 🕓 *Closed Mon. and Tues.*

L'Oca Giuliva

$$ | **EMILIAN** | Food, service, and ambience harmonize blissfully at this casual but elegant restaurant inside a 12th-century building. The chef shows a deft hand with area specialties and shines with the fish dishes. **Known for:** tasting menus; cappellacci di zucca (pumpkin-stuffed pasta); creative antipasti and seafood dishes. [$] *Average main: €18* ✉ *Via Boccacanale di Santo Stefano 38/40, Ferrara* ☎ *0532/207628* 🌐 *www.ristorantelocagiuliva.it* 🕓 *Closed Tues.*

Molto Più Che Centrale

$$ | **EMILIAN** | A winning combination of traditional and innovative dishes is the big draw at this stylish restaurant spread over two floors. With red and white walls adorned with splashy modern art, and elegant wooden tables and chairs, the ambience is colorful and contemporary without being garish. **Known for:** attentive waitstaff; upbeat, contemporary setting; local dishes with modern flourishes. [$] *Average main: €18* ✉ *Via Boccaleone 8, Ferrara* ☎ *0532/1880070* 🌐 *www.moltopiuchecentrale.it* 🕓 *Closed Thurs.*

★ **Quel Fantastico Giovedì**

$$ | **EMILIAN** | Locals and other cognoscenti frequent this sleek eatery just minutes away from Piazza del Duomo, where chef Gabriele Romagnoli uses prime local ingredients to create gustatory sensations on a menu that changes daily. Fish and seafood figure prominently among his dishes, such as with a *gratinato* (similar to a French au gratin) with seafood. **Known for:** excellent service; notable fish and seafood dishes; seasonal menu. [$] *Average main: €18* ✉ *Via Castelnuovo 9, Ferrara* ☎ *0532/760570* 🌐 *www.quelfantasticogiovedi.it* 🕓 *Closed Wed. No lunch Thurs.*

🛏 Hotels

Hotel Annunziata

$$ | **HOTEL** | Brightly colored fittings enliven the white-walled, hardwood-floor guest rooms—think minimalism with a splash—at this hotel on a quiet little piazza near the forbiddingly majestic Castello Estense. **Pros:** perfect location (you can't get much more central); terrific buffet breakfast; stellar staff. **Cons:** annex 500 feet from main building; some rooms have uninspiring views; few facilities and limited public spaces. [$] *Rooms from: €160* ✉ *Piazza Repubblica 5, Ferrara* ☎ *0532/201111* 🌐 *www.annunziata.it* 🛏 *27 rooms* 🍴 *Free Breakfast.*

★ **Locanda Borgonuovo**

$ | **B&B/INN** | In the early 18th century this lodging began life as a convent (later suppressed by Napoléon), but now it's a delightful city-center bed-and-breakfast, popular with performers at the city's Teatro Comunale. **Pros:** phenomenal breakfast featuring local foods and terrific cakes made in-house; knowledgeable local advice; bicycles can be borrowed for free. **Cons:** decor may be a bit over-fussy for some; must reserve far in advance as this place books quickly; steep stairs

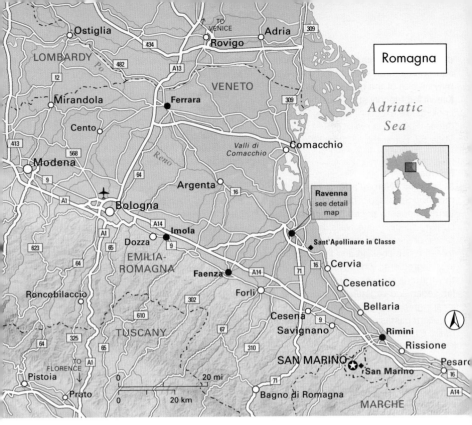

to reception area and rooms. $ *Rooms
from: €100* ✉ *Via Cairoli 29, Ferrara*
☎ *0532/211100* ⊕ *www.borgonuovo.com*
⇴ *5 rooms* ❛⊝❜ *Free Breakfast.*

Maxxim Hotel

$ | **HOTEL** | **FAMILY** | Though given a stylish
modern makeover, the courtyards, vaulted
brick lobby, and breakfast room of this
15th-century palazzo retain much of their
lordly Renaissance flair. **Pros:** beyond-help-
ful staff; tasteful modern makeover; good
choice for families. **Cons:** some bathrooms
are on the small side; occasional noise
from neighboring rooms; split-level loft
rooms impractical for some. $ *Rooms
from: €64* ✉ *Via Ripagrande 21, Ferrara*
☎ *0532/1770700* ⊕ *www.maxxim.it* ⇴ *40
rooms* ❛⊝❜ *Free Breakfast.*

Imola

*82 km (51 miles) south of Ferrara, 42 km
(26 miles) southeast of Bologna.*

Affluent Imola, with its wide and stately
avenues, lies on the border between
Emilia and Romagna. It was populated
as early as the Bronze Age, came under
Roman rule, and was eventually annexed
to the Papal States in 1504. Imola is best
known for its Formula One auto-racing
tradition: the San Marino Grand Prix was
held here every spring from 1981 until
2006. Auto racing as a serious sport in
Imola dates to 1953, when, with the
support of Enzo Ferrari, the racetrack just
outside the city center was inaugurated.
The venue sometimes returns to the
Formula One calendar, but you'll more
likely find yourself in Imola shopping for
its well-known ceramics or sampling

the cuisine at the town's world-famous restaurant, San Domenico.

GETTING HERE AND AROUND

Local trains from Bologna run often and take 20–30 minutes. If you're driving from Bologna, take the RA1 to the A14 (following signs for Ancona). Take the exit for Imola. If you're coming from Milan, you can catch the Frecciarossa to Bologna (a little over an hour), and then transfer to the local train.

VISITOR INFORMATION

CONTACT Imola Tourism Office. ✉ *Via Emilia 135,* ☎ *0542/602207* 🌐 *www.visitareimola.it.*

🍴 Restaurants

★ San Domenico

$$$$ | **MODERN ITALIAN** | Year after year this restaurant defends its position as one of Italy's most refined dining destinations, and heads of state, celebrities, and lovers of fine food venture here to savor chef Valentino Marcattilii's wondrous creations. Typical of these is his memorable *uovo in raviolo San Domenico,* in which a large raviolo is stuffed with a raw egg yolk—it cooks only a little, then spills out and mixes with Parmigiano-Reggiano, butter, and black truffles (depending on the season). **Known for:** impeccable service; raviolo filled with egg yolk; creative destination dining worth the price. [$] *Average main: €62* ✉ *Via G. Sacchi 1, Imola* ☎ *0542/29000* 🌐 *www.sandomenico.it* 🕒 *Closed Mon. No dinner Sun. Closed Sun. and Mon. June–Aug. No lunch Sat. June–Aug.*

Faenza

16 km (10 miles) southeast of Imola, 49 km (30 miles) southeast of Bologna.

In the Middle Ages, Faenza was the crossroads between Emilia-Romagna and Tuscany, and the 15th century saw many Florentine artists working in town. In 1509, when the Papal States took control, Faenza became something of a backwater. It did, however, continue its 12th-century tradition of making top-quality glazed earthenware. In the 16th century local artists created a color called *bianchi di Faenza* (Faenza white), which was widely imitated and wildly desired all over Europe. The Frenchified *faience,* referring to the color and technique, soon entered the lexicon, where it remains to this day. In the central **Piazza del Popolo,** dozens of shops sell local ceramics.

GETTING HERE AND AROUND

Trains run frequently from Bologna to Faenza, making the trip in 25–45 minutes. There's also sporadic service from Florence, a beautiful ride of under two hours. The walk to the centro storico, though easy, isn't especially interesting.

By car it takes about an hour from Bologna. Follow the SP253 to the RA1, at which point pick up on the A14/E45 heading in the direction of Ancona. Exit and take the SP8 into Faenza.

VISITOR INFORMATION

CONTACT Faenza Tourism Office. ✉ *Voltone della Molinella 2,* ☎ *0546/25231* 🌐 *www.prolocofaenza.it.*

👁 Sights

Museo Internazionale delle Ceramiche

ART MUSEUM | One of the largest ceramics museums in the world has a well-labeled, well-lit collection, with objects from the Renaissance among its highlights. Although the emphasis is clearly on local work, the rest of Italy and the globe are also represented. Don't miss the 20th- and 21st-century galleries, which prove that decorative arts often surpass their practical limitations and become genuinely sculptural. ✉ *Viale Baccarini 19, Faenza* ☎ *0546/697311* 🌐 *www.micfaenza.org* 🎟 *€10* 🕒 *Closed Mon.*

🍴 Restaurants

Marianaza

$$ | **ITALIAN** | A large open-hearth fireplace dominates this simple trattoria, and wonderful aromas of grilled meats and garlic greet you as you walk in. Marianaza successfully showcases the best of *la cucina romagnola* (the cuisine of Romagna): the extraordinary primi are mostly made with fresh pasta—tagliatelle or garganelli (egg-based and tubular)—while secondi rely heavily on the grill. **Known for:** Romagna specialties; fresh pasta; good-value grilled meats. [$] *Average main: €18* ✉ *Via Torricelli 21, Faenza* ☎ *0546/681461* 🌐 *www.marianaza.com* 🕒 *Closed Sun. and Wed.*

Rimini

70 km (43½ miles) southeast of Faenza, 52 km (32 miles) southeast of Ravenna, 121 km (75 miles) southeast of Bologna.

Rimini is one of the most popular summer resorts on the Adriatic Coast and one of the most popular in Italy. July and August are the most crowded, packed with people who don't mind crammed beaches and not-terribly-blue water. In the off-season (October through March), Rimini is a cold, windy fishing port with few places open. Any time of year, one of Rimini's least touristy areas is the port; rambling down the **Via Sinistra del Porto** or **Via Destra del Porto** past all the fishing boats, you're far from the crush of sunbathers.

The town stands at the junction of two great Roman consular roads, the Via Emilia and the Via Flaminia. In Roman times it was an important port, making it a strategic and commercial center. From the 13th century onward, Rimini was controlled by the Malatesta family, an unpredictable clan equally capable of grand gestures and savage deeds.

GETTING HERE AND AROUND

Trains run hourly from Ravenna to Rimini and take about an hour. By car from Ravenna, take the SS16/E55, then follow the SS3bis/E45/E55 in the direction of Roma/Ancona. Follow directions for Ancona Nord, then follow signs for Ancona. Take the A14/E55 to the Rimini Nord exit, then the SP136 to the SS16, and follow signs for the center of town. Alternatively, take the coastal road, SS16, which hugs the shoreline much of the way, passing through Cervia. Though only 52 km (32 miles), this scenic route is naturally slower (beware of fog in winter). The coast north of Rimini is lined with dozens of small resort towns, but only one really has any charm—the seaport of Cesenatico—the others are mini-Riminis, and in summer the narrow road is hopelessly clogged with traffic.

There's frequent train service (usually three or four trains per hour) from Bologna to Rimini. It takes one to two hours, depending on which train you choose. By car from Bologna, take the SP253 out of town, pick up the RA1, and then enter the A14 heading toward Ancona. Get off at the Rimini Nord exit, follow the SP136 to the SS16 to the center of town.

VISITOR INFORMATION

CONTACT Rimini Tourism Office. ✉ *Piazzale Federico Fellini 3,* ☎ *0541/53399* 🌐 *www.riminiturismo.it.*

👁 Sights

Arco d'Augusto

HISTORIC SIGHT | Rimini's oldest monument is the Arco d'Augusto, now stranded in the middle of a square just inside the city ramparts. It was erected in 27 BC, making it among the oldest surviving ancient Roman arches. ✉ *Largo Giulio Cesare at Corso d'Augusto, Rimini.*

Tempio Malatestiano

CHURCH | The Malatesta family constructed the Tempio Malatestiano, also called the Basilica Cattedrale, with a masterful facade by Leon Battista Alberti (1404–72). Inside, the chapel to the right of the high altar contains a wonderful (if faded) fresco by Piero della Francesca (1420–92) depicting Sigismondo Malatesta kneeling before a saint. The two greyhounds in the right corner are significantly less faded than the rest. ⊠ *Via IV Novembre 35, Rimini* ☎ *0541/1835101* ⊕ *www.diocesi. rimini.it* ✉ *Free.*

Restaurants

La Marianna

$$ | **ITALIAN** | It's all about fish at this welcoming spot, and aside from vegetable side dishes and dessert there's little on the menu that wasn't recently swimming (or lurking) in the sea. Locals flock here, and with good reason—the food is excellent, and the prices are reasonable. **Known for:** reasonable prices; lively outdoor dining; locally caught seafood across all courses. $ *Average main: €16* ⊠ *Viale Tiberio 19, Rimini* ☎ *0541/22530* ⊕ *www.trattorialamarianna.it.*

🛏 Hotels

Grand Hotel Rimini

$$$$ | **HOTEL** | **FAMILY** | This 1908 extravaganza, made famous by Federico Fellini in his film *Amarcord*, is grander than ever with ongoing restorations that keep the place completely current while maintaining its hyperluxe old-world charm. **Pros:** sumptuous buffet breakfast that starts early (7 am) and ends late (11 am); amenities including everything from a spa and a private beach to programs for children in summer; the American Bar. **Cons:** books up quickly in July and August; sea view rooms cost more; 1 km (½ mile) from Rimini's historic center. $ *Rooms from: €333* ⊠ *Parco Federico Fellini, Rimini* ☎ *0541/56000* ⊕ *www.grandhotelrimini. com* ⌘ *172 rooms* ⦿ *Free Breakfast.*

San Marino

20 km (12½ miles) southwest of Rimini, 139 km (86 miles) southeast of Bologna.

The world's smallest and oldest republic, as San Marino dubs itself, is surrounded entirely by Italy. It consists of three ancient castles perched on sheer cliffs rising implausibly out of the flatlands of Romagna, and a tangled knot of cobblestone streets below that are lined with tourist boutiques, cheesy hotels and restaurants, and gun shops. A visit here is justified, however, by the sweeping views from the castle of the countryside. The 3,300-foot-plus precipices will make jaws drop and acrophobes quiver.

Visiting San Marino in winter (off-season) increases the appeal of the experience, as tourist establishments shut down and you more or less have the castles to yourself. In August every inch of walkway on the rock is mobbed with sightseers. Don't worry about changing money, showing passports, and the like (although the tourist office in Piazza Garibaldi will stamp your passport for €5). San Marino is, for all practical purposes, Italy—except, that is, for its majestic perch, its lax gun laws, and its high national voter turnout rate.

GETTING HERE AND AROUND

To get to San Marino by car, take highway SS72 west from Rimini. From Borgo Maggiore, at the base of the rock, a cable car will whisk you up to the town. Alternatively, you can drive up the winding road; public parking is available. There is a regular bus service to and from Rimini, with service sometime every hour throughout the year (less frequent service on Sunday); a one-way ticket from Rimini to San Marino costs €5. The trip takes about 45 minutes.

VISITOR INFORMATION

CONTACT San Marino Tourism Office. ⊠ *Piazza Garibaldi,* ☎ *054/9885431* ⊕ *www. visitsanmarino.com.*

Sights

Piazza della Libertà

PLAZA/SQUARE | One must-see is the Piazza della Libertà, where the Palazzo Pubblico is guarded by soldiers in green uniforms. As you'll notice by peering into the shops along the old town's winding streets, the republic is famous for crossbows and other items (think fireworks or firearms) that are illegal almost everywhere else. ⊠ *San Marino.*

Tre Castelli

CASTLE/PALACE | San Marino's headline attractions are its Tre Castelli—medieval architectural wonders that appear on every coat of arms in the city—and some spectacular views. Starting in the center of town, walk a few hundred yards past the trinket shops, along a paved cliff-top ridge, from the 10th-century Rocca della Guaita to the 13th-century Rocca della Cesta (containing a museum of ancient weapons; worthwhile mostly for the views from its terraces and turrets) and finally to the 14th-century Rocca Montale (closed to the public), the most remote of the castles. Every step of the way affords spectacular views of Romagna and the Adriatic—it's said that on a clear day you can see Croatia. The walk makes for a good day's exercise, but is by no means arduous. Even if you arrive after visiting hours, it's supremely rewarding. ⊠ *San Marino* ☎ *0549/991369* ⊕ *www.cultura.sm* 🎫 *La Torre Guaita and La Torre Cesta €8.*

Ravenna

80 km (50 miles) northwest of San Marino, 93 km (58 miles) southeast of Ferrara.

A small, quiet, and well-heeled city, Ravenna has brick palaces, cobblestone streets, magnificent monuments, and spectacular Byzantine mosaics. The high point in its civic history occurred in the 5th century, when Pope Honorious moved his court here from Rome. Gothic kings Odoacer and Theodoric ruled the city until it was conquered by the Byzantines in AD 540. Ravenna later fell under the sway of Venice, and then, inevitably, the Papal States.

Because Ravenna spent much of its past looking east, its greatest art treasures show that Byzantine influence. Churches and tombs with the most unassuming exteriors contain within them walls covered with sumptuous mosaics. These beautifully preserved Byzantine mosaics put great emphasis on nature, which you can see in the delicate rendering of sky, earth, and animals. Outside Ravenna, the town of Classe hides even more mosaic gems.

GETTING HERE AND AROUND

By car from Bologna, take the SP253 to the RA1, and then follow signs for the A14/E45 in the direction of Ancona. From here, follow signs for Ravenna, taking the A14dir Ancona–Milano–Ravenna exit. Follow signs for the SS16/E55 to the center of Ravenna. From Ferrara the drive is more convoluted, but also more interesting. Take the SS16 to the RA8 in the direction of Porto Garibaldi, taking the Roma/Ravenna exit. Follow the SS309/E55 to the SS309dir/E55, taking the SS253 Bologna/Ancona exit. Follow the SS16/E55 into the center of Ravenna.

By train, there are one or two services hourly from Bologna, taking 70 minutes.

VISITOR INFORMATION

CONTACT Ravenna Tourism Office. ⊠ *Piazza San Francesco 7,* ☎ *0544/35755* ⊕ *www.turismo.ra.it.*

Sights

A combination ticket (available at ticket offices of the Basilica di San Vitale, the Museo Arcivescovile, and Sant'Apollinare Nuovo) admits you to four of Ravenna's important monuments: the Basilica di San Vitale, the Battistero Neoniano, the Museo

Arcivescovile, and Sant'Apollinare Nuovo. The Mausoleo di Galla Placidia may be added with a €2 reservation supplement. Start out early in the morning to avoid lines, and bear in mind that the months between March and mid-June are busy with school groups. A half day should suffice to explore the town; allowing at least half an hour each for the Mausoleo and the Basilica, and another couple of hours for sights in the outlying neighborhood of Classe, reachable by bus or bicycle.

★ Basilica di San Vitale

CHURCH | The octagonal church of San Vitale was built in AD 547, after the Byzantines conquered the city, and its interior shows a strong Byzantine influence. The area behind the altar contains the most famous works, depicting Emperor Justinian and his retinue on one wall, and his wife, Empress Theodora, with her retinue, on the opposite one. Notice how the mosaics seamlessly wrap around the columns and curved arches on the upper sides of the altar area.

■ TIP→ **School groups can sometimes swamp the site from March through mid-June.** ⊠ *Via San Vitale, off Via Salara, Ravenna* ☎ *0544/541688 for info, 800/303999 for info (toll-free)* ⊕ *www. ravennamosaici.it* ✉ *€11 combination ticket, includes 4–5 diocesan monuments.*

Battistero Neoniano

CHURCH | Next door to Ravenna's 18th-century cathedral, this baptistery has one of the town's most important mosaics. It dates from the beginning of the 5th century AD, with work continuing through the century. In keeping with the building's role, the great mosaic in the dome shows the baptism of Christ, and beneath are the Apostles. The lowest register of mosaics contains Christian symbols, the Throne of God, and the Cross. Note the naked figure kneeling next to Christ—he is the personification of the River Jordan. ⊠ *Piazza Duomo, Ravenna* ☎ *0544/541688 for info,*

800/303999 for info (toll-free) ⊕ *www. ravennamosaici.it* ✉ *€11 combination ticket, includes 4–5 diocesan monuments* ✍ *Reservations essential.*

Classis Ravenna–Museo della Città e del Territorio

OTHER MUSEUM | FAMILY | In Classe, a short distance outside Ravenna, this museum dazzlingly illustrates the history of Ravenna and its environs from the pre-Roman era to the Lombard conquest in AD 751. The museum occupies a refurbished sugar refinery, and with the help of multimedia presentations and panels in Italian and English, it chronicles the Roman, Ostrogoth, and Byzantine periods. Displays include bronze statuettes, stone sculptures, glassware, and mosaic fragments. A separate room summarizes the building's more recent history. It's an easy walk from Sant'Apollinare in Classe. ■ TIP→ **To get here from Ravenna, take Bus No. 4 from the station or the local train to Classe, or use the cycle path from the city center.** ⊠ *Via Classense 29, off SS71, Classe* ☎ *0544/473717* ⊕ *www.classisravenna.it* ✉ *€4.*

Domus dei Tappeti di Pietra

(House of the Stone Carpets)
RUINS | This archaeological site with lovely mosaics was uncovered in 1993 during digging for an underground parking garage near the 18th-century church of Santa Eufemia. Ten feet below ground level lie the remains of a Byzantine palace dating from the 5th and 6th centuries AD. Its beautiful and well-preserved network of floor mosaics displays elaborately designed patterns, creating the effect of luxurious carpets. ⊠ *Via Barbiani 16, enter through Sant'Eufemia church, Ravenna* ☎ *0544/473678* ⊕ *www. domusdeitappetidipietra.it* ✉ *€4.*

★ Mausoleo di Galla Placidia

CHURCH | The little tomb and the great church stand side by side, but the tomb predates the Basilica di San Vitale by at least 100 years: these two adjacent sights are decorated with the

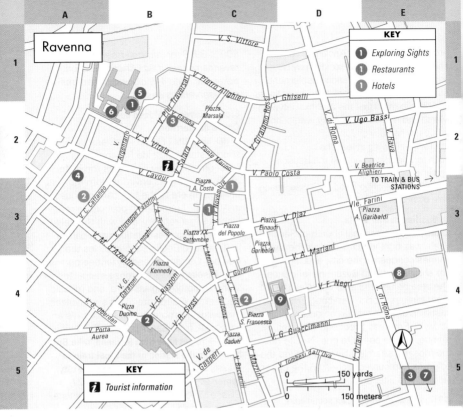

Ravenna

KEY
- ① Exploring Sights
- ① Restaurants
- ① Hotels

KEY
- 🛈 Tourist information

TO TRAIN & BUS STATIONS →

| 0 | 150 yards |
| 0 | 150 meters |

best-known, most elaborate mosaics in Ravenna. Galla Placidia was the sister of the Roman emperor Honorius, who moved the imperial capital to Ravenna in AD 402. This mid-5th-century mausoleum is her memorial.

The simple redbrick exterior only serves to enhance by contrast the richness of the interior mosaics, in deep midnight blue and glittering gold. The tiny central dome is decorated with symbols of Christ, the evangelists, and striking gold stars. Eight of the Apostles are represented in groups of two on the four inner walls of the dome; the other four appear singly on the walls of the two transepts. There are three sarcophagi in the tomb, none of which are believed to actually contain the remains of Galla Placidia.

■ TIP→ Visit early or late in the day to avoid the school groups that can sometimes swamp the Mausoleo from March through mid-June. ⊠ *Via San Vitale, 17, off Via Salara, Ravenna* ☎ *0544/541688 for info, 800/303999 for info (toll-free)* ⊕ *www.ravennamosaici.it* ⊠ *€11 combination ticket, includes 4–5 diocesan monuments (€2 supplement for mausoleum).*

Museo Nazionale di Ravenna (*National Museum of Ravenna*)

OTHER MUSEUM | Next to the Church of San Vitale and housed in a former Benedictine monastery, the museum contains artifacts from ancient Rome, Byzantine fabrics and carvings, and pieces of early Christian art. The collection is well displayed and artfully lighted. In the first cloister are marvelous Roman tomb slabs from excavations nearby; upstairs, you can see a reconstructed 18th-century pharmacy. ⊠ *Via San Vitale 17, Ravenna* ☎ *0544/213902* ⊕ *www.ravennantica.it/en/ravenna-national-museum-museo-nazionale-di-ravenna/* ⊠ *€6* ⊙ *Closed Mon.*

Sant'Apollinare in Classe

CHURCH | This church about 5 km (3 miles) southeast of Ravenna is landlocked now, but when it was built, it stood in the center of the busy shipping port known to the ancient Romans as Classis. The arch above and the area around the high altar are rich with mosaics. Those on the arch, older than the ones behind it, are considered superior. They show Christ in Judgment and the 12 lambs of Christianity leaving the cities of Jerusalem and Bethlehem. In the apse is the figure of Sant'Apollinare himself, a bishop of Ravenna, and above him is a magnificent Transfiguration against blazing green grass, animals in odd perspective, and flowers. ⊠ *Via Romea Sud 224, off SS71, Classe* ☎ *0544/527308* ⊠ *€5 or €9 including Classis Ravenna museum* ⊙ *Closed Mon.*

Sant'Apollinare Nuovo

CHURCH | The mosaics displayed in this church date from the early 6th century, making them slightly older than those in San Vitale. Since the left side of the church was reserved for women, it's only fitting that the mosaics on that wall depict 22 virgins offering crowns to the Virgin Mary. On the right wall, 26 men carry the crowns of martyrdom; they approach Christ, surrounded by angels. ⊠ *Via Roma 53, at Via Guaccimanni, Ravenna* ☎ *800/303999 for info (toll-free), 0544/541688 for info* ⊕ *www.ravennamosaici.it* ⊠ *€11 combination ticket, includes 4–5 diocesan monuments.*

Tomba di Dante

TOMB | Exiled from his native Florence, the author of *The Divine Comedy* died here in 1321, and Dante's tomb is in a small neoclassical building next door to the large church of St. Francis. The Florentines have been trying to reclaim their famous son for hundreds of years, but the Ravennans refuse to give him up, arguing that since Florence did not welcome Dante in life, it does not deserve him in death. Perhaps as penance, every September the Florentine government sends olive oil that's used to fuel the light hanging in the chapel's center. ⊠ *Via Dante Alighieri 9, Ravenna* ☎ *0544/215676* ⊠ *Free.*

Restaurants

Bella Venezia

$$ | ITALIAN | Pastel walls, crisp white tablecloths, and warm light provide the backdrop for some seriously good Romagnolo dishes. The menu offers local specialties, but also gives a major nod to Venice—Ravenna's conqueror of long ago. **Known for:** family owned and operated; outdoor dining; truffle dishes, depending on the season. $ *Average main: €17* ⊠ *Via IV Novembre 16, Ravenna* ☎ *0544/212746* ⊕ *www.ristorantebellavenezia.it* ⊘ *Closed Sun.*

Ca' de Vèn

$$ | ITALIAN | These buildings, joined by a glass-ceilinged courtyard, date from the 15th century, so the setting itself is reason enough to come; that the food is so good makes a visit here all the more satisfying. At lunchtime Ca' de Vèn teems with locals tucking in to *piadine* (a typical Romagnolo flatbread) stuffed or topped with various ingredients, and the grilled dishes—including *tagliata di pollo* (sliced chicken breast tossed with arugula and set atop exquisitely roasted potatoes)—are among the highlights. **Known for:** majestic, high-ceilinged lively setting; weekly menu of Romagnolo specialties; grilled meats. $ *Average main: €18* ⊠ *Via Corrado Ricci 24, Ravenna* ☎ *0544/30163* ⊕ *www.cadeven.it* ⊘ *Closed Mon.*

★ Osteria del Tempo Perso

$$ | ITALIAN | A couple of jazz-, rock-, and food-loving friends joined forces to open this smart little restaurant in the center. The interior's warm terra-cotta-sponged walls give off an orange glow, and wine bottles line the walls, interspersed with photographs of musical greats—but the food is what counts. **Known for:** house-made pastas; fine wine list; terrific seafood dishes. $ *Average main: €20* ⊠ *Via Gamba 12, Ravenna* ☎ *0544/215393* ⊕ *www.osteriadeltempoperso.it* ⊘ *No lunch weekdays.*

 Hotels

Albergo Cappello

$$ | HOTEL | Originally opened in the late 19th century and restored a century later, this small, charming place exhibits a Venetian influence, with Murano chandeliers hanging from the high coffered wood ceilings in common rooms. **Pros:** good location in historic area and near sights; wine bar and good restaurant; accommodating staff. **Cons:** occasional street noise in some rooms; parking sometimes hard to find; only seven rooms. $ *Rooms from: €132* ⊠ *Via IV Novembre 41, Ravenna* ☎ *0544/219813* ⊕ *www.albergocappello.it* ⇥ *7 rooms* ⦿ *Free Breakfast.*

Hotel Sant'Andrea

$ | B&B/INN | FAMILY | For a quiet and welcoming lodging on a residential street a stone's throw from the Basilica di San Vitale, look no further—it even has a delightful garden. **Pros:** quiet neighborhood; cheery and helpful staff; good-size guest rooms and family suites, some with terraces. **Cons:** few facilities; reception closes at 9 pm; can get a little noisy. $ *Rooms from: €120* ⊠ *Via Carlo Cattaneo 33, Ravenna* ☎ *0544/215564* ⊕ *www.santandreahotel.com* ⇥ *12 rooms* ⦿ *Free Breakfast.*

Performing Arts

Teatro di Tradizione Dante Alighieri

ARTS CENTERS | Operas and dance productions are staged here from November to April. If your Italian is up to it, you could also attend any of the theatrical productions. ⊠ *Via Mariani 2, Ravenna* ☎ *0544/249244* ⊕ *www.teatroalighieri.org.*

Chapter 12

FLORENCE

Updated by
Patricia Rucidlo

◉ **Sights**
★★★★★

🎫 **Restaurants**
★★★★★

🛏 **Hotels**
★★★★★

🏷 **Shopping**
★★★★★

🍸 **Nightlife**
★★★★☆

WELCOME TO FLORENCE

TOP REASONS TO GO

★ **Galleria degli Uffizi:** Italian Renaissance art doesn't get much better than this vast collection bequeathed in 1737 by the last Medici, Anna Maria Luisa.

★ **Brunelleschi's Dome:** His work of engineering genius is the city's undisputed centerpiece.

★ **Michelangelo's** *David*: One look, up close, and you'll know why this is one of the world's most famous sculptures.

★ **The view from Piazzale Michelangelo:** From this perch the city is laid out before you. The colors at sunset heighten the experience.

★ **Piazza Santa Croce:** After you've had your fill of Renaissance masterpieces, idle here and watch the world go by.

1 Around the Duomo. You're in the heart of Florence here. Among the numerous highlights are the city's greatest museum (the Uffizi) and arguably its most impressive square (Piazza della Signoria).

2 San Lorenzo. The complex of the basilica of San Lorenzo, the Palazzo Medici-Riccardi, and the Galleria dell'Accademia bears the imprints of the Medici and of Michelangelo, culminating in the latter's masterful statue *David*. Just to the north, the former convent of San Marco is an oasis of artistic treasures decorated with ethereal frescoes.

3 Santa Maria Novella. This part of town includes the train station, 16th-century palaces, and the city's swankest shopping street, Via Tornabuoni.

4 Santa Croce. The district centers on its namesake basilica, which is filled with the tombs of Renaissance (and other) luminaries. The area is also known for its leather shops.

5 The Oltrarno. Across the Arno you encounter the massive Palazzo Pitti and the narrow streets of the Santo Spirito neighborhood.

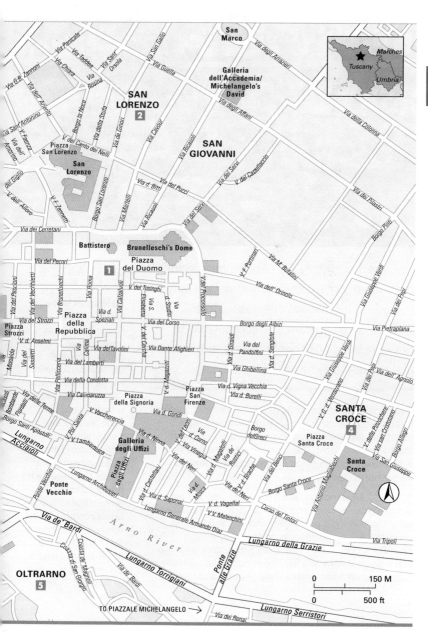

EATING AND DRINKING WELL IN FLORENCE

In Florence, simply prepared meats, grilled or roasted, are the culinary stars, usually paired with seasonal vegetables like artichokes or porcini. *Bistecca* (steak) is popular here, but there's plenty more that tastes great on the grill, too.

Traditionalists go for their gustatory pleasures in *trattorie* (casual restaurants) and *osterie* (down-home restaurants), places where decor is unimportant and place mats are mere paper. Culinary innovation comes slowly in this town, though some cutting-edge restaurants have been appearing.

By American standards, Florentines eat late: 1:30 or 2 pm is typical for lunch and 9 pm for dinner is considered early. Consuming a *primo* (first course), *secondo* (second course), and *dolce* (dessert) is largely a thing of the past. For lunch, many Florentines simply grab a panino and a glass of wine at a bar. Those opting for a simple trattoria lunch often order a plate of pasta and dessert.

STALE AND STELLAR

Stale bread is the basis for three classic Florentine primi: *pappa al pomodoro*, *ribollita*, and *panzanella*. Pappa is made with either fresh or canned tomatoes and that stale bread. Ribollita is a vegetable soup with *cavolo nero* (Tuscan kale) and cannellini beans, thickened with bread. Panzanella is reconstituted Tuscan bread combined with tomatoes, cucumber, and basil. They all are enhanced with a generous application of fragrant Tuscan olive oil.

A CLASSIC ANTIPASTO: CROSTINI DI FEGATINI

This beloved dish consists of a chicken-liver spread, presented warm or at room temperature, on toasted, garlic-rubbed bread. It can be served smooth, like a pâté, or in a chunkier, more rustic version. It's made by sautéing chicken livers with finely diced carrot and onion, enlivened with the addition of wine, broth, or Marsala reductions, and mashed anchovies and capers.

A CLASSIC SECONDO: BISTECCA FIORENTINA

The town's culinary pride and joy is a thick slab of beef, resembling a T-bone steak, from large white oxen called Chianina. The meat's slapped on the grill, seared on both sides, and served rare, sometimes with a pinch of salt.

A CLASSIC CONTORNO: CANNELLINI BEANS

Simply boiled, beans provide the perfect accompaniment to bistecca. The small white ones are best when they go straight from the garden into the pot. They should be anointed with a generous dose of Tuscan olive oil; the combination is oddly felicitous, and it goes a long way toward explaining why Tuscans are referred to as *mangiafagioli* (bean eaters) by other Italians.

A CLASSIC DOLCE: BISCOTTI DI PRATO

These are sometimes the only dessert on offer. *Biscotti* means twice-cooked (or, in this case, twice-baked). They are hard almond cookies that soften considerably when dipped languidly into *vin santo* ("holy wine"), a sweet dessert wine, or into a simple *caffè*.

A CLASSIC WINE: CHIANTI CLASSICO

This blend from the region just south of Florence relies mainly on the local, hardy sangiovese grape; it's aged for at least one year before hitting the market. (*Riserve*—reserve—is aged at least an additional six months.)

Chianti is usually the libation of choice for Florentines. Traditionalists opt for the younger, fruitier (and usually less expensive) versions often served in straw flasks. You can sample Chianti Classico all over town, and buy it in local supermarkets.

Its magical combination of beauty and history has drawn people to Florence for centuries, and then it draws them back again. It offers myriad moments of personal illumination before its palazzi, its churches, and its art museums, as well as in interaction with the people you meet there.

Florence has captivated visitors for ages now, probably ever since the powerful Medici family first staged jousts and later lavish pageants to celebrate their weddings. Its mostly sober beauty continued to attract people from all over Europe intent on taking in the achievements of the past on their Grand Tour of Europe. Sometimes this heady combination of art and beauty has proven overwhelming, as it did for French author and diplomat Stendhal in 1817, whose visit to the church of Santa Croce occasioned palpitations and a fainting spell. Today, however, visitors are more often overwhelmed by the press of their own numbers intent on taking it all in before moving on to the next stop on their tightly scheduled tours. Florence has always been visitor-friendly—the historical center of the city can be crossed on foot in less than half an hour, and the picturesque surrounding hills are a short bus ride away. But the flood of tourists has made the natives more reticent. A visitor is more likely to bump into or to exchange views with other visitors than with native Florentines, all busy catering to tourists' needs. Few Florentines, these days, can afford to live in the center where they work. Even the university has pulled out to a suburb. By day, the city is overrun

with busloads of day-trippers; come evening by droves of U.S. study-abroad students intent on immersion in the native *aperitivo* culture. Where have all the Italians gone, you wonder? Fear not, they still come out on Sundays to walk in family groups along the major shopping streets, school groups still pack museums, and they still hold parades in Renaissance costume to mark various historical or religious occasions. Caffè culture still thrives. All this will be revealed to the attentive visitor who sees past the crowds and takes the time to look around the corner onto a quieter street, piazza, or neighborhood.

Planning

Making the Most of Your Time

With some planning, you can see Florence's most famous sights in a couple of days. Start off at the city's most awe-inspiring architectural wonder, the **Duomo,** climbing to the top of the dome if you have the stamina (and are not claustrophobic: it gets a little tight going up and coming back down). On the same piazza, check out Ghiberti's bronze doors at the **Battistero.** (They're actually high-quality copies; the Museo dell'Opera del Duomo has the originals.) Set aside the afternoon for the **Galleria degli Uffizi,** making sure to reserve tickets in advance.

On Day 2, visit Michelangelo's *David* in the **Galleria dell'Accademia**—reserve tickets here, too. Linger in **Piazza della Signoria,** Florence's central square, where a copy of *David* stands in the spot the original occupied for centuries, then head east a couple of blocks to **Santa Croce,** the city's most artistically rich church. Double back and walk across Florence's landmark bridge, the **Ponte Vecchio.**

Do all that, and you'll have seen some great art, but you've just scratched the surface. If you have more time, put the **Bargello,** the **Museo di San Marco,** and the **Cappelle Medicee** at the top of your list. When you're ready for an art break, stroll through the **Boboli Gardens** or explore Florence's lively shopping scene, from the food stalls of the **Mercato Centrale** to the chic boutiques of the **Via Tornabuoni.**

HOURS

Florence's sights keep tricky hours. Some are closed Wednesday, some Monday, some every other Monday. Quite a few shut their doors each day (or on most days) by 2 in the afternoon. Things get even more confusing on weekends. Make it a general rule to check the hours closely for any place you're planning to visit; if it's someplace you have your heart set on seeing, it's worthwhile to call to confirm.

Here's a selection of major sights that might not be open when you'd expect (consult the Sights listings within this chapter for the full details). And be aware that, as always, hours can and do change. Also note that on the first Sunday of the month, all state museums are free. That means that the Accademia and the Uffizi, among others, do not accept

reservations. Unless you are a glutton for punishment (i.e., large crowds), these museums are best avoided on that day.

The **Accademia** and the **Uffizi** are both closed Monday. Note, too, that on the first Sunday of the month, all state museums, including these two, are free and do not accept reservations.

The **Bargello** is closed on Tuesday and the first, third, and last Sunday of the month. Otherwise, it's open from 8:45 am until 7 pm.

The **Battistero** is open daily 9 am to 7:30 pm.

The **Cappelle Medicee** are closed alternating Sundays and Mondays (those Sundays and Mondays when the Bargello is open).

The **Duomo** is closed on Sunday and is open from 10:15 am to 4:30 pm the rest of the week.

Museo di San Marco closes at 1:50 weekdays but stays open until 7 weekends—except for alternating Sundays and Mondays, when it's closed entirely.

Palazzo Medici-Riccardi is closed Wednesday.

RESERVATIONS

At most times of day a line of people snakes around the Uffizi. They're waiting to buy tickets, and you don't want to be one of them. Instead, call ahead for a reservation (☎ *055/294883*).

You'll be given a reservation number and an admission time—the sooner you call, the more time slots you'll have to choose from. Go to the museum's reservation door 10 minutes before the appointed hour (at least 30 minutes before in high season), give the clerk your number, pick up your ticket, and go inside. You'll pay €4 for this privilege, but it's money well spent.

You can also book through the ticketing website (⊕ *www.b-ticket.com/b-ticket/*

uffizi). The process takes some patience, but it works, and money-saving combo tickets are available as well. Use the same reservation service to book tickets for the Galleria dell'Accademia, where lines rival those of the Uffizi.

Reservations can also be made for the Palazzo Pitti, the Bargello, and several other sights, but they usually aren't needed—although, lately, in summer, lines can be long at Palazzo Pitti. An alternative strategy is to check with your hotel—many will handle reservations.

Getting Here and Around

AIR

To get into the city center from the airport by car, take the autostrada A11. A SITA bus will take you directly from the airport to the center of town. Buy the tickets within the train station.

AIR CONTACTS Aeroporto A. Vespucci.
☎ 055/30615 ⊕ *www.aeroporto.firenze. it*. **Aeroporto Galileo Galilei.** ☎ *050/849300* ⊕ *www.pisa-airport.com.*

BIKE AND MOPED

Brave souls (cycling in Florence is difficult at best) may rent bicycles at easy-to-spot locations at Fortezza da Basso, the Stazione Centrale di Santa Maria Novella, and Piazza Pitti. Otherwise, try **Alinari** (✉ *Via San Zanobi 38/r, San Marco* ☎ *055/280500*). You'll be up against hordes of tourists and those pesky *motorini* (mopeds). (For a safer ride, try Le Cascine, a former Medici hunting ground turned into a large public park with paved pathways.) The historic center can be circumnavigated via bike paths lining the *viali*, the ring road surrounding the area. If you want to go native and rent a noisy Vespa (Italian for "wasp") or other make of motorcycle or *motorino*, you can do so at **Massimo** (✉ *Via Campo d'Arrigo 16/r* ☎ *055/573689*).

BUS

Florence's flat, compact city center is made for walking, but when your feet get weary you can use the efficient bus system, which includes small electric buses making the rounds in the center. Buses also climb to Piazzale Michelangelo and San Miniato south of the Arno.

Maps and timetables are available for a small fee at the ATAF (Azienda Trasporti Area Fiorentina) booth next to the train station or for free at visitor information offices. Tickets must be bought in advance from tobacco shops, newsstands, automatic ticket machines near main stops, or ATAF booths. The ticket must be validated in the machine immediately upon boarding.

You have several ticket options, all valid for one or more rides on all lines. A €1.20 ticket is good for one hour from the time it is first canceled. A multiple ticket—four tickets, each valid for 70 minutes—costs €4.50. A 24-hour tourist ticket costs €5. Two-, three-, and seven-day passes are also available.

Long-distance buses provide inexpensive service between Florence and other cities in Italy and Europe. **SITA** (✉ *Via Santa Caterina da Siena 17/r* ☎ *055/47821*) is the major line.

CAR

Florence is connected to the north and south of Italy by the Autostrada del Sole (A1). It takes about 1½ hours of driving on scenic roads to get to Bologna (although heavy truck traffic over the Apennines often makes for slower going), about 3 hours to Rome, and 3–3½ hours to Milan. The Tyrrhenian Coast is an hour west on the A11.

An automobile in Florence is a major liability. If your itinerary includes parts of Italy where you'll want a car (such as Tuscany), pick the vehicle up on your way out of town.

TAXI

Taxis usually wait at stands throughout the city (in front of the train station and in Piazza della Repubblica, for example). You can also call radio dispatch (☎ *055/4390* or *055/4242*) for one to pick you up wherever you are.

The meter starts at €3.30 if you get a taxi at a stand or €5.40 if you call for one. Extra charges apply at night, on Sunday, and for luggage. Women out on the town after midnight are entitled to a 10% discount on the fare; you must, however, request it.

TRAIN

Florence is on the principal Italian train route between most European capitals and Rome, and within Italy it is served frequently from Milan, Venice, and Rome by Intercity (IC) and nonstop Eurostar trains. Avoid trains that stop only at the Campo di Marte or Rifredi station, which are not convenient to the city center.

TRAIN CONTACTS Stazione Centrale di Santa Maria Novella. ✉ *Piazza della Stazione, Santa Maria Novella* ☎ *055/892–2021 Trenitalia in Italy (fee for call)* ⊕ *www.trenitalia.com.*

Restaurants

Florence's popularity with tourists means that, unfortunately, there's a higher percentage of mediocre restaurants here than you'll find in most Italian towns (Venice, perhaps, might win that prize). Some restaurant owners cut corners and let standards slip, knowing that a customer today is unlikely to return tomorrow, regardless of the quality of the meal. So, if you're looking to eat well, it pays to do some research, starting with the recommendations here. Dining hours start at around 1 for lunch and 8 for dinner. Many of Florence's restaurants are small, so reservations are a must. You can sample such specialties as creamy fegatini (a chicken-liver spread) and

ribollita (minestrone thickened with bread and beans and swirled with extra-virgin olive oil) in a bustling, convivial trattoria, where you share long wooden tables set with paper place mats, or in an upscale ristorante with linen tablecloths and napkins.

Restaurant prices are the average cost of a main course at dinner or, if dinner is not served, at lunch. Restaurants reviews have been shortened. For full information, visit Fodors.com.

What it Costs in Euros			
$	$$	$$$	$$$$
AT DINNER			
under €15	€15–€24	€25–€35	over €35

Hotels

Florence is equipped with hotels for all budgets; for instance, you can find both budget and luxury hotels in the *centro storico* (historic center) and along the Arno. Florence has so many famous landmarks that it's not hard to find lodging with a panoramic view. The equivalent of the genteel *pensioni* of yesteryear can still be found, though they are now officially classified as "hotels." Generally small and intimate, they often have a quaint appeal that usually doesn't preclude modern plumbing. Florence's importance not only as a tourist city but also as a convention center and the site of the Pitti fashion collections guarantees a variety of accommodations.

The high demand also means that, except in winter, reservations are a must. If you find yourself in Florence with no reservations, go to **Consorzio ITA** (✉ *Stazione Centrale, Santa Maria Novella* ☎ *055/282893*). You must go there in person to make a booking.

Prices listed are for a standard double room in high season. Hotel reviews have been shortened. For full information, visit Fodors.com.

What it Costs in Euros			
$	$$	$$$	$$$$
FOR TWO PEOPLE			
under €125	€125–€200	€201–€300	over €300

Shopping

Window-shopping in Florence is like visiting an enormous contemporary-art gallery. Many of today's greatest Italian artists are fashion designers, and most keep shops in Florence. Discerning shoppers may find bargains in the street markets.

■TIP→ **Do not buy any knockoff goods from any of the hawkers plying their fake Prada (or any other high-end designer) on the streets. It's illegal, and fines are astronomical if the police happen to catch you. (You pay the fine, not the vendor.)**

Shops are generally open 9–1 and 3:30–7:30, and are closed Sunday and Monday mornings most of the year. Summer (June to September) hours are usually 9–1 and 4–8, and some shops close Saturday afternoon instead of Monday morning. When looking for addresses, you'll see two color-coded numbering systems on each street. The red numbers are commercial addresses and are indicated, for example, as "31/r." The blue or black numbers are residential addresses. Most shops take major credit cards and ship purchases, but because of possible delays it's wise to take your purchases with you.

Visitor Information

The Florence tourist office (☎ 039/055000 ⊕ *www.feelflorence. it*), also known as the APT, has branches at the airport, next to the Palazzo Medici-Riccardi, across the street from Stazione di Santa Maria Novella (the main train station), and at the Bigallo in Piazza del Duomo. The offices are generally open from 9 am until 7 pm. The multilingual staff will answer questions, give you directions, and provide information on the latest performing-arts happenings and other events. The website also provides information in English.

Around the Duomo

The heart of Florence, stretching from the Piazza del Duomo south to the Arno, is as dense with artistic treasures as any place in the world. Its churches, medieval towers, Renaissance palaces, and world-class museums and galleries contain some of the most outstanding achievements of Western art.

Much of the centro storico is closed to automobile traffic, but you still must dodge mopeds, cyclists, and masses of fellow tourists as you walk the narrow streets, especially in the area bounded by the Duomo, Piazza della Signoria, Galleria degli Uffizi, and the Ponte Vecchio. Via dei Calzaiuoli, between Piazza del Duomo and Piazza della Signoria, is the city's favorite *passeggiata* (constitutional).

◉ Sights

Bargello

ART MUSEUM | This building started out in the Middle Ages as the headquarters for the Capitano del Popolo (Captain of the People) during the Middle Ages and was later a prison. Today, it houses the Museo Nazionale, home to what is probably the finest collection of Renaissance sculpture in Italy. The remarkable masterpieces by Michelangelo (1475–1564), Donatello (circa 1386–1466), and Benvenuto Cellini (1500–71) are distributed amid an eclectic collection of arms, ceramics, and miniature bronzes, among other things. In 1401, Filippo Brunelleschi and Lorenzo Ghiberti competed to earn the most prestigious commission of the day: the decoration of the north doors of the Baptistery in Piazza del Duomo. ✉ *Via del Proconsolo 4, Bargello* ☎ *055/294883* ⊕ *www.museodelbargello.it* 🖃 *€12* ⊘ *Closed 2nd and 4th Mon. of the month.*

Battistero (*Baptistery*)

RELIGIOUS BUILDING | The octagonal Baptistery is one of the supreme monuments of the Italian Romanesque style and one of Florence's oldest structures. The round Romanesque arches on the exterior date from the 11th century, and the interior dome mosaics from the beginning of the mid-13th century are justly renowned, but they could never outshine the building's famed bronze Renaissance doors decorated with panels crafted by Lorenzo Ghiberti. Michelangelo declared them so beautiful that they could serve as the Gates of Paradise. ✉ *Piazza del Duomo, Duomo* ☎ *055/230–2885* ⊕ *duomo.firenze.it/it/home* 🖃 *Admission is via one of 3 combo tickets, each valid for 3 days: €30 Brunelleschi Pass (with Campanile, Cupola of the Duomo, Museo dell'Opera del Duomo, and Santa Reparata Basilica Cripta); €20 Giotto Pass (with Campanile, Museo dell'Opera, and Cripta); €15 Ghiberti Pass (with Museo dell'Opera and Cripta).*

Campanile

NOTABLE BUILDING | **FAMILY** | The Gothic bell tower designed by Giotto (circa 1266–1337) is a soaring structure of multicolor marble originally decorated with sculptures by Donatello and reliefs by Giotto, Andrea Pisano, and others (which are now in the Museo dell'Opera del Duomo). A climb of 414 steps rewards you with a close-up of Brunelleschi's cupola on the Duomo next door and a sweeping view of the city. ✉ *Piazza del Duomo, Duomo* ☎ *055/230–2885* ⊕ *duomo.firenze.it/it/home* 🖃 *Admission is via one of 2 combo tickets, each valid for 3 days: €30 Brunelleschi Pass (with Battistero, Cupola of the Duomo, Museo dell'Opera del Duomo, and Santa Reparata Basilica Cripta); €20 for Giotto Pass (with Battistero, Museo dell'Opera, and Cripta).* ⊘ *Closed Sun. morning.*

★ **Duomo** (*Cattedrale di Santa Maria del Fiore*)

CHURCH | In 1296, Arnolfo di Cambio was commissioned to build "the loftiest, most sumptuous edifice human invention could devise" in the Romanesque style. The immense Duomo was not completed until 1436, the year it was consecrated. The imposing facade dates only from the 19th century; its neo-Gothic style somewhat complements Giotto's genuine Gothic 14th-century campanile. The real glory of the Duomo, however, is Filippo Brunelleschi's dome, presiding over the cathedral with a dignity and grace that few domes to this day can match.

Brunelleschi's cupola was one of the great engineering breakthroughs of all time: most of Europe's later domes, including that of St. Peter's in Rome, were built employing Brunelleschi's methods, and today the Duomo has come to symbolize Florence in the same way that the Eiffel Tower symbolizes Paris. The interior is a fine example of Florentine Gothic, though much of the cathedral's best-known art has been moved to the nearby Museo dell'Opera del Duomo. ✉ *Piazza del Duomo, Duomo* ☎ *055/230–2885* ⊕ *duomo.firenze.it/it/home* 🖃 *Church is free. Admission to the cupola is via the €30 Brunelleschi Pass, a 3-day combo ticket that also includes the Battistero, Campanile, Museo dell'Opera del Duomo, and Santa Reparata Basilica Cripta.* ⊘ *Closed Sun.* ⚴ *Timed-entry reservations required for the cupola.*

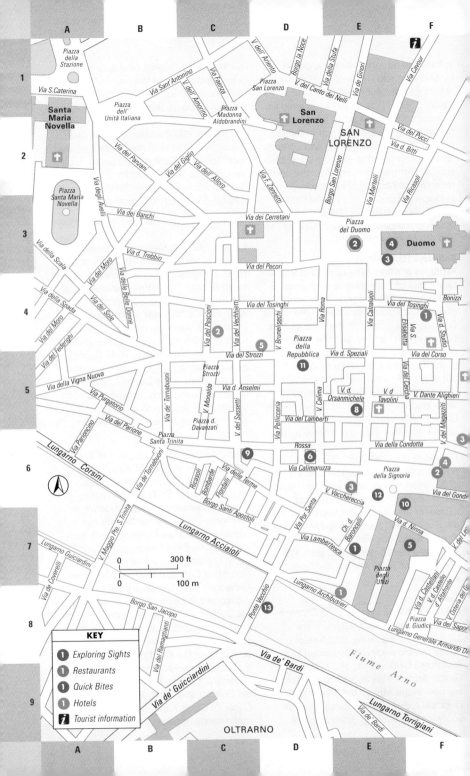

KEY

1 *Exploring Sights*

1 *Restaurants*

1 *Quick Bites*

1 *Hotels*

i *Tourist information*

Around the Duomo

Santa Maria degli Angeli

SAN GIOVANNI

Via Ricasoli

Via dei Servi

Via degli Affani

Via della Pergola

V. del Castellaccia

dei Servi

Via degli Affani

Via Nuova dei Caccini

Via M. Bufalini

Piazza Santa Maria Nuova

Via della Pergola

V. dell' Orinolo

v. F. Portinari

Via Sant' Egidio

Borgo Pinti

Via Fiesolana

V. del Proconsolo

Via dell' Orinolo

Borgo degli Albizi

Maggiore

Via d. Badesse

Via d. Giraldi

V. del Pandolfini

Via d. Sengiole

Crucifisso

Via Mattei Painieri

Via d. Rosa

Via dell' Agnolo

Via Ghibellina

Via dell Vecchia

Via del Burelli

Via Giuseppe Verdi

Via Ghibellina

V. G. d. Verrazano

Via del Fico

azza San enze

Via dell' Anguillara

Via Torta

Borgognona

Via dei Pepi

. Corno

Via de' Rustici

Borgo del Greci

Piazza Santa Croce

Via San Giuseppe

Vinegia

Via Magaloli

V. del Biache

Via del Benci

Santa Croce

el Neri

Borgo Santa Croce

. Mosca

Via del Neri

Cappella de'Pazzi

Via Antonio Magliabechi

V. del Vagellal

Corso del Tintori

iazza entana

V. Malenchini

Biblioteca Nazionale

Lungarno della Grazie

Piazza Cavalleggeri

Via Tripoli

Ponte alle Grazie

12

Florence AROUND THE DUOMO

★ Galleria degli Uffizi

ART MUSEUM | The Medici installed their art collections at Europe's first modern museum, open to the public (at first only by request) since 1591. Among the highlights are Paolo Uccello's *Battle of San Romano*; the *Madonna and Child with Two Angels* by Fra Filippo Lippi; *Birth of Venus* and *Primavera* by Sandro Botticelli; the portraits of the Renaissance duke Federico da Montefeltro and his wife Battista Sforza by Piero della Francesca; the *Madonna of the Goldfinch* by Raphael; Michelangelo's *Doni Tondo*; the *Venus of Urbino* by Titian; and the splendid *Bacchus* by Caravaggio.

Late in the afternoon is usually the least crowded time to visit. ■TIP➔ For a €4 fee, advance tickets (recommended) can be reserved by phone, online, or at the Uffizi reservation booth on the Piazza Pitti at least one day in advance of your visit. ⊠ *Piazzale degli Uffizi 6, Piazza della Signoria* ☎ *055/294883* ⊕ *www.uffizi.it* 🖼 *From €20* ☉ *Closed Mon.*

Mercato Nuovo (*New Market*)

MARKET | FAMILY | The open-air loggia, built in 1551, teems with souvenir stands, but the real attraction is a copy of Pietro Tacca's bronze *Porcellino* (which translates as "little pig" despite the fact the animal is, in fact, a wild boar). The sculpture is Florence's equivalent of the Trevi Fountain: put a coin in his mouth, and if it falls through the grate below (according to one interpretation), it means you'll return to Florence someday. What you're seeing is a copy of a copy: Tacca's original version, in the Museo Bardini, is actually a copy of an ancient Greek work. ⊠ *Via Por Santa Maria at Via Porta Rossa, Piazza della Repubblica* ☉ *Closed Sun.*

★ Museo dell'Opera del Duomo (*Cathedral Museum*)

ART MUSEUM | A seven-year restoration, completed in 2015, gave Florence one of its most modern, up-to-date museums. The exhibition space was doubled, and the old facade of the cathedral, torn down in the 1580s, was re-created with a 1:1 relationship to the real thing. Both sets of Ghiberti's doors adorn the same room. Michelangelo's *Pietà* finally has the space it deserves, as does Donatello's *Mary Magdalene*. ⊠ *Piazza del Duomo 9, Duomo* ☎ *055/230–2885* ⊕ *duomo.firenze.it/it/home* 🖼 *Admission is via one of 3 combo tickets, each valid for 3 days: €30 Brunelleschi Pass (with Battistero, Campanile, Cupola of the Duomo, and Santa Reparata Basilica Cripta); €20 Giotto Pass (with Battistero, Campanile, and Cripta); €15 Ghiberti Pass (with Battistero and Cripta)* ☉ *Closed 1st Tues. of month.*

Orsanmichele

CHURCH | This structure has served multiple purposes. Built in the 8th century as an oratory, in 1290, it was turned into an open-air loggia for selling grain. Destroyed by fire in 1304, it was rebuilt as a loggia-market. Between 1367 and 1380 its arcades were closed and two stories were added above. Finally, at century's end, it was turned into a church.

Although the interior contains a beautifully detailed 14th-century Gothic tabernacle by Andrea Orcagna (1308–68), its exterior that is most interesting. Niches contain sculptures (all copies) dating from the early 1400s to the early 1600s by Donatello and Verrocchio (1435–88), among others, which were paid for by the guilds. ⊠ *Via dei Calzaiuoli, Piazza della Repubblica* ☎ *055/284944* ⊕ *www.polomuseale.firenze.it* 🖼 *€2* ☉ *Closed Sun. and Mon. and Wed.–Fri.* ♿ *Reservations recommended.*

Palazzo Davanzati

CASTLE/PALACE | The prestigious Davizzi family owned this 14th-century palace in one of Florence's swankiest medieval neighborhoods (it was sold to the Davanzati in the 15th century). The place is a delight, as you can wander through the surprisingly light-filled courtyard and climb the steep stairs to the piano nobile (there's also an elevator), where the family did most of its living. The beautiful Sala dei Pappagalli (Parrot Room) is adorned with trompe-l'oeil tapestries and gaily painted birds. ⊠ *Piazza Davanzati 13, Piazza della Repubblica* ☎ *055/064–9460* ⊕ *www.polomuseale.firenze.it* ☜ *€6* ⊘ *Closed Mon. and 1st, 3rd, 5th Sun. of month.*

Palazzo Vecchio (*Old Palace*)

CASTLE/PALACE | FAMILY | Florence's forbidding, fortresslike city hall was begun in 1299, presumably designed by Arnolfo di Cambio, and its massive bulk and towering campanile dominate Piazza della Signoria. It was built as a meeting place for the guildsmen governing the city at the time; today, it is still City Hall. The main attraction is on the second floor, the opulently vast Sala dei Cinquecento (Room of the Five Hundred), named for the 500-member Great Council that met here. ⊠ *Piazza della Signoria* ☎ *055/276–8325* ⊕ *museicivicifiorentini.comune.fi.it* ☜ *From €13.*

Piazza della Repubblica

PLAZA/SQUARE | The square marks the site of an ancient forum, which was the core of the original Roman settlement and which was replaced in the Middle Ages by the Mercato Vecchio (Old Market). The current piazza, constructed between 1885 and 1895 as a neoclassical showpiece, is lined with outdoor cafés, affording an excellent opportunity for people-watching. ⊠ *Florence.*

Piazza della Signoria

PLAZA/SQUARE | This is by far the most striking square in Florence. It was here, in 1497 and 1498, that the famous "bonfire of the vanities" took place, when the fanatical Dominican friar Savonarola induced his followers to hurl their worldly goods into the flames. The statues in the square and in the 14th-century Loggia dei Lanzi on the south side vary in quality. Cellini's famous bronze *Perseus* holding the severed head of Medusa is certainly the most important. ⊠ *Florence.*

Ponte Vecchio (*Old Bridge*)

BRIDGE | This charmingly simple bridge was built in 1345 to replace an earlier bridge swept away by flood. Its shops first housed butchers, then grocers, blacksmiths, and other merchants. But in 1593, the Medici grand duke Ferdinand I, whose private corridor linking the Medici palace (Palazzo Pitti) with the Medici offices (the Uffizi) crossed the bridge atop the shops, decided that all this plebeian commerce under his feet was unseemly. So he threw out the butchers and blacksmiths and installed 41 goldsmiths and eight jewelers. The bridge has been devoted solely to these two trades ever since. The Corridoio Vasariano (⊠ *Piazzale degli Uffizi 6, Piazza della Signoria* ☎ *055/294883*), the private Medici elevated passageway, was built by Vasari in 1565. It was most likely designed so that the Medici family wouldn't have to walk amid the commoners. ⊠ *Florence.*

 Restaurants

Coquinarius

$$ | ITALIAN | This rustically elegant space, which has served many purposes over the past 600 years, offers some of the tastiest food in town at great prices. It's the perfect place to come if you aren't sure what you're hungry for, as they offer a little bit of everything: salad lovers will have a hard time choosing from among the lengthy list (the Scozzese, with poached chicken, avocado, and bacon, is a winner); those with a yen for pasta will face agonizing choices (the ravioli with pecorino and pears is particularly good). **Known for:** inconsistent service; reasonably priced wine list; marvelous salads. Ⓢ *Average main: €18* ⊠ *Via delle Oche 15/r, Duomo* ☎ *055/230–2153* ⊕ *www.coquinarius.it* ⊘ *Closed Sun.*

★ Gucci Osteria

$$$ | FUSION | Chef, artist, and visionary Massimo Bottura has joined forces with

Continued on page 559

THE DUOMO

FLORENCE'S BIGGEST MASTERPIECE

For all its monumental art and architecture, Florence has one undisputed centerpiece: the Cathedral of Santa Maria del Fiore, better known as the Duomo. Its cupola dominates the skyline, presiding over the city's rooftops like a red hen over her brood. Little wonder that when Florentines feel homesick, they say they have *"nostalgia del cupolone."*

The Duomo's construction began in 1296, following the design of Arnolfo di Cambio, Florence's greatest architect of the time. By modern standards, construction was slow and haphazard—it continued through the 14th and into the 15th century, with some dozen architects having a hand in the project.

In 1366, Neri di Fioravante created a model for the hugely ambitious cupola: it was to be the largest dome in the world, surpassing Rome's Pantheon. But when the time finally came to build the dome in 1418, no one was sure how—or even if—it could be done. Florence was faced with a 143 foot hole in the roof of its cathedral, and one of the greatest challenges in the history of architecture.

Fortunately, local genius Filippo Brunelleschi was just the man for the job. Brunelleschi won the 1418 competition to design the dome, and for the next 18 years he oversaw its construction. The enormity of his achievement can hardly be overstated. Working on such a large scale (the dome weighs 37,000 tons and uses 4 million bricks) required him to invent hoists and cranes that were engineering marvels. A "dome within a dome" design and a novel herringbone bricklaying pattern were just two of the innovations used to establish structural integrity. Perhaps most remarkably, he executed the construction without a supporting wooden framework, which had previously been thought indispensable.

Brunelleschi designed the lantern atop the dome, but he died soon after its first stone was laid in 1446; it wouldn't be completed until 1461. Another 400 years passed before the Duomo received its facade, a 19th-century neo-Gothic creation.

DUOMO TIMELINE

1296 Work begins, following design by Arnolfo di Cambio.

1302 Arnolfo dies; work continues, with sporadic interruptions.

1331 Management of construction taken over by the Wool Merchants guild.

1334 Giotto appointed project overseer, designs campanile.

1337 Giotto dies; Andrea Pisano takes leadership role.

1348 The Black Plague; all work ceases.

1366 Vaulting on nave completed; Neri di Fioravante makes model for dome.

1417 Drum for dome completed.

1418 Competition is held to design the dome.

1420 Brunelleschi begins work on the dome.

1436 Dome completed.

1446 Construction of lantern begins; Brunelleschi dies.

1461 Antonio Manetti, a student of Brunelleschi, completes lantern.

1469 Gilt copper ball and cross added by Verrocchio.

1587 Original facade is torn down by Medici court.

1871 Emilio de Fabris wins competition to design new facade.

1887 Facade completed.

WHAT TO LOOK FOR INSIDE THE DUOMO

The interior of the Duomo is a fine example of Florentine Gothic with a beautiful marble floor, but the space feels strangely barren—a result of its great size and the fact that some of the best art has been moved to the nearby **Museo dell'Opera del Duomo**.

Notable among the works that remain are two towering equestrian frescoes of famous mercenaries: Niccolò da Tolentino (1456) by Andrea del Castagno, and Sir John Hawkwood (1436) by Paolo Uccello. There's also fine terra-cotta work by Luca della Robbia. Ghiberti, Brunelleschi's great

rival, is responsible for much of the stained glass, as well as a reliquary urn with gorgeous reliefs. A vast fresco of the Last Judgment, painted by Vasari and Zuccari, covers the dome's interior. Brunelleschi had wanted mosaics to go there; it's a pity he didn't get his wish.

In the crypt beneath the cathedral, you can explore excavations of a Roman wall and mosaic fragments from the late 6th century; entry is near the first pier on the right. On the way down you pass Brunelleschi's modest tomb.

1. Entrance; stained glass by Ghiberti
2. Fresco of Niccolò da Tolentino by Andrea del Castagno
3. Fresco of John Hawkwood by Paolo Uccello
4. Dante and the Divine Comedy by Domenico di Michelino
5. Lunette: Ascension by Luca della Robbia
6. Above altar: two angels by Luca della Robbia. Below the altar: reliquary of St. Zenobius by Ghiberti
7. Lunette: Resurrection by Luca della Robbia
8. Entrance to dome
9. Bust of Brunelleschi by Buggiano
10. Stairs to crypt
11. Campanile

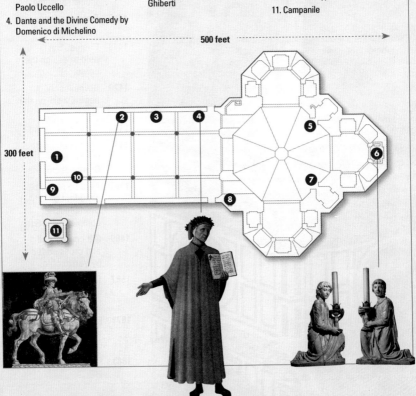

MAKING THE CLIMB

Climbing the 463 steps to the top of the dome is not for the faint of heart—or for the claustrophobic—but those who do it will be rewarded a smashing view of Florence (left). Keep in mind that the way up is also the way down, which means that while you're huffing and puffing in the ascent, people very close to you in a narrow staircase (below) are making their way down.

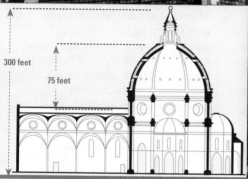

300 feet

75 feet

DUOMO BASICS

- Admission to the church is free, but there's a fee to visit the cupola, and timed-entry reservations are required.

- For an alternative to the dome, consider climbing the less trafficked campanile, which gives you a view from on high of the dome itself.

- Dress code essentials: covered shoulders, no short shorts, and hats off upon entering.

THE CRYPT

The crypt is worth a visit: computer modeling allows visitors to see its ancient Roman fabric and subsequent rebuilding. A transparent plastic model shows exactly what the earlier church looked like.

BRUNELLESCHI vs. GHIBERTI
The Rivalry of Two Renaissance Geniuses

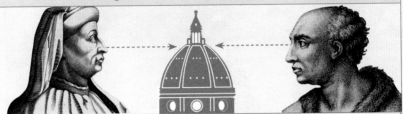

In Renaissance Florence, painters, sculptors, and architects competed for major commissions, with the winner earning the right to undertake a project that might occupy him (and keep him paid) for a decade or more. Stakes were high, and the resulting rivalries fierce—none more so than that between Filippo Brunelleschi and Lorenzo Ghiberti.

The two first clashed in 1401, for the commission to create the bronze doors of the Baptistery. When Ghiberti won, Brunelleschi took it hard, fleeing to Rome, where he would remain for 15 years. Their rematch came in 1418, over the design of the Duomo's cupola, with Brunelleschi triumphant. For the remainder of their lives, the two would miss no opportunity to belittle each other's work.

FILIPPO BRUNELLESCHI (1377–1446)

MASTERPIECE: The dome of Santa Maria del Fiore.

BEST FRIENDS: Donatello, whom he stayed with in Rome after losing the Baptistery doors competition; the Medici family, who rescued him from bankruptcy.

SIGNATURE TRAITS: Paranoid, secretive, bad tempered, practical joker, inept businessman.

SAVVIEST POLITICAL MOVE: Feigned sickness and left for Rome after his dome plans were publicly criticized by Ghiberti, who was second-in-command. The project proved too much for Ghiberti to manage on his own, and Brunelleschi returned triumphant.

MOST EMBARRASSING MOMENT: In 1434, he was imprisoned for two weeks for failure to pay a small guild fee. The humiliation might have been orchestrated by Ghiberti.

OTHER CAREER: Shipbuilder. He built a huge vessel, *Il Badalone*, to transport marble for the dome up the Arno. It sank on its first voyage.

INSPIRED: The dome of St. Peter's in Rome.

LORENZO GHIBERTI (1378–1455)

MASTERPIECE: The Gates of Paradise, the ten-paneled east doors of the Baptistery.

BEST FRIEND: Giovanni da Prato, an underling who wrote diatribes attacking the dome's design and Brunelleschi's character.

SIGNATURE TRAITS: Instigator, egoist, know-it-all, shrewd businessman.

SAVVIEST POLITICAL MOVE: During the Baptistery doors competition, he had an open studio and welcomed opinions on his work, while Brunelleschi labored behind closed doors.

OTHER CAREER: Collector of classical artifacts, historian.

INSPIRED: The Gates of Hell by Auguste Rodin.

The Gates of Paradise detail

Florence through the Ages

Guelph vs. Ghibelline. Although Florence can lay claim to a modest importance in the ancient world, it didn't come into its own until the Middle Ages. In the early 1200s the city, like most of the rest of Italy, was rent by civic unrest. Two factions, the Guelphs and the Ghibellines, competed for power. The Guelphs supported the papacy, and the Ghibellines supported the Holy Roman Empire. Bloody battles—most notably one at Montaperti in 1260—tore Florence and other Italian cities apart. By the end of the 13th century the Guelphs ruled securely, and the Ghibellines had been vanquished. This didn't end civic strife, however: the Guelphs split into the Whites and the Blacks for reasons still debated by historians. Dante, author of *The Divine Comedy*, was banished from Florence in 1301 because he was a White.

The Guilded Age. Local merchants had organized themselves into guilds by some time beginning in the 12th century. In 1250, they proclaimed themselves the *primo popolo* (literally, "first people"), making a landmark attempt at elective, republican rule. Though the episode lasted only 10 years, it constituted a breakthrough in Western history. Such a daring stance by the merchant class was a by-product of Florence's emergence as an economic powerhouse. Florentines were papal bankers; they instituted the system of international letters of credit; the gold florin became the international standard of currency. With this economic strength came a building boom. Sculptors such as Ghiberti and Donatello decorated the new churches; painters such as Giotto and Masaccio frescoed their walls.

Mighty Medici. Though ostensibly a republic, Florence was blessed (or cursed) with one very powerful family, the Medici, who came to prominence in 1434 and were initially the de facto rulers and then the absolute rulers of Florence for several hundred years. It was under patriarch Cosimo il Vecchio (1389–1464) that the Medici's position in Florence was securely established. Florence's golden age occurred during the reign of his grandson Lorenzo de' Medici (1449–92). Lorenzo was not only an astute politician but also a highly educated man and a great patron of the arts. Called "Il Magnifico" (the Magnificent), he gathered around him poets, artists, philosophers, architects, and musicians.

Lorenzo's son Piero (1471–1503) proved inept at handling the city's affairs. He was run out of town in 1494, and Florence briefly enjoyed its status as a republic while dominated by the Dominican friar Girolamo Savonarola (1452–98). After a decade of internal unrest, the republic fell and the Medici returned to power, but Florence never regained its former prestige. By the 1530s most of the major artistic talent had left the city—Michelangelo, for one, had settled in Rome. The now-ineffectual Medici, eventually attaining the title of grand dukes, remained nominally in power until the line died out in 1737, after which time Florence passed from the Austrians to the French and back again until the unification of Italy (1865–70), when it briefly became the capital under King Vittorio Emanuele II.

12

Florence AROUND THE DUOMO

the creative folk at Gucci to develop a marvelous menu that is both classic and innovative. Though he trained with Ducasse and Adrià, his major influence was his grandmother's cooking. **Known for:** outdoor seating in one of Florence's most beautiful squares; an ever-changing menu; tortellini in crema di Parmigiano Reggiano. [$] *Average main: €35* ✉ *Piazza della Signoria 10, Piazza della Signoria* ☎ *055/7592–7038* 🌐 *guccigarden.gucci.com.*

★ Rivoire
$$ | **ITALIAN** | One of the best spots in Florence for people-watching offers stellar service, light snacks, and terrific aperitivi. It's been around since the 1860s, and has been famous for its hot and cold chocolate (with or without cream) for more than a century. **Known for:** the view on the piazza; friendly bartenders; hot chocolate. [$] *Average main: €15* ✉ *Via Vacchereccia 4/r, Piazza della Signoria* ☎ *055/214412* 🌐 *rivoire.it/en* 🕒 *Closed Mon.*

Coffee and Quick Bites

★ 'ino
$ | **ITALIAN** | This is the perfect place to grab a bite and/or a glass of wine after a visit to the nearby Uffizi. Only the very best ingredients go into owner Alessandro Frassica's delectable panini. **Known for:** delicious bread; top-notch ingredients; interesting panini combinations. [$] *Average main: €8* ✉ *Via dei Georgofili 3/r–7/r, Piazza della Signoria* ☎ *055/214154* 🌐 *www.inofirenze.com* 🕒 *Closed Mon.*

Hotels

Hotel degli Orafi
$$$$ | **HOTEL** | A key scene in *A Room with a View* was shot in this pensione, which is today a luxury hotel adorned with chintz and marble. **Pros:** stellar Arno views; quiet location during the evenings; rooftop bar. **Cons:** somewhat pricey; on the path of many tour groups during the day; some street noise in river-facing rooms. [$] *Rooms from: €310* ✉ *Lungarno Archibusieri 4, Piazza della Signoria* ☎ *055/26622* 🌐 *www.hoteldegliorafi.it* 🛏 *50 rooms* 🍴 *Free Breakfast.*

Hotel Helvetia and Bristol
$$$$ | **HOTEL** | From the cozy yet sophisticated lobby with its stone columns to the guest rooms decorated with prints, you might feel as if you're a guest in a sophisticated manor house. **Pros:** central location; old-world charm; excellent restaurant. **Cons:** books up quickly; breakfast is not always included in the price of a room; rooms facing the street get some noise. [$] *Rooms from: €700* ✉ *Via dei Pescioni 2, Piazza della Repubblica* ☎ *055/26651* 🌐 *www.starhotelscollezione.com* 🛏 *89 rooms* 🍴 *Free Breakfast.*

Hotel Renaissance
$$ | **HOTEL** | Nestled in an old building just a stone's throw from the main civic square (Piazza Signoria), this charming little boutique hotel offers peace in quiet elegance. **Pros:** the staff; the location; the sumptuous breakfast. **Cons:** books up quickly; some street noise in some rooms; steps up to the elevator. [$] *Rooms from: €150* ✉ *Via della Condotta 4, Piazza della Signoria* ☎ *055/213996* 🌐 *www.hotelrenaissancefirenze.com* 🛏 *9 rooms* 🍴 *Free Breakfast.*

★ In Piazza della Signoria
$$$ | **B&B/INN** | In this home that is part of a 15th-century palazzo, a cozy feeling permeates the charming rooms, all of which are uniquely decorated and lovingly furnished; some have damask curtains, others fanciful frescoes in the bathroom. **Pros:** marvelous staff; some rooms easily accommodate three; tasty breakfast with a view of Piazza della Signoria. **Cons:** books up quickly during high season; some of the rooms have steps up into

showers and bathtubs; short flight of stairs to reach elevator. [$] *Rooms from: €300* ✉ *Via dei Magazzini 2, Piazza della Signoria* ☎ *055/239–9546* 🌐 *www.boutiquehotelinpiazza.com* 🛏 *13 rooms* 🍴 *Free Breakfast.*

Palazzo Vecchietti

$$$$ | HOTEL | If you're looking for a swank setting, and the possibility of staying in for a meal (each room has a tiny kitchenette), look no further than this hotel which, while thoroughly modern, dates to the 15th century. **Pros:** great service; public room has a Renaissance fireplace and high ceilings; central location. **Cons:** it's expensive; some street noise a possibility; no restaurant. [$] *Rooms from: €399* ✉ *Via degli Strozzi 4, Duomo* ☎ *055/230–2802* 🌐 *www.palazzovecchietti.com* 🛏 *14 rooms* 🍴 *Free Breakfast.*

Nightlife

Hard Rock Cafe

LIVE MUSIC | Hard Rock packs in young Florentines and travelers eager to sample the music hall chain's take on classic American grub. ✉ *Via De' Brunelleschi 1, Piazza della Repubblica* ☎ *055/277841* 🌐 *www.hardrock.com.*

Yab

DANCE CLUBS | Yab never seems to go out of style, though it increasingly becomes the haunt of Florentine high school and university students intent on dancing and doing vodka shots. ✉ *Via Sassetti 5/r, Piazza della Repubblica* ☎ *055/215160* 🌐 *www.yab.it.*

Performing Arts

Orchestra da Camera Fiorentina

MUSIC | This orchestra performs various concerts of classical music throughout the year at Orsanmichele, the grain-market–turned–church. ✉ *Via Monferrato 2, Piazza della Signoria* ☎ *055/783374* 🌐 *orchestradacamerafiorentina.it.*

Shopping

★ **Bernardo**

MEN'S CLOTHING | Come here for men's trousers, cashmere sweaters, and shirts with details like mother-of-pearl buttons. ✉ *Via Porta Rossa 87/r, Piazza della Repubblica* ☎ *055/283333* 🌐 *www.bernardofirenze.it.*

Cabó

MIXED CLOTHING | Missoni knitwear is the main draw at Cabó. ✉ *Via Porta Rossa 77–79/r, Piazza della Repubblica* ☎ *055/215774.*

Carlo Piccini

JEWELRY & WATCHES | Still in operation after four generations, this Florentine institution sells antique jewelry and makes pieces to order; you can also get old jewelry reset here. ✉ *Ponte Vecchio 31/r, Piazza della Signoria* ☎ *055/294768* 🌐 *www.fratellipiccini.com.*

Diesel

MIXED CLOTHING | Trendy Diesel started in Vicenza; its gear is on the "must have" list of many Italian teens. ✉ *Via degli Speziali 16/r, Piazza della Signoria* ☎ *055/239–9963* 🌐 *www.diesel.com.*

Gherardi

JEWELRY & WATCHES | Florence's king of coral, Gherardi has the city's largest selection of finely crafted pieces, as well as cultured pearls, jade, and turquoise. ✉ *Ponte Vecchio 36/r, Piazza della Signoria* ☎ *055/211809* 🌐 *www.gherardigioielli.it.*

Mandragora Art Store

MUSEUM SHOP | This is one of the first attempts in Florence to cash in on the museum-store craze. Look for reproductions of valued works of art and jewelry. ✉ *Piazza del Duomo 50/r, Duomo* ☎ *055/265–4384* 🌐 *www.mandragora.it.*

Mercato dei Fiori (*Flower Markete*)

MARKET | Every Thursday morning from September through June the covered loggia in Piazza della Repubblica hosts this lively market—a riot of plants, flowers, and difficult-to-find herbs. ⊠ *Piazza della Repubblica, Florence.*

Mercato del Porcellino

MARKET | FAMILY | If you're looking for cheery, inexpensive trinkets to take home, roam through the stalls under the loggia of the Mercato del Porcellino. ⊠ *Via Por Santa Maria at Via Porta Rossa, Piazza della Repubblica.*

Oro Due

JEWELRY & WATCHES | Gold jewelry and other beauteous objects are priced according to the level of craftsmanship and the value of gold bullion that day. ⊠ *Via Lambertesca 12/r, Piazza della Signoria* ☎ *055/292143.*

Patrizia Pepe

WOMEN'S CLOTHING | The Florentine designer has clothes for mostly really thin young people, especially for women with a tiny streak of rebelliousness. Sizes run extremely small. ⊠ *Piazza San Giovanni 12/r, Duomo* ☎ *055/264–5056* ⊕ *www.patriziapepe.com.*

★ Pegna

FOOD | This shop has been selling both Italian and non-Italian food since 1860. If you're tired of mozzarella and feel the need for some cheddar, this is the place to find it. ⊠ *Via dello Studio 8, Duomo* ☎ *055/282701* ⊕ *pegna.sangiustosrl.com.*

★ Penko

JEWELRY & WATCHES | Renaissance goldsmiths provide the inspiration for this dazzling jewelry with a contemporary feel. ⊠ *Via Ferdinando Zannetti 14–16/r, Duomo* ☎ *055/211661* ⊕ *www.paolopenko.com.*

Quercioli & Lucherini

LINGERIE | This shop has been vending high-quality clothing—the kind that goes next to bare skin—since 1895. Remember that luxury comes at a price. ⊠ *Via Porta Rossa 45/r, Piazza della Repubblica.*

San Lorenzo

A sculptor, painter, architect, and poet, Florentine native son Michelangelo was a consummate genius, and some of his finest creations remain in his hometown. The Biblioteca Medicea Laurenziana is perhaps his most fanciful work of architecture. A key to understanding Michelangelo's genius can be found in the magnificent Cappelle Medicee, where both his sculptural and architectural prowess can be clearly seen. Planned frescoes were never completed, sadly, for they would have shown in one space the artistic triple threat that he certainly was. The towering yet graceful *David*, perhaps his most famous work, resides in the Galleria dell'Accademia.

Sights

Basilica di San Lorenzo

CHURCH | Filippo Brunelleschi designed this basilica, as well as that of Santo Spirito in the Oltrarno, in the 15th century. He never lived to see either finished. The two interiors are similar in design and effect. San Lorenzo, however, has a grid of dark, inlaid marble lines on the floor, which considerably heightens the dramatic effect. Brunelleschi's Sagrestia Vecchia (Old Sacristy) has stucco decorations by Donatello; it's at the end of the left transept. ⊠ *Piazza San Lorenzo, San Lorenzo* ⊕ *sanlorenzofirenze.it* 🎫 *€7* ⊗ *Closed Sun.*

Biblioteca Medicea Laurenziana

(*Laurentian Library*)

LIBRARY | Michelangelo the architect was every bit as original as Michelangelo the sculptor. He was interested in experimentation, invention, and the expression of a personal vision that was at times highly idiosyncratic. It was never more idiosyncratic than in the Laurentian Library, begun in 1524 and finished in 1568 by Bartolomeo Ammannati. Its famous *vestibolo*, a strangely shaped anteroom, has had scholars scratching their heads for centuries. In a space more than two stories high, why did Michelangelo limit his use of columns and pilasters to the upper two-thirds of the wall? Why didn't he rest them on strong pedestals instead of on huge, decorative curlicue scrolls, which rob them of all visual support? Why did he recess them into the wall, which makes them look weaker still? The architectural elements give the room a soft, rubbery look that is one of the strangest effects ever achieved by 16th-century architecture. ⊠ *Piazza San Lorenzo 9, entrance to left of San Lorenzo, San Lorenzo* ⊕ *www. bmlonline.it* ⊠ *Special exhibitions €3* ⊗ *Check ahead on opening days and times as this site has seen temporary closures.*

Cappelle Medicee (*Medici Chapels*)
CHURCH | This magnificent complex includes the Cappella dei Principi, the Medici chapel and mausoleum begun in 1605 that kept marble workers busy for several hundred years, and the Sagrestia Nuova (New Sacristy), designed by Michelangelo and so called to distinguish it from Brunelleschi's Sagrestia Vecchia (Old Sacristy). Michelangelo received the commission for the New Sacristy in 1520 from Cardinal Giulio de' Medici, who later became Pope Clement VII. ⊠ *Piazza di Madonna degli Aldobrandini, San Lorenzo* ☎ *055/294883 reservations* ⊕ *www. cappellemedicee.it* ⊠ *€9* ⊗ *Closed Tues., and 1st, 3rd, and 5th Sun. of month.*

Galleria dell'Accademia
(*Accademia Gallery*)
ART MUSEUM | FAMILY | The collection of Florentine paintings, dating from the 13th to the 18th century, is largely unremarkable, but the sculptures by Michelangelo are worth the price of admission. The unfinished *Slaves*, fighting their way out of their marble prisons, were meant for the tomb of Michelangelo's overly demanding patron Pope Julius II. But the focal point is the original *David*,

commissioned in 1501 by the Opera del Duomo (Cathedral Works Committee), which gave the 26-year-old sculptor a leftover block of marble that had been ruined 40 years earlier by two other sculptors. ⊠ *Via Ricasoli 60, San Marco* ☎ *055/294883 reservations, 055/238–8609 gallery* ⊕ *www.polomuseale. firenze.it* ⊠ *€12* ⊗ *Closed Mon.*

★ **Mercato Centrale**
MARKET | FAMILY | Some of the food at this huge, two-story market hall is remarkably exotic. The ground floor contains meat and cheese stalls, as well as some very good bars that have panini. The upstairs food hall is eerily reminiscent of food halls everywhere, but the quality of the food served more than makes up for this. The downstairs market is closed on Sunday; the upstairs food hall is always open. ⊠ *Piazza del Mercato Centrale, San Lorenzo* ☎ *239–9798* ⊕ *www.mercato-centrale.it.*

Museo di Casa Martelli
HISTORIC HOME | The wealthy Martelli family, long associated with the all-powerful Medici, lived, from the 16th century, in this palace on a quiet street near the Basilica of San Lorenzo. The last Martelli died in 1986, and, in October 2009, the *casa-museo* (house-museum) opened to the public. It's the only nonreconstructed example of such a house in all of Florence, and for that reason alone it's worth a visit. The family collected art, and while most of the stuff is B-list, a few gems by Beccafumi, Salvatore Rosa, and Piero di Cosimo adorn the walls. ⊠ *Via Zanetti 8, San Lorenzo* ☎ *055/294883* ⊕ *www. polomuseale.firenze.it* ⊠ *€18* ⊗ *Closed Sun.–Fri.* ⊜ *Reservations essential.*

Museo di San Marco
ART MUSEUM | A former Dominican convent adjacent to the church of San Marco houses this museum, which contains many stunning works by Fra Angelico (circa 1400–55), the Dominican friar famous for his piety as well as for his painting. When the friars' cells were restructured

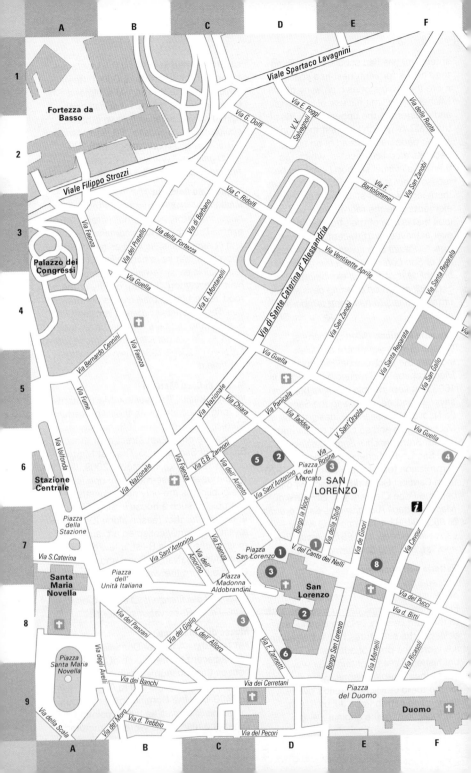

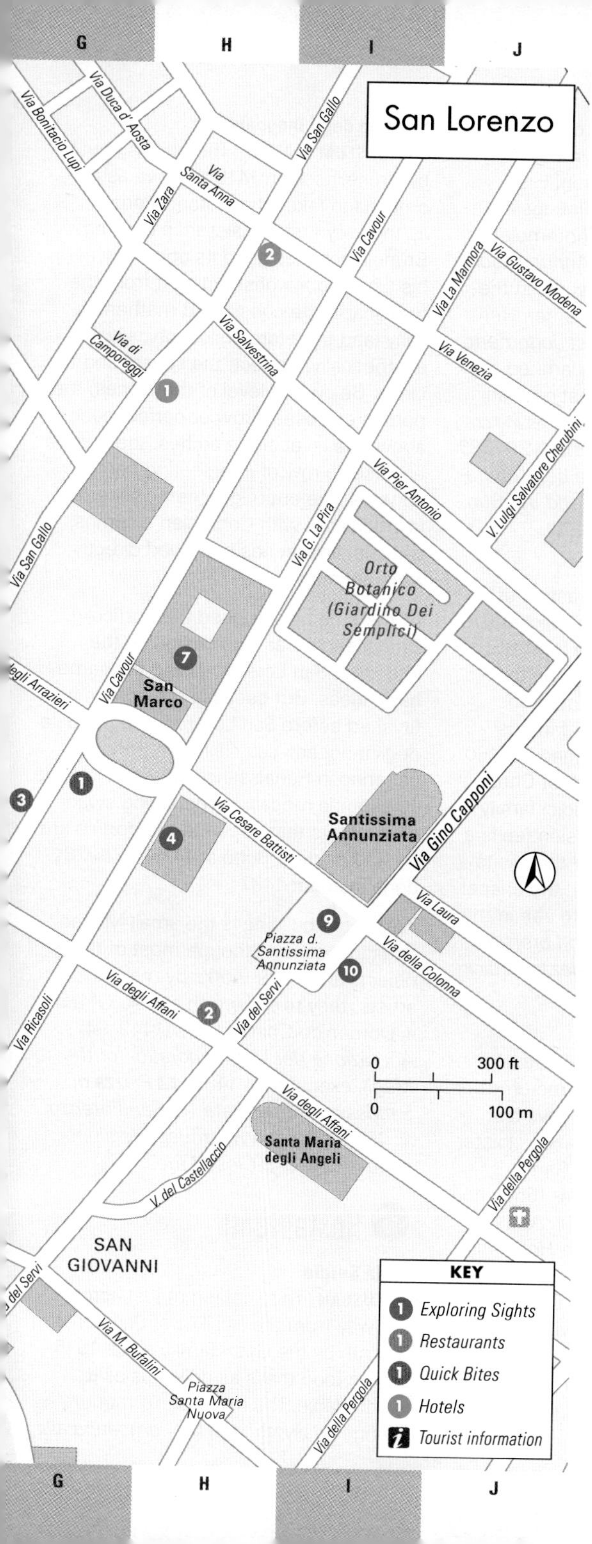

San Lorenzo

12

Florence SAN LORENZO

Orto Botanico (Giardino Dei Semplici)

San Marco

Santissima Annunziata

Piazza d. Santissima Annunziata

SAN GIOVANNI

Piazza Santa Maria Nuova

Santa Maria degli Angeli

0 ____ 300 ft
0 ____ 100 m

KEY

1 *Exploring Sights*
1 *Restaurants*
1 *Quick Bites*
1 *Hotels*
🛈 *Tourist information*

between 1439 and 1444, he decorated many of them with frescoes meant to spur religious contemplation. His unostentatious and direct paintings exalt the simple beauties of the contemplative life. Don't miss the famous *Annunciation*, on the upper floor, and the works in the gallery off the cloister as you enter. Here you can see his beautiful *Last Judgment*; as usual, the tortures of the damned are far more inventive and interesting than the pleasures of the redeemed. ⊠ *Piazza San Marco 1, San Lorenzo* ☎ *055/294883* ⊕ *www.polomusealetoscana.beniculturali.it* ⊠ *€8* ⊙ *Closed 1st, 3rd, and 5th Sun. and 2nd and 4th Mon. of month.*

Palazzo Medici-Riccardi

CASTLE/PALACE | The main attraction of this palace, begun in 1444 by Michelozzo for Cosimo de' Medici, is the interior chapel, the Cappella dei Magi, on the piano nobile (main floor). Painted on its walls is Benozzo Gozzoli's famous *Procession of the Magi*, finished in 1460 and celebrating both the birth of Christ and the greatness of the Medici family. Keep in mind that the admission fee is a bit pricey when you consider that visits are limited to 15 minutes and the chapel is the only interesting thing to see in the building. ⊠ *Via Cavour 1, San Lorenzo* ☎ *055/276–8224* ⊕ *www.palazzomediciriccardi.it* ⊠ *€10* ⊙ *Closed Wed.*

Santissima Annunziata

CHURCH | Dating from the mid-13th century, this church was restructured in 1447 by Michelozzo, who gave it an uncommon (and lovely) entrance cloister with frescoes by Andrea del Sarto (1486–1530), Pontormo (1494–1556), and Rosso Fiorentino (1494–1540). Another fresco is note is the very fine *Holy Trinity with St. Jerome* in the second chapel on the left. Done by Andrea del Castagno (circa 1421–57), it shows a wiry and emaciated St. Jerome with Paula and Eustochium, two of his closest followers. ⊠ *Piazza di Santissima Annunziata, San Lorenzo* ⊠ *Free.*

Spedale degli Innocenti

ART MUSEUM | FAMILY | The building built by Brunelleschi in 1419 to serve as an orphanage takes the historical prize as the very first Renaissance building. Brunelleschi designed its portico with his usual rigor, constructing it from the two shapes he considered mathematically (and therefore philosophically and aesthetically) perfect: the square and the circle. Below the level of the arches, the portico encloses a row of perfect cubes; above the level of the arches, the portico encloses a row of intersecting hemispheres. The entire geometric scheme is articulated with Corinthian columns, capitals, and arches borrowed directly from antiquity.

At the time he designed the portico, Brunelleschi was also designing the interior of San Lorenzo, using the same basic ideas. But because the portico was finished before San Lorenzo, the Spedale degli Innocenti can claim the honor of ushering in Renaissance architecture. The 10 ceramic medallions depicting swaddled infants that decorate the portico are by Andrea della Robbia (1435–1525/28), done in about 1487.

Within the building is the small Museo degli Innocenti. Although most of the objects are minor works by major artists, they're still worth a look. Of note is Domenico Ghirlandaio's (1449–94) *Adorazione dei Magi* (*Adoration of the Magi*), executed in 1488. ⊠ *Piazza di Santissima Annunziata 12, San Lorenzo* ☎ *055/20371* ⊕ *www.museodeglinnocenti.it* ⊠ *€13* ⊙ *Closed Tues.*

🍽 Restaurants

★ da Sergio

$ | TUSCAN | This restaurant just across the way from the Basilica of San Lorenzo and run by the Gozzi family since 1915 serves food that's as delicious as it is affordable. The menu short menu changes daily, though the *lombatina alla griglia* (grilled veal T-bone steak) is almost always available, and meat eaters should not miss it. **Known for:** terrific pastas; ever-changing menu; local favorite. $ *Average main: €10* ✉ *Piazza San Lorenzo 8/r, San Lorenzo* ☎ *055/281941* ⏾ *Closed Sun. No dinner Mon.–Thurs.*

La Mescita

$ | TUSCAN | Come early (or late) to grab a seat at this tiny spot frequented by Florentine university students and businesspeople, who come to enjoy the day's primi (the lasagna is terrific), perhaps followed by the *polpettone* (meat loaf) and tomato sauce. Though seats are cramped, and the wine is no great shakes, the service is friendly, and the food hits the spot. **Known for:** delicious pastas at rock-bottom prices; jovial staff; its longevity (it's been around since the 1920s). $ *Average main: €9* ✉ *Via degli Alfani 70/r, Florence* ☎ *347/795–1604* 🚫 *No credit cards* ⏾ *Closed Wed. No dinner.*

★ Mario

$ | TUSCAN | Florentines flock to this narrow, family-run trattoria near San Lorenzo to feast on Tuscan favorites served at simple tables under a wooden ceiling dating from 1536. A distinct cafeteria feel and genuine Florentine hospitality prevail: you'll be seated wherever there's room, which often means with strangers. **Known for:** festive atmosphere; roasted potatoes; grilled meats. $ *Average main: €13* ✉ *Via Rosina 2/r, corner of Piazza del Mercato Centrale, San Lorenzo* ☎ *055/218550* ⊕ *www.trattoriamario.com* ⏾ *Closed Sun. and Aug. No dinner.*

☕ Coffee and Quick Bites

Alfio e Beppe

$ | ITALIAN | Watch chickens roast over high flames while you decide which of the delightful side dishes you'd like to enjoy as well. Although this place is strictly takeout (there are no tables), it's open on Sunday when most places

are not. **Known for:** delicious roasted potatoes; roast chicken to go; good ribs. $ *Average main: €9* ✉ *Via Cavour 118–120/r, San Marco* ☎ *055/214108* ⏾ *Closed Sat.*

★ da Nerbone

$ | TUSCAN | This *tavola calda* (cafeteria) in the middle of the covered Mercato Centrale has been serving Florentines since 1872. Tasty primi and secondi are always available, as are *bolliti* (boiled beef sandwiches), but the cognoscenti come for the *panino con il lampredotto* (tripe sandwich)—best when it's prepared *bagnato* (with the bread quickly dipped in the tripe cooking liquid) and served slathered with the green and/or spicier red sauce. **Known for:** favorite dishes sell out fast; frequented by locals (and everyone else); tripe sandwich. $ *Average main: €10* ✉ *Mercato San Lorenzo, Florence* ⏾ *Closed Sun. No dinner.*

Shake

$ | ITALIAN | Handily located between Piazza San Marco and Piazza San Lorenzo, Shake serves up creative juices, tasty baked goods, wonderful salads, and great bowls. It's committed to sustainability and to keeping its carbon footprint small. **Known for:** remarkable way with juices (the De-Tox is especially good); courtyard seating; nice, cheerful staff. $ *Average main: €7* ✉ *Via Camillo Cavour 67/69r, San Lorenzo* ☎ *055/051–5418* ⊕ *www.shakecafe.bio* ⏾ *Closed Wed.*

🛏 Hotels

Antica Dimora Firenze

$$ | B&B/INN | Each simply furnished room in this *residenza* (guesthouse) is painted a different pastel color—peach, rose, powder-blue—and double-glazed windows ensure a peaceful night's sleep. **Pros:** ample DVD library; honor bar with Antinori wines; complimentary coffee, tea, and fresh fruit available all day in the sitting room. **Cons:** some might consider it too small; might be too removed for

some; books up quickly. $ *Rooms from:
€160* ✉ *Via San Gallo 72, San Marco*
☎ *055/462–7296* ⊕ *www.antichedimore-
fiorentine.it* ▭ *No credit cards* ⇆ *6 rooms*
⦿ *Free Breakfast.*

★ Antica Dimora Johlea

$$$ | **B&B/INN** | In addition to guest rooms
with four-poster beds and sweeping
drapes, this 19th-century palazzo has a
charming, flower-filled terrace where you
can sip a glass of wine while taking in a
view of Brunelleschi's cupola. **Pros:** great
staff; honor bar; cheerful rooms. **Cons:**
steps to breakfast room; staircase to
roof terrace is narrow; staff goes home
at 7:30. $ *Rooms from: €220* ✉ *Via San
Gallo 80, San Marco* ☎ *055/463–3292*
⊕ *www.antichedimorefiorentine.it* ⇆ *6
rooms* ⦿ *Free Breakfast.*

Firenze Number Nine

$$$ | **HOTEL** | At this elegant hotel, swank
reception rooms have comfortable
couches and contemporary artwork, and
guest rooms feature parquet floors, high
ceilings, and furnishings that combine Scandinavian sleekness with the
Italian love for fine fabric (think: damask
draperies). **Pros:** historic center location;
sumptuous breakfast; walk-in gym and
spa. **Cons:** books up quickly; might be
too trendy for some; some street noise.
$ *Rooms from: €300* ✉ *Via del Conti 9,
San Lorenzo* ☎ *055/293777* ⊕ *firenze-
numbernine.com* ⇆ *45 rooms* ⦿ *Free
Breakfast.*

Il Guelfo Bianco

$$ | **HOTEL** | The 15th-century building has
all modern conveniences, but Renaissance charm still shines in the high-ceil-
ing rooms. **Pros:** great staff; sumptuous
breakfast; beautiful floors made of either
parquet or marble. **Cons:** not all rooms are
well lit; might be too removed for some;
rooms facing the street can be noisy.
$ *Rooms from: €150* ✉ *Via Cavour 29,
San Marco* ☎ *055/288330* ⊕ *ilguelfobian-
co.it* ⇆ *40 rooms* ⦿ *Free Breakfast.*

Shopping

★ Baroni

FOOD | The cheese selection at Baroni
may be the most comprehensive in
Florence. It also sells high-quality truffle
products, vinegars, and other delicacies,
many of which are, or can be, packed
for shipping. ✉ *Mercato Central, enter
at Via Signa, San Lorenzo* ☎ *055/289576*
⊕ *www.baronialimentari.it.*

Mercato Centrale

MARKET | **FAMILY** | This huge indoor food
market offers a staggering selection of
all things edible. Downstairs is full of
vendors hawking their wares—meat,
fish, fruit, vegetables—upstairs (daily
8 am–midnight) is full of food stalls
serving up the best of what Italy has to
offer. ✉ *Piazza del Mercato Centrale,
San Lorenzo* ☎ *055/2399798* ⊕ *www.
mercatocentrale.it.*

Mercato di San Lorenzo

MARKET | **FAMILY** | The clothing and
leather-goods stalls of the Mercato di
San Lorenzo in the streets next to the
church of San Lorenzo have bargains for
shoppers on a budget. ✉ *Florence.*

Santa Maria Novella

Piazza Santa Maria Novella is a gorgeous,
pedestrian-only square, with grass (laced
with roses) and plenty of places to sit
and rest your feet. The streets in and
around the piazza have their share of
architectural treasures, including some
of Florence's most tasteful palaces.
Between Santa Maria Novella and the
Arno is Via Tornabuoni, Florence's swanki-
est shopping street.

Sights

Museo Novecento

ART MUSEUM | It began life as a 13th-cen-
tury Franciscan hostel offering shelter
to tired pilgrims. It later became a

convalescent home, and in the late 18th century it was a school for poor girls. Now the former Ospedale di San Paolo houses a museum devoted to Italian art of the 20th century. Admittedly, most of these artists are not exactly household names, but the museum is so beautifully well done that it's worth a visit. The second floor contains works by artists from the second half of the century; start on the third floor, and go directly to the collection of Alberto della Ragione, a naval engineer who was determined to be on the cutting edge of art collecting. ⊠ *Piazza Santa Maria Novella 10, Santa Maria Novella* ☎ *055/286132* ⊕ *www. museonovecento.it* ☎ *€9.50* ☉ *Closed Thurs.*

Museo Salvatore Ferragamo

ART MUSEUM | A shrine to footwear, the shoes in this dramatically displayed collection were designed by Salvatore Ferragamo (1898–1960) beginning in the early 20th century. Born in southern Italy, Ferragamo jump-started his career in Hollywood by creating shoes for the likes of Mary Pickford and Rudolph Valentino. He then returned to Florence and set up shop in the 13th-century Palazzo Spini Ferroni. The collection includes about 16,000 shoes, and those on display are frequently rotated. Special exhibitions are also mounted here and are well worth visiting—past shows have been devoted to Audrey Hepburn, Greta Garbo, and Marilyn Monroe. ⊠ *Via dei Tornabuoni 2, Santa Maria Novella* ☎ *055/356–2846* ⊕ *www.ferragamo.com* ☎ *€15.*

Museo Stibbert

ART MUSEUM | Frederick Stibbert (1838–1906), born in Florence to an Italian mother and an English father, liked to collect things. Over a lifetime of doing so, he amassed some 50,000 objects. This museum, which was also his home, displays many of them. He had a fascination with medieval armor, as well as costumes, particularly Uzbek costumes, which are exhibited in a room called the

Moresque Hall. These are mingled with an extensive collection of swords and guns. ⊠ *Via Federico Stibbert 26, Florence* ☎ *055/486049* ⊕ *www.museostibbert.it* ☎ *€8* ☉ *Closed Thurs.*

Palazzo Strozzi

CASTLE/PALACE | The Strozzi family built this imposing palazzo in an attempt to outshine the nearby Palazzo Medici. The exterior is simple, severe, and massive: it's a testament to the wealth of a patrician, 15th-century Florentine family. The interior courtyard is another matter altogether. It is here that the classical vocabulary—columns, capitals, pilasters, arches, and cornices—is given uninhibited and powerful expression. ⊠ *Via Tornabuoni, Piazza della Repubblica* ☎ *055/264–5155* ⊕ *www.palazzostrozzi.org* ☎ *Free.*

Santa Maria Novella

CHURCH | The facade of this church looks distinctly clumsy by later Renaissance standards, and with good reason: it is an architectural hybrid. The lower half was completed mostly in the 14th century and about 100 years later (around 1456), architect Leon Battista Alberti was called in to complete the job, adding architectural motifs in an entirely different style. Highlights include the 14th-century, stained-glass-rose window depicting the *Coronation of the Virgin*; the Cappella Filippo Strozzi, containing late-15th-century frescoes and stained glass by Filippino Lippi; and the *cappella maggiore*, displaying frescoes by Ghirlandaio. ⊠ *Piazza Santa Maria Novella 19, Santa Maria Novella* ☎ *055/219257 museo* ⊕ *www.smn.it/en* ☎ *€8* ☉ *Closed Sun. morning.*

Santa Trinita

CHURCH | Started in the 11th century by Vallombrosian monks and originally Romanesque in style, this church underwent a Gothic remodeling during the 14th century. (Remains of the Romanesque construction are visible on the interior front wall.) The major works are the fresco cycle and altarpiece in

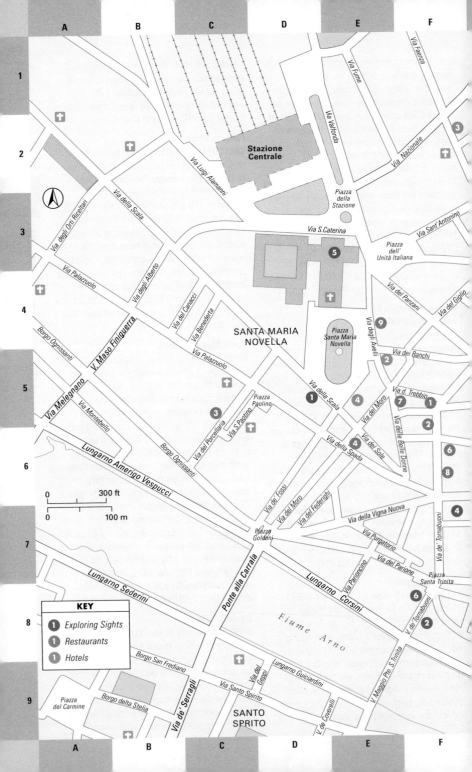

Santa Maria Novella

Sights ▼

1 Museo Novecento................. **D5**
2 Museo Salvatore Ferragamo...... **F8**
3 Museo Stibbert **G1**
4 Palazzo Strozzi **F7**
5 Santa Maria Novella **E4**
6 Santa Trinita........................ **F8**

Restaurants ▼

1 Buca Lapi............................ **F5**
2 Cantinetta Antinori **F6**
3 La Sostanza **C5**
4 La Spada............................ **E6**
5 Mangiafoco **G8**
6 Obicà **F6**
7 Osteria delle Belle Donne **E5**
8 Procacci **F6**
9 Vincanto **E4**

Hotels ▼

1 Gallery Hotel Art **G9**
2 Hotel L'Orologio **E5**
3 Nuova Italia **F2**
4 The Place Firenze.................. **E5**

the Cappella Sassetti, the second to the high altar's right, painted by Ghirlandaio between 1480 and 1485. His work here possesses graceful decorative appeal and proudly depicts his native city, as most of the cityscapes show 15th-century Florence in all its glory. The wall frescoes illustrate scenes from the life of St. Francis, and the altarpiece, depicting the *Adoration of the Shepherds,* veritably glows. ✉ *Piazza Santa Trinita, Santa Maria Novella* ⏲ *Closed Sun. 10:45–4.*

🍴 Restaurants

Buca Lapi
$$$$ | **ITALIAN** | The Antinori family started selling wine from their palace's basement in the 15th century, and, 600 years later, this *buca* (hole) is a lively, subterranean spot filled with Florentine aristocrats chowing down on what might be the best—and the most expensive—bistecca fiorentina (flavorful, lightly seasoned beef) in town. The classic Tuscan menu has the usual suspects: *crostino di cavolo nero* (black cabbage on toasted garlic bread), along with ribollita (vegetable, bean, and bread soup) and pappa al pomodoro (tomato and bread soup). **Known for:** gargantuan bistecca fiorentina; pet-friendly; adherence to Tuscan classics. [$] *Average main: €40* ✉ *Via del Trebbio 1* ☎ *055/213768* 🌐 *www.bucalapi.com/en* ⏲ *Closed Sun. No lunch.*

Cantinetta Antinori
$$$ | **TUSCAN** | After a morning of shopping on Via Tornabuoni, stop for lunch in this 15th-century palazzo, a place to see and be seen as well as to dine. The panache of the clientele is matched by that of the food, with dishes such as *tramezzino con pane di campagna al tartufo* (bread served with country pâté and truffles) and *insalata di gamberoni e gamberetti con carciofi freschi* (crayfish and prawn salad with shaved raw artichokes). **Known for:** outdoor seating in a 15th-century courtyard; most ingredients come from the family farm; chic clientele. [$] *Average main: €31* ✉ *Piazza Antinori 3, Santa Maria Novella* ☎ *055/292234* 🌐 *cantinetta-antinori.com/en* ⏲ *Closed Sun., 20 days in Aug., and Dec. 25–Jan. 6.*

★ La Sostanza
$$ | **TUSCAN** | Since opening its doors in 1869, this trattoria has been serving top-notch, unpretentious food to Florentines who like their bistecca very large and, of course, very rare, as that's the only way to eat it. The *tartino di carciofi* (artichoke tart) and the *pollo al burro* (chicken with butter) are signature dishes. **Known for:** Tuscan classics; no-frills, 19th-century decor; delicious desserts (especially the semifreddo). [$] *Average main: €16* ✉ *Via del Porcellana 25/r, Lungarno North* ☎ *055/212691* 💳 *No credit cards* ⏲ *Closed Sun.*

La Spada
$ | **ITALIAN** | **FAMILY** | Near Santa Maria Novella is La Spada. Walk in and inhale the fragrant aromas of meats cooking in the wood-burning oven. **Known for:** eat in or order takeout; adherence to Tuscan cuisine; grilled meats and aromatic pastas. [$] *Average main: €11* ✉ *Via della Spada 62/r, Santa Maria Novella* ☎ *055/218757* 🌐 *ristorantelaspada.it.*

★ Mangiafoco
$$ | **TUSCAN** | On a romantic medieval side street in the heart of the centro storico, this small restaurant serves Tuscan classics that reflect both the whims of the chef and what's in season. The menu features creative salads and pasta, meat, and truffle dishes, as well as *taglieri* (mixed meat and cheese plates) that are often served with jams made from Chianti, vin santo, or balsamic vinegar. **Known for:** great service; house-made breads and desserts; phenomenal wines by the glass or the bottle. [$] *Average main: €20* ✉ *Borgo Santi Apostoli 26/r, Santa Maria Novella* ☎ *055/265–8170* 🌐 *www.mangiafoco.com* ⏲ *Closed Wed.*

Obicà

$$ | ITALIAN | Mozzarella takes center stage at this sleek eatery on Florence's swankiest street. The cheese, along with its culinary cousin *burrata* (a fresh cheese filled with cream), arrives daily from southern Italy to become the centerpiece for various salads and pastas. **Known for:** outdoor seating in nice weather; outstanding pizza and desserts; mozzarella-laden menu. $ *Average main: €18* ⊠ *Via Tornabuoni 16, Santa Maria Novella* ☎ *055/277–3526* ⊕ *www.obica.com.*

Osteria delle Belle Donne

$$ | TUSCAN | Down the street from the church of Santa Maria Novella, this gaily decorated spot, always festooned with some sort of creative decoration (ropes of garlic and other vegetables have figured in the past) has an ever-changing menu and stellar service. The list of Tuscan standards is shaken up with alternatives such as *sedani con bacon, verza, e uova* (thick noodles sauced with bacon, cabbage, and egg); when avocados are ripe, they're on the menu, too, either with cold boiled shrimp or expertly grilled chicken breast. **Known for:** dessert; many dishes not typical of Tuscany; seasonal ingredients. $ *Average main: €19* ⊠ *Via delle Belle Donne 16/r, Santa Maria Novella* ☎ *055/238–2609* ⊕ *www. belledonneosteria.it.*

★ Procacci

$$ | ITALIAN | At this classy Florentine institution dating from 1885, try one of the truffle panini and swish it down with a glass of prosecco. **Known for:** serene (but tiny) space; excellent wines by the glass; pane tartufato. $ *Average main: €15* ⊠ *Via Tornabuoni 64/r, Santa Maria Novella* ☎ *055/211656* ⊕ *www.procacci1885.it.*

Vincanto

$$$ | ITALIAN | It opens at 11 am and closes at midnight: this is a rarity in Florentine dining. They do a little bit of everything here, including fine pastas, salads, pizzas, and even an American-style breakfast. **Known for:** outside terrace with views of a beautiful square; kitchen stays open; a wide-ranging menu. $ *Average main: €28* ⊠ *Piazza Santa Maria Novella 23/r, Santa Maria Novella* ☎ *055/2679300* ⊕ *www.ristorantevincanto.com.*

 # Hotels

Gallery Hotel Art

$$$$ | HOTEL | High design resides at this art showcase near the Ponte Vecchio, where sleek, uncluttered rooms are dressed mostly in neutrals but have luxe touches such as leather headboards and kimono robes. **Pros:** trendy atmosphere; the in-house Fusion Bar serves delightful cocktails; artistic touches. **Cons:** might be too trendy for some; books up quickly; some street noise. $ *Rooms from: €680* ⊠ *Vicolo dell'Oro 5, Santa Maria Novella* ☎ *055/27263* ⊕ *www.lungarnocollection. com/gallery-hotel-art* ⌐ *63 rooms* ❍❘ *Free Breakfast.*

Hotel L'Orologio

$$$ | HOTEL | The owner of this quietly understated, elegant hotel has a real passion for watches, which is why he chose to name his hotel after them (and why you will see them throughout the property). **Pros:** location; stunning breakfast room; great staff. **Cons:** holds conferences from time to time; gets the occasional tour group; some folks think it's too close to the train station. $ *Rooms from: €250* ⊠ *Piazza Santa Maria Novella 24, Santa Maria Novella* ☎ *055/277380* ⊕ *www. hotelorologioflorence.com* ⌐ *60 rooms* ❍❘ *Free Breakfast.*

Nuova Italia

$ | HOTEL | FAMILY | The genial Viti family oversees this property with clean and simple rooms near the train station and well within walking distance of the sights. **Pros:** reasonable rates; great for those on a budget; close to everything. **Cons:** some street noise; the neighborhood is highly trafficked; no elevator.

$ Rooms from: €119 ⊠ Via Faenza 26, Santa Maria Novella ☎ 055/287508 ⊕ www.hotel-nuovaitalia.com ⊗ Closed Dec. 20–Dec. 27 ⤸ 20 rooms ⦿ Free Breakfast.

★ The Place Firenze

$$$$ | HOTEL | Hard to spot from the street, this sumptuous place provides all the comforts of a luxe home away from home—expect soothing earth tones in the guest rooms, free minibars, crisp linens, and room service offering organic dishes. **Pros:** private, intimate feel; small dogs allowed; stellar staff. **Cons:** might be too trendy for some; books up quickly; breakfast at a shared table. $ Rooms from: €660 ⊠ Piazza Santa Maria Novella 7, Santa Maria Novella ☎ 055/264–5181 ⊕ www.theplacefirenze.com ⤸ 20 rooms ⦿ Free Breakfast.

✪ Performing Arts

Maggio Musicale Fiorentino

MUSIC | In 2014, a new music hall opened in the area now called the Parco della Musica (Music Park), which was designed by Paolo Desideri and associates. Maggio Musicale Fiorentino has taken up residence there, and continues to hold forth at the Teatro Comunale (⊠ Corso Italia 16, Lungarno North ☎ 055/287222). Within Italy you can purchase tickets from late April through July directly at the box office or by phone (☎ 055/277–9309). You can also buy them online. ⊠ Via Alamanni 39, Santa Maria Novella ☎ 055/200–1278 ⊕ www.maggiofiorentino.it.

Tuscany Hall

FESTIVALS | This large exhibition space, formerly Teatro Saschall, hosts many events throughout the year, including a big and boisterous Christmas bazaar run by the Red Cross, visiting rock stars, and trendy bands from all over Europe. ⊠ Lungarno Aldo Moro 3, Santa Maria Novella ☎ 055/650–4112 ⊕ www.tuscanyhall.it.

Shopping

Alberto Cozzi

STATIONERY | You'll find an extensive line of Florentine papers and paper products in this shop, where artisans also rebind and restore books and works on paper. Opening hours are tricky, so it's best to call before stopping by. ⊠ Via del Parione 35/r, Santa Maria Novella ☎ 055/294968.

★ Angela Caputi

JEWELRY & WATCHES | Angela Caputi wows Florentine cognoscenti with her highly creative, often outsize, acrylic jewelry. A small but equally creative collection of women's clothing made of fine fabrics is also on offer. ⊠ Borgo Santi Apostoli 44/46, Santa Maria Novella ☎ 055/292993 ⊕ www.angelacaputi.com.

Antica Officina del Farmacista Dr. Vranjes

PERFUME | Dr. Vranjes elevates aromatherapy to an art form with scents for the body and home. ⊠ Via della Vigna Nuova 30/r, Santa Maria Novella ☎ 055/094–5851 ⊕ www.drvranjes.it.

Brandimarte

HOUSEWARES | Most people want to buy gold when they come to Florence (for which it is justly famous). That said, Brandimarte, which has specialized in exquisitely crafted silver objects since 1955, is well worth a visit. ⊠ Via del Moro 92/r, Santa Maria Novella ☎ 349/422–0269 ⊕ www.brandimarte.com.

Cellerini

LEATHER GOODS | In a city where it seems just about everybody carries an expensive leather bag, Cellerini is an institution. ⊠ Via del Sole 9/r, Santa Maria Novella ☎ 055/282533 ⊕ www.cellerini.it.

Emilio Pucci

WOMEN'S CLOTHING | The aristocratic Marchese di Barsento, Emilio Pucci, became an international name in the late 1950s when the stretch ski clothes he designed for himself caught on with the dolce vita ("sweet life") crowd—his pseudopsychedelic prints and "palazzo pajamas" became all the rage. ⊠ *Via Tornabuoni 20–22/r, Santa Maria Novella* ☎ *055/265–8082* ⊕ *www.emiliopucci. com.*

Ferragamo

SHOES | This classy institution, in a 13th-century palazzo, displays designer clothing and accessories, though elegant footwear still underlies the Ferragamo success. ⊠ *Via Tornabuoni 14/r, Santa Maria Novella* ☎ *055/292123* ⊕ *store. ferragamo.com.*

Gatto Bianco

JEWELRY & WATCHES | This contemporary jeweler has breathtakingly beautiful pieces featuring semiprecious and precious stones. ⊠ *Borgo Santi Apostoli 12/r, Santa Maria Novella* ☎ *055/282989* ⊕ *www. gattobiancogioielli.com.*

Giotti

LEATHER GOODS | You'll find multiple lines of leather bags, wallets, and other accessories here. ⊠ *Piazza Ognissanti 3–4/r, Lungarno North* ☎ *055/294265* ⊕ *www. bottegagiotti.com/collection.*

★ Loretta Caponi

MIXED CLOTHING | Synonymous with Florentine embroidery, this shop sells luxury lace, linens, and lingerie that have earned the eponymous signora worldwide renown. There's also beautiful (and expensive) clothing for children. ⊠ *Via delle Belle Donne 28/r, Santa Maria Novella* ☎ *055/213668* ⊕ *www.lorettacaponi.it/en.*

★ Officina Profumo Farmaceutica di Santa Maria Novella

PERFUME | The essence of a Florentine holiday is captured in the sachets of this Art Nouveau emporium of herbal cosmetics and soaps that are made following centuries-old recipes created by friars. ⊠ *Via della Scala 16, Santa Maria Novella* ☎ *055/216276* ⊕ *www.smnovella.it.*

★ Pineider

STATIONERY | Although it has shops throughout the world, Pineider started out in Florence in 1774 and still does all its printing here. Stationery and business cards are the mainstay, but the stores also sell fine-leather desk accessories as well as a less stuffy, more lighthearted line of products. ⊠ *Piazza Rucellai 4/7/r, Santa Maria Novella* ☎ *055/284655* ⊕ *www.pineider.com.*

Principe

DEPARTMENT STORE | This Florentine institution sells casual clothes for men, women, and children at far-from-casual prices. It also has a great housewares department. ⊠ *Via del Sole 2, Santa Maria Novella* ☎ *055/292843* ⊕ *www. principedifirenze.com.*

Valli

FABRICS | Gifted seamstresses (and seamsters) should look no further than this place, which sells sumptuous silks, beaded fabrics, lace, wool, and tweeds by the meter. ⊠ *Via della Vigna Nuova 81/r, Santa Maria Novella* ☎ *055/282485* ⊕ *www.vallitessuti.com.*

Santa Croce

The Santa Croce quarter, on the southeast fringe of the historic center, was built up in the Middle Ages outside the second set of medieval city walls. The centerpiece of the neighborhood was (and is) the basilica of Santa Croce, which could hold great numbers of worshippers; the vast piazza could accommodate any overflow and also served as a fairground and, allegedly since the middle of the 16th century, as a playing field for no-holds-barred soccer games. A center of leatherworking since the Middle Ages, the neighborhood is still packed with leatherworkers and leather shops.

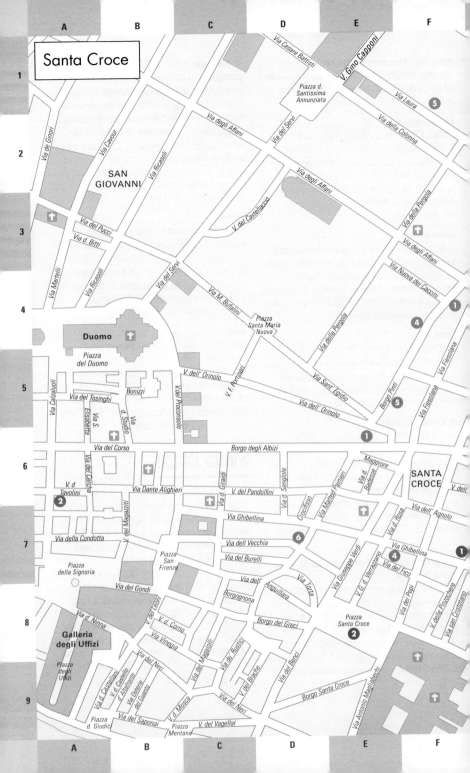

Sights ▼

1 Casa Buonarroti **F7**
2 Piazza Santa Croce................. **E8**
3 Santa Croce **H8**
4 Sinagoga........................... **H5**

Restaurants ▼

1 Antico Noè **E6**
2 Cibrèo Ristorante **H6**
3 Cibrèo Trattoria **H6**
4 Enoteca Pinchiorri................. **F7**
5 La Giostra.......................... **E5**
6 Pizzeria Caffè Italiano **D7**
7 Ruth's **H5**

Quick Bites ▼

1 da Rocco.......................... **I7**
2 Perché No!.......................... **A6**

Hotels ▼

1 Borgo Pinti.......................... **F4**
2 The Four Seasons **H1**
3 Hotel Regency **J2**
4 Monna Lisa.......................... **F4**
5 Morandi alla Crocetta.............. **F1**

12

Florence SANTA CROCE

Sights

Casa Buonarroti

ART MUSEUM | If you really enjoy walking in the footsteps of the great genius, you may want to complete the picture by visiting the Buonarroti family home. Michelangelo lived here from 1516 to 1525, and later gave it to his nephew, whose son, Michelangelo il Giovane (Michelangelo the Younger), turned it into a gallery dedicated to his great-uncle. The artist's descendants filled it with art treasures, some by Michelangelo himself. Two early marble works—the *Madonna of the Stairs* and *Battle of the Centaurs*—demonstrate his genius. ✉ *Via Ghibellina 70, Santa Croce* ☎ *055/241752* 🌐 *www.casabuonarroti.it* 🎫 *€8* 🕒 *Closed Tues.*

Piazza Santa Croce

PLAZA/SQUARE | Originally outside the city's 12th-century walls, this piazza grew with the Franciscans, who used it for public preaching. During the Renaissance, it hosted *giostre* (jousts), including one sponsored by Lorenzo de' Medici. Lined with many palazzi dating from the 15th and 16th centuries, the square remains one of Florence's loveliest and is a great place to people-watch. ✉ *Piazza Santa Croce, Santa Croce.*

★ Santa Croce

CHURCH | The collection of art within this Gothic church by far the most important of any church in Florence. The most famous works are the Giotto frescoes in the two chapels immediately to the right of the high altar. They illustrate scenes from the lives of St. John the Evangelist and St. John the Baptist (in the right-hand chapel), as well as those from the life of St. Francis (in the left-hand chapel). Among the church's other highlights are Donatello's *Annunciation*; 14th-century frescoes by Taddeo Gaddi (circa 1300–66) illustrating scenes from the life of the Virgin Mary; and Donatello's *Crucifix*, criticized by Brunelleschi for making Christ look like a peasant. ✉ *Piazza Santa Croce 16, Santa Croce* ☎ *055/246–6105 reservations* 🌐 *www.santacroceopera.it* 🎫 *Church and museum €8* 🕒 *Closed Tues.*

Sinagoga

SYNAGOGUE | Jews were well settled in Florence by the end of the 14th century. By 1574, however, they were required to live within the large "ghetto" at the north side of today's Piazza della Repubblica, by decree of Cosimo I. Construction of the modern Moorish-style synagogue began in 1874 as a bequest of David Levi, who wished to endow a synagogue "worthy of the city." Falcini, Micheli, and Treves designed the building on a domed Greek cross plan with galleries in the transept and a roofline bearing three distinctive copper cupolas visible from all over Florence. The exterior has alternating bands of tan travertine and pink granite, reflecting an Islamic style repeated in Giovanni Panti's ornate interior. ✉ *Via Farini 4, Santa Croce* ☎ *055/245252* 🌐 *www.firenzebraica.it/sinagoga* 🎫 *Synagogue and museum €7* 🕒 *Closed weekends and Jewish holidays.*

Restaurants

Antico Noè

$$ | **TUSCAN** | **FAMILY** | The short menu at the one-room eatery relies heavily on seasonal ingredients picked up daily at the market. Although the secondi are good, the antipasti and primi really shine, and the menu really comes alive during truffle and artichoke seasons (don't miss the grilled artichokes if they're available). **Known for:** porcini dishes; artichoke dishes; attention to seasonal vegetables. [$] *Average main: €18* ✉ *Volta di San Piero 6/r, Santa Croce* ☎ *055/234–0838* 🌐 *www.anticonoe.com* 🕒 *Closed 2 wks in Aug. No dinner Sun.*

★ Cibrèo Ristorante

$$$$ | TUSCAN | This upscale trattoria serves sumptuous options like the creamy crostini di fegatini (with a savory chicken-liver spread) and melt-in-your-mouth desserts. Many Florentines hail this as the city's best restaurant, and justifiably so—chef-owner Fabio Picchi knows Tuscan food better than anyone, and it shows. **Known for:** multilingual staff; no written menu; authentic Tuscan food. $ *Average main: €40* ✉ *Via A. del Verrocchio 8/r, Santa Croce* ☎ *055/234–1100* ⊕ *www.cibreo.com/en/cibreo-restaurant* ⊘ *Closed Sun. and Mon.*

Cibrèo Trattoria

$ | TUSCAN | This intimate trattoria, known to locals as Cibreino, shares its name and its kitchen with the famed Florentine restaurant but has a shorter, less-expensive menu. Save room for dessert, as the pastry chef has a deft hand with chocolate tarts. **Known for:** need to come early or late to avoid a wait; clever riffs on classic dishes; excellent meal at a moderate price. $ *Average main: €13* ✉ *Via dei Macci 122/r, Santa Croce* ☎ *055/234–1100* ⊕ *www.cibreo.com/en/cibreo-trattoria* ⊘ *Closed Sun., Mon., and July 25–Sept. 5.*

Enoteca Pinchiorri

$$$$ | ITALIAN | A sumptuous Renaissance palace with high, frescoed ceilings and bouquets in silver vases provides the backdrop for this restaurant, one of the most expensive in Italy. Some consider it one of the best, and others consider it inauthentic, as the cuisine extends far beyond Italian. **Known for:** exorbitantly high prices; wine cellar; creative food. $ *Average main: €90* ✉ *Via Ghibellina 87, Santa Croce* ☎ *055/242777* ⊕ *www.enotecapinchiorri.it* ⊘ *Closed Sun., Mon., and Aug. No lunch* 🜲 *Jacket required.*

★ La Giostra

$$$ | ITALIAN | This clubby spot, whose name means "carousel," was created by the late Prince Dimitri Kunz d'Asburgo Lorena and is now expertly run by Soldano, one of his twin sons. The ever-changing menu generally has vegetarian and vegan options. **Known for:** vegetarian and vegan options; carefully curated wine list; sublime tiramisu and a wonderfully gooey Sacher torte. $ *Average main: €30* ✉ *Borgo Pinti 12/r, Santa Croce* ☎ *055/241341* ⊕ *ristorantelagiostra.com* ⊘ *No lunch weekends.*

Pizzeria Caffè Italiano

$ | PIZZA | This small pizzeria is favored by locals. Come early to grab one of the few tables in front or round the back, and don't mind the fact that service here is intentionally rushed: turning tables is paramount. **Known for:** limited seating; local favorite; its limited (but very tasty) pizza offerings. $ *Average main: €10* ✉ *Via Isole delle Stinche 11/r, Santa Croce* ☎ *055/289080* ⊕ *caffeitaliano.it* ⊟ *No credit cards.*

Ruth's

$$ | TUSCAN | The only kosher–vegetarian restaurant in Tuscany is Ruth's, adjacent to Florence's synagogue. On the menu: inexpensive vegetarian and Mediterranean dishes and a large selection of kosher wines. **Known for:** nice wine list; friendly staff; harissa. $ *Average main: €15* ✉ *Via Farini 2/a, Santa Croce* ☎ *055/248–0888* ⊕ *www.kosheruth.com* ⊘ *No dinner Fri. No lunch Sat.*

☕ Coffee and Quick Bites

da Rocco

$ | TUSCAN | At one of Florence's biggest markets, you can grab lunch to go, or you can cram into one of the booths and pour from the straw-cloaked flask (wine here is *da consumo,* which means they charge you for how much you drink). Food is abundant, Tuscan, and fast; locals pack in. **Known for:** takeout; ever-changing menu; tasty food at rock-bottom prices. $ *Average main: €8* ✉ *Mercato Sant'Ambrogio, Piazza Ghiberti, Santa Croce* ☎ *339/838–4555*

🌐 *trattoria-da-rocco-lunch-restaurant.business.site* ⏱ *Closed Sun. No dinner.*

★ Perché No!

$ | **ICE CREAM** | **FAMILY** | What many consider the best gelateria in the centro storico embodies the "practice makes perfect" adage. It's been making ice cream since 1939. **Known for:** unusual flavors and vegan options; one of the oldest gelaterias in the city; gelati made daily. [$] *Average main: €3* ✉ *Via dei Tavolini 19r, Duomo* ☎ *055/239–8969* 🌐 *www.facebook.com/GelateriaPercheNo.*

Hotels

Borgo Pinti

$ | **B&B/INN** | Nuns of the Oblates of the Assumption run this convent holiday house, where some of the simple but spotlessly clean rooms have views of the Duomo's cupola, and others look out onto a garden where you are welcome to relax. **Pros:** great location and (mostly) quiet rooms; a soothing, somewhat untended garden; Mass held daily. **Cons:** rooms are frugal; rooms facing the street can be noisy; some have observed that there's hall noise. [$] *Rooms from: €88* ✉ *Borgo Pinti 15, Santa Croce* ☎ *055/234–6291* 🌐 *www.oblate.it* 🛏 *40 rooms* 🍴 *Free Breakfast.*

The Four Seasons

$$$$ | **HOTEL** | This 15th-century palazzo is perhaps the city's most luxurious hotel, where many guest rooms have original 17th-century frescoes, and an 11-acre garden is dotted with centuries-old trees. **Pros:** pool; Michelin-starred Il Palagio restaurant; state-of-the-art spa. **Cons:** small rooms; splashing children in the pool can be a nuisance for some; ultra-pricey. [$] *Rooms from: €1220* ✉ *Borgo Pinti 99e, Santa Croce* ☎ *055/26261* 🌐 *www.fourseasons.com/florence* 🛏 *117 rooms* 🍴 *No Meals.*

Hotel Regency

$$$$ | **HOTEL** | Though it's just 10 minutes from the Accademia and Michelangelo's *David,* this hotel—in a 19th-century mansion adorned with rich fabrics and period-appropriate furnishings—is a true retreat from the city's noise and crowds. **Pros:** faces one of the few green spaces in central Florence; lovely, on-site Relais le Jardin restaurant; quiet residential setting. **Cons:** books up quickly; rooms facing the park can be noisy; somewhat removed from the city center. [$] *Rooms from: €350* ✉ *Piazza d'Azeglio 3, Santa Croce* ☎ *055/245247* 🌐 *www.regency-hotel.com* 🛏 *31 rooms* 🍴 *Free Breakfast.*

★ Monna Lisa

$$ | **HOTEL** | Although some rooms are small, all are tastefully decorated and housed in a 15th-century palazzo that retains its original staircase and some of its wood-coffered ceilings. **Pros:** lavish buffet breakfast; pretty garden; cheerful, multilingual staff. **Cons:** thin walls have been noted; street noise in some rooms; rooms in annex are less charming than those in palazzo. [$] *Rooms from: €195* ✉ *Borgo Pinti 27, Santa Croce* ☎ *055/247–9751* 🌐 *www.monnalisa.it* 🛏 *48 rooms* 🍴 *Free Breakfast.*

★ Morandi alla Crocetta

$ | **B&B/INN** | You're made to feel like friends of the family at this charming and distinguished residence, furnished comfortably in the classic style of a gracious Florentine home and former convent. **Pros:** interesting, offbeat location near the sights; historic touches like fragments of a 17th-century fresco; affable staff. **Cons:** some say breakfast could be better; far from the "true" historical center; books up quickly. [$] *Rooms from: €115* ✉ *Via Laura 50, Santissima Annunziata* ☎ *055/234–4747* 🌐 *www.hotelmorandi.it* 🛏 *10 rooms* 🍴 *Free Breakfast.*

Continued on page 587

WHO'S WHO IN RENAISSANCE ART

Michelangelo. Leonardo da Vinci. Raphael. This heady triumvirate of the Italian Renaissance is synonymous with artistic genius. Yet they are only three of the remarkable cast of characters whose work defines the Renaissance, that extraordinary flourishing of art and culture in Italy, especially in Florence, as the Middle Ages drew to a close. The artists were visionaries, who redefined painting, sculpture, architecture, and even what it means to be an artist.

THE PIONEER. In the mid-14th century, a few artists began to move away the flat, two-dimensional painting of the Middle Ages. Giotto, who painted seemingly three-dimensional figures who show emotion, had a major impact on the artists of the next century.

THE GROUNDBREAKERS. The generations of Brunelleschi and Botticelli took center stage in the 15th century. Ghiberti, Masaccio, Donatello, Uccello, Fra Angelico, and Filippo Lippi were other major players. Part of the Renaissance (or "re-birth") was a renewed interest in classical sources—the texts, monuments, and sculpture of Ancient Greece and Rome. Perspective and the illusion of three-dimensional space in painting was another discovery of this era, known as the Early Renaissance. Suddenly the art appearing on the walls looked real, or more realistic than it used to.

Roman ruins were not the only thing to inspire these artists. There was an incredible exchange of ideas going on. In Santa Maria del Carmine, Filippo Lippi was inspired by the work of Masaccio, who in turn was a friend of Brunelleschi. Young artists also learned from the masters via the apprentice system. Ghiberti's workshop (bottega in Italian) included, at one time or another, Donatello, Masaccio, and Uccello. Botticelli was apprenticed to Filippo Lippi.

THE BIG THREE. The mathematical rationality and precision of 15th-century art gave way to what is known as the High Renaissance. Leonardo, Michelangelo, and Raphael were much more concerned with portraying the body in all its glory and with achieving harmony and grandeur in their work. Oil paint, used infrequently up until this time, became more widely employed: as a result, Leonardo's colors are deeper, more sensual, more alive. For one brief period, all three were in Florence at the same time. Michelangelo and Leonardo surely knew one another, as they were simultaneously working on frescoes (never completed) inside Palazzo Vecchio.

When Michelangelo left Florence for Rome in 1508, he began the slow drain of artistic exodus from Florence, which never really recovered her previous glory.

A RENAISSANCE TIMELINE

IN THE WORLD

Black Death in Europe kills one third of the population, 1347-50.

Joan of Arc burned at the stake, 1431.

IN FLORENCE

Dante, a native of Florence, writes The Divine Comedy, 1302-21.

Founding of the Medici bank, 1397.

Medici family made official papal bankers.

1434, Cosimo il Vecchio becomes de facto ruler of Florence. The Medici family will dominate the city until 1494.

1300

1400

IN ART

EARLY RENAISSANCE

Masaccio and Masolino fresco Santa Maria del Carmine, 1424-28.

GIOTTO (ca. 1267-1337)

Giotto fresoes in Santa Croce, 1320-25.

BRUNELLESCHI (1377-1446)

LORENZO GHIBERTI (ca. 1381-1455)

DONATELLO (ca. 1386-1466)

PAOLO UCCELLO (1397-1475)

FRA ANGELICO (ca. 1400-1455)

1334, 67-year-old Giotto is appointed chief architect of Santa Maria del Fiore, Florence's Duomo (below). He begins to work on the Campanile, which will be completed in 1359, after his death.

MASACCIO (1401-1428)

FILIPPO LIPPI (ca. 1406-1469)

Donatello sculpts his bronze David, ca. 144●

Fra Angelico frescoes friars' cells in San Marco, ca 1438-45.

Ghiberti wins the competition for the Baptistery doors (above) in Florence, 1401.

Uccello's Sir John Hawkwood, ca. 1436.

Brunelleschi wins the competition for the Duomo's cupola, 1418.

Gutenberg Bible is printed, 1455.

Columbus discovers America, 1492.

Martin Luther posts his 95 theses on the door at Wittenberg, kicking off the Protestant Reformation, 1517.

Constantinople falls to the Turks, 1453.

Machiavelli's Prince appears, 1513.

Copernicus proves that the earth is not the center of the universe, 1530-43.

Lorenzo "il Magnifico" (right), the Medici patron of the arts, rules in Florence, 1449-92.

Two Medici popes Leo X (1513-21) and Clement VII (1523-34) in Rome.

Catherine de' Medici becomes Queen of France, 1547.

1450   **1500**   **1550**

HIGH RENAISSANCE   MANNERISM

Fra Filippo Lippi's Madonna and Child, ca. 1452.

1508, Raphael begins work on the chambers in the Vatican, Rome.

Giorgio Vasari publishes his first edition of *Lives of the Artists*, 1550.

1504, Michelangelo's David is put on display in Piazza della Signoria, where it remains until 1873.

Michelangelo begins to fresco the Sistine Chapel ceiling, 1508.

Botticelli paints the Birth of Venus, ca. 1482.

BOTTICELLI (ca. 1444-1510)

LEONARDO DA VINCI (1452-1519)

RAPHAEL (1483-1520)

MICHELANGELO (1475-1564)

Leonardo paints The Last Supper (below) in Milan, 1495-98.

Giotto's Nativity Donatello's St. John the Baptist Ghiberti's Gates of Paradise

GIOTTO (CA. 1267-1337)
Painter/architect from a small town north of Florence.
He unequivocally set Italian painting on the course that led to the triumphs of the Renaissance masters. Unlike the rather flat, two-dimensional forms found in then prevailing Byzantine art, Giotto's figures have a fresh, life-like quality. The people in his paintings have bulk, and they show emotion, which you can see on their faces and in their gestures. This was something new in the late Middle Ages. Without Giotto, there wouldn't have been a Raphael.
In Florence: **Santa Croce; Uffizi; Campanile; Santa Maria Novella**
Elsewhere in Italy: **Scrovegni Chapel, Padua; Vatican Museums, Rome**

FILIPPO BRUNELLESCHI (1377-1446)
Architect/engineer from Florence.
If Brunelleschi had beaten Ghiberti in the Baptistery doors competition in Florence, the city's Duomo most likely would not have the striking appearance and authority that it has today. After his loss, he sulked off to Rome, where he studied the ancient Roman structures first-hand. Brunelleschi figured out how to vault the Duomo's dome, a structure unprecedented in its colossal size and great height. His Ospedale degli Innocenti employs classical elements in the creation of a stunning, new architectural statement; it is the first truly Renaissance structure.
In Florence: **Duomo; Ospedale degli Innocenti; San Lorenzo; Santo Spirito; Baptistery Doors Competition Entry, Bargello; Santa Croce**

LORENZO GHIBERTI (CA. 1381-1455)
Sculptor from Florence.
Ghiberti won a competition—besting his chief rival, Brunelleschi—to cast the gilded bronze North Doors of the Baptistery in Florence. These doors, and the East Doors that he subsequently executed, took up the next 50 years of his life. He created intricately worked figures that are more true-to-life than any since antiquity, and he was one of the first Renaissance sculptors to work in bronze. Ghiberti taught the next generation of artists; Donatello, Uccello, and Masaccio all passed through his studio.
In Florence: **Door Copies, Baptistery; Original Doors, Museo dell'Opera del Duomo; Baptistry Door Competition Entry, Bargello; Orsanmichele**

DONATELLO (CA. 1386-1466)
Sculptor from Florence.
Donatello was an innovator who, like his good friend Brunelleschi, spent most of his long life in Florence. Consumed with the science of optics, he used light and shadow to create the effects of nearness and distance. He made an essentially flat slab look like a three- dimensional scene. His bronze is probably the first free-standing male nude since antiquity. Not only technically brilliant, his work is also emotionally resonant; few sculptors are as expressive.
In Florence: **David, Bargello; St. Mark, Orsanmichele; Palazzo Vecchio; Museo dell'Opera del Duomo; San Lorenzo; Santa Croce**
Elsewhere in Italy: **Padua; Prato; Venice**

Fra Angelico's Déposition de Croix   Masaccio's Trinity   Filippo Lippi's Madonna and Child with Two Angels

PAOLO UCCELLO (1397-1475)
Painter from Florence.
Renaissance chronicler Vasari once observed that had Uccello not been so obsessed with the mathematical problems posed by perspective, he would have been a very good painter. The struggle to master single-point perspective and to render motion in two dimensions is nowhere more apparent than in his battle scenes. His first major commission in Florence was the gargantuan fresco of the English mercenary Sir John Hawkwood (the Italians called him Giovanni Acuto) in Florence's Duomo.
In Florence: **Sir John Hawkwood, Duomo; Battle of San Romano, Uffizi; Santa Maria Novella**
Elsewhere in Italy: **Urbino, Prato**

FRA ANGELICO (CA. 1400-1455)
Painter from a small town north of Florence.
A Dominican friar, who eventually made his way to the convent of San Marco, Fra Angelico and his assistants painted frescoes for aid in prayer and meditation. He was known for his piety; Vasari wrote that Fra Angelico could never paint a crucifix without a tear running down his face. Perhaps no other painter so successfully translated the mysteries of faith and the sacred into painting. And yet his figures emote, his command of perspective is superb, and his use of color startles even today.
In Florence: **Museo di San Marco; Uffizi**
Elsewhere in Italy: **Vatican Museums, Rome; Fiesole; Cortona; Perugia; Orvieto**

MASACCIO (1401-1428)
Painter from San Giovanni Valdarno, southeast of Florence.
Masaccio and Masolino, a frequent collaborator, worked most famously together at Santa Maria del Carmine. Their frescoes of the life of St. Peter use light to mold figures in the painting by imitating the way light falls on figures in real life. Masaccio also pioneered the use of single-point perspective, masterfully rendered in his His friend Brunelleschi probably introduced him to the technique, yet another step forward in rendering things the way the eye sees them. Masaccio died young and under mysterious circumstances.
In Florence: **Santa Maria del Carmine; Trinity, Santa Maria Novella**

FILIPPO LIPPI (CA. 1406-1469)
Painter from Prato.
At a young age, Filippo Lippi entered the friary of Santa Maria del Carmine, where he was highly influenced by Masaccio and Masolino's frescoes. His religious vows appear to have made less of an impact; his affair with a young nun produced a son, Filippino (Little Philip, who later apprenticed with Botticelli), and a daughter. His religious paintings often have a playful, humorous note; some of his angels are downright impish and look directly out at the viewer. Lippi links the earlier painters of the 15th century with those who follow; Botticelli apprenticed with him.
In Florence: **Uffizi; Palazzo Medici Riccardi; San Lorenzo; Palazzo Pitti**
Elsewhere in Italy: **Prato**

Botticelli's Primavera

Leonardo's Portrait of a Young Woman

Raphael's Madonna on the Meadow

BOTTICELLI (CA. 1444-1510)
Painter from Florence.
Botticelli's work is characterized by stunning, elongated blondes, cherubic angels (something he undoubtedly learned from his time with Filippo Lippi), and tender Christs. Though he did many religious paintings, he also painted monumental, nonreligious panels—his Birth of Venus and Primavera being the two most famous of these. A brief sojourn took him to Rome, where he and a number of other artists frescoed the Sistine Chapel walls.
In Florence:
Birth of Venus, Primavera, Uffizi; Palazzo Pitti
Elsewhere in Italy:
Vatican Museums, Rome

LEONARDO DA VINCI (1452-1519)
Painter/sculptor/engineer from Anchiano, a small town outside Vinci.
Leonardo never lingered long in any place; his restless nature and his international reputation led to commissions throughout Italy, and took him to Milan, Vigevano, Pavia, Rome, and, ultimately, France. Though he is most famous for his mysterious Mona Lisa (at the Louvre in Paris), he painted other penetrating, psychological portraits in addition to his scientific experiments: his design for a flying machine (never built) predates Kitty Hawk by nearly 500 years. The greatest collection of Leonardo's work in Italy can be seen on one wall in the Uffizi.
In Florence: **Adoration of the Magi, Uffizi**
Elsewhere in Italy: **Last Supper, Santa Maria delle Grazie, Milan**

RAPHAEL (1483-1520)
Painter/architect from Urbino.
Raphael spent only four highly productive years of his short life in Florence, where he turned out made-to-order panel paintings of the Madonna and Child for a hungry public; he also executed a number of portraits of Florentine aristocrats. Perhaps no other artist had such a fine command of line and color, and could render it, seemingly effortlessly, in paint. His painting acquired new authority after he came up against Michelangelo toiling away on the Sistine ceiling. Raphael worked nearly next door in the Vatican, where his figures take on an epic, Michelangelesque scale.
In Florence: **Uffizi; Palazzo Pitti**
Elsewhere in Italy: **Vatican Museums, Rome**

MICHELANGELO (1475-1564)
Painter/sculptor/architect from Caprese.
Although Florentine and proud of it (he famously signed his St. Peter's Pietà to avoid confusion about where he was from), he spent most of his 89 years outside his native city. He painted and sculpted the male body on an epic scale and glorified it while doing so. Though he complained throughout the proceedings that he was really a sculptor, Michelangelo's Sistine Chapel ceiling is arguably the greatest fresco cycle ever painted (and the massive figures owe no small debt to Giotto).
In Florence: **David, Galleria dell'Accademia; Uffizi; Casa Buonarroti; Bargello**
Elsewhere in Italy: **St. Peter's Basilica, Vatican Museums, and Piazza del Campidoglio in Rome**

🍸 Nightlife

Caffè Sant'Ambrogio
BARS | Come here when it's summer for outdoor seating with a view of an 11th-century church (Sant'Ambrogio) directly across the street. Come here at any time of the year for perfectly mixed drinks and a lively atmosphere filled with (mostly) locals. ⊠ *Piazza Sant'Ambrogio 7–8/r, Santa Croce* ☎ *055/247–7277.*

Jazz Club
LIVE MUSIC | Enjoy live music in this small basement club. ⊠ *Via Nuova de' Caccini 3, at Borgo Pinti, Santa Croce.*

Rex
BARS | A trendy, artsy clientele frequents this bar at aperitivo time. By 10 pm, the place is packed with mostly young folks sipping artful cocktails. ⊠ *Via Fiesolana 23–25/r, Santa Croce* ☎ *055/248–0331* ⊕ *www.rexfirenze.com.*

👜 Shopping

Mercato di Sant'Ambrogio
MARKET | FAMILY | It's possible to strike gold at this lively market, where clothing stalls abut those with fruits and vegetables. ⊠ *Piazza Ghiberti, off Via dei Macci, Santa Croce.*

Oreria
JEWELRY & WATCHES | The two women who run Oreria create divine designs using silver and semiprecious stones. Send suitors to purchase significant gifts here. ⊠ *Borgo Pinti 87/a, Santa Croce* ☎ *055/244708* ⊕ *www.oreria.net.*

Paolo Carandini
HOUSEWARES | Stop in here for exquisite leather picture frames, jewelry boxes, and desk accessories. ⊠ *Borgo Allegri 7/r, Santa Croce* ☎ *334/735–5954* ⊕ *www.paolocarandini.net.*

★ Scuola del Cuoio
LEATHER GOODS | Leatherworkers ply their trade at Scuola del Cuoio (Leather School), a consortium in the former dormitory of the convent of Santa Croce. High-quality, fairly priced jackets, belts, and purses are sold here. ⊠ *Piazza Santa Croce 16, Santa Croce* ☎ *055/244533* ⊕ *www.scuoladelcuoio.com.*

The Oltrarno

A walk through the Oltrarno (literally "the other side of the Arno") takes in two very different aspects of Florence: the splendor of the Medici, manifest in the riches of the mammoth Palazzo Pitti and the gracious Giardino di Boboli; and the charm of the Oltrarno, a slightly gentrified but still fiercely proud working-class neighborhood with artisans' and antiques shops.

👁 Sights

Giardino Bardini
GARDEN | Garden lovers, those who crave a view, and those who enjoy a nice hike should visit this lovely villa, whose history spans centuries. It had a walled garden as early as the 14th century; its "Grand Stairs"—a zigzag ascent well worth scaling—have been around since the 16th. The garden is filled with irises, roses, and heirloom flowers. It also has a Japanese garden and statuary. ⊠ *Via de'Bardini, San Niccolò* ☎ *055/263–8599* ⊕ *www.villabardini.it* 💶 *€10* 🕐 *Closed Mon. (with occasional exceptions).*

Giardino di Boboli *(Boboli Gardens)*
GARDEN | The main entrance to these gardens is from the right side of the courtyard of Palazzo Pitti. The landscaping began to take shape in 1549, when the Pitti family sold the palazzo to Eleanor of Toledo, wife of the Medici grand duke Cosimo I. A visit here can be disappointing because the gardens are somewhat sparse, but the pleasant walk offers excellent views. ⊠ *Piazza de' Pitti, Palazzo Pitti* ☎ *055/294883* ⊕ *www.uffizi.it/giardino-boboli* 💶 *€10* 🕐 *Closed 1st and last Mon. of month Nov.–May.*

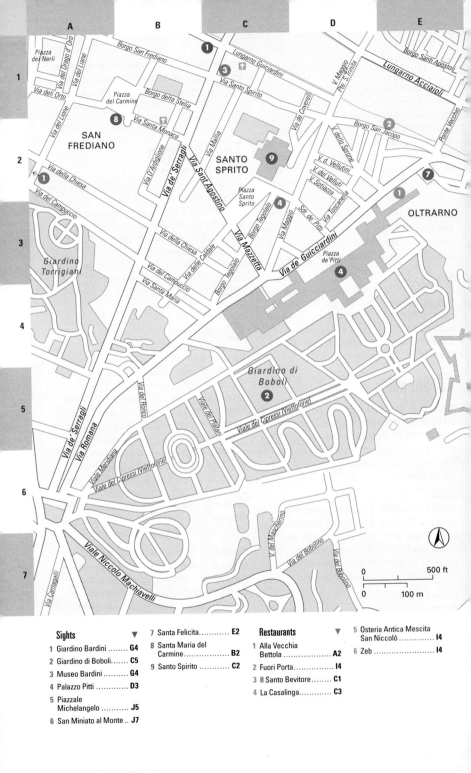

Sights ▼

7 Santa Felicita............. **E2**

8 Santa Maria del
Carmine.................. **B2**

9 Santo Spirito **C2**

1 Giardino Bardini **G4**

2 Giardino di Boboli....... **C5**

3 Museo Bardini **G4**

4 Palazzo Pitti **D3**

5 Piazzale
Michelangelo **J5**

6 San Miniato al Monte .. **J7**

Restaurants ▼

1 Alla Vecchia
Bettola **A2**

2 Fuori Porta................ **I4**

3 Il Santo Bevitore **C1**

4 La Casalinga............. **C3**

5 Osteria Antica Mescita
San Niccolò **I4**

6 Zeb **I4**

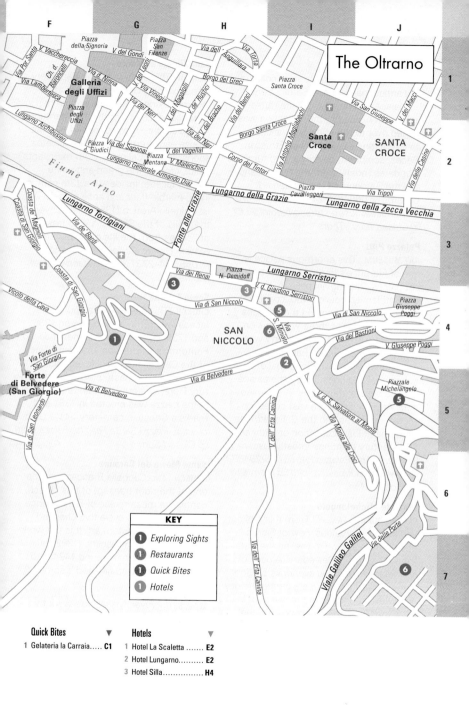

The Oltrarno

Museo Bardini

ART MUSEUM | The 19th-century collector and antiquarian Stefano Bardini turned his palace into his own private museum. Upon his death, the collection was turned over to the state and includes an interesting assortment of Etruscan pieces, sculpture, paintings, and furniture that dates mostly from the Renaissance and the Baroque. ⊠ *Via dei Renai 1, Oltrarno* 🕾 *055/234–2427* ⊕ *musefirenze. it/en/musei/museo-stefano-bardini* 🖅 *€7* ⊘ *Closed Tues.–Thurs.*

Palazzo Pitti

ART MUSEUM | This enormous palace is one of Florence's largest architectural set pieces. The original palazzo, built for the Pitti family around 1460, consisted of the main entrance and the sections extending as far as three windows on either side. In 1549, the property was sold to the Medici, and Bartolomeo Ammannati was called in to make substantial additions. Today, the palace houses several museums. The Museo degli Argenti displays a vast collection of Medici treasures and the Galleria d'Arte Moderna holds a collection of 19th- and 20th-century paintings, mostly Tuscan. ⊠ *Piazza Pitti, Palazzo Pitti* 🕾 *055/294883* ⊕ *www.uffizi.it/palazzo-pitti* 🖅 *From €16* ⊘ *Closed Mon.*

Piazzale Michelangelo

PLAZA/SQUARE | FAMILY | From this lookout you have a marvelous view of Florence and the hills around it, rivaling the vista from the Forte di Belvedere. A copy of Michelangelo's *David* overlooks outdoor cafés packed with tourists during the day and with Florentines in the evening. In May, the Giardino dell'Iris (Iris Garden) off the piazza is abloom with more than 2,500 varieties of the flower. The Giardino delle Rose (Rose Garden) on the terraces below the piazza is also in full bloom in May and June. ⊠ *Piazzale Michelangelo, San Niccolò.*

San Miniato al Monte

CHURCH | This abbey, like the Baptistery a fine example of Romanesque architecture, is one of the oldest churches in Florence, dating from the 11th century. A 12th-century mosaic topped by a gilt bronze eagle, emblem of San Miniato's sponsors, the Calimala (cloth merchants' guild), crowns the green-and-white marble facade. Inside are a 13th-century inlaid-marble floor and apse mosaic. Artist Spinello Aretino (1350–1410) covered the walls of the Sagrestia with frescoes of scenes from the life of St. Benedict. ⊠ *Viale Galileo Galilei, San Niccolò* 🕾 *055/234–2731* ⊕ *www.sanminiatoal-monte.it.*

Santa Felicita

CHURCH | This late-Baroque church (its facade was remodeled between 1736 and 1739) contains the Mannerist Jacopo Pontormo's *Deposition,* the centerpiece of the Cappella Capponi (executed 1525–28) and a masterpiece of 16th-century Florentine art. The granite column in the piazza was erected in 1381 and marks a Christian cemetery. ⊠ *Via Guicciardini, Piazza Santa Felicita, Palazzo Pitti* ⊘ *Closed Sun.*

Santa Maria del Carmine

CHURCH | The Cappella Brancacci, at the end of the right transept of this church, contains a masterpiece of Renaissance painting: a fresco cycle that changed the course of Western art. It is the work of Masaccio and Masolino (1383–circa 1447), who began it around 1424, and Filippino Lippi, who finished it some 50 years later.

It was, however, Masaccio's work that opened a new frontier for painting, as he was among the first artists to employ single-point perspective. His style predominates in the *Tribute Money,* on the upper-left wall; *St. Peter Baptizing,* on the upper altar wall; the *Distribution of Goods,* on the lower altar wall; and the *Expulsion of Adam and Eve,* on the chapel's upper-left entrance pier. The figures of Adam and

Eve possess a startling presence thanks to the dramatic way in which their bodies seem to reflect light. In their faces, you also see terrible shame and suffering depicted with a humanity rarely achieved in art. ⊠ *Piazza del Carmine, Santo Spirito* ☎ *055/276–8224 reservations* ⊕ *cultura.comune.fi.it/musei* ⊠ *€10* ⊙ *Closed Tues. and Thurs.* ⌕ *Reservations to visit the Cappella Brancacci are essential.*

Santo Spirito

CHURCH | The interior of this church is one of a pair designed in Florence by Filippo Brunelleschi in the early decades of the 15th century (the other is San Lorenzo). It was here that Brunelleschi supplied definitive solutions a major problem of interior Renaissance church design: how to build a cross-shape interior using classical architectural elements borrowed from antiquity. His solution was design the church so that all its parts were proportionally related. He believed that mathematical regularity and aesthetic beauty were flip sides of the same coin. ⊠ *Piazza Santo Spirito 30, Oltrarno* ☎ *055/210030* ⊕ *www.basilicasantospirito.it* ⌕ *Church: free. Tour: €2* ⊙ *Closed Wed.*

🍴 Restaurants

Alla Vecchia Bettola

$ | TUSCAN | The name doesn't exactly mean "old dive," but it comes pretty close. The recipes here come from "wise grandmothers" and celebrate Tuscan food in its glorious simplicity—prosciutto is sliced with a knife, grilled meats are tender, service is friendly, and the wine list is well priced and good. **Known for:** just outside the centro storico but worth the taxi ride; firmly Tuscan menu; grilled meats. 💲 *Average main: €14* ⊠ *Viale Vasco Pratolini, Oltrarno* ☎ *055/224158* ⊙ *Closed Sun. and Mon.*

★ Fuori Porta

$ | WINE BAR | What is, perhaps, the oldest and best wine bar in Florence serves cured meats and cheeses, as well as daily specials. Crostini and *crostoni*—grilled breads topped with a mélange of cheeses and meats—are the house specialty, but the verdure sott'olio are divine, too. **Known for:** changing daily specials; crostini and crostoni; lengthy wine list. 💲 *Average main: €11* ⊠ *Via Monte alle Croci 10/r, San Niccolò* ☎ *055/234–2483* ⊕ *www.fuoriporta.it.*

★ Il Santo Bevitore

$ | TUSCAN | Florentines and other lovers of good food flock to "The Holy Drinker" for tasty, well-priced dishes. Unpretentious white walls, dark wood furniture, and paper place mats provide the simple decor; start with the exceptional verdure sott'olio (vegetables in oil) or the terrina di fegatini (a creamy chicken-liver spread) before sampling any of the divine pastas. **Known for:** friendly waitstaff; delicious potato gratin; pasta. 💲 *Average main: €11* ⊠ *Via Santo Spirito 64/66r, Santo Spirito* ☎ *055/211264* ⊕ *www.ilsantobevitore. com* ⊙ *No lunch Sun.*

★ La Casalinga

$ | TUSCAN | *Casalinga* means "housewife," and this place, which has been around since 1963, has the nostalgic charm of a midcentury kitchen with Tuscan comfort food to match. If you eat ribollita anywhere in Florence, eat it here—it couldn't be more authentic. **Known for:** often packed; liver, Venetian style; ribollita. 💲 *Average main: €14* ⊠ *Via Michelozzi 9/r, Santo Spirito* ☎ *055/218624* ⊕ *www.trattorialacasalinga.it* ⊙ *Closed Sun., 1 wk at Christmas, and 3 wks in Aug.*

Osteria Antica Mescita San Niccolò

$ | TUSCAN | Always crowded—but always good and inexpensive—this osteria is next to the church of San Niccolò, and, if you sit in the lower part, you'll be in what was once a chapel dating from the 11th century. The subtle but dramatic background nicely complements the food, which is simple Tuscan at its best. **Known for:** outdoor seating in a small, lovely square; great, simple salads; delicious soup. [$] *Average main: €11* ✉ *Via San Niccolò 60/r, San Niccolò* ☎ *055/234–2836* 🌐 *www.osteriasanniccolo.it.*

Zeb

$$ | **TUSCAN** | "Zeb" stands for *zuppa e bollito* (soup and boiled things), but you can't go wrong with anything at this small *alimentari* (delicatessen). It's home-style Tuscan cuisine at its very best, served in unpretentious, intimate surroundings: there's room for only about 15 guests. **Known for:** lovely wine list; terrific pasta; fantastic soup. [$] *Average main: €17* ✉ *Via San Miniato 2, Oltrarno* ☎ *055/234–2864* 🌐 *www.zebgastronomia.com* ⏲ *Closed Wed. Nov.–Mar.: no dinner Sun.–Tues. Apr.–Oct.: no dinner Sun.*

Coffee and Quick Bites

Gelateria la Carraia

$ | **ICE CREAM** | **FAMILY** | Although it's a bit of a haul to get here (it's at the foot of Ponte Carraia, two bridges down from the Ponte Vecchio), you'll be well rewarded for doing so, with standard gelato flavors or creative options such as *limone con biscotti* (lemon sorbet with cookies). **Known for:** every flavor is delicious; generous €1 tasting cones; super-creamy gelato. [$] *Average main: €3* ✉ *Piazza Nazario Sauro 2, Santo Spirito* ☎ *055/280695* 🌐 *www.lacarraiagroup.eu.*

Hotels

Hotel La Scaletta

$$ | **HOTEL** | In addition to a tremendous view of the Boboli Gardens, this cozy pensione near the Ponte Vecchio and Palazzo Pitti has simply furnished but large rooms and a sunny breakfast room. **Pros:** in-house restaurant with stunning views; wonderful, multilingual staff; in a lively neighborhood. **Cons:** books up quickly; neighborhood can be noisy; small elevator, many steps. [$] *Rooms from: €152* ✉ *Via Guicciardini 13, Palazzo Pitti* ☎ *055/283028* 🌐 *www.hotellascaletta.it* 🛏 *36 rooms* 🍴 *Free Breakfast.*

Hotel Lungarno

$$$$ | **HOTEL** | Many rooms and suites here have private terraces that jut out over the Arno, granting stunning views of the Palazzo Vecchio and the Lungarno; a studio suite in a 13th-century tower preserves details like exposed stone walls and old archways, and looks over a little square with a medieval tower covered in jasmine. **Pros:** upscale without being stuffy; Borgo San Jacopo, its attached restaurant; lovely views of the Arno. **Cons:** walls can be thin; street noise happens; rooms without Arno views feel less special. [$] *Rooms from: €680* ✉ *Borgo San Jacopo 14, Oltrarno* ☎ *055/27261* 🌐 *www.lungarnocollection.com* 🛏 *67 rooms* 🍴 *Free Breakfast.*

Hotel Silla

$$ | **HOTEL** | Rooms in this 15th-century palazzo, entered via a courtyard with potted plants and sculpture-filled niches, are simply furnished; some have Arno views, others have stuccoed ceilings. **Pros:** in the middle of everything except the crowds; great breakfast; cordial, friendly staff. **Cons:** could use an update; small rooms; street noise. [$] *Rooms from: €130* ✉ *Via de' Renai 5, San Niccolò* ☎ *055/234–2888* 🌐 *www.hotelsilla.it* 🛏 *36 rooms* 🍴 *Free Breakfast.*

Shopping

★ **Giulio Giannini e Figlio**

STATIONERY | One of Florence's oldest paper-goods stores is *the* place to buy the marbleized stock, which comes in many shapes and sizes, from flat sheets to boxes and even on pencils. ✉ *Piazza Pitti 37/r, Oltrarno* ☎ *055/212621* 🌐 *www.giuliogiannini.com.*

★ Il Torchio

STATIONERY | Photograph albums, frames, diaries, and other objects dressed in handmade paper are high quality, and the prices lower than usual. ☒ *Via dei Bardi 17, San Niccolò* ☎ *055/234–2862* ⊕ *www. legatoriailtorchio.com.*

Maçel

WOMEN'S CLOTHING | Browse collections by lesser-known Italian designers, many of whom use the same factories as the A-list, at this women's clothing shop. ☒ *Via Guicciardini 128/r, Palazzo Pitti* ☎ *055/287355.*

★ Madova

HATS & GLOVES | Complete your winter wardrobe with a pair of high-quality leather gloves, available in a rainbow of colors and a choice of linings (silk, cashmere, and unlined), from Madova. It's been in business for 100 years. ☒ *Via Guicciardini 1/r, Palazzo Pitti* ☎ *055/239–6526* ⊕ *www.madova.com.*

Pitti Mosaici

HOUSEWARES | Stones are worked into exquisite tables, pictures, and jewelry at Pitti Mosaici, which continues the *pietre dure* tradition that was all the rage of 16th-century Florence. ☒ *Piazza dei Pitti 23/r, Palazzo Pitti* ☎ *055/282127* ⊕ *www. pittimosaici.com.*

Santo Spirito Flea Market

MARKET | FAMILY | The second Sunday of every month brings the Santo Spirito flea market. On the third Sunday of the month, vendors at the Fierucola organic fest sell such delectables as honeys, jams, spice mixes, and fresh vegetables. ☒ *Piazza Santo Spirito, Santo Spirito.*

A Side Trip from Florence

Fiesole

A half-day excursion to Fiesole, in the hills 8 km (5 miles) above Florence, gives you a pleasant respite from museums and a wonderful view of the city. From here the view of the Duomo gives you a new appreciation for what the Renaissance accomplished. Fiesole began life as an ancient Etruscan and later Roman village that held some power until it succumbed to barbarian invasions. Eventually it gave up its independence in exchange for Florence's protection. The medieval cathedral, ancient Roman amphitheater, and lovely old villas behind garden walls are clustered on a series of hilltops. A walk around Fiesole can take from one to two or three hours, depending on how far you stroll from the main piazza.

GETTING HERE AND AROUND

The trip from Florence by car takes 20–30 minutes. Drive to Piazza Liberta and cross the Ponte Rosso heading in the direction of the SS65/SR65. Turn right on to Via Salviati and continue on to Via Roccettini. Make a left turn to Via Vecchia Fiesolana, which will take you directly to the center of town. There are several possible routes for the two-hour walk from central Florence to Fiesole. One route begins in a residential area of Florence called Salviatino (Via Barbacane, near Piazza Edison, on the No. 7 bus route), and after a short time, offers peeks over garden walls of beautiful villas, as well as the view over your shoulder at the panorama of Florence in the valley.

VISITOR INFORMATION

CONTACT **Fiesole Tourism Office.** ☒ *Via Portigiani 3,* ☎ *055/596–1311* ⊕ *www. fiesoleforyou.it.*

Sights

Anfiteatro Romano (*Roman Amphitheater*)
RUINS | The beautifully preserved, 2,000-seat Anfiteatro Romano, near the Duomo, dates from the 1st century BC and is still used for summer concerts. To the right of the amphitheater are the remains of the Terme Romani (Roman Baths), where you can see the gymnasium, hot and cold baths, and rectangular chamber where the water was heated. ✉ *Via Portigiani 1, Fiesole* ☎ *055/596–1293* 🌐 *www.museidifiesole.it* 🎟 *€12, includes access to archaeological park and museums* 🕓 *Museo Bandini closed Mon.–Thurs.*

Badia Fiesolana
CHURCH | From the church of San Domenico it's a five-minute walk northwest to Fiesole's original cathedral. Dating from the 11th century, it was first the home of the Camaldolese monks. Thanks to Cosimo il Vecchio de'Medici, the complex was substantially restructured. The facade, never completed owing to Cosimo's death, contains elements of its original Romanesque decoration. ✉ *Via della Badia dei Roccettini 11, Fiesole* ☎ *055/46851* 🌐 *www.eui.eu* 🕓 *Closed Sat. afternoon and Sun.*

Duomo
CHURCH | A stark medieval interior yields many masterpieces. In the raised presbytery, the Cappella Salutati was frescoed by 15th-century artist Cosimo Rosselli, but it was his contemporary, sculptor Mino da Fiesole (1430–84), who put the town on the artistic map. The Madonna on the altarpiece and the tomb of Bishop Salutati are fine examples of the artist's work. ✉ *Piazza Mino da Fiesole, Fiesole.*

San Francesco
CHURCH | This lovely hilltop church has a good view of Florence and the plain below from its terrace and benches. Off the little cloister is a small, eclectic museum containing, among other things, two Egyptian mummies. Halfway up the hill you'll see sloping steps to the right; they lead to a fragrant wooded park with trails that loop out and back to the church. ✉ *Via San Francesco 13, Fiesole* ☎ *055/59175* 🌐 *www.fratifiesole.it* 🎟 *Free.*

Restaurants

La Reggia degli Etruschi
$$$ | **ITALIAN** | Atop a steep hill, en route to the church of San Francesco, this lovely little eatery is certainly worth the trek. Indulge in inventive reworkings of Tuscan classics, like the *mezzaluna di pera a pecorino* (little half-moon pasta stuffed with pear and pecorino) sauced with Roquefort and poppy seeds. **Known for:** small terrace with outdoor seating; good wine list and friendly service; out-of-the-way location. [$] *Average main: €25* ✉ *Via San Francesco 18, Fiesole* ☎ *333/355-6126* 🌐 *www.lareggiadeglietruschi.com.*

Hotels

Villa San Michele
$$$$ | **HOTEL** | The cypress-lined driveway provides an elegant preamble to this incredibly gorgeous (and very expensive) hotel nestled in the hills of Fiesole. **Pros:** exceptional convent conversion; shuttle bus makes frequent forays to and from Florence; stunning views. **Cons:** you must either depend on the shuttle bus or have a car; some rooms are small; money must be no object. [$] *Rooms from: €1715* ✉ *Via Doccia 4, Fiesole* ☎ *055/567–8200* 🌐 *www.belmond.com/hotels/europe/italy* 🕓 *Closed Nov.–Easter* 🛏 *45 rooms* 🍴 *Free Breakfast.*

Chapter 13

TUSCANY

Updated by
Patricia Rucidlo

◉ Sights	🍴 Restaurants	🛏 Hotels	🛍 Shopping	🍸 Nightlife
★★★★★	★★★★★	★★★★☆	★★★☆☆	★★★☆☆

WELCOME TO TUSCANY

TOP REASONS TO GO

★ **Piazza del Campo, Siena:** Sip a cappuccino or enjoy some gelato as you take in the spectacle in and of this shell-shape piazza.

★ **Piero della Francesca's True Cross frescoes, Arezzo:** If your Holy Grail is great Renaissance art, seek out these 12 enigmatic scenes in Arezzo's Basilica di San Francesco.

★ **San Gimignano:** Grab a spot at sunset on the steps of the Collegiata as flocks of swallows swoop in and out of the famous medieval towers.

★ **Wine tasting in Chianti:** Sample the fruits of the region's gorgeous vineyards, either at the wineries themselves or in the wine bars found in the towns.

★ **Leaning Tower of Pisa:** It may be touristy, but it's still a whole lot of fun to climb to the top and admire the view.

1 Lucca. See 16th-century ramparts.

2 Pisa. Its bell tower is known the world over.

3 Chianti. A picturesque wine region.

4 Volterra. Breathtaking hilltop views.

5 San Gimignano. Lovely hill town.

6 Colle di Val d'Elsa. Laid-back hill town.

7 Siena. An enchanting medieval city.

8 Arezzo. Visit for the sublime frescoes.

9 Cortona. Sits above the flat Valdichiana.

10 Montepulciano. Its higher altitude means cooler summers.

11 Pienza. An ideal city planned by Pope Pius II.

12 Montalcino. Famed for its robust red wine.

13 Abbazia di Sant'Antimo. A Romanesque abbey.

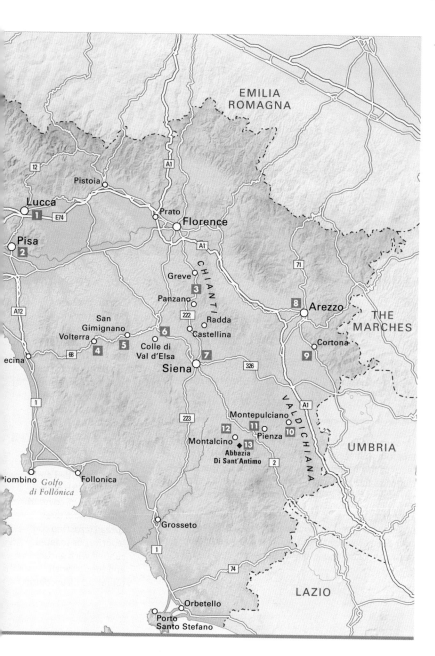

EMILIA ROMAGNA

A1

12

Pistoia

Lucca

1 E74

Prato

Florence

Pisa

2

A1

A12

CHIANTI

Greve

71

222

Panzano

3

Radda

8 Arezzo

San Gimignano

Castellina

THE MARCHES

Volterra

4 5

6

68

Colle di Val d'Elsa

7

Cortona

9

ecina

Siena

326

1

VALDICHIANA

A1

223

Montepulciano

11

UMBRIA

12

Pienza

10

Montalcino

13

Abbazia Di Sant'Antimo

2

iombino Golfo di Follónica

Follonica

Grosseto

1

74

LAZIO

Orbetello

Porto Santo Stefano

EATING AND DRINKING WELL IN TUSCANY

The influence of the ancient Etruscans—who favored the use of fresh herbs—is still felt in Tuscan cuisine three millennia later. Simple and earthy, Tuscan food celebrates the seasons with fresh vegetable dishes, wonderful bread-based soups, and meats perfumed with sage, rosemary, and thyme.

Throughout Tuscany there are excellent upscale restaurants that serve elaborate dishes, but to get a real taste of the flavors of the region, head for the family-run trattorias found in every town. The service and setting are often basic, but the food can be memorable.

Few places serve lighter fare at midday, so expect substantial meals at lunch and dinner, especially in out-of-the-way towns. Dining hours are fairly standard: lunch between 12:30 and 2, dinner between 7:30 and 10.

HOLD THE SALT

Tuscan bread is famous for what it's missing: salt. That's because it's intended to pick up seasoning from the food it accompanies, not be eaten alone. That doesn't mean Tuscans don't like to start a meal with bread, but usually it's prepared in some way. It can be grilled and drizzled with olive oil (*fettunta*), covered with chicken liver spread (*crostino con fegatini*), or toasted, rubbed with garlic, and topped with tomatoes (*bruschetta*).

AFFETTATI MISTI

The name, roughly translated, means "mixed cold cuts," and it's something Tuscans do exceptionally well. A platter of cured meats, served as an antipasto, is sure to include *prosciutto crudo* (cured pork, cut paper-thin) and *salame* (dry sausage, prepared in dozens of ways—some spicy, some sweet). The most distinctly Tuscan affettati are made from *cinta senese* (a once nearly extinct pig found only in the heart of the region) and *cinghiale* (wild boar, which roam all over Italy). You can eat these delicious slices unadorned or layered on a piece of bread.

PASTA

Restaurants throughout Tuscany serve dishes similar to those in Florence, but they also have their own local specialties. Many recipes are from the *nonna* (grandmother) of the restaurant's owner, handed down over time but never written down.

Look in particular for pasta creations made with *pici* (a long, thick, hand-rolled spaghetti). *Pappardelle* (a long, ribbonlike pasta noodle) is frequently paired with sauces made with game, such as *lepre* (hare) or cinghiale. In the northwest, a specialty of Lucca is *tordelli di carne al ragù* (meat-stuffed pasta with a meat sauce).

MEAT

Bistecca fiorentina (a thick T-bone steak, grilled rare) is the classic meat dish of Tuscany, but there are other specialties as well. Many menus will include *tagliata di manzo* (thinly sliced, roasted beef, drizzled with olive oil), *arista di maiale* (roast pork with sage and rosemary), and *salsiccia e fagioli* (pork sausage and beans). In the southern part of the region, don't be surprised to find *piccione* (pigeon), which can be roasted, stuffed, or baked.

WINE

Grape cultivation here also dates from Etruscan times, and vineyards are abundant, particularly in Chianti. The resulting medium-body red wine is a staple on most tables; however, you can select from a multitude of other varieties, including such reds as Brunello di Montalcino and Vino Nobile di Montepulciano and such whites as vermentino and vernaccia.

Super Tuscans (a fanciful name given to a group of wines by American journalists) now command attention as some of the best produced in Italy; they have great depth and complexity. The dessert wine vin santo is made throughout the region, and is often sipped with biscotti (twice-baked almond cookies), perfect for dunking.

Midway down the Italian peninsula, Tuscany (Toscana in Italian) is distinguished by rolling hills, snowcapped mountains, cypress trees, and miles of coastline on the Tyrrhenian Sea—which all adds up to gorgeous views at practically every turn.

The beauty of the landscape proves a perfect foil for the region's abundance of superlative art and architecture. It also produces some of Italy's finest wines and olive oils. The combination of unforgettable art, sumptuous landscapes, and eminently drinkable wines that pair beautifully with its simple food makes a trip to Tuscany something beyond special.

Many of Tuscany's cities and towns have retained the same fundamental character over the past 500 years. Civic rivalries that led to bloody battles centuries ago have given way to soccer rivalries. Renaissance pomp lives on in the celebration of local feast days and centuries-old traditions such as the Palio in Siena and the Giostra del Saracino (Joust of the Saracen) in Arezzo. Often, present-day Tuscans look as though they might have served as models for paintings produced hundreds of years ago. In many ways, the Renaissance lives on in Tuscany.

MAJOR REGIONS

Hill Towns Southwest of Florence. The search for the best tiny hill town always leads to San Gimignano, known as the "medieval Manhattan" for its 13th-century stone towers.

Southern Tuscany. Among the highlights of Tuscany's southern reaches are the wine-producing centers of Montalcino and Montepulciano.

Planning

Making the Most of Your Time

Tuscany isn't the place for a jam-packed itinerary. One of the greatest pleasures here is indulging in rustic hedonism, marked by long lunches and showstopping sunsets. Whether by car, by bike, or on foot, you'll want to get out into the glorious landscape, but it's smart to keep your plans modest. Set a church or a hill town or an out-of-the-way restaurant as your destination, knowing that half the pleasure is in getting there—admiring as you go the stately palaces, the tidy geometry of row upon row of grapevines, and the fields vibrant with red poppies, sunflowers, and yellow broom.

You'll need to devise a strategy for seeing the sights. Take Siena: this beautiful, art-filled town simply can't be missed; it's compact enough that you can see the major sights on a day trip, and that's exactly what most people do. Spend the night, though, and you'll get to see the town breathe a sigh and relax on the day-trippers' departure. In Pisa, the famous tower and the rest of the Camposanto are not only worth seeing but a must-see, a highlight of any trip to Italy. But nearby Lucca must not be overlooked either. In fact, this walled town has greater charms than Pisa does, making it a better choice for an overnight, so you should come up with a plan that takes in both places.

Getting Here and Around

BUS

Buses are a reliable but time-consuming means of getting around the region because they tend to stop in every town. Trains are a better option in virtually every respect when you're headed to Pisa, Lucca, Arezzo, and other cities with good rail service. But for most smaller towns, buses are the only option. Be aware that making arrangements for bus travel, particularly for a non–Italian speaker, can be a test of patience.

BUS CONTACTS Bus Italia. ⊕ www.fsbusitalia.it. **Tra-In.** ☎ 0577/204111 ⊕ www.trainspa.it.

CAR

Driving is the only way (other than hiking or biking) to reach many of Tuscany's small towns and vineyards. The cities west of Florence are easily accessed by the A11, which leads to Lucca and then to the sea. The A1 takes you south from Florence to Arezzo and Chiusi (where you turn off for Montepulciano). Florence and Siena are connected by a *superstrada* and also the scenic Via Cassia (SR2) and even more panoramic Strada Chiantigiana (SR222), both of which thread through Chianti, skirting rolling hills and vineyards. The hill towns north and west of Siena lie along superstradas and winding local roads—all are well marked, but you should still arm yourself with a good map.

TRAIN

Trains on Italy's main north–south rail line stop in Florence as well as Prato, Arezzo, and Chiusi. Another major line connects Florence with Pisa, and the coastal line between Rome and Genoa passes through Pisa as well. There's regular, frequent hourly service from Florence to Lucca, and several trips a day between Florence and Siena. Siena's train station is 2 km (1 mile) north of the *centro storico* (historic center), but cabs and city buses are readily available, as is a very handy funicular.

For other parts of Tuscany—Chianti, Montalcino, and Montepulciano, for example—you're better off traveling by bus or by car. Train stations, when they exist, are far from the historic centers (usually in the valleys below hill towns), and service is infrequent.

TRAIN CONTACT Trenitalia. ☎ 892021 toll-free in Italy ⊕ www.trenitalia.com.

Restaurants

A meal in Tuscany traditionally consists of five courses, and every menu you encounter will be organized along this plan of antipasto, primo, secondo, contorno, and dolce. The crucial rule of restaurant dining is that you should order at least two courses. Otherwise, you'll likely end up with a lonely piece of meat and no sides.

Prices in the dining reviews are the average cost of a main course at dinner, or, if dinner is not served, at lunch. Restaurant reviews have been shortened. For full information, visit Fodors.com.

Hotels

A visit to the Tuscan countryside is a trip into absolute beauty. There are plenty of good hotels in the larger towns, but the classic experience is to stay in one of the rural accommodations—often converted private homes, sometimes working farms or vineyards (known as *agriturismi*).

Although it's tempting to think you can stumble upon a little out-of-the-way hotel at the end of the day, you're better off not testing your luck. Make reservations before you go. If you don't have a reservation, you may be able to get help finding a room from the local tourist office.

Prices in the reviews are the lowest cost of a standard double room in high season. Hotel reviews have been shortened. For full information, visit Fodors.com.

What it Costs in Euros			
$	$$	$$$	$$$$
RESTAURANTS			
under €15	€15–€24	€25–€35	over €35
HOTELS			
under €125	€125–€200	€201–€300	over €300

Visitor Information

Many towns in Tuscany have tourist information offices, which can be useful resources for trip-planning advice (and sometimes maps). Such offices are typically open from 8:30 to 1 and 3:30 to 6 or 7; those in smaller towns are usually closed Saturday afternoon and Sunday, and often shut down entirely from early November through Easter.

The tourist information office in Greve is an excellent source for general information about the Chianti wine region and its hilltop towns. In Siena, the centrally located tourist office in Piazza del Campo has information about Siena and its province. Both offices book hotel rooms for a nominal fee. Offices in smaller towns can also be a good place to check if you need last-minute accommodations.

Lucca

Ramparts built in the 16th and 17th centuries enclose a charming fortress town filled with churches (99 of them), terra-cotta–roofed buildings, and narrow cobblestone streets, along which locals maneuver bikes to do their daily shopping. Here Caesar, Pompey, and Crassus agreed to rule Rome as a triumvirate in 56 BC; Lucca was later the first Tuscan town to accept Christianity. The town still has a mind of its own, and when most of Tuscany was voting communist as a matter of course, Lucca's citizens rarely followed suit. The famous composer Giacomo Puccini (1858–1924) was born here; he is celebrated during the summer Opera Theater and Music Festival of Lucca. The ramparts circling the centro storico are the perfect place to stroll, bicycle, or just admire the view.

GETTING HERE AND AROUND

You can reach Lucca easily by train from Florence; the centro storico is a short walk from the station. If you're driving, take the A11/E76.

VISITOR INFORMATION

CONTACT Lucca Tourism Office. ✉ *Piazzale Verdi, Lucca* ☎ *0583/583150* ⊕ *www. luccaturismo.it.*

Sights

Traffic (including motorbikes) is restricted in the walled historic center of Lucca. Walking is the best, most enjoyable way to get around. Or you can rent a bicycle; getting around on bike is easy, as the center is quite flat.

Duomo

CHURCH | The blind arches on the cathedral's facade are a fine example of the rigorously ordered Pisan Romanesque style, in this case happily enlivened by an extremely varied collection of small, carved columns. Take a closer look at the decoration of the facade and that of the portico below; they make this one of the most entertaining church exteriors in Tuscany.

The Gothic interior contains a moving Byzantine crucifix—called the Volto Santo, or Holy Face—brought here, according to legend, in the 8th century (though it probably dates from between the 11th and early 13th century). The masterpiece of the Sienese sculptor Jacopo della Quercia (circa 1371–1438) is the marble *Tomb of Ilaria del Carretto* (1407–08). ⊠ *Piazza San Martino 8, Lucca* ☎ *0583/490530* ⊕ *www.museocatte-dralelucca.it* ⊠ *€3.*

Museo Nazionale di Villa Guinigi

ART MUSEUM | Although this museum presents a noteworthy overview of Lucca's artistic traditions up through the 17th century, you might find few other visitors exploring its extensive collections of local Etruscan, Roman, Romanesque, and Renaissance art. It's all housed in the 15th-century former villa of the Guinigi family, on the eastern end of the historic center. ⊠ *Via della Quarquonia 4, Lucca* ☎ *0583/496033* ⊕ *www.polomusealetos-cana.beniculturali.it* ⊠ *€4* ☾ *Closed Mon. and 2nd, 4th, and 5th Sun. of month.*

★ Passeggiata delle Mura

CITY PARK | FAMILY | On nice days, the citizens of Lucca cycle, jog, stroll, or kick a soccer ball in this green, beautiful, and very large circular park. It's neither inside nor outside the city but rather right atop and around the ring of ramparts that defines Lucca. Sunlight streams through two rows of tall plane trees to dapple the *passeggiata delle mura* (walk on the walls), which is 4 km (2½ miles) long. Ten bulwarks are topped with lawns, many with picnic tables and some with play equipment for children. Be aware at all times of where the edge is—there are no railings, and the drop to the ground outside the city is a precipitous 40 feet. ⊠ *Lucca.*

Piazza dell'Anfiteatro Romano

PLAZA/SQUARE | FAMILY | Here's where the ancient Roman amphitheater once stood. Some of the medieval buildings built over the amphitheater retain its original oval shape and brick arches. ⊠ *Piazza Anfiteatro, Lucca.*

San Frediano

CHURCH | A 14th-century mosaic dec-orates the facade of this church just steps from the Anfiteatro. Inside are works by Jacopo della Quercia and Matteo Civitali (1436–1501), as well as the lace-clad mummy of St. Zita (circa 1218–78), the patron saint of household servants. ⊠ *Piazza San Frediano, Lucca* ☎ *349/844–0290* ⊕ *www.sanfredianoluc-ca.com* ⊠ *€3.*

San Michele in Foro

CHURCH | The facade here is even more fanciful than that of the Duomo. Its upper levels have nothing but air behind them (after the front of the church was built, there were no funds to raise the nave), and the winged archangel Michael, who stands at the very top, seems precarious-ly poised for flight. The facade, heavily restored in the 19th century, displays busts of such Italian patriots as Garibaldi and Cavour. Check out the superb Filip-pino Lippi (1457/58–1504) panel painting of Saints Jerome, Sebastian, Rocco, and Helen in the right transept. ⊠ *Piazza San Michele, Lucca* ⊕ *www.luccatranoi.it.*

Torre Guinigi

NOTABLE BUILDING | FAMILY | The tower of the medieval Palazzo Guinigi contains one of the city's most curious sights: a grove of ilex trees has grown at the top of the tower, and their roots have pushed their way into the room below. From the top you have a magnificent view of the city and the surrounding countryside. (Only the tower is open to the public, not the palazzo.) ⊠ *Via Sant'Andrea, Lucca* ☎ *0583/48090* ⊕ *www.comune.lucca. it* ⊠ *€5.*

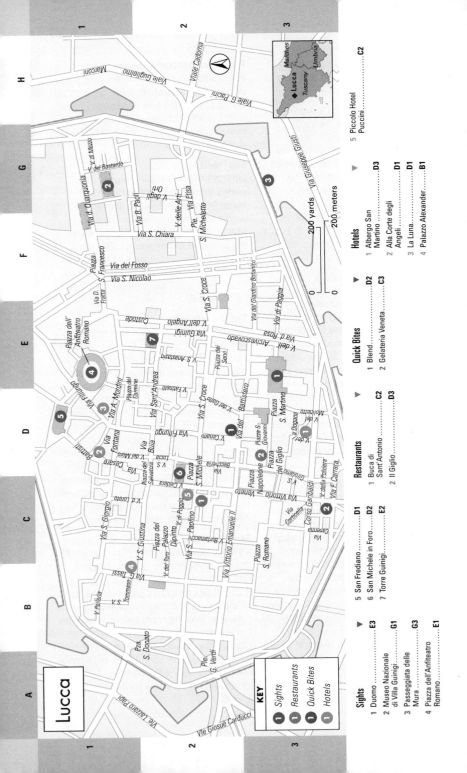

Lucca

KEY

- ① Sights
- ① Restaurants
- ① Quick Bites
- ① Hotels

🍴 Restaurants

★ Buca di Sant'Antonio

$$ | TUSCAN | The staying power of Buca di Sant'Antonio—it's been around since 1782—is the result of superlative Tuscan food brought to the table by waitstaff who don't miss a beat. The menu includes the simple but blissful *tortelli lucchesi al sugo* (meat-stuffed pasta with a tomato-and-meat sauce), as well as more daring dishes such as roast *capretto* (kid goat) with herbs. **Known for:** classy, family-run ambience; excellent sommelier; superlative pastas. $ *Average main: €20 ⊠ Via della Cervia 3, Lucca* ☎ *0583/55881* ⊕ *www.bucadisantonio.com* ☻ *Closed Mon., 1 wk in Jan., and 1 wk in July. No dinner Sun.*

★ Il Giglio

$$$ | TUSCAN | Divine, cutting-edge food and Tuscan classics are served in this one-room space, where in winter, there's a roaring fireplace and, in warmer months, there's outdoor seating on a pretty little piazza. If mushrooms are in season, try the *tacchoni con funghi,* a homemade pasta with mushrooms and a native herb called *nepitella.* A local favorite during winter is the *coniglio con olive* (rabbit stew with olives). **Known for:** the wine list, especially its selection of local wines; fine service; creative menu with seasonal ingredients. $ *Average main: €35 ⊠ Piazza del Giglio 2, Lucca* ☎ *0583/494508* ⊕ *www.ristorantegiglio.com* ☻ *Closed Wed. and 15 days in Nov. No dinner Tues.*

☕ Coffee and Quick Bites

Blend

$ | ITALIAN | If you're looking for a lovely spot to recharge, stop by this place (just around the corner from the Duomo), and have a fantastic sandwich, or a glass of wine, or a tasty salad, a coffee, or dessert. It's open from late morning to late in the evening. **Known for:** open late;

near the Duomo; good salads. $ *Average main: €7 ⊠ Piazza S. Giusto 8, Duomo.*

Gelateria Veneta

$ | ITALIAN | FAMILY | The outstanding gelato, sorbet, and ices, some of which are sugar-free, served here are prepared three times a day according to the same recipes used by the Arnoldo brothers when they opened the place in 1927. The pièces de résistance are frozen fruits stuffed with creamy filling: don't miss the apricot sorbet–filled apricot. **Known for:** delicious ices on a stick; sorbet-stuffed frozen fruits; longtime local favorite. $ *Average main: €3 ⊠ Via V. Veneto 74, Lucca* ☎ *0583/467037* ⊕ *www.gelateriaveneta.net* ☻ *Closed Nov.–Mar.*

Hotels

★ Albergo San Martino

$ | HOTEL | FAMILY | The brocade bedspreads of this inn in the heart of the centro storico are fresh and crisp; the proprietor is friendly; and the breakfast, served in a cheerful apricot room, is more than ample. **Pros:** comfortable beds; friendly staff; tucked away on a small, sunny square. **Cons:** slightly noisy during Lucca Music Festival; pleasant and stylish but not luxurious; parking is difficult. $ *Rooms from: €81 ⊠ Via della Dogana 9, Lucca* ☎ *0583/469181* ⊕ *www.albergosanmartino.it* ⬐ *18 rooms* ⦿ *No Meals.*

Alla Corte degli Angeli

$$ | B&B/INN | This charming hotel with a friendly staff is right off the main shopping drag, Via Fillungo. **Pros:** many rooms are connecting, making them good for families; fantastic on-site restaurant; great location. **Cons:** books up quickly; not all rooms are created equal; some rooms have tubs but no showers. $ *Rooms from: €180 ⊠ Via degli Angeli 23, Lucca* ☎ *0583/469204* ⊕ *www.allacortedegliangeli.it* ⬐ *21 rooms* ⦿ *Free Breakfast.*

La Luna

$$ | B&B/INN | On a quiet, airy courtyard close to the Piazza del Mercato, this hotel, run by the Barbieri family for more than four decades, occupies two renovated wings of an old building. **Pros:** professional staff; central location; the annex has wheelchair-accessible rooms. **Cons:** may be too central for some; street noise can be a bit of a problem; some rooms feel dated. $ *Rooms from: €175* ✉ *Corte Compagni 12, at Via Fillungo, Lucca* ☎ *0583/493634* ⊕ *www.hotellaluna.it* ⊘ *Closed Jan. 7–31* ⇆ *29 rooms* ¶ *Free Breakfast.*

Palazzo Alexander

$$ | HOTEL | This hotel, in a building dating from the 12th century, has public rooms with timbered ceilings, warm yellow walls, and brocaded chairs and guest rooms with high ceilings and still more of that glorious damask. **Pros:** intimate feel; a short walk from San Michele in Foro; gracious staff. **Cons:** might be too quiet for some; books up quickly; some complain of too-thin walls. $ *Rooms from: €160* ✉ *Via S. Giustina 48, Lucca* ☎ *0583/583571* ⊕ *www.hotelpalazzoalexander.it* ⇆ *13 rooms* ¶ *Free Breakfast.*

Piccolo Hotel Puccini

$ | HOTEL | Steps from the busy square and church of San Michele al Foro, this tranquil, affordable little hotel has rooms with hardwood floors and cheerfully patterned fabrics. **Pros:** upbeat, English-speaking staff; quiet, central location; good value. **Cons:** many wish the breakfast was more copious; some rooms are on the dark side; books up quickly. $ *Rooms from: €120* ✉ *Via di Poggio 9, Lucca* ☎ *0583/55421* ⊕ *www.hotelpuccini.com* ⇆ *14 rooms* ¶ *No Meals.*

🛍 Shopping

Lucca's justly famed olive oils are available throughout the city (and exported around the world).

★ Antica Bottega di Prospero

FOOD | Stop by this shop for top-quality local food products, including farro, dried porcini mushrooms, olive oil, and wine. ✉ *Via San Lucia 13, Lucca* ☎ *0583/494875.*

★ Caniparoli

CHOCOLATE | FAMILY | Chocolate lovers will be pleased with the selection of artisanal chocolates, marzipan delights, and gorgeous cakes. Creations become even more fanciful during two big Christian holidays: Christmas and Easter. ✉ *Via San Paolino 44, Lucca* ☎ *0583/53456* ⊕ *www.caniparolicioccolateria.it.*

★ Enoteca Vanni

WINE/SPIRITS | A huge selection of wines, as well as an ancient cellar, make this place worth a stop. For the cost of the wine only, tastings can be organized through the shopkeepers and are held in the cellar or outside in a lovely little piazza. All of this can be paired with affettati misti (sliced cured meats) and cheeses of the highest caliber. ✉ *Piazza San Salvatore 7, Lucca* ☎ *0583/491902* ⊕ *www.enotecavanni.com.*

★ Pasticceria Taddeucci

FOOD | FAMILY | A particularly delicious version of *buccellato*—the sweet, anise-flavored bread with raisins that is a Luccan specialty—is baked at Pasticceria Taddeucci. ✉ *Piazza San Michele 34, Lucca* ☎ *0583/494933* ⊕ *www.buccellatotaddeucci.com.*

🏃 Activities

A good way to spend the afternoon is to go biking around the large path atop the city's ramparts. There are two good spots right next to each other where you can rent bikes. The prices are about the same (about €16 per day and €4 per hour for city bikes) and they are centrally located, just beside the town wall.

Poli Antonio Biciclette

BIKING | FAMILY | This is the best option for bicycle rental on the east side of town. ✉ *Piazza Santa Maria 42, Lucca East* ☎ *0583/493787* ⊕ *www.biciclettepoli. com.*

Pisa

If you can get beyond the kitsch of the stalls hawking cheap souvenirs around the Leaning Tower, you'll find that Pisa has much to offer. Its treasures aren't as abundant as those of Florence, to which it is inevitably compared, but the cathedral-baptistery-tower complex of Piazza del Duomo, known collectively as the Campo dei Miracoli (Field of Miracles), is among the most dramatic settings in Italy.

Pisa may have been inhabited as early as the Bronze Age. It was certainly populated by the Etruscans and, in turn, became part of the Roman Empire. In the early Middle Ages this city on the Arno River flourished as an economic powerhouse—along with Amalfi, Genoa, and Venice, it was one of the four maritime republics. The city's economic and political power ebbed in the early 15th century as it fell under Florence's domination, though it enjoyed a brief resurgence under Cosimo I de' Medici in the mid-16th century. Pisa sustained heavy damage during World War II, but the Duomo and the Leaning Tower were spared, along with some other grand Romanesque structures.

GETTING HERE AND AROUND

Pisa is an easy hour's train ride from Florence. By car it's a straight shot on the Firenze–Pisa–Livorno ("Fi-Pi-Li") autostrada. The Pisa–Lucca train runs frequently and takes about 30 minutes.

VISITOR INFORMATION

CONTACT Pisa Tourism Office. ✉ *Piazza del Duomo 7, Pisa* ☎ *050/550100* ⊕ *www. turismo.pisa.it.*

Sights

Pisa, like many Italian cities, is best explored on foot, and most of what you'll want to see is within walking distance. The views along the Arno River are particularly grand and shouldn't be missed—there's a feeling of spaciousness that isn't found along the Arno in Florence.

As you set out, note that there are various combination-ticket options for sights on the Piazza del Duomo.

Battistero

NOTABLE BUILDING | This lovely Gothic baptistery, which stands across from the Duomo's facade, is best known for the pulpit carved by Nicola Pisano (circa 1220–84; father of Giovanni Pisano) in 1260. Every half hour, an employee will dramatically close the doors, then intone, thereby demonstrating how remarkable the acoustics are in the place. ✉ *Piazza del Duomo, Pisa* ☎ *050/835011* ⊕ *www. opapisa.it* 🎫 *From €7, discounts available if bought in combination with tickets for other monuments.*

Camposanto

CEMETERY | According to legend, the cemetery—a walled structure on the western side of the Piazza dei Miracoli—is filled with earth that returning Crusaders brought back from the Holy Land. Contained within are numerous frescoes, notably *The Drunkenness of Noah,* by Renaissance artist Benozzo Gozzoli (1422–97), and the disturbing *Triumph of Death* (14th century; artist uncertain), whose subject matter shows what was on people's minds in a century that saw the ravages of the Black Death. ✉ *Piazza del Duomo, Pisa* ☎ *050/835011* ⊕ *www. opapisa.it* 🎫 *From €7.*

Duomo

CHURCH | Pisa's cathedral brilliantly utilizes the horizontal marble-stripe motif (borrowed from Moorish architecture) that became common on Tuscan cathedrals. It is famous for the Romanesque panels on

Campo Santo translates literally to "holy field" because it's supposedly built around a shipload of sacred soil from Golgotha, the site where Jesus was crucified.

the transept door facing the tower that depict scenes from the life of Christ. The beautifully carved 14th-century pulpit is by Giovanni Pisano. ✉ *Piazza del Duomo, Pisa* ☎ *050/835011* ⊕ *www.opapisa.it.*

★ Leaning Tower (Torre Pendente)

NOTABLE BUILDING | FAMILY | Legend holds that Galileo conducted an experiment on the nature of gravity by dropping metal balls from the top of the 187-foot-high Leaning Tower of Pisa. Historians, however, say this legend has no basis in fact—which isn't quite to say that it's false. Work on this tower, built as a campanile (bell tower) for the Duomo, started in 1173. The lopsided settling began when construction reached the third story.

The architects attempted to compensate through such methods as making the remaining floors slightly taller on the leaning side, but the extra weight only made the problem worse. The settling continued, and, by the late 20th century, it had accelerated to such a point that many feared the tower would simply topple over, despite all efforts to prop it

up. The structure has since been firmly anchored to the earth. Work to restore the tower to its original tilt of 300 years ago was launched in early 2000 and finished two years later. This involved removing some 100 tons of earth from beneath the foundation.

Reservations, which are essential, can be made online or by calling the Museo dell'Opera del Duomo. It's also possible to arrive at the ticket office and book for the same day. Note, though, that children under eight aren't allowed to climb. ✉ *Piazza del Duomo, Pisa* ☎ *050/835011* ⊕ *www.opapisa.it* 🎟 *€20.*

Museo Nazionale di San Matteo

ART MUSEUM | On the north bank of the Arno, this museum contains some beautiful examples of local Romanesque and Gothic art. Despite the fact that it has stunning works by Donatello and Benozzo Gozzoli (among others), here you'll find very few other visitors. ✉ *Piazza Matteo in Soarta 1, Pisa* ☎ *050/541865* ⊕ *www. polomusealetoscana.beniculturali.it* 🎟 *€5* 🕐 *Closed Mon.*

Piazza dei Cavalieri

PLAZA/SQUARE | The piazza, with its fine Renaissance Palazzo dei Cavalieri, Palazzo dell'Orologio, and Chiesa di Santo Stefano dei Cavalieri, was laid out by Giorgio Vasari in about 1560. The square was the seat of the Ordine dei Cavalieri di San Stefano (Order of the Knights of St. Stephen), a military and religious institution meant to defend the coast from possible invasion by the Turks.

Also in this square is the prestigious Scuola Normale Superiore, founded by Napoléon in 1810 on the French model. Here graduate students pursue doctorates in literature, philosophy, mathematics, and science. In front of the school is a large statue of Ferdinando I de' Medici dating from 1596. On the extreme left is the tower where the hapless Ugolino della Gherardesca (died 1289) was imprisoned with his two sons and two grandsons—legend holds that he ate them. Dante immortalized him in Canto XXXIII of his *Inferno*. Duck into the Church of Santo Stefano (if you're lucky enough to find it open) and check out Bronzino's splendid *Nativity of Christ* (1564–65). ✉ *Piazza dei Cavalieri, Pisa.*

Santa Maria della Spina

CHURCH | Originally an oratory dating from the 13th century, this delicate, tiny church is a fine example of Tuscan Gothic architecture. It has been restored several times, including in 1996–98, after having been damaged by a flood. The results of a recent face-lift are grand. ✉ *Lungarno Gambacorti, Pisa* 🎟 *Free.*

🍴 Restaurants

La Pergoletta

$$ | **TUSCAN** | **FAMILY** | On an old town street named for its beautiful towers, this small, simple restaurant is in one such tower itself and is a place where Pisans come to celebrate. Three intimate rooms, one particularly charming with a pergola, are usually filled with locals eating dishes laced with imagination (curry and ginger often appear on the menu). **Known for:** gracious waitstaff; festive atmosphere; inventive, seasonal menu. [$] *Average main: €16* ✉ *Via delle Belle Torri 36, Pisa* ☎ *050/542458* 🌐 *www.ristorantelapergoletta.com* 🕒 *Closed Mon. and 1 wk in Aug. No lunch Sat.*

Osteria dei Cavalieri

$$ | **ITALIAN** | This charming, white-walled restaurant, a few steps from Piazza dei Cavalieri, is reason enough to come to Pisa. They can do it all here—serve up exquisitely grilled fish dishes, please vegetarians, and prepare *tagliata* for meat lovers. **Known for:** vegetable tasting menu; sea tasting menu; land tasting menu. [$] *Average main: €16* ✉ *Via San Frediano 16, Pisa* ☎ *050/580858* 🌐 *www.osteriacavalieri.pisa.it* 🕒 *No lunch Sat. Closed Sun., 2 wks in Aug., and Dec. 29–Jan. 7.*

★ **V. Beny**

$$$ | **TUSCAN** | Apricot walls hung with etchings of Pisa make this small, single-room restaurant warmly romantic. Husband and wife Damiano and Sandra Lazzerini have been running the place for two decades, and it shows in their obvious enthusiasm while talking about the menu (fish is a focus) and daily specials, which often astound. **Known for:** terrific wine list; gracious service; superb fish dishes. [$] *Average main: €27* ✉ *Piazza Gambacorti 22, Pisa* ☎ *050/25067* 🕒 *Closed Sun. and 2 wks in mid-Aug. No lunch Sat.*

★ **Vineria di Piazza**

$$ | **ITALIAN** | It's set in a lively, historic market square and frequented by locals. The menu adheres to Tuscan tradition, including high-quality bistecca fiorentina, but also indulges in some flights of fantasy, as evidenced by a whimsical dessert that riffs on a liquid Livornese classic. **Known for:** baccalà (salt cod) served in inventive ways; charming, energetic staff; inventive pasta dishes. [$] *Average main: €20* ✉ *Piazza delle Vettovaglie 13–15, Pisa* ☎ *330/441–6721.*

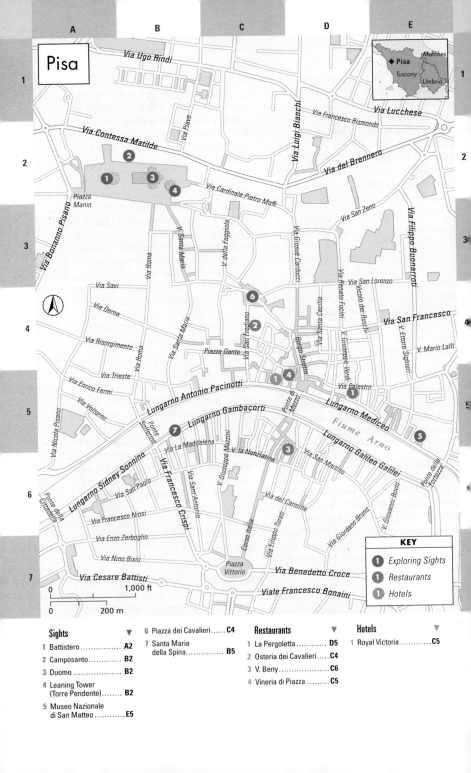

Pisa

Via Ugo Rindi
Via Lucchese
Via Francesco Rismondo
Via Luigi Bianchi
Via del Brennero
Via Contessa Matilde
Via Piave
Via Cardinale Pietro Maffi
Via San Zeno
Piazza Manin
Via Bonanno Pisano
V. Santa Maria
Via Roma
V. della Faggiola
Via Giusté Carducci
Via Filippo Buonarroti
Via San Lorenzo
Via Savi
Via Derna
Via San Frediano
Via Renato Fucini
Vicolo dei Ruschi
Via San Francesco
V. Ettore Sighieri
Via Risorgimento
Via Santa Maria
Piazza Dante
Via San Frediano
Borgo Stretto
Via Santa Cecilia
V. Giuseppe Verdi
V. Mario Lalli
Via Trieste
Via Enrico Fermi
Via Roma
Lungarno Antonio Pacinotti
Ponte di Mezzo
Via Palestro
Lungarno Mediceo
Via Volturno
Via Niccola Pisano
Lungarno Gambacorti
Fiume Arno
Lungarno Galileo Galilei
Ponte Solferino
Via La Maddalena
Via Giuseppe Mazzini
V. la Nunziatina
Via San Martino
Ponte della Fortezza
Lungarno Sidney Sonnino
Via San Paolo
Via Francesco Crispi
Via Sant'Antonio
V. Giuseppe Bruno
Ponte della Cittadella
Via Francesco Niosi
Via del Carmine
Via Giordano Bruno
Via Enzo Zerboglio
Corso Italia
Via Filippo Turati
Via Nino Bixio
Piazza Vittorio
Via Cesare Battisti
Via Benedetto Croce
Viale Francesco Bonaini

Pisa — Tuscany, Marches, Umbria

0 — 1,000 ft
0 — 200 m

KEY
1 Exploring Sights
1 Restaurants
1 Hotels

Hotels

Royal Victoria
$ | **HOTEL** | In a pleasant palazzo facing the Arno, a 10-minute walk from the Campo dei Miracoli, this hotel has room styles that range from the 1800s, complete with frescoes, to the 1920s; the most charming are in the old tower. **Pros:** friendly staff; old-world charm; lovely views of the Arno from many rooms. **Cons:** not all rooms have views of the Arno; rooms a little worn; rooms vary significantly in size. [$] *Rooms from: €95* ✉ *Lungarno Pacinotti 12, Pisa* ☎ *050/940111* 🌐 *www.royalvictoria.it* 🛏 *38 rooms* 🍴 *Free Breakfast.*

Performing Arts

Fondazione Teatro di Pisa
THEATER | Pisa has a lively performing-arts scene, most of which happens at the 19th-century Teatro Verdi. Music and dance performances are presented from September through May. Contact Fondazione Teatro di Pisa for schedules and information. ✉ *Via Palestro 40, Lungarni, Pisa* ☎ *050/941111* 🌐 *www.teatrodipisa.pi.it.*

Chianti

This is the heartland: both sides of the Strada Chiantigiana (SR222) are embraced by glorious panoramic views of vineyards, olive groves, and castle towers. Traveling south from Florence, you first reach the aptly named one-street town of Strada in Chianti. Farther south, the number of vineyards on either side of the road dramatically increases—as do the signs inviting you in for a free tasting. Beyond Strada lies Greve in Chianti, completely surrounded by wineries and filled with wineshops. There's art to be had as well: Passignano, west of Greve, has an abbey that shelters a 15th-century *Last Supper* by Domenico and Davide Ghirlandaio. Farther still, along the Strada Chiantigiana, are Panzano and Castellina in Chianti, both hill towns. It's from near Panzano and Castellina that branch roads head to the other main towns of eastern Chianti: Radda in Chianti, Gaiole in Chianti, and Castelnuovo Berardenga.

The Strada Chiantigiana gets crowded during the high season, but no one is in a hurry. The slow pace gives you time to soak up the beautiful scenery.

Greve in Chianti

40 km (25 miles) north of Siena, 28 km (17½ miles) south of Florence.

If there is a capital of Chianti, it is Greve, a friendly market town with no shortage of cafés, enoteche, and crafts shops lining its streets.

GETTING HERE AND AROUND

Driving from Florence or Siena, Greve is easily reached via the Strada Chiantigiana (SR222). SITA buses travel frequently between Florence and Greve. Tra-In and SITA buses connect Siena and Greve, but a direct trip is virtually impossible. There is no train service to Greve.

VISITOR INFORMATION

CONTACT Greve in Chianti Tourism Office. ✉ *Piazza Matteotti 11,* ☎ *055/854–6299* 🌐 *www.greve-in-chianti.info.*

Sights

Montefioralle
TOWN | A tiny hilltop hamlet, about 2 km (1 mile) west of Greve in Chianti, Montefioralle is the ancestral home of Amerigo Vespucci (1454–1512), the mapmaker, navigator, and explorer who named America. (His cousin-in-law, Simonetta, may have been the inspiration for Sandro Botticelli's *Birth of Venus,* painted sometime in the 1480s.) ✉ *Greve in Chianti.*

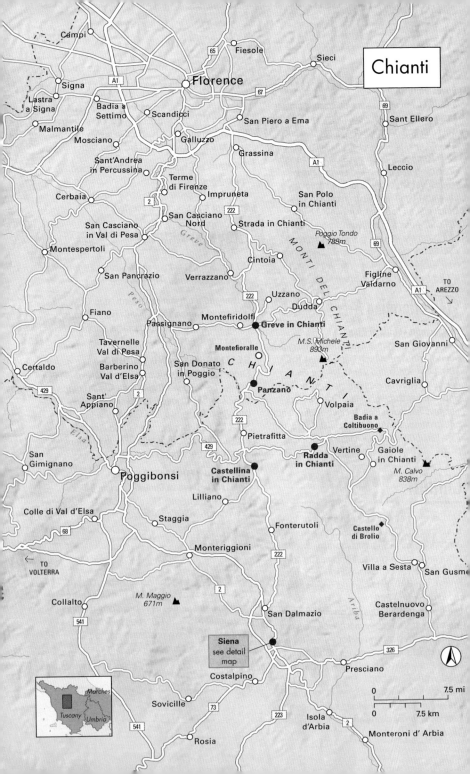

Piazza Matteotti

PLAZA/SQUARE | Greve's gently sloping and asymmetrical central piazza is surrounded by an attractive arcade with shops of all kinds. In the center stands a statue of the discoverer of New York harbor, Giovanni da Verrazzano (circa 1480–1527). Check out the lively market held here on Saturday morning. ✉ *Greve in Chianti.*

🍴 Restaurants

Enoteca Fuoripiazza

$$ | **TUSCAN** | Detour off Greve's flower-strewn main square for food that relies heavily on local ingredients (like cheese and salami produced nearby). The lengthy wine list provides a bewildering array of choices to pair with affettati misti (cured meats) or one of the primi (appetizers)—the pici (a thick, hand-rolled spaghetti) are deftly prepared here. **Known for:** attentively prepared food; local cheese and salami; alfresco dining. [$] *Average main: €15* ✉ *Via I Maggio 2, Greve in Chianti* ☎ *055/854–6313* 🌐 *www.enotecaristorantefuoripiazza.it* 🕒 *Closed Mon.*

★ Falorni

$ | **ITALIAN** | This institution—it's been around since 1806—began life as a butcher shop and, indeed, it still is. But it also has a little restaurant inside the shop which serves great *taglieri* (plates of mixed cured pork products, usually, though cheese does prominently figure as well). **Known for:** cured meats using centuries' old recipes; outdoor seating; great wines by the glass. [$] *Average main: €10* ✉ *Piazza G. Matteotti 66, Greve in Chianti* ☎ *055/853029* 🌐 *falorni.it.*

★ Ristoro di Lamole

$$ | **TUSCAN** | Up a winding road lined with olive trees and vineyards, this place is worth the effort it takes to find. The view from the outdoor terrace is divine, as is the simple, exquisitely prepared Tuscan cuisine—start with the bruschetta drizzled with olive oil or the sublime *verdure sott'olio* (marinated vegetables) before moving on to any of the fine secondi. **Known for:** your hosts Paolo and Filippo; sweeping view from the terrace; coniglio (rabbit) is a specialty. [$] *Average main: €20* ✉ *Via di Lamole 6, Località Lamole, Greve in Chianti* ☎ *055/854–7050* 🌐 *www.ristorodilamole.it* 🕒 *Closed Wed. and Nov.–Apr.*

🛏 Hotels

Albergo del Chianti

$$ | **B&B/INN** | **FAMILY** | Simple but pleasantly decorated bedrooms with plain modern cabinets and wardrobes and wrought-iron beds have views of the town square or out over the tile rooftops toward the surrounding hills. **Pros:** central location; swimming pool; best value in Greve. **Cons:** remote: a car is a necessity; small bathrooms; rooms facing the piazza can be noisy. [$] *Rooms from: €145* ✉ *Piazza Matteotti 86, Greve in Chianti* ☎ *055/853763* 🌐 *www.albergodelchianti.it* 🕒 *Closed Jan.–early Mar.* 🛏 *16 rooms* 🍽 *Free Breakfast.*

Castello Vicchiomaggio

$$ | **B&B/INN** | **FAMILY** | Stay in a fortified castle, which was built more than a millennium ago, was rebuilt during the Renaissance, and is now a charming inn and a prestigious wine estate where you can taste local vintages. **Pros:** spacious rooms; spectacular views; very helpful staff. **Cons:** might be too remote for some; you need a car to get around; some rooms lack air-conditioning. [$] *Rooms from: €185* ✉ *Via Vicchiomaggio 4, Località Vicchiomaggio, Greve in Chianti* ☎ *055/854079* 🌐 *www.vicchiomaggio.it* 🕒 *Closed Dec.–mid Mar.* 🛏 *15 rooms* 🍽 *Free Breakfast.*

★ Villa Bordoni

$$$ | **B&B/INN** | Scottish expats David and Catherine Gardner transformed a ramshackle, 16th-century villa into a stunning retreat where no two rooms are alike—all have stenciled walls; some have four-poster beds, others small mezzanines. **Pros:** splendidly isolated in the hills above Greve; wonderful hosts; beautiful decor. **Cons:** books up quickly; need a car to get around; on a long and bumpy dirt road. [$] *Rooms from: €240* ✉ *Via San Cresci 31/32, Greve in Chianti* ☎ *055/854–6230* 🌐 *www.villabordoni.com* 🕑 *Closed Dec.–Feb.* 🛏 *12 rooms* 🍴 *Free Breakfast.*

★ Villa Il Poggiale

$$ | **B&B/INN** | **FAMILY** | Renaissance gardens, beautiful rooms with high ceilings and elegant furnishings, a panoramic pool, and expert staff are just a few of the things that make a stay at this 16th-century villa memorable. **Pros:** beautiful gardens and panoramic setting; exceptionally professional staff; elegant historical building. **Cons:** it may be too isolated for some; some rooms face a country road and may be noisy during the day; private transportation necessary. [$] *Rooms from: €142* ✉ *Via Empolese 69, San Casciano Val di Pesa* ✣ *20 km (12 miles) northwest of Greve* ☎ *055/828311* 🌐 *www.villailpoggiale.it* 🕑 *Closed Jan. and Feb.* 🛏 *26 rooms* 🍴 *Free Breakfast.*

Panzano

7 km (4½ miles) south of Greve, 36 km (22 miles) south of Florence.

The magnificent views of the valleys of the Pesa and Greve Rivers easily make Panzano one of the prettiest stops in Chianti. The triangular Piazza Bucciarelli is the heart of the new town. A short stroll along Via Giovanni da Verrazzano brings you up to the old town, Panzano Alto, which is still partly surrounded by medieval walls. The town's 13th-century castle is now almost completely absorbed by later buildings (its central tower is now a private home).

GETTING HERE AND AROUND

From Florence or Siena, Panzano is easily reached by car along the Strada Chiantigiana (SR222). SITA buses travel frequently between Florence and Panzano. From Siena, the journey by bus is extremely difficult because SITA and Tra-In do not coordinate their schedules. There is no train service to Panzano.

Sights

San Leolino

CHURCH | Ancient even by Chianti standards, this hilltop church probably dates from the 10th century, but it was completely rebuilt in the Romanesque style sometime in the 13th century. It has a 14th-century cloister worth seeing. The 16th-century terra-cotta tabernacles are attributed to Giovanni della Robbia, and there's also a remarkable triptych (attributed to the Master of Panzano) that was executed sometime in the mid-14th century. Open days and hours are unpredictable; check with the tourist office in Greve in Chianti for the latest information. ✉ *Località San Leolino, Panzano* ✣ *3 km (2 miles) south of Panzano.*

Restaurants

★ Officina della Bistecca

$$$$ | **ITALIAN** | **FAMILY** | Local butcher and restaurateur, Dario Cecchini, has extended his empire of meat to include this space above his butcher's shop. In addition to two tasting menus—one heavily meat laden, the other with none—you'll find a house-made version of *giardiniera sott'olio* (pickled and preserved vegetables) that's second to none. **Known for:** enormously popular, especially in summer; performing waitstaff; convivial atmosphere. [$] *Average main: €50* ✉ *Via XX Luglio 11, Panzano* ☎ *055/852020* 🌐 *www.dariocecchini.com/officina* 🕑 *Closed Sun.*

★ Solociccia

$$$$ | **TUSCAN** | **FAMILY** | As at his other eateries, Dario Cecchini, Panzano's local merchant of meat, offers two set menus—one where beef products dominate every course and the other vegetarian.

The *musetto al limone e brodo vero* (an interesting salame served with stunning beef broth) kicks off the proceedings. **Known for:** party atmosphere; great service; choice of two set menus. $ *Average main: €40* ✉ *Via XX Luglio 11, Panzano* ☎ *055/852020* ⊕ *www.dariocecchini.com/solociccia* ⊗ *No dinner Mon.–Thurs.*

 Hotels

⭐ **Villa Le Barone**

$$$ | **B&B/INN** | Once the home of the Viviani della Robbia family, this 16th-century villa in a grove of ancient cypress trees retains many aspects of a private country dwelling, complete with homey guest quarters. **Pros:** beautiful location; great base for exploring the region; wonderful restaurant. **Cons:** a car is a must; 15-minute walk to nearest town; some rooms are a bit small. $ *Rooms from: €271* ✉ *Via San Leolino 19, Panzano* ☎ *055/852621* ⊕ *villalebarone. com* ⊗ *Closed Oct.–Easter* ⤴ *28 rooms* �🍴 *Free Breakfast.*

Radda in Chianti

26 km (15 miles) southeast of Panzano, 55 km (34 miles) south of Florence.

Radda in Chianti sits on a ridge stretching between the Val di Pesa and Val d'Arbia. It is easily reached by following the SR429 from Castellina. It's another one of those tiny villages with steep streets for strolling; follow the signs that point you toward the *camminamento medioevale,* a covered 14th-century walkway that circles part of the city inside the walls.

GETTING HERE AND AROUND
Radda can be reached by car from either Siena or Florence along the SR222 (Strada Chiantigiana), and from the A1 autostrada. Three Tra-In buses make their way from Siena to Radda. One morning SITA bus travels from Florence to Radda. There is no train service convenient to Radda.

VISITOR INFORMATION
CONTACT Radda in Chianti Tourism Office. ✉ *Piazza Castello 6,* ☎ *0577/738494* ⊕ *www.chianti.com.*

 Sights

Badia a Coltibuono
(Abbey of the Good Harvest)
WINERY | This Romanesque abbey has been owned by internationally acclaimed cookbook author Lorenza de' Medici's family for more than a century and a half (the family isn't related to the Florentine Medici). Wine has been produced here since the abbey was founded by Vallombrosan monks in the 11th century. Today, the family continues the tradition, making wines, cold-pressed olive oil, and various flavored vinegars. Don't miss the jasmine-draped courtyard and the inner cloister with its antique well. ✉ *Località Badia a Coltibuono, Gaiole in Chianti* ✛ *4 km (2½ miles) north of Gaiole* ☎ *0577/74481 tours* ⊕ *www. coltibuono.com* ✉ *Abbey €7* ⊗ *Closed Jan. 7–mid-Mar.*

⭐ Castello di Brolio
CASTLE/PALACE | If you have time for only one castle in Tuscany, this is it. At the end of the 12th century, when Florence conquered southern Chianti, Brolio became Florence's southernmost outpost, and it was often said, "When Brolio growls, all Siena trembles." It was built about AD 1000 and owned by the monks of the Badia Fiorentina. The "new" owners, the Ricasoli family, have been in possession since 1141. Bettino Ricasoli (1809–80), the so-called Iron Baron, was one of the founders of modern Italy and is said to have invented the original formula for Chianti wine.

Brolio, one of Chianti's best-known labels, is still justifiably famous. The grounds are worth visiting, and some of the guided tours do provide a glimpse of the castle's interior. The entrance fee includes a wine tasting in the enoteca.

A small museum, where the Ricasoli Collection is housed in a 12th-century tower, displays objects that relate the long history of the family and the origins of Chianti wine. There are various options for an overnight here. ✉ *Località Madonna a Brolio, Gaiole in Chianti* ✣ *2 km (1 mile) southeast of Gaiole* ☎ *0577/7301* 🌐 *www.ricasoli.com* 🎟 *€7 gardens* ⏲ *Closed Dec. Museum closed Mon.*

Palazzo del Podestà
GOVERNMENT BUILDING | Radda's town hall (aka Palazzo Comunale), in the middle of town, was built in the second half of the 14th century and has always served the same function. The 51 coats of arms (the largest is the Medici's) embedded in the facade represent the past governors of the town, but unless you have official business, the building is closed to the public. ✉ *Piazza Ferrucci 1, Radda in Chianti.*

Restaurants

Osteria Le Panzanelle
$ | **TUSCAN** | Silvia Bonechi's experience in the kitchen—with the help of a few precious recipes handed down from her grandmother—is one of the reasons for the success of this small restaurant in the tiny hamlet of Lucarelli; the other is the front-room hospitality of Nada Michelassi. These two *panzanelle* (women from Panzano) serve a short menu of tasty and authentic dishes at what the locals refer to as *il prezzo giusto* (the right price). **Known for:** unpretentious atmosphere; good wine list; fine home cooking. [$] *Average main: €13* ✉ *Località Lucarelli 29, Radda in Chianti* ✣ *8 km (5 miles) northwest of Radda on road to Panzano* ☎ *0577/733511* 🌐 *www.lepanzanelle.it* ⏲ *Closed Mon. and Jan. and Feb.*

Hotels

La Bottega di Giovannino
$ | **B&B/INN** | This is a fantastic place for the budget-conscious traveler, as rooms are immaculate and most have a stunning view of the surrounding hills. **Pros:** great location in the center of town; super value; close to restaurants and shops. **Cons:** basic decor; books up quickly; some rooms are small. [$] *Rooms from: €65* ✉ *Via Roma 6–8, Radda in Chianti* ☎ *0577/735601* 🌐 *www.labottegadigiovannino.it* 🛏 *9 rooms* 🍴 *No Meals.*

★ **La Locanda**
$$$ | **B&B/INN** | At an altitude of more than 1,800 feet, this converted farmhouse is probably the loftiest luxury inn in Chianti. **Pros:** idyllic setting; wonderful host; panoramic views. **Cons:** need a car to get around; isolated location; on a very rough gravel access road. [$] *Rooms from: €220* ✉ *Località Montanino di Volpaia, Radda in Chianti* ✣ *Off Via della Volpaia, 13 km (8 miles) northwest of Radda* ☎ *0577/738833* 🌐 *www.lalocanda.it* ⏲ *Closed mid-Oct.–mid-Apr.* 🛏 *7 rooms* 🍴 *Free Breakfast.*

Palazzo San Niccolò
$ | **HOTEL** | The wood-beam ceilings, terra-cotta floors, and some of the original frescoes of a 19th-century town palace remain, but the marble bathrooms have all been updated, some with Jacuzzi tubs. **Pros:** central location; pool (though a car is necessary to get there); friendly staff. **Cons:** some street noise in some rooms; room sizes vary; some rooms face a main street. [$] *Rooms from: €91* ✉ *Via Roma 16, Radda in Chianti* ☎ *0577/735666* 🌐 *www.hotelsanniccolo.com* ⏲ *Closed Nov.–Mar.* 🛏 *18 rooms* 🍴 *Free Breakfast.*

★ **Relais Fattoria Vignale**
$$ | **B&B/INN** | A refined and comfortable country house offers numerous sitting rooms with terra-cotta floors and attractive stonework, as well as wood-beamed

guest rooms filled with simple wooden furnishings and handwoven rugs. **Pros:** intimate public spaces; nice grounds and pool; excellent restaurant. **Cons:** a car is necessary; annex across a busy road; single rooms are small. $ *Rooms from: €170* ✉ *Via Pianigiani 9, Radda in Chianti* ☎ *0577/738300 hotel, 0577/738094 restaurant* 🌐 *www.vignale.it* 🕒 *Closed Nov.–Mar.* 🛏 *41 rooms* 🍴 *No Meals.*

Castellina in Chianti

13 km (8 miles) south of Panzano, 59 km (35 miles) south of Florence, 22 km (14 miles) north of Siena.

Castellina in Chianti—or simply Castellina—is on a ridge above three valleys: the Val di Pesa, Val d'Arbia, and Val d'Elsa. No matter what direction you turn, the panorama is bucolic. The strong 15th-century medieval walls and fortified town gate give a hint of the history of this village, which was an outpost during the continuing wars between Florence and Siena. In the main square, the Piazza del Comune, there's a 15th-century palace and a 15th-century fort constructed around a 13th-century tower. It now serves as the town hall.

GETTING HERE AND AROUND

As with all the towns along the Strada Chiantigiana (SR222), Castellina is an easy drive from either Siena or Florence. From Siena, Castellina is well served by the local Tra-In bus company. However, only one bus a day travels here from Florence. The closest train station is at Castellina Scalo, some 15 km (9 miles) away.

VISITOR INFORMATION

CONTACT Castellina in Chianti Tourism Office. ✉ *Via Ferruccio 40, Castellina in Chianti* ☎ *0577/741392.*

🍴 Restaurants

Albergaccio

$$$ | **TUSCAN** | The fact that the dining room can seat only 35 guests makes a meal here an intimate experience, and the ever-changing menu mixes traditional and creative dishes. In late September and October, *zuppa di funghi e castagne* (mushroom and chestnut soup) is a treat; grilled meats and seafood are on offer throughout the year. **Known for:** marvelous waitstaff; superb wine list; creative menu. $ *Average main: €25* ✉ *Via Fiorentina 63, Castellina in Chianti* ☎ *0577/741042* 🌐 *www.ristorantealbergaccio.com* 🕒 *Closed Tues. and Wed.*

Ristorante Le Tre Porte

$$ | **TUSCAN** | Grilled meat dishes are the specialty at this popular restaurant, with a bistecca fiorentina (served very rare, as always) taking pride of place; paired with grilled fresh porcini mushrooms when in season (spring and fall), it's a heady dish. The panoramic terrace is a good choice for dining in summer. **Known for:** fine wine list with lots of local bottles; their way with mushrooms; views from the terrace. $ *Average main: €18* ✉ *Via Trento e Trieste 4, Castellina in Chianti* ☎ *0577/741163* 🌐 *www.treporte.com* 🕒 *Closed Mon.–Wed.*

Sotto Le Volte

$$ | **TUSCAN** | As the name suggests, you'll find this small restaurant under the arches of Castellina's medieval walkway, and the eatery's vaulted ceilings make for a particularly romantic setting. The menu is short and eminently Tuscan, with typical soups and pasta dishes. **Known for:** attentive waitstaff; flair for Tuscan classics; unique setting. $ *Average main: €17* ✉ *Via delle Volte 14–16, Castellina in Chianti* ☎ *0577/741299* 🌐 *www.ristorantesottolevolte.it* 🕒 *Closed Wed. and Jan.–Mar.*

Sights

1 Duomo **B3**
2 Museo Etrusco Guarnacci .. **C4**
3 Pinacoteca . **B2**
4 Porta all'Arco Etrusco...... **B3**
5 Teatro Romano..... **B2**

Restaurants

1 Da Badò..... **D5**
2 Il Sacco Fiorentino... **B3**

Hotels

1 Etruria....... **B3**

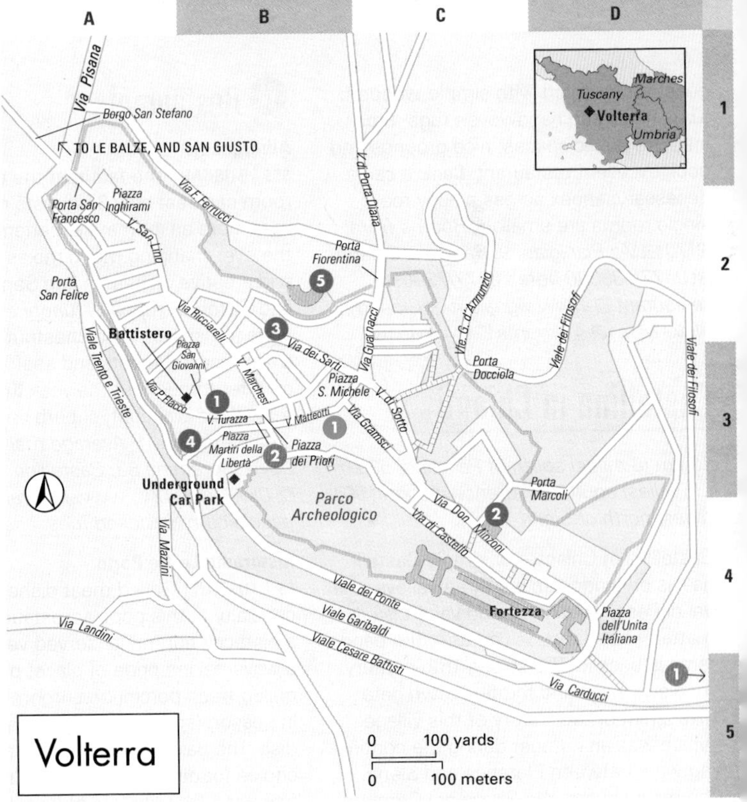

Hotels

★ Palazzo Squarcialupi
$$ | **B&B/INN** | In this lovely, 15th-century palace, spacious rooms have high ceilings, tile floors, and 18th-century furnishings, and many have views of the valley below. **Pros:** great location in town center; nice spa, pool, and grounds; elegant public spaces. **Cons:** rooms facing the street can experience some noise; across from a busy restaurant; on a street with no car access. [$] *Rooms from: €140* ✉ *Via Ferruccio 22, Castellina in Chianti* ☎ *0577/741186* 🌐 *www.squarcialupirelaxinchianti.com* 🕒 *Closed Nov.–Mar.* 🛏 *17 rooms* 🍴 *Free Breakfast.*

Volterra

30 km (18 miles) southwest of San Gimignano.

As you approach the town through bleak, rugged terrain, you can see that not all Tuscan hill towns rise above rolling green fields. Volterra stands mightily over Le Balze, a stunning series of gullied hills and valleys formed by erosion that has slowly eaten away at the foundation of the town—now considerably smaller than it was during its Etruscan glory days some 2000 years ago.

GETTING HERE AND AROUND

By car, the best route from San Gimignano follows the SP1 south to Castel San Gimignano and then the SS68 west to Volterra. Coming from the west, take the SS1, a coastal road to Cecina, then follow the SS68 east to Volterra. Either way, there's a long, winding climb at the end of your trip. Traveling to Volterra by bus or train is complicated; avoid it if possible, especially if you have lots of luggage. From Florence or Siena the journey by public transit is best made by bus and involves a change in Colle di Val d'Elsa. From Rome or Pisa, it is best to take the train to Cecina and then take a bus to Volterra or a train to the Volterra-Saline station. The latter is 10 km (6 miles) from town.

VISITOR INFORMATION

CONTACT Volterra Tourism Office. ⊠ *Piazza dei Priori 10,* ☎ *0588/86150* ⊕ *www. provolterra.it.*

Sights

Duomo

CHURCH | Behind the textbook 13th-century Pisan–Romanesque facade is proof that Volterra counted for something during the Renaissance, when many important Tuscan artists came to decorate the church. Three-dimensional stucco portraits of local saints are on the gold, red, and blue ceiling (1580) designed by Francesco Capriani, including St. Linus, the successor to St. Peter as pope and claimed by the Volterrans to have been born here.

The highlight of the Duomo is the brightly painted, 13th-century, wooden, life-size *Deposition* in the chapel of the same name. The unusual Cappella dell'Addolorata (Chapel of the Grieved) has two terra-cotta Nativity scenes; the depiction of the arrival of the Magi has a background fresco by Benozzo Gozzoli. ⊠ *Piazza San Giovanni, Volterra.*

★ Museo Etrusco Guarnacci

HISTORY MUSEUM | An extraordinary collection of Etruscan relics is made all the more interesting by clear explanations in English. The bulk of the collection is comprised of roughly 700 carved funerary urns. The oldest, dating from the 7th century BC, were made from tufa (volcanic rock). A handful are made of terra-cotta, but most—dating from the 3rd to 1st century BC—are done in alabaster. The urns are grouped by subject, and, taken together, they form a fascinating testimony about Etruscan life and death. ⊠ *Via Don Minzoni 15, Volterra* ☎ *0588/86347* ⊕ *www.comune.volterra. pi.it* 🖾 *From €8.*

Pinacoteca

ART MUSEUM | One of Volterra's best-looking Renaissance buildings contains an impressive collection of Tuscan paintings arranged chronologically on two floors. Head straight for Room 12, with Luca Signorelli's (circa 1445–1523) *Madonna and Child with Saints* and Rosso Fiorentino's later *Deposition*. Though painted just 30 years apart, they illustrate the shift in style from the early 16th-century Renaissance ideals to full-blown Mannerism: the balance of Signorelli's composition becomes purposefully skewed in Fiorentino's painting, where the colors go from vivid but realistic to emotively bright. Other important paintings in the small museum include Ghirlandaio's *Apotheosis of Christ with Saints* and a polyptych of the *Madonna and Saints* by Taddeo di Bartolo, which once hung in the Palazzo dei Priori. ⊠ *Via dei Sarti 1, Volterra* ☎ *0588/87580* ⊕ *www.comune. volterra.pi.it* 🖾 *From €8.*

Porta all'Arco Etrusco

RUINS | Even if a good portion of the arch was rebuilt by the Romans, three dark, weather-beaten, 4th-century-BC heads (thought to represent Etruscan gods) still face outward to greet those who enter here. A plaque on the outer wall recalls the efforts of the locals who saved the arch from destruction by filling it with stones during the German withdrawal at the end of World War II. ⊠ *Via Porta all'Arco, Volterra.*

Teatro Romano

RUINS | Just outside the walls, past Porta Fiorentina, are the ruins of the 1st-century-BC Roman theater, one of the best preserved in Italy, with adjacent remains of the Roman *terme* (baths). You can enjoy an excellent bird's-eye view of the theater from Via Lungo le Mura. ✉ *Viale Francesco Ferrucci, Volterra* 🎟 *€13* ⏲ *Closed weekdays Nov.–Mar.*

🍴 Restaurants

Da Badò

$ | **TUSCAN** | Family-run Da Badò—with Lucia in the kitchen and her sons, Giacomo and Michele, waiting tables—is the best place in town to eat traditional food elbow-to-elbow with locals. Lucia likes to concentrate on just a few dishes, so it won't take long to decide between the standards, all prepared with a sure hand. **Known for:** local favorite; small menu; excellent traditional dishes. [$] *Average main: €14* ✉ *Borgo San Lazzaro 9, Volterra* ☎ *0588/80402* 🌐 *www.trattoriadabado.com* ⏲ *Closed Wed.*

Il Sacco Fiorentino

$$ | **TUSCAN** | This lovely trattoria has been around for a long time, and with good reason. Here, they turn out Tuscan classics, relying heavily on the local cheese (pecorino) and local meats (especially wild boar, among others). **Known for:** excellent wine list; tranquil setting; three well-priced tasting menus. [$] *Average main: €16* ✉ *Via Giusto Turazza 13, Volterra* ☎ *0588/88537* ⏲ *Closed Wed.*

🛏 Hotels

Etruria

$ | **B&B/INN** | The rooms are modest, and there's no elevator, but the central location, the ample buffet breakfast, and the modest rates make this a good choice for those on a budget. **Pros:** great central location; tranquil garden with rooftop views; friendly staff. **Cons:** no elevator; books up quickly as it's good value; some rooms can be noisy during the day. [$] *Rooms from: €93* ✉ *Via Matteotti 32, Volterra* ☎ *0588/87377* 🌐 *albergoetruria.it* ⏲ *Closed Jan. and Feb.* 🛏 *15 rooms* 🍴 *Free Breakfast.*

San Gimignano

14 km (9 miles) northwest of Colle di Val d'Elsa, 38 km (24 miles) northwest of Siena, 54 km (34 miles) southwest of Florence.

When you're on a hilltop surrounded by soaring medieval towers silhouetted against the sky, it's difficult not to fall under the spell of San Gimignano. Its tall walls and narrow streets are typical of Tuscan hill towns, but it's the medieval "skyscrapers" that set the town apart from its neighbors. Today 14 towers remain, but at the height of the Guelph–Ghibelline conflict there was a forest of more than 70, and it was possible to cross the town by rooftop rather than by road.

Today San Gimignano isn't much more than a gentrified walled city, touristy but still very much worth exploring because, despite the profusion of cheesy souvenir shops lining the main drag, there's some serious Renaissance art to be seen here.

GETTING HERE AND AROUND

You can reach San Gimignano by car from the Florence–Siena superstrada. Exit at Poggibonsi Nord and follow signs for San Gimignano. Although it involves changing buses in Poggibonsi, getting to San Gimignano by bus from Florence is a relatively straightforward affair. SITA operates the service between Siena or Florence and Poggibonsi. From Siena, Tra-In offers direct service to San Gimignano several times daily. You cannot reach San Gimignano by train.

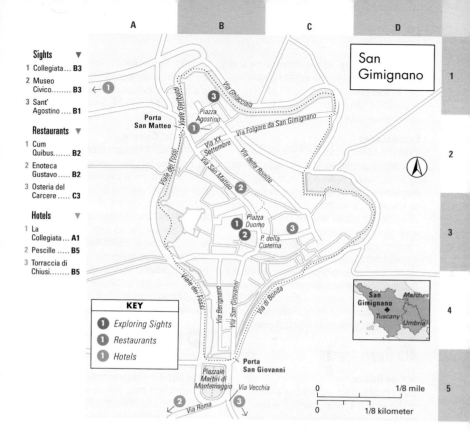

Sights ▼
1 Collegiata... **B3**
2 Museo Civico........ **B3**
3 Sant' Agostino **B1**

Restaurants ▼
1 Cum Quibus....... **B2**
2 Enoteca Gustavo **B2**
3 Osteria del Carcere **C3**

Hotels ▼
1 La Collegiata... **A1**
2 Pescille **B5**
3 Torraccia di Chiusi........ **B5**

San Gimignano

KEY

❶ *Exploring Sights*
❶ *Restaurants*
❶ *Hotels*

Porta San Matteo
Piazza Agostino
Via Ghiacciaia
Via Folgore da San Gimignano
Via XX Settembre
Via San Matteo
Via della Romite
Piazza Duomo
P. della Cisterna
Viale dei Fossi
Viale Garibaldi
Via Bergignano
Via San Giovanni
Via di Bonda
Porta San Giovanni
Piazzale Martiri di Montemaggio
Via Vecchia
Via Roma

San Gimignano
Tuscany
Marches
Umbria

0 ——— 1/8 mile
0 ——— 1/8 kilometer

VISITOR INFORMATION

CONTACT San Gimignano Tourism Office.
✉ *Piazza Duomo 1,* ☎ *0577/940008*
⊕ *www.sangimignano.com.*

👁 Sights

★ Collegiata

CHURCH | The town's main church is not officially a duomo (cathedral), because San Gimignano has no bishop. But behind the simple facade of the Romanesque Collegiata lies a treasure trove of fine frescoes, covering nearly every wall. Bartolo di Fredi's 14th-century fresco cycle of Old Testament scenes extends along one wall. Their distinctly medieval feel, with misshapen bodies, buckets of spurting blood, and lack of perspective, contrasts with the much more reserved scenes from the Life of Christ (attributed to 14th-century artist Lippo Memmi)

painted on the opposite wall just 14 years later. ✉ *Piazza Pecori 1–2, entrance on left side of church, San Gimignano* ☎ *0577/286300* ⊕ *www.duomosangimignano.it* 🎟 *€5* 🕐 *Closed Jan. 1, 15–31, and Nov. 15–30.*

Museo Civico

CASTLE/PALACE | The impressive civic museum occupies what was the "new" Palazzo del Popolo; the Torre Grossa is adjacent. Dante visited San Gimignano for only one day as a Guelph ambassador from Florence to ask the locals to join the Florentines in supporting the pope—just long enough to get the main council chamber named after him.

Upstairs, paintings by famous Renaissance artists Pinturicchio (*Madonna Enthroned*) and Benozzo Gozzoli (*Madonna and Child*), and two large *tondi* (circular paintings) by Filippino Lippi (circa

1457–1504) attest to the importance and wealth of San Gimignano. ✉ *Piazza Duomo 2, San Gimignano* ☎ *0577/990312* 🌐 *www.sangimignanomusei.it* 🎟 *€9 cumulative ticket.*

Sant'Agostino

CHURCH | Make a beeline for Benozzo Gozzoli's superlative 15th-century fresco cycle depicting scenes from the life of St. Augustine. The saint's work was essential to the early development of church doctrine. Benozzo's 17 scenes on the choir wall depict Augustine as a man who traveled and taught extensively in the 4th and 5th centuries. The 15th-century altarpiece by Piero del Pollaiolo (1443–96) depicts *The Coronation of the Virgin* and the various protectors of the city. ✉ *Piazza Sant'Agostino 10, San Gimignano* 🌐 *www.sangimignano.com* 🎟 *Free.*

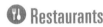

🍴 Restaurants

★ Cum Quibus

$$$ | ITALIAN | This is, without a doubt, one of the region's most creative restaurants—an intimate place with a menu that's Tuscan but not (it's rare to see bok choy incorporated into any dish, but here it's done with élan). Not a step is missed, and although it's possible to order à la carte, most opt for one of the tasting menus. **Known for:** amazing wine list with prices to suit all budgets; incorporation of non-Tuscan ingredients into Tuscan food; two marvelous tasting menus. [$] *Average main: €26* ✉ *Via San Martino 17, San Gimignano* ☎ *0577/943199* 🌐 *www.mktn.it/cumquibus* 🕒 *Closed Tues. and Jan. and Feb.*

Enoteca Gustavo

$ | WINE BAR | There's no shortage of places to try Vernaccia di San Gimignano, the justifiably famous white wine with which San Gimignano is often singularly associated. At this wine bar, run by energetic Maristella Becucci, you can buy a glass of Vernaccia di San Gimignano and sit down with a cheese plate or one of the fine crostini. **Known for:** quality products; fine list of wines by the glass; Maristella, who is a force of nature. [$] *Average main: €10* ✉ *Via San Matteo 29, San Gimignano* ☎ *0577/940057* 🕒 *Closed Tues.*

Osteria del Carcere

$$ | ITALIAN | Although it calls itself an *osteria* (tavern), this place much more resembles a wine bar, with a bill of fare that includes several different types of pâtés and a short list of seasonal soups and salads. The sampler of goat cheeses, which can be paired with local wines, should not be missed. **Known for:** housed in a former jail; inventive dishes; excellent chef-proprietor. [$] *Average main: €18* ✉ *Via del Castello 13, San Gimignano* ☎ *0577/941905* 🕒 *Closed Wed. and early Jan.–Mar. No lunch Thurs.*

🛏 Hotels

La Collegiata

$$$ | HOTEL | After serving as a Franciscan convent and then the residence of the noble Strozzi family, the Collegiata has been converted into a fine hotel, with no expense spared in the process. **Pros:** gorgeous views from terrace; wonderful staff; elegant rooms in main building. **Cons:** some rooms are dimly lit; service can be impersonal; long walk into town. [$] *Rooms from: €220* ✉ *Località Strada 27, San Gimignano* ✥ *1 km (½ mile) north of San Gimignano town center* ☎ *0577/943201* 🌐 *www.lacollegiata.it* 🕒 *Closed Nov.–Mar.* 🛏 *20 rooms* 🍽 *Free Breakfast.*

Pescille

$ | B&B/INN | A rambling farmhouse has been transformed into a handsome hotel with understated contemporary furniture in the bedrooms and country-classic motifs such as farm implements hanging on the walls in the bar. **Pros:** splendid views; 10-minute walk to town; quiet atmosphere. **Cons:** a vehicle is a must; there's an elevator for luggage but not for guests; furnishings a bit austere.

§ *Rooms from: €120 ⊠ Località Pescille, San Gimignano ⊕ 4 km (2½ miles) south of San Gimignano ☎ 0577/940186 ⊕ www.pescille.it ⊘ Closed mid-Oct.– Easter ↴ 38 rooms ⦿ Free Breakfast.*

Torraccia di Chiusi

$$ | B&B/INN | FAMILY | A perfect retreat for families, this tranquil hilltop agriturismo (farm stay) offers simple, comfortably decorated accommodations on extensive grounds 5 km (3 miles) from the hubbub of San Gimignano. **Pros:** great walking possibilities; delightful countryside view; family-run hospitality. **Cons:** might be too remote for some; need a car to get here; 30 minutes from the nearest town on a winding gravel road. § *Rooms from: €160 ⊠ Località Montauto, San Gimignano ☎ 0577/941972 ⊕ www.torracciadichiusi.it ↴ 11 rooms ⦿ Free Breakfast.*

Colle di Val d'Elsa

12 km (7 miles) west of Monteriggioni, 25 km (16 miles) northwest of Siena, 51 km (32 miles) south of Florence.

Most people pass through on their way to and from popular tourist destinations Volterra and San Gimignano—a shame, since Colle di Val d'Elsa has a lot to offer. It's another town on the Via Francigena that benefited from trade along the pilgrimage route to Rome. Colle got an extra boost in the late 16th century when it was given a bishopric, probably related to an increase in trade when nearby San Gimignano was cut off from the well-traveled road. The town is arranged on two levels, and from the 12th century onward the flat lower portion was given over to a flourishing papermaking industry; today the area is mostly modern, and efforts have shifted toward the production of fine glass and crystal.

GETTING HERE AND AROUND

You can reach Colle di Val d'Elsa by car on either the SR2 from Siena or the Florence–Siena superstrada. Bus service to and from Siena and Florence is frequent.

VISITOR INFORMATION

CONTACT Colle di Val d'Elsa Tourism Office. ⊠ *Piazza Arnolfo di Cambio 10,* ☎ *0577/292222 ⊕ www.terresiena.it.*

 Sights

Make your way from the newer lower town (Colle Bassa) to the prettier, upper part of town (Colle Alta). The best views of the valley are to be had from Viale della Rimembranza, the road that loops around the western end of town, past the church of San Francesco. The early-16th-century Porta Nuova was inserted into the preexisting medieval walls, just as several handsome Renaissance palazzi were placed into the medieval neighborhood to create what is now called the Borgo.

Chiesa di Santa Caterina

CHURCH | Visit this 15th-century church to view the excellent stained-glass window in the apse, executed by Sebastiano Mainardi (circa 1460–1513), as well as a haunting *Pietà* created by local artist Zacchia Zacchi (1473–1544). ⊠ *Via Campana 35, Colle di Val d'Elsa.*

Duomo

CHURCH | Several reconstructions have left little to admire of the once-Romanesque Duomo. Inside is the Cappella del Santo Chiodo (Chapel of the Holy Nail), built in the 15th century to hold a nail allegedly from the cross upon which Christ was crucified. (Perhaps it inspired the locals to go into the nail-making business, which became another of the town's flourishing industries.) ⊠ *Piazza del Duomo, Colle di Val d'Elsa.*

Museo San Pietro

ART MUSEUM | The museum of sacred art displays religious relics as well as triptychs from the Sienese and Florentine

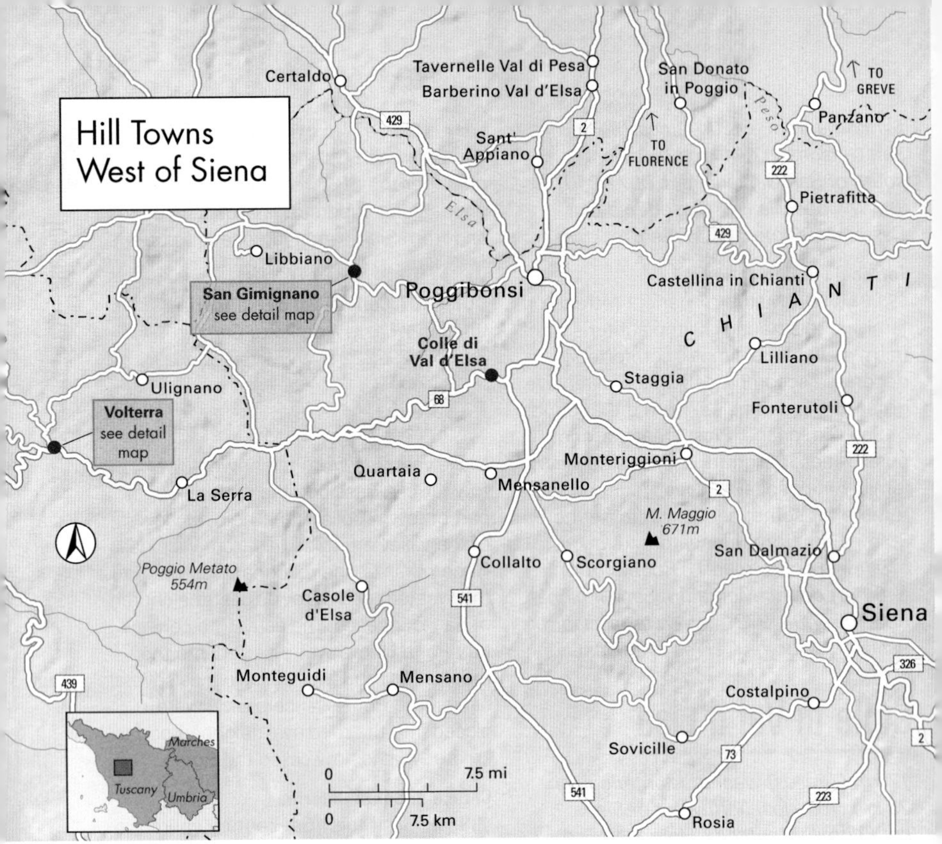
Hill Towns West of Siena
Certaldo
Tavernelle Val di Pesa
Barberino Val d'Elsa
San Donato in Poggio
TO GREVE
Panzano
Pesa
429
2
Sant' Appiano
TO FLORENCE
222
Pietrafitta
Elsa
429
Libbiano
San Gimignano
see detail map
Poggibonsi
Castellina in Chianti
CHIANTI
Colle di Val d'Elsa
Lilliano
Staggia
Ulignano
68
Fonterutoli
Volterra
see detail map
222
Monteriggioni
Quartaia
Mensanello
La Serra
2
M. Maggio 671m
San Dalmazio
Collalto
Scorgiano
Poggio Metato 554m
Casole d'Elsa
541
Siena
326
439
Monteguidi
Mensano
Costalpino
Marches
Tuscany
Umbria
Sovicille
73
2
0
7.5 mi
0
7.5 km
541
223
Rosia

schools dating from the 14th and 15th centuries. It also contains the town's tribute to Arnolfo di Cambio, with photos of the buildings he designed for other towns. Down Via del Castello, at Number 63, is the house-tower where Arnolfo was born in 1245. (It's not open to the public.) ✉ *Via Gracco del Secco 102, Colle di Val d'Elsa* ☎ *0577/286300* 🌐 *www.museisenesi.org* 🎟 *€9, includes the Museo Archeologico.*

Hotels

Palazzo San Lorenzo

$ | **B&B/INN** | A 17th-century palace in the historic center of Colle has rooms that exude warmth and comfort, with light-color wooden floors, soothingly tinted fabrics, and large windows. **Pros:** central location; extremely well maintained; indoor pool. **Cons:** a car is a necessity; some of the public spaces feel rather sterile; caters to business groups. [$] *Rooms from: €113* ✉ *Via Gracco del Secco 113, Colle di Val d'Elsa* ☎ *0577/923675* 🌐 *www.palazzosanlorenzo.it* 🛏 *48 rooms* 🍴 *Free Breakfast.*

Siena

With its narrow streets and steep alleys, a Gothic Duomo, a bounty of early Renaissance art, and the glorious Palazzo Pubblico overlooking its magnificent Campo, Siena is often described as Italy's best-preserved medieval city. It is also remarkably modern: many shops sell clothes by up-and-coming designers. Make a point of catching the *passeggiata* (evening stroll), when locals throng the Via di Città, Banchi di Sopra, and Banchi di Sotto, the city's three main streets.

Victory over Florence in 1260 at Montaperti marked the beginning of Siena's golden age. Even though Florentines avenged the loss 29 years later, Siena continued to prosper. During the following decades Siena erected its greatest buildings (including the Duomo); established a model city government presided over by the Council of Nine; and became a great art, textile, and trade center. All of these achievements came together in the decoration of the Sala della Pace in Palazzo Pubblico. It makes you wonder what greatness the city might have gone on to achieve had its fortunes been different, but in 1348 a plague decimated the population, brought an end to the Council of Nine, and left Siena economically vulnerable. Siena succumbed to Florentine rule in the mid-16th century, when a year-long siege virtually eliminated the native population. Ironically, it was precisely this decline that, along with Sienese pride, prevented further development, to which we owe the city's marvelous medieval condition today.

But although much looks as it did in the early 14th century, Siena is no museum. Walk through the streets and you can see that the medieval contrade—17 neighborhoods into which the city has been historically divided—are a vibrant part of modern life. You may see symbols of the *contrada* emblazoned on banners and engraved on building walls: Tartuca (turtle), Oca (goose), Istrice (porcupine), Torre (tower)—among others. The Sienese still strongly identify themselves with the contrada where they were born and raised; loyalty and rivalry run deep. At no time is this more visible than during the centuries-old Palio, a twice-yearly horse race held in the Piazza del Campo, but you need not visit then to come to know the rich culture of Siena, evident at every step.

GETTING HERE AND AROUND

From Florence, the quickest way to Siena is via the Florence–Siena superstrada. Otherwise, take the Via Cassia (SR2) for a scenic route. Coming from Rome, leave the A1 at Valdichiana, and follow the Siena–Bettole superstrada. SITA provides excellent bus service between Florence and Siena. Because buses are direct and speedy, they are preferable to the train, which sometimes involves a change in Empoli.

If you come by car, you're better off leaving it in one of the parking lots around the perimeter of town. Driving is difficult or impossible in most parts of the city center. Practically unchanged since medieval times, Siena is laid out in a "Y" over the slopes of several hills, dividing the city into *terzi* (thirds).

BUS CONTACT Tra-In. ☎ *0577/204111* ⊕ *www.trainspa.it.*

TIMING

It's a joy to walk in Siena—hills notwithstanding—as it's a rare opportunity to stroll through a medieval city rather than just a town. (There is quite a lot to explore, in contrast to tiny hill towns that can be crossed in minutes.) The walk can be done in as little as a day, with minimal stops at the sights. But stay longer and take time to tour the churches and museums, and to enjoy the streetscapes themselves. Many of the sites have reduced hours Sunday afternoon and Monday.

VISITOR INFORMATION

CONTACT Siena Tourism Office. ✉ *Piazza del Duomo 2* ☎ *0577/280551* ⊕ *www.terresiena.it.*

Sights

Battistero

RELIGIOUS BUILDING | The Duomo's 14th-century Gothic Baptistery was built to prop up the apse of the cathedral. There are frescoes throughout, but the highlight is a large bronze 15th-century baptismal font designed by Jacopo della Quercia. It's adorned with bas-reliefs by various artists, including two by Renaissance masters: the *Baptism of Christ* by Lorenzo Ghiberti (1378–1455) and the *Feast of Herod* by Donatello. ⊠ *Piazza San Giovanni, Città* ☎ *0577/286300* ⊕ *operaduomo.siena.it* ✉ *€13 combined ticket includes the Duomo, Cripta, and Museo dell'Opera.*

★ Cripta

CEMETERY | Routine excavation work revealed this crypt, which had been hidden for centuries under the grand *pavimento* (floor) of the Duomo and was opened to the public in 2003. In the late 13th century, an unknown master executed the crypt's breathtaking frescoes, which have sustained remarkably little damage and have retained their original colors. The *Deposition/Lamentation* proves that the Sienese school could paint emotion just as well as the Florentine school—and that it did so some 20 years before Giotto. ⊠ *Scale di San Giovanni, Città* ⚓ *Down steps to right side of cathedral* ☎ *0577/286300* ⊕ *operaduomo.siena.it* ✉ *€13 combined ticket includes the Duomo, Battistero, and Museo dell'Opera.*

★ Duomo

CHURCH | Siena's cathedral is one of the finest Gothic churches in Italy. The multi-color marbles and painted decoration are typical of the Italian approach to Gothic architecture—lighter and much less austere than the French. The amazingly detailed facade has few rivals. It was completed in two brief phases at the end of the 13th and 14th centuries. The statues and decorative work were designed by Nicola Pisano and his son Giovanni, although much of what's seen today are copies, the originals having been removed to the adjacent Museo dell'Opera Metropolitana. The gold mosaics are 18th-century restorations. The Campanile (no entry) is among central Italy's finest,

the number of windows increasing with each level, a beautiful and ingenious way of reducing the weight of the structure as it climbs to the heavens.

With its dark-green-and-white striping throughout and its illusionistic coffered and gilded dome, the Duomo's interior is simply striking. Look up at copies of Duccio's (circa 1255–1319) stained-glass panels; the originals, finished in 1288, are in the Museo dell'Opera and are the oldest examples of stained glass in Italy. The Duomo is most famous, though, for its inlaid-marble floors, which took almost 200 years to complete. More than 40 artists contributed to the magnificent work of 56 compositions depicting biblical scenes, allegories, religious symbols, and civic emblems. Although conserving the floors requires keeping them covered for much of the year, they are unveiled during September and October.

Also noteworthy is the Duomo's carousel pulpit, carved by Nicola Pisano around 1265; the Life of Christ is depicted on the rostrum frieze. In striking contrast to the nave's Gothic decoration are the well-preserved Renaissance frescoes in the Biblioteca Piccolomini, off the left aisle. Painted by Pinturicchio (circa 1454–1513) and completed in 1509, they depict events from the life of Aeneas Sylvius Piccolomini (1405–64), who became Pope Pius II in 1458.

The Duomo is grand, but the medieval Sienese people had even grander plans, namely, to use the existing church as a transept and build a new nave running toward the southeast, creating what would have been the world's largest church. Alas, only the side wall and part of the new facade were completed when the Black Death struck in 1348. The city subsequently fell into decline, funds dried up, and the plans were never carried out.

Indeed, the grand church project was actually doomed from the start—subsequent attempts to get it going revealed that the foundation was insufficient to bear the weight of the proposed structure. In any event, the unfinished new nave extending from the right side of the Duomo was ultimately enclosed to house the Museo dell'Opera. The Cripta was discovered during routine preservation work on the church. ⊠ *Piazza del Duomo, Città* ☎ *0577/286300* ⊕ *operaduomo.siena.it* ✉ *€13 combined ticket includes Cripta, Battistero, and Museo dell'Opera* ☞ *Last entrance is 30 mins before closing.*

★ Museo dell'Opera

ART MUSEUM | Part of the unfinished nave of what was to have been a new cathedral, the museum contains the Duomo's treasury and some of the original decoration from its facade and interior. The first room on the ground floor displays weather-beaten 13th-century sculptures by Giovanni Pisano (circa 1245–1318) that were brought inside for protection and replaced by copies, as was a tondo of the *Madonna and Child* (now attributed to Donatello) that once hung on the door to the south transept.

The masterpiece is unquestionably Duccio's *Maestà*, one side with 26 panels depicting episodes from the Passion, the other side with a *Madonna and Child Enthroned.* Painted between 1308 and 1311 as the altarpiece for the Duomo (where it remained until 1505), its realistic elements, such as the lively depiction of the Christ child and the treatment of interior space, proved an enormous influence on later painters. The work originally decorated the Duomo's high altar, before being displaced by Duccio's *Maestà.* There is a fine view from the tower inside the museum. ⊠ *Piazza del Duomo 8, Città* ☎ *0577/286300* ⊕ *operaduomo.siena.it* ✉ *€13 combined ticket includes the Duomo, Cripta, and Battistero.*

Palazzo Pubblico

GOVERNMENT BUILDING | The Gothic Palazzo Pubblico, the focal point of the Piazza del Campo, has served as Siena's town hall since the 1300s. It now also contains the Museo Civico, with walls covered in early Renaissance frescoes. The nine governors of Siena once met in the Sala della Pace, famous for Ambrogio Lorenzetti's frescoes called *Allegories of Good and Bad Government*, painted in the late 1330s to demonstrate the dangers of tyranny. The good government side depicts utopia, showing first the virtuous ruling council surrounded by angels and then scenes of a perfectly running city and countryside. Conversely, the bad government fresco tells a tale straight out of Dante. The evil ruler and his advisers have horns and fondle strange animals, and the town scene depicts the seven mortal sins in action.

The Torre del Mangia, the palazzo's famous bell tower, is named after one of its first bell ringers, Giovanni di Duccio (called Mangiaguadagni, or earnings eater). The climb up to the top is long and steep, but the view makes it worth every step. ⊠ *Piazza del Campo 1, Città* ☎ *0577/292232* ⊕ *www.comune.siena.it* ✉ *Museum €10, ticket sales end 30 mins before closing; tower €10, ticket sales end 45 mins before closing.*

★ Piazza del Campo

PLAZA/SQUARE | The fan-shape Piazza del Campo, known simply as Il Campo (The Field), is one of the finest squares in Italy. Constructed toward the end of the 12th century on a market area unclaimed by any contrada, it's still the heart of town. Its brickwork is patterned in nine different sections—representing each member of the medieval Council of Nine.

At the top of the Campo is a copy of the early 15th-century Fonte Gaia by Siena's greatest sculptor, Jacopo della Quercia. The 13 sculpted reliefs of biblical events and virtues that line the fountain are

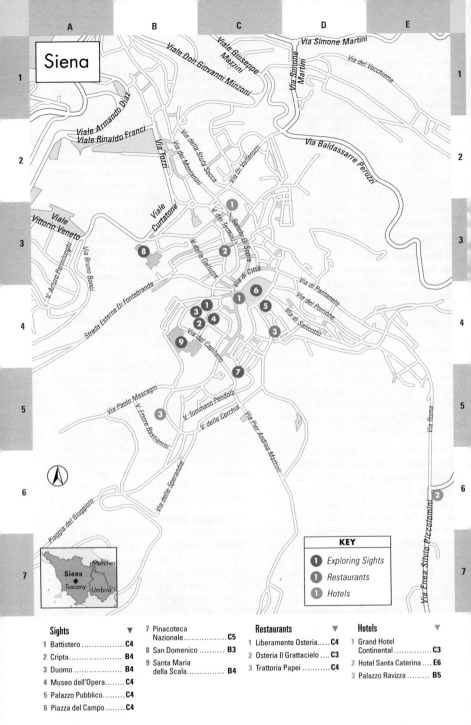

Siena

KEY

1 *Exploring Sights*

1 *Restaurants*

1 *Hotels*

19th-century copies; the originals are in the museum complex of Santa Maria della Scala. On Palio horse-race days (July 2 and August 16), the Campo and all its surrounding buildings are packed with cheering, frenzied locals and tourists craning their necks to take it all in. ⊠ *Piazza del Campo, Città.*

Pinacoteca Nazionale

ART MUSEUM | The superb collection of five centuries of local painting in Siena's national picture gallery can easily convince you that the Renaissance was by no means just a Florentine thing. Accordingly, the most interesting section of the collection, chronologically arranged, has several important firsts. Room 1 contains a painting of the *Stories of the True Cross* (1215) by the so-called Master of Tressa, the earliest identified work by a painter of the Sienese school, and is followed in Room 2 by late-13th-century artist Guido da Siena's *Stories from the Life of Christ,* one of the first paintings ever made on canvas (earlier painters used wood panels).

Rooms 3 and 4 are dedicated to Duccio, a student of Cimabue (circa 1240–1302) and considered to be the last of the proto-Renaissance painters. Ambrogio Lorenzetti's landscapes in Room 8 are among the first truly secular paintings in Western art. Among later works in the rooms on the floor above, keep an eye out for the preparatory sketches used by Domenico Beccafumi (1486–1551) for the 35 etched marble panels he made for the floor of the Duomo. ⊠ *Via San Pietro 29, Città* ☎ *0577/286143* ⊕ *pinacotecanazionale.siena.it* ⌛ *€8* ☉ *Closed Mon.*

San Domenico

CHURCH | Although the Duomo is celebrated as a triumph of 13th-century Gothic architecture, this church, built at about the same time, turned out to be an oversize, hulking brick box that never merited a finishing coat in marble, let alone a graceful facade. Named for the founder of the Dominican order, the church is now more closely associated with St. Catherine of Siena. Just to the right of the entrance is the chapel in which she received the stigmata. On the wall is the only known contemporary portrait of the saint, made in the late 14th century by Andrea Vanni (circa 1332–1414). Farther down is the famous Cappella delle Santa Testa, the church's official shrine.

On either side of the chapel are well-known frescoes by Sodoma (aka Giovanni Antonio Bazzi, 1477–1549) of *St. Catherine in Ecstasy.* Don't miss the view of the Duomo and town center from the apse-side terrace. ⊠ *Piazza San Domenico, Camollia* ☎ *0577/286848* ⊕ *www.basilicacateriniana.it.*

★ Santa Maria della Scala

ART MUSEUM | For more than 1,000 years, this complex across from the Duomo was home to Siena's hospital, but it now serves as a museum containing, among other things, Sienese Renaissance treasures. Restored 15th-century frescoes in the Sala del Pellegrinaio (once the emergency room) tell the history of the hospital, which was created to give refuge to passing pilgrims and others in need and to distribute charity to the poor. Incorporated into the complex is the church of the Santissima Annunziata, with a celebrated *Risen Christ* by Vecchietta (also known as Lorenzo di Pietro, circa 1412–80). Down in the dark, Cappella di Santa Caterina della Notte is where St. Catherine went to pray at night.

The displays—including the *bucchero* (dark, reddish clay) ceramics, Roman coins, and tomb furnishings—are clearly marked and can serve as a good introduction to the history of regional excavations. Be sure to visit the subterranean archaeological museum to see della Quercia's original sculpted reliefs from the Fonte Gaia. Although the fountain has been faithfully copied for the Campo, there's something incomparably beautiful about the real thing. ⊠ *Piazza del Duomo 2, Città* ☎ *0577/534511*

🌐 *www.santamariadellascala.com* 🎟 *€9* 🕑 *Closed Tues.*

🍴 Restaurants

Liberamente Osteria
$ | **ITALIAN** | Though the food here is rather good, the real reasons to come are the exquisitely crafted cocktails and the view, which just happens to be of Il Campo, arguably the prettiest square in all of Italy. Tasty little nibbles accompany the generously proportioned aperitivi. **Known for:** opens early (9 am) and closes late (2 am); facility with rum-based drinks; variations on the spritz. [$] *Average main: €7* ✉ *Il Campo 27, Siena* ☎ *0577/274733* 🌐 *www.liberamenteosteria.it.*

Osteria Il Grattacielo
$ | **TUSCAN** | If you're wiped out from too much sightseeing, consider a meal at this hole-in-the-wall restaurant where locals congregate for a simple lunch over a glass of wine. There's a collection of verdure sott'olio, a wide selection of affettati misti, and various types of frittatas—all of which can be washed down with the cheap, yet eminently drinkable, house red. **Known for:** usually filled with local men arguing about the Palio; earthy ambience; simple, good-value food. [$] *Average main: €10* ✉ *Via Pontani 8, Camollia* ☎ *331/742–2835* 🕑 *Closed Wed.*

Trattoria Papei
$ | **TUSCAN** | The menu hasn't changed for years, and why should it? This place, which has been in the Papei family for three generations, attracts both locals and visitors with basic but fine Sienese specialties and reasonable prices. **Known for:** outdoor seating; lively atmosphere; great place to sample local specialties. [$] *Average main: €13* ✉ *Piazza del Mercato 6, Città* ☎ *0577/280894* 🌐 *anticatrattoriapapei.com.*

🛏 Hotels

Grand Hotel Continental
$$$$ | **HOTEL** | Pope Alexander VII of the famed Sienese Chigi family gave this palace to his niece as a wedding present in 1600, and, through the centuries, it has been a private family home as well as a grand hotel—one that exudes elegance from its stately pillared entrance to its crisp-linen sheets. **Pros:** luxurious accommodations; first-rate concierge; great location on the main drag. **Cons:** breakfast costs extra; lots of noise if your room is street-side; sometimes stuffy atmosphere. [$] *Rooms from: €530* ✉ *Banchi di Sopra 85, Camollìa* ☎ *0577/56011* 🌐 *www.starhotelscollezione.com* 🔑 *51 rooms* 🍽 *No Meals.*

Hotel Santa Caterina
$$ | **B&B/INN** | Manager Lorenza Capannelli and her fine staff are welcoming, hospitable, enthusiastic, and go out of their way to ensure a fine stay; rooms in the back look out onto the garden or the countryside in the distance. **Pros:** friendly staff; breakfast in the garden; a short walk to center of town. **Cons:** 15-minute (easy) walk into the historic center; outside city walls; on a busy intersection. [$] *Rooms from: €134* ✉ *Via Piccolomini 7, San Martino* ☎ *0577/221105* 🌐 *www.hotelsantacaterinasiena.com* 🔑 *22 rooms* 🍽 *Free Breakfast.*

★ Palazzo Ravizza
$$ | **HOTEL** | This charming palazzo exudes a sense of an age gone by; its guest rooms have high ceilings, antique furnishings, and bathrooms decorated with hand-painted tiles. **Pros:** 10-minute walk to the center of town; professional staff and delightful restaurant; pleasant garden with a view beyond the city walls. **Cons:** somewhat removed from the center of things; some rooms are a little cramped; not all rooms have views. [$] *Rooms from: €129* ✉ *Pian dei Mantellini 34, Città* ☎ *0577/280462* 🌐 *www.palazzoravizza.it* 🔑 *41 rooms* 🍽 *Free Breakfast.*

Arezzo

63 km (39 miles) northeast of Siena, 81 km (50 miles) southeast of Florence.

Arezzo is best known for the magnificent Piero della Francesca frescoes in the church of San Francesco. It's also the birthplace of the poet Petrarch (1304–74), the Renaissance artist and art historian Giorgio Vasari, and Guido d'Arezzo (aka Guido Monaco), the inventor of contemporary musical notation. Arezzo dates from pre-Etruscan times, when around 1000 BC the first settlers erected a cluster of huts. Arezzo thrived as an Etruscan capital from the 7th to the 4th century BC, and was one of the most important cities in the Etruscans' anti-Roman 12-city federation, resisting Rome's rule to the last.

The city eventually fell and in turn flourished under the Romans. In 1248 Guglielmino degli Ubertini, a member of the powerful Ghibelline family, was elected bishop of Arezzo. This sent the city headlong into the enduring conflict between the Ghibellines (pro-emperor) and the Guelphs (pro-pope). In 1289 Florentine Guelphs defeated Arezzo in a famous battle at Campaldino. Among the Florentine soldiers was Dante Alighieri (1265–1321), who often referred to Arezzo in his *Divine Comedy*. Guelph–Ghibelline wars continued to plague Arezzo until the end of the 14th century, when Arezzo lost its independence to Florence.

GETTING HERE AND AROUND

Arezzo is easily reached by car from the A1, the main highway running between Florence and Rome. Direct trains connect Arezzo with Rome (2½ hours) and Florence (1 hour). Direct bus service is available from Florence, but not from Rome.

VISITOR INFORMATION

CONTACT Arezzo Tourism Office. ✉ *Piazza Libertà 1,* ☎ *0575/377678* ⊕ *www.arezzointuscany.it.*

Sights

★ Basilica di San Francesco

CHURCH | The famous Piero della Francesca frescoes depicting *The Legend of the True Cross* (1452–66) were executed on the three walls of the Capella Bacci, the apse of this 14th-century church. What Sir Kenneth Clark called "the most perfect morning light in all Renaissance painting" may be seen in the lowest section of the right wall, where the troops of Emperor Maxentius flee before the sign of the cross. Reservations are recommended June through September. ✉ *Piazza San Francesco 2, Arezzo* ☎ *0575/352727* ⊕ *www.pierodellafrancesca-ticketoffice.it* ☞ *€8.*

Duomo

CHURCH | Arezzo's medieval cathedral at the top of the hill contains a fresco of a tender *Maria Maddalena* by Piero della Francesca (1420–92); look for it in the north aisle next to the large marble tomb near the organ. Construction of the Duomo began in 1278 but twice came to a halt, and the church wasn't completed until 1510. The ceiling decorations and the stained-glass windows date from the 16th century. The facade, designed by Arezzo's Dante Viviani, was added later (1901–14). ✉ *Piazza del Duomo 1, Arezzo* ⊕ *www.diocesi.arezzo.it.*

Museo Archeologico

HISTORY MUSEUM | The Archaeological Museum in the Convento di San Bernardo, just outside the Anfiteatro Romano, exhibits a fine collection of Etruscan bronzes. The ticket allows admission to the Anfiteatro Romano. ✉ *Via Margaritone 10, Arezzo* ☎ *0575/20882* ⊕ *www.polomusealetoscana.beniculturali.it* ☞ *€6* ⊗ *Closed Wed. and Fri.–Sun.*

Piazza Grande

PLAZA/SQUARE | With its irregular shape and sloping brick pavement, framed by buildings of assorted centuries, Arezzo's central piazza echoes Siena's Piazza del Campo. Though not quite so magnificent,

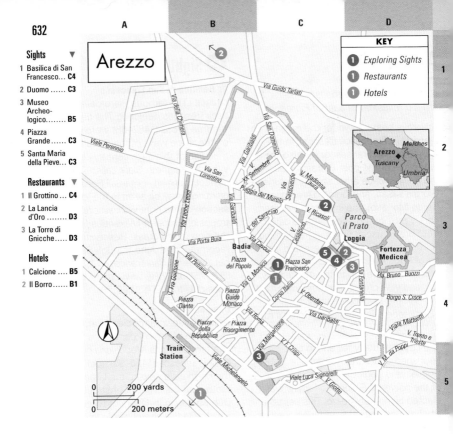

Sights ▼

1 Basilica di San Francesco... **C4**

2 Duomo **C3**

3 Museo Archeologico........ **B5**

4 Piazza Grande...... **C3**

5 Santa Maria della Pieve... **C3**

Restaurants ▼

1 Il Grottino ... **C4**

2 La Lancia d'Oro **D3**

3 La Torre di Gnicche..... **D3**

Hotels ▼

1 Calcione **B5**

2 Il Borro...... **B1**

KEY

🄸 Exploring Sights

🄸 Restaurants

🄸 Hotels

---

it's lively enough during the outdoor antiques fair the first weekend of the month and when the Giostra del Saracino (Saracen Joust), featuring medieval costumes and competition, is held here on the third Saturday of June and on the first Sunday of September. ✉ *Piazza Grande, Arezzo.*

Santa Maria della Pieve (*Church of Saint Mary of the Parish*)

CHURCH | The curving, tiered apse on Piazza Grande belongs to a church that was originally an early Christian structure—itself constructed over the remains of a Roman temple. The church was rebuilt in Romanesque style in the 12th century. The splendid facade dates from the early 13th century but includes granite Roman columns. A magnificent polyptych, depicting the Madonna and Child with four saints, by Pietro Lorenzetti (circa 1290–1348), embellishes the high altar. ✉ *Corso Italia 7, Arezzo.*

 **Restaurants**

Il Grottino

$ | **ITALIAN** | **FAMILY** | It's small, but the very cheery staff is only too happy to provide you with wonderful plates of typical Tuscan food. The kitchen stays open a little bit later than most, which makes this a perfect stop after seeing some of the amazing art that Arezzo has to offer. **Known for:** their soups (particularly the truffled potato/fungi); inventive desserts; surprisingly well-composed mixed salads. ⑤ *Average main: €14 ✉ Via della Madonna del Prato 1, Arezzo ☎ 0575/302537.*

La Lancia d'Oro

$$$ | **ITALIAN** | Fantastic food is to be had at this cheery, intimate trattoria with a view of Piazza Grande. An inventive menu has Tuscan classics; other dishes have unusual flavor combinations, and a superb wine list offers great pairings with all the food. **Known for:** desserts; stellar staff; fantastic pastas. $ *Average main: €26* ⊠ *Piazza Grande 18, Arezzo* ☎ *0575/21033* ⊕ *www. ristorantelanciadoro.it/en* ⊗ *Closed Mon. No dinner Sun.*

La Torre di Gnicche

$ | **ITALIAN** | Wine lovers shouldn't miss this wine bar/eatery, which is just off Piazza Grande and has more than 700 labels on its list. Seasonal traditional dishes, such as *acquacotta del casentino* (porcini mushroom soup) or *baccalà in umido* (salt-cod stew), are served in the simply decorated, vaulted dining room. **Known for:** outdoor seating in warm weather; an ever-changing menu; the extensive wine list, with many choices by the glass. $ *Average main: €9* ⊠ *Piaggia San Martino 8, Arezzo* ☎ *0575/352035* ⊕ *www.latorredignicche.it* ⊗ *Closed Wed. and Jan.*

 ## Hotels

★ Calcione

$ | **B&B/INN** | **FAMILY** | This six-century-old family estate (circa 1483) now houses sophisticated rustic lodgings; many of the apartments have open fireplaces, and the stone houses have a private pool (the rest share the estate pool). **Pros:** houses can sleep up to 17; quiet, beautiful, remote setting; private lakes for fishing and windsurfing. **Cons:** minimum two- to five-night stay in warmer months; no air-conditioning; private transportation is a must—nearest village is 8 km (5 miles) away. $ *Rooms from: €120* ⊠ *Località Il Calcione 102, Lucignano* ✛ *26 km (15 miles) southwest of Arezzo* ☎ *0575/837153* ⊕ *www.castellodelcalcione.com* ⤶ *30 rooms* ⦿| *No Meals.*

★ Il Borro

$$$$ | **HOTEL** | The location has been described as "heaven on earth," and a stay at this elegant Ferragamo estate—situated near a medieval village and with accommodations that include a 10-bedroom villa (rented out as a single unit) that was once a luxurious hunting lodge—is sure to bring similar descriptions to mind. **Pros:** exceptional service; unique setting and atmosphere; great location for exploring eastern Tuscany. **Cons:** very expensive; not all suites have country views; off the beaten track, making private transport a must. $ *Rooms from: €495* ⊠ *Località Il Borro 1* ✛ *Outside village of San Giustino Valdarno, 20 km (12 miles) northwest of Arezzo* ☎ *055/977053* ⊕ *www.ilborro.it* ⊗ *Closed Dec.–Mar.* ⤶ *61 rooms* ⦿| *Free Breakfast.*

🛍 Shopping

Ever since Etruscan goldsmiths set up their shops here more than 2,000 years ago, Arezzo has been famous for its jewelry. Today the town lays claim to being one of the world's capitals of jewelry design and manufacture, and you can find an impressive display of big-time baubles in the town center's shops.

Arezzo is also famous, at least in Italy, for its antiques dealers. The first weekend of every month, between 8:30 and 5:30, a popular and colorful flea market selling antiques and not-so-antique items takes place in the town's main square, **Piazza Grande,** and in the streets and parks nearby.

Cortona

29 km (18 miles) south of Arezzo, 79 km (44 miles) east of Siena, 117 km (73 miles) southeast of Florence.

Brought into the limelight by Frances Mayes's book *Under the Tuscan Sun* and a subsequent movie, Cortona is no longer the destination of just a few specialist art historians and those seeking

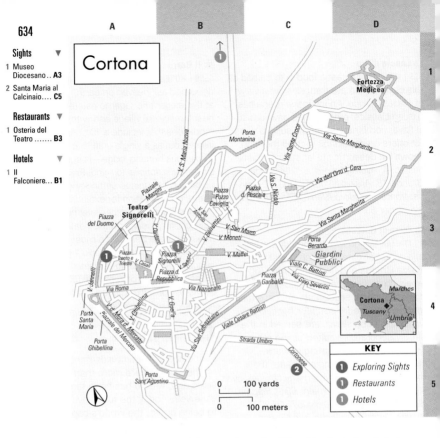

reprieve from busier tourist venues. The main street, Via Nazionale, is now lined with souvenir shops and fills with crowds during summer. Although the main sights of Cortona make braving the bustling center worthwhile, much of the town's charm lies in its maze of quiet backstreets. It's here that you will see laundry hanging from windows, find children playing, and catch the smell of simmering pasta sauce. Wander off the beaten track and you won't be disappointed.

GETTING HERE AND AROUND

Cortona is easily reached by car from the A1 autostrada: take the Valdichiana exit toward Perugia, then follow signs for Cortona. Regular bus service, provided by Etruria Mobilità, is available between Arezzo and Cortona (one hour). Train service to Cortona is made inconvenient by the location of the train station, in the valley 3 km (2 miles) steeply below the town itself. From there, you have to rely on bus or taxi service to get up to Cortona.

VISITOR INFORMATION

CONTACT Cortona Tourism Office. ✉ *Piazza Signorelli 9, Cortona* ☎ *0575/637223* ⊕ *www.comunedicortona.it.*

◉ Sights

Museo Diocesano

ART MUSEUM | Housed in part of the original cathedral structure, this nine-room museum has an impressive number of large, splendid paintings by native son Luca Signorelli (1445–1523), as well as a delightful *Annunciation* by Fra Angelico (1387/1400–55). The church was built between 1498 and 1505 and restructured by Giorgio Vasari in 1543. Frescoes depicting sacrifices from the Old Testament by Doceno (1508–56), based on designs by Vasari, line the walls. ✉ *Piazza Duomo 1, Cortona* ☎ *0575/62830* 🌐 *www.cortonamia.com* 🎫 *€6* 🕒 *Closed Mon.*

Santa Maria al Calcinaio

CHURCH | Legend has it that the image of the Madonna appeared on a wall of a medieval *calcinaio* (lime pit used for curing leather), the site on which the church was then built between 1485 and 1513. The linear gray-and-white interior recalls Florence's Duomo. Sienese architect Francesco di Giorgio (1439–1502) most likely designed the sanctuary: the church is a terrific example of Renaissance architectural principles. ✉ *Località Il Calcinaio 227, Cortona* ✣ *3 km (2 miles) southeast of Cortona's center.*

🍴 Restaurants

Osteria del Teatro

$$ | **TUSCAN** | Photographs from theatrical productions spanning many years line the walls of this tavern off Cortona's large Piazza del Teatro. The food is simply delicious—try the *filetto al lardo di colonnata e prugne* (beef cooked with bacon and prunes); service is warm and friendly. **Known for:** pretty dining room; lively atmosphere; food that's in season. [$] *Average main: €20* ✉ *Via Maffei 2, Cortona* ☎ *0575/630556* 🌐 *www.osteria-del-teatro.it* 🕒 *Closed Wed. and 2 wks in Nov.*

🛏 Hotels

★ **Il Falconiere**

$$$$ | **B&B/INN** | Accommodation options at this sumptuous property include rooms in an 18th-century villa, suites in the *chiesetta* (chapel, or little church), or for more seclusion, Le Vigne del Falco suites at the far end of the property. **Pros:** elegant, but relaxed; excellent service; attractive setting in the valley beneath Cortona. **Cons:** a car is a must; some find rooms in main villa a little noisy; might be too isolated for some. [$] *Rooms from: €500* ✉ *Località San Martino 370, Cortona* ✣ *3 km (2 miles) north of Cortona* ☎ *0575/612679* 🌐 *www.ilfalconiere.it* 🕒 *Closed Nov.–Jan.* 🛏 *33 rooms* 🍽 *Free Breakfast.*

Montepulciano

610 km (6 miles) northeast of Chianciano Terme, 65 km (40 miles) southeast of Siena, 114 km (70 miles) southeast of Florence.

Perched on a hilltop, Montepulciano is made up of a pyramid of redbrick buildings set within a circle of cypress trees. At an altitude of almost 2,000 feet, it is cool in summer and chilled in winter by biting winds sweeping down its spiraling streets. The town has an unusually harmonious look, the result of the work of three architects: Antonio da Sangallo "il Vecchio" (circa 1455–1534), Vignola (1507–73), and Michelozzo (1396–1472). The group endowed it with fine palaces and churches in an attempt to impose Renaissance architectural ideals on an ancient Tuscan hill town.

GETTING HERE AND AROUND

From Rome or Florence, take the Chiusi–Chianciano exit from the A1 (Autostrada del Sole). From Siena, take the SR2 south to San Quirico and then the SP146 to Montepulciano. Tra-In offers bus service from Siena to Montepulciano several times a day. Montepulciano's train station is in Montepulciano Stazione, 10 km (6 miles) away.

VISITOR INFORMATION

CONTACT Montepulciano Tourism Office. ✉ *Piazza Don Minzoni 1, Montepulciano* ☎ *0578/757341* 🌐 *www.prolocomontepulciano.it.*

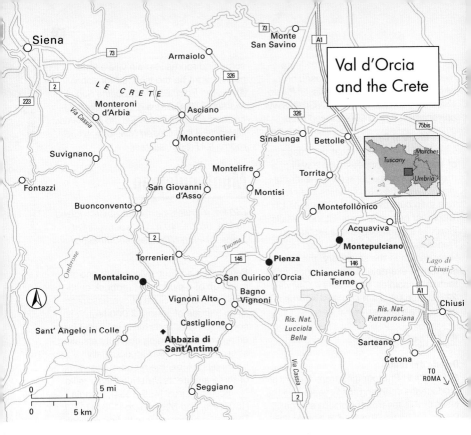

Val d'Orcia and the Crete

Sights

Duomo

CHURCH | The unfinished facade of Montepulciano's cathedral doesn't measure up to the beauty of its neighboring palaces. On the inside, however, its Renaissance roots shine through. The high altar has a splendid triptych painted in 1401 by Taddeo di Bartolo (circa 1362–1422), and you can see fragments of the tomb of Bartolomeo Aragazzi, secretary to Pope Martin V, that was sculpted by Michelozzo between 1427 and 1436. ⊠ *Piazza Grande, Montepulciano.*

Piazza Grande

PLAZA/SQUARE | Filled with handsome buildings, this large square on the heights of the old historic town is Montepulciano's pièce de résistance. ⊠ *Piazza Grande, Montepulciano.*

★ San Biagio

CHURCH | Designed by Antonio da Sangallo il Vecchio, and considered his masterpiece, this church sits on the hillside below the town walls and is a model of High Renaissance architectural perfection. Inside is a painting of the Madonna that, according to legend, was the only thing remaining in an abandoned church that two young girls entered on April 23, 1518. The girls saw the eyes of the Madonna moving, and that same afternoon so did a farmer and a cow, who knelt down in front of the painting. In 1963, the image was proclaimed the Madonna del Buon Viaggio (Madonna of the Good Journey), the protector of tourists in Italy. ⊠ *Via di San Biagio, Montepulciano* ☎ *0578/286300* ⊕ *www. tempiosanbiagio.it* 🎫 *€4.*

Restaurants

★ La Grotta

$$ | TUSCAN | You might be tempted to pass right by the innocuous entrance across the street from San Biagio, but you'd miss some fantastic food. This tasty menu relies heavily on local classics turned out to perfection. **Known for:** stellar service; local wine list; creative menu. $ *Average main: €22* ✉ *Via di San Biagio 15, Montepulciano* ☎ *0578/757479* ⊕ *www.lagrottamontepulciano.it* ⊘ *Closed Wed. and Jan. 15–Mar. 15.*

★ Osteria del Conte

$ | ITALIAN | As high in Montepulciano as you can get, just behind the Duomo, this small and intimate restaurant is expertly run by the mother-and-son team of Lorena and Paolo Brachi. Passionate about the food they prepare, both have a flair for the region's traditional dishes—the pici *all'aglione* (with garlic sauce) and the *filetto ai funghi porcini* (steak with porcini mushrooms) are mouthwateringly good. **Known for:** attentive service; good local wines; fine home cooking. $ *Average main: €13* ✉ *Via di San Donato 19, Montepulciano* ☎ *0578/756062* ⊕ *www.osteriadelconte.it* ⊘ *Closed Mon. No dinner Sun.*

🛏 Hotels

La Terrazza

$ | B&B/INN | FAMILY | On a quiet street in the upper part of town, these unpretentious lodgings are given sparkle by the welcoming and friendly service of the owners, Roberto and Vittoria Giardinelli. **Pros:** friendly family atmosphere; great value for money; quiet central location. **Cons:** books up quickly; no night porter; no air-conditioning. $ *Rooms from: €95* ✉ *Via del Piè al Sasso 16, Montepulciano* ☎ *0578/757440* ⊕ *www.laterrazzadimontepulciano.it* ⊅ *14 rooms* ⊚ *Free Breakfast.*

★ Podere Dionora

$$$ | B&B/INN | At this secluded and serene country inn, earth-tone fabrics complement antiques in the individually decorated rooms, all of which have functioning fireplaces. **Pros:** great views; bathrooms have a sauna and a whirlpool tub; attentive service. **Cons:** books up quickly; need a car to get around; long walk to the nearest town. $ *Rooms from: €280* ✉ *Via Vicinale di Poggiano 9, Montepulciano* ✚ *3 km (2 miles) east of Montepulciano town center* ☎ *0578/717496* ⊕ *www.dionora.it* ⊘ *Closed mid-Dec.–mid-Mar.* ⊅ *6 rooms* ⊚ *Free Breakfast.*

Pienza

12 km (7 miles) west of Montepulciano, 52 km (31 miles) southeast of Siena, 120 km (72 miles) southeast of Florence.

Pienza owes its appearance to Pope Pius II (1405–64), who had grand plans to transform his hometown of Corsignano—its former name—into a compact model Renaissance town. The man entrusted with the transformation was Bernardo Rossellino (1409–64), a protégé of the great Renaissance architectural theorist Leon Battista Alberti (1404–72). His mandate was to create a cathedral, a papal palace, and a town hall that adhered to the vainglorious pope's principles. Gothic and Renaissance styles were fused, and the buildings were decorated with Sienese paintings. The net result was a project that expressed Renaissance ideals of art, architecture, and civilized good living in a single scheme: it stands as an exquisite example of the architectural canons that Alberti formulated in the early Renaissance and that were utilized by later architects, including Michelangelo, in designing many of Italy's finest buildings and piazzas. Today the cool nobility of Pienza's center seems almost surreal in this otherwise unpretentious village, renowned for its smooth sheep's-milk pecorino cheese.

From Siena, drive south along the SR2 to San Quirico d'Orcia and then take the SP146. The trip should take just over an hour. Tra-In shuttles passengers between Siena and Pienza. There is no train service to Pienza.

VISITOR INFORMATION

CONTACT Pienza Tourism Office. ✉ Piazza Dante 18, ☎ 0578/748359 ⊕ www.pienza.info.

Sights

Duomo

CHURCH | This 15th-century cathedral was built by the architect Bernardo Rossellino (1409–64) under the influence of Leon Battista Alberti. The travertine facade is divided into three parts, with Renaissance arches under the pope's coat of arms encircled by a wreath of fruit. Inside, the cathedral is simple but richly decorated with Sienese paintings. The building's perfection didn't last long—the first cracks appeared immediately after it was completed, and its foundations have shifted slightly ever since as rain erodes the hillside behind. You can see this effect if you look closely at the base of the first pier as you enter the church and compare it with the last. ✉ Piazza Pio II, Pienza ☎ 0578/749071 ⊕ www.pienza.org.

Museo Diocesano

ART MUSEUM | This museum, which sits to the left of Pienza's Duomo, is small but has a few interesting papal treasures and rich Flemish tapestries. The most precious piece is a rare mantle that belonged to Pope Pius II: it's woven in gold and embellished with pearls and embroidered religious scenes. ✉ Corso Il Rossellino 30, Pienza ☎ 0578/749905 ⊕ www.palazzoborgia.it 🎟 From €5 ⊙ Closed Tues.

Palazzo Piccolomini

CASTLE/PALACE | In 1459, Pius II commissioned Bernardo Rossellino to design the perfect palazzo for his papal court. The architect took Florence's Palazzo Rucellai by Alberti as a model and designed this 100-room palace. Three sides of the building fit perfectly into the urban plan around it, while the fourth, looking over the valley, has a lovely loggia uniting it with the gardens in back. Guided tours departing every 30 minutes take you to the papal apartments, including a beautiful library, the Sala delle Armi (with an impressive weapons collection), and the music room, with its extravagant wooden ceiling forming four letter Ps, for Pope, Pius, Piccolomini, and Pienza. The last tour departs 30 minutes before closing. ✉ Piazza Pio II, Pienza ☎ 0577/286300 ⊕ www.palazzopiccolominipienza.it 🎟 €7 ⊙ Closed Tues. and early Jan.–mid-Feb. and mid-Nov.–late Nov.

🍴 Restaurants

★ Osteria Sette di Vino

$ | **TUSCAN** | Tasty dishes based on the region's cheeses are the specialty at this simple and inexpensive osteria on a quiet, pleasant, central square. Try versions of pici or the starter of radicchio baked quickly to brown the edges. **Known for:** awesome vegetable options; bean soup; pecorino tasting menu. 🅢 Average main: €7 ✉ Piazza di Spagna 1, Pienza ☎ 0578/749092 ⊙ Closed Wed., July 1–15, and Nov.

Montalcino

19 km (12 miles) northeast of Bagno Vignoni, 41 km (25½ miles) south of Siena, 109 km (68 miles) south of Florence.

Tiny Montalcino, with its commanding view from high on a hill, can claim an Etruscan past. It saw a fair number of travelers, as it was directly on the road from Siena to Rome. During the early

Climb to the top of La Fortezza for the views and then slake your thirst in the on-site enoteca.

Middle Ages it enjoyed a brief period of autonomy before falling under the orbit of Siena in 1201. Now Montalcino's greatest claim to fame is that it produces Brunello di Montalcino, one of Italy's most esteemed reds. Driving to the town, you pass through the brunello vineyards. You can sample the excellent but expensive red in wine cellars in town or visit a nearby winery, such as Fattoria dei Barbi, for a guided tour and tasting; you must call ahead for reservations.

GETTING HERE AND AROUND

By car, follow the SR2 south from Siena, then follow the SP45 to Montalcino. Several Tra-In buses travel between Siena and Montalcino daily, making a tightly scheduled day trip possible. There is no train service available.

VISITOR INFORMATION

CONTACT Montalcino Tourism Office.
✉ *Costa del Municipio 1, Montalcino* ☎ *0577/849331* ⊕ *www.prolocomontalcino.com.*

Sights

★ La Fortezza

CASTLE/PALACE | FAMILY | Providing refuge for the last remnants of the Sienese army during the Florentine conquest of 1555, the battlements of this 14th-century fortress are still in excellent condition. Climb the narrow, spiral steps for the 360-degree view of most of southern Tuscany. An on-site enoteca serves delicious snacks that pair beautifully with the local wines. ✉ *Piazzale Fortezza, Montalcino* ☎ *0577/849221* 🎫 *Fortress free, walls €4* 🕙 *Closed Mon. Nov.–Mar.*

Museo Civico e Diocesano d'Arte Sacra

ART MUSEUM | This fine museum is in a building that once belonged to 13th-century Augustinian friars. The ticket booth is in the glorious refurbished cloister, and the sacred art collection, gathered from churches throughout the region, is displayed on two floors in former monastic quarters. Although the art here might be called B-list, a fine altarpiece by Bartolo di Fredi (circa 1330–1410), the *Coronation* *of the Virgin,* makes dazzling use of gold. In addition, there's a striking 12th-century crucifix that originally adorned the high altar of the church of Sant'Antimo. Also on hand are many wood sculptures, a typical medium in these parts during the Renaissance. ✉ *Via Ricasoli 31, Montalcino* ☎ *0577/846014* 🌐 *www.museisenesi.org* 🎫 *€10* 🕓 *Closed Mon.–Thurs. Nov. 2–Dec. 24 and Jan. 7–Mar. 31.*

🍴 Restaurants

Il Grappolo Blu

$$ | **ITALIAN** | Any one of this restaurant's *piatti tipici* (typical plates) is worth trying, though the local specialty, pici all'aglione (thick, long noodles served with sautéed cherry tomatoes and many cloves of garlic), is done particularly well. The chef also has a deft touch with vegetables; if there's fennel on the menu, make sure to order it. **Known for:** convivial atmosphere; kind, caring staff; great quality and price. [$] *Average main: €15* ✉ *Scale di Via Moglio 1, Montalcino* ☎ *0577/847150* 🌐 *www.grappoloblu.it* 🕓 *Closed Wed.*

Taverna dei Barbi

$ | **TUSCAN** | This rustic taverna with a large stone fireplace is amid vineyards that produce excellent Brunello—as well as its younger cousin, Rosso di Montalcino—a few minutes south of Montalcino, in the direction of Sant'Antimo. The estate farm produces many of the ingredients used in the various soups and other traditional specialties. **Known for:** the superb staff; fantastic wines; heavenly aromas coming from grilled meat on a spit. [$] *Average main: €12* ✉ *Podere Podernuovo 170, Montalcino* ☎ *0577/84111* 🌐 *www.fattoriadeibarbi.it* 🕓 *Closed Wed. and Dec.–Feb.*

🛏 Hotels

★ Castiglion del Bosco

$$$$ | **RESORT** | This estate, one of the largest still in private hands in Tuscany, was purchased at the beginning of this century and meticulously converted into a second-to-none resort that incorporates a medieval *borgo* (village) and surrounding farmhouses and has luxurious suites, as well as opulent three- to five-bedroom villas, each with its own pool. **Pros:** exclusive and tranquil location; acclaimed golf course; breathtaking scenery. **Cons:** truly exorbitant prices; private transportation required; well off the beaten track, the nearest town is 12 km (7½ miles) away. [$] *Rooms from: €1852* ✉ *Località Castiglion del Bosco, Montalcino* ☎ *0577/191–3111* 🌐 *www.castigliondelbosco.com* 🛏 *53 units* 🍴 *Free Breakfast.*

Abbazia di Sant'Antimo

10 km (6 miles) south of Montalcino, 51 km (32 miles) south of Siena, 19 km (74 miles) south of Florence.

It's well worth your while to go out of your way to visit this 12th-century Romanesque abbey, as it's a gem of pale stone in the silvery green of an olive grove.

GETTING HERE AND AROUND

The Abbazia di Sant'Antimo, nestled below the town of Castelnuovo dell'Abate, is a 15-minute drive from Montalcino. Tra-In bus service is extremely limited, and the abbey cannot be reached by train.

👁 Sights

★ Abbazia di Sant'Antimo

CHURCH | The exterior and interior sculpture of this Romanesque abbey, dating from the 12th-century, is outstanding, particularly the nave capitals, a combination of French, Lombard, and even Spanish influences. The sacristy (seldom open) forms part of the primitive Carolingian church (founded in AD 781), its entrance flanked by 9th-century pilasters. The small vaulted crypt dates from the same period. ✉ *Castelnuovo dell'Abate* ☎ *0577/286300* 🌐 *www.antimo.it.*

Chapter 14

UMBRIA AND THE MARCHES

Updated by
Liz Humphreys

👁 **Sights**
★★★★☆

🍴 **Restaurants**
★★★★☆

🛏 **Hotels**
★★★★☆

🛍 **Shopping**
★★☆☆☆

🍸 **Nightlife**
★★☆☆☆

WELCOME TO UMBRIA AND THE MARCHES

TOP REASONS TO GO

★ **Palazzo Ducale, Urbino:** A visit here reveals more about the ideals of the Renaissance than a shelf of history books could.

★ **Assisi, shrine to St. Francis:** Recharge your soul in this rose-color hill town with a visit to the gentle saint's majestic basilica, adorned with great frescoes.

★ **Spoleto, Umbria's musical mecca:** Crowds descend and prices ascend here during summer's Festival dei Due Mondi, but Spoleto's hushed charm enchants year-round.

★ **Tantalizing truffles:** Are Umbria's celebrated "black diamonds" coveted for their pungent flavor, their rarity, or their power in the realm of romance?

★ **Orvieto's Duomo:** Arresting visions of heaven and hell on the facade and brilliant frescoes within make this Gothic cathedral a dazzler.

1 Perugia. Umbria's largest town, filled with university students.

2 Assisi. The fascinating city of St. Francis.

3 Gubbio. A medieval mountainous town in north Umbria.

4 Deruta. A 14th-century town famous for its ceramics.

5 Spello. A pretty hilltop town known for its cuisine.

6 Montefalco. A wine town nicknamed "balcony over Umbria."

7 Spoleto. Come to see the Piazza del Duomo.

8 The Valnerina. Valley of the River Nera.

9 Todi. Considered Umbria's prettiest hill town.

10 Orvieto. Carved out of volcanic rock and known for its cathedral.

11 Urbino. See the Palazzo Ducale here.

12 Loreto. Home to the House of the Virgin Mary.

13 Ascoli Piceno. A major producer of fruit and olives in the region.

EATING AND DRINKING WELL IN UMBRIA AND THE MARCHES

Central Italy is mountainous, and its food is hearty and straightforward, with a stick-to-the-ribs quality that sees hardworking farmers and artisans through a long day's work and helps them make the steep climb home at night.

In restaurants here, as in much of Italy, you're rewarded for seeking out the local cuisines, and you'll often find better and cheaper food if you're willing to stray a few hundred yards from the main sights. Spoleto is noted for its good food and service, probably a result of high expectations from the international arts crowd. For gourmet food, however, it's hard to beat Montefalco and Bevagna, which have both excellent restaurants and first-rate wine merchants.

A rule of thumb for eating well throughout Umbria is to order what's in season; stroll through local markets to see what's for sale. Also, a number of restaurants in the region offer *degustazione* (tasting) menus that give you a chance to try different local specialties without breaking the bank.

TASTY TRUFFLES

More truffles are found in Umbria than anywhere else in Italy. Spoleto and Norcia are prime territory for the *tartufo nero* (reddish-black interior and fine white veins), prized for its extravagant flavor and intense aroma.

The mild summer truffle, *scorzone estivo* (black outside and beige inside), is in season from May through December. The *scorzone autunnale* (burnt brown color and visible veins inside) is found from October through December.

OLIVE OIL

Nearly everywhere you look in Umbria, olive trees grace the hillsides. The soil of the Apennines allows the olives to ripen slowly, guaranteeing low acidity, a cardinal virtue of fine oil. Look for restaurants that proudly display their own oil, often a sign that they care about their food.

Umbria's finest oil is found in Trevi, where the local product is intensely green and fruity. You can sample it in the town's wine bars, which often offer olive-oil tastings.

PORK PRODUCTS

Much of traditional Umbrian cuisine revolves around pork. It can be cooked in wood-fired stoves, sometimes basted with a rich sauce made from innards and red wine. The roasted pork known as *porchetta* is grilled on a spit and flavored with fennel and herbs, leaving a crisp outer sheen.

In Norcia, the art of pork processing has been handed down through generations, so much so that charcuterie producers throughout Italy are often known as *norcini*. Don't miss *prosciutto di Norcia*, which is aged for two years.

LENTILS AND SOUPS

Throughout Umbria, look for *imbrecciata*, a soup of beans and grains, delicately flavored with local herbs.

The town of Castelluccio di Norcia is particularly known for its lentils and its farro (a grain used by the Romans, similar to wheat), as well as for the variety of beans used in its soups. Other ingredients that find their way into thick Umbrian soups are wild beet; sorrel; mushrooms; spelt; chickpeas; and the elusive, fragrant saffron, grown in nearby Cascia.

WINE

Sagrantino grapes are the star in Umbria's most notable red wines. For centuries they've been used in Sagrantino *passito*, a semisweet wine made by leaving the grapes to dry for a period after picking to intensify their sugar content. In recent decades, Montefalco Sagrantino *secco* (dry) has occupied the front stage. Both passito and secco have a deep, red-ruby color, with a full body and rich flavor.

The abundance of *enotecas* (wineshops and wine bars) has made it easier to arrange tastings. Many establishments also let you sample different olive oils on toasted bread, known as bruschetta. Some wine information centers, such as La Strada del Sagrantino in the town of Montefalco, will help set up appointments for tastings.

Birthplace of saints and home to some of the country's greatest artistic treasures, central Italy is a collection of misty green valleys and picture-perfect hill towns laden with centuries of history.

Umbria and the Marches are the Italian countryside as you've imagined it: verdant farmland, steep hillsides topped with medieval fortresses, and winding country roads. Orvieto's cathedral and Assisi's basilica are two of the most important sights in Italy, while Perugia, Todi, Gubbio, and Spoleto are rich in art and architecture.

East of Umbria, the Marches (Le Marche to Italians) stretch between the Apennines and the Adriatic Sea. It's a region of great turreted castles on high peaks defending passes and roads—a testament to the centuries of battle that have taken place here. Rising majestically in Urbino is a splendid palace, while the town of Ascoli Piceno can lay claim to one of the most beautiful squares in Italy.

MAJOR REGIONS

Umbria's largest town, **Perugia,** is home to some of Perugino's great frescoes. **Assisi,** the city of St. Francis, is a major pilgrimage site that retains its medieval hill-town character. The quiet towns lying around Perugia include **Deruta,** which produces exceptional ceramics. A massive castle towers over **Spoleto,** which is home to the Piazza del Duomo and Filippo Lippi frescoes in its cathedral.

Of central Italy's many hill towns, none has a more impressive setting than **Orvieto,** perched on a plateau 1,000 feet above the surrounding valley. East of Umbria, the steep, twisting roads of this region lead to well-preserved medieval

towns before settling down to the sandy beaches of the Adriatic.

Planning

Getting Here and Around

BUS
Perugia's bus station is in Piazza Partigiani, which you can reach by taking the escalators from the town center.

Local bus services between all the major and minor towns of Umbria are good. Some of the routes in rural areas are designed to serve as many places as possible and are, therefore, quite roundabout and slow. Schedules change often, so consult with local tourist offices before setting out.

BUS CONTACTS Flixbus. ⊕ *www.flixbus. com.* **Sulga.** ☎ *075/5009641* ⊕ *www. sulga.it.*

CAR
The steep hills and deep valleys that make Umbria and the Marches so idyllic also make for challenging driving. Fortunately, the area has an excellent, modern road network, but be prepared for tortuous roads if your explorations take you off the beaten track.

On the western edge of the region is the Umbrian section of the Autostrada del Sole (A1), Italy's principal north–south highway. It links Florence and Rome with

Orvieto and passes near Todi and Terni. The S3 intersects with the A1 and leads on to Assisi and Urbino. The Adriatica superhighway (A14) runs north–south along the coast, linking the Marches to Bologna and Venice.

Central Umbria is served by a major highway, the RA6, which passes along the shore of Lake Trasimeno and ends in Perugia. Assisi is served by the modern highway S75; the S75 connects to the S3 and S3bis, which cover the heart of the region. Major inland routes connect coastal A14 to large towns in the Marches, but inland secondary roads in mountain areas can be winding and narrow.

TRAIN

Several direct daily trains run by the Italian state railway, Trenitalia, link Florence and Rome with Perugia and Assisi, and local service to the same area is available from Terontola (on the Rome–Florence line) and from Foligno (on the Rome–Ancona line).

Intercity trains between Rome and Florence make stops in Orvieto. The main Rome–Ancona line passes through Narni, Terni, Spoleto, and Foligno.

Making the Most of Your Time

Umbria is a nicely compact collection of character-rich hill towns; you can settle in one, then explore the others, as well as the countryside and forest in between, on day trips.

Perugia, Umbria's largest and liveliest city, is a logical choice for your base, particularly if you're arriving from the north. If you want something a little quieter, virtually any other town in the region will suit your purposes; even Assisi, which overflows with bus tours during the day, is delightfully quiet in the evening and early morning. Spoleto and Orvieto are the most developed towns to the south,

but they're still of modest proportions. Charming Montefalco is a required stop for wine lovers.

If you have the time to venture farther afield, consider trips to Gubbio, northeast of Perugia, and Urbino, in the Marches. Both are worth the time it takes to reach them, and both make for pleasant overnight stays. In southern Umbria, Valnerina and the Piano Grande are out-of-the-way spots with the region's best hiking.

Festivals

If you want to attend an event, make arrangements in advance. During festival time, hotel rooms and restaurant tables are at a premium. A similar caveat applies for Assisi during religious festivals at Christmas, Easter, the feast of St. Francis (October 4), and Calendimaggio (May 1), when pilgrims arrive en masse.

★ Eurochocolate Festival

FESTIVALS | FAMILY | If you've got a sweet tooth and are visiting in fall, book early and head to Perugia for Europe's largest chocolate festival, held for 10 days in mid-October. ✉ *Ruggero d'Andreotto 19/E, Perugia* ☎ *075/5003838* ⊕ *www. eurochocolate.com.*

★ Festival dei Due Mondi

FESTIVALS | The annual event, held in late June and early July, is one of the most important cultural happenings in Europe, attracting big names in all branches of the arts, particularly music, opera, and theater. ✉ *Piazza del Commune 1,* ☎ *0743/776444* ⊕ *www.festivaldispoleto. com.*

★ Umbria Jazz Festival

FESTIVALS | One of the world's biggest jazz festivals attracts big names and big crowds to Perugia for 10 days in July and to Orvieto for five days in December or January. ✉ *Piazza Danti 28, Perugia* ☎ *075/5732432* ⊕ *www.umbriajazz.it.*

Restaurants

As befits a landlocked territory, the cuisine of Umbria is firmly based on local produce. Consequently, most restaurants in the region offer menus that are strictly seasonal, though locals have ensured that the food most associated with Umbria—*tartufi,* or truffles—is available year-round thanks to their mastery of freezing, drying, and preserving techniques.

Truffles are added to a variety of dishes, especially local pastas *stringozzi* (also written *strengozzi* or *strangozzi*) and *ombrichelli.* Lamb, pork, and boar are the most common meats consumed in Umbria, and lentils grown around Castelluccio are highly prized.

Seafood from the Adriatic predominates in the coastal Marches region, often made into *brodetto,* a savory fish soup. Inland, Ascoli Piceno is renowned for its stuffed green olives.

Restaurant prices are the average cost of a main course at dinner or, if dinner is not served, at lunch. Restaurant reviews have been shortened. For full information, visit Fodors.com.

Hotels

Virtually every older town, no matter how small, has some kind of hotel. A trend, particularly around Gubbio, Orvieto, and Todi, is to convert old villas, farms, and monasteries into first-class hotels. The natural splendor of the countryside more than compensates for the distance from town—provided you have a car. Hotels in town tend to be simpler than their country cousins, with a few notable exceptions in Spoleto, Gubbio, and Perugia.

Hotel prices are the lowest cost of a standard double room in high season. Hotel reviews have been shortened. For full information, visit Fodors.com.

What it Costs in Euros			
$	$$	$$$	$$$$
RESTAURANTS			
under €15	€15–€24	€25–€35	over €35
HOTELS			
under €125	€125–€200	€201–€300	over €300

Visitor Information

CONTACT Umbria Regional Tourism Office. ✉ *Piazza Matteotti 18,* ☎ *075/5736458* ⊕ *www.umbriatourism.it.*

Perugia

157 km (98 miles) southeast of Florence, 65 km (40 miles) east of Montepulciano.

Perugia is a majestic, handsome, wealthy city, and with its trendy boutiques, refined cafés, and grandiose architecture, it doesn't try to hide its affluence. A student population of around 30,000 means that the city, with a permanent population of about 165,000, is abuzz with activity throughout the year. Umbria Jazz, one of the region's most important music festivals, attracts music lovers from around the world every July, and Eurochocolate, the international chocolate festival, is an irresistible draw each October for anyone with a sweet tooth.

GETTING HERE AND AROUND

The best approach to the city is by train. The area around the station doesn't attest to the rest of Perugia's elegance, but buses running from the station to Piazza d'Italia, the heart of the old town, are frequent. If you're in a hurry, take the *minimetro,* a one-line subway, to Stazione della Cupa.

If you're driving to Perugia and your hotel doesn't have parking facilities, leave your car in one of the lots close to the center.

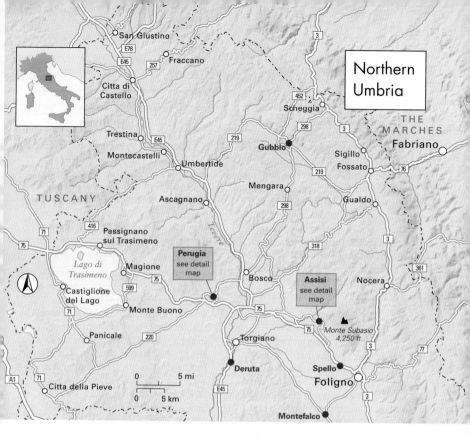

Electronic displays indicate the location of lots and the number of available spaces. If you park in the Piazza Partigiani, take the escalators that pass through the fascinating subterranean excavations of the city's Roman foundations and lead to the town center.

Sights

Collegio del Cambio (*Bankers' Guild Hall*)

HISTORIC SIGHT | These elaborate rooms, on the ground floor of the Palazzo dei Priori, served as the meeting hall and chapel of the guild of bankers and money changers. Most of the frescoes were completed by the most important Perugian painter of the Renaissance, Pietro Vannucci, better known as Perugino. He included a remarkably honest self-portrait on one of the pilasters. The iconography includes common religious themes, such

as the Nativity and the Transfiguration seen on the end walls. ⊠ *Corso Vannucci 25, Perugia* ☎ *075/5728599* ⊕ *www. collegiodelcambio.it* ⊡ *€5* ⊙ *Closed Sun. afternoon, also Mon. afternoon Nov.–Mar.*

Corso Vannucci

STREET | A string of elegantly connected palazzi expresses the artistic nature of this city center, the heart of which is concentrated along Corso Vannucci. Stately and broad, this pedestrian-only street runs from Piazza Italia to Piazza IV Novembre. Along the way, the entrances to many of Perugia's side streets might tempt you to wander off and explore. But don't stray too far as evening falls, when Corso Vannucci fills with Perugians out for their evening *passeggiata*, a pleasant predinner stroll that may include a pause for an aperitif at one of the many bars that line the street. ⊠ *Perugia*.

Umbria Through the Ages

The earliest inhabitants of Umbria, the Umbri, were thought by the Romans to be the most ancient inhabitants of Italy. Little is known about them: with the coming of Etruscan culture, the tribe fled into the mountains in the eastern portion of the region. The Etruscans, who founded some of the great cities of Umbria, were in turn supplanted by the Romans. Unlike Tuscany and other regions of central Italy, Umbria had few powerful medieval families to exert control over the cities in the Middle Ages—its proximity to Rome ensured that it would always be more or less under papal domination.

In the center of the country, Umbria has, for much of its history, been a battlefield where armies from north and south clashed. Hannibal destroyed a Roman army on the shores of Lake Trasimeno, and the bloody course of the interminable Guelph–Ghibelline conflict of the Middle Ages was played out here. Dante considered Umbria the most violent place in Italy. Trophies of war still decorate the Palazzo dei Priori in Perugia, and the little town of Gubbio continues a warlike rivalry begun in the Middle Ages—every year it challenges the Tuscan town of Sansepolcro to a cross-bow tournament. Today the bowmen shoot at targets, but neither side has forgotten that 500 years ago they were shooting at each other.

In spite of—or perhaps because of—this bloodshed, Umbria has produced more than its share of Christian saints. The most famous is St. Francis, the decidedly pacifist saint whose life shaped the Church of his time. His great shrine at Assisi is visited by hundreds of thousands of pilgrims each year. St. Clare, his devoted follower, was Umbria-born, as were St. Benedict, St. Rita of Cascia, and the patron saint of lovers, St. Valentine.

Duomo

CHURCH | Severe yet mystical, the Cathedral of San Lorenzo is most famous for being the home of the wedding ring of the Virgin Mary, stolen by the Perugians in 1488 from the nearby town of Chiusi. The ring, kept high up in a red-curtained vault in the chapel immediately to the left of the entrance, is stored under lock and key—15 locks, to be precise—most of the year. It's shown to the public on July 30 (the day it was brought to Perugia) and the second-to-last Sunday in January (Mary's wedding anniversary).

The cathedral itself dates from the Middle Ages, and has many additions from the 15th and 16th centuries. The most visually interesting element is the altar to the Madonna of Grace; an elegant fresco on a column at the right of the entrance of the altar depicts La Madonna delle Grazie. Sections of the church may be closed to visitors during religious services. ✉ Piazza IV Novembre, Perugia ☎ 075/5723832 ⊕ www.cattedrale.perugia.it 🎫 Museum €6 🕙 Museum closed Mon. Nov.–Mar.

★ Galleria Nazionale dell'Umbria

ART MUSEUM | The region's most comprehensive art gallery is housed on the fourth floor of the Palazzo dei Priori. The collection includes work by native artists—most notably Pintoricchio (1454–1513) and Perugino (circa 1450–1523). In addition to paintings, the gallery has frescoes, sculptures, and some superb examples of crucifixes from the 13th and 14th centuries. ✉ Corso

Vannucci 19, Piazza IV Novembre, Perugia ☎ *075/58668415* 🌐 *gallerianazionaledellumbria.it* 🎫 *€8* 🕒 *Closed Mon.*

Museo Archeologico Nazionale
HISTORY MUSEUM | An excellent collection of Etruscan artifacts from throughout the region sheds light on Perugia as a flourishing city long before it fell under Roman domination in 310 BC. Little else remains of Perugia's mysterious ancestors, although the Arco di Augusto, in Piazza Fortebraccio, the northern entrance to the city, is of Etruscan origin. ✉ *Piazza G. Bruno 10, Perugia* ☎ *075/5727141* 🌐 *www.musei.umbria.beniculturali.it* 🎫 *€5* 🕒 *Closed Mon.*

Palazzo dei Priori (*Palace of the Priors*)
GOVERNMENT BUILDING | A series of elegant, connected buildings serves as Perugia's city hall and houses three museums. The buildings string along Corso Vannucci and wrap around the Piazza IV Novembre, where the original entrance is located. The steps here lead to the Sala dei Notari (Notaries' Hall). Other entrances lead to the Galleria Nazionale dell'Umbria, the Collegio del Cambio, and the Collegio della Mercanzia.

The Sala dei Notari, which dates from the 13th century and was the original meeting place of the town merchants, had become the seat of the notaries by the second half of the 15th century. Wooden beams and an array of interesting frescoes attributed to Maestro di Farneto embellish the room. ✉ *Piazza IV Novembre 25, Perugia* 🎫 *Free.*

Rocca Paolina
HISTORIC SIGHT | A labyrinth of little streets, alleys, and arches, this underground city was originally part of a fortress built at the behest of Pope Paul III between 1540 and 1543 to confirm papal dominion over the city. Parts of it were destroyed after the end of papal rule, but much still remains. Begin your visit by taking the escalators that descend through the subterranean ruins from Piazza Italia down to Via Masi. In summer, this is the coolest place in the city. ✉ *Piazza Italia, Perugia* 🎫 *Free.*

🍴 Restaurants

Antica Trattoria San Lorenzo Simone Ciccotti
$$ | UMBRIAN | Both the food and the service are outstanding at this popular small, brick-vaulted eatery next to the Duomo. Particular attention is paid to adapting traditional Umbrian cuisine to the modern palate, and there's also a nice variety of seafood dishes on the menu, both à la carte and in good-value tasting menus—the *pacchero* (pasta with smoked eggplant, cod, and scampi) is a real treat. **Known for:** fish and truffle tasting menus; modernized versions of local recipes; impeccable service. [$] *Average main: €24* ✉ *Piazza Danti 19/a, Perugia* ☎ *075/5721956* 🌐 *anticatrattoriasanlorenzo.business.site* 🕒 *No lunch Sat.*

Dal Mi' Cocco
$$ | UMBRIAN | Favored by Perugia's university students, this casual spot with vaulted ceilings is fun, crowded, and inexpensive. Fixed-price meals change with the season and include starters, pasta, a main meat course, and dessert; each day of the week brings some new creation *dal cocco* (from the "coconut," or head) of the chef. **Known for:** abundant portions; honest prices; authentically casual feel. [$] *Average main: €15* ✉ *Corso Garibaldi 12, Perugia* ☎ *075/5732511* 🌐 *www.facebook.com/ristorantedalmicocco* 🕒 *Closed Mon. and late July–mid-Aug.*

★ Osteria a Priori
$ | MODERN ITALIAN | This charming wine-and-olive-oil shop with a restaurant (featuring vaulted ceilings and exposed brick) tucked into the back offers up small plates using ingredients with a "zero-kilometer" philosophy: everything comes from local and artisanal Umbrian producers. Regional cheeses, homemade

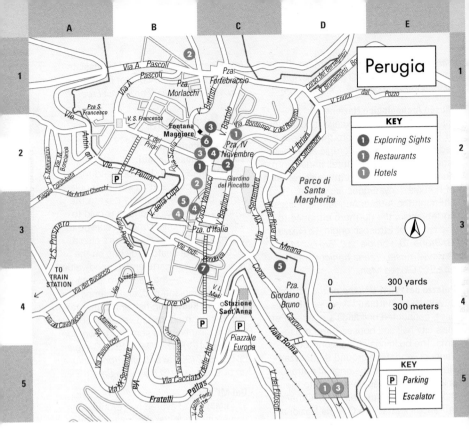

Perugia

KEY

- **1** Exploring Sights
- **1** Restaurants
- **1** Hotels

KEY

- **P** Parking
- Escalator

0 — 300 yards
0 — 300 meters

Sights ▼

1 Collegio del Cambio **C2**
2 Corso Vannucci..........**C2**
3 Duomo **C2**
4 Galleria Nazionale
 dell'Umbria **C2**
5 Museo Archeologico
 Nazionale.................**C4**
6 Palazzo dei Priori **C2**
7 Rocca Paolina............**C4**

Restaurants ▼

1 Antica Trattoria
 San Lorenzo
 Simone Ciccotti **C2**
2 Dal Mi' Cocco **B1**
3 Osteria a Priori...........**C2**
4 Ristorante
 La Rosetta **B3**
5 Ristorante
 La Taverna...............**B3**

Hotels ▼

1 Le Tre Vaselle
 Resort & Spa **D5**
2 Locanda della
 Posta **C3**
3 Posta Donini 1579 —
 UNA Esperienze **D5**
4 Sina Brufani **B3**

pastas, and slow-cooked meats steal the show, and, as might be expected, the selection of wine is top-notch. **Known for:** local, nontouristy atmosphere; knowledgeable servers; all Umbrian products. $ *Average main: €13* ✉ *Via dei Priori 39, Perugia* ☎ *075/5727098* ⊕ *www.osteriaapriori.it* ⊘ *Closed Sun.*

Ristorante La Rosetta

$$ | ITALIAN | The dining room of the hotel of the same name is a peaceful, elegant spot to get away from the bustle of central Perugia; in winter you dine inside under medieval vaults, and in summer, in the cool courtyard. The food is simple but reliable, and flawlessly served. **Known for:** professional service; refined versions of local meat dishes; elegant, old-fashioned setting. $ *Average main: €18* ✉ *Piazza Italia 19, Perugia* ☎ *075/3747858* ⊕ *www. ristorantelarosettaperugia.com.*

Ristorante La Taverna

$$$ | UMBRIAN | Medieval steps lead to a rustic two-story space where wine bottles and artful clutter decorate the walls. The regional menu features lots of delicious house-made pastas and grilled meats prepared by chef Claudio and served up in substantial portions, plus generous shavings of truffle in season. **Known for:** welcoming ambience; swift and efficient service; Umbrian specialties. $ *Average main: €25* ✉ *Via delle Streghe 8, off Corso Vannucci, Perugia* ☎ *075/5732536* ⊕ *www.ristorantelataverna.com* ⊘ *Closed Sun. and Mon.*

 Hotels

Le Tre Vaselle Resort & Spa

$$ | HOTEL | FAMILY | Rooms spread throughout four stone buildings are spacious and graced with floors of typical, red-clay, Tuscan tiles; olive groves surround the outdoor pool, and the indoor spa specializes in wine treatments. **Pros:** perfect for visiting the Torgiano wine area and Deruta; nice pool; friendly staff. **Cons:** service occasionally falters; amid

an uninspiring village; somewhat far from Perugia. $ *Rooms from: €149* ✉ *Via Garibaldi 48, Torgiano* ☎ *075/9880447* ⊕ *www.3vaselle.it* ⇌ *52 rooms* ⏐○⏐ *Free Breakfast.*

★ Locanda della Posta

$$ | HOTEL | This friendly, centrally located, converted 18th-century palazzo off the bustling pedestrian-only Corso Vannucci features spacious rooms soothingly decorated in muted colors; some include original frescoes and beamed ceilings. **Pros:** some fine views; exudes good taste and refinement; central location. **Cons:** no gym or spa; no real lobby; some street noise. $ *Rooms from: €139* ✉ *Corso Vannucci 97, Perugia* ☎ *075/5728925* ⊕ *www.locandadellapostahotel.it* ⇌ *17 rooms* ⏐○⏐ *Free Breakfast.*

★ Posta Donini 1579 — UNA Esperienza

$$ | HOTEL | FAMILY | Beguilingly comfortable guest rooms set on lovely grounds—where gardeners go quietly about their business—along with a small but charming spa and a well-regarded restaurant make this historical hotel south of Perugia worth a stay. **Pros:** plush atmosphere; great restaurant; a quiet and private getaway. **Cons:** parking area can get full; uninteresting village; outside Perugia. $ *Rooms from: €134* ✉ *Via Deruta 43, San Martino in Campo* ☎ *075/609132* ⊕ *www.postadonini.it* ⇌ *48 rooms* ⏐○⏐ *Free Breakfast.*

Sina Brufani

$$$ | HOTEL | Though a tad old-fashioned, this elegant, centrally located hotel dating from 1884 with a magnificent spa is the most upscale accommodation in town. **Pros:** wonderful location; excellent views from many rooms; unique spa area. **Cons:** service can be hit-or-miss; in-house restaurant not up to par; could use a refresh. $ *Rooms from: €284* ✉ *Piazza Italia 12, Perugia* ☎ *075/5732541* ⊕ *www.sinahotels.com* ⇌ *94 rooms* ⏐○⏐ *Free Breakfast.*

Nightlife

With its large student population, the city has plenty to offer in the way of bars and clubs. The best ones are around the city center, off Corso Vannucci.

Bottega del Vino

WINE BARS | This cozy wine bar offers a large selection of *vino* from around Italy as well as light meals; you can't go wrong with the *antipasti* (appetizers), cheese platter, or bruschetta. A live jazz band plays on Wednesday night. ⊠ *Via del Sole 1, Perugia* ☎ *075/5716181* ⊕ *www. labottegadelvino.net.*

★ Living Café

CAFÉS | Get the best views in town from the large terrace of this café-bar, attached to Ristorante del Sole. It's the most scenic spot in town for aperitivo; happy hour starts daily at 7 pm. ⊠ *Via della Rupe 1, Perugia* ☎ *075/5735031* ⊕ *www. ristorantesole.com.*

Zenoteca

WINE BARS | This informal hangout, with a living room atmosphere, serves up both Italian and international wines as well as craft beers. Regular live music nights draw an artsy crowd. ⊠ *Via Prospero Podiani 14, Perugia* ☎ *0324/6973490* ⊕ *zenoteca.business.site.*

🛍 Shopping

Stroll down any of Perugia's main streets, including Corso Vannucci, Via dei Priori, Via Oberdan, and Via Sant'Ercolano, and you'll see many well-known designer boutiques and specialty shops.

The most typical thing to buy is chocolate, which you can find almost anywhere. The best-known confections made by Perugina (now owned by Nestlé) are the chocolate-and-hazelnut-filled nibbles called Baci (literally, "kisses"). They're wrapped in silver foil that includes a sliver of paper, like the fortune in a fortune cookie, with multilingual romantic sentiments or sayings.

★ Chocostore by Eurochocolate

CHOCOLATE | The official store of the Eurochocolate festival sells bars, truffles, dipped fruits, and more chocolate goodies year-round. ⊠ *Piazza IV Novembre 7, Perugia* ☎ *075/5732885* ⊕ *www. eurochocolate.com/store.*

Perugina

CHOCOLATE | At Baci Perugina's original home, you'll find these iconic chocolates in all shapes and sizes, along with chocolate bars and candies. ⊠ *Corso Vannucci 101, Perugia* ☎ *075/5736677* ⊕ *www. sweetcityperugia.it.*

Assisi

28 km (17 miles) southeast of Perugia.

The small town of Assisi is one of the Christian world's most important pilgrimage sites and home of the Basilica di San Francesco—built to honor St. Francis (1182–1226) and erected swiftly after his death. The peace and serenity of the town are a welcome respite from the hustle and bustle of Italy's major cities.

GETTING HERE AND AROUND

Assisi lies on the Terontola–Foligno rail line, with almost hourly connections to Perugia and direct trains to Rome and Florence several times a day. The Stazione Centrale is 4 km (2½ miles) from town, with a bus service about every half hour.

Assisi is easily reached from the A1/E35 autostrada (Rome–Florence) and the SS75 highway. The walled town is closed to traffic, so cars must be left in the parking lots at Porta San Pietro, near Porta Nuova, or beneath Piazza Matteotti. Pay your parking fee at the *cassa* (ticket booth) before you return to your car to get a ticket to insert in the machine that will allow you to exit. It's a short but sometimes steep walk into the center of town; frequent minibuses (buy tickets

Assisi

KEY

1 Exploring Sights

1 Restaurants

1 Hotels

Steps

Sights ▶

1 Basilica
di San Francesco **A1**

2 Basilica di Santa
Chiara **F2**

3 Cattedrale di San
Rufino **F2**

4 Eremo delle Carceri **H2**

5 Santa Maria Sopra
Minerva **E2**

Restaurants ▶

1 Buca di
San Francesco **D2**

2 Osteria Piazzetta
dell'Erba **E2**

3 Ristorante Bar
San Francesco **B1**

4 Trattoria Pallotta
Assisi **E2**

Hotels ▶

1 Borgo Castello
Panicaglia **G1**

2 Castello di Petrata **G1**

3 Hotel Umbra **E2**

4 Nun Assisi Relais
& Spa Museum **G1**

from a newsstand or tobacco shop near where you park your car) make the rounds for weary pilgrims.

Sights

Assisi is pristinely medieval in architecture and appearance, owing in large part to relative neglect from the 16th century until 1926, when the celebration of the 700th anniversary of St. Francis's death brought more than 2 million visitors. Since then, pilgrims have flocked here in droves, and today several million arrive each year to pay homage. But not even the constant flood of visitors to this town of 28,000 residents can spoil the singular beauty of this significant religious center, the home of some of the Western tradition's most important works of art. The hill on which Assisi sits rises dramatically from the flat plain, and the town is dominated by a medieval castle at the very top.

Even though Assisi is sometimes besieged by busloads of sightseers who clamor to visit the famous basilica, it's difficult not to be charmed by the tranquility of the town and its medieval architecture. Once you've seen the basilica, stroll through the town's narrow winding streets to see beautiful vistas of the nearby hills and valleys peeking through openings between the buildings.

★ Basilica di San Francesco

CHURCH | The basilica isn't one church but two: the Gothic church on the upper level, and the Romanesque church on the lower level. Work on this two-tiered monolith was begun in 1228. Both churches are magnificently decorated artistic treasure houses, covered floor to ceiling with some of Europe's finest frescoes: the Lower Basilica is dim and full of candlelight shadows, while the Upper Basilica is bright and airy.

In the Upper Church, the magnificent frescoes from 13th-century Italian painter Giotto, painted when he was only in his twenties, show that he was a pivotal artist in the development of Western painting. He broke away from the stiff, unnatural styles of earlier generations to move toward realism and three-dimensionality. The Lower Church features frescoes by celebrated Sienese painters Simone Martini and Pietro Lorenzetti, as well as by Giotto (or his assistants). The basilica's dress code is strictly enforced—no bare shoulders or bare knees are permitted. ⊠ *Piazza di San Francesco, Assisi* ☎ *075/8190084* ⊕ *www.sanfrancescoassisi.org* ⊡ *Free.*

Basilica di Santa Chiara

CHURCH | The lovely, wide piazza in front of this church is reason enough to visit. The red-and-white-striped facade frames the piazza's panoramic view over the Umbrian plains. Santa Chiara is dedicated to St. Clare, one of the earliest and most fervent of St. Francis's followers and the founder of the order of the Poor Ladies— or Poor Clares—which was based on the Franciscan monastic order. The church contains Clare's body, and in the Cappella del Crocifisso (on the right) is the cross that spoke to St. Francis. A heavily veiled nun of the Poor Clares order is usually stationed before the cross in adoration of the image. ⊠ *Piazza Santa Chiara, Assisi* ☎ *075/812216* ⊕ *www.assisisantachiara. it* ⊡ *Free.*

Cattedrale di San Rufino

CHURCH | St. Francis and St. Clare were among those baptized in Assisi's Cattedrale, which was the principal church in town until the 12th century. The baptismal font has since been redecorated, but it's possible to see the crypt of St. Rufino, the bishop who brought Christianity to Assisi and was martyred on August 11, 238 (or 236 by some accounts), as well as climb to the bell tower. Admission to the crypt includes the small Museo della Cattedrale, with its detached frescoes and artifacts. Visits to the crypt on weekends must be reserved at least one day in advance;

see the website for details. ✉ *Piazza San Rufino, Assisi* ☎ *075/812712* 🌐 *www.assisimuseodiocesano.it* 🎟 *Church free, crypt and museum €4, bell tower and museum €4, bell tower €2* 🕒 *Bell tower and museum closed Wed.*

Eremo delle Carceri

RELIGIOUS BUILDING | About 4 km (2½ miles) east of Assisi is a monastery set in a dense wood against Monte Subasio: the Hermitage of Prisons. This was the place where St. Francis and his followers went to "imprison" themselves in prayer. The only site in Assisi that remains essentially unchanged since St. Francis's time, the church and monastery are the kinds of tranquil places that St. Francis would have appreciated. The walk out from town is very pleasant, and many trails lead from here across the wooded hillside of Monte Subasio (now a protected forest), with beautiful vistas across the Umbrian countryside. True to their Franciscan heritage, the friars here are entirely dependent on alms from visitors. ✉ *Via Eremo delle Carceri 38, 4 km (2½ miles) east of Assisi, Assisi* ☎ *075/812301* 🌐 *www.santuarioeremodellecarceri.org* 🎟 *Donations accepted.*

Santa Maria Sopra Minerva

CHURCH | Dating from the time of the Emperor Augustus (27 BC–AD 14), this structure was originally dedicated to the Roman goddess of wisdom, and in later times it was used as a monastery and prison before being converted into a church in the 16th century. The expectations raised by the perfect classical facade are not met by the interior, which was subjected to a thorough Baroque transformation in the 17th century. ✉ *Piazza del Comune 14, Assisi* ☎ *075/812361* 🎟 *Free.*

🍴 Restaurants

Buca di San Francesco

$ | **UMBRIAN** | In summer, dine in a cool green garden; in winter, under the low brick arches of the cozy cellars. The unique settings and the first-rate (though straightforward) fare make this central restaurant one of Assisi's busiest; try the namesake homemade spaghetti *alla buca,* served with a roasted mushroom sauce. **Known for:** warm and welcoming service; historical surroundings; cozy atmosphere. [$] *Average main: €12* ✉ *Via Eugenio Brizi 1, Assisi* ☎ *075/812204* 🌐 *buca-di-san-francesco.business.site* 🕒 *Closed Mon. and 10 days in late July.*

★ **Osteria Piazzetta dell'Erba**

$$ | **UMBRIAN** | Hip service and sophisticated presentations attract locals, who enjoy Italian cuisine with unusual twists (think porcini mushroom risotto with blue cheese and blueberries), a nice selection of salads—unusual for an Umbrian restaurant—plus sushi options and intriguing desserts. The enthusiastic young team keep things running smoothly and the energy high. **Known for:** intimate ambience; inventive dishes; friendly staff. [$] *Average main: €18* ✉ *Via San Gabriele dell'Addolorata 15/b, Assisi* ☎ *075/815352* 🌐 *www.osteriapiazzettadellerba.it* 🕒 *Closed Mon. and a few wks in Jan. or Feb.*

Ristorante Bar San Francesco

$$ | **UMBRIAN** | An excellent view of the Basilica di San Francesco from the covered terrace is just one reason to patronize this traditional restaurant, where Umbrian dishes are made with aromatic locally grown herbs. Menus change seasonally and include a fine selection of pastas and mains; appetizers and desserts are also especially good. **Known for:** pleasant staff; tasty seasonal dishes; prime Assisi location. [$] *Average main: €20* ✉ *Via di San Francesco 52, Assisi* ☎ *075/813302* 🌐 *www.ristorantesanfrancesco.com.*

Trattoria Pallotta Assisi

$$ | **UMBRIAN** | At this homey, family-run trattoria with a crackling fireplace and stone walls, the women do the cooking, and the men serve the food; try the *strangozzi alla pallotta* (thick spaghetti with a pesto of olives and mushrooms). Connected to the restaurant is an inn whose eight rooms have firm beds and some views across the rooftops of town. **Known for:** fast and courteous service; delicious meat plates, including pigeon and rabbit; traditional local dishes. $ *Average main: €18* ⊠ *Vicolo della Volta Pinta 3, Assisi* ☎ *075/8155273* ⊕ *www. trattoriapallotta.it* ☺ *Closed Tues.*

Hotels

Advance reservations are essential at Assisi's hotels between Easter and October and over Christmas. Latecomers are often forced to stay in the modern town of Santa Maria degli Angeli, 8 km (5 miles) away. As a last-minute option, you can always inquire at restaurants to see if they're renting out rooms.

Until the early 1980s, pilgrim hostels outnumbered ordinary hotels in Assisi, and they present an intriguing and economical alternative to conventional lodgings. They're usually called *conventi* or *ostelli* ("convents" or "hostels") because they're run by convents, churches, or other Catholic organizations. Rooms are spartan but peaceful. Check with the tourist office for a list.

★ Borgo Castello Panicaglia

$$$ | **HOTEL** | **FAMILY** | This rustic-chic, 17-room hotel between Assisi and Gubbio, dating from 1266 but thoroughly modernized inside, is a relaxing base for exploring the pretty Umbrian countryside. **Pros:** extremely family-friendly atmosphere; modern amenities in a historical building; tasty and inventive meals. **Cons:** location is quite rural; no spa; need a car to get around the area. $ *Rooms from: €208* ⊠ *Località Panicaglia, Nocera* ⊕ *24 km (15 miles) northeast of Assisi* ☎ *0742/81663* ⊕ *www.borgocastellopanicaglia.com* ⇆ *17 rooms* ⊚ *Free Breakfast.*

★ Castello di Petrata

$$ | **HOTEL** | Wood beams and sections of exposed medieval stonework add a lot of character to this 14th-century fortress, while creature comforts make each individually decorated room a delightful retreat. **Pros:** great views of town and country; peaceful pool; medieval character. **Cons:** limited choices in restaurant; far from Assisi town center; slightly isolated. $ *Rooms from: €142* ⊠ *Via Petrata 25, Assisi* ☎ *075/815451* ⊕ *www.castello-petrata.it* ☺ *Closed Sun.–Thurs. Jan. and Feb.* ⇆ *20 rooms* ⊚ *Free Breakfast.*

Hotel Umbra

$ | **HOTEL** | Rooms on the upper floors of this charming 16th-century town house near Piazza del Comune look out over the Assisi rooftops to the valley below, as does the sunny, vine-covered terrace. **Pros:** very central; excellent valley views from some rooms; pleasant small garden. **Cons:** uninspiring breakfasts; some small rooms; difficult parking. $ *Rooms from: €110* ⊠ *Via degli Archi 6, Assisi* ☎ *075/812240* ⊕ *www.hotelumbra.it* ☺ *Closed Nov.–late Mar.* ⇆ *24 rooms* ⊚ *Free Breakfast.*

★ Nun Assisi Relais & Spa Museum

$$$$ | **HOTEL** | Within walking distance of Assisi's restaurants and shops, this monastery built in 1275 has been converted into a thoroughly contemporary, high-end place to stay with a fabulous spa carved out of 2,000-year-old Roman baths. **Pros:** fantastic blend of the historical and modern; wonderful place to relax; excellent restaurant. **Cons:** split-level rooms with stairs difficult for those with mobility issues; on-site parking costs extra; on the expensive side. $ *Rooms from: €385* ⊠ *Via Eremo delle Carceri 1A, Assisi* ☎ *075/8155150* ⊕ *www.nunassisi.com* ⇆ *18 rooms* ⊚ *Free Breakfast.*

Continued on page 662

ASSISI'S BASILICA DI SAN FRANCESCO

The legacy of St. Francis, founder of the Franciscan monastic order, pervades Assisi. Each year the town hosts several million pilgrims, but the steady flow of visitors does nothing to diminish the singular beauty of one of Italy's most important religious centers. The pilgrims' ultimate destination is the massive Basilica di San Francesco, which sits halfway up Assisi's hill, supported by graceful arches.

The basilica is not one church but two. The Romanesque Lower Church came first; construction began in 1228, just two years after St. Francis's death, and was completed within a few years. The low ceilings and candlelit interior make an appropriately solemn setting for St. Francis's tomb, found in the crypt below the main altar. The Gothic Upper Church, built only half a century later, sits on top of the lower one, and is strikingly different, with soaring arches and tall stained-glass windows (the first in Italy). Inside, both churches are covered floor to ceiling with some of Europe's finest frescoes: the Lower Church is dim and full of candlelit shadows, and the Upper Church is bright and airy.

VISITING THE BASILICA

THE LOWER CHURCH

The most evocative way to experience the basilica is to begin with the dark Lower Church. As you enter, give your eyes a moment to adjust. Keep in mind that the artists at work here were conscious of the shadowy environment—they knew this was how their frescoes would be seen.

In the first chapel to the left, a superb fresco cycle by Simone Martini depicts scenes from the life of St. Martin. As you approach the main altar, the vaulting above you is decorated with the Three Virtues of St. Francis (poverty, chastity, and obedience) and St. Francis's Triumph, frescoes attributed to Giotto's followers. In the transept to your left, Pietro Lorenzetti's Madonna and Child with St. Francis and St. John sparkles when the sun hits it. Notice Mary's thumb; legend has it Jesus is asking which saint to bless, and Mary is pointing to Francis. Across the way in the right transept, Cimabue's Madonna Enthroned Among Angels and St. Francis is a famous portrait of the saint. Surrounding the portrait are painted scenes from the childhood of Christ, done by the assistants of Giotto. Nearby is a painting of the crucifixion attributed to Giotto himself.

You reach the crypt via stairs midway along the nave—on the crypt's altar, a stone coffin holds the saint's body. Steps up from the transepts lead to the cloister, where there's a gift shop, and the treasury, which contains holy objects.

THE UPPER CHURCH

The St. Francis fresco cycle is the highlight of the Upper Church. (See facing page.) Also worth special note is the 16th-century choir, with its remarkably delicate inlaid wood. When a 1997 earthquake rocked the basilica, the St. Francis cycle sustained little damage, but portions of the ceiling above the entrance and altar collapsed, reducing their frescoes (attributed to Cimabue and Giotto) to rubble. The painstaking restoration is ongoing. ⚠ The dress code is strictly enforced—no bare shoulders or bare knees.

FRANCIS, ITALY'S PATRON SAINT

St. Francis was born in Assisi in 1181, the son of a noblewoman and a well-to-do merchant. His troubled youth included a year in prison. He planned a military career, but after a long illness Francis heard the voice of God, renounced his father's wealth, and began a life of austerity. His mystical embrace of poverty, asceticism, and the beauty of man and nature struck a responsive chord in the medieval mind; he quickly attracted a vast number of followers. Francis was the first saint to receive the stigmata (wounds in his hands, feet, and side corresponding to those of Christ on the cross). He died on October 4, 1226, in the Porziuncola, the secluded chapel in the woods where he had first preached the virtue of poverty to his disciples. St. Francis was declared patron saint of Italy in 1939, and today the Franciscans make up the largest of the Catholic orders.

THE UPPER CHURCH'S ST. FRANCIS FRESCO CYCLE

The 28 frescoes in the Upper Church depicting the life of St. Francis are the most admired works in the entire basilica. They're also the subject of one of art history's biggest controversies. For centuries they thought to be by Giotto (1267-1337), the great early Renaissance innovator, but inconsistencies in style, both within this series and in comparison to later Giotto works, have thrown their origin into question. Some scholars now say Giotto was the brains behind the cycle, but that assistants helped with the execution; others claim he couldn't have been involved at all.

Two things are certain. First, the style is revolutionary—which argues for

Giotto's involvement. The tangible weight of the figures, the emotion they show, and the use of perspective all look familiar to modern eyes, but in the art of the time there was nothing like it. Second, these images have played a major part in shaping how the world sees St. Francis. In that respect, who painted them hardly matters.

Starting in the transept, the frescoes circle the church, showing events in the saint's life (and afterlife). Some of the best are grouped near the church's entrance—look for the nativity at Greccio, the miracle of the spring, the death of the knight at Celano, and, most famously, the sermon to the birds.

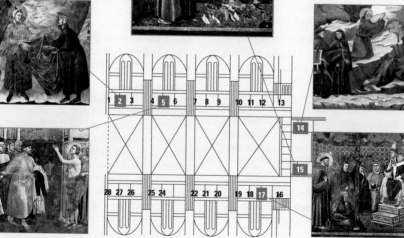

The St. Francis fresco cycle
1. Homage of a simple man
2. Giving cloak to a poor man
3. Dream of the palace
4. Hearing the voice of God
5. Rejection of worldly goods
6. Dream of Innocent III
7. Confirmation of the rules
8. Vision of flaming chariot
9. Vision of celestial thrones
10. Chasing devils from Arezzo
11. Before the sultan
12. Ecstasy of St. Francis
13. Nativity at Greccio
14. Miracle of the spring
15. Sermon to the birds
16. Death of knight at Celano
17. Preaching to Honorius III
18. Apparition at Arles
19. Receiving the stigmata
20. Death of St. Francis
21. Apparition before Bishop Guido and Fra Agostino
22. Verification of the stigmata
23. Mourning of St. Clare
24. Canonization
25. Apparition before Gregory IX
26. Healing of a devotee
27. Confession of a woman
28. Repentant heretic freed

Gubbio

39 km (24 miles) northeast of Perugia, 92 km (57 miles) east of Arezzo.

There's something otherworldly about this jewel of a medieval town, tucked away on the slopes of Monte Ingino. Even in the height of summer, the so-called Città del Silenzio (City of Silence) stays comparatively cool, and its dramatically steep streets remain relatively serene. At Christmas, kitsch is king. From December 7 to January 10, colored lights are strung down the mountainside in a shape resembling an evergreen, creating the world's largest Christmas tree.

Parking in the central Piazza dei Quaranta Martiri—named for 40 hostages murdered by the Nazis in 1944—is easy and secure. It's wise to leave your car there and explore the narrow streets on foot.

GETTING HERE AND AROUND

If you're driving from Perugia, take the SS318, which rises steeply up toward the Gubbio hills. The trip will take you 40 to 50 minutes. The closest train station is Fossato di Vico, about 20 km (12 miles) from Gubbio. Daily buses connect the train station with the city, a 30-minute trip. There are also many buses a day that leave from Perugia's Piazza Partigiani, the main Perugia bus terminal.

VISITOR INFORMATION

CONTACT Gubbio Tourism Office. ⊠ *Via Repubblica 15,* ☎ *075/922–0693* ⊕ *www. ilikegubbio.com.*

Sights

Basilica di Sant'Ubaldo

CHURCH | Gubbio's famous *ceri*—three 16-foot-tall pillars crowned with statues of Saints Ubaldo, George, and Anthony—are housed in this basilica atop Monte Ingino. The pillars are transported to the Palazzo dei Consoli on the first Sunday of May, in preparation for the Festa dei Ceri, one of central Italy's most spectacular festivals. ⊠ *Via Monte Ingino 5, Gubbio* ☎ *075/9273872* ⊕ *diocesigubbio. it* ✉ *Free.*

Duomo di Gubbio

CHURCH | Set on a narrow street on the highest tier of the town, the Duomo dates from the 13th century, with some Baroque additions—in particular, a lavishly decorated bishop's chapel. ⊠ *Via Ducale, Gubbio* ☎ *075/922138* ⊕ *diocesigubbio.it* ✉ *Free.*

Funivia Colle Eletto

TRANSPORTATION | FAMILY | For a bracing ride to the top of Monte Ingino (where you can see the Basilica di Sant'Ubaldo), hop on the funicular that climbs the hillside just outside the city walls at the eastern end of town. It's more like an oversize metal birdcage than a cable car, and it's definitely not for those who suffer from vertigo. Operating hours vary considerably from month to month; check the funicular's website. ⊠ *Via San Girolamo, Gubbio* ☎ *075/9273881* ⊕ *www.funiviagubbio.it* ✉ *€6 round-trip.*

Palazzo dei Consoli

HISTORY MUSEUM | Gubbio's striking Piazza Grande is dominated by this medieval palazzo, attributed to a local architect known as Gattapone, who is still much admired by today's residents (though some scholars have suggested that the palazzo was in fact the work of another architect, Angelo da Orvieto). In the Middle Ages, the Parliament of Gubbio assembled in the palace, which has become a symbol of the town and now houses a museum with a collection famous chiefly for the Tavole Eugubine—seven bronze tablets that are written in the ancient Umbrian language, employing Etruscan and Latin characters, and that provide the best key to understanding this obscure tongue.

Also in the museum is a fascinating miscellany of rare coins and earthenware pots. A lofty loggia provides exhilarating views over Gubbio's roofscape and beyond. For a few days at the beginning of May, the palace also displays the famous ceri, the ceremonial wooden pillars at the center of Gubbio's annual festivities. ✉ *Piazza Grande, Gubbio* ☎ *075/9274298* 🌐 *www.palazzodeiconsoli.it* 🎟 *€7.*

Palazzo Ducale

CASTLE/PALACE | This scaled-down copy of the Palazzo Ducale in Urbino (Gubbio was once the possession of that city's ruling family, the Montefeltro) contains a small museum and a courtyard. Some of the public rooms offer magnificent views. ✉ *Via Federico da Montefeltro 2, Gubbio* ☎ *075/9275872* 🌐 *www.musei.umbria.beniculturali.it* 🎟 *€5* 🕒 *Closed Mon.*

🍴 Restaurants

Ristorante Grotta dell'Angelo

$$ | **UMBRIAN** | In summer, the handful of outdoor tables are in high demand at this rustic trattoria, which is situated in a hotel of the same name at the lower part of the old town near the main square. The menu features simple local specialties, including *capocollo* (a type of salami), *stringozzi* (Umbrian wheat pasta), and lasagna *tartufata* (with truffles). **Known for:** homey atmosphere; good antipasti and grilled meats; reasonable prices. [$] *Average main: €15* ✉ *Via Gioia 47, Gubbio* ☎ *075/9271747* 🌐 *www.grottadellangelo.it* 🕒 *Closed Tues. and Jan. 7–Feb. 7.*

★ **Taverna del Lupo**

$$ | **UMBRIAN** | One of the city's most famous taverns has a menu that includes such indulgences as lasagna made in the Gubbian fashion, with ham and truffles, and the *suprema di faraono* (guinea fowl in a delicately spiced sauce); save room for the excellent desserts. The restaurant also has two fine wine cellars and an extensive wine list. **Known for:** good wine list; alluring presentation; wide menu choice. [$] *Average main: €20* ✉ *Via Ansidei 21, Gubbio* ☎ *075/9274368* 🌐 *www.tavernadellupo.it.*

🛏 Hotels

★ **Castello di Petroia**

$ | **HOTEL** | This atmospheric, 12th-century castle 15 km (9 miles) from Gubbio has spacious, antiques-filled, individually decorated rooms—some with decorated or beamed ceilings and stained glass, many with whirlpool tubs—as well as excellent in-house breakfasts and dinners. **Pros:** charming atmosphere; seasonal outdoor swimming pool; lovely breakfast buffet with handmade cakes and jams. **Cons:** temperature can be difficult to regulate in guest rooms; beds could be comfier; decor is on the simple side. [$] *Rooms from: €120* ✉ *Località Petroia, Gubbio* ☎ *075/920287* 🌐 *www.petroia.it* 🕒 *Closed early Jan.–late Mar.* 🛏 *13 rooms* 🍴 *Free Breakfast.*

Hotel Bosone Palace

$ | **HOTEL** | A former palace is now home to an elegant, if faded, hotel, where elaborate frescoes grace the ceilings of the two enormous suites and delightful breakfast room. **Pros:** friendly welcome; low rates; excellent location. **Cons:** can hear church bells ringing during the night; rooms and bathrooms on the small side; needs a refresh. [$] *Rooms from: €62* ✉ *Via XX Settembre 22, Gubbio* ☎ *075/9220688* 🌐 *www.hotelbosone.com* 🕒 *Closed early Jan. and Feb.* 🛏 *30 rooms* 🍴 *No Meals.*

Deruta

19 km (11 miles) southeast of Perugia, 60 km (37 miles) southwest of Gubbio.

This 14th-century hill town is most famous for its ceramics. A drive through the countryside to visit the workshops is a good way to spend a morning, but be sure to stop in the medieval town itself.

GETTING HERE AND AROUND

From Perugia, follow the directions for Rome and the E45 highway; Deruta has its own exits. There are also buses from Perugia that take about 30 minutes to reach Deruta.

VISITOR INFORMATION

CONTACT Deruta Tourism Office. ✉ *Via Biordo Michelotti 27,* ☎ *075/9728612* ⊕ *visitderuta.com.*

 Sights

Museo Regionale della Ceramica (*Regional Ceramics Museum*)

HISTORY MUSEUM | It's only fitting that Deruta is home to an impressive ceramics museum, which is housed in the 14th-century former convent of San Francesco. Panels in Italian and English explain artistic techniques and production processes, and the more than 6,000 items on display constitute the country's largest collection of Italian ceramics. The most notable are Renaissance vessels made using the *lustro* technique, which originated in Arab and Middle Eastern cultures some 500 years before coming into use in Italy in the late 1400s and which incorporates crushed precious materials such as gold or silver to create a rich, lustrous finish. ✉ *Largo San Francesco, Piazza del Consoli 12, Deruta* ☎ *075/9711000* ⊕ *www.museocerami-cadideruta.it* 🎟 *€7, includes Pinacoteca Comunale* ⊗ *Closed Tues. and Wed.*

Pinacoteca Comunale

ART MUSEUM | The 14th-century Palazzo dei Consoli houses Deruta's Municipal Picture Gallery, open only on Sunday. The rich collection displayed over two floors includes frescoes and paintings by the Renaissance artists Perugino and L'Alunno, among other works from local churches. Upstairs, the Pascoli Collection features 17th- and 18th-century canvases, donated by a descendant of the prominent art collector and writer Lione Pascoli. Artists represented include

Giovanni Battista Gaulli, Sebastiano Conca, and Francesco Trevisani. ✉ *Piazza dei Consoli 12, Deruta* ☎ *075/9711000* ⊕ *www.museoceramicadideruta.it* 🎟 *€7, includes Museo Regionale Della Cerami-ca* ⊗ *Closed Mon.–Sat.*

 Shopping

Deruta is home to dozens of ceramics shops that offer a range of items, including extra pieces commissioned by well-known British and North American tableware manufacturers. A drive along Via Tiberina Nord takes you past one shop after another. If you ask, most owners will take you to see where they actually throw, bake, and paint their wares.

Spello

30 km (19 miles) southeast of Perugia, 12 km (7 miles) southeast of Assisi, 33 km (21 miles) north of Spoleto.

With well-appointed hotels, this hilltop town at the edge of Monte Subasio, just a short drive or train ride from Perugia or Assisi, makes an excellent base for exploring the region. Spello's art scene includes first-rate frescoes by Pinturicchio and Perugino, and contemporary artists can be observed at work in studios around town. If antiquity is your passion, the town also has some intriguing Roman ruins. And the warm, rosy-beige tones of the local *pietra rossa* stone on the buildings brighten even cloudy days.

GETTING HERE AND AROUND

Spello is an easy half-hour drive from Perugia. From the E45 highway, take the exit toward Assisi and Foligno. Merge onto the SS75 and take the Spello exit. There are also regular trains on the Perugia–Assisi line. Spello is 1 km (½ mile) from the train station, and it's a short, steep walk up to Porta Consolare.

From Porta Consolare, continue up the steep main street, which begins as Via

Consolare and changes names several times as it crosses the little town. It also follows the original Roman road, so, as it curves around, you'll see winding medieval alleyways to the right and more uniform, Roman-era blocks to the left.

Sights

Santa Maria Maggiore

CHURCH | The two great Umbrian artists hold sway in this 16th-century basilica. Pinturicchio's vivid frescoes in the Cappella Baglioni (1501) are striking for their rich colors, finely dressed figures, and complex symbolism. Among his finest works are the *Nativity, Christ Among the Doctors* (on the far left side is a portrait of Troilo Baglioni, the prior who commissioned the work), and the *Annunciation* (look for Pinturicchio's self-portrait in the Virgin's room). The artist painted them after he had already won great acclaim for his work in the Palazzi Vaticani in Rome for Borgia Pope Alexander VI. Two pillars on either side of the apse are decorated with frescoes by Perugino (circa 1450–1523). Hours to visit the cappella may be limited and vary by season; see the website for details. ✉ *Piazza Matteotti 18, Spello* ☎ *0742/301792* 🌐 *www.smariamaggiore.com* 🎟 *€3 for Cappella Baglioni.*

Hotels

Hotel Palazzo Bocci

$ | HOTEL | Lovely sitting areas, a reading room, bucolic ceiling and wall frescoes, and a garden terrace all add quiet, elegant charm to this slightly faded 14th-century property, where you could settle in for a week and take a cooking course or have the staff book you a bicycle or a horseback excursion. **Pros:** central location; abundant breakfasts; splendid views of the valley from public areas and some rooms. **Cons:** needs a spruce-up; not all rooms have views; noisy in summer months. [$] *Rooms from: €103* ✉ *Via Cavour 17, Spello* ☎ *0742/301021* 🌐 *www.palazzobocci.com* 🛏 *23 rooms* 🍴 *Free Breakfast.*

La Bastiglia

$ | HOTEL | Polished wood planks and handwoven rugs have replaced the rustic flooring of a former grain mill, and comfortable sitting rooms and cozy bedrooms are filled with a mix of antique and modern pieces. **Pros:** lovely terrace restaurant; fine views from top-floor rooms, some with terraces; leisure and wellness facilities. **Cons:** can use an overall refresh; no elevator and plenty of steps, so pack light; some shared balconies. [$] *Rooms from: €110* ✉ *Via Salnitraria 15, Spello* ☎ *0742/651277* 🌐 *labastiglia.com* 🕓 *Closed 3 wks in Jan.* 🛏 *34 rooms* 🍴 *Free Breakfast.*

Montefalco

18 km (11 miles) south of Spello, 34 km (21 miles) south of Assisi, 48 km (30 miles) southeast of Perugia.

Nicknamed the "balcony over Umbria" for its high vantage point over the valley that runs from Perugia to Spoleto, Montefalco began as an important Roman settlement along the Via Flaminia. The town owes its current name ("Falcon's Mount") to Emperor Frederick II (1194–1250). Obviously a greater fan of falconry than Roman architecture, he destroyed the ancient town, which was known as Coccorone, in 1249, and built in its place what would later become Montefalco. Aside from a few fragments incorporated in a private house just off Borgo Garibaldi, no traces remain of the old Roman center.

However, Montefalco has more than its fair share of interesting art and architecture and is well worth the drive up the hill. It's also a good place to stop for a meal, as is nearby Bevagna. You need go no farther than the main squares to find a restaurant or bar with a hot meal, and most establishments—both simple and sophisticated—offer a splendid combination of history and small-town hospitality.

GETTING HERE AND AROUND

If you're driving from Perugia, take the E45 toward Rome. Take the Foligno exit, then merge onto the SP445 and follow it into Montefalco. The drive takes around 50 minutes. The nearest train station is in Foligno, about 7 km (4½ miles) away. From there you can take a taxi or a bus into Montefalco.

VISITOR INFORMATION

CONTACT La Strada del Sagrantino. ✉ *Piazza del Comune 17,* ☎ *0742/378490* 🌐 *www.stradadelsagrantino.it.*

🍴 Restaurants

★ Enoteca L'Alchimista

$$ | **UMBRIAN** | "The Alchemist" is an apt name, as the chef's transformations are magical, and everything can be paired with wines from the restaurant's extensive selection. Though pasta, veggie, and meat dishes change seasonally, the homemade gnocchi in Sagrantino sauce, always on offer, wins raves from guests, plus all the delicious desserts are made on the premises. **Known for:** refined but relaxed dining; congenial setting and atmosphere; extensive wine list. [$] *Average main: €18* ✉ *Piazza del Comune 14, Montefalco* ☎ *0742/378558* 🌐 *www.ristorantealchimista.it* ⏲ *Closed Tues.*

★ Redibis

$$ | **MODERN ITALIAN** | Housed in a Roman theater—built in the 1st century AD but brought up-to-date with mid-century modern furniture and sleek chandeliers—this restaurant has an atmosphere that's as unique as the food. The seasonally changing menu, featuring mainly zero kilometer products, aims to adapt ancient ingredients like Roveja wild peas of Colfiorito to sophisticated modern tastes, while offering a fine selection of Umbrian wines. **Known for:** beautifully presented dishes; focus on local producers; fascinating cavelike atmosphere. [$] *Average main: €23* ✉ *Via dell'Anfiteatro 3, Bevagna* ✣ *8 km (5 miles) northwest of Montefalco* ☎ *0742/362120* 🌐 *www.foodie.bio* ⏲ *Closed Tues.*

🛏 Hotels

★ Palazzo Bontadosi Hotel & Spa

$$ | **HOTEL** | This charming boutique hotel, set in an 18th-century palace overlooking the main square, has spacious, individually decorated rooms, where original frescoes and beamed ceilings contrast with modern furnishings and some bathrooms have deep soaking tubs. **Pros:** sophisticated, design-focused vibe; friendly service; spa in medieval cellars has a private Turkish bath and soaking pool. **Cons:** small breakfast selection; no gym; rooms facing the square can be noisy. [$] *Rooms from: €161* ✉ *Piazza del Comune 19, Montefalco* ☎ *0742/379357* 🌐 *hotelbontadosi.it* 🛏 *12 rooms* 🍽 *Free Breakfast.*

Villa Pambuffetti

$$ | **HOTEL** | If you want to be pampered in the refined atmosphere of a private villa, this is the spot, with the warmth of a fireplace in the winter, a pool to cool you down in summer, and cozy reading nooks and guest rooms year-round. **Pros:** peaceful gardens; excellent dining room; cooking courses offered. **Cons:** dated feel; grounds could be better kept; outside the town center. [$] *Rooms from: €140* ✉ *Viale della Vittoria 20, Montefalco* ☎ *0742/379417* 🌐 *www.villapambuffetti.it* 🛏 *15 rooms* 🍽 *Free Breakfast.*

Spoleto

24 km (15 miles) southeast of Montefalco, 46 km (29 miles) south of Assisi, 63 km (39 miles) southeast of Perugia, 80 km (50 miles) east of Orvieto.

For most of the year, Spoleto is one more in a pleasant succession of sleepy hill towns, resting regally atop a mountain.

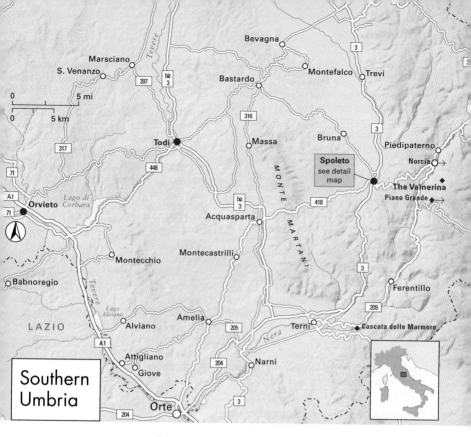

But for more than two weeks every summer the town shifts into high gear for a turn in the international spotlight during the Festival dei Due Mondi (Festival of Two Worlds), an extravaganza of theater, opera, music, painting, and sculpture.

As the world's top artists vie for honors, throngs of art aficionados vie for hotel rooms. If you plan to spend the night in Spoleto during the festival, make sure you have confirmed reservations, or you may find yourself scrambling at sunset.

Spoleto has plenty to lure you during the rest of the year as well: the final frescoes of Filippo Lippi, beautiful piazzas and streets with Roman and medieval attractions, and superb natural surroundings with rolling hills and a dramatic gorge. Spoleto makes a good base for exploring all of southern Umbria, as Assisi, Orvieto,

and the towns in between are all within easy reach.

GETTING HERE AND AROUND

Spoleto is an hour's drive from Perugia. From the E45 highway, take the exit toward Assisi and Foligno, then merge onto the SS75 until you reach the Foligno Est exit. Merge onto the SS3, which leads to Spoleto. There are regular trains on the Perugia–Foligno line. From the train station it's a 15-minute uphill walk to the center, so you may want to take a local bus or a taxi.

VISITOR INFORMATION

CONTACT Spoleto Tourism Office. ✉ *Largo Ferrer 6,* ☎ *0743/218620* ⊕ *www. comune.spoleto.pg.it.*

Sights

The walled city is set on a slanting hill-side, with the most interesting sections clustered toward the upper portion. Parking options inside the walls include Piazza Campello (just below the Rocca) on the southeast end, Via del Trivio to the north, and Piazza San Domenico on the west end. You can also park at Piazza della Vittoria farther north, just outside the walls, or at one of several well-marked lots near the train station. If you arrive by train, you can walk 1 km (½ mile) from the station to the entrance to the lower town. Regular bus connections are every 15–30 minutes.

Like most other towns with narrow, winding streets, Spoleto is best explored on foot. Bear in mind that much of the city is on a steep slope, so there are lots of stairs and steep inclines. The well-worn stones can be slippery even when dry; wear rubber-sole shoes for good traction.

Several pedestrian walkways cut across Corso Mazzini, which zigzags up the hill, and three escalators connect the main car parks with the upper town. A €9.50 Spoleto Card, sold at any of the town's museums, allows you entry to all the main museums and galleries over seven days.

Casa Romana (Roman House)
RUINS | Spoleto became a Roman colony in the 3rd century BC, but the best excavated remains date from the 1st century AD. Best preserved among them is the Casa Romana. According to an inscription, it belonged to Vespasia Polla, the mother of Emperor Vespasian (one of the builders of the Colosseum and perhaps better known by the Romans for taxing them to install public toilets, later called "Vespasians"). The rooms, arranged around a large central atrium built over an *impluvium* (rain cistern), are decorated with black-and-white geometric mosaics. ⊠ *Palazzo del Municipio, Via di Visiale 9,*

Spoleto ☎ *0743/40255* ⊕ *www.spoleto-card.it* ✉ *€3; included with Spoleto Card* ⊙ *Closed Tues.*

★ Duomo di Spoleto (*Spoleto Cathedral*)
CHURCH | The 12th-century Romanesque facade received a Renaissance face-lift with the addition of a loggia in a rosy pink stone, creating a stunning contrast in styles. One of the finest cathedrals in the region is lit by eight rose windows that are especially dazzling in the late afternoon sun. The original floor tiles remain from an earlier church destroyed by Frederick I (circa 1123–90). Above the church's entrance is Bernini's bust of Pope Urban VIII (1568–1644), who had the church redecorated in 17th-century Baroque; fortunately he didn't touch the 15th-century frescoes painted in the apse by Fra Filippo Lippi (circa 1406–69) between 1466 and 1469. These immaculately restored masterpieces—the *Annunciation, Nativity,* and *Dormition*—tell the story of the life of the Virgin. The *Coronation of the Virgin,* adorning the half dome, is the literal and figurative high point. Portraits of Lippi and his assistants are on the right side of the central panel.

The Florentine artist-priest, "whose colors expressed God's voice" (the words inscribed on his tomb), died shortly after completing the work. His tomb, which you can see in the right transept (note the artist's brushes and tools), was designed by his son, Filippino Lippi (circa 1457–1504). ⊠ *Piazza del Duomo 2, Spoleto* ☎ *0577/286300* ⊕ *www.duomo-spoleto.it* ✉ *Free; €5 for audio guide.*

La Rocca Albornoz
CASTLE/PALACE | Built in the mid-14th century for Cardinal Egidio Albornoz, this massive fortress served as a seat for the local pontifical governors, a tangible sign of the restoration of the Church's power in the area when the pope was ruling from Avignon. Several popes spent time here, and, in 1499, one of them, Alexander VI, sent his capable teenage daughter, Lucrezia Borgia (1480–1519),

to serve as governor for three months. The Gubbio-born architect Gattapone (14th century) used the ruins of a Roman acropolis as a foundation and took materials from many Roman-era sites, including the Teatro Romano.

La Rocca's plan is long and rectangular, with six towers and two grand court-yards, an upper loggia, and grand interior reception rooms. In the largest tower, Torre Maestà, you can visit an apartment with some interesting frescoes. The fortress also contains the Museo Nazionale del Ducato, 15 rooms dedicated to the art of the duchy of Spoleto during the Middle Ages. If you phone in advance, you may be able to secure an English-speaking guide. ✉ *Piazza Campello, Spoleto* ☎ *0743/224952* 🖥 *€8, including the Museo Nazionale del Ducato; included with Spoleto Card.*

★ Palazzo Collicola Arti Visive

ART MUSEUM | Spoleto's compact but delightful modern art museum, housed in an 18th-century palace, features a fine collection of works from Italian contemporary artists, including renowned Spoleto sculptor Leoncillo and Umbria-based American sculptor Barbara Pepper. International artists such as Alexander Calder and Richard Serra, are also represented, and an entire room is devoted to a large-scale wall drawing by Sol Lewitt. The Appartamento Nobile is a reproduction of an 18th-century nobleman's house, and the Pictures Gallery has paintings from the 16th to 19th centuries. ✉ *Piazza Collicola 1, Spoleto* ☎ *0743/46434* ⊕ *www. palazzocollicola.it* 🖥 *€9; included with Spoleto Card* 🕙 *Closed Tues. and Wed.*

★ Ponte delle Torri (*Bridge of the Towers*)

BRIDGE | Standing massive and graceful through the deep gorge that separates Spoleto from Monteluco, this 14th-century bridge is one of Umbria's most photographed monuments, and justifiably so. Built over the foundations of a Roman-era aqueduct, it soars 262 feet above the forested gorge—higher than the dome

of St. Peter's in Rome. Though you can't walk across the bridge as it's being repaired due to earthquake damage, it's still a must-see, particularly on a starry night. ✉ *Via del Ponte, Spoleto* 🖥 *Free.*

Teatro Romano

RUINS | FAMILY | The Romans who colonized the city in 241 BC constructed this small theater in the 1st century AD; for centuries afterward it was used as a quarry for building materials. The most intact portion is the hallway that passes under the *cavea* (stands). The rest was heavily restored in the early 1950s and serves as a venue for Spoleto's Festival dei Due Mondi. The theater was the site of a gruesome episode in Spoleto's history: during the medieval struggle between Guelph (papal) and Ghibelline (imperial) forces, Spoleto took the side of the Holy Roman Emperor. Afterward, 400 Guelph supporters were massacred in the theater, their bodies burned in an enormous pyre. In the end, the Guelphs were triumphant, and Spoleto was incorporated into the states of the Church in 1354. Through a door in the west portico of the adjoining building is the Museo Archeologico, with assorted artifacts found in excavations primarily around Spoleto and Norcia. The collection contains Bronze Age and Iron Age artifacts from Umbrian and pre-Roman eras. The highlight is the stone tablet inscribed on both sides with the Lex Spoletina (Spoleto Law). Dating from 315 BC, this legal document prohibited the desecration of the woods on the slopes of nearby Monteluco. ✉ *Piazza della Libertà, Spoleto* ☎ *0743/223277* ⊕ *www.spoletocard.it* 🖥 *€4, included with Spoleto Card* 🕙 *Closed Mon. and Tues.*

 Restaurants

Il Tartufo

$$ | UMBRIAN | As the name indicates, dishes prepared with truffles are the specialty here—don't miss the risotto al tartufo. Incorporating the ruins of a

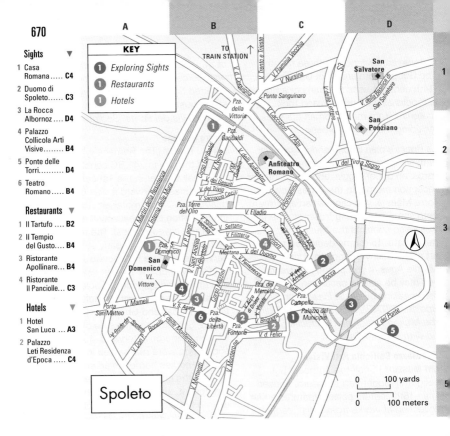

Roman villa, the surroundings are rustic on the ground floor and more modern upstairs; in summer, tables appear outdoors, and the traditional fare is spiced up to appeal to the cosmopolitan crowd attending (or performing in) the Festival dei Due Mondi. **Known for:** abundant portions, well presented; charming staff; recipes incorporating truffles. $ *Average main:* €18 ⊠ *Piazza Garibaldi 24, Spoleto* ☎ *0743/40236* ⊕ *www.ristoranteiltartufo. it* ⊗ *Closed Mon. and early Jan.–early Feb. No dinner Sun.*

Il Tempio del Gusto

$$ | UMBRIAN | In charming shabby-chic environs, this welcoming eatery near the Arco di Druso (ancient Roman arch) serves up Italian with a subtle twist. Along with an extensive selection of thoughtfully chosen Umbrian wines, you'll find lots of veggie options, mounds

of truffles in season, and, to finish things off, a superlative version of Spoleto sponge cake. **Known for:** quaint setting; friendly atmosphere; flavorful Umbrian cuisine. $ *Average main:* €16 ⊠ *Via Arco di Druso 11, Spoleto* ☎ *0743/47121* ⊕ *www.iltempiodelgusto.com* ⊗ *Closed Thurs.*

★ Ristorante Apollinare

$$ | UMBRIAN | Low wooden ceilings and flickering candlelight make this monastery from the 10th and 11th centuries Spoleto's most romantic spot; in warm weather, you can dine under a canopy on the piazza. The kitchen serves sophisticated, innovative variations on local dishes, including long, slender strengozzi pasta with such toppings as cherry tomatoes, mint, and a touch of red pepper or (in season) porcini mushrooms or truffles. **Known for:** impeccable service; intimate and elegant setting; modern versions of traditional Umbrian dishes. $ *Average main: €22* ✉ *Via Sant'Agata 14, Spoleto* ☎ *0743/223256* ⊕ *www.ristoranteapollinare.it* ⊗ *Closed Tues.*

Ristorante Il Panciolle

$ | UMBRIAN | A small garden filled with lemon trees in the heart of Spoleto's medieval quarter provides one of the most appealing settings you could wish for. Dishes, which change throughout the year, might include pastas served with asparagus or mushrooms, as well as grilled meats; more expensive dishes prepared with fresh truffles are also available in season. **Known for:** panoramic terrace; affable staff; authentic local cuisine. $ *Average main: €14* ✉ *Via del Duomo 3/5, Spoleto* ☎ *0743/45677* ⊕ *www.ilpanciolle.it* ⊗ *Closed Wed. Sept.–Mar.*

 Hotels

★ Hotel San Luca

$ | HOTEL | Hand-painted friezes decorate the walls of the spacious guest rooms, and elegant comfort is the grace note throughout—you can sip afternoon tea in oversize armchairs by the fireplace or take a walk in the sweet-smelling rose garden. **Pros:** very helpful staff; close to escalators for exploring city; spacious rooms. **Cons:** can feel soulless in winter; restaurant only open for groups; outside the town center. $ *Rooms from: €104* ✉ *Via Interna delle Mura 21, Spoleto* ☎ *0743/223399* ⊕ *www.hotelsanluca.com* ⇌ *35 rooms* ¶⊙¶ *Free Breakfast.*

★ Palazzo Leti Residenza d'Epoca

$ | HOTEL | Fabulously landscaped gardens, complete with fountains and sculptures, along with panoramic views provide a grand entrance to this late-13th-century residence turned charming hotel high up in Spoleto's old town. **Pros:** feels like a private hideaway; friendly owners happy to help; unbeatable views. **Cons:** few amenities (no restaurant, gym, or spa); often booked

far in advance; reaching on-site parking can be tricky. $ *Rooms from: €120* ✉ *Via degli Eremiti 10, Spoleto* ☎ *0743/224930* ⊕ *www.palazzoleti.com* ⇌ *12 rooms* ¶⊙¶ *Free Breakfast.*

The Valnerina

The Valnerina is 27 km (17 miles) southeast of Spoleto.

The Valnerina (the valley of the River Nera, to the southeast of Spoleto) is the most beautiful of central Italy's many well-kept secrets. The twisting roads that serve the rugged landscape are poor, but the drive is well worth the effort for its forgotten medieval villages and dramatic mountain scenery.

GETTING HERE AND AROUND

You can head into the area from Terni on the S209, or on the SP395 bis north of Spoleto, which links the Via Flaminia (SS3) with the middle reaches of the Nera Valley through a tunnel.

 Sights

Cascata delle Marmore

WATERFALL | FAMILY | The road east of Terni (SS3 Valnerina) leads 10 km (6 miles) to the Cascata delle Marmore (Waterfalls of Marmore), which, at 541 feet, are the highest in Europe. A canal was dug by the Romans in the 3rd century BC to prevent flooding in the nearby agricultural plains. Nowadays, the waters are often diverted to provide hydroelectric power for Terni, reducing the roaring falls to an unimpressive trickle, so check with the information office at the falls (there's a timetable on its website) or with Terni's tourist office before heading here.

On summer evenings, when the falls are in full spate, the cascading water is floodlit to striking effect. The falls are usually at their most energetic at midday and at around 4 pm. This is a good place for hiking, except in December and

Hiking the Umbrian Hills

Magnificent scenery makes the heart of Italy excellent walking, hiking, and mountaineering country. In Umbria, the area around Spoleto is particularly good; several pleasant, easy, and well-signed trails begin at the far end of the Ponte alle Torri bridge over Monteluco. From Cannara, an easy half-hour walk leads to the fields of Pian d'Arca, the site of St. Francis's sermon to the birds.

For slightly more arduous walks, follow the saint's path uphill from Assisi to the Eremo delle Carceri, and then continue along the trails that crisscross Monte Subasio. At 4,250 feet, the treeless summit affords views of Assisi, Perugia, far-off Gubbio, and the distant mountain ranges of Abruzzo. For even more challenging hiking, the northern reaches of the Valnerina are exceptional; the mountains around Norcia should not be missed.

Throughout Umbria and the Marches, most recognized trails are marked with the distinctive red-and-white blazes of the Club Alpino Italiano. Tourist offices are a good source for walking and climbing itineraries to suit all ages and levels of ability, and bookstores, *tabacchi* (tobacconists), and *edicole* (newsstands) often have maps and guides that detail the best area routes. Wear comfortable walking shoes or hiking boots, depending on your route, and bring plenty of water.

January, when most trails may be closed. ✉ *SP79, Terni* ✣ *10 km (6 miles) east of Terni* ☎ *0744/67561* 🌐 *www.cascatadellemarmore.info* 🎫 *€10.*

Norcia

TOWN | The birthplace of St. Benedict, Norcia is best known for its Umbrian pork and truffles, which you can sample at shops throughout town. Norcia exports truffles to France and hosts a truffle festival, Nero Norcia, every February. Though the town itself is still under reconstruction following a devastating 2016 earthquake, the surrounding mountains provide spectacular hiking. ✣ *42 km (25 miles) east of Spoleto, 67 km (42 miles) northeast of Terni.*

★ Piano Grande

VIEWPOINT | A spectacular mountain plain 25 km (15 miles) to the northeast of the valley, Piano Grande is a hang glider's paradise and a wonderful place for a picnic or to fly a kite. It's also nationally famous for the quality of the lentils grown here, which are a traditional part of every Italian New Year's feast. ✉ *Teramo* 🎫 *Free*

Hotels

★ Palazzo Seneca

$$ | **HOTEL** | The Bianconi family oversees this elegant hotel, which is housed in a 16th-century palace—just around the corner from Norcia's main square—and features stone floors, vaulted ceilings, and a Michelin-star restaurant. **Pros:** lots of style and charm; central location; fabulous restaurant (book well in advance). **Cons:** no parking at the hotel; breakfast not up to par; no gym. [$] *Rooms from: €178* ✉ *Via Cesare Battisti 12, Norcia* ☎ *0743/817434* 🌐 *www.palazzoseneca.com* 🛏 *24 rooms* 🍴 *Free Breakfast.*

Todi

34 km (22 miles) south of Perugia, 34 km (22 miles) northeast of Orvieto, 46 km (29 miles) northwest of Spoleto.

As you stand on Piazza del Popolo, looking out onto the Tiber Valley below, it's easy to see why Todi is often described as Umbria's prettiest hill town. Legend has it that the town was founded by the Umbri, who followed an eagle who had stolen a tablecloth. They liked this lofty perch so much that they settled here for good. The eagle is now perched on the insignia of the medieval palaces in the main piazza.

GETTING HERE AND AROUND

Todi is best reached by car, as the town's two train stations are way down the hill and connected to the center by infrequent bus service. From Perugia, follow the E45 toward Rome. Take the Todi/Orvieto exit, then follow the SS79 bis into Todi. The drive takes around 40 minutes.

VISITOR INFORMATION

CONTACT Todi Tourism Office. ✉ *Piazza del Popolo 29–30,* ☎ *0758/895–6227* ⊕ *www.visitodi.eu.*

 Sights

Duomo di Todi (*Todi Cathedral*)

CHURCH | One end of the Piazza del Popolo is dominated by this 12th-century Romanesque-Gothic masterpiece, built over the site of a Roman temple. The simple facade is enlivened by a finely carved rose window. Look up at that window as you step inside and you'll notice its peculiarity: each "petal" of the rose has a cherub's face in the stained glass. Also take a close look at the capitals of the double columns with pilasters: perched between the acanthus leaves are charming medieval sculptures of saints—Peter with his keys, George and the dragon, and so on. You can see the rich brown tones of the wooden

choir near the altar, but unless you have binoculars or request special permission in advance, you can't get close enough to see all the exquisite detail in this Renaissance masterpiece of woodworking (1521–30). The severe, solid mass of the Duomo is mirrored by the Palazzo dei Priori (1595–97) across the way. ✉ *Piazza del Popolo 1, Todi* ☎ *0335/5420520* ⊕ *www.chiesaditodi.it* ⊠ *Free.*

Piazza del Popolo

PLAZA/SQUARE | Built above the Roman Forum, Piazza del Popolo is Todi's high point, a model of spatial harmony with stunning views onto the surrounding countryside. In the best medieval tradition, the square was conceived to house both the temporal and the spiritual centers of power. ✉ *Todi* ⊠ *Free.*

 **Restaurants**

★ Pane & Vino

$$ | ITALIAN | This charmingly rustic restaurant in Todi's historic center specializes in "dishes of the past" made from local ingredients. Choose from a fine selection of meat and cheese antipasti, house-made pastas and soups, and hearty meat dishes—accompanied by truffles in season—along with tempting daily specials, served with well-priced wines from a comprehensive list. **Known for:** focus on organic products from small producers; friendly, knowledgeable service; fabulous selection of wines from across Italy. $ *Average main: €16* ✉ *Via Augusto Ciuffelli 33, Todi* ☎ *075/8945448* ⊕ *panevinotodi.com* ⊗ *Closed Wed.*

Ristorante Umbria

$$ | UMBRIAN | Todi's most popular restaurant for more than four decades is reliable for its sturdy country food and the wonderful view from its terrace; because it has only 16 tables outside, make sure you reserve ahead. In winter, try lentil soup, risotto with saffron and porcini mushrooms, or wild boar with polenta; steaks, accompanied by a rich dark-brown wine sauce, are good any time of year. **Known for:** friendly atmosphere; terrific vista from terrace; traditional Umbrian dishes. [$] *Average main: €15* ✉ *Via San Bonaventura 13, Todi* ☎ *075/8942737* 🌐 *www.ristoranteumbria.it* 🕓 *Closed Tues. and 3–4 wks in Jan. and Feb.*

Hotels

★ Relais Todini
$$$ | **HOTEL** | Inside a 14th-century manor house 9 km (6 miles) southeast of Todi, this elegant hotel sits adjacent to working vineyards (don't forget to sample the Todini wines) and features such welcome amenities as a spa, outdoor pool, and gym. **Pros:** quiet location; walking paths around the grounds; lots of relaxing public spaces, including a spa. **Cons:** reception not staffed 24/7; priced on the high side; decor feels a bit worn. [$] *Rooms from: €210* ✉ *Frazione Collevalenza, Todi* ☎ *075/887521* 🌐 *www.relaistodini.com* 🕓 *Closed weekdays Nov.–Mar.* 🛏 *12 rooms* 🍴 *Free Breakfast.*

Residenza D'Epoca San Lorenzo Tre
$ | **HOTEL** | Magnificent valley views are paired with 19th-century charm at this property filled with paintings, antique furnishings, and period knickknacks. **Pros:** old-world atmosphere; spectacular views; excellent central location. **Cons:** small, basic bathrooms; long flight of steps to enter; few modern amenities. [$] *Rooms from: €105* ✉ *Via San Lorenzo 3, Todi* ☎ *075/8944555* 🌐 *www.sanlorenzo3.it* 🕓 *Closed Nov.–mid-Apr.* 🛏 *6 rooms* 🍴 *Free Breakfast.*

Orvieto

30 km (19 miles) southwest of Todi, 78 km (48 miles) southwest of Perugia, 81 km (51 miles) west of Spoleto.

Carved from an enormous plateau of volcanic rock high above a green valley, Orvieto has natural defenses that made the high walls seen in many Umbrian towns unnecessary. The Etruscans were the first to settle here, digging a honeycombed network of more than 1,200 wells and storage caves out of the soft stone.

The Romans attacked, sacked, and destroyed the city in 283 BC. Since then, it has grown up out of the rock into an enchanting maze of alleys and squares. Orvieto was solidly Guelph in the Middle Ages, and, for several hundred years, popes sought refuge in the city, at times needing protection from their enemies, at times seeking respite from the summer heat in Rome.

When painting his frescoes inside the Duomo, Luca Signorelli asked that part of his contract be paid in Orvietan wine, and he was neither the first nor the last to appreciate the region's popular white. In past times, the caves carved underneath the town were used to ferment the Trebbiano grapes used in making Orvieto Classico. Although local wine production has moved out to more traditional vineyards, you can still while away the afternoon with tastings at any number of shops in town.

GETTING HERE AND AROUND

Orvieto is well connected by train to Rome, Florence, and Perugia. It's also adjacent to the A1 autostrada that runs between Florence and Rome. Parking areas in the upper town tend to be crowded. A better idea is to follow the signs for the Campo Della Fiera parking lot, then take the escalators or elevator that carry people up the hill.

VISITOR INFORMATION

The Carta Orvieto Unica (single ticket) is expensive but a great deal if you want to visit everything. For €20 you get admission to nine museums and monuments, including the three major sights in town—Cappella di San Brizio (at the Duomo), Museo Etrusco Claudio Faina, and Orvieto Underground—along with entry to the Torre del Moro, with views of Orvieto, plus a bus and funicular pass. You can buy the card online or at any of the included museums.

CONTACT Orvieto Tourism Office. ✉ *Piazza del Duomo 24,* ☎ *0763/341772* 🌐 *www.liveorvieto.com.*

Sights

★ Duomo di Orvieto (*Orvieto Cathedral*)
CHURCH | Orvieto's stunning cathedral was built to commemorate the Miracle at Bolsena. In 1263, a young priest who questioned the miracle of transubstantiation (in which the Communion bread and wine become the flesh and blood of Christ) was saying Mass at nearby Lago di Bolsena. A wafer he had just blessed suddenly started to drip blood, staining the linen covering the altar. Thirty years later, construction began on a duomo in Orvieto to celebrate the miracle and house the stained altar cloth.

The cathedral's interior is rather vast and empty; the major works are in the transepts. To the left is the Cappella del Corporale, where the square linen cloth (*corporale*) is kept in a golden reliquary that's modeled on the cathedral and inlaid with enamel scenes of the miracle. In the right transept is the Cappella di San Brizio, which holds one of Italy's greatest fresco cycles, notable for its influence on Michelangelo's *Last Judgment*, as well as for the extraordinary beauty of the figuration. In these works, a few by Fra Angelico and most by Luca Signorelli, the damned fall to hell, demons breathe fire and blood, and Christians are martyred. The Museo dell'Opera dell Duomo next to the cathedral is worth a short visit to see its small collection of historical paintings and sculptures. ✉ *Piazza del Duomo, Orvieto* ☎ *0763/342477* 🌐 *www.opsm.it* 🎫 *€5, including Cappella di San Brizio and Museo dell'Opera dell Duomo; included with Carta Unica.*

Museo Etrusco Claudio Faina
HISTORY MUSEUM | This superb private collection, beautifully arranged and presented, goes far beyond the usual smattering of local remains displayed at many museums. The collection is particularly rich in Greek- and Etruscan-era pottery, from large Attic amphorae (6th–4th century BC) to Attic black- and red-figure pieces to Etruscan *bucchero* (dark-reddish clay) vases. Other interesting items include a 6th-century sarcophagus and a substantial display of Roman-era coins. ✉ *Piazza del Duomo 29, Orvieto* ☎ *0763/341216* 🌐 *museofaina.it* 🎫 *€6* ⏲ *Closed Tues.*

Orvieto Underground
RUINS | **FAMILY** | More than just about any other town, Orvieto has grown from its own foundations. The Etruscans, the Romans, and those who followed dug into the tufa (the same soft volcanic rock from which catacombs were made) to create more than 1,000 separate cisterns, caves, passages, storage areas, and production areas for wine and olive oil. Much of the tufa removed was used as building blocks for the city that exists today, and some was partly ground into pozzolana, which was made into mortar. You can see the labyrinth of dugout chambers beneath the city on the Orvieto Underground tour, which runs daily at 11, 12:15, 4, and 5:15 (more frequently in busy periods), departing from Piazza del Duomo 23. ✉ *Piazza del Duomo 23, Orvieto* ☎ *0763/340688* 🌐 *www.orvietounderground.it* 🎫 *Tours €7; included with Carta Unica.*

Pozzo della Cava
RUINS | If you're short on time but want a quick look at the cisterns and caves beneath the city, head for the Pozzo della Cava, an Etruscan well for spring water. On a walk through nine excavated caves you can see the fascinating ruins of medieval houses and unearthed archaeological artifacts. ✉ *Via della Cava 28, Orvieto* ☎ *0763/342373* 🌐 *www.pozzodellacava.it* 🎫 *€4; included with Carta Unica.*

Restaurants

Le Grotte del Funaro

$$ | **UMBRIAN** | Dine inside tufa caves under central Orvieto, where the two windows afford splendid views of the hilly countryside. The traditional Umbrian food is reliably good, with simple grilled meats and vegetables and pizzas—oddly, though, the food is outclassed by an extensive wine list, with top local and Italian labels and quite a few rare vintages. **Known for:** good choice of wines; crusty pizzas; unusual setting. $ *Average main: €16* ⊠ *Via Ripa Serancia 41, Orvieto* ☎ *0763/343276* ⊕ *www. grottedelfunaro.com* ⊗ *Closed Mon. and 10 days in July.*

Ristorante Maurizio

$$ | **UMBRIAN** | Off a busy pedestrian street near the Duomo, this welcoming, family-owned restaurant has an ultracontemporary look but is actually housed in a 14th-century medieval building with arched ceilings. The Martinelli family's own products, including balsamic vinegar, olive oil, and pasta, are used in their robustly flavored dishes, and you can also sample their well-regarded Montefalco wines. **Known for:** local wines; traditional Umbrian dishes; complimentary balsamic vinegar tasting to start. $ *Average main: €16* ⊠ *Via del Duomo 78, Orvieto* ☎ *0763/341114* ⊕ *www.ristorante-maurizio.com.*

Trattoria La Grotta

$ | **UMBRIAN** | The vaulted, plant-filled dining area—where white walls are adorned with paintings, antique vases, and other knickknacks—makes a congenial setting for this small, rustic-style trattoria, which is lauded for its homemade pasta, perhaps with an artichoke, duck, or wild-boar sauce. Roast lamb, veal, and pork are all also good, and the desserts are supplied by Orvieto's most eminent pasticceria. **Known for:** warm and welcoming service; fresh, local ingredients; tasty homemade pastas. $ *Average main: €14* ⊠ *Via Luca Signorelli 5, Orvieto* ☎ *0763/341348* ⊕ *www.trattorialagrottaorvieto.com* ⊗ *Closed Tues.*

 Hotels

Eremito

$$$$ | **ALL-INCLUSIVE** | For a more spiritual slant to your vacation, spend a night or two at this "modern monastery," where you'll sleep in a cell, eat vegetarian food by candlelight, practice yoga, and relax in a whirlpool tub. **Pros:** chance to meet other travelers; lovely scenery; truly getting away from it all. **Cons:** very simple accommodations (and no Wi-Fi); need a car to get there; on the pricey side. $ *Rooms from: €370* ⊠ *Località Tarina 2, Parrano* ⊹ *28 km (17 miles) north of Orvieto* ☎ *0763/891010* ⊕ *www.eremito. com* ⊠ *14 rooms* ⊙ *All-Inclusive.*

Hotel Palazzo Piccolomini

$ | **HOTEL** | This 16th-century family palazzo has been beautifully restored, with inviting public spaces and handsome guest quarters where contemporary surroundings are accented with old beams, vaulted ceilings, and other distinctive touches. **Pros:** private parking; good location; efficient staff. **Cons:** some rooms and bathrooms are small; four-star category not completely justified; underwhelming breakfasts. $ *Rooms from: €120* ⊠ *Piazza Ranieri 36, Orvieto* ☎ *0763/341743* ⊕ *www.palazzopiccolomini.it* ⊗ *Closed Jan. and Feb.* ⊠ *33 rooms* ⊙ *Free Breakfast.*

★ Locanda Palazzone

$$$ | **HOTEL** | Spending the night in this 13th-century building just 5 km (3 miles) northwest of Orvieto is like staying in a sophisticated country home, albeit one with vineyard views, a private chef, and two-level rooms with modern furnishings. **Pros:** tranquil surroundings; tasty meals served nightly; extremely friendly owners and staff. **Cons:** split-level rooms can be difficult for those with mobility issues or young children; limited public

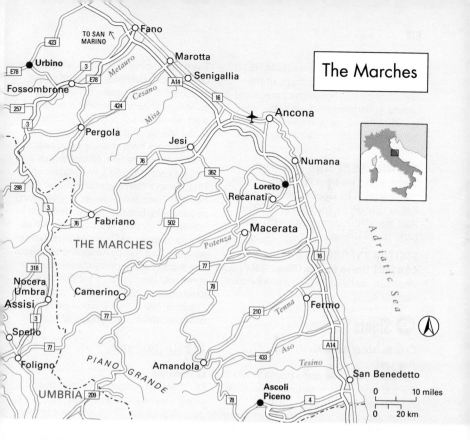

spaces to lounge in; no à la carte menus.
$ Rooms from: €239 ⊠ Località Rocca
Ripesena 68, Orvieto ☎ 0763/393614
⊕ www.locandapalazzone.it ⤳ 7 rooms
🍴 Free Breakfast.

Urbino

*230 km (143 miles) east of Florence, 116
km (72 miles) northeast of Perugia, 75
km (47 miles) north of Gubbio.*

Majestic Urbino, atop a steep hill with a
skyline of towers and domes, is something of a surprise to come upon. Though
quite remote, it was once a center of
learning and culture almost without
rival in western Europe. The town looks
much as it did in the glory days of the
15th century: a cluster of warm brick
and pale stone buildings, all topped with

russet-color tile roofs. The focal point
is the immense and beautiful Palazzo
Ducale.

The city is also home to the small but
prestigious Università di Urbino—one of
the oldest in the world—so its streets are
usually filled with students, and it has the
usual college town array of bookshops,
bars, and coffeehouses. In summer, the
Italian student population is replaced by
foreigners who come to study Italian
language and arts at several prestigious,
private, fine-arts academies.

Urbino's fame rests on the reputation of
three of its native sons: Duke Federico
da Montefeltro (1422–82), the enlightened warrior-patron who built the Palazzo
Ducale; Raffaello Sanzio (1483–1520),
or Raphael, one of the most influential
painters in history and an embodiment
of the spirit of the Renaissance; and the

architect Donato Bramante (1444–1514), who translated the philosophy of the Renaissance into buildings of grace and beauty. Unfortunately there's little work by either Bramante or Raphael in the city, but the duke's influence can still be felt strongly.

GETTING HERE AND AROUND

Take the SS3 bis from Perugia, and follow the directions for Gubbio and Cesena. Exit at Umbertide and take the SS219, then the SS452, and at Calmazzo, the SS73 bis to Urbino.

VISITOR INFORMATION

CONTACT Urbino Tourism Office. ✉ *Via Puccinotti 35,* ☎ *0722/2613* 🌐 *www.turismo.marche.it.*

👁 Sights

Casa Natale di Raffaello (*House of Raphael*)
HISTORIC HOME | This is the house in which the painter was born and where he took his first steps in painting, under the direction of his artist father. There's some debate about the fresco of the Madonna here; some say it's by Raphael, whereas others attribute it to the father—with Raphael's mother and the young painter himself standing in as models for the Madonna and Child. ✉ *Via Raffaello 57, Urbino* ☎ *0722/320105* 🌐 *www.casaraffaello.com* 🎫 *€4.*

★ Palazzo Ducale di Urbino (*Ducal Palace*)
ART MUSEUM | The Palazzo Ducale holds a place of honor in the city. If the Renaissance was, ideally, a celebration of the nobility of man and his works, of the light and purity of the soul, then there's no place in Italy, the birthplace of the Renaissance, where these tenets are better illustrated. From the moment you enter the peaceful courtyard, you know you're in a place of grace and beauty, and the harmony of the building indeed reflects the high ideals of the time. The palace houses the Galleria Nazionale delle Marche (National Museum of the Marches), with a superb collection of paintings, sculpture, and other objets d'art. Some pieces originally belonged to the Montefeltro family; others were brought here from churches and palaces throughout the region. Masterworks include Paolo Uccello's *Profanation of the Host,* Titian's *Resurrection* and *Last Supper,* and Piero della Francesca's *Madonna of Senigallia.* But the gallery's highlight is Piero's enigmatic work long known as *The Flagellation of Christ.* Much has been written about this painting, and although few experts agree on its meaning, most agree that this is one of the painter's masterpieces. ✉ *Piazza Rinascimento 13, Urbino* ☎ *0722/2760* 🌐 *www.gallerianazionalemarche.it* 🎫 *€8* 🕒 *Closed Mon.*

🍴 Restaurants

La Fornarina
$$ | **ITALIAN** | Locals often crowd this small, two-room trattoria near the Piazza della Repubblica. The specialty is meaty country fare, such as *coniglio* (rabbit) and *vitello alle noci* (veal cooked with walnuts) or *ai porcini* (with mushrooms); there's also a good selection of pasta dishes. **Known for:** hospitable staff; welcoming atmosphere; excellent starters. [$] *Average main: €18* ✉ *Via Mazzini 14, Urbino* ☎ *0722/320007.*

★ Osteria Angolo Divino
$$ | **ITALIAN** | Chef Tiziano Rossetti helms this long-standing restaurant in the center of Urbino, where tradition still reigns supreme. Elegant versions of regional dishes feature lots of local ingredients, including truffles, forest mushrooms, game, and pork, along with a wine list focused on small producers from the Marche. **Known for:** traditional osteria-style decor; quality cuisine with experimental elements; calm and pleasant ambience. [$] *Average*

main: €23 ✉ Via S. Andrea 14, Urbino ☎ 0722/327559 🌐 www.tizianorossetti.com/osterialangolodivino ⏲ Closed Wed. No lunch Thurs.

Hotels

Hotel Bonconte

$ | HOTEL | Just inside the city walls and close to the Palazzo Ducale, this hotel has pleasant, if worn, rooms decorated with a smattering of antiques; those in front also have views of the valley below Urbino. **Pros:** pleasant views; good breakfast; central but away from the bustle. **Cons:** rooms and public spaces getting a bit shabby; some rooms are cramped; an uphill walk to town center. [$] *Rooms from: €110 ✉ Via delle Mura 28, Urbino ☎ 0722/2463 🌐 www.viphotels.it 🛏 23 rooms 🍴 No Meals.*

Loreto

150 km (93 miles) northeast of Perugia, 121 km (75 miles) southeast of Urbino.

There's a strong Renaissance feel to this hilltop town, which is home to one of the most important religious sites in Europe, the Santuario della Santa Casa (House of the Virgin Mary). Bramante and Sansovino gave the church its Renaissance look, although many other artists helped create its special atmosphere.

Today, the town revolves around the religious calendar. If you can be here on December 10, you will witness the Feast of the Translation of the Holy House, when huge bonfires are lighted to celebrate the miraculous arrival of the house in 1295.

GETTING HERE AND AROUND

If you're driving from Perugia, take the SS318 and then the SS76 highway to Fabriano and then on to Chiaravalle, where it merges with the A14 autostrada. The drive takes around two hours. Trains also go to Loreto, but the station is about a mile outside the town center. Regular buses leave from the station to the center.

VISITOR INFORMATION

CONTACT Loreto Tourism Office. ✉ *Via Solari 3,* ☎ *071/970276* 🌐 *www.turismo.marche.it.*

Sights

★ **Basilica della Santa Casa**

CHURCH | Loreto is famous for one of the best-loved shrines in the world: the Santuario della Santa Casa (House of the Virgin Mary), within the Basilica della Santa Casa. Legend has it that angels moved the house from Nazareth, where the Virgin Mary was living at the time of the Annunciation, to this hilltop in 1295. The reason for this sudden and divinely inspired move was that Nazareth had fallen into the hands of Muslim invaders, who the angelic hosts viewed as unsuitable keepers of this important shrine.

The house itself consists of three rough stone walls contained within an elaborate marble tabernacle. Built around this centerpiece is the giant Basilica of the Holy House, which dominates the town. Millions of pilgrims come to the site every year (particularly at Easter and on the December 10 Feast of the Holy House), and the little town of Loreto can become uncomfortably crowded.

Many great Italian architects—including Bramante, Antonio da Sangallo the Younger (1483–1546), Giuliano da Sangallo (circa 1445–1516), and Sansovino (1467–1529)—contributed to the design of the basilica. It was begun in the Gothic style in 1468 and continued in Renaissance style through the late Renaissance. ✉ *Piazza della Madonna 1, Loreto* ☎ *071/9747155* 🌐 *www.santuarioloreto.it* 🎟 *Free.*

Ascoli Piceno

156 km (97 miles) southeast of Perugia, 88 km (55 miles) south of Loreto.

Ascoli Piceno sits in a valley ringed by steep hills and cut by the Tronto River. In Roman times, it was one of central Italy's best-known market towns. Today, with almost 52,000 residents, it's a major fruit and olive producer, making it one of the most important towns in the region.

Despite growth during the Middle Ages and at other times, the streets in the town center continue to reflect the grid pattern of the ancient Roman city. You'll even find the word *rua,* from the Latin *ruga,* used for "street" instead of the Italian *via.* Now largely closed to traffic, the city center is great to explore on foot.

GETTING HERE AND AROUND

From Perugia, take the SS75 to Foligno, then merge onto the SS3 to Norcia. From here, take the SS4 to Ascoli Piceno. There are also trains, but the journey would be quite long, taking you from Perugia to Ancona, 105 km (65 miles) to the north, before changing for Ascoli Piceno.

VISITOR INFORMATION

CONTACT Ascoli Piceno Tourism Office. ✉ *Piazza Aringo 7,* ☎ *0736/298916* 🌐 *www.visitascoli.it.*

Sights

Piazza del Popolo

PLAZA/SQUARE | The heart of the town is the majestic Piazza del Popolo, dominated by the Gothic church of San Francesco and the Palazzo del Popolo, a 13th-century town hall that contains a graceful Renaissance courtyard. The square functions as the living room of the entire city and at dusk each evening is packed with people strolling and exchanging news and gossip—the sweetly antiquated ritual called a passeggiata—performed all over the country. ✉ *Ascoli Piceno* 🎟 *Free.*

Hotels

Hotel Pennile

$ | **HOTEL** | This modern, affordable, family-run hotel in a quiet residential area outside the old city center is pleasantly set amid a grove of olive trees. **Pros:** peaceful environment; easy parking; a good budget option. **Cons:** can hear some noise from other rooms; no restaurant; distance from town center. [$] *Rooms from: €75* ✉ *Via G. Spalvieri 13/A, Ascoli Piceno* ☎ *0736/41645* 🌐 *www.hotelpennile.it* 🛏 *33 rooms* 🍴 *Free Breakfast.*

Chapter 15

NAPLES AND CAMPANIA

Updated by
Nick Bruno and Fergal Kavanagh

15

⊙ **Sights**
★★★★★

🍴 **Restaurants**
★★★★★

🛏 **Hotels**
★★★★☆

🛍 **Shopping**
★★★★☆

🍸 **Nightlife**
★★★★☆

WELCOME TO NAPLES AND CAMPANIA

TOP REASONS TO GO

★ **Naples, Italy's most operatic city:** Walk through the energy, chaos, and beauty that is Spaccanapoli, the city's historic artery, and you'll create an unforgettable memory.

★ **Pompeii:** The excavated ruins of Pompeii offer a unique, occasionally spooky glimpse into everyday life—and sudden death—in Roman times.

★ **"The Living Room of the World":** Pose oh-so-casually with the beautiful people on La Piazzetta, the central crossroads of the island of Capri—a stage-set square that always seems ready for a gala performance.

★ **Ravello:** High above the famously blue Bay of Salerno, this Amalfi Coast charmer is a contender for the title of "most beautiful village in the world."

★ **Positano, a world made of stairs:** Built like a vertical amphitheater, Positano's only job is to look enchanting on the Amalfi Coast—and it does that very well.

1 **Naples.** Italy's third-largest city is lush, chaotic, friendly, amusing, confounding, and very beautiful.

2 **Herculaneum.** The famous archaeological site was once a wealthy seaside resort.

3 **Pompeii.** The most famous dig of all—the one that arguably kick-started archaeological studies—is Pompeii.

4 **Vesuvius.** Dominating the skyline southeast of Naples is the destructive Vesuvius caldera.

5 **Oplontis.** Fascinating lesser-known ruins.

6 **Ischia.** More than twice the size of Capri, lesser-known Ischia has volcanic-sand beaches, thermal hot-spring spas, and fewer day-trippers.

7 **Procida.** Sun, cliffs, and sea combine to create the distinctive atmosphere so memorably immortalized in the film *Il Postino*.

8 **Capri.** The rocky island mixes natural beauty and dolce vita glamour.

9 **Sorrento.** Perched over the Bay of Naples with an incomparable view of Mt. Vesuvius, this Belle Époque resort town is sheer delight.

10 **Positano.** The ultimate pastel-brushed, tumbling-to-the-seaside village moves between sophisticated-luxe, beachcomber casual, and selfie-reverential posing.

11 **Conca Dei Marini.** Put on the map by 1960s jet-setters, this tiny but exceedingly picturesque harbor hideaway rubs shoulders with the luminous Emerald Grotto.

12 **Amalfi.** This buzzy resort is threaded with beguiling, rambling passages, testimony to its Norman and Arab-Sicilian past. The glory of the city's days as a medieval maritime republic is most evident in its fantastic cathedral.

13 **Ravello.** Just beyond the Valley of the Dragon lies Ravello, perched "closer to the sky than the sea" atop Monte Cereto and set over the breathtaking Bay of Salerno. Ravello is one of Italy's most beautiful towns.

14 **Paestum.** With its Greek temples and Roman ruins in flowery meadows, this vision of a lost city makes a rousing finale to any Grand Tour.

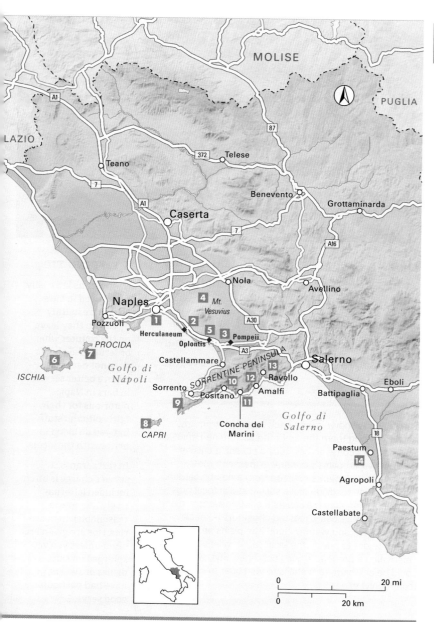

EATING AND DRINKING WELL IN NAPLES AND CAMPANIA

Think of Neapolitan food and you conjure up images of pasta, pizza, and tomatoes. The stereotype barely scratches the surface of what's available in Naples—to say nothing of the rest of Campania, where the cuisine reflects an enormously diverse landscape.

The region is known for its enclaves of gastronomy, notable among them the tip of the Sorrentine Peninsula. You may well come across *cucina povera*, a cuisine inspired by Campania's *contadino* (peasant) roots, with all the ingredients sourced from a nearby garden. Expect to see roadside stalls selling stellar local produce, including *annurca* apples (near Benevento), giant lemons (Amalfi Coast), roasted chestnuts (especially near Avellino), and watermelons (the plains around Salerno). Try to get to one of the local *sagre*, village feasts celebrating a *prodotto tipico* (local specialty), which could be anything from snails to wild boar to cherries to (commonly) wine.

A TIPPING TIP

Neapolitans are easily recognized in bars elsewhere in Italy by the tip they leave on the counter when ordering. This habit does not necessarily ensure better service in bars in Naples, notorious for their fairly offhand staff, but you do blend in better with the locals.

In restaurants, a service charge is often included (alternatively, 5%–10% is reasonable). In pizzerias, tips are given less often unless you've splurged on side dishes or sweets, or have had particularly good service.

PIZZA

Naples is the undisputed homeland of pizza, and you'll usually encounter it here in two classic forms: *margherita* and *marinara*. Given the larger-than-your-plate portions of standard pizzas, some choose to ask for a *mignon* (kids' portion), or even to share, divided between two plates. Take-away outlets in most town centers sell pizza by the slice, along with the usual range of fried *arancini* (rice balls) and *crocchè di patate* (potato fritters).

COFFEE

Given the same basic ingredients—coffee grounds, water, a machine—what makes *caffè* taste so much better in Naples than elsewhere remains a mystery. If you find the end product too strong, ask to have it with a dash of milk (caffè *macchiato*) or a little diluted (caffè *lungo*). Many bars serve with sugar already added, so if you want it without, request *senza zucchero* or *amaro*.

BUFFALO

Long feted for the melt-in-your-mouth mozzarella cheese made from its milk (pictured below), the river buffalo is also the source of other culinary delights. Throughout the region, look for buffalo ricotta and mascarpone, as well as buffalo *provola* and *scamorza*, which may be lightly smoked (resulting in a golden crust). Caserta has more mature *nero di bufala* (aged like sheep's cheese), while around Salerno you'll find smoked *caciocavallo* cheese as well as *carne di bufala* (buffalo meat).

THE ORAL TRADITION

Locals in Campania like to bypass the restaurant menu and ask what the staff recommend. Take this approach and you'll often wind up with a daily special or the house specialty. Although you're unlikely to get multilingual staff outside the larger hotels and main tourist areas, the person you talk to will spare no effort to get the message across.

WINE

Wine in Campania has an ancient pedigree. Some say fancifully that Campania's undisputed king of reds, the *aglianico*, got its name from the word "Hellenic"; and *fiano*, the primary white grape, closely resembles the Roman variety *apianus*. Horace, the Latin poet, extolled the virtues of drinking wine from Campania. A century later, Pliny the Elder was harsher in his judgment.

In recent decades, though, Campania has gained respect for its boutique reds. Due to the rugged landscape, small farms, and limited mechanization, prices can be relatively high, but the quality is high as well.

A region of evocative names—Capri, Sorrento, Pompeii, Positano, Amalfi—Campania conjures up visions of cliff-shaded, sapphire-hue coves, sun-dappled waters, and mighty ruins. More travelers visit this corner than any other in southern Italy, and it's no wonder.

Home to Vesuvius, the area's unique geology is responsible for Campania's photogenic landscape. A spectacular coastline stretches out along a deep blue sea, punctuated by rocky islands.

Through the ages, the area's temperate climate, warm sea, fertile soil, and natural beauty have attracted Greek colonists, then Roman emperors—who called the region "Campania Felix," or "the happy land"—and later Saracen raiders and Spanish invaders. The result has been a rich and varied history, reflected in everything from architecture to mythology. The highlights span millennia: the near-intact Roman towns of Pompeii and Herculaneum, the Greek temples in Paestum, the Norman and Baroque churches in Naples, the white-dome fisherman's houses of Positano, the dolce vita resorts of Capri. Campania piles them all onto one mammoth must-see sandwich.

The region's complex identity is most intensely felt in its major metropolis, Naples. Few who visit remain ambivalent. You needn't participate in the mad whirl of the city, however. The best pastime in Campania is simply finding a spot with a stunning view and indulging in *il dolce far niente* ("the sweetness of doing nothing").

MAJOR REGIONS

Volcanic ash and mud preserved the Roman towns of **Herculaneum** and **Pompeii** almost exactly as they were on the day **Mt. Vesuvius** erupted in AD 79, leaving them not just archaeological ruins but museums of daily life in the ancient world. The two cities and the volcano that buried them can be visited from either Naples or Sorrento, thanks to the Circumvesuviana, the suburban railroad that provides fast, frequent, and economical service.

Capri may get star billing among the islands that line the Bay of Naples, but **Ischia** and **Procida** also have their own lower-key appeal. Once entirely dependent on its thermal springs, Ischia is now the archaeological front-runner in the bay, thanks to the noted museum in Lacco Ameno. Procida has opened up to tourism, sparking rejuvenation through culture as *Capitale Italiana della Cultura 2022*, while opening access to its chief natural asset, the unspoiled isle of Vivara.

As the hub for a whole banquet of must-see sites—Pompeii and Naples to the north, Capri to the west, and the Amalfi Coast to the south—the beautiful, Belle Époque resort town of **Sorrento** is unequaled. The rest of the Sorrentine Peninsula, with plains and limestone outcroppings, watchtowers and Roman ruins, groves and beaches, monasteries and villages, winding paths leading to isolated coves, and panoramic views of the bays of both Naples and Salerno, remains relatively undiscovered.

One of the most gorgeous places on Earth is the corner of the Campania region called the Amalfi Coast. The justly famed jewels along the water are **Positano**, **Amalfi**, and **Ravello**. Considering the natural splendor of this region, it's no surprise that it has some of the most beautiful beaches in the world. White, sunbaked villages rise above cliffs hollowed out with grottoes and crystal lagoons lapped by emerald green water. Larger beaches, like those in Positano and Amalfi, are easily accessible, but the magic often lies in finding hidden coves and scenic spots, such as the picture-perfect Marina di Praia.

Planning

Making the Most of Your Time

In Campania there are three primary travel experiences: Naples, with its restless exuberance; the resorts (Capri, Sorrento, the Amalfi Coast), dedicated to leisure and indulgence; and the archaeological sites (Pompeii, Herculaneum, Paestum), where the ancient world is frozen in time. Each is wonderful in its own way. If you have a week, you can get a good taste of all three. With less time, you're better off choosing between them rather than stretching yourself thin.

Pompeii, being a day trip, is the simplest to plan for. To get a feel for Naples, you should give it a couple of days at a minimum. The train station makes a harsh first impression (an overhaul has softened the blow), but the city grows on

you as you take in the sights and interact with the locals.

That said, many people bypass Naples and head right for the resorts. These places are all about relaxing—you'll miss the point if you're in a rush. Although Sorrento isn't as spectacular as Positano or Capri, it makes a good base because of its central location.

DISCOUNTS AND DEALS
Government-run sites are free on the first Sunday of each month—good for those on a budget, but less so for avoiding crowds. The **Campania ArteCard** with app entitles users to free or discounted admission to about four dozen museums and monuments in Naples and beyond. These are the main passes: Naples, three days (€21), has two sights included and up to 50% off the rest, plus transportation; Campania region, three days (€32), including Pompeii and other Bay of Naples sights and Ravello and Paestum with two sights included and others up to 50% off, plus transportation; Campania region, seven days (€34), with five sights included and many others up to 50% off, but no transportation. For longer stays the new 365 Gold Pass allows two entries to principle attractions and up to 50% off entry to others over an entire year (€43). Other benefits (which vary depending on the pass) include discounts on audio guides, theater and ferry tickets, city tours, and other activities. Visitors aged 18–25 receive generous discounts (10 free admissions) with the three-day Napoli Young card (€12) and 365 Gold Pass Young (€33) for entry to the ArteCard circuit sights over a year.

Confusingly, in 2019 the e-commerce-driven **Naples Pass** (app only) was introduced in conjunction with ArteCard. It includes some free sights, tours and transport (except the Lite), adding discounts. A warning: the poorly written, biased guide nudges the user to use certain affiliated businesses. It's pricey too: the cheapest three-day option

Naples Pass Lite is €49 while the seven-day Whole Campania is €88. For more information, visit the ⊕ *www.campaniartecard.it* and ⊕ *www.naplespass.eu,* or the tourist office in the Piazza Garibaldi station, which distributes a helpful booklet about the various passes.

Getting Here and Around

BOAT

Several companies offer a variety of fast craft and passenger and car ferries connecting the islands of Capri, Ischia, and Procida with Naples and Pozzuoli year-round. Hydrofoils and other fast craft leave from Naples's Molo Beverello, adjacent to Piazza Municipio, with some departures in high season also from Mergellina, about 1½ km (1 mile) west of Piazza Municipio. Slower car ferries leave from the berths at Calata Porta di Massa, a 10-minute walk, or three-minute shuttle bus ride, east of Molo Beverello.

Information on departures is published every day in the local paper, *Il Mattino.* Alternatively, ask at the tourist office or at the port, check websites, or contact these companies directly. Always double-check schedules in stormy weather.

BOAT CONTACTS Caremar.
☎ *081/18966690* ⊕ *www.caremar. it.* **Navigazione Libera del Golfo.** (*NLG*) ☎ *081/8071812 Sorrento office, 081/5520763 Naples Port office* ⊕ *www. navlib.it.* **SNAV.** ☎ *081/4285555* ⊕ *www. snav.it.*

BUS

Within Campania there's an extensive network of local buses, although finding information about it can be trying.

BUS CONTACT SITA Buses.
☎ *342/6256442* ⊕ *www.sitasudtrasporti. it.*

CAR

You can get along fine without a car in Campania, and there are plenty of reasons not to have one. Much of Naples is pedestrianized, meaning motorized arteries are often bottlenecked; you can't bring a car to Capri (except in winter, when everything's closed); and parking in the towns of the Amalfi Coast is hard to come by and expensive.

Italy's main north–south route, the A1 (aka the Autostrada del Sole), connects Rome with Naples and Campania. In good traffic the drive to Naples from Rome takes a little more than two hours. The A3 autostrada, a somewhat perilous continuation of the A1, runs south from Naples through Campania and into Calabria. Herculaneum (Ercolano) and Pompeii (Pompei) both have marked exits off the A3. For Vesuvius, take the Portici Ercolano exit. For the Sorrento Peninsula and the Amalfi Coast, exit at Castellammare di Stabia. To get to Paestum, take the A3 to the Battipaglia exit, and follow the road to Capaccio Scalo–Paestum. Roads on the Sorrento Peninsula and Amalfi Coast are narrow and twisting, but they have outstanding views.

If you come to Naples by car, find a garage, agree on the rate, and leave it there for the duration of your stay. (If you park on the street, you run the risk of theft.)

NAPLES GARAGE CONTACTS Petraglia. ✉ *Via Ferraris 42, Piazza Garibaldi* ☎ *081/3602840* ⊕ *www.garagepetraglia. it* Ⓜ *Garibaldi.*

TAXI

You may be able to hail a taxi if you see one driving, but your best bet is to call Radio Taxi or ask someone at your hotel to book one. Taxi ranks can be found outside the central Piazza Garibaldi train station and the port (Molo Beverello), as well as throughout the city. Watch out for overcharging at three locations: the airport, the railway station, and the hydrofoil marina. The fixed rate (be sure to ask for *tariffa predeterminata*!) from the airport to the central station is €18, which covers three people, two large pieces of luggage, and two small pieces. City Airport Taxis offers a private service.

Ask for *il tariffario*, the tariff information sheet of the Comune di Napoli with common fixed-rate journeys when taking a taxi, as drivers may invent an exorbitant price, even hiding the tariff sheet—trips around the city should cost €8–€10. You can of course request that the meter is switched on; this often results in your paying less. Taxis charge approximately €3.50 initially (more on Sunday, holidays, and after 10 pm), then €0.05 per 48 meters (or 8 seconds of idling). A copy of the latest tariff sheet can be downloaded at ⊕ *www.comune.napoli. it/taxi*. Other options besides Radio Taxi include Consorttaxi (☎ *081/2222*), La Partenope (☎ *081/0101*), and La 570 (☎ *081/5707070*). In summer, many cabs in Naples have no air-conditioning, so you can bake if caught in a traffic jam.

TAXI CONTACTS City Airport Taxis.
⊕ *www.city-airport-taxis.com*. **Radio Taxi Napoli.** ☎ *081/8888* ⊕ *www.taxinapoli.it*.

TRAIN

There are up to five trains every hour between Rome and Naples. Both the Alta Velocità Frecciarossa and Italo trains (the fastest types of train service) make the trip in a little more than an hour, with the Intercity taking two. All trains to Naples stop at the refurbished but forever scuzzy Stazione Centrale.

The efficient (though run-down) suburban Circumvesuviana runs from Naples's Porta Nolana and stops at Stazione Centrale before continuing to Herculaneum, Pompeii, and Sorrento. Travel time between Naples and Sorrento on the Circumvesuviana line is about 75 minutes.

For ticketing purposes, the region is divided into travel zones by distance from Naples. If you're traveling from Naples to anywhere else in Campania, be sure to ask for a *biglietto integrato*. It's slightly more expensive than the direct ticket (about €1 more), but there will be no need to buy a separate ticket for your subway, tram, or bus ride to the train station as the biglietto integrato covers the whole journey. An integrato ticket to Herculaneum costs €2.70, to Pompeii €3.50, and to Sorrento €4.90.

TRAIN CONTACTS Circumvesuviana.
☎ *800/211388* ⊕ *www.eavsrl.it*. **Trenitalia and Italo.** ✉ *Piazza Garibaldi*, ☎ *892021 Trenitalia, in Italy: fee, 06/68475475 Trenitalia, from abroad, 892020 Italo, in Italy: fee, 06/89371892 Italo, from abroad* ⊕ *www.trenitalia.com, www.italotreno.it*.

Restaurants

As the birthplace of pizza, Naples prides itself on its vast selection of pizzerias, the most famous of which—Da Michele (where Julia Roberts filmed her pizza scene in *Eat Pray Love*) or Sorbillo— deserve the designation of "incomparable." Many Neapolitans make lunch their big meal of the day, and then have a pizza for supper.

Dining on the Amalfi Coast, Capri, Ischia, and Procida revolves largely around seafood. Dishes are prepared using the short, rolled handmade *scialatielli* or large *paccheri* pasta and adorned with local *vongole* (clams) or *cozze* (mussels) and other shellfish. Octopus, squid, and the fresh fish of the season are always on the menu for the second course. Cetara has been famous for its *alici* (anchovies) since Roman times, and even produces alici bread. Eateries range from beachside trattorias to beacons of fine dining with stupendous views.

Restaurant prices are the average cost of a main course at dinner, or, if dinner is not served, at lunch. Restaurant reviews have been shortened. For full information, visit Fodors.com.

Hotels

Most parts of Campania have accommodations in all price categories, but they tend to fill up in high season, so reserve well in advance. In summer, on the coast and the islands, hotels that serve meals often require you to take half board.

Prices in the reviews are the lowest cost of a standard double room in high season. Hotel reviews have been shortened. For full information, visit Fodors.com.

What it Costs in Euros			
$	$$	$$$	$$$$
RESTAURANTS			
under €15	€15–€24	€25–€35	over €35
HOTELS			
under €125	€125–€200	€201–€300	over €300

Tours

City Sightseeing

BUS TOURS | FAMILY | Close to the port, beside the main entrance to Castel Nuovo, is the terminal for double-decker buses belonging to City Sightseeing. For €23 you can take two different excursions, giving you reasonable coverage of the downtown sights and outlying attractions like the Museo di Capodimonte. ✉ *Piazza Municipio, Naples* ☎ *055/961237, 39/3248114807 WhatsApp/Cellphone* ⊕ *www.city-sightseeing.it/naples.*

Lino Tour

GUIDED TOURS | Lino Tour offers tailor-made tours of the attractions in and around Naples. ✉ *Naples* ☎ *081/8772244* ⊕ *www.linotourcarservice.com.*

Naples

Located under the shadow of Vesuvius, Naples is the most vibrant city in Italy—a steaming, bubbling, reverberating minestrone in which each block is a small village and everything seems to be a backdrop for an opera not yet composed.

It's said that northern Italians vacation here to remind themselves of the time when Italy was *molto italiana—really* Italian. In this respect, Naples (Napoli in Italian) doesn't disappoint: Neapolitan rainbows of laundry wave in the wind over alleyways, mothers caress children, men break out into impromptu arias at sidewalk cafés, and street scenes offer an intricate theater of human exchanges.

Everywhere contrasting elements of faded gilt and romance, grandeur and squalor form a pageant of pure *Napoletanità*, a distillation of *Italianità*—Italy at its most Italian.

As the historic capital of the region known as Campania, Naples has been perpetually and tumultuously in a state of flux. Neapolitans are instinctively the most hospitable of people, and they've often paid a price for being so, having unwittingly extended a warm welcome to wave after wave of invaders. Lombards, Goths, Normans, Swabians, Spanish viceroys and kings, and Napoleonic generals arrived in turn; most of them proved to be greedy and self-serving. Still, if these foreign rulers bled the populace dry with taxes, they left the impoverished city with a rich architectural inheritance.

GETTING HERE AND AROUND

Public transportation in Naples is decent, and includes two subway lines, three funiculars, and a multitude of buses. Tickets cost €1.10 per journey (€1.30 on Metro Linea 2), but a Ticket Integrato Campania costs €1.60 and is valid for 90 minutes on all transport for as far as Pozzuoli to the west and Portici to the east; €4.50 buys a *biglietto giornaliero* (all-day ticket).

Now with a couple of art-decorated stations (Toledo and Università) voted among Europe's most attractive, Naples's Metropolitana provides fairly frequent service and can be the fastest way to get across the traffic-clogged city. Linea 1, Metropolitana Collinare, links the hill area of the Vomero and beyond with the National Archaeological Museum and Piazza Municipio near the port, as well as Stazione Centrale. The older Linea 2 stretches from the train station to Pozzuoli. Trains on both lines run 5:45 am–11 pm. To check journey costs and download the app visit ⊕ *www.unicocampania.it.*

Bus service is viable, especially with the introduction of larger buses on the regular R1, R2, R3, and R4 routes. Electronic signs display wait times at many stops. Three tram routes now thread through the streets with new tram rolling stock introduced in 2020, but the service is unreliable and regularly suspended.

VISITOR INFORMATION

The numerous tourist offices in Naples aren't always open when they claim to be, but most are generally open Monday–Saturday 8:30–8 (Sunday 8:30–2) except where noted. The AACST specializes in information on old Naples but generally just supplies brochures. A second office, which is closed on Sunday, is handily located inside the Palazzo Reale. There's an EPT (Ente Provinciale per il Turismo; open daily 9–6) office in Stazione Centrale staffed by a welcoming team of helpers. Pick up a free map and the latest "Art in Campania" brochure listing key venues and possible savings through the Campania ArteCard.

CONTACTS I Naples. ⊠ *Piazza del Gesù 7, Centro Storico* ☎ *081/5512701* ⊕ *www.inaples.it.*

Centro Storico

To experience the true essence of Naples, you need to explore the Centro Storico, an unforgettable neighborhood that is the heart of old Naples. This is the Naples of peeling building facades and hanging laundry, with small alleyways fragrant with fresh flowers laid at the many shrines to the Blessed Virgin. Here the cheapest pizzerias in town feed the locals like kings, and the raucous street carnival of Neapolitan daily life is punctuated with oases of spiritual calm. All the contradictions of Naples—splendor and squalor, palace and slum, triumph and tragedy—meet here and sing a full-throated chorale.

Sights

Duomo

CHURCH | Although the cathedral was established in the 1200s, the current building was erected a century later and has since undergone radical changes—especially during the Baroque period. Inside, the 350-year-old wooden ceiling is supported by 110 ancient columns salvaged from pagan buildings. The 4th-century church of Santa Restituta, incorporated into the cathedral, was redecorated in the late 1600s in the Baroque style, though the mosaics in the Battistero (Baptistery) are claimed to be the oldest in the Western world. In the Cappella del Tesoro di San Gennaro, multicolor marbles and frescoes honor St. Januarius, the miracle-working patron saint of Naples. Three times a year his dried blood is believed to liquefy during rites in his honor. The most spectacular painting is Ribera's *San Gennaro in the Furnace* (1647), depicting the saint emerging unscathed from the furnace. The Museo del Tesoro di San Gennaro houses a rich collection of treasures associated with the saint. ⊠ *Via Duomo 149, Centro Storico* ☎ *081/449097 Duomo, 081/294980* ⊕ *www.museosangennaro.it* ☜ *Cappella del Tesoro di San*

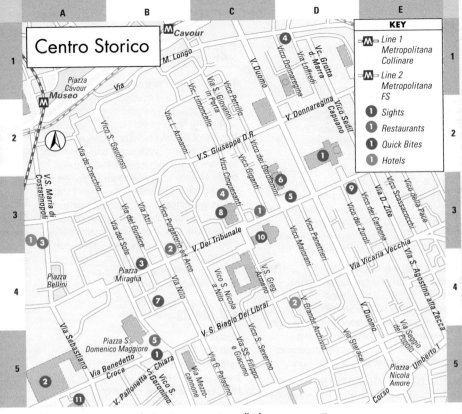

Centro Storico

Sights ▼

1	Duomo	**D2**
2	Gesù Nuovo	**A5**
3	LAPIS Museum	**B4**
4	Madre	**D1**
5	The Madonna and Pistol	**D3**
6	Monumento Nazionale dei Girolamini	**D3**
7	Museo Cappella Sansevero	**B4**
8	Napoli Sotterranea	**C3**
9	Pio Monte della Misericordia	**D3**
10	San Lorenzo Maggiore	**C3**
11	Santa Chiara	**A5**

Restaurants ▼

1	Di Matteo	**C3**
2	Gino Sorbillo	**B3**
3	L'Etto	**A3**
4	Le Sorelle Bandiera	**C3**
5	Palazzo Petrucci Pizzeria	**B5**

Quick Bites ▼

1	Scaturchio	**B5**

Hotels ▼

1	Costantinopoli 104	**A3**
2	Hotel Palazzo Decumani	**D4**

Gennaro €4; museum and chapel €10
Ⓜ Duomo, Cavour.

Gesù Nuovo

CHURCH | A stunning architectural contrast
to the plain Romanesque frontage of
other nearby churches, the oddly faceted
stone facade of this elaborate Baroque
church dates to the late 16th century.
Originally a palace, the building was
seized by Pedro of Toledo in 1547 and
sold to the Jesuits with the condition the
facade remain intact. Recent research
has revealed that the symbols on the
stones out front are Aramaic musical
notes that produce a 45-minute concerto.
Behind the entrance is Francesco Solime-
na's action-packed *Heliodorus' Eviction
from the Temple*. The bulk of the interior
decoration took more than 40 years and
was completed only in the 18th century.
You can find the work of familiar Baroque
sculptors (Naccherino, Finelli) and
painters inside. The gracious *Visitation*
above the altar in the second chapel
on the right is by Massimo Stanzione,
who also contributed the fine frescoes
in the main nave: they're in the presby-
tery (behind and around the main altar).
✉ *Piazza Gesù Nuovo, Centro Storico*
☎ 081/5578111 Ⓜ *Dante*.

★ LAPIS Museum

RUINS | FAMILY | The beautifully restored
17th-century Basilica di Pietrasanta, a
Cosimo Fanzago Baroque masterpiece
built on the site of the Roman Temple
of Diana, hosts regular multimedia
exhibitions, but the star attraction here
is the underground visit to a section of
Naples's oldest aqueduct. Four tours a
day descend 40 meters below the busy
Via dei Tribunali to large lavishly illuminated cisterns hewed from excavated tuff
two millennia ago, still filled with running
water (thanks to a collaboration with the
city's waterworks). A quarter-mile stroll
east through the tunnels takes you to
where up to a thousand Neapolitans at
a time huddled when the air-raid sirens
sounded during World War II, often

returning to the surface to find their
houses destroyed by Allied or German
bombs. Nowadays there's a lift—the only
archaeological elevator in Naples—to
whisk you back up to the 21st century.
✉ *Piazzetta Pietrasanta 17/18, Centro Storico* ☎ 081/19230565 ⊕ *www.
lapismuseum.com* 🎫 €10 Ⓜ *Dante*.

The Madonna and Pistol

PUBLIC ART | This piece is by controversial
street artist Banksy. Located on the wall
of the birthplace of 17th-century philosopher Giambattista Vico, a stencilled *La
Madonna con la Pistola* sits beside a
religious shrine to the Virgin Mary. Fans
of street art can take a tour of the city's
other interesting graffiti by contacting
Napoli Paint Stories. ✉ *Piazza Gerolomini,
Centro Storico* ⊕ *www.napolipaintstories.
it* Ⓜ *Cavour*.

Madre (*Museum of Contemporary Art
Donnaregina*)

ART GALLERY | With 86,111 square feet of
exhibition space, a host of young and
helpful attendants, and occasional late-
night events, the Madre is one of the
most visited museums in Naples. Most
of the artworks on the first floor were
installed in situ by their creators, but the
second-floor gallery exhibits works by
international and Italian contemporary
artists. The museum also hosts tempo-
rary shows by major international artists.
✉ *Via Settembrini 79, San Lorenzo,
Centro Storico* ☎ 081/19978017 ⊕ *www.
madrenapoli.it/en* 🎫 €8 ⊘ Closed Tues.
Ⓜ *Cavour*.

Monumento Nazionale dei Girolamini

RELIGIOUS BUILDING | *I Girolamini* is anoth-
er name for the Oratorians, followers
of St. Philip Neri, to whom the splendid church I Girolamini is dedicated.
The church is part of a larger complex
managed as the Monumento Nazionale
dei Girolamini. The Florentine architect
Giovanni Antonio Dosio designed I Girolamini, which was erected between 1592
and 1619; the dome and facade were
rebuilt (circa 1780) in the most elegant

neoclassical style after a design by Ferdinando Fuga. Inside the entrance wall is Luca Giordano's grandiose fresco (1684) of Christ chasing the money changers from the temple. The intricate carved-wood ceiling, damaged by Allied bombs in 1943, has now been restored to its original magnificence. ⊠ *Via Duomo 142, Centro Storico* ☎ *081/294444* ⊕ *www.bibliotecadeigirolamini.beniculturali.it* 🎟 *€8* Ⓜ *Cavour.*

★ Museo Cappella Sansevero

(*Sansevero Chapel Museum*)
NOTABLE BUILDING | The dazzling funerary chapel of the Sangro di Sansevero princes combines noble swagger, overwhelming color, and a touch of the macabre—which expresses Naples perfectly. The chapel was begun in 1590 by Prince Giovan Francesco di Sangro to fulfill a vow to the Virgin if he were cured of a dire illness. The seventh Sangro di Sansevero prince, Raimondo, had the building modified in the mid-18th century and is generally credited for its current Baroque styling, the noteworthy elements of which include the splendid marble-inlay floor. ⊠ *Via Francesco de Sanctis 19, off Vicolo Domenico Maggiore, Centro Storico* ☎ *081/5518470* ⊕ *www.museosansevero.it* 🎟 *€8* ⊗ *Closed Tues.* Ⓜ *Dante.*

Napoli Sotterranea (*Underground Naples*)
HISTORIC SIGHT | **FAMILY** | Fascinating 90-minute tours of a portion of Naples's fabled underground city provide an initiation into the complex history of the city center. Efforts to dramatize the experience—amphoras lowered on ropes to draw water from cisterns, candles given to navigate narrow passages, objects shifted to reveal secret passages—combine with enthusiastic English-speaking guides to make this particularly exciting for older children. Be prepared on the underground tour to go up and down many steps and crouch in very narrow corridors. ⊠ *Piazza San Gaetano 68, along Via dei Tribunali, Centro Storico*

☎ *081/296944* ⊕ *www.napolisotterranea. org* 🎟 *€10* Ⓜ *Dante, Cavour.*

★ Pio Monte della Misericordia

RELIGIOUS BUILDING | One of the Centro Storico's defining sites, this octagonal church was built around the corner from the Duomo for a charitable institution seven noblemen founded in 1601. The institution's aim was to carry out acts of Christian charity like feeding the hungry, clothing the poor, nursing the sick, sheltering pilgrims, visiting prisoners, and burying the indigent dead—acts immortalized in the history of art by Caravaggio's famous altarpiece depicting the *Sette Opere della Misericordia* (*Seven Acts of Mercy*). Pride of place is given to the great Caravaggio above the altar. ⊠ *Via Tribunali 253, Centro Storico* ☎ *081/446973* ⊕ *www.piomontedellamisericordia.it* 🎟 *€8* ⊗ *Closed Sun. afternoon* Ⓜ *Cavour, Duomo.*

★ San Lorenzo Maggiore

RELIGIOUS BUILDING | The church of San Lorenzo features a very unmedieval facade of 18th-century splendor. Due to the effects and threats of earthquakes, the church was reinforced and reshaped along Baroque lines in the 17th and 18th centuries. Begun by Robert d'Anjou in 1270 on the site of a previous 6th-century church, the church has a single, barnlike nave that reflects the Franciscans' desire for simple spaces with enough room to preach to large crowds. A grandiose triumphal arch announces the transept, and the main altar (1530) is the sculptor Giovanni da Nola's masterpiece; this is a copy of the original, now disappeared, pedestal. Also found here is the church's most important monument: the tomb of Catherine of Austria (circa 1323), by Tino da Camaino, among the first sculptors to introduce the Gothic style into Italy. ⊠ *Via dei Tribunali 316, Centro Storico* ☎ *081/2110860* ⊕ *www.laneapolissotterrata.it* 🎟 *Excavations and museum €9* Ⓜ *Cavour, Dante.*

★ Santa Chiara

RELIGIOUS BUILDING | Offering a stark and telling contrast to the opulence of the nearby Gesù Nuovo, Santa Chiara is the leading Angevin Gothic monument in Naples. The fashionable house of worship for the 14th-century nobility and a favorite Angevin church from the start, the church of St. Clare was intended to be a great dynastic monument by Robert d'Anjou. His second wife, Sancia di Majorca, added the adjoining convent for the Poor Clares to a monastery of the Franciscan Minors; this was the first time the two sexes were combined in a single complex. Built in a Provençal Gothic style between 1310 and 1328 (probably by Gagliardo Primario) and dedicated in 1340, the church had its aspect radically altered in the Baroque period. A six-day fire started by Allied bombs on August 4, 1943, put an end to all that. Around the left side of the church is the **Chiostro delle Clarisse**, the most famous cloister in Naples. ⊠ *Piazza Gesù Nuovo, Centro Storico* ☎ *081/5516673* ⊕ *www. monasterodisantachiara.it* 🖃 *Museum and cloister €6* 🕙 *Closed Sun. afternoon* Ⓜ *Dante, Università.*

 Restaurants

★ Di Matteo

$ | PIZZA | Every pizzeria along Via dei Tribunali is worth the long wait—and trust us, all the good ones will be jam-packed—but just one can claim to have served a U.S. president: Bill Clinton enjoyed a margherita here when the G8 was held in Naples in 1994. Today the superlative *pizzaioli* (pizza makers) turn out a wide array of pizzas, all to the utmost perfection. **Known for:** top value, including filling pizza fritta (fried); funny pics of Clinton and the "Pizzaiolo del Presidente" Ernesto Cacialli in 1994; functional decor and pizzaioli working at front. $ *Average main: €6* ⊠ *Via Tribunali 94, Centro Storico* ☎ *081/455262* ⊕ *www. pizzeriadimatteo.com* Ⓜ *Cavour, Dante.*

Gino Sorbillo

$ | PIZZA | FAMILY | There are a few restaurants called Sorbillo along Via dei Tribunali; this is the one with the crowds waiting outside and is world-renowned. Order the same thing the locals come for: a basic Neapolitan pizza (try the unique pizza al pesto or the stunningly simple marinara—just tomatoes and oregano). **Known for:** head honcho Gino is a celebrity and pizza ambassador; leave your name at the door and listen to be called; the crowd waiting outside. $ *Average main: €10* ⊠ *Via dei Tribunali 32, Centro Storico* ☎ *081/446643* ⊕ *www.sorbillo.it* 🕙 *Closed Sun.* Ⓜ *Dante.*

Le Sorelle Bandiera

$ | PIZZA | For a mere €8, you can eat under a bust of Queen Margherita herself, otherwise known as the Pizza Queen, whose name inspired the traditional pizza. The dough here is kept in a tufa-stone area, allowing the restaurant to claim it is "geothermal." The slightly upmarket pizza is served on tables, which are set with majolica tiling unearthed during the excavation of the historic San Paolo convent, which was once located on the same corner as the restaurant, thus bolstering the sense of authenticity. **Known for:** outside seating area; geothermal pizza; lovely majolica-tiled tables. $ *Average main: €8* ⊠ *Vico Cinquesanti 33, Centro Storico* ☎ *081/19503535* ⊕ *www.lesorellebandiera.com* Ⓜ *Cavour, Dante.*

L'Etto

$ | SOUTHERN ITALIAN | The premise of this innovative eatery is to weigh the delicacies diners choose from the adventurous buffet and charge by the pound. In recent times they have introduced a menu of fixed-price bowls, a Neapolitan variation of Hawaiian poke—the *squisita* (exquisite) includes rice, octopus, onions, and cherry tomatoes, and there is also a vegan option. **Known for:** selling meals by the pound; communal eating area; Neapolitan poke. $ *Average main: €14* ⊠ *Via Santa Maria di Costantinopoli 102,*

Centro Storico ☎ 081/19320967 ⊕ www. ettoexperience.it ⊗ No dinner Thurs. Ⓜ Dante, Museo.

Palazzo Petrucci Pizzeria

$ | PIZZA | In a 17th-century mansion facing the grand Piazza San Domenico Maggiore, Palazzo Petrucci doesn't lack for dramatic settings for dining—under the vaulted ceiling of the former stables, near the pizzaiolo and oven action, outside in the piazza, or on the roof terrace at giuglia (obelisk) di San Domenico level. Expect classic pizze, pizze fritte, and some unusual topping combinations, alongside heaped salads and antipasti. **Known for:** craft beer, pizze fritte, and vegan options; atmospheric views and sounds over the piazza; grandest palazzo venue for a pizza feast. ⓢ Average main: €10 ⊠ Piazza San Domenico Maggiore 5–7, Centro Storico ☎ 081/5512460 ⊕ www.palazzopetruccipizzeria.it ⊗ Closed 2 wks in Aug. Ⓜ Dante.

☕ Coffee and Quick Bites

★ Scaturchio

$ | CAFÉ | Established in 1905, this Neapolitan institution on Spaccanapoli is a buzzy place to sample some of the finest pastries in town—plus it also makes classic savory dishes, ice cream, and mighty decent coffee. **Known for:** zucchine a scapece, arancini, and other savory bites; Ministeriale liquor-filled chocolates; sumptuous babà, sfogliatelle, and pastiera. ⓢ Average main: €6 ⊠ Piazza San Domenico Maggiore 19, Centro Storico ☎ 081/551 6944 ⊕ www.scaturchio.it.

Hotels

Costantinopoli 104

$$ | HOTEL | An oasis of what Italians call stile liberty (Art Nouveau style), with impressive stained-glass fittings and striking artwork, this serene, elegant hotel is well placed for touring the Museo Archeologico Nazionale and the Centro Storico. **Pros:** pool (a rarity in

Neapolitan hotels) and garden; convenient Centro Storico location; pleasant service. **Cons:** some rooms suffer from nightlife disturbance from Piazza Bellini; can be difficult to find; rooms getting dated. ⓢ Rooms from: €184 ⊠ Via Costantinopoli 104, Centro Storico ☎ 081/5571035 ⊕ costantinopoli104.it ⇄ 19 rooms ⑪ Free Breakfast Ⓜ Museo.

★ Hotel Palazzo Decumani

$$ | HOTEL | This contemporary upscale hotel near the Centro Storico's major sights occupies an early-20th-century palazzo, but you won't find heavy, ornate furnishings—the emphasis is on light and space, both in short supply in old Naples. **Pros:** guests-only lounge-bar; service on par with fancier hotels; large rooms and bathrooms. **Cons:** soundproofing not the best; some may find decor a tad sparse; can be hard to find—follow signs from Corso Umberto. ⓢ Rooms from: €180 ⊠ Piazzetta Giustino Fortunato 8, Centro Storico ☎ 081/4201379 ⊕ www.palazzodecumani.com ⇄ 28 rooms ⑪ Free Breakfast Ⓜ Duomo.

🛍 Shopping

Ferrigno

CRAFTS | Shops selling Nativity scenes cluster along the Via San Gregorio Armeno off Spaccanapoli, and they're all worth a glance. The most famous is Ferrigno. Although Maestro Giuseppe Ferrigno died in 2008, the family business continues, still faithfully using 18th-century techniques. ⊠ Via San Gregorio Armeno 8, Centro Storico ☎ 081/5523148 ⊕ www.arteferrigno.it Ⓜ Cavour, Duomo.

Ospedale delle Bambole

TOYS | FAMILY | In the courtyard of the 16th-century Palazzo Marigliano is this world-famous hospital for dolls. In business since 1850, it's a wonderful place to take kids (and their injured toys). It's closed Sunday. ⊠ Via San Biagio dei Librai

39, Centro Storico ☎ *081/18639797* ⊕ *os-pedaledellebambole.com* Ⓜ *Duomo.*

Museo Archeologico Nazionale

It's only fitting that the Museo Archeologico Nazionale—the single most important and remarkable museum of Greco-Roman antiquities in the world (in spite of itself, some observers say)—sits in the upper *decumanus,* or neighborhood, of ancient Neapolis, the district colonized by the ancient Greeks and Romans. Happily, it's almost always open (its core collection, that is). But if two hours is your limit for gazing at ancient art, nearby you can discover some of the lesser-known delights of medieval and Renaissance Naples, along with the city's lush botanical gardens. Along the way are churches that are repositories for magnificent 15th- and 16th-century art and sculpture.

👁 Sights

★ **Museo Archeologico Nazionale** (*National Museum of Archaeology*)

HISTORY MUSEUM | Also known as MANN, this legendary museum has experienced something of a rebirth in recent years. Its unrivaled collections include world-renowned archaeological finds that put most other museums to shame, from some of the best mosaics and paintings from Pompeii and Herculaneum to the legendary Farnese collection of ancient sculpture. The core masterpiece collection is almost always open to visitors, while seasonal exhibitions feature intriguing cultural events, collaborations, and contemporary artists. Some of the newer rooms, covering archaeological discoveries in the Greco-Roman settlements and necropolises in and around Naples, have helpful informational panels in English. ✉ *Piazza Museo 19, Centro Storico* ☎ *081/4422111* ⊕ *mannapoli.it* 🎟 *€15* 🕑 *Closed Tues.* Ⓜ *Museo.*

Toledo

Naples's setting on what is possibly the most captivating bay in the world has long been a boon for its inhabitants—the expansive harbor has always brought great mercantile wealth to the city—and, intermittently, a curse. Throughout history, a who's who of Greek, Roman, Norman, Spanish, and French despots has quarreled over this gateway to Campania. Each set of conquerors recognized that the area around the city harbor—today occupied by the Molo Beverello hydrofoil terminal and the 1928 Stazione Marittima—functioned as a veritable welcome mat to the metropolis and consequently should be a fitting showcase of regal authority. This had become imperative because of explosive population growth, which, by the mid-16th century, had made Naples the second-largest city in Europe, after Paris. With the mass migration of the rural population to the city, Naples had grown into a capricious, unplanned, disorderly, and untrammeled capital. Thus, the central aim of the ruling dynasties became the creation of a *Napoli nobilissima*—a "most noble" Naples.

👁 Sights

★ **Castel Nuovo**

CASTLE/PALACE | Known to locals as Maschio Angioino, in reference to its Angevin builders, this imposing castle is now used more for marital than military purposes—a portion of it serves as a government registry office. A white four-tiered triumphal entrance arch, ordered by Alfonso of Aragon after he entered the city in 1443 to seize power from the increasingly beleaguered Angevin Giovanna II, upstages the building's looming Angevin stonework. Across the courtyard within the castle is the Sala Grande, also known as the Sala dei Baroni, which has a stunning vaulted ceiling 92 feet high. ✉ *Piazza Municipio, Toledo* ☎ *081/7957722* ⊕ *castelnuovo.comune.*

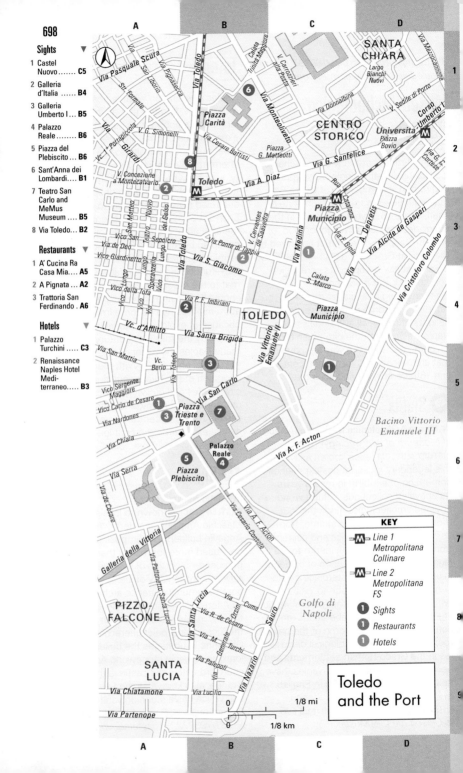

napoli.it, www.timelinenapoli.it 🖃 *From €6, tours €10* 🕙 *Closed Sun.* Ⓜ *Municipio.*

Galleria Umberto I
NOTABLE BUILDING | The galleria was erected during the "cleanup" of Naples following the devastating cholera epidemic of 1884. With facades on Via Toledo—the most animated street in Naples at the time—the structure, built between 1887 and 1890 according to a design by Emanuele Rocco, had a prestigious and important location. 🖃 *Entrances on Via San Carlo, Via Toledo, Via Santa Brigida, and Via Verdi, Toledo* Ⓜ *Toledo.*

Gallerie d'Italia
ART GALLERY | Once the headquarters of the Banco di Napoli, this vast 20th-century building houses a small museum that's worth seeking out for its outstanding collection of 17th- and 18th-century paintings. Relocated from the nearby 17th-century Palazzo Zevallos Stigliano in 2022, the star attraction is Caravaggio's last work, *The Martyrdom of Saint Ursula.* The saint here is, for dramatic effect, deprived of her usual retinue of a thousand followers. On the left, with a face of pure spite, is the king of the Huns, who has just shot Ursula with an arrow after his proposal of marriage has been rejected. Free lunchtime concerts are sometimes held in the atrium of the palazzo. 🖃 *Via Toledo 177, Toledo* 🕾 *800/454229* ⊕ *www.gallerieditalia.com* 🖃 *€5* 🕙 *Closed Mon.* Ⓜ *Toledo.*

★ Palazzo Reale
CASTLE/PALACE | A leading Naples showpiece created to express Bourbon power and values, the Palazzo Reale dates from 1600. Renovated and redecorated by successive rulers, once lorded over by a dim-witted king who liked to fire his hunting rifles at the birds in his tapestries, it is filled with salons designed in the most lavish 18th-century Neapolitan style. The Spanish viceroys originally commissioned the palace, ordering the Swiss architect Domenico Fontana to build a new residence for King Philip III, should he

chance to visit Naples. He died in 1621 before ever doing so. 🖃 *Piazza Plebiscito, Toledo* 🕾 *081/5808255, 848/082408 schools and guided tours* ⊕ *www.palazzorealedinapoli.org* 🖃 *€6* 🕙 *Closed Wed.* Ⓜ *Toledo, Municipio.*

Piazza del Plebiscito
PLAZA/SQUARE | After spending time as a parking lot, this square was restored in 1994 to one of Napoli Nobilissima's most majestic spaces, with a Doric semicircle of columns resembling St. Peter's Square in Rome. The piazza was erected in the early 1800s under the Napoleonic regime, but after the regime fell, Ferdinand, the new King of the Two Sicilies, ordered the addition of the Church of San Francesco di Paola. On the left as you approach the church is a statue of Ferdinand and on the right one of his father, Charles III, both of them clad in Roman togas. Around dusk, floodlights come on, creating a magical effect. A delightful sea breeze airs the square, and most days one corner becomes an improvised soccer stadium where local youths emulate their heroes. 🖃 *Piazza Plebiscito, Toledo* Ⓜ *Toledo, Municipio.*

★ Sant'Anna dei Lombardi
CHURCH | Long favored by the Aragonese kings, this church, simple and rather anonymous from the outside, houses some of the most important ensembles of Renaissance sculpture in southern Italy. Begun with the adjacent convent of the Olivetani and its four cloisters in 1411, it was given a Baroque makeover in the mid-17th century by Gennaro Sacco.

To the left of the Ligorio Altar is the Mastrogiudice Chapel, whose altar contains precious reliefs of the Annunciation and *Scenes from the Life of Jesus* (1489) by Benedetto da Maiano, a great name in Tuscan sculpture. On the other side of the entrance is the Piccolomini Chapel, with a *Crucifixion* by Giulio Mazzoni (circa 1550), a refined marble altar (circa 1475), a funerary monument to Maria d'Aragona by another prominent Florentine sculptor,

Antonello Rossellino (circa 1475), and on the right, a rather sweet fresco of the Annunciation by an anonymous follower of Piero della Francesca. ✉ *Piazza Monteoliveto 15, Toledo* ☎ *081/4420039* 🌐 *www.santannadeilombardi.com* 🎫 *Side chapels, oratory, and sacristy €6* 🕒 *Side chapels, oratory, and sacristy closed Sun. morning* [M] *Dante.*

Teatro San Carlo and MeMus Museum

PERFORMANCE VENUE | Out of all the Italian opera houses, La Scala in Milan is the most famous, but San Carlo is more beautiful, and Naples is, after all, the most operatic of cities. The neoclassical structure, designed by Antonio Niccolini, was built in a mere nine months after an 1816 fire destroyed the original. Many operas were composed for the house, including Donizetti's *Lucia di Lammermoor* and Rossini's *La Donna del Lago*. In the theater, nearly 200 boxes are arranged on six levels, and the 12,000-square-foot stage permits large-scale productions. ✉ *Via San Carlo 101–103, Toledo* ☎ *081/7972331 ticket office, 081/7972412 tours, 081/7972449 MeMus* 🌐 *www.teatrosancarlo.it* 🎫 *From €6* 🕒 *MeMus closed Wed. and Aug.* [M] *Municipio.*

Via Toledo

HISTORIC DISTRICT | Sooner or later you'll wind up at one of the busiest commercial arteries, also known as Via Roma, which is thankfully closed to through traffic—at least along the stretch leading from the Palazzo Reale. Don't avoid dipping into this parade of shops and coffee bars where plump pastries are temptingly arranged. ✉ *Via Toledo, Toledo* [M] *Toledo.*

🍴 Restaurants

A' Cucina Ra Casa Mia

$ | SOUTHERN ITALIAN | Just off bustling Via Toledo on the basalti flagstones of a narrow Quartieri Spagnoli street, this small trattoria does superb-value, classic Neapolitan dishes. Take a seat at one of the small tables with checkered tablecloths and ask the amiable staff about the day's freshest seafood, meat, and vegetable dishes, while taking in the atmospheric surroundings. **Known for:** veggie and gluten-free options; fresh seafood pasta dishes; homey place popular with locals. [$] *Average main: €13* ✉ *Via Carlo De Cesare 14, Toledo* ☎ *081/4976297* 🌐 *www.acucinaracasamia.it* 🕒 *Closed Tues.*

A Pignata

$ | SOUTHERN ITALIAN | A hidden gem in the Quartieri Spagnoli, A Pignata is a favorite with locals for its typical Neapolitan cooking. The antipasta is a meal in itself but save space for the grilled calamari or baccalà *alla Siciliana*, made with potatoes, tomatoes, olives, and capers. **Known for:** sumptuous local dishes; a favorite with locals; relaxed atmosphere. [$] *Average main: €12* ✉ *Vico Lungo del Gelso 110/112, Toledo* ☎ *081/413526* 🌐 *www.trattoriapignata.it* 🕒 *Closed Mon.* [M] *Toledo.*

Trattoria San Ferdinando

$$$ | SOUTHERN ITALIAN | This cheerful trattoria seems to be run for the sheer pleasure of it, and chatting locals give it a buzzy Neapolitan atmosphere. Try the excellent fish or the traditional (but cooked with a lighter modern touch) pasta dishes, especially those with *verdure* (fresh leafy vegetables) or with *patate con la provola* (potatoes and smoked mozzarella). **Known for:** near Teatro San Carlo; popular with locals in the evening, so reserve ahead; excellent, fresh seafood specialties. [$] *Average main: €25* ✉ *Via Nardones 117, Toledo* ☎ *081/421964* 🌐 *www.trattoriasanferdinando.com* 🕒 *Closed Sun. and last 3 wks of Aug. No dinner Sat. and Mon.* [M] *Toledo, Municipio.*

Hotels

Palazzo Turchini

$ | **HOTEL** | Just a few minutes' walk from the Castel Nuovo, Palazzo Turchini is one of the city center's more attractive smaller hotels. **Pros:** good location for the port; rooftop terrace; more intimate than neighboring business hotels. **Cons:** rooms on the small and stuffy side; rooms a tad businesslike; close to a busy traffic hub. $ *Rooms from: €118* ✉ *Via Medina 21, Toledo* ☎ *081/5510606* ⊕ *www. palazzoturchini.it* ⤳ *27 rooms* ⫽ *Free Breakfast* Ⓜ *Municipio.*

Renaissance Naples Hotel Mediterraneo

$$ | **HOTEL** | A modern, efficient business hotel, the Mediterraneo is within walking distance of both the Teatro San Carlo and the Centro Storico. **Pros:** convenient to the port; good for those who want a modern hotel; attractive rooftop breakfast terrace. **Cons:** not for those who want historic atmosphere; some of the rooms are poorly maintained; in a busy part of town. $ *Rooms from: €180* ✉ *Via Nuova Ponte di Tappia 25, Toledo* ☎ *081/7970001* ⊕ *www.mediterraneo-napoli.com, www.marriott.com* ⤳ *189 rooms* ⫽ *Free Breakfast* Ⓜ *Toledo, Municipio.*

🛍 Shopping

Ascione

JEWELRY & WATCHES | A family firm established in 1855 and known for its traditionally made coral jewelry and artwork, Ascione has a showroom/gallery on the second floor of a shabby wing of the Galleria Umberto. A hidden secret, aficionados should not miss the guided tour (€5, book ahead) describing the company's rich history, with displays including Egypt's King Farouk's elaborate wedding gift to his bride Farida and what many consider the most beautiful cameo in existence. ✉ *Piazzetta Matilde Serao 19, Piazza Municipio* ☎ *081/4211111* ⊕ *www.ascione.it* Ⓜ *Municipio.*

Chiaia, Santa Lucia, and Nearby

The Lungomare is the city's grandest stretch of waterfront. In the 19th century, Naples's waterfront harbored the picturesque quarter that was called Santa Lucia, a district dear to artists and musicians and known for its fishermen's cottages. The fishermen were swept away when an enormous landfill project extended the land out to what is now Via Nazario Sauro and Via Partenope, the address for some of Naples's finest hotels. Huge stretches of the waterfront are blessedly traffic-free, only enhancing their distinctly Neapolitan charm. The area also boasts the chic Chiaia neighborhood surrounding Piazza dei Martiri and the gilded 19th-century Villa Pignatelli.

Sights

Castel dell'Ovo (*Castle of the Egg*)

CASTLE/PALACE | The oldest castle in Naples, the 12th-century Castel dell'Ovo dangles over the Porto Santa Lucia on a thin promontory. Built atop the ruins of an ancient Roman villa, the castle these days shares its views with some of the city's top hotels. Its gigantic rooms, rock tunnels, and belvederes over the bay are among Naples's most striking sights. Some rooms are given over to temporary art and photography shows. The castle's name comes from the poet Virgil, who is supposed to have hidden inside the ancient villa an egg that had protective powers as long as it remained intact. The belief was taken so seriously that to quell the people's panic after Naples suffered an earthquake, an invasion, and a plague in quick succession, its monarch felt compelled to produce an intact egg, solemnly declaring it to be the Virgilian original. ✉ *Santa Lucia waterfront, Via Eldorado 3, off Via Partenope, Santa Lucia* ☎ *081/7956180* ⌾ *Free.*

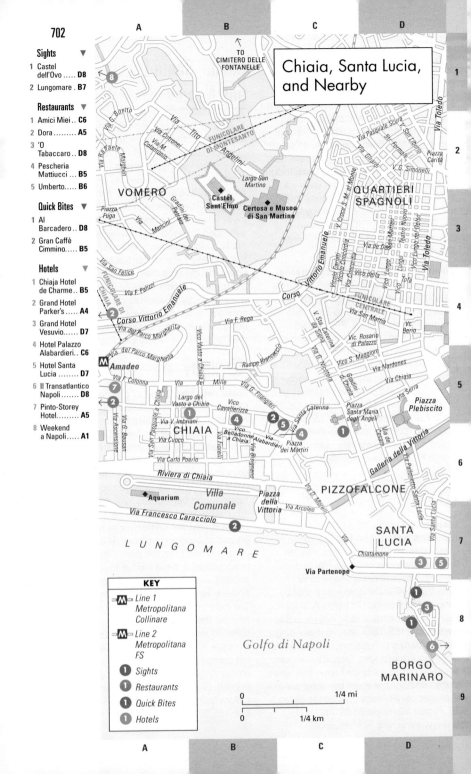

702

Sights ▼

1 Castel dell'Ovo **D8**
2 Lungomare . **B7**

Restaurants ▼

1 Amici Miei .. **C6**
2 Dora **A5**
3 'O Tabaccaro .. **D8**
4 Pescheria Mattiucci ... **B5**
5 Umberto **B6**

Quick Bites ▼

1 Al Barcadero .. **D8**
2 Gran Caffè Cimmino **B5**

Hotels ▼

1 Chiaja Hotel de Charme .. **B5**
2 Grand Hotel Parker's **A4**
3 Grand Hotel Vesuvio **D7**
4 Hotel Palazzo Alabardieri .. **C6**
5 Hotel Santa Lucia **D7**
6 Il Transatlantico Napoli **D8**
7 Pinto-Storey Hotel **A5**
8 Weekend a Napoli **A1**

Chiaia, Santa Lucia, and Nearby

VOMERO

Castel Sant'Elmo

Certosa e Museo di San Martino

Largo San Martino

QUARTIERI SPAGNOLI

Piazza Carità

TO CIMITERO DELLE FONTANELLE

Corso Vittorio Emanuele

FUNICOLARE CENTRALE

Amadeo

CHIAIA

Piazza dei Martiri

Piazza Santa Maria degli Angeli

Piazza Plebiscito

PIZZOFALCONE

Riviera di Chiaia

Aquarium

Villa Comunale

Piazza della Vittoria

Via Francesco Caracciolo

SANTA LUCIA

Via Partenope

L U N G O M A R E

Chiatamone

BORGO MARINARO

Golfo di Napoli

KEY

Ⓜ Line 1 Metropolitana Collinare

Ⓜ Line 2 Metropolitana FS

① Sights

① Restaurants

① Quick Bites

① Hotels

0   1/4 mi
0   1/4 km

★ **Lungomare** (*Seafront*)

PROMENADE | The first thing Mayor Luigi de Magistris did after his 2011 election was to banish traffic from the city's seafront. Strolling, skating, or biking along Via Caracciolo and Via Partenope with Capri, Mt. Vesuvius, and the Castel dell'Ovo in your sights is a favorite Neapolitan pastime. ✉ *Via Caracciolo, Chiaia.*

🍴 Restaurants

Amici Miei

$$$ | **SOUTHERN ITALIAN** | Favored by meat eaters who can't abide another bite of bream, this dimly lit cozy dining den is known for dishes such as tender carpaccio with fresh artichoke hearts. There are also excellent house-made pasta selections, including orecchiette with chickpeas or *alla barese* (with chewy green turnips), but the highlights are the extravagant grilled meat plates. **Known for:** superb, friendly service befitting the name; Art Nouveau decorative flourishes; a choice of quality meat dishes. [$] *Average main: €25* ✉ *Via Monte di Dio 78, Chiaia* ☎ *081/7646063* 🌐 *www.ristoranteamicimiei.com* 🕓 *Closed Mon. and late July–early Sept. No dinner Sun.* [M] *Chiaia.*

Dora

$$$ | **SEAFOOD** | Despite its location up an unpromising-looking *vicolo* (alley) off the Riviera di Chiaia, this small restaurant has achieved cult status for its seafood platters. It's remarkable what owner-chef Renato can produce in his tiny kitchen: start with linguine *alla Dora,* laden with local seafood and fresh tomatoes, and perhaps follow up with grilled *pezzogna* (blue-spotted bream). **Known for:** great service; simple, attractive nautical-theme decor; freshest seafood, both raw and cooked. [$] *Average main: €26* ✉ *Via Fernando Palasciano 30, Chiaia* ☎ *081/680519* 🌐 *www.ristorantedora.it* 🕓 *Closed Mon.* [M] *San Pasquale.*

'O Tabaccaro

$ | **SEAFOOD** | If you're trying to keep to a budget but want to enjoy a seafood feast alongside the yachts of the Borgo Marinaro harbor, head to this former tobacco store. While your eyes feast on all the pretty boats, the Lungomare hotels, the Castel dell'Ovo, and Vesuvius, you can savor classic Neapolitan seafood spaghetti or an *impepata di cozze* (mussels with pepper and garlic). **Known for:** family service; portside dining; relatively inexpensive fare. [$] *Average main: €13* ✉ *Via Luculliana 28, Santa Lucia* ☎ *081/7646352.*

★ **Pescheria Mattiucci**

$$ | **SOUTHERN ITALIAN** | In the evening, this fourth-generation fish shop becomes a trendy spot to enjoy an aperitif and a light meal. If you want to experience superb Neapolitan sushi and cold wine while sitting on a buoy stool, get here early: service is 7:30–10:30. **Known for:** fish lunches; intimate and small place, so get here early or call ahead for dinner; pescheria counter displaying today's catch. [$] *Average main: €15* ✉ *Vico Belledonne a Chiaia 27, Chiaia* ☎ *081/2512215* 🌐 *www.pescheriamattiucci.com* 🕓 *Closed Sun. and Mon.* [M] *San Pasquale.*

★ **Umberto**

$$ | **SOUTHERN ITALIAN** | Run by the Di Porzio family since 1916, Umberto is one of the city's classic restaurants, combining the classiness of its neighborhood, Chiaia, and the friendliness one finds in other parts of Naples. Try the *paccheri 'do tre dita* ("three-finger" pasta with octopus, tomato, olives, and capers); it bears the nickname of the original Umberto, who happened to be short a few digits. **Known for:** classic Neapolitan meat sauce alla Genovese; charming hosts; authentic Pizza DOC (smaller, with chunky cornicione rim). [$] *Average main: €17* ✉ *Via Alabardieri 30–31, Chiaia* ☎ *081/418555* 🌐 *www.umberto.it* 🕓 *No lunch Mon.* [M] *Chiaia.*

Coffee and Quick Bites

Al Barcadero

$ | **SOUTHERN ITALIAN** | Located below the walkway to Castel dell'Ovo, Al Barcadero is a romantic outdoor setting for a snack and a coffee or aperitif. Take a break at one of the tables and gaze at Mt. Vesuvius beyond the masts of the nearby luxury yachts. **Known for:** light snack beside the castle; the city's most romantic setting; portside outdoor seating. [$] *Average main: €5* ✉ *Banchina Santa Lucia 2, Santa Lucia* ☎ *333/2227023 mobile* 🌐 *www.albarcaderonapoli.blogspot.com.*

Gran Caffè Cimmino

$ | **CAFÉ** | Connoisseurs often say the most refined pastries in town can be found at Gran Caffè Cimmino. Many of the city's lawyers congregate here, to celebrate or commiserate with crisp, light cannoli; airy lemon eclairs; choux paste in the form of a mushroom laced with chocolate whipped cream; and delightful wild-strawberry tartlets. **Known for:** terrace for watching Chiaia's finest; babà to die for; Neapolitan breakfast favorite. [$] *Average main: €3* ✉ *Via G. Filangieri 12/13, Chiaia* ☎ *081/418303* [M] *Chiaia.*

Hotels

Chiaja Hotel de Charme

$ | **HOTEL** | This 18th-century palazzo has a great location and its apartments, all on the first floor, have plenty of atmosphere. **Pros:** good location near Piazza del Plebiscito and the Palazzo Reale; some antiques in guest rooms; on a bustling pedestrian-only street. **Cons:** entrance up a flight of stairs; even with a/c, some rooms get hot in summer; no views in a town with some great ones. [$] *Rooms from: €89* ✉ *Via Chiaia 216, Chiaia* ☎ *081/415555* 🌐 *www.hotelchiaia.it* 🛏 *33 rooms* 🍴 *Free Breakfast* [M] *Chiaia.*

Grand Hotel Parker's

$$$ | **HOTEL** | A little up the hill from Chiaia, with fine views of the bay and distant Capri, this landmark hotel, first opened in 1870, continues to serve up a supremely elegant dose of old-style atmosphere to visiting VIPs. **Pros:** excellent restaurant; historic hotel; fabulous views. **Cons:** terrace sometimes closed when hosting weddings; not quite as grand as it once was; a very long walk or taxi ride from city center and seafront. [$] *Rooms from: €250* ✉ *Corso Vittorio Emanuele 135, Chiaia* ☎ *081/7612474* 🌐 *www.grandhotelparkers.it* 🛏 *79 rooms* 🍴 *Free Breakfast.*

★ **Grand Hotel Vesuvio**

$$$$ | **HOTEL** | You'd never guess from the modern exterior that this is the oldest of the city's great seafront hotels—the place where Enrico Caruso died, where Oscar Wilde dallied with lover Lord Alfred Douglas, and where Bill Clinton charmed the waitresses—fortunately, the spacious, soothing interior compensates for what's lacking on the outside. **Pros:** luxurious atmosphere; directly opposite Borgo Marinaro; historic setting and traditionally furnished rooms. **Cons:** not all rooms have great views; reception staff can be snooty; spa and pool cost extra. [$] *Rooms from: €400* ✉ *Via Partenope 45, Santa Lucia* ☎ *081/7640044* 🌐 *www.vesuvio.it* 🛏 *160 rooms* 🍴 *Free Breakfast.*

★ **Hotel Palazzo Alabardieri**

$$ | **HOTEL** | Just off the chic Piazza dei Martiri, this is a solid choice among the city's smaller smart hotels—with comfortable guest rooms and a fab location for sights, shopping, and eating. **Pros:** impressive public salons; polite, pleasant staff; central yet quiet location. **Cons:** small rooms; cell reception and a/c are patchy; no sea view. [$] *Rooms from: €178* ✉ *Via Alabardieri 38, Chiaia* ☎ *081/415278* 🌐 *www.palazzoalabardieri.it* 🛏 *44 rooms* 🍴 *Free Breakfast* [M] *Chiaia.*

Hotel Santa Lucia
$$ | **HOTEL** | Neapolitan lungomare enchantment can be yours if you stay at this luxurious, quietly understated hotel that overlooks the port immortalized in the song "Santa Lucia." Hundreds of boats bob in the water, seafood restaurants line the harbor, and the medieval Castel dell'Ovo presides over it all. **Pros:** great views from most rooms; fab pastries and baked goods; proximity to the port is convenient for trips to the islands. **Cons:** not near a metro stop; extra charges at breakfast; rooms can be small. [$] *Rooms from: €200* ✉ *Via Partenope 46, Santa Lucia* ☎ *081/7640666* 🌐 *www.santalucia.it* 🛏 *85 rooms* 🍴 *Free Breakfast.*

★ Il Transatlantico Napoli
$$ | **B&B/INN** | Enjoying perhaps the most enchanting setting in all of Naples, this modestly priced hotel tops many travelers' dream list of places to stay. **Pros:** fabulous location and views; boat hire available; reasonable prices for maritime-style rooms. **Cons:** sometimes loud music in the Borgo; no elevator; dated furniture and fabrics. [$] *Rooms from: €140* ✉ *Via Luculliana 15, Santa Lucia* ☎ *081/7648842* 🌐 *www.transatlanticonapoli.com* 🛏 *8 rooms* 🍴 *No Meals.*

Pinto-Storey Hotel
$ | **HOTEL** | The name combines a 19th-century Englishman who fell in love with Naples with a certain Signora Pinto; together they went on to establish this hotel that overflows with warmth, charm, and late-19th-century (but fully renovated) decor. **Pros:** safe neighborhood; traditional Anglophile atmosphere; near public transit. **Cons:** two-night minimum in high season; no views; not close to major sights. [$] *Rooms from: €100* ✉ *Via G. Martucci 72, Chiaia* ☎ *081/681260* 🌐 *www.pintostorey.it* 🛏 *6 rooms* 🍴 *No Meals* [M] *Piazza Amedeo.*

★ Weekend a Napoli
$ | **B&B/INN** | Patrizia and Paolo run this homey upscale B&B in a handsome stile-liberty (Italian Art Nouveau) palazzo on the well-to-do Vomero hill. **Pros:** residential Vomero atmosphere; passionate, knowledgeable hosts; home baking and cozy lounge. **Cons:** away from the downtown sights; some rooms have steps to mezzanine beds; basic rooms lack light and are noisy. [$] *Rooms from: €120* ✉ *Via Enrico Alvino 157, Vomero* ☎ *081/5781010* 🌐 *weekendanapoli.com* 🕒 *Closed Jan.* 🛏 *6 rooms* 🍴 *Free Breakfast.*

🍸 Nightlife

★ Enoteca Belledonne
WINE BARS | Between 8 and 9 in the evening, it seems as though the whole upscale Chiaia neighborhood has descended into this tiny space for an aperitivo. The small tables and low stools are notably uncomfortable, but the cozy atmosphere and the pleasure of being surrounded by glass-front cabinets full of wine bottles with beautiful labels more than makes up for it. Excellent local wines are available by the glass at great prices. ✉ *Vico Belledonne a Chiaia 18, Chiaia* ☎ *081/403162* 🌐 *www.enotecabelledonne.it* [M] *San Pasquale.*

🛍 Shopping

Marinella
MEN'S CLOTHING | Count the British royal family among the customers of this shop that has been selling old-fashioned made-to-measure ties for more than 100 years. ✉ *Via Riviera di Chiaia 287, Chiaia* ☎ *081/7642365* 🌐 *www.emarinella.eu* [M] *Chiaia, San Pasquale.*

Tramontano
LEATHER GOODS | Since 1865, this place has been crafting fine leather luggage, bags, belts, and wallets. ✉ *Via Chiaia 143, Chiaia* ☎ *081/414837* 🌐 *www.tramontano.it* [M] *Chiaia.*

Piazza Garibaldi

The first place many see in Naples thanks to the city's main train station, there is not a lot to hold your attention here. Recently completely rebuilt, it now features a swanky new underground shopping mall based around the train station, but is still a gathering point for street sellers and hawkers and is best avoided at night. The surrounding area has some notable churches as well as the famed Porta Capuana, one of the historic gates to the city walls.

🍴 Restaurants

Da Michele

$ | PIZZA | You may recognize Da Michele from the movie *Eat Pray Love*, but for more than 140 years before Julia Roberts arrived, this place was a culinary reference point. Despite offering only two types of pizza—marinara (with tomato, garlic, and oregano) and Margherita (with tomato, mozzarella, and basil)—plus a small selection of drinks, it still manages to draw long lines. **Known for:** long lines outside the humble, historic HQ; marinara and Margherita only; pizza purists' favorite. $ *Average main: €6* ✉ *Via Sersale 1/3, off Corso Umberto, between Piazza Garibaldi and Piazza Nicola Amore, Piazza Garibaldi* ☎ *081/5539204* ⊕ *www.damichele.net* ⊗ *Closed Sun. and 2 wks in Aug.* Ⓜ *Garibaldi, Duomo.*

Mimì alla Ferrovia

$$ | NEOPOLITAN | Patrons of this Neapolitan institution have included the filmmaker Federico Fellini and that truly Neapolitan comic genius and self-styled aristocrat, Totò. It's in a fairly seedy area so take a taxi, especially at night, but it's worth it to sample Mimì's classics such as pasta e fagioli and the sea bass *al presidente*, baked in a pastry crust and enjoyed by visiting Italian presidents. **Known for:** fresh fish on display from the market; classic Neapolitan dishes; crammed with washed-out photos of Italian VIPs. $ *Average main: €18* ✉ *Via A. D'Aragona 19/21, Piazza Garibaldi* ☎ *081/5538525* ⊕ *www.mimiallaferrovia.it* ⊗ *Closed Sun. and last wk in Aug.* Ⓜ *Garibaldi.*

Capodimonte and Vomero

The Parco di Capodimonte is the crowning point of the vast mountainous plain that slopes down through the city to the waterfront area. Nearly 5 km (3 miles) removed from the crowds in the Centro Storico, it is enjoyed by locals and visitors alike as a favored escape from the overheated city center. With views over the entire city and bay, the park was first founded in the 18th century as a hunting preserve by Charles of Bourbon. Before long, partly to house the famous Farnese collection that he had inherited from his mother, he commissioned a spectacular Palazzo Reale for the park. Today this palace is the Museo di Capodimonte, which contains among its treasures the city's greatest collection of Old Master paintings.

To the west is the largely residential Vomero. From the balcony belvedere of the Museo di San Martino, a rich spread of southern Italian amplitude fills the eye: hillsides dripping with luxuriant greenery interspersed with villainously ugly apartment houses, streets short and narrow—leading to an unspeakable as well as unsolvable traffic problem—countless church spires and domes, and far below, the reason it all works, the intensely blue Bay of Naples. To tie together the lower parts with Vomero, everyone uses the *funicolare*—the funicular system that runs on four separate routes up and down the hill.

⊙ Sights

Castel Sant'Elmo

CASTLE/PALACE | Perched on the Vomero, this massive castle is almost the size of a small town. Built by the Angevins in the 14th century to dominate the port and the old city, it was remodeled by the Spanish in 1537. The parapets, configured in the form of a six-pointed star, provide fabulous views. The whole bay lies on one side; on another, the city spreads out like a map, its every dome and turret clearly visible; to the east is slumbering Vesuvius. Once a major military outpost, the castle these days hosts occasional cultural events. Its prison, the Carcere alto di Castel Sant'Elmo, is the site of the Museo del Novecento Napoli, which traces Naples's 20th-century artistic output, from the Futurist period through the 1980s. ⊠ *Largo San Martino, Vomero* ☎ *848/800288, 081/5587708* ⊕ *www. beniculturali.it/luogo/castel-sant-elmo-e-museo-del-novecento-a-napoli* ⊠ *€5* ☉ *Museo del Novecento closed Tues.*

★ Certosa e Museo di San Martino

RELIGIOUS BUILDING | Atop a rocky promontory with a fabulous view of the entire city and majestic salons that would please any monarch, the Certosa di San Martino is a monastery that seems more like a palace. This *certosa,* or charter house, started in 1325, was so sumptuous that by the 18th century Ferdinand IV was threatening to halt the religious order's government subsidy. Although the Angevin heritage can be seen in the pointed arches and cross-vaulted ceiling of the **Certosa Church**, over the years dour Gothic was traded in for varicolored Neapolitan Baroque. Highlights include the **Cappella del Tesoro**, with Luca Giordano's ceiling fresco of Judith holding aloft Holofernes's head and Jusepe de Ribera's masterful *Pietà*; architect and sculptor Cosimo Fanzago's polychrome marble work in the **Chiostro Grande** (Great Cloister); the **Quarto del Priore** (Prior's Quarters), an extravaganza of salons

filled with frescoes, majolica-tile floors, and paintings; and the Sezione Presepiale, the world's greatest collection of Christmas cribs. ⊠ *Piazzale San Martino 8, Vomero* ☎ *081/2294503* ⊕ *www. beniculturali.it/luogo/certosa-e-museo-di-san-martino* ⊠ *€6* ☉ *Closed Wed.* Ⓜ *Vanvitelli.*

★ Museo di Capodimonte

ART MUSEUM | The grandiose, 18th-century, neoclassical, Bourbon royal palace houses fine and decorative art in 124 rooms. The main galleries on the first floor are devoted to the Farnese collection, as well as work from the 13th to the 18th century, including many pieces by Dutch masters, as well as an El Greco and 12 Titian paintings. On the second floor look for stunning paintings by Simone Martini (circa 1284–1344) and Caravaggio (1573–1610). ⊠ *Via Miano 2, Capodimonte* ☎ *081/7499111, 848/800288* ⊕ *capodimonte.cultura.gov. it, www.amicidicapodimonte.org* ⊠ *€14* ☉ *Closed Wed.*

Nightlife

Fonoteca

BARS | By day the city's best independent record store, by night this is *the* place to hear eclectic tunes and mingle in Vomero. They serve decent bar snacks, pasta dishes, cakes, and drinks. ⊠ *Via Morghen 31, Vomero* ☎ *081/5560338* ⊕ *www. fonoteca.net* Ⓜ *Vanvitelli.*

Herculaneum

10 km (6 miles) southeast of Naples.

A visit to the archaeological site of Herculaneum neatly counterbalances the hustle of its larger neighbor, Pompeii. Although close to the heart of busy Ercolano—indeed, in places right under the town—the ancient site seems worlds apart.

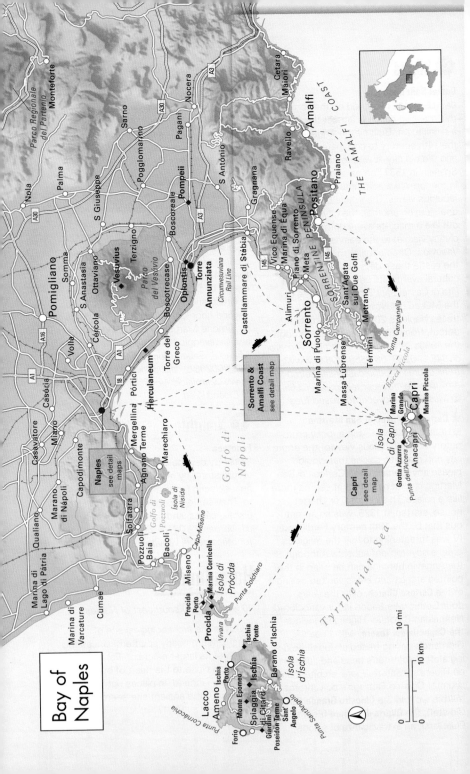

GETTING HERE AND AROUND

To get to Herculaneum by car, take the A3 Naples–Salerno autostrada and exit at Ercolano. Follow signs for the "Scavi" (excavations). The Circumvesuviana railway connects Herculaneum to Naples, Portici, Torre del Greco, Torre Annunziata, Pompeii, and Sorrento.

 Sights

★ Herculaneum Ruins

RUINS | Lying more than 50 feet below the present-day town of Ercolano, the ruins of Herculaneum are set among the acres of greenhouses that make this area an important European flower-growing center. In AD 79, the gigantic eruption of Vesuvius, which also destroyed Pompeii, buried the town under a tide of volcanic mud. The semiliquid pyroclastic surge seeped into the crevices and niches of every building, covering household objects, enveloping textiles and wood, and sealing all in a compact, airtight tomb. Excavation began in 1738 under King Charles of Bourbon, using tunnels. Digging was interrupted but recommenced in 1828, continuing into the following century. Today less than half of Herculaneum has been excavated. With contemporary Ercolano and the unlovely Resina Quarter sitting on top of the site, progress is limited. From the ramp leading down to Herculaneum's well-preserved edifices, you get a good overall view of the site, as well as an idea of the amount of volcanic debris that had to be removed to bring it to light.

About 5,000 people lived in Herculaneum when it was destroyed, many of them fishermen and craftsmen. Among the recent poignant discoveries of human remains was that of the blood-stained skeleton of a 40-something man found on the old beach in 2020. Experts believe he may have been trying to escape the 750°F–950°F atomic-bomb-like blast. He is clutching a small leather bag with a wooden box, from which a ring is protruding.

Although Herculaneum had only one-third the population of Pompeii and has been only partially excavated, what has been found is generally better preserved. In some cases you can even see the original wooden beams, doors, and staircases. Unfortunately, the Villa dei Papiri (Villa of Papyri) is currently closed to the public— this excavation outside the main site was built by Julius Caesar's father-in-law (with a replica built by Paul Getty in Malibu almost 2,000 years later). The building is named for almost 2,000 carbonized papyrus scrolls dug up here in the 18th century, leading scholars to believe that this may have been a study center or library. Also worth special attention are the carbonized remains within the Casa del Tramezzo di Legno (House of the Wooden Partition).

Be sure to stock up on refreshments beforehand; there is no food at the archaeological site. At the entrance, pick up a free map showing the gridlike layout of the dig, which is divided into numbered blocks, or insulae. Splurge on an audio guide app via ⊕ *www.ercolano. tours* (€10; adult and children's versions): the standard audio guide (€8 for one, €13 for two) may be available for those without a smartphone. You can also join a group with a local guide (around €15 per person). Most of the houses are open, and a representative cross section of domestic, commercial, and civic buildings can be seen. Check the website for the latest openings and news of recent excavation discoveries. ⊠ *Corso Resina 6, Ercolano* ☎ *081/7777008* ⊕ *ercolano. beniculturali.it* ✉ *€13* ⊗ *Closed Wed.*

Museo Archeologico Virtuale (MAV)

HISTORY MUSEUM | FAMILY | With dazzling "virtual" versions of Herculaneum's streets and squares and a multidimensional simulation of Vesuvius erupting, Herculaneum's 1st-century-meets-the-21st-century museum is a must for kids and adults alike. After stopping at the ticket office you descend, as in an excavation, to a floor below.

You'll experience Herculaneum's Villa dei Papiri before and (even more dramatically) during the eruption, courtesy of special effects: enter "the burning cloud" of AD 79; then emerge, virtually speaking, inside Pompeii's House of the Faun, which can be seen both as it is and as it was for two centuries BC. The next re-creation is again Villa dei Papiri. Then comes a stellar pre- and postflooding view of Baia's Nymphaeum, the now-displaced statues arrayed as they were in the days of Emperor Claudius, who commissioned them.

Visitors here are invited to take a front-row seat for "Day and Night in the Forum of Pompeii," with soldiers, litter-bearing slaves, and toga-clad figures moving spectrally to complete the spell; or to make a vicarious visit to the Lupanari brothels, their various pleasures illustrated in graphic virtual frescoes along the walls. A wooden model of Herculaneum's theater, its virtual re-creation, reminds us that it was here that a local farmer, while digging a well, first came across what proved to be not merely a single building, but a whole town. Equally fascinating are the virtual baths. There's also a 3D film of Vesuvius erupting, replete with a fatalistic narrative and cataclysmic special effects: the words of Pliny the Younger provide a timeless commentary while the floor vibrates under your feet. ✉ *Via IV Novembre 44, Ercolano* ☎ *081/7776843* ⊕ *www.museomav.it* 💶 *€10* 🕑 *Closed Mon. and Tues. Oct.–Feb.*

Pompeii

22 km (14 miles) southeast of Naples, 17 km (10½ miles) southeast of Herculaneum.

Mention Pompeii and most travelers think of ancient Roman villas, prancing bronze fauns, plaster casts of writhing Vesuvius victims, and the fabled days of the emperors.

GETTING HERE AND AROUND

To get to Pompeii by car, take the A3 Napoli–Salerno highway to the Pompei exit and follow signs for the nearby "Scavi." There are numerous guarded parking lots near the Porta Marina, Piazza Essedra, and Anfiteatro entrances, where you can leave your vehicle for a fee.

Pompeii has two central Circumvesuviana railway stations served by two separate train lines. The Naples–Sorrento train stops at "Pompei Scavi–Villa dei Misteri," 100 yards from the Porta Marina ticket office of the archaeological site, while the Naples–Poggiomarino train stops at Pompei Santuario, more convenient for the Santuario della Madonna del Rosario and the hotels and restaurants in the modern town center. A third Ferrovie della Statale (FS) train station south of the town center is only convenient if arriving from Salerno or Rome.

 Sights

★ **Pompeii**

RUINS | Petrified memorial to Vesuvius's eruption in 79 AD, Pompeii is the largest, most accessible, and most famous excavation anywhere. Ancient Pompeii had a population of 10,000–20,000 and covered about 170 acres on the seaward end of the Sarno Plain. Today it attracts more than 2 million visitors every year, but if you come in the quieter late afternoon, you can truly fall under the site's spell. Highlights include the Foro (Forum), which served as Pompeii's cultural, political, commercial, and religious hub; homes that were captured in various states by the eruption of Vesuvius, including the Casa del Poeta Tragico (House of the Tragic Poet), a typical middle-class residence with a floor mosaic of a chained dog, and the Casa dei Vettii (House of the Vettii), the best example of a wealthy merchant's home; the Villa dei Misteri (Villa of the Mysteries), a palatial abode with many fresco-adorned rooms; and the Anfiteatro (Amphitheater), built

Planning for Your Day in Pompeii

Getting There

The archaeological site of Pompeii has its own stop (Pompei–Villa dei Misteri) on the Circumvesuviana line to Sorrento, close to the main entrance at the Porta Marina, which is the best place from which to start a tour. If, like many visitors every year, you get the wrong train from Naples (stopping at the other "Pompei" station), all is not lost. There's another entrance to the excavations at the far end of the site, just a seven-minute walk to the Amphitheater.

Admission

Single tickets cost €16 (€10 reduced afternoon admission fee from 3:30 pm) and are valid for one full day. The site is open April–October, daily 9–7 (last admission at 5:30; although check ahead as it's closed Monday from early autumn through early June); and November–March, daily 9–5 (last admission at 3:30). For more information call ☎ 081/8575347 or visit ⊕ www.pompeiisites.org.

What to Bring

The only restaurant inside the site is both overpriced and busy, so bring along water and snacks. There are some shady, underused picnic tables outside the Porta di Nola, to the northeast of the site. Luggage is not allowed in the site.

Timing

Visiting Pompeii does have its frustrating aspects: many buildings are blocked off by locked gates, and enormous group tours tend to clog up more popular attractions. But the site is so big that it's easy to lose yourself. To really see the site, you'll need four or five hours, a bit less if you hire a guide.

To get the most out of Pompeii, rent an audio guide and opt for one of the three itineraries (two hours, four hours, or six hours). If hiring a guide, make sure the guide is registered for an English tour and standing inside the gate; agree beforehand on the length of the tour and the price, and prepare yourself for sound bites of English mixed with dollops of hearsay. For a higher-quality (and more expensive) full-day tour, try Context Travel (⊕ www.contexttravel.com).

around 70 BC. Consider renting an €8 audio guide and opt for one of the three itineraries (two hours, four hours, or six hours) available at Porta Marina. If hiring a guide, agree beforehand on the length of the tour and the price. ⊠ Pompei ☎ 081/8575347 ⊕ www.pompeiisites.org 🎫 From €16 ☞ Tickets available online at www.ticketone.it/en/artist/scavi-pompei/.

Vesuvius

8 km (5 miles) northeast of Herculaneum, 16 km (10 miles) east of Naples.

Vesuvius may have lost its plume of smoke for now, but it has lost none of its fascination—especially for those who live in the towns around the cone.

GETTING HERE AND AROUND

To arrive by car, take the A3 Napoli–Salerno autostrada to the Torre del Greco exit and follow Via E. De Nicola from the tollbooth and then signs for the Parco Nazionale del Vesuvio.

Vesuvio Express operates a shuttle-bus service (€10) departing every 40 minutes from Ercolano Circumvesuviana station. The vehicles thread their way rapidly up back roads, reaching the top in 20 minutes. Allow at least three hours for the journey, including a 30-minute walk to the crater on a soft cinder track.

BUS CONTACT Vesuvio Express. ✉ *Piazzale Stazione Circumvesuviano 7,* ☎ *081/7393666* ⊕ *vesuvioexpress.info.*

 Sights

Mt. Vesuvius

VOLCANO | Although Vesuvius's destructive powers are on hold, the threat of an eruption remains ever present. Seen from the other side of the Bay of Naples, Vesuvius appears to have two peaks: on the northern side is the steep face of Monte Somma, possibly part of the original crater wall in AD 79; to the south is the present-day cone of Vesuvius, which has actually formed within the ancient crater. The AD 79 cone would have been considerably higher, perhaps peaking at around 9,000 feet. The upper slopes bear the visible scars left by 19th- and 20th-century eruptions, the most striking being the lava flow from 1944 lying to the left (north side) of the approach road from Ercolano on the way up.

As you tour the cities that felt the volcano's wrath, you may be overwhelmed by the urge to explore Vesuvius itself, and it's well worth the trip. The view when the air is clear is magnificent, with the curve of the coast and the tiny white houses among the orange and lemon blossoms. When the summit becomes lost in mist, though, you'll be lucky to see your hand in front of your face. If you

notice the summit clearing—it tends to be clearer in the afternoon—head for it. If possible, see Vesuvius after you've toured the ruins of buried Herculaneum to appreciate the magnitude of the volcano's power. Admission to the crater includes a compulsory guide, usually a young geologist who speaks a smattering of English. At the bottom you'll be offered a stout walking stick (a small tip is appreciated when you return it). The climb can be tiring if you're not used to steep hikes. Because of the volcanic stone you should wear athletic or sturdy shoes, not sandals. ☎ *081/7775720, 081/8653911* ⊕ *www.parconazionaledelvesuvio.it* ⊠ *€10* ⊘ *Tickets in advance at vesuviopark.vivaticket.it.*

Oplontis (Torre Annunziata)

20 km (12 miles) southeast of Naples, 5 km (3 miles) west of Pompeii.

Surrounded by the fairly drab 1960s urban landscape of Torre Annunziata, Oplontis justifies its reputation as one of the more mysterious archaeological sites to be unearthed in the 20th century. The villa complex has been imaginatively ascribed—from a mere inscription on an amphora—to Nero's second wife, Poppaea Sabina. Her family was well known among the landed gentry of neighboring Pompeii, although, after a kick in the stomach from her emperor husband, she died some 15 years before the villa was overwhelmed by the eruption of 79.

GETTING HERE AND AROUND

By car, take the A3 Napoli–Salerno autostrada to the Torre Annunziata exit. Follow Via Veneto west, then turn left onto Via Sepolcri for the excavations. By train, take the Circumvesuviana railway to Torre Annunziata, the town's modern name (€2.80 from Naples).

Continued on page 720

ANCIENT POMPEII
TOMB OF A CIVILIZATION

The site of Pompeii, petrified memorial to Vesuvius's eruption in AD 79, is the largest, most accessible, and probably most famous of excavations anywhere.

A busy commercial center with a population of 10,000–20,000, ancient Pompeii covered about 170 acres on the seaward end of the fertile Sarno Plain. Today Pompeii is choked with both the dust of 25 centuries and more than 2 million visitors every year; only by escaping the hordes and lingering along its silent streets can you truly fall under the site's spell. On a quiet backstreet, all you need is a little imagination to picture life in this ancient town. Come in the late afternoon when the site is nearly deserted and you will understand the true pleasure of visiting Pompei.

A FUNNY THING HAPPENS ON THE WAY TO THE FORUM

as you walk through Pompeii. Covered with dust and decay as it is, the city seems to come alive. Perhaps it's the familiar signs of life observed along the ancient streets: bakeries with large ovens just like those for making pizzas, *thermopolia* (snack bars) tracks of cart wheels cut into the road surface, graffiti etched onto the plastered surfaces of street walls. But a glance up at Vesuvius, still brooding over the scene like an enormous headstone, reminds you that these folks—whether imagined in your head or actually wearing a mantle of

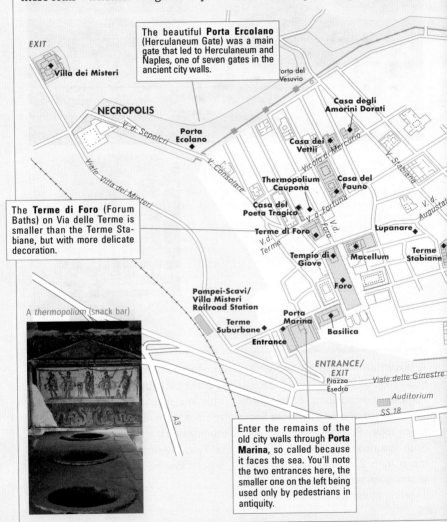

The beautiful **Porta Ercolano** (Herculaneum Gate) was a main gate that led to Herculaneum and Naples, one of seven gates in the ancient city walls.

The **Terme di Foro** (Forum Baths) on Via delle Terme is smaller than the Terme Stabiane, but with more delicate decoration.

A *thermopolium* (snack bar)

Enter the remains of the old city walls through **Porta Marina**, so called because it faces the sea. You'll note the two entrances here, the smaller one on the left being used only by pedestrians in antiquity.

EXIT
Villa dei Misteri
Porta del Vesuvio
NECROPOLIS
V. d. Sepolcri
Porta Ecolano
Casa degli Amorini Dorati
Casa dei Vettii
Vicolo di Mercurio
V. Stabiana
V. Consolare
Thermopolium Caupona
Casa del Fauno
Viale Villa dei Misteri
Casa del Poeta Tragico
V. d. Fortuna
V. d. Foro
V. d. Augustali
Terme di Foro
Lupanare
V. d. Terme
Tempio di Giove
Macellum
Terme Stabiane
Foro
Pompei-Scavi/ Villa Misteri Railroad Station
Porta Marina
Terme Suburbane
Basilica
Entrance
ENTRANCE/ EXIT
Piazza Esedra
Viale delle Ginestre
Auditorium
SS 18
A3

lava dust—have not taken a breath for centuries. The town was laid out in a grid pattern, with two main intersecting streets. The wealthiest took a whole block for themselves; or built a house and rented out the front rooms, facing the street, as shops.

Pompeii's cemetery, or Necropolis

There were good numbers of tabernae (taverns) and thermopolia on almost every corner, and frequent shows at the amphitheater.

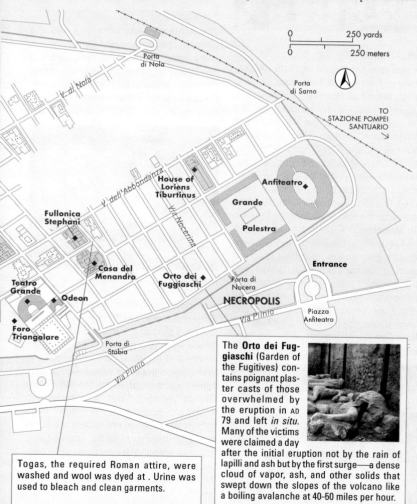

0 ——— 250 yards
0 ——— 250 meters

Porta di Nola

V. di Nola

Porta di Sarno

TO STAZIONE POMPEI SANTUARIO

House of Loriens Tiburtinus

V. dell'Abbondanza

Via Nocerina

Anfiteatro

Grande Palestra

Fullonica Stephani

Casa del Menandro

Orto dei Fuggiaschi

Porta di Nocera

Entrance

Teatro Grande

Odeon

NECROPOLIS

Via Plinio

Piazza Anfiteatro

Foro Triangolare

Porta di Stabia

Via Plinio

The **Orto dei Fuggiaschi** (Garden of the Fugitives) contains poignant plaster casts of those overwhelmed by the eruption in AD 79 and left *in situ*. Many of the victims were claimed a day after the initial eruption not by the rain of lapilli and ash but by the first surge—a dense cloud of vapor, ash, and other solids that swept down the slopes of the volcano like a boiling avalanche at 40–50 miles per hour.

Togas, the required Roman attire, were washed and wool was dyed at . Urine was used to bleach and clean garments.

PUBLIC LIFE IN ANCIENT POMPEII

Forum

THE CITY CENTER

As you enter the ruins at Porta Marina, make your way uphill to the **Foro** (Forum), which served as Pompeii's commercial, cultural, political, and religious center. You can still see some of the two stories of colonnades that used to line the square. Like the ancient Greek *agora* in Athens, the Forum was a busy shopping area, complete with public officials to apply proper standards of weights and measures. Fronted by an elegant three-column portico on the eastern side of the forum is the **Macellum**, the covered meat and fish market dating to the 2nd century BC; here vendors sold goods from their reserved spots in the central market. It was also in the Forum that elections were held, politicians let rhetoric fly, speeches and official announcements were made, and worshippers crowded around the **Tempio di Giove** (Temple of Jupiter), at the northern end of the forum.

Basilica

On the southwestern corner is the **Basilica**, the city's law court and the economic center. These rectangular aisled halls were the model for early Christian churches, which had a nave (central aisle) and two side aisles separated by rows of columns. Standing in the Basilica, you can recognize the continuity between Roman and Christian architecture.

THE GAMES

The **Anfiteatro** (Amphitheater) was the ultimate in entertainment for Pompeians and offered a gamut of experiences, but essentially this was for gladiators rather than wild animals. By Roman standards, Pompeii's amphitheater was quite small (seating 20,000). Built in about 70 BC,

Amphitheater

making it the oldest extant permanent amphitheater in the Roman world, it was oval and divided into three seating areas. There were two main entrances—at the north and south ends—and a narrow passage on the west called the Porta Libitinensis, through which the dead were probably dragged out. A wall painting found in a house near the theater (now in the Naples Museum) depicts the riot in the amphitheater in AD 59 when several citizens from the nearby town of Nocera were killed. After Nocerian appeals to Nero, shows were suspended for three years.

Fresco of Pyramus and Thisbe in the House of Loreius Tiburtinus

BATHS AND BROTHELS

In its day, Pompeii was celebrated as the Côte d'Azur, the Fire Island of the ancient Roman empire. Evidence of a Sybaritic bent is everywhere—in the town's grandest villas, in its baths and rich decorations, and murals reveal ing a wor-ship of hedonism. Satyrs, bacchantes, hermaphrodites, and acrobatic couples are pictured.

The first buildings to the left past the ticket turnstiles are the **Terme Suburbane** (Suburban Baths), built—by all accounts without permission—right up against the city walls. The baths have eyebrow-raising frescoes in the *apodyterium* (changing room) that strongly suggest that more than just bathing and massag-ing went on here.

On the walls of **Lupanari** (brothels) are scenes of erotic games in which clients could engage. The **Terme Stabiane** (Stabian Baths) had underground furnaces, the heat from which circulated beneath the floor, rose through flues in the walls, and escaped through chimneys. The sequence of the rooms is standard: changing room (apoditerium), tepid (tepidarium), hot (cali-darium), and cold (frigidarium). A vigorous massage with oil was followed by rest, and conversation.

Thanks to those deep layers of pyroclastic deposits from Vesuvius that protected the site from natural wear and tear over the centuries, graffiti found in Pompeii provide unique insights into the sort of things that the locals found important 2,000 years ago. A good many were personal and lend a human dimension to the disaster that not even the sights can equal.

At the baths: **"What is the use of having a Venus if she's made of marble?"**

At the entrance to the front lavatory at a private house: **"May I always and everywhere be as potent with women as I was here."**

On the Viale ai Teatri: **"A copper pot went missing from my shop. Anyone who returns it to me will be given 65 bronze coins."**

In the Basilica: **"A small problem gets larger if you ignore it."**

PRIVATE LIFE IN ANCIENT POMPEII

The facades of houses in Pompeii were relatively plain and seldom hinted at the care and attention lavished on the private rooms within. When visitors arrived they passed the shops and entered an atrium, from which the occupants received air, sunlight, and rainwater, the latter caught by the *impluvium*, a rectangular-shaped receptacle under the sloped roof. In the back was a receiving room, the *tablinum*, and behind was another open area, the peristyle.

House of Paquius Proculus

Life revolved around this uncovered inner courtyard, with rows of columns and perhaps a garden with a fountain. The atrium was surrounded by *cubicula* (bedrooms) and the *triclinium* (dining area). Interior floors and walls were covered with colorful marble tiles, mosaics, and frescoes.

Several homes were captured in various states by the eruption of Vesuvius, each representing a different slice of Pompeiian life. The **Casa del Fauno** (House of the Faun) displayed wonderful mosaics, now at the Museo Archeologico Nazionale in Naples. The **Casa del Poeta Tragico** (House of the Tragic Poet) is a typical middle-class house. On the floor is a mosaic of a chained dog and the inscription *cave canem* ("Beware of the dog"). The **Casa degli Amorini Dorati** (House of the Gilded Cupids) is an elegant, well-preserved home with original decorations. Many paintings and mosaics were executed at **Casa del Menandro** (House of Menander), a patrician's villa named for a fresco of the Greek playwright. Two blocks beyond the Stabian Baths you'll notice on the left the current digs at the **Casa dei Casti Amanti** (House of the Chaste Lovers). A team of plasterers and painters were at work here when Vesuvius erupted, redecorating one of the rooms and patching up the cracks in the bread oven near the entrance—possibly caused by tremors a matter of days before.

Small Garden

Triclinium — Owner's Quarters

Kitchen — Servant's Quarters

Secondary Atrium

Entrance

Garden

Atrium

Impluvium

Peristyle

CASA DEI VETTII

The **House of the Vettii** (temporarily closed for restoration) is the best example of a house owned by wealthy *mercatores* (merchants). It contains vivid murals—a magnificent pinacoteca (picture gallery) within the very heart of Pompeii. The scenes here—except for those in the two wings off the atrium—were all painted after the earthquake of AD 62. Once inside, look at the delicate frieze around the wall of the   (on the right of the peristyle garden as you enter from the atrium), depicting cupids engaged in various activities, such as selling oils and perfumes, working as goldsmiths and metalworkers, acting as wine merchants, or performing in chariot races. Another of the main attractions in the Casa dei Vettii is the small cubicle beyond the kitchen area (to the right of the atrium) with its faded erotic frescoes now protected by Perspex screens.

UNLOCKING THE VILLA DEI MISTERI

Villa dei Misteri

There is no more astounding, magnificently memorable evidence of Pompeii's devotion to the pleasures of the flesh than the frescoes on view at the **Villa dei Misteri** (Villa of the Mysteries), a palatial abode 400 yards outside the city gates, northwest of Porta Ercolano. Unearthed in 1909, this villa had many beautiful rooms painted with frescoes; the finest are in the *triclinium*. Painted in the most glowing Pompeiian reds and ochers, the panels may relate the saga of a young bride (Ariadne) and her initiation into the mysteries of the cult of Dionysus, who was a god imported to Italy from Greece and then given the Latin name of Bacchus. The god of wine and debauchery also represented the triumph of the irrational—of all those mysterious forces that no official state religion could fully suppress.

Pompeii's best frescoes, painted in glowing reds and oranges, retain an amazing vibrancy.

The Villa of the Mysteries frescoes were painted circa 50 BC, most art historians believe, and represent the peak of the Second Style of Pompeiian wall painting. The triclinium frescoes are thought to have been painted by a local artist, although the theme may well have been copied from an earlier cycle of paintings from the Hellenistic period. In all there are 10 scenes, depicting children and matrons, musicians and satyrs, phalluses and gods. There are no inscriptions (such as are found on Greek vases), and after 2,000 years historians remain puzzled by many aspects of the triclinium cycle. Scholars endlessly debate the meaning of these frescoes, but anyone can tell they are among the most beautiful paintings left to us by antiquity. In several ways, the eruption of Vesuvius was a blessing in disguise, for without it, these masterworks of art would have perished long ago.

Sights

Oplontis

RUINS | For those overwhelmed by the throngs at Pompeii, a visit to the site of Oplontis offers a chance for contemplation and intellectual stimulation. What has been excavated so far of the Villa of the Empress Poppaea covers more than 75,000 square feet, and because the site is bound by a road to the west and a canal to the south, its full extent may never be known.

Complete with porticoes, a large peristyle, a pool, baths, and extensive gardens, the villa is thought by some to have been a school for young philosophers and orators. You have to visit to appreciate the full range of Roman wall paintings; one highlight is found in Room 5, a sitting room that overlooked the sea. ⊠ *Via Sepolcri 1, Torre Annunziata* ☎ *081/8575347* ⊕ *www.pompeiisites.org* ⊠ *From €5* ⊗ *Closed Tues.*

Ischia

45 mins by hydrofoil, 90 mins by car ferry from Naples, 60 mins by ferry from Pozzuoli.

Although Capri leaves you breathless with its charm and beauty, Ischia (pronounced "EES-kee-ah"), also called Isola Verde (Green Island)—not, as is often believed, because of its lush vegetation, but for its typical green tuff rock—takes time to cast its spell. In fact, an overnight stay is not long enough; you have to look harder here for the signs of antiquity, the traffic can be reminiscent of Naples, and the island displays all the hallmarks of rapid, uncontrolled urbanization. Ischia does have many jewels, though. There are the wine-growing villages beneath the lush volcanic slopes of Monte Epomeo, and unlike Capri, the island enjoys a life of its own that survives when the tourists head home.

Ischia is volcanic in origin, with thermal springs said to cure whatever ails you. Today the island's main industry, tourism, revolves around the more than 100 thermal baths, most of which are attached to hotels.

Much of the 37 km (23 miles) of coastline are punctuated with a continuum of *stabilimenti balneari* (private bathing establishments) in summer. However, there are also lots of public beaches set against the scenic backdrop of Monte Epomeo and its verdant slopes.

GETTING HERE AND AROUND

Ischia is well connected with the mainland in all seasons. The last boats leave for Naples and Pozzuoli at about 8 pm (though in the very high season there is a midnight sailing), and you should allow plenty of time for getting to the port and buying a ticket. Ischia has three ports—Ischia Porto, Casamicciola, and Forio (hydrofoils only)—so you should choose your ferry or hydrofoil according to your destination. Non-Italians can bring cars to the island relatively freely. Up-to-date schedules are published at ⊕ *www. traghetti-ischia.info.*

Ischia's bus network reaches all the major sites and beaches on one of its 18 lines. The principal lines are CD and CS, circling the island in clockwise and counterclockwise directions—in the summer months runs continue until after midnight. The main bus terminus is in Ischia Porto at the start of Via Cosca, where buses run by the company EAV radiate out around the island. There are also convenient *fermate* (stops) at the two main beaches—Citara and Maronti—with timetables displayed at the terminus. Tickets cost €1.50 per ride, €1.80 for 100 minutes. A one-day pass is €4.50, a seven-day pass €14.50. Note that conditions can get hot and crowded at peak beach-visiting times.

VISITOR INFORMATION

CONTACT Azienda Autonoma di Cura, Soggiorno e Turismo. ✉ Via Iasolino 7, ☎ 081/5074211 ⊕ www.agenziaturismo-campania.it.

 Sights

Forio

TOWN | FAMILY | The far-western and southern coasts of Ischia are more rugged and attractive than other areas. Forio, at the extreme west, has a waterfront church, Chiesa del Soccorso, and is a good spot for lunch or dinner. ■ TIP→ **Head to the whitewashed Soccorso church to watch a gorgeous sunset—perhaps the best spot on the island to do so.** ✉ Forio.

Giardini Poseidon Terme

HOT SPRING | FAMILY | The largest spa on the island has the added boon of a natural sauna hollowed out of the rocks. Here you can sit like a Roman senator on stone chairs recessed in the rock and let the hot water cascade over you. With countless thermally regulated pools, promenades, and steam pools, plus lots of kitschy toga-clad statues of the Caesars, Poseidon exerts a special pull on tourists, many of them grandparents shepherding grandchildren. On certain days, the place is overrun with people, so be prepared for crowds and wailing babies. ✉ Citara Beach, Forio ☎ 081/9087111 ⊕ www.giardiniposeidon-terme.com ☞ €35 all day Apr.–June and Oct. and Nov., €40 July–Sept. ⊗ Closed Nov.–mid-Apr.

Ischia Ponte

NEIGHBORHOOD | FAMILY | Most of the hotels are along the beach in the part of town called Ischia Ponte, which gets its name from the *ponte* (bridge) built by Alfonso of Aragon in 1438 to link the picturesque castle on a small islet offshore with the town and port. For a while the castle was the home of Vittoria Colonna,

poetess, granddaughter of Renaissance Duke Federico da Montefeltro (1422–82), and platonic soul mate of Michelangelo, with whom she carried on a lengthy correspondence. You'll find a typical resort atmosphere in this area: countless cafés, shops, and restaurants, and a 1-km (½-mile) fine-sand beach. ✉ Ischia Ponte.

Ischia Porto

TOWN | FAMILY | This is the island's largest town and the usual point of debarkation. It's no workaday port, however, but rather a lively resort with plenty of hotels, the island's best shopping area, and low, flat-roof houses on terraced hillsides overlooking the water. Its narrow streets and villas and gardens are framed by pines. ✉ Ischia Porto.

Monte Epomeo

VOLCANO | The inland town of Fontana is the base for excursions to the top of this long-dormant volcano that dominates the island landscape. You can reach its 2,589-foot peak in less than 1½ hours of relatively easy walking. ✉ Ischia.

★ **Sant'Angelo**

TOWN | FAMILY | On the southern coast, this is a charming village with a narrow path leading to its promontory; the road doesn't reach all the way into town, so it's free of traffic. It's a five-minute boat ride from the beach of Maronti, at the foot of cliffs. ✉ Sant'Angelo.

 Restaurants

Da Cocò

$$ | SOUTHERN ITALIAN | This inviting restaurant with a terrace is on the causeway that links the Aragonese castle to the rest of Ischia. It's renowned for its fresh seafood, which is highly prized by the Ischitani: shoreline classics dominate, including the antipasto *polipo con patate* (octopus with potatoes) and primo summer favorite *spaghetti allo scoglio*. **Known for:** good spot to just sit with an aperitivo

and nibbles; deliciously light lemon and almond cake; magical setting near the castello. [$] *Average main: €21* ✉ *Via Aragonese 1, Ischia Ponte* ☎ *081/981823* ⏲ *Closed Jan. and Feb.*

O' Padrone Dò Mare

$$ | **SOUTHERN ITALIAN** | In a gorgeous seaside location just off the pedestrian stretch, this is the ideal place to enjoy fresh seafood—the name, "owner of the sea," says it all. For more than 75 years, O' Padrone Dò Mare has been an institution on the island, and locals and visitors crowd the terrace. **Known for:** local institution; spot-on fritto misto di mare seafood medley; cracking harbor views. [$] *Average main: €15* ✉ *Corso A. Rizzoli 6, Lacco Ameno* ☎ *081/900244* ⏲ *Closed Nov.–Mar.*

★ **Umberto a Mare**

$$$ | **SOUTHERN ITALIAN** | This iconic eatery has occupied the space below the Santuario del Soccorso since 1936, when the original Umberto began to grill the local catch on the seafront. The setting is divine, with a terrace overlooking the Bay of Citara and the green tuff *scogli innamorati* (lovers' rocks). **Known for:** decades-long reputation for exquisite seafood; changing displays of artworks; breathtaking sunset sea views. [$] *Average main: €26* ✉ *Via Soccorso 8, Forio* ☎ *081/997171* 🌐 *www.umbertoamare.it* ⏲ *Closed Nov.–Mar.*

Coffee and Quick Bites

Ice da Luciano

$ | **ITALIAN** | A stop here for some gelato is a must upon arriving in Ischia Ponte. **Known for:** inexpensive prices; large selection; the best ice cream on the island. [$] *Average main: €2* ✉ *Via Luigi Mazzella 140, Ischia Ponte* ☎ *081/0123228* 🌐 *www.facebook.com/icedaluciano.*

Hotels

★ **Albergo Il Monastero**

$$ | **HOTEL** | The Castello Aragonese, on its own island, is the unrivaled location for this unique hotel with a peaceful ambience and simple but comfortable rooms overlooking the Mediterranean. **Pros:** stunning views and peaceful garden; great restaurant on terrace; situated inside the castle. **Cons:** some may not like the understated decor; perhaps too far from the town's action; a long way from the entrance to your room. [$] *Rooms from: €150* ✉ *Castello Aragonese 3, Ischia Ponte* ☎ *081/992435* 🌐 *www.albergoilmonastero.it* ⏲ *Closed Nov.–late Apr.* 🛏 *21 rooms* 🍴 *Free Breakfast.*

Albergo L'Approdo

$$ | **HOTEL** | A short walk from Casamicciola's port, spas, and town center, this small hotel has a fine array of facilities and guest rooms with private terraces. **Pros:** wonderful elevated views; pool perched above bay; great beauty treatments. **Cons:** showers are tiny; not quite in the town; the beach is across a busy road. [$] *Rooms from: €134* ✉ *Via Eddomade 29, Casamicciola Terme* ☎ *081/3330190* 🌐 *www.albergolapprodo.it* 🛏 *38 rooms* 🍴 *Free Breakfast.*

★ **Mezzatorre Resort & Spa**

$$$$ | **HOTEL** | Far from the madding, sunburned crowds—in a sleekly renovated former fortress on Punta Cornacchia above the Bay of San Montano—this luxurious getaway tempts its privileged guests to stay put and *relax*, with a glamorous heated pool overlooking a storybook cove, fine restaurants, spa treatments, and hundreds of pretty pine and pomegranate trees. **Pros:** tranquil retreat with wonderful views; private bay; good restaurants and spa. **Cons:** far from the action; pricey; very isolated. [$] *Rooms from: €680* ✉ *Via Mezzatorre 23, Forio* ☎ *081/986111* 🌐 *www.mezzatorre.it* ⏲ *Closed Nov.–Apr.* 🛏 *52 rooms* 🍴 *Free Breakfast.*

Procida

35 mins by hydrofoil, 1 hr by car ferry from Naples.

Lying barely 3 km (2 miles) from the mainland and 10 km (6 miles) from the nearest port (Pozzuoli), Procida is an island of enormous contrasts. It's the most densely populated island in Europe—just more than 10,000 people crammed into less than 2 square miles—and yet there are oases like Marina Corricella and Vivara, which seem to have been bypassed by modern civilization. The inhabitants of the island—the Procidani—have an almost symbiotic relationship with the Mediterranean: many join the merchant navy, others either fish or ferry vacationers around local waters. And yet land traffic here can be more intense than on any other island in the Bay of Naples.

GETTING HERE AND AROUND

Procida's ferry timetable caters to the many daily commuters who live on the island and work in Naples or Pozzuoli. The most frequent—and cheapest—connections are from the Port of Pozzuoli. After stopping at Procida's main port, Marina Grande (also called Sancio Cattolico), many ferries and hydrofoils continue on to Ischia, for which Procida is considered a halfway house.

Sights

★ Marina Corricella

TOWN | FAMILY | Perched under the citadel of the Terra Murata, the Marina Corricella is Procida's most memorable sight. Singled out for the waterfront scenes in *Il Postino* (*The Postman,* the 1995 Oscar winner for Best Foreign Film), this fishermen's cove is one of the most eye-popping villages in Campania—a rainbow-hued, horizontal version of Positano, comprising hundreds of traditional Mediterranean-style stone houses threaded by numerous *scalatinelle* (staircase streets). ✉ *Procida.*

Restaurants

La Conchiglia

$$ | SOUTHERN ITALIAN | A meal at this restaurant, on the beach about a half-mile east of Corricella, encapsulates Procida's seaside simplicity. Lapping waves and views of the marina and Capri form the backdrop for the fresh seafood and vegetable creations. **Known for:** boat trips and bathing nearby; freshest ingredients; beachside views and breezes through open windows. [$] *Average main: €20* ✉ *Via Pizzaco 10, Procida* ☎ *081/8967602* 🌐 *www.laconchigliaristorante.com* 🕒 *Closed mid-Nov.–Mar.*

Coffee and Quick Bites

Bar Dal Cavaliere

$ | CAFÉ | This busy café-bar has outside seating on the *basalti* flagstones with views of the port, so you can watch the boats coming in and out while munching on sfogliatella, panino, or a semi-freddo. **Known for:** stuzzichini snacks with beers and aperitivi; near the ferry port; pastries sold by weight—great for groups. [$] *Average main: €5* ✉ *Via Roma 42, Marina Grande, Procida* ☎ *081/8101074.*

Capri

Gorgeous grottoes, soaring conical peaks, caverns great and small, plus villas of the emperors and thousands of legends brush Capri with an air of whispered mystery. Emperor Augustus was the first to tout the island's pleasures by nicknaming it Apragopolis (City of Sweet Idleness), and Capri has drawn escapists of all kinds ever since. Ancient Greek and Roman goddesses were moved aside by the likes of Jacqueline Onassis, Elizabeth Taylor, and Brigitte Bardot, who made the island into a paparazzo's playground in the 1960s. Today, new generations of glitterati continue to answer the island's call.

Life on Capri gravitates around the two centers of Capri Town (on the saddle between Monte Tiberio and Monte Solaro) and Anacapri, higher up (902 feet). The main road connecting Capri Town with the upper town of Anacapri is well plied by buses. On arriving at the main harbor, the Marina Grande, everyone heads for the famous funicular, which ascends (and descends) several times an hour. Once you're lofted up to Anacapri by bus, you can reach the island heights by taking the spectacular chairlift that ascends to the top of Monte Solaro (1,932 feet) from Anacapri's town center. Within Capri Town and Anacapri foot power is the preferred mode of transportation, as much for convenience as for the sheer delight of walking along these gorgeous streets and roads.

GETTING HERE AND AROUND

Capri is well connected with the mainland in all seasons, though there are more sailings April–October. Hydrofoils, Sea Cats, and similar vessels leave from Molo Beverello (below Piazza Municipio) in Naples, while far less frequent car ferries leave from Calata Porta di Massa, 1,000 yards to the east. There's also service to and from Sorrento's Marina Piccola. Much of Capri is pedestrianized, and a car is a great hindrance, not a help.

Several ferry and hydrofoil companies ply the waters of the Bay of Naples, making frequent trips to Capri. Schedules change from season to season; the tourist office's website (⊕ *www.capritourism. com*) gives updated departure times. However, you can't return to Naples after the last sailing (11 pm in high season, often 8 pm or even earlier in low season). There's little to be gained—sometimes nothing—from buying a round-trip ticket, which will just tie you down to the return schedule of one line. However, book in advance in spring and summer for a Sunday return to the mainland.

VISITOR INFORMATION

CONTACTS Azienda Autonoma di Cura, Soggiorno e Turismo. ⊠ *Piazza Umberto I,* ☎ *081/8370686* ⊕ *www.capritourism. com.*

 # Sights

★ Anacapri

TOWN | A tortuous road leads up to Anacapri, the island's "second city," about 3 km (2 miles) from Capri Town. To get here you can take a bus either from Via Roma in Capri Town or from Marina Grande (both €2), or a taxi (about €30 one-way; agree on the fare before starting out). Crowds are thick down Via Capodimonte leading to Villa San Michele and around Piazza Vittoria, the square where you catch the chairlift to the top of Monte Solaro. Via Finestrale leads to the noted **Le Boffe quarter,** centered on the Piazza Diaz. Le Boffe owes its name to the distinctive domestic architecture prevalent here, which uses vaults and sculpted groins instead of crossbeams. Elsewhere, Anacapri is quietly appealing. It's a good starting point for walks, such as the 80-minute round-trip journey to the **Migliara Belvedere,** on the island's southern coast. ⊠ *Anacapri.*

Capri Town

TOWN | On arrival at the port, pick up the excellent map of the island at the tourist office. You may have to wait for the funicular railway (€2 one-way) to Capri Town, some 450 feet above the harbor. So this might be the time to splurge on an open-top taxi—it could save you an hour in line and a sweaty ride packed into a tiny, swaying bus. From the upper station, walk out into Piazza Umberto I, better known as the Piazzetta, the island's social hub. ⊠ *Capri.*

Certosa di San Giacomo

HISTORIC SIGHT | An eerie atmosphere hangs around neglected corners of this once-grand, palatial complex between the Castiglione and Tuoro hills, which

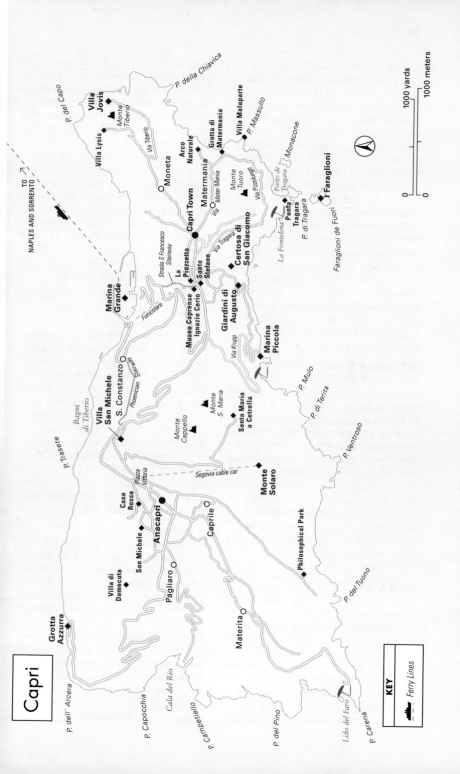

Capri

KEY
~~~ Ferry Lines

1000 yards
1000 meters

TO NAPLES AND SORRENTO

P. del Capo
P. della Chiavica
Villa Jovis
Monte Tiberio
Via Tiberio
Villa Lysis
Moneta
Arco Naturale
Grotta di Matermania
Villa Malaparte
P. Massullo
Matermania
Via Matermania
Capri Town
Via Matermania
Monte Tuoro
Via Pizzolungo
Porto de Tragara
Monacone
Strada S Francesco Stairway
La Piazzetta
Santo Stefano
Certosa di San Giacomo
Via Tragara
Punta Tragara
Faraglioni
Via Tragara
La Fontelina
Museo Caprense Ignazio Cerio
Giardini di Augusto
P. di Tragara
Faraglioni de Fuori
Marina Grande
Funicolare
Bagni di Tiberio
Villa San Michele
S. Constanzo
Phoenician Stairway
Via Krupp
Marina Piccola
P. Mulo
Monte S. Maria
Santa Maria a Cetrella
Monte Cappello
P. di Terita
P. Trasete
Segovia cable car
Piazza Vittoria
Monte Solaro
P. Ventroso
Casa Rossa
Anacapri
Caprile
Philosophical Park
P. del Tuono
San Michele
Pagliaro
Villa di Damecuta
Grotta Azzurra
Materita
P. dell' Arcea
Cala del Rio
P. Capocchia
P. Campetiello
P. del Pino
Lido del Faro
P. Carena

was for centuries a Carthusian monastery dedicated to St. James. It was founded between 1371 and 1374, when Queen Giovanna I of Naples gave Count Giacomo Arcucci, her secretary, the land and the means to create it. The count himself then became devoutly religious and retired here until his death. After the monastery was sacked by the pirates Dragut and Barbarossa in the 16th century, it was thoroughly restored and rebuilt—thanks in part to heavy taxes exacted from the populace. The Quarto del Priore hosts occasional art exhibitions from international artists, but the showstopper here is the Museo Diefenbach, with restored large canvases by influential German painter K.W. Diefenbach, who visited Capri in 1899 and stayed until his death in 1913. ⊠ *Via Certosa, Capri* ☎ *081/8376218* 🖾 *€6, with audio guide* ☉ *Closed Mon.*

★ Giardini di Augusto
(*Gardens of Augustus*)

GARDEN | From the terraces of this beautiful public garden, you can see the village of Marina Piccola below—restaurants, cabanas, and swimming platforms huddle among the shoals—and admire the steep, winding Via Krupp, actually a staircase cut into the rock. Friedrich Krupp, the German arms manufacturer, loved Capri and became one of the island's most generous benefactors. Sadly, the path down to Marina Piccola is closed indefinitely due to the danger of rockfalls. ⊠ *Via Matteotti, beyond monastery of San Giacomo, Capri* 🖾 *€1.*

Grotta Azzurra

CAVE | Only when the Grotta Azzurra was "discovered" in 1826, by the Polish poet August Kopisch and Swiss artist Ernest Fries, did Capri become a tourist destination. The watery cave's blue beauty became a symbol of the return to nature and revolt from reason that marked the Romantic era, and it soon became a required stop on the Grand Tour. In reality, the grotto had long been a local

landmark. During the Roman era—as testified by the extensive remains, primarily below sea level, and several large statues now at the Certosa di San Giacomo—it had been the elegant, mosaic-decorated nymphaeum of the adjoining villa of Gradola. Historians can't quite agree if it was simply a lovely little pavilion where rich patricians would cool themselves or truly a religious site where sacred mysteries were practiced. The water's extraordinary sapphire color is caused by a hidden opening in the rock that refracts the light. At highest illumination the very air inside seems tinted blue. Locals say the afternoon light is best from April to June, and the morning in July and August.

The Blue Grotto can be reached from Marina Grande or from the small embarkation point below Anacapri on the northwest side of the island, accessible by bus from Anacapri. If you're pressed for time, however, skip this sometimes frustrating and disappointing excursion. You board one boat to get to the grotto, then transfer to a smaller boat that takes you inside. If there's a backup of boats waiting to get in, you'll be given precious little time to enjoy the gorgeous color of the water and its silvery reflections. ⊠ *Capri* 🖾 *From €15 from Marina Grande via various companies, then €14 by rowboat with Coop. Battellieri* ☉ *Closed if the sea is even minimally rough.*

★ I Faraglioni

NATURE SIGHT | Few landscapes set more artists dreaming than that of the famous Faraglioni—three enigmatic, pale-ocher limestone colossi that loom out of the sea just off the Punta Tragara on the southern coast of Capri. Soaring almost 350 feet above the water, the Faraglioni have become for most Italians a beloved symbol of Capri and have been poetically compared to Gothic cathedrals or modern skyscrapers. The first rock is called Faraglione di Terra, since it's attached to the land; at its base is the famous restaurant and bathing lido Da Luigi, where a beach mattress may accompany the luncheon menu. The second is called Faraglione di Mezzo, or Stella, and little boats can often be seen going through its picturesque tunnel, which was caused by sea erosion. The rock farthest out to sea is Faraglione di Scopolo and is inhabited by a wall lizard species with a striking blue belly, considered a local variant by biologists although legend has it that they were originally brought as pets from Greece to delight ancient Roman courtiers. ⊠ End of Via Tragara, Capri.

★ Marina Piccola

BEACH | FAMILY | A 10-minute ride from the main bus terminus in Capri (Piazzetta d'Ungheria), Marina Piccola is a delightfully picturesque inlet that provides the Capresi and other sun worshippers with their best access to reasonable beaches and safe swimming. The entire cove is lined with *stabilimenti*—elegant bathing lidos where the striped cabanas are often air-conditioned and the bodies can be Modigliani-sleek. The most famous of these lidos (there's a fee to use the facilities), found closest to the Faraglioni, is La Canzone del Mare, once presided over by the noted British music-hall singer Gracie Fields and for decades favored by the smart set, including Noël Coward and Emilio Pucci (who set up his first boutique here). La Canzone del Mare's seaside restaurant offers a dreamy view of the Faraglioni and a luncheon here, although pricey, can serve as an indelible Capri moment. Jutting out into the bay at the center of the marina is the Scoglio delle Sirene, or Sirens' Rock—a small natural promontory—which the ancients believed to be the haunt of the Sirens, the mythical temptresses whose song seduced Odysseus in Homer's *Odyssey*. This rock separates the two small beaches: Pennaulo, to the east, and Marina di Mulo, site of the original Roman harbor, to the west. The small church, Chiesa di Sant'Andrea, was built in 1900 to give the local fishermen a place of worship. ⊠ *Via Marina Piccola, Capri.*

★ Monte Solaro

VIEWPOINT | An impressive limestone formation and the highest point on Capri (1,932 feet), Monte Solaro affords gasp-inducing views toward the bays of both Naples and Salerno. A serene 13-minute chairlift ride will take you right to the top (refreshments available at the bar), where you can launch out on a number of scenic trails on the western side of the island. Picnickers should note that even in summer it can get windy at this height, and there are few trees to provide shade or refuge. ⊠ *Piazza Vittoria, Anacapri* ☎ *081/8371428* ⊕ *www.capriseggiovia.it* 🎟 *€9 one-way, €12 return* ⊗ *Closed chairlift in adverse weather.*

★ Villa Jovis

RUINS | In Roman times, Capri was the site of 12 spacious villas, but Villa Jovis is both the best preserved and the largest, occupying nearly 23,000 square feet. Named in honor of the ancient Roman god Jupiter, or Jove, the villa of the emperor Tiberius is riveted to the towering Rocca di Capri like an eagle's nest overlooking the strait separating Capri from Punta Campanella, the tip of the Sorrentine Peninsula. A powerful reminder of the importance of the island in Roman times, the site is even more compelling because of the accounts of the latter years of Tiberius's reign between AD 27 and 37, written by authors and near-contemporaries Suetonius and Tacitus. The Salto di Tiberio (Tiberius's Leap) is where ancient gossips believed Tiberius had enemies (among them his discarded lovers and even unfortunate cooks) hurled over the precipice into the sea some 1,000 feet below. From La Piazzetta allow 45 minutes each way for the walk to this site. ⊠ *Via A. Maiuri, Capri* ☎ *081/8374549* 🎟 *€6, with audio guide* ⊗ *Closed Jan. and Feb. and Tues. Oct.–Mar.*

★ Villa San Michele

HISTORIC HOME | From Anacapri's Piazza Vittoria, picturesque Via Capodimonte leads to Villa San Michele, the charming former home of Swedish doctor and philanthropist Axel Munthe (1857–1949), and which Henry James called "the most fantastic beauty, poetry, and inutility that one had ever seen clustered together." At the ancient entranceway to Anacapri at the top of the Scala Fenicia, the villa is set around Roman-style courtyards, marble walkways, and atria. Rooms display the doctor's varied collections, which range from bric-a-brac to antiquities. Medieval choir stalls, Renaissance lecterns, and gilded statues of saints are all part of the setting, with some rooms preserving the doctor's personal memorabilia. A spectacular pergola path overlooking the entire Bay of Naples leads from the villa to the famous Sphinx Parapet, where an ancient Egyptian sphinx looks out toward Sorrento. ✉ *Viale Axel Munthe 34, Anacapri* ☎ *081/8371401* 🌐 *www.villasanmichele.eu* 🎫 *€10.*

🍴 Restaurants

Al Grottino

$$ | **SOUTHERN ITALIAN** | In a 14th-century building close to the Piazzetta, this small, friendly, family-run restaurant has arched ceilings, autographed photos of famous patrons, and lots of atmosphere. Specialties include scialatielli *ai fiori di zucchine e gamberetti* (with zucchini flowers and shrimp) and *cocotte* (house-made pasta with mussels, clams, and shrimps), but the owner delights in taking his guests through the menu of regional dishes. **Known for:** gluten-free options; Caprese specialties with the freshest ingredients; good value for Capri. [$] *Average main: €20* ✉ *Via Longano 27, Capri* ☎ *081/8370584* 🌐 *www.ristorantealgrottino.net* 🕓 *Closed Nov.–late Mar.*

Aurora

$$$ | **SOUTHERN ITALIAN** | Often frequented by celebrities, whose photographs adorn the walls inside and out, the island's oldest restaurant offers courtesy and *simpatia* (irrespective of your star status), a sleekly minimalist interior, and tables outside along a chic thoroughfare. The cognoscenti start by sharing a pizza *all'Acqua*—thin-crust, with mozzarella and a sprinkling of *peperoncino* (chili)—but the *gnocchetti al pesto con fagiolini croccanti e pinoli* (dumplings with pesto, beans, and pine nuts) and house-made sweets are good, too. **Known for:** incredible wine cellar and choice; Papà Gennaro's unusually light pizza all'Acqua; historic jet-set hangout. [$] *Average main: €28* ✉ *Via Fuorlovado 18/22, Capri* ☎ *081/8370181* 🌐 *auroracapri.com* 🕓 *Closed Nov.–Easter.*

Barbarossa

$$ | **SOUTHERN ITALIAN** | Take the staircase behind Piazza Vittoria's bus stop to the covered terrace of this ristorante-pizzeria with panoramic views of the Barbarossa castle and the sea. The no-frills ambience belies the quality of the à la carte *cucina*: besides *pizze* they specialize in local dishes—including risotto *con gamberi a limone* (shrimp with lemon). **Known for:** chef's semifreddi and other dessert specials; lively function room during events; authentic (certified) Vera Pizza Napoletana. [$] *Average main: €17* ✉ *Piazza Vittoria 1, Anacapri* ☎ *081/8371483* 🌐 *www.ristorantebarbarossa.com.*

★ Da Gelsomina

$$$ | **SOUTHERN ITALIAN** | Amid its own terraced vineyards with inspiring views to the island of Ischia and beyond, this is much more than just a well-reputed restaurant. The owner's mother was a friend of Axel Munthe, and he encouraged her to open a food kiosk, which evolved into Da Gelsomina; today the specialties include *pollo a mattone,* chicken grilled on bricks, and locally caught rabbit. **Known for:** fresh produce and wine from their verdant gardens; chicken grilled on bricks; opened in the 1960s with family links to Axel Munthe. [$] *Average main: €35* ✉ *Via Migliara 72, Anacapri* ☎ *081/8371499* 🌐 *www.dagelsomina.com* 🕓 *Closed Nov.–Mar.*

★ Il Solitario

$$ | NEOPOLITAN | Tucked away from Via G. Orlandi, there's always a warm, relaxed family welcome and deliciously simple Caprese food here. **Known for:** grilled fish and meat; cheery dining room and leafy pergola; sumptuous ravioli. $ *Average main: €16* ⊠ *Via Giuseppe Orlandi 96, Anacapri* ☎ *081/8371382* ⊕ *www.ilsolitarioanacapri.com* ⊘ *No dinner Sun.*

La Canzone del Mare

$$$ | SOUTHERN ITALIAN | Although it's not primarily a restaurant, a luncheon dominated by fresh seafood and vegetables in the covered pavilion of this legendary bathing lido of the Marina Piccola is Capri at its most picture-perfect. With two seawater pools, a rocky beach, and I Faraglioni in the distance, it was the erstwhile haunt of Gracie Fields, Emilio Pucci, Noël Coward, and any number of 1950s and '60s glitterati. **Known for:** famous dolce vita–era haunt, now very crowded; sunset wine and peaches served with stuzzichini (appetizers); open terrace overlooking Marina Piccola. $ *Average main: €35* ⊠ *Via Marina Piccola 93, Capri* ☎ *081/8370104* ⊕ *www.lacanzonedelmare.com* ⊘ *No dinner. Closed Oct.–mid-Apr.*

★ La Capannina

$$$ | SOUTHERN ITALIAN | Near the busy piazzetta and long one of Capri's most celebrity-haunted restaurants, La Capannina has a discreet flower-decked veranda that's ideal for dining by candlelight. Specialties change daily depending on the season, but the menu always includes ravioli capresi, linguine con lo scorfano (with scorpion fish), and an exquisite "Pezzogna" (sea bream cooked whole and topped with a layer of potatoes). **Known for:** seafood dishes; wine bar next door; walls strewn with photos of celebrity clientele. $ *Average main: €26* ⊠ *Via Le Botteghe 12b, Capri* ☎ *081/8370732* ⊕ *www.capanninacapri.com* ⊘ *Closed Nov.–mid-Mar.*

La Fontelina

$$$ | SOUTHERN ITALIAN | Given its position right on the water's edge, seafood is almost de rigueur here, but also expect fabulous fresh vegetable creations like *polpette di melanzane* (eggplant fritters), and then dip into the vegetable buffet. La Fontelina also functions as a lido, with steps and ladders into fathoms-deep blue water, and this location—accessible on foot from Punta Tragara or by boat from Marina Piccola (10 minutes; €25 up to four passengers)—makes it a good place to spend a delightfully comatose day. **Known for:** chef Mario's daily seafood specials; shuttle boat from Marina Piccola; lunch stop for beach-club bathers. $ *Average main: €28* ⊠ *Via Faraglioni 2, Capri* ☎ *081/8370845* ⊕ *www.fontelina-capri.com* ⊘ *No dinner. Closed mid-Oct.–Easter.*

Le Grottelle

$$$ | SOUTHERN ITALIAN | This extremely informal trattoria enjoys a distinctive setting up against limestone rocks not far from the Arco Naturale, with the kitchen in a cave at the back. Whether you stumble over it (and are lucky enough to get a table) or intentionally head for it after an island hike, Le Grottelle will prove memorable, thanks to the ambience, the views of Li Galli islands, and a menu that includes ravioli and local rabbit but is best known for seafood dishes such as linguine *con gamberetti e rucola* (with shrimp and arugula). **Known for:** cool grotto interiors; seafood dishes; breathtaking cliff-clinging location. $ *Average main: €25* ⊠ *Via Arco Naturale 13, Capri* ☎ *081/8375719* ⊘ *Closed Nov.–mid-Mar.*

☕ Coffee and Quick Bites

★ Buonocore

$ | ITALIAN | FAMILY | Follow your nose to this legendary, sweet-smelling Caprese fave for breakfast, beach picnics, and on-the-hoof snacks. Buonocore lures you down its steps on a Capri Town lane with all manner of pizza, panini, gelati, and paste, including their speciality almond and lemon Caprilú biscotti. **Known for:** very popular so may have to fare la coda; small pizze to take away; tempting smells of freshly made cones and pastries. Ⓢ *Average main: €8* ✉ *Via Vittorio Emanuele 35, Capri Town* ☎ *081/8377826.*

 # Hotels

⭐ Caesar Augustus

$$$$ | **HOTEL** | A favorite of the Hollywood set, this landmark villa hotel is a Caprese paradise thanks to its breathtaking perch atop a cliff; its grand gardens, terraces, and pool; and its charming, casual-chic rooms with their plump chairs and fragrant bouquets. **Pros:** serene terrace views; infinity pool; summer concerts on-site. **Cons:** pricey; no kids under 12 allowed; a bit far from the action for some. Ⓢ *Rooms from: €700* ✉ *Via G. Orlandi 4, Anacapri* ☎ *081/8373395* ⊕ *www.caesar-augustus.com* ⊘ *Closed Nov.–mid-Apr.* ⇆ *55 rooms* ⦙◉⦙ *Free Breakfast.*

⭐ Capri Palace Jumeirah

$$$$ | **RESORT** | This Anacapri icon with unique design, spa, exquisite food, and luxurious retreat atmosphere throughout has amassed a noted art collection and even launched a fashion and home line and hosted A-list cultural events. **Pros:** noted art collection; award-winning spa and dining; stunning (and sometimes surprising) design. **Cons:** service can be slow; some may find the quiet Anacapri location removed from the action (and water); all that glam comes at a price. Ⓢ *Rooms from: €725* ✉ *Via Capodimonte 14, Anacapri* ☎ *081/9780111* ⊕ *www.capripalace.com* ⊘ *Closed mid-Oct.–mid-Apr.* ⇆ *78 rooms* ⦙◉⦙ *Free Breakfast.*

⭐ Capri Tiberio Palace

$$$$ | **HOTEL** | Offering guests comfort, style, luxury, and sigh-inducing views since the 19th century, this hotel is a short walk from the piazzetta—near the action, but not quite in the thick of it.

Pros: friendly staff; traditional and kosher restaurant; pure luxury. **Cons:** tiny gym; the pool is too close to the restaurant; no port-to-door guest shuttle. Ⓢ *Rooms from: €599* ✉ *Via Croce 11–15, Capri* ☎ *081/9787111* ⊕ *www.capritiberiopalace.com* ⊘ *Closed Nov.–mid-Apr.* ⇆ *54 rooms* ⦙◉⦙ *Free Breakfast.*

⭐ J. K. Place

$$$$ | **HOTEL** | Occupying an 1876 villa above Marina Grande harbor, southern Italy's most glamorous hotel makes other Capri accommodations seem dull. **Pros:** exquisite pool; free shuttle to town; pleasant walk to the magical Tiberio beach. **Cons:** pool visible from main road; only for high rollers; expensive. Ⓢ *Rooms from: €1182* ✉ *Via Provinciale Marina Grande 225, Capri* ☎ *081/8384001* ⊕ *www.jkcapri.com* ⊘ *Closed mid-Oct.–mid-Apr.* ⇆ *22 rooms* ⦙◉⦙ *Free Breakfast.*

La Tosca

$$ | **HOTEL** | Up a tiny side street above the Certosa, this simple, quiet hotel offers unassuming vibes, terrace views, and reasonable rates. **Pros:** simple, unadorned charm; quiet spot near Capri Town; pleasant, helpful owner. **Cons:** rooms might seem to lack panache; books up early; not all rooms have good views. Ⓢ *Rooms from: €165* ✉ *Via Birago 5, Capri* ☎ *081/8370989* ⊕ *www.latoscahotel.com* ⊘ *Closed Nov.–Feb.* ⇆ *11 rooms* ⦙◉⦙ *Free Breakfast.*

⭐ Punta Tragara

$$$$ | **HOTEL** | Designed by Le Corbusier, this former private villa was the site of a secret wartime meeting between Churchill and Eisenhower; today, it's one of Capri's most beautiful hotels, with a breathtaking location on Punta Tragara; public areas adorned with baronial fireplaces, gilded antiques, and travertine marble; and guest rooms that are simultaneously sumptuous and cozy-casual. **Pros:** decadent and luxurious; two gorgeous pools; wonderful views of the famed Faraglioni rocks. **Cons:** small gym; some find the style dated (others find it a

plus); a 15-minute walk from the center. $ *Rooms from: €950* ✉ *Via Tragara 57, Capri* ☏ *081/8370844* ⊕ *www.hoteltragara.com* ⊙ *Closed mid-Oct.–mid-Apr.* ⇘ *44 rooms* ⦿⧠ *Free Breakfast.*

Quisisana

$$$$ | HOTEL | Some say Capri has three villages: Capri Town, Anacapri, and this landmark hotel, which looms large in island mythology, attracts utterly devoted guests, and has an enormous lobby and theater-cum-convention center that are 1930s jewels designed by noted modernist Gio Ponti. **Pros:** luxe atmosphere on a large scale; top spa facilities; stumbling distance from La Piazzetta. **Cons:** not quite as ritzy as in bygone days; convention-size and far from cozy; minimum three- or five-night stay some periods. $ *Rooms from: €490* ✉ *Via Camerelle 2, Capri* ☏ *081/8370788* ⊕ *www.quisisana.com* ⊙ *Closed Nov.–mid-Mar.* ⇘ *147 rooms* ⦿⧠ *Free Breakfast.*

Villa Krupp

$$ | B&B/INN | Occupying a beautiful house overlooking the idyllic Gardens of Augustus, this hostelry (once the home of Maxim Gorky, whose guests included Lenin) has comfy beds in plain but spacious rooms, some of which have south-facing terraces and awesome views. **Pros:** a historical home; much-needed porter service; stunning views. **Cons:** breakfast doesn't match the views; simple rooms; a lot of steps to negotiate. $ *Rooms from: €170* ✉ *Viale Matteotti 12, Capri* ☏ *081/8370362* ⊕ *www.villakrupp.com* ⊙ *Closed mid-Oct.–mid-Apr.* ⇘ *12 rooms* ⦿⧠ *Free Breakfast.*

Villa Sarah

$$$ | HOTEL | This yellow, two-story, Mediterranean-style hostelry—complete with Capri's signature round windows and a setting amid lovely gardens in a pleasant residential district—has lots of Caprese spirit and simple but homey and brightly accented rooms that will make you feel like a guest in a private villa. **Pros:**

gorgeous pool; unfussy decor; lush gardens. **Cons:** small pool; many rooms tiny; a long and steep climb from the Piazzetta. $ *Rooms from: €250* ✉ *Via Tiberio 3/a, Capri* ☏ *081/8377817* ⊕ *www.villasarah.it* ⊙ *Closed Nov.–Mar.* ⇘ *20 rooms* ⦿⧠ *Free Breakfast.*

Sorrento

50 km (31 miles) south of Naples.

Winding along a cliff above a small beach and two harbors, the town is split in two by a narrow ravine formed by a former mountain stream. To the east, dozens of hotels line busy Via Correale along the cliff—many have "grand" included in their names, and some indeed are. To the west, however, is the historic sector, which still enchants. It's a relatively flat area, with winding, stone-paved lanes bordered by balconied buildings, some joined by medieval stone arches. The bustling, coach- and car-traffic–fringed central piazza is named after the poet Torquato Tasso, born here in 1544. Away from the vehicles this part of town is a delightful place to walk through. Craftspeople are often at work in their stalls and shops and are happy to let you watch; in fact, that's the point. Music spots and bars cluster in the side streets near Piazza Tasso.

GETTING HERE AND AROUND

From downtown Naples, take a Circumvesuviana train from Stazione Centrale (Piazza Garibaldi) or a hydrofoil from Molo Beverello. If you're coming directly from the airport in Naples, pick up a direct bus to Sorrento. By car, take the A3 Naples–Salerno autostrada, exiting at Castellammare, and then following signs for Penisola Sorrentina, then for Sorrento.

VISITOR INFORMATION

CONTACT Azienda Autonoma di Soggiorno Sorrento-Sant'Agnello. ✉ *Via L. De Maio 35,* ☏ *081/8074033.*

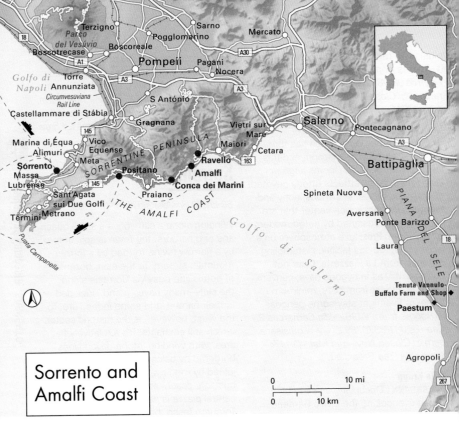

Sorrento and Amalfi Coast

 Sights

Convento di San Francesco

RELIGIOUS BUILDING | Near the Villa Comunale gardens and sharing its view over the Bay of Naples, the convent is celebrated for its 12th-century cloister. Filled with greenery and flowers, the Moorish-style cloister has interlaced pointed arches of tufa rock, alternating with octagonal columns topped by elegant capitals, supporting smaller arches. The combination makes a suitably evocative setting for summer concerts and theatrical presentations. The church portal is particularly impressive, with the 16th-century door (moved from a church across the road in 1947) featuring intarsia (inlaid) work. The interior's 17th-century decoration includes an altarpiece, by a student of Francesco Solimena, depicting St. Francis receiving the stigmata. The convent is now an art school, where students' works are often exhibited. ⊠ *Piazza S. Francesco, Sorrento* ☎ *081/8781269* ⌖ *Free.*

Marina Grande

MARINA/PIER | Close to the historic quarter (but not that close—many locals prefer to use the town bus to shuttle up and down the steep hill), the port, or *borgo*, of the Marina Grande is Sorrento's fishing harbor. In recent years it has become unashamedly touristy, with outdoor restaurants and cafés encroaching on what little remains of the original harbor. Most establishments down here are geared to the English-speaking market—expect a "good evening" rather than a "buona sera" as you enter. The marina still remains a magical location for an evening out on the waterfront, but if you're interested in a dip—given the dubious sea-water quality here and the cramped conditions—head out instead toward Massa Lubrense and Nerano. Don't confuse this harbor with Marina Piccola, at the base of the cliff, below Piazza Tasso and the Hotel Excelsior Vittoria; that's the area where ferries and hydrofoils dock. ✉ *Via del Mare, Sorrento.*

Museo Correale di Terranova

ART MUSEUM | In an 18th-century villa with a lovely garden, on land given to the patrician Correale family by Queen Joan of Anjou in 1428, this museum is a highlight of Sorrento and a must for connoisseurs of the *seicento* (17th century). It has an eclectic private collection amassed by the count of Terranova and his brother—one of the finest devoted to Neapolitan paintings, decorative arts, and porcelains. Magnificent 18th- and 19th-century inlaid tables by Giuseppe Gargiulo, Capodimonte porcelains, and rococo portrait miniatures are reminders of the age when pleasure and delight were everything in wealthy circles. Also on view are regional Greek and Roman archaeological finds, medieval marble work, glasswork, Old Master paintings, and 17th-century majolicas—even the poet Tasso's death mask. The building itself is fairly charmless, with few period rooms, but the garden offers an allée of palm trees, citrus groves, floral nurseries, and an esplanade with a panoramic view of the Sorrento Coast. ✉ *Via Correale 50, Sorrento* ☎ *081/8781846* 🌐 *www.museocorreale.it* 🎟 *€8, €13 with guide* 🕒 *Closed Mon.*

Sedile Dominova

NOTABLE BUILDING | Enchanting showpiece of the Largo Dominova—the little square that is the heart of Sorrento's historic quarter—the Sedile Dominova is a picturesque open loggia with expansive arches, balustrades, and a green-and-yellow-tile cupola, originally constructed in the 16th century. The open-air structure is frescoed with 18th-century trompe-l'oeil columns and the family coats of arms, which once belonged to the *sedile* (seat), the town council where nobles met to discuss civic problems as early as the Angevin period. Today Sorrentines still like to congregate around the umbrella-topped tables near the tiny square. ✉ *Largo Dominova, at Via S. Cesareo and Via P.R. Giuliani, Sorrento* 🎟 *Free.*

Villa Comunale

VIEWPOINT | The largest public park in Sorrento sits on a cliff top overlooking the entire Bay of Naples. It offers benches, flowers, palms, and people-watching, plus a seamless vista that stretches from Capri to Vesuvius. From here steps lead down to Sorrento's main harbor, the Marina Piccola. ✉ *Adjoining church of San Francesco, Sorrento.*

🍴 Restaurants

Da Emilia

$$ | **SOUTHERN ITALIAN** | Near the steps of the Marina Grande, this reliable choice for seafood (established in 1947) might not be Sorrento's most visually prepossessing place, but its homespun, family feel—complete with wooden tables and checked tablecloths—is a refreshing change from the town's (occasionally pretentious) elegance. **Known for:** family run; harbor terrace above the rocks; tasty and fresh seafood combos like mussels with Sorrentine lemons. [$] *Average main: €21* ✉ *Via Marina Grande 62, Sorrento* ☎ *081/8072720* 🌐 *www.daemilia.it* 🕒 *Closed Nov.–Feb.*

★ **Don Alfonso 1890**

$$$$ | **SOUTHERN ITALIAN** | A gastronomic giant and pioneer in upscale farm-to-table cuisine (it even grows its own produce on a small farm nearby), Don Alfonso is considered one of Italy's best restaurants. It's a family affair, with mamma (Livia) handling the dining room, papà (former chef Alfonso Iaccarrino) tending to the organic plot, one son working as the current chef (preparing classic dishes alongside edgier creations), and the other serving as maître d'. **Known for:** Punta

Campanella local garden produce; slow food pioneer; stellar tasting menus. $ *Average main: €160* ✉ *Corso Sant'Agata 13, Sant'Agata sui Due Golfi* ⊹ *SITA Bus to via Nastro Verde or taxi from Sorrento.* ☎ *081/8780026* ⊕ *www.donalfonso.com* ⊘ *Closed Mon. and Tues. and Nov.–Apr. No lunch weekdays.*

★ Ristorante Bagni Delfino

$$ | SOUTHERN ITALIAN | At this informal, waterside restaurant and snack bar, you won't see many locals—they're unlikely to be impressed by the four-language menus—but the seafood platters are fresh and flavorful, and you can eat alfresco in the sunshine or inside a glass-enclosed dining area with a nautical motif. You can even go for a swim (just please, wait an hour or so after eating!). **Known for:** great views of the Marina Grande and beyond; terrace beside a sunbathing/swimming jetty; bountiful portions. $ *Average main: €22* ✉ *Via Marina Grande 216, Sorrento* ☎ *081/8782038* ⊕ *www. ristoranteildelfinosorrento.com* ⊘ *Closed Nov.–Mar.*

★ Ristorante Museo Caruso

$$$$ | SOUTHERN ITALIAN | Sorrentine favorites, including *acquerello* (fresh fish appetizer) and ravioli with crab and zucchini sauce, are tweaked creatively here. The staff is warm and helpful, the singer on the sound system is the long-departed "fourth tenor" himself, and the operatic memorabilia (including posters and old photos of Caruso) is displayed in a flattering blush-pink light. **Known for:** tasting menus and a few à la carte choices; Torna a Surriento and the Neapolitan songbook; Caruso memorabilia aplenty. $ *Average main: €40* ✉ *Via S. Antonino 12, Sorrento* ☎ *081/8073156* ⊕ *www. ristorantemuseocaruso.com.*

Ristorante 'o Parrucchiano La Favorita

$$ | SOUTHERN ITALIAN | Opened in 1868 by an ex-priest ('*o parrucchiano* means "the priest" in the local dialect), this restaurant serves classic Sorrentine cuisine in an enchanting 19th-century setting: a

sprawling, multilevel greenhouse, packed with tables and chairs amid fruit trees and enough tropical foliage to fill a Victorian conservatory. **Known for:** gorgeous setting but may disappoint food-wise; signature cannelloni created in 1870; fecund greenhouse and terrace foliage and fruit. $ *Average main: €24* ✉ *Corso Italia 71, Sorrento* ☎ *081/8781321* ⊕ *www.parrucchiano.com* ⊘ *Closed Wed. mid-Nov.–mid-Mar.*

☕ Coffee and Quick Bites

★ A'Marenna

$ | ITALIAN | FAMILY | Run with enthusiasm and love by two young Sorrentine women, this small rustic-styled bakery and bistro makes generously filled panini using fresh ingredients on ciabatta and *panuozzo* pizza-dough bread. It's also a fab spot to linger with some local wine and a cheese platter. **Known for:** vegan and veggie options; local wines; friendly service. $ *Average main: €7* ✉ *Via Tasso 23, Sorrento* ☎ *081/18495183.*

Hotels

★ Bellevue Syrene

$$$$ | HOTEL | This luxurious retreat, magnificently set on a bluff high over the Bay of Naples, is one of Italy's most legendary hotels, complete with Art Deco touches throughout; lounges and salons decorated with avant-garde artwork and trompe-l'oeil frescoes; and guest rooms that range from sleekly modern to sumptuously fanciful. **Pros:** impeccable design elements; half board available; elegant common areas. **Cons:** small pool; parking is €25 a day; very expensive. $ *Rooms from: €550* ✉ *Piazza della Vittoria 5, Sorrento* ☎ *081/8781024* ⊕ *www.bellevue.it* ⊘ *Closed Jan.–Mar.* ⇥ *49 rooms* ⊚ *Free Breakfast.*

★ Excelsior Vittoria

$$$$ | HOTEL | Overlooking the Bay of Naples, this luxurious Belle Époque dream has been in the same family since 1834, which means that public spaces are virtual museums—with elegant Victorian love seats and *stile liberty* (Art Nouveau) ornamentation—and guest rooms are spacious, with soigné furnishings and balconies and terraces that overlook gardens or the bay. **Pros:** beyond the protected gates, you're in the heart of town; grand spaces and handsome furnishings; gardens buffer city noise. **Cons:** front desk can be cold; some rooms are comparatively small; not all rooms have sea views. $ *Rooms from: €746* ⊠ *Piazza Tasso 34, Sorrento* ☎ *081/8777111* ⊕ *www.exvitt.it* ⊗ *Closed Jan.–Mar.* ⇛ *83 rooms* ¶ *Free Breakfast.*

La Favorita

$$$$ | HOTEL | The lobby might be a glamorous white-on-white extravaganza of Caprese columns, tufted sofas, shimmering crystal chandeliers, silver ecclesiastical objects, and gilded Baroque mirrors, but the charming staff ensure the vibe is elegantly casual, the guest rooms are well equipped and spacious, and the rooftop pool area has magnificent bay and Vesuvius vistas. **Pros:** central location; idyllic garden; beautiful terrace. **Cons:** rooms near the bar noisy after midnight; lack of decent air-conditioning and room thermostat control; no views to speak of from guest rooms. $ *Rooms from: €439* ⊠ *Via T. Tasso 61, Sorrento* ☎ *081/8782031* ⊕ *www.hotellafavorita. com* ⊗ *Closed Jan.–Mar.* ⇛ *85 rooms* ¶ *Free Breakfast.*

Settimo Cielo

$$$ | HOTEL | Even if your wallet won't allow a stay at one of Sorrento's grand hotels, Settimo Cielo—although dated and a hike away on Capo Sorrento—provides gorgeous views, pretty gardens, and a swimming pool. **Pros:** plenty of parking; balcony options; wonderful sea and Vesuvio views. **Cons:** walls not soundproofed; basic, dated rooms and below-par breakfast; 15-minute walk along busy road into Sorrento. $ *Rooms from: €260* ⊠ *Via Capo 27, Sorrento* ☎ *081/8781012* ⊕ *www.hotelsettimocielo.com* ⇛ *20 rooms* ¶ *Free Breakfast.*

Positano

14 km (9 miles) east of Sorrento, 57 km (34 miles) south of Naples.

When John Steinbeck visited Positano in 1953, he wrote that it was difficult to consider tourism an industry because "there are not enough [tourists]." Alas, there are more than enough now, and the town's vertical landscape with pastel-hue houses, drapes of bright pink bougainvillea, and sapphire-blue sea make it easy to understand why.

The most photographed fishing village in the world, this fabled locale is home to some 4,000 Positanesi, who are joined daily by hordes arriving from Capri, Sorrento, and Amalfi. The town clings to the Monti Lattari with arcaded, cubist buildings, set in tiers up the mountainside, in shades of rose, peach, purple, and ivory.

GETTING HERE AND AROUND
SITA buses leave from the Circumvesuviana train station in Sorrento. Buses also run from Naples and, in summer, Rome. There is a ferry from Sorrento in the summer months.

A word of advice: wear comfortable walking shoes and be sure your back and legs are strong enough to negotiate those picturesque but daunting and ladderlike *scalinatelle*. In the center of town, where no buses can go, you're on your own from Piazza dei Mulini. To begin your explorations, make a left turn onto the boutique-flanked Via dei Mulini and head down to the Palazzo Murat, Santa Maria Assunta, and the beach—one of the most charming walks of the coast.

VISITOR INFORMATION
CONTACT Ufficio di Turismo - Comune di Positano. ⊠ *Via Regina Giovanna 13,* ☎ *334/9118563.*

Marina Grande Beach in Positano is a nice, long stretch of sand that attracts a cosmopolitan crowd.

Sights

Palazzo Murat

NOTABLE BUILDING | Past a bevy of resort boutiques, head to Via dei Mulini to view the prettiest garden in Positano: the 18th-century courtyard of the Palazzo Murat, named for Joachim Murat, who sensibly chose the palazzo as his summer residence. This was where Murat, designated by his brother-in-law Napoléon as king of Naples in 1808, came to forget the demands of power and lead a simpler life. He built this grand abode (now a hotel) near the church of Santa Maria Assunta, just steps from the main beach. ⊠ *Via dei Mulini 23, Positano* ☎ *089/875177* ⊕ *www.palazzomurat.it.*

Santa Maria Assunta

CHURCH | The Chiesa Madre, or parish church of Santa Maria Assunta, lies just south of the Palazzo Murat, its green-and-yellow majolica dome topped by a perky cupola visible from just about anywhere in town. Built on the site of the former Benedictine abbey of St. Vito,

the 13th-century Romanesque structure was almost completely rebuilt in 1700. The last piece of the ancient mosaic floor can be seen under glass behind the altar. Note the carved wooden Christ, a masterpiece of devotional religious art, with its bathetic face and bloodied knees, on view before the altar. At the altar is a Byzantine 13th-century painting on wood of Madonna with Child, known popularly as the Black Virgin. A replica is carried to the beach every August 15 to celebrate the Feast of the Assumption. Legend claims that the painting was once stolen by Saracen pirates, who, fleeing in a raging storm, heard a voice from on high saying, "*Posa, posa*" (Put it down, put it down). When they placed the image on the beach near the church, the storm calmed, as did the Saracens. Embedded over the doorway of the church's bell tower, set across the tiny piazza, is a medieval bas-relief of fishes, a fox, and a pistrice (the mythical half-dragon, half-dog sea monster). This is one of the few relics of the medieval abbey of Saint Vito. The oratorio houses historic statues from the sacristy; renovations to the crypt have unearthed part of an extensive Roman villa buried by the AD 79 eruption. ✉ *Piazza Flavio Gioia, Positano* ☎ *089/875480* 🌐 *www.chiesapositano.it.*

Spiaggia Grande

BEACH | **FAMILY** | The walkway from the Piazza Flavio Gioia leads down to Spiaggia Grande, Positano's main beach, bordered by an esplanade and some of the town's busiest restaurants. Surrounded by the spectacular amphitheater of houses and villas that leapfrog up the hillsides of Monte Comune and Monte Sant'Angelo, this remains one of the most picturesque beaches in the world. **Amenities:** food and drink; lifeguards; showers; toilets; water sports. **Best for:** swimming. ✉ *Spiaggia Grande, Positano.*

★ **Via Positanesi d'America**

PROMENADE | **FAMILY** | Just before the ferry ticket booths to the right of Spiaggia Grande, a tiny road that is the loveliest seaside walkway on the entire coast rises up and borders the cliffs leading to Fornillo Beach. The road is named for the town's large number of 19th-century emigrants to the United States—Positano virtually survived during World War II thanks to the money and packages their descendants sent back home. Halfway up the path lies the Torre Trasìta (Trasìta Tower), the most distinctive of Positano's three coastline defense towers. Now a residence occasionally available for summer rental, the tower was used to spot pirate raids. As you continue along the Via Positanesi d'America, you'll pass a tiny inlet and an emerald cove before Fornillo Beach comes into view. ✉ *Via Positanesi d'America, Positano.*

🍴 Restaurants

Il Ritrovo

$$ | **SOUTHERN ITALIAN** | **FAMILY** | In the tiny town square of Montepertuso, 1,500 feet up the mountainside from Positano (call for the free shuttle service to and from), the Ritrovo has been noted for its cucina for more than 20 years. The menu showcases food from both the sea and the hills: try the scialatielli *ai frutti di mare* accompanied by well-grilled vegetables; the house specialty *zuppa saracena,* a paella-like affair brimming with assorted seafood; and the lemon tiramisu, perhaps paired with one of 80 different kinds of a homemade liqueur, including carob and chamomile options. **Known for:** amiable padrone Salvatò, who also runs a cooking school; trademark zuppa saracena (seafood soup); airy, tranquil mountainside location. [$] *Average main: €23* ✉ *Via Montepertuso 77, Montepertuso* ☎ *089/812005* 🌐 *www.ilritrovo.com* 🕒 *Closed mid-Jan.–mid-Feb.*

Lo Guarracino

$$ | **SOUTHERN ITALIAN** | This partly arbor-covered restaurant is a romantic place to enjoy scialatielli di mare (seafood pasta) above the waves, with a terrace vista that takes in the cliffs, the sea, the Li Galli islands, Spiaggia del Fornillo, and Torre Clavel. **Known for:** romantic Robinson Crusoe–esque terrace; family-made liquori digestivi including a wild-herb number (agrumi); seafood and wood-fired pizza. [$] *Average main: €24* ✉ *Via Positanesi d'America 12, Positano* ☎ *089/875794* 🌐 *www.loguarracinopositano.it* 🕒 *Closed Jan.–Mar.*

Next2

$$$ | **SOUTHERN ITALIAN** | Wrought-iron gates open from scenic Via Pasitea into Next2's *bianco e nero*–chic courtyard, replete with a cocktail bar and a whiff of edgy, youthful swagger. You can watch the talented *squadra* at work in the open kitchen crafting elegant, subtly flavored creations such as the caprese starter, the seared tuna *secondo,* and—for those with bigger, bolder appetites—the *frittura di mare* (fried seafood medley). **Known for:** cocktails with novel, fresh infusions; delectable dessert pairings such as pear and walnut ice cream; exquisite-looking small-portioned dishes. [$] *Average*

main: €28 ✉ *Via Pasitea 242, Positano* ☎ *089/8123516* 🌐 *next2.it* 🕒 *No lunch.*

Coffee and Quick Bites

Paradise Lounge Bar

$ | **SANDWICHES** | **FAMILY** | With an outdoor terrace overlooking the Spiaggia Grande, this is an ideal stop for a coffee, a sandwich, or an ice cream. By night, MTV music pumps from the stereo and the clamor of sporting events blares from the four large-screen TVs, as movers, groovers, and soccer fans from around the globe sip cocktails after a hard day on the beach. **Known for:** pastries, pizza, and panini; warm counter service; fab gelato artigianale. [$] *Average main: €5* ✉ *Via del Saracino 32, Positano* ☎ *089/811915* 🕒 *Closed Mon.*

Hotels

Hotel Eden Roc

$$$ | **HOTEL** | The closest hotel to the Sponda bus stop, this luxury property (perfect for either couples or families) has spectacular views and service and spacious, pastel-hue guest rooms—all with terraces overlooking the town and some with whirlpool tubs. **Pros:** large rooms; good on-site amenities (gym, steam bath, wellness center, rooftop pool); magical views. **Cons:** some rooms are dated; a bit of a climb from the town center; on the main road (take care as you exit the hotel). [$] *Rooms from: €290* ✉ *Via G. Marconi 110, Positano* ☎ *089/875844* 🌐 *www.edenroc.it* 🕒 *Closed mid-Nov.–Feb.* 🛏 *25 rooms* 🍴 *Free Breakfast.*

Hotel L'Ancora

$$$$ | **HOTEL** | Set back a little from the main road and a short walk up from the main beach, this hotel has commanding views and bright guest rooms decorated with local artwork and boldly patterned mosaic tile. **Pros:** bright and sunny; not far from the Sponda bus stop; all rooms have balconies or terraces and sea views. **Cons:** some rooms lack views; no on-site pool; a slight climb from the main drag. [$] *Rooms from: €500* ✉ *Via Cristoforo Colombo 36, Positano* ☎ *089/875318* 🌐 *www.hotelancorapositano.com* 🕒 *Closed Nov.–Mar.* 🛏 *18 rooms* 🍴 *Free Breakfast.*

La Fenice

$$$ | **HOTEL** | This tiny, unpretentious hotel on the outskirts of Positano beckons with bougainvillea-laden views, castaway cottages, and a turquoise seawater pool—all perched over a private beach where a boat can whisk you away to Capri. **Pros:** small private beach with kayaks; secluded pool; family owned. **Cons:** lots of steps; roadside rooms are small and noisy; a 10-minute walk to town. [$] *Rooms from: €230* ✉ *Via G. Marconi 4, Positano* ☎ *089/875513* 🌐 *www.lafenicepositano.com* 🕒 *Sometimes closed Dec.–Feb.* 🛏 *14 rooms* 🍴 *Free Breakfast.*

★ Le Sirenuse

$$$$ | **HOTEL** | As legendary as its namesake sirens, this 18th-century palazzo has long set the standard for luxury in Italian hotels: it opened in 1951 with just 12 rooms (John Steinbeck stayed here while writing "Positano" for *Harper's Bazaar* in 1953) and now sprawls over eight floors, where extravagantly stylish guest rooms are accented with antiques and fine linens. **Pros:** unrivaled views, including from poolside terrace; gorgeous artworks around every corner; many rooms have whirlpool tubs. **Cons:** can be noisy; lower-priced rooms are small; a bit of a climb from the town center. [$] *Rooms from: €2128* ✉ *Via Cristoforo Colombo 30, Positano* ☎ *089/875066* 🌐 *www.sirenuse.it* 🕒 *Closed Nov.–Mar.* 🛏 *58 rooms* 🍴 *Free Breakfast.*

Palazzo Murat

$$$$ | **HOTEL** | A central-yet-secreted location, an infinity pool below the cupola of Santa Maria Assunta, and a magical bougainvillea-draped patio garden are among the things that make the Murat an extraordinary place to stay. **Pros:** once

a regal residence; shops and passeggiata on the doorstep; stunning garden and surroundings. **Cons:** not all balconies secluded; constant stream of curious day-trippers; only five rooms have seaside views. $ *Rooms from: €650* ✉ *Via dei Mulini 23, Positano* ☎ *089/875177* ⊕ *www.palazzomurat.it* ⊘ *Closed Nov.– Mar.* ⤴ *31 rooms* ⦿ *Free Breakfast.*

Ⓨ Nightlife

La Zagara

COCKTAIL LOUNGES | Come evening, things heat up at this bar and pasticceria where a local pianist tickles the ivories and summer sees DJ jams on the leafy terrace. ✉ *Via dei Mulini 8, Positano* ☎ *089/875964* ⊕ *www.lazagara.com.*

L'Africana

DANCE CLUBS | Off a mile-long footpath from the Marina del Praia—or accessed via an elevator from Statale 163—L'Africana is a golden-oldie classic from the 1960s. With an open-to-the-sea atmosphere, a cave for a dance floor, and wildish shows with partial nudity, you can party the night away here, as Jackie Kennedy once did. The nightclub runs boats from Positano on Saturday— transfer can also be arranged from other points along the coast. Just ring them to get picked up. ✉ *Via Terramare 2, Praiano* ☎ *089/874858, 351/8112728 cell phone* ⊕ *www.africanafamousclub.com.*

Conca dei Marini

13 km (8 miles) east of Positano, 29 km (18 miles) east of Sorrento.

A longtime favorite of the off-duty rich and famous, Conca dei Marini (the name means "seafarers' basin") hides many of its charms, as any sublime hideaway should. On a curve in the road sits the village's most noteworthy attraction, the Emerald Grotto.

⊚ Sights

Grotta dello Smeraldo (*Emerald Grotto*)
NATURE SIGHT | FAMILY | The tacky road sign, squadron of tour buses, Dean Martino–style boatmen, and free-form serenading (Andrea is the king of the grotto crooners) scream tourist trap, but there is, nevertheless, a compelling, eerie *bellezza* in the rock formations and luminous waters here. The karstic cave was originally part of the shore, but the lowest end sank into the sea. Intense greenish light filters into the water from an arch below sea level and is reflected off the cavern walls. You visit the Grotta dello Smeraldo, which is filled with huge stalactites and stalagmites, on a large rowboat. Don't let the boatman's constant spiel detract from the experience— just tune out and enjoy the sparkles, shapes, and brilliant colors. The light at the grotto is best from noon to 3 pm. You can take an elevator from the coast road down to the grotto, or in the summer you can drive to Amalfi and arrive by boat (€10, excluding the grotto's €6 admission fee). Companies in Positano, Amalfi, and elsewhere along the coast provide passage to the grotto, but consider one of the longer boat trips that explore Punta Campanella, Li Galli, and the more secluded spots along the coast. ✉ *Via Smeraldo, west of Capo di Conca, Conca dei Marini* ☎ *089/831535* 🎫 *€6* ⊘ *Closed in adverse weather conditions.*

🛏 Hotels

★ Monastero Santa Rosa Hotel & Spa

$$$$ | HOTEL | One of Italy's most exclusive retreats—in a 17th-century monastery on dramatic coastal cliffs—this boutique hotel has just 20 rooms, all with vaulted ceilings, Italian antiques, modern amenities, sumptuous bathrooms, and dazzling views framed by Mediterranean gardens. **Pros:** excellent service; gorgeous gardens and infinity pool; meticulously restored property with spa. **Cons:** a bit remote;

some rooms could be more spacious; out of reach for many budgets. $ *Rooms from: €902* ⊠ *Via Roma 2, Conca dei Marini* ☎ *089/8321199* ⊕ *www.monasterosantarosa.com* ⊙ *Closed Nov.–mid-Apr.* ⇌ *20 rooms* ⭐ *Free Breakfast.*

Amalfi

18 km (11 miles) east of Positano, 35 km (22 miles) east of Sorrento.

At first glance, it's hard to imagine that this resort destination was one of the world's great naval powers, and a sturdy rival of Genoa and Pisa for control of the Mediterranean in the 11th and 12th centuries. Once the seat of the Amalfi Maritime Republic, the town is set in a verdant valley of the Lattari Mountains, with cream-color and pastel-hue buildings tightly packing a gorge on the Bay of Salerno. The harbor, which once launched the greatest fleet in Italy, now bobs with ferries and blue-and-white fishing boats. The main street, lined with shops and *pasticcerie,* has replaced a raging mountain torrent, and terraced hills flaunt the green and gold of lemon groves. Bearing testimony to its great trade with Tunis, Tripoli, and Algiers, Amalfi remains honeycombed with Arab-Sicilian cloisters and covered passages. In a way Amalfi has become great again, showing off its medieval glory days with sea pageants, convents-turned-hotels, ancient paper mills, covered streets, and its glimmering cathedral.

GETTING HERE AND AROUND

From April to October the optimal way to get to Amalfi is by ferry from Salerno. SitaSud buses run from Naples and Sorrento throughout the year. By car, take the Statale 163 (Amalfitana) from outside Sorrento or Salerno, or take the Angri exit on the A3 autostrada and cross the mountainous Valico di Chiunsi.

 Sights

★ Duomo di Sant'Andrea

CHURCH | Complicated, grand, delicate, and dominating, the 9th-century Amalfi cathedral has been remodeled over the years with Romanesque, Byzantine, Gothic, and Baroque elements, but retains a predominantly Arab-Norman style. Built around 1266 as a burial ground for Amalfi's elite, the cloister, the first stop on a tour of the cathedral, is one of southern Italy's architectural treasures. Its flower-and-palm-filled quadrangle has a series of exceptionally delicate intertwining arches on slender double columns. The chapel at the back of the cloister leads into the 9th-century basilica, now a museum housing sarcophagi, sculpture, Neapolitan goldsmiths' artwork, and other treasures from the cathedral complex. Steps from the basilica lead down into the Cripta di Sant'Andrea (Crypt of St. Andrew). The cathedral above was built in the 13th century to house the saint's bones, which came from Constantinople. Following the one-way traffic up to the cathedral, you can admire the elaborate polychrome marbles and painted, coffered ceilings from its 18th-century restoration. ⊠ *Piazza Duomo, Amalfi* ☎ *089/871324* ⊕ *museodiocesanoamalfi.it* 🎫 *€4* ⊙ *Generally closed early Jan. and Feb. except for daily services.*

★ Museo della Carta (*Paper Museum*)

HISTORY MUSEUM | **FAMILY** | Uphill from town, the Valle dei Mulini (Valley of the Mills) was for centuries Amalfi's center for papermaking, an ancient trade learned from the Arabs, who learned it from the Chinese. Beginning in the 12th century, former flour mills were converted to produce paper made from cotton and linen. The paper industry was a success, and by 1811 more than a dozen mills here, with more along the coast, were humming. Natural waterpower ensured that the handmade paper was cost-effective. Yet, by the late 1800s the industry had moved to Naples and other more geographically accessible areas. Flooding in 1954 closed most of the mills for good, and many have been converted into private housing. The Museo della Carta (Museum of Paper) opened in 1971 in a 15th-century mill. Paper samples, tools of the trade, old machinery, and the audio-visual presentation are all enlightening. You can also participate in a paper-making laboratory. ✉ *Via delle Cartiere 23, Amalfi* ☎ *089/8304561* 🌐 *www.museodellacarta.it* 🎫 *€5, includes guided tour; €7 with paper-making experience* 🕒 *Closed Feb. and Mon. Nov.–Jan.*

🍴 Restaurants

La Caravella

$$$$ | **SOUTHERN ITALIAN** | Opened in 1959 and southern Italy's first restaurant to earn a Michelin star (in 1966), this atmospheric place—graced with frescoes, marble floors, vibrant ceramics, and fresh flowers—once had a gilded guest list that included Andy Warhol and Federico Fellini. The menu maintains dishes favored 50 years ago (picture slices of fish grilled in lemon leaves marinated with an almond and wild fennel sauce); there's also a tasting menu, but don't miss the antipasti. **Known for:** wine-dealer expertise; cheerful dining room; the Mezzogiorno's pioneering fine-dining eatery. [$] *Average main: €60* ✉ *Via Matteo Camera 12, near Arsenale, Amalfi* ☎ *089/871029* 🌐 *www.ristorantelacaravella.it* 🕒 *Closed Tues. and Nov. and Jan.*

☕ Coffee and Quick Bites

Andrea Pansa

$ | **CAFÉ** | Amalfi's historic pasticceria is famed for its candied fruits and assortment of tempting Neapolitan pastries. If you have no time to linger and indulge at their piazza tables, order at the bar for a cheaper stand-up coffee and *sfogliatella* pastry fix. **Known for:** excellent but pricey; delizia di limone cake; historic facade and interiors on Piazza Duomo. [$] *Average main: €5* ✉ *Piazza Duomo 40, Amalfi* ☎ *089/871065* 🌐 *www.pasticceriapansa.it.*

🛏 Hotels

Albergo Sant'Andrea

$$ | **HOTEL** | Just across from the magnificent steps leading to Amalfi's cathedral, this tiny, family-run *pensione* has a cute "Room with a View" lobby that's as big as a Victorian closet and guest rooms (most overlooking the Duomo) that range from cozy to vast. **Pros:** great location on the main square; friendly, reliable budget option; divine Duomo views. **Cons:** on the piazza, so expect noise; simple, dated decor; steep flight of steps to entrance. [$] *Rooms from: €150* ✉ *Via Duca Mansone I, Amalfi* ☎ *089/871145* 🌐 *www.albergosantandrea.it* 🕒 *Closed Feb. and Mar.* 🛏 *8 rooms* 🍽 *Free Breakfast.*

★ Grand Hotel Convento di Amalfi

$$$$ | **HOTEL** | This fabled medieval monastery was lauded by such guests as Longfellow and Wagner, and though recently modernized, it still retains some of its historic charm, including Victorian lecterns, Savonarola chairs, and a celebrated Arab-Sicilian cloister; once stark monk cells are now comfy contemporary guest room cocoons, some with wicker settees and beds. **Pros:** a slice of paradise; sublime terrace and garden walkways; impeccable service. **Cons:** limited dining options; a 10-minute walk to town; traditionalists will miss some of its old-world charm. [$] *Rooms from: €1071* ✉ *Via Annunziatella 46, Amalfi* ☎ *089/8736711* 🌐 *www.ghconventodiamalfi.com* 🕒 *Closed Jan.–mid-Mar.* 🛏 *53 rooms* 🍽 *Free Breakfast.*

👜 Shopping

Leading off from Piazza Duomo is the main street of Amalfi, Via Lorenzo d'Amalfi, which is lined with some of the loveliest shops on the coast. While it can be crowded during the day, be sure to take a stroll along here in the evening.

Ravello

5 km (3 miles) northeast of Amalfi, 40 km (25 miles) northeast of Sorrento.

Positano may focus on pleasure, and Amalfi on history, but cool, serene Ravello revels in refinement. Thrust over the S163 and the Bay of Salerno on a mountain buttress, below forests of chestnut and ash, above terraced lemon groves and vineyards, it early on beckoned the affluent with its island-in-the-sky views and secluded defensive positioning. Gardens out of the *Arabian Nights,* pastel palazzi, tucked-away piazzas with medieval fountains, architecture ranging from Romano-Byzantine to Norman-Saracen, and those sweeping blue-water, blue-sky vistas have inspired a panoply of large personalities. Today, many visitors flock here to discover this paradisiacal place, some to enjoy the town's celebrated two-month-long summer music festival (the Ravello Festival; ⊕ *www.ravellofestival. com*), others just to stroll through the hillside streets to gape at the bluer-than-blue panoramas of sea and sky.

GETTING HERE AND AROUND

Buses from Amalfi make the 20-minute trip along white-knuckle roads. From Naples, take the A3 Naples–Salerno autostrada; then exit at Angri and follow signs for Ravello. The journey takes about 75 minutes. Save yourself the trouble of driving by hiring a car and driver.

VISITOR INFORMATION

CONTACT Azienda Autonoma Soggiorno e Turismo. ⊠ *Piazza Fontana Moresca, 10,* ☎ *089/857096.*

👁 Sights

Auditorium Oscar Niemeyer

ARTS CENTER | Crowning Via della Repubblica and the hillside, which overlooks the spectacular Bay of Salerno, Auditorium Niemeyer is a startling piece of modernist architecture. Designed with a dramatically curved, all-white roof by the Brazilian architect Oscar Niemeyer (designer of Brasília), it was conceived as an alternative indoor venue for concerts, including those of the famed summer Ravello Festival, and is now also used as a cinema. The subject of much controversy since its first conception back in 2000, it raised the wrath of some locals who denounced such an ambitious modernist building in medieval Ravello. They need not have worried. The result, inaugurated in 2010, is a design masterpiece—a huge, overhanging canopied roof suspended over a 400-seat concert area, with a giant eye-shape window allowing spectators to contemplate the extraordinary bay vista during performances. ⊠ *Via della Repubblica 12, Ravello.*

★ Duomo

CHURCH | Ravello's first bishop, Orso Papiciò, founded this cathedral, dedicated to San Pantaleone, in 1086. Rebuilt in the 12th and 17th centuries, it retains traces of medieval frescoes in the transept, an original mullioned window, a marble portal, and a three-story 13th-century bell tower playfully interwoven with mullioned windows and arches. The 12th-century bronze door has 54 embossed panels depicting Christ's life, and saints, prophets, plants, and animals, all narrating biblical lore. Ancient columns divide the nave's three aisles, and treasures include sarcophagi from Roman times and paintings by the southern Renaissance artist Andrea da Salerno. Most impressive are the two medieval pulpits: the earlier one is inset with a mosaic scene of Jonah and the whale, while the more famous one opposite boasts exquisite mosaic work

Ravello's History

The town itself was founded in the 9th century, under Amalfi's rule. Residents prospered from cotton tussled with the superpower republic and elected their own doge in the 11th century; Amalfitani dubbed them *ribelli* (rebels). In the 12th century, with the aid of the Norman King Roger, Ravello even succeeded in resisting Pisa's army for a couple of years, though the powerful Pisans returned to wreak destruction along the coast. Even so, Ravello's skilled seafaring trade with merchants and Moors from Sicily and points east led to a burgeoning wealth, which peaked in the 13th century, when there were 13 churches, four cloisters, and dozens of sumptuous villas. Neapolitan princes built palaces and life was privileged.

Ravello's bright light eventually diminished, first through Pisa's maritime rise in the 14th century, then through rivalry between its warring families in the 15th century. When the plague cast its shadow in the 17th century, the population plummeted from upward of 30,000 to perhaps a couple of thousand souls, where it remains today. When Ravello was incorporated into the diocese of Amalfi in 1804, a kind of stillness settled in. Despite the decline of its power and populace, Ravello's cultural heritage and special loveliness continued to blossom. Gardens flowered and music flowed in the ruined villas, and artists, sophisticates, and their lovers filled the crumbling palazzi. Grieg, Wagner, D. H. Lawrence, Chanel, Garbo and her companion, conductor Leopold Stokowski, and then, slowly, tourists, followed in their footsteps.

and six twisting columns sitting on lion pedestals. In the crypt is the **Museo del Duomo**, which displays 13th-century treasures from the reign of Frederick II of Sicily. ⊠ *Piazza del Duomo, Ravello* ☎ *089/858311* 💳 *€3.*

Giardini del Vescovo (*Monsignore*)
GARDEN | A onetime bishop's residence that dates from at least the 12th century, the Villa Episcopio (formerly Villa di Sangro) today hosts concerts and exhibitions and has an open-air theater in its splendid gardens—the same gardens where André Gide found inspiration for his novel *The Immoralist*, where Italy's King Vittorio Emanuele III abdicated in favor of his son in 1944, and where Jackie Kennedy enjoyed breaks from her obligations as First Lady during a much publicized 1962 visit. Wheelchair access is via a new ramp on via San Giovanni del Toro. ⊠ *Via Richard Wagner/Via dei Episcopio, Ravello* 💳 *Free.*

Mamma Agata
SCHOOL | If you fancy learning how to make some of the things you've been eating, Mamma Agata, who has cooked for Elizabeth Taylor, Federico Fellini, Jackie Kennedy, and Marcello Mastroianni, will take you into her kitchen—with the almost obligatory stunning view—and walk you through the preparation of the area's pasta dishes and sweets. A morning session is followed by lunch—that you will have seen made. ⊠ *Piazza San Cosma 9, Ravello* ☎ *089/857845* ⊕ *www. mammaagata.com* 💳 *Cooking class and lunch cost €250* ⊙ *Closed weekends, and Nov.–mid-Mar.*

★ **Museo del Corallo** (*Coral Museum*)
ART MUSEUM | To the left of the Duomo, the entrance to this private museum is through the tempting shop CAMO, and both are the creation of master-craftsman-in-residence Giorgio Filocamo.

The museum celebrates the venerable tradition of Italian workmanship in coral, harvested in bygone centuries from the gulfs of Salerno and Naples and crafted into jewelry, cameos, and figurines. The fascinating collection, not confined solely to coral work, includes a painting of Sisto IV from the 14th century. Look also in particular for a carved Christ from the 17th century, for which the J. Paul Getty Museum offered $525,000 in 1987 (the offer was refused), and a tobacco box covered in cameos, one of only two in the world. There is also a statue of the Madonna dating to 1532. Giorgio has crafted coral for Pope John Paul II, the Clintons, and Princess Caroline, as well as numerous Hollywood stars. ⊠ *Piazza Duomo 9, Ravello* ☎ *089/857461* ⊕ *www. museodelcorallo.com* 🎫 *Free.*

★ Villa Cimbrone

GARDEN | To the south of Ravello's main square, a somewhat hilly 15-minute walk along Via San Francesco brings you to Ravello's showstopper, the Villa Cimbrone, whose dazzling gardens perch 1,500 feet above the sea. This medieval-style fantasy was created in 1905 by England's Lord Grimthorpe and made world famous in the 1930s when Greta Garbo found sanctuary from the press here. The Gothic *castello-palazzo* sits amid idyllic gardens that are divided by the grand Avenue of Immensity pathway, leading in turn to the literal high point of any trip to the Amalfi Coast—the **Belvedere of Infinity**. This grand stone parapet, adorned with stone busts, overlooks the entire Bay of Salerno and frames a panorama the late writer Gore Vidal, a longtime Ravello resident, described as the most beautiful in the world. The villa itself is now a five-star hotel. ⊠ *Via Santa Chiara 26, Ravello* ☎ *089/857459* ⊕ *www. villacimbrone.it* 🎫 *€7.*

★ Villa Rufolo

GARDEN | Directly off Ravello's main piazza is the Villa Rufolo, home to some of the most spectacular gardens in Italy, framing a stunning vista of the Bay of Salerno, often called the "bluest view in the world." If one believes the master storyteller Boccaccio, the villa was built in the 13th century by Landolfo Rufolo, whose immense fortune stemmed from trade with the Moors and the Saracens. Norman and Arab architecture mingle in a welter of color-filled gardens so lush the composer Richard Wagner used them as inspiration for Klingsor's Garden, the home of the Flower Maidens, in his opera *Parsifal.* Beyond the Arab-Sicilian cloister and the Norman tower lie the two terrace gardens. The lower one, the "Wagner Terrace," is often the site of Ravello Festival concerts. Highlights of the house are its Moorish cloister—an Arabic-Sicilian delight with interlacing lancet arcs and polychromatic palmette decoration—and the 14th-century Torre Maggiore, or Klingsor's Tower. ⊠ *Piazza del Duomo, Ravello* ☎ *089/857621* ⊕ *www.villarufolo.it* 🎫 *€7, extra charge for concerts.*

🍴 Restaurants

Vittoria

$$ | PIZZA | FAMILY | Just south of the Duomo, this airy, unfussy place with coved stone ceilings is a good bet for an informal bite. The *pizza al forno di legna* with fresh toppings is the star attraction: locals praise it, and even Gore Vidal allegedly approved. **Known for:** Campanian classics, including seafood frittura and eggplant parmigiana; very popular with locals and tourists; extensive menu. $ *Average main: €20* ⊠ *Via dei Rufolo 3, Ravello* ☎ *089/857947* ⊕ *www.ristorantepizzeriavittoria.it.*

🛏 Hotels

Hotel Parsifal

$$ | HOTEL | In 1288, this diminutive property overlooking the coastline housed an order of Augustinian friars; today the intact cloister hosts travelers intent on enjoying themselves under the coved ceilings of the former *eremitani scalzi* (shaved hermit) cells. **Pros:** staying in a former Ravello convent; open year-round; charming manager and his family dote on Americans. **Cons:** minimum three-night stay in some periods; tiny rooms; some may not like the '70's vibe. $ *Rooms from: €190 ⊠ Viale Gioacchino d'Anna 5, Ravello ☎ 089/857144 ⊕ www.hotelparsifal.com ↝ 17 rooms ⦿ Free Breakfast.*

Hotel Rufolo

$$$ | HOTEL | FAMILY | The quarters might be snug and simply furnished, but many have balconies with gorgeous sea and sky vistas framed by the palm trees of the Villa Rufolo, just below the hotel. **Pros:** parking included in room rates; beautiful views over Villa Rufolo; great pool and spa services. **Cons:** dated decor; overpriced: paying for the location; car park clutters the entrance. $ *Rooms from: €275 ⊠ Via San Francesco 1, Ravello ☎ 089/857133 ⊕ www.hotelrufolo.it ☉ Closed Jan.–Mar. ↝ 34 rooms ⦿ Free Breakfast.*

★ Hotel Villa Cimbrone

$$$$ | HOTEL | Suspended over the azure sea and set amid legendary rose-filled gardens, this Gothic-style castle was once home to Lord Grimthorpe and a hideaway for Greta Garbo; since the 1990s, it's been an exclusive if pricey visitors haven, with guest rooms ranging from palatial to cozy. **Pros:** gorgeous pool and views; top-rated restaurant; surrounded by beautiful gardens. **Cons:** special place comes at a price; daily arrival of respectful day-trippers; a longish hike from town center (porters can help with luggage). $ *Rooms from: €750 ⊠ Via Santa Chiara 26, Ravello ☎ 089/857459 ⊕ www.villacimbrone.com ☉ Closed Nov.–mid-Apr. ↝ 19 rooms ⦿ Free Breakfast.*

Villa Amore

$$$ | HOTEL | A 10-minute walk from the Piazza Duomo, this secluded hotel with a garden is family run and shares the same exhilarating view of the Bay of Salerno as Ravello's most expensive hotels. **Pros:** wonderful views; good-value restaurant; inexpensive alternative to its illustrious neighbors. **Cons:** long flight of steps to reach entrance; some rooms are very cramped and without views; away from the main drag. $ *Rooms from: €210 ⊠ Via dei Fusco 5, Ravello ☎ 089/857135 ⊕ www.villaamore.it ☉ Closed Nov.–Mar. ↝ 12 rooms ⦿ Free Breakfast.*

Paestum

99 km (62 miles) southeast of Naples.

For history buffs, a visit to Campania is not complete without seeing the ancient ruins of Paestum. A visit to the ruins to stroll past the incredibly well-preserved temples and see the top-notch collection at the Museo Nazionale is a great day trip from the Amalfi Coast or Naples.

GETTING HERE AND AROUND

By car, take the A3 autostrada south from Salerno, take the Battipaglia exit to SS18. Exit at Capaccio Scala. You can also take a CSTP or SCAT bus (departs hourly) or an FS train from Salerno. The archaeological site is a 10-minute walk from the station.

VISITOR INFORMATION

CONTACT Azienda Autonoma Soggiorno e Turismo di Paestum. (*Paestum Tourist Office*) ⊠ *Via Magna Grecia 887, ☎ 0828/811016 ⊕ www.infopaestum.it.*

Sights

★ Greek Temples

RUINS | One of Italy's most majestic sights lies on the edge of a flat coastal plain: the remarkably preserved Greek temples of Paestum. This is the site of the ancient city of Poseidonia, founded by Greek colonists probably in the 6th century BC. When the Romans took it over in 273 BC, they Latinized the name to Paestum and changed the layout of the settlement, adding an amphitheater and a forum. Much of the archaeological material found on the site is displayed in the Museo Nazionale, and several rooms are devoted to the unique tomb paintings—rare examples of Greek and pre-Roman pictorial art—discovered in the area.

At the northern end of the site opposite the ticket barrier is the Tempio di Cerere (Temple of Ceres). Built in about 500 BC, it is thought to have been originally dedicated to the goddess Athena. Follow the road south past the Foro Romano (Roman Forum) to the Tempio di Nettuno (Temple of Poseidon), a showstopping Doric edifice with 36 fluted columns and an entablature (the area above the capitals) that rivals those of the finest temples in Greece. Beyond is the so-called Basilica. It dates from the early 6th century BC. The name is an 18th-century misnomer, though, since it was, in fact, a temple to Hera, the wife of Zeus. Try to see the temples in the early morning or late afternoon when the stone takes on a golden hue. ✉ *Via Magna Grecia, Paestum* ☎ *0828/811023 ticket office* 🌐 *www.museopaestum.beniculturali.it* 🎫 *Site and museum: Mar.–Nov. €12, Dec.–Feb. €6.*

★ Tenuta Vannulo—Buffalo Farm and Shop

FARM/RANCH | **FAMILY** | Foodies, families, and the curious flock to this novel farm attraction that celebrates humane animal husbandry, organic mozzarella di bufala, and other wonderful products. A tour of the ranch run by the Palmieri family—headed by the serene octogenerian Antonio—brings you nose to glistening snout with probably the most pampered buffalo in the world. Some 600 of them wallow in pools, get a mechanical massage, and flap their ears to classical music. The shop/restaurant is the place to taste and take away cheese, ice cream, yogurt, chocolate, and leather products. ✉ *Contrada Vannulo, Via Galileo Galilei 101, Capaccio, Paestum* ☎ *0828/727894* 🌐 *www.vannulo.it* 🎫 *€5 guided tours; book in advance.*

Hotels

Azienda Agrituristica Seliano

$$ | **B&B/INN** | At this working farm about 3 km (2 miles) from Paestum's Greek temples, befriend the resident dogs so they will accompany you on country walks or bike rides, and opt for half-board to enjoy home-produced mozzarella and rich buffalo stew; you'll dine at a table with other guests before withdrawing to your charming wood-beamed guest room in one of the 19th-century baronial buildings. **Pros:** a great taste of a working farm; cooking classes; a banquet every evening. **Cons:** rustic, dated decor; not for non–dog fans; confusing to find. [$] *Rooms from: €140* ✉ *Via Seliano, Paestum* ☎ *0828/723634* 🌐 *www.agriturismoseliano.it* 🕒 *Closed Nov.–Mar.* 🛏 *14 rooms* 🍴 *Free Breakfast.*

Chapter 16

PUGLIA, BASILICATA, AND CALABRIA

16

Updated by
Nick Bruno

 Sights
★★★☆☆

 Restaurants
★★★★★

 Hotels
★★★☆☆

 Shopping
★★☆☆☆

 Nightlife
★☆☆☆☆

WELCOME TO PUGLIA, BASILICATA, AND CALABRIA

TOP REASONS TO GO

★ **A wander through Sassi:** The Basilicata town of Matera is endowed with one of the most unusual landscapes in Europe—a complex network of ancient cave dwellings partially hewn from rock, some of which now house chic bars and restaurants.

★ **A trip to peasant-food heaven:** Dine on Puglia's famous puree of fava beans with chicory and olive oil in a humble country restaurant.

★ **Lecce and its Baroque splendors:** The beautiful, friendly city of Lecce might be known for its peculiar brand of fanciful Baroque architecture, but it's not yet famous enough to have lost its Pugliese charm.

★ **The trulli of the Valle d'Itria:** Strange conical houses—many of them still in use—dot the rolling countryside of Puglia, centering around Alberobello, a town still composed almost entirely of these *trulli.* They must be seen to be believed.

1 Bari. An atmospheric *centro storico* is a highlight of this busy Adriatic port.

2 Trani. Don't miss this harbor town's stunning cathedral.

3 Polignano a Mare. Steep cliffs draw thrill-seekers and those looking to relax overlooking gorgeous inlets.

4 Castel del Monte. This town's octagonal, eponymous fortress is mysterious.

5 Mattinata. The Gulf of Manfredonia beaches here will dazzle you.

6 Vieste. The spectacular Gargano Promontory is the site of this resort town.

7 Alberobello. It's hard not to be enchanted by Alberobello's fairy-tale stone trulli.

8 Ostuni. The so-called Città Bianca (White City) is perched above azure waters.

9 Ceglie Messapica. The heart of this town is beguilingly medieval.

10 Martina Franca. Lose yourself in a maze of alleys and piazzas.

11 Taranto. An engaging archaeological museum is the main draw of this port town with a naval base.

12 Lecce. Here, it's all about Baroque beauty and lively locals.

13 Otranto. Look out over the sea from Otranto's medieval fortress.

14 Gallipoli. This fishing town is famed for its island *borgo antico.*

15 Matera. The so-called City of Sassi is filled with the intriguing cave dwellings.

16 Maratea. The mountains here seem to fall into the sea.

17 Diamante. This Calabrese resort is lively.

18 Castrovillari. For hiking, this gateway to mountainous Pollino National Park is a great hub.

19 Cosenza. Come to explore attractive medieval sights.

20 Camigliatello. The mountainous Sila National Park surrounds this town.

21 Crotone. The Treasure of Hera is among Crotone's draws.

22 Tropea. Gorgeous beaches will beckon you to Tropea.

23 Reggio Calabria. This busy port city plays footsie with Sicily.

EATING AND DRINKING WELL IN PUGLIA, BASILICATA, AND CALABRIA

The Mediterranean diet was born in the South of Italy. The cuisine here is based on seasonal local produce, so don't expect to find, say, grapes in May or watermelon in November, although the mild climate and fertile soil, linked to modern farming methods, mean that most vegetable products have a long growing season.

Traditional cuisine reflects its peasant origins, with hearty homemade pasta, thick bean soups, and grilled meat and fish. The emphasis, though, is on vegetables, with zucchini, eggplant, beans, sweet peppers, and at least a dozen varieties of tomatoes transformed into imaginative dishes. Naturally, the local olive oil is never lacking on the table. Dribbled over soup or a thick chunk of bread, it can transform the plainest dish into a gourmet treat. One defining principle of Italian cooking is to use excellent ingredients in simple preparations. That philosophy reaches its purest expression here.

FABULOUS FAVA

Puré di fave e cicorielle, a puree of fava beans topped with sautéed chicory, is unique to Puglia and Basilicata. The simple recipe has been prepared here for centuries and continues to be a staple of the local diet. The dried favas are soaked overnight, cooked with potatoes, seasoned with salt and olive oil, and served warm with wild green chicory, often with a sprinkling of ground *peperoncino* (chili pepper). Mix it together before eating, and wash it down with a glass of *primitivo* or *aglianico*.

MEAT

In addition to its excellent beef, Basilicata is known for its *salsicce lucane* (sausages), seasoned with salt, cayenne pepper, and fennel seeds. Enormous grills are a feature of many of the region's restaurants, infusing the dining area with the aroma of freshly cooked meat. Adventurous eaters in Puglia should look for *turcinieddhri* (a blend of lamb's innards) and *pezzetti di cavallo* (braised horse meat).

PASTA

Puglia is the home of orecchiette with *cime di rapa* (broccoli rabe) and olive oil, a melodious dish that's wondrous in its simplicity. Try also cavatelli and *strascinati* (rectangles of pasta with one rough side and one smooth side).

PEPPERS

Calabria is known for its use of little hot peppers that can range from a mild sprinkling in tomato sauce to the tongue-scorching *'nduja* (spicy pork salami) paste. Local cured meats like *soppressata* (dried spicy salami) and *salsiccia piccante* (hot sausage), often sold by street vendors on a roll with peppers, onions, french fries, and mayonnaise, are all spiced with peperoncini.

SEAFOOD

Fish can be grilled (*alla griglia*), baked (*al forno*), roasted (*arrosto*), or steamed (*in umido*). Among the highlights are delicate *orata* (sea bream), branzino (sea bass), *gamberi rossi* (sweet red shrimp), and calamari. Puglia is the home of *cozze pelose* (hairy-shelled mussels), and Calabria's version of sushi is freshly caught *ricci di mare* (sea urchins), considered a delicacy—and an aphrodisiac!

WINES

Puglia produces around 17% of Italy's wine, more than the output of Australia. In the past, most of it was *vino sfuso* (jug wine), but over the past 15 years, producers have been concentrating on quality—with impressive results. The ancient *primitivo* grape (an ancestor of California's zinfandel) yields strong, heady wines like Primitivo di Manduria. The *negroamaro* grape is transformed into palatable *rosati* (rosés), as well as the robust Salice Salentino. Pair a dessert with the sweet red Aleatico di Puglia or Moscato di Trani.

In Basilicata, producers use the *aglianico* grape to outstanding effect in the prestigious Aglianico del Vulture. In Calabria, they've worked wonders with *gaglioppo*.

Venture off the traffic-filled highways and explore the countryside of Italy's boot, made up of three separate regions—Puglia, Basilicata, and Calabria—each one with its own character. This is Italy's deep south, where whitewashed buildings stand silently over three turquoise seas, castles guard medieval alleyways, and grandmothers dry their handmade orecchiette in the afternoon heat.

At every turn, these three regions boast dramatic scenery. Geographical divides have preserved an astonishing cultural and linguistic diversity that's unequaled elsewhere on the Italian mainland. Southern Italians are extremely proud of their hometowns and will gladly direct you to some forgotten local chapel in an olive grove, an unmarked monument, or an obscure work of art.

One of southern Italy's most popular vacation destinations is the Gargano Promontory, where safe sandy shores and secluded coves are nestled between whitewashed coastal towns and craggy limestone cliffs. You'll also find many beautiful stretches of sandy beaches along the coast of the Salento Peninsula and the Mediterranean shoreline of Calabria and Basilicata.

MAJOR REGIONS

Bari and the Adriatic Coast. The busy port of Bari offers architectural nuggets in its labyrinthine old quarter. In nearby Trani a distinctive Apulian-Romanesque church stands by the sea, while Polignano a Mare has cliff-top medieval charm above sparkling waters. For a unique excursion, head to Castel del Monte, home to an enigmatic 13th-century octagonal castle.

The Gargano Promontory. Amid the Foresta Umbra's landscape of craggy limestone, pine trees, and scrubby Mediterranean *macchia* (underbrush) are the beguiling coastal resorts of Vieste and Mattinata.

The Trulli District. The inland area southeast of Bari has a mostly flat, rock-strewn terrain that's been given over to olive cultivation. The area is also interspersed with idiosyncratic limestone habitations called *trulli*. The center of the Trulli District is Alberobello in the enchanting Valle d'Itria. Amid this fairy-tale-like landscape are the dazzling whitewashed hilltop market towns of Martina Franca, Ceglie Messapica, and Ostuni.

The Salento Penninsula. South of the Trulli District the monotony of endless olive trees is redeemed by an alluring coastline of dramatic sandstone cliffs and intimate fishing towns such as Otranto and Gallipoli. Taranto has a captivating archaeological museum amid its rusty, industrial surroundings, while Lecce is an oasis of grace and sophistication, with swirling Baroque architecture and a lively cultural scene.

Basilicata. Occupying the instep and part of the heel of Italy's boot, this and the neighboring Calabria region formed part of Magna Graecia, southern Italy's Greek colonies. Today, Basilicata attracts travelers in search of bucolic settings, great food, and archaeological treasures. The village of Aliano was made famous by writer Carlo Levi (1902–75). Matera, a recently rejuvenated city with Baroque splendor, is built on the side of a ravine honeycombed with Sassi that have been transformed into swanky homes, restaurants, and hotels. On a spectacularly mountainous section of the Tyrrhenian coast is the gorgeous resort Maratea.

Calabria. Italy's southernmost mainland region has fantastic beaches in lively resort communities such as Tropea and Diamante. Castrovillari, Cosenza, and Camigliatello are great rustic bases for exploring the Sila Mountains and Pollino National Park. Crotone was a major ancient cultural center, and, toward Sicily, the busy port of Reggio Calabria is home to two arresting ancient Greek statues, the *Bronzi di Riace.*

Planning

Making the Most of Your Time

If your priority is relaxing on the beach, plan on a few days at a seaside resort in one of the Gargano Promontory's fishing villages, such as Peschici, Rodi Garganico, and Vieste, and perhaps a further stay at one of the Calabrian coastal resorts, such as Diamante or Tropea, or Maratea in Basilicata.

Otherwise, choose a base like Polignano a Mare or Trani, especially if you land or dock in Bari. Take day trips out to the Valle d'Itria, or to the remarkable octagonal Castel del Monte. Then head east along the Adriatic route (SS16), stopping to see the idyllic hilltop Ostuni before continuing on to Lecce, where you'll want to spend at least two to three nights exploring the city's Baroque wonders and taking a day trip down to Otranto and Gallipoli.

Next, take regional roads and the Via Appia (SS7) to reach Matera, whose Sassi cave dwellings are a southern Italian highlight; allow at least two nights here. Then it's back out to the SS106 to Calabria, along the coast dotted with ancient Greek settlements, as far as Tropea. At this point, cut inland on the SS107 across the Sila Massif, stopping at the hill resort of Camigliatello or carrying on to the more vibrant lowland Cosenza. Reggio Calabria is worthwhile just to see the celebrated Riace bronzes.

Getting Around

BUS

There is direct, if not always frequent, service between most destinations within Calabria, Puglia, and Basilicata. In many cases, bus service is the backup when problems with train service arise. Matera is linked with Bari by frequent Ferrovie Appulo Lucane trains and buses and with Taranto by SITA bus. In Calabria the Romano bus company runs a regular service between various towns. Ferrovie della Calabria operates many of the local routes.

BUS CONTACTS Bus Romano.
☎ *0962/21709* ⊕ *www.autolineeromano.com.* **Ferrovie della Calabria.**
☎ *0961/896306 Catanzaro Stazione,* ⊕ *www.ferroviedellacalabria.it.*
SITA. ☎ *0835/385007 Matera Office,*
080/5790111 Puglia Regional Office, Bari,

0971/506811 Basilicata Regional Office, Potenza ⊕ *www.sitasudtrasporti.it.*

CAR

Although roads are generally good in the south, and major cities are linked by fast autostradas, driving here is a major test of navigation skills. Driving into the center of many cities and towns can be particularly complicated, owing to mazes of one-way streets, pedestrianized zones, and limited parking facilities. The good news is that you can bypass many communities via ring roads. Also, if you're staying at an in-town hotel, check with the staff about parking: the more upscale properties often have garage facilities or valet services for guests.

If you're squeamish about getting lost, don't drive at night in the countryside—roads can be confusing without the visual aid of landmarks, and GPS is far from infallible. Also, Bari, Brindisi, and Reggio Calabria are notorious for car thefts and break-ins. In these cities, don't leave valuables in the car, and find a guarded parking space if possible.

The toll-free A3 autostrada (Napoli–Reggio Calabria) links Naples to the south, with major exits at Sicignano (for the interior of Basilicata and Matera), Cosenza (the Sila Massif and Crotone), and Pizzo (for Tropea). Parts of the A3 in northern Calabria cross uplands more than 3,000 feet high, and snow chains may be required during winter months. In the summer and during holiday weekends this is the main north–south route for Italy's sun seekers, so factor in plenty of time for delays and avoid peak travel times.

Take the SS18 for coastal destinations on the Tyrrhenian side and the E90 for the Ionian, alongside various state roads that crisscross toward the Adriatic. Given speed detectors and driver-tracking technology, it's best to stick to speed limits and be careful not to enter ZTL (*zona a traffico limitato*) restricted traffic areas

(cameras are set up in towns such as Matera and Altamura): you'll be spared an unwelcome ticket when you get home.

TRAIN

Trenitalia runs to Calabria, either following the Ionian Coast as far as Reggio Calabria or swerving inland to Cosenza and the Tyrrhenian Coast. Italo runs high-speed services along the coasts to Bari and Reggio Calabria.

CONTACTS Ferrovie Appulo Lucane. ☎ *080/5725421 Bari Centrale, 800/050500 numero verde (toll-free)* ⊕ *www.ferrovieappulolucane.it.* **Ferrovie Sud-Est.** ☎ *800/079090 numero verde (toll-free)* ⊕ *www.fseonline.it.* **Italo.** ☎ *892020* ⊕ *www.italotreno.it/ en.* **Trenitalia.** ☎ *892021 (within Italy), 06/68475475 (from outside Italy)* ⊕ *www. trenitalia.com.*

Restaurants

Italy's southern region is home to numerous restaurants that feature home cooking or Slow Food–inspired menus, which boils down to everything is made with the freshest ingredients. Meals are meant to be enjoyed at leisure, however, and service is not swift. Whether you decide to dine in a well-known restaurant or at a humble country trattoria, plan to give some thought to your menu choices (it's expected) and ask questions (also expected).

Restaurant prices are the average cost of a main course at dinner, or, if dinner is not served, at lunch. Restaurant reviews have been shortened. For full information, visit Fodors.com.

Hotels

Hotels in the region range from grand upscale establishments to small and stylish bijou inns to family-run rural *agriturismi* (country hostelries, often part of farms) that compensate for a lack of amenities with their famous southern hospitality. *Fattorie* and *masserie* (small farms and grander farm estates) offering accommodations are listed at local tourist offices.

In beach areas such as the Gargano Promontory and Salento, campgrounds and bungalow lodgings are ubiquitous and popular with families and budget travelers. Note that many seaside hotels open up just for the summer season, when they often require several-day stays with full or half board. And do remember that in a region like this—blazingly hot in summer and chilly in winter—air-conditioning and central heating can be important.

Hotel prices are the lowest cost of a standard double room in high season. Hotel reviews have been shortened. For full information, visit Fodors.com.

What it Costs in Euros			
$	**$$**	**$$$**	**$$$$**
RESTAURANTS			
under €15	€15–€24	€25–€35	over €35
HOTELS			
under €125	€125–€200	€201–€300	over €300

Bari

260 km (162 miles) southeast of Naples, 450 km (281 miles) southeast of Rome.

The biggest city in the region, Bari is a major port and a transit point for travelers catching ferries across the Adriatic to Greece, Croatia, and Albania. It's also a cosmopolitan city with one of the most interesting historic centers in the region. In recent years, it has become a major center of pilgrimage for Russian Orthodox visitors, due to its connection with St. Nicholas, the patron saint of

Russia, as well as of Bari. The old quarter of the city, around the basilica and the harbor castle, is a lively maze of white-washed alleyways buzzing with bars, cafés, restaurants, and crafts shops. Most of the modern town is set out in a logical 19th-century grid, following the designs of Joachim Murat (1767–1815), Napoléon's brother-in-law and King of the Two Sicilies. The heart is **Piazza della Libertà**, where old and young gather in the evenings to stroll up and down and see and be seen.

GETTING HERE AND AROUND

By car, take the Bari-Nord exit from the A14 autostrada. Bari's train station is a hub for Puglia-bound trains. Alitalia and Ryanair fly to Bari Airport from Rome and Milan. Bari and Milan are also connected by easyJet and Wizz Air.

VISITOR INFORMATION

CONTACT Infopoint Turistico Bari. ✉ *Piazza del Ferrarese 29, Bari* ☎ *080/0805242244* ⊕ *www.viaggiareinpuglia.it.*

 Sights

★ **Bari Vecchia and Via Sparano**

HISTORIC DISTRICT | FAMILY | By day, you can lose yourself in the maze of white alleyways in Bari Vecchia, the old town stretching along the harbor, now humming with restaurants, cafés, and crafts shops. Residents tend to leave their doors wide open, so you catch a glimpse into the daily routine of southern Italy: matrons hand-rolling orecchiette, their grandchildren home from school for the midday meal, and workers busy patching up centuries-old arches and doorways. Back in the new town, join the evening passeggiata on pedestrian-only Via Sparano, then, when night falls, saunter out among the outdoor bars and restaurants in Piazza Mercantile, past Piazza Ferrarese at the end of Corso Vittorio Emanuele. ✉ *Via Sparano, Bari.*

Puglia, Past and Present

Puglia has long been inhabited and invaded. On sea voyages to their colonies and trading posts in the west, the ancient Greeks invariably headed for Puglia first—it was the shortest crossing—before filtering southward into Sicily and westward to the Tyrrhenian Coast. In turn, the Romans—often bound in the opposite direction—were quick to recognize the strategic importance of the peninsula. Later centuries would see a procession of other empires raiding or colonizing Puglia: Byzantines, Saracens, Normans, Swabians, Turks, and Spaniards all swept through, each group leaving their mark. Romanesque churches and the powerful castles built by 13th-century Holy Roman Emperor Frederick II (who also served as king of Sicily and Jerusalem) are among the most impressive buildings in the region. Frederick II, dubbed "Stupor Mundi" (Wonder of the World) for his wide-ranging interests in literature, science, mathematics, and nature, was one of the foremost personalities of the Middle Ages.

The region experienced a huge economic revival after decades of neglect following World War II. Since then, EU funding, state incentive programs, and irrigation subsidies have helped Puglia to become Italy's top regional producer of wine, with the remainder of land devoted to olives, citrus, and vegetables. The main ports of Bari, Brindisi, and Taranto are thriving economic centers, though there remain serious problems of unemployment and poverty. However, the much-publicized arrival of thousands of asylum seekers from Eastern Europe and beyond has not significantly destabilized these cities (as had been feared), and economic and political refugees have dispersed throughout Italy. Today, despite several years of region-wide *recessione*, an air of prosperity still wafts through the smarter streets of Lecce, Trani, and smaller towns like Otranto and Peschici.

★ Basilica di San Nicola

CHURCH | The 11th-century Basilica di San Nicola, overlooking the sea in the *città vecchia* (old city), houses the bones of St. Nicholas, the inspiration for Santa Claus. His relics were stolen from Myra, in present-day Turkey, by a band of sailors from Bari and are now buried in the crypt. Because St. Nicholas is also the patron saint of Russia, the church draws both Roman Catholic and Russian Orthodox pilgrims; souvenir shops in the area display miniatures of the Western saint and his Eastern counterpart side by side. ⊠ *Largo Abate Elia 13, Piazza San Nicola, Bari* ☎ *080/5737111* ⊕ *www. basilicasannicola.it.*

Castello Svevo

CASTLE/PALACE | Looming over the cathedral is the symbol of Bari: huge Castello Svevo, which houses a number of archaeological and art collections within its evocative courtyards, towers, and rooms. The current building dates from the time of Holy Roman Emperor Frederick II (1194–1250), who rebuilt an existing Norman-Byzantine castle to his own exacting specifications. Designed more for power than beauty, it looks out beyond the cathedral to the small Porto Vecchio (Old Port). Inside are displays that include plaster-cast reproductions of the city's sculptural riches, Byzantine archaeological finds, photo collections from Bari's past, and historic ceramics and other precious objects. ⊠ *Piazza Federico*

Il di Svevia, Bari ☎ *080/8869304* ⊕ *www. musei.puglia.beniculturali.it* ✉ *€6; €9 during exhibitions* ⊘ *Closed Tues.*

Cattedrale di San Sabino

CHURCH | Bari's 12th-century cathedral is the seat of the local bishop and was the scene of many significant political marriages between important families in the Middle Ages. The cathedral is dedicated to San Sabino, a 6th-century bishop who apparently lived to be 105. The architecture reflects the Romanesque style favored by the Normans of that period. ✉ *Piazza dell'Odegitria, Bari* ☎ *080/5210605* ⊕ *www.arcidiocesibaribitonto.it.*

 ## Restaurants

Ristorante al Pescatore

$$$ | SEAFOOD | In the lively heart of the old town, opposite the castle, stands one of Bari's best seafood restaurants. The interior is rather sparse, with whitewashed walls and a vaulted ceiling, and the dining room can be crowded and noisy, but during the summer you can sit on the quieter outdoor veranda. **Known for:** ricci di mare—a taste of the Puglian sea; lively atmosphere with tables packed together; seafood antipasto (crudo misto). $ *Average main: €27* ✉ *Piazza Federico II di Svevia 6/8, Bari* ☎ *080/5237039.*

Ristorante Opera

$$ | SOUTHERN ITALIAN | Don't be put off by its nondescript modernist street location, as Opera delivers a well-crafted menu of superb-value seafood dishes, from sushi-style antipasti to beautifully prepared fillets of sea bream. The always innovative food is served on gorgeous arty tableware in the smart yet welcoming contemporary space or on the street-side terrace outside. **Known for:** freshest seafood with a twist; innovative vegetarian options; loved by locals and families. $ *Average main: €17* ✉ *Via Nicolo' Piccinni 151, Bari* ☎ *340/1774153 mobile* ⊘ *Closed Mon. and Sun. dinner.*

 ## Coffee and Quick Bites

★ Caffè Vergnano 1882 Amendola

$ | SOUTHERN ITALIAN | Grand stone rooms and a pretty terrazza sprouting olive trees make this a flexible and fab venue to breakfast, brunch, and lunch—and to socialize with evening drinks. As well as a constant stream of excellent coffee, they do a selection of pastries, great-value daily specials (pasta for just €6), and various snacks. **Known for:** evening buffet and DJ sets; daily pasta, grilled meat, and veggie dishes; historic stone building and courtyard seating. $ *Average main: €8* ✉ *Via Amendola 128/B, Bari* ☎ *080/5586586.*

Hotels

Palace Hotel

$$ | HOTEL | Common areas in this downtown landmark (est. 1956) have bright color schemes and Baroque touches, and the spacious guest rooms have balconies and marble-lined bathrooms. **Pros:** convenient location near the medieval old town; garage facilities; comfortable, modern rooms. **Cons:** some bathrooms and rooms desperately need updating; large, busy hotel (can feel impersonal); mainly geared to conferences and business clients. $ *Rooms from: €150* ✉ *Via Lombardi 13, Bari* ☎ *080/5216551* ⊕ *www.palacehotelbari.com* ➦ *195 rooms* ⦿ *Free Breakfast.*

Trani

43 km (27 miles) northwest of Bari.

Trani has a harbor filled with fishing boats and a quaint old town with cobblestone streets, gleaming medieval churches, and palazzi built from local limestone. The town is also justly famous for its sweet dessert wine, Moscato di Trani. It's smaller than the other ports along this coast.

Puglia

ISOLE
TREMITI
I Cameronio
ISOLE S.
DOMINO

TO TERMOLI

Adriatic Sea

Vieste
Mattinata
Monte Sant'Angelo
Manfredonia
L'Annunziata
Golfo di
Manfredonia
Foresta Umbra
Rodi Garganico
Peschici
San Giovanni Rotondo
GARGANO PROMONTORY
Lago di Varano
San Severo
Lucera
Foggia
Cerignola
Zapponeta
Barletta
Andria
Corato
Trani
Castel del Monte
Spinazzola
Gravina in Puglia
Santeramo in Colle
Altamura
Matera
Gioia del Colle
Molfetta
Bari
Polignano a Mare
Grotte di Castellana
TRULLI DISTRICT
Alberobello
Locorotondo
Martina Franca
Fasano
Ostuni
Ceglie Messapica
Grottaglie
Massafra
Taranto
Mare Piccolo
Mare Grande
Castellaneta Marina
Lido di Metaponto
Scanzano
Golfo di Taranto
Brindisi
Mesagne
Via Appia
Francavilla Fontana
Campi
Manduria
Lecce
Maglie
Nardo
Gallipoli
SALENTO
Otranto
Santa Cesarea Terme
Castro
Leuca

PUGLIA
BASILICATA
LUCANO
Potenza
Melfi
S. Angelo dei Lombardi
CAMPANIA
Ariella
Battipaglia
Eboli
Salerno
Golfo di
TO NAPLES

KEY
Ferry lines

30 miles
50 km

0   0

GETTING HERE AND AROUND

By car, take the Trani exit from the A14 autostrada. Frequent trains run from Bari.

VISITOR INFORMATION

CONTACT Info Point Trani. ⊠ *Palazzo Palmieri, Piazza Trieste 10, Trani* ☎ *375/5575405 mobile and WhatsApp messaging, 0883/588830* ⊕ *www.prolocotrani.it.*

Sights

Castello Svevo

CASTLE/PALACE | One of Frederick II's most imposing fortresses, the quadrangular Trani Castle guarded the Adriatic sea route throughout the Middle Ages. It was the scene of several royal weddings of the Swabian and Anjou houses, as well as the place of imprisonment for life of Siffridina, Countess of Caserta, who had supported the losing Swabian dynasty against Charles I of Anjou. In the early 20th century it became a state prison and remained so until 1974. The ground floor contains a museum telling the story of the castle alongside archaeological finds, sculpture, and a wealth of ceramics. ⊠ *Piazza Re Manfredi 14, Trani* ☎ *0883/506603* 🎟 *€5* 🕑 *Closed Mon. and Tues. and Sun. in Nov.*

★ Cattedrale

CHURCH | The stunning pinkish-white 11th-century cathedral, considered one of the finest in Puglia, is built on a spit of land jutting into the sea. Dedicated to St. Nicholas the Pilgrim, it was a favorite place of prayer for crusaders embarking for war in the Holy Land. Its lofty bell tower can be visited, and guided tours arranged by request at the nearby Museo Diocesiano and via the website calendar slots; the views are worth the climb. ⊠ *Piazza Duomo, Trani* ☎ *0883/500293* ⊕ *www.cattedraletrani.it* 🎟 *Free, bell tower €5.*

Museo Sinagoga Sant'Anna (*Synagogue Street and Sant'Anna Museum*)

SYNAGOGUE | In the 12th century one of the largest Jewish communities in southern Italy flourished here, and on Via Sinagoga two of the four synagogues still stand. The 13th-century Scolanova has been reconverted to a synagogue after a long period as a Christian church, while the former Sant'Anna now houses a museum of Trani's Jewish history. ■**TIP**→ **Contact the Trani Tourism Office to set up tours and visits.** ⊠ *Via La Guidea 24, corner of Via San Martino, Trani* ☎ *0883/582470* ⊕ *www.fondazioneseca.it* 🎟 *Donations accepted.*

Polo Museale Trani

OTHER MUSEUM | Four floors of the handsome 18th-century Palazzo Lodispoto, near the Duomo, contain two very different collections: the Museo Diocesano showcases Trani's wealth of religious artifacts, while the Museo della Macchina per Scrivere follows the evolution of the typewriter. Among the highlights in the former are fragments from the 6th-century basilica, medieval and Baroque architectural elements, and funereal treasures commissioned by Charles I of Anjou on the death of his son Philip. The latter collection has 400 examples of typewriters from around the world, including some iconic Olivetti models as well as those used to type Braille, Arabic, and Japanese. A reasonably priced café serves drinks and pastries. ⊠ *Palazzo Lodispoto, Piazza Duomo 8/9, Trani* ☎ *0883/582470* ⊕ *www.fondazioneseca.it* 🎟 *Free* 🕑 *Closed Mon.*

Hotels

Ibis Styles Trani

$ | **HOTEL** | Although this hotel caters mainly to business travelers, its location near the main sights in Trani's historic center makes it a decent value option for tourists. **Pros:** close to the train station and the old town; parking in hotel garage; wheelchair accessible. **Cons:** breakfast disappointing; noise from trains; functional but somewhat basic. $ *Rooms from: €68* ⊠ *Corso Imbriani 137, Trani* ☎ *0883/588010* ⊕ *www.accorhotels.com* ⌐ *46 rooms* ⎮◎⎮ *Free Breakfast.*

★ Palazzo Filisio

$ | HOTEL | Superbly positioned in front of the Duomo on a quiet seaside piazza, this small, handsome, beautifully maintained hotel has guest rooms with contemporary wooden furniture, white and azure fabrics, and marbled bathrooms. **Pros:** right next to the cathedral; most rooms have sea views; superb breakfast and restaurant. **Cons:** books up in high season; often occupied by wedding parties; no parking outside hotel. $ *Rooms from: €120* ⊠ *Via M. Reginaldo Giuseppe Maria Addazi 2, Trani* ☎ *0883/500931* ⊕ *www. palazzofilisio.it* ◷ *Restaurant closed Mon.* ⌐ *10 rooms* ⎮◎⎮ *Free Breakfast.*

Polignano a Mare

35 km (22 miles) southeast of Bari, 14 km (9 miles) north of Castellana.

This well-preserved, whitewashed old town, perched on limestone cliffs overlooking the Adriatic, makes an atmospheric base for exploring the surrounding area. Film crews and adrenaline junkies come to experience the town's spectacular cliff-diving championships, which usually take place in late September.

GETTING HERE AND AROUND

From Bari, take the Polignano exit from the SS16. Frequent trains run from Bari.

VISITOR INFORMATION

CONTACT Polignano Tourism Office. ⊠ *Via Martiri Di Dogali 2, Polignano a Mare* ☎ *080/4252336* ⊕ *www.viaggiarein-puglia.it.*

 Restaurants

Antica Trattoria Comes Dal 1926

$$ | SOUTHERN ITALIAN | FAMILY | Run by genial Giuseppe, this family-run trattoria serves classic seafood dishes in a relaxed, modern dining room. Freshly netted catch are heaped on hearty plates, like *insalata di mare* (seafood salad), seafood cavatelli pasta, and grilled *gamberoni* (prawns). **Known for:** big helpings, big value; cold cuts, cheeses, and Angus steaks; superb Pugliese seafood antipasti. $ *Average main: €17* ⊠ *Via Pompeo Sarnelli 14, Polignano a Mare* ☎ *080/4248888* ◷ *Closed Wed.*

Hotels

Borgobianco Resort & Spa

$$$$ | RESORT | FAMILY | Housed in a handsome masseria farmhouse building, this countryside resort provides a tranquil base for relaxing by the pool, eating alfresco in courtyards and terrace, and spa pampering. **Pros:** cool, whitewashed luxury in tranquil location; gorgeous pool, spa, and outdoor spaces; shuttle bus to town. **Cons:** decor could be a tad soulless for some; service can be patchy; town not in easy walking distance. $ *Rooms from: €321* ⊠ *Contrada Casello Cavuzzi, Polignano a Mare* ☎ *080/2049060* ⊕ *borgobianco.it* ⌐ *48 rooms* ⎮◎⎮ *Free Breakfast.*

Hotel Covo dei Saraceni

$$ | HOTEL | It would be difficult to find a more romantic location than that occupied by this hotel, dramatically perched on the rocks above the narrow cove of Polignano. **Pros:** magnificent sea views; spa center in the hotel; decent buffet breakfast. **Cons:** some rooms and bathrooms small with odd layouts; some rooms have views of parking lot; popular for wedding receptions (can be busy). $ *Rooms from: €190* ⊠ *Via Conversano 1, Polignano a Mare* ☎ *080/4241177* ⊕ *www.covodeisaraceni.com* ⌐ *32 rooms* ⎮◎⎮ *Free Breakfast.*

The imposing Castel del Monte is a 13th-century structure built by Emperor Frederick II on land he inherited from his mother, Constance of Sicily.

Castel del Monte

56 km (35 miles) southwest of Bari.

The isolated Norman Castel del Monte dominates the surrounding countryside from the top of a 1,778-foot-high hill. The nearest town is Andria, 17 km (10½ miles) away, largely modern and congested—avoid traffic by taking the ring road around it.

GETTING HERE AND AROUND

Take the Andria-Barletta exit from the A14 autostrada, then follow the SS170dir to Castel del Monte. From April through October (and weekends November–March) there's a daily minibus service from Piazza Bersaglieri d'Italia in Andria.

VISITOR INFORMATION

CONTACT Castel del Monte Tourism Office. ⊠ *Via Vespucci 114, Andria* ☎ *0883/592283* ⊕ *www.proloco.andria. ba.it.*

Sights

★ Castel del Monte

CASTLE/PALACE | Crowning an isolated hill 1,778 feet above sea level in the heart of the Alta Murgia National Park, this enigmatic octagonal fortress, built by Frederick II in the first half of the 13th century, has puzzled historians and researchers for centuries. Rooms are arranged in a seemingly illogical sequence through eight towers around a central courtyard. Recent interpretations suggest it was an elaborate cultural center conceived by Frederick to study various scientific disciplines of the Western and the Arabic worlds. Umberto Eco used it as his inspiration for riddles in *The Name of the Rose.* ⊠ *On signposted minor road, 17 km (10½ miles) south of Andria, Andria* ☎ *327/9805551* ⊕ *www.casteldelmonte. beniculturali.it* ⊠ *€7, €10 when there's an exhibition.*

Mattinata

138 km (86 miles) northwest of Bari.

The town of Mattinata is a good center for hikes in the Foresta Umbra and for visiting the Santuario di San Michele. It also has attractive stretches of sandy beach.

GETTING HERE AND AROUND

From Foggia (the chief city in Puglia's northernmost province), take the winding SS89. Regular buses leave from Foggia's train station.

VISITOR INFORMATION

CONTACT Info Point Mattinata. ⊠ *Palazzo Mantuano, Via delle Camelie, Mattinata* ☎ *0884/597291 municipal office* ⊕ *www.comune.mattinata.fg.it.*

Sights

Foresta Umbra

NATURE PRESERVE | In the middle of the Gargano Promontory is the majestic Foresta Umbra (Shady Forest), a dense growth of beech, maple, pine, and oak generally found in more northerly climates, thriving here because of the altitude, which reaches 3,200 feet above sea level. Between the trees in this national park are occasional dramatic vistas opening out over the Golfo di Manfredonia. There are nature trails and picnic areas easily reached from Vieste, Peschici, and Mattinata. ⊠ *Visitor center, Laghetto Umbra, SP52bis, Monte Sant'Angelo* ☎ *0884/708578 national park* ☉ *Visitor center closed Oct.–Easter.*

Santuario di San Michele

RELIGIOUS BUILDING | Pilgrims have flocked to the mountain community of Monte Sant'Angelo for nearly 1,500 years— among them St. Francis of Assisi and crusaders setting off for the Holy Land from the then-flourishing port of Manfredonia. Monte Sant'Angelo is centered on the Santuario di San Michele, built over the grotto where the archangel Michael is believed to have appeared before shepherds in the year 490. Walk down a long series of steps to get to the grotto itself; on its walls you can see the hand tracings left by pilgrims. The Sanctuary was declared a UNESCO World Heritage site in 2011. To learn more about the history and myth surrounding the site visit the adjoining Musei TECUM. ⊠ *Via Reale Basilica 127, Monte Sant'Angelo* ☎ *0884/561150* ⊕ *www.santuariosan-michele.it* ☞ *Musei TECUM €5.*

Restaurants

Trattoria dalla Nonna

$$$ | SEAFOOD | FAMILY | Waves lap at the shore just inches from your table at this elegant but unpretentious trattoria, which often has a cozy fireplace ablaze in winter. You must follow a narrow twisting lane to get here, but it's worth the effort for specialties like the raw seafood antipasto, which features shellfish you might not find anywhere else. **Known for:** also run a B&B; fabulous sea views; unique cozze pelose mussels. $ *Average main: €26* ⊠ *Contrada Funni al Lido, Località Funni, off the main road (watch for signs), Mattinata* ☎ *0884/559205* ⊕ *www.dallanonna.it* ☉ *No lunch Tues.*

Hotels

Baia delle Zagare

$$ | HOTEL | Overlooking one of the Gargano Peninsula's loveliest bays, this secluded cluster of whitewashed buildings houses simply furnished modern rooms, some of which have balconies. **Pros:** incredible views and location; access to wonderful beach; fab pool and gardens. **Cons:** lots of steps; rooms may be a tad sparse for some; impossible to get to without a car. $ *Rooms from: €165* ⊠ *Litoranea Mattinata–Vieste, Mattinata* ☎ *0884/550155* ⊕ *www.hotelbaiadellezagare.it* ☉ *Closed Oct.–mid May* ⇨ *143 rooms* ○ *Free Breakfast.*

Vieste

93 km (58 miles) northeast of Foggia, 179 km (111 miles) northwest of Bari.

This large whitewashed town jutting off the tip of the spur of Italy's boot is an attractive place to wander around. Although curvy mountain roads render it slightly less accessible from autostradas and main rail stations than, say, Mattinata, it is, nevertheless, a good base for exploring Gargano. The resort attracts legions of tourists in summer, some bound for the Isole Tremiti, a tiny archipelago connected to Vieste by regular ferries.

GETTING HERE AND AROUND

If you're driving from Foggia, take the winding SS89. Regular buses leave from Foggia's train station.

VISITOR INFORMATION

CONTACT IAT Vieste Tourism Office. ✉ *Piazza John Fitzgerald Kennedy, Vieste* ☎ *0884/708806* 🌐 *www.viaggiarein-puglia.it.*

Sights

Castello Svevo

CASTLE/PALACE | Originally built by Frederick II, this impressive structure was enlarged by the Spanish to defend against attacks from the Turks, and it has remained a military base ever since. It is only open to the public for guided visits and temporary exhibitions and events; call ahead for the latest information. ✉ *Via Duomo, Vieste* ☎ *0884/708806* 🌐 *www.viesteturismo.com.*

Museo Civico Archeologico Michele Petrone

HISTORY MUSEUM | Opened in 2019 and housed in the Beata Vergine degli Angeli convent, next to the church of SS. Sacramento, this small but stimulating municipal museum consists mainly of Greco-Roman artifacts excavated in the area. Multimedia displays bring to life handsome amphorae, Roman bathhouse bronze statuary, and finds from the necropolis at nearby Villa di Santa Maria di Merino. ✉ *Lungomare A. Vespucci, Vieste* ☎ *0884/712223* 🎟 *Free* ⏲ *Closed weekends.*

Restaurants

★ Al Dragone

$$$ | **SOUTHERN ITALIAN** | Dine on exquisite Gargano fare at this atmospheric eatery set in a natural grotto just next to the cathedral in the heart of the old center. The menu is dominated by locally caught fish, and although dishes draw on traditional recipes, you can expect the occasional innovation. **Known for:** impressive wine cellar and cigar selection; gorgeous setting; beautifully crafted seafood dishes. [$] *Average main: €26* ✉ *Via Duomo 8, Vieste* ☎ *0884/701212* 🌐 *www.aldragone.it* ⏲ *Closed mid-Oct.–Mar. 1.*

Hotels

★ Navircri

$ | **B&B/INN** | **FAMILY** | Run by the friendly *famiglia* De Mauro, this modern B&B ticks all the boxes for those seeking great value in a tranquil, scenic setting near the beach. **Pros:** fab rooftop pool and Jacuzzi; immaculate rooms; great breakfast spread, including homemade jams. **Cons:** minimum night stays in high season; one triple doesn't have a balcony; having to walk to town and beach might not appeal to some. [$] *Rooms from: €70* ✉ *Via Saragat, Vieste* ☎ *0884/705022* 🌐 *www.bbnavicri.it* 🛏 *6 rooms* 🍴 *Free Breakfast.*

Alberobello

59 km (37 miles) southeast of Bari, 45 km (28 miles) north of Taranto.

With more than 1,000 trulli along its steep, narrow streets, Alberobello has been designated a UNESCO World Heritage site. It is one of the more popular

and well-established destinations in Puglia, and has some excellent restaurants (and some less-than-excellent trinket shops).

GETTING HERE AND AROUND

By car, take the Monopoli exit from the SS16, follow the SP237 to Putignano, then SS172 to Alberobello. Trains run half-hourly from Bari to Putignano, where you then take a bus. The journey takes around two hours.

VISITOR INFORMATION

CONTACT Alberobello Tourism Office. ✉ *Via Monte Nero 1, Alberobello* ☎ *348/8972795 mobile* 🌐 *www.prolocoalberobello.it.*

Sights

Alberobello–Martina Franca Road
SCENIC DRIVE | The trulli in Alberobello itself are impressive, but the most scenic concentration of these unique conical structures is along a 15-km (9-mile) stretch of the SS172 (Alberobello–Martina Franca) through the tranquil Valle d'Itria. Stop to visit some of the area's vineyards and oil mills—many of which have a welcoming open-door policy—surrounded by vast groves of ancient gnarled olive trees. ✉ *Alberobello.*

Trullo Sovrano
MUSEUM VILLAGE | **FAMILY** | Although this 18th-century house, Alberobello's largest trullo, originally belonged to a wealthy family, it has been furnished in a traditional style, providing insight into what everyday life was like in these unique beehive constructions. Guided tours are included with admission; there's an information center and shop, and gastronomic events are held in the garden. Check out the classic film *Casanova '70*, starring Marcello Mastroianni and Moira Orfei, which was partly filmed in and around the trullo. ✉ *Piazza Sacramento 10, Alberobello* ✥ *Follow Corso Vittorio Emanuele up past the obelisk and basilica* ☎ *080/4326030* 🌐 *www.trullosovrano.eu* 🎫 *€2.*

Restaurants

Il Poeta Contadino
$$$ | **SOUTHERN ITALIAN** | There are actually two eateries here, but far superior is the well-regarded Poeta Contadino, which specializes in regional cooking with a creative twist and offers a refined dining experience amid candlelight that casts shadows on ancient stone walls. If you're on a budget, though, the more affordable Osteria del Poeta also serves bite-size traditional dishes. **Known for:** extensive wine list; stunning vaulted ceiling; exquisite seafood and meat dishes. [$] *Average main: €28* ✉ *Via Indipendenza 21–27, Alberobello* ☎ *080/4321917* 🌐 *www.ilpoetacontadino.it* 🕓 *Closed Thurs.*

★ L'Aratro
$$ | **SOUTHERN ITALIAN** | Welcoming and rustic, this eatery is set inside adjoining trulli, complete with dark-wood beams, whitewashed walls, and a patio for summer dining. It's a certified Slow Food restaurant, so local ingredients figure prominently in the traditional, often seasonal dishes. **Known for:** gorgeous trulli venue; classic regional fare; diligent use of local produce. [$] *Average main: €23* ✉ *Via Monte San Michele 25–29, Alberobello* ☎ *080/4322789* 🌐 *www.ristorantearatro.it.*

Coffee and Quick Bites

Principotto
$ | **SOUTHERN ITALIAN** | **FAMILY** | For a great-value on-the-hoof snack, pop into this tiny, popular place for filled *panzerotti* (deep-fried pockets), *friselle* (crunchy durum-wheat bread), and *schiacciatella Romana* (pizza-like flatbread). Check the board for daily specials, including meaty ragù sauces and seafood like *polpi* (octopus) to fill your freshly fried pockets. **Known for:** bar next door for a vino accompaniment; cime di rapa and other Pugliese produce; buzzy place with crowds spilling out. [$] *Average*

main: €6 ✉ Via Bissolati 16, Alberobello ☎ 347/4529922 ⏲ Closed Thurs.

Hotels

★ Le Alcove

$$$ | **HOTEL** | This cluster of trulli has been transformed into luxury suites with original architectural features, modern comforts, and tasteful flourishes that make everything seem straight out of a lifestyle-magazine spread. **Pros:** centrally located near the Trullo Sovrano; heated floors; quaint, unusual accommodations. **Cons:** some rooms have a narrow, awkward metal staircase to upper areas; three rooms aren't in the main building; rooms are rather small. *[$] Rooms from: €260 ✉ Piazza Ferdinando IV 7, Alberobello ☎ 080/4323754 🌐 www.lealcove.it 🛏 9 rooms 🍴 Free Breakfast.*

Ostuni

50 km (30 miles) west of Brindisi, 85 km (53 miles) southeast of Bari.

This sun-bleached medieval town lies on three hills not far from the coast. From a distance, Ostuni is a jumble of blazing white houses and churches spilling over a hilltop and overlooking the sea. Don't be surprised if you hear a lot of English and German spoken in the cobbled streets. The Città Bianca (White City), as it is called, has cast its spell on a large number of British and German nationals, who have bought second homes here. That doesn't mean that the town has lost its local flavor; fairs, religious festivals, and colorful traditional events are held as always with the same enthusiasm and fervor.

GETTING HERE AND AROUND

By car, take the Ostuni exit from the SS16. Trenitalia runs frequent trains from Bari. The station, however, is 5 km (3 miles) from the town—there is almost hourly local bus service.

VISITOR INFORMATION

CONTACT Info-Point Ostuni. *✉ Corso Mazzini 8, Ostuni ☎ 0831/339627.*

Sights

Ostuni Old Town

HISTORIC DISTRICT | Known as the Città Bianca for its dazzling white buildings and cobbled streets, Ostuni commands stupendous views out over the coast and the surrounding plain. Its unpolluted sea and clean beaches have earned it international Blue Flag recognition since 2008. The surrounding countryside contains a number of interesting 17th- and 18th-century masserie, many of which have been converted into agriturismi. *✉ Ostuni 🌐 www.viaggiareinpuglia.it.*

Piazza Libertà

PLAZA/SQUARE | The city's main square divides the new town to the west and the old town to the east. The triangular piazza contains the town symbol: the towering Guglia di Sant'Oronzo (Spire of St. Oronzo), named after the patron of Ostuni, in whose honor an elaborate festival is held every year in late August. *✉ Ostuni 🌐 www.viaggiareinpuglia.it.*

Beaches

★ Torre Guaceto

BEACH | The transparent water and chalky sand of this marine reserve extend 12 miles along the coast and 4 miles inland, where the wetlands are a haven for wildlife. Those seeking a spectacular walk in an unspoiled expanse head to the Spiaggia delle Conchiglie, which consists of tiny white shells. Note: it's protected and off-limits to bathers. A shuttle bus operates from the main car park. **Amenities:** food and drink; lifeguards; parking (fee); toilets. **Best for:** snorkeling; sunrise; sunset; swimming; walking. *✉ Riserva Naturale di Torre Gauceto, Ostuni 🌐 www.riservaditorreguaceto.it.*

🍴 Restaurants

Osteria del Tempo Perso

$$ | SOUTHERN ITALIAN | On an old-town side street, this laid-back restaurant occupies two caves, where ancient rough-hewn stone walls contrast with elegant table settings. The service is friendly, and local, seasonal dishes include antipasti mainstays like eggplant Parmesan or salumi di Martina Franca, as well as both meat and fish *secondi*. **Known for:** local meat, including donkey; excellent changing menu; house-made pasta with classic Pugliese sauces. Ⓢ *Average main: €22* ⊠ *Via G. Tanzarella Vitale 47, Ostuni* ☎ *0831/304819* ⊕ *www.osteriadeltemposperso.com* ⊘ *Closed Mon. Sept.–June.*

Hotels

Hotel Relais Sant'Eligio

$ | HOTEL | Nestled in a valley just below Ostuni and surrounded by venerable olive trees, this stylish adaptation of a 16th-century posthouse—with characteristic stone archways and roughcasted walls—has whitewashed, simply furnished guest rooms whose beds have wrought-iron headboards. **Pros:** pleasant, modern environment with touches of old-world charm; fab views; free parking at hotel. **Cons:** showers lack decent water pressure; limited breakfast choice; outside the city walls and short walk uphill to the old center of Ostuni. Ⓢ *Rooms from: €115* ⊠ *Via Giosuè Pinto 50, Ostuni* ☎ *0831/1985171* ⊕ *www.santeligiorelais.it* ⇢ *22 rooms* ❚❉❚ *Free Breakfast.*

La Terra Hotel

$$ | B&B/INN | It doesn't get more historic than this 14th-century noble residence, where spacious, tastefully decorated rooms and a cocktail-perfect, colonnaded rooftop loggia offer character and comfort aplenty. **Pros:** inside the walls of the old city, near all sights; some rooms have superb views; great seafood restaurant. **Cons:** standard rooms look a bit tired; street can be noisy in high season; parking outside town (with shuttle service). Ⓢ *Rooms from: €163* ⊠ *Via Gaspare Petrarolo 16, Ostuni* ☎ *0831/336651* ⊕ *www.laterrahotel.it* ⇢ *17 rooms* ❚❉❚ *Free Breakfast.*

Ceglie Messapica

11 km (7 miles) southwest of Ostuni, 18 km (11 miles) southeast of Martina Franca.

With its 14th-century Piazza Vecchia, tattered Baroque balconies, and lordly medieval castles, the little whitewashed town of Ceglie Messapica is the epitome of everyone's notion of the sleepy southern Italian town. Situated at the center of the triangle formed by Taranto, Brindisi, and Fasano, this town was once the military capital of the region, and often defended itself against invasions from the Taranto city-state, which wanted to clear a route to the Adriatic. Nowadays, Ceglie Messapica is a gourmet destination, with a surprising number of excellent restaurants.

GETTING HERE AND AROUND

By car, take the Ostuni exit from the SS16, and follow the SP22 to Ceglie Messapica. Ferrovie del Sud-Est runs frequent bus and train connections from Bari.

VISITOR INFORMATION

CONTACT Info-Point Ceglie Messapica. ⊠ *Via G. Elia 16, Ceglie Messapica* ☎ *0831/371003* ⊕ *www.ceglieturismo.it.*

🍴 Restaurants

Al Fornello Da Ricci

$$$ | SOUTHERN ITALIAN | The cuisine served in the elegant dining room of this restaurant, complete with a verdant garden and run by a local couple—both creative chefs—marries exotic influences with tradition. It's a great place to splurge on a tasting menu; note, though, that hours can be erratic, especially during

winter months, so call ahead. **Known for:** friendly service; magical outside space; imaginative dishes. $ *Average main: €28* ✉ *Via delle Grotte 11, Ceglie Messapica* ☎ *0831/377104* ⊕ *www.antonellaricci-nodsookar.it* ⊗ *Closed Mon. and Tues.*

★ Cibus
$ | **SOUTHERN ITALIAN** | Amid the stone vaults and vine-leafy, light-dappled courtyard of this highly acclaimed old-town osteria turned Slow Food destination, the freshest Pugliese meat and produce are transformed into exquisite tapas-like dishes. Be sure to ask the amiable owner to show you his wine cellar and equally impressive cheese larder, where he personally controls the maturing process. **Known for:** noteworthy wine and cheese; friendly service and Slow Food ethos; gorgeous setting. $ *Average main: €14* ✉ *Via Chianche di Scarano, Ceglie Messapica* ☎ *0831/388980* ⊕ *www. ristorantecibus.it* ⊗ *Closed Tues.*

Martina Franca

29 km (18 miles) southwest of Ostuni, 36 km (22 miles) north of Taranto.

Martina Franca is a beguiling town with a dazzling mixture of medieval and Baroque architecture in the light-color local stone. Developed as a military stronghold in the 14th century, all that remains of the defensive walls are the four gates that divide the old part from the modern suburbs. Lose yourself in the maze of twisting white alleyways, where erstwhile palaces jostle with ancient churches and narrow stairways leading up to humbler abodes. No longer a little-known backwater, the centro storico can be crowded with sightseers on the weekends. The positive side is that this has led to the emergence of top-quality restaurants, and you'll be spoiled for choice. Each July into early August, the town hosts the Valle d'Itria music festival, which showcases classical music and opera.

GETTING HERE AND AROUND
By car, take the Fasano exit from the SS16, then follow the SS172. The Ferrovie Sud-Est runs frequent trains and buses from Bari and Taranto.

VISITOR INFORMATION
CONTACT Martina Franca Tourism Office. ✉ *Via Dott. Adolfo Ancona 5, Martina Franca* ☎ *366/1266045* ⊕ *www.proloco-martinafranca.it.*

Sights

Basilica di San Martino
CHURCH | A splendid example of southern Italian Baroque architecture, the basilica contains rows of lavishly decorated altars in polychrome marbles, as well as treasures like the silver statues of the two patron saints, San Martino and Santa Comasia. To the right of the main altar note the illuminated niche with the sculpture of the Madonna Pastorella as a shepherd girl in a gown of cloth-of-gold, defending Christ's flock from demons. The elaborately sculpted facade is dominated by a dramatic image of St. Martin with his prancing horse in a shell-shape niche. Some interesting MuBA (Museo Basilica) exhibits in the adjacent Palazzo Stabile tell the story of Martina Franca through religious art and artifacts. ✉ *Via Vittorio Emanuele 30, Martina Franca* ☎ *080/4302664* ⊕ *www.muba-sanmartino.it* ⊠ *€3 museum; €2 for guided tour* ⊗ *Museum closed Mon.*

Restaurants

★ Garibaldi Bistrot
$$ | **MODERN ITALIAN** | **FAMILY** | The location—right on the piazza by the Duomo, with tables outside and a cool whitewashed dining room inside—is what initially draws people to this restaurant. But it's the tasty Pugliese produce used in simple salads, antipasti, pasta dishes, and classic seafood or meat mains that keeps people coming back. **Known for:** great value and service; stunning spot on

the piazza; heaping salads and bountiful bruschetta. $ *Average main: €18* ⊠ *Piazza Plebiscito 13, Martina Franca* ☏ *080/4837987.*

Taranto

100 km (62 miles) southeast of Bari, 40 km (25 miles) south of Martina Franca.

Taranto (stress the first syllable) was an important port even in Greek times, and it's still Italy's largest naval base. It lies toward the back of the instep of the boot on the broad Mare Grande bay, which is connected to a small internal Mare Piccolo basin by two narrow channels, one artificial and one natural. The old town is a collection of palazzi (in varying states of decay) along narrow cobblestone streets on an island between the two bodies of water, linked by causeways to the modern city, which stretches inward along the mainland. Circumnavigating the city can be quite tricky, with a confusing series of junctions and overpasses; take it as slowly as you can and follow the signs for the centro storico, where the main sights are situated.

GETTING HERE AND AROUND

By car, the A14 autostrada takes you almost directly to Taranto. Trenitalia runs frequent trains from Bari and Brindisi.

VISITOR INFORMATION

CONTACT Infopoint Taranto. ⊠ *Piazza Castello, Taranto* ☏ *389/9935679* ⊕ *www.prolocoditaranto.wordpress.com.*

 Sights

Castel Sant'Angelo

CASTLE/PALACE | The monumental Castel Sant'Angelo, more commonly referred to as the Castello Aragonese, guards the drawbridge leading from the island center of Taranto to the newer city on the mainland. The castle is occupied by the Italian navy, but it's open to the public, and navy personnel conduct regular,

free guided tours. The castle, built in its present form by King Ferdinand of Aragon, king of Naples, in the 15th century, contains ruins of older Greek, Byzantine, and Norman constructions as well as the Renaissance Chapel of San Leonardo. ⊠ *Piazza Castello 4, Taranto* ☏ *099/7753438* ⊕ *www.castelloaragonesetaranto.com* 🎟 *Free.*

★ MArTA – Museo Archeologico Nazionale Taranto

OTHER MUSEUM | Taranto's outstanding National Archaeological Museum (MArTA) occupies the historic premises of the ex-monastery of San Pasquale. The museum dates from 1887, and its collection of Greek and Roman antiquities is considered to be one of the most important in Italy. Many artifacts were discovered in the vicinity, testifying to the city's centuries-old importance as a port. Admire the rich cache of tomb goods, including magnificent gold jewelry, polychrome terra-cotta, objects in ivory and bone, and rare colored glass. A display of Jewish, Christian, and Muslim funeral epitaphs, dating from the 4th to 11th century, demonstrate the peaceful coexistence of the three religions in this multicultural Mediterranean hub from the Byzantine era to the Middle Ages. ⊠ *Via Cavour 10, Taranto* ☏ *099/4532112* ⊕ *www.museotaranto.beniculturali.it* 🎟 *€8.*

San Domenico Maggiore

CHURCH | Taranto's most important monument is the ancient church and monastery of San Domenico in the heart of the centro storico. Situated on the narrow strip of land that divides Taranto's two bays, Mare Piccolo and Mare Grande, the present, rather neglected church rises over the ancient Greek acropolis of Taranto where the city is considered to have originated. The statue of Our Lady of Sorrows, much venerated by the local people, stands in the last chapel on the left. Pop into the beautiful 13th-century cloister for a moment's respite from sightseeing. ⊠ *Via Duomo 33, Taranto*

☎ *099/4713511* 🎟 *Free* ⏲ *Erratic hrs; cloister closed Sun.*

🍴 Restaurants

Al Gatto Rosso

$$$ | SOUTHERN ITALIAN | Set in a handsome *Stile Liberty* (Art Nouveau) palazzo, with outdoor seating and a smart, minimalist dining room, the well-regarded "Red Cat" has been serving elegant seafood since 1952. The third-generation owner and head chef is renowned for his innovative dishes using the freshest fish and seasonal vegetables. **Known for:** near MArTA; delicious gelato and semifreddo desserts; raw seafood antipasti. [$] *Average main: €26* ✉ *Via Cavour 2, Taranto* ☎ *340/5337800* 🌐 *www.ristorantegattorosso.com* ⏲ *Closed Mon.*

🛏 Hotels

Hotel Europa

$$ | HOTEL | The views are fantastic from this Belle Époque palazzo—situated on a point jutting out over Mar Piccolo, across from the old town—and most of the high-ceilinged guest rooms have little balconies where you can watch naval ships mingle with fishing boats in the port. **Pros:** great location overlooking the bay; some mini-apartments with kitchenettes; short walk to MArTA. **Cons:** tricky parking in such a busy area; steep stairs to mezzanine areas in some rooms; rooms a bit old-fashioned and on the small size. [$] *Rooms from: €140* ✉ *Via Roma 1, Taranto* ☎ *099/4525994* 🌐 *www.hoteleuropataranto.it* 🛏 *43 rooms* 🍴 *Free Breakfast.*

Hotel L'Arcangelo

$ | HOTEL | Set in a handsome 17th-century palazzo on slightly scruffy but charming Piazza Fontana, this self-styled "boutique hotel" has limestone walls, coved ceilings and warm off-white hues throughout, with many guest rooms having sea or church views and terraces. **Pros:** central piazza location near San Nicola church; fish restaurants nearby; gorgeous roof terrace. **Cons:** noise from piazza; some corners dated; area undergoing renovation works. [$] *Rooms from: €86* ✉ *Piazza Fontana, angolo via Garibaldi 3, Taranto* ☎ *099/4715940* 🌐 *www.hotelarcangelotaranto.it* 🛏 *11 rooms* 🍴 *Free Breakfast.*

Lecce

40 km (25 miles) southeast of Brindisi, 87 km (54 miles) east of Taranto.

Lecce is the crown jewel of the Mezzogiorno. The city is called "the Florence of the south," but that term doesn't do justice to Lecce's uniqueness in the Italian landscape. Although its pretty boutiques, lively bars, bustling streets, laid-back student cafés, and evening passeggiata draw comparisons to the cultural capitals of the north, Lecce's impossibly intricate Baroque architecture and its hyperanimated crowds are distinctively southern. The city is a cosmopolitan oasis two steps from the idyllic Otranto–Brindisi coastline and a hop from the olive groves of Puglia. Relatively undiscovered by foreign tourists, Lecce exudes an optimism and youthful joie de vivre unparalleled in any other Baroque showcase.

Summer is a great time to visit, when courtyards and piazzas throughout the city host dramatic productions or performances by rock and pop stars. Baroque music concerts are often held in Lecce's beautiful churches and cultural spaces.

GETTING HERE AND AROUND

By car from Bari, take the main coast road via Brindisi and continue along the SS613 to Lecce. Frequent trains run along the coast from Bari and beyond. The closest airport is in Brindisi.

VISITOR INFORMATION
CONTACT Lecce Tourism Office. ✉ Corso Vittorio Emanuele II 16, Lecce ☎ 0832/682985 ⊕ www.turismo.ilecce.it/infopoint.

◉ Sights

★ Duomo

CHURCH | Dominating a vast square concealed by a maze of alleyways, Lecce's magnificent cathedral of Santa Maria Assunta never fails to take visitors by surprise. The goal when building the 17th-century structure was to stun the faithful with a vision of opulence and power. Its sheer theatricality still leaves viewers open-mouthed, especially at night when the entire piazza is illuminated like a stage set. Constructed in rosy local stone, the church is flanked by the ornate Bishops' Palace (1694), the seminary, whose first-floor Museum of Sacred Art (MuDAS) displays curious wooden and papier-mâché sculptures alongside brooding Caravaggio-esque paintings of the "Neapolitan School." Adding to this melodious architectural scene is the 236-foot-high bell tower, which dominates the centro storico skyline. Tickets must be booked at chieselecce.it; purchase a **LeccEcclesiae ticket** (valid for 15 days) to see the Duomo and crypt, MuDAS, Churches of San Matteo and Santa Chiara, and the Basilica of Santa Croce. ✉ Piazza Duomo, off Corso Vittorio Emanuele II, Lecce ☎ 0832/308557 ⊕ www.cattedraledilecce.it 🎫 Duomo €6; LeccEcclesiae ticket €9.

Fondazione Biscozzi Rimbaud

ART GALLERY | Contemporary and modern art enthusiasts should seek out this 2018-established collection lovingly amassed since the late '60s by a wealthy Pugliese couple, which foregrounds their passions for the region's leading artists. Among the 200-plus works, striking geometric and abstract paintings and sculpture between 1950–80 predominate. The permanent exhibits are a wonderful introduction to masters of modernismo italiano and less well-known Pugliese artists from Burri to Zorio, while temporary shows and cultural events make it a vibrant cultural and educational hub. ✉ Piazzetta Baglivi 4, Lecce ☎ 0832/1994743 ⊕ www.fondazionebiscozzirimbaud.it 🎫 €5 ☾ Closed Mon.

Museo Faggiano

HISTORY MUSEUM | FAMILY | Wannabe restauranteur Luciano Faggiano excavated a new lifelong archaeological passion project and fascinating discoveries when he bought this building and investigated the blocked toilet back in the year 2000. After initially finding a false floor that led to a Messapian tomb that predates Christ by two centuries, more digging with the help of family and friends unearthed incredible artifacts including Roman devotional bottles, ancient vases, a ring with Christian symbols, medieval relics, and dusty frescoes. With encouragement and help from the Lecce government and university, an atmospheric homespun museum was born that allows visitors to explore the layers of history beneath the regions seemingly mundane masonry and toilet cisterns. ✉ Via Ascanio Grandi 56, Lecce ☎ 0832/300528 ⊕ www.museofaggiano.it 🎫 €5.

Piazza Sant'Oronzo

PLAZA/SQUARE | This is the buzzing hub of Lecce's social life in the heart of the maze of pedestrianized alleyways lined with cafés, little restaurants, and crafts shops. Named after Oronzo, the city's patron saint, who crowns a Roman column that once marked the end of the Via Appia Antica, the piazza is also occupied by another city symbol, the somewhat odd-looking 17th-century Sedile, formerly the town hall but now an art and exhibition center. The piazza revolves around the sunken hemicycle of the old Anfiteatro Romano, where the rows of seats are clearly visible. ✉ Piazza Sant'Oronzo, Lecce.

Santa Croce

CHURCH | Although Lecce was founded before the time of the ancient Greeks, it's often associated with the term *Barocco leccese,* the result of a citywide impulse in the 17th century to redo the town in an exuberant fashion. But this was Baroque with a difference: generally, such architecture is heavy and monumental, but here it took on a lighter, more fanciful air, and the church of Santa Croce is a fine example, along with the adjoining Palazzo della Prefettura. The facade is a riot of sculptures of saints, angels, leaves, vines, and columns—all in glowing local honey-color stone, creating an overall lighthearted effect. ✉ *Via Umberto I 3, Lecce* ☎ *0832/241957* 🌐 *basilicasantacrocelecce.it* 🎫 *Church €6; LeccEcclesiae ticket €9.*

🍴 Restaurants

Alle Due Corti

$$ | **SOUTHERN ITALIAN** | **FAMILY** | Renowned local culinary experts run this cove-ceilinged trattoria, where traditional Salentine cuisine is treated with both respect and originality. The white-walled interior is stark, but there's plenty of character in the simple, tasty fare and the gregarious chatter of local families. **Known for:** Anthony Bourdain dined here for his Parts Unknown series; hearty, tasty Pugliese food; cookery courses. [$] *Average main: €17* ✉ *Corte dei Giugni 1, corner of Via Prato 42, Lecce* ☎ *0832/242223* 🌐 *www.alleduecorti.com* 🕒 *Closed Sun.*

Corte dei Pandolfi

$$ | **SOUTHERN ITALIAN** | Choose from a vast list of Salento's best wines, and feast on an unparalleled spread of artisanal *salumi* (cured meats) and local cheeses accompanied by delicious local honey and *mostarda* (preserved fruit). The seasonally changing menu of primi and secondi includes vegetarian specialties. **Known for:** buzzing courtyard; classic coved ceilings mix with contemporary minimalism; vegetarian specialists. [$] *Average main: €18* ✉ *Corte dei Pandolfi 3, Lecce* ☎ *0832/332309* 🌐 *www.cortedeipandolfi.com* 🕒 *No lunch Mon.*

Le Zie Trattoria Casereccia

$$ | **SOUTHERN ITALIAN** | **FAMILY** | Local families favor this tiny old-fashioned trattoria, where no-frills charm is matched by wholesome, unfussy food. *Cucina casereccia* (home-cooked) specialties include *polpo in teglia* (stewed octopus), *baccalà al forno* (baked salt cod), and the ubiquitous rustic *purè di fave e cicoria* (bean puree with wild chicory). **Known for:** best to book ahead; genuine local color and cuisine; warm hospitality. [$] *Average main: €17* ✉ *Via Costadura 19, Lecce* ☎ *0832/245178* 🕒 *Closed Mon. No dinner Sun.*

☕ Coffee and Quick Bites

Caffè Alvino

$ | **SOUTHERN ITALIAN** | This historic caffè-gelateria is in the heart of Lecce, with handsome interiors and seating out on Piazza Sant'Oronzo. From early morning to late at night this is a buzzy place where Leccesi come to meet and refuel on classic Salentino pastries like *pasticciotti* and *zeppole*. **Known for:** centrally located; great coffee and gelato; arguably the best pastries in town. [$] *Average main: €7* ✉ *Piazza Sant'Oronzo 30, Lecce* ☎ *0832/246748.*

🛏 Hotels

★ 8piuhotel

$ | **HOTEL** | **FAMILY** | Its design is more "international style" than "rustic Pugliese," but this hotel offers superb value, combining contemporary creature comforts with fancy tech. **Pros:** fitness center and guest cycles; on-site restaurant, Negroamaro; abundant breakfast. **Cons:** tech overload; a bit out of town; lack of local character might not appeal to some. [$] *Rooms from: €119* ✉ *Viale del Risorgimento, Lecce* ☎ *0832/306686*

⊕ www.8piuhotel.com ⤳ 83 rooms
†◎† Free Breakfast.

Patria Palace

$$$ | **HOTEL** | Lecce's grandest hotel—impeccable from top to bottom, with vaulted ceilings, frescoes, and antique furnishings—also happens to have a stellar location in front of the monumental Santa Croce Basilica, the crown jewel of Lecce Baroque. **Pros:** many sumptuous, high-ceilinged rooms; valet parking for guests; fabulous roof terrace. **Cons:** style of the lobby doesn't match that of the handsome facade; some rooms outdated and less grand; a few rooms overlook noisy backstreets. $ *Rooms from: €279* ⊠ *Piazzetta Riccardi 13, Lecce* ☎ *0832/245111* ⊕ *www.patriapalace.com* ⤳ *67 rooms* †◎† *Free Breakfast.*

Risorgimento Resort Lecce

$$ | **HOTEL** | Although this hotel has been a centro storico landmark since 1880, it feels unmistakably 21st century, with modern decor and vibrant color schemes. **Pros:** highly professional staff; wellness spa; spacious guest rooms. **Cons:** tiny gym; may be noisy in rooms at the front; smart, international-style hotel without much local atmosphere. $ *Rooms from: €156* ⊠ *Via Augustus Imperatore 19, Lecce* ☎ *0832/246311* ⊕ *www.risorgimentoresort.it* ⤳ *47 rooms* †◎† *Free Breakfast.*

Otranto

36 km (22 miles) southeast of Lecce, 188 km (117 miles) southeast of Bari.

In one of the first great Gothic novels, Horace Walpole's *The Castle of Otranto*, published in 1764, the English writer immortalized this city and its mysterious medieval fortress, and indeed Otranto (stress the first syllable) has had more than its share of dark thrills. As the easternmost point in Italy—and, therefore, closest to the Balkan Peninsula—it's often borne the brunt of foreign invasions, including the massacre of 800 citizens by the Moors in 1480 because they refused to give up their faith. From here, you can see across the sea to Albania on a clear day. If you are a fan of the Neolithic, you will be interested in the Grotta dei Cervi, a few miles down the coast. The walls of the cave are covered with hundreds of prehistoric images, painted with red ocher and black bat guano.

GETTING HERE AND AROUND

By car from Lecce, take the southbound SS16 and exit at Maglie. To follow the coast, take the SS53 from Lecce, then follow the SS611 south. There's regular train service from Lecce on Ferrovie del Sud-Est.

VISITOR INFORMATION

CONTACT I.A.T. Otranto Tourism Office. ⊠ *Piazza Castello, Otranto* ☎ *0836/801436* ⊕ *www.comune.otranto.le.it.*

Sights

Castello Aragonese

CASTLE/PALACE | The massive Aragonese Castle is considered a masterpiece of 16th-century military architecture. Rebuilt by the Spanish viceroy Don Pedro di Toledo in 1535 after it was badly damaged in the siege of Otranto (1480), when invading Ottoman armies destroyed the city, its impressive walls and bastions dominate the port and seashore. Escape the heat with a walk around its cool interiors that snake around its recently landscaped moats. Various art and photographic exhibitions are held here in the summer. ⊠ *Piazza Castello, Otranto* ☎ *0836/801436, 0836/210094* ⊕ *www.comune.otranto.le.it* ⊠ *€3.*

Cattedrale

CHURCH | By far the best sight in Otranto is the cathedral, Santa Maria Annunziata, consecrated in 1088. Its highlight is a 12th-century Pantaleone mosaic: covering the entire length of the nave, the sanctuary, and the apse, it depicts scenes from the Old Testament and traditional medieval chivalric tales and animals set alongside a Tree of Life. The walls behind the main altar are lined with glass cases containing the skulls and tibias of the 800 martyrs of Otranto, slain by the Ottomans after the seige of 1480 for not renouncing their faith. ✉ *Piazza Basilica, Otranto* ☎ *0836/801436* 🌐 *www.comune.otranto.le.it.*

Hotels

Corte di Nettuno

$$ | **HOTEL** | Handily moored near the marina and the castello, this hotel has a nautical theme with wrought-iron gates in the shape of waves, a statue of the sea god Neptune at the entrance, the owner's maritime antiques throughout, and guest rooms accented by shades of blue. **Pros:** good location near the marina and sights; decent food; quirky decor full of artsy surprises. **Cons:** lackadaisical service in low season; clinical feel in some dated and gloomy rooms; some people may find the sea theme overly eccentric. [$] *Rooms from: €170* ✉ *Via Madonna del Passo, Otranto* ☎ *0832/351321* 🌐 *www.cdshotels.it* 🕒 *Closed Nov.–Mar.* 🛏 *28 rooms* 🍴 *Free Breakfast.*

Masseria Montelauro

$$$ | **B&B/INN** | **FAMILY** | Beautifully restored, with high-style interiors, this 19th-century former masseria is an oasis of comfort just a short drive from lovely Otranto. **Pros:** interesting building; friendly, helpful service; lovely grounds and pool. **Cons:** some rooms rather stuffy; food is pricey; a car is absolutely necessary. [$] *Rooms from: €245* ✉ *SP358, Otranto* ☎ *0836/806203* 🌐 *www.masseriamontelauro.it* 🕒 *Closed Nov.–Apr.* 🛏 *29 rooms* 🍴 *Free Breakfast.*

Gallipoli

37 km (23 miles) south of Lecce, 190 km (118 miles) southeast of Bari.

The fishing port of Gallipoli, on the eastern tip of the Golfo di Taranto, is divided between a new town, on the mainland, and the beautiful fortified *borgo antico* (old town) across a 17th-century bridge, crowded onto its own small island in the gulf. The Greeks called it Kallipolis ("the fair city"), the Romans Anxa. Like the infamous Turkish town of the same name on the Dardanelles, the Italian Gallipoli occupies a strategic location and thus was repeatedly attacked through the centuries—by the Normans in 1071, the Venetians in 1484, and the British in 1809. Today life in Gallipoli revolves around fishing. Boats in primary colors breeze in and out of the bay during the day, and Gallipoli's fish market, below the bridge, throbs with activity all morning.

GETTING HERE AND AROUND

From Lecce, take the SS101. From Taranto, follow the coastal SS174. Frequent trains run from Lecce.

VISITOR INFORMATION

CONTACT Gallipoli Tourism Office. ✉ *Via Kennedy, Gallipoli* ☎ *0833/264283* 🌐 *www.prolocogallipoli.it.*

Sights

Castello Aragonese

CASTLE/PALACE | The massive bulk of Gallipoli's castle guards the entrance to the island of the borgo antico, which is linked to the new town by a bridge. Rising out of the sea, the present fortress, dating from the 17th to 18th century, is built on the foundations of an earlier Byzantine citadel. It has four towers, plus a separate fifth known as the Rivellino, where open-air shows are held in summer. A visit allows grandstand sea views, but there's little to see inside between exhibitions. ✉ *Rampa*

Castello, Gallipoli ☎ *0833/262775* 🌐 *www.castellogallipoli.it* 🎫 *€7* 🕒 *Closed Mon., and Tues.–Sun. 1–3.*

Duomo

CHURCH | In the center of the borgo antico, Gallipoli's Duomo is a notable Baroque cathedral from the late 17th century, dedicated to Sant'Agata, patron saint of the city. Built in local limestone, the ornate facade is matched by an equally elaborate interior with columns and altars in fine polychrome marble and paintings by leading local Gallipoli and Neapolitan maestros of the time. Particularly interesting are the stone carvings that depict episodes from the city's history. ✉ *Via Duomo 1, Gallipoli* ☎ *0833/261987* 🌐 *www.cattedralegallipoli.it.*

La Purità

CHURCH | A fine example of Gallipoli Baroque, the 17th-century Church of Santa Maria della Purità stands at the end of the borgo antico overlooking famed Purità Beach. It contains an eye-popping wealth of art and decoration, including the painting at the high altar by Luca Giordano, intricately carved wooden choir stalls, and a 19th-century majolica pavement. ✉ *Riviera Nazario Sauro, Gallipoli* ☎ *0833/261699.*

Beaches

★ Beaches of Gallipoli

BEACH | FAMILY | Ample swimming and clean, fine-grained sand make Gallipoli's beaches a good choice for families. The 5-km (3-mile) strand reaches from Punta Pizzo to Lido San Giovanni and is divided among a series of bathing establishments, all of which provide sun beds, umbrellas, showers, changing facilities, and snack bars. Parco Gondar hosts a fun fair and music events. Water-sports equipment can be bought or rented at the waterfront shops in town. **Amenities:** food and drink; lifeguards; parking (fee); showers; toilets; water sports. **Best for:** partiers; snorkeling; sunset; swimming; walking; windsurfing. ✉ *Gallipoli* 🌐 *www.prolocogallipoli.it.*

Restaurants

Trattoria La Vinaigrette

$$ | SEAFOOD | Within shell-like earshot of the sea, this professionally run trattoria with sleek white interiors and a panoramic terrace serves some of the finest seafood in the Salento. Expect classic Pugliese salty preparations like *crudi, grigliate,* and *fritture* (raw, grilled, and fried) beautifully cooked and elegantly presented. **Known for:** pick from the freshest catch on display; sea views and sushi-like crudi like tuna tartare; well-considered wine list. [$] *Average main: €21* ✉ *Riviera Armando Diaz 75, Gallipoli* ☎ *0833/264501* 🌐 *www.lavinaigrette.it.*

Hotels

★ Relais Corte Palmieri

$$ | HOTEL | Set in an aristocratic 18th-century house in the center of the borgo antico and near Purità Beach, the Relais Corte Palmieri has been tastefully renovated to meet modern standards while preserving its frescoes, mosaics, antique doors, and other historical features. **Pros:** individually decorated rooms; on-site spa; roof garden with spectacular views. **Cons:** noisy rooms street-side and near breakfast room; parking is mighty tricky in narrow alleys; difficult to reach. [$] *Rooms from: €170* ✉ *Corte Palmieri 3, Gallipoli* ☎ *0833/265318* 🌐 *www.relaiscortepalmieri.it* 🕒 *Closed late Oct.–late Mar. or early Apr.* 🛏 *20 rooms* 🍴 *Free Breakfast.*

Matera

62 km (39 miles) south of Bari.

This town of unique Sassi (cave dwellings) is one of southern Italy's most intriguing places. The so-called New Town is full of elegant Baroque churches, palazzi, and broad piazzas, which are filled to bursting during the evening passeggiata. It's perched on the verge of a steep gully crowded with ancient rock churches, some of which you can tour, and other Sassi converted into modern-day homes as well as hotels and restaurants. This is a particularly good time to visit: Matera's designation as the European Capital of Culture for 2019 reenergized the community with investment, cultural initiatives, and plenty of buzz.

GETTING HERE AND AROUND
From Bari, take the SS96 to Altamura, then the SS99 to Matera. Roughly one train per hour (Ferrovie Appulo Lucane) leaves Bari Centrale for Matera.

VISITOR INFORMATION
CONTACT Proloco Matera Città dei Sassi (Tourism Office). ☒ *Via Ridola 60, Matera* ☎ *328/9333548* ⊕ *www.prolocomatera2019.it.*

Sights

★ Duomo
CHURCH | Matera's splendidly restored cathedral, dedicated to the Madonna della Bruna and Sant'Eustachio, was built in the late 13th century and occupies a prominent position between the two Sassi. Lavishly decorated, it has a typical Puglian Romanesque flavor; inside, there's a recovered fresco, probably painted in the 14th century, showing scenes from the Last Judgment. On the Duomo's facade the figures of Sts. Peter and Paul stand on either side of a sculpture of Matera's patron, the Madonna della Bruna. ☒ *Piazza Duomo, Matera* ☎ *0835/332012.*

Museo Nazione di Matera (MNM) - Domenico Ridola Archaeological Museum
HISTORY MUSEUM | Named after local 19th-century medical doctor Domenico Ridola, who investigated archaeological sites in the surrounding area, this seat of the MNM highlights his excavations of the remains of Paleolithic and Neolithic settlements, as well as a richly endowed 4th-century-BC tomb. Ridola's finds are on view in the museum, which is housed in the former monastery of Santa Chiara. The collection includes an extensive selection of prehistoric and classical artifacts, notably Bronze Age implements and beautifully decorated red-figure pottery from Magna Graecia. ☒ *Via Ridola 24* ☎ *0835/310058* ⊕ *www.museonazionaledimatera.it* ⊡ *€5.*

Museo Nazione di Matera (MNM) - Museo Nazionale d'Arte Medievale e Moderna della Basilicata
ART MUSEUM | Housed within the handsome 17th-century Palazzo Lanfranchi, this part of the MNM is divided into three contrasting thematic sections: Sacred Art, Collectibles, and Contemporary Art. You may want to skim through the many restored artifacts from Basilicata's churches and the 300-plus works of the Neapolitan school: the main attraction are the paintings of Carlo Levi and his must-stop-to-absorb humanist masterpiece *Lucania '61.* ☒ *Piazza G. Pascoli 1, Matera* ☎ *0835/310058* ⊕ *www.museonazionaledimatera.it* ⊡ *€4.*

MUSMA (Museo della Scultura Contemporanea)
ART GALLERY | Amid otherworldly cave interiors, medieval courtyards, frescoed corners, and the grand spaces of 17th-century Palazzo Pomarici, this museum charts the evolution of Italian sculpture from the early 1800s to the present. Innovative curation, atmospheric lighting, and eerie acoustics make for a one-of-a-kind gallery experience. ☒ *Palazzo Pomarici, Via San Giacomo, Matera* ☎ *366/9357768* ⊕ *www.musma.it* ⊡ *€7.*

San Giovanni Battista
CHURCH | Considered a jewel of medieval architecture, the 13th-century Romanesque church of San Giovanni Battista was restored to its pre-Baroque simplicity in 1926. The elaborately carved portal is a riot of entwining stone vines, flowers, leaves, human figures, and allegorical creatures. Inside, the three naves

are flanked by columns crowned with capitals, each one decorated with symbolic animal forms and other images—no two are alike. ✉ *Via San Biagio, Matera* ☎ *0835/334182.*

★ Sassi di Matera

HISTORIC DISTRICT | Matera's Sassi are piled chaotically atop one another down the sides of a steep ravine. Some date from Paleolithic times, when they were truly just caves. Over time, they were transformed into enclosed houses, which once presented the Dante-esque vision of squalor and poverty that was graphically described in Carlo Levi's 1945 memoir, *Christ Stopped at Eboli*. In the 1960s, most inhabitants moved into ugly apartment blocks. The 1993 designation as a UNESCO World Heritage site, however, resulted in a cleanup and gentrification, with hotels, bars, and restaurants taking over many structures. From the upper town, the Strada Panoramica walk offers stellar views of the two areas known as **Sasso Caveoso** and **Sasso Barisano**. Feel free to wander down amid the troglodytic abodes, which, in the words of travel writer H. V. Morton in his *A Traveller in Southern Italy*, "resemble the work of termites rather than of man." There are also more than 100 *chiese rupestri*, or rock-hewn churches, some of which have medieval frescoes and a few of which are open to the public. The most spectacular is **Santa Maria de Idris**, right on the edge of the Sasso Caveoso, near the ravine. Guided tours can be arranged through the tourist office. ✉ *Sasso Caveoso, Matera* ⊕ *www.prolocomatera2019.it.*

★ Storica Casa Grotta di Vico Solitario

MUSEUM VILLAGE | Head to this house-museum in the Sasso Caveoso district for moving insights into what peasant life was like in a limestone cave dwelling. The cramped quarters are filled with traditional utensils and furniture, the belongings of its last inhabitants, who left in 1956 as part of a forced relocation of some 15,000 Sassi residents to apartment blocks. With its rainwater cistern, hand loom, storage niches, and tiny kitchen area and other living spaces (for both the family and their animals), the cave also demonstrates the ingenuity that made living here possible. ✉ *Vicinato di vico Solitario 11, Matera* ☎ *0835/310118* ⊕ *www.casagrotta.it* 🎫 *€5.*

🍴 Restaurants

Il Terrazzino

$$ | **SOUTHERN ITALIAN** | The dining area is carved out of a cliff, and the terrace overlooks the famous Sassi ravine. From both you can enjoy such rustic specialties as *foglie d'ulivo* (stuffed olive leaves), *zuppa di grano e ceci* (cheese and chickpea soup), and *pignata* (lamb stew with seasonal vegetables). **Known for:** interesting interiors (including a spectacular three-level wine cellar); classic Basilicata meat dishes and fresh pasta; stupendous views. 🅢 *Average main: €18* ✉ *Vico S. Giuseppe 7, Matera* ☎ *0835/332503* ⊕ *www.ilterrazzino.org* ⊗ *Closed Tues.*

★ Vitantonio Lombardo

$$$$ | **MODERN ITALIAN** | An open kitchen and contemporary table lamps heighten the culinary theater of Matera's fanciest restaurant, set in a cool, minimalist Rione Sassi grotto. The chef's innovative tasting menus feature vibrant seasonal creations served on artsy ceramics and in wooden bowls. **Known for:** exquisite bread and olive oil; imaginative, changing tasting menu; glass-screened wine cellar. 🅢 *Average main: €120 for 6-course tasting menu* ✉ *Via Madonna delle Virtù 13/14, Matera* ☎ *0835/335475* ⊕ *www.vlristorante.it* ⊗ *Closed Tues. No lunch Wed.*

☕ Coffee and Quick Bites

I Vizi degli Angeli - Laboratorio di Gelateria Artigianale

$ | **SOUTHERN ITALIAN** | **FAMILY** | As befitting the "artisan gelato laboratory" moniker, this whitewashed parlor with vibrant colors has an array of vegan-friendly and alchemical ice-cream combos. Among the more unusual "angels" vices' flavors served in *coppe* (tubs) and freshly made *coni* (cones) are pineapple and ginger, lavender and liquorice. **Known for:** refreshing granita di melone; fruity frullati; icy frappè and caffè shakerato. [$] *Average main: €4* ✉ *Via Domenico Ridola 36, Matera* ☎ *0835/310637* 🌐 *www.ivizidegliangeli.it.*

Hotels

★ Locanda di San Martino

$$ | **HOTEL** | Situated at the bottom of the Sassi ravine on Via Fiorentini (limited car access), the Locanda is a more upscale cave-dwelling hotel, with all modern comforts, including an elevator to whisk you up the cliff to your room. **Pros:** convenient location if you come by car; on-site ancient Roman–style spa; comfortable rooms. **Cons:** spa may be a tad intimate for some; limited parking nearby; rooms reached via outdoor walkway. [$] *Rooms from: €160* ✉ *Via Fiorentini 71, Matera* ☎ *0835/256600* 🌐 *www.locandadisanmartino.it* 🛏 *40 rooms* 🍴 *Free Breakfast.*

★ Palazzo Margherita

$$$$ | **HOTEL** | On the main square in the town of Francis Ford Coppola's ancestors, a large palazzo has been transformed (by French designer Jacques Grange) into Basilicata's top lodging, complete with hidden gardens, spacious porticoes, frescoed ceilings, and Moroccan-tile floors. **Pros:** professional, courteous staff; spacious rooms with lots of high-tech gadgetry; a garden pool. **Cons:** not much to do in Bernalda; private transport needed; film-star prices. [$] *Rooms from: €640* ✉ *Corso Umberto 64, Matera* ✣ *A 40-min drive south of Matera: take the SS7 out of Matera heading for Potenza and then join the SS407 for Metaponto and Taranto. Look for the turnoff to Bernalda after 25 km (16 miles)* ☎ *0835/549060* 🌐 *www.thefamilycoppolahideaways.com/en/palazzo-margherita* 🛏 *9 rooms* 🍴 *Free Breakfast.*

Palazzo Viceconte

$$ | **HOTEL** | If cave dwelling isn't your style, consider staying at this hotel in a former aristocratic residence—a lovingly restored property, where each unique guest room showcases oil paintings, antiques, and high vaulted frescoed ceilings. **Pros:** an easy walk to most of the main sights; suites are especially spacious; on a quiet square. **Cons:** breakfast may disappoint; exorbitant parking rates; rooms vary considerably in size. [$] *Rooms from: €194* ✉ *Via San Potito 7, Matera* ☎ *0835/330699* 🌐 *www.palazzoviceconte.it* 🛏 *14 rooms* 🍴 *Free Breakfast.*

Sant'Angelo Resort

$$$ | **HOTEL** | Authentic rough-hewn walls and arches contrast with chic furnishings and modern amenities at this Sassi hotel, created by interior designer Stefano Tardito and situated across a piazza from the Church of San Pietro Caveoso. **Pros:** unrivaled views; a more luxurious cave-dwelling experience; atmospheric rooms with minimalist design. **Cons:** lack of natural light; can feel stuffy and humid at times; no elevator and many steps to climb. [$] *Rooms from: €260* ✉ *Piazza San Pietro Caveoso, Matera* ☎ *0835/314010* 🌐 *www.santangeloresort.it* 🛏 *21 rooms* 🍴 *Free Breakfast.*

Maratea

217 km (135 miles) south of Naples.

The high, twisty road into the Maratea region affords breathtaking glimpses of the turquoise sea and a gigantic statue of Cristo Redentore (reminiscent of the one in Rio de Janeiro) atop a hill. Steep crags separate the area into villages that include Maratea Porto, Marina di Maratea, Fiumicello, and Cersuta. The main inland town of Maratea proper is a tumble of cobblestone streets, where the ruins of a much older settlement (Maratea Antica) can be seen. Between the rocky headlands, there's no shortage of secluded beaches, which can get crowded in August. A summer minibus service connects all the different points once or twice an hour.

GETTING HERE AND AROUND

By car, take the Lagonegro exit from the A3 autostrada and continue along the SS585. Intercity, regional, and seasonal high-speed Frecciarossa trains from Reggio Calabria and Naples stop at Maratea. In the summer months there's a bus linking the train station to the upper town 4 km (2½ miles) away.

VISITOR INFORMATION

CONTACT APT Maratea (Azienda di Promozione Turistica). ✉ *Piazza Vitolo, Maratea* ☎ *0973/030366* 🌐 *www.aptbasilicata.it.*

Beaches

Cala Jannita

BEACH | FAMILY | Maratea's dramatic rock topography is best experienced from this fab little bay and its Spiaggia Nera (Black Beach) with sparkling limpid waters and striking dark, volcanic pebbles. Bring sandals or shoes as it's a tricky approach. **Amenities:** food and drink; lifeguards; parking; showers; toilets. **Best for:** swimming. **TIP→ For a kayak adventure around Maratea's beaches and sea caves visit www.flymaratea.it, which also offers guided treks for all abilities.** ✉ *Maratea* ☎ *348/8930031.*

Restaurants

Da Cesare

$$ | SOUTHERN ITALIAN | With an open kitchen and a veranda—so you can keep an eye on both the chef and the azure waters of the Golfo di Policastro—there's always something to see at this family-run seafood restaurant. Even better: it serves some of the freshest catch in town, with specialties like linguine *con nero di seppia* (with cuttlefish ink sauce), grilled squid, and *grigliata mista* (mixed grilled fish and seafood). **Known for:** prominent position on coastal road; open veranda with views; seafood dishes aplenty. [$] *Average main: €21* ✉ *Via Nazionale Cersuta 52, on the SS18 (main coast road) in village of Cersuta, about 5 km (3 miles) north of Maratea, 3 km (2 miles) south of Acquafredda, Maratea* ☎ *0973/871840* ⏲ *Closed Thurs. Nov.–Mar.*

Hotels

Villa Cheta Elite

$$ | HOTEL | FAMILY | This Stile Liberty villa in the seaside village of Acquafredda has original features and period pieces, a tranquil garden, a pool where you can idle the days away, and a flowery terrace for sunset dining. **Pros:** surrounded by Mediterranean greenery; lovely Art Nouveau building; beautiful coast and mountain views. **Cons:** steps to entrance and Porticello beach; popular in high season; hotel is quite remote, so shops and the town require a car. [$] *Rooms from: €150* ✉ *Via Timpone 46, Maratea* ☎ *0973/878134* 🌐 *www.villacheta.it* ⏲ *Closed Oct.–Apr.* 🛏 *22 rooms* 🍴 *Free Breakfast.*

Diamante

51 km (32 miles) south of Maratea, 225 km (140 miles) south of Naples.

A lively and attractive little resort on Calabria's north Tyrrhenian Coast, Diamante styles itself as "the town of murals and peperoncini." The old town center is accessed over a bridge across the Corvino River, which runs through town to the sea. The maze of alleyways and whitewashed houses is covered in murals by both local and international artists, many featuring fishing and religious themes, while strings of bright-red chili pods hang from doorways and balconies. The pedestrianized seafront promenade is the town hub, lined with small shops, ice cream parlors, and bars. Flanking the broad palm-lined promenade are sparkling beaches to the north and south and interesting archaeological remains in the nearby Cirella district. September's annual Peperoncino Festival brings spicy cultural and gastronomic events. During the summer months the Occhio Marino (€18) glass-walled boat allows passengers to view the marine wildlife in and around the nearby island of Cirella; while the S'Aligusta motorboat (€25) explores the sea caves of Isola di Dino. Visit ⊕ *www.prolocodiamante.it/escursioni*.

GETTING HERE AND AROUND

Driving from Maratea, take the SS18; from Cosenza, take the SS107 to Paola, then the SS18. Regional trains leave from Naples a few times a day, with regular service from Paola and Cosenza.

VISITOR INFORMATION

CONTACT Proloco Diamante & Cirella. ⊠ *Via Gullo 1, Diamante* ☎ *0985/81130* ⊕ *www.prolocodiamante.it.*

 **Restaurants**

A' Cucchiarella

$$ | SEAFOOD | FAMILY | One of Diamante's most popular restaurants, in the old town center just off the seafront promenade, has atmospheric stone interiors. In the summer, sidewalk tables are the perfect relaxed place to watch the evening *passeggiata* while savoring inventive fish dishes. **Known for:** handsome stone-walled dining rooms and a terrace; good vegetarian options; exceptional seafood with arty presentation. ⑤ *Average main: €18* ⊠ *Via Cavour 6, Diamante* ☎ *0985/877287* ◷ *No lunch Mon.–Thurs. Closed Oct.–Mar.*

La Guardiola

$$ | ITALIAN | FAMILY | With its own private beach on the Diamante Riviera, La Guardiola is a great spot to go for a swim, enjoy a relaxing lunch, and indulge in a siesta under a beach umbrella. The menu has many pizza options, as well as dishes focusing on the catch of the day—perhaps spaghetti with sea urchins, fish-stuffed ravioli, or *stufata di alici alla diamantese* (fresh anchovy stew). **Known for:** beachside views and sunsets; evenings can be lively, with music and televised soccer matches; spicy pizza al peccati di gola with 'nduja (Calabrese pork salumi). ⑤ *Average main: €16* ⊠ *Lungomare Riviera Bleu, Diamante* ☎ *0985/876759* ⊕ *www.laguardioladiamante.it.*

 Hotels

Grand Hotel San Michele

$$ | HOTEL | Set in a Belle Époque–style villa surrounded by gardens, atop a cliff near the village of Cetraro, the San Michele offers Mediterranean charm and old-style elegance. **Pros:** beautiful setting; pool and private beaches; 9-hole golf course. **Cons:** isolated, if you lack your own transport; breakfast lacks variety; some garden levels accessed by steps. ⑤ *Rooms from: €160* ⊠ *Località Bosco 8/9, Cetraro* ☎ *0982/91012* ⊕ *www.san-michele.it* ◷ *Closed Nov.–Easter* �“ *65 rooms* ⦿ *Free Breakfast.*

Hotel Ferretti

$ | HOTEL | FAMILY | A visual standout on the coast just outside Diamante, this gleaming, white, 1970s wedding-cake structure is a good base for a relaxing stay away from the crowds and bustle. **Pros:** overlooks the sea; quirky architecture and decor; beach, pool, and tennis court. **Cons:** food is underwhelming; extra costs for leisure facilities; modernist style might not appeal to everyone. ⑤ *Rooms from: €115* ⊠ *Via Poseidone 171, Diamante* ☎ *0985/81428* ⊕ *www.ferrettihotel.it* ➚ *52 rooms* ⦿ *Free Breakfast.*

Castrovillari

68 km (43 miles) northeast of Diamante, 75 km (48 miles) northwest of Cosenza.

Stress the first *i* when you pronounce the name of this provincial Calabrian city, nestled in the deep valley beneath 7,375-foot Mt. Pollino. The town is notable as a venue for summer's Calabria-wide Peperoncino Jazz Festival (🌐 *www.peperoncinojazzfestival.com*). Its synagogue, which you can visit, dates from the early Middle Ages; its San Giuliano church from the 16th century. The excellent restaurant La Locanda di Alia has also made Castrovillari something of a gastronomic destination.

The city is also a great jumping-off point for exploring both the Albanian-speaking village of Cìvita and Pollino National Park, Italy's biggest national park and a walkers' paradise.

GETTING HERE AND AROUND

By car, take the A3 autostrada and exit at Frascineto-Castrovillari. Ferrovie della Calabria runs around four buses per day from Cosenza.

Sights

Parco Nazionale del Pollino

NATIONAL PARK | **FAMILY** | Italy's largest national park straddles Calabria and Basilicata, rises to over 7,000 feet at Serra Dolcedorme, and offers many opportunities for outdoors enthusiasts. Its ancient wooded valleys are home to Europe's oldest tree, a 1,230-year-old Heldreich's pine. Pollino has been recognized as a UNESCO Global Geopark for its geological importance: its central massif peaks were formed by the collision of sedimentary Apennine limestone and the metamorphic and sedimentary geology of the Calabrian Arch. There are five summits all over 6,562 feet, the highest point being Serra Dolcedorme at 7,438 feet above sea level, the highest point of the Southern Apennines. It's the only peak from where it's possible to see three seas: the Ionian, the Tyrrhenian, and the Adriatic. Hiking trails dot the landscape with excursions for most abilities—and there are popular picnicking viewpoints, often near *rifugi* (rustic hostels that tend to offer food). The Rifugio Biagio Longo near Castrolvillari is a good bet for those seeking to explore. Consult the park and Club Alpino websites for the latest info and guided excursions. For a more leisurely introduction, head to Rotonda in neighboring Basilicata, where the park headquarters and infopoint can put you in touch with outdoor centers and guides for rafting, hiking, climbing, and skiing. ✉ *Via Cairoli 80, Castrovillari* ☎ *334/1005054 Club Alpino Italiano–Sezione di Castrovillari, 0973/669311 Ente Parco Nazionale del Pollino Infopoint* 🌐 *parcopollino.it; www.caicastrovillari.it.*

Restaurants

★ La Locanda di Alia

$$$ | **MODERN ITALIAN** | International food magazines have lauded this restaurant, where the wine cellar is well stocked and renowned chef-owner Gaetano Alia incorporates local produce and imaginative twists into the Calabrese dishes on the changing menu. La Locanda also has guest rooms in its adjoining Alia Jazz Hotel, which is surrounded by a lush garden and has a swimming pool. **Known for:** gorgeous setting with a leafy terrace; candele pasta with spicy Calabrese 'nduja sauce; award-winning but unpretentious cuisine. [$] *Average main: €26* ✉ *Via Ietticelli 55, off the main street in Castrovillari (look for signs), Castrovillari* ☎ *0981/46370* 🕒 *No dinner Sun.*

Hotels

Alia Jazz Hotel

$ | **B&B/INN** | In addition to a theme that honors the international jazz festival held in the town every summer, the hospitable inn adjoining acclaimed Locanda di Alia restaurant has small but well-appointed and uniquely decorated guest rooms, each with a little sitting area and a modern bath equipped with a hydro-massage tub. **Pros:** peaceful setting and informal atmosphere; local art in rooms; fabulous homemade cakes, jams, and other culinary treats. **Cons:** some rooms have a mezzanine-level bedroom; rooms can be gloomy in winter; rooms in a row all at ground level. [$] *Rooms from: €90* ✉ *Via Ietticelli 55, Castrovillari* ☎ *0981/46370* 🌐 *aliahotel.business.site* 🛏 *14 rooms* 🍴 *Free Breakfast.*

Cosenza

75 km (48 miles) southeast of Diamante, 185 km (115 miles) northeast of Reggio Calabria.

A construction boom in the 1950s and '60s encased Cosenza's medieval city—which winds up the hillsides between the Busento and Crati Rivers—in a sprawling, traffic-clogged modern town. Nevertheless, the steep, stair-filled centro storico truly hails from another age: wrought-iron balconies overlook narrow alleyways lined with old-fashioned storefronts and bars. The palazzi that line the route to the 12th-century Duomo, a UNESCO World Heritage monument, once housed nobility but today serve as studio spaces for many artists and artisans. The medieval castle, open to the public, crowns Pancrazio Hill, where the views of the town and the surrounding countryside are magnificent.

Cosenza is also the gateway to the cool and silent forests of the Sila mountains and villages like Rende (only 13 km [8 miles] away) and the Pollino National Park area (less than 80 km [50 miles]).

GETTING HERE AND AROUND

By car, take the Cosenza exit from the A3 autostrada. By train, change at Paola or Napoli on the main Rome–Reggio Calabria line. Regional trains run from Naples. Ferrovie della Calabria runs buses from Spezzano della Sila, Castrovillari, and Camigliatello.

VISITOR INFORMATION

CONTACT Cosenza Tourist Office. ✉ *Piazza XI Settembre, Cosenza* ☎ *0984/813015, 328/1754422 mobile* 🌐 *www.cosenzaturismo.com.*

Sights

Castello Svevo

CASTLE/PALACE | Castello Normanno Svevo crowns Pancrazio Hill above the old city, and the uphill walk rewards with wonderful views across to the Sila Mountains. Its origins are lost to memory: it may have been built by the Byzantines or the Saracens, and, before he was ousted by Normans, it was the residence of the Arab caliph Saati Cayti. What is known is that the castle takes its name from the great Swabian emperor Frederick II (1194–1250), who added two octagonal towers. Although extensively restored and open to the public, with audio guide/tablet tours (€1–€2) and occasional cultural events, the castle shows the ravages of successive earthquakes and a lightning strike that ignited gunpowder once stored within. ✉ *Via del Castello, Colle Pancrazio, Cosenza* ☎ *0984/1811234* 🌐 *www.castellocosenza.it* 🎟 *€4* 🕒 *Closed Mon.*

Duomo

CHURCH | Cosenza's original Duomo, probably built in the middle of the 11th century, was destroyed by an earthquake in 1184. A new cathedral was consecrated in the presence of Emperor Frederick II in 1222. After many Baroque additions, later alterations have restored some of the Provençal Gothic style. Inside, on the left of the main altar, you'll see the lovely monument to Isabella of Aragon, who died after falling from her horse en route to France in 1271. ✉ *Piazza del Duomo 1,*

Cosenza ☎ 0984/77864 ⊘ Closed daily 12:30 pm–4 pm.

Museo Diocesano di Cosenza

HISTORY MUSEUM | Situated between the archbishop's palace and the Duomo, the museum contains paintings, silverware, vestments, and other precious objects collected by the archbishops of Cosenza over centuries. Look for the filigreed silver cup known as "the Pope," two ivory statuettes attributed to the School of Michelangelo, the 15th-century "Torquemada" chalice, and paintings by Luca Giordano, Andrea Vaccaro, and Giuseppe Pascaletti. The heart of the museum contains the emblem of Cosenza and the city's greatest treasure: a unique reliquary cross dating back to the 13th century, which was donated by Frederick II of Swabia on the occasion of the consecration of the cathedral in 1222. ✉ Piazza Aulo Giano Parrasio 16, Cosenza ☎ 0984/687750 ⊕ www.museodiocesanocosenza.it ⊠ Free ⊘ Closed Mon.–Sat. 12:30 pm–3 pm, and Sun. (except by appointment).

Restaurants

Calabria Bella

$ | SOUTHERN ITALIAN | FAMILY | Don't let the small, unimposing entrance or the rusticity fool you: the clientele of this family-run restaurant nestled by the steps to the Duomo often includes celebrities. Cuisine is typical of the region, with ingredients like porcini mushrooms from the Sila forests and strigoli (bladder-campion seedpods) from nearby fields. **Known for:** generous house antipasto Calabria Bella; rustic interior and piazza seating; excellent, robust cucina calabrese. $ Average main: €14 ✉ Piazza Duomo 20, Cosenza ☎ 0984/793531 ⊕ www.ristorantecalabriabella.it.

★ Hippocampus

$$$ | SEAFOOD | Renowned for its simply crafted dishes made with the freshest seasonal catch, Cosenza's best seafood restaurant has (appropriately enough) a minimalist, blue-and-white, nautical-theme interior. Guided by a waiter, you might start with a selection of antipasti to share, followed by a classic pasta allo scoglio and a main fritto misto di mare (medley of fried seafood). **Known for:** unfussy, welcoming vibe; a chef happy to create vegetarian dishes; exceptional, superfresh seafood. $ Average main: €25 ✉ Via Piave 33, Cosenza ☎ 0984/22103 ⊘ Closed Mon. No dinner Sun.

Hotels

Royal Hotel

$ | HOTEL | Like most hotels in Cosenza, the Royal caters mainly to a business clientele, yet it's nevertheless a good choice for a stopover: what it lacks in local flavor, it makes up for with functional whitewashed decor, spacious bathrooms, and reasonable room rates. **Pros:** close to pedestrian-only shopping area; good customer service; free parking. **Cons:** can be busy during events; beige '70s time-capsule decor in parts; 20-minute walk from centro storico. $ Rooms from: €75 ✉ Via delle Medaglie d'Oro 1, Cosenza ☎ 0984/412165 ⊕ www.hotelroyalcosenza.it ⬐ 34 rooms ⍾ Free Breakfast.

Camigliatello

30 km (19 miles) east of Cosenza.

Lined with chalets, Camigliatello is one of the Sila Massif's major resort towns. Most of the Sila isn't mountainous at all; rather, it's an extensive, sparsely populated plateau with areas of thick forest. There was, at one point, considerable deforestation, but in 1968 the area received a special designation as the Parco Nazionale della Sila, and strict rules have limited the felling of timber, which has allowed the forests to regenerate. There are well-marked trails through pine

Take a break from sightseeing and enjoy the great outdoors in La Fossiata nature preserve.

and beech woods and ample opportunities for horseback riding. Autumn sees droves of locals hunting mushrooms and gathering chestnuts; winter brings crowds to nearby ski slopes.

GETTING HERE AND AROUND

By car, take the Cosenza Nord exit from the A3 autostrada, then follow the SS107, or if you are following the SS106 along the Ionian Coast, branch off at Sibari and follow the signs.

VISITOR INFORMATION

CONTACT Proloco Camigliatello Tourism Office. ⊠ *Via Roma 5, Camigliatello* ☎ *0984/452850* ⊕ *www.prolococamigli-atello.it.*

Sights

Il Treno della Sila

TRAIN/TRAIN STATION | FAMILY | In spring and summer, this narrow-gauge steam railway takes visitors through stunning countryside from Moccone to San Nicola (at 4,600 feet) via Camigliatello. The journey takes 40–50 minutes and costs €18 online or €20 on the train; check the website for schedules. ⊠ *Via Forgitelle 11, Camigliatello* ☎ *328/2391117* ⊕ *www.trenodellasila.it.*

★ Parco Nazionale della Sila—La Fossiata

NATIONAL PARK | Calabria's granite plateau of Sila National Park is a wonderful place for lovers of the wild outdoors. Rising to nearly 7,000 feet at its highest peak, Botte Donato, the park was inaugurated in 2002, with forests, valleys, and rivers home to 175 species of vertebrates, including the park's now protected symbol, *il lupo*, the wolf. A couple of miles east of Campigliatello is Lago Cecita, a good starting point for exploring La Fossiata, a lovely wooded conservation area within the park that has a rich variety of trees, some centuries old. The forestry commission office in nearby Cupone can provide tourist information, maps, and assistance, such as arranging guides. ⊠ *Via Nazionale, Lorica di San Giovanni in Fiore, Camigliatello* ☎ *0984/537109 Forestry Commission Office* ⊕ *www.parcosila.it* ⊗ *Office closed weekends.*

Hotels

Tasso

$ | HOTEL | FAMILY | On the edge of Camigliatello, less than 1 km (½ mile) from the ski slopes, this hotel is in a peaceful, picturesque location. **Pros:** beautiful surroundings; conveniently located near the ski area; lively evening and family entertainment. **Cons:** dated bathrooms; scant breakfast choice lacking Calabrese products; nondescript architecture and out-of-date decor. $ *Rooms from: €90* ✉ *Via Torquato Tasso, Camigliatello* ☎ *0984/578113* ⊕ *www.hoteltasso.it* ⇘ *82 rooms* ⭤ *Free Breakfast.*

Crotone

105 km (65 miles) east of Cosenza, 150 km (94 miles) northeast of Locri.

One of the most important Magna Graecia colonies in Italy, Crotone was a major cultural center in the 5th century BC, when it was the home of thinkers like philosopher and mathematician Pythagoras. Sadly, modern development has eclipsed much of its former beauty, but it preserves something of an old-town feel, with its imposing 16th-century castle and an archaeological museum of some importance. Its coastal waters, stretching to Capo Rizzuto, make up Italy's largest protected marine area; and the island Castle Le Castella, 15 km (9 miles) from Crotone, is a vision out of a fairy tale.

GETTING HERE AND AROUND

By car, take the Cosenza Nord exit from the A3 autostrada, then follow the SS107. There are regular trains from Sibari.

VISITOR INFORMATION

CONTACT Proloco Crotone Tourism Office. ✉ *Via Molo Sanità 2, Crotone* ☎ *329/8154963* ⊕ *www.prolocolecastella.it.*

Sights

Museo Archeologico Nazionale

HISTORY MUSEUM | Constructed to house the treasures found at the Sanctuary of Hera Lacinia, as well as many antiquities recovered from the surrounding seabed, the museum is situated in the heart of the old city of Crotone, close to the seafront castle. The most precious part of the collection is the so-called Treasure of Hera, with the goddess's finely wrought gold diadem and belt pendant. You can also see the rare 5th-century-BC bronze *askos* (container for oil) in the form of a mermaid, illegally exported to the United States and subsequently recovered by the Italian government from the Getty Museum in California. ✉ *Via Risorgimento 121, Crotone* ☎ *0962/23082* ⊕ *musei.calabria.beniculturali.it* 🎫 *€4* ⊘ *Closed Mon.*

★ Museo e Parco Archeologico Nazionale di Capo Colonna

RUINS | Il Santuario di Hera Lacinia (Sanctuary of Hera Lacinia) was once one of the most important shrines of Magna Graecia. Only one column remains standing, but the site (known as Capo Colonna because of that single pillar) occupies a stunning position on a promontory 11 km (7 miles) south of the town of Crotone. The ruins are part of a vast park, which also contains a well-appointed museum documenting finds from prehistory to the Roman era. The sanctuary itself, which dates from the 7th century BC, is fenced off for safety reasons, but a walkway allows viewing. ✉ *Via Michele Di Donato, Capo Colonna, Crotone* ☎ *0962/934814* ⊕ *musei.calabria.beniculturali.it* 🎫 *Free* ⊘ *Closed Mon.*

Beaches

★ Capo Rizzuto—Spiagge Rosse

BEACH | FAMILY | If practicalities and time allow, make the short trip toward Capo Rizzuto just down the coast for some of the most fabulous bathing and snorkeling in the region. Among its bays and protected marine reserve waters is Spiagge Rosse, whose orange-red sand beach and crystalline waters make it the most alluring on this stretch of coast. **Amenities:** food and drink; lifeguards; parking (free); showers; toilets. **Best for:** snorkeling; swimming. ⊠ *Contrada Fratte, Capo Rizzuto, Crotone.*

 Hotels

Hotel Helios

$ | HOTEL | On the coastal road between Crotone and Capo Colonna, a little out of town and just 8 km (5 miles) from the Sanctuary of Hera Lacinia, the '70s-style Helios has crystal clear shores nearby and a fab pool, terrace, restaurant, and snack bar—all on-site. **Pros:** elevated sea views; on bus route into town and open year-round; efficient, courteous staff. **Cons:** rooms need a refresh; no minibar; uninspiring architecture. $ *Rooms from: €85* ⊠ *Viale Magna Grecia at Via Makalla 2, Crotone* ☎ *0962/901291* ⊕ *www.helioshotels.it* ⤴ *42 rooms* ꙳⃝ *Free Breakfast.*

Tropea

120 km (75 miles) southwest of Cosenza, 107 km (66 miles) north of Reggio Calabria.

Ringed by cliffs and wonderful sandy beaches, the Tropea promontory is still just beginning to be discovered by foreign tourists. The main town of Tropea, its old palazzi built in simple golden stone, easily wins the contest for prettiest town on Calabria's Tyrrhenian Coast. On a clear day the seaward views from the waterfront promenade take in Stromboli's cone and at least four of the other Aeolian Islands; you can visit them by motorboat, departing daily in summer. Accommodations are good, and beach addicts won't be disappointed by the choice of magnificent sandy bays within easy reach. The beach beside Santa

Maria dell'Isola is said to be one of the Mediterranean's most beautiful, but there are other fine beaches south at Capo Vaticano and north at Briatico.

GETTING HERE AND AROUND

By car, exit the A3 autostrada at Pizzo and follow the southbound SP6/SS522. Frequent trains depart daily from Lamezia Terme.

VISITOR INFORMATION

CONTACT Proloco Tropea Tourism Office. ⊠ *Piazza Ercole 19–23, Tropea* ☎ *0963/61475* ⊕ *www.prolocotropea.eu.*

 Sights

Cattedrale

CHURCH | In Tropea's beguiling warren of lanes, seek out the old Norman cathedral, whose main altar contains the locally revered icon of the Madonna di Romania, protectress of the city. Also of interest are the imposing 14th-century "Black Crucifix," in one of the side chapels, and the adjoining Museo Diocesano, which contains an archaeological section and a collection of sacred art, including a life-size statue of Santa Domenica in solid silver, dating from 1738. ■ **TIP→ November through March, the cathedral is open for church services only, but if you're quiet and respectful, you can probably sneak a peek.** ⊠ *Largo Duomo, Tropea* ☎ *0963/61034* 🎫 *Cathedral free, Museo Diocesano €2* ⊙ *Closed Nov.–Mar., except for services.*

★ Santa Maria dell'Isola

VIEWPOINT | The sanctuary of Santa Maria dell'Isola is the symbol of Tropea, and it is easy to see why. Perched high on a rocky promontory and accessible only by a winding flight of stone steps cut into the cliff side, it dominates the sea view from Piazza Ercole, the main town square. Believed to date from the 4th century AD, it has been rebuilt many times and took its present form in the 18th century, after it was damaged by an earthquake. The inside of the church is unadorned, but visitors can climb up to the roof to admire the splendid view or wander through the pleasant garden set on the rocks behind the building. The beach below the rock is considered to be among the most beautiful in Italy. ✉ *Largo Marina dell'Isola, Tropea* ☎ *347/2541232* 🎟 *Church free, garden €2.*

Beaches

★ Marasusa

BEACH | FAMILY | The most famous of Calabria's beaches is backed by sheer cliffs topped by Tropea's stacked buildings—seemingly growing out of the rock. Beyond this popular vacation destination stretch sits the gleaming island promontory sanctuary of Santa Maria dell'Isola. For bathers, snorkelers, and frolickers the light-hued sand is quite fine underfoot and the greenish-blue waters are wonderful. Adding to the drama is the smoking cone of island volcano Stromboli on the western horizon. **Amenities:** lifeguards; parking (free); showers; toilets. **Best for:** snorkeling; surfing; swimming; windsurfing. ✉ *Via Lungomare, Tropea.*

Restaurants

Osteria Antico Androne

$$ | SOUTHERN ITALIAN | With intimate tables around the interior courtyard and mezzanine of the 18th-century Palazzo Teotino, this osteria is a truly atmospheric place to dine. The menu is a mix of traditional local dishes and classic southern Italian pasta combinations—with subtle Tropeana twists here and there. **Known for:** meat and vegetarian options; Calabrese fileja pasta with Tropea onions; grilled and fried seafood. [$] *Average main: €19* ✉ *Via Boiano 6, Tropea* ☎ *349/2887969* ⏲ *Closed Mon.*

Pimm's

$$ | SOUTHERN ITALIAN | Since the 1960s, this basement restaurant in the historic center has offered Tropea's top seafood dining experience, with such specialties as pasta with monkfish and almond pesto, smoked swordfish and prawns on red Tropea onions, and gnocchi filled with tiny clams and creamed pistachio nuts. The splendid sea views from the rear windows (ask for the *tavolo in nicchia panoramica*) are a surprising—and substantial—reason to head here. **Known for:** book a window table for the azure views; perched high above the beach; excellent fresh seafood. [$] *Average main: €20* ✉ *Largo Migliarese 2, at the foot of Corso Vittorio Emanuele, Tropea* ☎ *0963/666105.*

Hotels

★ Hotel Rocca della Sena

$$$ | HOTEL | Overlooking Tropea's golden sands and azure waters, this intimate, self-styled boutique hotel—with modern, quirky, equatorial-themed rooms—is a reliable option. **Pros:** tranquil location on Tropea's periphery; a terrace with a large whirlpool bath; fab sea views. **Cons:** some may find the LED mood lighting and furnishings tacky; lack of bar menu options; standard rooms on the cramped and gloomy side. [$] *Rooms from: €206* ✉ *Via Paolo Orsi, Tropea* ☎ *0963/62374* 🌐 *www.hotelroccadellasena.it* ⏲ *Closed Nov.–early Apr.* 🛏 *12 rooms* 🍴 *Free Breakfast.*

Villa Paola

$$$ | HOTEL | Converted from an elegant 16th century Franciscan convent and immersed in gorgeous, flowery grounds and cloisters on the outskirts of Tropea, this pastel-hued retreat-style hotel has stylish, minimalist interiors and wonderful tranquil terraces replete with infinity pool and breathtaking views. **Pros:** large beds and quality linen bedding; elevated views over Tropea and the sea; warm Calabrese staff. **Cons:** a 15-minute walk from the beach; occasional weddings may break the exclusive retreat feel; perhaps lacks the full five-star facilities and attentiveness. [$] *Rooms from: €285* ✉ *Contrada Paola 6, Tropea* ☎ *0963/62370*

⊕ *www.villapaolatropea.it* 🛏 *10 rooms* ❤️ *Free Breakfast.*

Reggio Calabria

115 km (71 miles) south of Tropea, 499 km (311 miles) south of Naples.

This raw city is one of Italy's busiest ports, where you can find not only container ships and cranes but also a wonderful *lungomare* (promenade) made for lazy passeggiatas. Hydrofoils for Sicily depart from here; vehicle-carrying ferries depart from Villa San Giovanni, 13 km (8 miles) north.

Reggio Calabria is also a great base for visiting *borghi* (historic villages) like the beautiful town of Stilo, which is known for being the birthplace and home of the philosopher Tommaso Campanella (1568–1639), whose magnum opus was the socialistic *La Città del Sole* (*The City of the Sun*, 1602). Stilo is 138 km (86 miles) northeast of Reggio Calabria, along the Ionian coastal road, SS106. Regular trains run from Lamezia Terme.

GETTING HERE AND AROUND
The A3 autostrada runs directly to Reggio Calabria. A dozen direct trains depart from Naples and Rome daily. There are daily flights from all over Italy and seasonal services from around Europe.

VISITOR INFORMATION
CONTACT I.A.T. Reggio Calabria Tourism Office. ✉️ *Via Venezia 1, Reggio Calabria* ☎️ *0965/21010* ⊕ *turismo.reggiocal.it.*

👁 Sights

★ Museo Nazionale della Magna Grecia
HISTORY MUSEUM | Reggio Calabria is home to one of southern Italy's most important archaeological museums. Its prize exhibit, of course, is the two ancient Greek statues known as the Bronzi di Riace, which were discovered by an amateur deep-sea diver off Calabria's Ionian Coast in 1972. After a lengthy but necessary conservation effort, these 5th-century-BC statues of two Greek warriors, thought to be the work of either Pheidias or Polykleitos, now take pride of place in their special temperature-controlled room, complete with earthquake-resistant bases. ✉️ *Piazza de Nava 26, Reggio Calabria* ☎️ *0965/613988* ⊕ *www.museoarcheologicoreggiocalabria.it* 🎟️ *€8* 🕐 *Closed Mon.*

Hotels

Excelsior Grand Hotel
$ | HOTEL | Inviting modern decor, all the amenities one expects from a top international hotel, and a prime location near the town's seafront make this a popular choice with business travelers as well as tourists. **Pros:** centrally located near Museo Nazionale della Magna Grecia; near the beach; rooftop restaurant with views and truly unique dishes. **Cons:** some rooms are tiny; street noise in some rooms; standard business hotel decor. 💲 *Rooms from: €110* ✉️ *Via Vittorio Veneto 64, Reggio Calabria* ☎️ *0965/812211* ⊕ *www.grandhotelexcelsiorrc.it* 🛏 *84 rooms* ❤️ *Free Breakfast.*

★ Hotel Medinblu
$ | HOTEL | The sleek, contemporary guest rooms at this hotel in an imaginatively renovated 1915 palazzo are warmed up a bit by fabrics with bold prints; fabulous public areas include a spacious, chic roof terrace and cocktail bar that serve aperitivi. **Pros:** central location; rooftop breakfast and seasonal evening concerts; warm, professional customer service. **Cons:** some may find decor lacks character; traffic noise in some rooms; hotel's garage a short walk away. 💲 *Rooms from: €122* ✉️ *Via Demetrio Tripepi 98, Reggio Calabria* ☎️ *0965/312982* ⊕ *www.hotelmedinblu.com* 🛏 *33 rooms* ❤️ *Free Breakfast.*

Chapter 17

SICILY

Updated by
Robert Andrews, Ros Belford,
Jennifer V. Cole, Craig McKnight,
and Rochelle Del Borrello

◉ Sights	🍴 Restaurants	🛏 Hotels	🛍 Shopping	🍸 Nightlife
★★★★☆	★★★★★	★★★★☆	★★☆☆☆	★★☆☆☆

WELCOME TO SICILY

TOP REASONS TO GO

★ **Taormina, Sicily's most beautiful resort:** The view of the sea and Mt. Etna from its jagged cactus-covered cliffs is as close to perfection as a panorama can get.

★ **A walk on Siracusa's Ortigia Island:** Classical ruins rub elbows with faded seaside palaces and fish markets in Sicily's most striking port city, where the Duomo is literally built atop an ancient Greek temple.

★ **Palermo's palaces, churches, and crypts:** Virtually every great European empire ruled Sicily's strategically positioned capital at some point, and it shows most of all in the diverse architecture, from Roman to Byzantine to Arab-Norman.

★ **Valley of the Temples, Agrigento:** This stunning set of ruins is proudly perched above the sea in a grove full of almond trees; not even in Athens will you find Greek temples this finely preserved.

1 **Palermo.**

2 **Monreale.**

3 **Segesta.**

4 **Erice.**

5 **Trapani.**

6 **Marsala.**

7 **Selinunte.**

8 **Agrigento.**

9 **Enna.**

10 **Piazza Armerina.**

11 **Caltagirone.**

12 **Ragusa.**

13 **Modica.**

14 **Scicli.**

15 **Noto.**

16 **Siracusa.**

17 **Catania.**

18 **Acireale.**

19 **Mt. Etna.**

20 **Taormina.**

21 **Castelmola.**

22 **Messina.**

23 **Lipari.**

24 **Salina.**

25 **Panarea.**

26 **Stromboli.**

27 **Filicudi.**

28 **Cefalù.**

Stromboli 26

Panarea 25

Salina 24 27 **Filicudi**

Alicudi 23 **Lipari**

AEOLIAN IS. **Vulcano**

Mare Tirreno

Villa San Giovanni

Milazzo

Capo d'Orlando A20 22 **Messina**

Palermo 1

Bagheria **Barcellona Pozzo di Gotto**

Cefalù A20 28 116 **Reggio Calabria**

Termini Imerese *TYRRHENIAN COAST*

Randazzo 120 **Castelmola**

A19 21 20 **Taormina**

189 19 **Mt. Etna 3,323m** A18 *Mare Ionio*

Adrano 284

Paterno 18 **Acireale**

Enna A19

Caltanissetta 9 17 **Catania**

640

Canicatti 10 **Piazza Armerina** 417

grigento 8 **Caltagirone** 194 **Augusta**

123 11

115 626 16 **Siracusa**

Licata 115 **Ortygia**

Gela 12 **Ragusa** 124

Vittoria 13 **Modica** 15 **Noto**

Scicli 14

diterráneo **Pachino**

A20

A19

A19

646

640

A18

EATING AND DRINKING WELL IN SICILY

Sicilian cuisine is one of the oldest in existence, with records of cooking competitions dating to 600 BC. Food in Sicily today reflects the island's unique cultural mix, imaginatively combining fish, fruits, vegetables, and nuts with Italian pastas and Arab and North African elements—couscous is a staple in Palermo.

It's hard to eat badly here. From the lowliest of *trattorias* to the most highfalutin *ristorante*, you'll find classic dishes that have long been staples of the family dinner table—basically pasta and seafood. In more formal restaurants, you'll find greater attention to detail and a more sophisticated atmosphere, while less pretentious trattorias tend to be family-run affairs, often without so much as a menu to guide you. There's also a new wave of creative restaurants that have come up with interesting versions of old standbys, using local and often organic ingredients and changing their menus with the season. No matter where you choose to eat in the most gregarious of regions in the most convivial of countries, you can expect a lively dining experience.

SICILIAN MARKETS

Sicily's natural fecundity is evident wherever you look, from the prickly pears sprouting on roadsides, to the slopes of vineyards and citrus groves covering the interior, to the ranks of fishing boats moored in every harbor. You can come face-to-face with this bounty in the clamorous street markets of Palermo and Catania. Here, you'll encounter teetering piles of olives and oranges, enticing displays of cheeses and meats, plus pastries and sweets of every description.

WINES

The earthy *nero d'avola* grape bolsters many of Sicily's traditionally sunny, expansive reds, and it's often softened with fruity, bright *frappato* to make Sicily's only DOCG wine, Cerasuolo di Vittoria. Red wines from around Mt. Etna that use the grapes *nerello mascalese* and *nerello cappuccio* have also gained renown. Sicily produces crisp white varieties, too, such as *carricante, catarratto bianco, inzolia,* and *grillo.* When it comes to sweet accompaniments, the small island of Pantelleria produces the smooth *passito* dessert wine, made from *zibibbo* grapes, while the Aeolian Islands are known for Malvasia delle Lipari.

DELICIOUS FISH

Pasta *con le sarde,* with fresh sardines, olive oil, raisins, pine nuts, and wild fennel gets a different treatment at every restaurant. Grilled *tonno* (tuna) and *orata* (dorado) are coastal staples, while delicate *ricci* (sea urchins) are a specialty. King, however, is *pesce spada* (swordfish), best enjoyed *marinato* (marinated), *affumicato* (smoked), or as the traditional *involtini di pesce spada* (roulades).

LOCAL SPECIALTIES

In Catania, you'll be offered *caserecci alla Norma* (a short pasta with a sauce of tomato, eggplant, salted ricotta, and basil). The *mandorla* (bitter almond), the pride of Agrigento, plays into everything from risotto *alle mandorle* (with almonds, butter, Grana cheese, and parsley) to incomparable almond granita—an absolute must in summer. Pistachios (pronounced *pistakkio*) produced around Bronte, on the lower slopes of Etna, go into pasta sauces as well as ice cream and granita, while capers from the Aeolian Islands add zest to salads and fish sauces.

SNACKS

Two favorite Sicilian snacks are *arancini* ("little oranges," or rice croquettes with a cheese or meat filling), and *panelle* (seasoned chickpea flour boiled to a paste, cooled, sliced, and fried). Other tidbits to look out for include special foods associated with festivals, such as the ominously named *ossa dei morti* ("bones of the dead," or rolled almond cookies). But the most eye-catching of all are the *frutta martorana*: sweet marzipan confections shaped to resemble fruits and temptingly arrayed in bars and *pasticcerie* (pastry shops). The Baroque town of Modica is famous for its chocolate, produced using an Aztec recipe.

The island of Sicily has an abundance of history. Some of the world's best-preserved Byzantine mosaics stand adjacent to magnificent Greek temples and Roman amphitheaters. Add the spectacular sight of Mt. Etna plus Sicily's unique cuisine—mingling Arab and Greek spices, Spanish and French techniques—and you understand why visitors continue to be drawn here.

Sicily has beckoned seafaring wanderers since the trials of Odysseus were first sung in Homer's *Odyssey*—an epic that is sometimes called the world's first travel guide. Strategically poised between Europe and Africa, this mystical land of three corners and a fiery volcano once hosted two of the most enlightened capitals of the West: Siracusa and Palermo. And it has been a melting pot of every great civilization on the Mediterranean—Greek and Roman, then Arab and Norman, and finally French, Spanish, and Italian. Invaders through the ages weren't just attracted by its strategic location, however; they recognized a paradise in Sicily's deep blue skies and temperate climate, in its lush vegetation and rich marine life—all of which prevail to this day.

In modern times, the traditional graciousness and nobility of the Sicilian people have survived alongside the destructive influences of the Mafia under Sicily's semiautonomous government. The island has more recently emerged as something of an international travel hot spot, drawing increasing numbers of visitors. Brits and Germans flock in ever-growing numbers to Agrigento and Siracusa, and in high season Chinese and American tour groups seem to outnumber the locals in Taormina and the Baroque hill towns. And yet, in Sicily's windswept heartland, vineyards, olive groves, and lovingly kept dirt roads leading to family farmhouses still tie Sicilians to the land and to tradition, forming a happy connectedness that can't be defined by economic measures.

Planning

When to Go

Sicily's high season (mid-June through mid-September) is hot, expensive, and busy. During the peak season from late July to late August, beaches are crowded, and hotels and restaurants are often booked up, so advance reservations are necessary—often several weeks or even months for hotels and a day or two for restaurants.

April–May and mid-September–October are the ideal months for more temperate weather, more elbow room on the beaches, and more capacity and availability at hotels and restaurants. Just keep in mind the Easter period (lasting a few days around Good Friday) can be very busy, and some resort destinations may close in October.

The winter months of November through March see many places outside the cities closed, if only for a few weeks, while tourist facilities at most of Sicily's beach resorts and on all the offshore islands shut down for the entire period. Flights, accommodation rates, and car rentals are at their lowest at this time of year, but bear in mind that November and December see a lot of rain while January and February are the coldest months.

Getting Here and Around

AIR

There are frequent internal flights from Milan, Rome, and other regional airports to Sicily's two major airports, Palermo's Falcone Borsellino Airport (PMO) and Catania's Fontanarossa Airport (CTA) as well as to Trapani-Birgi's Vincenzo Florio Airport (TPS).

CONTACTS Catania-Fontanarossa Airport. ✉ *Via Fontanarossa, Catania* ☎ *095/7239111* ⊕ *www. aeroporto.catania.it/en.* **Palermo Airport.** ☎ *800/541880* ⊕ *www.aeroportodipalermo.it.* **Aeroporto Vincenzo Florio Trapani Birgi.** ✉ *Contrada Birgi Nivaloro, Trapani* ☎ *0923/610111* ⊕ *www.airgest.it.*

BUS

Air-conditioned buses connect major and minor cities in Sicily and are often faster and more convenient than local trains—still single track on many stretches—but also slightly more expensive. Various companies serve different routes. SAIS runs frequently between Palermo and Catania, Messina, and other cities, in each case arriving at and departing from near the train stations.

BUS CONTACTS Cuffaro. ☎ *091/6161510* ⊕ *www.cuffaro.info.* **SAIS.** ☎ *800/211020 toll-free* ⊕ *www.saisautolinee.it.*

CAR

Driving is the ideal way to explore Sicily. Modern highways circle and bisect the island, making all main cities easily reachable. Along the north coast, the A20 autostrada (also known as E90) connects Messina, Cefalù, and Palermo while along the eastern coast, Messina, Taormina, Catania, and Siracusa are linked by the A18/E45. Running through the interior, from Catania to west of Cefalù, is the A19; threading west from Palermo, the A29/E933 runs to Trapani, with a leg stretching down to Mazara del Vallo. In general, the south side of the island is less well served, though the extension of the A18 to Gela is under construction, while stretches of the SS115 west of Agrigento are relatively fast and traffic-free. The A18 and A20 autostradas are subject to tolls. You'll likely hear stories about the dangers of driving in Sicily. In the big cities—especially Palermo, Catania, and Messina—streets can be a honking mess, with lane markings and stop signs taken as mere suggestions; you can avoid the chaos by driving through at off-peak times or on weekends. However, once outside the urban areas and resort towns, most of the highways and regional state roads are a driving enthusiast's dream—they're winding, sparsely populated, and reasonably well maintained, with striking new views around many bends. Obviously, don't leave valuables in your car, and make sure baggage is stowed out of sight, if possible.

TRAIN

There are direct express trains from Rome to Palermo, Catania, and Siracusa. The Rome–Palermo and Rome–Siracusa trips take at least 11 hours. After Naples, the run is mostly along the coast, so try to book a window seat on the right if you're not on an overnight train. At Villa San Giovanni, in Calabria, the train is separated and loaded onto a ferryboat to cross the strait to Messina—a favorite for kids.

There are no high-speed lines within Sicily, but main lines connect Messina, Taormina, Siracusa, Catania, and Palermo. The Messina–Palermo run, along the northern coast, and Messina–Taormina, along the eastern coast, are especially scenic. Secondary lines are generally very slow and may be unreliable. For schedules, check the website of the Italian state railway, Trenitalia.

TRAIN CONTACT Trenitalia. ☎ *892021 in Italy, 06/68475475 outside Italy* ⊕ *www. trenitalia.com.*

Restaurants

As befits a major city, Palermo has a huge selection of interesting and varied restaurants, while Catania is best known for its high-quality seafood. In the tourist-heavy coastal towns, dining can be hit or miss, while inland there has been a mini-explosion of new-wave gourmet restaurants in the Baroque towns of Ragusa, Modica, and especially Noto, as well as some intriguing options popping up on Mt. Etna.

In the west of the island, expect to find a Sicilian variant of North African couscous on the menus, often made with seafood and well worth sampling. In the countryside, *agriturismi* (farm B&Bs), country hotels, and wineries are your best bets for a good meal.

Restaurant reviews are the average cost of a main course at dinner, or, if dinner is not served, at lunch. Restaurant reviews have been shortened. For full information, visit Fodors.com.

Hotels

High-quality and boutique hotels tend to be confined to the major cities and resorts of Palermo, Catania, Taormina, and Siracusa. The southeast towns of Modica, Ragusa, and Noto also offer some very classy and charming accommodations but are mostly small in scale. B&Bs exist everywhere, with the greatest choice in Palermo, Catania, and Taormina, including both period and more modern designer places. Beach resorts tend to have a range of options, while rural lodgings may include the odd swanky estate but are mostly confined to agriturismi (rural bed-and-breakfasts), ranging from quite basic to extensive spreads, and usually offering all-inclusive, full-board plans that can make for some of Sicily's most memorable meals.

Hotel reviews are the lowest cost of a standard double room in high season. Hotel reviews have been shortened. For full information, visit Fodors.com.

What it Costs in Euros

	$	$$	$$$	$$$$
RESTAURANTS				
	under €15	€15–€24	€25–€35	over €35
HOTELS				
	under €125	€125–€200	€201–€300	over €300

Palermo

Once the intellectual capital of southern Europe, Palermo has always been at the crossroads of civilization. Favorably located on a crescent bay at the foot of Monte Pellegrino, it has attracted almost every culture touching the Mediterranean world. To Palermo's credit, it's absorbed these diverse cultures into a unique personality that's at once Arab and Christian,

Byzantine and Roman, Norman and Italian. The city's heritage encompasses all of Sicily's varied ages, but its distinctive aspect is its Arab-Norman identity, an improbable marriage that, mixed in with Byzantine and Jewish elements, resulted in resplendent works of art. These are most notable in its churches, from small jewels such as San Giovanni degli Eremiti to larger-scale works such as the cathedral. No less noteworthy than the architecture is Palermo's chaotic vitality, on display at some of Italy's most vibrant outdoor markets, public squares, street bazaars, and food vendors, and, above all, in its grand, discordant symphony of motorists, motorcyclists, and pedestrians that triumphantly climaxes in the new town center each evening with Italy's most spectacular passeggiata.

Sicily's capital is a multilayered, vigorous metropolis with a strong historical profile; approach it with an open mind. You're likely to encounter some frustrating instances of inefficiency and, depending on the season, stifling heat. If you have a car, park it in a garage as soon as you can, and don't take it out until you're ready to depart.

Palermo is easily explored on foot, but you may choose to spend a morning taking a bus tour to help you get oriented. The Quattro Canti, or Four Corners, is the hub that separates the four sections of the old city: La Kalsa (the old Arab section) to the southeast, Albergheria to the southwest, Capo to the northwest, and Vucciria to the northeast. Each of these is a tumult of activity during the day, though at night the narrow alleys empty out and are best avoided in favor of the more animated avenues of the new city north of Teatro Massimo. Sights to see by day are scattered along three major streets: Corso Vittorio Emanuele, Via Maqueda, and Via Roma. The tourist information office in Piazza Bellini will give you a map and a valuable handout that lists opening and closing times, which sometimes change with the seasons.

GETTING HERE AND AROUND

Palermo is home to one of Sicily's two major international airports, Aeroporto di Falcone Borsellino at Punta Raisi, 30 km (18 miles) west of town, and as such is a main gateway for those arriving in Sicily by plane. Along with international flights, there are regular connections from and to other Italian cities such as Milan, Rome, and Naples, as well as to Sicily's far-flung isles of Pantelleria and Lampedusa.

Trains run from the station below Palermo's airport to the city center every half hour or so, with tickets dispensed from machines. Don't forget to validate your ticket before travel by punching it at one of the station's machines. Prestia e Comandè buses run every 30 minutes to Piazza Ruggero Settimo in the city center. A taxi from Palermo's airport to the center should cost €40–€50, while shared taxis cost €8 per person, with drop-offs at a range of points within the city (though you may have to wait for the minimum of five passengers before setting off). Journey time by taxi or bus between Palermo airport and city center is 30 minutes to one hour, depending on traffic; by train, it's around one hour, with stops within walking distance of Palazzo Reale and Via della Libertà before reaching the main station.

You'll find you can walk to most spots within central Palermo, though it's worth taking advantage of city bus services, run by AMAT, for longer stretches—for example, between the main train station and Piazza Castelnuovo (Bus 101); between the main train station and Piazza dell'Indipendenza, for the Palazzo Reale (Bus 109); and out to Monreale (Bus 389 from Piazza dell'Indipendenza) and Mondello (Bus 806 from the Politeama or Viale della Libertà).

Bus tickets can be purchased from kiosks and shops showing the AMAT sticker and cost €1.40 for any journeys made within 90 minutes (timed from when you punch your ticket in the machine onboard the bus); €3.50 for tickets lasting an entire day; €6 for tickets lasting two days; €8 for three days; and €16.50 for a week.

VISITOR INFORMATION

CONTACTS Palermo Tourism Office. ⊠ Piazza Bellini, Quattro Canti ☎ 091/7408020 Piazza Bellini, 091/591698 airport ⊕ www.cittametropolitana.pa.it/turismo.

 Sights

Catacombe dei Cappuccini

CEMETERY | The spookiest sight in all of Sicily, this 16th-century catacomb houses over 8,000 corpses of men, women, and young children—some in tombs but many mummified and preserved—hanging in rows on the walls, divided by social caste, age, or gender. Most wear signs indicating their names and the years they lived, and many are Capuchin friars, who were founders and proprietors of this bizarre establishment from 1599 to 1911. The site is still managed by the nearby Capuchin church, but was closed to new corpses when an adjacent cemetery was opened, making the catacombs redundant. Though memorable, this is not a spot for the faint of heart; children might be frightened or disturbed. ⊠ Piazza Cappuccini 1, off Via Cappuccini, Near Palazzo Reale ☎ 091/6527389 ⊕ www. catacombepalermo.it ☜ €3.

Cattedrale

CHURCH | This church is a lesson in Palermitano eclecticism—originally Norman (1182), then Catalan Gothic (14th to 15th century), then fitted out with a Baroque and neoclassical interior (18th century). Its turrets, towers, dome, and arches come together in the kind of meeting of diverse elements that King Roger II (1095–1154), whose tomb is inside along

with that of Frederick II, fostered during his reign. The exterior is more intriguing than the interior, but the back of the apse is gracefully decorated with interlacing Arab arches inlaid with limestone and black volcanic tufa. It's possible to visit the cathedral's roof for some fabulous city views. ⊠ Corso Vittorio Emanuele, Palermo ☎ 091/334373 ⊕ www.cattedrale.palermo.it ☜ Free; €12 treasury, crypt, royal tombs, and roof visit; €7 treasury, crypt, and tombs; €2 royal tombs only.

Chiesa del Gesù

CHURCH | It is more than worth the short detour from the lively Ballarò Market to step into the serene Baroque perfection of Chiesa del Gesù (Church of St. Mary of Gesù). The ornate church was built by the Jesuits not long after their arrival in Palermo in the late 16th century, and was constructed at the site of their religious seat in the city, so the chuch is also sometimes known as Casa Professa (mother house). The interior is almost completely covered with intricate marble bas-reliefs and elaborate black, tangerine, and cream stone work. The splendid church was severely damaged in World War II, but careful restoration has returned it to its shiny, swirling glory. ⊠ Piazza Casa Professa 21, Palermo ☎ 338/4512011 ☜ Free.

★ La Martorana (Santa Maria dell'Ammiraglio)

CHURCH | One piazza over from the dancing nymphs of Fontana Pretoria, this church, with its elegant Norman campanile, was erected in 1143 but had its interior altered considerably during the Baroque period. High along the western wall, however, is some of the oldest and best-preserved mosaic artwork of the Norman period. Near the entrance is an interesting mosaic of King Roger II being crowned by Christ. In it Roger is dressed in a bejeweled Byzantine stole, reflecting the Norman court's penchant for all things Byzantine. Archangels along the ceiling

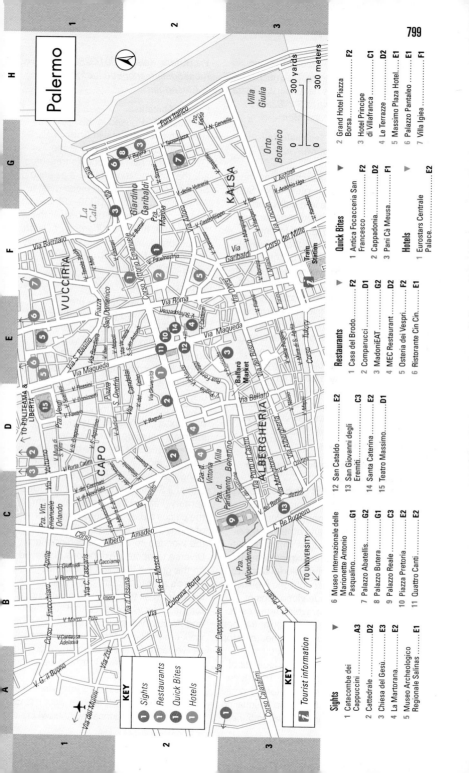

Palermo

KEY

- ⓵ Sights
- ⓵ Restaurants
- ⓵ Quick Bites
- ⓵ Hotels

KEY

🛈 Tourist information

▶ **Sights**

1	Catacombe dei Cappuccini	A3
2	Cattedrale	D2
3	Chiesa del Gesù	E3
4	La Martorana	E2
5	Museo Archeologico Regionale Salinas	E1
6	Museo Internazionale delle Marionette Antonio Pasqualino	G1
7	Palazzo Abatellis	G2
8	Palazzo Butera	G1
9	Palazzo Reale	C3
10	Piazza Pretoria	E2
11	Quattro Canti	E2
12	San Cataldo	E2
13	San Giovanni degli Eremiti	C3
14	Santa Caterina	E2
15	Teatro Massimo	D1

▶ **Restaurants**

1	Casa del Brodo	F2
2	Comparucci	D1
3	MadoniEAT	G2
4	MEC Restaurant	D2
5	Osteria dei Vespri	F2
6	Ristorante Cin Cin	E1

▶ **Quick Bites**

1	Antica Focacceria San Francesco	F2
2	Cappadonia	D2
3	Pani Cà Meusa	F1

▶ **Hotels**

1	Eurostars Centrale Palace	E2
2	Grand Hotel Piazza Borsa	F2
3	Hotel Principe di Villafranca	C1
4	Le Terrazze	D2
5	Massimo Plaza Hotel	E1
6	Palazzo Pantaleo	E1
7	Villa Igiea	F1

300 yards

300 meters

wear the same stole wrapped around their shoulders and arms. The much plainer San Cataldo is next door. ⊠ *Piazza Bellini 3, Quattro Canti* ☏ *345/8288231* 🖾 *€2* 🕙 *Closed Sun. and Mon.*

Museo Archeologico Regionale Salinas (*Salinas Regional Museum of Archaeology*)

HISTORY MUSEUM | This archaeology museum is the oldest public museum in Sicily, with a small but excellent collection, including a marvelously reconstructed Doric frieze from the Greek temple at Selinunte, which reveals the high level of artistic culture attained by the Greeks in Sicily some 2,500 years ago. There are also lion's head water spouts from 480 BC, as well as other excavated pieces from around Sicily, including Taormina and Agrigento, which make up part of an informative exhibition on the broader history of the island. After admiring the artifacts, wander through the two plant-filled courtyards, and be sure to check the website for special culture nights, when the museum is open late to host musical performances. ⊠ *Piazza Olivella 24, Via Roma, Olivella* ☏ *091/6116807* 🖾 *€6* 🕙 *Closed Mon.*

Museo Internazionale delle Marionette Antonio Pasqualino

OTHER MUSEUM | FAMILY | This collection of more than 4,000 masterpieces showcasing the traditional Opera dei Pupi (puppet show), both Sicilian and otherwise, will delight visitors of all ages with their glittering armor and fierce expressions. The free audio guide to the colorful displays is only available in Italian, but the well-designed exhibits include video clips of the puppets in action, which requires no translation. There are also regular live performances in the museum's theater (stop by or call in advance to check times), which center on the chivalric legends of troubadours of bygone times. The museum can be hard to find: look for the small alley just off Piazzetta Antonio Pasqualino 5. ⊠ *Piazzetta Antonio Pasqualino 5, near*

Via Butera, Kalsa ☏ *091/328060* 🌐 *www. museodellemarionette.it/en* 🖾 *€5* 🕙 *Closed Sat.*

Palazzo Abatellis

ART MUSEUM | Housed in this late-15th-century Catalan Gothic palace with Renaissance elements is the Galleria Regionale. Among its treasures are the *Annunciation* (1474), a painting by Sicily's prominent Renaissance master Antonello da Messina (1430–79), and an arresting fresco by an unknown 15th-century painter, titled *The Triumph of Death,* a macabre depiction of the plague years. ⊠ *Via Alloro 4, Kalsa* ☏ *091/6230011* 🖾 *€8* 🕙 *Closed Mon.*

★ Palazzo Butera

ART MUSEUM | Dating from the 18th century but closed for most of the last four decades, the Palazzo Butera has reopened following a complete facelift and conversion into one of Sicily's (and Italy's) most imaginative museum collections. Its labyrinthine rooms now display a heady mixture of old and new art. The collection's strength lies in its bold juxtapositions, with works by an international roster of experimental modern artists of the likes of Gilbert and George, and David Tremlett, exhibited alongside classical landscapes and graceful Sicilian furniture from the 19th century. Painted ceilings remain from the palace's Baroque beginnings, some of them artfully peeled back to reveal the wooden construction behind them. Diverse temporary exhibitions displayed on the ground floor add to the mix. There's a lot to take in, but if you need a break from all the hectic creativity, head for the terrace, accessed from the second floor, which provides benches and a walk around one of the two courtyards as well as views over the harbor. You can get even better views from the viewing platform reached from the roof, while further up, steps lead to a lofty view of the harbor, Monte Pellegrino, and, inland, the whole of the Conca d'Oro bowl in which the city sits. ✉ *Via Butera 18, Kalsa* ☎ *091/7521754* ⊕ *www.palazzobutera.it* ✈ *€7.50* ⊗ *Closed Mon.*

★ **Palazzo Reale** (*Royal Palace*)
CASTLE/PALACE | This historic palace, also called Palazzo dei Normanni (Norman Palace), was the seat of Sicily's semiautonomous rulers for centuries; the building is a fascinating mesh of 10th-century Norman and 17th-century Spanish structures. Because it now houses the Sicilian Parliament, parts of the palace are closed to the public from Tuesday to Thursday when the regional assembly is in session. The must-see Cappella Palatina (Palatine Chapel) remains open. Built by Roger II in 1132, it's a dazzling example of the harmony of artistic elements produced under the Normans and the interweaving of cultures in the court. Here the skill of French and Sicilian masons was brought to bear on the decorative purity of Arab ornamentation and the splendor of 11th-century Greek Byzantine mosaics. The interior is covered with glittering mosaics and capped by a splendid 10th-century Arab honeycomb stalactite wooden ceiling. Biblical stories blend happily with scenes of Arab life—look for one showing a picnic in a harem—and Norman court pageantry.

Upstairs are the royal apartments, including the Sala di Re Ruggero (King Roger's Hall), decorated with ornate medieval mosaics of hunting scenes—an earlier (1120) secular counterpoint to the religious themes seen elsewhere. During the time of its construction, French, Latin, and Arabic were spoken here, and Arab astronomers and poets exchanged ideas with Latin and Greek scholars in one of the most interesting marriages of culture in the Western world. From Friday to Monday, the Sala is included with entry to the palace or chapel; it sometimes hosts special art exhibits. ✉ *Piazza del Parlamento, Near Palazzo Reale* ☎ *091/7055611* ⊕ *www.federicosecondo.*

org ✈ *€19 Fri.–Mon.; €16 Tues.–Thurs.* ⊗ *Royal Apartments closed Tues.–Thurs.*

Piazza Pretoria
FOUNTAIN | The square's centerpiece, a lavishly decorated fountain with 500 separate pieces of sculpture and an abundance of nude figures, so shocked some Palermitans when it was unveiled in 1575 that it got the nickname "Fountain of Shame." It's even more of a sight when illuminated at night. ✉ *Piazza Pretoria, Quattro Canti.*

Quattro Canti
STREET | The Four Corners is the decorated intersection of two main thoroughfares: Corso Vittorio Emanuele and Via Maqueda. Four rather exhaust-blackened Baroque palaces from Spanish rule meet at concave corners, each with its own fountain and representations of a Spanish ruler, patron saint, and one of the four seasons. Today it's often a venue for buskers and other street performers. ✉ *Palermo.*

San Cataldo
CHURCH | Three striking Saracenic scarlet domes mark this church, built in 1154 during the Norman occupation of Palermo. The church now belongs to the Knights of the Holy Sepulchre and has a spare but intense stone interior. ✉ *Piazza Bellini 3, Kalsa* ☎ *091/6077111* ✈ *€2.50.*

San Giovanni degli Eremiti
CHURCH | Distinguished by its five reddish-orange domes and stripped-clean stone interior, this 12th-century church was built by the Normans on the site of an earlier mosque—one of 200 that once stood in Palermo. The emirs ruled Palermo for nearly two centuries and brought to it their passion for lush gardens and fountains. One is reminded of this while sitting in San Giovanni's delightful cloister of twin half columns, surrounded by palm trees, jasmine, oleander, and citrus trees. ✉ *Via dei Benedettini 14–20, Near Palazzo Reale* ☎ *091/6515019* ✈ *€6.*

Santa Caterina

CHURCH | The walls of this splendid Baroque church (1596) in Piazza Bellini are covered with extremely impressive decorative 17th-century inlays of precious marble. There is also a bakery selling delicacies made using the nuns' recipes. ✉ *Piazza Bellini, Quattro Canti* ☎ *091/2713837* 🌐 *www.monasterosanta-caterina.com* 🎟 *€3; €10 combined ticket, includes church, monastery, and rooftop.*

Teatro Massimo

PERFORMANCE VENUE | Construction of this formidable neoclassical theater, the largest in Italy, was started in 1875 by Giovanni Battista Basile and completed by his son Ernesto in 1897. A reconstruction project started in 1974 ran into severe delays, and the facility remained closed until just before its centenary, in 1997. Its interior is as glorious as ever, but the exterior remains more famous thanks to *The Godfather Part III*, which ended with a famous shooting scene on the theater's steps. Visits, by 30-minute guided tour only, are available in five languages, including English. ✉ *Piazza Verdi 9, at top of Via Maqueda, Olivella* ☎ *091/6053267 tours, 091/8486000, 091/6053580 ticket office* 🌐 *www.teatromassimo.it* 🎟 *€10.*

🍴 Restaurants

Casa del Brodo

$$ | **SICILIAN** | On the edge of the Vucciria, this is one of Palermo's oldest restaurants, dating back to 1890, and still dear to the hearts of locals for its wintertime namesake dish, tortellini *in brodo* (in beef broth), the specialty of the house. There's an extensive antipasto buffet, and you can't go wrong with the *fritella di fave, piselli,*and *carciofi e ricotta* (fried fava beans, peas, artichokes, and ricotta). **Known for:** good choice of meat dishes; tortellini in brodo; large selection of antipasti. [$] *Average main: €15* ✉ *Corso Vittorio Emanuele 175, Vucciria* ☎ *091/321655* 🌐 *www.casadelbrodo.it* 🕓 *Closed Jan., Tues. in Oct.–May, and Sun. in June–Sept.*

★ Comparucci

$ | **PIZZA** | One of Palermo's best modern pizzerias serves delicious Neapolitan pies from a big oven in the open kitchen—the genius is in the crust, which is seared in a matter of seconds. The owners make their money on a quick turnover (so don't expect a long, leisurely meal), but the pizza is delicious and the place often serves until midnight—later than almost any other restaurant in the neighborhood. **Known for:** late-night dining; outdoor seating in summer; pizza, pizza, and more pizza. [$] *Average main: €8* ✉ *Via Messina 36e, Libertà* ☎ *091/6090467* 🌐 *www.comparucci.it* 🕓 *No lunch.*

★ MadoniEAT

$ | **SICILIAN** | Only the finest agricultural produce of the nearby Madonie mountains goes into the simple but fabulous dishes served in this informal eatery attached to the Palazzo Butera art gallery. The frequently changing menu—dependent on the season and what's available from their suppliers—might include chicken breasts in orange sauce and almonds; vegetarian meatballs with ricotta cheese; or sausages braised in red wine with kale. **Known for:** seasonal, fresh, and locally produced ingredients; gourmet sandwiches; convenient for lunch after a visit to Palazzo Butera. [$] *Average main: €11* ✉ *Palazzo Butera, Via Butera 20, Kalsa* ☎ *091/7521749* 🌐 *www.madonieat.com* 🕓 *Closed Mon. and 2 wks in Jan. No dinner.*

★ MEC Restaurant

$$$$ | **SICILIAN** | Here's a novelty for Palermo in the form of a superb modern restaurant located within a museum dedicated to Steve Jobs and Apple products, a surprisingly successful combination; you not only have the ability to revisit ancient IT devices and learn about the history of the tech company, but the food is pretty excellent. Each of the dishes is a revelation, from the sea-urchin ice cream to the ravioli with stewed veal cheek and the lamb sirloin, while vegetarian options are as good as any that Palermo has to offer. **Known for:** restaurant and museum in one gorgeous historic building; attentive service; innovative modern dishes. [$] *Average main: €40* ✉ *Via Vittorio Emanuele 452, Quattro Canti* ☎ *091/9891901* 🌐 *www.mecrestaurant.it* 🕑 *Closed Sun. No lunch.*

Osteria dei Vespri

$$$ | **SICILIAN** | This popular eatery occupies a cozy-but-elegant space on an unheralded piazza in the historic city center and splits its offerings between the winter menu (November–March) with traditional osteria fare, and a special larger tasting menu built around seasonal ingredients for the summer. Local seafood is a big draw here, and the housemade pastas won't disappoint, especially when paired with a selection from the extensive wine list. **Known for:** impressive wine cellar; local seafood; tasting menus with local ingredients. [$] *Average main: €25* ✉ *Piazza Croce dei Vespri 6, Kalsa* ☎ *091/6171631* 🌐 *www.osteriadeivespri.it* 🕑 *No dinner Sun. No lunch Mon. in Nov.–Apr.*

Ristorante Cin Cin

$$ | **SICILIAN** | The Sicilian-born owner of this charming restaurant near Palermo's main shopping street is known for creating lighter and more modern versions of traditional Sicilian dishes, including exemplary pasta with ultrafresh seasonal ingredients and creative takes on seafood-based main dishes. Don't miss the signature dessert, a heavenly semifreddo with flavors like pistachio and cinnamon, chocolate and hazelnut, and Marsala wine and raisin—and perhaps learn some of the secrets with a chef's private cooking class. **Known for:** top-notch cooking classes; delicious semifreddo; modernized Sicilian flavors. [$] *Average main: €16* ✉ *Via Manin 22, Libertà* ☎ *091/6124095* 🌐 *www.ristorantecincin.com* 🕑 *Closed Sun. and Feb. No lunch.*

Coffee and Quick Bites

Antica Focacceria San Francesco

$ | **SICILIAN** | Turn-of-the-20th-century wooden cabinets, marble-top tables, and cast-iron ovens characterize this neighborhood bakery, celebrated for its Sicilian snacks and inexpensive meals. The big pot on the counter holds the delicious regional specialty *pani cà meusa* (boiled calf's spleen with caciocavallo cheese and salt), but the squeamish can opt for chickpea fritters or an enormous arancina (stuffed, fried rice ball). **Known for:** meat and pasta specialties; historic atmosphere; Sicilian street food. [$] *Average main: €12* ✉ *Via A. Paternostro 58, Kalsa* ☎ *091/320264* 🌐 *www.anticafocacceria.it* 🕑 *Closed Jan. and Feb.*

Cappadonia

$ | **ICE CREAM** | **FAMILY** | After experiencing the cozy but basic trattorias located down Palermo's twisting alleyways, take a sweet break at this modern gelateria along the main drag, which serves exceptional gourmet ice cream. The flavors change with the seasons, but don't miss the tangerine sorbetto that bursts with sweet citrus tang or the classic zabaglione custard. **Known for:** central location; delicious ice cream; seasonal flavors. [$] *Average main: €3* ✉ *Via Vittorio Emanuele 401, Palermo* ☎ *392/5689784, 392/5759351* 🌐 *cappadonia.it* 🕑 *Closed Nov.–Feb.*

Pani Cà Meusa

$ | **SANDWICHES** | A civic institution facing Palermo's old fishing port, this standing-room-only joint has been serving its titular calf's spleen sandwich for more than 70 years. The original owner's grandsons still produce this local specialty sprinkled with a bit of salt and some lemon and served with or without cheese to a buzzing crowd of Palermo's well-weathered elders. **Known for:** no seating; a bit of Sicilian history; calf's spleen sandwich that might be the best in town. [$] *Average main: €2* ✉ *Via Cala 62, Porta Carbone, Kalsa* ☎ *091/323433* 🕑 *Closed Sun.*

Hotels

★ Eurostars Centrale Palace

$ | **HOTEL** | A stone's throw from Palermo's main historic sites, this is the only hotel in the heart of the old town that was once a stately private palace; built in 1717, it weaves old-world charm with modern comfort. **Pros:** great rooftop restaurant; comfortable rooms; location in the center of it all. **Cons:** some rooms have no views; very limited parking; showing its age a bit. [$] *Rooms from: €116* ✉ *Corso Vittorio Emanuele 327, Quattro Canti* ☎ *091/336666* 🌐 *www.eurostarscentralepalace.com* 🛏 *104 rooms* 🍴 *Free Breakfast.*

Grand Hotel Piazza Borsa

$$ | **HOTEL** | Cleverly converted from three historic buildings—a bank, a palazzo, and a monastery—this hotel is ideally located in a quiet corner of the old town, just off the central axis of Corso Vittorio Emanuele. **Pros:** quiet but central location; wellness center with fitness equipment, rare for Sicily hotels; interesting architecture. **Cons:** building feels a bit sterile; some noise issues in rooms; somewhat indifferent staff. [$] *Rooms from: €145* ✉ *Via dei Cartari 18, Kalsa* ☎ *091/320075* 🌐 *piazzaborsa.it* 🛏 *127 rooms* 🍴 *Free Breakfast.*

Hotel Principe di Villafranca

$$ | **HOTEL** | Contemporary art mixed with antique furnishings, creamy marble floors, and vaulted ceilings evoke a luxurious private home in a residential area near Palermo's glitzy shopping district. **Pros:** appealing design; quiet, center-adjacent location; well-maintained building. **Cons:** immediate surroundings lack character; car park has just four spaces; some rooms and bathrooms on the small side. [$] *Rooms from: €148* ✉ *Via G. Turrisi Colonna 4, Libertà* ☎ *091/6118523* 🌐 *www.principedivillafranca.it* 🛏 *32 rooms* 🍴 *Free Breakfast.*

★ Le Terrazze

$ | **B&B/INN** | Although just steps from the bustling Cattedrale area, complete calm envelops this small, beautifully restored B&B, named for its five lush roof terraces, all with sublime views. **Pros:** convenient location; period-style rooms; in summer, breakfast is served on the glorious rooftop. **Cons:** Wi-Fi sometimes patchy; books up quickly; parking can be difficult. [$] *Rooms from: €110* ✉ *Via Pietro Novelli 14, Albergheria* ☎ *091/6520866, 320/4328567* 🌐 *www.leterrazzebb.it* 💳 *No credit cards* 🛏 *2 rooms* 🍴 *Free Breakfast.*

Massimo Plaza Hotel

$$ | **HOTEL** | Small and select, this hotel enjoys one of Palermo's best locations—opposite the Teatro Massimo, on the border of the old and new towns—and has guest rooms that are spacious, comfortably furnished, and well insulated from the noise on pedestrianized Via Maqueda. **Pros:** central location; tasty breakfast made to order; low-season bargains. **Cons:** cheaper rooms have no views; in pedestrian zone, so vehicles have to keep their distance; 21 steps (no elevator) up to the rooms. [$] *Rooms from: €191* ✉ *Via Maqueda 437, Olivella* ☎ *091/325657* 🌐 *www.massimoplazahotel.com* 🛏 *11 rooms* 🍴 *Free Breakfast.*

★ Palazzo Pantaleo

$ | **B&B/INN** | Accessed from a quiet courtyard situated between Palermo's two great theaters, with large, airy rooms and a charming host, this top-floor apartment is part of a beautifully renovated palazzo dating from the mid-19th century. **Pros:** pleasant and welcoming host; free private parking; very close to airport bus stop. **Cons:** a little hard to find; occasional noise intrusion from other guests; often booked up. [$] *Rooms from: €110* ✉ *Via Ruggero Settimo 74, Libertà* ☎ *335/7006091* 🌐 *www.palazzopantaleo.it* 🛏 *7 rooms* 🍴 *Free Breakfast.*

★ Villa Igiea

$$$$ | HOTEL | Although recently renovated, this grande dame set in a private tropical garden at the edge of the bay—a local landmark for a century—still maintains a somewhat faded aura of luxury and comfort and retains its essential character. **Pros:** secluded setting; free shuttle to city center in the summer; historic building with lots of atmosphere. **Cons:** a bit far from Palermo attractions; no amenities in the nearby area; price range out of reach for most. $ *Rooms from: €680* ✉ *Salita Belmonte 43, Palermo* ☎ *091/2570050* ⊕ *villa-igiea.com* ⊙ *Closed early Nov.–mid-Mar.* ↩ *100 rooms* ¶⊙¶ *Free Breakfast.*

Nightlife

BARS AND CAFÉS

★ Bocum Fuoco

COCKTAIL LOUNGES | This multilevel cocktail bar between the Vucciria market and the marina is serious about mixology and has created a dedicated oasis in the city's trendiest area. Linger over complex cocktails while lounging on vintage chairs under sparkling chandeliers, all while rubbing elbows with Palermo's cool crowd as records spin on the retro turntable in the corner. A short menu of pasta, meat, and seafood dishes is also available. ✉ *Via dei Cassari 6, Vucciria* ☎ *091/332009* ⊕ *www.bocum.it.*

Santa Monica

PUBS | Immensely popular with the twenty- and thirtysomething crowd, who belly up to the bar for pizza, crepes, and excellent German-style draft beer, this pub is also a good place to watch televised soccer. ✉ *Via E. Parisi 7, Libertà* ☎ *091/324735* ⊕ *www.santamonicaristorante.it.*

Performing Arts

CONCERTS AND OPERA

★ Teatro Massimo

CONCERTS | As the biggest theater in Italy, Teatro Massimo is truly larger than life. Concerts and operas are presented throughout the year, though in summer concerts are usually held outdoors. An opera at the Massimo is an unforgettable Sicilian experience. ✉ *Piazza Verdi, at top of Via Maqueda, Palermo* ☎ *091/6053580 tickets, 091/8486000 general information, 091/6053267 tours* ⊕ *www. teatromassimo.it* 🎟 *Performances from €22, tours €8.*

PUPPET SHOWS

Figli d'Arte Cuticchio Association

PUPPET SHOWS | FAMILY | Palermo's tradition of puppet theater holds an appeal for children and adults alike, and street artists often perform outside the Teatro Massimo in summer. One of the most celebrated examples of the folk tradition is performed by the Figli d'Arte Cuticchio association, which hosts classic puppet shows from September to June. ✉ *Via Bara all'Olivella 95, Olivella* ☎ *091/323400* ⊕ *www.figlidartecuticchio. com* 🎟 *€10.*

Shopping

Ballarò Market

MARKET | Wind your way through the Albergheria district and this historic market, where the Saracens did their shopping in the 11th century—joined by the Normans in the 12th. The market's name is said to come from nearby Monreale, named Bahlara when Arab traders resided there, and it remains faithful to their original commerce of fruit, vegetables, and grain. These days the stalls are dotted with bars and outdoor restaurants where you can sample the produce, but the market has lost none of its authenticity—just keep a close eye on your belongings in the crowd. And go early: the action dies out by 4 pm most days.

✉ *Ballarò Market, Albergheria* ✛ *Between La Martorana and Quattro Canti.*

Enoteca Picone

WINE/SPIRITS | The best wineshop in town has been family run for four generations and stocks a fantastic selection of Sicilian and national wines. Although service can be curt, you can taste a selection of wines by the glass in the front of the store. There are tables in the back, where meats and cheeses are also served. ✉ *Via Marconi 36, Libertà* ☎ *091/331300* ⊕ *www.enotecapicone.it.*

Pasticceria Alba

FOOD | One of the most famous sweets shops in Italy, this is the place to find pastry favorites like cannoli and cassata siciliana, as well as excellent gelato in summer. There is also an on-site restaurant pizzeria. ✉ *Piazza Don Bosco 7/C, off Via della Libertà near La Favorita Park, Libertà* ☎ *091/309016* ⊕ *www.baralbadonbosco.it.*

Vucciria Market

MARKET | It's easy to see how this market got its name—*vucciria* translates to "voices" or "hubbub." Though now just as frequented by tourists as it is by locals, Palermo's most established outdoor market, in the heart of the old town, is a maze of side streets around Piazza San Domenico, where hawkers deliver incessant chants from behind stands brimming with mounds of olives, blood oranges, fennel, and long-stem artichokes. Morning is the best time to see the market in full swing, but it takes on more of a street food atmosphere at night, when no-name bars open to sell cheap cocktails to the crowds gathering around the smoking grills that are wheeled outside after dark. ✉ *Vucciria Market, Vucciria.*

Monreale

10 km (6 miles) southwest of Palermo.

Only a short drive or bus ride from Palermo, the sleepy town of Monreale is well worth the effort of a visit just to see the spectacular gold mosaics inside its Duomo. Try to arrive early in the morning or later in the afternoon to avoid the tour bus hordes.

GETTING HERE AND AROUND

You can reach Monreale on frequent AMAT buses that depart from Palermo's Piazza Indipendenza or on AST buses from Piazza Giulio Cesare, outside the central station. From Palermo, drivers can follow Corso Calatafimi west, though the going can be slow. Park in the car park a little way outside Monreale's center.

 Sights

Cloister

RELIGIOUS BUILDING | The lovely cloister of the abbey adjacent to the Duomo was built at the same time as the church but enlarged in the 14th century. The beautiful enclosure is surrounded by 216 intricately carved double columns, every other one decorated in a unique glass mosaic pattern. Afterward, don't forget to walk behind the cloister to the belvedere, with stunning panoramic views over the Conca d'Oro (Golden Conch) valley toward Palermo. ✉ *Piazza del Duomo, Monreale* ☎ *091/7489995* 🎫 *€6; €10 with Duomo.*

★ Duomo

CHURCH | Monreale's splendid cathedral is lavishly executed with mosaics depicting events from the Old and New Testaments. It's a glorious fusion of Eastern and Western influences, widely regarded as the finest example of Norman architecture in Sicily. After the Norman conquest of Sicily, the new princes showcased their ambitions through monumental building projects. William II (1154–89) built the church complex with a cloister and palace between 1174 and 1185, employing Byzantine craftsmen.

The major attraction is the 68,220 square feet of glittering gold mosaics decorating the cathedral interior. Christ Pantocrator dominates the apse area; the nave contains narratives of the Creation; and scenes from the life of Christ adorn the walls of the aisles and the transept. The painted wooden ceiling dates from 1816–37 while the roof commands a great view (a reward for climbing 172 stairs). The wood and metal organ, the only one in Europe with six keyboards and 10,000 pipes, was restored after lightning damage in 2015, and played by Mick Jagger on a private visit in 2021.

Bonnano Pisano's bronze doors, completed in 1186, depict 42 biblical scenes and are considered among the most important medieval artifacts still in existence. Barisano da Trani's 42 panels on the north door, dating from 1179, present saints and evangelists. ⊠ *Piazza del Duomo, Monreale* ⊕ *www.monrealeduomo.it* ⊠ *€4; €10 with Cloister.*

Segesta

70 km (43 miles) northeast of Corleone, 85 km (53 miles) southwest of Palermo.

Segesta is the site of one of Sicily's most impressive temples, constructed on the side of a barren windswept hill overlooking a valley of giant fennel. Virtually intact today, the temple is considered by some to be finer in its proportions and setting than any other Doric temple left standing.

GETTING HERE AND AROUND

At least four Tarantola e Cuffaro buses travel from Trapani to Segesta every day but Sunday. About as many trains from Palermo and Trapani stop at the Segesta–Tempio station, a 20-minute uphill walk

from Segesta. The site is easily reached via the A29 autostrada.

BUS CONTACT Tarantola e Cuffaro.
☎ *0924/31020* ⊕ *www.tarantolacuffaro.it.*

Sights

★ **Tempio Dorico** (*Doric Temple*)
RUINS | Segesta's imposing temple was actually started in the 5th century BC by the Elymians, who may have been refugees from Troy—or at least non-Greeks, since it seems they often sided with Carthage. In any case, the style of the temple is in many ways Greek, but it was never finished; the walls and roof never materialized, and the columns were never fluted.

Wear comfortable shoes, as you need to park your car in the lot at the bottom of the hill and walk about five minutes up to the temple. If you're up for a longer hike, a little more than 1 km (½ mile) away near the top of the hill are the remains of a fine theater with impressive views, especially at sunset, of the plains and the Bay of Castellammare (there's also a shuttle bus to the theater for €2 that leaves every 15–30 minutes). Concerts and plays are staged here in summer. ⊠ *Calatafimi-Segesta* ☎ *0924/952356* ⊕ *www.parcodisegesta.com* ⊠ *€6.*

Erice

38 km (24 miles) south of San Vito Lo Capo, 15 km (9 miles) northeast of Trapani.

Perched 2,450 feet above sea level, Erice is an enchanting medieval mountaintop aerie of palaces, fountains, and cobblestone streets. Shaped like an equilateral triangle, the town was the ancient landmark Eryx, dedicated to Aphrodite (Venus). When the Normans arrived, they built a castle on Monte San Giuliano, where today there's a lovely public park with benches and belvederes offering

striking views of Trapani, the Egadi Islands offshore, and, on a very clear day, Cape Bon and the Tunisian coast. Because of Erice's elevation, clouds conceal much of the view for most of winter. Sturdy shoes (for the cobblestones) and something warm to wear are recommended.

GETTING HERE AND AROUND

Make your approach via Trapani, which is on the A29 autostrada and well connected by bus and train with Marsala and Palermo. In late March to early January, a *funivia* runs from the outskirts of Trapani to Erice (Monday 2–9, Tuesday to Friday 8:30–8, weekends 9:30–8:30; extended hours from late June to mid-September; see ⊕ *www.funiviaerice.it* for details). Going by car or bus from Trapani takes around 40 minutes. By car, take the route via Valderice, not the "direct route," to avoid an extremely winding and steep country road. Buses depart from the terminal on Trapani's Piazza Malta.

 Restaurants

Monte San Giuliano

$$ | SICILIAN | At this traditional restaurant located on a side street near the main piazza, you can sit on a tree-lined patio overlooking the sea or in the white-walled dining room and munch on free panelle (chickpea fritters) while waiting for your main dish, which will be served tableside, spooned from the cooking pots to your plate by the friendly staff. The pastas are exemplary (there are even gluten-free options), but the specialty is the seafood couscous, served with a bowl of fish broth on the side. **Known for:** extensive and interesting wine list; charming setting; great pasta and couscous. $ *Average main: €16* ✉ *Vicolo San Rocco 7, Erice* ☎ *334/1396763, 0923/869595* ⊕ *www.montesangiuliano. it* ⊗ *Closed Mon., 6 wks in Jan. and Feb., and 4 wks in Nov. and Dec.*

☕ Coffee and Quick Bites

★ La Tonda Fritta

$ | SICILIAN | Arancine—fried rice balls— are ubiquitous all over Sicily, but rarely do you find them prepared while you wait or offered in such a range as in this little snack shop near Porta Trapani. The menu lists more than 35 varieties, which include swordfish, smoked salmon, and curry fillings, as well as vegetarian and vegan options. **Known for:** more than 35 types of arancine; fast service; great snacks on the go. $ *Average main: €3* ✉ *Via Vittorio Emanuele 100, Erice* ☎ *328/1378708* ⊕ *www.la-tonda-fritta. jimdosite.com* ⊗ *Closed Nov.–Feb.*

Pasticceria Grammatico

$ | BAKERY | Fans of Sicilian sweets make a beeline for this place, run by Maria Grammatico, who gained international fame with *Bitter Almonds,* her life story of growing up in a convent orphanage cowritten with Mary Taylor Simeti. Her almond-paste creations are works of art, molded into striking shapes, including dolls and animals. **Known for:** uniquely shaped desserts; nice views; delicious sweets. $ *Average main: €5* ✉ *Via Vittorio Emanuele 14, Erice* ☎ *0923/869390* ⊕ *www.mariagrammatico.it.*

🛏 Hotels

Hotel Elimo

$ | HOTEL | Like the town of Erice itself, the Hotel Elimo is old-fashioned and yet full of charm; eccentric knickknacks and artwork fill the lobby, and the homey guest rooms are all different, many boasting terraces with views of either the cobblestone streets or the valleys below (when they're not shrouded in clouds). **Pros:** convenient location; great on-site restaurant; lots of character. **Cons:** noise in some rooms; small bathrooms; rooms can feel a bit musty. $ *Rooms from: €85* ✉ *Via Vittorio Emanuele 75, Erice* ☎ *0923/869377* ⊕ *www.hotelelimo.*

it ☾ *Closed Jan. and Feb.* ⇱ *21 rooms* ⎢◎⎢ *Free Breakfast.*

Moderno

$ | **HOTEL** | This delightful hotel has a creaky old feel to it, but that's part of the charm—the lobby area, scattered with books, magazines, and tchotchkes, calls to mind an elderly relative's living room; but the rooms themselves are simple, light, and comfortable. **Pros:** central location; well-regarded restaurant; great rooftop terrace. **Cons:** old-fashioned feel not for everyone; street-facing rooms can be noisy; very modest rooms. Ⓢ *Rooms from: €90* ✉ *Via Vittorio Emanuele 67, Erice* ☎ *0923/869300* ⊕ *www.hotelmodernoerice.it* ⇱ *40 rooms* ⎢◎⎢ *Free Breakfast.*

 # Shopping

Ceramica Ericina

CERAMICS | Among Italians, Erice is known for the quality and delicate floral designs of its majolica ceramics, well represented in this ceramics store off Piazza San Domenico, one of the best in town. ✉ *Via Gian Filippa Guarnotti 20, Erice* ☎ *0923/869126.*

Trapani

11 km (7 miles) southwest of Erice, 30 km (19 miles) northwest of Segesta, 75 km (47 miles) southwest of Palermo.

The provincial capital of Trapani (both province and city share the same name) was originally founded by the ancient Elymians, who claimed descent from the Trojans, as a port for Eryx (Erice). Its Greek name, Drepanon, meaning "sickle," refers to the long, curving limb of land trailing into the sea on which the city is built. Much of its later wealth was founded on the salt pans lying to the south that are still active today.

Although the outskirts of town are uninspiring, Trapani's old town has a busy, buzzy feel to it, especially in the evenings when families crowd the main, pedestrianized Corso Vittorio Emanuele and bars and restaurants spill onto the street. Via Garibaldi, linking the old and new districts, is also a busy shopping and promenading thoroughfare. North of the hydrofoil port, the old Jewish quarter is a warren of somewhat down-at-heel alleys centered on the 16th-century Palazzo della Giudecca on Via della Giudecca.

Linked to Palermo and Mazara del Vallo by autostrada A20, the town has its own airport and is also an important nexus for trips to Erice, Mozia, San Vito Lo Capo, and the Egadi Islands.

GETTING HERE AND AROUND

Trapani's airport is located in Birgi, 15 km (9 miles) to the south. The town is linked to Palermo by the A29 autostrada and by infrequent slow trains. Most using public transport travel on the much faster bus services, which all terminate at Piazza Malta, though fast buses from the airport, Palermo, Palermo airport, and Agrigento also make a stop at the ferry and hydrofoil port.

With much of the old town closed to traffic and available parking spots hard to find, drivers should take advantage of the large and inexpensive car park on Piazza Vittorio Emanuele, at the bottom of Via Garibaldi. The old town is easy to negotiate on foot, though visitors to the Museo Pepoli and Santuario Annunziata should either drive or make use of the frequent city bus services.

Tickets to the Egadi islands can be picked up from the ticket offices at the port or from the Egatour agency, which also offers island tours, tickets for Pantelleria, and bus tickets.

AIRPORT CONTACT Trapani–Birgi Airport. ✉ *Trapani* ☎ *0923/610111* ⊕ *www.airgest.it.*

Sights

Museo Regionale Pepoli

ART MUSEUM | Trapani's foremost museum collection is located in a former Carmelite monastery that was attached to the important religious site of Santuario dell'Annunziata. The art sections take in some excellent examples of medieval and Renaissance art, including statuary by Antonello Gagini and a painting by Titian. Among the archaeological exhibits is a selection of low-key finds from Mozia and Selinunte. There's also a guillotine from 1800, and a good collection of memorabilia from Garibaldi's Sicilian campaign against the Bourbons in 1860.

The usual entrance to the museum is in the Villa Pepoli public garden; when this is closed enter from Via Madonna, behind the garden. ✉ *Via Conte Agostino Pepoli 180, Trapani* ☎ *0923/553269* 🎫 *€6* 🕒 *Closed Mon.*

Restaurants

Ai Lumi

$ | **SICILIAN** | This popular restaurant on the pedestrianized Corso Vittorio Emanuele occupies some former stables, though the modern art on the walls and its candlelit tables evoke far more romantic associations. Dishes are predominantly local and sea-based, like a delicious fish couscous, *ghiotta di pesce misto* (mixed seafood in a rich sauce of tomatoes, olives, and capers), and swordfish involtini (roulades) served with orange. **Known for:** quirky interiors; fast service; delicious local dishes. [$] *Average main: €14* ✉ *Corso Vittorio Emanuele 75, Trapani* ☎ *0923/872418.*

Coffee and Quick Bites

★ **Meno Tredici**

$ | **ICE CREAM** | **FAMILY** | There's a regular trickle of locals to this gelateria conveniently located opposite the hydrofoil port. Most opt for the local favorite: ice cream in a brioche with a couple of wafer biscuits poking out. **Known for:** tangy ice creams; tasty desserts; thirst-quenching granitas. [$] *Average main: €3* ✉ *Via Staiti 61, Trapani* ☎ *0923/1781797* 🌐 *www.gelateriamenotredici.it.*

Hotels

Room of Andrea

$$ | **HOTEL** | A 19th-century palazzo is now home to this hotel opposite a public garden in central Trapani, which provides pampering accommodation in swish surroundings. **Pros:** characterful surroundings and decor; small rooftop pool; good location. **Cons:** better rooms are overpriced in high season; no hotel parking; most rooms lack much of a view. [$] *Rooms from: €139* ✉ *Viale Regina Margherita 31, Trapani* ☎ *0923/365728* 🌐 *www.roomofandrea.it* 🛏 *45 rooms* 🍴 *Free Breakfast.*

Marsala

30 km (19 miles) south of Trapani.

Marsala is readily associated with its world-famous, richly colored eponymous fortified wine, and your main reason for stopping may be to visit some of the many wineries in the area and sample the product. But this quiet seaside town, together with the nearby island of Mozia, was also once the main Carthaginian base in Sicily: it was from here that Carthage fought for supremacy over the island against Greece and Rome, leaving behind intriguing archaeological sites. In 1773, a British merchant named John Woodhouse happened upon the town and discovered that the wine here was as good as the port long imported by the British from Portugal. Two other wine merchants, Whitaker and Ingram, rushed in, and by 1800 Marsala was exporting wine all over the British Empire.

Later in the 18th century, Marsala played a significant role in the Risorgimento, the movement for Italian liberty. It was here that the swashbuckling national hero Giuseppe Garibaldi landed in 1860 with his thousand Redshirts to begin the campaign to oust the Bourbons from southern Italy.

GETTING HERE AND AROUND
Buses and trains from Palermo, Trapani, and Castelvetrano stop in Marsala. Drivers can take the coastal SS115.

VISITOR INFORMATION
CONTACT Marsala Tourism Office. ✉ *Via XI Maggio 100,* ☎ *0923/714097* ⊕ *www. turismocomunemarsala.com.*

Sights

★ Donnafugata Winery
WINERY | A respected Sicilian wine producer, the 160-year-old Donnafugata Winery is open for tastings and tours of its *cantina* (wine cellar); reservations are required and can be made online or by phone. It's an interesting look at the wine-making process in Sicily, and it ends with a sampling of several whites and reds, an optional food pairing, and a chance to buy a bottle. Don't miss the delicious, full-bodied red Mille e Una Notte, and the famous Ben Ryè Passito di Pantelleria, a sweet dessert wine made from dried grapes. ✉ *Via Sebastiano Lipari 18, Marsala* ☎ *0923/724245* ⊕ *www.donnafugata.it* 🎫 *Tastings from €24* 🕓 *Closed Sun.*

★ Marsala Salt Pans
SCENIC DRIVE | Driving along the flat and winding coast road north of Marsala, you'll soon come across the extraordinary series of salt pans glistening in the shallows of Sicily's largest lagoon, the Stagnone di Marsala. The shallow depth of the lagoon, ranging from 2 to 6 feet, has made it perfect for the production of salt, and it has been put to this purpose since Phoenician times. The sheer flatness of the scene is varied only by the conical heaps of salt and a scattering of the disused windmills once used to supply power. The scene is still and quiet most of the time, but you'll sometimes see pockets of activity, with full wheelbarrows of salt being hauled to the conveyor belts that create the mounds. The stacks of earthenware tiles you'll see everywhere are used to weigh down the salt to prevent it being from blown away by gusts of wind. It's an extremely photogenic tableau, with the light changing through the day and Mozia and the Egadi archipelago looming through the haze.

The narrow coastal road is one-way for much of its length, and the cycle track running alongside it enables the area to be comfortably toured on two wheels. ✉ *Marsala.*

Museo Archeologico Baglio Anselmi
HISTORY MUSEUM | A sense of Marsala's past as a Carthaginian stronghold is captured by the well-preserved Punic warship displayed in this museum, along with some of the amphorae and other artifacts recovered from the wreck. The vessel, which was probably sunk during the great sea battle that ended the First Punic War in 241 BC, was dredged up from the mud near the Egadi Islands in the 1970s. There's also a good display of maritime and archaeological finds, as well as some Roman ruins with mosaics just beyond the museum's doors. ✉ *Lungomare Boeo 30, Marsala* ☎ *0923/952535* 🎫 *€4* 🕓 *Closed Mon.*

Selinunte

35 km (22 miles) southeast of Mazara del Vallo, 114 km (71 miles) southwest of Palermo.

Numerous ruined Greek temples perch on a high, undulating plateau overlooking the Mediterranean at Selinunte (or Selinus). The town is named after a local variety of wild celery (*Apium graveolens* or *petroselinum*) that in spring grows in profusion among the ruined columns and overturned capitals. Although the nearest village of Marinella di Selinunte is a rather unremarkable seaside resort, there are some very nice places to stay just inland as well as some good beaches, including Porto Palo and the wild dunes of the Foce del Belice nature reserve. Although many travelers treat Selinunte as a quick stop between the temples of Segesta and Agrigento, the area makes a very pleasant holiday base.

GETTING HERE AND AROUND

Selinunte is a half-hour drive from Mazara del Vallo, and an 85-minute drive from Agrigento, which means it can be easily visited via car as a day trip from any of the towns south along the coast. Getting here by public transport is trickier. There are five buses daily to Selinunte from the town of Castelvetrano, 11 km (7 miles) north, which is itself accessible from Palermo by bus and train.

Sights

★ Greek Temple Ruins

RUINS | Selinunte was one of the most important colonies of ancient Greece, recently discovered to have been home to the largest industrial quarter found in any ancient European city. Founded in the 7th century BCE, the city became the rich and prosperous rival of Segesta, making its money on trade and manufacturing ceramics. When in 409 BCE Segesta turned to the Carthaginians for help in vanquishing their rival, the Carthaginians sent an army to destroy Selinunte. The temples were demolished, the city was razed, and 16,000 of Selinunte's inhabitants were slaughtered. Archaeologists recently discovered pots with the remains of food inside, proof that some were in the middle of eating when the attackers arrived. The remains of Selinunte are in many ways unchanged from the day of its sacking—burn marks still scar the Greek columns, and much of the site still lies in rubble at its exact position of collapse. The original complex held seven temples scattered over two sites separated by a harbor. Of the seven, only one—reconstructed in 1958—is whole. **■ TIP→ This is a large archaeological site, so you might make use of the private navetta (shuttle) to save a bit of walking. Alternatively, if you have a car, you can visit the first temples close to the ticket office on foot and then drive westward to the farther site. Be prepared to show your ticket at various stages.** ✉ *SS115, Marinella Selinunte* ✣ *13 km (8 miles) southeast of Castelvetrano* ☎ *0924/46277* 🎟 *€6.*

Restaurants

★ Da Vittorio

$$ | SEAFOOD | Located right on the beach at Porto Palo, Da Vittorio is something of a local legend, highly regarded and much loved by everyone from wine and olive oil makers to celebrating families. The focus is on fresh fish and seafood, with pasta for the first course, and grilled fish for a second, all enhanced with traditional Sicilian flavors such as capers, almonds, and wild fennel. **Known for:** open all year long; creative seafood on the beach; neighborhood institution since the 1960s. [$] *Average main: €16* ✉ *Via Friuli Venezia Giulia 9, Marinella Selinunte* ☎ *0925/78381* 🌐 *www.ristorantevittorio.it* ⏲ *Closed mid-Dec.–mid-Jan.*

Agrigento

8 km (5 miles) northeast of Porto Empedocle, 128 km (80 miles) south of Palermo.

Agrigento owes its fame almost exclusively to its stunning ancient Greek temples—though it was also the birthplace of playwright Luigi Pirandello (1867–1936) and the setting for the Montelusa scenes of Andrea Camilleri's Inspector Montalbano books. For fans of the books in particular, the old town is an evocative place for a wander, culminating in a visit to nuns for an almond pastry and the fascinating Museo di Santo Spirito. There is much to fascinate and intrigue in the area around Agrigento, too, both in the rural hinterland and along the coast south to Licata, scene of the Allied landings of 1943.

GETTING HERE AND AROUND

If you're driving, take the A19 autostrada to Caltanissetta, follow the SS640 to Agrigento. Motorists can also access the town easily via the coastal SS115 and, from Palermo, by the SS189. Buses and trains run from Enna, Palermo, and Catania; both bus and train stations are centrally located.

VISITOR INFORMATION

CONTACT Agrigento Tourism Office. ✉ *Via Empedocle 73,* ☎ *0922/20391* ⊕ *www. visitsicily.info.*

 Sights

Monastero di Santo Spirito

RELIGIOUS BUILDING | First built in 1299, these cloisters and courtyard, up the hill above the Valle dei Templi near the modern city, are open to the public. However, most visitors stop by the adjacent abbey for a treat and tour of the church, so be sure to ring the doorbell and try the chewy almond cookies. On special occasions, there may be *kus-kus dolce*—a sweet dessert dish made from pistachio nuts, almonds, and chocolate—that the Cistercian nuns learned from Tunisian servants back in the 13th century. ✉ *Cortile Santo Spirito 9, off Via Porcello, Agrigento* ☎ *0922/1552737, 349/4792401* ⊕ *www.monasterosspirito.wixsite.com/ agrigento.*

★ Valle dei Templi

RUINS | The temples of Agrigento, a UNESCO World Heritage site, are considered to be some of the finest and best-preserved Greek temples in the world. Whether you first come upon the valley in the early morning light, bathed by golden floodlights after sunset, or in

January and February when the valley is awash in the fragrant blossoms of thousands of almond trees, it's easy to see why Akragas (Agrigento's Greek name) was celebrated by the poet Pindar as "the most beautiful city built by mortals." The temples were originally erected as a showpiece to flaunt the Greek victory over Carthage, and they have since withstood a later sack by the Carthaginians, mishandling by the Romans, and neglect by Christians and Muslims.

Although getting to, from, and around the dusty ruins of the Valle dei Templi is pretty easy, this important archaeological zone still deserves several hours. The temples are a bit spread out, but the valley is all completely walkable and usually toured on foot. However, since there's only one hotel (Villa Athena) that's close enough to walk to the ruins, you'll most likely have to drive to reach the site. The best place to park is at the entrance to the temple area. The site, which opens at 8:30 am, is divided into western and eastern sections, linked by a bridge. The best way to see them both is to park at the Temple of Juno entrance and walk downhill through the eastern zone, across the footbridge into the western zone, and then return back uphill, so that you see everything again but from a different angle and in a different light. The best time to go is a couple of hours before sunset, although if you are in Agrigento in high summer you might want to consider a night visit; the gates open a short while before sunset, with the temples floodlit as night falls.

You'll want to spend time seeing the eight pillars of the Tempio di Ercole (Temple of Hercules) that make up Agrigento's oldest temple complex, dating from the 6th century BC. The Tempio di Giunone (Temple of Juno) at the top of the hill is perhaps the most beautiful of all the temples, partly in ruins and commanding an exquisite view of the valley (especially at sunset). The low wall of mighty stone blocks in front of it was an altar on which animals were sacrificed as an offering to the goddess. Next down the hill is the almost perfectly complete Tempio della Concordia (Temple of Concord), perhaps the best-preserved Greek temple currently in existence, thanks to having been converted into a Christian church in the 6th century, and restored back to being a temple in the 18th century. Below it is the valley's oldest surviving temple, the Temple of Hercules, with nine of its original 38 columns standing, the rest tumbled around like a child's upended bag of building bricks.

Continuing over the pedestrian bridge, you reach the Tempio di Giove (Temple of Jupiter). Meant to be the largest temple in the complex, it was never completed, but it would have occupied approximately the site of a soccer field. It was an unusual temple, with half columns backing into a continuous wall, and 25-foot-high telamon, or male figures, inserted in the gaps in between. A couple of the telamon have been roughly reassembled horizontally on the ground near the temple. Beyond is the so-called Temple of Castor and Pollux, prettily picturesque, but actually a folly created in the 19th century from various columns and architectural fragments. ✉ *Zona Archeologica, Via dei Templi, Agrigento* ☎ *0922/1839996* 🌐 *www.parcovalledeitempli.it* 🎫 *€10, €14 with museum (free 1st Sun. of month).*

🍴 Restaurants

★ Il Re di Girgenti
$$ | **SICILIAN** | You might not expect to find an ultramodern—even hip—place to dine within a few minutes' drive of Agrigento's ancient temples, yet Il Re di Girgenti offers up pleasing versions of Sicilian classics in a trendy, country-chic atmosphere (think funky black-and-white tile floors mixed with shelves lined with old-fashioned crockery) popular with young locals. The thoughtful wine list offers good prices on both local wines and those from throughout Sicily. **Known for:** delightful wine selections; contemporary setting with lovely views; Sicilian dishes with a twist. [$] *Average main: €22* ✉ *Via Panoramica dei Templi 51, Agrigento* ☎ *0922/401388* 🌐 *www.ilredigirgenti.it* 🕓 *Closed Tues.*

Trattoria dei Templi
$$ | **SICILIAN** | Along a road on the way up to Agrigento proper from the temple area, this vaulted family-run restaurant serves up tasty traditional food, namely daily house-made pasta specials and plenty of fresh fish dishes, all prepared with Sicilian flair. Your best bet is to ask the advice of brothers Giuseppe and Simone, the owners and chief orchestrators in the restaurant, who can also help select a Sicilian wine to pair with your meal. **Known for:** good choice of local wines; fresh fish; exceptional antipasti, like carpaccio of cernia (grouper). [$] *Average main: €18* ✉ *Via Panoramica dei Templi 15, Agrigento* ☎ *0922/403110* 🕓 *Closed Sun.*

🛏 Hotels

Foresteria Baglio della Luna
$$ | **HOTEL** | In the valley below the temples, fiery sunsets and moonlight cast a glow over the ancient 12th-century watchtower at the center of this farmhouse-hotel complex, which is composed of stone buildings surrounding a peaceful geranium- and ivy-filled courtyard and the garden beyond. **Pros:** quiet setting; top-notch restaurant; pretty gardens. **Cons:** location a bit remote; no pool; hotel a little dark inside. [$] *Rooms from: €145* ✉ *Via Serafino Amabile Guastella 1, Agrigento* ☎ *0922/511061* 🌐 *www.bagliodellaluna.com* 🕓 *Closed Dec.–Feb.* 🛏 *23 rooms* 🍽 *Free Breakfast.*

★ Villa Athena
$$$$ | **HOTEL** | The 18th-century Villa Athena, updated into a sleek, luxurious place to stay, complete with gorgeous manicured gardens and swimming

pool, holds a privileged position directly overlooking the Temple of Concordia, a 10-minute walk away—an amazing sight both during the day and when it's lit up at night. **Pros:** unbeatable location for the Valle dei Templi, with phenomenal temple views; plenty of free parking; good restaurant and spa. **Cons:** lack of information on local attractions; very expensive compared to other area options; lobby on the small side. $ *Rooms from: €420* ✉ *Via Passeggiata Archeologica 33, Agrigento* ☎ *0922/596288* 🌐 *www.hotelvillaathena.it* 🛏 *27 rooms* 🍴 *Free Breakfast.*

Enna

33 km (21 miles) northwest of Piazza Armerina.

Deep in Sicily's interior, the fortress city of Enna (altitude 2,844 feet) commands exceptional views of the surrounding rolling plains, and, in the distance, Mt. Etna. It's the highest provincial capital in Italy and, thanks to its central location, is nicknamed the "Navel of Sicily." Virtually unknown by tourists and relatively untouched by industrialization, this lively town charms and prospers in a distinctly old-fashioned Sicilian way. Its surrounding towns and areas are also well worth exploring, and will take you even further off the beaten track.

Due to its historic lack of tourists, the most appealing lodgings are outside town. Those short on time will discover that Enna makes a good stopover for a touch of sightseeing with lunch, as it is right along the autostrada about halfway between Palermo and Catania.

GETTING HERE AND AROUND

Just off the A19 autostrada, Enna is easily accessible by car. With the train station 5 km (3 miles) below the upper town, the most practical public transportation is by the efficient bus service from Palermo or Catania.

Sights

Castello di Lombardia

CASTLE/PALACE | Enna's narrow, winding streets are dominated at one end by the impressive cliff-hanging Castello di Lombardia, rebuilt by Frederick II to create an expansive summer residence on the foundations of an ancient Sicani fort raised more than 2,000 years ago. While there is little to see inside the castle, climb up the tower for great views from the dead center of the island—on a very clear day, you can see to all three coasts. Immediately to the south you see Lake Pergusa (dry, in late summer), now almost swallowed by Enna's sprawling suburbs and the racetrack around its perimeter. According to Greek mythology, this was where Persephone was abducted by Hades. While a prisoner in his underworld realm she ate six pomegranate seeds, and was therefore doomed to spend half of each year there. For the ancients, she emerged at springtime, triggering a display of wildflowers that can still be admired all over Sicily. ✉ *Piazza di Castello di Lombardia, Enna* 🌐 *www.icastelli.it/it/sicilia/enna/enna/castello-di-lombardia-a-enna* 🎟 *From €3 combined ticket with Torre di Federico II.*

Piazza Vittorio Emanuele

PLAZA/SQUARE | In town, head straight for Via Roma, which leads to Piazza Vittorio Emanuele—the center of Enna's shopping scene and evening passeggiata. The attached **Piazza Crispi,** dominated by what used to be the grand old Hotel Belvedere, affords breathtaking panoramas of the hillside and smoking Etna looming in the distance. The bronze fountain in the middle of the piazza is a reproduction of Gian Lorenzo Bernini's famous 17th-century sculpture *The Rape of Persephone,* a depiction of Hades abducting Persephone. ✉ *Piazza Vittorio Emanuele, Enna.*

Rocca di Cerere (*Rock of Demeter*)
VIEWPOINT | The Greek cult of Demeter, goddess of the harvest, was said to have centered on Enna, where its adherents built a temple atop the Rocca di Cerere, protruding out on one end of town next to the Castello di Lombardia. The spot enjoys spectacular views of the expansive countryside and windswept Sicilian interior. ⊠ *Enna* ☎ *93/5504717* ⊕ *www. roccadicereregeopark.it.*

Torre di Federico II
VIEWPOINT | This mysterious octagonal tower stands above the lower part of town and has been celebrated for millennia as marking the exact geometric center of the island—thus the tower's (and the city's) nickname, Umbilicus Siciliae (Navel of Sicily). Climb the 97 steps of the spiral staircase for views over the city and beyond. ⊠ *Enna* ⊕ *www.torredienna.it* ☎ *From €2, combined ticket with Castello di Lombardia.*

 Restaurants

Centrale
$ | **SICILIAN** | Housed in an old palazzo, this casual place has served meals since 1889 and famously keeps a medieval specialty, *controfiletto all'Ennese* (a veal fillet with onions, artichokes, guanciale, and white wine), on the menu, in addition to a range of slightly more modern seasonal dishes. Choose from a decent selection of Sicilian wines to accompany your meal while you take in the large mirrored wall and local pottery. **Known for:** atmospheric outdoor terrace in summer; classic Sicilian dishes and local wines; antipasti buffet. $ *Average main: €13* ⊠ *Piazza VI Dicembre 9, Enna* ☎ *0935/500963* ⊕ *www.ristorantecentrale.net* ☉ *No lunch Sat. in Sept.–Mar.*

Piazza Armerina

30 km (18 miles) northwest of Caltagirone.

Crowned by a mighty cathedral, the medieval hill town of Piazza Armerina is a magnificent sight from afar. Up close, the historic center's crumbling yellow-stone architecture with Sicily's trademark bulbous balconies creates quite an effect despite a feeling of dilapidation and abandonment (most locals have moved to the modern suburbs). It is a place to visit rather than stay, with the most appealing lodging options in the surrounding countryside.

Piazza Armerina is most famous for the ancient Roman mosaics down the road at Villa Romana del Casale, but lovers of ancient history may be even more entranced by the huge and rarely visited Greek town of Morgantina and the incredible finds from the site, which once graced the galleries of the Getty museum in Malibu, California.

GETTING HERE AND AROUND
Piazza Armerina is linked to Catania, Enna, and Palermo by regular buses, with less frequent buses also connecting to Caltagirone. There's no train station.

VISITOR INFORMATION
CONTACT Piazza Armerina Tourism Office. ⊠ *Via Monsignore Sturzo 3,* ☎ *338/8524872.*

Sights

★ **Villa Romana del Casale**
(*Imperial Roman Villa*)
HISTORIC HOME | The exceptionally well-preserved Imperial Roman Villa is thought to have been a hunting lodge of the emperor Maximian (3rd–4th century AD) and offers some of the best mosaics of the Roman world, artfully covering more than 12,000 square feet. The excavations were not begun until 1950, and most of the wall

decorations and vaulting have been lost, but the shelter over the site hints at the layout of the original building. The mosaics were probably made by North African artisans; they're similar to those in the Tunis Bardo Museum, in Tunisia. The entrance was through a triumphal arch that led into an atrium surrounded by a portico of columns, which line the way to the *thermae*, or bathhouse. It's colorfully decorated with mosaic nymphs, a Neptune, and enslaved people massaging bathers. The peristyle leads to the main villa, where in the Salone del Circo you look down on mosaics illustrating scenes from the Circus Maximus in Rome. A theme running through many of the mosaics—especially the long hall flanking one entire side of the peristyle courtyard—is the capturing and shipping of wild animals, which may have been a major source of the owner's wealth. Yet the most famous mosaic is the floor depicting 10 girls wearing the ancient equivalent of bikinis, going through what looks like a fairly rigorous set of training exercises. ⊠ *SP15, Contrada Casale, 4 km (2½ miles) southwest of Piazza Armerina,* ☎ *0935/680036 ticket office, 0935/687667 office* ⊕ *www.piazzaarmerina.org* ☙ *€10 (free 1st Sun. of month).*

Restaurants

★ Al Fogher

$$ | **MODERN ITALIAN** | This culinary beacon in Sicily's interior features ambitious—and successful—dishes with the creative flair of chef Angelo Treno, whose unforgettable pastas topped with truffles or caviar, for example, offer a decidedly different expression of traditional regional ingredients. The unassuming and elegant dining room is inside an old railway house and is the perfect place to enjoy a bottle from the 500-label wine list; in cold weather, you can cozy up to a fireplace, but the terrace is the place to be in summer. **Known for:** well-thought-out wine list; local ingredients; sophisticated preparations. $ *Average main: €18*

⊠ *Contrada Bellia, near SS117 bis, Aidone exit, about 1 km (½ mile) north of Piazza Cascino, Piazza Armerina* ☎ *0935/684123* ⊕ *alfogher.sicilia.restaurant* ☉ *No dinner Sun. No lunch Mon.*

Caltagirone

72 km (41 miles) northeast of Licata.

Built over three hills, Caltagirone's functional modern periphery gives way to an imposing, if slightly run-down, Baroque town center. The town is one of the main centers of Sicily's ceramics industry, evidenced by churches and palazzi featuring majolica decorations on their balustrades, domes, windowsills, and facades. The best-known sight is the monumental Scala Santa Maria del Monte.

GETTING HERE AND AROUND

Driving is the best way to get to Caltagirone. Regular buses from Catania stop in the lower town, which is a pleasant stroll from the center. Connections by bus with other towns in Sicily are infrequent, and train connections are even worse.

VISITOR INFORMATION

CONTACT Caltagirone Tourism Office. ⊠ *Via Volta Libertini 3,* ☎ *0933/53809* ⊕ *www. cittadicaltagirone.it.*

Sights

Museo della Ceramica

OTHER MUSEUM | Caltagirone was declared a UNESCO World Heritage site for its ceramics as well as for its numerous Baroque churches. Although the museum offers little information in English about the beautiful items displayed in its many glass cases, you can still see one of Sicily's most extensive ceramics collections, ranging from Neolithic finds to red-figure pottery from 5th-century BC Athens and 18th-century terra-cotta Nativity figures. ⊠ *Via Roma, inside Giardini Pubblici, Caltagirone* ☎ *0933/58418, 0933/58423* ⊕ *www.*

poloregionalecatania.net/home/caltagirone_museo_it ⌚🖼 €4.

★ Scala Santa Maria del Monte

VIEWPOINT | While you can see examples of Caltagirone's long ceramic tradition throughout the city, the most impressive display can be found in the 142 individually decorated tiled steps of this monumental staircase leading up to the neglected Santa Maria del Monte church. On July 24 (the feast of San Giacomo, the city's patron saint) and again on August 15 (the feast of the Assumption), the stairs are illuminated with candles that form a tapestry design. Months of work go into preparing the 4,000 *coppi*, or cylinders of colored paper, that hold oil lamps—then, at 9:30 pm on the nights of July 24, July 25, August 14, and August 15, a squad of hundreds of youngsters (tourists are welcome to participate) spring into action to light the lamps, so that the staircase flares up all at once. ⌧ *Begins at Piazza Municipio, Caltagirone.*

Shopping

Improntibarre Handcraft & Design Laboratory

CERAMICS | Of the numerous ceramics shops in Caltagirone's old center, this one 13 steps up Caltagirone's fabled ceramic staircase is one of the best, selling eye-catching work with a modern aesthetic that is inspired by the town's long artisan tradition. ⌧ *Scala Santa Maria del Monte 5, Caltagirone* ☎ *0933/24427* ⊕ *www.improntabarre.it.*

Ragusa

21 km (13 miles) northwest of Modica.

Ragusa, a modern city with a beautiful historic core, is known for some great local red wines and wonderful cheese—a creamy, doughy, flavorful version of *caciocavallo*, made by hand every step of the way. It also has some wonderful Baroque buildings with fabulous vantage points throughout its narrow, twisty, and steep old town.

GETTING HERE AND AROUND

Trains and buses leave from Siracusa four or five times daily.

VISITOR INFORMATION

CONTACT Ragusa Tourism Office. ⌧ *Piazza della Repubblica,* ☎ *0932/684780.*

Sights

Basilica di San Giorgio

CHURCH | Designed by Rosario Gagliardi in 1738, the duomo is a fine example of the Sicilian Baroque. ⌧ *Salita Duomo 15, Ragusa* ☎ *0932/220085* ⊕ *www.diocesidiragusa.it.*

Giardino Ibleo

GARDEN | Set on the edge of the old town, Giardino Ibleo is a tranquil public garden lined with palm trees and dotted with fountains and churches along stone paths. The ambling walkways skirt the cliff side and offer dramatic views of the valley below. ⌧ *Via Giardino, Ragusa* ☎ *0932/652374.*

Ragusa Ibla

HISTORIC DISTRICT | The lovely historic center of Ragusa, known as Ibla, was completely rebuilt after the devastating earthquake of 1693. Its tumble of buildings are perched on a hilltop and suspended between a deep ravine and a sloping valley. The tiny squares and narrow lanes make for pleasant meandering, but expect plenty of stairs. ⌧ *Ragusa.*

 Restaurants

Duomo

$$$$ | SICILIAN | In an understated palazzo on a cobblestone street near the Duomo, star chef Ciccio Sultano prepares imaginative and beautifully plated splurge-worthy dinners and a four-course set lunch menu (a terrific value) that include unforgettable variations on classic Sicilian cuisine. Although dishes can be ordered à la carte, tasting menus convey a fuller sense of the chef's signature style, which uses the finest ingredients from around the island in subtly extravagant combinations. **Known for:** intimate and elegant setting; imaginative wine pairings; spaghettone with yellowtail tuna and carrot sauce. $ *Average main: €45* ✉ *Via Capitano Bocchieri 31, Ragusa* ☎ *0932/651265* ⊕ *www.cicciosultano. it* ⊗ *Closed early Jan.–late Feb. and Sun. No lunch Mon., except in Aug. and Dec. 26–Jan. 6.*

Locanda Gulfi

$$ | SICILIAN | On the grounds of the expansive Gulfi winery, which produces well-regarded organic wines, you'll find a unique place for a sophisticated lunch or dinner, with sweeping views of the Chiaramonte hills and vineyards (about a half-hour drive north of Ragusa). The chef skillfully uses local ingredients to prepare Sicilian dishes with a twist in the modern dining room which features handblown chandeliers and a design-focused black-and-red color scheme; in warmer months, enjoy your meal on the lovely terrace. **Known for:** vineyard views and an inn to stay the night; renowned Gulfi wine; seasonal, local Sicilian dishes. $ *Average main: €18* ✉ *C. da. Patria, Chiaramonte Gulfi* ☎ *0932/928081 reservations, 0932/921654 winery* ⊕ *www. locandagulfi.it.*

 Hotels

★ Eremo della Giubiliana

$$ | B&B/INN | Set in the countryside, a 20-minute drive from Ragusa, this charming family-run monastery-turned-hotel features friendly service and a relaxed but luxurious vibe, with unique rooms in former monks' chambers that vary in size and lay-out but are all quiet and well-appointed. **Pros:** peaceful atmosphere; top-notch service; rooms filled with character. **Cons:** no other nearby eateries due to remote location; restaurant food

could be better for the price; grounds, while lovely, could use better upkeep. $ *Rooms from: €200* ✉ *Contrada Giubiliana, Marina di Ragusa* ☎ *0932/669119* ⊕ *www.eremodellagiubiliana.it* ⇥ *24 rooms* ⦿ *Free Breakfast.*

★ Locanda Don Serafino

$$ | HOTEL | This small boutique hotel offers contemporary rooms and excellent service inside a historic manor house in the heart of Ragusa Ibla. **Pros:** modern design in a historic setting; valet parking service; incredibly attentive staff. **Cons:** steep stairs limit the accessibility of some rooms; some rooms are a few doors down from the main building; bathrooms can be small or quirky. $ *Rooms from: €160* ✉ *Via XI Febbraio 15, Ragusa* ☎ *0932/220065 hotel, 0932/248778 restaurant* ⊕ *www.locandadonserafino.it* ⇥ *11 rooms* ⦿ *Free Breakfast.*

Modica

37 km (23 miles) west of Noto.

Modica and Ragusa are the two chief cities in Sicily's smallest province (also called Ragusa), and the centers of a region known as Iblea. The dry, rocky, and gentle countryside filled with canyons and grassy knolls is a unique landscape for Sicily. In Modica, the main artery—Corso Umberto I—is lined with shops and restaurants and is in the valley at the bottom of the town (called Modica Bassa), while the old town of Modica Alta is built atop a ridge. That's part of this UNESCO-listed area's charm; it's a joy to wander its steep 14th-century lanes traversed by endless staircases and lined with Baroque architecture. Modica is also famed for its chocolate—don't miss trying it at one of the many stores on Corso Umberto I.

Trains leave from Siracusa six times a day, while buses from Catania, Siracusa, Ragusa, and Noto also stop in Modica on a regular basis.

CONTACT Modica Tourism Office. ⊠ *Corso Umberto I 141,* ☎ *346/6558227.*

Sights

Cattedrale di San Pietro

CHURCH | Statues of the apostles line the staircase of Modica's cathedral, which was originally constructed in the 14th century, then rebuilt in an impressive Baroque style following its destruction in the 1693 earthquake. ⊠ *Corso Umberto I 120,* ☎ *0932/941074* ⊕ *www.scoprimodica.it/cosa-vedere/le-chiese/san-pietro* 🎟 *Free.*

★ Chiesa di San Giorgio

CHURCH | This lovely Baroque church in Modica Alta, dating from after the 1693 earthquake, is reached by climbing 250 steps that crisscross in a monumental staircase leading up to the main doors. It's worth the effort for the amazing views over the old town. ⊠ *Corso San Giorgio, Modica* ☎ *0932/941279* ⊕ *www.scoprimodica.it/cosa-vedere/le-chiese/san-giorgio* 🎟 *Free.*

Museo del Cioccolato di Modica

OTHER MUSEUM | There is an abundance of choice when it comes to indulgent desserts in Sicily, but the chocolate of Modica—cooked at a low temperature and possessed of a distinctive granular texture—is prized above all others. It feels only natural, then, to find a museum in the center of the old town dedicated to the local sweet. The small exhibits (with English translations) follow the history of chocolate in general, before describing the way cacao beans first arrived in Modica, and how they were traditionally processed by being ground on a board made of volcanic stone. There is also an eccentric collection of

sculptures and celebrity portraits made entirely of chocolate. ⊠ *Corso Umberto I 149, 1st fl., behind Museo Civico, Modica* ☎ *347/4612771* ⊕ *museociccolatomodica.business.site* 🎟 *€3* ⊗ *Closed Mon.*

 Restaurants

★ Accursio Ristorante

$$$$ | SICILIAN | This intimate Michelin-starred restaurant is a fantastic option if you are staying in Modica overnight. Forget the usual starchy tablecloths and formal service, this place is all about the food, with the chef cooking his own personal takes on classic Sicilian dishes, including options like Trucioli pasta with cheese fondue, lemon, and capers; grilled lettuce with pork cheek, caviar, and walnuts; and cannoli with ricotta cheese and cotton candy for dessert.
Known for: equally extensive and more affordable lunch menu; Michelin-starred food at reasonable prices; relaxed atmosphere. $ *Average main: €120* ⊠ *Via Grimaldi 41, Modica* ☎ *0932/941689* ⊕ *www.accursioristorante.it* ⊗ *Closed Mon. No dinner Sun.*

 Coffee and Quick Bites

Caffè dell'Arte

$ | ITALIAN | FAMILY | Across the street from the Museo del Cioccolato, this small coffee bar makes excellent granita. The shaved ice is often eaten for breakfast in the summer months with a soft brioche, and the toasted almond flavor here is particularly good. **Known for:** casual outdoor seating; great almond granita; best hot chocolate in town. $ *Average main: €5* ⊠ *Corso Umberto I 114* ☎ *0932/943257* ⊕ *caffedellarte.it* ⊗ *Closed Tues.*

Pasticceria Di Lorenzo

$ | BAKERY | FAMILY | Wood lined and unadorned, this family-run pastry shop is one of the best places to try Modica's signature crescent-shape cookies, the *'mpanatigghi.* These soft cookies are filled with a mixture of chocolate, almonds, and veal, a combination that works surprisingly well. The meat was added to the cookies as a way of making the snacks more nutritious on long voyages. **Known for:** specialty cookies; family run; chocolate squares that resemble the city's cobblestones. [$] *Average main: €5* ✉ *Corso Umberto I 225, Modica* ☎ *0932/945324* 🌐 *www.pasticceriadilorenzo.it* 🕒 *Closed Wed.*

Shopping

Modica is famous for its chocolate, which uses an ancient Aztec technique. Made at a low heat, it has a grainier consistency than most. It's actually more difficult to find a shop here that doesn't sell the local chocolate, usually in a wide variety of flavors.

★ Antica Dolceria Bonajuto
CHOCOLATE | Bonajuto is the oldest chocolate producer in town, dating from 1880. This busy shop on Modica Bassa's main street lets you sample many varieties of their delightful product before you buy, and also makes renowned cannoli and candied orange peel. ✉ *Corso Umberto I 159, Modica* ☎ *0932/941225* 🌐 *www.bonajuto.it.*

Scicli

44 km (27 miles) west of Noto.

Overshadowed by its larger neighbors, Modica and Ragusa, Scicli is a Baroque beauty in its own right and one of the eight villages designated by UNESCO in the Val di Noto. In recent years, it has entered Italian popular culture as the filming location of the hugely popular Montalbano series, but its decorated stone palaces and unique Madonna delle Milizie (Virgin Mary of Militias) will delight visitors who may not yet know the Sicilian detective show.

GETTING HERE AND AROUND

Buses from Siracusa, Ragusa (by way of Modica), and Noto stop in Scicli on a regular basis.

Sights

Chiesa di San Bartolomeo
CHURCH | An enchanting fusion of the Baroque and rococo lies behind the lace grate doors of this church on the edge of the town's historic center. Inside the single-nave church is a wooden nativity scene that dates back to the 16th century. ✉ *Via S. Bartolomeo, Scicli* 🎟 *Free.*

Chiesa di San Matteo
VIEWPOINT | Scicli is a city of honey-hued churches, all built after the devastating earthquake in the 17th century. The church of San Matteo is abandoned, but it's well worth climbing the shallow stairs up the steep hillside to take in the panoramic views of Scicli's old town from the terrace in front of the church. ✉ *Via San Matteo 9, Scicli.*

Chiesa di Sant'Ignazio
CHURCH | Founded in the 17th century as a Jesuit church, this was rebuilt following the 1693 earthquake. Housing the remains of Scicli's patron saint Guglielmo the hermit, a side chapel also hosts the life-size papier-mâché statue of the Madonna *su cavallo* (on a horse), the Madonna delle Milizie. This is paraded through the streets on the last Saturday in May to celebrate her feast day. ✉ *Piazza Italia, Scicli* ☎ *0932/931278.*

Noto

38 km (23 miles) southwest of Siracusa.

If Siracusa's Baroque beauties whet your appetite for that over-the-top style, head to Noto, a UNESCO World Heritage site. Lying about 40 minutes away on the A18, the compact and easy-to-navigate city is doable as a day trip—though staying overnight lets you see the lovely buildings glow in the setting sun after the tourist hordes have departed. Despite being decimated by an earthquake in 1693 and rebuilt in the prevailing fashion of the day, Noto has remarkable architectural integrity. A prime example of design from the island's Baroque heyday, it presents a pleasing ensemble of honey-color buildings, strikingly uniform in style but never dull. Simply walking Corso Vittorio Emanuele, the pedestrianized main street, qualifies as an aesthetic experience.

GETTING HERE AND AROUND

Trains leave from Siracusa at least eight times daily (fewer trains on Sunday); there are also four trains a day from Ragusa, though the station is a bit outside of town. Buses depart numerous times a day from Siracusa, Catania, and Ragusa.

VISITOR INFORMATION

CONTACT Noto Tourism Office. ✉ *Corso Vittorio Emanuele 135,* ☎ *339/4816218* 🌐 *www.notoinforma.it.*

Sights

★ Cattedrale di San Nicolò

CHURCH | Noto's domed cathedral (divine in more ways than one) is an undisputed highlight of the extraordinary Baroque architecture for which the town is world-famous. Climb the monumental staircase to get a glimpse of the interior—restored over a 10-year period after the dome collapsed in 1996—which is simple compared to the magnificent exterior, but still worth a look. ✉ *Corso Vittorio Emanuele,* ☎ *0931/835286* 🌐 *www.diocesinoto.it.*

Palazzo Nicolaci di Villadorata

CASTLE/PALACE | For a rare insight into the lifestyle of social climbers in the 18th century, this palace is a must-see. It contains about 90 rooms belonging to the noble Nicolaci family, and although only some are on view to the public, they include a splendid frescoed ballroom. Outside the palace, note the gorgeous balconies featuring mythical creatures. ✉ *Via Corrado Nicolaci, Noto* ☎ *338/7427022* 🌐 *www.palazzonicolaci.it* 🎫 *€4.*

Restaurants

Anche gli Angeli

$$ | ITALIAN | Part concept store, part bar, and part fine gourmet dining experience, this unique eatery is built into a grotto underneath the Chiesa di San Carlo and specializes in deceptively simple grilled dishes and contemporary cocktails. There's live music on the weekends, but it's quite laid-back and unobtrusive. **Known for:** high-end takes on local meat dishes; excellent drinks; beautiful design under historic arched ceiling. [$] *Average main: €18* ✉ *Via Arnaldo da Brescia 2, Noto* ☎ *0931/576023* 🌐 *www.anchegli-angeli.it.*

★ Ristorante Crocifisso

$$ | SICILIAN | Considered by many as one of Noto's best restaurants, getting to Crocifisso is a bit of a hike as it's away from Noto's tourist area and up a hill only accessible by many steps. However, intrepid diners will be rewarded with one of the Baroque town's finest restaurants, serving traditional dishes presented in a contemporary style in a beautiful modern dining room. **Known for:** fantastic wine selection with a focus on Sicilian and natural wines; superlative house-made pastas; new takes on classic Sicilian dishes. [$] *Average main: €18* ✉ *Via Principe Umberto 48, Noto* ☎ *0931/968608* 🌐 *www.ristorantecrocifisso.it* 🕒 *Closed mid-Jan.–late Feb. and Wed. No lunch Thurs.*

★ Ristorante Manna

$$ | SICILIAN | The plain exterior here gives no hint of the sleek, cool design inside this welcoming restaurant just off of Noto's main street where all of the dishes—from fresh pastas to creative seafood and exceptional daily specials—shine a light on local premium

Walk inside the Ear of Dionysius, the Greek god of wine, fertility, ritual madness, and religious ecstasy.

ingredients. Although the small outdoor patio allows for great people-watching, it's inside that the restaurant really shines; the chic multilevel dining area highlights modern art, a stylish complement to the restaurant's thoroughly modern food. **Known for:** cool, contemporary setting; delightful staff; modern, creative Sicilian cuisine. *Average main: €18 Via Rocco Pirri 19, Noto 0931/836051 www.mannanoto.it Closed Nov., Jan., and Tues.*

Coffee and Quick Bites

Caffè Sicilia

$ | **BAKERY** | When you need a break from the architectural eye candy, indulge in an edible sweet (and a restorative coffee or granita) at this wondrous cake shop. Their cannoli and gelato are particularly highly rated and considered some of the best in the country. **Known for:** house-made ice cream; delicious cannoli; perfect almond granita. *Average main: €5 Corso Vittorio Emanuele 125, Noto 0931/835013 www.caffesicilia.it Closed mid-Jan.–mid-Mar.*

Hotels

Gagliardi Boutique Hotel

$$$ | **HOTEL** | For an unbeatable location only a block from the main pedestrian street, visitors to Noto can't do better than this hotel with an industrial vibe and spacious minimalist rooms accented with chandeliers—all inside a former 18th-century palace. **Pros:** extremely central location; large rooms and good public spaces; friendly service. **Cons:** short on amenities (no restaurant, spa, or pool); iffy Wi-Fi connection; only one room has a bathtub. *Rooms from: €228 Via Silvio Spaventa 41, Noto 0931/839730 www.gagliardihotel.com 11 rooms Free Breakfast.*

Siracusa

Siracusa, known to English speakers as Syracuse, is a wonder to behold. One of the great ancient capitals of Western civilization, the city was founded in 734 BC by Greek colonists from Corinth and soon grew to rival—and even surpass—Athens in splendor and power. It became the largest, wealthiest city-state in the West and a bulwark of Greek civilization. Although Siracusa lived under tyranny, rulers such as Dionysius filled their courts with Greeks of the highest cultural stature—among them the playwrights Aeschylus and Euripides and the philosopher Plato. The Athenians, who didn't welcome Siracusa's rise, set out to conquer Sicily, but the natives outsmarted them in what was one of the greatest military campaigns in ancient history (413 BC). The city continued to prosper until it was conquered two centuries later by the Romans.

Present-day Siracusa still has some of the finest examples of Baroque art and architecture; dramatic Greek and Roman ruins; and a Duomo that's the stuff of legend—a microcosm of the city's entire history in one building. The modern city also has a wonderful, lively Baroque old town worthy of extensive exploration, as well as pleasant piazzas, outdoor cafés and bars, and a wide assortment of excellent seafood. There are essentially two areas to explore in Siracusa: the Parco Archeologico (Archaeological Zone) on the mainland, and the island of Ortigia (spelled Ortygia by English speakers), the ancient city first inhabited by the Greeks, which juts out into the Ionian Sea and is connected to the mainland by two small bridges. Ortigia has become increasingly popular with tourists, and although it's filled with lots of modern boutiques (and tourist shops), it still retains its charm despite the crowds.

GETTING HERE AND AROUND

On the main train line from Messina and Catania, Siracusa is also linked to Catania and the nearby Val di Noto by frequent buses.

Although Ortigia is a compact area and a pleasure to amble around without getting unduly tired, mainland Siracusa is a grid of wide modern avenues. At the northern end of Corso Gelone, above Viale Paolo Orsi, the orderly grid gives way to the ancient quarter of Neapolis, where the sprawling Parco Archeologico is accessible from Viale Teracati (an extension of Corso Gelone). East of Viale Teracati, about a 10-minute walk from the Parco Archeologico, the district of Tyche holds the archaeological museum and the church and catacombs of San Giovanni, both off Viale Teocrito (drive or take a taxi or city bus from Ortigia). Coming from the train station, it's a 15-minute trudge to Ortigia along Via Francesco Crispi and Corso Umberto. If you're not up for that, take one of the free electric buses leaving every 10 minutes from the station around the corner.

VISITOR INFORMATION

CONTACT Siracusa Tourism Office. ✉ *Via Roma 31, Ortygia* ☎ *800931/055500* ⊕ *www.siracusaturismo.net.*

Archaeological Zone

 Sights

Catacomba di San Giovanni

RUINS | Not far from the Archaeological Park, off Viale Teocrito, the catacombs below the church of San Giovanni are one of the earliest known Christian sites in the city. Inside the crypt of San Marciano is an altar where St. Paul preached on his way through Sicily to Rome. The frescoes in this small chapel are mostly bright and fresh, though some dating from the 4th century AD show their age. To visit the catacombs, you must take a 45-minute guided tour (included with

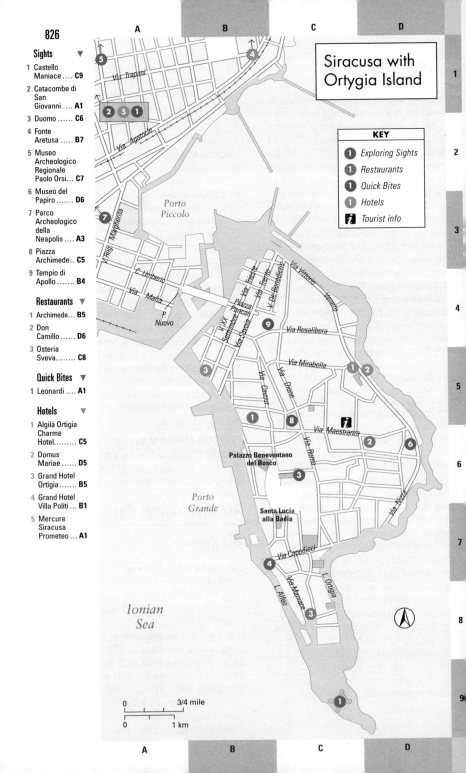

Sights ▼

1 Castello
  Maniace **C9**

2 Catacombe di
  San
  Giovanni **A1**

3 Duomo **C6**

4 Fonte
  Aretusa **B7**

5 Museo
  Archeologico
  Regionale
  Paolo Orsi... **C7**

6 Museo del
  Papiro **D6**

7 Parco
  Archeologico
  della
  Neapolis **A3**

8 Piazza
  Archimede.. **C5**

9 Tempio di
  Apollo **B4**

Restaurants ▼

1 Archimede... **B5**

2 Don
  Camillo **D6**

3 Osteria
  Sveva........ **C8**

Quick Bites ▼

1 Leonardi **A1**

Hotels ▼

1 Algilà Ortigia
  Charme
  Hotel......... **C5**

2 Domus
  Mariae **D5**

3 Grand Hotel
  Ortigia....... **B5**

4 Grand Hotel
  Villa Politi ... **B1**

5 Mercure
  Siracusa
  Prometeo ... **A1**

Siracusa with Ortygia Island

KEY

1 Exploring Sights

1 Restaurants

1 Quick Bites

1 Hotels

ℹ Tourist info

Porto Piccolo

Porto Grande

Palazzo Beneventano del Bosco

Santa Lucia alla Badia

Ionian Sea

0 — 3/4 mile
0 — 1 km

the admission price), which leaves about every half hour and is conducted in Italian and English. ✉ *Piazza San Giovanni, Tyche* ☎ *0931/64694* ⊕ *www.kairos-web.com* 🖂 *€8* ⊙ *Closed daily 12:30–2:30 and Mon. in winter.*

Museo Archeologico Regionale Paolo Orsi

HISTORY MUSEUM | The impressive collection of Siracusa's splendid archaeological museum is organized by region and time period around a central atrium and ranges from Neolithic pottery to fine Greek statues and vases. Compare the Landolina Venus—a headless goddess of love who rises out of the sea in measured modesty (a 1st-century-AD Roman copy of the Greek original)—with the much earlier (300 BC) elegant Greek statue of Hercules in Section C. Of a completely different style is a marvelous fanged Gorgon, its tongue sticking out, that once adorned the cornice of the Temple of Athena to ward off evildoers. ✉ *Viale Teocrito 66, Tyche* ☎ *0931/489514* ⊕ *www.regione.sicilia.it/beniculturali/ museopaoloorsi* 🖂 *€10; combined ticket with Parco Archeologico della Neapolis €22; additional fees for special exhibitions* ⊙ *Closed Mon.*

★ Parco Archeologico della Neapolis

RUINS | Siracusa is most famous for its dramatic set of Greek and Roman ruins, which are considered to be some of the best archaeological sites in all of Italy and should be combined with a stop at the Museo Archeologico. If the park is closed, go up Viale G. Rizzo from Viale Teracati to the belvedere overlooking the ruins, which are floodlit at night.

Before the park's ticket booth is the gigantic Ara di Ierone (Altar of Hieron), which was once used by the Greeks for spectacular sacrifices involving hundreds of animals. The first attraction in the park is the Latomia del Paradiso (Quarry of Paradise), a lush tropical garden full of palm and citrus trees. This series of quarries served as prisons for the defeated Athenians, who were enslaved;

the quarries once rang with the sound of their chisels and hammers. At one end is the famous **Orecchio di Dionisio (Ear of Dionysius)**, with an ear-shape entrance and unusual acoustics inside, as you'll hear if you clap your hands. The legend is that Dionysius used to listen in at the top of the quarry to hear what the enslaved people were plotting below.

The **Teatro Greco** is the chief monument in the Archaeological Park. Indeed it's one of Sicily's greatest classical sites and the most complete Greek theater surviving from antiquity. Climb to the top of the seating area (which could accommodate 15,000) for a fine view: all the seats converge upon a single point—the stage—which has the natural scenery and the sky as its backdrop. Hewn out of the hillside rock in the 5th century BC, the theater saw the premieres of the plays of Aeschylus, and Greek tragedies are still performed here every year in May and June. Above and behind the theater runs the Via dei Sepulcri, in which streams of running water flow through a series of Greek sepulchers.

The well-preserved and striking Anfiteatro Romano (Roman Amphitheater) reveals much about the differences between the Greek and Roman personalities. Where drama in the Greek theater was a kind of religious ritual, the Roman amphitheater emphasized the spectacle of combative sports and the circus. This arena is one of the largest of its kind and was built around the 2nd century AD. The corridor where gladiators and beasts entered the ring is still intact, and the seats (some of which still bear the occupants' names) were hauled in and constructed on the site from huge slabs of limestone. ✉ *Viale Teocrito, entrance on Via Agnello, Archaeological Zone* ☎ *0931/66206* ⊕ *www.regione.sicilia. it/beniculturali/museopaoloorsi* 🖂 *€17, combined ticket with Museo Archeologico €22; free 1st Sun. of month.*

Coffee and Quick Bites

Leonardi

$ | **BAKERY** | For some great Sicilian cakes and ice cream on your way to the Archaeological Park, visit this bar-cum-pasticceria. It's popular with locals, so you may have to line up for your cakes during holiday times. **Known for:** handy location near the Archaeological Park; a favorite of locals; great coffee and cakes. $ *Average main: €3* ⊠ *Viale Teocrito 123, Siracusa* ☎ *0931/61411* ⊕ *www.pasticcerialeonardi.com.*

🛏 Hotels

Grand Hotel Villa Politi

$$ | **HOTEL** | Winston Churchill, European royalty, and other VIPs have frequented the grand 18th-century Villa Politi, and although it's now a little faded, it retains a sense of charm and elegance with rococo furnishings alongside modern luxuries like comfy beds. **Pros:** excellent service; expansive outdoor pool and nearby private beach; free parking in the hotel lot. **Cons:** not as sparkling and fresh as in the past; not many restaurants in the neighborhood; a fair distance from the sights of Ortigia. $ *Rooms from: €180* ⊠ *Via M. Politi 2, Archaeological Zone* ☎ *0931/412121* ⊕ *www.villapoliti.com* ⏎ *100 rooms* ❘○❘ *Free Breakfast.*

Mercure Siracusa Prometeo

$$ | **HOTEL** | This spot occupies a glass-fronted building along the busy Viale Teracati and, like most other hotels in the same chain, it's a slick operation with first-rate amenities. **Pros:** two-minute walk from the archaeological site of Neapolis; good parking; swimming pool on the roof. **Cons:** €10 breakfast; a long way from the island of Ortigia; chain hotel with little character. $ *Rooms from: €150* ⊠ *Viale Teracati 20, Tyche* ☎ *0931/464646* ⊕ *www.hotelmercuresiracusa.com* ⏎ *93 rooms* ❘○❘ *No Meals.*

Performing Arts

Teatro Greco (*Greek Theater*)

THEATER | From early May to mid-July, Siracusa's ancient Teatro Greco stages performances of classical tragedy and comedy. Tickets range €36–€73, with a small discount if you buy the ticket in person. ⊠ *Via del Teatro Greco, Archaeological Zone* ☎ *0931/487248 ticket office* ⊕ *www.indafondazione.org.*

Ortigia

👁 Sights

Castello Maniace

CASTLE/PALACE | The southern tip of Ortigia island is occupied by this castle built by Frederick II (1194–1250), from which there are fine sea views (until recently, it was an army barracks). There's also a small museum with information about the castle's history and artifacts found during excavations, though English translations are limited. ⊠ *Via del Castello Maniace 51, Ortygia* ☎ *0931/4508211* ⊕ *aditusculture.com/biglietti/sicilia/siracusa/castello-maniace-siracusa* 🎫 *€7.*

★ Duomo

RELIGIOUS BUILDING | Siracusa's Duomo is an archive of more than 2,000 years of island history, and has creatively incorporated ruins through the many time periods it has survived, starting with the bottommost, where excavations have unearthed remnants of Sicily's distant past, when the Siculi inhabitants worshipped their deities here. During the 5th century BC (the same time Agrigento's Temple of Concord was built), the Greeks erected a temple to Athena over it, and in the 7th century, Siracusa's first Christian cathedral was built on top of the Greek structure. The massive columns of the original Greek temple were incorporated into the present structure and are clearly visible, embedded in the exterior wall along Via Minerva. The Greek columns were also used to dramatic advantage inside, where on one side they form chapels connected by elegant wrought-iron gates. The Baroque facade, added in the 18th century, displays a harmonious rhythm of concaves and convexes. In front, the sun-kissed stone piazza is encircled by pink and white oleanders and elegant buildings ornamented with filigree grillwork, and is typically filled with frolicking children and street musicians. Check with the tourist office for guided tours of its underground tunnels, which are located to the right when you stand facing the cathedral. ⊠ *Piazza del Duomo, Ortygia* ☎ *0931/65328* ⊕ *arcidiocesi.siracusa.it/chiesa-cattedrale* ⌦ *€2.*

Fonte Aretusa

FOUNTAIN | A freshwater spring, the Fountain of Arethusa, sits next to the sea, studded with Egyptian papyrus that's reportedly natural. This anomaly is explained by a Greek legend that tells how the nymph Arethusa was changed into a fountain by the goddess Artemis (Diana) when she tried to escape the advances of the river god Alpheus. She fled from Greece, into the sea, with Alpheus in close pursuit, and emerged in Sicily at this spring. It's said if you throw a cup into the Alpheus River in Greece, it will emerge here at this fountain, which is home to a few tired ducks and some faded carp—but no cups. If you want to stand right by the fountain, you need to gain admission through the aquarium; otherwise look down on it from Largo Aretusa. ⊠ *Largo Aretusa, Ortygia* ⊹ *Off promenade along harbor* ☎ *0931/65861* ⊕ *www.fontearetusasiracusa.it* ⌦ *€5* ⊘ *Closed Tues.*

Museo del Papiro

OTHER MUSEUM | Housed in the 16th-century former convent of Sant'Agostino, the small but intriguing Papyrus Museum uses informative exhibits and videos to demonstrate how papyri are prepared from reeds and then painted—an ancient tradition in the city. Siracusa, it seems, has the only climate outside the Nile Valley in which the papyrus plant—from which the word "paper" comes—thrives. ⊠ *Via Nizza 14, Ortygia* ☎ *0931/22100* ⊕ *www.museodelpapiro.it* ⌦ *€5* ⊘ *Closed Mon.*

Piazza Archimede

PLAZA/SQUARE | The center of this piazza has a Baroque fountain, the Fontana di Diana, festooned with fainting sea nymphs and dancing jets of water. Look for the Chiaramonte-style **Palazzo Montalto,** an arched-window gem just off the piazza on Via Montalto. ⊠ *Piazza Archimede, Ortygia.*

Tempio di Apollo

RUINS | Scattered through the piazza just across the bridge to Ortigia are the ruins of a temple dedicated to Apollo, which dates back to the 6th century BC. A model of this is in the Museo Archeologico. In fact, little of this noble Doric temple remains except for some crumbled walls and shattered columns; the window in the south wall belongs to a Norman church that was built much later on the same spot. ⊠ *Largo XXV Luglio, Ortygia* ⌦ *Free.*

 Restaurants

Archimede

$$ | PIZZA | Although the restaurant gets decidedly mixed reviews, the Archimede pizzeria offers well-made pizzas with classical names, such as the Teocrite, topped with fresh tomato, mozzarella, garlic, onion, and basil. For those who can't face the full-size offerings, minipizzas are also available (albeit at the same price), and everyone should find enough space to sample one of the many bottled beers on the menu. **Known for:** good beer selection; reasonable prices; satisfying pizzas. Ⓢ *Average main: €15* ⊠ *Via Gemmellaro 8, Ortygia* ☎ *0931/69701.*

★ Don Camillo

$$ | SICILIAN | A gracious series of delicately arched rooms at this beloved local eatery are lined with wine bottles and sepia-tone images of the old town. À la carte preparations bring together fresh seafood and inspired creativity: sample, for instance, the sublime spaghetti *delle Sirene* (with sea urchin and shrimp in butter) or *gamberoni* (prawns) prepared, unexpectedly (and wonderfully), in pork fat. If you want, you can put yourself in the hands of the chef and opt for one of the exquisite tasting menus, which start at €70 excluding wine. **Known for:** fantastic wine list; helpful service; fish, meat, and vegetarian tasting menus. $ *Average main: €20 ⊠ Via Maestranza 96, Ortygia* ☎ *0931/67133* ⊕ *www.ristorantedoncamillosiracusa.it* ⊗ *Closed Sun., 2 wks in Jan., and 2 wks in July.*

Osteria Sveva

$$ | SICILIAN | At this slow-food tavern, conveniently located right behind the Castello Maniace, you can sit back and enjoy both surf and turf dishes in the studiously modern but minimalist surroundings. One major plus is that you can order half portions of several pasta dishes or opt for a secondo, like the unusual *pesce in crosta di patate* (grilled fish in a potato crust)—all served on hand-painted ceramic ware. **Known for:** charming setting on a square; good-value meals; authentic Sicilian dishes. $ *Average main: €15 ⊠ Piazza Federico di Svevia 1, Ortygia* ☎ *0931/24663* ⊗ *Closed Jan., Nov., and Wed. mid-Sept.–June. No lunch June–Sept.*

 ## Hotels

★ Algilà Ortigia Charme Hotel

$$$$ | HOTEL | It's hard to say what's more charming about this boutique hotel: its location overlooking the sea on the edge of the old town, or its delightful interiors, including guest rooms done up in country-chic style, with a mix of modern amenities (Bulgari toiletries, free minibar) and antique touches (wood-beamed ceilings, hand-painted tiles in the bathroom). **Pros:** wonderfully central location; eager-to-please service with valet parking (fee); prime water views. **Cons:** not all rooms have sea views; lots of stairs could be an issue for some; no spa, pool, or gym. $ *Rooms from: €328 ⊠ Via Vittorio Veneto 93, Ortygia* ☎ *0931/465186* ⊕ *www.algila.it* ⊅ *54 rooms* ⦿ *Free Breakfast.*

★ Domus Mariae

$$ | HOTEL | On Ortigia's eastern shore, this hotel, in an unusual twist, is owned by Ursuline nuns, who help to make the mood placid and peaceful, but the elegant accommodations are far from monastic. **Pros:** nice breakfast; enthusiastic staff; gorgeous sea views and rooftop terrace. **Cons:** small rooms and not all rooms have sea views; not much street parking near the hotel; stairs to climb. $ *Rooms from: €149 ⊠ Via Vittorio Veneto 76, Ortygia* ☎ *0931/60087* ⊕ *www.domusmariaebenessere.com* ⊅ *12 rooms* ⦿ *Free Breakfast.*

Grand Hotel Ortigia

$$$ | HOTEL | An elegant though somewhat old-fashioned design of inlaid wood furniture and stained-glass windows prevails in the guest rooms at this venerable institution, which has enjoyed a prime position on the Porto Grande at the base of Ortigia since 1890. **Pros:** wonderful seafront views from the restaurant; convenient location; private parking (a rarity on Ortigia). **Cons:** Wi-Fi weak in some rooms; small bathrooms; back rooms have no view. $ *Rooms from: €247 ⊠ Viale Mazzini 12, Ortygia* ☎ *0931/464611* ⊕ *www.grandhotelortigia.it* ⊅ *57 rooms* ⦿ *Free Breakfast.*

Shopping

★ Ortygia Street Market

MARKET | This historic food market is still the daily shopping center for residents of Ortigia and mainland Siracusa. Seafood stalls display the catch of the day, ranging from local clams that you'll find in most restaurants to sea urchins that normally only appear on the more expensive menus. Even in the colder months, the vegetable and fruit stalls are still vibrant and inviting. One thing to look out for is the local Pachino tomato. It has protected status and can be found fresh, dried, or reduced to a gloriously intense thick paste used in pasta. Intertwined within the stalls are several local bars where you can rest and take in the hustle and bustle of local Italian food culture. The market is open every day except for Sunday, from 7 am to 1:45 pm. ⊠ *Vicolo Bagnara, Ortygia* ☎ *No phone.*

Catania

210 km (130 miles) southeast of Palermo, 60 km (37 miles) north of Siracusa.

The chief wonder of Catania, Sicily's second city, is that it's there at all. Nearly every century has seen its share of tragedy for the Catanesi: a Greek tyrant that cast the population out, another who sold the majority of the citizens into slavery, Carthaginians who drove the successive occupants away once again. Each time, the city was rebuilt, only to meet more destruction. The plague hit hard in the Middle Ages, severely decimating the population. Mt. Etna erupted in 1669, with a mile-wide stream of lava covering part of the city, and just 25 years after that, a disastrous earthquake forced Catania to begin again.

Today Catania is in the midst of yet another resurrection—this time from crime, filth, and urban decay. Although the city remains loud and full of traffic, signs of gentrification are everywhere. The elimination of vehicles from the Piazza del Duomo and the main artery of Via Etnea, and the cleaning of many of the historic buildings have added to its newfound charm. Home to what is arguably Sicily's best university, Catania is full of youthful

exuberance, which comes through in its designer bistros, the chic osterias that serve wine, and the trendy boutiques that have cropped up all over town. Even more impressive is the vibrant cultural life.

GETTING HERE AND AROUND

Catania is well connected by bus and train with Messina, Taormina, Siracusa, Enna, and Palermo. The airport of Fontanarossa serves as a transportation hub for the eastern side of the island. From here you can get buses to most major destinations without going into the city center. The Alibus runs a loop from the airport through the city center (*€4; approximately every 25 minutes*).

Within the city, use the AMTS bus service (*€1; ⊕ www.amts.ct.it*), which also connects to outlying areas such as Aci Castello. The website can be difficult to use, but the AMT Catania app offers useful route suggestions, online ticket purchasing, and timetables—and it's available in English. Catania also has an underground Metro line (*€1; ⊕ www.circumetnea.it*), but with only 10 stations centered on the downtown area, it's often easier to just walk.

VISITOR INFORMATION

CONTACT Catania Tourism Office. ⊠ *Via Etnea 63/65,* ☎ *095/4014070* ⊕ *turismo.cittametropolitana.ct.it.*

 Sights

Amenano River

NATURE SIGHT | This underground river flows beneath much of Catania. You can glimpse it at the Fontana dell'Amenano, but the best place to experience the river is at the bar-restaurant A Putia dell'Ostello. Here you can sit at an underground table as swirls of water rush by. If you're not planning to stay for a drink, someone from the bar will sell you a €1 ticket to walk into the cavelike seating area. Aside from the underground river, the bar area above ground is a lively, fun spot to hang out on a Monday evening when many other places are closed. ✉ *Piazza Currò 6, Catania* ☎ *095/7233010* ⊕ *aputiadellostel-lo.business.site.*

Cattedrale di Sant'Agata (Duomo)

CHURCH | Giovanni Vaccarini designed the contrasting black lava and white limestone facade of city's cathedral, which dominates the Piazza del Duomo and which houses the tomb of composer Vincenzo Bellini. Also of note are the three apses of lava that survive from the original Norman structure and a fresco from 1675 in the sacristy that portrays Catania's submission to Etna's eruption. Guided tours of the cathedral, which is dedicated to Catania's protector, are available in English if reserved at least a week in advance. The cathedral's treasures are on view in the Museo Diocesano Catania (www.museodiocesanocatania.com), and underneath the cathedral are the ruins of Greco-Roman baths. ✉ *Piazza del Duomo, bottom end of Via Etnea, Catania* ☎ *095/320044, 339/4859942 for tours* ⊕ *www.cattedralecatania.it* 🎫 *Museum €7, sacristy €2, baths €5; combined ticket €10.*

Centro Storico

HISTORIC DISTRICT | Black lava stone from Etna, combined with largely Baroque architecture, give Catania's historic center a very distinctive feel. After Catania's destruction by lava and earthquake at the end of the 17th century, the city was rebuilt and its informal mascot "U Liotru" (an elephant carved out of lava balancing an Egyptian obelisk) was placed outside the cathedral as a kind of talisman. This square also marks the entrance to Catania's famous *pescheria* (fish market) and is one of the few points in the city where you can see the Amenano River above ground. Another point of interest is Via Garibaldi, which runs from Piazza del Duomo up toward the impressively huge Porta Garibaldi, a black-and-white triumphal arch built in 1768 to commemorate the marriage of

Ferdinando I. Also of note in the center are Castello Ursino, which is now a museum, the Greco-Roman theater off Via Vittorio Emanuele II, and the Roman amphitheater in Piazza Stesicoro. ✉ *Catania.*

Via Etnea

STREET | With the ever-looming volcano perfectly framed at the end of the road, this main street is lined with cafés and stores selling high-street jewelry, clothing, and shoes. At sunset, it plays host to one of Sicily's most enthusiastic passeggiatas, in which Catanesi of all ages take part. It is closed to automobile traffic (other than buses, taxis, and police) until 10 pm during the week and all day on weekends. ✉ *Via Etnea, Catania.*

Restaurants

★ Km.0

$$ | SICILIAN | For the best of what's locally in season, look to chef Marco Cannizzaro and his 25-seat fine-dining restaurant. Harvested from Etna to the Ionian Sea, the primary ingredients of the area simply shine in his hands: Nerello mascelese grapes show up as rich sauces, wild greens harvested from the slopes of Etna make their way into risottos or stuffed into tender calamari meatballs, and donkey, an economical protein staple of the area, is transformed into flavorful and refined tartare. **Known for:** fine dining with a neighborhood feel; four-, five-, or seven-course tasting menus; Robiola-stuffed smoked onion with strawberry. 💲 *Average main: €22* ✉ *Via Antonino Longo 26, Catania* ☎ *347/7327788* ⊕ *www.km0ristorante. com* 🕐 *Closed Wed. yr-round and Sun. in summer.*

★ Oasi Frutti di Mare da Nitto

$ | SEAFOOD | Located in the Ognina port, the little Nitto empire has exploded: what began as a mobile market in the 1960s (from the back of a Piaggio Ape) is now a standing fresh fish market and series of restaurants. Locals line up outside the little market to get their daily catch, while next door the fast-casual restaurant serves some of the best-prepared seafood in the area, including squid ink pastas, skewers of grilled fish, and raw seafood platters. **Known for:** tuna agrodolce, a sweet-and-sour tuna dish studded with pine nuts and raisins; fresh-off-the-boat seafood; vivacious atmosphere. $ *Average main: €12 ⊠ Piazza Mancini Battaglia 6, Catania ☎ 095/491165 ⊕ www.nittopescheria.it.*

Coffee and Quick Bites

Caffè del Duomo

$ | **CAFÉ** | Dive right into the hustle and bustle of Catania at Caffè del Duomo, which has handmade cookies and cakes and a great local atmosphere. The piazza-front location is the main draw, but the fantastic cannoli are another reason to stop for coffee and watch the world go by. **Known for:** typical Sicilian breakfast; handmade treats; great spot for people-watching. $ *Average main: €5 ⊠ Piazza Duomo 11–13, Catania ☎ 095/7150556 ⊕ www.caffedelduomocatania.com.*

★ Scirocco Sicilian Fish Lab

$ | **SEAFOOD** | In the heart of the fish market, you'll find the best *fritto misto* in the area. Walk up to the little counter on the stone balcony overlooking the action and place your order for a paper cone of fried seafood made with the lightest and crispiest batter. **Known for:** superfresh seafood; fast service; unique seafood sandwiches called tramezzini. $ *Average main: €9 ⊠ Piazza Alonzo di Benedetto 7, Catania ☎ 095/8365148 ⊕ www.sciroccolab.com.*

Hotels

★ Palazzo Marletta

$$$ | **HOTEL** | Baroque architecture punctuates the city, and one of the best ways to see it up close is with a stay at Palazzo Marletta, a private palace turned plush

hotel. **Pros:** copious breakfast; arrangement with a local car valet service for parking; prime location just off the Duomo. **Cons:** can be difficult to navigate the historic district if arriving by car; modern rooms lack some of the charm of historic ones; some of the bathrooms have little privacy. $ *Rooms from: €252 ⊠ Via Erasmo Merletta 7, Catania ☎ 380/2160253 ⊕ www.palazzomarletta.it ⤳ 7 rooms ⦿| Free Breakfast.*

Una Hotel Palace

$$ | **HOTEL** | For great views of Etna, this centrally located hotel overlooking Catania's main shopping street has a rooftop terrace where you can enjoy breakfast or take in the scenery during happy hour over a cocktail and antipasti buffet. **Pros:** amazing rooftop views; eager-to-please staff; extremely central location. **Cons:** fee for parking; some noisy rooms; bit of a generic feel. $ *Rooms from: €126 ⊠ Via Etnea 218, Catania ☎ 095/2505111 ⊕ www.gruppouna.it/esperienze/palace-catania ⤳ 94 rooms ⦿| Free Breakfast.*

Nightlife

First Lounge Bar

BEER GARDENS | Breathing new life into the San Berillo district, First is an outdoor lounge-bar with a beer garden feel, original street art, and walls covered in potted plants. Stop in for a craft beer or a cocktail in the previously forgotten back alleys a few minutes from Teatro Massimo Bellini, and you will also likely be treated to art installations or live DJ sets, depending on the constantly updated cultural calendar of events. ⊠ *Via Martinez 13, Catania ☎ 320/7633921.*

🛍 Shopping

I Dolci di Nonna Vincenza

FOOD | The selection of almond-based delights here may be small, but everything is fresh and phenomenally good. Ask for boxes of mixed cookies by weight, add in some marzipan treats dedicated to Catania's patron, Sant'Agata, and enjoy the grab-bag selection at your leisure later. International shipping is available. This is the original and most historic location, but other stores can be found on Via San Giuseppe la Rena and Piazza Mancini Battaglia. ⊠ *Palazzo Biscari, Piazza San Placido 7, Catania* ☏ *095/7151844* ⊕ *www.dolcinonnavincenza.it.*

★ Outdoor Fish and Food Market

MARKET | Beginning behind the Fontana Amenano at the corner of Piazza Duomo and spreading westward between Via Garibaldi and Via Transito, this is one of Italy's most memorable markets. It's a feast for the senses, with ricotta, fresh produce, endless varieties of meats, thousands of just-caught fish (some still wriggling), plus a symphony of vendor shouts to fill the ears. The market is at its best in early morning and finishes up around 1 pm. It's open every day except Sunday. ⊠ *Corner of Piazza Duomo, Catania.*

Acireale

6 km (4 miles) north of Aci Trezza, 16 km (10 miles) north of Catania.

Acireale sits amid a clutter of rocky pinnacles and lush lemon groves. The craggy coast is known as the Riviera dei Ciclopi, after the legend narrated in *The Odyssey* in which the blinded Cyclops, Polyphemus, hurled boulders at the retreating Ulysses, thus creating spires of rock, or *faraglioni* (pillars of rock rising dramatically out of the sea). Tourism has barely taken off here, so it's a good destination if you feel like putting some distance between yourself and the busloads of tourists in Taormina, or if seeking an easy day trip from Catania. And though the beaches are rocky, there's good swimming here, too.

GETTING HERE AND AROUND

Buses arrive frequently from Taormina and Catania. Acireale is on the main coastal train route, though the station is a long walk south of the center. Local buses pass every 20 minutes or so.

VISITOR INFORMATION

CONTACT Acireale Tourism Office.
⊠ *Via Oreste Scionti 15, Acireale* ☏ *095/891999, 095/895249.*

Sights

Belvedere di Santa Caterina

VIEWPOINT | Lord Byron (1788–1824) visited the Belvedere di Santa Caterina to look out over the Ionian Sea during his Italian wanderings. Today, the viewing point is south of the old town, near the Terme di Acireale, off SS114, and is a tranquil spot for photos or quiet reflection on one of the several benches positioned toward the water. ⊠ *Off SS114, Acireale.*

Duomo

CHURCH | With its cupola and twin turrets, Acireale's Duomo is an extravagant Baroque construction dating from the 17th century. In the chapel to the right of the altar, look for the 17th-century silver statue of Santa Venera (patron saint of Acireale) by Mario D'Angelo, and the early-18th-century frescoes by Antonio Filocamo. ⊠ *Piazza del Duomo, Acireale* ☏ *095/601102* ⊕ *www.diocesiacireale.it.*

Santa Maria La Scala

TOWN | A half-hour walk (or a very twisty drive) from Acireale's center, this picturesque harbor, with lava stone steps leading to the water, is filled with fishermen unloading brightly colored boats. Inexpensive lunches are served in the many restaurants along the harbor; your fresh fish dish is priced by weight. ⊠ *Santa Maria La Scala, Acireale.*

Restaurants

★ La Grotta

$$$ | SEAFOOD | With its dining room set in a cave above the harbor of Santa Maria La Scala, this rustic trattoria specializes in seafood. Try the *insalata di mare* (a selection of delicately boiled fish served with lemon and olive oil), pasta with clams or cuttlefish ink, or fish grilled over charcoal. **Known for:** unique cave setting; superfresh seafood; the catch of the day. $ *Average main: €26* ✉ *Via Scalo Grande 46, Acireale* ☎ *095/7648153* ⊕ *www. ristorantelagrotta.info* ⊘ *Closed Tues. and late Oct.*

Coffee and Quick Bites

Gran Caffè Eldorado

$ | CAFÉ | The delicious ice creams and *granita di mandorla* (almond granita) at Eldorado are a must-visit when in Acireale. Just steps from the cathedral, it makes for a nice *pausa caffè* during a day of sightseeing. **Known for:** friendly staff; wonderful desserts; great ice creams. $ *Average main: €3* ✉ *Corso Umberto 3, Acireale* ☎ *347/9717926* ⊕ *www.grancaffeeldorado.it.*

Performing Arts

Teatro dell'Opera dei Pupi

PUPPET SHOWS | FAMILY | Although it has died out in most other parts of the island, the puppet-theater tradition carries on in Acireale with a small but informative free exhibit at the Museo Opera dei Pupi, which recounts the history of the art and displays the puppets once used in widely beloved local performances. ✉ *Via Nazionale per Catania 195, Acireale* ☎ *095/7648035* ⊕ *www.operadeipupi. com* 🎟 *€10 for guided tours, €15 for shows.*

Mount Etna

30 km (19 miles) northwest of Acireale, 35 km (22 miles) north of Catania, 64 km (40 miles) southwest of Taormina.

The first time you see Mt. Etna, whether it's trailing clouds of smoke or emitting fiery streaks of lava, is certain to be unforgettable. The best-known symbol of Sicily and one of the world's major active volcanoes, Etna is the largest and highest volcano in Europe—the cone of the crater rises 11,014 feet above sea level. Etna is so important to locals that she's often affectionately called Mamma Etna. Although you'll get wonderful vantage points of Etna from Taormina, Castelmola, and Catania in particular, it also makes a rewarding day or overnight trip to see the mountain up close, with a hike or climb; you can find routes suitable for every fitness level. It's also become a popular destination for wine lovers thanks to the many boutique wineries on its slopes; most accept visitors with an appointment.

GETTING HERE AND AROUND

Reaching the lower slopes of Mt. Etna is easy, either by car or by bus from Catania. Getting to the more interesting, higher levels requires taking one of the stout four-wheel-drive minibuses that leave from Piano Provenzana on the north side and from Rifugio Sapienza on the south side. A cable car, called the Funivia dell'Etna, from Rifugio Sapienza takes you part of the way.

CABLE CAR Funivia dell'Etna. ✉ *Rifugio Sapienza* ☎ *095/914141, 095/914142* ⊕ *www.funiviaetna.com.*

TOURS

Club Alpino Italiano

ADVENTURE TOURS | This is a great resource to discover Mt. Etna climbing and hiking guides for those who have some experience and don't want a lot of hand-holding. ✉ *Via Messina 593/a, Catania* ☎ *340/2326542* ⊕ *www.caicatania.it.*

Eastern Sicily, the Tyrrhenian Coast, and the Aeolian Islands

TO NAPLES
TO NAPLES
TO TROPEA

Stromboli

AEOLIAN ISLANDS

Panarea

ALICUDI **Filicudi**
Salina

Tyrrhenian Sea

Lipari

Vulcano

Golfo di Milazzo

Milazzo
Villa San Giovanni
A3
Messina
Reggio Calabria

CAPO D'ORLANDO
St Agata di Militello
113
A20
Patti
113
114
106
116
Cefalù
TYRRHENIAN COAST
113
A20
Caldura
116
185
A18

Pizzo Carbonara
117
Randazzo
Castelmola
Taormina
120
120
Bronte
Linguaglossa
Nicosia
Mount Etna
Milo
Giardini-Naxos
Riposto
A19
121
Adrano
Barone di Villagrande
Giarre
Zafferana Etnea
Trecastagni
Santa Maria La Scala
Biancavilla
Nicolosi
Acireale
Enna
192
Paterno
Aci Castello
Caltanisetta
Aci Trezza
Villa Romana del Casale
288
Catania
191
Casale
Piazza Armerina
417
Golfo di Catania
626
117b
Mazzarino
385
Agnone
Palagonia
194
E45
Caltagirone
124
Lentini
Augusta
Vizzini
Euryalus
Gela
Palazzolo Acreide
194
124
A18
115
Vittoria
124
Siracusa with Ortigia Island
see detail map
Golfo di Gela
Ragusa
Comiso
115
Noto
Avola
Modica
Golfo di Noto
TO MALTA
Scicli
19
E45
Pachino
CAPO PASSERO

Ionian Sea

KEY
🚢 Ferry lines
⛷ Ski Area

0   20 m
0   20 km

Etna Wine School

FOOD AND DRINK TOURS | For a comprehensive overview of the wine world on Mt. Etna, look to Benjamin North Spencer, an American-born wine expert, Etna resident, and author of *The New Wines of Mount Etna*. He and his team offer half-day and full-day courses suitable for professionals and casual enthusiasts alike. You'll visit a vineyard, taste wines based on Carricante and Nerello Mascalese grapes, eat local delicacies, and learn about Etna wine-making traditions at the source. ☎ *347/3348782* ⊕ *www. etnawineschool.com* ✉ *½-day tours €140 per person.*

★ Etna Experience

ADVENTURE TOURS | Your answer to all things outdoors in the area, Etna Experience offers sailing tours between Catania and Aci Trezza, full-day hikes to volcanic caves and the Alcantara gorges, half-day sunset hikes, and the signature Mount Etna Summit tour, which includes high-level trekking up to 10,800 feet to get you as close to the crater as humanly possible. ☎ *349/3053021* ⊕ *www.etnaexperience.com* ✉ *From €44 per person.*

Gruppo Guide Etna Nord

ADVENTURE TOURS | This group offers more personalized (and more expensive) services than others, including excursions well suited to novice climbers. Be sure to reserve ahead of time. ✉ *Piazza Attilio Castrogiovanni 19, Linguaglossa* ☎ *095/7774502, 348/0125167* ⊕ *www. guidetnanord.com.*

VISITOR INFORMATION

CONTACT Nicolosi Tourism Office. (*Porta dell'Etna*) ✉ *Piazza Vittorio Emanuele,* ☎ *095/914488* ⊕ *www.nicolosietna.it.*

Sights

★ Barone di Villagrande

WINERY | At the oldest winery on Etna, the expansive terrace shaded by oak trees looks out over vineyards and down to the sea. The staff offers friendly and informative tours (with excellent English) followed by a tasting of five wines with food pairings or a more formal lunch. Reservations are required. There are also four charming guest rooms overlooking the vineyards for overnight stays. ✉ *Via del Bosco 25, Milo* ☎ *095/7082175* ⊕ *www.villagrande.it* ✉ *€25 tour and tasting.*

Circumetnea

TRAIN/TRAIN STATION | Instead of climbing up Mt. Etna, you can circle it on this private railroad, which runs between Catania and Riposto, with a change at Randazzo. By following the base of the volcano, the Circumetnea stretches out a 31-km (19-mile) journey along the coastal road to 114 km (71 miles). The line was first constructed between 1889 and 1895 and remains small, slow, and single track, but it has some dramatic vistas of the volcano and goes through lava fields. The one-way trip takes about 3½ hours, with departures every 90 minutes or so. After you've made the trip, you can get back to where you started from on the much quicker, but less scenic, conventional rail service between Riposto and Catania. ✉ *Via Caronda 352, Catania* ☎ *095/541111* ⊕ *www.circumetnea.it* ✉ *€8 one-way* ⊘ *Closed Sun.*

★ Mt. Etna

VOLCANO | Affectionally called Idda (or "she" in Sicilian dialect), Etna is basically always active, and occasionally there are airspace closures due to the spewing ash. But for the locals who live in her shadow, Etna is not some ever-present doomsday reminder. She's a living part of the dynamic landscape, loved and revered.

In 387 BC, Plato sailed in just to catch a glimpse of it; in the 9th century AD, the first granita of all time was shaved off its snowy slopes; in 1669, it erupted continuously for four months and lava flows reached Catania; and in the 21st century, the volcano still grabs headlines on an annual basis. Significantly notable eruptions have occurred in the modern era, such as in 1971 (when lava buried the Etna Observatory), in 1981 (when the village of Randazzo narrowly missed destruction), in 2001 (when there was a large flank eruption), in 2002 (when a column of ash spewed that could be seen from space), and in 2008 (when the eruption lasted 417 days and triggered some 200 earthquakes). In February and March 2021, she erupted 11 times in a matter of three weeks, scattering windblown ash throughout the towns below, including Catania. Traveling to the proximity of the crater depends on Mt. Etna's temperament, but you can walk up and down the enormous lava dunes and wander over its moonlike surface of dead craters. The rings of vegetation change markedly as you rise, with vineyards and pine trees gradually giving way to growths of broom and lichen. ✉ *Parco dell'Etna* ☎ *095/821111* 🌐 *www.parcoetna.it.*

🍴 Restaurants

★ Cave Ox

$ | **ITALIAN** | This casual osteria is frequented by local winemakers who come for pizza dinners and rustic daily lunch specials, but most visitors are smitten with the small but amazing cellar focused on Etna natural wines. Everything's fresh, simple, and delicious—and made to pair with one of the delightful wines suggested by owner and wine enthusiast Sandro. **Known for:** local winemaker crowd; filling lunches and pizza dinners; superlative selection of natural wines from Etna. [$] *Average main: €12* ✉ *Via Nazionale Solicchiata 159* ☎ *0942/986171* 🌐 *www.caveox.it* ⏲ *Closed Tues.*

★ Shalai

$$ | **MODERN ITALIAN** | You might not expect to find a thoroughly contemporary restaurant on the slopes of Mt. Etna, but Shalai, in the boutique hotel of the same name, is truly a modern oasis, where young chef Giovanni Santoro prepares updated and beautifully presented versions of Sicilian classics. For the full Michelin-starred experience, choose from the six-course meat or fish tasting menus; to finish, the deconstructed cannoli are a true delight. **Known for:** excellent wine list; delicious tasting menus; innovative modern Sicilian dishes. [$] *Average main: €24* ✉ *Via Marconi 25, Linguaglossa* ☎ *095/643128* 🌐 *www.shalai.it* ⏲ *No lunch weekdays.*

🛏 Hotels

★ Monaci delle Terre Nere

$$$$ | **HOTEL** | This cozy boutique hotel in the foothills of Mt. Etna features spacious rustic-chic rooms on a working organic farm with vineyards, along with an elegant Slow Food–inspired restaurant. **Pros:** eco-conscious atmosphere and policies; pool with countryside views; delicious food and wine. **Cons:** bathrooms can be quite minimalist; no televisions in bedrooms; accommodations may be a little quirky for some. [$] *Rooms from: €370* ✉ *Via Monaci, Zafferana Etnea* ☎ *095/7083638* 🌐 *www.monacidelleterrenere.it* ⏲ *Closed Jan.–mid-Mar.* 🛏 *27 rooms* 🍴 *Free Breakfast.*

Taormina

35 km (22 miles) north of Riposto, 54 km (34 miles) northeast of Catania.

The view of the sea and Mt. Etna from Taormina's jagged, cactus-covered cliffs is as close to perfection as a panorama can get—especially on clear days, when the snowcapped volcano's white puffs of smoke rise against the blue sky. Even when overrun with tourists, its natural beauty is hard to dispute. Writers have extolled Taormina's charms almost since it was founded in the 6th century BC by Greeks from nearby Naxos; Goethe and D.H. Lawrence were among its well-known enthusiasts. The town's boutique-lined main streets get old pretty quickly, but the many hiking paths that wind through the beautiful hills surrounding Taormina promise a timeless alternative. A trip up to stunning Castelmola (whether on foot or by car) should also be on your itinerary. It should be noted that in general, Taormina becomes a ghost town in January and February, with almost every hotel and restaurant closed.

GETTING HERE AND AROUND
Buses from Messina or Catania arrive near the center of Taormina, while trains from these towns pull in at the station at the bottom of the hill. Local buses bring you the rest of the way. A cable car takes passengers up the hill from a parking lot about 2 km (1 mile) north of the train station.

VISITOR INFORMATION
CONTACT Taormina Tourism Office.
⊠ *Piazza Santa Caterina,* ☎ *0942/23243* ⊕ *www.comune.taormina.me.it.*

 # Sights

Castello Saraceno
VIEWPOINT | An unrelenting 20-minute walk up the Via Crucis footpath takes you to the church of the Madonna della Rocca, hollowed out of the limestone rock. Above it towers the 1,000-year-old stone walls of Castello Saraceno, which is built on the site of earlier Greek and Roman fortifications. Although the gate to the castle has been locked for decades, it's worth the climb just for the panoramic views. ⊠ *Monte Tauro, Taormina.*

Funivia
OTHER ATTRACTION | Taormina Mare and the Bay of Mazzarò are accessible by a funivia, or suspended cable car, that glides past incredible views on its way down to the beach at Mazzarò. It departs every 15 minutes, until 8 pm. In June, July, and August, the normal hours are extended until 1 am. ⊠ *Via L. Pirandello, downhill from town center toward bus station, Taormina* ☎ *0942/23906* ⊕ *www. taorminaservizipubblici.it* 🎫 *€3 one-way, €10 day ticket.*

Palazzo Corvaja
NOTABLE BUILDING | Many of Taormina's 14th- and 15th-century palaces have been carefully preserved. Especially beautiful is the Palazzo Corvaja, with characteristic black-lava and white-limestone inlays. Today it houses the tourist office and a museum dedicated to Sicilian art and traditions. ⊠ *Largo Santa Caterina, Taormina* ☎ *0942/620198.*

★ Teatro Greco
RUINS | The Greeks put a premium on finding impressive locations to stage their dramas, such as Taormina's hillside Teatro Greco. Beyond the columns, you can see the town's rooftops spilling down the hillside, the arc of the coastline, and Mt. Etna in the distance. The theater was built during the 3rd century BC and rebuilt by the Romans during the 2nd century AD. Its acoustics are exceptional: even today a stage whisper can be heard in the last rows. In summer, many music and dance performances are held in the Teatro Greco after sunset, when the marvelous vistas of the sparkling Ionian Sea are shrouded in darkness, but the glow of Sicily's most famous volcano can sometimes be seen in the distance. ⊠ *Via Teatro Greco, Taormina* ☎ *0942/23220* ⊕ *www.parconaxostaormina.com* 🎫 *€10.*

★ Villa Comunale
GARDEN | Stroll down Via Bagnoli Croce from the main Corso Umberto to the Villa Comunale to enjoy the stunning views from the seaside city's best terrace walkways. Also known as the Parco Duca di Cesarò, the lovely public gardens were designed by Florence Trevelyan Cacciola, a Scottish lady "invited" to leave England following a romantic liaison with the future Edward VII (1841–1910). Arriving in Taormina in 1889, she married a local professor and devoted herself to the gardens, filling them with native Mediterranean and exotic plants, ornamental pavilions, and fountains. ⊠ *Via Bagnoli Croce, Taormina.*

Beaches

Taormina Mare

BEACH | Below the main city of Taormina is Taormina Mare, where summertime beachgoers jostle for space on a pebble beach against the scenic backdrop of the aptly named Isolabella. The first section of beach is reserved for expensive resorts but the far end, next to Isolabella, has a large free area. The tiny "beautiful island" of Isolabella was once a private residence, but is now a nature preserve reached by walking along a narrow rocky path and visited for a small fee of €4. **Amenities:** none. **Best for:** walking. ⊠ *Taormina Mare, Taormina* ⊕ *www. parconaxostaormina.com* ⊠ *€4 for Isola Bella.*

 Restaurants

L'Arco dei Cappuccini

$$ | SEAFOOD | Just off Via Costantino Patricio, by the far side of the Cappuccini arch, lies this diminutive restaurant. Outdoor seating and an upstairs kitchen help make room for a few extra tables—a necessity, as locals are well aware that neither the price nor the quality is equaled elsewhere in town. **Known for:** a great wine list; authentic local cooking; fine inexpensive dining. $ *Average main: €16* ⊠ *Via Cappuccini 7, off Via Costantino Patricio, Taormina* ☎ *392/2442484* ⊕ *www.arcodeicappuccini.com* ⏱ *Closed Feb.*

Osteria RossoDiVino

$$ | SICILIAN | Run by two sisters, this intimate restaurant in a cobblestone courtyard just before the old city gate is one of the friendliest in town, with creative daily menus highlighting house-made pastas, seasonal produce from the market, and freshly caught fish; seating is primarily outdoors on the patio (bug spray is provided, if mosquitoes become an issue). As the name suggests, wine is a specialty, so let them recommend a glass or bottle. **Known for:** delicious

modern Sicilian food; excellent wine choices; daily-changing menus. $ *Average main: €18* ⊠ *Vico de Spuches 8, Taormina* ☎ *0942/628653* ⏱ *Closed Jan. and Feb and Tues.*

★ Trattoria Il Barcaiolo

$$$ | SEAFOOD | Just behind the public beach in Mazzarò Bay, this intimate little terrace restaurant is shrouded by an enormous old grapevine and looks out onto postcard-perfect views of paradise. Since 1981, the family-owned trattoria has been serving pristine seafood to discerning locals and in-the-know tourists. **Known for:** swordfish carpaccio with citrus and capers; cassata and cannoli for dessert; extensive wine list. $ *Average main: €25* ⊠ *Via Castelluccio 43, Taormina* ☎ *379/2089564* ⊕ *www.barcaiolo. altervista.org* ⏱ *Closed Tues.*

Coffee and Quick Bites

Pasticceria Etna

$ | BAKERY | Fans of marzipan will delight at the range of almond sweets on offer here in the shape of the ubiquitous *fico d'India* (prickly pear) and other fruit. A block of almond paste makes a good souvenir—you can bring it home to make an almond latte or granita. **Known for:** house-made granita; fresh cannoli; almond sweets. $ *Average main: €2* ⊠ *Corso Umberto I 112, Taormina* ☎ *0942/24735* ⊕ *www.pasticceriaetna.com.*

Hotels

★ Belmond Grand Hotel Timeo

$$$$ | HOTEL | On a princely perch overlooking the town, the Greek theater, and the bay, this truly grand hotel, Taormina's oldest, wears a graceful patina that suggests la dolce vita, with a splash of Baroque and a dash of Mediterranean design in the lobby, which has tile- and brickwork walls and vaulted ceilings. **Pros:** feeling of indulgence; exemplary service; amazing location with fantastic views. **Cons:** spa is on the small side;

lower category rooms only have partial views; very expensive. $ *Rooms from: €900* ✉ *Via Teatro Greco 59, Taormina* ☎ *0942/6270200* ⊕ *www.belmond.com/ grand-hotel-timeo-taormina* ☉ *Closed Jan.–mid-Mar.* 🛏 *70 rooms* ◐ *Free Breakfast.*

★ Belmond Villa Sant'Andrea

$$$$ | HOTEL | FAMILY | In a prime location on its own private beach at Taormina Mare, this elegant hotel in a late-1800s villa offers phenomenal views of the water, attentive service, and luxurious and comfortable guest rooms. **Pros:** glorious private beach; free shuttle service to Taormina town; flawless service. **Cons:** pricey food and drinks; spa is small; limited on-site parking. $ *Rooms from: €900* ✉ *Via Nazionale 137, Taormina* ☎ *0942/6271200* ⊕ *www.belmond.com/ villa-sant-andrea-taormina-mare* ☉ *Closed Nov.–mid-Apr.* 🛏 *70 rooms* ◐ *Free Breakfast.*

Hotel Metropole Taormina

$$$$ | HOTEL | This trendy boutique hotel boasts a prime location, with the main shopping street of Corso Umberto on one side and sea views on the other. **Pros:** most rooms are suites; amazing views from restaurant and pool; lovely spa and public areas. **Cons:** not all rooms have good views; expensive overall, with high prices particularly in the bar; bathrooms can be small and dark. $ *Rooms from: €432* ✉ *Corso Umberto 154, Taormina* ☎ *0942/24013* ⊕ *www. hotelmetropoletaormina.it* ☉ *Closed Jan.–Mar.* 🛏 *23 rooms* ◐ *Free Breakfast.*

Hotel Villa Paradiso

$$$ | HOTEL | On the edge of the town's historic center, overlooking lovely public gardens and facing the sea, this under-the-radar family-run hotel was renovated in 2021, but still maintains its antique furnishings, paintings, and Persian rugs, as well as its delightful service, good rooftop restaurant, and Etna views from many guest rooms. **Pros:** good value; great rooftop views; free shuttle bus to beach. **Cons:** beach club fee is extra; only three free parking spaces (paid parking nearby); not all rooms have views. $ *Rooms from: €259* ✉ *Via Roma 2, Taormina* ☎ *0942/23921* ⊕ *www.hotel-villaparadisotaormina.com* 🛏 *37 rooms* ◐ *Free Breakfast.*

★ San Domenico Palace, A Four Seasons Hotel

$$$$ | HOTEL | The sweeping views of the castle, the sea, and Mt. Etna from this converted 14th-century Dominican monastery will linger in your mind, along with the equally memorable levels of luxury and wonderful food in the hotel's highly lauded restaurant, Principe Cerami. **Pros:** strong sense of history and grandeur; quiet and restful; gorgeous infinity pool with amazing views. **Cons:** beach access through partner affiliates; parking €50 per day; very expensive. $ *Rooms from: €1200* ✉ *Piazza San Domenico 5, Taormina* ☎ *0942/613111* ⊕ *www.fourseasons. com/taormina* ☉ *Closed early Jan.–mid-Mar.* 🛏 *111 rooms* ◐ *Free Breakfast.*

Castelmola

5 km (3 miles) west of Taormina.

Although many believe that Taormina has the most spectacular views, tiny Castelmola—floating 1,800 feet above sea level—takes the word "scenic" to a whole new level. Along the cobblestone streets within the ancient walls, 360-degree panoramas of mountain, sea, and sky are so ubiquitous that you almost get used to them (but not quite). Collect yourself with a sip of the sweet almond wine (best served cold) made in local bars, or with lunch at one of the humble pizzerias or panino shops.

A 10-minute drive on a winding but well-paved road leads from Taormina to Castelmola; you must park in one of the public lots below the village and walk up to the center, only a few minutes away. On a nice day, hikers are in for a treat if they make the trip from Taormina on foot instead. It's a serious uphill climb, but the 1½-km (¾-mile) path offers breathtaking views, which compensate for the somewhat poor maintenance of the path itself. You'll begin at Porta Catania in Taormina, with a walk along Via Apollo Arcageta past the Chiesa di San Francesco di Paola on the left. The Strada Comunale della Chiusa then leads past Piazza Andromaco, revealing good views of the jagged promontory of Cocolonazzo di Mola to the north. Allow around an hour for the ascent, a half hour for the descent. There's another, slightly longer (2-km [1-mile]) path that heads up from Porta Messina past the Roman aqueduct, Convento dei Cappuccini, and the northeastern side of Monte Tauro. You could take one up and the other down. In any case, avoid the midday sun, wear comfortable shoes, and carry plenty of water with you.

GETTING HERE AND AROUND
Regular buses bound for Castelmola leave from Taormina's bus station on Via Pirandello.

Sights

★ Castello Normanno
RUINS | In all of Sicily there may be no spot more scenic than atop Castello Normanno, reached by a set of steep staircases rising out of the town center. From here you can gaze upon two coastlines, smoking Mt. Etna, and the town spilling down the mountainside. The area was fortified by the Byzantines in the 9th century and was later rebuilt by the Normans, but all that stands today are the remains of the 16th-century castle walls. Come during daylight hours to take full advantage of the vista. ⊠ *Castello Normanno, Castelmola* ⊕ *www.comune-castelmola.it.*

Restaurants

Il Vicolo
$ | SICILIAN | Located on a side street, this trattoria is one of the simpler dining choices in town, and also one of the better ones—what it lacks in views it makes up for with a pleasant rustic ambience plus a great selection of handmade pasta and, in the evening, *forno a legna* (from a wood-fired oven). In winter, pizzas are served weekends only. **Known for:** signature squid ragù; pasta and pizza; cozy environs. $ *Average main: €12* ⊠ *Via Papa Pio IX 26, Castelmola* ☎ *0942/28481* ⊗ *Closed Tues. Sept.–June and 2 wks late Jan.–early Feb.*

Hotels

Villa Sonia
$$ | HOTEL | Many guest rooms at this well-situated hotel have private terraces with gorgeous grab-the-camera views of Etna without the crowds (or high prices) of nearby Taormina. **Pros:** bus stop to Taormina outside door; friendly service; on-site sauna and pool. **Cons:** iffy Wi-Fi; not much to do in the evening; some rooms are quite small. $ *Rooms from: €139* ⊠ *Via Porta Mola 9, Castelmola* ☎ *0942/28082* ⊕ *www.hotelvillasonia.com* ⊗ *Closed Nov.–mid-Dec. and early Jan.–mid-Mar* ⇥ *44 rooms* ⊗ *Free Breakfast.*

Nightlife

Bar Turrisi
BARS | Truly one of the most infamous places to have a drink in all of Italy, this humorous bar has cozy nooks and crannies on three levels—all decked out with phallic images of every size, shape, and color imaginable, from bathroom wall murals inspired by the brothels of ancient Greece to giant wooden carvings honoring Dionysus. If you can get past the design choices, the roof terrace has extraordinary views of Taormina and the

coast, while a limited selection of hearty pasta dishes are served inside. ✉ *Piazza del Duomo 19, Castelmola* ☎ *0942/28181* ⊕ *www.turrisibar.it.*

Messina

42 km (26 miles) north of Savoca, 94 km (59 miles) northeast of Catania, 237 km (149 miles) east of Palermo.

Messina's ancient history recounts a series of disasters, but the city once vied with Palermo in a bid to become the island's capital, developing a fine university, a bustling commercial center, and a thriving cultural environment. At 5:20 am on December 28, 1908, Messina was reduced from a flourishing metropolis of 120,000 to a heap of rubble, shaken to pieces by an earthquake that turned into a tidal wave; 80,000 people died as a result, and the city was almost completely leveled. As you approach by ferry, you won't notice any outward indication of the disaster, just the modern countenance of a 3,000-year-old city. The somewhat flat look is a precaution of seismic planning: tall buildings are not permitted.

GETTING HERE AND AROUND

Frequent hydrofoils and ferries carry passengers, cars, and trains across the Strait of Messina from Villa San Giovanni, from just below the train station. There are also regular hydrofoil departures for foot passengers from Reggio Calabria. Cruise ships also stop in Messina's port.

From within Sicily, Messina is easily reachable by car, as it sits just off the E45 autostrada from Catania and the E90 autostrada from Palermo. There are regular train and bus services from both cities as well.

VISITOR INFORMATION

CONTACT Messina Tourism Office. ✉ *Via dei Mille 270, Messina* ☎ *090/7761048, 090/776146* ⊕ *turismoecultura.cittametropolitana.me.it.*

Sights

Duomo

CHURCH | The reconstruction of Messina's Norman and Romanesque cathedral, originally built by the Norman king Roger II and consecrated in 1197, has retained much of the original plan—including a handsome crown of Norman battlements, an enormous apse, and a splendid wood-beamed ceiling. The adjoining bell tower contains one of the largest and most complex mechanical clocks in the world: constructed in 1933, it has a host of gilded automatons (a roaring lion and crowing rooster among them) that spring into action every day at the stroke of noon, lasting for 12 minutes.

Don't miss the chance to climb the bell tower itself. As you head up the internal stairs, you'll see the system of levers and counterweights that operates the movements of the gilded bronze statues that parade through the open facade high over the Duomo's square. At the top, an open-air terrace offers 360-degree views of Messina and the Strait. ✉ *Piazza del Duomo 29, Messina* ☎ *090/66841* ⊕ *www.diocesimessina.it* ✆ *Clock tower €4.*

 Restaurants

★ A Cucchiara

$$ | MODERN ITALIAN | A light nautical theme permeates this stone-walled restaurant, where the open kitchen provides theater and owner Peppe Giamboi takes the stage as a gustatory storyteller, roaming from table to table. The menu is constantly changing, but you'll find excellent work with vegetables (a rarity in Sicily) and really lovely preparations of local cod. **Known for:** locally, sustainably sourced seafood; robust wine program;

elegant food in a relaxed, welcoming atmosphere. $ *Average main: €18* ⊠ *Strada San Giacomo 19, Messina* ☎ *090/711023* ⊕ *www.ristoranti.messina. it* ⊙ *Closed Sun.*

Lipari

2 hours, 10 minutes from Milazzo by ferry, 1 hour by hydrofoil; 60–75 minutes from Reggio di Calabria and Messina by ferry.

The largest and most developed of the Aeolians, Lipari welcomes you with distinctive pastel-color houses. Fields of spiky agaves dot the northernmost tip of the island, Acquacalda, indented with pumice and obsidian quarries. In the west is San Calogero, where you can explore hot springs and mud baths. From the red-lava base of the island rises a plateau crowned with a 16th-century castle and a 17th-century cathedral.

GETTING HERE AND AROUND

Ferries and hydrofoils from Milazzo, which is 41 km (25 miles) west of Messina, stop here. There's also ferry service from Reggio di Calabria and Messina. On the island, if you plan to explore extensively, you should rent a car or a scooter. Lipari is the largest of the Aeolians and navigating it can be difficult without your own mode of transport.

 Sights

★ Museo Archeologico Regionale Eoliano

HISTORY MUSEUM | This vast, multibuilding museum is terrific, with an intelligently arranged collection of prehistoric finds— some dating as far back as 4000 BC— from various sites in the archipelago, as well as Greek and Roman artifacts, including an outstanding collection of Greek theatrical masks, and even interesting information on volcanoes. Basic descriptions about the exhibits are provided in English and Italian, though

more comprehensive information is in Italian only. That said, there is so much to see, the museum is worth at least a few hours of your time. ⊠ *Via Castello 2, Lipari* ☎ *090/9880174* ⊠ *€6.*

★ Vulcano

ISLAND | True to its name, the island of Vulcano has a profusion of fumaroles sending up jets of hot vapor, although the volcano itself has long been dormant. Visitors come to soak in the strong-smelling sulfur springs or to sunbathe and walk on some of the archipelago's best beaches, though the volcanic black sand can be off-putting at first glance. Ascend to its crater (1,266 feet above sea level) on muleback for eye-popping views, or take a boat ride into the grottoes around the volcano's base. From Capo Grillo, you can see all the Aeolians. ⊠ *Vulcano.*

 Restaurants

★ Osteria San Bartolo

$$ | **ITALIAN** | Chef Danilo Conti started with a passion for wine and subsequently grew deeper respect for the soil of his home territory. The dishes at his osteria just steps from the port in Lipari are clean and balanced—the opposite of fussy—but primarily celebrate the fishing and agricultural traditions of the island; think lime-scented carpaccio of swordfish and pasta with anchovies, wild fennel, and orange zest. **Known for:** stuffed calamari; showcasing the best of both sea and land; natural wine (chef owns a wine shop a few doors down). $ *Average main: €16* ⊠ *Via Francesco Crispi 109, Lipari* ☎ *090/8961317* ⊕ *www.sanbartolovineriaedispensa.com* ⊙ *Closed Wed.*

🛏 **Hotels**

Hotel Villa Enrica

$$ | **HOTEL** | This hotel's hillside position gives it one of the best views on the island, looking south over Marina Lunga and the castle, and it seems like nearly every part of the hotel (from rooms to

common areas) takes advantage of that vista. **Pros:** cliff-side infinity pool with snack bar for light lunches; free shuttle service to beach; heated hydromassage pool. **Cons:** service can be slow; often hosts events so can get crowded with nonguests; needs updating. $ *Rooms from: €132 ⊠ Strada Serra Pirrera 11, Lipari ☎ 090/9880826 ⊕ www.hotelvillae-nricalipari.com ⊗ Closed mid-Oct.–Easter ⇌ 20 rooms ⦿ No Meals.*

Les Sables Noirs

$$$ | **HOTEL** | Named for the black sands of the beach it sits in front of, this luxury hotel is superbly sited on the beautiful Porto di Ponente and its cool modern furnishings and inviting pool and spa induce a sybaritic mood. **Pros:** stunning beachfront location; quick five-minute walk to town; delicious breakfasts. **Cons:** the spa is not included in the price; five-night minimum stay in August; no on-site restaurant. $ *Rooms from: €240 ⊠ Porto di Ponente, Vulcano ☎ 090/9850 ⊕ www.lessablesnoirs.it ⊗ Closed mid-Oct.–Apr. ⇌ 53 rooms ⦿ Free Breakfast.*

Salina

50 minutes from Lipari by ferry, 20 minutes by hydrofoil.

The second largest of the Aeolians, Salina is also the most fertile, which accounts for its excellent Malvasia wine. Salina is the archipelago's lushest and highest island, too: Mt. Fossa delle Felci rises to more than 3,000 feet and offers a challenging two-hour hike to the summit, and the vineyards and fishing villages along its slopes add to the allure. Pollara, in the west of the island, has capitalized on its fame as one of the locations in the 1990s cult movie *Il Postino* (*The Postman*) and is an ideal location for sunset watching and an evening passeggiata on well-maintained paths along the volcanic terrain.

GETTING HERE AND AROUND

Ferries and hydrofoils arrive here from Alicudi, Lipari, Panarea, and Stromboli. Note that there are two ports on Salina: Santa Marina Salina and Rinella. Not all ferries and hydrofoils arrive at both ports, so double-check your tickets and timetables. Once on the island, you can get around by taxi, or rent a car or a scooter. The island's bus service, C.I.T.I.S. (€1.90 one-way), runs reliably and on time between the island's towns.

TOURS
Sogno Eoliano

BOAT TOURS | Though the island's verdant hills beckon, Salina is best experienced by water. Native son Samuele, with a sparkling smile and easy charm, navigates the sea on his 21-foot boat, taking guests on excursions ranging from a two-hour aperitivo sunset cruise to Pollara Bay to full-day trips to neighboring islands. He grew up on the sea (and fishes during the off-season), so he knows these waters intimately and that comes through in his tours, which are all customizable according to your specific interests. Prices start at €150 for up to five people. ⊠ *Salina ☎ 331/9928032 ⊕ www.sognoeoliano.it ⊟ From €150.*

🍴 Restaurants

★ Da Alfredo

$ | **SICILIAN** | Starting in 1968, the mini-empire of owner Alfredo Olivieri was built one granita and one *pane cunzato* at a time, and no summer on Salina is complete without a stop at his little shop off the Marina Garibaldi piazza in Lingua. You'll find all the classic granita flavors (almond, coffee, lemon, pistachio), but it's the seasonal fruits that shine here: mulberry, fig, wild blackberries, watermelon, and cantaloupe. **Known for:** charismatic owner; joyous atmosphere; seasonally focused granita. $ *Average main: €11 ⊠ Via Marina Garibaldi, Santa Marina, Salina ☎ 090/9843980 ⊗ Closed Oct.–Apr.*

Hotels

★ Principe di Salina

$$$ | **HOTEL** | Awash in white with vibrant pops of color, this family-run boutique property that hugs the Malfa hillside defines barefoot chic. **Pros:** house-made breads and pastries; excellent wine and cocktail list; Ortigia bath products. **Cons:** restaurant closed to external guests; no kids under age 10; not directly on the sea. [$] *Rooms from: €250* ✉ *SP 182 3, Malfa, Salina* ☎ *090/9844415* 🌐 *www.principedisalina.it* 🕒 *Closed mid-Oct.–late Apr.* 🛏 *12 rooms* 🍴 *Free Breakfast.*

Panarea

2 hours from Lipari by ferry, 25–50 minutes by hydrofoil; 30 minutes from Salina by hydrofoil.

Panarea is the second smallest of the islands but has some of the most dramatic scenery, including wild caves carved out of rock and dazzling flora. The exceptionally clear water and the richness of life on the seafloor make Panarea especially suitable for underwater exploration. The outlying rocks and islets make a gorgeous sight, and you can enjoy the panorama on an easy excursion to the small Bronze Age village at Capo Milazzese.

GETTING HERE AND AROUND

Ferries and hydrofoils arrive here from Lipari, Salina, and Naples. For a splurge, you can book a helicopter flight with Air Panarea (🌐 *www.airpanarea.com*) from Milazzo, Catania, Taormina, or even Palermo. The Milazzo flight is 18 minutes and costs €1,300 for five people. Once on the island, you'll need to rely on walking, Vespas, or electric golf carts to get around—cars are banned.

Hotels

Hotel Raya

$$$$ | **HOTEL** | Although some visitors say it's resting on past laurels, Raya is perfectly in keeping with the elite style of Panarea—discreet and expensive, with a pool and terrace that enjoy views over the sea toward Stromboli. **Pros:** great views of Stromboli; lovely pool area; hippie-chic ambience. **Cons:** in need of renovations; uphill trudge to rooms; snooty staff. [$] *Rooms from: €500* ✉ *Via San Pietro, Panarea* ☎ *090/983013* 🌐 *www.hotelraya.it* 🕒 *Closed mid-Oct.–mid-Apr.* 🛏 *34 rooms* 🍴 *Free Breakfast* ☞ *No young children allowed.*

Stromboli

3 hours, 45 minutes from Lipari by ferry, 65–90 minutes by hydrofoil; 80 minutes from Salina by hydrofoil; 9 hours from Naples by ferry, 5 hours by hydrofoil.

This northernmost of the Aeolians consists entirely of the cone of an active volcano. The view from the sea—especially at night, as an endless stream of glowing red-hot lava flows into the water—is unforgettable. Stromboli is in a constant state of mild dissatisfaction, and every now and then its anger flares up, so following a devastating eruption on July 3, 2019, which killed a hiker, authorities do not allow any ascents to the principal crater. The main town has a small selection of reasonably priced hotels and restaurants, and a choice of lively clubs and cafés. In addition to the island tour, excursions might include boat trips around the sea stack of Strombolicchio, which is all that remains of the original volcano that gave rise to Stromboli. At night boats offer trips to see the Sciara del Fuoco, the lava channel that rises out of the blue waters.

GETTING HERE AND AROUND

Ferries and hydrofoils arrive here from Lipari, Salina, and Naples. Once on the island, you'll need to navigate by foot, or you can book one of the golf cart taxis located near the port.

TOURS

★ MagmaTrek

ADVENTURE TOURS | You can freely hike the volcano up to 951 feet, but for anything beyond that (up to the 1,312 foot) safe limit, you'll need an authorized guide. MagmaTrek offers five-hour hikes (€25) that get you as close as humanly possible to the volcanic activity as you ascend approximately 5 miles up the flanks of Stromboli. They provide the mandatory helmets, but you should be sure to pack sturdy walking shoes. ✉ *Via Vittorio Emanuele, Stromboli* ☎ *090/9865768* 🌐 *www.magmatrek.it* 🕒 *Closed Nov.–mid-Nov.*

Pippo Navigazione

BOAT TOURS | The best way to see Stromboli's eruptions is with a boat tour such as those run by Pippo Navigazione. Boat trips include three-hour day cruises and night tours that explore the area where the lava reaches the sea. Trips start at €25 per person for groups up to 30 people. You can also book private excursions. ✉ *Porto Scari, Stromboli* ☎ *348/0559296 Giovanni, 339/2229714 Giovanni's mother* 🎟 *From €25.*

Filicudi

30–60 minutes from Salina and Lipari by hydrofoil; 2 hours from Cefalù and Palermo, 2 hours from Milazzo, and 10 hours from Naples by ferry.

Just a dot in the sea, Filicudi is famous for its unusual volcanic rock formations, the enchanting Grotta del Bue Marino (Grotto of the Sea Ox), and the crumbled remains of a prehistoric village at Capo Graziano. The island, which is spectacular for walking and hiking, is still a truly undiscovered, restful haven, and has a handful of hotels and *pensioni* as well as some more informal rooms with families who put up guests. Car ferries are available only in summer.

GETTING HERE AND AROUND

Ferries and hydrofoils arrive throughout the year from Salina and Lipari, and also in summer from Palermo, Cefalù, Milazzo, and Naples. Once you've arrived, you can rent a car or a scooter at the port. You can also find the minibus taxi of D&G Servizio Navetta (☎ *347/7575916*) usually waiting at the port.

🛏 Hotels

La Canna

$$ | HOTEL | Set above the tiny port and commanding fabulous views of sea and sky from its flower-filled terrace, this hotel offers small but adequate guest rooms, kept clean and tidy by the family-friendly staff. **Pros:** relaxing pool and lounge area; great views; family-friendly atmosphere. **Cons:** no Wi-Fi in guest rooms; half board required in peak season; an uphill climb from the port. [$] *Rooms from: €160* ✉ *Via Rosa 43, Filicudi Porto* ☎ *090/9889956* 🌐 *www.lacannahotel.it* 🕒 *Closed mid-Oct.–mid-Apr.* 🛏 *14 rooms* 🍴 *No Meals.*

Cefalù

39 km (22 miles) northeast of Caccamo.

The jewel of the Tyrrhenian Coast is no doubt Cefalù, a classically appealing old Sicilian town built on a spur jutting out into the sea.

The city's medieval origins have left behind many interesting historical sites to explore. The Palazzo Maria in Piazza Duomo and the Osteria Magno in Corso Ruggero are palaces that date back to the 13th century. They were both owned by the Ventimiglia family, an influential aristocratic family that dominated and owned most of the agricultural wealth of this part of the island in the middle ages.

Another piece of history here is the medieval washhouse. Carved out of rustic lava stone and used until the early 20th century, the ancient bathhouse is home to a series of basins fed by the waters of the Cefalino River, which flow out from 22 iron lion-shape mouths. Here, you can get a sense of how life was in Sicily in the Middle Ages.

Cefalù's historical heritage continues with remnants of the Baroque period from the 18th century, which gave birth to the elaborate decorations and style that are quite unique to Sicily. There are the ornate facades of the church of the Monte della Pietà, which dates from 1716, and the stunning Church of Purgatory (1668). The town's historical center is dotted with endless portholes, squares, facades, and architectural details.

GETTING HERE AND AROUND

Trains and buses run between Palermo and Messina, and stop at the station about a 10-minute walk from town. Drivers can take the A20 autostrada, though the traffic going in and out of Cefalù can be heavy in summer and the 50-minute train ride from Palermo may be the better option.

VISITOR INFORMATION

CONTACT Cefalù Tourism Office. ✉ *Corso Ruggeri 77,* ☎ *0921/421050* 🌐 *www.cefalu.it.*

Sights

Duomo

CHURCH | Cefalù is dominated by a massive headland—*la rocca*—and a 12th-century Romanesque Duomo, which is one of the finest Norman cathedrals in Italy. Roger II began the church in 1131 as an offering of thanks for having been saved here from a shipwreck. Its mosaics rival those of Monreale. (Whereas Monreale's Byzantine Christ figure is an austere and powerful image, emphasizing Christ's divinity, the Cefalù Christ is softer, more compassionate, and more human.)
At the Duomo you must be respectfully attired—no shorts or beachwear permitted. ✉ *Piazza del Duomo, Cefalù* ☎ *0921/922021* 🌐 *www.cattedraledicefalu.com* 🎟 *Cloister €3* 🕒 *Cloister closed weekends.*

Restaurants

Al Porticciolo

$$ | **SICILIAN** | Nicola Mendolia's seaside restaurant is comfortable, casual, and faithfully focused on food—primarily pizza, but with an extensive selection of seafood, pasta, and meat, too. Dark, heavy wooden tables create a comfortable environment filled with a mix of jovial locals and businesspeople, though you may opt to dine on the spacious terrace. **Known for:** lovely terrace overlooking the water; local seafood; high-quality pizza. [$] *Average main: €17* ✉ *Via C. Ortolani di Bordonaro 66, Cefalù* ☎ *0921/921981* 🌐 *www.alporticcioloristorante.com.*

Hotels

Kalura

$$$ | **HOTEL** | **FAMILY** | This modern hotel is on a small promontory in Caldura, 2 km (1 mile) east of Cefalù, a few minutes away by taxi or a 30-minute walk, and offers bright and cheerful rooms, many with balconies overlooking the sea. **Pros:** beautiful sea views; family-friendly environment; good swimming. **Cons:** minimum stay of two to seven nights in high season; Wi-Fi only in lobby; outside town. [$] *Rooms from: €209* ✉ *Via V. Cavallaro 13, Cefalù* ☎ *0921/421354* 🌐 *www.hotel-kalura.com* 🕒 *Closed mid-Nov.–mid-Mar.* 🛏 *84 rooms* 🍴 *Free Breakfast.*

SARDINIA

Updated by
Robert Andrews

👁 **Sights**
★★★☆☆

🍴 **Restaurants**
★★★★☆

🛏 **Hotels**
★★★★☆

🛍 **Shopping**
★★☆☆☆

🍸 **Nightlife**
★☆☆☆☆

WELCOME TO SARDINIA

TOP REASONS TO GO

★ **Relax on idyllic beaches:** Covering more than 1,200 miles of coastline, Sardinia's beaches beckon with their turquoise waters, white sand, and rippled dunes.

★ **Discover natural beauty:** A network of trails explores Sardinia's resplendent mountains, deep gorges, lush forests, and cascading waterfalls.

★ **Explore charming towns and villages:** From coastal towns to rural villages, the island is dotted with a variety of settlements that take pride in their history and tradition. Each has its own culture, cuisine, and unique way of life.

★ **Dive or snorkel the outer reefs:** Crystalline waters, warm weather, and outer reefs make Sardinia a paradise for underwater adventurers. Sunken ships and marine reserves provide the ideal place to discover marine life.

★ **Savor Sardinian delicacies:** From pasta and prosciutto to lamb and cheese, the island's cuisine is sure to satisfy any appetite.

1 Cagliari. Sardinia's capital is a hive of cultural attractions, dining hot spots, and glamorous shops.

2 Pula. Just south of Cagliari, Pula is home to resorts, beaches, and a major archaeological site.

3 Sant'Antioco. A significant archaeological site and museum merit a visit on this west-coast island, once a major Carthaginian base.

4 San Pietro. This offshore isle makes a perfect bolt-hole, with its lively port and undeveloped beaches.

5 Costa Verde. A high, cliffy coastline and alluring beaches are the main attractions on Sardinia's "Green Coast."

6 Barumini. The island's ancient and enigmatic nuraghic culture are showcased at Su Nuraxi, just outside Barumini.

7 Oristano. Little visited by tourists, this provincial center makes an appealing base for the nearby Sinis Peninsula.

8 Tharros. Explore Carthaginian and Roman ruins at this site near the town of Oristano.

9 Nuoro. The largest inland town is a must-see for anyone interested in Sardinia's traditional culture.

10 Fonni. Near the island's highest peaks, Fonni makes an ideal hiking base.

11 Alghero. Alghero's historic center is a warren of traffic-free lanes lined with lively bars, shops, and restaurants.

12 Sassari. Sardinia's second city has an engaging old quarter.

13 Castelsardo. This former north coast stronghold is renowned for its basketware.

14 Santa Teresa Gallura. On the island's northern tip, this resort is surrounded by excellent beaches.

15 La Maddalena. Garibaldi's former home is a highlight of any tour of this archipelago.

16 Porto Cervo. Day-trippers are drawn to this jet-setter enclave on the famed Costa Smeralda.

17 Olbia. Sardinia's northern gateway is a short drive from some of Italy's most exclusive hotels and beaches.

FRANCE

Santa Teresa Gallura · La Maddalena · Palau · Porto Cervo · Arzachena · Golfo Aranci · Olbia · Golfo di Olbia · COSTA SMERALDA · Bassacutena · Tempio Pausania · Telti · Monti · Padru · Castelsardo · Sedini · Chiaramonti · Oschiri · Buddusò · Siniscola · Sorso · Ozieri · Bultei · Bitti · Sas Linnas Siccas · Orosei · Monte Ortobene · Dorgali · Cala Gonone · Nuoro · Orotelli · Fonni · Tortolì · Bari Sardo · Oristano · Asuni · Laconi · Nurallao · Barumini · Su Nuraxi · Furtei · Muravera · Monastir · Dolianova · Villasor · Cagliari · Villasimius · Sarroch · Pula · Chia

Punta Caprara · ISOLA ASINARA · Stintino · Golfo dell'Asinara · Porto Torres · Sassari · Alghero · Villanova Monteleone · Padria · Bosa · Tresnuraghes · Macomer · Abbasanta · Cabras · Tharros · Golfo di Oristano · Marrubiu · Uras · Porto Palma · COSTA VERDE · Guspini · Piscinas · Samassi · Buggerru · Iglesias · Portoscuso · Carloforte · ISOLA SAN PIETRO · Sant'Antioco · ISOLA SANT'ANTIOCO · Golfo di Palmas · Capo Teulada · Carbonia · Giba · Capo Spartivento

Golfo di Orosei · Golfo di Cagliari

90 · 133 · 427 · 125 · 200 · 127 · 199 · 125 · 392 · 199 · 131 · 291 · 597 · 389 · 125 · 105 · 292 · 131 · 49 · 129 · 389 · 128 · 292 · 131 · 388 · 128 · 389 · 125 · 198 · 126 · 125 · 197 · 128 · 197 · 126 · 131 · 130 · 125 · 126 · 293 · 195 · 195

0   10 mi
0   10 km

EATING AND DRINKING WELL IN SARDINIA

Wining and dining in Sardinia is not just a richly delicious experience, it's also a way to have a close-up encounter with the history, geography, and cultural traditions of the island. Sardinian food has its own culinary identity, a complex and eclectic mix that makes for mouthwatering and often revelatory dishes.

Sardinia's proximity to North Africa and its long Spanish occupation mean that elements of both cultures can be found in the island's kitchens, including couscous and paella. There are also strong regional variations within Sardinia itself, as well as a traditional division between the land-based fare of the interior and the fresh seafood on the coasts. Wherever you go here, you'll find a strong emphasis on seasonal ingredients and ancient cooking techniques.

BREADS, CHEESES, AND SWEET SPECIALTIES

Sardinia has a strong tradition of bread making and is famous for crispy paper-thin *pane carasau* flatbread (*carta di musica* in Italian).

Ever wondered about all those sheep roaming the rugged slopes of the interior? They're there to produce the raw materials for Italy's original and best pecorino. It's ubiquitous in Sardinia, and comes in various strengths and consistencies.

Sardinian desserts include *sospiri* (morsels of almond dough stuffed with citrus-infused almond paste), *torrone di mandorle* (almond nougat), and *seadas* (cheese-filled pastries topped with honey, also called *sebadas*). The *candelaus*, a fruit-and-almond dessert, and sweet ricotta-stuffed *pardula* cakes are popular in Cagliari. Unmissable is *amaro di corbezzolo,* made by bees that suck nectar from a plant known as *arbutus,* the tree strawberry.

MEAT

The most popular meat dishes are veal, roast *agnello* (lamb), and *porcheddu* (spit-roasted suckling pig). *Cavallo,* or *carne equino* (horse meat), is also commonly found on restaurant menus, particularly in Sassari, where it's generally served in the form of a *bistecca* (thin steak). Donkey (*asino*) and wild boar (*cinghiale*) are other Sardinian specialties. Sometimes cinghiale is roasted on a spit or prepared using the ancient Sardinian technique of *incarralzadu,* for which it's placed in a large hole lined with fragrant myrtle leaves. Another option is *suppa quata,* a hearty soup that's made from beef broth, bread, and aged pecorino cheese.

SEAFOOD

Whole fish are best eaten roasted or grilled, though you may also find

them sautéed in pasta or incorporated into *copaxa de peix,* a fish soup from Alghero. The most famous Alghero dish is lobster, known as *langouste* or *aragosta.* Lobster doesn't appear on restaurant menus in winter—fortunately, the very time when *riccio di mare* (sea urchin), another local specialty, is best enjoyed. Winter is also the best season for *bottarga,* the dried, cured roe of gray mullet or tuna.

STARTERS

Opt for antipasti *di mare* or *di terra* to kick off your meal. Traditional pastas include *malloreddus* (small shells), *culurgiones* (ravioli), and *maccarones de busa* (thick pasta twists). Homemade pastas might be topped with a wild-boar sauce; *fregola,* a semolina pasta, is often served with *arselle* (clams).

WINE

Among the whites, the dry *torbato* of the Alghero Coast and the slightly sparkling *vermentino* from Gallura are standouts. The Oristano region produces the dry, sherrylike *vernaccia* (unrelated to the Tuscan variety), Bosa produces amber-tone *malvasia,* and Barbagia is one of the best sources of *cannonau,* a red wine with an ancient pedigree. The traditional liqueur *mirto,* which makes a fine after-dinner drink, is made from native wild myrtle berries.

The second-largest island in the Mediterranean, Sardinia remains unique and enigmatic with its rugged coastline and white-sand beaches, dramatic granite cliffs, and mountainous inland tracts. Glamorous resorts lie within a short distance of quiet, medieval villages, and ruined castles and ancient churches testify to an eventful history.

But although conquerors from all directions—Phoenicians, Carthaginians, Romans, Catalans, Pisans, Piemontese—have left their traces, no outside culture has had a dominant impact. Pockets of foreign influence persist along the coasts, but inland, a proud Sardinian culture flourishes.

As a travel destination, Sardinia's identity is split: the island has some of Europe's most expensive resorts, but it's also home to pristine terrain untouched by commercial development. Fine sand and clean waters draw summer sun worshippers to beaches that rank among the Mediterranean's best. Most famous are those along the Costa Smeralda (Emerald Coast), where the ultrarich have anchored their yachts since the 1960s.

Apart from the glamorous shores and upscale locales found in the east, most of Sardinia's coast is rugged and unreachable, a jagged series of wildly beautiful inlets accessible only by sea. Inland, Sardinia remains shepherd's country, silent and stark.

MAJOR REGIONS

Cagliari and the Southern Coast. Sardinia's capital and largest city, Cagliari (pronounced *cahl*-yah-ree) contains the island's principal art and archaeology museums as well as an intact old citadel with lofty views of the sea, lagoons, and mountains. To the southwest is Pula, an inland resort within easy reach of good beaches and the excavations at Nora.

Su Nuraxi to the Costa Smeralda. Inland and north of Cagliari, explore the apogee of the island's prehistoric nuraghic civilization at Su Nuraxi, just outside the village of Barumini. Northwest of here, Oristano makes an ideal stopover for exploring the ruins at Tharros. In the mountainous interior, Nuoro has a first-rate ethnographic museum highlighting Sardinia's traditional culture. The rugged granite landscape of Sardinia's northeast is probably best known for the Costa Smeralda, a short strip of elite hotels and beaches.

Planning

Getting Here and Around

AIR

Flying is by far the fastest and easiest way to get to the island. Sardinia's major airport, Aeroporto di Elmas, is in Cagliari, with smaller ones at Alghero (Aeroporto Fertilia) and Olbia (Aeroporto Costa Smeralda).

CONTACTS Aeroporto di Alghero. ⊠ *Regione Nuraghe Biancu* ☎ *079/935011* ⊕ *www.aeroportodialghero.it.* **Aeroporto di Cagliari.** ⊠ *Via dei Trasvolatori,* ☎ *070/211211* ⊕ *www.cagliariairport.it.* **Aeroporto di Olbia Costa Smeralda.** ⊠ *Strada Statale Orientale Sarda,* ☎ *0789/563444* ⊕ *www.geasar.it.*

BUS

Cagliari is linked with the other towns of Sardinia by a network of buses. All major cities and most local destinations are served by ARST. City buses in Cagliari, Olbia, Alghero, and Sassari operate on the same system as those on the mainland: either buy your ticket first, at a tobacco shop, ticket booth, or machine, and punch it in the machine on the bus, or buy on board incurring a supplementary charge.

CONTACTS ARST. ☎ *351/8374226 in Italy, daily 7 am–8 pm* ⊕ *www.arst.sardegna. it.* **Cagliari Bus Station.** ⊠ *Piazza Matteotti,* ☎ *070/6671824.*

CAR

Sardinia is about 270 km (167 miles) long from north to south, which takes three to four hours to drive on main roads; it's roughly 120 km (75 miles) across, but there are no fast east–west routes. Most of the ferries that connect the island with the mainland transport cars.

Roads are generally in good condition, with clear signposting. Superstrada double-lane routes are well developed.

Expect winding inland mountain and coastal roads with hairpin turns. Most gas stations are closed in the afternoon, at night, and on Sunday, though at those times you can still use cards to automatically gas up. Try to avoid driving at night, when mountain roads are particularly hazardous and roadside facilities are infrequent, especially in the east. Fog and snow may be issues in winter.

TRAIN

Trenitalia, or Ferrovie dello Stato (FS), is the national railway of Italy. You can plan itineraries, purchase tickets, and look for special deals online. The Stazione Centrale in Cagliari is next to the bus station on Piazza Matteotti. There are fairly good connections between Olbia, Cagliari, Sassari, and Oristano. Service on the few other local lines is infrequent and slow. The fastest train between Olbia and Cagliari takes 3½ hours. Local trains run by ARST connect Sassari with Alghero (around 40 minutes).

If you can stand a little agitation and are a fan of slow travel, consider taking a trip on the rickety old narrow-gauge railroad operated by Trenino Verde della Sardegna through the island's interior. The service, which started as a public transport utility in 1893, now only runs during the high season in the form of tourist excursions that take in some of Sardinia's most panoramic landscapes. The main Trenino Verde routes run from the village of Mandas (linked to Cagliari by local trains) to either Sadali or Laconi, and from Arbatax, a small port on the island's east coast, to the mountain village of Gairo; each is a full-day excursion taking 9–11 hours, and each includes guided tours of some of the places en route plus lunch stops. There are one to four departures weekly between late April and late September.

CONTACTS Trenitalia. ☎ *892021 in Italy, 06/68475475 from outside Italy* ⊕ *www. trenitalia.com.*

When to Go

The best time to visit Sardinia is Easter through September. European vacationers flock to the island for sunshine in July and August. Expect to pay the highest rates during these two peak summer months, when roads, tourist sites, and beaches are most crowded. Nature is at its most exuberant during the spring, while from September to October, when accommodations start to shut down for the year, you'll find end-of-season deals and fewer tourists. During the winter months, the smaller resorts can resemble ghost towns—with closed restaurants, hotels, and shops.

Restaurants

The full range of eateries can be found in every Sardinian town, from pizzerias to gourmet restaurants, and you'll be especially spoiled for choice in the island's capital, Cagliari, and the resort of Alghero, where good-value fixed-price menus are common. Seafood is ubiquitous, though the most authentic Sard cuisine is based on land products, such as lamb, boar, and suckling pig, not to mention mushrooms, artichokes, and other seasonal produce. Note that, as in other parts of Italy, fish dishes are often priced according to weight (usually by the *etto,* or 100 grams). Many places close in winter; in summer, book ahead to be sure of a table.

Restaurant reviews are the average cost of a main course at dinner, or, if dinner is not served, at lunch. Restaurant reviews have been shortened. For full information, visit Fodors.com.

Hotels

In Sardinia, there are numerous luxury resorts with stunning beachfront vistas, bed-and-breakfast inns in medieval villages, private villas tucked away on lush hills, modern hotels in the trendy capital, and farmhouses on tranquil mountainsides. During summer months, the most popular destination on the island is the Costa Smeralda in the east. High demand during July and August raises nightly rates to an astronomical range, above €1,500 for the most deluxe accommodations. Find more reasonable hotel rates in other parts of the island, which are equally breathtaking and less crowded. Plan dates well in advance, as many hotels close at the end of September until the following April or May.

Hotel reviews are the lowest cost of a standard double room in high season. Hotel reviews have been shortened. For full information, visit Fodors.com.

What it Costs in Euros			
$	$$	$$$	$$$$
RESTAURANTS			
under €15	€15–€24	€25–€35	over €35
HOTELS			
under €125	€125–€200	€201–€300	over €300

Tours

Visos Viaggi

PRIVATE GUIDES | This travel agent and tour operator specializes in individual tours and villa and hotel accommodations. ✉ *Via Puccini 41, Cagliari* ☎ *070/658772* ⊕ *www.visosviaggi.com.*

Cagliari

268 km (166 miles) south of Olbia.

Known in the local dialect as Casteddu, the island's capital has a warren of pedestrianized streets at its heart and a range of impressive Italianate architecture, from modern to medieval. The city comprises nearly 160,000 people and has a busy commercial port and waterfront with broad avenues and arched arcades, while the old hilltop citadel (called, simply, Castello) makes a good starting point to a visit, not least for the Museo Archeologico located here. The imposing Bastione di Saint Remy and Mercato di San Benedetto (one of the best fish markets in Italy) are both must-sees.

GETTING HERE AND AROUND

The easiest way to arrive in Cagliari is by plane or boat. From the airport, it's easy to get into the city center by train. You can also rent a car at the airport; booking before arrival is highly recommended. If you arrive by boat, travel from Palermo (Sicily), Civitavecchia (Rome), or Naples. The port is near the city center.

Piazza Matteotti is the terminal for long-distance buses and Cagliari's city buses, which are operated by Consorzio Trasporti e Mobilità (CTM). Buy city bus tickets (€1.30 for a ticket valid for 90 minutes, or €3.30 for an all-day ticket) at the kiosk or machine here before boarding. From nearby Via Roma or Piazza Yenne, you can pick up the circular Bus 7, useful for reaching the old quarter in the upper town. If you don't mind the steep walk, you could get there on foot (about 10 minutes from Piazza Yenne), but you can't drive there—only residents' cars are allowed. Most of Cagliari's restaurants and bars are located in the Marina area, near the port, which is only accessible on foot.

CONTACT Consorzio Trasporti e Mobilità. ✉ *Cagliari* ☎ *070/20911* ⊕ *www.ctm-cagliari.it.*

VISITOR INFORMATION

CONTACT Cagliari Tourism Office. ✉ *Palazzo Civico, Piazza Matteotti, Cagliari* ☎ *338/6498498, 070/6777397* ⊕ *www.cagliariturismo.it/en.*

Sights

Anfiteatro Romano

RUINS | This substantial amphitheater arena dating from the 2nd century AD attests to the importance of this area to the Romans. You can tour the seating area but not (at least for the time being) the underground passages. ■**TIP**➔ **The site isn't suitable for people with mobility impairments. If you don't want to enter it, good views can be had from Viale Sant'Ignazio.** ✉ *Viale Sant'Ignazio da Laconi, Cagliari* ☎ *366/2562826* ⊕ *www.beniculturalicagliari.it* ⊠ *€3* ⊗ *Closed Mon., Tues., Thurs., and Sat.*

Castello

VIEWPOINT | Perched over the vast expanse of Cagliari and its port, this hillside quarter has narrow streets that hold ancient monuments and piazzas amid apartments with wash hung out to dry on elaborate wrought-iron balconies. The most impressive entrance is through the commanding late-19th-century archway of the Bastione di St. Remy on Piazza Costituzione. Entering this way means climbing numerous steps; if this is a problem, walk up Viale Regina Elena to find an elevator. At the top is an impressive panorama of the cityscape and the Gulf of Cagliari. From Piazza Palazzo, holding Cagliari's cathedral, you can walk to Piazza Indipendenza and the 14th-century limestone St. Pancras Tower, a twin of the nearby Elephant Tower. ✉ *Cagliari* ⊕ *www.comune.cagliari.it/portale.*

Duomo

CHURCH | The Cattedrale di Santa Maria, also known as the Duomo, was begun in the 12th century, but major renovation in the 17th century and reconstruction during the mid-1930s have left little of the original medieval church. The tiers of columns on the facade resemble those of medieval Romanesque Pisan churches, but only sections of the central portal, the bell tower, and the two side entrances are from the 13th century.

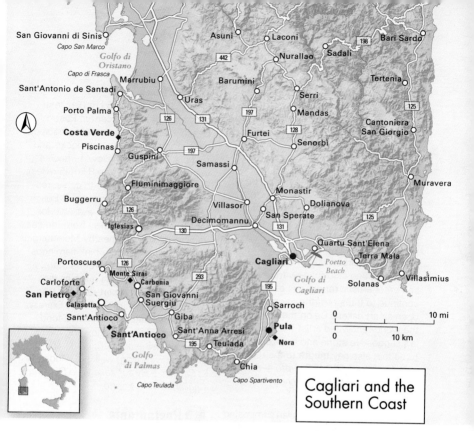

Look for one of the most memorable features inside—the oversize marble pulpit sculpted in the 1300s and divided in half to fit into the church nave; it now lies on either side of the main entrance. ✉ *Piazza Palazzo, Cagliari* ☎ *070/663837* ⊕ *www.duomodicagliari.it* ⊗ *Closed 1–4 pm Mon.–Sat. Closed 1–4:30 pm Sun.*

Museo Archeologico

HISTORY MUSEUM | Built within the walls of the Pisan castle erected in the early 1300s, Cagliari's archaeological museum is the world's foremost authority on Sardinia's ancient nuraghic civilization, named after the curious stone towers, or nuraghi, that are unique to the island. Archaeologists date most of these enigmatic structures to about 1300–1200 BC, the same time the ancient Israelites were establishing themselves in Canaan. Among the highlights on display are bronze statuettes from nuraghic towers and tombs, and the much-celebrated Giganti di Mont'e Prama, giant nuraghic stone statues representing warriors and boxers, unearthed in the 1970s and only recently restored and displayed to the public. ✉ *Cittadella dei Musei, Piazza Arsenale, Cagliari* ☎ *070/655911* ⊕ *www. museoarcheocagliari.beniculturali.it* ✉ *€9* ⊗ *Closed Mon.*

Orto Botanico

GARDEN | **FAMILY** | Located just below Cagliari's amphitheater, the city's Botanical Garden offers a welcome refuge from the summer's heat, and a shady spot for a pause from sightseeing. The 12-acre site is managed by Cagliari university and includes plants from all over the Mediterranean as well as Africa and further afield, plus herbariums, ponds, and a scattering of Roman remains, notably cisterns, tanks, and a well. As the only green space in the city center, it's ideal for kids to let off steam, and perfect for a picnic. Guided tours are also available (book ahead). ✉ *Viale Sant'Ignazio da Laconi 11, Cagliari* ☎ *070/6753512* 🌐 *sites.unica.it/hbk* 🎫 *€4* ⏲ *Closed Mon.*

San Sperate

MUSEUM VILLAGE | Considered a *paese museo,* a "museum village," this small town 20 km (12 miles) northwest of Cagliari has houses whose walls have been brightened with murals by local artists and some well-known Italian painters. The first murals were painted in the 1960s, and colorful new trompe-l'oeil and other artistic renderings of daily life continue to transform the town into an open-air art gallery. Be on the lookout for the world-renowned artist Pinuccio Sciola's suggestive stone and bronze sculptures that also pay tribute to the region's ancient history. ✉ *San Sperate* ✥ *SP4, off SS131* 🌐 *www.sansperate.net.*

Torre dell'Elefante

HISTORIC SIGHT | Part of Cagliari's imposing Pisan defenses, this medieval fortified tower was built in 1307 by Giovanni Capula as one of the main entrances to the Castello quarter. It is named after the small carving of an elephant visible on one wall. The side facing the old citadel was left entirely open, allowing you to view the series of wooden stairs and landings inside without climbing a step. If you are tempted to climb to the top, you'll be rewarded by a fabulous panorama of the city and its surrounding lagoons. Tours are available every hour. The structure is the twin of Torre San Pancrazio, located near the archaeological museum and currently closed for renovation work. ✉ *Via Santa Croce, Cagliari* ☎ *366/2562826* 🌐 *www.beniculturalicagliari.it* 🎫 *€3* ⏲ *Closed Mon.*

Beaches

★ Poetto Beach

BEACH | FAMILY | Only 5 km (3 miles) southeast of the city center, Poetto Beach is one of the most enticing spots to relax in summer for both locals and tourists. Its clean, shallow, turquoise waters stretch for some 8 km (5 miles), and the beach is lined with cafés, restaurants, snack bars, and parks. Beach chairs and umbrellas are available for rent for around €15. Away from the sea, you can explore the nearby Molentargius lagoon, and admire the pink flamingos that nest in the marshy reeds there. **■ TIP→ Poetto is easy to reach on the frequent public transport services: take Bus PF, PQ, or, in summer, Poetto Express, from Piazza Matteotti. Amenities:** food and drink; lifeguards; showers; toilets; parking (fee in summer); water sports. **Best for:** swimming; walking; windsurfing. ✉ *Cagliari* ✥ *By car, take Viale Diaz from Cagliari to Viale Poetto.*

Restaurants

★ Dal Corsaro

$$$$ | ITALIAN | This elegant but simply furnished Michelin-starred restaurant near the port offers modern and creative Italian haute cuisine on two wide-ranging tasting menus (€110 and €145 per person), consisting of a series of dishes that are only revealed when presented to your table (any food allergies can be communicated beforehand). Dal Corsaro shares its chef, Stefano Deidda, and kitchen with the adjacent, more casual Fork bistro, where the à la carte and prix-fixe lunch menus include such mouthwatering dishes as lobster salad with burrata and fried fennel bread, seafood stew, and risotto with chicory, pig's cheek, and cannonau wine; there's a separate oyster menu, too. **Known for:** good-value lunches at next-door Fork; surprise dishes; adventurous and sophisticated cuisine. [$] *Average main: €110* ✉ *Viale Regina Margherita 28,*

Cagliari ☎ *070/664318* 🌐 *www.stefanodeidda.it* 🕓 *Closed Mon. and 2 wks in Jan. No lunch at Dal Corsaro.*

Sa Ide e S'Ollia

$$ | **ITALIAN** | Take a tour of contemporary Sardinian gastronomy in this trendsetting place that has become a huge hit with the *cagliaritani*. You can choose between eating à la carte or the small dishes offered on the tasting menus (€27, €32, and €37, including desserts and nonalcoholic drinks), which might include such bold pairings as *ravioli di cernia con fragole e gamberi* (fish ravioli with strawberries and prawns), *spezzatino di maiale con le cozze* (pork stew with mussels), and *cappuccino di seppie in crema di patate e bottarga* (cuttlefish with creamed potatoes and mullet roe). **Known for:** good-value set menus; enthusiastic service; innovative food pairings. [$] *Average main: €17* ✉ *Corso Vittorio Emanuele II 370, Cagliari* ☎ *346/8586574, 347/7618240* 🕓 *Late May–Oct., no lunch Sun.; Nov.–late May, no dinner Tues. and Sun.*

Su Cumbidu

$$ | **ITALIAN** | A meal at this restaurant in Cagliari's lively Marina quarter, near the port, makes for a quick and affordable introduction to Sardinia's rural cuisine. Dishes can be ordered as part of a fixed-price meal or separately, and portions are large, so go easy on antipasti to leave room for main courses of lamb, sausage, and the famous Sardinian *maialetto* (roast suckling pig, aka porcheddu). **Known for:** range of set-price menus; casual, friendly atmosphere; traditional meat-based dishes. [$] *Average main: €15* ✉ *Via Napoli 13, Cagliari* ☎ *070/670712* 🌐 *www.sucumbidu.com.*

Coffee and Quick Bites

Antico Caffè

$$ | **ITALIAN** | The gilded Antico Caffè once served as an intellectual haunt for famous writers like D.H. Lawrence and Grazia Deledda, who won the Nobel Prize in Literature in 1926. **Known for:** swift lunches; convenient location; traditional ambience. [$] *Average main: €20* ✉ *Piazza Costituzione 10/11, Cagliari* ☎ *070/658206* 🌐 *www.anticocaffe1855.it.*

Caffè Svizzero

$ | **ITALIAN** | Entering this antique, vaulted, and frescoed bar a stone's throw from the port is like stepping back into the 19th century. Order a steaming cappuccino, a glass of the local vermentino, or a freshly squeezed fruit juice, and nibble on a panino, a pizzetta, or a pastry. **Known for:** great pastries; courteous staff; historic interior. [$] *Average main: €5* ✉ *Largo Carlo Felice 6–8, Cagliari* ☎ *070/664578* 🕓 *Closed Sun.*

Hotels

Hotel Regina Margherita

$$ | **HOTEL** | Close to the port and the main downtown sights, this large, modern hotel attracts both vacationers and businesspeople with a quiet, friendly ambience and spacious, sober rooms. **Pros:** central location; free parking; higher rooms have harbor views. **Cons:** breakfast sometimes disappoints; few leisure facilities; lacks local character. [$] *Rooms from: €147* ✉ *Viale Regina Margherita 44, Cagliari* ☎ *070/670342* 🌐 *www.hotelreginamargherita.com* 🛏 *100 rooms* 🍴 *Free Breakfast.*

Il Gallo Bianco

$ | **B&B/INN** | A broad sun terrace and white, plant-filled decor make this sleek boutique hotel a good choice, as do the spacious and surprisingly quiet—given the busy location—guest rooms, all of which have modern baths and some of which have private balconies. **Pros:** sun terrace; central location near the train and bus stations; friendly staff. **Cons:** no parking; neighborhood is traffic-heavy and a bit run-down; breakfast is a bit basic. [$] *Rooms from: €123* ✉ *Via Roma 237, Cagliari* ☎ *070/6848527, 334/9533149* 🌐 *www.gallobiancocagliari.it* 🛏 *16 rooms* 🍴 *Free Breakfast.*

La Ghirlanda

$ | B&B/INN | At this quiet haven in the heart of the Marina quarter, the spacious, high-ceilinged rooms are decorated with taste and restraint with period furnishings redolent of the 19th century, making you feel as if you're a guest at a palazzo. **Pros:** elegant rooms; convenient location near the port and bus and train stations; reasonable rates. **Cons:** books up quickly; no parking; no views from the rooms. $ *Rooms from: €85* ⊠ *Via Lodovico Baylle 7, Cagliari* ☎ *351/5364248* ⊕ *www.bnblaghirlanda.com* ⊐ *3 rooms* ¡○¡ *Free Breakfast.*

Pensione Vittoria

$$ | B&B/INN | The airy white rooms, period-style furnishings, and ceramic flooring make this third-floor pension directly opposite the port cozy and characterful. **Pros:** clean rooms; family atmosphere; central location near port. **Cons:** shabby entrance; no parking; breakfast is not served in the hotel. $ *Rooms from: €125* ⊠ *Via Roma 75, Cagliari* ☎ *349/4473556, 070/667970* ⊕ *www.hotelbjvittoria.it* ⊐ *14 rooms* ¡○¡ *Free Breakfast.*

★ T Hotel

$ | HOTEL | In the vicinity of Parco di Monte Claro, about a 15-minute taxi or bus ride from Cagliari's center, this trendy hotel offers contemporary styling and upscale guest rooms in a 15-floor circular tower with sweeping city views. **Pros:** great views from most rooms; outstanding service; free parking. **Cons:** constant bustle in public areas; spa facilities can get busy; 2 km (1¼ miles) from port. $ *Rooms from: €119* ⊠ *Via Dei Giudicati 66, Cagliari* ☎ *070/47400* ⊕ *www.thotel.it* ⊐ *207 rooms* ¡○¡ *Free Breakfast.*

▼ Nightlife

Al Merlo Parlante

PUBS | This backstreet *birroteca* ("beer bar") has been dispensing distinguished brews for the last 40 years, and is a favorite haunt of students and beer aficionados of all ages. Local Sardinian craft beers and lagers and ales from around the world feature on its extensive and changing menu, many of them hand-pulled. The list of panini is almost equally long, and nachos are also served. ⊠ *Via Portoscalas 69, Cagliari* ☎ *339/3693612.*

Caffè dell'Elfo

CAFÉS | A central yet secluded location (off Piazza Yenne) and a casual ambience attract local professionals and artists, who linger in the evening over good wine, snacks, and conversation. It's closed during the day and all Sunday; open hours may be reduced in winter. ⊠ *Salita Santa Chiara 4/6, off Piazza Yenne, Cagliari* ☎ *070/682399.*

Caffè Libarium Nostrum

CAFÉS | A dim bohemian haunt full of wooden beams and brick-lined nooks and crannies, Libarium Nostrum is one of Cagliari's coolest café-bars. It's an occasional venue for live music and DJs, but the real draw is the outdoor terrace high atop medieval ramparts, the perfect spot for enjoying cocktails and sunset views. Panini and other snacks are available. It stays open late, and is closed Monday in winter. ⊠ *Via Santa Croce 33/35, Cagliari* ☎ *346/5220212.*

⊕ Performing Arts

The Teatro Lirico stages concerts with local and well-known European artists throughout the year. See www.teatrolirico dicagliari.it or contact the tourist office for information.

⊖ Shopping

Cagliari's best shopping street—full of boutiques and specialty shops for clothes, shoes, bags, and jewelry—is **Via Manno,** just up from the port off Piazza Yenne. Via Manno climbs to Piazza Costituzione, from where **Via Garibaldi** trails back downhill, where you'll find an equally good range of slightly cheaper stores.

ISOLA

CRAFTS | Located within the T Hotel, the Istituto Sardo Organizzazione Lavoro Artigiano is a government-sponsored cooperative of artisans. Look for hand-made ceramics, woven and wooden goods, baskets, metalwork, and beautiful gold filigree or precious stone jewelry. ⊠ T Hotel, Via Dei Giudicati 66, Cagliari ☎ 070/47400 ⊕ www.isolacagliari.com.

Sapori di Sardegna

OTHER SPECIALTY STORE | Drop into this shop for Sardinian food products, including local wines, artisanal biscuits, pecorino cheeses, carasau flatbread, honey, and olives. There's a great range of items, and the English-speaking staff are always willing to help you out. If you want to sample some of the foodstuffs first, try the branches nearby at *Pipette*, Via dei Mille 8, and *Sabores*, Via Baylle 6, where snacks and full meals are served. ⊠ *Vico dei Mille 1, Cagliari* ☎ *070/6848747* ⊕ *www.saborescagliari.com.*

 Activities

WINDSURFING

Windsurfing Club Cagliari

WINDSURFING | **FAMILY** | Sardinia has some of Europe's best windsurfing spots. This outfit located in Cagliari's beach resort of Poetto provides advice and courses for everyone from beginners to experts. ⊠ *Viale Marina Piccola, Cagliari* ☎ *070/372694* ⊕ *www.windsurfingclub. it.*

Pula

29 km (18 miles) southwest of Cagliari, 314 km (195 miles) southwest of Olbia.

Resort villages sprawl along the coast southwest of the capital, which has its share of fine scenery and good beaches. On the marshy shoreline between Cagliari's Aeroporto di Elmas and Pula, huge flocks of flamingos are a common sight. Beaches and lodging catering to summer crowds are concentrated 4 km (2½ miles) south of Pula, a little more than 1½ km (1 mile) south of Nora, in a conglomeration that makes up Santa Margherita di Pula. 19 km (12 miles) southwest of Pula at Chia is one of Sardinia's most magnificent coastal stretches, with white-sand beaches, turquoise waters, placid coves, and powdery dunes.

GETTING HERE AND AROUND

From Cagliari, drive approximately 40 km (25 miles) on the SS195. Follow directions for Pula/Chia. From Olbia, take SS131 toward Cagliari-Sassari; then, follow SS554 toward Pula/Chia. The journey is approximately 300 km (190 miles).

 Sights

★ Nora

MUSEUM VILLAGE | The narrow promontory outside Pula was the site of a Phoenician, Carthaginian, and then, later, Roman settlement that was first inhabited some 2,800 years ago. Nora was a prime location as a stronghold and an important trading town; Phoenician settlers scouted for good harbors, cliffs to shelter their craft from the wind, and an elevation from which they could defend themselves. An old Roman paved road passes the temple ruins, which include baths, a Roman theater, and an amphitheater now reserved for summer music festivals. ⊠ *3 km (2 miles) south of Pula, Pula* ☎ *070/9209366* ⊕ *www.nora.beniculturali.unipd.it* 🖃 *€8.*

Sant'Efisio

CHURCH | The simple 11th-century church at the base of the Nora promontory is key to one of the island's most colorful annual events. Don't be put off by the inappropriate modern frontage added to the building in 2021—the interior retains its ancient character. A four-day procession during the Festa di Sant'Efisio accompanies a statue of the martyred St.

Efisius all the way from Cagliari to here and back again. The event culminates in a huge parade of costumed Sardinians and decorated *traccas* (ox-drawn carriages) along Cagliari's main avenue. Try to catch this if you're in southern Sardinia from May 1 to May 4. ✉ *Nora Beach, 3 km (2 miles) south of Pula, Pula* ☎ *389/1675008, 347/1436054* ⏲ *Closed weekdays and Sat. morning.*

Beaches

★ Chia Beach

BEACH | **FAMILY** | Although there is a perfectly serviceable sandy beach right outside the archaeological site of Nora, infintely more enticing is the series of long expanses of sand 18 km (11 miles) farther south toward the cape of Capo Spartivento, Sardinia's southernmost tip. **Amenities:** food and drink; lifeguards; toilets; parking (fee in summer). **Best for:** swimming. ✉ *Santa Margherita di Pula* ✣ *By car, head south down the SS195 past Santa Margherita di Pula.*

Restaurants

Su Furriadroxu

$ | **ITALIAN** | Amid the lime and lemon trees in this courtyard trattoria in the center of Pula, you'll find down-home Sard cooking at its most authentic, with the accent firmly on meat dishes. The menu (in the local Campidanese dialect, with Italian and English translations) lists a selection of meaty fare, with pride of place going to the most famous of island dishes, porceddu (roast suckling pig), which you'll find displayed sizzling on a spit to satisfy the most purist of local gourmands. **Known for:** carnivorous feast; traditional outdoor setting; authentic Campidanese cooking. [$] *Average main: €13* ✉ *Via XXIV Maggio 11, Pula* ☎ *070/9246148* 🌐 *www.sufurriadroxu.it* ⏲ *Closed Wed. June–Sept., Tues. and Wed. Oct.–May. No lunch Mon.–Sat. No dinner Sun.*

Hotels

★ Conrad Chia Laguna Sardinia

$$$$ | **RESORT** | Now relaunched under Hilton's Conrad banner, the Chia Laguna hotel still has its captivating position overlooking Monte Cogoni beach and the sleek expanse of Chia lagoon, and its five-star facilities are geared to maximizing guests' enjoyment of these natural advantages. **Pros:** choice of fine restaurants; proximity to some of Sardinia's best beaches; first-class facilities. **Cons:** extravagant room rates and extras; remote location; not always child-friendly. [$] *Rooms from: €676* ✉ *Via dei Fenicotteri 52, Chia* ☎ *070/92393000* 🌐 *www.hilton.com* 🛏 *107 rooms* 🍴 *Free Breakfast.*

Costa dei Fiori

$$$$ | **HOTEL** | **FAMILY** | Worry and stress seem to melt away upon arriving at this beach hideaway, where modern guest rooms with stone floors, big windows, and rural Sardinian touches are surrounded by peaceful gardens planted with pines and palms. **Pros:** great leisure facilities; good low-season rates; lovely grounds. **Cons:** the beach may disappoint; you need a car; poor road access. [$] *Rooms from: €321* ✉ *SS195 Km 33, Santa Margherita di Pula* ☎ *070/9245333* 🌐 *www.costadeifiori.it* ⏲ *Closed Oct.–early May* 🛏 *82 rooms* 🍴 *Free Breakfast.*

★ Faro Capo-Spartivento

$$$$ | **HOTEL** | Atop a cliff at the end of a rocky track on Sardinia's southernmost tip, a working lighthouse dating from 1856 contains this unusual hotel—a self-described "door suspended between the sky and the sea"—where it's easy to switch off and tune out amid luxurious surroundings. **Pros:** select and secluded; unique character and setting; excellent restaurant. **Cons:** extravagant rates; hard to find; remote and isolated location. [$] *Rooms from: €924* ✉ *Viale Spartivento* ✣ *5 km (3 miles) southwest of Chia* ☎ *393/8276800* 🌐 *www.farocapospartivento.com* 🛏 *10 rooms* 🍴 *Free Breakfast.*

Is Molas Resort

$ | **HOTEL** | **FAMILY** | If you love golf and stargazing, then the place to stay in southern Sardinia is this peaceful hotel, with 70 Mediterranean-style rooms and a 27-hole golf complex. **Pros:** immediate access to golf course; tranquil setting with rural views; freshwater pool. **Cons:** poor soundproofing in some rooms; isolated location; lacks charm. [$] *Rooms from: €119* ✉ *SS195, Pula* ☎ *070/9241006* 🌐 *www.ismolas.it* 🕒 *Closed Nov.–May* 🛏 *70 rooms* 🍴 *Free Breakfast.*

Is Morus Relais

$$$ | **RESORT** | **FAMILY** | A luxurious, palm-filled garden enclave laced with undulating paths, the Is Morus sits on a sandy cove and has all the amenities of a fine beach resort. **Pros:** lovely grounds; attentive staff; large pool and poolside grill restaurant. **Cons:** disappointing beach; needs modernizing; food overall could be improved. [$] *Rooms from: €300* ✉ *SS195, Km 37.4, Santa Margherita di Pula* ☎ *070/921596, 070/921171* 🌐 *www.ismorus.it* 🕒 *Closed mid-Oct.–early May* 🛏 *62 rooms* 🍴 *Free Breakfast.*

Sant'Antioco

75 km (47 miles) west of Pula, 100 km (62 miles) west of Cagliari.

Off Sardinia's southwest coast is the sleepy island of Sant'Antioco—the most hectic activity seems to be the silent repairing of nets by local fishermen who have already pulled in their daily catch. It has become a popular holiday spot because of its good beaches. The island has been connected to the mainland since Roman times by a causeway that's still standing (the modern causeway that you cross runs parallel).

GETTING HERE AND AROUND

Sant'Antioco is about 90 minutes from Cagliari by bus or car. Drive on the SS130 as far as Iglesias, then the SS126 in the direction of Carbonia and Sant'Antioco.

Sights

Calasetta

TOWN | On the island of Sant'Antioco, off the southwestern coast of Sardinia, the fishing village and port of Calasetta draws visitors year-round for its beautiful beaches and fresh-seafood dishes. The pristine beaches of Spiaggia Grande and Le Saline, alternating with rocky areas, dunes, and local vegetation, form a rugged paradise. Founded by Ligurian settlers who worked as coral and tuna fishermen, Calasetta is connected daily by ferry boats with the smaller island of San Pietro, which also keeps intact its Ligurian cultural history and dialect. ✉ *10 km (6 miles) northwest of Sant'Antioco town, Sant'Antioco.*

Carbonia

MINE | If you like to seek out the esoteric, explore the rugged inland hills and town of Carbonia, less than 30 minutes' drive from Sant'Antioco and about an hour by car or train from Cagliari. Built in 1938 by Mussolini to serve as an administrative center of a once booming coal-mining area, its time-frozen architecture—ordered rows of workers' houses around a core of monumental public buildings on the broad Piazza Roma—has been called an urban UFO set down in the Sardinian landscape. ✉ *S126 at S78, Carbonia.*

Iglesias

TOWN | Perched at about 600 feet in the southwest hills of the island, this authentic Sardinian town 35 km (22 miles) north of Sant'Antioco has two notable medieval churches: the Cattedrale di Santa Chiara and Madonna delle Grazie. The town is famous for its theatrical, Spanish-inflected Easter festivities. A short drive away, on the Costa Verde, you can enjoy unspoiled, uncrowded beaches, including the beautiful Masua cove at Porto Cauli beach. ✉ *27 km (16 miles) north of Carbonia, Iglesias* ☎ *0781/274507 tourist office* 🌐 *www.visitiglesias.comune.iglesias.ca.it.*

Monte Sirai

RUINS | Just outside Carbonia and stra-
tegically positioned atop a plateau that
provides views inland and far out to sea,
the remains of one of Sardinia's most
important Carthaginian military strong-
holds were discovered by chance in 1962.
The walls of Mt. Sirai were erected around
375 BC, and they continued to function
as impregnable fortress barriers until the
Roman conquest in 238 BC. ⊠ *Off SS126,
Km 17, Località Sirai ⊹ 1 km (½ mile)
north of Carbonia, direction Sant'Antioco*
☏ *0781/1888256 office, 345/8886058
museum, 345/7559751 site* ⊕ *www.
carboniamusei.it* ⊠ *Site €6, museum €6,
or €10 for both* ⊙ *Closed Mon.*

Zona Archeologica

RUINS | The chief point of interest in
Sant'Antioco island's eponymous main
town is the Archaeological Zone at the
top of the old section, which has terrific
views of the Sardinian mainland. Here
you can see a *tophet*—a Punic sanctuary,
necropolis, and burial site—which is
scattered with urns that contained the
cremated remains of stillborn children.
Below the site is Sant'Antioco's excellent
archaeological museum that showcases
artifacts from the tophet as well as from
the Neolithic, Byzantine, and Roman
eras. You can also visit a nearby ethnographic collection and a Piedmontese
fort. Various combined tickets are available. ⊠ *Via Sabatino Moscati, Sant'Antioco*
☏ *0781/82105, 389/7962114* ⊕ *www.
mabsantantioco.it* ⊠ *Archaeological
zone €4, museum €6, combined tickets
for both €7, ethnographic collection €3,
Piedmontese fort €3.*

San Pietro

5 km (3 miles) northwest of Sant'Antioco.

A ferry at the small northern port of Calasetta connects Sant'Antioco with Carloforte, the main town on the smaller island
of San Pietro. This classic little Italian port

and its surrounding coastline are a favorite
of wealthy Cagliarians, many of whom
have built weekend cottages here. The
best views are from Capo Sandalo, on
San Pietro's rugged western coast, but
head to the island's southern tip for the
beaches. During daylight hours the ferry
departs approximately hourly in summer
and every 90 minutes in winter—the trip
takes 30 minutes.

GETTING HERE AND AROUND

Car ferries operated by Delcomar
connect San Pietro with Calasetta on
Sant'Antioco, or Portoscuso near Iglesias
on the Sardinian mainland. Round-trip
tickets are about €10 per person, €20 for
a car.

CONTACT Delcomar. ☏ *800/195344*
⊕ *www.delcomar.it.*

Hotels

Hotel Hieracon

$ | HOTEL | This Art Nouveau–style hotel
with modern whitewashed rooms sits on
the harbor in Carloforte. **Pros:** helpful English-speaking staff; good location; pretty
internal garden. **Cons:** poorly maintained;
few sea-facing rooms; cheaper rooms are
cramped. Ⓢ *Rooms from: €91* ⊠ *Corso
Cavour 62, Carloforte* ☏ *0781/854028*
⊕ *www.hotelhieracon.com* ⊙ *Closed
early Oct.–late Apr.* ⇱ *23 rooms* ⦿ *Free
Breakfast.*

Costa Verde

80 km (50 miles) northwest of Cagliari.

If you've come to Sardinia in search of
untrammeled wilderness and sweeping
sands as far as the eye can see, this
semideserted coast is the place to find
them. Hidden away in the forgotten
southwest corner of the island, the Costa
Verde, or Green Coast, is a succession of
cliffs and beaches, many of them accessible only by bumpy, unpaved tracks. The
effort is worth it. The dune-backed sands

shelter rare grasses and birdlife, and the area offers magnificent swimming along stretches of beach that seem endless.

GETTING HERE AND AROUND

The best way to access the Green Coast is by car, though roads can be dangerously steep and winding. Take precautions and drive during daytime, also because roads and exits are poorly lit. Roads designated "SS" are developed freeways with fast-flowing traffic.

You can approach one of the most evocative stretches of the coast, Piscinas, either from the town of Guspini, on the straggling S126, or from a turnoff a couple of miles farther south, which leads through the abandoned mining town of Ingurtosu. It's a strange, ghostly cluster of chimneys and workers' dwellings, forlorn amid the encroaching scrubland. Drive down the dirt track another 10 km (6 miles) or so, through woods of juniper, to reach the sea.

Barumini

65 km (40 miles) north of Cagliari.

Take a detour along good roads into Sardnia's interior to visit the extraordinary stone village-fortress of Su Nuraxi, just outside the quiet village of Barumini.

GETTING HERE AND AROUND

The best way to reach Su Nuraxi is by car. From the capital, follow SS131 to SS197. Direct buses to the site are few and far between.

 Sights

★ Su Nuraxi

RUINS | FAMILY | The most extensive of the island's 7,000 discovered nuraghi, Su Nuraxi is on the UNESCO World Heritage list. Concentric rings of thick stone walls conceal dark chambers and narrow passages in a central beehive-shape tower. In the ruins of the surrounding village there

are benches, ovens, wells, and other Bronze Age remnants. Tours start every 30 minutes and last about 50 minutes. The same ticket includes entry to a museum and exhibition center in Barumini.

■ TIP ➜ **If you're driving from SS131, don't be misled to other, lesser nuraghi—follow the signs all the way to Barumini.** ⊠ *Viale Su Nuraxi, Barumini ⊹ SP5 Barumini– Tuili, 1 km (½ mile) west of Barumini* ☎ *070/9368128* ⊕ *www.fondazionebarumini.it* ☑ *€14.*

Oristano

25 km (16 miles) north of Giara di Gesturi, 93 km (58 miles) northwest of Cagliari.

The elegant and compact old quarter of this provincial center off the tourist track exudes a distinct serenity. Oristano's evening passeggiata teems with vivacious children and has a relaxed friendliness about it.

GETTING HERE AND AROUND

Oristano is easily accessible and well connected to other major areas of Sardinia by car, train, or bus. Trains and buses between Cagliari, Sassari, Olbia, and Nuoro stop here several times per day. The central bus station is in the city center, the train station on the outskirts, a short bus or taxi ride away. By car, turn off the SS131 highway for Oristano. The part-pedestrianized old center is easily negotiable on foot.

VISITOR INFORMATION

CONTACT Oristano Tourist Office. ⊠ *Piazza Eleonora 19, Oristano* ☎ *0783/308691* ⊕ *www.gooristano.com.*

 Sights

Cabras

BEACH | FAMILY | Fishermen pole round-bottomed rush boats through shallow ponds teeming with eels, crayfish, and wildlife in the extensive marshlands

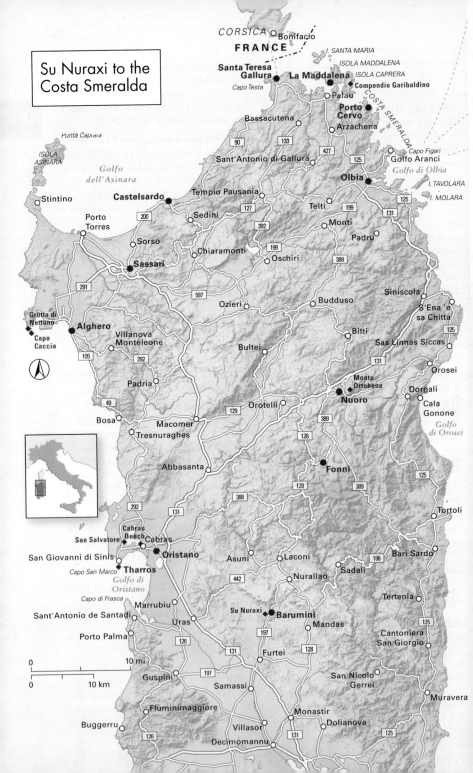

outside this 11th-century town. Make a stop at the archaeological museum here for its awe-inspiring nuraghic statues, then drive north and west into the Sinis Peninsula to access the pristine beaches of Is Arutas, Maimoni, and Mari Ermi, characterized by fine white quartzified sand grains. ✉ *SP3 off SP1, 10 km (6 miles) northwest of Oristano, Cabras.*

🍴 Restaurants

Cocco e Dessi
$$ | **ITALIAN** | The building dates from 1925 but the interior shows a diversity of styles, with the main dining area (one of five) inside a glass gazebo. Dishes featuring fresh catches of the day, vegetables, and herb-infused sauces are complemented by pizzas and pastas—just save room for a dessert of crème caramel topped with walnuts and chocolate or pastry with Chantilly cream and berries. **Known for:** great pizzas; convivial setting; quirky decor. [$] *Average main: €19* ✉ *Via Tirso 31, Oristano* ☎ *0783/252648* 🌐 *www.coccoedessi.it.*

Ristorante Craf da Banana
$$ | **ITALIAN** | The brick walls, dim lighting, and arched ceilings here make you feel as if you've stepped into a wine cellar. Aged photographs of Oristano's Sa Sartiglia jousting festival and specialty dishes from Oristano and Montiferru do a good job capturing local flavor. **Known for:** cozy, romantic atmosphere; historical setting; traditional Sardinian dishes. [$] *Average main: €17* ✉ *Via de Castro 34, Oristano* ☎ *0783/70669* 🌐 *www.ristorantecrafdabanana.com* 🕒 *No lunch Sun. June–Sept. No dinner Sun. Oct.–May.*

Trattoria Gino
$ | **SEAFOOD** | Light-color walls lined with bottles of wine and simple rows of tables deck out the single room of Trattoria Gino, beloved by locals, especially at lunch, and run by the same family for nearly a century. Although the lobster is a memorable splurge, consider trying the antipasto *di mare* (mixed seafood appetizer) or spaghetti *ai ricci* (with sea urchins). **Known for:** cordial, attentive service; reasonable prices; honest, local cooking. [$] *Average main: €14* ✉ *Via Tirso 13, Oristano* ☎ *0783/71428* 🕒 *Closed Sun. and mid-Aug.–mid-Sept.*

☕ Coffee and Quick Bites

Bar Pasticceria Eleonora
$ | **CAFÉ** | Steps from the tourist office, you can take a refreshing afternoon break with a coffee and a pastry or panino. The friendly café has outdoor tables on the corner of Piazza Eleonora, which retains an old-world charm thanks to a neoclassical town hall, a marble monument to Giudichessa Eleonora carved by the Florentine sculptor Ulisse Cambi in 1881, and the 18th-century Mameli palace with its beautiful wrought-iron balconies. **Known for:** central people-watching spot; outdoor seating; traditional local flavor. [$] *Average main: €8* ✉ *Piazza Eleonora d'Arborea 1, Oristano* ☎ *0783/71454* 🕒 *Closed Sun. and evenings.*

🛏 Hotels

Mariano IV Palace Hotel
$ | **HOTEL** | This central downtown hotel has a reassuringly old-fashioned style, with its grand, columned exterior and elegant neoclassical lobby hung with chandeliers. **Pros:** convenient location; low online rates; good restaurant. **Cons:** no parking for cars; caters mostly to business travelers; dated feel. [$] *Rooms from: €90* ✉ *Piazza Mariano 50, Oristano* ☎ *0783/360101* 🌐 *www.hotelmarianoiv.com* 🛏 *81 rooms* 🍴 *Free Breakfast.*

Residenza d'Epoca Regina d'Arborea
$$ | **HOTEL** | One floor of a 19th-century palazzo, next to the town hall on Oristano's traffic-free main square, has been tastefully converted into a small but stylish guest house, with rich furnishings, chandeliers, antique murals, and domed ceilings. **Pros:** period character;

helpful hosts; central location. **Cons:** not suitable for children; no car access possible; few facilities. $ *Rooms from: €144* ⊠ *Piazza Eleonora d'Arborea 4, Oristano* ☎ *0783/302101* ⊕ *www.reginadarborea. it* ⊗ *Closed 10 days in Dec.* ⌐ *6 rooms* ⫶◎⫶ *Free Breakfast.*

Activities

BIKING
Bike Or
BIKING | Oristano and the flat terrain surrounding it is ideal for cycling, in particular the Sinis peninsula to the north and west, which ranks as Sardinia's most rewarding area for exploring on two wheels. Bike Or has a range of bikes to rent that can be delivered to and collected from a location of your choosing, and also arranges guided cycling excursions. ⊠ *Oristano* ☎ *349/3967335* ⊕ *www. bikeor.it.*

Tharros

16 km (10 miles) west of Oristano, 52 km (32 miles) northwest of Barumini.

Spread across a thin tongue of land that dangles off the Sinis Peninsula, the archaeological site of Tharros ranks as one of Sardinia's most important Phoenician, Carthaginian, and Roman settlements. It's not hard to understand why this evocative site was selected by the ancients, given its sweeping views across the Gulf of Oristano, its defensibility, and the shelter it provides vessels. Founded around 800 BC, the city was finally abandoned in the 11th century AD, in favor of Oristano.

GETTING HERE AND AROUND
Whether you're heading to Tharros from the north or south, follow the SS131 to Oristano. Drive through Oristano toward Cabras, branching off on SP6 for San Giovanni di Sinis and Tharros. There's frequent bus service from Oristano.

Sights

Museo Civico di Cabras
HISTORY MUSEUM | This lagoon-side archaeological museum displays many of the better-preserved urns and other artifacts recovered from nearby excavation sites, including Tharros. It is also the main home of the Giganti di Mont'e Prama—unique nuraghic stone statues recovered from the Sinis Peninsula in the 1970s but only recently viewable in their restored state. The visit takes about an hour. Buy a combination ticket to see the Museo Civico and the ruins at Tharros. ⊠ *Via Tharros 121, off SP6, 10 km (6 miles) northwest of Oristano, Cabras* ☎ *0783/290636* ⊕ *www.museocabras.it* ⛭ *€7; €10 combined ticket, includes Tharros.*

Tharros
RUINS | **FAMILY** | The spectacular site of the Carthaginian and Roman city of Tharros was, like Nora to the south, chosen because it commanded the best views of the gulf and could provide an easy escape route if inland tribes threatened. The Phoenician-Punic city planning here includes sophisticated water channeling and masonry foundations. Two reconstructed Corinthian columns stand as testament to the site's Roman history, and there are baths visible and mosaic fragments from the Roman city. ⊠ *Off SP6, 16 km (10 miles) west of Oristano, 113 km (70 miles) northwest of Cagliari, San Giovanni di Sinis* ☎ *0783/370019* ⊕ *www.tharros. sardegna.it* ⛭ *€7; €10 combined ticket, includes Museo Civico di Cabras; tower €4* ⊗ *Closed Mon. early Jan.–Mar.*

Nuoro

107 km (67 miles) northeast of Tharros, 181 km (113 miles) north of Cagliari.

The strongly traditional but somewhat nondescript provincial capital of Nuoro stands on the edge of the Gennargentu massif, home to the island's highest peaks (6,000 feet). Not much happens here; you can do some shopping amid strolling locals, or try the local Barbagia sausage, which is great.

GETTING HERE AND AROUND

From Cagliari, the drive to Nuoro takes about two hours. Take the SS131 toward Sassari/Oristano/Nuoro, then continue on SS131 DCN toward Nuoro/Olbia. After 55 km (34 miles), turn off, following signs for Nuoro Centro until you reach Nuoro.

VISITOR INFORMATION

CONTACT Nuoro Tourism Office. ✉ *Piazza Italia 8,* ☎ *0784/238878.*

Sights

Monte Ortobene

MOUNTAIN | About 7 km (4 miles) northeast of Nuoro is Monte Ortobene, a granite peak at 2,900 feet offering lofty views over the gulch below. Here you can also see up close the imposing bronze statue of the Rendentore, or Christ the Redeemer, overlooking the valley. Pilgrimages and Masses take place in summer here. Picnic tables make this a favorite spot for an alfresco lunch throughout the year. The mountain is easily reachable from Nuoro by bus or car via SP45. ✉ *Nuoro* 🌐 *www.comune.nuoro.it.*

★ **Museo Etnografico Sardo**

HISTORY MUSEUM | This ethnographic collection is a must for anyone interested in the cultural context of Sardinia's customs and traditions. Among the 8,000 items in the museum's collection, you can view domestic and agricultural implements, splendid jewelry, traditional musical instruments, and dozens of local costumes. Audio guides are available, and guided tours can be booked. The nearby park on Sant'Onofrio Hill affords magnificent views over Nuoro and the surrounding country. **TIP→ Entry to the museum is free on the first Sunday of the month.** ✉ *Via A. Mereu 56, Nuoro* ☎ *0784/257035* 🌐 *www.isresardegna.it* 🎟 *€5* 🕓 *Closed Mon.*

En Route

On the way to the archaeological ruins in Tharros you pass the ghost town of **San Salvatore**, revived briefly in the 1960s as a locale for spaghetti Westerns and since abandoned, except for a few days every summer, when it is the focus of a religious festival. The saloon from the movie set still stands. Among the dunes past San Salvatore are large huts formerly used by fishermen and now much in demand as vacation homes. The 5th-century church of **San Giovanni di Sinis**, on the Sinis Peninsula, is claimed to be the oldest Christian church in Sardinia.

Restaurants

★ **Il Portico**

$$ | **ITALIAN** | Brotherly love (and ownership) and quality seafood are among the things that make this old-town restaurant so exceptional. Modern artwork, stone pillars, and arched ceilings help to provide a fitting setting for the predominantly traditional cuisine livened up with modern elements. **Known for:** welcoming atmosphere; locals' choice; innovative takes on traditional cuisine. [$] *Average main: €15* ✉ *Via Mons. Bua 13, Nuoro* ☎ *0784/232909* 🌐 *www.ilporticonuoro.it* 🕓 *Closed Mon., 2 wks July–Aug., and 2 wks Jan.–Feb. No dinner Sun.*

Il Rifugio

$$ | **ITALIAN** | **FAMILY** | At this family-run local spot, the rustic dining area—with terra-cotta floors, brick pillars, and a wood-burning stove—is packed nearly every night. The service, presentation, and wine list are as exceptional as the food: only the freshest local meats and cheeses are served, and all the dishes are made from scratch, including the pizza, the pasta, and the ice cream drizzled with honey. **Known for:** amiable staff; unpretentious but expertly prepared local dishes; lively and convivial air. $ *Average main: €17* ✉ *Via A. Mereu 28/36, Nuoro* ☎ *0784/232355* ⊕ *www.trattoriarifugio.com* ⊗ *Closed Wed.*

Hotels

Casa Solotti

$ | **B&B/INN** | You don't have to venture far out of Nuoro to appreciate its magnificent mountainous setting, and mountain views don't get much grander than from this excellent lodging immersed in the oak forests of Monte Ortobene. **Pros:** beautiful mountain views; terrific breakfasts; warm and friendly hospitality. **Cons:** few facilities; not ideal for anyone with impaired mobility; remote spot. $ *Rooms from: €70* ✉ *Località Monte Ortobene, Nuoro* ☎ *0784/33954, 328/6028975* ⊕ *www.casasolotti.it* ⊗ *Closed mid-Nov.–late Dec. and late Jan.–late Mar.* ⇘ *6 rooms* ⦿| *Free Breakfast.*

Euro Hotel

$ | **HOTEL** | Centrally located, this simple block-style hotel—more or less standard for provincial Nuoro—is ideal for a stopover; rooms are spacious and clean, with parquet flooring and modern amenities. **Pros:** amiable staff; near train station; ample parking. **Cons:** no restaurant; outdated rooms; not much character. $ *Rooms from: €81* ✉ *Via Trieste 62, Nuoro* ☎ *0784/34071* ⊕ *www.eurohotelnuoro.it* ⇘ *54 rooms* ⦿| *Free Breakfast.*

Su Gologone Experience Hotel

$$$$ | **HOTEL** | Just southeast of Nuoro, in the foothills of the Supramonte range, Su Gologone combines luxury with rural flavor in guest rooms that feel like country retreats (exposed beams, wooden chests, traditional Sardinian fabrics) and a rustic restaurant that pairs local cannonau reds with such Sardinian specialties as maccarones de busa (thick homemade pasta twists), culurgiones (ravioli),

suckling pig, and, for dessert, sebadas (fried-dough pockets stuffed with cheese and lemon peel). **Pros:** locally influenced restaurant; museumlike decor; great location for hiking in the Supramonte Valley. **Cons:** poorly maintained; many stairs to negotiate; used by groups and wedding parties. $ *Rooms from: €328* ✉ *Località Su Gologone, Oliena* ☎ *0784/287512* ⊕ *www.sugologone.it* ⊗ *Closed early Nov.–mid-Apr.* ⇘ *68 rooms* ⦿| *Free Breakfast.*

Fonni

30 km (19 miles) south of Nuoro, 137 km (85 miles) south of Olbia.

In the heart of the Barbagia region, Fonni is the highest town on the island. This mountainous district, including Monte Spada and the Bruncu Spina refuge on the Gennargentu massif, is Sardinia's most primitive. Life in some villages seems not to have changed much since the Middle Ages.

GETTING HERE AND AROUND

To reach Fonni, the highest town in Sardinia, drive (or hire a car and driver) or take a bus from Nuoro. There is no train service.

From Nuoro, take SS389 from the junction of Mamoiada, or take SS128 to the town of Gavoi. From Cagliari, follow SS131, exiting toward the village of Ottana. Continue on SS128, turning at Fonni. From Sassari, follow SS131 south, turning east onto SS129 at Macomer. Continue on SS128, following signs for Fonni.

Hotels

Hotel Sa Orte

$ | **HOTEL** | Close to the highest peaks of the Gennargentu range in the center of Sardinia, this hotel, a palazzo in the center of Fonni, provides a warm welcome at any time of the year. **Pros:** generous breakfasts; convenient for mountain excursions; affable staff. **Cons:** no views; restaurant food is patchy; some rooms are small and dark. $ *Rooms from: €80* ✉ *Via Roma 14, Fonni* ☎ *0784/58020* ⊕ *www.hotelsaorte.it* ⤳ *33 rooms* ℐ○ℐ *Free Breakfast.*

Shopping

Special candies made from honey and nougat are sold in hilltop **Tonara,** 15 km (9 miles) southwest of Fonni.

In the mountain village of **Aritzo,** about 45 km (28 miles) south of Fonni, high up in the Barbagia, look for handcrafted wooden utensils and furniture.

Alghero

137 km (85 miles) southwest of Olbia.

A tourist-friendly town of about 45,000 inhabitants, with a distinctly Spanish flavor, Alghero is also known as "Barcelonetta" (Little Barcelona) for its strong Catalan ties. Rich wrought-iron scrollwork decorates balconies and screened windows; Spanish motifs appear in stone portals and bell towers.

Besides its historic architectural gems, the fortified city is well worth a visit to simply stroll and discover local culture and the boutiques lining its narrow cobblestone lanes. Pick up an "Alghero Ticket" allowing free entry into all Alghero's principal sights at the tourist office or one of the participating attractions (€25, or €50 for a family ticket).

GETTING HERE AND AROUND

Alghero International Airport is 15 km (9 miles) from the city center, which you can reach by car, taxi, or public transport. Regional buses and local trains connect the town with Sassari, and there are buses to local villages. The closest passenger port to Alghero is Porto Torres, approximately 40 km (25 miles)

away, with links to Genoa, Civitavecchia (Rome), Corsica, and France.

VISITOR INFORMATION

CONTACT Alghero Tourism Office. ✉ *Via Cagliari 2,* ☎ *079/979054* ⊕ *www. algheroturismo.eu.*

Sights

Capo Caccia

NATURE SIGHT | Head 25 km (16 miles) west of Alghero for the spectacular heights of the imposing limestone headland of Capo Caccia. The rugged promontory, blanketed by thick maquis, forms part of the Porto Conte nature reserve and is home to deep caves such as the Grotta di Nettuno. Close by are the beaches of Porto Ferro, Cala Viola, and, on the beautiful Porto Conte inlet, Cala Dragunara. ✉ *Alghero* ☎ *079/945005* ⊕ *www.algheroparks.it.*

★ **Grotta di Nettuno** (*Neptune's Cave*)
CAVE | **FAMILY** | At the base of a sheer cliff, the pounding sea has carved an entrance to a vast fantastic cavern filled with stunning water pools, stalactites, and stalagmites. The dramatic cave and coves, discovered by fishermen in the 18th century, are popular tourist attractions for their sheer natural beauty. You must visit with a guide; tours start on the hour. It's possible to reach the caves by boat or by land. Between April and October, boat trips depart regularly from the port of Alghero for €16 round-trip (admission to the grotto is extra). To reach the grotto by land, you can descend the 654 dizzying steps of Escala del Cabirol ("Goat Steps"), which are cut into the steep cliff here. ■**TIP**➔ **By public bus from Alghero's Via Catalogna, the trip to the top of the stairway takes about 50 minutes. Allow 15 minutes for the descent by foot.** ✉ *Off SP55, 13 km (8 miles) west of Alghero, Alghero* ☎ *079/946540 office, 345/7418361 grotto* ⊕ *www.grottadinettuno.it* ⌸ *€14* ⊘ *Closed in rough seas.*

Museo del Corallo
OTHER MUSEUM | The coast around Alghero is one of the Mediterranean's most abundant sources of red coral, the subject of this entertaining and informative museum housed in a Liberty-era villa near Piazza Sulis. Old photographs and films show the process of harvesting the substance, and there are impressive displays of coral jewelry and ornaments. ✉ *Via Venti Settembre 8, Alghero* ☎ *079/4134690* 🌐 *www.museialghero.it* 🎟 *€5* 🕒 *Closed Tues.*

Museo Diocesano d'Arte Sacra (*Diocesan Museum of Sacred Art*)
RELIGIOUS BUILDING | This cathedral museum is housed in a 13th-century church designed in the Catalan Gothic style. The usual assortment of religious treasures—paintings, wooden sculptures, and bronze statues—is on display; look for the masterful 16th-century Catalan silverware, forged with intricate ancient motifs. Call ahead to check opening times. ✉ *Via Maiorca 1, Alghero* ☎ *079/9733041* 🎟 *€5.*

Beaches

Le Bombarde and Lazzaretto Beaches
BEACH | **FAMILY** | A couple of kilometers north of Alghero's old town, backed by pine woods, Maria Pia beach offers a convenient though unspectacular spot for an afternoon of bathing and sunbathing, but if you don't mind going farther afield, head for the altogether superior beaches of Le Bombarde and Lazzaretto, on adjacent inlets 10 kms (6 miles) west of town. Sheltered from the wind and fully equipped with bars and facilities for renting pedalos and canoes, the beaches are similar in style—both curves of soft sand studded with a few rocks, and both packed in August. ■ **TIP→ The beaches are easy to reach on the frequent tourist bus service, Il Trottolo.** **Amenities:** food and drink; lifeguards; sunloungers; showers; toilets; parking (fee in summer); water sports. **Best for:** swimming; snorkeling; windsurfing. ✉ *Alghero* ✣ *By car, take Via Garibaldi and then SS127bis north and west along the coast toward Fertilia.*

🍴 Restaurants

Il Pavone
$$ | **ITALIAN** | Fresh flowers on white linen tablecloths add color to the bright glass-enclosed dining area of this delightful eatery on busy Piazza Sulis; gold-framed paintings and oversize wine bottles capped in wax add Italian charm—as does the seasonally changing menu of pasta and seafood dishes such as tagliolini with mullet roe, artichokes, and pecorino cheese, or potato-stuffed culurgiones topped with sheep's cheese, dried tomatoes, and wild rocket. The four-course prix-fixe menu (€55) includes an appetizer, two tastings of pasta, two of seafood, and a traditional dessert, with coffee to follow. **Known for:** attentive and knowledgeable service; impressive wine list; delicious mains and desserts. [$] *Average main: €22* ✉ *Piazza Sulis 3, Alghero* ☎ *079/979584* 🌐 *www.ilpavone-ristorante.com* 🕒 *Closed Mon. and 2 wks in Nov. No dinner Sun. late Nov.–Mar.*

La Lepanto
$$ | **SEAFOOD** | A covered veranda by the seafront marks out Alghero's top seafood restaurant, an expansive and sunny room complete with crustacean-filled aquarium. Summer sees crowds of both locals and tourists, many of whom come for the specialty aragosta (lobster) cooked different ways, including *alla catalana* (with tomato and onions) or with ricotta foam, parsley, basil, and tomato. **Known for:** central location; bright interior with covered veranda seating; superior seafood in all its forms. [$] *Average main: €20* ✉ *Via Carlo Alberto 135, Alghero* ☎ *079/979116* 🌐 *www.lalepanto.com.*

Mabrouk
$$$$ | **ITALIAN** | There's always a lively crowd at this backstreet trattoria, where diners pack into three rooms to enjoy

the same multicourse set menu. If this seems limiting, think again—you'll be presented with a range of fresh, delicious, seasonally appropriate dishes (perhaps prawns, squid, swordfish, or sea bass) in abundant portions. **Known for:** vivacious atmosphere; fresh seafood; prix-fixe menus with unlimited drinks. [$] *Average main: €50* ✉ *Via Santa Barbara 4, Alghero* ☎ *340/4035349* 🕑 *Closed Oct.–Apr. No lunch.*

☕ Coffee and Quick Bites

Bar Pasticceria Ciro

$ | **ITALIAN** | For a delicious cannolo, fruit tart or *bignè* (cream puff), local cognoscenti make a beeline for this traditional bar and pastry shop, where the sweet delights displayed are made with the lightest pastry and the freshest fillings. Good coffees, ice creams, and sandwiches are also available, and there are tables inside and out back. **Known for:** cordial service; old-fashioned style; light pastries. [$] *Average main: €5* ✉ *Via Sassari 35/b, Alghero* ☎ *079/979960* 🕑 *Closed Mon.*

Cafè Latino

$ | **ITALIAN** | In prime position on Alghero's broad city walls, with views down to the yachting marina and across to Capo Caccia, this makes a wonderful place to pause by day or night with a spritz or fruit juice. The menu has a number of food items, too. **Known for:** friendly service; good selection of snacks and cocktails; superb views over the port. [$] *Average main: €10* ✉ *Bastioni Magellano 10, Alghero* ☎ *079/6766044* 🌐 *www.cafelatino.it* 🕑 *Closed Jan.–mid-Feb. and Tues. mid-Feb.–May and Oct.–Dec.*

Gelateria K2

$ | **ITALIAN** | Traditional and more unusual flavors jostle for space at this highly rated ice-cream parlor, an obligatory stop on any passeggiata in the old town. Among the favorites are fig, nocciola (hazelnut), and pistachio. **Known for:** ample choice; lactose- and gluten-free options; superb flavors. [$] *Average main: €4* ✉ *Via Roma 73, Alghero* ☎ *340/2809307* 🕑 *Closed Nov.–Mar.*

🛏 Hotels

San Francesco Heritage Hotel

$$ | **B&B/INN** | The only hotel located in Alghero's central Catalan quarter occupies an ex-convent once attached to the church of San Francesco. **Pros:** historic ambience; breakfast in the cloister; central location. **Cons:** no parking nearby; not a good choice for kids; no frills or extras. [$] *Rooms from: €128* ✉ *Via Machin 2, Alghero* ☎ *079/980330* 🌐 *www.sanfrancescohotel.com* 🕑 *Closed Oct.–Mar.* 🛏 *21 rooms* 🍴 *Free Breakfast.*

Smy Carlos V Alghero

$$$$ | **HOTEL** | **FAMILY** | On the shore boulevard opposite the Villa Las Tronas and 15 minutes from the airport, this grand, modern hotel (pronounced "Carlos Quinto") has an array of gardens and terraces, as well as a saltwater pool with sea views and a separate children's pool. **Pros:** wonderful vistas; rates drop in low season; good-size pool. **Cons:** dated in parts; sometimes falls short of five-star standards; large-hotel atmosphere. [$] *Rooms from: €328* ✉ *Lungomare Valencia 24, Alghero* ☎ *079/9720600* 🌐 *www.smyhotels.com* 🛏 *188 rooms* 🍴 *Free Breakfast.*

★ **Villa Las Tronas Hotel & Spa**

$$$$ | **HOTEL** | A stunning mansion dating from the 1880s has been transformed into this elegant secluded hotel that blends gold tapestries, crystal chandeliers, marble floors, canopy-draped beds, vaulted ceilings, and other Belle Époque treasures with modern amenities such as a luxury spa with a gym and an illuminated pool. **Pros:** promontory setting with regal sea views; luxury spa; incredible service. **Cons:** very expensive; no meat dishes served at dinner; usually a three-night minimum stay June–September. [$] *Rooms from: €420* ✉ *Lungomare*

Valencia 1, Alghero ☎ *079/981818*
⊕ *www.hotelvillalastronas.it* ⤶ *24 rooms*
† ⊙† *Free Breakfast.*

Nightlife

Poco Loco

LIVE MUSIC | For live music, bowling, or just a slice of pizza, this long-standing establishment has been a fixture for generations of Alghero's youth. The music is mainly jazz, blues, and rock, while a range of beers and cocktails are served as well as pizza cooked in a wood oven and dispensed by the meter. ⊠ *Via Gramsci 8, Alghero* ☎ *079/983604* ⊕ *www.pocolocoalghero.com.*

Shopping

De Filippis

JEWELRY & WATCHES | On the so-called Riviera del Corallo, Alghero has long been famed for its coral products, fashioned into elegant jewelry. This shop, with three outlets within a few yards of each other in the old town, has an impressive range of bracelets, brooches, and necklaces. ⊠ *Via Carlo Alberto 23, Alghero* ☎ *079/979394* ⊕ *www.defilippis.it.*

Activities

BOATING AND SAILING

Lega Navale Italiana

BOATING | This state-sponsored organization has information on the island's sailing facilities, as well as everything associated with maritime activity. ⊠ *Banchina del Porto R. Catardi, Alghero* ☎ *079/984093* ⊕ *www.leganavale.it.*

Sassari

34 km (21 miles) northeast of Alghero, 212 km (132 miles) north of Cagliari.

With a population of about 130,000, Sassari, the island's second-largest city, is an important university town and administrative center, notable for its history of intellectualism and bohemian student culture. Look for downtown vendors of *fainè*, a pizzalike chickpea-flour pancake glistening with olive oil, which is a Genoese and Sassarese specialty. The mazelike old town is blissfully isolated from the chaotic traffic swirling through the newer neighborhoods—Sassari is the hub of several highways and secondary roads leading to various coastal resorts, among them Stintino and Castelsardo.

GETTING HERE AND AROUND

Sassari can be reached by plane, ferry, train, bus, or car. The nearest airport is Alghero-Fertilia, about 30 km (19 miles) from Sassari. Inexpensive buses can get you to the center of Sassari. The closest port is Porto Torres, about 20 km (12½ miles) away, connected by ferry to Spain, France, Genoa, and Civitavecchia (Rome). Frequent bus and train services operate between Sassari and Cagliari, Olbia, and Alghero.

VISITOR INFORMATION

CONTACT Sassari. ⊠ *Via Sebastiano Satta 13,* ☎ *079/2008072* ⊕ *turismosassari.it.*

Sights

Duomo

CHURCH | The highly ornate stone Duomo is Sassari's must-see sight. The cathedral, dedicated to St. Nicolas (of Santa Claus inspiration), took more than half a millennium to build: the foundations were laid in the 12th century, and the Spanish colonial–style facade was completed in the 18th. Of particular interest in the plainer interior are the ribbed Gothic vaults, the 14th-century painting of the Madonna del Bosco on the high altar, and the early-19th-century tomb of Placido Benedetto di Savoia, the uncle of united Italy's first king. ⊠ *Piazza Duomo 3, Sassari* ☎ *079/233185* ⊡ *Free.*

🍴 Restaurants

L'Assassino

$$ | ITALIAN | Get a true taste of regional cuisine at this family-run trattoria in the old town. The menu is not for the squeamish or for vegetarians: horse, donkey, and—one of the stand-outs—roasted suckling pig feature prominently, as do typical Sassarese dishes such as *trippa alla parmigiana* (tripe with Parmesan), *lumaconi in rosso* (snails in a rich tomato sauce), and *cordula con piselli* (sheep's intestines with peas). **Known for:** pleasant courtyard seating in summer; superb roasted suckling pig; authentic local dishes. [$] *Average main: €16* ✉ *Via Pettenadu 19, Sassari* ☎ *079/233463* 🌐 *www.trattoriatipica.sassari.it* 🕒 *Closed Mon. lunch Oct.–May.*

Castelsardo

32 km (20 miles) northeast of Sassari.

The seaside citadel of Castelsardo is surmounted by an impressive fortress, which now contains a museum highlighting the basketware for which the town is famous. Wandering the upper town's maze of steep alleys is a delight, as is browsing the numerous shops in the lower town. Good souvenirs include not only woven baskets but also rugs and wrought-iron items. On the road into Castelsardo from the east, note the **Roccia dell'Elefante** (Elephant Rock), which was hollowed out by primitive man to be used as a burial chamber. The local name for this type of structure is *domus de janas* (literally, "fairy house").

GETTING HERE AND AROUND

Castelsardo is a 40-minute drive from Sassari on SS200. Frequent ARST buses also connect the two towns. Cars cannot enter Castelsardo's historic center, though you can drive part of the way up from Piazza La Pianedda. Parking is extremely limited, however, and if you're fit enough to tackle the steep streets you're best off leaving your car in the lower town and walking up.

VISITOR INFORMATION

CONTACT Castelsardo Tourism Office. ✉ *Via Pietro Sassu 1, Castelsardo* ☎ *079/4780931.*

👁 Sights

Museo dell'Intreccio Mediterraneo

CASTLE/PALACE | Castelsardo is best known in Sardinia for its intricate and colorful basketwork, numerous examples of which can be seen in the stores lining the main road and on the walls of the old center. The Museo dell'Intreccio Mediterraneo, located in the formidable old castle that dominates the town, puts it all into context, displaying a diverse range of woven baskets, bottles, trays, and fishing equipment. The well preserved castle was the Sardinian base of the powerful Doria family in the middle ages, and has replicas of catapults and other medieval weaponry on the walls; try to time your visit to be here at sunset for the unforgettable views. The castle stays open till midnight and beyond in July and August, and your entry ticket includes admission to a museum dedicated to Castelsardo and its Genoan origins, housed in an old Franciscan convent. ✉ *Via Marconi, Castelsardo* ☎ *079/6014769* 🌐 *www.mimcastelsardo.it* 🎫 *€5.*

Santa Teresa Gallura

100 km (62 miles) northeast of Sassari, 65 km (41 miles) northwest of Olbia.

At the northern tip of Sardinia, Santa Teresa Gallura retains the relaxed, carefree air of a former fishing village. Nearby beaches rival those farther down the coast yet somehow aren't as crowded with tourists.

GETTING HERE AND AROUND

Ferry crossings from Bonifacio in Corsica operated by Moby Lines run up to four times per day. The trip lasts about 50 minutes.

By car, you can drive from Olbia following the SS125 in the direction of Arzachena-Palau. At the fork in Palau, turn left to Santa Teresa Gallura. Continue for 25 km (16 miles). From Cagliari, follow SS131 to Sassari. Before the city center, exit at Sassari Latte Dolce, heading in the direction of Platamona/Castelsardo, which leads to the scenic coastal road Porto Torres–Santa Teresa.

From Alghero, follow SS291 until Sassari. Continue toward Porto Torres until you reach the northern part of the island.

There are frequent bus connections with Olbia, but there is no train station in Santa Teresa Gallura. The nearest main-line train station is in Olbia.

FERRY CONTACTS Moby Lines. ✉ *Santa Teresa Gallura* 🌐 *www.mobylines.com.*

VISITOR INFORMATION

CONTACT Santa Teresa Gallura Tourist Office. ✉ *Piazza Vittorio Emanuele 24, Santa Teresa Gallura* ☎ *0789/740986* 🌐 *www.santateresagalluraturismo.com.*

🛏 Hotels

Hotel Canne al Vento

$ | B&B/INN | Family-run Canne al Vento has been a quiet, cheerful haven in town since the late 1950s. **Pros:** abundant and memorable breakfasts; clean and orderly rooms; personal, friendly service. **Cons:** no elevator for upper-floor rooms; on a main road; few facilities. [$] *Rooms from: €80* ✉ *Via Nazionale 23, Santa Teresa Gallura* ☎ *0789/754219* 🌐 *www.hotelcannealvento.com* 🛏 *22 rooms* 🍴 *Free Breakfast.*

Hotel Corallaro

$$$ | HOTEL | FAMILY | A brief walk from the town center, this hotel occupies a panoramic spot right by the splendid Rena Bianca beach and has functional rooms—most of them spacious, a few of them with balconies and sea views. **Pros:** welcoming management and staff; airy rooms with plenty of storage space; steps away from the beach. **Cons:** attracts groups; steep uphill walk to town center; rooms with sea views and balconies fill up early. [$] *Rooms from: €234* ✉ *Spiaggia Rena Bianca, Santa Teresa Gallura* ☎ *0789/755475* 🌐 *www.hotelcorallaro.it* ⏲ *Closed mid-Oct.–early May* 🛏 *81 rooms* 🍴 *Free Breakfast.*

La Maddalena

45 km (20 miles) northwest of Olbia, 68 km (42 miles) northeast of Castelsardo.

From the port of Palau you can visit the archipelago of La Maddalena, seven granite islands embellished with aromatic scrub and wind-bent pines. The most significant of the handful of sites to see here is Giuseppe Garibaldi's home and tomb. Explore the lively port (also called La Maddalena), then head to one of several picture-postcard coves, the perfect spot for a picnic and to rejuvenate after your journey to the archipelago.

GETTING HERE AND AROUND

The only way to get to this small island is by boat or ferry. From Olbia, take a bus or drive to Palau, then catch the ferry to La Maddalena. During the day, car ferries make the 3-km (2-mile) trip two to four times an hour. The town center is right in front of the dock. Local buses are available for accessing the beaches, although the island is best explored by scooter or bike.

VISITOR INFORMATION

CONTACT La Maddalena Tourist Office. ✉ *Via XX Settembre 47, La Maddalena* ☎ *0789/736321.*

⊙ Sights

★ Compendio Garibaldino

HISTORIC HOME | FAMILY | Pilgrims from around the world converge on the Compendio Garibaldino, a complex on the island of Caprera that contains not only the restored home of Giuseppe Garibaldi (1807–82) but also his tomb. The national hero and military leader who laid the groundwork for the unification of Italy in 1861 lived a simple life as a farmer on Caprera, the island that he eventually owned. Exhibits include a collection of weaponry, numerous items of furniture belonging to the family, Garibaldi's famous red shirt, and the poncho he wore during his South American campaigns. The grounds contain the hero's tomb alongside those of his family, all surrounded by the olive grove that he planted. There are explanatory panels in Italian and English, and visitors can also download an app providing more comprehensive information. A combined ticket takes in the Memoriale Giuseppe Garibaldi, 4 km (2½ miles) away, a multimedia museum housed within a stern fortress dating from 1895, that chronicles the swashbuckling career of the Italian hero.

To visit the Compendio and Memoriale, take the ferry from Palau to Isola Maddalena, from where a causeway bridge crosses to Caprera. Note that visits to the Compendio Garibaldino must always be booked ahead for a specific time slot. A tour of the house and grounds should take less than an hour. ■ TIP→ **Caprera island is now a nature reserve, its woods and Mediterranean scrub crisscrossed by a network of waymarked trails that offer great opportunities for scenic walks and picnics.** ⊠ 7 km (4½ miles) east of Isola Maddalena, Caprera, La Maddalena ☎ 0789/727162 for information, 335/7505401 for booking visits ⊕ www.compendiogaribaldino.it ⊠ €7; €11 combined ticket includes Memoriale Giuseppe Garibaldi ⊙ Usually closed Mon. Apr.–Oct., Sun.

Nov.–Mar. (check first) ⚓ Book ahead for Compendio Garibaldino.

Porto Cervo

35 km (22 miles) southeast of La Maddalena, 30 km (19 miles) north of Olbia.

Sardinia's northeastern coast is fringed with low cliffs, inlets, and small bays. This has become an upscale vacationland, with glossy resorts such as Baia Sardinia and Porto Rotondo just outside the confines of the famed Costa Smeralda. Some of Italy's most expensive hotels are here, and magnificent yachts anchor in the waters of Porto Cervo. Golf courses, yacht clubs, and numerous alfresco restaurants and bars cater to those who want to see and be seen.

GETTING HERE AND AROUND

Porto Cervo is accessible by boat, car, taxi, and bus. Buses run regularly from Olbia and Palau.

Whichever airport or port of entry into Sardinia you choose, head to Olbia. By car, follow SS125 north toward Arzachena and Costa Smeralda. After 10 km (6 miles), turn right onto SP73 toward Porto Rotondo/Porto Cervo. Continue on SP94 and turn onto SP59 to Porto Cervo. The trip takes about 30 minutes.

⊕ Beaches

The beaches around the Costa Smeralda are some of the most exclusive in Europe, and they don't disappoint—with fine golden sand sheltered by red cliffs and fronting azure waters. Many can only be reached by boat, and there are regular launches from Porto Cervo. Rentals of sun beds and towels are as expensive as you'd expect.

Spiaggia del Principe

BEACH | FAMILY | Among the less developed of the Costa Smeralda's five-star beaches, the Spiaggia del Principe is tucked well away from the crowds, mainly because it is not so readily accessible as some of the others. The rewards, however, are all the greater. Edged by jagged, gold-tinted rocks, the beach has fine white sand and water ranging from emerald to a Caribbean shade of turquoise. Access from the car park is tricky—a 10-minute walk along a rough path (stout sneakers needed)—but a tuk-tuk service is sometimes on hand for a small charge. **Amenities:** food and drink; toilets; parking (fee in summer). **Best for:** swimming; walking. ✉ *Porto Cervo* ✥ *3 km (2 miles) east of Cala di Volpe on Via Romazzino and Via delle Mimose.*

🍴 Restaurants

I Frati Rossi
$$$ | **ITALIAN** | In the hills above Porto Cervo, this soothing hideaway—where a sheltered terrace looks out onto a verdant garden—is a great place to take a break from the coast's glossy trappings. Recommended antipasti include *sa cannacca* (dried sausage with pecorino cheese) and octopus salad with potatoes; *ravioli di cernia e carciofi* (homemade ravioli with grouper fish, artichokes, and truffle) is a great pasta choice; and the grilled fish is an excellent main. **Known for:** terrace seating with garden views; tasty seafood dishes; secluded dining. [$] *Average main: €30* ✉ *Via Paolino Azara, Pantogia, off SP59, Pantogia* ☎ *0789/94395* 🌐 *www.fratirossi.it* 🕑 *Closed Nov.–early Jan. No dinner Sun. and Mon. early Jan.–Easter. No lunch Mon.*

🛏 Hotels

★ Cala di Volpe
$$$$ | **RESORT** | Long a magnet for the beautiful people, this hyperglamorous Marriott Luxury Collection hotel was designed by Jacques Couëlle to resemble an ancient Sardinian fishing village, complete with its own covered bridge; the exterior is complemented by a rustic-elegant interior with beamed ceilings, terra-cotta floors, Sardinian arts and crafts, and porticoes overlooking the Cala di Volpe Bay. There's an Olympic-size saltwater pool, boat service to a private beach, and access to the Pevero Golf Club. **Pros:** stunning architecture and grounds; professional staff; luxurious ambience. **Cons:** car necessary; astronomical rates for room, additional amenities, drinks, and meals; some rooms disappoint. [$] *Rooms from: €1900* ✉ *Cala di Volpe, Porto Cervo* ☎ *800/4484066 toll-free, 0789/976111* 🌐 *www.caladivolpe.com* 🕑 *Closed mid-Oct.–mid-May* 🛏 *121 rooms* 🍽 *Free Breakfast.*

Cervo Hotel, Costa Smeralda Resort
$$$$ | **HOTEL** | Designed in 1962 by the architect Luigi Vietti, this Marriott Sheraton property—next to the busy piazzetta in the car-free heart of Porto Cervo—features low Mediterranean buildings with Spanish tile roofs surrounding a large pool and garden and spacious, white adobe rooms, most with a terrace, that have colorfully painted wood furniture and slip-covered sofas. **Pros:** open year-round; shuttle service to private beach; prime central location. **Cons:** very expensive rates and extras; most rooms and bathrooms are relatively small; no elevator. [$] *Rooms from: €513* ✉ *Waterfront, Porto Cervo* ☎ *800/4484066 toll-free, 0789/931111* 🌐 *www.hotelcervocostasmeralda.com* 🛏 *80 rooms* 🍽 *Free Breakfast.*

Nibaru
$$ | **HOTEL** | Amid lush gardens on a secluded inlet, this complex of pinkish-red brick buildings with tiled roofs has the feel of a small resort—albeit one with fewer amenities and lower prices than most of the Costa Smeralda's full-scale resorts. **Pros:** courteous staff; close to good beaches; nice pool. **Cons:** a car is necessary; no sea view; no restaurant. [$] *Rooms from: €193* ✉ *Località Cala di Volpe, Porto Cervo* ☎ *0789/96038* 🌐 *www.hotelnibaru.it* 🕑 *Closed Oct.–mid-May* 🛏 *53 rooms* 🍽 *Free Breakfast.*

Petra Segreta Resort and Spa
$$$$ | **HOTEL** | Sea and mountain views, top-quality cuisine, and chic and spacious guest rooms are the main draws at this romantic boutique hotel outside the picturesque village of San Pantaleo. **Pros:** tranquil mountainside setting with spectacular views; two good restaurants; blend of traditional surroundings and modern amenities. **Cons:** not suitable for families; remote and isolated; three-night minimum stay July and August. [$] *Rooms from: €504* ✉ *Via Buddeu, Olbia* ☎ *0789/1876441* 🌐 *www.petrasegretaresort.com* 🕓 *Closed Nov.–Apr.* 🛏 *25 rooms* 🍴 *Free Breakfast.*

Activities

BOATING AND SAILING

Yacht Club Costa Smeralda
SAILING | The Aga Khan IV founded this yacht club with some local associates in 1967 in order to promote nautical activities. The club provides use of its pool, restaurant, bar, and guest rooms to those with memberships at associated yacht clubs. Watch for regattas from June to September, and check out the YCCS Sailing School, which organizes courses on dinghies and cabin cruisers. ✉ *Via della Marina, Porto Cervo* ☎ *0789/902200* 🌐 *www.yccs.it.*

GOLF

Pevero Golf Course
GOLF | Designed by Robert Trent Jones Sr. and opened in 1972, Pevero is a world-class course with some of Europe's most beautiful fairways. Stretching nearly 6½ km (4 miles) between the Gulf of Pevero and Cala di Volpe (Bay of Foxes), it provides challenging playing conditions that incorporate 70 bunkers, several rock formations, and vegetation. The dress code is formal in the upscale club house. Note that the course and club house are closed on Monday and Tuesday between November and February. ✉ *Località Cala di Volpe 20, Porto Cervo* ☎ *0789/976400* 🌐 *www.peverogolfclub.com* 🎟 *€100–€160, depending on season; €60 for club car* ⛳ *18 holes, 6700 yards, par 72.*

Olbia

30 km (19 miles) south of Porto Cervo.

Amid the resorts of Sardinia's northeastern coast, Olbia, a town of about 60,000, is a lively little seaport and port of call for mainland ferries at the head of a long, wide bay.

GETTING HERE AND AROUND

The main airport, Olbia–Costa Smeralda, is only 1½ km (1 mile) from the town center. Inexpensive city buses and taxis are available outside the terminal. Trains operate between Olbia and Cagliari and take about four hours.

The Olbia–Isola Bianca harbor provides daily connections with the Italian mainland, less than 300 km (186 miles) away. Regular ferries arrive from Genoa, Piombino, Civitavecchia (Rome), and Livorno. Most ferries take 6–10 hours.

VISITOR INFORMATION

CONTACT Olbia. ✉ *Via Dante 1,* ☎ *0789/52206* 🌐 *www.helloolbia.com.*

Sights

Basilica San Simplicio
CHURCH | Olbia's little basilica, a short walk from the main Corso Umberto I, is the city's unmissable sight. The simple granite structure dates from the 11th century, part of the great Pisan church-building program, using pillars and columns recycled from Roman buildings. The basilica has a bare, somewhat somber interior; its three naves are separated by a series of Romanesque arches, and fragments of frescoes are visible behind the altar. **TIP→ Recent renovations of the monument have unearthed the remains of a Greek and Roman necropolis, which is now open to the public (the entrance is in the**

car park beneath the piazza). ✉ *Piazza San Simplicio, Olbia* ☎ *345/6328150* 🌐 *www.museumtempioampurias.it.*

🍴 Restaurants

Il Gambero

$$ | **ITALIAN** | This backstreet trattoria has a strong rustic flavor, its two rooms adorned with brass cooking pots, colorful embroideries, old photographs, and agricultural knickknacks. The menu, too, has a local focus and might include tagliolini pasta with squid ink, artichokes, and prawns or sliced tuna with rocket and strawberries. **Known for:** informal but discreet service; fresh, local meat and seafood dishes; simple, rustic decor. [$] *Average main: €18* ✉ *Via Lamarmora 6, Olbia* ☎ *0789/23874* 🌐 *ristorante-il-gambero-seafood-restaurant.business.site* 🕓 *Closed Mon.*

☕ Coffee and Quick Bites

Café Cosimino

$ | **ITALIAN** | At the heart of Olbia life since 1905, this popular café and wine bar with tables in the town's central piazza occupies a great position for a pause or a snack while exploring the town. Pastas, salads, and panini are served alongside a good range of wines and beers, and it stays open late. **Known for:** social hub; late opening; range of local wines. [$] *Average main: €8* ✉ *Piazza Regina Margherita 3, Olbia* ☎ *320/1414952.*

🛏 Hotels

La Locanda del Conte Mameli

$$ | **HOTEL** | Housed in a remodeled palazzo built at the end of the 19th century for the count after which it is named, this small and select hotel occupies a quiet location on a traffic-free backstreet just a few steps from Corso Umberto. **Pros:** small hotel with personal service; central but quiet location; antique furnishings. **Cons:** no parking; some rooms are slightly cramped and gloomy; tricky to access by car. [$] *Rooms from: €139* ✉ *Via delle Terme 8, Olbia* ☎ *0789/23008* 🌐 *www.lalocandadelcontemameli.com* 🛏 *11 rooms* 🍴 *Free Breakfast.*

Index

Photo Credits

Front Cover: Rudi1976 / Alamy Stock Photo [Description: Autumn in Alps. Beautiful St. Magdalena village with Dolomites mountains in a gorgeous Val di Funes valley, South Tyrol, Italian Alps at autumn]. **Back cover, from left to right:** Viviane Teles. Bensliman/Shutterstock. Steven Lee/Shutterstock. **Spine:** Baloncici/Shutterstock. **Interior, from left to right:** Freesurf69/ Dreamstime (1). Shaiith/Dreamstime (2-3). ChiccoDodiFC FotoOk.it (5). **Chapter 1: Experience Italy:** Minnystock/Dreamstime (10-11). Mapics/Dreamstime (12-13). Carso80/ shutterstock (13). Pcruciatti/Shutterstock (13). Vladimir Korostyshevskiy/Shutterstock (14). Kimberly A F/shutterstock (14). Renata Sedmakova/shutterstock (14). Chen Min Chun/ shutterstock (14). Janoka82 (15). Jaroslaw Pawlak/shutterstock (15). Mi.Ti./shutterstock (16). Inguaribile Vlaggiatore/shutterstock (16). Alessandro Cristiano/shutterstock (16). Parilov/shutterstock (16). Cheryl Ramalho/iStockphoto (17). Alexirina27000/Dreamstime (18). Siempreverde22/Dreamstime (18). Gaspar Janos/shutterstock (18). Andrei Molchan/ shutterstock (18). Bucha Natallia/shutterstock (19). Anibal Trejo/shutterstock (19). Marianceccarelli/iStockphoto (20). Cge2010/shutterstock (20). Cge2010/ shutterstock (20). Stefano Garau/shutterstock (20). Omas_Photo/shutterstock (21). Canadastock/Shutterstock (28). StevanZZ/Shutterstock (29). Vololikeno/shutterstock (30). Marcin Krzyzak/shutterstock (30). Tour Liguria by Volver (30). Poludziber/shutterstock (30). Franco Cappellari/ Pugliapromozione (31). Fokke baarssen/shutterstock (31). Roman Babakin/shutterstock (31). Lucamato/iStockphoto (31). Daniela marchi/Castiglion del Bosco (32). Alessandro Moggi (33). Phant/Shutterstock (34). Boris Stroujko/Shutterstock (34). R.Nagy/Shutterstock (34). Nattee Chalermtiragool/Shutterstock (35). Luxerendering/Shutterstock (35). Mazerath/Shutterstock (36). Giannis Papanikos/Shutterstock (37). Taste Bologna (38). Montese Cooking Experiences (38). Monni & Pirisi/Tasting Sardinia (38). Joaquin Corbalan P/shutterstock (39). Dr. Ronald Pitcock/Cook with us in Rome (39). AndrewSoundarajan/iStockphoto (40). AndreaAstes/ iStockphoto (40). Robert Zehetmayer/Dreamstime (40). LizCoughlan/shutterstock (40). Venezia, Palazzo Ducale (41). **Chapter 3: Rome:** AngeloCampus (71). EricaDuecy (74). AngeloCampus (75). Lisay/iStockphoto (75). Michelangelo, Public domain, via Wikimedia Commons (98-99). Public Domain (98). RPBaiao/Shutterstock (100). Michelangelo [CC BY-SA 3.0]/Wikimedia Commons (102-103). Michelangelo [CC BY-SA 3.0]/Wikimedia Commons (104-105). **Chapter 4: Side Trips from Rome:** Marco Rubino/Shutterstock (165). Ragemax/shutterstock (165). **Chapter 5: Venice:** Paul D'Innocenzo2008 (187). Paul D'Innocenzo2008 (190). Jess_h / Shutterstock (191). Iz89 / Shutterstock (191). Catarina Belova/Shutterstock (198-199). Olaf Unger/ Shutterstock (200). Lybid/Shutterstock (200). Zvonimir Atletic/Shutterstock (200). ArTono/Shutterstock (200). Zoltan Tarlacz/Shutterstock (200). SvetlanaSF/Shutterstock (201). Don Mammoser/Shutterstock (201). Viacheslav Lopatin/Shutterstock (202). ArTono/Shutterstock (202). Viacheslav Lopatin/Shutterstock (202). Evgeny Shmulev/Shutterstock (203). Marco Rubino/Shutterstock (204). ilozavr/Shutterstock (204). Minnystock/Dreamstime (248). **Chapter 6: The Veneto and Friuli–Venezia Giulia:** Wojtek Buss/age fotostock (255). Francesco Majo (258). Michele Bella (259). Danilo Donadoni (259). **Chapter 7: The Dolomites:** Angelami/ fototeca Trentino (303). Danilo Donadoni (306). Plmrue/ Dreamstime (307). Cubolmages srl / Alamy (307). Elena Brunelli/shutterstock (332). Pridalo/shutterstock (337). **Chapter 8: Milan, Lombardy, and the Lakes:** Worldscapes/age fotostock (347). Danilo Donadoni (350). Nagy Julia/Shutterstock (351). Valerio Pardi (351). Alexandre Rotenberg/shutterstock (388). Gambarini Gianandrea/shutterstock (390). **Chapter 9: Piedmont and the Valle d'Aosta:** RostislavGlinskyPhotography (417). S74/Shutterstock (420). Danilo Donadoni (421). Piga&catalano (421). Mikhail Varentsov/shutterstock (442). **Chapter 10: The Italian Riviera:** Silvano audisio/Shutterstock (449). Zagorulko Inka/Shutterstock (452). Ubik (453). Maxsala/ Dreamstime (453). Oana Dragan/iStockphoto (459). Whatafoto/Shutterstock (460). Borut Trdina/iStockphoto (460). ELEPHOTOS/Shutterstock (460). Nightcap/Shutterstock (460). Sannga Park (461). Aliaksandr Antanovich/Shutterstock (461). Viviane Teles (461). Valeria Cantone/ shutterstock (493). **Chapter 11: Emilia–Romagna:** Cristiano Palazzini / Shutterstock (495). Matz Sjoberg/agefotostock (498). Matz Sjoberg/agefotostock (499). Franco pizzochero (499). ESstock/Shutterstock (511). Piccerella/iStockphoto (512). Alessia Pierdomenico/ Shutterstock (512). Consorzio del Prosciutto di Parma (512). Parma 040 by http://www.flickr.com/photos/nordelch/6198040562/ Attribution-ShareAlike License (512). Grischa Georgiew/iStockphoto/Thinkstock (512). Consorzio del Formaggio Parmigiano-Reggiano (513). Consorzio del Formaggio Parmigiano-Reggiano (513). Roberto A Sanchez/iStockphoto (513). M Laky/Shutterstock (513). Consorzio del Formaggio Parmigiano-Reggiano (513). AGF Srl / Alamy Stock Photo (514). Verysmallplanet/Shutterstock (514). ESstock/Shutterstock (515). Foodlove/Shutterstock (515). Giorgio Morara/Shutterstock (515). Claudio Baldini/Shutterstock (515). **Chapter 12: Florence:** Alysta/ Shutterstock (539). Thekovtun/Shutterstock (542). Paolo Gallo / Alamy Stock Photo (543). Restock images/ Shutterstock (543). George Diamonds/Shutterstock (554-555). Skovalsky/Shutterstock (557). AlfioGiannotti (557). Rough Guides / Alamy (557). Kritskaya/Shutterstock (558). Everett Collection/Shutterstock (581). Everett Collection/Shutterstock (581). Marzolino/Shutterstock (581). Romas_Photo/Shutterstock (582). Steve Allen/Shutterstock (582). Giannit/Dreamstime (583). Karl Allen Lugmayer/Shutterstock (583). MisterStock/Shutterstock (583). Yuri Turkov/Shutterstock (583). Public Domain (584). Flickr/virtusincertus (584). CYSUN/ Shutterstock (584). Flickr/jean louis mazieres (585). Flickr/Deb Nystrom (585). Bill Perry/Shutterstock (585). Planet Art (Own) (586). Planet Art (Own) (586). Planet Art (Own) (586). **Chapter 13: Tuscany:** Cornelia Doerr (595). Kuvona/Dreamstime (598). Marco scataglini (599). Nico tondini (599). Kiev.Victor/shutterstock (608). Simona Bottone/shutterstock (639). **Chapter 14: Umbria and the Marches:** Honza Hruby/shutterstock (641). B&Y Photography / Alamy (644). 5 second Studio / Shutterstock (645). Doco Dalfiano (645). StevanZZ/Shutterstock (659). Threerivers11/Dreamstime (660). Fototeca ENIT (All) (661). **Chapter 15: Naples and Campania:** Stephenmiller1 (681). Look Die Bildagentur der Fotografen GmbH / Alamy (684). Bon Appetit / Alamy (685). Cubolmages srl / Alamy (685). Wjarek/Shutterstock (713). Superstock (713). Kated/Shutterstock (714). Antonina Tadeush/ Shutterstock (715). Balounm/Shutterstock (715). Ivan bastien/Shutterstock (716). Freevideophotoagency/ Shutterstock (716). Boris Stroujko/ Shutterstock (716). Leonid Andronov/Shutterstock (717). Katie Hamlin (718). Alfiya Safuanova/Shutterstock (719). Laszlo Konya/dreamstime (736). **Chapter 16: Puglia, Basilicata, and Calabria:** JosĖ Fuste Raga/age fotostock (747). Jcartwright01/Dreamstime (750). Fanfo/ Dreamstime (751). Davide cerati (751). Fabio Dell/shutterstock (761). Marco Fine/shutterstock (784). **Chapter 17: Sicily:** Peeter Viisimaa/ iStockPhoto (789). Yadid Levy (792). Yadid Levy (793). ChiccoDodiFC FotoOk.it (793). Vvoe/shutterstock (824). **Chapter 18: Sardinia:** Eva Bocek/shutterstock (849). Marmo81/Shutterstock (852). Marmo81/Shutterstock (853). Oxana Denezhkina/Shutterstock (853). Travelwild/ shutterstock (855). **About Our Writers:** All photos are courtesy of the writers except for the following: Liz Shemaria, courtesy of Ian Tuttle; Laura Itzkowitz, coutesy of Annie Ojile. *Every effort has been made to trace the copyright holders, and we apologize in advance for any accidental errors. We would be happy to apply the corrections in the following edition of this publication.*

Fodor's ESSENTIAL ITALY 2023

Publisher: Stephen Horowitz, *General Manager*

Editorial: Douglas Stallings, *Editorial Director;* Jill Fergus, Amanda Sadlowski, *Senior Editors;* Kayla Becker, Brian Eschrich, Alexis Kelly, *Editors;* Angelique Kennedy-Chavannes, *Assistant Editor*

Design: Tina Malaney, *Director of Design and Production;* Jessica Gonzalez, Senior *Designer;* Erin Caceres, *Graphic Design Associate*

Production: Jennifer DePrima, *Editorial Production Manager;* Elyse Rozelle, *Senior Production Editor;* Monica White, *Production Editor*

Maps: Rebecca Baer, *Senior Map Editor;* David Lindroth, Mark Stroud (Moon Street Cartography), *Cartographers*

Photography: Viviane Teles, *Senior Photo Editor;* Namrata Aggarwal, Neha Gupta, Payal Gupta, Ashok Kumar, *Photo Editors;* Eddie Aldrete, *Photo Production Intern;* Kadeem McPherson, *Photo Production Associate Intern*

Business and Operations: Chuck Hoover, *Chief Marketing Officer;* Robert Ames, *Group General Manager;* Devin Duckworth, *Director of Print Publishing*

Public Relations and Marketing: Joe Ewaskiw, *Senior Director of Communications and Public Relations*

Fodors.com: Jeremy Tarr, *Editorial Director;* Rachael Levitt, *Managing Editor*

Technology: Jon Atkinson, *Director of Technology;* Rudresh Teotia, *Lead Developer*

Writers: Robert Andrews, Ros Belford, Nick Bruno, Jennifer Cole, Rochelle Del Borrello, Liz Humphreys, Laura Itzkowitz, Fergal Kavanaugh, Natalie Kennedy, Craig McKnight, Patricia Rucidlo, Liz Shemaria, Erla Zwingle

Editors: Jill Fergus (lead editor), Kayla Becker, Amanda Sadlowski, Douglas Stallings

Production Editor: Elyse Rozelle

5th Edition

ISBN 978-1-64097-549-1

ISSN 2476-0692

All details in this book are based on information supplied to us at press time. Always confirm information when it matters, especially if you're making a detour to visit a specific place. Fodor's expressly disclaims any liability, loss, or risk, personal or otherwise, that is incurred as a consequence of the use of any of the contents of this book.

SPECIAL SALES
This book is available at special discounts for bulk purchases for sales promotions or premiums. For more information, e-mail SpecialMarkets@fodors.com.

PRINTED IN THE UNITED STATES OF AMERICA

10 9 8 7 6 5 4 3 2

About Our Writers

Born of Sicilian stock, **Robert Andrews** has been living and working in various parts of Italy for most of his adult life. He has written articles and guidebooks on this multifaceted peninsula, and provides travel consultancy services as well as leading individual and small-group tours in Sicily and Sardinia. For this edition, Robert updated the Sardinia and Sicily chapters.

Nick Bruno is an Italy specialist and frequent Fodor's contributor. As well as authoring and updating books and features, he makes radio packages for the BBC. A lifelong interest in history and Italian language has led to a project researching his paternal Italian family during the Il Ventennio Fascista period. Nick updated the Experience; Travel Smart; Veneto and Friuli-Venezia Giulia; Puglia, Basilicata, and Calabria; Naples and Campania; and Venice chapters. Follow him on Instagram and Twitter @nickjgbruno and ⊕ *barbruno. com.*

Liz Humphreys is a transplant to Europe from New York City, where she edited for media companies including Condé Nast and Time Inc. Since then she's written for publications including *Condé Nast Traveler, Michelin Green Guides,* and *Forbes Travel Guide.* Liz has an advanced certificate in wine studies from WSET (Wine & Spirit Education Trust), which comes in handy when exploring her beloved Italian wine regions. Liz updated the Dolomites; Piedmont and the Valle D'Aosta; Umbria and the Marches; and Venice. Follow her @winederlust_wanderings.

Patricia Rucidlo holds master's degrees in Italian Renaissance history and art history. She is also a licensed tour guide in Florence and also works in Lucca. When she's not extolling the virtues of a Pontormo masterpiece or angrily defending the Medici, you can find her leading food and wine tours in Florence and environs. Patricia updated the chapters of Florence, Tuscany, Emilia-Romagna, and the Italian Riviera.

Liz Shemaria is an Italy-based journalist and third-generation Northern Californian who has trekked solo in Himalaya, interviewed artists in military-ruled Burma, and once rode an overnight train across Egypt on her birthday. She has contributed to more than a dozen travel and news publications including Fodor's guidebooks, *AFAR, BBC Travel,* and *Roads & Kingdoms.* Spontaneous dance parties are essential to her creative process. For this edition, Liz updated the Milan, Lombardy, and the Lakes chapter. Follow her on Instagram @lizshemaria.

Ros Belford lived full-time in Sicily for 12 years, raising her daughters on the Aeolian island of Salina. She now spends her time between Sicily, Florence, and her home in Cambridge, England. She's the *Telegraph*'s luxury hotel expert for Cornwall and Sicily. She worked on Sicily.

Freelance writer **Jennifer Cole** worked on Sicily covering the Aeolian Islands and Mt. Etna and Eastern Sicily.

About Our Writers

 Rochelle Del Borrello is an Italian-Australian writer from Perth, Western Australia. Rochelle has lived in Sicily since 2002 and has written extensively about the island. Rochelle publishes her thoughts and musings on her blog Sicily Inside and Out (⊕ *www. sicilyinsideandout.com*). She worked on Sicily.

 Laura Itzkowitz is a freelance writer and editor based in Rome with an MFA in creative writing and a passion for covering travel, arts and culture, lifestyle, design, food and wine. Her writing has appeared in *Travel + Leisure*, *Architectural Digest*, *Vogue*, *GQ*, *Departures*, *AFAR*, and others. Laura updated the Rome and Rome Side Trips chapters. Follow her on Instagram and Twitter @lauraitzkowitz.

 Fergal Kavanagh travels extensively throughout Italy with his Tune Into English Roadshow, where he teaches English through pop music (⊕ *www.tuneintoenglish.com*). In his 25 years in the country there is hardly a town square he has not passed through. He updated Naples and Campania.

Originally from California, **Natalie Kennedy** moved to Rome planning to stay for only a year, but has now called the Eternal City home for nearly a decade and runs a popular blog about Roman life (⊕ *www. anamericanin-rome.com*). For this edition she updated Rome.

Craig McKnight was originally born in northeast England, and has had a love of Italy since childhood. After a change of career, he is now based as a teacher in Reggio Calabria, which gives him the time to explore Sicily and Calabria, and to write and blog about both. Craig worked on Sicily.

 Erla Zwingle has been a contributor to *National Geographic* since 1982 and wrote their guidebook to Venice, as well as writing for other publications including *Smithsonian* and *Esquire*. She lives in Venice and writes a blog called "Venice: I am not making this up." She updated Venice.